Michael G. Aamodt

Industrial/Organizational
Psychology
An Applied Approach

9e

✦ Cengage

Australia • Brazil • Canada • Mexico • Singapore • United Kingdom • United States

***Industrial/Organizational Psychology:
An Applied Approach,* Ninth Edition**
Michael G. Aamodt

Senior Vice President, Higher Education &
Skills Product: Erin Joyner

Product Director: Laura Ross

Product Manager: Cazzie Reyes

Vendor Content Manager: Valarmathy
Munuswamy, Lumina Datamatics, Ltd.

Product Assistant: Jessica Witczak

Manufacturing Planner: Ron Montgomery

Digital Delivery Quality Partner: Allison
Marion

Inventory Analyst: Seth Cohn

Intellectual Property Analyst: Deanna Ettinger

Intellectual Property Project Manager:
Ilakkiya Jayagopi

Production Service: Lumina Datamatics, Ltd.

Art Director and Cover Designer: Angela
Sheehan

Cover Image: alphaspirit.it/Shutterstock.com

For product information and technology assistance, contact us at
**Cengage Customer & Sales Support, 1-800-354-9706
or support.cengage.com.**

For permission to use material from this text or product, submit all
requests online at **www.copyright.com**.

Library of Congress Control Number: 2021923937

ISBN: 978-0-357-65834-5

Cengage
200 Pier 4 Boulevard
Boston, MA 02210
USA

Cengage is a leading provider of customized learning solutions
with employees residing in nearly 40 different countries and sales
in more than 125 countries around the world. Find your local
representative at: **www.cengage.com**.

To learn more about Cengage platforms and services, register or
access your online learning solution, or purchase materials for your
course, visit **www.cengage.com**.

Printed at CLDPC, USA, 09-23

This edition is dedicated to my mother-in-law, Joanne Hicks, who continues to demonstrate a kind spirit in spite of the complexities of getting a little older.

Brief Contents

Contents

Chapter 4   **Employee Selection: Recruiting and Interviewing**   **117**

Chapter 7   Evaluating Employee Performance

Chapter 15   Stress Management: Dealing with the Demands of Life and Work   533

Appendix   Working Conditions and Human Factors   575

Preface

To Students

I can't imagine a career better than industrial/organizational (I/O) psychology; it has something for everyone. You can be a scientist, a detective, a lawyer, an adviser, a statistician, an inventor, a writer, a teacher, a mentor, a trainer, a high-stakes gambler, a motivator, a humanitarian, or an engineer—or all at the same time. In no other field can you experience such challenging opportunities, earn an excellent salary, and derive the satisfaction of bettering the lives of others.

I wrote this book because there was a strong need for a text that would appeal directly to undergraduates without sacrificing scholarship. Our field is so exciting, yet the existing texts do not reflect that excitement. This book contains many real-world examples that illustrate important points; humor to make your reading more enjoyable; and charts and tables that integrate and simplify such complicated issues as employment law, job satisfaction, work motivation, and leadership.

In writing this book, I tried to strike a balance between research, theory, and application. In addition to the fundamental theories and research in I/O psychology, you will find such practical applications as how to write a résumé, survive an employment interview, write a job description, create a performance appraisal instrument, and motivate employees.

Student Friendly!

To make your reading easier, humor, stories, and real-world examples are used. The text is written at a level designed to help you understand the material rather than at a level designed to show off the author's vocabulary. The feedback I have received indicates that students actually *enjoy* reading this text!

To help you learn, *innovative charts* such as those found in Chapters 3, 8, 9, 10, and 13 integrate the main points of the chapter. At the beginning of each chapter, a list of *learning objectives* helps organize your thinking for what you are about to read. On each page, *key terms* are defined in the margins. At the end of each chapter, a *chapter summary* reminds you of the important points you learned, and *critical thinking questions* test the depth of your new knowledge.

To help you apply the material to whatever career you choose, each chapter contains a Career Workshop Box that provides tips on how to use the chapter information to help your career, a case study of an actual situation experienced by a real organization, and a Focus on Ethics Box that presents an ethical dilemma related to the chapter material.

Two Books in One!

Your instructor has access to both a workbook containing applied exercises and a statistics primer that they can distribute to students at no additional cost. Each chapter comes with exercises to help you apply what you have learned. Thus, not only will you read about I/O psychology, but you will also get the opportunity to experience it as well.

You will take psychological tests, conduct the critical incident technique, solve case studies, analyze situations, prepare for an interview, and create a structured interview.

To Instructors

Instructor Resources

Additional instructor resources for this product are available online. Instructor assets include an Instructor's Manual, PowerPoint slides, a test bank powered by Cognero, a workbook, and a Statistics Primer. Sign up or sign in at **www.cengage.com** to search for and access this product and its online resources.

Instructor's Manual

The instructor's manual contains a variety of resources to aid instructors in preparing and presenting text material in a manner that meets their personal preferences and course needs. It presents chapter-by-chapter suggestions and resources to enhance and facilitate learning.

PowerPoint® Slides

These vibrant Microsoft PowerPoint lecture slides for each chapter assist you with your lecture by providing concept coverage using content directly from the textbook.

Cengage Learning Testing, powered by Cognero®

Cognero is a flexible online system that allows you to author, edit, and manage test bank content as well as create multiple test versions in an instant. You can deliver tests from your school's learning management system, your classroom, or wherever you want!

Workbook

This workbook contains exercises related to psychological tests, case studies, and interviews.

Understanding Statistics Primer

This resource provides students with a brief guide to understanding the statistics they encounter in journal articles, technical reports, and conference presentations.

New to This Edition

- More examples of diversity efforts spread throughout the text
- Enhanced discussion of the history of I/O psychology
- Revised discussion of conducting salary equity analyses
- Updates on changes in employment law
- Updated discussion on employee recruitment
- Enhanced discussion of considering an applicant's criminal history
- New material on expectancy charts
- Increased discussion of virtual interviews, meetings, and communication
- New discussion of the four-drive theory of human nature
- Enhanced discussion of working at home
- Updated use of technology examples
- Updated references and examples in every chapter

Acknowledgments

I am grateful to the excellent staff at Cengage Learning, including vendor project manager Sheila Moran and associate product manager Cazzie Reyes. I am especially grateful to Valarmathy Munuswamy of Lumina Datamatics for working so diligently and patiently in getting the text through production. The quality of this edition was greatly enhanced by the thoughtful responses of Jolene Goh who served as a subject matter expert to ensure accuracy and provide additional examples.

I would like to thank the reviewers of previous editions, whose comments and suggestions continue to make the text stronger: Sheree Barron, Georgia College and State University; Elizabeth Boyd, Indiana University–Purdue University Indianapolis; Jay Brand, Haworth Inc.; Robert Bubb, Auburn University; Linda Butzin, Owens Community College; Maureen Conard, Sacred Heart University; George Cook, University of Rochester; Daniel DeNeui, University of Southern Oregon; Jim Diefendorff, University of Akron; Elizabeth Erffmeyer, Western Kentucky University; Armando Estrada, Washington State University; Evan Finer, College of Lake County; Donald Fisher, Southwest Missouri State; Mary Fox, University of Maryland; Mark Frame, University of Texas at Arlington; Alisha Francis, Northwest Missouri State University; Dean Frost, Portland State University; William Gaeddert, SUNY-Plattsburgh; David Gilmore, University of North Carolina at Charlotte; Matthew Grawitch, St. Louis University; George Hampton, University of Houston; Paul Hanges, University of Maryland; Kathy Hanish, Iowa State University; Donald Hantula, Temple University; Steven Hurwitz, Tiffin University; Brian Johnson, University of Tennessee at Martin; Scott Johnson, John Wood Community College; Harold Kiess, Framingham State College; Jean Powell Kirnan, The College of New Jersey; Janet Kottke, California State University at San Bernardino; Charles Lance, University of Georgia; Laurie Lankin, Mercer University; Paul Lloyd, Southwest Missouri State University; Janine Miller Lund, Tarrant County College; Alexandra Luong, University of Minnesota; James Mitchel, LIMRA International; Paul Nail, Southwestern Oklahoma State University; Christopher Nave, Rutgers University; Craig Parks, Washington State University; Charles Pierce, University of Memphis; Marc Pratarelli, Colorado State University-Pueblo; Juan Sanchez, Florida International University; Steven Scher, Eastern Illinois University; Ken Schultz, California State University, San Bernardino; Eugene Sheehan, University of Northern Colorado; William Siegfried, University of North Carolina at Charlotte; Sharmin Spencer, University of Illinois; Ross Steinman, Widener University; Keith Syrja, Owens Community College; Todd Thorsteinson, University of Idaho; and Tiffani Tribble, College of Mount Union.

I would also like to thank my family, friends, and students for accommodating my time spent writing and for all their ideas and support. I appreciate my colleagues Eric Dunleavy, Emilee Tison, Mark Nagy, Kayo Sady, Michael Surrette, and David Cohen, who patiently allowed me to bounce ideas off them, vent, and ask dumb questions. Thanks also to my SIOP, IPMA, IPAC, and SHRM colleagues for their insight and stories. There is no way I can properly express my gratitude to my mentor, Dr. Wilson W. Kimbrough, who taught me much more than facts and theories, and to Dr. Al Harris and Dr. Daniel Johnson, who have been so supportive throughout my career.

Finally, I thank my wife, Bobbie, and son, Josh, for their love and emotional support. Most of the time, writing a book is an enjoyable process. However, during the times I was stressed or confused (an increasingly common occurrence), my family was always patient and understanding. I could not have done this, or much of anything, without them. I would also like to thank Bobbie for her contributions in helping write the stress chapter, the section on organizational culture, several of the Career Workshop Boxes, and all of the Focus on Ethics Boxes.

Michael G. Aamodt

About the Author

Mike is a professor emeritus of industrial/organizational psychology at Radford University in Radford, Virginia. In 2009, after 26 years of teaching at RU, Mike took advantage of an early retirement option and joined DCI Consulting Group as a principal consultant.

Mike received his B.A. in psychology from Pepperdine University in Malibu, California, and both his M.A. and Ph.D. from the University of Arkansas. Over the years, Mike has taught courses in employee selection, job analysis, compensation, employee training and development, organizational psychology, organizational influence, organizational politics, and forensic psychology. Mike has received teaching awards as a graduate student at the University of Arkansas and as a professor at Radford University. Mike is the recipient of the 2020 Stephen E. Bemis Memorial Award for Excellence.

As a researcher, Mike has published over 65 journal articles and book chapters and presented many papers at professional conferences. He is the author of *Applied Industrial/Organizational Psychology*, now in its ninth edition, *Research in Law Enforcement Selection, I/O Psychology in Action, Understanding Statistics in I/O Psychology*, and *Human Relations in Business*. Mike is on the editorial boards of the *Journal of Police and Criminal Psychology* and *Criminal Justice and Behavior*.

In over 35 years as a trainer and a consultant, Mike has helped a wide variety of organizations deal with such issues as employee selection, performance evaluation, down-sizing, organizational change, compensation, and motivation. He is considered one of the nation's experts in police psychology. Mike's fast-paced and humorous presentation style makes him a frequently requested speaker throughout the region.

Mike is an active member in many organizations, including SIOP, SHRM, IPAC, and the Society for Police and Criminal Psychology.

In his spare time, Mike likes to make lame attempts at being athletic, cook what at times turn out to be edible meals, travel, and scuba dive. He lives in Pulaski, Virginia, with his wife, Bobbie. Mike and Bobbie have a son, Josh, who is an attorney in northern Virginia, but they continue to love him anyway.

Chapter

1

Introduction to I/O Psychology

Learning Objectives

1-1 Define I/O psychology.

1-2 Describe what I/O psychologists do.

1-3 Summarize the history of I/O psychology.

1-4 List the admissions requirements for graduate programs in I/O psychology.

1-5 Explain the importance of conducting research.

1-6 Describe how to evaluate I/O psychology research.

1-7 Differentiate various research methods.

Wouldn't it be wonderful if all employees loved their jobs so much that they couldn't wait to get to work and were so well suited and trained that their performances were outstanding? Well, this is the ultimate goal of industrial psychology. Unfortunately, not every employee will enjoy their job, and not every employee will do well on a job. In this book, you will learn the techniques developed by industrial/organizational (I/O) psychologists that lead toward the goal of a happy and productive workforce.

Before we can talk about these techniques, several areas must be discussed so that you will have the basics to help you better understand the rest of the book. This chapter has two distinct sections. The first section provides a brief overview of the field of I/O psychology; the second section discusses the research methods that will be mentioned throughout the text.

1-1 The Field of I/O Psychology

Differences Between I/O and Business Programs

Industrial/organizational psychology A branch of psychology that applies the principles of psychology to the workplace.

Perhaps the best place to begin a textbook on I/O psychology is to look at the field itself. **Industrial/organizational psychology** is a branch of psychology that applies the principles of psychology to the workplace. The purpose of I/O psychology is "to enhance the dignity and performance of human beings, and the organizations they work in, by advancing the science and knowledge of human behavior" (Rucci, 2008).

For example, principles of learning are used to develop training programs and incentive plans, principles of social psychology are used to form work groups and understand employee conflict. Principles of motivation and emotion are used to motivate and satisfy employees. The application of psychological principles is what best distinguishes I/O psychology from related fields typically taught in business colleges. Although many of the topics covered in this text are like those found in a human resource management (HRM) or organizational behavior text, the main difference between I/O psychology and business fields is that I/O psychology examines factors that affect the *people* in an organization, as opposed to the broader aspects of running an organization such as marketing channels, transportation networks, and cost accounting (Kimbrough, Durley, & Muñoz, 2005). As you can tell from the typical graduate courses listed in Table 1.1, business (MBA) programs examine such areas as accounting, economics, and marketing, whereas I/O programs focus almost exclusively on issues involving the people in an organization (Moberg & Moore, 2011).

Scientist-practitioner model A teaching model in which students are trained first to be scientists and second to be able to apply the science of their field to find solutions to real-world problems.

I/O psychology relies extensively on research, quantitative methods, and testing techniques. I/O psychologists are trained to use empirical data and statistics rather than intuition to make decisions. I/O psychologists are not clinical psychologists who happen to be in industry, and they do not conduct therapy for workers. There are psychologists working for organizations and helping employees with such problems as drug and alcohol misuse, but these are counselors rather than I/O psychologists. A factor that helps differentiate I/O psychology from other branches of psychology is the reliance on the **scientist-practitioner model**. That is, I/O psychologists act as scientists when they conduct research and as practitioners when they work with actual organizations. In addition, I/O psychologists act as scientist-practitioners when they apply research findings so the work that they perform with organizations will be of high quality and enhance an organization's effectiveness.

One reason that I/O psychology continually increases in popularity is that, perhaps more than in any other field, professionals in the field can have a positive impact on the lives of other people. To support this last statement, let us examine a typical day in the life of a typical person:

Work	8 hours
Commute to work	1 hour
Watch TV	3 hours
Sleep	8 hours
Prepare and eat meals	2 hours
Other	2 hours

With the possible exception of sleeping, people spend more time at their jobs than at any other activity in life. (And sometimes these two activities overlap!) Thus, it makes sense that people who are happy with and productive at their jobs will lead more fulfilling lives than people unhappy with their jobs. If a person is unhappy at work for

Table 1.1 Comparison of Commonly Required Courses in I/O Psychology and MBA Programs

Course	Program Type I/O (%)	Program Type MBA (%)
Research methods	90	6
Quantitative methods	82	50
Employee selection	80	0
Organizational psychology/behavior	80	48
Psychometrics/test construction	62	0
Training & development	60	2
Performance appraisal	38	2
Finance	0	94
Marketing	0	90
Corporate strategies and policies	4	82
Accounting	0	78
Information systems	0	68
Economics	0	66
Operations management	0	56
Culture/global/international business	12	42
Ethics	20	36

Source: Adapted from Moberg & Moore (2011).

eight hours a day, the residual effects of this unhappiness will affect the quality of that person's family and leisure life as well.

From a societal perspective, I/O psychologists can also improve the quality of life by increasing employee effectiveness, which reduces the cost of sold goods by improving product quality. This in turn reduces repair and replacement costs by improving organizational efficiency, which can result in decreases in inefficient activities such as waiting in line.

Thus, I/O psychology can improve the quality of life at levels equal to, and often exceeding, those of fields such as counseling psychology and medicine. So even though I/O psychologists earn a good salary, the real benefits to the field involve the positive impacts on the lives of others.

Major Fields of I/O Psychology

Though the goal of I/O psychology is to increase the productivity and well-being of employees, there are two approaches as to how this can be accomplished. The industrial approach (the "I" in I/O psychology) focuses on determining the competencies needed to perform a job, staffing the organization with employees who have those competencies, and increasing those competencies through training. The organizational approach (the "O" in I/O psychology) creates an organizational structure and culture that will motivate employees to perform well, give them the necessary information to do their jobs, and provide working conditions that are safe and result in an enjoyable and satisfying work/life environment.

Personnel Psychology

Personnel psychology The field of study that concentrates on the selection and evaluation of employees.

I/O psychologists and human resource management professionals involved in **personnel psychology** study and practice in such areas as analyzing jobs, recruiting applicants, selecting employees, determining salary levels, training employees, and evaluating employee performance. Professionals working in these areas choose existing tests or create new ones that can be used to select and promote employees. These tests are then constantly evaluated to ensure that they are both fair and valid.

Personnel psychologists also analyze jobs to obtain a complete picture of what each employee does, often assigning monetary values to each position. After obtaining complete job descriptions, professionals in personnel psychology construct performance-appraisal instruments to evaluate employee performance.

Psychologists in this area also examine various methods that can be used to train and develop employees. People within this subfield usually work in a training department of an organization and are involved in such activities as identifying the organization's training needs, developing training programs, and evaluating training success.

Organizational Psychology

Organizational psychology The field of study that investigates the behavior of employees within the context of an organization.

Psychologists involved in **organizational psychology** are concerned with the issues of leadership, job satisfaction, employee motivation, organizational communication, conflict management, organizational change, and group processes within an organization. Organizational psychologists often create and conduct surveys of employee attitudes to get ideas about what employees believe are an organization's strengths and weaknesses. Usually serving in the role of a consultant, an organizational psychologist makes recommendations on ways problem areas can be improved. For example, low job satisfaction might be improved by allowing employees to participate in making certain company decisions, and poor communication might be improved by implementing an employee suggestion system.

Organization development professionals implement organization-wide programs designed to improve employee performance. Such programs might include team building, restructuring, and employee empowerment.

Human Factors/Ergonomics

Human factors A field of study concentrating on the interaction between humans and machines.

Psychologists studying **human factors** concentrate on workplace design, human-machine interaction, ergonomics, and physical fatigue and stress. These psychologists frequently work with engineers and other technical professionals to make the workplace safer and more efficient. Sample activities in this subfield have included designing the optimal way to assemble products, designing the most comfortable chair, and investigating the optimal work schedule.

Brief History of I/O Psychology

Considering that the field of psychology itself has been around for only a relatively short time (since 1879), it is not surprising that I/O psychology has a correspondingly short history. Although various experts disagree about the precise beginning of I/O psychology, as shown in Table 1.2, it is generally thought to have started either in

Table 1.2   Important Events in I/O Psychology

Year	Event
1903	Walter Dill Scott publishes *The Theory of Advertising*
1911	Walter Dill Scott publishes *Increasing Human Efficiency in Business*
	Frederick Winslow Taylor publishes *The Principles of Scientific Management*
1913	Hugo Münsterberg publishes *Psychology and Industrial Efficiency* (German version published in 1910)
1917	*Journal of Applied Psychology first published*
1918	World War I provides I/O psychologists with first opportunity for large-scale employee testing and selection
1921	First Ph.D.s in I/O psychology awarded to Bruce Moore and Merrill Ream at Carnegie Tech
1932	First I/O text written by Morris Viteles
1933	Hawthorne studies published
1937	American Association for Applied Psychology established
1939	The Dictionary of Occupational Titles (DOT) was first published by the U.S. Employment Service
1945	Society for Industrial and Business Psychology established as Division 14 of the American Psychological Association (APA) with 130 members
1951	Marion Bills elected as the first woman president of Division 14
1960	Division 14 renamed as Society for Industrial Psychology, membership exceeds 700
1963	Equal Pay Act passed
1964	Civil Rights Act passed First issue of The Industrial-Organizational Psychologist (TIP) published
1970	Division 14 membership exceeds 1,100
1971	B. F. Skinner publishes *Beyond Freedom and Dignity*
1980	Division 14 membership exceeds 1,800
1982	Division 14 renamed Society for Industrial and Organizational Psychology (SIOP)
1986	Society for Industrial and Organizational Psychology (SIOP) holds first annual national conference separate from APA meeting
1989	Supreme Court sets conservative trend and becomes more "employer friendly"
1990	Americans with Disabilities Act passed SIOP membership exceeds 2,800
1991	Civil Rights Act of 1991 passed to overcome 1989 conservative Supreme Court decisions
1997	SIOP celebrates golden anniversary at its annual conference in St. Louis
2000	SIOP membership exceeds 5,700
2005	Office of Federal Contract Compliance Programs (OFCCP) and Equal Employment Opportunity Commission (EEOC) become more aggressive in fighting systemic discrimination
2008	The journal *Industrial and Organizational Psychology: Perspectives on Science and Practice* begins publication as an official journal of SIOP
2009	Lilly Ledbetter Fair Pay Act and Americans with Disabilities Act Amendment Act (ADAAA) passed
2010	SIOP membership exceeds 8,000; SIOP members narrowly vote to keep the name Society for Industrial Organizational Psychology rather than change the name to the Society for Organizational Psychology
2013	OFCCP issues new regulations affecting the hiring of military veterans and individuals with disabilities
2020	SIOP membership exceeds 7,500 Global COVID-19 pandemic results in a tremendous increase in employees working remotely and the SIOP conference being held virtually

1903, when Walter Dill Scott wrote *The Theory of Advertising*, in which psychology was first applied to business; in 1910, when Hugo Münsterberg wrote *Psychology and Industrial Efficiency*, which was first published in English in 1913; in 1911, when Scott wrote the book *Increasing Human Efficiency in Business* (Koppes & Pickren, 2007) or when Taylor published *The Principles of Scientific Management*, which emphasized a fourfold philosophy of management, including personnel selection and training (Van De Water, 1997). Regardless of the official starting date, I/O psychology was born in the early 1900s. In addition to Scott Taylor, and Münsterberg, pioneers in the field include James Cattell, Walter Bingham, Arthur Kornhauser, Louis Thurstone, John Watson, Marion Bills, and Lillian Gilbreth (DiClemente & Hantula, 2000; Vinchur & Koppes Bryan, 2021). Interestingly, the term "industrial psychology" was seldom used prior to World War I. Instead, the common terms for the field were "economic psychology," "business psychology," and "employment psychology" (Koppes & Pickren, 2007).

I/O psychology made its first big impact during World War I. Because of the large number of soldiers who had to be assigned to various units within the armed forces, I/O psychologists were employed to test recruits and then place them in appropriate positions. The testing was accomplished mainly through the **Army Alpha** and **Army Beta** tests of mental ability. The Alpha test was used for recruits who could read and the Beta test for recruits who could not read. The higher scoring recruits were assigned to officer training, and the lower scoring to the infantry. John Watson, who is better known as a pioneer in behaviorism, served as a major in the U.S. Army in World War I and developed perceptual and motor tests for potential pilots (DiClemente & Hantula, 2000). I/O psychologists, along with engineers such as Henry Gantt, were responsible for increasing the efficiency with which cargo ships were built, repaired, and loaded (Van De Water, 1997). While women were infrequently directly involved with World War I, after attending graduate school at the University of Chicago, Mary Holmes Steven Hayes consulted and conducted research on personnel issues on the Committee on Classification of Personnel in the Army (Koppes, 1997). I/O psychologists helped select aviators in Italy; gunners and pilots in France; and pilots, radio operators and drivers in Germany (Vinchur, 2018).

Though certainly not an I/O psychologist, inventor Thomas A. Edison understood the importance of selecting the appropriate employees for the job requirements. In 1920, Edison created a 163-item knowledge test that he administered to over 900 applicants. The test and its passing score were so difficult that only 5% of the applicants passed! You will learn more about Edison's test in the Applied Case Study at the end of Chapter 6.

Two of the most interesting figures in the early years of I/O psychology were the husband-and-wife team of Frank Gilbreth and Lillian Moller Gilbreth. The Gilbreths were among the first, if not the first, scientists to improve productivity and reduce fatigue by studying the motions used by workers. Frank began his career as a contractor and became famous for developing improvements in bricklaying that reduced the number of motions needed to lay a brick from 18 to 4½. Lillian, received her Ph.D. from Brown University in 1915—a rare achievement for a woman at that time. As a couple, they had 12 children, and the efficiency methods they used to raise their children while having busy careers were the inspiration for the book and the movie *Cheaper by the Dozen* (the 1950 version of the movie). After Frank's death in 1924 at the age of 55, Lillian continued her consulting with industry, as the Great Depression forced companies to find ways to reduce costs and be more productive. In 1935, she became a professor of management and engineering at Purdue University, the first woman to hold such a position.

During these early years, I/O psychology thrived outside of the United States. Prominent psychologists who applied psychology to problems in industry outside the United States included Jules Suter and Franziska Baumgarten-Tramer in Switzerland; Bernard Muscio and Alfred Martin in Australia; Walter Moede, William Stern, Otto

Army Alpha An intelligence test developed during World War I and used by the army for soldiers who can read.

Army Beta An intelligence test developed during World War I and used by the army for soldiers who cannot read.

Frank and Lillian Gilbreth were two pioneers in I/O psycholog.

Lipmann, and Emil Kraepelin in Germany; Jean-Marie Lahy in France; Isaak Shipil'rein in Russia; Edward Webster and Gerald Cosgrave in Canada; and Cyril Burt, Charles Myers, and Sir Frederick Bartlett in Great Brittan (Feitosa & Sim, 2021, Vinchur & Koppes Bryan 2021; Warr, 2007).

Zickar and Gibby (2021) note that the early years of I/O psychology were characterized by four themes: an emphasis on production and efficiency, an emphasis on statistical analysis, a focus on employee selection, and a balance between science and practice Frederick Taylor pioneered the use of financial incentives to increase employee job performance and productivity, as noted in his first article released in 1895, A Piece Rate System, Being a Step Toward Partial Solution of the Labor Problem (Van De Water, 1997). His efforts in studying production and efficiency throughout the years led to his nomination as president of the American Society of Mechanical Engineers (ASME) in 1906, in which he presented his 26 years of research on increasing employee productivity.

In the early years of I/O psychology, psychologists were involved in the selection process of a variety of jobs including apprentices, stenographers, streetcar drivers, tram operators, teachers, clerical and office employees, military personnel, and ammunition inspectors (Vinchur, 2021) Marion Almira Bills, who received her PhD from Bryn Mawr College and developed a proficiency for personnel selection, examined the effectiveness of selection tests and criteria used to hire stenographers through predictive validity studies. She concluded that more measures would result in a higher chance of successful personnel selection (Koppes, 1997).

In the 1930s, I/O psychology greatly expanded its scope. Until then, it had been involved primarily in improving productivity through the selection and placement of employees and the application of financial incentives. An exception to this emphasis was a chapter in a book, *Industrial Psychology*, by Morris Viteles on work motivation in which he called for the study of worker motives and attitudes (Latham & Budworth, 2021). However, later in the 1930s, when the findings from the famous **Hawthorne studies** were published, psychologists became more involved in the quality of the work environment, as well as the attitudes of employees. The Hawthorne studies, which were conducted at the Hawthorne plant of the Western Electric Company in the United States demonstrated that employee behavior was complex and that the interpersonal interactions between managers and employees played a tremendous role in employee behavior. The Hawthorne studies were initially designed to investigate such issues as the effects of lighting levels, work schedules, wages, temperature, and rest breaks on employee performance.

Much to the surprise of the researchers, the actual work conditions did not affect productivity in the predicted manner. That is, there were times when productivity improved after work conditions were made worse, and times when productivity decreased after work conditions were made better. After interviewing employees and studying the matter further, the researchers realized that employees changed their behavior and became more productive *because* they were being studied and received attention from their managers, a condition that is now commonly referred to as the **Hawthorne effect.** Additionally, the six employees in the small test group received incentives for productivity and were protected from layoffs, advantages that the other employees did not receive (Highhouse, 2021). Perhaps the major contribution of the Hawthorne studies was that it inspired psychologists to increase their focus on human relations in the workplace and to explore the effects of employee attitudes (Olson, Verley, Santos, & Salas, 2004).

The 1940s brought World War II and with it, the extensive use of I/O psychologists to support the war effort, especially in Germany and Great Britain. In addition to cognitive ability and aptitude tests, I/O psychologists began using such selection methods as life history, interviews, and leaderless group discussions (Vinchur, 2021). Interest in identifying effective leaders, especially in the military, and finding ways to motivate employees beyond the use of financial incentives also increased during this decade (Latham & Budworth, 2021; Zaccaro, Day, & Hedrick, 2021) Training methods, including job instructional training, were also emphasized greatly during this time period, and companies and university-based centers began establishing R&D departments for research and training (Katzell & Austin, 1992).

The 1950s were associated with further advancements in employee selection, most importantly the assessment center and biodata. Interviews and application blank data were the most popular selection methods (Vinchur, 2021). These methods are discussed in detail in Chapters 4 and 5. New theories and subsequent research on employee motivation and satisfaction continued to increase in the 1950s.

The 1960s were characterized by the passage of several major pieces of civil rights legislation, which are discussed in Chapter 3. These laws focused the attention of HR professionals on developing fair selection techniques. As a result, the need for I/O psychologists greatly increased. The 1960s were also characterized using sensitivity training and T-groups (laboratory training groups) for managers (Carson, Lanier, Carson, & Guidry, 2000).

The 1970s brought great strides in the understanding of many organizational psychology issues that involved employee satisfaction and motivation. The decade also saw the development of many theories about employee behavior in organizations. B. F. Skinner's (1971) *Beyond Freedom and Dignity* resulted in the increased use of behavior-modification techniques in organizations. The study of goal setting on employee behavior was also a major component of the 1970s (Latham & Budworth, 2021).

The 1980s and 1990s brought four major changes to I/O psychology. The first involved an increased use of fairly sophisticated statistical techniques and methods of

Hawthorne studies A series of studies, conducted at the Western Electric plant in Hawthorne, Illinois, that have come to represent any change in behavior when people react to a change in the environment.

Hawthorne effect When employees change their behavior due solely to the fact that they are receiving attention or are being observed.

analysis. This change is evident if one compares journal articles written in the 1960s with those written since 1980. More recent articles use such complex statistical techniques as path analysis, structural equation modeling, meta-analysis, hierarchical linear modeling (HLM), multivariate analysis of variance (MANOVA), and causal modeling. Prior to the 1970s, simpler statistical techniques such as t-tests and analysis of variance (ANOVA) were used (unless you have taken a statistics course, these methods probably are not familiar to you). This reliance on statistics explains why students enrolled in an I/O psychology doctoral program take at least five statistics courses as part of their education.

A second change concerned a new interest in the application of cognitive psychology to industry. For example, articles written about performance appraisal in the 1970s primarily described and tested new methods for evaluating employee performance. In the 1980s and early 1990s, however, many articles approached the performance appraisal issue by examining the thought process used by managers when they conduct such appraisals.

The third change was the increased interest in occupational health psychology, a field that applies psychological principles to improve, "the quality of work-life and promoting the safety, health, and well-being of people at work" (Hammer & Brady, 2021).

The final major change in the 1980s and 1990s came about when I/O psychologists took a renewed interest in developing methods to select employees. In the 1960s and 1970s, the courts were still interpreting the major civil rights acts of the early 1960s, with the result that I/O psychologists took a cautious approach in selecting employees. By the mid-1980s, however, the courts became less strict, and a wider variety of selection instruments was developed and used. Examples of these instruments include cognitive ability tests, personality tests, biodata, and structured interviews. Other changes during the 1980s and 1990s that had significant I/O psychology–related effects included massive organizational downsizing, greater concern for diversity and gender issues, an increasing older population in the workforce, increased concern about the effects of stress, and the increased emphasis on such organizational development interventions as total quality management (TQM), reengineering, and employee empowerment.

In the 2000s, perhaps the greatest influence on I/O psychology is the rapid advances in technology. Many tests and surveys are now administered online, employers recruit and screen applicants online; job seekers use such social media outlets as Twitter, LinkedIn, and Facebook to find jobs; I/O psychologists increasingly focus on "big data" and artificial intelligence, employees are being trained and meetings are being held virtually rather than in person.

Another important factor impacting I/O psychology is the changing demographic makeup of the workforce. Women are increasingly entering the workforce and taking on managerial roles; Hispanics and Latino/as are now the largest underrepresented groups in the United States; Asian Americans are the fastest-growing segment of the U.S. population; and an increasing number of workers, vendors, and customers have English as their second language. Thus, diversity and inclusion issues will continue to be an important factor in the workplace.

The global economy is also affecting the role of I/O psychology. As many manufacturing jobs are shifted to developing countries with lower wages, there will be an increased emphasis on service jobs requiring human relations skills. As an increasing number of employees work in other countries (as expatriates) and as rates of immigration (both documented and undocumented) increase, efforts must keep pace to understand various cultures, and training must be conducted so that employees and managers can successfully work not only in other countries, but at home with expatriates from other countries.

Other factors that are impacting I/O psychology, especially due to the global COVID-19 pandemic, include high unemployment rates, movements toward flexible work schedules, family-friendly work policies, accommodation of an increasing number of employees with childcare and older adult-care responsibilities, flatter organizational structures with fewer management levels, population shifts from urban to suburban locations, and increasing costs of health-care benefits. In addition, potential changes in the retirement age for Social Security may result in employees working into their late sixties.

The long-term effects of the COVID-19 global pandemic are yet to be determined. Many employees liked working from home and organizations realized that working virtually has advantages for both the employee and the organization.

Employment of I/O Psychologists

It is useful to examine some of the broad areas in which I/O psychologists work. As shown in Table 1.3, I/O psychologists typically work in one of four settings: colleges and universities, consulting firms, the private sector, and the public sector. As one might expect, I/O psychologists who work at colleges and universities typically teach and conduct research, although some work as administrators (e.g., deans, provosts, vice presidents).

I/O psychologists who work in consulting firms help a wide variety of organizations become more productive by helping them select a high quality and diverse workforce, designing systems that will motivate employees while treating them fairly, creating efficient and effective training plans for employees, and ensuring that organizations treat applicants and employees in a legal and ethical manner. Consulting firms range in size from one-person organizations to large consulting firms employing hundreds of consultants. Some consulting firms specialize in one area of I/O psychology (e.g., employee selection, diversity, attitude surveys), whereas others offer a range of services.

I/O psychologists who work in the private and public sectors perform similar duties as consultants, but they do so in vastly different environments. I/O psychologists who work in the private sector work for a single company such as IBM, Microsoft, and FedEx, whereas consultants work with many companies. I/O psychologists in the public sector work for a local, state, or federal government agency. Though the private sector historically paid more than the public sector, many employees believe the higher job stability of the public sector offsets the potential for lower pay. Though master's- and doctoral-level graduates can be found in all employment areas, Ph.D.s are much more likely to be employed in an academic setting; master's-level graduates are more often employed as HR generalists, data analysts, trainers, and compensation analysts.

As you can tell by the job titles listed in Table 1.4, there are many careers in I/O psychology, including entry-level jobs to presidents and CEOs of large companies. Whether one wants to work in the public or private sector, work with data or work with people, spend the day talking, writing, or analyzing, there is some job or the

Table 1.3   Employment Settings of I/O Psychologists

| | **Highest Degree Obtained** | |
Employment Setting	**M.A.**	**Ph.D.**
Education	3%	45%
Private sector	76%	43%
Public sector	8%	7%
Nonprofit	12%	6%

Source: SIOP (2020).

Table 1.4 Job Titles of I/O Psychologists

Chairman and CEO	Industrial-organizational psychologist
City manager	Manager of leadership and development
Compensation analyst	Personnel manager
Compensation manager	President
Consultant	Professor
Data scientist	Recruiter
Director of organizational effectiveness	Research analyst
Director of training and development	Research scientist
Director of workforce planning	Research psychologist
Director of assessment and selection	Senior partner
EEO/Diversity specialist	Staffing manager
Employee relations manager	Trainer
HR director	Training coordinator
HR generalist	Training manager
HR representative	Vice president for human resources
HR specialist	Vice president for organizational development
HR supervisor	

other in I/O psychology that fits everyone. Given such great opportunities, it is not surprising that the Bureau of Labor Statistics released data that job opportunities for I/O psychologists are estimated to grow by 12.8% from 2018 to 2028.

As of 2020, the median salary was $88,900 for master's-level positions and $125,000 for doctoral-level positions (SIOP, 2020). Current information about I/O salaries can be found at the website of the Society for Industrial and Organizational Psychology (SIOP) at www.siop.org.

Educational Requirements and Types of Programs

Although people with bachelor's degrees can find employment in the HRM field, having a master's or doctoral degree certainly increases employment and career opportunities. Obtaining a master's degree in I/O psychology takes between one and two years after the completion of a bachelor's degree. Admission requirements vary greatly from school to school, but an undergraduate grade point average (GPA) of at least 3.0 and a score of 300 on the **Graduate Record Exam (GRE)**, which is the graduate school version of the Scholastic Aptitude Test, or SAT, that students in the United States typically take after high school, are not uncommon prerequisites (Nagy, Schroeder, & Aamodt, 2005). Advice for getting into graduate school can be found in the Career Workshop Box.

Graduate Record Exam (GRE) A standardized admission test required by most psychology graduate schools.

Types of Graduate Programs

Master's degree programs come in two varieties: those that are part of a Ph.D. program and those that terminate at the master's degree. Schools with **terminal master's degree programs** do not have Ph.D. programs, and a master's degree is the highest that can be earned at such schools. Schools with doctoral programs offer both master's degrees and Ph.D.s. Terminal programs are best suited for students wanting an applied HR position in

Terminal master's degree programs Graduate programs that offer a master's degree but not a Ph.D.

an organization (although many students in terminal degree programs go on to earn their doctorates at other universities). These programs usually have less stringent entrance requirements and provide more financial aid and individual attention to master's students than do Ph.D. programs. Doctoral programs, on the other hand, usually have more well-known faculty members and better facilities and research funding. Doctoral programs are best suited for students who eventually want to teach, do research, or consult.

Master's Programs.   Completion of most master's programs requires about 40 hours of graduate coursework (Nagy et al., 2005). Although 15 to 18 hours is considered a full undergraduate semester load, 9 to 12 hours is considered a full graduate load. In addition to coursework, many programs require a student to complete a thesis, which is usually an original research work created and conducted by the student. The thesis is completed in the second year of graduate school.

Most programs also allow the student to complete an **internship** or **practicum** with an organization. These internship requirements vary by program. Depending on the university, students may work 10 hours per week at an organization during their last semester of graduate school, do their internships in the summer between their first and second years, or take a semester off to work full time with an organization.

Finally, most programs require a student to pass a comprehensive oral and/or written examination before graduation. These exams usually are taken during the final semester and cover material from all of the courses taken during the graduate program.

Internship A situation in which a student works for an organization, either for pay or as a volunteer, to receive practical work experience.

Practicum A paid or unpaid position with an organization that gives a student practical work experience.

Career Workshop   Getting into Graduate School

Although different graduate programs often emphasize different entrance requirements, most place some weight on GRE scores, GPA, letters of recommendation, and previous research or professional experience. With this in mind, following the advice below should increase your chances of being selected for a graduate program.

- Take extra mathematics and English courses. The main GRE test consists of three sections: quantitative reasoning, verbal reasoning, and analytical writing. There is also a separate test tapping knowledge of psychology that is required by some psychology graduate programs. The quantitative reasoning portion requires knowledge of algebra, geometry, and some trigonometry. Thus, often the only way to do well on this section is to take extra courses in these subjects. Taking English courses in reading comprehension, writing, and vocabulary will help your score on the verbal reasoning and analytical writing sections. It is important to understand that the GRE is a test of knowledge, not intelligence. Thus, with extra coursework, you can improve your scores. as it may have been a while since you have studied these topics.
- Study for your GRE and get a good night's sleep before you take the test. You may not be able to learn much new material by studying, but you can at least refresh your memory about material that you have already learned but may have forgotten. Remember that your GRE score is an

important factor that helps determine your admission to graduate program so prepare for it accordingly.

- Take at least one psychology course in each of the areas of statistics, experimental methods, abnormal psychology, personality, developmental psychology, social psychology, physiological psychology, sensation and perception, learning, and cognitive psychology; each area is covered in the GRE's psychology portion.
- Make sure that you have at least three people who can write positive letters of recommendation for you, at least one of which should be from a professor (Stone & Sanders, 2020). Getting an A in a professor's class is not enough to expect a good letter that will carry weight with an admissions committee. Let the professors get to know you as both student and person. Edited to specify undergraduate thesis. You might want to consider completing an undergraduate thesis through an independent study research project. Most professors allow undergraduate students to join their research lab and undertake a project of their own. This not only demonstrates to graduate programs that you have proficiency and expertise in research, but also allows your undergraduate professor to get to know you professionally, resulting in better and more complete letters of recommendation.
- Get involved! Conduct independent research projects, join professional clubs, get an internship related to your field— anything to demonstrate your desire to be a professional.

Completing a master's degree program in I/O psychology is tough, but it can lead to excellent employment and professional benefits.

Doctoral Programs.   Obtaining a Ph.D. is more difficult than obtaining a master's, with the typical doctoral program taking five years to complete (Rentsch, Lowenberg, Barnes-Farrell, & Menard, 1997). The first two years of a doctoral program involve taking a wide variety of courses in psychology. In most programs, the student does not concentrate on I/O courses until the third and fourth years. In addition to a thesis, a student working toward a Ph.D. must complete a **dissertation.** No formal definition distinguishes a thesis from a dissertation. The major differences, however, are that the dissertation is broader in scope, longer, and requires more original and independent effort than the thesis (Riddle & Foster, 1997). Doctoral programs also involve a series of comprehensive exams that are similar to, but more extensive than, the exams taken in a master's program. Information on programs is available from the SIOP at www.siop.org.

Dissertation A formal research paper required of most doctoral students to graduate.

1-2 Research in I/O Psychology

Now that you have a good idea about the field of I/O psychology, it is time to learn the essentials of one of the foundations of the upcoming chapters: research. This section does not provide an in-depth discussion of research techniques and procedures, but it gives you enough information so that you can understand the method that was used when a study is mentioned in the text.

Why Conduct Research?

Though you might not go on to careers as a researcher, understanding research and statistics is important for several reasons.

Answering Questions and Making Decisions

As mentioned earlier in the chapter, one of the characteristics of I/O psychology is its extensive use of research and statistics. Although there are many reasons for this reliance on research, the most important is that research ultimately saves organizations money. To many of you, this last statement may seem a bit insensitive. Keep in mind, however, that for most organizations, the most important thing is the bottom line. If I/O psychologists are not able to save the company considerably more money than it pays for their salary and expenses, they will be without a job.

These monetary savings can result from many factors, including increased employee satisfaction, increased productivity, and fewer accidents. There are a multitude of ways that organizations have deployed I/O psychologists to the workplace to save money. An excellent example of this is from a study conducted by IBM in 2013, which revealed the importance of training and development in an organization. The study found that employees are 62% more likely to stay if they have received adequate training. With employee turnover and attrition costing organizations up to a trillion dollars annually according to a Gallup study, research in the workplace has been proven to be a powerful tool in saving organizations from spending more money than needed.

Research and Everyday Life

Research confronts us on an almost daily basis, both at home and on the job. As a student, you will encounter research throughout this and other courses. As a professional, you will receive advertisements and sales pitches containing references to research supporting a particular product. At home, you read the results of political polls and are bombarded with advertisements trumpeting the effectiveness of weight loss techniques or claiming that "nine out of ten dentists" recommend a product. Understanding research helps you to critically listen and analyze results of these studies to make more intelligent decisions. After all, you would hate to buy a fitness product based on the results of poorly conducted research!

When I was an undergraduate at Pepperdine University in Malibu, California, the students attempted to hold the first dance ever at the university. Until this point, dancing was prohibited, and the students wanted the prohibition removed. The dance proposal came under heavy attack by the church sponsoring the university as well as by several administrators. An opponent of the dance proposal wrote a letter to the school newspaper citing research "that in a study of Catholic confessionals, nine out of ten fallen women had their downfall on the dance floor." When confronted with this devastating piece of research, we pulled out our trusty experimental psychology books and, using our finely honed research skills, challenged the validity of the study on such grounds as the poorly defined dependent variable (What is a fallen woman?), the sample size (How many women fell?), and the question of whether the study actually existed (there is no way the Catholic Church would allow a study of confessionals). After our impressive critique, the administration gave in, and we were allowed to hold our dance off of campus but advertise it on campus. If you consider allowing 200 students with no rhythm to dance as a victory, then our superior knowledge of research made us victors.

It's a crazy story. But the fact that people actually used such research to support their point underscores the importance of understanding research.

Common Sense Is Often Wrong

Often, there is a temptation not to conduct research because the answer to a question is "common sense." Unfortunately, common sense is not so common and is often wrong. Until the end of the fifteenth century, it was common sense that the world was flat and that a person sailing toward the horizon would fall off the planet. Until late in twentieth century, common sense said that women employees could not perform as well as men. In other words, many of our commonsense policies have been, and continue to be, wrong.

As a good example, imagine taking a multiple-choice test. After finishing the test, you go back and read question 32 but can't decide if you should stick with your original response of "b" or change it to "c." What would you do? Most students respond with what they have always been told: *Stick with your first answer.* If you stuck with this piece of common advice, you probably would miss the question. Thirty-three studies investigating this question concluded that contrary to common sense, the majority of the time, an answer will be changed from wrong to right (Kruger, Wirtz, & Miller, 2005). Another victory for research over common sense!

Considerations in Conducting Research
Ideas, Hypotheses, and Theories

The first step in conducting research is to decide *what to research*. Though the majority of I/O psychology research is conducted to test the accuracy of theories, many research ideas stem from a person starting a sentence with "I wonder. . . ." For example, a manager might say, "I wonder why some of my employees can't get to work on time"; an employee might say, "I wonder if I could assemble more parts if my chair were higher"; or a supervisor might say, "I wonder which of my employees is the best to promote." All three seem to be ordinary questions, but each is just as valid and important in research as those asked by a professor in a university. Thus, everyone is a researcher at heart, and conducting some form of research to answer a question will undoubtedly lead to a better answer than could be obtained by guesswork alone.

Once a question has been asked, the next step is to form a **hypothesis**—an educated prediction about the answer to a question. This prediction is usually based on a **theory,** previous research, or logic. For example, as shown in Figure 1.1, a researcher is curious about the effect of noise on employee performance (the question) and believes that high levels of noise will result in decreased performance (the hypothesis). The prediction is based on the theory that distracting events reduce the ability to concentrate. To find out if the hypothesis is correct, the researcher would need to conduct a study.

If the results support the hypothesis, it becomes important to test the theory. In psychology, there are often competing theories that predict the same outcome, but for different reasons. Take the situation depicted in Figure 1.2 as an example. An I/O psychologist wants to know which method of recruiting employees is best. The psychologist predicts that employee referrals will result in longer employee tenure (employees staying with the company) than will the other recruitment methods.

Though they are sure about their hypothesis, they are not sure about the reason, as there are four possible theories or explanations for the hypothesis:

1. Applicants referred by a current employee will stay with the company longer because they were given an accurate picture of the job and the company by the person telling them about the job (realistic job preview theory).
2. The personalities of applicants using employee referrals are different than the personalities of applicants using other methods to find jobs (differential recruitment-source theory).

Hypothesis An educated prediction about the answer to a research question.

Theory A systematic set of assumptions regarding the cause and nature of behavior.

Figure 1.1
Hypothesis Example 1

Does all this noise affect my employees' performance?	High levels of noise will increase the number of errors made in assembling electronic components.	Noise causes a distraction, making it difficult to concentrate.
Idea or question	*Hypothesis or prediction*	*Theory or explanation*
	What will happen	**Why it will happen**

Figure 1.2
Hypothesis Example 2

What employee recruitment source is best?	Employee referrals will result in employees who stay with the company longer than will the other recruitment methods.	1. Realistic job preview theory 2. Differential recruitment-source theory 3. Personality similarity theory 4. Socialization theory
Idea or question	*Hypothesis or prediction*	*Theory or explanation*
	What will happen	**Why it will happen**

3. Friends have similar personalities; thus, if one person has the type of personality that makes them want to stay with their current job, their friend should also like the job in question (personality similarity theory).
4. Employees who know someone in a workplace are more quickly absorbed into the informal system, receive coaching, and have their social needs met (socialization theory).

Thus, even though a study might support a hypothesis, it is still important to determine *why* the hypothesis is true. In this example, it would be necessary to conduct further studies to determine which of the four theories, if any, best explains the results. This is important because our ability to understand and use the best theory allows us to develop new methods to improve productivity in the workplace. In this example, if the first theory were true, we would give every applicant a realistic job preview. If the third theory were true, we would encourage current successful employees to recruit their friends.

At times, forming a hypothesis can be difficult. In some cases, no previous research has been conducted or theory proposed that would suggest a clear hypothesis about the answer to a question. For example, a student of mine wanted to see if personality was related to handwriting neatness. They couldn't find any research on handwriting neatness, much less on the relationship between personality and handwriting. There were also no theories or logical reason to predict what types of personalities would write a particular way. So, the researcher conducted an *exploratory study* without a hypothesis—a practice that is not uncommon but is viewed as just the first step by scientists. If exploratory studies are used, follow-up studies should then be conducted to confirm the results of the exploratory study.

In other cases, it is difficult to form a hypothesis because a prediction could go either way. For example, another of my students was curious about whether a recommendation letter written by an important person (such as a senator) would be more influential than one written by a professor (Hey, I thought professors were important!). The student had trouble forming a hypothesis because there were as many reasons that a reference by an important person would be more influential as there were reasons that such a reference would be less influential.

At times, a hypothesis may not be supported by a study even though the logic and theory behind it is correct. Often, a poor research design is the culprit. Other times, it is because the topic is more complicated than originally thought. When studying a topic, psychologists wish for simple answers. Unfortunately, most situations in life are not simple. For example, psychologists have been trying for years to understand aggression and violence. They have postulated many theories for why people are violent: genetics, brain abnormalities, learning, and frustration, to name a few. Some studies support these reasons, but others don't. Why the lack of consistency? Because no one theory by itself is the answer. Each of the theories is partially true in that each explains violence in certain people under certain circumstances. Furthermore, violent behavior may be the result of a combination of several factors, each of which by itself will not result in violence.

Confused? I hope not. The purpose of the preceding discussion is to show you the complexity of research. At times, many theories may explain a particular behavior. At other times, behavior can be predicted, but the reason for the behavior may not be known. At still other times, we have questions but can't predict what the answer will be. This complexity of life is what makes research fun.

Literature Reviews

Once a research idea has been created, the next step is to search the literature for similar research. This search is important because if the question you are interested in answering has already been researched in 20 studies, it is probably not necessary for you to conduct a new study. As a graduate student, it took me a while to realize that most of my research ideas that were "so brilliant, no one else could have thought of them" had already been conducted several times over. I guess the moral of this story is, don't forget about your university library, even after you have finished school. I would venture to say that most of the questions you will have can be answered by a quick visit to the library website or a thorough online search; it is not necessary, or smart, to constantly reinvent the wheel.

Even if your specific question has not been researched before, the probability is high that similar forms of research have been conducted. This research is useful even though it does not directly answer your question, because it can provide some good ideas on how to conduct your study.

Literature reviews can be conducted in many ways, the most common of which are using such electronic databases as *PsycINFO* and *Academic Search Complete*, browsing through journals, searching the reference sections of related articles, and asking other researchers (Tubré, Bly, Edwards, Pritchard, & Simoneaux, 2001).

When reviewing the literature, you are likely to encounter four types of periodicals: journals, **bridge publications**, trade magazines (listed in Table 1.5), and magazines. **Journals** consist of articles written by researchers directly reporting the results of a study. Journals can be difficult to read (and boring) but are the best source of unbiased and accurate, peer-reviewed information about a topic. The leading journals in I/O psychology include the *Journal of Applied Psychology, Journal of Business and Psychology, Industrial and Organizational Psychology, Personnel Psychology, Journal of Occupational Health Psychology, and Journal of Organizational Behavior* (Landers, 2018).

Bridge publications are designed to "bridge the gap" between academia and the applied world. Articles in these publications are usually written by professors about a topic of interest to practitioners, but they are not as formal or statistically complex as articles in journals. Examples of bridge publications relevant to I/O psychology are *Academy of Management Executive, Harvard Business Review*, and *Organizational Dynamics.*

Trade magazines contain articles usually written by professional writers who have developed expertise in a given field. The main audience for trade magazines is practitioners in the field. Trade magazines present the research on a topic in an easy-to-understand format; however, the articles in these publications do not cover all the research on a topic and can be somewhat biased. *HR Magazine* and *Training* are examples of I/O-related trade magazines.

You may already be familiar with **magazines** such as *People, Time*, and *Cat Fancy.* These periodicals are designed firstly to entertain, and then to inform. Magazines are good sources of ideas but terrible sources to use in support of a scientific hypothesis. Magazine articles are often written by professional writers who do not have training in the topic and thus little expertise in what they are writing about. As a result, the "scientific" information in magazines is often wrong.

As most of you have already discovered, the Internet contains a wealth of information on just about every topic. As useful as online research is, a word of caution

Bridge publication A publication with the goal of bridging the gap between the research conducted by academics and the practical needs of practitioners.

Journals A written collection of articles describing the methods and results of new research.

Trade magazines A collection of articles for those "in the biz," about related professional topics, seldom directly reporting the methods and results of new research.

Magazines An unscientific collection of articles about a wide range of topics.

Table 1.5   List of I/O Psychology Periodicals

Journals

Academy of Management Journal

Academy of Management Review

Administrative Science Quarterly

Applied Ergonomics

Applied H.R.M. Research

Applied Psychological Measurement

Applied Psychology: An International Review

Ergonomics

Human Factors

Human Performance

Industrial and Organizational Psychology: Perspectives on Science and Practice

International Journal of Selection and Assessment

International Journal of Training and Development

Journal of Applied Psychology

Journal of Applied Social Psychology

Journal of Business and Psychology

Journal of Consulting Psychology: Practice & Research

Journal of Management

Journal of Occupational Health Psychology

Journal of Organizational Behavior

Journal of Personnel Psychology

Journal of Vocational Behavior

Organizational Behavior and Human Decision Processes

Personnel Assessment and Decisions

Personnel Psychology

Personnel Review

Public Personnel Management

South African Journal of Industrial Psychology

Bridge Publications

Academy of Management Executive

Harvard Business Review

Organizational Dynamics

The Psychologist Manager Journal

Trade Magazines

Diversity Executive

HR Magazine

Personnel

Training

T+D Magazine (Training plus Development Magazine)

---

is in order. There is no review of information placed online to ensure that it is accurate. For example, I was once involved with a project in which we were trying to profile the people who were setting off church fires across the United States. Because our first step was to get a list of church fires, we searched online and found three webpages on church burnings. One was from *USA Today* and had a rather complete listing of church burnings, one was from a left-wing group, and the other was from a right-wing group. As you can imagine, the left- and right-wing pages listed only churches that confirmed their hypotheses about why the churches were burned. Had we used only one of these webpages, we would have made an inaccurate profile.

A problem with relying on secondary sources such as the Internet is that one cannot be sure if the information in a secondary source accurately reflects the information in the primary source. In the field of psychology, two excellent examples of this lack of accuracy are the use of the "little Albert" story to demonstrate the role of classical conditioning in learning phobias and the use of the Kitty Genovese story to demonstrate the lack of bystander intervention. In reviews of the accuracy of textbook information, Harris (1979) found many errors in the secondary accounts of little Albert as did Manning, Levine, and Collins (2007) with what really happened to Kitty Genovese. For example, whereas Harris (1979) found that two texts indicated little Albert was conditioned to fear a rabbit rather than a rat, many texts incorrectly included such postconditioning stimuli as a teddy bear, a white furry glove, a fur pelt, a cat, and Albert's aunt and three texts described how Watson removed little Albert's fear of the rat, although no such reconditioning was actually done.

Manning and her colleagues (2007) compared the myth of the attack on Genovese to what actually happened and found numerous discrepancies between the story and reality. For example, most textbooks as well as an early newspaper article mention the 38 witnesses who saw the attack yet did nothing to help. Not only is there no evidence that there were 38 eyewitnesses, but there is evidence that at least two of the witnesses took action and called the police.

The Location of the Study

Once a research idea has been created and a hypothesis has been formed, you must decide whether to conduct the study in the laboratory or in the field.

Laboratory Research.   Often when one hears the word *research*, the first thing that comes to mind is an experimenter in a white coat running subjects in a basement laboratory. Few experimenters actually wear white coats, but 32% of I/O psychology research is conducted in a laboratory (Roch, 2008). Usually, this is done at a university, but research is also conducted in such organizations as AT&T, the U.S. Office of Personnel Management, and Microsoft.

One disadvantage of **laboratory research** is **external validity,** or **generalizability,** of results to organizations in the "real world." An example of this issue involves research about employee selection methods. It is not uncommon in such research for subjects to view a résumé or a video of an interview and make a judgment about a hypothetical applicant. The problem: Is the situation similar enough to actual employment decisions made in the real world, or is the laboratory environment so controlled and hypothetical that the results will not generalize to situations outside of the laboratory? Although the answers to these questions have not been resolved, research is often conducted in laboratories because researchers can control many variables that are not of interest in the study, leading to more conclusive results.

Field Research.   Another location for research is away from the laboratory and out in the "field," which could be the assembly line of an automotive plant, the secretarial pool of a large insurance company, or the interviewing room at a personnel agency. **Field research** has a problem opposite to that of laboratory research. What field research obviously gains in external validity it loses in control of extraneous variables that are not of interest to the researcher (*internal validity*).

Does the location of a study make a difference? It can. A meta-analysis by Reichard and Avolio (2005) found that leadership training was more effective in laboratory studies than in field studies and Gordon and Arvey (2004) found that age bias was stronger in laboratory settings than in field settings. In general, however, a meta-analysis concluded that in I/O psychology, laboratory studies and field studies tend to show similar findings (Mitchell, 2012).

Field research can provide researchers with an ethical dilemma. Psychologists require that subjects participate in studies of their own free will—a concept called **informed consent.** In laboratory studies, informed consent is seldom an issue because potential subjects are told the nature and purpose of a study, their right to decline participation or withdraw from participation, the risks and benefits of participating, limits of confidentiality, and who they can contact with questions (Salkind, 2019). They are then asked to sign an informed consent form indicating that they understand their rights as subjects and have chosen to voluntarily participate.

Laboratory research Research that is conducted in a laboratory setting that can be controlled more easily than research conducted in a field setting.

External validity The extent to which research results can be expected to hold true outside the specific setting in which they were obtained.

Generalizability Like external validity, the extent to which research results hold true outside the specific setting in which they were obtained.

Field research Research conducted in a natural setting as opposed to a laboratory.

Informed consent The formal process by which subjects give permission to be included in a study.

In field studies, however, obtaining informed consent can not only be difficult but change the way people behave.

For example, suppose we think that making a supervisor's office more pleasant looking will increase the number of employees who visit the supervisor's office. After decorating five supervisors' offices with plants and paintings and making five other supervisors' offices look messy and cold, we use a video camera to record the number of office visitors. Would the results of our study be affected if we told our employees that they were going to be part of a study? Probably so.

Based on our ethical guidelines, informed consent can be waived only when the research involves minimal risk to the participants, the waiver will not adversely affect the rights of the participants, and the research could not be carried out without the waiver (Ilgen & Bell, 2001a).

When studies involve negative consequences for a subject, as would be the case if we subjected employees to intense heat to study the effects of temperature, informed consent can be waived only if the importance of the study outweighs the negative consequences. Universities have **institutional review boards** to monitor research to ensure ethical treatment of research participants. These review boards pay close attention to *confidentiality*. Because the data collected in research can be of a sensitive nature (e.g., performance ratings, salaries, test scores), researchers ensure confidentiality by using subject ID numbers rather than names and avoiding discussion of individual participants.

Ilgen and Bell (2001b) explored whether authors in industrial and organizational psychology journals believed that their studies necessitated a review by the institutional review board. Interestingly, this study resulted in 68% of the authors responding "no", and ultimately only 44% reported that they did, in fact, submit their research plans to institutional review boards. The authors of this study gave several reasons for the percentage of institutional review board submissions, including confusion about exactly what constituted as research to be reviewed, and a lack of established professional relationship between researchers and their institutional review boards.

The Research Method to Be Used

After deciding the location for the research, the researcher must determine which type of research method to use. The choices include experiments, quasi-experiments, archival research, observations, surveys, and meta-analyses.

Experiments.   As you might recall from your general psychology course, the experimental method is the most powerful of all research methods because it is the only one that can determine **cause-and-effect relationships.** Thus, if it is important to know whether one variable produces or causes another variable to change, then the **experiment** is the only method that should be used.

Two characteristics define an experiment: (1) **manipulation** of one or more independent variables and (2) random assignment of subjects to experimental and control conditions. If either of these characteristics is missing, a research project cannot be called an experiment; instead, it is called a *quasi-experiment*, a *study*, a *survey*, or an *investigation*.

In an experiment, the researcher intentionally manipulates one or more aspects of the question of interest, called the **independent variable,** and measures the changes that occur because of that manipulation, called the **dependent variable.** For example, as shown in Table 1.6, a researcher might randomly assign 100 employees to receive customer service training and 100 employees to receive no training. Following the training program, the researcher looks at the change in customer spending. In this example, training is the independent variable (what was manipulated), and customer spending is the dependent variable (what was expected to change because of the

Institutional review boards A committee designated to ensure the ethical treatment of research subjects.

Cause-and-effect relationships The result of a well-controlled experiment about which the researcher can confidently state that the independent variable caused the change in the dependent variable.

Experiment A type of research study in which the independent variable is manipulated by the experimenter.

Manipulation The alteration of a variable by an experimenter in expectation that the alteration will result in a change in the dependent variable.

Independent variable The manipulated variable in an experiment.

Dependent variable The measure of behavior that is expected to change as a result of changes in the independent variable.

Table 1.6   Example of an Experimental Design

Received Customer Service Training in September	Average Customer Sales per Employee		
	August	**October**	**Change**
Yes	$3,200	$4,700	$1,500
No	$3,100	$3,500	$ 400

independent variable). The employees who received the training are collectively called the **experimental group,** and the employees who did not receive the training are collectively called the **control group.**

Suppose we were interested in finding out whether applicants who include a cover letter with a résumé have a better chance of being hired than applicants who don't include a cover letter. We could study this issue by observing job applicants at a specific company and comparing the hiring rates of applicants who included a cover letter with the hiring rates of those that did not include a cover letter. We might find that a higher percentage of applicants who included a cover letter were hired than those that did not, but we could not conclude that including the cover letter *caused* the higher rate of being hired; something other than the cover letter may be at work. Perhaps applicants who include a cover letter are more conscientious than those who do not, and it is actually the higher level of conscientiousness that increased their chances of being hired. Remember that correlation does not necessarily equal causation.

Now if we want to determine that cover letters influence job offers (and thus, determine a causal relationship), we must manipulate the variable of interest and hold all other variables as constant as possible. How could we turn this into an experiment? Let us take 100 people and randomly assign 50 of them to include a cover letter and assign the other 50 to not include a cover letter with their resume. Each subject then goes through an interview with an HR director. Afterward, we compare the hiring recommendation of our two groups. In this case, the independent variable is the inclusion of a cover letter and the dependent variable is the hiring recommendation.

Even though this particular research design is not very sophisticated and has some problems (Can you spot them?), the fact that we manipulated whether the applicant included a cover letter gives us greater confidence that the cover letter was the cause of the hiring decision. Even though the results of experiments provide more confidence regarding cause-and-effect relationships, ethical and practical considerations do not always make experimental designs possible.

Suppose we wish to study the effect of loud noise on worker performance. To make this an experimental design, we could have 50 subjects work on an assembly line while being subjected to very loud noise and 50 subjects work on an assembly line with no noise. Two months later, we compare the productivity of the two groups. But what is wrong with this study? In addition to having lower productivity, the high-noise group now has poorer hearing—not a very ethical-sounding experiment (yes, the pun *was* intended).

Quasi-Experiments.   Even though researchers prefer to use experiments, it is not always possible. **Quasi-experiments** are then used. As an example, let's go back to our noise study. Because we cannot manipulate the level of noise, we will instead test the noise level of 100 manufacturing plants and compare the average productivity of plants with lower noise levels with that of plants with higher noise levels. As you can easily notice, this is not as good a research design as the unethical experiment that we created earlier. There are too many variables other than noise that could account for any differences found in productivity; however, given the circumstances, it still provides us with more information than we had before the study.

Quasi-experiments are often used to evaluate the results of a new program implemented by an organization. For example, an organization that had instituted a childcare center wanted to identify whether the center had any effect on employee absenteeism. To find the answer, the organization compared absenteeism levels from the year before the center was introduced with the absenteeism levels for the year following the implementation; the organization found that both absenteeism and turnover had decreased.

Although it is tempting to conclude that the childcare center was a success, such a conclusion would not be prudent. Many other variables might have caused the reduction. As shown in Table 1.7, the organization implemented several other progressive programs during the same period. Thus, the decrease in absenteeism and turnover could have been the result of other programs or some combination of programs. Furthermore, the economy changed, and jobs became more difficult to obtain. Workers may have reduced their absentee rates out of fear of being fired, and turnover may have been reduced because employees realized that few jobs were available. In addition, the weather improved in the second year, which meant workers were rarely unable to get to work Recall that field studies have high external validity but low internal validity. Because it has been conducted out in the "field", researchers were not able to control these extraneous variables that might have affected the results of the study..

Taken by itself, we would certainly not want to rely on the results of our quasi-experiment. But if 10 other researchers conduct separate quasi-experiments to study the same question and find similar results, we might feel confident enough to make changes or reach conclusions based on the available research evidence.

Archival Research.   Another research method that is commonly used in I/O psychology is **archival research.** Archival research involves using previously collected data or records to answer a research question. For example, if we want to know what distinguishes productive workers from unproductive workers, we could look in the personnel files to see whether the backgrounds of productive workers have common characteristics not shared by unproductive workers. Or, if we want to determine if people on the night shift had more turnover than people on the day shift, we could get information on shift and turnover from the company records. Archival research has many desirable features, such as not being obtrusive or expensive, but it also has severe drawbacks (Shultz, Hoffman, & Reiter-Palmon, 2005). Records in files are not always accurate and are not always kept up to date. Furthermore, the type of data needed by a researcher may not be in the archives because the data were never recorded in the first place.

As an undergraduate, I was involved with an archival study designed to determine why some students in an executive Master of Business Administration (MBA) program dropped out while others completed their coursework. What was supposed to be an easy job of getting records from a few files turned into a nightmare. The records of more than 300 students were scattered in storage rooms in three locations in Southern California and were not filed in any order. Furthermore, almost every student had at least one important item missing from their files. Needless to say, these problems kept the results of the study from being as accurate as desired. Now, however, the virtual storage of information has greatly increased the potential for archival research.

Surveys.   Another method of conducting research is to *ask* people their opinion on some topic. Surveys might ask employees about their attitudes toward the organization,

Archival research
Research that involves the use of previously collected data.

Table 1.7 Why Nonexperimental Studies are Difficult to Interpret: The Childcare Center

Date	Absenteeism %	External Factor	Internal Factor
1/21	2.8	—	—
2/21	3.1	—	—
3/21	4.7	Unemployment rate at 4.1%	—
4/21	4.7	—	—
5/21	4.8	—	—
6/21	6.7	Main highway closed	—
7/21	6.5	—	—
8/21	4.9	Highway reopens	—
9/21	4.5	—	—
10/21	4.4	—	—
11/21	8.7	Terrible snowstorm	—
12/21	5.3	—	—
1/22	5.3	—	Childcare center started
2/22	5.2	—	—
3/22	5.1	—	Flextime program started
4/22	2.0	Local unemployment rate hits 9.3%	—
5/22	2.0	—	—
6/22	2.0	—	—
7/22	1.8	—	Wellness program started
8/22	1.8	—	—
9/22	2.0	—	New attendance policy
10/22	2.1	—	—
11/22	4.0	Mild weather	—
12/22	4.2	Mild weather	—

Note: Absenteeism rate in 2021 before childcare center = 5.09% rate in 2022 after childcare center = 3.01%.

HR directors about their opinions regarding the best recruitment method, or managers about the success of their childcare centers.

Surveys can be conducted via a variety of methods such as mail, personal interviews, phone, email, and online. Additionally, such methods as the interview can vary in the extent to which the questions are being asked by a live person, voice or video recording, computer assisted interviewing, or self-administered paper questionnaire. When selecting a survey method, it is important to consider whether the intended population can access the medium of the survey (e.g., access to email, access to an online connection, access to a phone with a landline), whether they will agree to complete the survey (e.g., survey length), and the extent to which the person will provide honest and accurate answers. For example, a survey focused on the effects of aging should not use an online survey, as the Pew Internet and American Life Project telephone survey found that 27% of Americans over 65 did not use online databases compared to fewer than 3% of adults age 18 to 49 in 2019. Likewise, a survey of drug usage or criminal behavior should not use face-to-face interviews, as people are more likely to admit to having engaged in sensitive activities when the questions are not asked by a live person (Tourangeau & Yan, 2007).

A multinational study by Church (2001) found some interesting results regarding survey methods. Employees from the United States, Japan, and France preferred automated phone response technology, whereas employees in Germany, Italy, and the United Kingdom preferred the traditional paper-and-pencil method. Employees completing the survey online were more likely to leave items blank than were employees using a paper-and-pencil format.

Although a high response rate is essential for trust to be placed in survey results, survey response rates have been on the decline (Anseel, Lievens, Schollaert, & Choragwicka, 2010). Based on the meta-analysis results of Anseel et al. (2010), response rates can be increased by:

- Notifying participants in advance that they will be receiving a survey
- Providing monetary or non-monetary incentives; making the incentive contingent on returning the survey does not greatly improve response rates
- Personalizing the survey through such means as an original signature or addressing the participant in a cover letter
- Ensuring that survey responses will be anonymous by using identification numbers
- Having a university sponsor the survey
- Distributing the survey in person rather than through the mail

Contrary to popular belief, providing incentives and sending reminders do not increase survey responses (Anseel et al., 2010). It seems that people respond because they are interested in expressing their opinions rather than receiving an incentive.

Well-designed survey questions are easy to understand; use simple language, do not ask about hypothetical situations, and keep the questions relatively short in length. Care must be taken in choosing the words used in each question. Peterson and West (2015) provide an excellent example of the importance of how a question is worded. Education Next conducted a survey asking parents questions about education. One of the questions in the survey asked about support for school vouchers. In separate surveys, Education Next asked the question in two different ways:

> *A proposal has been made that would give all families with children in public schools a wider choice, by allowing them to enroll their children in private schools instead, with government helping to pay the tuition. Would you favor or oppose this proposal?*

> *A proposal has been made that would use government funds to pay the tuition of all students who choose to attend private schools. Would you favor or oppose this proposal?*

Forty-six percent of the respondents favored the proposal in the first question that emphasized "choice" versus only 26% that favored the proposal in the second question that emphasized government funding.

A final issue involving surveys is the extent to which responses to the survey questions are accurate. This issue is especially important when asking about sensitive or controversial issues. That is, if I ask whether you believe that men and women are equally qualified to be managers, would you tell the truth if you thought men were better qualified? Would people honestly respond to questions about their former drug use, poor performance at work, or unethical behavior? Probably not! But they do seem to be accurate when reporting such things as height and body weight (Imrhan, Imrhan, & Hart, 1996). A good example of people not being truthful in surveys occurred when researchers from Harris Interactive asked 1,006 adults in 2010 if they regularly washed their hands after using a public restroom; 96% said yes. However, when researchers observed 6,028 people in restrooms, less than 85% washed their hands.

Inaccurately responding to survey questions is not always an intentional attempt to be dishonest. Instead, inaccurate responses can be the result of a person not actually understanding the question, or knowing the correct answer to a question. For example, an employee might respond to a question about attendance by stating they had missed three days of work in the past year when in fact they missed five. Were they lying, or just mistaken about their attendance record?

An interesting investigation into the accuracy of survey responses was a meta-analysis of studies comparing self-reported grade point averages and SAT scores with the actual scores (Kuncel, Credé, & Thomas, 2005). The meta-analysis indicated that the self-reported GPAs and SAT scores correlated highly with actual scores (.90 for college GPA and .82 for SAT scores). Although the scores were highly correlated, there was a tendency for the self-reported GPAs and SAT scores to be higher than the actual scores.

Meta-Analysis. **Meta-analysis** is a statistical method of reaching conclusions based on previous research. Prior to meta-analysis, a researcher interested in reviewing the literature on a topic would read all the available research and then make a rather subjective conclusion based on the articles. With meta-analysis, the researcher goes through each article, determines the **effect size** for each article, and then finds a statistical average of effect sizes across all articles. A meta-analysis results in one number, called the **mean effect size,** which indicates the effectiveness of some variable.

Correlation coefficients (r) are used as the effect size when researchers are interested in the positive or negative *relationship* between two variables, and many studies use correlation as their statistical test. Examples include studies looking at the relationship between personality and job performance, integrity test scores and employee theft, and the relationship between job satisfaction and performance.

A **difference score** (d) is used as the effect size when researchers are looking at the *difference* between two groups. Examples are studies looking at the effectiveness of a training method, the effect of goal setting, and the effects of shift work. The d score indicates the number of standard deviations in which the two groups differ. For example, imagine that a study investigating the effect of a new training program on employee sales performance found an effect size of $d = .50$ for the training intervention. This would mean that employees who went through the training had sales half a standard deviation higher than employees not receiving the training. Effect sizes can be interpreted in two ways: by comparing them to norms or directly applying them to a particular situation. Although it is commonly written that effect sizes (d) less than .40 are small; those between .40 and .80 are moderate, and those higher than .80 are

---

Effect size Used in meta-analysis, a statistic that indicates the amount of change caused by an experimental manipulation.

Meta-analysis A statistical method for cumulating research results.

Mean effect size Used in meta-analysis, a statistic that is the average of the effect sizes for all studies included in the analysis.

Correlation coefficients A statistic, resulting from performing a correlation, that indicates the magnitude and direction of a relationship.

Difference score A type of effect size used in meta-analysis that is signified by the letter *d* and indicates how many standard deviations separate the mean score for the experimental group from the control group.

considered large (Cohen, 1988). It is important to note that these numbers are "rules of thumb" (i.e., general guidelines based on practical experience rather than theory); the actual **practical significance** of an effect size depends on many factors and even a small effect size can result in great monetary savings for an organization (in Chapter 6, we will discuss some formulas that can be used to better understand the practical significance of an effect size). The average effect size for an organizational intervention is .44 (Guzzo, Jette, & Katzell, 1985).

When directly applying an effect size to a particular situation, you need to know the **standard deviation** of the variable in question. This standard deviation is then multiplied by the effect size from the meta-analysis to yield a meaningful score. Confused? Perhaps an example would help.

Suppose employees at a John Deere manufacturing plant miss an average of 9.5 days of work per year with a standard deviation of 3.6 days. John Deere is considering a new incentive system to improve attendance that a meta-analysis indicates has an effect size of .32 in reducing absenteeism. What can John Deere expect to gain from this incentive system? By multiplying their absenteeism standard deviation (3.6 days) by the effect size from the meta-analysis (.32), John Deere can expect the incentive system to reduce absenteeism by an average of 1.15 days per employee (3.6 × .32 = 1.15). Alternatively, if the attendance data for employees at General Motors were an average of 13.4 days per year missed with a standard deviation of 9.6, it could expect an annual reduction in absenteeism of 1.79 days per employee (9.6 × .32 = 3.07). John Deere and General Motors would each have to decide if the predicted reduction in savings, 1 day per person for John Deere and 3 days per person for General Motors, is worth the cost of the incentive system.

A complete discussion of meta-analysis is beyond the scope of this book and probably beyond your interest as well. It is important, however, that you be able to interpret the outcomes of meta-analyses because they are used in this text and are the current standard when reviewing previous research. Points to keep in mind as you read the text:

- Because meta-analyses summarize all the available studies on a topic, a reference to a meta-analysis should carry more weight than a reference to only one or two studies.
- When describing meta-analysis results in this text, I will often include the effect size at the end of a sentence. For example, I might write, "References are not good predictors of performance, $r = .18, p = .27$." The symbol r indicates the actual correlation from the meta-analysis. The symbol p, also known as *rho*, is the correlation after it has been corrected for factors that can reduce the size of a correlation. These factors are called artifacts, and you can learn more about them in the meta-analysis chapter of the statistics primer that was written to accompany this text and available through your Companion Website (Aamodt, Surrette, & Cohen, 2010). Rho is often referred to as the *corrected* correlation or the *true* correlation.

Subject Samples

Decisions also must be made regarding the size, composition, and method of selecting the subjects who will serve as the sample in a study. Although it is nice to have a large sample for any research study, a large sample size is not necessary if the experimenter can choose a random sample and control for many of the extraneous variables. In fact, properly conducted surveys need only about 1,000 participants to generalize survey results to the entire U.S. population (Deane, 1999).

The method of selecting the sample is certainly dependent on the nature of the organization. A small organization will probably be forced to use all its employees, which means that the sample will be small but highly representative of the intended population. For economical and practical reasons, a large organization will select only certain employees to participate in a study rather than use the entire workforce. The problem then becomes one of which employees will participate.

If the study involves a questionnaire, it is no problem to randomly select a desired number of employees and have them complete the survey. If, however, the study is more elaborate, such as investigating the effects of lighting on performance, it would be difficult to randomly select employees. That is, it would not be practical to have one employee work under high levels of light while the person next to them is uninvolved with the experiment. If we decide to have one plant work with high levels of light and another with lower levels, what we gain in practicality we lose in randomness and control. So we try to strike a balance between practicality and experimental rigor.

To increase experimental rigor and decrease the costs of conducting research, many studies are conducted at universities using students as subjects rather than employees. In fact, college students served as subjects in 46% of research studies published in four leading I/O journals (Roch, 2008). This use of students has led to considerable debate regarding the generalizability of university research; that is, do students behave in the same fashion as employees? Some authors (e.g., Sears, 1986) point out that compared with adults, college students are younger, more educated, and more egocentric; possess a less formulated sense of self; and have a stronger need for peer approval. Because of these differences, it makes sense that students would behave differently from adults who are in the working world.

Research on this issue, however, is mixed. Some researchers have found differences between student subjects and professional subjects, but others have not (Bordens & Abbott, 2014). For example, in a meta-analysis investigating the relationship between personality and team performance, the personality traits of agreeableness and conscientiousness predicted team performance when professionals were used as subjects but not when students were used as subjects (Peeters, Van Tuijl, Rutte, & Reymen, 2006). Likewise, Gordon and Arvey (2004) found that students and professionals differed in research on age bias. However, in a meta-analysis of the relationship between locus of control (the extent to which a person believes they had control over their life) and work outcome, Ng, Sorensen, and Eby (2006) found that the relationship was similar whether the subjects were employees or students. Because students and professionals do not always respond the same way in studies, it is important to keep in mind that studies using students as research subjects may not generalize to the real world.

A final important issue concerns the method used to recruit subjects. To obtain the best research results, it is important to use a **random sample** so that the sample will be as representative as possible. This means that if a survey is randomly sent to 100 employees, the research will be most accurate only if all employees return the survey, or the ones that do, are representative of the entire organization. The problem is that researchers are unlikely to get a 100% return rate if study participation is voluntary, and the ethics of the American Psychological Association (APA) require that participation be voluntary. With voluntary participation, it is possible that those who do not participate in the study might differ from those who chose to participate This is called self-selection bias, in which participants that have been voluntarily selected are a non-random sample with nonprobability sampling. Thus, it is essential to include questions that will allow the researchers to determine if those

Random sample A sample in which every member of the relevant population had an equal chance of being chosen to participate in the study.

who participated are similar to the organization as a whole on such variables as race, gender, age, and tenure. Although random samples are best, they are rarely used in I/O psychology research (Landers & Behrend, 2015).

Because obtaining random samples is very difficult, especially in industry, many studies use a **convenience sample**, samples that are easily available to the researcher, and then randomly assign subjects to the various experimental conditions. Commonly used convenience samples in I/O psychology research include college students; online panels; crowdsourcing/Amazon Mechanical Turk; and snowball, network (emails sent through social networks), and organizational samples (Landers & Behrend, 2015). With **random assignment,** each subject in a nonrandom sample is randomly *assigned* to a particular experimental condition. For example, in a study designed to test the effectiveness of a training method, 60 subjects agree to participate in the study. Thirty of the subjects are randomly assigned to the group receiving training; another 30 are randomly assigned to the control group that does not receive training. Random assignment is important when using convenience samples, as research indicates that random and nonrandom assignment result in different outcomes (Shadish & Ragsdale, 1996). If random assignment is a better method than nonrandom assignment, why would a researcher not randomly assign participants? Usually because of limitations placed on the researcher. For example, if a union contract stipulated that employees with longer tenure had first choice in the shift they worked, a researcher studying the effects of shift work could not randomly assign employees to various shifts.

Running the Study

When all of these decisions have been made, it is finally time to run the study and collect data. To ensure that data are collected in an unbiased fashion, it is important that all instructions to the subjects be stated in a standardized fashion and at a level that is understandable. Once the subject is finished with their participation, they should be **Debriefing,** or told the purpose of the experiment and be given a chance to ask questions about their participation.

Statistical Analysis

After all data have been collected, the results are statistically analyzed. A discussion of statistics is beyond the scope of this book, but it is important to understand why statistics are used. Statistical analysis helps us determine how confident we are that our results are real and did not occur by chance alone. For example, if we conducted a study in a classroom in which we compared the average age of students on the left side of the room with that of students on the right side of the room, we would no doubt get a difference. That is, the average age of the students on the right would not be exactly the same as that of the students on the left. If we did not conduct a statistical analysis of our data, we would conclude that people on the right side are older than people on the left side. Perhaps we could even develop a theory about our results!

Does this sound ridiculous? Of course it does. But it points out the idea that any set of numbers we collect will in all probability be different. The question is, are they *significantly* different? Statistical analysis provides the answer by determining the probability that our results were due to chance. In psychology, we use the .05 level of

Convenience sample A nonrandom research sample that is used because it is easily available.

Random assignment The random, unbiased assignment of subjects in a research sample to the various experimental and control conditions.

Debriefing Informing the subject in an experiment about the purpose of the study in which they were a participant and providing any other relevant information.

significance: If our analysis indicates that the probability that our findings resulted from chance is 5% or less, we consider our results to be statistically significant. Although the .05 level of significance is the most commonly used, some researchers have suggested that we should be more flexible and use either more conservative or more liberal levels, depending upon the situation (Bordens & Abbott, 2014).

At this point, a caution must be made about the interpretation of significance levels. Significance levels indicate only the level of confidence we can place on a result being the product of chance. They say nothing about the strength of the results. Thus, a study with results significant at the .01 level does not necessarily show a stronger effect than a study with results significant at the .05 level of confidence.

To determine the strength of a finding, we use the effect size, discussed earlier in the section on meta-analysis. Significance levels tell us the *statistical significance* of a study, and effect sizes (combined with logic) tell us the *practical significance* of a study.

For example, suppose we conduct a study comparing the SAT scores of men and women high school students. Based on a sample of five million students, we find that men average 1,059 and women 1,058. With such a huge sample size, we will probably find that the two means are statistically different. However, with only a 1-point difference between the two groups on a test with a maximum score of 1,600, we would probably not place much practical significance in the difference.

Correlation.   It is necessary to discuss one particular statistic—correlation—because it is so widely used in I/O psychology and throughout this book. **Correlation** is a statistical procedure that enables a researcher to determine the *relationship* between two variables—for example, the relationships found between an employment test and future employee performance; job satisfaction and job attendance; or performance ratings made by workers and supervisors. It is important to understand that correlational analysis does not necessarily say anything about causality.

Why does a correlation coefficient not indicate a cause-and-effect relationship? Because a third variable, an **intervening variable,** often accounts for the relationship between two variables. Take the example often used by psychologist David Schroeder. Suppose there is a correlation of +.80 between the number of ice cream cones sold in New York during August and the number of babies that die during August in India. Does eating ice cream kill babies in another nation? No, that would not make sense. Instead, we look for that third variable that would explain our high correlation. In this case, the answer is clearly the summer heat.

Another interesting example was provided by Mullins (1986) in a presentation about the incorrect interpretation of correlation coefficients. Mullins pointed out that data show a strong negative correlation between the number of cows per square mile and the crime rate. With his tongue firmly planted in his cheek (i.e., he was joking), Mullins suggested that New York City could rid itself of crime by importing millions of heads of cattle. Of course, the real interpretation for the negative correlation is that crime is greater in urban areas than in rural areas.

A good researcher should always be cautious about variables that seem related. The point should be clear. Just because two events occur at the same time or seem to be related does not mean that one event or variable causes another.

Correlation A statistical procedure used to measure the relationship between two variables.

Intervening variable A third variable that can often explain the relationship between two other variables.

The result of correlational analysis is a number called a correlation coefficient. The values of this coefficient range from -1 to $+1$; the further the coefficient is from zero, the greater the relationship between two variables. That is, a correlation of .40 shows a stronger relationship between two variables than a correlation of .20. Likewise, a correlation of $-.39$ shows a stronger relationship than a correlation of $+.30$. The $(+)$ and $(-)$ signs indicate the *direction* of the correlation. A positive $(+)$ correlation means that as the values of one variable increase, so do the values of a second variable. For example, we might find a positive correlation between intelligence and scores on a classroom exam. This would mean that the more intelligent the student, the higher their score will be on the exam.

A negative $(-)$ correlation means that as the values of one variable increase, the values of a second variable decrease. For example, we would probably find a negative correlation between the number of beers that you drink the night before a test and your score on that test. In I/O psychology, we find negative correlations between job satisfaction and absenteeism, age and reaction time, and nervousness and interview success.

1-3 Ethics in Industrial/Organizational Psychology

Organizations and employees are faced with ethical dilemmas every day. Ethical dilemmas are ambiguous situations that require a personal judgment of what is right or wrong because there are no rules, policies, or laws guiding such decisions. Individuals often rely on their morals and personal values, which often leads to different decisions by different people in similar situations. Because people have different backgrounds that impact their personal values and how they define a particular situation, the decision that one person makes may be very different than what another one makes.

For example, suppose you want to sell your car. You know that your car has been in several accidents and has had a lot of work done on it. Do you share that information with a prospective buyer? There is no law or policy that says you must. In fact, most people would say that unless the buyer specifically asks you that question you shouldn't bring it up at all. Is it morally wrong or unfair not to share this information? Based on an individual's value system, the answer may be "yes," it is morally wrong, or "no," it's not morally wrong.

In life, we often encounter two types of ethical dilemmas: Type A and Type B.

In a Type A dilemma, there is a high level of uncertainty as to what is right or wrong, there appears to be no best solution, and there are both positive and negative consequences to a decision. For example, many people would say that drug research that uses animals to test new drugs is unethical, because it is morally wrong to hurt any living creature. Others would say that new drugs could save millions of lives and that it would be morally wrong *not* to make and test drugs that could potentially save human lives. As you can see, there seems to be no one best answer, as there are both negative and positive consequences in making this decision.

In a Type B dilemma, also called "rationalizing dilemmas," the difference between right and wrong is much clearer than in a Type A dilemma. Usually, individuals know what is right but choose the solution that is most advantageous to themselves. For example, choosing not to tell a prospective buyer about any past damage that occurred with a car for sale would have the most advantages for the seller. Type B dilemmas are called rationalizing dilemmas because individuals "rationalize" they are right because "everyone else does it." For example, many students will say that they have cheated at least one time on a test. Most of those students would agree that it is morally wrong to cheat. So, why have so many done it? They rationalize that "for just this one time" it is okay and that it is not hurting anyone. And they convince themselves that because everyone else is doing it, it must be okay. This ability to rationalize is why unethical behavior is so common in organizations. For example, a 2017 survey done by Careerbuilder.com found that 40% of workers called in sick when they weren't actually sick. In a survey by the Ethics Resource Center in 2013, 41% of workers surveyed reported witnessing unethical behavior from others, including such things as "borrowing" work supplies and taking them home, stealing pencils and other equipment, using sick leave when they weren't sick, abuse of employees by management, and coming in late and leaving early.

At the end of each successive chapter in this textbook, you will be presented with some ethical dilemmas for which you are asked to discuss and answer questions. Using the information from this section, decide whether you think those situations are ethical or unethical. There is no right or wrong answer. Compare your thoughts and ideas with other classmates to get a clear perspective of how difficult it is to get everyone to make the same decision when faced with an ethical dilemma as opposed to a decision that is guided by law or policy.

On the Job ▶ Applied Case Study

Conducting Research at the Vancouver (British Columbia) International Airport Authority, Canada

The Vancouver International Airport, located in Richmond, British Columbia, is Canada's second-busiest airport; serving over 26.4 million passengers in 2019. It has twice been named the top airport in North America for overall customer satisfaction. Thus, it takes great pride in its employees and their performance.

The Airport Authority oversees more than 550 employees in such areas as project management, finance, human resources, engineering, communications, and emergency preparedness. Employees working for the airlines, stores, and restaurants are not part of the Airport Authority; this is because they are employees of private companies.

To reduce costs and increase productivity, the Vancouver Airport Authority designed a wellness program for its employees. The program, called *Fitness and Balance*, comprised many components, including seminars on such topics as smoking cessation and stress management; health-related newsletters and announcements; outdoor-activity days in which employees and their families could hike, skate, or walk; and discounts at fitness facilities. To determine the effectiveness of this program, the Airport Authority collected data and found that absenteeism dropped from 4.07% to 2.55% and that the number of annual injuries dropped from 22 to 6.

- How would you have designed the study to determine the effectiveness of the wellness program?

- What outcome measures other than absenteeism and injuries might you use?

- What ethical or practical considerations need to be considered when collecting and reporting data in a study such as this one?

More information on this case can be found at Canada's government website page on Healthy Living:
http://www.phac-aspc.gc.ca/pau-uap/fitness/work/study_vancouver_e.html

Chapter Summary

In this chapter you learned:

- The field of I/O psychology consists of three major subfields: personnel psychology, organizational psychology, and human factors. Industrial psychologists work in a variety of settings including industry, government, education, and consulting firms.
- The field of I/O psychology began in the early 1900s and has grown rapidly since then: Division 14 of the APA began in 1945 with 130 members and now has over 8,000 members.
- World War I, World War II, the Hawthorne studies, civil rights legislation, new technology, and changing demographics have had important impacts on I/O psychology.
- At least a bachelor's degree is required to find employment in the field, and median salaries currently are around $80,750 at the master's level and $103,200 at the Ph.D. level.
- Research is important so that I/O psychologists can make the best decisions.
- Decisions must be made regarding what to research, the location of the research (laboratory or field), the research method that will be used (experimental method, nonexperimental method, survey, archival research, meta-analysis), the sample that will be used, and the statistics that will be selected to analyze the research data.

Key Terms

Industrial/organizational psychology   (2)
Scientist-practitioner model   (2)
Personnel psychology   (4)
Organizational psychology   (4)
Human factors   (4)
Army Alpha   (6)
Army Beta   (6)
Hawthorne studies   (8)
Hawthorne effect   (8)
Graduate Record Exam (GRE)   (11)
Terminal master's degree programs   (11)
Internship   (12)
Practicum   (12)
Dissertation   (13)
Hypothesis   (15)
Theory   (15)
Bridge publication   (17)
Journals   (17)
Trade magazines   (17)
Magazines   (17)
Laboratory research   (19)
External validity   (19)
Generalizability   (19)
Field research   (19)

Informed consent   (19)
Institutional review boards   (20)
Cause-and-effect relationships   (20)
Experiment   (20)
Manipulation   (20)
Independent variable   (20)
Dependent variable   (20)
Experimental group   (21)
Control group   (21)
Quasi-experiments   (21)
Archival research   (22)
Effect size   (25)
Meta-analysis   (25)
Mean effect size   (25)
Correlation coefficients   (25)
Difference score   (25)
Practical significance   (26)
Standard deviation (SD)   (26)
Random sample   (27)
Convenience sample   (28)
Random assignment   (28)
Debriefed   (28)
Correlation   (29)
Intervening variable   (29)

Questions for Review

1. What were the important events that shaped the field of I/O psychology?
2. What role will demographic changes play in how we hire and manage employees?
3. If you wanted to pursue a career in I/O psychology, what would you need to do between now and graduation to make this career possible?
4. How are theories and hypotheses different?
5. Is a random sample really better than a convenience sample? Why or why not?
6. When would you use a quasi-experiment rather than an experiment?
7. Why don't correlations between two variables indicate that one caused the other?

Chapter

2

Job Analysis and Evaluation

Learning Objectives

2-1 Explain the definition and uses of job analysis.

2-2 Create a job description.

2-3 Describe the job analysis process.

2-4 Differentiate the various job analysis methods.

2-5 Describe the job evaluation process.

2-6 Explain the concept of pay equity.

Job analysis The process of identifying how a job is performed, the conditions under which it is performed, and the personal requirements it takes to perform the job.

I n 1585, 15 English settlers established a colony on Roanoke Island near what is now the Outer Banks of the North Carolina coast in the United States. When John White arrived at Roanoke Island in 1590, he found no trace of the colony and only the word, Croatan, carved on a tree. To this day, it is not known what happened to the settlers of the Lost Colony of Roanoke.

Many theories have been put forth to explain the fate of the lost colony—one theory is that the members of the colony were not prepared to survive in the new continent; that is, the group consisted of politicians, soldiers, and sailors. Although worthy individuals were sent to the New World, few had the necessary training and skills to survive. In fact, the colony might have survived if settlers with more appropriate skills, such as farmers, had been sent instead of the traditional explorer types. Thus, a better match between job requirements and personnel might have saved the colony.

Does this sound far-fetched? Perhaps so, but the story does underscore the importance of a process called *job analysis*—gathering and analyzing information about the work an employee performs, the conditions under which the work is performed, and the worker characteristics needed to perform the work under the identified conditions.

2-1 Job Analysis

Importance of Job Analysis

A thorough job analysis, also called work analysis (Wilson, Bennett, Gibson, & Alliger, 2012), is the foundation for almost all human resources activities. It is difficult to imagine how one could write **job descriptions**, select employees, evaluate performances, or conduct training programs without knowing the tasks an employee performs, the conditions under which they are performed, and the competencies needed to perform the tasks. A thorough job analysis provides such information.

> **Job description** A written summary of the tasks performed in a job, the conditions under which the job is performed, and the requirements needed to perform the job.

Writing Job Descriptions

One of the written products of a job analysis is a job description—a brief, two- to five-page summary of the tasks and job requirements found in the job analysis. In other words, job analysis is the *process* of determining the work activities and requirements, and a job description is the written *result* of the job analysis. Job analyses and job descriptions serve as the basis for many HR activities, including employee selection, evaluation, training, and work design.

Employee Selection

It is difficult to imagine how an employee can be selected unless there is a clear understanding of the tasks to be performed and the competencies needed to perform those tasks. By identifying such requirements, it is possible to select tests or develop interview questions to determine whether a particular applicant possesses the necessary knowledge, skills, and abilities to carry out the requirements of the job. Although this seems like common sense, the discussion of the unstructured employment interview that you will read about in Chapter 4 demonstrates that many non-job-related variables such as height and physical attractiveness are sometimes used to select employees.

Training

Again, it is difficult to see how employees can be trained unless the requirements of the job are known. Job analyses yield lists of job activities that can be systematically used to identify the requirements of a job in order to create training programs.

Personpower Planning

One important but seldom employed use of job analysis is to determine *worker mobility* within an organization. That is, if individuals are hired for a particular job, to what other jobs can they expect to eventually be promoted and become successful? Many organizations have a policy of promoting the person who performs the best in the job immediately below the one in question. Although this approach has its advantages, it can result in the so-called **Peter Principle**: that is, promoting employees until they eventually reach their highest level of incompetence (Peter & Hull, 1969). For example, consider an employee who is the company's best salesperson. Even though this person is known to be excellent in sales, it is not known what type of supervisor they will be. Promotion solely based on sales performance does not guarantee that the individual will do well as a supervisor. Suppose, however, that job analysis results are used to compare all jobs in the company to the supervisor's job. Instead of promoting the person in the

> **Peter Principle** The idea that organizations tend to promote good employees until they reach the level at which they are not competent—in other words, their highest level of incompetence.

job immediately below the supervisor, we promote the best employee from the most similar job—that is, a job that already involves much of the same knowledge, skills, and abilities as the supervisor's job. With this approach, there is a better match between the person being promoted and the requirements of the job.

Performance Appraisal

Another important use of job analysis is the construction of a performance appraisal instrument (Roch & Williams, 2012). As in employee selection, evaluating employee performance must be job related. Employees are often evaluated with forms that use such vague categories as "dependability," "knowledge," and "initiative." The use of specific, job-related categories leads to more accurate performance appraisals that are better accepted not only by employees but also by the courts (Foster, Dunleavy, Campion, & Steubing, 2008). In addition, when properly administered and utilized, job-related performance appraisals can be a powerful tool for identifying gaps in employee knowledge, skills, and abilities, and serve as a guide for the creation of training and development opportunities.

Job Classification

Job analysis enables a human resources professional to classify jobs into groups based on similarities in requirements and duties. Job classification is useful for determining pay levels, transfers, and promotions. The growth of employment opportunities in the field of Big Data in the 21st century is an excellent demonstration of the constantly-evolving nature of job requirements that necessitate methodical job classifications. While organizations raced to secure the most promising talent in the industry, this proved to be a difficult task as the job descriptions were seemingly left up to subjective interpretations of the organization's needs (De Mauro, Greco, Grimaldi, & Ritala, 2018). Research showed that there was a definitive gap between the most notable Big Data jobs and their required knowledge, skills, and abilities (Song & Zhu, 2015). In this case, there was a clear need for the establishment of job classifications in order to effectively attract and compensate talent in this field.

Job Evaluation

Job analysis information can also be used to determine the *worth* of a job. Job evaluation will be discussed in greater detail later in this chapter.

Job Design

Job analysis information can be used to determine the optimal way in which a job should be performed. That is, what would be the best way for an employee to sit at their computer or what would be the best way for a warehouse person to lift boxes? By analyzing a job, wasted and unsafe motions can be eliminated, resulting in higher productivity and reduced numbers of job injuries. A job design was mentioned in Chapter 1 with the example of Frank Gilbreth, who, after studying the inconsistency with which brick masons did their work, was able to reduce from 18 to 4½ the number of motions needed to lay a brick.

Compliance with Legal Guidelines

As will be discussed in greater detail in Chapter 3, any employment decision must be based on job-related information. One legally acceptable way to directly determine job relatedness is by job analysis. No law specifically requires a job analysis, but several important guidelines and court cases mandate job analysis for all practical purposes.

Uniform Guidelines Federal guidelines used to guide an employer in establishing fair selection methods.

First, the ***Uniform Guidelines*** on Employee Selection Procedures (UGESP, 1978)—the HR principles designed to ensure compliance with federal standards—contain several direct references to the necessity of job analysis. Even though the *Uniform Guidelines* are not law, courts have granted them "great deference" (Morgeson, Brannick, & Levine, 2020). The importance of job analysis is also discussed in the *Principles for the Validation and Use of Personnel Selection Procedures* (SIOP, 2018), a document that provides guidance from professionals in the field of I/O psychology regarding the employee selection process.

Second, several court cases have discussed the concept of job relatedness. For example, in *Griggs v. Duke Power* (1971), employment decisions were based in part upon applicants' possession of a high school diploma. Because a higher percentage of Black applicants than White applicants did not meet this requirement, smaller percentages of Black applicants were hired and promoted. Thus, a suit was filed against the Duke Power Company charging that a high school diploma was not necessary to carry out the demands of the job. The U.S. Supreme Court agreed with Griggs, stating that the company had indeed not established the job relatedness of the high school diploma requirement.

Although not specifically mentioning the term "job analysis," the decision in *Griggs* was the first to address the issue of job relatedness. Subsequent cases such as *Albermarle v. Moody* (1975), *Chance v. Board of Examiners* (1971), *Guardians v. Civil Service* (1980), and *Kirkland v. New York State Department of Correctional Services* (1974) further established the necessity of job relatedness and the link between it and job analysis. For a job analysis to withstand legal scrutiny, it is essential that the job analysis process and results be well documented (Gutman & Dunleavy, 2012).

Organizational Analysis

Job analysis interview Obtaining information about a job by talking to a person performing it.

During the course of their work, job analysts often become aware of certain problems within an organization. For example, during a **job analysis interview**, an employee may indicate that they do not know how they are evaluated or to whom they are supposed to report. The discovery of such lapses in organizational communication can then be used to correct problems and help an organization function better. For example, while conducting job analysis interviews of credit union positions, job analyst Deborah Peggans discovered that none of the workers knew how their job performances were evaluated. This discovery let the organization know it had not done an adequate job of communicating performance standards to its employees.

Writing a Good Job Description

As mentioned earlier, one of the most useful results of a job analysis is the job description. A job description is a relatively short summary of a job and should be about two to five pages in length. This suggested length is not really typical of most job descriptions used in industry; they tend to be only of one page. But for a job description to be of value, it must describe a job in enough detail that decisions about activities such as selection and training can be made. Such decisions probably cannot be made if the description is only one page long.

Though I/O psychologists believe that job descriptions should be detailed and lengthy, many professionals in organizations resist such efforts. These professionals worry that listing each activity will limit their ability to direct employees to perform tasks not listed on the job description. The concern is that an employee, referring to the job description as support, might respond, "It's not my job." This fear, however, can be countered with two arguments. The first is that duties can always be added to a job description, which can, and should, be updated on a regular basis. The second is that the phrase "and performs other job-related duties as assigned" should be included in the job description. In fact, one employer has a policy stating that the university can require employees to perform any duties not on the employees' job descriptions for a period not to exceed three months. After three months, the duty must either be eliminated or permanently added to the employee's job description, at which time a review will also be made to determine if the addition is significant enough to merit a salary increase.

Job descriptions can be written in many ways, but the format discussed here has been used successfully for many jobs and is a combination of methods used by many organizations and is consistent with the format suggested by Hurtz and Wright (2012) for work descriptions. A job description should contain the following eight sections: a job title, a brief summary, work activities, tools and equipment used, the work context, performance standards, compensation information, and personal requirements.

Job Title

A job title is important for several reasons. An accurate title describes the nature of the job, its power and status level, and the competencies needed to perform the job (Martinez, Laird, Martin, & Ferris, 2008). When industrial psychologist David Faloona started a new job at Washington National Insurance in Chicago, his official title was "psychometric technician." Unfortunately, none of the other workers knew what he did. To correct that problem, his title was changed to "personnel assistant," and supervisors then began consulting with him on human resources related problems. A job analysis that I conducted provides another example. After analyzing the position of "secretary" for one credit union, I found that the duties performed were actually those of a position that other credit unions labeled "loan officer." This change in title resulted in the employee's receiving a higher salary.

An accurate title also aids in employee selection and recruitment. If the job title indicates the true nature of the job, potential applicants for a position will be better able to determine whether their skills and experience match those required for the job. In the example given in the previous paragraph, applicants for a secretary's job in the usual sense might not possess the lending and decision-making skills needed by a loan officer.

When conducting a job analysis, it is not unusual for an analyst to discover that some workers do not have job titles. Job titles provide workers with some form of identity. Instead of just saying that they are a "worker at the foundry," an employee can say that they are a "welder" or a "machinist." At most universities, students receiving financial aid are called "work-study students" rather than "clerks," "data entry specialists," or "mail sorters." This inaccurate title might cause some students to think that they are supposed to study as they work rather than photocopy exams or input data.

Job titles can also affect perceptions of a job's status and worth. For example, job descriptions containing gender-neutral titles such as "administrative assistant" are evaluated as being worth more money than ones containing titles with a female sex linkage (e.g., "executive secretary") (Naughton, 1988). As another example, Smith, Hornsby, Benson, and Wesolowski (1989) had subjects read identical job descriptions that differed only in the status of the title. Jobs with higher-status titles were evaluated as being worth more money than jobs with lower-status titles. Some authors, however, have questioned the gender effects associated with titles (Mount & Ellis, 1989; Rynes, Weber, & Milkovich, 1989).

Though some organizations allow their employees to create their own titles, it is important that employees who are doing the same job have the same title and that the title accurately reflect the nature of the job. Broad titles such as "Office Support

Worker" often ignore potential salary market differences and responsibility differences found in more specific titles such as administrative assistant, secretary, and accounting clerk. In conducting salary equity analyses, it is not unusual to find that compensation differences between two people in the same job title are because, although they share the same title, they are performing very different work. This is especially true in IT jobs in which two employees with the tile of Software Programmer II could be programming very different types of software.

Brief Summary

The summary need be only a paragraph in length but should briefly describe the nature and purpose of the job. This summary can be used in external and internal job postings.

Work Activities

The work activities section lists the tasks and activities that the worker will be involved in. These tasks and activities should be organized into meaningful categories to make the job description easy to read and understand. The category labels are also convenient to use in the brief summary. Refer to the sample job description in Table 2.1: the 66 work activities performed by the bookkeeper are divided into seven main areas: accounting, clerical, teller, share draft, collections, payroll and data processing, and financial operations.

Tools and Equipment Used

A section should be included that lists all the tools and equipment used to perform the work activities in the previous section. Even though tools and equipment may have been mentioned in the activities section, placing them in a separate section makes their identification simpler. Information in this section is used primarily for employee selection and training. That is, an applicant can be asked if they know how to use Microsoft Word and Excel and if they have a valid driver's license.

Job Context

This section describes the environment in which the employee works and mentions stress level, work schedule, physical demands, level of responsibility, temperature, number of coworkers, degree of danger, and any other relevant information. This information is especially important in providing applicants with disabilities with information they can use to determine their ability to perform a job under a particular set of circumstances.

Work Performance

The job description should outline standards of performance. This section contains a relatively brief description of how an employee's performance is evaluated and what work standards are expected of the employee.

Compensation Information

Grade A cluster of jobs of similar worth.

This section of the job description should contain information on the salary **grade**, whether the position is exempt, and the compensable factors used to determine salary. These concepts will be described later in the chapter. The employee's actual salary or salary range should *not* be listed on the job description but can be listed later in a job posting.

Job Competencies

This section contains what are commonly called **job specifications** or **competencies**. These are the **knowledge**, skills, abilities, and **other characteristics** (**KSAOs**) (such as interest, personality, and training) that are necessary to be successful on the job. Competencies are determined by deciding what types of KSAOs are needed to perform the tasks identified in the job analysis. These KSAOs can be determined through a combination of logic, research, and use of specific job analysis techniques discussed later in this chapter.

The competencies section should be divided into two subsections. The first contains KSAOs that an employee must have at the time of hiring, commonly referred to as "Needed at entry". The second subsection contains the KSAOs that are an important part of the job but can be obtained after being hired. The first set of KSAOs is used for employee selection and the second for training purposes (Wooten, 1993).

Preparing for a Job Analysis

Prior to conducting a job analysis, several decisions must be made that will influence how it is conducted.

Who Will Conduct the Analysis?

Typically, a job analysis is conducted by a trained individual in the Human Resources department, but it can also be conducted by job incumbents, supervisors, or external consultants. If job incumbents or supervisors are used, then it is essential that they be thoroughly trained in job analysis procedures. The *Uniform Guidelines* state that a job analysis must be "professionally conducted," and a job analyst certainly cannot be called a professional unless they have been trained. In addition, research indicates that analysts who have been trained produce slightly different results from those produced by untrained analysts (Cellar, Curtis, Kohlepp, Poczapski, & Mohiuddin, 1989; Surrette, Aamodt, & Johnson, 1990).

Time is always an issue when using supervisors or incumbents. Telling a supervisor to "write job descriptions in your spare time" is not likely to go over well. Thus, supervisors and employees will need to be released from other duties—a situation that is seldom possible.

The state of Virginia developed a system in which all employees were asked to follow set guidelines and write their own job descriptions. The system itself was well conceived, but employees were not given enough job analysis training, which resulted in substantial confusion and, in some cases, inaccurate job descriptions.

Consultants are a good choice for conducting a job analysis because they are well trained and have extensive experience. The main drawback, though, is their expense. Consultants typically charge between $100 and $500 per hour based on their degree, experience, and reputation. Given that 10 hours is probably the least amount of time that will be spent analyzing the simplest job, and the most complex jobs can take months of analysis, an organization must carefully weigh the benefits of consultants against their cost.

An interesting alternative to consultants is the use of college interns. Graduate students from I/O psychology programs tend to have job analysis training and experience and can be employed for a relatively small cost. For example, many I/O graduate programs have projects in which graduate students obtain job analysis experience by conducting job analyses for companies as well as for such local nonprofit agencies as school systems, towns, police departments, and hospitals (Kottke, Shultz, & Aamodt, 2020). In this way, graduate students obtain experience,

Table 2.1 Example of a Job Description

Bookkeeper
True Value Credit Union

Job Summary
Under the general supervision of the office manager, the bookkeeper is responsible for all of the accounting duties of the office. Specifically, the bookkeeper is responsible for keeping all financial records accurate and up to date; processing loans; and preparing and posting statements, reports, and bonds.

Work Activities
The work activities of the Bookkeeper are divided into seven main functional areas:

Accounting Activities
- Prepares quarterly income statements
- Maintains and posts all transactions in the general ledger
- Pays credit union bills
- Prepares statistical reports
- Updates undivided earnings account
- Prepares and files tax returns and statements
- Completes IRA forms and reports in cooperation with CUNA
- Annually computes Cumis Bond
- Balances journal and cash records

Clerical Activities
- Looks up members' account information when requested
- Answers phone
- Makes copies of transactions for members
- Drafts statements of account to members
- Prints certificates of deposit
- Picks up, sorts, and disperses credit union mail
- Sorts checks or copies of checks in numerical order
- Orders supplies
- Prepares reports and minutes from board meetings
- Maintains and updates files for members
- Prepares correspondence
- Enters change-of-address information into the computer

Teller Activities
- Enrolls new members
- Opens and closes accounts for new members Reconciles accounts
- Issues money orders and traveler's checks
- Conducts history of accounts
- Processes and issues receipts for transactions
- Asks for identification if person making transaction is not known
- Orders new or replacement checks for members
- Prints and issues checks
- Makes proper referrals

Share Draft Activities
- Deducts fee from member's account when a share is returned
- Processes statements for share draft accounts
- Issues stop payments and sends copy of form to member
- Deducts fee in form of an overdraft when more than three transfers have occurred for any one member in a month
- Checks and records share drafts or additions from previous day

- Receives share draft totals for each member from CUNA data
- Decides on an individual basis whether overdrafts will be covered by credit union
- Determines if overdrafts on account have been paid
- Checks to see if share drafts have cleared
- Telephones Bank when a member does not have enough money to cover a share draft

Collections Activities
- Withholds money from member's check to meet loan payments
- Decides if a member who has a delinquent loan will be able to take money out of account
- Locates and communicates with members having delinquent loans
- Completes garnishee form to send to courts on delinquent loans
- Resubmits garnishee form once every three months until delinquent loan has been paid in full by member
- Makes collection on delinquent loans
- Checks on previous member's address and current job to see if loan payments can be made
- Determines number and length of time of delinquent loans
- Sends judgment form to court, which sends it to delinquent member
- If a member is delinquent, finds out if they are sick or on vacation

Payroll and Data-Processing Activities
- Checks and verifies payroll run for all necessary deductions
- Reads and interprets reports
- Computes and subtracts deductions from payroll
- Sets up and changes deduction amounts for payroll savings plan
- Computes payroll
- Runs daily trial balances and transaction registers
- Loads paper into printer
- Makes backup copies of all daily computer transactions
- Runs quarterly and/or monthly statements

Financial Operations Activities
- Scans business/financial environment to identify potential threats and opportunities
- Makes recommendations to the board regarding investments
- Invests all excess money into accounts that will earn interest
- Computes profits and amounts to be used for investments
- Prepares statements of financial condition and federal operating fee report
- Obtains enough funds for day-to-day operation of branch
- Notifies and makes available investment funds to the NCUA

Tools and Equipment Used
- Calculator
- Microsoft Word and Excel
- Printer
- Motor vehicle
- Photocopy machine
- Safe
- Telephone
- Security check writer

Job Context
The bookkeeper spends the majority of time making entries in and balancing journals and ledgers. The workday is spent in a climate-controlled office with four coworkers. Physical demands are minimal and sitting is required for most of the day. Work hours are Monday–Friday from 8:00 a.m. to 5:00 p.m., with an unpaid hour for lunch. No weekend or holiday work is required, and overtime seldom occurs. Psychological stress is usually low but becomes moderate when dealing with an angry customer.

(Continued)

Table 2.1   Example of a Job Description (*Continued*)

Work Performance

The bookkeeper is evaluated annually by the office manager using the credit union's standard performance appraisal system. To receive an excellent performance appraisal, the bookkeeper should:

- Maintain neat and accurate records
- Meet all deadlines
- Maintain an orderly office
- Make sure all ledgers and journals balance
- Perform duties of other jobs when the need arises
- Have a good attendance record

Compensation Information

Grade: 6

FLSA Status: Not exempt

Job Competencies

Upon hire, the bookkeeper must:

- Have a high school diploma and a basic knowledge of math and grammar
- Have a valid driver's license
- Understand financial documents
- Be able to make limited financial decisions
- Have completed advanced coursework in accounting and finance
- Be skilled in using Microsoft Excel and Word

After hire, the bookkeeper must:

- Learn general office procedures
- Learn the style of credit union accounting procedures and regulations
- Learn how to complete the various forms

---

and the organizations receive professional-quality job analyses and job descriptions at a reduced cost.

How Often Should a Job Description Be Updated?

The typical answer to this tough question is that a job description should be updated if a job changes significantly. With high-tech jobs, this is probably fairly often. Recall the earlier example of the expansion of employment opportunities in the field of Big Data, which came about in the early 21st century. The rapid advances in technology resulted in the creation of new techniques and software for these jobs, requiring constant updates to job descriptions for these positions (De Mauro et al., 2018). However, with jobs such as package handling, the job might not change substantially for 20 years. A study by Vincent, Rainey, Faulkner, Mascio, and Zinda (2007) compared the stability of job descriptions at intervals of 1, 6, 10, 12, and 20 years. After one year, 92% of the tasks listed in the old and updated job descriptions were the same, dropping to 54% after 10 years. As one would expect, the stability of tasks performed, the tools and equipment used, and KSAOs needed to perform the job varied by the complexity of the job.

Job crafting A process in which employees unofficially change their job duties to better fit their interests and skills.

An interesting reason that job descriptions change across time is **job crafting**—the informal changes that employees make in their jobs (Wrzesniewski & Dutton, 2001). That is, it is common for employees to quietly expand the scope of their jobs to add tasks they want to perform and to remove tasks that they don't want to perform. In a study of sales representatives, 75% engaged in job crafting in just one year (Lyons, 2008)!

Further investigation conducted on job crafting has uncovered numerous benefits to not only the organization, but also the employees. Researchers have found that allowing employees to make these informal changes to their job can lead to a positive work identity (Wrzesniewski & Dutton, 2001), enhanced job satisfaction, and a positive increase in organizational outcomes (Tims & Bakker, 2010).

Which Employees Should Participate?

For organizations with relatively few people in each job, it is advisable to have all employees participate in the job analysis. In organizations in which many people perform the same job (e.g., teachers at a university, assemblers in a factory, nurses in a hospital), every person need not participate. If every incumbent is not going to participate, the question becomes, "How many people need to be included in the job analysis?" This is a difficult question, one that I normally answer by advising job analysts to keep interviewing incumbents until they do not hear anything new. Anecdotally, this seems to be after the third or fourth incumbent for a particular job. Although a job analyst may stop hearing new information after only a few interviews, it is often advisable to continue to conduct more interviews so that the job analysis results will better survive a legal challenge.

The answer to this question to some extent depends on whether the job analysis will be committee-based or field-based. In a committee-based job analysis, a group of subject-matter experts (people who are knowledgeable about the job and include job incumbents, supervisors, customers, and upper-level management) meet to generate the tasks performed, the conditions under which they are performed, and the KSAOs needed to perform them. In a field-based job analysis, the job analyst individually interviews/observes several incumbents out in the field. Taken together, the results of four studies (Ash, Levine, Higbee, & Sistrunk, 1982; Maurer & Tross, 2000; O'Leary, Rheinstein, & McCauley, 1990; Tannenbaum & Wesley, 1993) suggest that committee-based job analyses yield similar results to field-based job analyses.

Rouleau and Krain (1975) developed a table to estimate how many incumbents should be included in a job analysis; their recommendation is that a committee-based approach should have one session of 4 to 6 incumbents for jobs having fewer than 30 incumbents and two to three sessions for jobs with higher numbers of incumbents. Green and Stutzman (1986) have suggested a minimum of 3 incumbents, and Gael (1988) has suggested 6 to 10. Unfortunately, no research is available to verify the accuracy of these estimates.

Beatty (1996) compared the results of job analysis samples of 10, 15, 20, and 212 incumbents in a federal law enforcement position. His results indicated that the job tasks and job requirements resulting from the use of 10 versus 212 incumbents were nearly identical. These results support and extend those found by Fletcher, Friedman, McCarthy, McIntyre, O' Leary, and Rheinstein (1993) and Pass and Robertson (1980), who found that job analysis samples of 10 and 20 yielded comparable results.

Mullins (1983) had 97 campus police officers at 13 universities generate critical incidents as part of a job analysis. The results indicated that no new incidents appeared after examining the incidents from the first three universities. Furthermore, after examining the incidents supplied by the first 19 incumbents, no new incidents or categories appeared.

After the number of participants has been determined, a decision needs to be made about which *particular employees* will participate. If every employee will not participate, the same sampling rules used in research should be used in job analysis. That is, as discussed in Chapter 1, participants should be selected in as random a way as practical yet still be representative. The reason for this, according to research, is that employee differences in gender, race, job performance level, experience, job enjoyment, and personality can at times result in slightly different job analysis outcomes.

Job Competence.   Sanchez, Prager, Wilson, and Viswesvaran (1998) and Mullins and Kimbrough (1988) found that high-performing employees generated different job analysis outcomes than did low-performing employees; Ansoorian and Shultz (1997) found moderate differences in physical effort made by employees with varying levels of expertise; and both Landy and Vasey (1991) and Prien, Prien, and Wooten (2003) found that more experienced employees rated tasks differently than less experienced employees. However, Mailhot (1996) and Conley and Sackett (1987) did not find any differences in job analysis ratings made by employees of different performance levels.

If higher-performing employees generate different job analysis results than lower-performing employees, a tough decision must be made regarding which employees to include in the job analysis. On the one hand, it would be nice to include a representative sample of employees. On the other hand, do we really want to write a job description and select future employees based on how poorly performing employees do their jobs?

Race.   Aamodt, Kimbrough, Keller, and Crawford (1982); Schmitt and Cohen (1989); Veres, Green, and Boyles (1991); and Landy and Vasey (1991) report small but significant differences in the ways in which White and Black incumbents viewed their jobs. For example, Landy and Vasey found that White police officers administered first aid more often and Black officers were more involved in sweeps and raids related to widespread narcotics use. Veres et al. (1991) found that job analysis ratings were related not only to the race of the incumbent but to the race of the incumbent's coworkers.

Gender.   Landy and Vasey (1991) found possible differences in the ways men and women viewed their jobs. Because gender was confounded with experience, they were not able to draw any definite conclusions. Schmitt and Cohen (1989) found that male middle-level managers were more often involved in budgetary or finance-related tasks than were their female counterparts. Ansoorian and Schultz (1997) found no differences in the physical-effort ratings assigned by male and female incumbents. Walion and Baker (2018) found that male and female police officers differed in how they rated the frequency and importance of tasks.

Education Level.   Landy and Vasey (1991) found that police officers with only a high school diploma were less involved in court activities than were their more educated counterparts.

Personality.   Cucina, Vasilopoulos, and Sehgal (2005) found that the personality of the incumbent was related to the personality traits rated by the incumbent to be important to the job. That is, extroverted incumbents rated such traits as friendliness, leadership ability, and ambition as being important for the job whereas conscientious incumbents rated such traits as work ethic and attention to detail as being important. Similarly, Ford, Truxillo, Wang, and Bauer (2008) found that extroverts and people high in agreeableness were likely to inflate task and KSAO ratings.

Viewpoint.   It should be no surprise that people with different perspectives on the job (e.g., incumbent, supervisor, customer) produce different job analysis results. For example, Mueller and Belcher (2000) found that incumbents (fire captains) and their supervisors (fire chief, deputy fire chiefs, and division chiefs) produced different task ratings during a job analysis of the fire captain position. Truxillo, Paronto, Collins, and Sulzer (2004) found differences in ratings provided by police officers and district attorneys of the criticality of different aspects of report writing for reports written by police officers. Wagner (1950) conducted a job analysis of dentists and found that patients generated more incidents where patient–dentist relationship was critical, whereas dentists reported more technical-proficiency incidents. Likewise, Fisher and Greenis (1996) and Andersson and Nilsson (1964) found differences in the critical incidents generated by managers, incumbents, and customers.

The consideration of which employees are chosen to participate is an important issue because a job can often be performed in several ways. If people in different age groups perform equally well on a job, yet perform the job in different ways, the job analyses must contain information about both styles. For example, suppose research indicates that older supervisors lead by setting goals and being directive and younger supervisors use more of a participative approach. Consequently, a job analysis conducted only on younger supervisors would result in a different set of KSAOs than a job analysis using both older and younger supervisors. Because job analysis is the basis for every personnel decision, equal opportunity efforts seem to begin as early as the job analysis.

The issue of using the best employees or the typical employees is also important. During a job analysis at a large printing factory, it was discovered that one employee performed their job differently from the employees on the other two shifts. Further investigation revealed that the one employee was also rated much higher in job performance than the other two. Thus, it appeared that the logical thing to do was write the job analysis results based on the way the best employee performed the job and then retrain the other two.

What Types of Information Should Be Obtained?

An important decision concerns the *level of specificity*. That is, should the job analysis break a job down into very minute, specific behaviors (e.g., "tilts arm at a 90-degree angle" or "moves foot forward three inches"), or should the job be analyzed at a more general level ("makes financial decisions," "speaks to clients")? Although most jobs are analyzed at levels somewhere between these two extremes, there are times when the level of analysis will be closer to one end of the spectrum than the other. Wilson (2012) advises that because highly specific information in a job analysis becomes obsolete more quickly than general information, a job analysis should identify only information as specific as necessary to meet the goals of the project.

For some jobs that involve intricate work, extensive and expensive efforts have been undertaken to identify the optimal way in which tasks should be performed. For example, in a window manufacturing plant, job analysis determined that many more windows could be mounted in frames by lifting the glass just six inches and then sliding it into place, than by lifting the glass higher and placing it in the frame. In such a situation, the work obviously must be performed in a specific manner for the greatest financial savings. Thus, the job analysis is more effective at a more detailed level.

A related decision addresses the issue of *formal versus informal* requirements. Formal requirements for an administrative assistant might include preparing PowerPoint presentations or entering data into Excel. Informal requirements might involve making coffee or picking up the boss's children from school. Including informal requirements has the advantages of identifying and eliminating duties that may be illegal or unnecessary. For example, suppose a job analysis reveals that an administrative assistant in one department picks up the boss's children from school and takes them to a daycare center. This is an important finding because the company may not want this to occur. However, because the manager makes $200,000 per year, the company may prefer that the lower-paid administrative assistant rather than the higher-paid executive take an hour a day to pick up the children. If this task is in the job description, an applicant will know about this duty in advance and can decide before accepting the job whether it is acceptable.

In addition, informal requirements (e.g., picking up mail) may need to be made more formal to reduce potential confusion regarding who is responsible for the task. At one credit union, a continued source of bickering involved whose job or whose turn it was to pick up the mail, especially when the weather was bad and post office parking became limited. This problem could have been eliminated if the task were assigned to one individual.

Conducting a Job Analysis

Although there are many ways to conduct a job analysis, the goal of most job analyses is to identify the tasks performed in a job, the conditions under which the tasks are performed, and the KSAOs needed to perform the tasks under the conditions identified. This section will begin with a commonly used strategy for conducting a job analysis and conclude with descriptions of alternative methods.

Step 1: Identify Tasks Performed

The first step in conducting a job analysis is to identify the major job dimensions and the tasks performed for each dimension, the tools and equipment used to perform the tasks, and the conditions under which the tasks are performed. This information is usually gathered by obtaining previous information on the job, interviewing job incumbents, observing performance, or performing the job itself.

Some jobs require tremendous attention to detail

Hisham Ibrahim/PhotoDisc/Getty Images

Subject-matter experts (SMEs) Sources such as supervisors and incumbents who are knowledgeable about a job.

Job analyst The person conducting the job analysis.

SME conference A group job analysis interview consisting of subject-matter experts (SMEs).

Gathering Existing Information. Prior to interviewing incumbents, it is always a good idea to gather information that has already been obtained. For example, one might gather existing job descriptions, task inventories, and training manuals. This information might come from the organization with which you are working, other organizations, trade publications, and journal articles. Examples of external sources are occupational and career information systems such as O*NET, employment advertisements, certification and training resources, and technical and research reports (Dierdorff, 2012).

Interviewing Subject-Matter Experts. The most common method of conducting a job analysis is to interview **subject-matter experts (SMEs)**. SMEs are people who are knowledgeable about the job and include job incumbents, supervisors, customers, and upper-level management. Job analysis interviews differ greatly from employment interviews in that the purpose of the job analysis interview is to obtain information about the job itself rather than about the person doing the job. Job analysis interviews come in two main forms: individual and group. In the individual interview, the **job analyst** interviews only one employee at a time. In the group interview, or **SME conference**, a larger number of employees are interviewed together. As mentioned earlier in this chapter, individual interviews tend to yield similar results to group interviews.

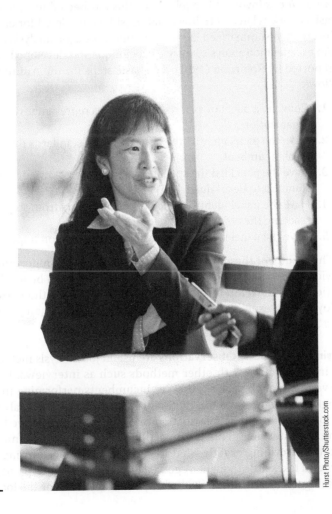

Interviews are a common job analysis technique

Hurst Photo/Shutterstock.com

Regardless of whether individual or group interviews are used, certain guidelines should be followed that will make the interview go more smoothly.

1. *Prepare* for the interview by announcing the job analysis to the employees well in advance and by selecting a quiet and private interview location.
2. *Open* the interview by establishing rapport, putting the worker at ease, and explaining the purpose of the interview.
3. *Conduct* the interview by asking open-ended questions, using easy-to-understand vocabulary, and allowing sufficient time for the employee to talk and answer questions. Avoid being condescending and disagreeing with the incumbent.

Most workers are proud of their jobs and are willing to describe them in great detail. Once the initial apprehensions and jitters are over, most job analysis interviews go well. A good way to start the actual interview is by asking the employee to describe what they do from the moment they first start work to the moment they end their workday. A question such as this provides some structure for the employee in recalling the various aspects of their job and also provides the interviewer with many follow-up questions and areas that will provide additional information.

With a committee-based approach, a committee of SMEs meets to brainstorm the *major duties* involved in a job. Once this has been done, the committee identifies the tasks (work-related activities) that must be completed for each of the duties. The results are then summarized in job descriptions or a job analysis report.

An excellent job analysis interview technique was developed by Ammerman (1965) and reported by Robinson (1981). The basic steps for the **Ammerman technique** are as follows:

1. Convene a panel of experts that includes representatives from all levels of the organization.
2. Have the panel identify the objectives and standards that are to be met by the ideal incumbent.
3. Have the panel list the specific behaviors necessary for each objective or standard to be attained.
4. Have the panel identify which of the behaviors from step 3 are "critical" to reaching the objective.
5. Have the panel rank-order the objectives based on importance.

The results of these procedures will yield a set of important objectives and the behaviors necessary to meet them. These behaviors can be used to create employee selection tests, develop training programs, or evaluate the performance of current employees. An example of Ammerman-style objectives and behaviors is shown in Figure 2.1.

Observing Incumbents. **Observations** are useful job analysis methods, especially when used in conjunction with other methods such as interviews. During a job analysis observation, the job analyst observes incumbents performing their jobs in the work setting. The advantage to this method is that it lets the job analyst see the worker do their job and thus obtain information that the worker may have forgotten to mention during the interview. This is especially important because many employees have difficulty describing exactly what they do; to them, performing their job is second nature and takes little thought. A good demonstration of this point is people's difficulty in naming the location of individual keys on a keyboard or the location of gears when

Ammerman technique A job analysis method in which a group of job experts identifies the objectives and standards to be met by the ideal worker.

Observations A job analysis method in which the job analyst watches job incumbents perform their jobs.

Figure 2.1

Example of Ammerman Technique Objectives and Tasks for a Bank Teller

Cross-sell bank products.
- Study daily rate charts.
- Explain new products to customers.

Balance drawer within 30 minutes at end of day.
- Accurately count money.
- Trial balance drawer during downtimes.

Comply with federal and state regulations.
- Notify federal government of cash transactions in excess of $10,000.
- Treat customers equally regardless of age, race, gender, or national origin.

Accurately complete paperwork.
- Obtain all necessary information from customers.
- Obtain all necessary signatures.

Make each customer feel a "part of the family."
- Know each customer's name.
- Refer to customers by their first names.
- Smile and greet each customer.

they drive. We all type and shift gears without thinking (well, most of us do), but quickly describing to another person the location of the V key on our keyboard or "Reverse" on our manual transmission console is difficult.

The method's disadvantage is that it can be obtrusive. Observing someone without their knowing is difficult. Think of the jobs at which you have worked; there is seldom anyplace from which an analyst could observe without being seen by employees. This is a problem because once employees know they are being watched, their behavior changes, which keeps an analyst from obtaining an accurate picture of the way jobs are done. When I was in college and working third shift at a bookbinding factory, the company hired an "efficiency expert" to analyze our performance. The expert arrived in a three-piece suit, armed with a stopwatch and clipboard. He stuck out like a sore thumb! You can bet that for the two weeks the efficiency expert observed us, we were ideal employees (I can even remember calling my supervisor "sir") because we knew he was watching. Once he left, we went back to being our normal time-wasting, soda-drinking, wise-cracking selves.

Job Participation. One can analyze a job by actually performing it. This technique, called **job participation**, is especially effective because it is easier to understand every aspect of a job once you have done it yourself. The technique is easily used when the analyst has previously performed the job. An excellent example would be a supervisor who has worked their way up through the ranks. As mentioned earlier, the problem with using a supervisor or an incumbent is that neither has been trained in job analysis techniques.

A professional job analyst can also perform an unfamiliar job for a short period of time, although this, of course, is limited to certain occupations that involve quick training and minimal consequences from an error. Brain surgery would probably not be good to analyze using this method.

The analyst should spend enough time on the job to properly sample work behavior in addition to job difficulty. Yet spending long periods of time can be expensive and still not guarantee that all aspects of behavior will be covered. Psychologist Wayman Mullins used job participation techniques to analyze the job of a firefighter. Mullins spent two weeks living at the fire station and performing all the duties of a firefighter. The only problem during this two-week period—no fires. If Mullins had not already

Job participation A job analysis method in which the job analyst actually performs the job being analyzed.

had a good idea of what a firefighter did, he would have concluded that the most important duties were sleeping, cleaning, cooking, and playing cards!

Step 2: Write Task Statements

Once the tasks have been identified, the next step is to write the task statements that will be used in the **task inventory** and included in the job description. As shown in Table 2.2, at the minimum, a properly written task statement must contain an *action* (what is done) and an *object* (to which the action is done). Often, task statements will also include such components as *where* the task is done, *how* it is done, *why* it is done, and *when* it is done.

Here are some characteristics of well-written task statements:

- One action should be done to one object. If the statement includes the word "and," it may have more than one action or object. For example, the statement "Writes correspondence to be sent to vendors" has one action and one object. However, "Writes, files, and sends correspondence to vendors" contains three very different actions (writes, files, sends).
- Task statements should be written at a level that can be read and understood by a person with the same reading ability as the typical job incumbent.
- All task statements should be written in the same tense.
- The task statement should include the tools and equipment used to complete the task.
- Task statements should not be competencies (e.g., "Be a good writer").
- Task statements should not be a policy (e.g., "Treats people nicely").
- The statement should make sense by itself. That is, "Makes photocopies" does not provide as much detail as "Makes photocopies of student exams when requested by professors," which indicates what types of materials are photocopied and for whom they are copied.
- For those activities that involve decision making, the level of authority should be indicated. This level lets the incumbent know which decisions they can make on their own and which decisions need approval from a higher level.

Research has differentiated between two methods for generating task statements: "decomposed strategies", in which job analysts gather detailed information about each discrete element of a job activity, or "holistic strategies", in which the job analysis information tends to be more abstract and broader (Cornelius, Lyness, 1980). The decomposed strategy is more time-consuming and expensive than the holistic strategy, but often provides a higher reliability by simplifying any judgment required by the job analysis respondents. Researchers have contended that the use of the holistic strategy for generating task statements is one of the more contentious topics in job analysis (Harvey & Wilson, 2000). It has also been suggested that a few

Table 2.2 Writing Effective Task Statements

Poorly Written Task Statement	Properly Written Task Statement
Makes purchase requests	Makes purchase requests to the purchasing department by entering the request into the University Purchasing System
Drives	Drives a five-speed truck to make food deliveries within the city of Toledo
Locks hall doors	Uses master key to lock hall doors at midnight so that nonresidents cannot enter the residence hall

tasks not part of a job be placed into the task inventory; data from incumbents who rate these irrelevant tasks as part of their job are removed from the job analysis due to their carelessness (Green & Stutzman, 1986). Including "bogus tasks" is probably a good idea. Pine (1995) included five such items in a 68-item task inventory for corrections officers and found that 45% reported performing at least one of the bogus tasks. For example, a task inventory might include "operates a Gonkulator" or "uses PARTH program to analyze data" even though no such machine or computer program actually exists. A study by Dierdorff and Rubin (2007) found that incumbents who are low in cognitive ability and are confused about their work role (role ambiguity) are the most likely to endorse the bogus tasks on a task inventory.

Step 3: Rate Task Statements

Task analysis The process of identifying the tasks for which employees need to be trained.

Once the task statements have been written, the next step is to conduct a **task analysis**—using a group of SMEs to rate each task statement on the frequency and the importance or criticality of the task being performed. For example, consider the task *accurately shoots a gun*. For a police officer, this task occurs infrequently (most officers never discharge their weapon on the job during their entire career), but when it does, its importance is paramount. If a frequency scale alone were used, shooting a gun might not be covered in training. Although many types of scales can be used, research suggests that many of the scales tap similar types of information (Sanchez & Fraser, 1992); thus, using the two scales of frequency of occurrence and importance shown in Table 2.3 should be sufficient. In fact, rather than asking for ratings of frequency of occurrence or relative time spent on a task, some researchers advise that the task inventory should simply ask, "Do you perform this task?" (Wilson & Harvey, 1990). Raters tend to agree on ratings of task importance but not on time spent (Lindell, Clause, Brandt, & Landis, 1998).

After a representative sample of SMEs rates each task, the ratings are organized into a format like that shown in Table 2.4. Tasks will not be included in the *job description* if their average frequency rating is 0.5 or below. Tasks will not be included in the final *task inventory* if they have either an average rating of 0.5 or less on *either* the frequency (F) or importance (I) scales or an average combined rating (CR) of less than 2. Using these criteria, tasks 1, 2, and 4 in Table 2.4 would be included in the job description, and tasks 2 and 4 would be included in the final task inventory used in the next step of the job analysis.

Step 4: Determine Essential KSAOs

Once the task analysis is completed and a job analyst has a list of tasks that are essential for the proper performance of a job, the next step is to identify the KSAOs needed to perform the tasks.

Table 2.3   Example of Task Inventory Scales

Frequency

0	Task is not performed as part of this job.
1	Task is seldom performed.
2	Task is occasionally performed.
3	Task is frequently performed.

Importance

0	Unimportant: There would be no negative consequences if the task was not performed or if the task was not performed properly.
1	Important: Job performance would be diminished if the task was not completed properly.
2	Essential: The job could not be performed effectively if the incumbent did not properly complete this task.

Table 2.4   Example of Task Inventory Scales

Task #	Cooper			Farrah Fowler			Combined Average		
	F	+ I	= CR	F	+ I	= CR	F	+ I	= CR
1	2	0	2	3	0	3	2.5	0.0	2.5
2	2	2	4	2	1	3	2.0	1.5	3.5
3	0	0	0	0	0	0	0.0	0.0	0.0
4	3	2	5	3	2	5	3.0	2.0	5.0

Skill Proficiency to perform a particular task.

- **Knowledge** is a body of information needed to perform a task.
- A **skill** is the proficiency to perform a learned task.
- An **ability** is a basic capacity for performing a wide range of different tasks, acquiring knowledge, or developing a skill.
- **Other characteristics** include such personal factors as personality, willingness, interest, and motivation and such tangible factors as licenses, degrees, and years of experience.

Currently, KSAOs are commonly referred to as *competencies*. In the old days, KSAOs were called job specifications (job specs). Though there may be some disagreement among I/O psychologists, the terms "KSAOs," "competencies," and "job specs" can be used interchangeably and there is no real difference among the three (other than which term is in vogue). When competencies are tied to an organization's strategic initiatives and plans rather than to specific tasks, the process is called *competency modeling*.

To refer to our example of a police officer accurately shooting a gun (skill), the police officer would need to hold the gun properly and allow for such external conditions as the target distance and wind conditions (knowledge), and have the hand strength, steadiness, and vision necessary to hold the gun, pull the trigger, and aim properly (abilities). To carry the gun, the officer would need to have a weapons certification (other characteristic). Determining important KSAOs can be done in one of two ways: logically linking tasks to KSAOs or using prepackaged questionnaires.

To logically link KSAOs to tasks, a group of SMEs brainstorm the KSAOs needed to perform each task. For example, a group of police officers might consider the task of "writing accident reports" and determine that grammar skills, spelling skills, and knowledge of accidents are the KSAOs needed for a police officer to perform this task.

Once the list of essential KSAOs has been developed, another group of SMEs is given the list and asked to rate the extent to which each of the KSAOs is essential for performing the job. If a scale such as that shown in Table 2.5 is used, KSAOs with an average score of .5 or less are eliminated from further consideration.

As you can see in Table 2.5, it is also important for the SMEs to determine when each KSAO is needed. Using data from the table, KSAOs that receive average ratings of 2.5 or higher will be part of the employee selection process as they will be needed-at-entry, KSAOs with average ratings between 1.5 and 2.49 will be taught at the police academy, and KSAOs with average ratings between .5 and 1.49 will be learned on the job during the officer's probationary period.

Rather than using the previously discussed process, KSAOs, or competencies, can be identified using such structured methods as the Job Components Inventory (JCI), Threshold Traits Analysis (TTA), Fleishman Job Analysis Survey (F-JAS), Critical

Incident Technique (CIT), and the Personality-Related Position Requirements Form (PPRF). Each of these will be discussed in detail later in the chapter.

Step 5: Selecting Tests to Tap KSAOs

Once the important KSAOs have been identified, the next step is to determine the best methods to tap the KSAOs needed at the time of hire. These methods will be used to select new employees and include such methods as interviews, work samples, ability tests, personality tests, reference checks, integrity tests, biodata, and assessment centers. These methods, and how to choose them, will be discussed in detail in Chapters 4, 5, and 6.

The average ratings obtained from step 4 will be used to weight test scores. That is, a test tapping a KSAO with a rating of 2.9 should receive more weight than a test tapping a KSAO with a rating of 2.5.

Using Other Job Analysis Methods

In the previous pages, the most common method for conducting a job analysis was discussed. Though this method provides great information, it can be rather lengthy and unstructured. To save time, increase structure, or supplement information obtained from interviews, observations, and task analysis, other job analysis methods are available. These methods tend to provide information on one of four specific factors that are commonly included in a job description: worker activities, tools and equipment used, work environment, and competencies.

Methods Providing General Information About Worker Activities

Using the strategy discussed previously yields *specific* information about the tasks and activities performed by an incumbent in a *particular job*. Though such detailed information is ideal, obtaining it can be both time-consuming and expensive. As an alternative, several questionnaires have been developed to analyze jobs at a more general level. This general analysis saves time and money and allows jobs to be more easily compared with one another than is the case if interviews, observations, job participation, or task analysis is used.

Position Analysis Questionnaire. The **Position Analysis Questionnaire (PAQ)** is a structured instrument developed at Purdue University by McCormick, Jeanneret, and Mecham (1972), and is still commercially available. The current version of the PAQ contains 300 items organized into six main dimensions: information input, mental processes, work output, interpersonal activities, job context, and other job-related

Position Analysis Questionnaire (PAQ) A structured job analysis method developed by McCormick.

Table 2.5   Scales Used to Rate KSAOs for Law Enforcement

Importance of KSAO

0	KSAO is **not needed** for satisfactory completion of the academy or for satisfactory job performance.
1	KSAO is **helpful** for satisfactory completion of the academy or for satisfactory job performance.
2	KSAO is **important/essential** for satisfactory completion of the academy or for satisfactory job performance.

When KSAO Is Needed

0	KSAO is not needed.
1	KSAO is needed after completion of field training.
2	KSAO is needed after completion of the academy.
3	KSAO is needed at the time of hire.

variables such as work schedule, pay, and responsibility (Morgeson, Brannick, & Levine, 2020). In the sample PAQ page shown in Figure 2.2, notice that the level of analysis is fairly general. That is, the PAQ tells us if a job involves interviewing but does not indicate the type of interviewing that is performed (interviewing job applicants versus

Figure 2.2

Example of
PAQ Questions

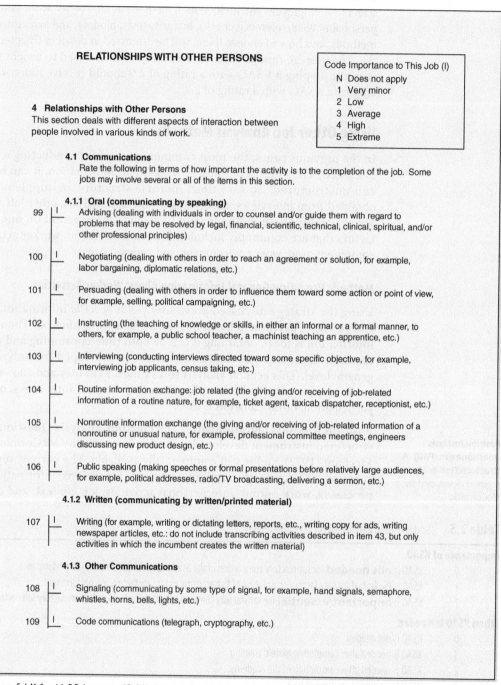

RELATIONSHIPS WITH OTHER PERSONS

Code Importance to This Job (I)
N Does not apply
1 Very minor
2 Low
3 Average
4 High
5 Extreme

4 Relationships with Other Persons
This section deals with different aspects of interaction between people involved in various kinds of work.

4.1 Communications
Rate the following in terms of how important the activity is to the completion of the job. Some jobs may involve several or all of the items in this section.

4.1.1 Oral (communicating by speaking)

99 I Advising (dealing with individuals in order to counsel and/or guide them with regard to problems that may be resolved by legal, financial, scientific, technical, clinical, spiritual, and/or other professional principles)

100 I Negotiating (dealing with others in order to reach an agreement or solution, for example, labor bargaining, diplomatic relations, etc.)

101 I Persuading (dealing with others in order to influence them toward some action or point of view, for example, selling, political campaigning, etc.)

102 I Instructing (the teaching of knowledge or skills, in either an informal or a formal manner, to others, for example, a public school teacher, a machinist teaching an apprentice, etc.)

103 I Interviewing (conducting interviews directed toward some specific objective, for example, interviewing job applicants, census taking, etc.)

104 I Routine information exchange: job related (the giving and/or receiving of job-related information of a routine nature, for example, ticket agent, taxicab dispatcher, receptionist, etc.)

105 I Nonroutine information exchange (the giving and/or receiving of job-related information of a nonroutine or unusual nature, for example, professional committee meetings, engineers discussing new product design, etc.)

106 I Public speaking (making speeches or formal presentations before relatively large audiences, for example, political addresses, radio/TV broadcasting, delivering a sermon, etc.)

4.1.2 Written (communicating by written/printed material)

107 I Writing (for example, writing or dictating letters, reports, etc., writing copy for ads, writing newspaper articles, etc.: do not include transcribing activities described in item 43, but only activities in which the incumbent creates the written material)

4.1.3 Other Communications

108 I Signaling (communicating by some type of signal, for example, hand signals, semaphore, whistles, horns, bells, lights, etc.)

109 I Code communications (telegraph, cryptography, etc.)

Source: E. J. McCormick, P. R. Jeannert, and R. C. Mecham. (1969). *Position Analysis Questionnaire*, Purdue Research Foundation, West Lafayette, Indiana 47907.

interviewing a witness to a crime) or how the interview is conducted. Thus, the results would be difficult to use for functions such as training or performance appraisal.

The PAQ offers many advantages. It is inexpensive and takes relatively little time to use. It is one of the most standardized job analysis methods, has acceptable levels of reliability, and its results for a particular position can be compared through computer analysis with thousands of other positions.

Although the PAQ has considerable support, research indicates its strengths are also the source of its weaknesses. The PAQ's instructions suggest that incumbents using the questionnaire have education levels between grades 10 and 12. Research has found, however, that the PAQ questions and directions are written at the college graduate level (Ash & Edgell, 1975); thus, many workers may not be able to understand the PAQ. This is one reason developers of the PAQ recommend that trained job analysts complete the PAQ rather than the employees themselves.

In addition, the PAQ was designed to cover all jobs; but limited to 300 questions and six dimensions, it has not proven very sensitive. For example, a homemaker and a police officer have similar PAQ profiles (Arvey & Begalla, 1975). Similar profiles also are obtained regardless of whether an analyst observes the job or just looks at a job title or a job description (Morgeson, et al., 2020).

Finally, having a large amount of information about a job yields the same results as having little information (Surrette et al., 1990). Although these studies speak favorably about the reliability of the PAQ, they also provide cause for worry because the PAQ appears to yield the same results regardless of how familiar the analyst is with a job.

Job Structure Profile. A revised version of the PAQ was developed by Patrick and Moore (1985). The major changes in the revision, which is called the **Job Structure Profile (JSP)**, include item content and style, new items to increase the discriminatory power of the intellectual and decision-making dimensions, and an emphasis on having a job analyst, rather than the incumbent, use the JSP. Research by JSP's developers indicates that the instrument is reliable, but little research has been conducted on the JSP since 1985.

Job Elements Inventory. Another instrument designed as an alternative to the PAQ is the **Job Elements Inventory (JEI)**, developed by Cornelius and Hakel (1978). The JEI contains 153 items and has a readability level appropriate for an employee with only a tenth-grade education (Cornelius, Hakel, & Sackett, 1979). Research comparing the JEI with the PAQ indicates that the scores from each method are very similar (Harvey, Friedman, Hakel, & Cornelius, 1988); Additionally, a survey comparing personnel selection specialists' familiarity with and attitudes toward different methods of job analysis found that the study respondents were more familiar with, and tended to favor, the job elements inventory method when compared to the Position Analysis Questionnaire (Levine, Ash, & Bennett, 1980); thus, the JEI may be a better replacement for the difficult-to-read PAQ. But as mentioned with the JSP, much more research is needed before conclusions can be confidently drawn.

Functional Job Analysis. Functional Job Analysis (FJA) was initially designed by Sidney Fine (1955) as a method that could be used by the federal government to analyze and compare thousands of jobs. The FJA process begins in a similar manner to many job analysis methods: a small group of subject matter experts meets to identify the key functions of a job (what gets done) as well as the tasks performed to complete each function (Cronshaw, 2012). What makes FJA unique, is that once the SMEs have identified these functions and tasks, they assign a percentage of time the incumbent spends on

Job Structure Profile (JSP) A revised version of the Position Analysis Questionnaire (PAQ) designed to be used more by the job analyst than by the job incumbent.

Job Elements Inventory (JEI) A structured job analysis technique developed by Cornelius and Hakel that is similar to the Position Analysis Questionnaire (PAQ) but easier to read.

Functional Job Analysis (FJA) A job analysis method developed by Fine that rates the extent to which a job incumbent is involved with functions in the categories of data, people, and things.

three functions: data (information and ideas), people (clients, customers, and coworkers), and things (machines, tools, and equipment). An analyst is given 100 points to allot to the three functions. The points are usually assigned in multiples of 5, with each function receiving a minimum of 5 points. Once the points have been assigned, the highest level at which the job incumbent functions is then chosen from the chart shown in Table 2.6.

Methods Providing Information About Tools and Equipment

Job Components Inventory.   To take advantage of the PAQ's strengths while avoiding some of its problems, Banks, Jackson, Stafford, and Warr (1983) developed the **Job Components Inventory (JCI)** for use in England. The JCI consists of more than 400 questions covering five major categories: tools and equipment, perceptual and physical requirements, mathematical requirements, communication requirements, and decision making and responsibility. It is the only job analysis method containing a detailed section on tools and equipment.

Published research on the JCI is not abundant. But it does appear to be a useful technique, with research indicating that it is reliable (Banks & Miller, 1984), can differentiate between jobs (Banks et al., 1983), can cluster jobs based on their similarity to one another (Stafford, Jackson, & Banks, 1984) and, unlike the PAQ, is affected by the amount of information available to the analyst (Surrette et al., 1990).

Methods Providing Information About the Work Environment

The techniques discussed so far provide information about the activities that are performed and the equipment used to perform them. The job analyst still needs information about the conditions under which the activities are performed. For example, two employees might perform the task "delivers packages," yet one might do it by manually carrying 50-pound packages outside in very hot or cold weather whereas the other delivers 5-pound packages by driving a golf cart through an air-conditioned warehouse. To obtain information about the work environment, a job analyst might use the **AET**, an acronym for "Arbeitswissenschaftliches Erhebungsverfahren zur Tätigkeitsanalyse" (try saying this three times!), which means "ergonomic job analysis procedure." By *ergonomic*, we mean that the instrument is primarily concerned with the relationship between the

Job Components Inventory (JCI) A structured job analysis technique that concentrates on worker requirements for performing a job rather than on specific tasks.

AET An ergonomic job analysis method developed in Germany (*Arbeitswissenschaftliches Erhebungsverfahren zur Tätigkeitsanalyse*).

Table 2.6   Data, People, and Things Levels

Data	People	Things
0 Synthesizing	0 Mentoring	0 Setting up
1 Coordinating	1 Negotiating	1 Precision working
2 Analyzing	2 Instructing	2 Operating-controlling
3 Compiling	3 Supervising	3 Driving-operating
4 Computing	4 Diverting	4 Manipulating
5 Copying	5 Persuading	5 Tending
6 Comparing	6 Speaking	6 Feeding-offbearing
	7 Serving	7 Handling
	8 Taking instructions	
	9 Helping	

worker and work objects. Developed in Germany by Rohmert and Landau (1983), the AET is a 216-item, standardized questionnaire that analyzes a job along the dimensions shown in Table 2.7. Sample items from the AET can be found in Table 2.8. Although the AET appears to be a useful method for obtaining certain types of job analysis information, there has not been enough published research to draw any real conclusions.

Methods Providing Information About Competencies

Occupational Information Network. The **Occupational Information Network (O*NET)** is a national job analysis system created by the federal government in 1998 (and continually updated) to replace the *Dictionary of Occupational Titles* (**DOT**), which had been in use since the 1930s (Levine & Oswald, 2012). O*NET is a major advancement in understanding the nature of work, in large part because its developers understood that jobs can be viewed at four levels: economic, organizational, occupational, and individual. As a result, O*NET has incorporated the types of information obtained in many job analysis techniques.

Table 2.7 AET Dimensions

Part A Work System Analysis
1 Work objects
    1.1 material work objects (physical condition, special properties of the material, quality of surfaces, manipulation delicacy, form, size, weight, dangerousness)
    1.2 energy as work object
    1.3 information as work object
    1.4 human, animals, plants as work objects
2 Equipment
    2.1 working equipment
        2.1.1 equipment, tools, machinery to change the properties of the work objects
        2.1.2 means of transport
        2.1.3 controls
    2.2 other equipment
        2.2.1 displays, measuring instruments
        2.2.2 technical aids to support human sense organs information
        2.2.3 work chair, table, room
3 Work environment
    3.1 Physical environment
        3.1.1 environmental influences
        3.1.2 dangerousness of work and risk of occupational diseases
    3.2 Organizational and social environment
        3.2.1 temporal organization of work
        3.2.2 position in the organization of work sequence
        3.2.3 hierarchical position in the organization
        3.2.4 position in the communication system

    3.3 Principles and methods of remuneration
        3.3.1 principles of remuneration
        3.3.2 methods of remuneration

Part B Task Analysis
1 Tasks relating to material work objects
2 Tasks relating to abstract work objects
3 Human-related tasks
4 Number and repetitiveness of tasks

Part C Demand Analysis
1 Demands on perception
    1.1 mode of perception
        1.1.1 visual
        1.1.2 auditory
        1.1.3 tactile
        1.1.4 olfactory
        1.1.5 proprioceptive
    1.2 absolute/relative evaluation of perceived information
    1.3 accuracy of perception
2 Demands for decision
    2.1 complexity of decision
    2.2 pressure on time
    2.3 required knowledge
3 Demands for response/activity
    3.1 body postures
    3.2 static work
    3.3 heavy muscular work
    3.4 light muscular work
    3.5 strenuousness and frequency of movements

AET = Arbeitswissenschaftliches Erhebungsverfahren zur Tätigkeitsanalyse = ergonomic job analysis procedure.
Rohmert, W., and Landau, K. (1983). *A new technique for job analysis*. New York: Taylor & Francis. Reprinted with permission of the publisher.

Table 2.8   Sample AET Items

CNO	CC
1.1.7	Weight
	Answer questions 22–24 indicating the individual proportions of *time* during which the incumbent performs tasks involving work materials of *different* weights.
22	D *Low* weight
	objects weighing up to 1 kg can normally be manipulated with fingers or hands.
23	D *Medium* weight
	1–10 kg can normally be manipulated with hands.
24	*Heavy* weight
	more than 10 kg can partly be manipulated by one person without using additional auxiliaries, partly including the use of handling equipment and hoisting machines
1.1.8	Danger
	Answer questions 25–30 indicating the individual proportions of *time* during which the incumbent performs tasks involving *dangerous work materials*
25	D Work materials that are *explosive*
	E.g., explosives and igniting mixtures, ammunition, fireworks
26	D Work materials that are conductive to fire or inflammable
	E.g., petrol, technical oils, lacquers, and varnishes
27	D Work materials that are *poisonous or caustic*
	E.g., basic chemicals, chemical-technical materials, plant protectives, cleaning materials
28	D Work materials that are *radioactive*
	E.g., uranium concentrate, nuclear materials
29	D Work materials that are irritating skin or mucous membrane
	E.g., quartz, asbestos, Thomas meal, flax, raw cotton
30	D Work materials causing other health hazards
	If characteristic I is rated D = 5, continue with characteristic 34.

AET = Arbeitswissenschaftliches Erhebungsverfahren zur Tätigkeitsanalyse = ergonomic job analysis procedure.
Rohmert, W., and Landau, K. (1983). *A new technique for job analysis.* New York: Taylor & Francis. Reprinted with permission of the publisher.

As of 2021, O*NET contained detailed information on 923 occupations. As a result of this extensive collection of information, many job analysts use O*NET as an early source of information for their job analyses. O*NET includes information about the occupation (generalized work activities, detailed work activities, work context, tools used, technology skills needed, organizational context) and the worker characteristics (ability, occupational interests, knowledge, work styles, work values, skills, education, credentials) needed for success in the occupation. The O*NET also includes information about such economic factors as labor demand, related occupations, labor supply, salaries, and occupational trends. This information can be used by employers to select new employees and by applicants who are searching for careers that match their skills, interests, and economic needs. O*NET-based information can be obtained at http://onetonline.org.

Critical Incident Technique.   The **Critical Incident Technique (CIT)** was developed and first used by John Flanagan and his students at the University of Pittsburgh in the late

Critical Incident Technique (CIT) The job analysis method developed by John Flanagan that uses written reports of good and bad employee behavior.

1940s and early 1950s. The CIT is used to discover actual incidents of job behavior that make the difference between a job's successful or unsuccessful performance (Flanagan, 1954). This technique can be conducted in many ways, but the basic procedure is as follows:

1. Job incumbents each generate between one and five incidents of both excellent and poor performance that they have seen on the job. These incidents can be obtained using logbooks, questionnaires, or interviews; research has shown that the method used makes little difference (Campion, Greener, & Wernli, 1973), although questionnaires are usually used because they are the easiest. A convenient way to word requests for critical incidents is by asking incumbents to think of times they saw workers perform in an especially outstanding way and then to write down exactly what occurred. Incumbents are then asked to do the same for times they saw workers perform poorly. This process is repeated as needed. Two examples of critical incidents are shown in Table 2.9.

2. Job experts examine each incident and decide whether it is an example of excellent or poor behavior. This step is necessary because approximately 5% of incidents initially cited as poor examples by employees are actually good examples and vice versa (Aamodt, Reardon, & Kimbrough, 1986). For example, in a job analysis of the position of university instructor, a few students described their worst teachers as those who lectured from material not included in their textbooks. A committee of faculty members and students who reviewed the incidents determined that lecturing from nontext material actually was excellent. Thus, the incidents were counted as examples of excellent rather than poor performance.

3. The incidents generated in the first stage are then given to three or four incumbents to sort into an unspecified number of categories. The incidents in each category are then read by the job analyst, who combines, names, and defines the categories.

4. To verify the judgments made by the job analyst in procedure 3, three other incumbents are given the incidents and category names and are asked to sort the incidents into the newly created categories. If two of the three incumbents sort an incident into the same category, the incident is considered part of that category. Any incident that is not agreed upon by two sorters is either thrown out or placed in a new category.

5. The numbers of both types of incidents sorted into each category are then tallied and used to create a table like Table 2.10. The categories provide the important dimensions of a job, and the numbers provide the relative importance of these dimensions.

The CIT is an excellent addition to a job analysis because the actual critical incidents can be used for future activities such as performance appraisal and training. The CIT's greatest drawback is that its emphasis on the difference between excellent and poor performance ignores routine duties. Thus, the CIT cannot be used as the sole method of job analysis.

Job Components Inventory. In addition to information about tools and equipment used on the job, which were discussed earlier, the JCI also provides information about the perceptual, physical, mathematical, communication, decision making, and responsibility skills needed to perform the job.

Table 2.9   Critical Incident Examples

1. About a year ago, I was driving home from school and had a flat tire. I was having trouble changing the tire when the police officer stopped and helped me. The officer then followed me to the nearest gas station to make sure that I didn't have any more trouble. Most cops probably wouldn't have done a darn thing to help.

2. I got pulled over for doing 45 in a 25-mph zone. Instead of just writing me up, the cop told me what a jerk I was for speeding and that if they ever saw me speed again, I would get more than a ticket.

Table 2.10   CIT Categories and Frequencies for Excellent and Poor Resident Assistants

Category	Excellent	Poor	Total
Interest in residents	31	19	19
Availability	14	27	41
Responsibility	12	20	32
Fairness	18	10	28
Self-adherence to the rules	0	28	28
Social skills	19	7	26
Programming	13	7	20
Self-confidence	12	8	20
Rule enforcement	4	14	18
Authoritarianism	1	16	17
Counseling skills	12	4	16
Self-control	5	2	7
Confidentiality	1	2	3

Threshold Traits Analysis (TTA) A 33-item questionnaire developed by Lopez that identifies traits necessary to successfully perform a job.

Threshold Traits Analysis.   An approach similar to the JCI is the **Threshold Traits Analysis (TTA)**, which was developed by Lopez, Kesselman, and Lopez (1981). This method is available only by hiring a particular consulting firm (Lopez and Associates), but its unique style makes it worthy of mentioning. The TTA questionnaire's 33 items identify the traits that are necessary for the successful performance of a job. The 33 items cover five trait categories: physical, mental, learned, motivational, and social. An example of an item from the TTA can be found in Figure 2.3. The TTA's greatest advantages are that it is short and reliable and can correctly identify important traits (Lopez et al., 1981). The TTA's greatest disadvantage is that it is not available commercially, and therefore organizations might not be able to afford the additional expense of hiring the consulting firm. Because the TTA also focuses on traits, its main uses are in the development of an employee selection system or a career plan (Lopez, Rockmore, & Kesselman, 1980).

Fleishman Job Analysis Survey (F-JAS) A job analysis method in which jobs are rated on the basis of the abilities needed to perform them.

Fleishman Job Analysis Survey.   Based on more than 30 years of research (Fleishman & Reilly, 1992a), the **Fleishman Job Analysis Survey (F-JAS)** requires incumbents or job analysts to view a series of abilities such as the one shown in Figure 2.4 and to rate the level of ability needed to perform the job. These ratings are performed for 73 distinct cognitive, physical, psychomotor, sensory-perceptual, and social/interpersonal abilities

Problem Solving

Job Functions Include	Incumbent Must
Processing information to reach specific conclusions, answering problems, adapting and assessing ideas of others, and revising into workable form.	Analyze information and, by inductive reasoning, arrive at a specific conclusion or solution (trait also known as *convergent thinking, reasoning*).

Level	Job Activities That Require Solving	Level	Incumbent Must Solve
0	Very minor problems with fairly simple solutions (running out of supplies or giving directions).	0	Very minor problems with fairly simple solutions.
1	Problems with known and limited variables (diagnosing mechanical disorders or customer complaints).	1	Problems with known and limited variables.
2	More complex problems with many known variables (programming or investment analysis).	2	Problems with many known and complex variables.
3	Very complex and abstract problems with many unknown variables (advanced systems design or research).	3	Very complex and abstract problems with many unknown variables.

Figure 2.3
Sample from Threshold Traits Analysis Questionnaire

Source: Adapted from Lopez, F. M., Kesselman, G. A., and Lopez, F. E. (1981). An empirical test of a trait-oriented job analysis technique. *Personnel Psychology*, 34, 479–502.

and knowledge (Caughron, Mumford, & Fleishman, 2012). The F-JAS is easy to use by incumbents or trained analysts, demonstrates acceptable levels of reliability, and is supported by years of research. Its advantages over TTA are that it is more detailed, is commercially available, is available in several languages, and can be completed online.

Figure 2.4
Fleishman Job Analysis Survey Example

How Written Comprehension Is Different from Other Abilities		
Written Comprehension: Involves **reading** and **understanding written** words and sentences.	vs.	*Oral Comprehension:* Involves **listening to** and **understanding** words and sentences spoken by others. *Oral Expression* and *Written Expression:* Involve **speaking** or **writing** words and sentences so others will understand.

Requires understanding complex or detailed information that is in writing, contains unusual words and phrases, and involves fine distinctions in meaning among words.

7 — Understand an instruction book on repairing a missile guidance system
6
5
Understand an apartment lease
4
3

Requires understanding short or simple written information that contains common words and phrases.

2
Understand signs on the highway
1

Job Adaptability Inventory. The **Job Adaptability Inventory (JAI)** is a 132-item inventory developed by Pulakos, Arad, Donovan, and Plamondon (2000) that taps the extent to which a job incumbent needs to adapt to situations on the job. The JAI has eight dimensions:

1. Handling emergencies or crisis situations
2. Handling work stress
3. Solving problems creatively
4. Dealing with uncertain and unpredictable work situations
5. Learning work tasks, technologies, and procedures
6. Demonstrating interpersonal adaptability
7. Demonstrating cultural adaptability
8. Demonstrating physically oriented adaptability

The JAI has excellent reliability and has been shown to distinguish among jobs (Pulakos, Arad, Donovan, & Plamondon, 2000).

Personality-Related Position Requirements Form (PPRF). The **Personality-Related Position Requirements Form (PPRF)** was developed by Raymark, Schmit, and Guion (1997) to identify the personality types needed to perform job-related tasks. The PPRF consists of 107 items tapping 12 personality dimensions that fall under the "Big 5" personality dimensions (openness to experience, conscientiousness, extroversion, agreeableness, and emotional stability). Though more research is needed, the PPRF is reliable and shows promise as a useful job analysis instrument for identifying the personality traits necessary to perform a job.

Performance Improvements Characteristics (PIC). Like the PPRF, the 48 questions on the PIC help determine which of the seven main personality traits are needed to perform a given job. Research on the PIC indicates that it has acceptable reliability and can differentiate between jobs (Foster, Gaddis, & Hogan, 2012.).

Evaluation of Methods

In the previous pages, many job analysis methods were presented. To help compare the methods, Table 2.11 summarizes the potential uses for each method. Any time there are multiple methods for something, a logical question is, "Which one is best?" Unfortunately, there is no clear answer to this question in job analysis. The best method to use in analyzing a job appears to be related to the end use of the job analysis information.

That is, different methods are best for different uses—*worker-oriented methods* (in which the focus is on the attributes required to perform the job), such as the CIT, JCI, and TTA, are the best for employee selection and performance appraisal; *job-oriented methods* (in which the focus is on the tasks involved in performing the job), such as task analysis, are best for work design and writing job descriptions. To get the most out of a job analysis, several techniques should be used so that information on each of the job description sections can be obtained.

From a legal perspective, courts have ruled that job analysis is necessary (Sparks, 1988) and that acceptable job analyses should (1) use several up-to-date sources, (2) be conducted by experts, (3) use many job incumbents, and (4) cover the entire range of worker activities and qualifications (Thompson & Thompson, 1982).

Other than a meta-analysis demonstrating that job analysis ratings of specific tasks are more reliable than ratings of general work activities (Dierdorff & Wilson, 2003), little research directly comparing job analysis methods has been conducted. This lack of research is primarily because direct comparison of methods is virtually impossible: Each method yields results that differ in both the number and type of dimensions. Thus, the comparative research that has been conducted has focused on opinions of job analysts.

Survey research by Levine, Ash, and their colleagues (Levine, Ash, & Bennett, 1980; Levine, Ash, Hall, & Sistrunk, 1983) has found the following:

1. The PAQ is seen as the most standardized technique and the CIT the least standardized.
2. The CIT takes the least amount of job analyst training and task analysis the most.
3. The PAQ is the least costly method and the CIT the most.
4. The PAQ takes the least amount of time to complete and task analysis the most.
5. Task analysis has the highest-quality results and TTA the lowest.
6. Task analysis reports are the longest and job-elements reports the shortest.
7. The CIT has been rated the most useful and the PAQ the least.
8. Task analysis gives the best overall job picture and the PAQ the worst.

Table 2.11 Comparison of the Output of the Types of Information Gained from Various Job Analysis Methods?

Job Analysis Method	Job Description Section						
	Specific Tasks	General Duties	Tools	Job Context	Performance	Compensation	Competencies
Interview	X	X	X	X	X	X	X
Observation	X	X	X	X			X
Job participation	X	X	X	X			X
PAQ		X		X			X
JSP		X		X			X
JEI		X		X			X
FJA		X					
JCI			X				X
AET				X			
O*NET		X					X
CIT		X					X
TTA							X
F-JAS							X
JAI							X
PPRF							X

PAQ = Position Analysis Questionnaire; JSP = Job Structure Profile; JEI = Job Elements Inventory; FJA = Functional Job Analysis; JCI = Job Components Inventory;

AET = Arbeitswissenschaftliches Erhebungsverfahren zur Tätigkeitsanalyse = ergonomic job analysis procedure; O*NET = Occupational Information Network; CIT = Critical Incident Technique; TTA = Threshold Traits Analysis; F-JAS = Fleishman Job Analysis Survey; JAI = Job Adaptability Inventory; PPRF = Personality-Related Position Requirements Form.

Keep in mind, however, that these findings were based on users' opinions rather than on actual empirical comparison and that many of the newer (post-1980) job analysis methods were not included in the Levine and Ash studies.

2.2 Job Evaluation

Job evaluation The process of determining the monetary worth of a job.

Internal pay equity The extent to which employees within an organization are paid fairly compared with other employees within the same organization.

Once a job analysis has been completed and a thorough job description written, it is important to determine how much employees in a position should be paid. This process of determining a job's *worth* is called **job evaluation**. A job evaluation is typically done in two stages: determining internal pay equity and determining external pay equity.

Determining Internal Pay Equity

Internal pay equity involves comparing jobs within an organization to ensure that the people in jobs worth the most money are paid accordingly. The difficulty in this process, of course, is determining the worth of each job. Because a complete discussion of all

Should employees in dangerous jobs be compensated for the increased risk?

Kim Steele/PhotoDisc/Getty Images

job evaluation methods is beyond the scope of this text, we will stick to a discussion of the most used method.

Step 1: Determining Compensable Job Factors

The first step in evaluating a job is to decide what factors differentiate the relative worth of jobs. Possible **compensable job factors** include the following:

- Level of responsibility
- Physical demands
- Mental demands
- Education requirements
- Training and experience requirements
- Working conditions

The philosophical perspectives of the job evaluator can affect these factors. Some evaluators argue that the most important compensable factor is responsibility and that physical demands are unimportant. Others argue that education is the most important. The choice of compensable factors thus is often more philosophical than empirical.

Step 2: Determining the Levels for Each Compensable Factor

Once the compensable factors have been selected, the next step is to determine the levels for each factor. For a factor such as education, the levels are easy to determine (e.g., high school diploma, associate's degree, bachelor's degree). For factors such as responsibility, a considerable amount of time and discussion may be required to determine the levels.

Step 3: Determining the Factor Weights

Because some factors are more important than others, weights must be assigned to each factor and to each level within a factor. Here is the process for doing this:

1. A job evaluation committee determines the total number of points that will be distributed among the factors. Usually, the number is some multiple of 100 (e.g., 100, 500, 1,000) and is based on the number of compensable factors. The greater the number of factors, the greater the number of points.
2. Each factor is weighted by assigning several points. The more important the factor, the greater the number of points that will be assigned.
3. The number of points assigned to a factor is then divided into each of the levels. If 100 points had been assigned to the factor of education, then 20 points (100 points/5 degrees) would be assigned to each level. An example of this procedure is shown in Table 2.12. The job evaluation committee takes the job descriptions for each job and assigns points based on the factors and degrees created in the previous steps.
4. The total number of points for a job is compared with the salary currently being paid for the job. This comparison is typically graphed in a fashion like the **wage trend line** shown in Figure 2.5. Wage trend lines are drawn based on the results of a regression formula in which salary is predicted by the number of job analysis points. Jobs whose point values fall well below the line (as with Job D in Figure 2.5) are considered underpaid ("green circled") and are immediately assigned higher salary levels. Jobs with point values well above the line (as with Job H) are considered overpaid ("red circled") and the salary level is decreased once current jobholders leave.

Table 2.12   Example of Completed Job Evaluation Results

Factors	Points
Education (200 points possible)	
High school education or less	40
Two years of college	80
Bachelor's degree	120
Master's degree	160
Ph.D.	200
Responsibility (300 points possible)	
Makes no decisions	75
Makes decisions for self	150
Makes decisions for 1–5 employees	225
Makes decisions for more than 5 employees	300
Physical demands (90 points possible)	
Lifts no heavy objects	30
Lifts objects between 25 and 100 pounds	60
Lifts objects more than 100 pounds	90

Determining External Pay Equity

External equity The extent to which employees within an organization are paid fairly compared with employees in other organizations.

With **external equity**, the worth of a job is determined by comparing the job to the external market (other organizations). External equity is important if an organization is to attract and retain employees. In other words, it must be competitive with the compensation plans of other organizations. That is, a fast-food restaurant that pays cooks $12 an hour will probably have trouble hiring and keeping high-caliber employees if other fast-food restaurants in the area pay $17 an hour.

Figure 2.5
Example of a Wage Trend Line

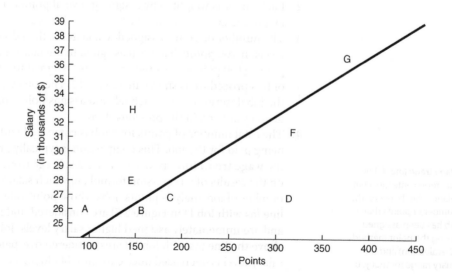

Salary surveys A questionnaire sent to other organizations to see how much they are paying their employees in positions similar to those in the organization sending the survey.

To determine external equity, organizations use **salary surveys**. Sent to other organizations, these surveys ask how much an organization pays its employees in various positions. An organization can either construct and send out its own survey or use the results of surveys conducted by trade groups or private companies specializing in conducting salary surveys. Most organizations choose the last two options. Based on the survey results such as those shown in Table 2.13, an organization can decide where it wants to be in relation to the compensation policies of other organizations (often called *market position*). That is, an organization might choose to offer compensation at higher levels to attract the best applicants as well as keep current employees from going to other organizations. Other organizations might choose to pay at the "going rate" so that they have a reasonable chance of competing for applicants, even though they will often lose the best applicants to higher-paying organizations. Market position is most important in a good economy where jobs are plentiful and applicants have several job options.

Roanoke County, Virginia, in the United States, provides an excellent example of the importance of market position. The county was concerned about the high turnover rate of its police dispatchers and undertook a study to determine the reason for the problem. Possible reasons were thought to be working conditions, location, reputation, and pay. The study revealed that most of the turnover was due to a neighboring city paying its dispatchers $2,500 more per year. This resulted in Roanoke County dispatchers resigning after a year of experience to take a higher-paying job only five miles away. Adjusting the salary greatly reduced the turnover rate.

Keep in mind that job evaluation concerns the worth of the *job itself*, not the worth of a *person* in the job. For example, suppose a salary survey reveals that the going rate for a job falls within the range of $30,000 to $40,000, and an organization, deciding to be at the upper end of the market, sets its range for the position at $37,000 to $42,000. Decisions must then be made regarding where in the $5,000 range each particular employee will be paid. This decision is based on such factors as years of experience, years with the company, special skills, education, local cost of living, and performance level.

Table 2.13   Example of Salary Survey Results

Position	# orgs with Position	Number of Employees	Weighted Average	Salary Range				
				Low	Q1	Median	Q3	High
Assembly/Production								
Foreperson	18	286	$23.21	12.67	19.96	22.67	28.69	37.44
Machinist	9	419	$20.83	10.28	17.79	19.63	22.09	26.80
Production control planner	9	36	$19.73	17.64	19.68	21.63	24.59	37.44
Production worker	15	3,487	$18.91	9.49	13.24	16.05	16.62	24.27
Quality control inspector	10	45	$15.23	11.00	13.84	15.01	21.31	24.18
Maintenance								
Janitor	10	322	$12.00	8.85	10.02	11.15	12.04	20.81
Maintenance person A	17	112	$15.90	10.65	11.54	15.97	20.40	27.78
Mechanic	11	382	$19.80	12.99	18.10	19.30	21.27	25.98

We have earlier discussed the amount of money a job is worth: this amount is called **direct compensation**. Employees are also compensated in other ways, such as pay for time not worked (e.g., holidays, vacation, sick days), deferred income (e.g., Social Security and pension plans), health protection such as medical and dental insurance, and perquisites ("perks") such as a company car (Martocchio, 2017). Consequently, a job with a direct compensation of $30,000 might actually be worth more than one at $35,000 because of the indirect compensation package.

Determining Sex, Race, and Ethnicity Equity

In addition to analyses of internal and external equity, pay audits should also be conducted to ensure that employees are not paid differently based on sex, race, or ethnicity. For organizations with 50 or more employees and federal contracts more than $50,000, salary equity analyses are mandatory each year. The Office of Federal Contract Compliance Programs (OFCCP) monitors these analyses to ensure that they are conducted and that federal contractors are not discriminating based on pay.

Salary equity studies are required because national statistics indicate there are substantial sex and race/ethnicity differences in average salary. On average, full-time female workers in 2019 made only 81.5% of what full-time male workers were paid. On average, Black and Hispanic/Latinx workers made less than Asian and White workers. As shown in Table 2.14, the pay gap, which was narrowing for many years, seems to have stagnated at approximately 82% for women. In 2020, the gap between

Table 2.14 Trends of Salary Level of Women as a Percentage of Men's Salaries and Minorities as a Percentage of White Workers' Salaries

Year	Women to Men	Black to White Workers	Hispanic to White Workers	Asian to White Workers
2020	82.3	79.2	75.6	130.6
2019	81.5	77.8	74.7	124.2
2018	81.1	75.8	74.2	119.5
2017	81.8	76.6	73.6	117.2
2016	81.9	78.7	72.4	118.4
2015	81.1	76.8	72.3	118.9
2010	81.2	79.9	69.9	111.8
2005	81.0	77.3	70.1	112.1
2000	76.9	80.3	72.9	104.2
1995	75.5	77.5	73.5	
1990	71.9	77.6	71.7	
1985	68.1	77.8	75.8	
1980	64.2	78.8	78.2	

Source: U.S. Department of Labor (www.bls.gov).
Note: Percentages are based on weekly earnings for full-time employees.

White workers and other race/ethnicity groups was 79.2% for Black workers and 75.6% for Hispanic/Latinx workers. It should be noted that Asian workers make more money than do the other ethnic and racial groups.

Research indicates that all but about 6% of the gap between men and women can be explained by such factors as differences in jobs and men being in the workforce longer, having a higher percentage of full-time jobs, and working more hours in a year (CONSAD, 2009; Wall, 2000). Thus, differences in pay are often less an issue of pay discrimination by organizations than one of vocational choice and educational opportunity discrimination. Because of the sex and race/ethnicity gaps in pay, several states (e.g., California, Colorado, Hawaii) have passed laws making it illegal to ask about an applicant's salary history. Furthermore, because men are more inclined to negotiate such things as starting salaries than are women (Babcock & Laschever, 2008; Kugler, Tamara, Reif, & Brodbeck, 2014; Stuhlmacher & Walters, 1999), organizations such as reddit and Fathom Healthcare either ban or limit salary negotiations during the hiring process (Sammer, 2015). Such limitations are becoming increasingly common. Although a complete discussion on this topic goes beyond the scope of this book, an excellent assortment of articles and links on this issue can be found at http://www.swcollege.com/bef/policy_debates/gender.html.

For some advice on salary negotiation, refer to the Career Workshop Box.

Conducting a Sex and Race Salary Equity Study

The first step in conducting a salary equity analysis for an organization is to place jobs into what are called Similarly Situated Employee Groups (SSEG). The OFCCP defines similarly situated employees as those that:

> "would be expected to be paid the same based on: (a) job similarity (e.g., tasks performed, skills required, effort, responsibility, working conditions and complexity); and (b) other objective factors such as minimum qualifications or certifications."

Creating SSEGs takes considerable time, as one needs to use salary grades to determine similarity of worth and use job descriptions to determine similarity of tasks performed, skills required, effort, responsibility, working conditions and complexity. An SSEG can be something as narrow as a grade and job title (e.g., 10–Mechanical Engineer I; 8–Financial Analyst) or something broader such as a grade and job family (e.g., 10–Engineering; 8–Finance). During OFCCP audits or litigation, there is often considerable disagreement about what are appropriate SSEGS.

Once the SSEGs have been created, the next step is to conduct statistical analyses to determine if within each SSEG, there are statistically significant sex or race/ethnicity differences in pay after controlling for legitimate factors thought to be related to pay (e.g., experience, education, performance).

Two types of statistical analyses are typically used: regression and Fisher's exact tests. For smaller SSEGs, a Fisher's exact test is used to compare gender and race differences in the percentage of employees above the median salary for the SSEG. If there are at least 30 employees in the SSEG and at least 5 employees in each sex or race group (i.e., 5 men and 5 women; as of 2021, separate analyses for people identifying as nonbinary were not legally required nor commonly conducted), this can be done through a statistical technique called *regression*.

Toward the end of this chapter, you learned that one of the main causes of salary inequity between men and women is that men are more likely to negotiate salaries than are women. It is important for a job applicant to understand that most salary offers are negotiable. Most organizations have a pay range in which employee salaries must fall for each job. For example, the range for an accountant at IBM might be $50,000 to $60,000. An applicant will never get less than the $50,000 or more than the $60,000. The negotiation determines where in that $10,000 range you will fall. Here are some thoughts for negotiating:

- Know what the job is worth. All public organizations and some private organizations will make their salary ranges available to applicants. If they don't, you can use information from salary surveys and your university career placement office to help you find information about salary ranges for a type of job. Good online sources include www.jobstar.org, www.salary.com, and www. salaryexpert.com.
- Ask your career placement center about the typical starting salaries for graduates in your field from your university.
- Know what you need to earn. Think about the cost of living and your expenses (e.g., rent, utilities, student loans, car payment). That will give you an idea about the minimum salary you will accept. There are times when the offer you get is not negotiable and is below what you need to survive. In such cases, you must turn down the offer.

- Know what you are worth. If you have experience, graduated from a top school, were a top student in your university, or have unique skills, you are worth more than the typical applicant. If you are asked in an interview about your expected starting salary, you might use this information to respond, "The typical salary for accounting majors at our university is $28,000. Because I have done an internship and was one of the top students in our department, my expectation is to start above $30,000."
- Don't be afraid to negotiate. When the organization makes an offer, counter with a higher amount. In doing so, be realistic and base your offer on logic and facts. Explain why you think an increased starting salary is justifiable. If you graduated with no experience and a 2.01 GPA, you probably have little room to negotiate above the bottom of the range.
- When the job market is tight and employers cannot find good applicants, your value is higher.
- In addition to salary, there are times when you can negotiate such things as vacation time, starting dates, and other benefits.

With regression, the first step is to enter your merit variables into the equation to determine what percentage of individual differences in pay they explain. The second step in the equation is to enter sex (coded 0 for men, 1 for women) to determine whether, after controlling for the merit variables, an employee's sex is significantly related to pay. That is, suppose the average salary for men in our Grade 10 – Engineering SSEG is $77,000 and for women $74,000. It may be that this $3,000 difference can be explained by the fact that the average man in the SSEG has been with the organization five years longer than the average woman in the SSEG. The results of the regression will determine if the $3,000 salary difference can be fully explained, partially explained, or not explained by differences in the merit variables.

If the results of the regression analysis indicate that the merit variables do not explain sex or race/ethnicity differences in salary, one still cannot conclude that discrimination has occurred. It could be that there are valid factors involved in the differences (e.g., the economy at the time of hire) that were not entered into the regression. However, in the absence of a valid explanation, salary adjustments may be in order.

Salary adjustments are determined by entering the merit variables for each employee into a regression equation to estimate what the employees "should" be making. For this approach to be reliable, the merit variables should account for a statistically significant percentage of the individual differences in salary. An employee whose actual salary is two standard errors below their predicted salary is considered to be an outlier and a potential candidate for a salary adjustment. I realize that this process is complicated and highly statistical, but that is the nature of salary equity analysis, and salary equity analyses are becoming an important function performed by human resource departments as both the EEOC and OFCCP as well as many states are paying increasing attention to potential salary discrimination. The process can be made substantially easier by using software such as *EEOPay* or *COMPARE*, which are designed for such purposes.

On the Job ▶ Applied Case Study

National Board of Veterinary Medical Examiners

To become a veterinarian, a person must pass the North American Veterinary Licensing Exam (NAVLE), a 360-item national exam typically taken after graduation from veterinary school. Examples of questions on the exam include the following:

1. Which of the following is the most common cause of maxillary sinusitis in the horse?
   (A) Bacterial lower respiratory tract disease extending into the sinus
   (B) Infection and abscessation of a tooth root extending into the sinus
   (C) Inhaled foreign bodies lodging in the sinus
   (D) Puncture wounds extending into the maxillary sinus
2. An African gray parrot that is presented for necropsy is suspected to have psittacosis. Which of the following findings is most likely to confirm the diagnosis?
   (A) Hepatomegaly and splenomegaly on gross examination
   (B) Identification of the causative organism by Gram's stain
   (C) Isolation and identification of *Chlamydia psittaci*

   (D) Presence of acid-fast organisms in the liver

To ensure that this national exam covers the important information needed to be a veterinarian, the National Board of Veterinary Medical Examiners decided to conduct a job analysis of the position of entry-level veterinary practitioner. Given that there are over 60,000 veterinarians throughout the country, this was indeed a daunting task. This number is compounded by the fact that veterinarians work in a variety of settings such as private practice, governmental agencies, veterinary medicine colleges, pharmaceutical companies, zoos, and research laboratories. Furthermore, major job duties can range from direct health care to research to disease control.

1. How would you conduct such a large-scale job analysis?
2. In determining the sample of veterinarians that would participate in the job analysis, what factors (e.g., region of the country) would you need to consider?
3. How many veterinarians would you include in your job analysis?
4. Which job analysis method would you use?

There is no question that executives are compensated well. And there has always been a gap between executives and workers. But this gap is widening. In 2019, the highest-paid CEO in the nation made about 1,085 times the wage of the average worker! In 2019, the typical CEO in the United States made 320 times the wage of the average worker.

The top-five CEOs in 2020 earned the following amounts through salaries and stock options:

- Elon Musk, CEO, Tesla.: $595.3 million
- Tim Cook, CEO, Apple: $133.7 million
- Thomas Rutledge, CEO, Charter Communications: $116.9 million
- Joseph Ianniello, CEO, CBS Entertainment: $116.6 million
- Sumit Singh, CEO, Chewy, Inc.: $108.25 million

CEOs and other executives say that high compensation buys better performance from them, which includes their ability to create new jobs for workers in communities that might otherwise have high unemployment. The job factors usually used to decide such compensation include the level of responsibility, education requirements, experience, and sometimes working conditions.

There are advocates and opponents for these high compensation packages. On the one hand, the level of education, experience, and responsibility greatly differentiates CEOs and executives from the average worker. Publicly traded companies are accountable to their stockholders. So, these executives are being paid to make money for the company and its stockholders. And to make money, the company must significantly compensate its executives for high performance.

On the other hand, these high compensation packages could come at the expense of the workers who actually make the product or deliver a service to consumers. As executives continue to be compensated at higher and higher levels for their performance, the focus of increasing wages and salaries for the average worker may decline if the company does not have some set standards of values and ethics. And, as your textbook says, the choice of compensable factors is often more philosophical than empirical—which means this level of compensation may not be necessary to motivate executives to perform well.

What Do You Think?

- Are CEOs being paid too much or are they worth the high compensation packages they receive?
- Is it ethical or fair that a CEO receives a bonus when employees are being laid off or having their benefits reduced?
- Does high compensation for CEOs actually increase company performance?
- Should a company's number one focus be on making money for its shareholders?
- What might be other ethical factors surrounding this issue?

Chapter Summary

In this chapter you learned:

- Job analysis provides the foundation for such areas as performance appraisal, employee selection, training, and job design.
- A properly written job description contains a job title, a brief summary, an extensive list of work activities, a list of tools and equipment, information about the work context, compensation information, performance standards, and personal requirements.
- Before a job analysis begins, decisions must be made about the type of information that will be obtained, who will conduct the job analysis, and who will participate in it.
- The typical job analysis involves interviewing and observing subject-matter experts (SMEs) to determine tasks that are performed, the conditions under which they are performed, the tools and equipment needed to perform them, and the knowledge, skills, abilities, and other characteristics (KSAOs) needed to perform them.

- Although no job analysis method is always better than others, each is better for certain purposes. For example, the Position Analysis Questionnaire (PAQ) is an excellent method for compensation uses, and the Critical Incident Technique (CIT) is an excellent method for performance appraisal.
- Job evaluation is the process of assigning a monetary value to a job.
- Internal equity, external equity, and comparable worth are important pay issues that must be addressed during any job evaluation.

Key Terms

Job analysis (35)
Job descriptions (36)
Peter Principle (36)
Uniform Guidelines (38)
Job analysis interview (38)
Grade (40)
Job specifications (41)
Knowledge (41)
Other characteristics (41)
KSAOs (41)
Competencies (41)
Job crafting (44)
Subject-matter experts (SMEs) (49)
Job analyst (49)
SME conference (49)
Ammerman technique (50)
Observations (50)
Job participation (51)
Task inventory (52)
Task analysis (53)
Skill (54)
Position Analysis Questionnaire (PAQ) (55)

Job Structure Profile (JSP) (57)
Job Elements Inventory (JEI) (57)
Functional Job Analysis (FJA) (57)
Job Components Inventory (JCI) (58)
AET (58)
Occupational Information Network (O*NET) (59)
Dictionary of Occupational Titles (DOT) (59)
Critical Incident Technique (CIT) (60)
Threshold Traits Analysis (TTA) (62)
Fleishman Job Analysis Survey (F-JAS) (62)
Job Adaptability Inventory (JAI) (64)
Personality-Related Position Requirements Form (PPRF) (64)
Job evaluation (66)
Internal pay equity (66)
Compensable job factors (67)
Wage trend line (67)
External equity (68)
Salary surveys (69)
Direct compensation (70)

Questions for Review

1. Why is job analysis so important?
2. What are the main sections of a job description?
3. Would a job analyst expect to find gender and race differences in the way employees perform the duties of their jobs? Why or why not?
4. How should a task statement be written?
5. Why are there so many job analysis methods?
6. Research indicates that the average salary for women in the United States is about 80% of the average salary for men. Why is this?
7. Is external pay equity more important than internal pay equity? Why or why not?

Chapter

3

Legal Issues in Employee Selection

Learning Objectives

3-1 Describe the legal process involving employment law.

3-2 Identify what classes of people are protected by federal law.

3-3 Determine the legality of an employment practice.

3-4 Explain the concept of adverse impact.

3-5 Define affirmative action.

3-6 Describe the important issues involving employee privacy rights.

Equal Employment Opportunity Commission (EEOC) A branch of the Department of Labor charged with investigating and prosecuting complaints of employment discrimination.

In the field of human resources (HR), it is not a question of *whether* you will get sued by an applicant or former employee but *when* and *how often*. In 2020 alone, 67,488 discrimination complaints were filed with the **Equal Employment Opportunity Commission (EEOC)**, resulting in more than $439.2 million in awards and settlements. These statistics should convince anyone entering the human resources field that knowledge of employment law is essential (updated statistics can be obtained on the U.S. Equal Employment Opportunity Commission website at www.eeoc.gov/eeoc/statistics/enforcement/index.cfm).

3-1 The Legal Process

To know whether a given employment practice is legal, it is important to understand the legal process as it relates to employment law in the United States. The first step in the legal process is for some legislative body, such as the U.S. Congress or a state legislature, to pass a law. If a law is passed at the federal level, states may pass laws that *expand* the rights granted in the federal law; states may not, however, pass laws that will *diminish* the rights granted in federal legislation. For example, if Congress passed a law that gave parents six months of parental leave, a state or local government could pass a law extending the leave to eight months, but it could not reduce the amount of parental leave to less than the mandated six months. Thus, to be on firm legal ground, it is important to be aware of state and local laws as well as federal legislation.

Once a law has been passed, situations occur in which the intent of the law is not clear. For example, a law might be passed to protect employees with disabilities. Two years later, an employee is denied promotion because they have high blood pressure. The employee may file a charge against the employer claiming discrimination based on a disability. They may claim that high blood pressure is a disability but that they can still work despite the disability and consequently deserve the promotion. The organization, on the other hand, might claim that high blood pressure is not a disability and that even if it were, an employee with high blood pressure could not perform the job. It would then be up to the courts to decide.

Resolving the Complaint Internally

Grievance system A process in which an employee files a complaint with the organization and a person or committee within the organization makes a decision regarding the complaint.

Before a complaint can be filed with the EEOC, an employee must utilize whatever internal resolution process is available within the organization. As a result, most organizations have formal policies regarding how discrimination complaints will be handled internally. Typically, these policies involve such forms of alternative dispute resolution (ADR) as a grievance process, mediation, and arbitration. ADR will be discussed in greater detail in Chapter 13, but a brief description is provided here. With a **grievance system**, employees take their complaints to an internal committee that decides regarding the complaints. If employees do not like the decision, they can then take their complaints to the EEOC. With **mediation**, employees and the organization meet with a neutral third party who tries to help the two sides reach a mutually agreed upon solution. If they cannot reach a solution, the complaint can be taken to arbitration or to the EEOC. The EEOC has begun to strongly recommend mediation as a solution to discrimination complaints, in part because 96% of employers who tried mediation said they would try it again, and data indicate that the time taken to resolve a dispute through mediation is less than half that of going through more formal channels (Tyler, 2007) However, research has found that while 89% of employees consent to mediation sponsored through the EEOC, only 31% of organizations actually follow through (Goldman, Pearsall, Gilliland, & Shapiro, 2007).

Mediation A method of resolving conflict in which a neutral third party is asked to help the two parties reach an agreement.

Arbitration A method of resolving conflicts in which a neutral third party is asked to choose which side is correct.

Binding arbitration A method of resolving conflicts in which a neutral third party is asked to choose which side is correct and in which neither party is allowed to appeal the decision.

With **arbitration**, the two sides present their case to a neutral third party who then decides as to which side is right. Arbitration and mediation differ in that the neutral third party *helps* the two sides reach an agreement in mediation, whereas in arbitration, the neutral third party *makes* the decision. If **binding**

What to Do If You Feel You Are Being Discriminated Against at Work

There may be times during your career when you believe you are being treated unfairly based on your sex, race, ethnicity, age, religion, disabilities, or national origin. If you feel you have been discriminated against or are being harassed in the workplace, consider the following advice provided by consultant Bobbie Raynes:

- Most organizations have policies explaining how employees should handle situations in which they have been harassed or discriminated against. Refer to your organization's policy manual for guidance.
- Document what occurred, when it occurred, and who was involved.
- Report the situation to your supervisor or the human resources director. (If it is your supervisor who has harassed or discriminated against you, take your concerns directly to the HR director.)
- Some employees have gone directly to the person who did the harassing or discriminating to see if they can work out the situation without getting others involved. However, this step works only if you feel comfortable with it. You are under no obligation to go directly to that person.
- Remember that there are time limits involved in reporting discrimination or harassment situations.

- Consider mediation to resolve the situation. This process includes a neutral third party who meets with all parties involved in the incident, as well as the human resources director, to discuss how best to resolve the situation. The mediator will not decide who is right or wrong. The mediator's goal is to help all parties consider options, other than legal options, for resolving past and future problems. Research shows that 90% of all workplace disputes that go through mediation are amicably resolved without help from the courts. This process can be less stressful than going to court and will often preserve workplace relationships.
- If mediation is not an option and/or the organization seems unwilling to address the situation, another option is to file a complaint with the EEOC.
- Being discriminated against or harassed is a very upsetting experience and can cause anger, anxiety, depression, or other feelings. Even if the matter is handled amicably, you may still have some of these feelings. Consider using the organization's employee assistance program (EAP) to talk to a counselor about your feelings. If the organization does not have an EAP, seek a counselor outside of the organization.

Nonbinding arbitration A method of resolving conflicts in which a neutral third party is asked to choose which side is correct but in which either party may appeal the decision.

arbitration is used, neither side can appeal the decision. If **nonbinding arbitration** is used, the parties can either accept the decision or take the case to court. Through a number of landmark decisions, the U.S. Supreme Court has ruled favorably of enforcing arbitration agreements – that is, the applicant or aggrieved employee is not allowed to take a complaint to the EEOC or to court if an organization has a policy of mandatory arbitration. The few notable cases (*Southland Corp v. Keating* (1984), *Allied-Bruce Terminix Cos., Inc v. Dobson* (1995), *Gilmer v. Interstate/Johnson Lane Corp.* (1991), and *Circuit City Stores v. Adams* (2001)) culminated in this ruling, fueling an ongoing debate over arbitration agreements and how to interpret them in the workplace (McCandless, 2002).

Filing a Discrimination Charge

As shown in Figure 3.1, a charge of discrimination is usually filed with a government agency. A state agency is used if the alleged violation involves a state law. A federal agency, usually the EEOC, handles alleged violations of federal law. An EEOC complaint must be filed within 180 days of the discriminatory act, but within 300 days if the complainant has already filed a complaint with a state or local fair employment practice agency. The government agency will try to notify the employer within 10 days

Discrimination suits are common in organizations.

Comstock/Stockbyte/Getty Images

about the complaint, obtain further information from both parties if necessary, and review the charge to determine whether it has merit.

It is important to note that the Lilly Ledbetter Fair Pay Act, signed into law by President Barack Obama in 2009 following the U.S. Supreme Court decision on the *Ledbetter v. Goodyear Tire and Rubber Co.* case, clarified that the 180-day period for filing a lawsuit alleging pay discrimination begins at the time of the last paycheck rather than when the employee's salary was determined. Take, for example, a situation in which two equally qualified applicants, Mary and John, were both hired on January 1, 2021. Mary's starting salary was $60,000; John's was $80,000. On January 1, 2022, Mary discovers that she is making less than John and considers filing a discrimination lawsuit. Prior to the Ledbetter Act, she would not be able to do so because the decision regarding her salary was made 360 days ago, outside of the 180-day statute of limitations. However, because the Ledbetter Act changed the focus from the date of the decision to the date of the last paycheck, she would not be time-barred from filing her lawsuit.

Outcomes of an EEOC Investigation

Charge Does Not Have Merit

If, after reviewing a complaint, the governmental agency does not find merit, one of two things can happen based on whether the person filing the complaint accepts the decision. If the complainant accepts the decision, the process ends. If the complainant

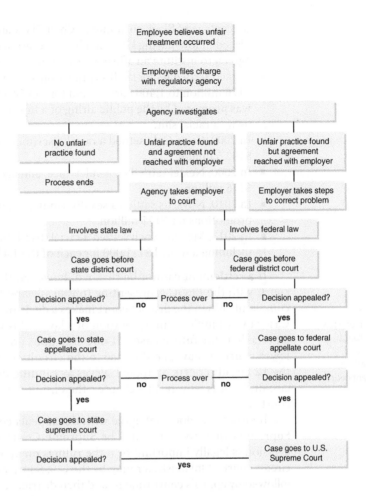

Figure 3.1
Legal Process in Employment Law

does not accept the decision, they are issued a "right to sue" letter that entitles them to hire a private attorney and file the case themself.

Charge Has Merit

If the EEOC believes that the discrimination charge has merit, it will try to work out a settlement between the claimant and employer without taking the case to court. These settlements might include an employer offering a job or promotion to the person filing the complaint, the payment of back wages, and the payment of compensatory or punitive damages. These settlements can range in size from a few dollars to more than $100 million:

- In 2020, Walmart settled a sex discrimination case for $20 million.
- In 1993, the Shoney's restaurant chain settled a racial discrimination case for $132.5 million. Most of the money went to approximately 10,000 Black workers who either worked for or were denied employment with Shoney's over a seven-year period. The size of the settlement was based not only on the high number of victims but also on the severity of the discrimination. For example, the number of Black employees in each restaurant was limited to the

percentage of Black customers. When Black applicants were hired, they were placed in low-paying kitchen jobs. In addition to the $132.5 million, Shoney's agreed to institute an affirmative action program over the next 10 years.

- Texaco settled its racial discrimination suit in 1996 by agreeing to pay $176 million to 1,400 current and former Black employees. The settlement was prompted by the public airing of a tape recording of a Texaco executive using a racial slur.
- In 2000, Coca-Cola settled a racial discrimination case for a record $192.5 million.
- In 2000, Nextel settled its gender, race, and age discrimination suit for $176 million.
- In 2010, Novartis settled a sex discrimination suit involving pay and promotions for $175 million.
- In 2013, Merrill Lynch settled a racial discrimination case for $160 million, including a record $111,000 for each of the 1,433 class members.

Case law The interpretation of a law by a court through a verdict in a trial, setting precedent for subsequent court decisions.

If a settlement cannot be reached, however, the case goes to a federal district court, with the EEOC representing (physically and financially) the person filing the complaint. When the district court makes a decision, the decision becomes **case law**. Case law is a judicial interpretation of a law and is important because it establishes a precedent for future cases. If one side does not like the decision rendered in a lower court, it may take the case to the circuit court of appeal. A ruling by one of the 12 circuit courts of appeal serves as binding case law only for that particular circuit. That is why, in this chapter, the circuit is identified along with most of the court cases.

If either side does not agree with the appeals court decision, it can ask the U.S. Supreme Court to review it. The Supreme Court will consider a case only if the decision is legally important or if the rulings on an issue are inconsistent across the circuit courts. Obviously, a ruling by the U.S. Supreme Court carries the most weight, followed by appeals court rulings, and then district court rulings.

3-2 Determining Whether an Employment Decision Is Legal

At first glance, the legal aspects of making employment decisions seem complicated. After all, there are many laws and court cases that apply to employment decisions. The basic legal aspects, however, are not that complicated. Use the flowchart in Figure 3.2 to make the process easier to understand as each stage is discussed.

Does the Employment Practice Directly Refer to a Member of a Federally Protected Class?

An employment practice is any decision that affects an employee. Employment practices include hiring, training, firing, promoting, assigning employees to shifts, determining pay, disciplining, and scheduling vacations. Thus, *any* decision made by an employer has the potential for legal challenge.

The first step in determining the legality of an employment practice is to decide whether the practice directly refers to a member of a protected class.

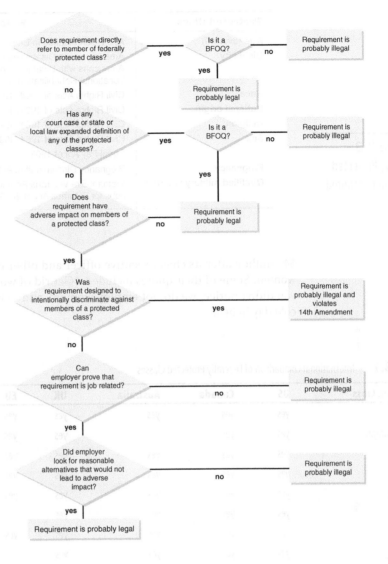

Figure 3.2
Determining Whether an Employment Process Is Legal

The flowchart contains the following elements:

Does requirement directly refer to member of federally protected class? — **yes** → Is it a BFOQ? — **no** → Requirement is probably illegal

Is it a BFOQ? — **yes** → Requirement is probably legal

Does requirement directly refer to member of federally protected class? — **no** ↓

Has any court case or state or local law expanded definition of any of the protected classes? — **yes** → Is it a BFOQ? — **no** → Requirement is probably illegal

Is it a BFOQ? — **yes** ↓ → Requirement is probably legal

Has any court case or state or local law expanded definition of any of the protected classes? — **no** ↓

Does requirement have adverse impact on members of a protected class? — **no** → Requirement is probably legal

Does requirement have adverse impact on members of a protected class? — **yes** ↓

Was requirement designed to intentionally discriminate against members of a protected class? — **yes** → Requirement is probably illegal and violates 14th Amendment

Was requirement designed to intentionally discriminate against members of a protected class? — **no** ↓

Can employer prove that requirement is job related? — **no** → Requirement is probably illegal

Can employer prove that requirement is job related? — **yes** ↓

Did employer look for reasonable alternatives that would not lead to adverse impact? — **no** → Requirement is probably illegal

Did employer look for reasonable alternatives that would not lead to adverse impact? — **yes** ↓

Requirement is probably legal

Protected class Any group of people for whom protective legislation has been passed.

A **protected class** is any group of people for which protective legislation has been passed. A federally protected class is any group of individuals specifically protected by *federal* law. A list of U.S. federally protected classes is shown in Figure 3.3. Table 3.1 shows the similarity of protected classes in the United States and in selected other countries. In Canada, there are no federally protected classes; each province makes its own employment law. Thus, the protected classes listed for Canada in Table 3.1 are those protected by law in *all* provinces and territories. A complete list of provincially protected classes can be found in the Appendix at the end of the book.

Though one would assume that few employers in the twenty-first century would intentionally make employment decisions based on a person's sex, race, national origin, color, age, religion, or disability, there are hundreds of organizations each year that do exactly that. For example, in 2001, Rent-A-Center settled a sex discrimination case for

Figure 3.3

Federally Protected Classes in the United States

Protected Class	Federal Law
Age (over 40)	Age Discrimination in Employment Act
Disability	Americans with Disabilities Act Americans with Disabilities Amendments Act Vocational Rehabilitation Act of 1973
Race	Civil Rights Acts of 1964, 1991
National origin	Civil Rights Acts of 1964, 1991
Religion	Civil Rights Acts of 1964, 1991
Sex	Civil Rights Acts of 1964, 1991 Equal Pay Act of 1963
Pregnancy	Pregnancy Discrimination Act
Qualified military veterans	Vietnam-Era Veterans Readjustment Assistance Act of 1974 Jobs for Veterans Act of 2002

$47 million after its chief executive officer and other managers discriminated against women. Some of their quotes included, "Get rid of women any way you can," "In case you didn't notice, we do not employ women," and "The day I hire a woman will be a cold day in hell."

Table 3.1 International Comparison of Federally Protected Classes

Protected Class	US	Canada	Australia	UK	EU	Mexico	Japan
Race	yes	yes	yes	yes	yes	yes	
National origin	yes	yes		yes	yes	yes	yes
Sex	yes	yes	yes	yes	yes	yes	yes
Age	yes	yes	yes	yes	yes	yes	yes
Disability	yes	yes	yes	yes	yes	yes	yes
Color	yes	yes	yes	yes		yes	
Religion	yes	yes	yes	yes	yes	yes	yes
Pregnancy	yes	yes	yes	yes		yes	yes
Veteran status	yes						
Marital status		yes	yes	yes		yes	
Sexual orientation	yes	yes	yes	yes	yes	yes	
Political beliefs			yes			yes	yes
Familial status		yes	yes				
Gender identity	yes	yes	yes	yes			
Criminal conviction			yes				
National extraction			yes				
Social origin			yes				
Medical record			yes				
Trade union activity			yes				
Social status							yes

Race

Based on the Civil Rights Acts of 1866, 1964, and 1991, as well as the **Fifth** and **Fourteenth Amendments** to the U.S. Constitution, it is illegal to discriminate against a person based on **race**. The five races recognized by the federal government are Black (Not of Hispanic origin), White (Not of Hispanic origin), Asian, Native Hawaiian or Other Pacific Islander, and American Indian or Alaskan Native. Hispanic and Latino/a are considered ethnicities.

The *equal protection clauses* of the Fifth and Fourteenth Amendments mandate that no federal or state agency may deny a person equal protection under the law. This implies that a government may not *intentionally* discriminate or allow intentional discrimination to take place. Because any suit filed under the Fifth or Fourteenth Amendment must demonstrate intent, they are not often invoked.

The Civil Rights Acts of 1964 (known as Title VII) and 1991 extended the scope of the Fifth and Fourteenth Amendments to the private sector and to local governments. Title VII, Section 703, makes it illegal for employers with more than 15 employees and for labor unions, employment agencies, state and local governmental agencies, and educational institutions to

- fail or refuse to hire or to discharge any individual, or otherwise to discriminate against any individual with respect to their compensation, terms, conditions, or privileges of employment, because of such individual's race, color, religion, sex, or national origin; or
- limit, segregate, or classify their employees in any way which would deprive or tend to deprive any individual of employment opportunities or otherwise adversely affect their status as an employee because of an individual's race, color, religion, sex, or national origin.

Unlike the Fifth and Fourteenth Amendments, the Civil Rights Acts do not require that the employment practice discriminate intentionally to be deemed as potentially illegal. Instead, proof of discrimination is determined through statistical analysis of selection rates and by the presence or absence of adverse impact, which will be discussed in detail later in the chapter.

The Civil Rights Acts have also been interpreted by the courts to cover the "atmosphere" of an organization, which includes such behavior as sexual harassment (*Broderick v. Ruder*, 1988; *Brundy v. Jackson*, 1971); age harassment (*Louis v. Federal Prison Industries*, 1986); race harassment (*Hunter v. Allis-Chalmers*, 1986); and religious harassment (*Abramson v. William Paterson College of New Jersey*, 2001).

An interesting example of courts considering the atmosphere of the organization is the case of *Forbes v. ABM Industries* (2005). Cheryl Forbes was a top-producing manager who accused the company of using subtle political ploys to create an atmosphere in which women could not be successful. Some of these ploys included area managers going to dinner with male managers but not with female managers, employees being encouraged to bypass female managers and go directly to their subordinates, and rumors being started about female managers. The jury found in favor of Forbes, and a Washington State appeals court upheld the jury award of over $4 million for sexual discrimination and harassment.

Color

Also protected by the Civil Rights Acts is color. Though commonly used as a synonym for race, the reference to color protects individuals against discrimination based specifically on variations in skin color. For example, in the 1989 case of *Walker v. Secretary of the Treasury*, a district court found that a darker-skinned Black supervisor at the Internal Revenue Service illegally fired a lighter-skinned Black employee. In a similar case, Applebee's Neighborhood Bar and Grill paid a $40,000 settlement to a dark-skinned Black employee who complained that his lighter-skinned Black manager made disparaging remarks about his skin color (Mirza, 2003).

Sex

The Civil Rights Acts, as well as the Equal Pay Act of 1963, prohibit discrimination based on sex. The courts have ruled that intentional discrimination against either women or men is illegal (*Diaz v. Pan American Airways*, 1991). Included in the definition of sex are sexual stereotypes. That is, it would be illegal to not hire a female applicant because she looks or dresses too masculine (*Lewis v. Heartland Inns of America*, 2010). In 2020, the U.S. Supreme Court ruled that the Civil Right Act prohibition on sex discrimination also applied to gay, lesbian, bisexual, and transgender employees (*Bostock v. Clayton County*, 2020, and *Altitude Express, Inc. v. Zarda*, 2020).

National Origin

National origin is protected under the Civil Rights Acts. Note that Hispanics are protected under national origin, not race. Claims of discrimination based on national origin have increased greatly over the past few years. One of the most common complaints is about "English-only" or "understandable-English" speaking requirements. The courts have generally ruled that language requirements are legal if they are job related and intended to ensure safety or promote job related communication (Steingold, 2019) and limited to communication during "company time" rather than on breaks An example of one such debate centers around the psycholinguistic argument that language choice is not always deliberate. However, in the case of Garcia v. Gloor, 1980, the courts ruled that because the aggrieved employee was bilingual, it was therefore a deliberate act to speak Spanish instead of English at work. This case, amongst others, established the precedence of legal language requirements in the workplace (McCalips, 2001).

A good example of an illegal "English-only" language requirement was a case that resulted in a nearly $1 million settlement between the EEOC and the Delano Regional Medical Center in 2012. The hospital forbade Filipino employees from speaking Tagalog, yet allowed other employees to speak in languages such as Spanish. The employees were told that the hospital would install cameras, if necessary, to monitor their use of English.

Religion

Also protected under the Civil Rights Acts is religion. It is illegal to use an individual's religion as a factor in an employment decision unless the nature of the job is religious. For example, the Catholic Church can require its priests to be Catholic but cannot require this of its clerical staff. The Civil Rights Acts also require organizations to make accommodations for religious beliefs unless to do so would be an undue hardship. The accommodation failures most cited in the 2,404 complaints of religious discrimination filed in 2020 with the EEOC are those involving days of worship, worship practices, and religious attire.

Days of Worship.   Many religions forbid their members from working on particular days. For example, Seventh-day Adventists and Orthodox Jews cannot work from sundown Friday to sundown Saturday, and members of the Greek Orthodox Church cannot work on Sunday. Such nonwork *requirements* should not be confused with *preferences* for nonwork on days of worship (e.g., Protestants working on Sunday or Christmas; attending a morning rather than an evening worship service), as the courts have ruled that an employee's preference does not need to be accommodated (*Dachman v. Shalala*, 2001; *Tiano v. Dillard Department Stores*, 1998).

Days of worship are often easily accommodated by scheduling employees without religious restrictions to work on those days. When there are only a few employees, scheduling rotations, or "shift swapping," can be used to reduce, but not eliminate, the number of days of worship that an employee might have to miss. Accommodations become legally unreasonable when there are no coworkers available, overtime will have to be paid to cover an employee's day of worship, or another employee's seniority or collective bargaining rights have been violated. However, with a little ingenuity and proper explanations of an employee's religious requirements, reasonable accommodations can usually be made.

The case of Eddie Kilgore provides an example of a poorly handled case of religious accommodation. Kilgore had been employed for 18 years by Sparks Regional Medical Center in Arkansas when he was suddenly ordered to be on call on Saturdays. As a Seventh-day Adventist, he was forbidden to work on Saturdays, a requirement long known by his employer. When Kilgore refused the Saturday work, he was fired. Kilgore filed a suit for religious discrimination and a jury awarded him $100,000 and his former job back.

Worship Practices. Two practices, in particular, can cause potential problems: prayer and fasting. Some religions require members to pray at certain times. For example, followers of Islam perform the Salat ritual prayer five times daily: at sunrise, noon, afternoon, sunset, and night. Because each prayer can take 15 minutes (including preparation such as hand washing), organizations such as fast-food restaurants and retail stores often have difficulty accommodating every prayer request. Fasting requirements can also pose problems. For example, followers of Islam must refrain from food and drink from sunrise to sunset during the 30-day period of Ramadan. Though Muslim employees are available to work, their endurance and performance may be most affected during the latter part of the day. Thus, fasting can be accommodated by having dangerous, strenuous, or complicated work performed earlier in the day or scheduling Muslim employees for earlier hours. A good example of this practice occurred in 2010 when Ramadan fell during the period in which "two-a-day" football practices were held at most U.S. high schools. Fordson High School in Dearborn, Michigan, whose student body is predominantly Muslim, moved its football practices from daytime to 11:00 p.m. so that players could drink water while they practiced.

Though fasts and prayer are the most common worship practices that need accommodation, they are certainly not the only ones. For example, because Jehovah's Witnesses cannot celebrate birthdays or nonreligious holidays, their lack of participation in an office birthday party or celebration is often viewed by uninformed coworkers as an "attitude problem." The traditional office Christmas party in which Christmas decorations are hung, a tree is decorated, inexpensive presents are exchanged among employees, and alcohol and food are served provides a great example of potential religious diversity issues. Would such a party offend people who don't celebrate Christmas? Are there employees whose religion would prohibit them from attending the party? Is the food served consistent with the dietary restrictions of groups such as Muslims, Hindus, Buddhists, and Jews?

Religious Attire. Because many religions require their members to wear certain attire, potential conflicts can occur when an organization wants employees to have a uniform appearance, either to promote a company image or to keep customers happy. Because of this desire for employees to look alike, complaints of religious discrimination regarding religious attire have been made. A good example is the complaint filed by the EEOC against Abercrombie & Fitch. Abercrombie had a dress code called the "look policy" which included a ban on any headwear. Samantha Elauf, as required by her Muslim religion, wore a scarf to her interview and was not hired because the company thought it would be required to accommodate Elauf's wearing of a scarf. The U.S. Supreme Court ruled this practice to be illegal (*EEOC v. Abercrombie & Fitch*, 2015). The courts have also supported face-piercing for members of the Church of Body Modification (*Cloutier v. Costco Wholesale*, 2004).

If, however, the religious apparel creates the potential of danger to the employee or others (e.g., a bracelet getting caught in a piece of machinery or a head covering preventing the wearing of a safety helmet), the courts have been clear that banning such apparel is legal. For example, in *EEOC v. GEO Group, Inc.* (2010), the court upheld the prison's zero-tolerance policy for employees wearing nonissued headgear (e.g., hats, scarves). The policy was challenged by three female Muslim employees who claimed that their religion required that they wear a *khimar* (religious head scarf). The prison responded by stating that such headgear posed a safety risk, as it made it easier to smuggle contraband, made it more difficult to visually identify a prison employee, and the *khimar* could be used by inmates to strangle the employee. Consistent with its ruling in a similar case (*Webb v. City of Philadelphia*, 2009), the U.S. Court of Appeals for the Third Circuit ruled that the prison's safety concerns took precedence over the employee's religious rights.

Grooming standards can also be a source of religious discrimination. For example, UPS had a policy that male employees in supervisory or customer contact positions could not have hair below their collar and could not have a beard. The EEOC claimed that such a policy discriminated against Sikhs, Muslims, Rastafarians, and other religious groups. In 2018, UPS settled the case for $4.9 million.

Age

Age Discrimination in Employment Act (ADEA) A federal law that, with its amendments, forbids discrimination against an individual who is over the age of 40.

The **Age Discrimination in Employment Act (ADEA)** and its later amendments forbid an employer or union from discriminating against an individual over the age of 40. In part, this act was designed to protect older workers from employment practices aimed at reducing costs by firing older workers with higher salaries and replacing them with lower-paid younger workers. Such legislation is important because, despite evidence to the contrary, people often view older workers as being less competent than younger workers (Bal, Reiss, Rudolph, & Baltes, 2011). To file suit under this act, an individual must demonstrate that they are in the specified age bracket, has been discharged or demoted, was performing the job adequately at the time of discharge or demotion, and has been replaced by a younger worker, even if the younger worker is older than 40 (*O'Connor v. Consolidated Coin Caterers*, 1996). All employment practices (e.g., hiring, placement, promotion, layoffs, demotions, compensation) are covered by the ADEA.

Though mandatory retirement ages are allowed in certain circumstances (e.g., 70 years for college professors), they are usually illegal. Practices that favor older workers are not illegal (Guerin & Barreiro, 2019).

Age discrimination is also a factor in countries outside the United States. As shown in Table 3.1, many countries have age discrimination laws. In the European Union, practices that have an adverse impact on older workers may be illegal. For example, the common practice of hiring younger workers by recruiting at colleges and universities (called "milk runs" in the United Kingdom) may no longer be allowed (Gomm, 2005).

Disability

Discrimination against people with disabilities by the federal government or by federal contractors is forbidden by the **Vocational Rehabilitation Act of 1973**, and discrimination against people with disabilities by any other employer with 15 or more employees is forbidden by the **Americans with Disabilities Act (ADA)**. In 2013, the OFCCP revised its rules under Section 503 of the Vocational Rehabilitation Act and began requiring federal contractors in 2014 to ask job applicants to identify if they had a disability and set a utilization goal (not a quota) that at least 7% of a contractor's employees should be individuals with disabilities.

The ADA, signed into law by President George H. W. Bush in 1990, is the most important piece of employment legislation since the 1964 Civil Rights Act. An amendment to the ADA, the ADA Amendments Act (ADAAA), was signed into law by President George W. Bush in 2008. The ADA requires organizations with 15 or more employees to make "reasonable accommodation for the physically and mentally disabled, unless to do so would impose an undue hardship." Though Congress did not provide a list of disabilities, it did define "disability" as

1. a physical or mental impairment that substantially limits one or more of the major life activities of an individual;
2. a record of such impairment; or
3. being regarded as having such an impairment.

For the first part of the definition, *major life activities* include such things as walking, hearing, and speaking. The ADAAA expanded the list of major life activities to include the operation of major bodily functions (e.g., digestive, bowel, bladder). A condition that keeps a person from working a *particular* job, as opposed to all jobs or a class of jobs, is not a disability (*Toyota v. Williams*, 2002). Examples of disabilities defined by case law by case law or the U.S. Department of Labor are blindness, paralysis, asthma, muscular dystrophy, and various learning disabilities such as dyslexia. Conditions not considered by the courts to be disabilities have included fear of heights, color blindness, hypertension, depression, temporary illnesses such as pneumonia, sprained ankles, being 20 pounds overweight, carpal tunnel syndrome, and wearing glasses.

The second part of the definition was designed to protect people who were once disabled but no longer are. Examples include individuals recovering from an alcohol use disorder, cancer patients in remission, people who spent time in a mental health facility, and individuals with a previous substance abuse disorder who have successfully completed treatment.

The final part of the definition protects individuals who don't have a disability but are regarded or treated as if they do. Examples of people protected under this clause are those with facial scarring or severe burns. In an interesting case (*Johnson v. Apland & Associates*, 1997), the U.S. Court of Appeals for the Seventh Circuit ruled that a man missing 18 teeth had a right to file an ADA suit on the grounds that he was regarded as having a disability. The case was sent back to the lower court to determine whether this perception actually "substantially" limited "one or more major life activit[ies]."

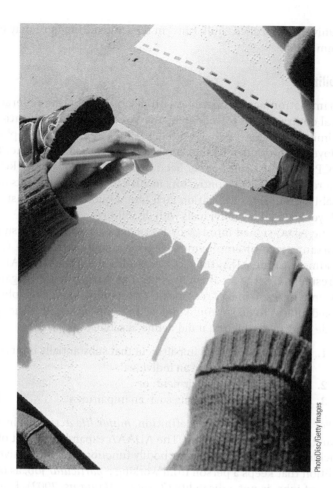

Accommodations, such as providing Braille versions of tests, are sometimes necessary.

The ADAAA expanded this part of the definition, clarified that if an impairment was expected to last less than six months, it would not be considered a disability, and clarified that employers do not need to provide reasonable accommodation to employees who are *regarded* as being disabled. The ADA does not require an organization to hire or give preference to individuals with disabilities, only that persons with disabilities be given an equal chance and that reasonable attempts be made to accommodate their disabilities. Although there are no guidelines regarding what can be considered "reasonable," accommodations can include providing readers or interpreters, modifying work schedules or equipment, and making facilities more accessible. In spite of the fact that the majority of accommodations cost less than $500 (Job Accommodation Network, 2020), many employees are reluctant to ask for, and many organizations are reluctant to provide, accommodations (Baldridge & Veiga, 2001).

In an interesting case demonstrating that many organizations do not comply with the spirit of the ADA, in 2005 a jury awarded $8 million to Dale Alton, an applicant for a customer service position who asked EchoStar Communications to accommodate his blindness by providing him with a computer program, Job Access with Speech (JAWS), that translates text into speech. When Alton first applied for the job, EchoStar told him not to bother because the company was "not set up to handle blind people."

If a disability keeps a person from performing the "essential functions" of a job identified during a job analysis or poses a direct threat to their own or others' safety, the person does not have to be hired or retained (Zink, 2002). Furthermore, the Seventh Circuit Court of Appeals ruled that an organization is not required to make significant changes in the essential functions of a job to accommodate an employee with disabilities (*Ammons v. Aramark Uniform Services*, 2004). For example, in *Caston v. Trigon Engineering* (1993), a district court ruled that a woman with dissociative identity disorder was unable to perform her job as an environmental engineer. In another case (*DiPompo v. West Point*, 1991), a district court ruled that an applicant with dyslexia, though considered disabled, was not able to perform essential job functions such as inspecting vehicles and buildings for the presence of dangerous materials and recording information such as work schedules and emergency calls. In *Calef v. Gillette Company* (2003), the First Circuit Court of Appeals ruled that although Fred Calef had attention deficit/hyperactivity disorder, his threatening behavior and inability to handle his anger was not protected. In *Ethridge v. State of Alabama* (1994), a district court ruled that a police applicant with restricted use of his right hand could not perform the essential job functions because he was unable to shoot in a two-handed position (Weaver stance).

An interesting and well-publicized ADA case was that of golfer Casey Martin (*Martin v. PGA Tour*, 2000). Martin had Klippel-Trènaunay-Weber syndrome in his right leg. Because this syndrome made it difficult for Martin to walk on the golf course, he requested an accommodation that he be allowed to use a golf cart. The Professional Golfers Association (PGA) denied the request, arguing that walking is an "essential function" of golf, and thus, using a cart would not be a reasonable accommodation. The U.S. Supreme Court ruled in favor of Martin's contention that walking was not an essential function of golf and that allowing Martin to use a cart was not an unreasonable accommodation.

Pregnancy

Pregnancy Discrimination Act A 1978 federal law protecting the rights of pregnant women.

The **Pregnancy Discrimination Act** states that "women affected by pregnancy, childbirth, or related medical conditions shall be treated the same for all employment related purposes, including receipt of benefit programs, as other persons not so affected but similar in their ability or inability to work." Simply put, this act requires pregnancy to be treated as any other short-term disability (Guerin & Barreiro, 2019). For example, in 2020, Walmart settled a case for $14 million after the EEOC claimed that Walmart did not offer the same light duty work accommodation to 3,995 pregnant employees that they did for similar employees who were not pregnant (*EEOC v. Walmart*, 2020).

Family and Medical Leave Act (FMLA) Passed in 1993, the FMLA provides 12 weeks of unpaid leave for birth, adoption, or serious illness of a child, parent, spouse, or the employee. All organizations that physically employ 50 or more people within a 70-mile radius of one another are covered by the act.

In the case of *California Federal Savings and Loan Association v. Guerra* (1987), the U.S. Supreme Court expanded the scope of the law. Pregnant employees may receive better treatment than other persons with disabilities but cannot receive worse treatment. In 2020, 2,698 charges of pregnancy discrimination were filed with the EEOC. Many of the rights provided in the Pregnancy Discrimination Act have been greatly expanded by the **Family Medical Leave Act (FMLA)**, which will be discussed later in this chapter. Some states (e.g., California, Colorado, Illinois) require employers to offer leave to employees who are unable to work because of their pregnancy.

Military Veteran Status

Vietnam-Era Veterans Readjustment Assistance Act (VEVRAA) A 1974 federal law that mandates that federal government contractors and subcontractors take affirmative action to employ and promote Vietnam-era veterans.

Due to the large-scale discrimination in the 1960s and 1970s against soldiers returning from duty in Vietnam, Congress passed the **Vietnam-Era Veterans Readjustment Assistance Act (VEVRAA)** in 1974. This act mandates any federal contractor or subcontractor with more than $100,000 in federal government contracts to take affirmative action to employ and promote Vietnam-era veterans. VEVRAA was amended by the 2002 **Jobs for Veterans Act** to increase the coverage of VEVRAA to include disabled veterans, veterans who have recently left the service (within three years), and veterans who participated in a U.S. military operation for which an Armed Forces Service Medal was awarded. In 2021, the OFCCP updated their VEVRAA enforcement rules and set a "target" that a federal contractor's workforce should consist of at least 5.6% qualified veterans (OFCCP will update this target each year). Because providing affirmative action to qualified veterans will likely result in adverse impact against women, federal contractors must walk a fine line in how they recruit and hire veterans.

Is the Requirement a BFOQ?

Employment decisions based on membership in a protected class (e.g., "We will not hire women because they are not strong enough to do the job") are illegal unless the employer can demonstrate that the requirement is a **bona fide occupational qualification (BFOQ)**.

If a job can be performed only by a person in a particular class, the requirement is considered a BFOQ. Actually, some jobs can be performed only by a person of a particular sex; for instance, only men can be a sperm donor. The courts have ruled that sex is a BFOQ for such jobs as bathroom attendants and prison guards (Guerin & Barreiro, 2019). However, there are very few jobs in our society that can be performed only by a person of a particular race, gender, or national origin. Take, for example, a job that involves lifting 75-pound crates. Although it is true that on average, men are stronger than women, a company cannot set a men-only requirement. The real BFOQ in this example is strength, not gender. Thus, restricting employment to men would be illegal.

The courts have clearly stated that a BFOQ must involve the ability to perform the job, not satisfy a customer's or client's preferences. For example:

- In *Geraldine Fuhr v. School District of Hazel Park, Michigan* (2004), the Sixth Circuit Court of Appeals ruled that the *preference* that a man rather than a woman coach a boys' basketball team was not a BFOQ.
- In *Diaz v. Pan American Airways* (1991), the court ruled that even though airline passengers prefer female flight attendants, the nature of the business is to transport passengers safely, and males can perform the essential job functions as well as females.
- In 1989, Caesar's Casino in Atlantic City was fined $250,000 for removing Black and female card dealers from a table to appease a high-stakes gambler who preferred White male dealers.

One of the few exceptions to the BFOQ requirement seems to be grooming standards. It is not unusual for an organization to have separate dress codes and grooming standards for men and women. Though different standards based on sex would appear to violate the law, the courts have generally upheld them (Fowler-Hermes, 2001; *Jespersen v. Harrah's Casino*, 2005) if the separate codes were equally burdensome. However, following the U.S. Supreme Court's decision in *Bostock v. Clayton County* (2020) that the Title VII definition of sex includes LGBTQ individuals, the EEOC and the courts may take another look at the separate grooming standard issue.

Perhaps the most interesting of the BFOQ cases was the EEOC complaint against Hooters, the restaurant chain famous for its chicken wings and scantily clad waitresses. Hooters allowed only women to be servers and claimed that it was a BFOQ due to the restaurant's unique atmosphere. In fact, a Hooters spokesman was quoted as saying that the restaurant doesn't sell food, it sells (female) sex appeal, and to have female sex appeal, you have to be female. The EEOC disagreed; and in an unusual settlement, Hooters agreed to pay $3.75 million to a group of men who were not hired, and the EEOC agreed to let Hooters continue to hire only women for the server positions.

Has Case Law, State Law, or Local Law Expanded the Definition of Any of the Protected Classes?

An employment decision may not violate a federal law, but it may violate one of the many state and local laws that have been passed to protect additional groups of people. For example, at the state level:

- Two states (California and New York) and the District of Columbia forbid discrimination based on a person's political affiliation or activities.
- Six states (Louisiana, Missouri, New Hampshire, Oklahoma, South Dakota, West Virginia) and the District of Columbia outlaw discrimination based on off duty use of tobacco products.
- Twenty-two states (California, Colorado, Connecticut, Delaware, Hawaii, Illinois, Iowa, Maine, Maryland, Massachusetts, Minnesota, Nevada, New Hampshire, New Jersey, New Mexico, New York, Oregon, Rhode Island, Utah, Vermont, Washington, and Wisconsin) and the District of Columbia prohibit discrimination by private and public employers based on sexual orientation; and twelve states (Alaska, Arizona, Delaware, Indiana, Kentucky, Louisiana, Michigan, Montana, North Carolina, Ohio, Pennsylvania, and Virginia) only prohibit discrimination by public employers.
- Twenty-two states (Alaska, California, Connecticut, Delaware, Florida, Hawaii, Illinois, Maryland, Michigan, Minnesota, Montana, Nebraska, New Hampshire, New Jersey, New Mexico, New York, North Dakota, Ohio, Oregon, Virginia, Washington, and Wisconsin) and the District of Columbia forbid discrimination based on marital status.

At the local level:

- Santa Cruz, California, outlaws discrimination based on height and physical appearance.
- Discrimination based on sexual orientation is prohibited in over 185 cities and counties.
- Cincinnati, Ohio, prohibits discrimination against people of Appalachian heritage.

In addition to state and local laws, the definitions of protected classes can be expanded or narrowed by court decisions. As discussed previously, these decisions become case law. For example, in a variety of cases, the courts have ruled that the definition of disability should be expanded to include obesity but not former drug use.

Does the Requirement Have Adverse Impact on Members of a Protected Class?

Adverse impact An employment practice that results in members of a protected class being negatively affected at a higher rate than members of the majority class. Adverse impact is usually determined by the four-fifths rule.

If the employment practice does not refer directly to a member of a protected class, the next step is to determine whether the requirement *adversely affects* members of a protected class. **Adverse impact** means that a particular employment decision results in negative consequences more often for members of one race, sex, or national origin than for members of another race, sex, or national origin. For example, an employee selection requirement of a college degree would lead to a lower percentage of Black applicants being hired compared with White applicants. Thus, even though such a requirement does not mention Black individuals (a protected class), it does adversely impact them because according to U.S. Census data, in 2019, 37.6% of White individuals had bachelor's degrees or higher compared with 23.7% of Black individuals. Though adverse impact analyses have traditionally been limited to groups protected by the 1964 Civil Rights Act, the U.S. Supreme Court ruled in 2005 that employees could file adverse impact charges based on age, which is protected under the ADEA (*Roderick Jackson v. Birmingham Board of Education*, 2005).

The courts use two standards to determine adverse impact: statistical significance and practical significance. Experts believe that both standards should be met for a finding of adverse impact (Cohen, Aamodt, & Dunleavy, 2010). The statistical significance burden is met if a plaintiff can demonstrate that the differences in selection rates for two groups (e.g., men and women) would not have occurred by chance alone. Statistics used to make this determination include the standard deviation test, chi-square, and Fisher's exact test.

If the statistical test suggests that the selection rate differences would probably not have occurred by chance, the next step is to use a test of practical significance. That is, is the difference between the two groups at a level high enough to suggest potential discrimination? Although there are several methods of determining practical significance, the most common is probably the **four-fifths rule**. With the four-fifths rule, the percentage of applicants hired from one group (e.g., women, Hispanic individuals) is compared to the percentage of applicants hired in the most favored group (e.g., men, White individuals). If the percentage of applicants hired in the disadvantaged group is less than 80% of the percentage for the advantaged group, adverse impact is said to have occurred.

Four-fifths rule When the selection ratio for one group (e.g., females) is less than 80% (four-fifths) of the selection ratio for another group (e.g., males), adverse impact is said to exist.

It is important to keep in mind that adverse impact refers to *percentages* rather than raw numbers. For example, as shown in Table 3.2, if 25 of 50 male applicants are hired, the hiring percentage is 50%. If 10 women applied, at least 4 would need to be hired to avoid adverse impact. Why only four? Because the hiring percentage for women must be at least 80% of the hiring percentage for men. Because the male-hiring percentage in this case is 50%, the hiring percentage for women must be at least four-fifths (80%) of 50%. Thus, $.50 \times .80 = .40$, indicating that at least 40% of all female applicants need to be hired to avoid adverse impact and a potential charge of unfair discrimination. With 10 applicants, this results in hiring at least 4.

Adverse impact is typically computed separately for race and sex. That is, an organization would not compute hiring rates for White men or Black women. Instead, hiring rates have typically been computed for men and for women and then be computed separately for White applicants and for Black applicants. However, government regulatory practices are changing and there is an increasing concern about discrimination due to the intersection of sex and race.

Table 3.2   Adverse Impact Example

	Sex	
	Male	**Female**
Applicants	50	10
Hires	25	4
Selection ratio	.50	.40

It is illegal to *intentionally* discriminate against White individuals and men, but employment practices that result in adverse impact against White individuals and men, although technically illegal, are probably not illegal in practice. No court has upheld an adverse impact claim by a White applicant. For example, it was mentioned previously that requiring a college degree adversely impacts Black applicants because 36.6% of White applicants have at least a bachelor's degree compared with 23.7% of Black applicants and 16.8% of Hispanic applicants. Though 54.7% of Asian Americans have college degrees, a White applicant could not realistically win a discrimination charge based on adverse impact. However, the OFCCP has entered into conciliation agreements with federal contractors accused of practices resulting in adverse impact against White applicants.

Though determining the adverse impact of a test seems simple—which is done by comparing the hiring rates (hires ÷ applicants) of two groups—the actual nuts and bolts of the calculations can get complicated, and it is common that plaintiffs and defendants disagree on who is considered an "applicant" and who is considered a "hire." For example, as shown in Table 3.3, if a person applying for a job does not meet the minimum qualifications, they are not considered as an applicant in adverse impact calculations. For example, if a plumber applies for a job as a brain surgeon, they lack the minimum qualifications for the job—a medical degree.

There are three criteria for a minimum qualification: it must be needed to perform the job, and not merely be a preference; it must be formally identified and communicated prior to the start of the selection process; and it must be consistently applied. As you can imagine, with such criteria, there is much room for disagreement.

Was the Requirement Designed to Intentionally Discriminate Against a Protected Class?

If an employment practice does not refer directly to a member of a protected class but adversely affects a protected class, the courts will look closely at whether the practice was initiated to intentionally reduce the pool of qualified minority[1] applicants. For example, suppose a city requires all its employees to live within the city limits. The city believes that this is a justifiable requirement because salaries are paid by tax dollars, and town employees should contribute to that tax base. Though such a requirement is not illegal, the court might look deeper to see if the tax base

---

1   Please note that the terms "minorities" and "nonminorities" are used in this text to be consistent with the terms used in employment law in in federal regulations. References to "underrepresented groups" or specific minority groups rather than the umbrella term "minorities" may be more inclusive/appropriate/preferred in everyday conversations.

Table 3.3 Who Is an Applicant and Who Is a Hire?

Who is an Applicant?

    Count as an applicant

        Those meeting minimum qualifications

    Remove from calculation

        Those who did not meet minimum qualifications

        Those who are not eligible to apply

            Former employees who were terminated (if this is company policy)

            Former employees who did not wait the required time to apply (if this is company policy)

            Duplicate applications within a specified period of time

        Those who are no longer interested

            Found another job

            No longer interested in the job

            Declined or did not show up for the interview

Who is a Hire?

    Both hires and offers count

    Hires

        Hired and reported to work

        Hired but did not report to work

        Hired but failed drug test or background test

    Offers

        Offered job but declined

was in fact the reason for the residency requirement. That is, if the city population was 99% White and the population of the surrounding area was 90% Black, the court might argue that the residency requirement was a subtle way of discriminating against minorities.

Though such subtle requirements are probably no longer common in the employment sector, they have been used throughout history. For example, before the 1970s, some states required voters to pass a "literacy test" to be eligible to vote. Though the stated purpose of the test was to ensure that voters would make intelligent and educated decisions, the real purpose was to reduce the number of minority voters.

Can the Employer Prove That the Requirement Is Job Related?

As shown in the flowchart in Figure 3.2, if our employment practice does not result in adverse impact, it is probably legal. If adverse impact does result, then the burden of proof shifts to the employer to demonstrate that the employment practice is either **job related** or exempt from adverse impact. Before discussing these two strategies, two points need to be made. First, adverse impact is a fact of life in personnel selection. Almost any hiring test is going to have adverse impact on some protected class, though some may have less adverse impact than others.

Second, the burden of proof in employment law is different than in criminal law. In criminal law, a defendant is innocent until proven guilty. In employment law, both the

Job related The extent to which a test or measure taps a knowledge, skill, ability, behavior, or other characteristic needed to successfully perform a job.

1991 Civil Rights Act and the court's ruling in *Griggs v. Duke Power* (1972) shift the burden of proof: Once adverse impact is established, an employer (the defendant) is considered guilty unless it can prove its innocence by establishing the job relatedness of the test.

Valid Testing Procedures

An employment practice resulting in adverse impact may still be legal if the test is job related (valid) and as long as reasonable attempts have been made to find other tests that might be just as valid but have less adverse impact (refer to the flowchart in Figure 3.2). For example, if an employer uses a cognitive ability test to select employees, there is a strong possibility that adverse impact will occur (this impact was discussed in a widely-circulated and cited article by Hunter and Hunter (1984)). If the employer can demonstrate, however, that the cognitive ability test predicts performance on the job and that no other available test measuring a similar construct with less adverse impact will predict performance as well, the use of the test is probably justified. Terpstra, Mohamed, and Kethley (1999) conducted a review of federal court cases to investigate the degree of litigation surrounding several frequently used selection devices. The researchers found that between 1978 to 1997, there were 28 court cases that challenged the legality of cognitive ability tests, second only to the unstructured interview. A more in-depth discussion of validity strategies is found in Chapter 6.

An interesting example of adverse impact and job relatedness comes from the town of North Miami, Florida. For 30 years, North Miami required that police recruits be able to swim. Although the requirement seemed logical given that the town is located next to the ocean, it had adverse impact against Black recruits. When the town looked further at the job relatedness of the requirement, it discovered that North Miami officers seldom entered the water for rescues: only eight times from 1986 to 2004. Because swimming was an infrequent activity and the swimming requirement resulted in adverse impact, in 2004 North Miami eliminated the swimming ability as a requirement for the job of police officer.

Exceptions

Bona Fide Seniority System.   An organization that has a long-standing policy of promoting employees with the greatest seniority or laying off employees with the least seniority can continue to do so even though adverse impact occurs. For a seniority system to be considered bona fide, the *purpose* of the system must be to reward seniority; not to discriminate (Twomey & Greene, 2020). That is, if an organization established a seniority system to protect male employees, it would not be considered bona fide.

National Security.   In certain circumstances, it is legal for an employer to discriminate against a member of a particular national origin or other protected class when it is in the best interest of the nation's security to do so. For example, for years Russian citizens living in the United States were prohibited from working in any defense-related industry.

Veteran's Preference Rights.   Most civil service jobs provide extra points on tests for veterans of the armed forces. For example, in Fort Worth, Texas, veterans who apply for city jobs get five points added to their exam score. Because most people in the military are men, awarding these extra points for military service results in adverse impact against women. However, according to the Civil Rights Act of 1964, such practices by public agencies are exempt from legal action as long as the veteran's preference is the result of a government regulation.

Did the Employer Look for Reasonable Alternatives That Would Result in Lesser Adverse Impact?

As shown in Figure 3.2, if an employer proves a test is job related, the final factor looked at by the courts is the extent to which the employer looked for other valid selection tests that would have less adverse impact. For example, if an organization wanted to use a particular cognitive ability test, did it explore such alternatives as education level or other cognitive ability tests that would be just as valid but would have less adverse impact?

3-3 Harassment

An issue of growing concern in the workplace is sexual harassment. In 2019, 26,221 complaints of harassment were filed with the EEOC; 7,514 of these were for sexual harassment. Of these 7,514, 16.8% were filed by men. Of harassment claims filed with the EEOC, approximately 33% involve racial harassment, 29% sexual harassment, and 38% harassment of other protected classes. In 2016, an EEOC task force estimated that between 25% and 85% of women have experienced sexual harassment in the workplace (Feldblum & Lipnic, 2016). These percentages increase when employees are the sole representative of their gender (called *gender pioneers*) or consist of a small minority of the employees in a particular work setting (called *gender isolates*) (Niebuhr & Oswald, 1992).

Harassment is not an issue limited to the United States. Though the United States has taken the lead in preventing and punishing harassment, Canada, the United Kingdom, Australia, New Zealand, Ireland, and the European Union also have laws prohibiting sexual harassment (Gutman, 2005).

Though the following discussion focuses on sexual harassment, the courts have ruled that racial, religious, disability, and age harassment are also illegal (e.g., *Crawford v. Medina General Hospital*, 1996; *Lanman v. Johnson County, Kansas*, 2004). For example:

- In 2020, Porous Materials settled a race, sex and national origin harassment suit for $93,000. A manager called employees from other countries "terrorists" and told immigrants to leave America.
- In 2013, the Los Angeles Police Department settled a racial harassment suit for $1.5 million. The harassment included racially offensive comments and pranks. For example, when Earl Wright asked to leave work early one day, his supervisor responded, "Why? You got go pick watermelons?" On a different occasion, Wright's supervisor gave him a cake with a fried chicken leg and a piece of watermelon on top.
- In 2004, Fairfield Toyota in California settled an EEOC charge of religion (Muslim), color (dark-skinned), and national origin (Afghan) harassment for $550,000. Supervisors and other employees commonly referred to seven Afghan Muslim employees as "the bin Laden gang" and "camel jockeys."

Types of Harassment

Legally, sexual harassment can take one of two forms: *quid pro quo* or *hostile environment.*

Quid Pro Quo

Quid pro quo A type of sexual harassment in which the granting of sexual favors is tied to an employment decision.

With **quid pro quo**, the granting of sexual favors is tied to such employment decisions as promotions and salary increases. An example of a quid pro quo case of harassment is a supervisor who tells the secretary that they must sleep with the supervisor to keep their job. In quid pro quo cases, a *single* incident is enough to constitute sexual harassment and result in the organization being liable for legal damages (Gutman, 2005).

Hostile Environment

Hostile environment A type of harassment characterized by a pattern of unwanted conduct related to gender that interferes with an individual's work performance.

In a **hostile environment** case, sexual harassment occurs when an unwanted *pattern* of conduct related to *gender* unreasonably interferes with an individual's work performance. Though men and women differ in their perceptions of what constitutes harassment (Rotundo, Nguyen, & Sackett, 2001), the courts have ruled that such conduct can include comments, unwanted sexual or romantic advances, or the display of demeaning posters, signs, or cartoons (*Jenson v. Eveleth Taconite Co.*, 1993).

Pattern of Behavior. For conduct to be considered sexual harassment based on a hostile environment, the U.S. Supreme Court has ruled that the conduct must be a *pattern* of behavior rather than an isolated incident (*Clark County School District v. Breeden*, 2001). It would not be harassment to ask a coworker for a date, even if the coworker does not agree to the date. It becomes harassment if the coworker *continually* makes unwanted romantic or sexual overtures or repeatedly makes inappropriate remarks.

Based on Sex. To be considered sexual harassment, conduct must be due to the *sex* of the employee. That is, but for the sex of the employee, would the conduct have occurred? For example, in *Christopher Lack v. Wal-Mart* (2001), the Fourth Circuit Court of Appeals ruled that a supervisor's lewd and vulgar language and jokes were not sexual harassment because they were made both to men and to women. The Courts of Appeal for the Seventh (*Holman v. Indiana Department of Transportation*, 2000) and Eighth (*Jenkins v. Southern Farm Bureau Casualty*, 2002) Circuits have made similar rulings. Members of a police department consistently referring to female officers as "babes" or "honey" would be an example of sexual harassment because the comments are based on sex and are demeaning to the female officers. A male officer calling a female officer "stupid" would be an example of rude behavior, but not sexual harassment because the nature of the comment was not based on sex.

In 1998, the U.S. Supreme Court considered whether an employee can sexually harass a member of the same sex. That is, if a male makes sexual comments or improperly touches another male, is this a case of sexual harassment? In the case of *Oncale v. Sundowner Offshore Services* (1998), the Supreme Court said yes. As a roustabout on an oil platform, Joseph Oncale was subjected to sexual threats and battery by other male roustabouts. After getting no help from his supervisor, Oncale quit his job and filed suit, eventually reaching the Supreme Court. The key to the *Oncale* ruling was that the harassment was due to Oncale's *sex* (he was harassed because he was a *male*), not his *sexual orientation*.

It should be pointed out that employers should not tolerate harassment of any type. Protected classes are a legal concept rather than a moral one, and few human resources professionals would argue against the idea that employers have a moral obligation to provide a workplace free of harassment.

Negative to the Reasonable Person.   Any pattern of behavior based on sex that causes an employee discomfort might constitute sexual harassment. In *Harris v. Forklift Systems* (1993), the U.S. Supreme Court found that a male supervisor's comments such as, "Let's go to the Holiday Inn and negotiate your raise," and, "You're just a dumb-ass woman" constituted harassment, even though the female employee did not suffer any great psychological damage or "have a nervous breakdown."

Organizational Liability for Sexual Harassment

In cases of quid pro quo harassment of its employees, an organization will always be liable. In hostile environment cases, however, the U.S. Supreme Court has ruled that an organization can avoid liability by showing that it "exercised reasonable care to prevent and correct promptly any sexually harassing behavior" or that the complainant did not take reasonable advantage of the corrective opportunities provided by the organization (*Burlington Industries v. Ellerth*, 1998; *Faragher v. City of Boca Raton*, 1998).

Preventing Sexual Harassment

In determining an organization's liability for the sexual harassment of its employees, the courts look first at the organization's attempts to prevent this behavior. To avoid liability, the organization must have a well-conceived policy regarding sexual harassment, must have communicated that policy to its employees (*Frederick v. Sprint*, 2001), and must have enforced that policy (*MacGregor v. Mallinckrodt, Inc.*, 2004). The policy must explain the types of harassment (*Smith v. First Union National Bank*, 2000) and include a list of the *names* of the company officials to whom an employee should report any harassment (*Gentry v. Export Packaging*, 2001). It is important to note that organizations are also responsible for harassment committed by vendors, customers, and other third parties.

Correcting Sexually Harassing Behavior

If an employee complains of sexual harassment, it is essential that the organization investigate the complaint quickly and then promptly take any necessary action to rectify the situation and punish the offender. To reduce an organization's liability for sexual harassment, Jacobs and Kearns (2001) advise the following:

- All complaints, no matter how trivial or far-fetched they appear, must be investigated.
- The organization's policy must encourage victims to come forward and afford them multiple channels or sources through which to file their complaint.
- Complaints must be kept confidential to protect both the accused and the accuser. Information from the investigation should be kept in a file separate from the employee's personnel file.
- Action must be taken to protect the accuser during the time the complaint is being investigated. Actions might include physically separating the two parties or limiting the amount of contact between them.
- Both the accused and the accuser must be given due process, and care must be taken to avoid an initial assumption of guilt.
- The results of the investigation must be communicated in writing to both parties.
- The severity of the punishment (if any) must match the severity of the violation.

As mentioned previously, the proper handling of a sexual harassment complaint can protect an employer from legal liability. In such cases as *Linda Roebuck v. Odie Washington* (2005) and *Rheineck v. Hutchinson Technology* (2001), courts of appeal ruled that the organization was not liable for sexual harassment because it investigated the complaint in a timely manner and then took prompt corrective action against the harasser. In contrast, in *Intlekofer v. Turnage* (1992), the court of appeals found the Veterans Administration liable for harassment because it ignored nearly two dozen complaints by an employee and refused to take corrective action against the harasser.

However, the concern for prompt action should not deny the accused due process. In 1997, a jury awarded an employee accused of sexual harassment $26.6 million. The employee was fired by Miller Brewing Company for discussing an episode of the TV show *Seinfeld* in which Jerry Seinfeld forgot the name of a date (Delores) but remembered that it rhymed with a female body part. The jury ruled that a reasonable person would not have been offended by the discussion, and thus Miller Brewing went too far in firing the accused employee.

Rather than being *reactive* to sexual harassment complaints, it is in the best interests of an organization to be *proactive* and prevent harassment. Proactive steps include having a strong organizational policy against harassment (*Frederick v. Sprint*, 2001) and training employees about behavior that constitutes harassment.

In addition to the obvious legal costs, sexual harassment has other financial ramifications for an organization. Sexual harassment results in higher levels of turnover, greater absenteeism, and lower levels of productivity (Munson, Hulin, & Drasgow, 2000; Pratt, Burnazi, LePla, Boyce, & Baltes, 2003; Willness, Steel, & Lee, 2007).

3-4 Family Medical Leave Act

In 1993, Congress passed the Family Medical Leave Act, or FMLA, which entitles eligible employees to a minimum of 12 weeks of unpaid leave each year to deal with the following family matters:

- Births, adoptions, or placement for foster care
- To care for a child, parent, or spouse with a serious health condition
- For employee's own serious health condition that makes them unable to perform the job

In 2008, President George W. Bush signed the National Defense Authorization Act that amended the FMLA to provide 26 weeks of unpaid leave for a spouse, child, parent, or next of kin to care for a member of the military.

All public agencies and private organizations with 50 or more employees physically employed within a 70-mile radius of one another are covered by the act. Employers can decide if they want to define the eligibility period as a calendar year (i.e., January through December) or as a rolling 12-month period measured backward from the date an employee uses any FMLA leave. If the employer does not define its eligibility period in the employee handbook, the method most favorable to the employee will be in force (*Dodaro v. Village of Glendale Heights*, 2003).

Employees are eligible if they

1. work for a covered employer;
2. have worked for the organization for at least one year; and
3. have worked at least 1,250 hours over the previous 12 months.

Because the FMLA allows employees to take leave for the *serious illness* of a child, parent, spouse, or themselves, there has been some debate about how serious an illness has to be to qualify. The Department of Labor defines a serious health condition this way:

- Any period of incapacity of more than three consecutive calendar days *and* at least two visits to a health-care provider *or* one visit and issuance of prescription medicine (or)
- Any period of incapacity due to a chronic serious health condition requiring periodic treatment covering an extended period of time (or)
- Any period of absence to receive multiple treatments for a condition that would result in a three+-day period of incapacity if left untreated.

On the basis of this definition, the courts have ruled such conditions as an ear infection (*Juanita Caldwell v. Kentucky Fried Chicken*, 2000) or a cold/flu (*Miller v. AT&T*, 2001; *Rose Rankin v. Seagate Technologies*, 2001) could be serious.

If employees take advantage of family or medical leave, the organization must continue the employees' health care coverage and guarantee them that when they return, they will either have the same or an equivalent position. In return, employees must provide a doctor's certification and give 30 days' notice if the leave is foreseeable (e.g., birth or adoption). Employees on FMLA leave from one company cannot work at another job (moonlight) during that period (*Pharakhone v. Nissan North America, Inc., and Rodney Baggett*, 2003).

To protect employers from potential problems in complying with the FMLA, Congress allows them to exempt their key employees from using it. "Key employees" are the highest-paid 10% in the organization. Other than record-keeping headaches, however, the FMLA has not resulted in many hardships for most organizations.

3-5 Affirmative Action

Reasons for Affirmative Action Plans

Affirmative action The process of ensuring proportional representation of employees based on variables such as race and gender.

Organizations have **affirmative action** plans for one of four reasons, two of which are involuntary and the other two voluntary (Robinson, Allen, & Abraham, 1992).

Involuntary: Government Regulation

Most affirmative action requirements are the result of Presidential Executive Order 11246. This order, as well as sections of several laws, requires federal contractors and subcontractors with more than 50 employees to submit an annual EEO-1 Report and requires federal contractors and subcontractors with at least one federal contract more than $50,000 to have formal affirmative action plans. Most state and local governments also have such requirements, although the number of employees and dollar amounts of contracts will differ. These mandatory affirmative action plans typically involve analyses of all major job groups (e.g., managers, professionals) and indicate which job groups have under-representations of the protected classes, as well as goals and plans for overcoming such under-representations.

Involuntary: Court Order

When a court finds a public agency such as a police or fire department guilty of not hiring or promoting enough members of a protected class, it can order the agency to begin an affirmative action program. As previously discussed, this program may involve increased recruitment efforts or may entail specific hiring or promotion goals.

Voluntary: Consent Decree

If a discrimination complaint has been filed with a court, a public agency can "voluntarily" agree to an affirmative action plan rather than have a plan forced on it by the court. With a consent decree, the agency agrees that it has not hired or promoted enough members of a protected class and is willing to make changes. The specific nature of these changes is agreed upon by the group filing the complaint and the agency that is the subject of the complaint. This agreement is then approved and monitored by the court.

Voluntary: Desire to Be a Good Citizen

Rather than wait for a discrimination complaint, many organizations develop affirmative action and diversity programs out of a desire to be good citizens. That is, they want to voluntarily ensure that their employment practices are fair to all groups of people.

Affirmative Action Strategies

Although most people associate affirmative action with hiring goals or quotas, there are actually four main affirmative action strategies.

Monitoring, Hiring, and Promotion Statistics

One of the primary affirmative action strategies is for organizations to monitor their hiring, placement, and promotion rates for men and women and Whites and minorities. Though such monitoring is a good idea for all organizations, it is mandatory for federal contractors, for banks, and for educational institutions that receive federal funds. Such organizations must write affirmative action plans in which they monitor adverse impact as well as compare the percentages of women and minorities in the organization with the percentages of women and minorities in the qualified workforce.

Intentional Recruitment of Minority Applicants

A common affirmative action strategy is to target underrepresented groups for more extensive recruitment. Such efforts might include advertising in print publications and websites with a minority readership, recruiting at predominantly minority or female universities, visiting minority communities, or paying current employees a bonus for recruiting a member of a protected class.

A related technique is to establish training programs designed to train or teach minority applicants the skills needed to obtain employment with the organization. For example, Hogan and Quigley (1994) found that providing a six-week exercise program would result in fewer female applicants failing physical ability tests for positions such as firefighter.

Identification and Removal of Employment Practices Working Against Minority Applicants and Employees

A third affirmative action strategy, and the heart of most diversity initiatives, is to identify and remove practices that might discourage minority applicants from applying to an organization, being promoted within an organization, or remaining with an organization. Such practices might involve company policy, supervisor attitudes, training opportunities, succession planning, availability of mentors and role models, or the way in which an organization is decorated. For example, it is a common practice for police applicants to receive information and obtain employment applications from the police department itself. However, minority applicants may be uncomfortable with the idea of going to a police station and asking White police officers for information and application materials. As a result, an easy affirmative action strategy would be to have employment applications available only at the city's human resources office.

When I presented this example to a meeting of police chiefs, the overwhelming response was, "How can someone be a cop if they don't feel comfortable going to a police station?" I responded that it is uncomfortable for anyone to go into a new environment, much less one with the stigma associated with a police station. I then told the group a story of how scared I was when, back in high school, I had to go to a police station to register a car rally that our school group was having. I still recall the icy stare and gruff voice of the desk sergeant, which quickly turned my legs to jelly. When a few others in the crowd joined in with similar stories, it drove home the point that there are many things, seemingly trivial, that deter others from applying for jobs.

Preferential Hiring and Promotion of Minorities

This is certainly the most controversial and misunderstood of the affirmative action strategies. Under this strategy, minority applicants will be given preference over an equally qualified nonminority applicant. It is important to note that in no way does affirmative action require an employer to hire an unqualified minority over a qualified nonminority. Instead, affirmative action requires employers to monitor their employment records to determine whether minority groups are underrepresented. If they are, affirmative action requires that an organization do the best it can to remedy the situation. One such remedy might be preferential hiring and promotion.

Legality of Preferential Hiring and Promotion Plans

Recently, the courts have indicated that any form of preferential hiring or promotion must undergo a "strict scrutiny analysis," in which the plan must be narrowly tailored and meet a compelling government interest (Gutman, 2004). The various courts have ruled that achieving diversity in such settings as a university (*Grutter v. Bollinger*, 2003) and a police department (*Petit v. City of Chicago*, 2003) are compelling government interests.

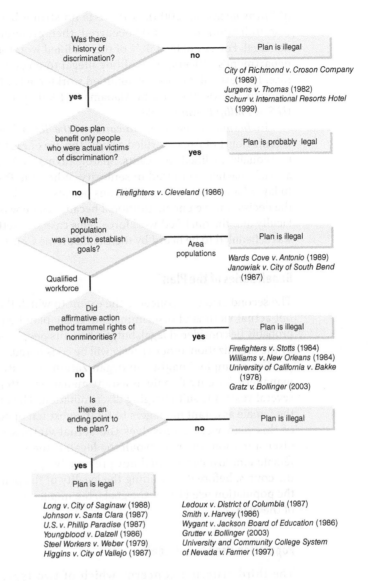

Figure 3.4
Determining the Legality of an Affirmative Action Plan

If the plan does not meet a compelling government interest, it is illegal. If it does meet a compelling government interest, as shown in Figure 3.4, the courts use five criteria to "strictly scrutinize" the extent to which an affirmative action plan involving preferential hiring is narrowly tailored. It is always legal to monitor employment statistics, actively recruit minorities, and remove barriers discouraging women and minorities from being hired or staying with an organization.

The five criteria used to assess an affirmative action plan are history of the organization, beneficiaries of the plan, population to be considered, impact on the nonminority group, and the end point of the plan.

A History of Discrimination

The first criterion examined is whether there has been a history of discrimination by a particular organization (*Western States Paving v. Washington State Department of Transportation*, 2005). If there is no strong basis in evidence to indicate that discrimination has recently occurred, then preferential hiring is neither necessary nor legal. For example, if 30% of the qualified workforce is Black, as is 30% of a police department's officers, it would be illegal to engage in preferential hiring based on race. However, if 25% of the qualified workforce is Black and there are no Black state troopers (as was the case in Alabama in 1980), preferential hiring could be justified (*U.S. v. Phillip Paradise*, 1987).

In *Taxman v. Board of Education of the Township of Piscataway* (1996), the Third Circuit Court of Appeals ruled against the use of race as a factor to break a tie between two equally qualified applicants. Sharon Taxman, a White teacher, and Debra Williams, a Black teacher, were tied in seniority. When the Piscataway School Board decided to lay off a teacher, it kept Williams because she was Black. The appeals court ruled the decision to be unconstitutional because there was no racial disparity between the faculty and the qualified workforce. This case was settled in 1997, a few days before it was scheduled to be heard by the U.S. Supreme Court.

Beneficiaries of the Plan

The second criterion concerns the extent to which the plan benefits people who were not actual victims of discrimination. If the plan benefits only actual victims, it will probably be considered legal, but if it benefits people not directly discriminated against by the organization, other criteria will be considered.

For example, imagine an organization consisting of 100 male, but no female, managers. Twenty female assistant managers, after being denied promotions for several years, file suit charging discrimination. The organization agrees to hire ten of the female assistant managers to fill the next ten openings. Because the beneficiaries of this plan were themselves the actual victims of the organization's previous discrimination, the plan would be legal. If the plan, however, involved promoting female employees who had not previously applied for the management positions, the courts, before determining the legality of the plan, would consider three factors: the population used to set the goals, the impact on nonminorities, and the end point of the plan.

Population Used to Set Goals

The third criterion concerns which of two types of populations was used to statistically determine discrimination and to set affirmative action goals. With area populations, an organization compares the number of minorities in the general area with the number of minorities in each position in the organization. If a discrepancy occurs, the organization sets hiring goals to remedy the discrepancy. For example, if 80% of the area surrounding an organization is Hispanic but only 20% of the salaried workers in the organization are Hispanic, the organization might set hiring goals for Hispanics at 90% until the workforce becomes 80% Hispanic.

Although the use of area population figures has been traditional, Supreme Court decisions have declared them inappropriate. Instead, the population that must be used in goal setting is that of the **qualified workforce** in the area rather than the area population as a whole.

For example, several southern states are under court supervision to increase the number of minority faculty in their public universities. Rather than a goal consistent

Qualified workforce The percentage of people in a given geographic area who have the qualifications (skills, education, etc.) to perform a certain job.

with the percentage of Black individuals in the United States (roughly 12%), the goal of 7% is based on the qualified workforce—Black individuals with doctoral degrees. This example is important because it illustrates that the courts are not unreasonable when it comes to setting affirmative action goals. They realize that a university cannot hire minorities in numbers equal to the national population because a lower percentage of minorities than nonminorities have doctorates.

Another example is the case of *City of Richmond v. Croson* (1989). Because 50% of the Richmond population is from a minority group, the city required that contractors receiving city funds subcontract at least 30% of their work to minority-owned businesses. The J. A. Croson Company received a contract with the city but was unable to subcontract the required 30% because there were not enough minority-owned businesses in the city. The U.S. Supreme Court found Richmond's plan illegal because the goal of 30% was based on the area population rather than the percentage of relevant qualified minority-owned businesses (less than 5%). The U.S. Supreme Court ruled similarly in *Adarand v. Pena* (1995).

Impact on Nonminorities

The fourth criterion used by courts to determine the legality of an affirmative action program is whether the remedy designed to help minorities is narrowly tailored: Does the plan "unnecessarily trammel" the rights of nonminorities? That is, a plan that helps women cannot deny the rights of men. Preference can be given to a qualified minority over a qualified nonminority, but an unqualified minority can never be hired over a qualified nonminority.

Affirmative action becomes controversial when an organization realizes it has discriminated against a particular protected group. For example, police and fire departments have long been staffed by White men. In some cases, this composition has been accidental; in others it has been intentional. To remedy such situations, police and fire departments often set goals for minority hiring. These goals are objectives and are not to be confused with quotas, which *require* a certain percentage of minorities to be hired. This is an important distinction, as the 1991 Civil Rights Act forbids the use of quotas.

Should only a small number of minority applicants test highly enough to be considered qualified, the organization is under no obligation to hire unqualified applicants. In fact, if an organization hires unqualified minorities over qualified nonminorities, hires a lesser-qualified minority over a more qualified nonminority, or sets unreasonable goals, it can be found guilty of reverse discrimination. For example, in *Bishop v. District of Columbia* (1986), the U.S. Court of Appeals ruled that reverse discrimination occurred when a Black battalion chief was promoted ahead of five higher-ranking White deputy chiefs. The court ruled the promotion to be illegal because it was the result of political pressure rather than qualifications and previous job performance. A similar decision was reached in *Black Firefighters Association v. City of Dallas* (1994), when the U.S. Court of Appeals ruled that "skip promotions" were not legal.

In *Higgins v. City of Vallejo* (1987), however, the U.S. Court of Appeals ruled that promotion of a minority applicant with the third-highest score over a nonminority applicant with the highest score was legal. The court's decision was based on the idea that even though the two applicants had different scores, they were close enough to be considered "equally qualified." When two candidates are equally qualified, affirmative action needs can be taken into consideration to decide which of the candidates will be chosen. As one can imagine, the question of how close different qualifications need to be before two candidates are no longer considered equal is difficult to answer. In Chapter 6, methods to answer this question, such as banding and passing scores, will be discussed.

U.S. Supreme Court cases involving affirmative action confirm what you have learned in the previous discussion; both cases involved preferential treatment of minorities in the admission practices at the University of Michigan: *Grutter v. Bollinger* (2003) involved law school admissions, and *Gratz v. Bollinger* (2003) involved undergraduate admissions. In both cases, the Supreme Court ruled that increasing diversity was a compelling government interest. In the *Grutter* case, the Court ruled that using race as one of many factors in admissions decisions was narrowly tailored and did not trammel the rights of nonminorities. In the *Gratz* case, however, the Court ruled that automatically giving points to an applicant because of their race was not narrowly tailored and thus was illegal. Taken together, the two cases reinforce previous case law (*Regents of University of California v. Bakke*, 1978) that the legality of preferential hiring will be determined on a case-by-case basis and that the plan must be narrowly tailored and not trammel the rights of nonminorities. Interestingly, a Gallup poll in 2013 reported that 67% of respondents opposed an affirmative action plan for admission practices into higher education institutions, even if it trammeled the rights of nonminorities. However, the same poll also found that Americans might not actually grasp the concept of affirmative action plans, because 58% of respondents also said that they favored affirmative action plans for underrepresented groups.

End Point of the Plan

The fifth and final criterion concerns setting an end point for the plan. That is, an affirmative action plan cannot continue indefinitely; it must end when certain goals have been obtained. For example, in *Detroit Police Officers Association v. Coleman Young* (1993), the U.S. Court of Appeals ruled that an affirmative action plan that had been utilized for 19 years had resulted in its intended goal: 50% of the Detroit police department was minority. Continuing the plan would be illegal, reasoned the Court, because it would now result in a substantial hardship on nonminority-group applicants. The court also reasoned that should the percentage of minorities in the department drop in the future, the preferential hiring plan could be reinstated.

Unintended Consequences of Affirmative Action Plans

Though affirmative action and diversity programs are an important tool in ensuring equal opportunity, they can result in some unintended negative consequences for people hired or promoted as the result of affirmative action (Caleo & Heilman, 2019). Research indicates that employees hired due to affirmative action programs are perceived by coworkers as less competent (Heilman, Block, & Lucas, 1992; Heilman, Block, & Stathatos, 1997), tend to devalue their own performance (Gillespie & Ryan, 2012; Heilman & Alcott, 2001; Leslie, Mayer, & Kravitz 2014), and behave negatively toward others who are hired based on affirmative action programs (Heilman, Kaplow, Amato, & Stathatos, 1993). These effects can be reduced when applicants are given positive information about their abilities (Heilman et al., 1993; Kravitz et al., 1997) and when the term "diversity initiative" rather than "affirmative action" is used (Awad, 2013). Not surprisingly, women and ethnic minorities hold more positive views toward affirmative action than do men and nonminorities (Harrison, Kravitz, Mayer, Leslie, & Lev-Arey, 2006). With these studies in mind, it is essential that an organization be sensitive about how it promotes and implements its diversity and affirmative action efforts. It is also important to consider affirmative action plans in multinational corporations. With increased remote work opportunities and organizations shifting towards integrating international talent into the workplace, research has begun to investigate the perceptions of such plans through different cultural perspectives. For example, in researching the difference in perception of affirmative action plans between American and Indian cultures, Combs and Nadkarni (2005) found that Indian employees tended to view beneficiaries of an affirmative action plan less favorably than American employees. This study, amongst others, highlight the importance of considering different cultural perspectives when implementing affirmative action plans in the workplace as well.

3-6 Privacy Issues

As discussed previously in the chapter, an employment practice is illegal if it results in adverse impact and is not job related. An employment practice can also be illegal if it unnecessarily violates an individual's right to privacy.

Fourth Amendment The amendment to the U.S. Constitution that protects against unreasonable search or seizure; the amendment has been ruled to cover such privacy issues as drug testing, locker and office searches, psychological testing, and electronic surveillance.

The **Fourth Amendment** to the U.S. Constitution protects citizens against unreasonable search or seizure by the government. Its importance to I/O psychology is in drug testing and locker searches. Several courts have ruled that drug testing is considered a "search" and that therefore, to be legal in the public sector, drug testing programs must be reasonable and with cause. It is important to understand that the Fourth Amendment is limited to public agencies such as state and local governments. Private industry is not restricted from drug testing by the Fourth Amendment but government regulation may require drug testing (e.g., for trucking companies and railroads), but drug testing and searches by a private organization must be conducted in "good faith and with fair dealing."

Drug-Free Workplace Act Requires federal contractors to maintain a drug-free workplace.

Generally, employers are free (even encouraged by the government) to test job applicants for current drug use. In fact, the federal **Drug-Free Workplace Act** requires employers with federal contracts of $100,000 or more to maintain a drug-free workplace. Furthermore, such states as Alabama, Arkansas, Florida, and Georgia provide discounts on workers' compensation rates to employers with a drug-free workplace program (Steingold, 2019).

Drug Testing

Many state laws allow employers to test *job applicants* for drug use, especially if the testing is done after a conditional offer of hire. Even in states that have decriminalized marijuana, employers have the right to have a drug free workplace (Steingold, 2019). Drug testing of *current employees* by a *public agency* is more complicated and must be based on "reasonable suspicion" and with "just cause." Based on prior cases, reasonable suspicion means that there is reason to suspect that employees are using drugs at work (Goldstein, 2000). Such suspicion can be produced from a variety of sources, including "tips" that employees are using drugs (*Copeland v. Philadelphia Police Department*, 1989; *Feliciano v. Cleveland*, 1987; *Garrison v. Justice*, 1995), accidents or discipline problems (*Allen v. City of Marietta*, 1985; *Burnley v. Railway*, 1988), actual observation of drug usage (*Everett v. Napper*, 1987), or physical symptoms of being under the influence (*Connelly v. Newman*, 1990).

The legality of random drug testing in the public sector is a murky area. When considering it, the courts consider the extent to which the special needs of the employer outweigh the employees' right to privacy. For example, in *Local 6000 v. Janine Winters* (2004), the Sixth Circuit Court of Appeals ruled that random drug testing of probation and parole officers was justified, the Tenth Circuit Court of Appeals supported random testing of corrections officers in a juvenile detention center (Washington v. Unified Government of Wyandotte County, 2017), and in *National Treasury Employers Union v. Von Rabb* (1989), the U.S. Supreme Court ruled that random testing of customs officials involved in drug interdiction efforts was legal.

Traditionally, the courts consider the degree to which an employee's behavior affects the safety and trust of the public as a factor in deciding whether the needs of the employer outweigh the employee's right to privacy. For example, air traffic controllers (*Government Employees v. Dole*, 1987) and teachers (*Knox County Education Association v. Knox County Board of Education*, 1998) have been deemed to be responsible for the safety of the public, but school bus attendants have not (*Jones v. McKenzie*, 1987).

Other factors taken into consideration by the courts include the accuracy of the drug tests and the care and privacy taken during the testing (*Hester v. City of Milledgeville*, 1986; *Triblo v. Quality Clinical Laboratories*, 1982). The issue of privacy is an especially interesting one because employees who use drugs often try to "cheat" on their drug tests (Cadrain, 2003a). Attempts at cheating include bringing in "clean" urine that has been taken or purchased from a friend, or diluting the urine sample with soap, toilet water, or other chemicals. Strangely enough, to help applicants cheat on their drug tests, one company markets a product called the "Original Whizzinator," a prosthetic penis containing a four-ounce bag of dehydrated drug-free urine and an organic heating pad to keep the urine at body temperature (Cadrain, 2003a).

To stop such attempts, some organizations have required those to be tested to strip so that they cannot bring anything into the test area; they also may require that the employee be observed while they provide the urine specimen. Testing conditions such as these would be allowed only under the most serious situations involving national security.

Two other important issues are the appeal process (*Harvey v. Chicago Transit Authority*, 1984) and the confidentiality of test results (*Ivy v. Damon Clinical Laboratory*, 1984). Employees must be given the opportunity to have their specimens retested and to explain why their tests were positive even though they may not have taken illegal drugs.

Thus, for a drug testing program to be legal, the organization must have reason to suspect drug usage, the job must involve the safety or trust of the public, the testing process must be accurate and reasonably private, the results should be handled in a confidential manner, and employees who test positive must be given opportunities to appeal and undergo rehabilitation. A detailed discussion of the use and validity of drug testing for employee selection can be found in Chapter 5.

Office and Locker Searches

Office and locker searches are allowed under the law if they are reasonable and with cause (*O'Conner v. Ortega*, 1987). Allowing employees to place their own locks on lockers, however, removes the right of the organization to search the locker.

Psychological Tests

An employment test may be illegal if its questions unnecessarily invade the privacy of an applicant. At most risk are psychological tests originally developed to measure psychopathology. These tests often include questions about such topics as religion and sexual preference that some applicants feel uncomfortable answering. In *Soroka v. Dayton Hudson* (1991), three applicants for store security guard positions with Target Stores filed a class action suit after taking a 704-item psychological test (Psychscreen). The applicants believed some of the questions, a few of which are shown in Table 3.4, violated their right to privacy guaranteed by the California constitution.

Table 3.4 Do These True-False Questions Violate an Applicant's Right to Privacy?

I go to church almost every week.

I am very religious.

I believe there is a God.

My sex life is satisfactory.

I like to talk about sex.

I have never indulged in any unusual sex practices.

Though the two sides reached a settlement prior to the case being decided by the U.S. Supreme Court, the case focused attention on the questions used in psychological testing. Of particular concern to I/O psychologists was that the tests were scored by a consulting firm, and Target Stores never saw the individual answers to the questions. It instead received only overall scores indicating the applicant's level of emotional stability, interpersonal style, addiction potential, dependability, and socialization. The finding by courts that use of the test was an invasion of privacy was troubling to psychologists, who routinely make decisions based on overall test scores rather than the answers to any one particular question (Brown, 1993).

Electronic Surveillance

Almost 90% of organizations in the United States use electronic surveillance or monitor their employees' behavior, email, Internet usage, or telephone conversations. The idea behind this electronic monitoring is that unproductive behavior can be tracked and potential legal problems (e.g., inappropriate email, insider trading) or theft of trade secrets can be prevented.

A 2018 survey by Alfresco found that

- 87% of employers monitor their employees' emails;
- 70% monitor their employees' web browser history; and
- 34% look at their employees' social media accounts.

If employers are going to monitor their employees' internet use, Steingold (2019) advises that they:

- Create a policy stating that company computers are for business use only;
- Communicate that policy to employees and let the employees that software has been installed to monitor their web browsing;
- Inform employees that violation of the policy will result in disciplinary action; and
- Get the employees to sign a statement saying that they have read and understand the policy and agree to it.

The First Circuit Court of Appeals has ruled that video surveillance is not an invasion of privacy because employees do not have an expectation of privacy while working in open areas (*Vega-Rodriguez v. Puerto Rico Telephone*, 1997). However, in 2009, the California Supreme Court ruled that placing a hidden video camera in the office - whether its purpose is to record the employee or not - constitutes an invasion of privacy (*Hernandez v. Hillsides, Inc.*, 2009). This ruling is consistent with the recommendations from Steingold (2019) in which employers are advised to communicate to employees if there is software with surveillance capabilities installed in the office. Furthermore, several district courts have ruled that organizations can monitor their employees' email or search their computer files (*Gary Leventhal v. Lawrence Knapek*, 2001), especially when the employees have been told that monitoring is part of organizational policy (Leonard & France, 2003; Raynes, 1997).

Chapter Summary

In this chapter you learned:

- Discrimination complaints are filed with the EEOC.
- A variety of federal laws forbid discrimination based on sex, race (Black, White, Asian, Native American or Alaskan Native, Native Hawaiian or Other Pacific Islander), national origin, color, religion, disability, age (over 40), pregnancy, and qualified veteran status.
- The legality of an employment practice is determined by such factors as the presence of adverse impact and the job relatedness of the employment practice.
- Adverse impact is usually determined by the four-fifths rule.
- Organizations can be held liable for the sexual harassment of their employees. This harassment can take the form of quid pro quo or a hostile environment.
- Affirmative action consists of a variety of strategies, such as intentional recruitment of minority applicants, identification and removal of employment practices working against minority applicants and employees, and preferential hiring and promotion.
- Employers need to be cautious about violating employee privacy rights regarding drug testing, office and locker searches, psychological testing, and electronic surveillance.

Key Terms

Equal Employment Opportunity Commission (EEOC) (77)
Grievance system (78)
Mediation (78)
Arbitration (78)
Binding arbitration (78)
Nonbinding arbitration (79)
Case law (82)
Protected class (83)
Fifth Amendment (85)
Fourteenth Amendments (85)
Race (85)
Age Discrimination in Employment Act (ADEA) (88)
Vocational Rehabilitation Act of 1973 (89)
Americans with Disabilities Act (ADA) (89)

Pregnancy Discrimination Act (91)
Family and Medical Leave Act (FMLA) (91)
Vietnam-Era Veterans Readjustment Assistance Act (VEVRAA) (91)
Jobs for Veterans Act (92)
Bona fide occupational qualification (BFOQ) (92)
Adverse impact (94)
Four-fifths rule (94)
Job related (96)
Quid pro quo (99)
Hostile environment (99)
Affirmative action (102)
Qualified workforce (106)
Fourth Amendment (109)
Drug-Free Workplace Act (109)

Questions for Review

1. What would make an employment practice a BFOQ?
2. Is affirmative action still needed? Why or why not?
3. Why do public employees have more privacy rights than private employees?
4. If an employee asks out a coworker, is this sexual harassment? Would your answer be different if the employee were a supervisor rather than a coworker? Why or why not?
5. Would a color-blind person be considered disabled under the ADA? Why or why not?

Appendix Canadian Employment Law by Province

Protected Class	Province											
	Alb	**BC**	**Man**	**Ont**	**NB**	**NF**	**NS**	**NWT**	**PEI**	**Queb**	**SAS**	**Yukon**
Race	yes	yes	yes	yes	yes	yes	yes	yes	yes	yes	yes	yes
Sex	yes	yes	yes	yes	yes	yes	yes	yes	yes	yes	yes	yes
Disability	yes	yes	yes	yes	yes	yes	yes	yes	yes	yes	yes	yes
Color	yes	yes	yes	yes	yes	yes	yes	yes	yes	yes	yes	yes
Religion	yes	yes	yes	yes	yes	yes	yes	yes	yes	yes	yes	yes
Marital status	yes	yes	yes	yes	yes	yes	yes	yes	yes	yes	yes	yes
Pregnancy	yes	yes	yes	yes	yes	yes	yes	yes	yes	yes	yes	yes
National origin	no	no	yes	yes	yes	yes	yes	yes	yes	yes	yes	yes
Age	18+	19–65	all	18–65	all	19–65	all	all	all	all	18–64	all
Sexual orientation	yes	yes	yes	yes	yes	yes	yes	yes	yes	yes	yes	yes
Drug/alcohol dependence	yes	yes	yes	yes	yes	yes	yes	no	yes	yes	yes	no
Ancestry/place of origin	yes	yes	yes	yes	yes	no	no	yes	no	no	yes	yes
Political beliefs	no	yes	yes	no	yes	yes	yes	yes	yes	yes	no	yes
Familial status	yes	yes	yes	yes	yes	yes	yes	yes	yes	yes	yes	yes
Association	No	no	yes	yes	yes	no	yes	no	yes	no	no	yes
Criminal conviction	No	yes	no	yes	no	no	no	no	no	yes	no	yes
Language	No	no	no	yes	no	no	no	no	no	yes	no	yes
Social condition	No	no	yes	no	yes	yes	no	yes	no	yes	no	no
Source of income	yes	no	yes	no	no	yes	no	yes	yes	no	no	yes
Citizenship	No	no	no	yes	no	yes	no	no	no	no	no	no
Receipt of public assistance	No	no	no	no	no	no	no	no	no	no	yes	no

Keystone RV Company, Goshen, Indiana

For safety reasons, Keystone RV in Goshen, Indiana, had a zero-tolerance policy regarding drug misuse at its manufacturing plant. In 2005, the company received complaints from police that its employees were using drugs during breaks. To deal with the problem, Keystone closed the plant for a day to test its 125 employees and then fired the 28 who tested positive for drugs and the 6 who refused to be tested. Keystone transferred 20 employees from another facility to handle the new shortage of employees while it quickly filled the open positions from nearly 2,000 applicants who heard the news about the firings and wanted to work there.

- Based on what you learned in this chapter, do you think Keystone handled the situation properly? Why or why not?

- What legal considerations would come into play when randomly testing and then firing employees in a private company?

- What could Keystone have done to prevent its employees from using drugs at work in the first place?

You read in this chapter that drug testing, office and locker searches, psychological testing, and electronic surveillance are legal, with few restrictions. Genetic screening checks for genetic abnormalities in healthy people at risk for developing certain diseases in the future. This type of screening can be used to screen job applicants and employees who may be likely to develop disease if exposed to certain worksite substances such as chemicals or radiation. And even though President George W. Bush signed the Genetic Information Nondiscrimination Act on May 21, 2008, that prohibits employers from firing, refusing to hire or otherwise discriminating against workers based on genetic information, there is still fear that it will be used for just that reason.

Genetic screening, according to its supporters, can keep both employee and employer safe. Research has identified about 50 genetic disorders that could increase a person's susceptibility to toxins or chemicals. For example, people with sickle cell trait could be at risk for sickle cell anemia if exposed to carbon monoxide or cyanide. Genetic screening could reduce certain people's chances of getting such diseases, which would spare them from spending thousands of dollars in medical bills and from premature death. Employers would benefit from the savings incurred from less workers' compensation payments, health-care premiums, low productivity, and high absenteeism and turnover. And job applicants don't have to agree to the screening. According to defenders of this practice, those applicants have the right to seek employment elsewhere.

Another practice related to privacy is electronic surveillance. Electronic surveillance such as email, Internet, and telephone monitoring, and use of video cameras is a proactive step toward catching potentially harmful or illegal behaviors by employees. For example, by monitoring internal emails, management can learn about inappropriate emails of a sexual or discriminatory nature directed toward a specific employee or employees and can take immediate action to stop this behavior. And this type of monitoring can help employers more fairly evaluate employee performance, because managers are able to track both good and bad behaviors throughout the day by monitoring emails, Internet usage, and telephone conversations. For example, there is software that can be used to view an employee's screen while they are working, count keystrokes of data entry personnel to track speed and reliability, and track the amount of time an employee's computer remains idle. This type of software is beneficial to both employees and employers. Proponents for such practices in the workplace say that these types of practices can protect and help employees, consumers and/or companies.

Many opponents of such practices in the workplace say that there are many issues involved with these practices, one of which is employee privacy. Critics state that there are certain aspects of an employee's personal life, both at work and at home, that should not be available to employers, such as personal phone conversations or personal emails. Although making personal phone conversations or personal emails may cut into company time, it is unrealistic to think that there are never times when it is necessary for an employee to do such personal things during work hours.

Although some amount of employee monitoring, if used properly, may be useful to evaluate employees' performance, critics say there should be a limit to how much monitoring can be done. Information that is gathered can be stored and used against the employee many years later, which could impact an employees' potential promotion within the company or their references when applying to other companies. And it is not necessary that managers watch everything employees do to be able to fairly evaluate their performance. Some limits should be imposed, by law, including some mechanism that can warn employees when they are being monitored so that they will not be engaging in activities of a private matter.

As for genetic testing, this will remain an ongoing debate. Opponents state that such screening violates the Fourteenth Amendment to the Constitution, which provides equal protection to all people (not just healthy ones) and states that all people should be treated fairly. They state that a person's health is a private matter and should not be under scrutiny of potential or actual employers. If companies find out that applicants or employees are at risk for certain diseases, these applicants and employees will be treated differently from those who are not at risk. Not only is that breaking the law, according to critics, it is unfair, and therefore, unethical treatment of a certain class of people. Other objections to genetic testing include the fact that the validity and reliability of such tests have not been established, and the fear that the information gained from the genetic tests could fall into the hands of health-care providers, who can then reject some people who may never actually end up with a disease from adequate health care coverage.

What Do You Think?

- Do you think the legal reasons for these workplace practices outweigh the ethical responsibilities of organizations?

- Are companies being unfair, and therefore, unethical by engaging in such activities?

- What are the ethical responsibilities to employees from companies who chose to use such practices?

- What are some other ethical dilemmas that you think could arise from such practices?

- Conduct an online search on the Genetic Information Nondiscrimination Act signed by President Bush. Do you think that act is fair to employers and employees? Why or why not?

Employee Selection: Recruiting and Interviewing

Learning Objectives

4-1 Know how to recruit applicants.

4-2 Explain why the traditional, unstructured interview doesn't work.

4-3 Construct a valid, structured interview.

4-4 Perform well when being interviewed.

4-5 Write a résumé and a cover letter.

In the television version of the motion picture *The Enforcer*, the actor Clint Eastwood, who was portraying the detective Harry Callahan, upon learning that he has been transferred from homicide to personnel, replies, "Personnel—only idiots work in personnel!" Although this statement is a bit strong, it represents the attitude many people held about the field of human resources. That is, if you can't do anything else, you can always work in human resources.

The image of the human resources (HR) field has been greatly enhanced in recent years, however, for the most part by its application of modern, scientific principles in employee selection and by the realization that properly designed employee selection procedures can save organizations a lot of money.

Chapters 4, 5, and 6 will focus on issues associated with recruiting, screening, selecting, and hiring employees. In this chapter, we will first explore ways to recruit employees and explain job-hunting methods, and then discuss interviewing techniques as well as offer some tips that you can use to help find and obtain a desired job. Chapter 5 will discuss non-interview selection techniques used by I/O psychologists and Chapter 6 will conclude with a discussion of how to evaluate the various selection techniques.

As shown in Figure 4.1, certain steps can be taken to successfully choose employees. Some of the steps are designed to attract excellent applicants to the organization, others are designed to select the best applicants, and still others are designed to give applicants a good image not only of the organization but of the job search process in general. Keep in mind that for most job openings, many more people will apply than will be hired. If you multiply the number of people who are not hired by the number of job openings each year, a lot of people will be in contact with a particular organization. Those people not hired are potential customers, with friends who are also potential customers. Furthermore, applicants not hired for one position may turn out to be well qualified for future positions with the organization. Leaving them with a positive image of the company should be a priority.

4-1 Employee Recruitment

Recruitment The process of attracting employees to an organization.

An important step in selecting employees is **recruitment**: attracting people with the right qualifications (as determined in the job analysis) to apply for the job. As you will see in the first section of this chapter, recruitment methods have changed tremendously over the past 30 years. Thirty years ago, most employees were recruited through advertisements run in newspapers and trade publications. Today, the Internet serves as a primary source for both employers advertising jobs as well as applicants searching for jobs. As you read about the various recruitment methods, keep in mind that, although some methods are used more than others, the degree of use depends on such factors as the nature of the job and the size of the organization. That is, the small downtown business will likely recruit employees differently than will such large organizations as Microsoft, Amazon, and Tyson Foods.

External recruitment Recruiting employees from outside the organization.

Internal recruitment Recruiting employees already employed by the organization.

Although most of our discussion will focus on recruiting new employees to the organization (**external recruitment**), it is important to understand that many jobs are filled by transferring or promoting someone from within the organization (**internal recruitment**). Many organizations first advertise employment openings for two weeks to current employees. If no qualified applicants are found, the organizations then advertise outside. Federal contractors are an exception to this option as they must post all job openings with state employment agencies to meet their affirmative action requirements for qualified veterans.

Internal promotions can be either competitive or noncompetitive. Noncompetitive promotions usually involve "career progression" positions in which employees move from a position such as Engineer I to Engineer II to Engineer III and so on as they gain experience and knowledge and can perform more complex work. The number of promotions in a given year is not limited and employees do not compete with other employees. At universities, a good example of a career progression for faculty would be the promotion from Assistant Professor to Associate Professor and finally to Professor. Career progression promotions usually result in a change of title as well as an increase in salary. A study conducted by LinkedIn in 2020 found that the global pandemic COVID-19 led to a year-over-year increase of internal recruitment by nearly 20%.

With competitive promotions, several internal applicants compete with one another (and sometimes with external applicants) for a limited number of higher positions. For example, 20 Amazon employees might compete for an assistant warehouse manager position. Internal promotions can be a great source of motivation, but if an organization always promotes employees from within, it runs the risk of having a stale workforce that is devoid of the many ideas that new employees bring with them from their previous employment settings. Heavy reliance on internal sources is thought to perpetuate the racial, gender, and age composition of the workforce. Thus, a balance between promoting current employees and hiring outside applicants is needed.

Media Advertisements
Newspaper Ads

Running ads in periodicals such as local newspapers or professional journals is a declining method of recruiting employees. In fact, in a study of 108,000 external hires in large organizations, Crispin and Mehler (2013) found that, in 2012, only 2.3% of external hires were recruited through print media, compared to 28.7% from a similar survey in 1997. Such a decline is consistent with a 2007 survey in which recruiters rated print advertising as one of the least effective recruitment methods (SHRM, 2007). These findings demonstrate the huge change in recruiting that has occurred in the past decade: In 2002, recruiters rated newspaper advertising as one of the most effective avenues of applicant recruitment (Gere, Scarborough, & Collison, 2002)!

Writing Recruitment Ads. Although little research is available, there is plenty of expert advice on the best way for an employer to write recruitment advertisements. Research on recruitment ads indicates the following findings:

- Ads containing realistic information about the job, rather than information that is "too good to be true," increase applicant attraction to the organization (Thorsteinson, Palmer, Wulff, & Anderson, 2004).
- Ads containing detailed descriptions of the job and organization provide applicants with an idea of how well they would fit into an organization and result in positive thoughts about it (Roberson, Collins, & Oreg, 2005). Additionally, an applicant's perceived fit of a job emerged as a strong predictor of applicant attraction throughout the recruitment stages, highlighting the importance of accurately describing the job responsibilities and organizational culture (Uggerslev, Fassina, & Kraichy, 2012).
- Ads containing information about the selection process affect the probability that applicants will apply for a job. For example, ads stating that an in-person interview will be used to select employees result in applicants being more likely to apply for a job than ads indicating that grade point average (GPA) will be a factor (Reeve & Schultz, 2004).

Figure 4.1
Steps in Selecting Employees

Job analysis

↓

Selection of testing methods

↓

Test validation

↓

Recruitment

↓

Screening

↓

Testing

↓

Selecting

↓

Hiring/ rejecting

A trend in help-wanted advertising has been the use of creative, high-energy ads (Levit, 2008). By using innovative advertising, On-Line Software tripled the number of applicants who responded to its help-wanted ad for secretarial positions. Hyundai's innovative ad cost only $5,000 and had almost 2,000 responses to advertised positions. Some organizations have tried to recruit employees by making fun of the job openings. Here are some examples:

- FH Company, a Norwegian importer and distributor, ran a help-wanted advertisement reading, "Tiresome and boring wholesale company seeks indolent people with a total lack of service mindedness for a job that is completely without challenge."
- A national sales company advertised that they were "interested in hiring five semi-obnoxious pushy sales pros for a very boring repetitive job of selling. Our current sales staff is the laziest group of individuals that you'll ever see drag themselves to work 5 days a week to decide whether to complain about the weather, coffee, thermostat or the manager."

Thus, the same techniques and imagination used in product advertisements may increase the recruitment yield from help-wanted ads.

Electronic Media

Although not common, some organizations find that using electronic media such as TV and radio ads is an effective recruitment tool. For example, CarMax ran a national television campaign to publicize its career opportunities. In addition to generating applicants, the commercials are an excellent public relations vehicle. In the public sector, the military has been very active in television recruitment: For example, the Marine Corps currently runs commercials featuring the "Battle to Belong" slogan and the Army has commercials featuring its slogan, "What's Your Warrior." Who can forget the classic "The Few. The Proud. The Marines," "Be all that you can be," and "An army of one" commercials?

The potential advantage to using electronic media for recruitment is that the average person spends considerable time each day watching TV, listening to the radio, and viewing social media. Furthermore, different types of radio stations (e.g., rock, rap, classical, country, oldies, news) reach different types of audiences, and thus radio ads can be easily targeted to the desired audience. For example, Harris Trucking often advertises its openings for drivers on radio stations playing country music. The radio ads are used not only to recruit new drivers but to thank current drivers for doing such a good job. Some organizations have even shown help-wanted videos during movie previews at theaters.

Point-of-Purchase Methods

Point-of-purchase method A recruitment method in which help-wanted signs are placed so that they can be viewed by people who visit the organization.

The **point-of-purchase method** of recruitment is based on the same "POP" (point-of-purchase) advertising principles used to market products to consumers. For example, consider shopping at a local grocery store. As you push your cart through one aisle, you come across a special display for potato chips, in the next aisle a display for cookies. When you get to the checkout stand, items such as the *National Enquirer*, candy, and batteries are conveniently placed so you can examine them while you wait in line. The idea is to get you to buy more items once you are already in the store.

In employee recruitment, job vacancy notices are posted in places where customers or current employees are likely to encounter them: store windows, bulletin boards, restaurant placemats, and the sides of trucks. The advantages to this method are that

Career Workshop   How to Be Successful at a Job Fair

Prior to the Job Fair

- Make sure your résumé is current and print several copies to give to employers. If there are going to be a variety of jobs, create several types of résumés that focus on each category of job. Bring these copies in a professional-looking folder. Consider printing business cards to bring as well.
- Try to get a list of the organizations that will be attending the job fair so that you can research them prior to the job fair. What does the organization do? What types of jobs do they have? You will probably not have the time to speak with every employer so strategically select which ones on which you want to concentrate.
- Develop a 30-second introduction of yourself that you can use when you approach an employer.
- Dress professionally yet comfortably.

During the Job Fair

- Approach the employer and smile, make eye contact, and shake their hand.

- Introduce yourself and use your 30-second introduction to describe who you are inform the employer about the types of jobs you are looking for.
- Using the research you conducted prior to the job fair, ask questions about the employer. Be sure to ask the employer how you can apply for a job.
- Provide the employer with a copy of your résumé.
- Thank the employer and ask for a business card. You might want to take notes after the meeting with the employer, such as any relevant information about questions that you asked.

After the Job Fair

- Email the employer, telling them it was nice meeting them and that you are interested in their organization. This is where the notes that you have taken on the employer's business card will come in handy. Be sure to reference any relevant information that you discussed with the employer in your email.
- Apply for the jobs in which you are interested.

it is inexpensive and that it is targeted toward people who frequent the business and enjoy the organization's products. The disadvantage is that only a limited number of people are exposed to the sign.

Cabela's, a retail chain specializing in hunting and fishing goods, is an excellent example of an organization that recruits current customers for job openings. Because Cabela's needs employees with extensive knowledge of hunting and fishing, they find it much easier to hire customers who already have interest and knowledge than to train new employees from scratch. In addition to targeting current customers, Cabela's also lures in hunting and fishing clubs whose members are not only potential employees, but potential customers as well. A perk that also helps recruit avid hunters and fishermen is product discounts and a policy that allows sales staff to take a product home for 60 days so that they can provide customers with accurate opinions about the product (Taylor, 2007).

Keurig is another company that tries to hire its "super fans." Not only do these customers become great employees who can answer customer questions, they provide ideas for new products and services.

Because of the difficulty in obtaining employees, many fast-food restaurants are using unusual point-of-purchase techniques. Wendy's has printed announcements of job openings on its cash-register receipts ("Now hiring smiling faces"), as do Target and Home Depot; Domino's Pizza placed help-wanted ads on its pizza boxes; and Kentucky Fried Chicken placed flyers in food bags asking the customer to "join our KFC family." Because Store 24 had difficulty recruiting manager trainees, it took the unique approach of placing a help-wanted advertisement on one side of its milk cartons. The cost of the recruitment campaign was minimal, as the company already bore the expense of creating and printing the milk cartons. Other examples of innovative recruitment methods include Lauriat's Books placing a job posting and mini-résumé on a bookmark; the clothing store Rugged Wearhouse putting help-wanted signs in its dressing rooms; retail chain IKEA Australia placed job ads featuring career opportunities in the instruction packets that go home with the customer; and both SmithKline and Prudential Insurance posting help-wanted ads on billboards in the Philadelphia area.

Recruiters
Campus Recruiters

Many organizations send recruiters to college campuses to answer questions about themselves and interview students for available positions. Not surprisingly, the behavior and attitude of recruiters can greatly influence applicants' decisions to accept jobs that are offered (Breaugh, 2008; Chapman, Uggerslev, Carroll, Piasentin, & Jones, 2005).

Due to cost considerations, many employers have cut back on the use of on-campus recruiting. As a result, an increasing number of colleges are organizing **virtual job fairs**, in which their students and alumni can use the web to communicate with recruiters from hundreds of organizations at one time. In a virtual job fair, applicants can talk to or text a recruiter, learn more about the company, and submit résumés. 70% of talent professionals assert that virtual recruiting will take over as the new standard for hiring, in a study conducted by LinkedIn in 2020.

Outside Recruiters

More than 38% of organizations use such outside recruiting sources as private employment agencies, public employment agencies, and **executive search firms** (SilkRoad, 2017). Private employment agencies and executive search firms are designed to make a profit from recruitment activities, whereas public employment agencies are operated by state and local public agencies and are strictly nonprofit.

Employment Agencies and Search Firms
Employment Agencies

Employment agencies operate in one of two ways. They charge either the company or the applicant when the applicant takes the job. The amount charged usually ranges from 10% to 30% of the applicant's first-year salary.

From an organization's perspective, there are few risks in using an employment agency that charges the applicant for its services. That is, if the employment agency cannot find an appropriate candidate, the organization has not wasted money. But if the employment agency is successful, the organization gets a qualified employee at no cost.

Employment agencies are especially useful if an HR department is overloaded with work or if an organization does not have an individual with the skills and experience needed to select employees properly. The disadvantage of employment agencies is that a company loses some control over its recruitment process and may end up with undesirable applicants. Remember, most "counselors" at employment agencies are hired because of their skill in sales, not because of their solid background in personnel selection. In fact, one employment agency turned down one of its own job applicants because the applicant had earned a degree in personnel management. During the interview, the head of the agency told the applicant, "We are not really looking for a personnel professional. What we want is the type of person who could sell aluminum siding to the owner of a brick home."

Virtual job fairs A job fair held on campus in which students can "tour" a company online, ask questions of recruiters, and electronically send résumés.

Executive search firms Employment agencies, often also called headhunters, that specialize in placing applicants in high-paying jobs.

Employment agency An organization that specializes in finding jobs for applicants and finding applicants for organizations looking for employees.

The applicant can seldom go wrong using an employment agency. If the fee is charged to the company, the applicant gets a job at no cost. However, even if the fee is charged to the applicant, the applicant may still benefit. For example, suppose you are having difficulty finding a job, and an employment agency finds you a good job paying $60,000 per year. Spending $6,000 to obtain a good job might be worthwhile because every month of unemployment is costing you $5,000 in lost income. So, the fee is essentially one month's salary that you would not have earned anyway without the job.

Executive Search Firms

Executive search firms, better known as "headhunters," differ from employment agencies in several ways. First, the jobs they represent tend to be higher-paying, non-entry-level positions such as executives, engineers, and computer programmers. Second, reputable executive search firms always charge their fees to organizations rather than to applicants. Third, fees charged by executive search firms tend to be about 30% of the applicant's first-year salary.

A word of caution about both employment agencies and executive search firms: Because they make their money on the number of applicants they place, they tend to exert tremendous pressure on applicants to take jobs that are offered. But applicants are not obligated to take jobs and should not be intimidated about turning down a position that appears to be a poor match.

Public Employment Agencies

Public employment agency An employment service operated by a state or local government, designed to match applicants with job openings.

The third type of outside recruitment organization is state and local employment agencies. These **public employment agencies** are designed primarily to help the unemployed find work, but they often offer services such as career advisement and résumé preparation. From the organization's perspective, public employment agencies can be of great value in filling blue-collar and clerical positions. Not only is there no cost involved in hiring the applicants, but often government programs are also available that will help pay training costs. There are many organizations that do all of their recruiting and screening for laborer and clerical positions exclusively with state employment agencies.

Many public employment agencies have made finding jobs easier by placing kiosks in locations such as shopping malls and public buildings. Applicants can use the kiosks to search for local job openings and get information on how they can apply for the jobs. Recruiting kiosks are increasingly being used by employers that receive large numbers of walk-in applicants. Rather than speaking to a receptionist, potential job applicants can use the kiosk located in the company lobby, shopping mall, or state employment agency to search for current job openings and then apply electronically to jobs for which they are qualified.

Employee Referrals

Employee referral A method of recruitment in which a current employee refers a friend or family member for a job.

Another way to recruit is by **employee referral**, in which current employees recommend family members and friends for specific job openings. Surveys investigating this referral method indicate that about 78% of private organizations use employee referrals in some way and that employee referrals were the top source of newly hired employees (SilkRoad, 2017, 2018). This success may in part, be due to the increased ease of making referrals through social media networks such as LinkedIn, Twitter, and Facebook.

Some organizations are so convinced of the attractiveness of this method that they provide financial incentives to employees who recommend applicants who are hired. For example, Integrated Systems Consulting Group gave $3,000 and a chance to win a vacation in Hawaii to employees referring successful applicants. Ondeck gave employees a $2,000 bonus for referring applicants who got hired; Temporary Associates in Illinois gave $250 college scholarships to students who recommended applicants for seasonal positions; 7-Eleven offered employees $1,000 for recommending potential field consultants; Sybase ran a referral campaign in which employees whose referrals resulted in an interview were entered in a raffle for such prizes as a TV, five cases of beer, 36 Baby Ruth bars, and a hammock; InMobi gave employees the opportunity to wins trips to places such as Bali and Hawaii for successful referrals; DigitalOcean not only gave employees $3,000 for a successful referral but also donated $1,500 toward the employee's favorite charity; and White Memorial Medical Center provided recommenders of successful employees free maid service for a full year. The average amount of such bonuses offered by organizations is between $1,000 and $2,500 (WorldatWork, 2016).

The typical time period that a new employee must stay with the company before the referring employee is eligible for a bonus is three months (WorldatWork, 2016). Stewart, Ellenburg, Hicks, Kremen, & Daniel, 1990 found no relationship between the size of the bonus and the number of referrals, nor did they find that organizations offering referral bonuses received more referrals than did organizations not offering bonuses. Though such a finding might be surprising, 42% of employees said they made a referral to help a friend, and another 24% said they made the referral to help their employer. Only 24% reported making the referral for the incentive (Lachnit, 2001).

In general, research indicates that employee referrals are an excellent recruitment source. Employee referrals are more likely to be hired and have longer tenure with an organization than are employees recruited through other means (Brown, Setren, & Topa, 2013; Burks, Cowgill, Hoffman, & Housman, 2015; Zottoli & Wanous, 2000).

Although the idea of employee referrals sounds good, not all referrals are the same. Aamodt and Carr (1988) and Rupert (1989) compared the success of employees who had been referred by current successful and unsuccessful employees and found that employees referred by successful employees had longer tenure than did employees who had been referred by unsuccessful employees. Thus, only those referrals made by successful employees should be considered. This finding, explained by social psychology research, indicates that our friends tend to be similar to us in characteristics such as personality, values, and interests. If a particular employee is a good employee, then the same characteristics that make them a good employee are probably shared by their friends and family. The same would be true of an unsuccessful employee.

Even though referrals by successful employees are a good recruitment avenue, the similarity of friends can also pose some problems. The biggest is that our friends also tend to be the same gender, race, and national origin as we are. For example, Mouw (2002) found that 88% of the friends of White employees and 92% of the friends of Black employees are of the same race, and 50% of job applicants used their social networks to help find a job.

Thus, if an organization uses employee referrals and the organization consists predominantly of White men, it is possible that it will hire fewer Black individuals or women than an organization whose employees are more diverse. Thus, even though the organization didn't intend to discriminate, the consequences of its recruitment policy may have that effect. However, organizations such as Alpine Banks of Colorado have used this similarity bias to their advantage by asking its bilingual employees to refer bilingual applicants. Similarly, Wegmans Food Markets encourages employees to refer family members so much so that as of 2009, 7,000 of the organization's 37,000 employees were related to at least one person on the company payroll (Owens, 2009).

Direct Mail

Because **direct mail** has been successful in product advertising, several organizations have used it to recruit applicants, especially those who are not actively job hunting. With direct-mail recruitment, an employer typically obtains a mailing list and sends help-wanted letters or brochures to people through the mail. Although direct-mail recruitment seems to be an "old school" technique, it is still used as it reaches audiences such as passive job seekers that many electronic methods such as job boards do not. For example, in 2021, the U.S. Postal Service used a direct mail campaign to recruit letter carriers.

One California branch of Allstate Insurance had been using newspaper advertisements and getting limited response. However, from a single mailing of 64,000 letters that explained the career opportunities available at Allstate to current policyholders, the company received more than 500 calls and was able to hire 20 new employees. Union Special, an Illinois manufacturer of sewing machines, had difficulty filling 10 engineering positions, so they direct-mailed 3,300 cards to Chicago-area engineers at a cost of about $5,000. As a result, the company received 100 responses and conducted 30 interviews. A third company that successfully used direct-mail recruitment is Bank of America. To save money, Bank of America did something different from Allstate and Union Special. Instead of sending a special recruitment mailing, Bank of America included recruitment literature in the regular monthly mailing of bank statements to its customers.

Direct-mail recruiting is especially useful for positions involving specialized skills. For example, Minor's Landscape Services in Texas had difficulty finding licensed irrigators, so the company located a list of people in Texas who had irrigation licenses and sent letters to each person on the list. The company found 20 qualified candidates and was able to fill both of its openings. Likewise, Doctors Community Hospital in Maryland used direct mail to fill a night-shift pharmacy position in a record three days. Defense Force Recruitment used direct mail to successfully recruit engineers.

Because passive applicants are different from those actively seeking jobs, employers using a direct-mail approach need to increase their availability to the applicants. That is, instead of having interested applicants apply through the normal online process, the recruiter should provide an email address and phone number through which the applicants can directly contact the recruiter.

Internet

The Internet continues to be a major source of recruitment. According to Morelli and Illingworth (2019), internet recruiting efforts usually take one of four forms: employer-based websites, job boards, social networking sites, and job marketplaces.

Employer-Based Websites

With employer-based websites, an organization lists available job openings and provides Information about itself and the minimum requirements needed to apply to a particular job. Though the level of sophistication varies across organization websites, on most, applicants can upload their résumés, answer questions designed to screen out unqualified applicants, and then actually take employment tests. On many sites, the tests are instantly scored, and if the applicant is deemed qualified, interviews are scheduled electronically.

Rock Bottom restaurants (Rock Bottom Brewery, Old Chicago pizza, Chop House, Walnut Brewery, and Sing Sing nightclub) provide an excellent example of an employer using an automated hiring system. Applicants can apply for jobs and complete personality inventories online at home, at a Rock Bottom restaurant, or at a career fair. The system automatically screens for work eligibility, scores the tests, and sends messages to restaurant managers letting them know when a high-quality applicant has applied. The system even suggests interview questions the manager should ask a particular applicant (e.g., Why did you have a five-month gap between jobs in 2020?). Since using the new online system, turnover has gone down.

Research indicates that the effective employer-based websites contain information that is detailed and credible, are easy to navigate, are aesthetically pleasing, are interactive, and contain videos of employee testimonials regarding the company (Allen, Mahto, & Otondo, 2007; Breaugh, 2008). Including employee testimonials from racially and ethnically diverse employees can enhance an organization's diversity efforts (Walker, Feild, Giles, Armenakis, & Bernerth, 2009).

As is the case with print media, the look and content of a web recruitment page or advertisement greatly influences applicant reactions. A study by Dineen, Ling, Ash, and DelVecchio (2007) found that web-based job postings were most effective when the posting was aesthetically pleasing *and* contained customized information about the job and the company. Aesthetics or content by themselves were not enough to influence applicant reactions.

Many organizations are expanding the traditional web approach by blogging and posting videos on YouTube. Blogging allows recruiters to more informally discuss an organization's career opportunities and corporate culture with potential applicants. The blog will usually include links to the organization's official employment website. Recruiting videos posted on YouTube allow applicants to get gain information about an organization as well as insight into its culture.

Job Boards

A job board is a private company whose website lists job openings for hundreds or thousands of organizations and résumés for millions of applicants. The largest Internet recruiter, Indeed, had more than 250 million visitors per month in 2020.

Employers are finding that there are many advantages to using job boards compared with traditional newspaper help-wanted ads. Perhaps the biggest advantage is the cost; depending on the geographic location, advertisement size, and length of the ad run, advertising in a major city newspaper can be 10 times more expensive than Internet recruiting. Internet recruiting reaches more people over a larger geographic area than do newspaper ads, and whereas the Sunday edition is the main newspaper recruitment tool, "every day is Sunday" on the Internet. Though the Internet changes every day, these were the leading recruitment websites in 2020:

www.indeed.com
www.Glassdoor.com
www.monster.com
www.LinkedIn.com

In addition to the large job boards previously mentioned, there are job boards that are specific to a particular industry or skill set. For example, AllRetailJobs.com not surprisingly specializes in retail jobs, Adrants specializes in advertising jobs, and ClearanceJobs contains jobs in which the applicant needs a security clearance.

Social Media

One of the greatest change in employee recruitment has been the increased use of social media outlets such as LinkedIn, Facebook, and Twitter. The various sites primarily differ on the audiences they reach: Facebook reaches friends and family, LinkedIn reaches professional connections, and Twitter reaches people related by similar interests such as a favorite celebrity, hobby, or occupation.

With LinkedIn, an applicant can search for job openings by company and can email or message professional connections to see if they know of job openings. A recruiter with a job opening can search profiles for people with the desired skills and experience, post job openings for applicants to find, and can email connections about an opening. With Twitter, applicants can connect to people that they may not know but share similar interests. Applicants can learn about job openings, read Tweets from people who work for an organizations, and send Tweets asking for information about a company or about potential job openings. On Facebook, applicants can inform their networks about status changes such as moving or losing a job or about job openings with their company.

According to Vaughn, Petersen, and Gibson (2019), social media provides a variety of benefits to both the job seeker and the hiring organization. For the job seeker, social media provides a platform to market their background, experience, and skills and increases the number of job opportunities to which they are exposed. For the hiring organization, social media allows the opportunity to target potential applicants who have particular skills or characteristics, provides access to a large number of applicants, reduces recruiting costs, and provides a large amount of information about the applicant that can be used for screening purposes.

Job Marketplaces

Job marketplaces, such as Glassdoor, are websites in which former or current employees can post reviews of what it is like to work for a particular employer. Potential applicants can search for job openings, read employee reviews about the organizations with the job openings, obtain information about the salaries paid by organizations for that job, and actually apply for a job opening. Job marketplaces are a powerful recruitment tool, and researchers have discussed its potential for moving toward a global labor market (Beerepoot & Lambregts, 2015). While it seems like there are largely still various obstacles in becoming the new standard, such as gender-bias in selection outcomes, job marketplaces such as oDesk can serve as an alternate source of recruitment for organizations.

Job Fairs

Job fairs A recruitment method in which several employers are available at one location so that many applicants can obtain information at one time.

Job fairs are used by many organizations to provide information in a personal fashion to as many applicants as possible. Job fairs are typically conducted in one of three ways. In the first, many types of organizations have booths at the same location. For example, a multiemployer job fair sponsored by the Birmingham, Alabama Chamber of Commerce drew over 600 applicants and 45 employers. Your college probably has one or two of these job fairs each year, in which dozens of organizations send representatives to discuss employment opportunities with students and to collect résumés. In addition, representatives usually hand out company literature and souvenirs such as T-shirts, yardsticks, and cups. If you haven't been to a campus job fair, contact your career services center to see when they are scheduled on your campus.

Job fairs are also held when an event or disaster occurs that affects local employment. Following the September 11, 2001, attack on the World Trade Center, a job fair for displaced workers attracted more than 25,000 job seekers. Similar fairs were held for airline workers in Philadelphia and Pittsburgh (Gelbart, 2001). Similarly, in the rebuilding process in the aftermath of Hurricane Katrina, a multiemployer job fair called "West of the Connection" was held in the New Orleans area. To overcome the social gathering restrictions caused by the COVID-19 pandemic in 2020, 10 employers in Shenandoah County, Virginia, held a virtual job fair that was attended by more than 60 job seekers.

The second type of job fair has many organizations in the same field in one location. For example, an education job fair in Honolulu, Hawaii, in 2011 had 50 private and public schools attend to recruit new teachers. The advantage to this type of job fair is that with a single employment field represented, each visitor is a potential applicant for every organization. The drawback, of course, is that each organization must compete directly with the other organizations at the fair.

The third approach to a job fair is for an organization to hold its own. Here are some examples:

- Gaylord Palms in Kissimmee, Florida, held a job fair attended by more than 12,000 people interested in the resort's 1,400 job openings.
- LG Chem in Holland, Michigan, had more than 800 job seekers attend its job fair held to fill 100 production positions at its new plant.
- Microsoft held a job fair in Atlanta that attracted 3,000 people, and Concentra Corporation held an "open house" that attracted more than 100 applicants and resulted in four job openings being filled.

Although this approach is certainly more expensive than multiemployer job fairs, it has the advantage of focusing the attention of the applicants on only one company.

Special Recruit Populations
Increasing Applicant Diversity

Many organizations make special efforts to recruit women and underrepresented groups. Efforts include recruiting at historically Black colleges and universities (HBCUs), developing targeted intern positions, and highlighting the organization's openness to diversity in recruitment materials (e.g., including affirmative action statements, displaying pictures of employees from underrepresented groups, and using recruiters from underrepresented groups). Research by Avery and McKay (2006) indicates that a key to recruiting underrepresented applicants is how they perceive the diversity of the organization during a site visit. That is, underrepresented applicants look at how many underrepresented individuals they see, what positions they are in, and how well they perceive the quality of the interaction between underrepresented and non-underrepresented employees.

Nontraditional Sources

When traditional recruitment methods are unsuccessful, many organizations look for potential applicants from nontraditional sources. Here are a few examples:

- Manpower Incorporated, in Chandler, Arizona; the Chicago Police Department; and the Hackensack, New Jersey, Police Department formed partnerships with local churches that resulted in successful hires (Tyler, 2000).

- IBM, Google, Morgan Stanley, and Cisco Systems developed recruitment strategies and such LGBTQIA+−friendly benefits as domestic partner benefits to recruit and retain LGBTQIA+ employees.
- In 2019, Jefferson County, Alabama sponsored a job fair for individuals previously incarcerated that was attended by 75 organizations.
- Cub Foods in Illinois hires people with intellectual disabilities to serve as baggers in their grocery stores, and at rug maker Habitat International in Tennessee, over 80% of the employees have a physical or intellectual disability (Andrews, 2005).
- To solve the driver-shortage problem, many trucking companies are trying to hire married couples to be team drivers. To better entice them, trucks are enhanced to include larger sleeping berths and appliances such as microwave ovens (Taylor, 2007).

Recruiting "Passive" Applicants

Apart from the direct-mail approach, and at times, the use of executive recruiters, most of the recruiting methods previously discussed in this chapter deal with applicants who are actively seeking work. Because "the best" employees are already employed, recruiters try to find ways to identify this hidden talent and then convince the person to apply for a job with their company.

One such approach is for recruiters to build relationships with professional associations for each of the fields in which they recruit. For example, SIOP would be the professional association for I/O psychologists, the Society for Human Resource Management (SHRM) for HR professionals, and the American Compensation Association (ACA) for compensation professionals. Recruiters would then attend the association's conferences, read their newsletters and magazines, and scan the association's website to identify the best candidates then approach those people about applying for a job (Overman, 2007).

Evaluating the Effectiveness of Recruitment Strategies

Considering the number of potential recruitment sources, it is important to determine which source is the best to use. Such an evaluation can be conducted in several ways. As shown in Figure 4.2, one method is to examine the *number of applicants* each recruitment source yields. That is, if a newspaper ad results in 100 applicants and an in-store sign results in 20 applicants, newspaper ads could be considered the better method.

Using the number of applicants as the measure of success may be appropriate when the emphasis is simply getting enough bodies to fill the job openings, but looking

Figure 4.2
Evaluating the Effectiveness of Recruitment Strategies

Criterion	Recruitment Sources		
	Advertisements	Referrals	Walk-ins
Number of applicants	40	30	10
Number qualified	10	15	5
Number hired	2	7	1
Number successful	0	4	1

only at the number of applicants does not take into account the cost of the recruitment campaign. Thus, a second method for evaluating the success of a recruitment campaign is to consider the **cost per applicant**, which is determined by dividing the number of applicants by the amount spent for each strategy. Continuing with the previous example, suppose our newspaper ad cost $200 and yielded 10 applicants and our in-store sign cost $5 and yielded 2 applicants. The cost per applicant for the newspaper ad would be $20, whereas the cost per applicant for the in-store sign would be just $2.50. Using this method of evaluation, the in-store sign would be best as long as it generated the number of applicants needed by the organization. But if the organization needs to hire 10 new employees and there are only 2 applicants for jobs, this recruitment strategy by itself is not effective.

Cost per applicant The amount of money spent on a recruitment campaign divided by the number of people that subsequently apply for jobs as a result of the recruitment campaign.

Although the cost-per-applicant evaluation method is an improvement on the applicant-yield method, it too has a serious drawback. An organization might receive a large number of applicants at a relatively low cost per applicant, but none may be qualified for the job. Therefore, the third and fourth strategies would be to look at either the *number of qualified applicants* or the **cost per qualified applicant**.

Another method for evaluating the effectiveness of various recruitment sources, and perhaps the best one, looks at the number of successful employees generated by each recruitment source. This is an effective method because, as shown in Figure 4.3, every applicant will not be qualified, nor will every qualified applicant become a successful employee.

Cost per qualified applicant The amount of money spent on a recruitment campaign divided by the number of qualified people that subsequently apply for jobs as a result of the recruitment campaign.

A final method for evaluating recruitment source effectiveness is to look at the number of individuals from underrepresented groups and women that applied for the job and were hired. It is not uncommon for large organizations to hold recruiters accountable for their efforts in attracting a diverse applicant pool. Though there has not been much research on this topic, Kirnan, Farley, and Geisinger (1989) found that women and Black individuals were more likely to use formal sources of recruitment (e.g., newspaper ads, job fairs) than were men and White individuals.

To determine differences in recruitment-source effectiveness, a meta-analysis conducted by Zottoli and Wanous (2000) first categorized recruitment methods as being from either an inside source (employee referrals, rehires) or an outside source (advertisements, employment agencies, school placement offices, recruiters). They found that employees recruited through inside sources stayed with the organization longer (higher tenure) and performed better than employees recruited through outside sources. Several theories might explain the superiority of inside sources.

The first theory suggests that rehires or applicants who are referred by other employees receive more accurate information about the job than do employees

1. Why should I hire you?
2. What do you see yourself doing five years from now?
3. What do you consider your greatest strengths and weaknesses?
4. How would you describe yourself?
5. What college subjects did you like best? Least?
6. What do you know about our company?
7. Why did you decide to seek a position with the company?
8. Why did you leave your last job?
9. What do you want to earn five years from now?
10. What do you really want to do in life?

Figure 4.3

Commonly Asked Unstructured Employment Interview Questions

recruited by other methods (Wanous, 1980). This theory has been supported in research by McManus and Baratta (1992), Conard and Ashworth (1986), and Breaugh and Mann (1984), who found that applicants referred by current employees received not only more information but also more accurate information about the job than did applicants recruited through other channels.

The second theory postulates that differences in recruitment-source effectiveness are the result of different recruitment sources reaching and being used by different types of applicants (Schwab, 1982). Although some research has supported this theory of individual differences (Breaugh & Mann, 1984; Swaroff, Barclay, & Bass, 1985; Taylor & Schmidt, 1983), other research has not (Breaugh, 1981). In fact, no variables have *consistently* distinguished users of one recruitment method from users of another method. Furthermore, the typical person looking for a job uses a wide variety of job search strategies. To underscore this point, think of the part-time jobs you have held. How did you find out about each one? Was it the same method each time? As you can see, it is unlikely that a certain type of person responds only to newspaper ads, whereas another type goes only to employment agencies.

A third theory might better explain the finding that employee referrals result in greater tenure than do other recruitment strategies. This theory, cited earlier in the discussion on employee referral programs, has its roots in the literature on interpersonal attraction, which indicates that people tend to be attracted to those who are similar to themselves (Kassin, Fein, & Markus, 2014). If true—and research strongly suggests it is—then an employee recommending a friend for a job will more than likely recommend one similar to themselves. Thus, it would make sense that a person who is happy with their job would recommend a person who, because of their similarity to the incumbent, should also be happy with the job. Likewise, an unhappy employee would recommend similar friends who would also be unhappy and would probably have short tenure with the organization.

This theory has not been heavily researched, but it has been supported by two studies. As discussed earlier, both Aamodt and Carr (1988) and Rupert (1989) found that long-tenured employees referred applicants who, after being hired, stayed on their jobs longer than applicants who were referred by short-tenured employees. No significant differences were found when job performance was examined instead of tenure.

4-2 Realistic Job Previews

Realistic job preview (RJP) A method of recruitment in which job applicants are told both the positive and the negative aspects of a job.

Because recruitment sources have only a slight effect on tenure of future employees, using other methods during the recruitment process may be helpful in recruiting applicants who will be successful. One such method is the **realistic job preview (RJP)**. RJPs involve giving an applicant an honest assessment of a job. For example, instead of telling the applicant how much fun they will have working on the assembly line, the recruiter honestly tells them that although the pay is well above average, the work is often boring and there is little chance for advancement.

The logic behind RJPs is that even though telling the truth scares away many applicants (Saks, Wiesner, & Summers, 1996), especially the most qualified ones (Bretz & Judge, 1998), the ones who stay will not be surprised about the job. Because they know what to expect, informed applicants will tend to stay on the job longer than applicants who did not understand the nature of the job. As one would imagine, RJPs have the greatest impact on applicants who have little knowledge or unrealistic expectations about a job or company and who are also in a financial position that they can actually decline a job offer (Breaugh, 2008).

RJPs are also thought to be effective because they communicate to the applicant that the company is willing to be honest, and thus can be trusted. In fact, in a meta-analysis investigating why RJPs might be successful in reducing turnover, Earnest, Allen, and Landis (2011) found that the perception of company honesty was the prime driver of RJP success.

In a meta-analysis of 40 RJP studies, Phillips (1998) found that although RJPs result in lower turnover, higher job satisfaction, and better performance, the size of the effect is rather small. The meta-analysis also suggested that RJPs will be most effective if they are given in an oral rather than a written format, and if they are given to the applicant at the time of the job offer rather than earlier in the recruitment process or after the job offer has been accepted. The Earnest et al. meta-analysis also found that the effect size for reducing turnover was small and that an oral presentation was best but found that an RJP given after hire was as effective, if not more so, than one given prehire.

In another meta-analysis, Shetzer and Stackman (1991) found that RJPs discussing opportunities for career advancement ($d = .19$) were more effective than ones without a career component ($d = .05$). These two meta-analyses indicate that RJPs, especially if they are conducted orally and contain a career component, may be useful in the recruitment process.

A variation of the RJP is a technique called an **expectation-lowering procedure (ELP)**. Unlike an RJP, which focuses on a particular job, an ELP lowers an applicant's expectations about work and expectations in general (Buckley et al., 2002). For example, an RJP might include a statement such as, "This job is performed in a very small space, in high levels of heat, with few opportunities for social interaction," whereas an ELP might include a statement such as:

> "We often start a new job with high expectations, thinking the job will be perfect. As you will discover, no job is perfect and there will be times when you become frustrated by your supervisor or your coworkers. Prior to accepting this job, be sure to give some thought regarding whether this job and our organization will meet the expectations that you have. Also, give some thought to whether your expectations about work are realistic."

Expectation-lowering procedure (ELP) A form of RJP that lowers an applicant's expectations about the various aspects of the job.

4-3 Effective Employee Selection Techniques

If the recruitment process was successful, an organization will have several applicants from which to choose. At this point, many techniques can be used to select the best person from this pool of applicants. In the remainder of this chapter, we will discuss the employment interview. In Chapter 5, such methods as reference checks, assessment centers, biodata, psychological tests, and physical ability tests will be discussed.

Effective employee selection systems share three characteristics: They are valid, they reduce the chance of a legal challenge, and they are cost-effective. A valid selection test is one that is based on a job analysis (content validity), predicts work-related behavior (criterion validity), and measures the construct it purports to measure (construct validity). As you will recall from Chapters 2 and 3, selection tests will reduce the chance of a legal challenge if their content appears to be job related (face validity), the questions don't invade an applicant's privacy, and adverse impact is minimized.

Ideal selection tests are also cost-effective in terms of the costs to purchase or create, to administer, and to score. With these characteristics in mind, let's begin our discussion of selection techniques with the employment interview.

4-4 Employment Interviews

Employment interview A method of selecting employees in which an interviewer asks questions of an applicant and then makes an employment decision based on the answers to the questions as well as the way in which the questions were answered.

Undoubtedly, the most commonly used method to select employees is the **employment interview** (Chambers & Arnold, 2015). In fact, if you have ever applied to any part-time and summer jobs, most of those jobs were obtained after you went through an interview process. You might even remember the sweaty palms that went along with the interview. In all likelihood, the interviews you have been through could be labeled "traditional" or "unstructured" and must be distinguished from the structured interviews that will be discussed in this chapter. In a study of interview questions, Huffcutt, Conway, Roth, and Stone (2001) found that most interview questions try to reveal information about one of seven constructs:

- Personality
- Mental ability
- Knowledge and skills
- Social skills
- Interests and preferences
- Organizational fit
- Physical attributes

Types of Interviews

Perhaps a good place to start a discussion on interviews is to define the various types. Interviews vary on three main factors: structure, style, and medium.

Structure

Structured interviews Interviews in which questions are based on a job analysis, every applicant is asked the same questions, and there is a standardized scoring system so that identical answers are given identical scores.

Unstructured interview An interview in which applicants are not asked the same questions and in which there is no standard scoring system to score applicant answers.

The structure of an interview is determined by the source of the questions, the extent to which all applicants are asked the same questions, and the structure of the system used to score the answers. A **structured interview** is one in which (1) the source of the questions is a job analysis (job-related questions), (2) all applicants are asked the same questions, and (3) there is a standardized scoring key to evaluate each answer. An **unstructured interview** is one in which interviewers are free to ask anything they want (e.g., Where do you want to be in five years? What was the last book you read?), are not required to have consistency in what they ask of each applicant and may assign numbers of points at their own discretion. Interviews vary in their structure, and rather than calling interviews structured or unstructured, it might make more sense to use terms such as *highly structured* (all three criteria are met), *moderately structured* (two criteria are met), *slightly structured* (one criterion is met), and *unstructured* (none of the three criteria are met). The research is clear that highly structured interviews are more reliable and valid than interviews with less structure (Huffcutt & Arthur, 1994; Huffcutt, Culbertson, & Weyhrauch, 2013). That is, structured interviews have been proven to be a better job predictor than unstructured interviews. Researchers posit that this is due to structured interviews having standardization across applicants, and also the ability to gain a wide variety of applicant information (McDaniel, Whetzel, Schmidt, & Maurer, 1994).

Style

The style of an interview is determined by the number of interviewees and number of interviewers. *One-on-one interviews* involve one interviewer interviewing one applicant. *Serial interviews* involve a series of single interviews. For example, the HR manager might interview an applicant at 9:00 a.m., the department supervisor interviews the applicant at 10:00 a.m., and the vice president interviews the applicant at 11:00 a.m. *Return* interviews are similar to serial interviews with the difference being a passing of time between the first and subsequent interview. For example, an applicant might be interviewed by the HR manager and then brought back a week later to interview with the vice president. *Panel interviews* have multiple interviewers asking questions and evaluating answers of the same applicant at the same time, and *group interviews* have multiple applicants answering questions during the same interview. Of course, one could put together several combinations such as a *serial-panel-group interview*.

Medium

Interviews also differ in the extent to which they are done in person. In *face-to-face interviews*, both the interviewer and the applicant are in the same room. Face-to-face interviews provide a personal setting and allow the participants to use both visual and vocal cues to evaluate information. *Telephone interviews* are often used to screen applicants but do not allow the use of visual cues (not always a bad thing). *Video-conference interviews* are conducted virtually through software such as Zoom, Teams, and GoToMeeting. The applicant and the interviewer can hear and see each other, but the setting is not as personal, nor is the image and vocal quality of the interview usually as sharp as in face-to-face interviews. *Written interviews* involve the applicant answering a series of written questions and then sending the answers back through regular mail or through email. A study from 2003 found that most final selection decisions were made through the face-to-face interview (Chapman & Webster, 2003), whereas almost 20 years later, the shift toward more technology-focused mediums are very apparent as organizations race to adapt to the advances in technology.

Advantages of Structured Interviews

Though some HR professionals think they are using a structured interview because they ask the same questions of everyone, it is the job relatedness and standardized scoring that most distinguish the structured from the unstructured interview. The distinction is an important one because meta-analyses (Huffcutt & Arthur, 1994; McDaniel, Whetzel, Schmidt, & Maurer, 1994) clearly indicate that interviews high in structure are more valid than unstructured interviews. This is true even when the interview is conducted over the phone (Schmidt & Rader, 1999). Furthermore, research (Campion, Campion, & Hudson, 1994; Cortina, Goldstein, Payne, Davison, & Gilliland, 2000) indicates that structured interviews can add predictive power (called *incremental validity*) to the use of cognitive ability tests.

From a legal standpoint, structured interviews are viewed more favorably by the courts than are unstructured interviews (Williamson, Campion, Malos, Roehling, & Campion, 1997). There are two probable reasons for this. One, structured interviews are based on a job analysis. A review of interview research by Campion, Palmer, and Campion (1997) concluded that interviews based on a job analysis will be more valid and legally defensible than ones not based on a job analysis. Two, structured interviews result in substantially lower adverse impact than do unstructured interviews

(Alonso, Moscoso, & Salgado, 2017; Huffcutt & Roth, 1998; Levashina, Hartwell, Morgeson, & Campion, 2014). In part, this is because unstructured interviews concentrate on general intelligence, education, and training, whereas structured interviews tap job knowledge, job skills, applied mental skills, and interpersonal skills (Huffcutt, Conway, Roth, & Stone, 2001). A further advantage to structured interviews is that the racial and gender similarity issues mentioned previously as a problem with unstructured interviews do not appear to greatly affect structured interviews (Buckley, Jackson, Bolino, Veres, & Feild, 2007; McCarthy, Van Iddekinge, & Campion, 2010).

Although structured interviews are considered superior to unstructured ones, applicants perceive structured interviews to be more difficult (Gilmore, 1989). Furthermore, because the interview is so structured, applicants may feel that they did not have the chance to tell the interviewer everything they wanted to (Gilliland & Steiner, 1997).

Problems with Unstructured Interviews

Why does the unstructured interview seem *not* to predict future employee performance? Researchers have investigated this question for several years and have identified eight factors that contribute to the poor reliability and validity of the unstructured interview: poor intuitive ability, lack of job relatedness, primacy effects, contrast effects, negative-information bias, interviewer-interviewee similarity, interviewee appearance, and nonverbal cues.

Poor Intuitive Ability

Interviewers often base their hiring decisions on "gut reactions," or intuition. However, people are not good at using intuition to predict behavior: research indicates that human intuition and clinical judgment are inaccurate predictors of a variety of factors ranging from future employee success (Kuncel, Klieger, Connelly, & Ones, 2013) to the detection of deception (Aamodt, 2008). And contrary to what many HR professionals think, there are no individual differences in interviewers' ability to predict future performance (Pulakos, Schmitt, Whitney, & Smith, 1996). That is, research does not support the idea that some interviewers are able to predict behavior, whereas others are not. Divorce rates provide an excellent example of this poor predictive ability. Couples involved in romantic relationships spend, on average, two years together before getting married. Despite this time together, 50% of all marriages fail—an important reason for which is lack of compatibility. So, if after two years of "interviewing" a prospective spouse, we make the wrong choice 50% of the time, is it logical to assume that after spending only 15 minutes interviewing an applicant, we can predict how well they will get along with the varied members of an organization?

Lack of Job Relatedness

Research by Bolles (2020) has identified the most common questions asked by interviewers. As you can see in Figure 4.4, these questions are not related to any particular job. Furthermore, the proper answers to these questions have not been empirically determined. Research has shown which answers HR professionals prefer (Bolles, 2020), but preference for an answer does not imply that it will actually predict future performance on the job. As discussed earlier in this and preceding chapters, information that is used to select employees *must* be job related if it is to have any chance of predicting future employee performance. In addition to not being job related,

Question Type	Example
Clarifier	I noticed a three-year gap between two of your jobs. Could you tell me about that? You were a bench hand at AT&T. What is that?
Disqualifier	Can you work overtime without notice? Do you have a valid driver's license?
Skill-level determiner	Several months after installing a computer network, the client calls and says that nothing will print on the printer. What could be going wrong?
Past-focused (behavioral)	When you are dealing with customers, it is inevitable that you are going to get someone angry. Tell us about a time when a customer was angry with you. What did you do to fix the situation?
Future-focused (situational)	Imagine that you told a client that you would be there at 10:00 a.m. It is now 10:30 and there is no way you will be finished with your current job until 11:30. You are supposed to meet with another client for lunch at noon and then be at another job at 1:15 p.m. How would you handle this situation?
Organizational fit	What type of work pace is best for you? Describe your experience working with a culturally diverse group of people.

Figure 4.4
Types of Structured Interview Questions

many questions asked by interviewers are illegal (e.g., "Are you married?" or "Do you have any health problems?"). Interestingly, most interviewers who ask illegal questions know that they are illegal (Dew & Steiner, 1997).

Primacy Effects

Primacy effects The fact that information presented early in an interview carries more weight than information presented later.

Research suggests that **primacy effects**, or "first impressions," in the interview are important. Some research indicates that information presented prior to the interview (Dougherty, Turban, & Callender, 1994) or early in the interview carries more weight than does information presented later in the interview (Farr, 1973). Furthermore, a 2015 CareerBuilder survey found that about 50% of interviewers determine within five minutes whether they think an applicant will be a good fit for the position. These survey results are supported by several studies (Barrick, Swider, & Stewart, 2010; Giluk, Stewart, & Shaffer; 2008; Stewart, Dustin, Shaffer, & Giluk, 2008; Swider, Barrick, & Harris, 2016) that found significant correlations between interviewer ratings made after a few minutes of rapport building and the final interview rating.

However, one study (Raymark et al., 2008) found that only 5% of interviewers made up their mind in the first minute and only 31% within the first five minutes. Thus, most interviewers take at least five minutes to make their decisions. As one would imagine, the time taken by interviewers to make a decision was influenced by several factors, such as the degree to which the interview is structured, the behavior of the interviewee, and the interview dimensions being tapped. Regardless of when an interviewer makes their decision, there is no relationship between the length of an interview and how well the interview predicts performance (Thorsteinson, 2014).

To reduce potential primacy effects, interviewers are advised to make repeated judgments throughout the interview rather than one overall judgment at the end of the interview. That is, the interviewer might rate the applicant's response after each question or series of questions rather than waiting until the end of the interview to make a single rating or judgment.

Contrast Effects

Contrast effect When the performance of one applicant affects the perception of the performance of the next applicant.

With the **contrast effect**, the interview performance of one applicant may affect the interview score given to the next applicant (Kopelman, 1975; Oduwole, Morgan, & Bernardo, 2000; Wexley, Sanders, & Yukl, 1973). If a terrible applicant precedes an average applicant, the interview score for the average applicant will be higher than if no applicant or a very qualified applicant preceded them. In other words, an applicant's performance is judged in relation to the performance of previous interviewees. Thus, it may be advantageous to be interviewed immediately after someone who has done poorly.

Research by Wexley, Yukl, Kovacs, and Sanders (1972) found that interviewers who were trained to be aware of the occurrence of contrast effects were able to reduce them. Other researchers (Landy & Bates, 1973), however, have questioned whether the contrast effect actually plays a significant role in the interview process. A related phenomenon called the uniqueness effect was also shown to influence the interview score (Roulin, Bangerter, & Yerly, 2011). This study found that applicants that provided unique answers to traditional interview questions received higher evaluations and were more likely to receive a job offer, as when compared to applicants who provided non-unique, but qualitatively comparable, answers.

Negative-Information Bias

Negative-information bias The fact that negative information receives more weight in an employment decision than does positive information.

Negative information apparently weighs more heavily than positive information (Bocketti, Hamilton, & Maser, 2000; Rowe, 1989). **Negative-information bias** seems to occur only when interviewers aren't aware of job requirements (Langdale & Weitz, 1973). It seems to support the observation that most job applicants are afraid of being honest in interviews for fear that one negative response will cost them their job opportunities.

This lack of honesty may be especially evident in the interview, where the face-to-face nature of the process increases the odds that an applicant would respond in such a way as to look better to the interviewer. In a study conducted to increase the honesty of applicants during the interview process, Martin and Nagao (1989) had applicants interview for a job in one of four conditions. In the first, applicants read written interview questions and then wrote their responses to the questions. In the second condition, applicants were "interviewed" by a computer. In the third condition, applicants were interviewed face-to-face by an interviewer who behaved warmly; and in the fourth condition, applicants were interviewed by an interviewer who seemed cold. As expected, Martin and Nagao found that applicants were more honest in reporting their GPAs and their SAT scores under the nonsocial conditions that involved paper-and-pencil and computer interviewing. Thus, one might increase the accuracy of information obtained in the interview by reducing social pressure and using written or computerized interviews.

Interviewer-Interviewee Similarity

In general, research suggests that an interviewee will receive a higher score (Howard & Ferris, 1996) if they are similar to the interviewer in terms of personality (Foster, 1990), attitude (Frank & Hackman, 1975), gender (Foster, Dingman, Muscolino, & Jankowski, 1996), or race (McFarland, Ryan, Sacco, & Kriska, 2004; Prewett-Livingston et al., 1996). However, a study by Sacco, Scheu, Ryan, and Schmitt (2003) found that the method used to analyze interview data is a factor in whether similarity matters. Sacco et al. found that when using a traditional approach (d scores) to analyze their findings, interviewers gave higher ratings to same-race interviewees. When a more sophisticated method was used (hierarchical linear models), neither racial nor sex similarity affected interview scores. Thus, further research is needed to accurately determine the importance of similarity in unstructured interview decisions.

Interviewee Appearance

Meta-analyses (Barrick, Shaffer, & DeGrassi, 2009; Hosoda, Stone-Romero, & Coats, 2003; Steggert, Chrisman, & Haap, 2006) indicate that, in general, physically attractive applicants have an advantage in interviews over less attractive applicants, and applicants who dress professionally receive higher interview scores than do more poorly dressed applicants.

The appearance bias extends to weight, as research (Kutcher & Bragger, 2004; Pingitore, Dugoni, Tindale, & Spring, 1994; Roehling, Pichler, & Bruce, 2013; Rudolph, Wells, Weller, & Baltes, 2009) indicates that applicants who are people diagnosed with obesity receive lower interview scores and are less likely to be hired and are offered lower salaries than their leaner counterparts. The interviewee's appearance, it seems, is a potent hiring factor.

Nonverbal Cues

Nonverbal communication Factors such as eye contact and posture that are not associated with actual words spoken.

A meta-analysis by Barrick et al. (2009) found that the use of appropriate **nonverbal communication** is highly correlated with interview scores. Appropriate nonverbal cues include such things as smiling and making appropriate eye contact (Levine & Feldman, 2002). Not surprisingly, meta-analysis results indicate that structured interviews are not as affected by nonverbal cues as are unstructured interviews (Barrick et al., 2009). Meta-analysis results also indicate that the appropriate use of such verbal cues as tone, pitch, speech rate, and pauses is also related to higher interview scores (Barrick et al., 2009).

Although many more studies and variables could be listed, this discussion shows that the interview contains many sources of bias that are not job related. Remember that one of the major purposes of the employment interview is to determine which applicant will be the most successful in performing a job. To determine this, decisions must be based on ability to do the job and not on such variables as physical attractiveness and similarity.

Creating a Structured Interview

To create a structured interview, information about the job is obtained (job analysis) and questions are created that are designed to find out the extent to which applicants' skills and experiences match those needed to successfully perform the job. These questions are incorporated into an interview form used by all interviewers for all applicants. Examples of good and bad answers are located next to the questions to help an interviewer score the answers given by applicants.

Determining the KSAOs to Tap in the Interview

The first step in creating a structured interview is to conduct a thorough job analysis and write a detailed job description. As discussed in Chapter 2, the job analysis should identify the tasks performed, the conditions under which they are performed, and the competencies needed to perform the tasks. The second step is to determine the best way to measure an applicant's ability to perform each of the tasks identified in the job analysis. Some of the competencies can be appropriately measured in an interview; others will need to be tapped through such methods as psychological tests, job samples, assessment centers, references, background checks, and training and experience ratings (these other methods will be thoroughly discussed in Chapter 5). For example, suppose a job description for a receptionist indicated that the primary tasks included typing reports, filing correspondence, answering the phone, and dealing with people visiting the organization. Typing ability might best be measured with a typing test, filing correspondence with a filing test, answering the phone with a job sample, and customer service with an interview question. The important point here is that not every competency can or should be tapped in an interview.

Creating Interview Questions

Clarifier A type of structured interview question that clarifies information on the résumé or application.

Disqualifier A type of structured interview question in which a wrong answer will disqualify the applicant from further consideration.

Skill-level determiner A type of structured-interview question designed to tap an applicant's knowledge or skill.

Future-focused question A type of structured interview question in which applicants are given a situation and asked how they would handle it.

Situational question A structured-interview technique in which applicants are presented with a series of situations and asked how they would handle each one.

As shown in Figure 4.5, there are six types of interview questions: clarifiers, disqualifiers, skill-level determiners, past-focused, future-focused, and organizational fit. **Clarifiers** allow the interviewer to clarify information in the résumé, cover letter, and application, fill in gaps, and obtain other necessary information. Because each applicant's résumé and cover letter are unique, specific clarifiers are not standard across applicants. For example, an interviewer may need to ask one applicant to explain what they won the McArthur Award for and another applicant what they were doing during a two-year gap between jobs. **Disqualifiers** are questions that must be answered a particular way or the applicant is disqualified. For example, if a job requires that employees work on weekends, a disqualifier might be, "Are you available to work on weekends?" If the answer is no, the applicant will not get the job.

Skill-level determiners tap an interviewee's level of expertise. For example, if an applicant says they are proficient in Microsoft Word, an interviewer might ask some questions about the word processing program. If an applicant claims to be fluent in Spanish, the interviewer might want to ask them a few questions in Spanish.

Future-focused questions, also called **situational questions**, ask an applicant what they would do in a particular situation. As shown in Table 4.1, the first step in creating situational questions is to collect critical incidents, a technique you learned in Chapter 2. These incidents are then rewritten into questions that will be used during the interview. It is important that these questions can be answered with the applicant's current knowledge. That is, asking police applicants situational questions in which they would need knowledge

Table 4.1   Creating Situational Interview Questions

The Critical Incident

A customer entered a bank and began yelling about how the bank had messed up their account. They became so angry that they began to swear, saying that they would not leave the bank until the problem was solved. Unfortunately, the computer was down and the teller could not access the needed information.

The Question

You are working as a teller and have a long line of waiting customers. One customer runs to the front of the line and yells that they bounced a check and was charged $20, which caused other checks to bounce. They then swear at you and tell you that they will not leave until the problem is solved. You are unable to check on their account because the information is at another branch. What would you do?

The Benchmark Answers

5   Because I do not have the information and the line is long, I would call my supervisor and have them talk to the customer in their office away from everyone else.

4   While trying to calm them down, I would call my supervisor.

3   I would try to calm them down and explain to them that the computer is down.

2   I would explain that I cannot help them because the computer is down, and ask them to come back later.

1   I would tell them to get to the end of the line and wait their turn.

---

of police procedures would not be appropriate because they won't learn this information until they graduate from the police academy. After creating the questions, the next step is to create a scoring key. This step will be discussed later in the chapter.

Past-focused questions, sometimes referred to as **patterned-behavior description interviews (PBDIs)**, differ from situational interview questions by focusing on *previous* behavior rather than future intended behavior. That is, applicants are asked to provide specific examples of how they demonstrated job-related skills in previous jobs (Janz, Hellervik, & Gilmore, 1986). Although future-focused and past-focused interview questions have different orientations, interviewees who do well on one type typically do well on the other (Campion et al., 1994; Cohen & Scott, 1996). However, scores on past-focused questions are better predictors of performance in higher-level positions than are future-focused questions (Huffcutt, Roth, Conway, & Klehe, 2004; Huffcutt, Weekley, Wiesner, DeGroot, & Jones, 2001; Pulakos & Schmitt, 1995).

Rather than trying to predict future performance, **organizational-fit questions** tap the extent to which an applicant will fit into the culture of an organization or with the leadership style of a particular supervisor. For example, some organizations are very policy-oriented, whereas others encourage employees to use their initiative. Some supervisors are very task-oriented, whereas others are more person-oriented. The idea behind organizational-fit questions is to make sure that the applicant's personality and goals are consistent with those of the organization.

Creating a Scoring Key for Interview Answers

Once interview questions are created, the next step is to create a key to score applicants' answers to the questions. Though answers to some questions can be scored as being right or wrong (e.g., "Do you have to pay an employee overtime for working over 8 hours in a day?"), as shown in Table 4.2, there are two main methods of scoring most answers: typical-answer approach and key-issues approach.

Right/Wrong Scoring.   Some interview questions, especially skill-level determiners, can be scored simply based on whether the answer given was correct or incorrect. For example, consider the question posed to an interviewee in the United States, "As a server, can you

---

Past-focused questions A type of structured-interview question that taps an applicant's experience.

Patterned-behavior description interviews (PBDIs) A structured interview in which the questions focus on behavior in previous jobs.

Organizational-fit questions A type of structured-interview question that taps how well an applicant's personality and values will fit with the organizational culture.

Right/wrong scoring A method of scoring interview questions in which the answer is either right or wrong (e.g., What is the legal drinking age in Virginia?).

Table 4.2   Scoring Examples

Typical-Answer Approach

1   I would tell them to get to the end of the line and wait their turn.
2   I would explain to them that I cannot help them because the computer is down and ask them to come back later.
3   I would try to calm them down and explain to them that the computer is down.
4   I would call my supervisor.
5   Because I do not have the information and the line is long, I would call my supervisor and have them talk to the customer in their office away from everyone else.

Key-Issues Approach

_____   Acknowledged the long line and the concern for other customers
_____   Recognized the need to calm the customer
_____   Recognized the need to get the customer away from the other customers
_____   Recognized that help could not be immediately given because the computer was down
_____   Was not confrontational with the customer

---

give a glass of wine to a 16-year-old if their parents are present and give permission?" If the interviewee answers no, they would get a point for a correct answer. If they answer yes, they would not get a point. If the question type being asked was a disqualifier (e.g., Can you work weekends?), the wrong answer would actually disqualify the individual from further consideration rather than merely result in no points being awarded.

Typical-Answer Approach.   The idea behind the **typical-answer approach** is to create a list of all possible answers to each question, have subject-matter experts (SMEs) rate the favorableness of each answer, and then use these ratings to serve as benchmarks for each point on a five-point scale. Though some scoring keys have only one benchmark answer for each point on the scale, research by Buchner (1990) indicates that increasing the number of **benchmark answers** will greatly increase the scoring reliability. Because the number of possible answers to any question is probably finite, it might be a good idea at this stage to brainstorm all possible answers to a question and then benchmark each of the answers. This approach would result in 10 or so benchmarked answers per question rather than the traditional 5.

Key-Issues Approach.   A problem with the typical-answer approach is that there are many possible answers to a question, and applicants often provide answers that could fit parts of several different benchmarks. To correct this problem, the **key-issues approach** can be used. In this approach, SMEs create a list of key issues they think should be included in the perfect answer. For each key issue that is included, the interviewee gets a point. The key issues can also be weighted so that the most important issues get more points than the less important issues.

Psychologist Pete DiVasto uses the key-issues approach when he interviews applicants for law enforcement positions. In one of his questions, he asks applicants to imagine that they are a police officer and have received a call about a possible break-in at a store. Upon arrival, the officer notices the following: a police car in the parking lot with its lights flashing, an officer on the ground next to the police car, an alarm going off in the store, and a person running from the store. DiVasto then asks the applicant what they would do in that situation. The key issues in a good answer include indicating that a police officer is hurt and needs help, an understanding that the person running could be dangerous but could also be a victim, the realization that backup is needed, and articulation of a good rationale for choosing to either help the police officer first or attend to the person running.

When scoring interviews, it is appropriate to have a system to evaluate an applicant's nonverbal cues, especially when the job involves interpersonal skills. Such scoring is supported by research demonstrating that an applicant's nonverbal cues in interviews can predict job performance (Barrick et al., 2008; Burnett & Motowidlo, 1998; DeGroot & Motowidlo, 1999).

Conducting the Structured Interview

Though it is common to use a panel interview, research suggests that interviews will best predict performance when one trained interviewer is used for all applicants (Huffcutt & Woehr, 1999). The first step in conducting the interview is to build rapport; do not begin asking questions until applicants have had time to "settle their nerves." Building rapport is an important step, as it results in the applicant feeling more positive about the interview (Chapman & Zweig, 2005).

Once an applicant feels at ease, set the agenda for the interview by explaining the process. Most applicants have not been through a structured interview, so it is important to explain the types of questions that will be asked and point out that each interviewer will be taking notes and scoring the answers immediately after the interviewee has responded. After the agenda has been established, ask the interview questions. You may want to have only one person ask all the questions or have each panel member ask some questions. It is important to score each answer after it has been given. Once the questions have been asked, provide information about the job and the organization. Such information might include salary and benefits, the job duties, opportunities for advancement, a history of the organization, and so on. Then, answer any questions the applicant might have. It is a good idea at this point to say something like, "We have asked you a lot of questions but may not have asked you about things you want to tell us. Is there any information you would like to tell us that we did not ask about?" End the interview on a pleasant note by complimenting the interviewee ("It was a pleasure meeting you") and letting them know when you will be contacting the applicant about job offers. At the conclusion of the interview, the scores from the questions are summed and the resulting figure is the applicant's interview score.

4-5 Job Search Skills

Though the orientation of this and the next chapter is on selecting employees, it is important that you master the skills necessary to obtain a job. The following three sections provide advice on how to interview, write a cover letter, and write a résumé.

Successfully Surviving the Interview Process

Even though the unstructured employment interview has many problems, the odds are high that a person being considered for a job will undergo such an interview. Research and experience both indicate that applicants can take several steps to increase their interview scores. One of the most important of these steps is to obtain training on how to interview. Research by Maurer and his colleagues (Maurer, Solamon, Andrews, & Troxtel, 2001; Maurer, Solamon, & Troxtel, 1998) has shown that such training can increase an applicant's score on structured interviews. Receiving interview training and practicing interviewing skills are good ways to reduce interview anxiety. Reducing anxiety is important, as research indicates that there is a negative correlation between interviewee anxiety and interview performance (McCarthy & Goffin, 2004; McCarthy & Saks, 2008).

Scheduling the Interview

Contrary to popular advice, neither day of week nor time of day affect interview scores (Aamodt, 1986; Willihnganz & Myers, 1993). What will affect the score, however, is *when* applicants arrive for the interview. If they arrive late, the score will be drastically lower (Lantz, 2001). In fact, in a study I conducted many years ago (Aamodt, 1986), no applicant who arrived late was hired. No differences, however, have been found in interview scores based on whether an applicant arrives on time or five or ten minutes early. Therefore, the interview can be scheduled for any time of the day or week, but the applicant must not be late!

Before the Interview

Learn about the organization (Freiberger, 2013). Recall from Figure 4.4 that one of the most commonly asked unstructured interview questions ("What do you know about our company?") is used to determine the applicant's knowledge of the organization. Not only does this advice make sense, but research has found that an applicant's knowledge significantly correlates with the interview rating (Aamodt, 1986) and that interview preparation significantly correlates with being asked back for a second interview (Caldwell & Burger, 1998). Organizations are especially impressed if an applicant knows its products and services, future needs, major problems faced, and philosophy or mission.

A former student of mine tells the story of an interview for a managerial position that they had with Allstate Insurance. The night before the interview, they read all the available information on Allstate on the Internet. During the interview, they were asked why they wanted to work for Allstate. They replied that they were active in the community and was attracted to Allstate because of its "Helping Hands" community program—which they had read about the night before. The interviewer was greatly impressed and spent the next 10 minutes describing the program and its importance. The interview was a success in part because the applicant had done their homework.

During the Interview

Most suggestions about how best to behave in an interview take advantage of the interviewer biases discussed in this chapter. Nonverbal behaviors should include a firm handshake, eye contact, smiling, and head nodding. Desired verbal behaviors include asking questions, subtly pointing out how you are like the interviewer, not asking about the salary, not speaking slowly, and not hesitating before answering questions. Keep in mind that first impressions are the most important.

As a method of saving travel expenses associated with face-to-face interviews, many organizations interview applicants through a videoconference in which an applicant uses software such as Zoom, GoToMeeting, or Skype and is interviewed by employers who may be hundreds or thousands of miles away. Although the previous interview advice still holds for videoconference interviews, some additional advice includes speaking loudly, keeping hand and arm movements to a minimum, looking directly at the camera, and dressing in conservative, solid colors. It is also important to ensure that there is adequate lighting and a strong Internet connection. The background, whether it is the actual background or a virtual background, be professional.

After the Interview

Immediately following the interview, write a brief email thanking the interviewer for their time, indicating that you look forward to hearing from them, and adding or clarifying information that you forgot to mention in the interview. This is a nice touch certainly cannot hurt.

Writing Cover Letters

Cover letters A letter that accompanies a résumé or job application.

Cover letters tell an employer that you are attaching or enclosing your résumé and would like to apply for a job. There is considerable debate regarding the importance of cover letter. Some experts believe a cover letter is no longer necessary and other experts think a cover letter gives an applicant an edge. Regardless, a well-written cover letter will not be a negative and might actually be a positive.

April 18, 2022

Mr. John Smith
Alco, Inc.
217 West Street
Johnson, VA 24132

Dear Mr. Smith:

Enclosed is a copy of my résumé. Please consider me for the position of welder that was advertised in the *Roanoke Times and World News*.

For several reasons, I believe that I am qualified for your position. First, I have six years of welding experience in an industrial setting. Second, I am a very dependable worker, as shown by the fact that I have missed only two days of work in the last five years. Finally, I am available to work any shift at any of your three plants.

I look forward to hearing from you. I can best be reached after 3:00 p.m. on weekdays and anytime on weekends.

Sincerely,

Andrew S. Jones

Figure 4.5
Example of a Cover Letter

Cover letters should never be longer than one page. As shown in the sample cover letters in Figures 4.6, cover letters contain a salutation, four basic paragraphs, and a closing signature.

Salutation

If possible, get the name of the person to whom you want to direct the letter. If you aren't sure of the person's name, contact the company and simply ask for the name of the person (have it spelled) to whom you should send your résumé. Do not refer to the person by their first name (e.g., Dear Sarah). If you can't get the person's name, a safe salutation is "Dear Human Resource Director." Avoid phrases such as "Dear Sir or Madam" or "To Whom It May Concern."

Paragraphs

The opening paragraph should be one or two sentences long and communicate three pieces of information: the fact that your résumé is enclosed, the name of the job you are applying for, and how you know about the job opening (such as a website or from a friend). The second paragraph states that you are qualified for the job and provides about three reasons why. This paragraph should be only four or five sentences in length and should not rehash the content of your résumé. The third paragraph explains why you are interested in the particular company to which you are applying. The final paragraph closes your letter and provides information on how you can best be reached. Though your phone number will be on your résumé, this paragraph is a good place to tell the employer the best days and times to reach you.

July 15, 2022

Ms. Maria Duffie, Director
Human Resource Department
Raynes Cosmetics, Inc.
69 Beall Avenue
Amityville, NY 00312

Dear Ms. Duffie:

Enclosed is a copy of my résumé. Please consider me for the position of sales representative that was advertised this past Sunday in the *Washington Post*. As you can see below, my qualifications are a good match for the requirements stated in your advertisement.

Your Requirements

Bachelor's degree
Two years of sales experience
History of success in sales
Strong clerical skills

My Qualifications

B.A. in marketing from Radford University
Five years of sales experience
Received three sales awards at L.L. Bean
A.A.S. in secretarial science
Three years of clerical experience
55 words per minute typing speed

I am especially interested in working for your company because I have used your products for over ten years and thus am familiar with both your product line and the high quality of your cosmetics.

I am looking forward to hearing from you. Please feel free to call me at home after 6:00 p.m. or at work from 8:00 a.m. until 5:00 p.m. Because L.L. Bean is downsizing, my employer will not mind your calling me at work.

Sincerely,

Mable Leane

Mable Leane
2345 Revlon Blvd.
Avon, VA 24132
Home: (540) 555–5678
Work: (540) 555–7676
mimi@aol.com

Figure 4.6

Example of a
Customized Cover
Letter

Signature

Above your signature, use words such as "cordially" or "sincerely." "Yours truly" is not advised, and words such as "Love," "Peace," or "Hugs and snuggles" are strongly discouraged.

HR professional GeGe Beall provides job applicants with the following tips about cover letters:

- Avoid sounding desperate and don't beg (I really need a job bad! Please, please, please hire me!).
- Avoid grammar and spelling errors. Employers view cover letters and résumés as examples of the best work applicants can produce. If your cover letter contains errors, an employer will be concerned about the quality of your regular work.

- Avoid officious words or phrases. Don't use a 25-cent word when a ten-cent word will do. Not only will employers be unimpressed by a large vocabulary, but applicants using "big words" often misuse them. As an example, one applicant tried to describe his work productivity by saying that his writings were "voluptuous," rather than "voluminous," as we think he meant to say.
- Don't discuss personal circumstances such as "I find myself looking for a job because I am recently divorced." Employers are interested in only your qualifications.
- If possible, tailor your letter to each company. Standard cover letters are efficient but not as effective as those written specifically for each job you are applying for.
- Don't write your cover letter with the letterhead of your current employer. Ensure that you have used the correct name of the organization throughout the letter or email.

Writing a Résumé

Résumés A formal summary of an applicant's professional and educational background.

Résumés are summaries of an applicant's professional and educational background. Although résumés are commonly requested by employers, little is known about their value in predicting employee performance. Some studies have found that when an interviewer reads a résumé before interviewing an applicant, the validity of the employment interview may actually be *reduced* (Dipboye, Stramler, & Fontenelle, 1984; Phillips & Dipboye, 1989). Beyond these studies, however, it is unclear how much predictive value, if any, résumés have.

Résumés may not predict performance partly because they are intended to be advertisements for an applicant. Companies that specialize in résumé design openly brag about their ability to "make your strengths more obvious and your weaknesses hard to find." As a result, many résumés contain inaccurate information. In a review of surveys on résumé fraud, Aamodt and Williams (2005) found that the median estimate was that 25% of résumés contained inaccurate information.

Contrary to popular belief, there is no one best way to write a résumé. Because people have such different backgrounds, a format that works for one individual may not work for another. Therefore, this section will provide only general advice about writing a résumé; the rest is up to you.

Characteristics of Effective Résumés

One of the most frustrating aspects of writing a résumé is that asking 100 people for advice results in 100 different opinions. However, though there are many *preferences*, there are really only three *rules* that must be followed in writing résumés:

1. *The résumé must be attractive and easy to read.* To achieve this, try to leave at least a 1-inch margin on all sides, and allow plenty of white space; that is, do not "pack" information into the résumé by using smaller fonts and margins. A résumé can have great content, but if the "package" is not attractive, few employers will want to read it. This rule is hardly surprising, as physical attractiveness provides a first impression for many activities, such as interviewing, dating, and purchasing products.
2. *The résumé cannot contain typing, spelling, grammatical, or factual mistakes.* When Walter Pierce, Jr., was a personnel officer for Norfolk Southern

Corporation, his boss received a résumé from an excellent applicant who was applying for a job as a computer programmer. Even though the applicant had outstanding credentials, the personnel director would not even offer him an interview, because the applicant had misspelled two words on his résumé. A similar story is told by Dick Williams, general manager of N&W Credit Union. He once received two cover letters stapled together—both referring to the résumé that wasn't there. To make matters worse, four words were misspelled. I could tell you more horror stories, but the point should be clear: Do not make any careless mistakes!

3. *The résumé should make the applicant look as qualified as possible—without lying.* This is an important rule in determining what information should be included. If including hobbies, summer jobs, and lists of courses will make you look more qualified for *this particular job*, then by all means, include them.

If a résumé follows these three rules—it looks nice, it doesn't contain mistakes, and it makes the applicant look as good as possible—then it is an effective résumé. Opinions to the contrary (such as "use boldface type instead of underlining" or "outline your duties instead of putting them in a paragraph") probably represent differences in individual references rather than any major problem with the résumé. Some excellent examples of résumés can be found at: https://resumegenius.com/blog/resume-help/how-to-write-a-resume.

Impression Formation and Writing Résumés

In writing a résumé, one should take advantage of certain impression-formation principles. For example, the résumé should begin with a short summary of your strengths. This section takes advantage of the impression-formation principles of *priming* (preparing the reader for what is to come), *primacy* (early impressions are most important), and *short-term memory limits* (the list should not be longer than seven items).

The next section of the résumé should contain information about either your education or your experience—whichever is strongest for you. The design of the education section is intended to provide an organizational framework that will make it easier for the reader to remember the contents. In deciding which information to put into these two sections, three impression-management rules should be used: relevance, unusualness, and positivity. If information is *relevant* to your desired career, it probably should be included. For example, you might mention that you have two children if you are applying for a position in day care or elementary school teaching, but not if you are applying for a job involving a lot of travel. How far back should one go in listing jobs? Using the principle of relevance, the answer would be far enough back to include all relevant jobs. It is certainly acceptable to list hobbies if they are relevant.

Unusual information should be included when possible, as people pay more attention to it than to typical information. A problem for college seniors is that their résumés look identical to those of their classmates. That is, most business majors take the same classes, belong to the same clubs, and have had similar part-time jobs. To stand out from other graduates, an applicant needs something unusual, such as an internship, an interesting hobby, or an unusual life experience (e.g., spent a year in Europe, rode a bike across the country).

Though it is advisable to have unusual information, the information must also be *positive*. It probably would not be a good idea to list unusual information such as "I've been arrested more times than anyone in my class" or "I enjoy bungee jumping without cords." The unacceptability of these two examples is obvious, and few applicants would make the mistake of actually placing such information on their résumés; however, more subtle items can have the same effect. For example, suppose you enjoy hunting and are a member of the Young Democrats on campus. Including this item might make a negative impression on those who oppose hunting. Include only information that most people will find positive (such as Red Cross volunteer, worked to help finance education, etc.), and avoid information that may be viewed negatively, such as political affiliation, religion, and dangerous hobbies.

Averaging versus adding model A model proposed by Anderson that postulates that our impressions are based more on the average value of each impression than on the sum of the values for each impression.

Of the many positive activities and accomplishments that you could list, list only your best. Do not list everything you have done; research by Spock and Stevens (1985) found that it is better to list a few great things, rather than a few great things and many good things. This finding is based on Anderson's (1965) **averaging versus adding model** of impression formation, which implies that activity quality is more important than quantity. It is neither necessary nor desirable to list all of your coursework.

On the Job — Applied Case Study

Recruitment at the Borgata Hotel Casino and Spa

The Borgata Hotel Casino and Spa was about to open the first new resort in Atlantic City in 13 years. The 2,000-room casino and resort needed to hire 5,000 employees across hundreds of positions. To find enough high-quality employees, the Borgata engaged in a creative recruitment campaign that resulted in 30,000 well-qualified job applicants.

- How would you have conducted such an extensive recruitment campaign?
- What factors would affect not only the number of available applicants but the quality as well?
- How would you handle the practical aspects of receiving and screening the 30,000 applications?

Focus on Ethics — The Ethics of Recruiting and Hiring Based on Physical Appearance

Harvard economics professor Robert Barro believes that physical appearance is always a bona fide worker qualification as long as customers and coworkers think that it is. That is, if customers want to be served by physically attractive people and coworkers prefer working with physically attractive people, then it should be okay for companies to recruit and hire based on an individual's looks.

When people refer to someone's "looks" or "physical appearance," they are generally referring to that person's height, weight, and facial symmetry (i.e., high cheekbones vs. no visible cheekbones; small nose vs. big or bulbous nose). Because looks are subjective, beauty really is in the eyes of the beholder. In the United States, as well as other countries, physically attractive people are often judged based on their external characteristics, rather than such internal characteristics as personality and ability. And it appears that many employers want employees who are tall and strong (for men), small/petite (for women), with no visible body fat, and a physically attractive face. Even those HR professionals who know better can often fall into the "looks" trap when recruiting and hiring.

Although some cities have laws against discrimination of applicants based on their height, weight, and/or physical appearance (e.g., San Francisco, CA; Santa Cruz, CA; Washington, DC), basically, there is no real federal protection from appearance-based discrimination unless it singles out applicants based on race, gender, or age.

The hiring professionals at the Borgata Hotel Casino and Spa in Atlantic City, New Jersey, embrace this philosophy. Applicants for positions of servers are told that once hired, their weight cannot increase by more than 7%. This means that a 125-pound woman cannot gain more than eight pounds over her tenure at the company.

Defenders of the right to hire based on looks say that physically attractive people are perceived as smarter, more successful, more sociable, more dominant, and as having higher self-esteem. And customers would rather be helped by those types of employees instead of by the less attractive ones. The assumption is that the more physically attractive employees a company has, the more clients or customers that business will attract. This, of course, means more money for the company. And, the more money the company brings in, the higher the salaries employees can earn. So, according to the defenders, it's a win-win situation. Well, win-win for the physically attractive people, anyway.

And speaking of salaries: In 2005, the Federal Reserve Bank of St. Louis reviewed the correlation between looks and wages. The research showed that workers with below average looks earned, on average, 9% less per hour than above average looking workers. Above average looking employees earn 5% more than their average looking coworkers. And Fortune 500 companies seem to hire male CEOs that are about 6 feet tall, which is 3" taller than the average man.

Competency and the ability to do the job are often overlooked when emphasis is placed on looks. Although these physically attractive people may be able to do the job, there may be less attractive people denied a position who could do the job more successfully.

What Do You Think?

- Do you see any potential ethical dilemmas of recruiting and hiring based on looks? If so, what are they?

- Is it ethical to take a less skilled applicant over a more skilled one just because one is more attractive than the other?

- Is it fair or ethical for places like Borgata Casino and Spa to refuse employment to less than average looking employees?

- Is there a more ethical way to balance the rights of companies to have attractive people and the rights of people who are perceived as unattractive?

- Do you think that more states and cities should make laws against discrimination of people based on their looks?

Chapter Summary

In this chapter you learned:

- Employees can be recruited by a variety of methods, including help-wanted advertisements, employee referrals, employment agencies, the Internet, point-of-purchase methods, direct mail, and job fairs.
- The traditional, unstructured interview isn't valid, because of such factors as lack of job relatedness, poor interviewer intuition, contrast effects, negative-information bias, use of nonverbal cues, interviewer-interviewee similarity, and primacy effects.
- The structured interview is a valid predictor of employee performance because it is based on a job analysis, all applicants are asked the same questions, and applicant answers are scored with a standardized scoring procedure.
- To perform well when being interviewed, you need to be on time, learn about the company, dress neatly, and use appropriate nonverbal behavior.

Key Terms

Questions for Review

1. Why are employee referrals an effective means of recruitment?
2. Describe the principles one should follow to write an effective help-wanted ad.
3. If the unstructured interview is so bad, why is it still used so often?
4. Is the key-issues approach to scoring interview questions better than the typical-answer approach? Why or why not?
5. What psychological principles of impression formation are important to consider when writing a résumé?

Chapter

5

Employee Selection: References and Testing

Learning Objectives

5-1 Explain why references typically don't predict performance.

5-2 Choose the right type of employment test for a particular situation.

5-3 Describe the different types of tests used to select employees.

5-4 Create and score a biodata instrument.

5-5 Write a well-designed rejection letter.

I n Chapter 4, interviews and résumés were described as the most commonly used methods to screen and select employees. Although these methods are the most commonly used, they are certainly not the best. In this chapter, we discuss several other techniques that are preferred by industrial psychologists to select employees.

5-1 Predicting Performance Using References and Letters of Recommendation

In psychology, a common belief is that the best predictor of future performance is past performance. Thus, if an organization wants to hire a salesperson, the best applicant might be a successful salesperson who held jobs that were similar to the one for which they are now applying.

Verifying previous employment is not difficult, but it can be difficult to verify the *quality* of previous performance. I recently watched the National Football League's draft of college players and was envious of the fact that professional football teams can assess a player's previous performance by watching game films. That is, they do not have to rely on other coaches' opinions. Instead, the scouts can watch literally every minute a player has spent on the field while in college.

Unfortunately, few applicants bring "game films" of their previous employment performances. Instead, an employer must obtain information about the quality of previous performance by relying on an applicant's references, either by calling those references directly or asking for letters of recommendation from previous employers. The Career Workshop Box tells how to ask for a letter of recommendation.

Before discussing this topic further, it might be a good idea to differentiate among *reference checks*, *references*, and *letters of recommendation*. A **reference check** is the process of confirming the accuracy of information provided by an applicant. A **reference** is the expression of an opinion, either orally or through a written checklist, regarding an applicant's ability, previous performance, work habits, character, or potential for future success. The content and format of a reference are determined by the person or organization asking for the reference. A **letter of recommendation** is a letter expressing an opinion regarding an applicant's ability, previous performance, work habits, character, or potential for future success. The content and format of a letter of recommendation are determined by the letter writer.

Reference check The process of confirming the accuracy of résumé and job application information.

Reference The expression of an opinion, either orally or through a written checklist, regarding an applicant's ability, previous performance, work habits, character, or potential for future success.

Letter of recommendation A letter expressing an opinion regarding an applicant's ability, previous performance, work habits, character, or potential for success.

Reasons for Using References and Recommendations
Confirming Details on a Résumé

Résumé fraud The intentional placement of untrue information on a résumé.

As mentioned in Chapter 4, it is not uncommon for applicants to engage in **résumé fraud**—lying on their résumés about what experience or education they actually have. Thus, one reason to check references or ask for letters of recommendation is simply to confirm the truthfulness of information provided by the applicant. An excellent example of résumé fraud is the bizarre 1994 assault against figure skater Nancy Kerrigan arranged by the late Shawn Eckardt, the bodyguard of Kerrigan's skating rival Tonya Harding (this story is featured in the 2017 movie *I, Tonya*). Harding hired Eckardt as her bodyguard because his résumé indicated he was an expert in counterintelligence and international terrorism, had graduated from an elite executive protection school, and had spent four years "tracking terrorist cells" and "conducting a successful hostage retrieval operation" (Meehan, 1994). After the attack against Kerrigan, however, a private investigator discovered that Eckardt never graduated from a security school and would have been 16 during the time he claimed he was in Europe saving the world from terrorists. The president of a school he did attend stated that he "wouldn't hire Eckardt as a bodyguard in a lifetime"—an opinion that would have been discovered had Harding checked Eckardt's references.

Résumé fraud may not initially seem like a great problem, but consider these examples:

- In 2019, Veronica Hilda Theriault from Australia, was sentenced to prison for lying on her résumé about her education and prior employment. Not only did she lie on her résumé, but she also posed as a former employer and gave herself an excellent reference and she used a photo of supermodel Kate Upton on her LinkedIn profile!
- In 2014, a Polk State College professor, David Broxterman, was fired when the university discovered that he had lied about having a Ph.D. from the University of South Florida (USF). What helped give him away after five years at Polk State? He misspelled the word "Board" on his fake diploma and used the wrong middle name when forging the USF president's signature on the diploma. If being fired wasn't bad enough, Broxterman was convicted of grand theft and sentenced to five years in prison; the State charged that his salary was stolen because he got his job through fraud.
- In 2012, Yahoo CEO, Scott Thompson, resigned after it was discovered that his claim of having a degree in computer science wasn't true, although he did have a bachelor's degree in accounting.
- In 2008, *Dinner: Impossible* host Robert Irvine was fired from the Food Network after a newspaper reported that Irvine's claims of designing Princess Diana's wedding cake and being a chef at the White House were not true. Apparently, the Food Network didn't think such a falsehood was too serious, as they rehired Irvine later that same year.
- In April 2005, Federiqkoe DiBritto was fired from his $100,000 job as a fundraiser at UCLA after it was discovered that his résumé listed phony credentials. This was not the first time DiBritto had engaged in résumé fraud; he had also doctored his credentials so that he could obtain previous jobs as a Catholic

priest, a youth counselor, and the executive director of the Southern California chapter of the National Kidney Foundation.

- In May 2002, Sandra Baldwin was forced to resign as chair of the U.S. Olympic Committee, when it was discovered she had lied on her résumé about having a Ph.D.

These stories are tragic and may not be typical of résumé-fraud cases, but in a 2018 HR.Com survey, 95% of employers believe that it is enough of a problem to merit reference checks. In a survey of employers in the United Kingdom, 25% said that they had withdrawn job offers in the past year after discovering that applicants had lied on their applications, and another 23% said they had fired current employees after discovering résumé fraud (Reade, 2005). In 2006, legislators in the State of Washington thought résumé fraud was so much of a problem that they passed a law in which claiming a fake degree is a Class C felony, punishable by up to $10,000 in fine or five years in prison. Oregon, New Jersey, and North Dakota also have laws making it illegal to use a fake degree. Such consequences seem fair when résumé fraud can lead to wasted resources and time on an organization's part. Researchers found that résumé fraud is a predictor of reduced job performance, as well as an increase in workplace deviance (Henle, Dineen, & Duffy, 2019).

Checking for Discipline Problems

A second reason to check references or obtain letters of recommendation is to determine whether the applicant has a history of such discipline problems as poor attendance, sexual harassment, and violence. Such a history is important for an organization to discover to avoid future problems as well as to protect itself from a potential charge of **negligent hiring**. If an organization hires an applicant without checking their references and background and they later commit a crime while in the employ of the organization, the organization may be found liable for negligent hiring if the employee has a criminal background that would have been detected had a background check been conducted.

Negligent hiring A situation in which an employee with a previous criminal record commits a crime as part of their employment.

Negligent-hiring cases are typically filed in court as common-law cases, or torts. These cases are based on the premise that an employer has the duty to protect its employees and customers from harm caused by its employees or products. In determining negligent hiring, courts look at the nature of the job. Organizations involved with the safety of the public, such as police departments and day-care centers, must conduct more thorough background and reference checks than organizations such as retail stores. Such checks are important, as demonstrated by a study done by a reference-checking firm, which found that 23% of applicants had undisclosed criminal backgrounds (EmployeeScreenIQ, 2014).

For example, a child-care center in California hired an employee without checking his references. A few months later, the employee sexually abused a child at the center. The employee had a criminal record of child abuse that would have been discovered with a simple call to his previous employer. As one would expect, the court found the employer guilty of negligent hiring because the employer had not taken "reasonable care" in ensuring the well-being of its customers.

In Virginia, an employee of a grocery store copied the address of a female customer from a check she had written to the store. The employee later went to the customer's home and raped her. In this example, a case for negligent hiring could not be made because the company had contacted the employee's previous employment references and had found no reason not to hire him. Because there was nothing to discover and because the store had taken reasonable care to check its employees, it was not guilty of negligent hiring.

Discovering New Information About the Applicant

Employers use a variety of methods to understand the personality and skills of job applicants; references and letters of recommendation certainly can be two of these methods. Former employers and professors can provide information about an applicant's work habits, character, personality, and skills. Care must be taken, however, when using these methods because the opinion provided by any particular reference may be inaccurate or purposefully untrue. For example, a reference might describe a former employee as "difficult to work with," implying that everyone has trouble working with the applicant. It may be, however, that only the person providing the reference had trouble working with the applicant. This is an important point because every one of us probably knows people we don't get along with, even though, all things considered, we are basically good people. Thus, reference checkers should always obtain specific behavioral examples and try to get consensus from several references.

It is not uncommon for employers to search an applicant's name online to find more information about the applicant. A CareerBuilder.com survey of employers found that in 2018, 70% of them used social networking sites to discover applicant information. Potential job applicants should carefully monitor what is on their blogs or social network sites, as 57% of organizations reported that they eliminated a job candidate on the basis of information that was found on the web. Interestingly, according to the same CareerBuilder.com survey, 47% of employees are less likely to call an applicant for an interview if the applicant does not have an online presence. Reasons given include having an expectation of an online presence, as well as the employer wanting to gather more information prior to conducting the interview.

Background check firm Good Egg provides an extensive analysis of an applicant's social media presence. Good Egg reviews all of the applicant's social media posts and provides a report of how many posts involved each of the following negative communications:

- Hate speech
- Insults and bullying
- Narcotics
- Obscene language
- Self-harm
- Threats of violence
- Toxic language
- Drug-related images
- Explicit/racy images
- Violent images

The Good Egg report actually includes copies of the posts!

Predicting Future Performance

In psychology, a common belief is that the best predictor of future performance is past performance. References and letters of recommendation are ways to try to predict future performance by looking at past performance.

Even though references are commonly used to screen and select employees, they have not been successful in predicting future employee success. In fact, a meta-analysis found that the average uncorrected **validity coefficient** for references/letters of recommendation and performance is only .18, with a **corrected validity** of .29 (Aamodt & Williams, 2005). This low validity is largely due to four main problems with references and letters of recommendation: leniency, knowledge of the applicant, low reliability, and extraneous factors involved in writing and reading such letters.

Validity coefficient The correlation between scores on a selection method (e.g., interview, cognitive ability test) and a measure of job performance (e.g., supervisor rating, absenteeism).

Corrected validity A term usually found with meta-analysis, referring to a correlation coefficient that has been corrected for predictor and criterion reliability and for range restriction. Corrected validity is sometimes called "true validity."

Leniency.   Research is clear that most letters of recommendation are positive: Fewer than 1% of references rate applicants as below average or poor (Aamodt & Williams, 2005). Because we have all worked with terrible employees at some point in our lives, it would at first seem surprising that references typically are so positive. But keep in mind that *applicants choose their own references*! Even Adolf Hitler, serial killer Aileen Wuornos, and terrorist Osama bin Laden would have been able to find three people who could provide them with favorable references.

Figure 5.1 shows how coworkers' attitudes toward an employee affect the references they give that person. In the first situation, all of the applicant's eight coworkers have positive feelings about the applicant. Thus, if we ask for references from two coworkers, both would be positive *and* representative of the other six coworkers. In situation 2, most coworkers have neutral regard for the applicant, with two having positive feelings and two having negative feelings. In this situation, however, both references chosen by the applicant would be positive and *more favorable* than most coworkers' attitudes. In situation 3, only two of eight people like the applicant—yet the two reference letters will be the same as in the first and second situations, even though most coworkers have negative feelings about our applicant. In situation 4, no one likes our applicant. In this case, our request for references would either keep the person from applying for our job or force the applicant to find references from somewhere else. But if we *require* work-related references, they probably, but not necessarily, would be negative because research has shown that coworkers *are* willing to say negative things about unsatisfactory employees (Grote, Robiner, & Haut, 2001).

Although coworkers are willing to say negative things about unsatisfactory employees, *confidentiality concerns* can hold them back. By law, students have a right to see their reference letters, but most sign waivers such as that shown in Figure 5.2 to encourage reference providers to be more candid. This increased candidness was demonstrated in research that found that people providing references tend to be less lenient when applicants waive their right to see a reference letter (Ceci & Peters, 1984; Shaffer & Tomarelli, 1981). That is, when a person writing a reference letter knows that the applicant is allowed to see the letter, the writer is more inclined to provide a favorable evaluation. With this in mind, a colleague of mine almost completely discounts any recommendation letters for which the waiver is not signed.

A third cause of leniency stems from the *fear of legal ramifications*. A person providing references can be charged with defamation of character (slander if the reference is oral, libel if written) if the content of the reference is both untrue and made with malicious intent. This fear keeps many organizations from providing references at all (Kleiman & White, 1991). However, people providing references are granted what is called a *conditional* or *qualified privilege*, which means that they have the right to

Situation	Positive	Neutral	Negative
1	👤👤👤👤👤👤👤👤		
2	👤👤	👤👤👤👤	👤👤
3	👤👤		👤👤👤👤👤👤
4			👤👤👤👤👤👤👤👤

Figure 5.1
Coworkers' Attitudes
Toward Employee

Statement of Release

_____   _____
Name of person asked to write   Date
this recommendation

I request that you complete this recommendation form, which I understand will become a part of my file in the Radford University Graduate College. I further understand:

(1) that this recommendation statement from you will be a candid evaluation of my scholarship, work habits, and potential;

(2) that the completed statement will be sent to the Radford University Graduate College; and

(3) that it will be held in confidence from me and the public by the Radford University Graduate Office.

_____   _____
Applicant's name (print)   Applicant's signature

Figure 5.2
A Typical Reference Waiver

Negligent reference An organization's failure to meet its legal duty to supply relevant information to a prospective employer about a former employee's potential for legal trouble.

express their opinion provided they believe what they say is true and have reasonable grounds for this belief (Ryan & Lasek, 1991; Zink & Gutman, 2005). Furthermore, the person providing the reference must have a common interest with the applicant (e.g., employer-employee, professor-student) and the statement must be limited to this common interest (Steingold, 2019). One way to avoid losing a defamation suit is to provide only behavioral information in a reference. That is, rather than saying, "This employee is a jerk," you might say, "This employee was warned three times about yelling at other employees and four employees requested that they not have to work with the employee in question." To reduce the possibility of a lawsuit, 72% of organizations have applicants sign a waiver stating that they will not sue the company for checking references nor the people providing references (Burke, 2005).

Several companies have emerged that make their living by contacting companies to see what they will say about former employees. These firms are hired by applicants who are concerned that their former employer might be providing a negative reference. These "reference detectives" contact the former employer under the guise of being a company considering hiring the former employee. The reference information is then passed on to the client, who has the option of filing a defamation suit if they don't like what is being said (Cadrain, 2004).

Because an employer can be guilty of negligent hiring for not contacting references, a former employer also can be guilty of **negligent reference** if it does not provide relevant information to an organization that requests it. For example, if a bank fires an employee for theft and fails to divulge that fact to another bank that is thinking of hiring the person, the former employer may be found liable if the employee steals money at their new bank.

Many years ago, based on several letters of recommendation, our department hired a part-time instructor. Two weeks after he started the job, we discovered that he had to return to his home in another state to face charges of stealing drugs from his former employer, a psychology department at another university. We were upset because neither of the references from his former job mentioned the charges. After a rather heated conversation with one of the references, we learned that the applicant was the son of the department chairman and that the faculty were afraid to say anything that would anger their boss.

These last examples show why providing references and letters of recommendations can be so difficult. On the one hand, a former employer can be charged with slander or libel if it says something bad about an applicant that cannot be proven. On the other hand, an employer can be held liable if it does not provide information about a potentially dangerous applicant. Because of these competing responsibilities, many organizations will confirm only employment dates and salary information unless a former employee has been convicted of a criminal offense that resulted in termination. The use of professional reference-checking companies can help alleviate this problem.

Knowledge of the Applicant. A second problem with letters of recommendation is that the person writing the letter often does not know the applicant well, has not observed all aspects of an applicant's behavior, or both. Professors are often asked to provide recommendations for students whom they know only from one or two classes. Such recommendations are not likely to be as accurate and complete as those provided by professors who have had students in several classes and perhaps worked with them outside the classroom setting.

Even in a work setting in which a supervisor provides the recommendation, they often do not see all aspects of an employee's behavior (Figure 5.3). Employees often act very differently around their supervisors than they do around coworkers and customers. Furthermore, as Figure 5.3 shows and as will be discussed in greater detail in Chapter 7, those behaviors that a reference writer actually recalls are only a fraction of the behaviors actually occurring in the presence of the person writing the recommendation.

Reliability. The third problem with references and letters of recommendation involves the *lack of agreement* between two people who provide references for the same person. Research reveals that reference **reliability** is only .22 (Aamodt & Williams, 2005). The problem with reliability is so severe that there is more agreement between recommendations written *by the same person* for two different applicants than between two people writing recommendations *for the same person* (Aamodt & Williams, 2005). Thus, letters of recommendation may say more about the person writing the letter than about the person for whom it is being written.

This low level of reliability probably results from the point cited earlier that a reference writer has not seen all aspects of an applicant's behavior. Thus, a reference provided by a professor who has observed an applicant in a classroom may not agree with a reference provided by a supervisor who has observed the same applicant in a work setting. Although there may be good reasons for the low levels of reliability in reference letters that limit their validity, research has yet to answer this question: If two references do not agree, which one should be taken the most seriously?

Extraneous Factors. The fourth problem with letters of recommendation concerns extraneous factors that affect their writing and evaluation. Research has indicated that the method used by the letter writer is often more important than the actual content. For example, Knouse (1983), but not Loher, Hazer, Tsai, Tilton, and James

Reliability The extent to which a score from a test or from an evaluation is consistent and free from error.

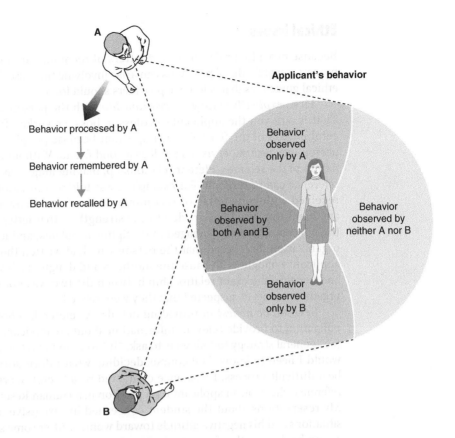

Figure 5.3
A Reference Writer Often Lacks Competent Knowledge of an Employee's Behavior

Applicant's behavior

Behavior processed by A

Behavior remembered by A

Behavior recalled by A

Behavior observed only by A

Behavior observed by both A and B

Behavior observed by neither A nor B

Behavior observed only by B

A

B

(1997), found that letters that contained specific examples were rated higher than letters that contained generalities. Mehrabian (1965) and Weins, Jackson, Manaugh, and Matarazzo (1969) found that even though most letters of recommendation are positive, letters written by references who like applicants are longer than those written by references who do not. This is important because research (Loher et al.,1997; Liu, Minsky, Ling, & Kyllonen, 2009) found that the longer the recommendation letter, the more positively the letter was perceived.

A promising approach to increasing the validity of references is to increase the structure of the reference check. This can be done by conducting a job analysis and then creating a reference checklist that is tied directly to the job analysis results. When such a process is used, research has demonstrated higher levels of predictability (McCarthy & Goffin, 2001; Taylor, Pajo, Cheung, & Stringfield, 2004; Zimmerman, Triana, & Barrick, 2010). Another extraneous factor that impacts the validity of recommendation letters is the difference between the way letters are written for different genders. Current published research in this area has focused on the difference specifically between men and women (McCarthy & Goffin, 2001; Madera, Hebl, & Martin, 2009). Qualitative studies have shown the use of stereotypical gender-related phrases and language, such as the description of applicants as "feminine" and "masculine" (Watson, 1987). Additionally, when comparing between letters written for men and women, researchers found that they leaned more favorably toward men, including having more standout adjectives (e.g., remarkable), and were much longer (Trix & Psenka, 2003).

As this discussion illustrates, references and letters of recommendation often are not great predictors of performance. But with further refinement and research, methods using increased structure may increase the predictive abilities of references.

Ethical Issues

Because providing references and letters of recommendation is a rather subjective process, several ethical problems can arise involving their use. Raynes (2005) lists three ethical guidelines that reference providers should follow.

First, *explicitly state your relationship* with the person you are recommending. That is, are you the applicant's professor, boss, coworker, friend, relative, or some combination of the five? This is important because people often have dual roles: A person may be a supervisor as well as a good friend. Without understanding the exact nature of the referee–referent relationship, making judgments about the content of a reference can be difficult. For example, I was told of a situation in which an applicant received a glowing letter of recommendation from a coworker and in which the applicant was hired in part due to the strength of that letter. Within a few months, the new employee was engaged in discipline problems, and it was only then that the organization discovered that the person who had written the glowing letter was the applicant's daughter. Because the mother's and daughter's last names were different and because the exact relationship between the two was not stated in the letter, the organization never suspected that they were related.

Second, *be honest* in providing details. A referee has both an ethical and legal obligation to provide relevant information about an applicant. A good rule of thumb (i.e., general strategy to follow) is to ask, "If I were in the reference seeker's shoes, what would I need to know?" Of course, deciding what information to provide can often be a difficult process. I was once contacted by a Secret Service agent conducting a reference check on an applicant for a position in a Human Resources (HR) department. My reservations about the student concerned his excessive use of alcohol in social situations and his negative attitude toward women. After some soul searching (as much as can be done with a federal agent staring at you), I decided to provide information about the student's attitude toward women, as I thought it was relevant to an HR job, but not to mention the social drinking problem. Had the student been an applicant for a position as an agent, I would have mentioned the drinking. I'm not sure that my decision was correct, but the example demonstrates the dilemma of balancing the duty to provide information to the reference seeker with a duty to treat an applicant fairly.

Finally, let the *applicant see your reference* before sending it, and give them the chance to decline to use it. Such a procedure is fair to the applicant and reduces the referee's liability for any defamation charge. Though this last piece of advice seems wise, it can result in some uncomfortable discussions about the content of references that are not positive.

5-2 Predicting Performance Using Applicant Training and Education

For many jobs, it is common that applicants must have a minimum level of education or training to be considered. That is, an organization might require that managerial applicants have an MBA to pass the initial applicant screening process. A meta-analysis by Ng and Feldman (2009) found that better educated employees had higher performance, were more likely to engage in organizational citizenship behaviors, less likely to be absent, and less likely to engage in on-the-job substance abuse than were employees with lower levels of education. A meta-analysis of the relationship between education and police performance found that education was a valid predictor of performance in the police academy ($r = .26, \rho = .38$) and performance on the job ($r = .17, \rho = .28$) and added incremental validity to cognitive ability tests (Aamodt, 2004).

Meta-analyses indicate that a student's GPA can predict job performance (Roth, BeVier, Switzer, & Schippmann, 1996), training performance (Dye & Reck, 1989), promotions (Cohen, 1984), salary (Roth & Clarke, 1998), and graduate school performance (Kuncel, Hezlett, & Ones, 2001). GPA is most predictive in the first few years after graduation (Roth et al., 1996). As with many measures of cognitive ability, the use of GPA will result in high levels of adverse impact (Roth & Bobko, 2000). Another factor complicating the use of education and GPA to select employees is the increased use of homeschooling; data from the National Home Education Research Institute indicated that in 2020, more than 4 million children were being homeschooled in the United States, up from 1.1 million in 2003.

5-3 Predicting Performance Using Applicant Knowledge

Job knowledge tests A test that measures the amount of job-related knowledge an applicant possesses.

Used primarily in the public sector, especially for promotions, **job knowledge tests** are designed to measure how much a person knows about a job. For example, applicants for a bartender position might be asked how to make a martini or a White Russian, and applicants for an HR position might be asked about conducting a job analysis. These tests are similar to the exams given several times a semester in a college class. They are typically given in multiple-choice fashion for ease of scoring, but they also can be written in essay format or given orally in a job interview. Common examples of job knowledge tests include tests of computer programming knowledge, knowledge of electronics, and knowledge of mechanical principles. Standardized job knowledge tests are commonly used by state licensing boards for such occupations as lawyers and psychologists.

A meta-analysis by Dye, Reck, and McDaniel (1993) indicates that job knowledge tests are good predictors of both training performance ($r = .27, p = .47$) and on-the-job performance ($r = .22, p = .45$). Because of their high face validity, they are positively accepted by applicants (Robertson & Kandola, 1982). Even though job knowledge tests do a good job of predicting performance, they often result in adverse impact (Brodin, 2018) and can be used only for jobs in which applicants are expected to have job knowledge at the time of hire or promotion.

5-4 Predicting Performance Using Applicant Ability

Ability A basic capacity for performing a wide range of different tasks, acquiring knowledge, or developing a skill.

Ability tests tap the extent to which an applicant can learn or perform a job-related skill. Ability tests are used primarily for occupations in which applicants are not expected to know how to perform the job at the time of hire. Instead, new employees will be taught the necessary job skills and knowledge. Examples of such occupations include police officers, firefighters, and military personnel. For example, cognitive ability would enable a police cadet to obtain knowledge of search-and-seizure laws; psychomotor ability (dexterity) would enable an administrative assistant to type fast or an assembler to rapidly assemble electronic components; perceptual ability would enable a mail clerk to distinguish zip codes or a textile worker to distinguish colors; and physical ability would enable a firefighter to learn how to climb a ladder or carry a victim from a burning building.

Cognitive Ability

Cognitive ability Abilities involving the knowledge and use of information such as math and grammar.

Cognitive ability includes such dimensions as oral and written comprehension, oral and written expression, numerical facility, originality, memorization, reasoning (mathematical, deductive, inductive), and general learning. Although there are many facets of cognitive ability, they all share a common construct called general mental ability or *g* (Ones, Dilchert, Viswesvaran, & Selgado, 2017). Cognitive ability is related to employee performance across job type, job complexity, and country (Ones et al., 2017).

Cognitive ability tests Tests designed to measure the level of intelligence or the amount of knowledge possessed by an applicant.

Cognitive ability tests are commonly used because they are excellent predictors of employee performance and training performance in the United States and in many countries (Ones et al., 2017; Salgado, Anderson, Moscoso, Bertua, & De Fruyt, 2003; Schmidt & Hunter, 1998), are easy to administer, and are relatively inexpensive. Cognitive ability is thought to predict work performance in two ways: by allowing employees to quickly learn job-related knowledge and by processing information resulting in better decision-making. Though cognitive ability tests are thought by many to be the most valid method of employee selection, especially for complex jobs, they certainly have some drawbacks. Perhaps the most crucial of these is that they result in high levels of adverse impact (Roth, BeVier, Bobko, Switzer, & Tyler, 2001) and often lack face validity. This adverse impact has been theorized by research to be due to a number of racially unequal conditions that contribute to developmental conditions, such as: availability of learning materials, home environment, and maternal sensitivity (Cottrell, Newman, & Roisman, 2015). Because cognitive ability tests have the highest level of adverse impact of any employee-selection method, it is not surprising that they also are frequently challenged in court. As you learned in Chapter 3, an organization can still use a test with adverse impact if it can show that it is related to performance, and cognitive ability tests that have been properly developed and validated usually survive legal challenges (Shoenfelt & Pedigo, 2005). However, defending lawsuits, even if the company wins, can be expensive.

Another drawback to cognitive ability tests is the difficulty of setting a passing score. That is, how much cognitive ability do you need to perform well in a particular job? Should we always give preference to the smartest applicant or is there a point at which increased cognitive ability doesn't help? The On the Job case study at the end of this chapter will give you a good opportunity to explore this question further.

Though meta-analyses suggest that cognitive ability is one of the best predictors of performance across all jobs (Salgado et al., 2003; Schmidt & Hunter, 1998), the results of job-specific meta-analyses raise some doubt about this assumption. For example, in a meta-analysis of predictors of law enforcement performance, Aamodt (2004) found cognitive ability to be significantly related to performance, but the corrected validity ($\rho = .27$) was not nearly as high as that reported in the general meta-analysis by Schmidt and Hunter ($\rho = .51$). Similar results were found by Vinchur, Schippmann, Switzer, and Roth (1998) in their meta-analysis of predictors of performance for salespeople: Cognitive ability was significantly related to supervisor ratings ($\rho = .31$) but not to actual sales performance ($\rho = -.03$). Thus, further meta-analyses on specific occupations are still needed before we can conclude that cognitive ability is one of the best predictors for all jobs.

One of the most widely used cognitive ability tests in industry is the **Wonderlic Personnel Test**. The short amount of time (12 minutes) necessary to take the test, as well as the fact that it can be administered in a group setting, makes it popular. Sample items from the Wonderlic are shown in Figure 5.4. Other popular cognitive tests are the Miller Analogies Test, the Quick Test, Harver's Cognitive Ability Assessment, Criteria Cognitive Aptitude Test, Employee Aptitude Survey, and Raven Progressive Matrices.

A potential breakthrough in cognitive ability tests is the Siena Reasoning Test (SRT). The developers of this test theorized that the large race differences in scores on traditional cognitive ability tests were due to the knowledge needed to understand the questions rather than the actual ability to learn or process information (intelligence). Take, for example, the analogy, *Colt is to horse as _____ is to dog.* To correctly answer this question, one must have prior knowledge of animals as well as the ability to do analogies. To reduce the reliance on previous knowledge, the SRT items contain nonsense words and words that are commonly known (e.g., lamp, couch). A study comparing the SRT with other cognitive ability tests found that not only did the SRT predict college grades and work performance at least as well as traditional cognitive ability tests, but almost eliminated the racial differences in test scores (Ferreter, Goldstein, Scherbaum, Yusko, & Jun, 2008). Much more research, however, will need to be conducted to determine the utility of the SRT.

A type of test related to cognitive ability is the situational judgment test. In this test, applicants are given a series of situations and asked how they would handle each one. These situations cover such topics (constructs) as leadership skills, interpersonal skills, personality tendencies, teamwork, and job knowledge (Christian, Edwards, & Bradley, 2010). A meta-analysis by McDaniel, Morgeson, Finnegan, Campion, and Braverman (2001) found that situational judgment tests correlated highly with cognitive ability tests ($r = .46$) and with job performance ($r = .34$). Though situational judgment tests are correlated with cognitive ability, this combination is more valid than either test alone (Clevenger, Pereira, Wiechmann, Schmitt, & Harvey, 2001).

Perceptual Ability

Perceptual ability consists of vision (near, far, night, peripheral), color discrimination, depth perception, glare sensitivity, speech (clarity, recognition), and hearing (sensitivity, auditory attention, sound localization) (Fleishman & Reilly, 1992b). Abilities from this dimension are useful for such occupations as machinist, cabinet maker, die setter, and tool and die maker.

An interesting example of the importance of monitoring ability testing is provided in a study by Padgett (1989), who was hired to determine vision requirements for a municipal fire department. Prior to Padgett's study, national vision standards for firefighters had been set without any empirical research. The standards stipulated that firefighters needed a minimum uncorrected vision of 20/40 and could not wear contact lenses because they might be "blown out of their eyes."

After conducting his study of actual job-related duties, however, Padgett discovered that the minimum vision needed to perform firefighting tasks was 20/100 if the person wore glasses and that there was no minimum if the person wore contacts. The difference in requirements for contacts and glasses was because certain duties might result in a loss of glasses, but it was very unlikely a firefighter would lose contacts while performing a task requiring acute vision. As a result of this study, many qualified applicants who had been turned away because of the archaic vision requirements were allowed the chance to become firefighters.

An example of a perceptual ability test is shown in Figure 5.5.

WONDERLIC

PERSONNEL TEST

FORM II

NAME _____   _____

(Please Print)   Date

READ THIS PAGE CAREFULLY. DO EXACTLY AS YOU ARE TOLD.
DO NOT TURN OVER THIS PAGE UNTIL YOU ARE
INSTRUCTED TO DO SO.

PROBLEMS MUST BE WORKED WITHOUT THE AID OF A CALCULATOR
OR OTHER PROBLEM-SOLVING DEVICE.

This is a test of problem-solving ability. It contains various types of questions. Below is a sample question correctly filled in.

PLACE
ANSWERS
HERE

REAP is the opposite of
    1 obtain.   2 cheer.   3 continue.   4 exist.   5 <u>sow.</u>

[5]

The correct answer is "sow." (It is helpful to underline the correct word.) The correct word is numbered 5. Then write the figure 5 in the brackets <u>at the end of the line.</u>

Answer the next sample question yourself.

Paper sells for 23 cents per pad. What will 4 pads cost?

[_____]

The correct answer is 92¢. There is nothing to underline so just place "92¢" in the brackets.

Here is another example:

MINER   MINOR — Do these words
    1 have similar meanings?   2 have contradictory meanings?   3 mean neither the same nor opposite?

[_____]

The correct answer is "mean neither the same nor opposite," which is number 3, so all you have to do is place a figure "3" in the brackets <u>at the end of the line.</u>

When the answer to a question is a letter or a number, put the letter or number in the brackets.
All letters should be printed.

This test contains 50 questions. It is unlikely that you will finish all of them, but do your best. After the examiner tells you to begin, you will be given exactly 12 minutes to work as many as you can. Do not go so fast that you make mistakes since you must try to get as many right as possible. The questions become increasingly difficult, so do not skip about. Do not spend too much time on any one problem. The examiner will not answer any questions after the test begins.

Now, lay down your pencil and wait for the examiner to tell you to begin!

> *Do not turn the page until you are told to do so.*

Source: E. F. Wonderlic Personnel Test, Inc., Northfield, IL.

Figure 5.4
Wonderlic Personnel Test

2. SPATIAL RELATIONS (SR)

This is a test of Spatial Relations. Following are patterns which can be folded into figures. You are to choose which figure can be correctly made by folding the pattern and then darken the answer space above it. Only one of the four figures is correct for each pattern shown. Practice on these examples.

Example 1:

Example 2:

In Example 1, the first figure, the cube, is correct. You should have darkened the answer space above the first figure. In Example 2, all of the figures are correct in shape, but only one of them is shaded correctly. The last figure is correct.

Remember the surfaces you are shown in the pattern must always be the outside of the folded figure.

When the signal is given turn the page over and begin. Work as quickly and as carefully as you can.

NOTE: If you change an answer, mark a heavy "X" on the answer you wish to change, then darken the correct answer.

You will have 5 minutes to complete this section.

DO NOT TURN THIS PAGE UNTIL YOU ARE TOLD TO DO SO.

Source: CAPS, EdiTS, San Diego, California 92107.

Figure 5.5
Perceptual Ability Test

Psychomotor Ability

Psychomotor ability includes finger dexterity, manual dexterity, control precision, multilimb coordination, response control, reaction time, arm-hand steadiness, wrist-finger speed, and speed-of-limb movement (Fleishman & Reilly, 1992b). Psychomotor abilities are useful for such jobs as carpenter, police officer, sewing-machine operator, post office clerk, and truck driver. An example of a psychomotor test is shown in Figure 5.6.

Physical Ability

Physical ability tests are often used for jobs that require physical strength and stamina, such as police officer, firefighter, and lifeguard. It has been estimated that 28% of employees in the United States work at physically demanding jobs (Gebhardt & Baker, 2017), and wage growth and employment opportunities in manual labor jobs surpassed STEM jobs between 2013–2018 (U.S. Bureau of Labor Statistics, Occupational Employment Statistics).. If physical ability tests are going to be part of the selection process, ergonomic and environmental conditions must be identified as part of the job analyses. These conditions can be measured by something as simple as measuring the number of steps an employee must climb or as complex as the amount of oxygen consumed (Gebhardt & Baker, 2017).

Physical ability is measured in one of two ways: job simulations and physical agility tests. With a job simulation, applicants actually demonstrate job-related physical behaviors. For example, firefighter applicants might climb a ladder and drag a 48-pound hose 75 feet across a street, police applicants might fire a gun and chase down a suspect, and lifeguard applicants might swim 100 yards and drag a drowning victim back to shore. Though job simulations are highly content valid, from a financial or safety perspective they can be impractical (Hoover, 1992).

Testing the physical ability of police applicants is an excellent example of this impracticality. Job analyses consistently indicate that the physical requirements of police officers can be divided into two categories: athletic and defensive. *Athletic requirements* are easy to simulate because they involve such behaviors as running, crawling, and pulling. *Defensive requirements*, however, are difficult to safely and accurately simulate because they involve such behaviors as applying restraining holds, kicking, and fending off attackers. One can imagine the liability and safety problems of physically attacking applicants to see if they could defend themselves.

Because of the difficulty in using simulations to measure these last types of behaviors, physical ability tests are used. Instead of simulating defensive behaviors, tests are developed that measure the basic abilities needed to perform these behaviors. Tests commonly used to measure the abilities needed to perform defensive behaviors include push-ups, sit-ups, and grip strength. Research has shown that there are nine basic physical abilities (Fleishman & Reilly, 1992b):

- dynamic strength (strength requiring repetitions)
- trunk strength (stooping or bending over)
- explosive strength (jumping or throwing objects)
- static strength (strength not requiring repetitions)
- dynamic flexibility (speed of bending, stretching, twisting)
- extent flexibility (degree of bending, stretching, twisting)
- gross body equilibrium (balance)
- gross body coordination (coordination when body is in motion)
- stamina (ability to exert effort over long periods of time)

8. MANUAL SPEED AND DEXTERITY (MSD)

This is a test of Manual Speed and Dexterity. Following is a series of arrows arranged in columns. You are to draw straight vertical lines connecting the tips of the adjacent arrows.

Start each line at the tip of the top arrow and draw to the tip of the bottom arrow. Make sure that you touch both arrow tips without crossing the tips into the shaded area. Start at the top of each column and work down making sure the lines you draw are straight, heavy and dark. Practice on the following examples:

When the signal is given turn the page over and begin. Work as quickly and as accurately as you can. Your score will depend on both speed and accuracy. You will have 5 minutes to complete this section.

DO NOT TURN THIS PAGE UNTIL YOU ARE TOLD TO DO SO.

Source: CAPS, EdiTS, San Diego, California 92107.

Figure 5.6
Psychomotor Ability Test

Because physical ability tests often have adverse impact against women (Courtright, McCormick, Postlethwaite, Reeves, & Mount, 2013; Hough, Oswald, & Ployhart, 2001), they have been criticized on three major points: job relatedness, passing scores, and the time at which they should be required.

Job Relatedness

Though few people would disagree that it is *better* for a police officer to be strong and fit than weak and out of shape, many argue whether it is *necessary* to be physically fit. Critics of physical agility testing cite two reasons for questioning the necessity of physical agility: current out-of-shape police officers and technological alternatives. Currently, many police officers are overweight, slow, and out of shape (according to a report released by the U.S. Federal Bureau of Investigation in 2014, 80% of law enforcement staff are overweight), yet they perform safely and at high levels. Furthermore, there is research to suggest that physical size is not related to police safety (Griffiths & McDaniel, 1993). Thus, critics argue that physical agility is not an essential part of the job. This is especially true due to technological advances in policing. As an example, Sollie and Sollie (1993) presented data showing that the use of pepper spray in Meridian, Mississippi, almost completely reduced the need for officers to physically restrain intoxicated or physically aggressive suspects. However, supporters of physical ability testing cite studies demonstrating significant relationships between isometric strength tests and supervisor ratings of employee physical ability (Blakley, Quiñones, Crawford, & Jago, 1994). Such discrepancies in research findings demonstrate the importance of conducting studies to determine the importance of physical ability for any particular job. Research has shown that physical ability tests not only predict job performance but can result in fewer injuries and lower turnover (Gebhardt & Baker, 2017).

Passing Scores

A second problem with physical ability tests is determining passing scores; that is, how fast must an applicant run or how much weight must be lifted to pass a physical ability test? Passing scores for physical ability tests are set based on one of two types of standards: relative or absolute. Relative standards indicate how well an individual scores compared with others in a group such as women, police applicants, or current police officers. The advantage to using relative standards is that adverse impact is eliminated because people are measured against others in the same group individuals are only compared with people of the same gender. The problem with relative scales, however, is that a female applicant might be strong compared with other women, yet not strong enough to perform the job. Furthermore, relative standards based on protected classes (e.g., sex, race) were made illegal by the 1991 Civil Rights Act (although technically illegal, the Justice Department has not enforced the ban against gender-specific physical standards). In contrast, absolute passing scores are set at the minimum level needed to perform a job. For example, if a police officer needs to be able to drag a 170-pound person from a burning car, 170 pounds becomes the passing score. As one can imagine, the problem comes in determining the minimum amounts. That is, how fast does an officer *need* to run to adequately perform the job? Because people come in all sizes, how many pounds does an officer *need* to be able to drag?

When the Ability Must Be Present

A third problem with physical ability requirements is the point at which the ability must be present. Most police departments require applicants to pass physical ability tests on the same day other tests are being completed. However, the applicant doesn't need the strength or speed until they are actually in the academy or on the job. Furthermore, applicants going through an academy show significant increases in physical ability and fitness by the end of the academy (Henderson, Berry, & Matic, 2007). Showing awareness of this problem, cities such as San Francisco and Philadelphia provide applicants with a list of physical abilities that will be required of them once they arrive at the academy. Applicants are then given suggestions on how they can get themselves into the proper condition. Some cities even hold conditioning programs for applicants! Such policies reduce adverse impact by increasing the ability of women applicants to meet the minimal physical requirements of the job (Gebhardt & Baker, 2017).

5-5 Predicting Performance Using Applicant Skill

Rather than measuring an applicant's current knowledge or potential to perform a job (ability), some selection techniques measure the extent to which an applicant already has a job-related skill. The two most common methods for doing this are the work sample and the assessment center.

Work Samples

With a work sample, the applicant performs actual job-related tasks. For example, an applicant for a job as automotive mechanic might be asked to fix a torn fan belt; a bookkeeper applicant might be asked to balance a ledger; a teacher applicant might be asked to give a lecture; and a truck-driver applicant might be asked to back a truck up to a loading dock.

Work samples are excellent selection tools for several reasons. First, because they are directly related to job tasks, they have excellent content validity. Second, scores from work samples tend to predict actual work performance and thus have excellent criterion validity (Callinan & Robertson, 2001; Roth, Bobko, & McFarland, 2005). Third, because job applicants can see the connection between the job sample and the work performed on the job, the samples have excellent face validity and thus are challenged less often in civil service appeals or in court cases (Whelchel, 1985). Finally, work samples have lower racial differences in test scores than do written cognitive ability tests (Roth, Bobko, McFarland, & Buster, 2008), although the actual extent of the difference is still under debate (Bobko, Roth, & Buster, 2005). The main reason for not using work samples is that they can be expensive to both construct and administer. For this reason, work samples are best used for well-paying jobs for which many employees will be hired.

Assessment Centers

Assessment center A method of selecting employees in which applicants participate in several job-related activities, at least one of which must be a simulation, and are rated by several trained evaluators.

An **assessment center** is a selection technique characterized by the use of multiple assessment methods that allow multiple assessors to actually *observe* applicants perform simulated job tasks (Joiner, 2002). Its major advantages are that assessment methods are all job-related and multiple trained assessors help to guard against many (but not all) types of selection bias. According to the International Task Force on Assessment Center Guidelines (2015), for a selection technique to be considered an assessment center, it must meet the following requirements:

- The assessment center activities must be based on the results of a thorough job analysis.
- Behaviors displayed by participants must be classified into meaningful and relevant categories such as behavioral dimensions, attributes, characteristics, aptitudes, qualities, skills, abilities, competencies, or knowledge.
- Multiple assessment techniques must be used, and the assessments must provide information about the applicant that was determined as being important in the job analysis.
- At least one of the assessment techniques must be a job simulation.
- A dimension-by-exercise matrix must be developed.
- Multiple trained assessors must be used.
- Behavioral observations must be documented at the time the applicant behavior is observed.
- Assessors must prepare a report of their observations.
- The procedures for administering the assessment center must be standardized such that each person going through the assessment center has an equal opportunity to demonstrate their skills.

Although early assessment centers were conducted in person, as with many of the assessment methods discussed in this chapter, most assessment exercises can be administered remotely through **unproctored internet-based testing** (UIT; Arthur & Traylor, 2019). With UIT, test takers have the freedom to select the time, place, and device in which to take the assessment (Arthur, Keiser, & Doverspike, 2018; Arthur & Traylor, 2019).

Development and Components

Although many different techniques may be used in assessment centers, the basic development and types of exercises are fairly standard. The first step in creating an assessment center is, of course, to do a job analysis (Caldwell, Thornton, & Gruys, 2003). From this analysis, exercises are developed that measure different aspects of the job. Common exercises include the in-basket technique, simulations, work samples, leaderless group discussions, structured interviews, personality and ability tests, and business games. Each of these techniques can be used by itself, but only when several are used in combination do they become part of an assessment center. The typical assessment center has four or five exercises, takes two to three days to complete, and costs about $2,000 per applicant. Once the exercises have been developed, assessors are chosen to rate the applicants going through the assessment center. These assessors typically hold positions two levels higher than those being assessed and spend one day being trained (Eurich, Krause, Cigularov, & Thornton, 2009; Spychalski, Quiñones, Gaugler, & Pohley, 1997).

The In-Basket Technique.

The **in-basket technique** is designed to simulate the types of daily information that appear on a manager's or employee's desk. The technique takes its name from the wire baskets typically seen on office desks. Usually these baskets have two levels: the "in" level, which holds paperwork that must be handled, and the "out" level, which contains completed paperwork.

During the assessment center, examples of job-related paperwork are placed in a basket, and the job applicant is asked to go through the basket and respond to the paperwork as if they were actually on the job. Examples of such paperwork might include a phone message from an employee who cannot get their car started and does not know how to get to work or an email from the accounting department stating that an expense voucher is missing.

Unproctored internet-based testing An assessment method that can be taken virtually at any time and place and on the device of the applicant's choosing.

In-basket technique An assessment center exercise designed to simulate the types of information that daily come across a manager's or employee's desk in order to observe the applicant's responses to such information.

The applicant is observed by a group of assessors, who score the applicant on several dimensions, such as the quality of the decision, the manner in which the decision was carried out, and the order in which the applicant handled the paperwork—that is, did they start at the top of the pile or did they start with the most important tasks? Research on the reliability and validity of the in-basket technique provides modest support for its usefulness (Whetzel, Rotenberry, & McDaniel, 2014).

Simulations. Simulation exercises are the real backbone of the assessment center because they enable assessors to observe an applicant "in action." **Simulations**, which can include such diverse activities as role-plays and work samples, place an applicant in a situation that is as similar as possible to one that will be encountered on the job. To be effective, simulations must be based on job-related behaviors and should be reasonably realistic.

A good example of a role-playing simulation is an assessment center used by a large city to hire a new police chief. The job analysis revealed that an important activity for the police chief was to hold press conferences. The assessment center included an exercise in which the candidate was given information about an officer-involved shooting. The candidate was then asked to make a brief statement to the press and answer reporters' questions. The candidate's performance was scored on their presentation skills, the extent to which proper information was included, and the accuracy and appropriateness of the answers to the reporter's questions.

Many simulations can be administered virtually. For example, a company hiring a computer programmer might assign the job applicant to write a program that accomplishes a particular goal; a consulting firm might ask an applicant to analyze a set of data, and a call center might provide an applicant with three simulated calls from a customer and ask them to respond to the calls.

The development and administration of simulation exercises can be expensive and take months to develop (Adler, Boyce, Martin, & Dreibelbis, 2019), but prepackaged exercises can be purchased at a much lower price. Though simulation exercises can be expensive, the cost may be money well spent, as simulations result in lower adverse impact than do traditional paper-and-pencil tests (Schmitt & Mills, 2001). Additionally, high-fidelity and low-fidelity simulations (such as assessment centers and situational judgment tests, respectively) have been shown to have incremental validity over the knowledge test (Lievens & Patterson, 2011).

Work Samples. Usually, when a simulation does not involve a situational exercise, it is called a **work sample**. Work samples were discussed earlier in this section but are listed again here because they are common assessment center exercises.

Leaderless Group Discussions. In this exercise, applicants meet in small groups and are given a job-related problem to solve or a job-related issue to discuss. For example, supervisory applicants might be asked to discuss ways to motivate employees, or resident assistant applicants might be asked to discuss ways to reduce noise in residence halls. No leader is appointed, hence the term "**leaderless group discussion.**" As the applicants discuss the problem or issue, they are individually rated on such dimensions as cooperativeness, leadership, and analytical skills. There are various factors that influence the validity and reliability of leaderless group discussions, including sex, group size, whether candidates have been coached, and the leadership potential of other candidates in the same group (Bass, Klubeck, & Wurster, 1953; Kaess, Witryol, & Nolan, 1961).

Business Simulation Games. **Business simulation games** are exercises that allow the applicant to demonstrate such attributes as creativity, decision making, and ability

Simulations An exercise designed to place an applicant in a situation that is similar to the one that will be encountered on the job.

Work samples A method of selecting employees in which an applicant is asked to perform samples of actual job-related tasks.

Leaderless group discussion A selection technique, usually found in assessment centers, in which applicants meet in small groups and are given a problem to solve or an issue to discuss.

Business simulation games An exercise, usually found in assessment centers, that is designed to simulate the business and marketing activities that take place in an organization.

to work with others. A business game in one assessment center placed computer programming applicants into small groups and asked them to develop a proposal for a new iPhone application. The proposal had to include the target audience, the cost and time needed to create the app, and potential marketing strategies. Unfortunately, there is currently little research on the extent to which scores from these games predict future work performance (Weidner & Short, 2019).

Gamified Assessments. A recent change in the development and administration of assessment center exercises is the **gamification** of such exercises as simulations, work samples, and business simulation games. Gamification is the application of game-like elements such as progress bars, point scoring, and competition with others to traditional assessments (Weidner & Short, 2019). In addition to making it more interesting to take an assessment, gamification allows for the collection of detailed data on an applicant's physical, perceptual, and cognitive skills as well as elements of the applicant's personality. In addition to the gamification of traditional assessments, data from recreational games While this is a relatively novel development and requires further investigation, emerging research has shown promising results in establishing construct validity of gamified assessments (Georgiou, Gouras, & Nikolaou, 2019) has been used to measure a person's personality and values (Weidner & Short, 2019).

Gamification The application of game-like elements to traditional assessments.

Evaluation of Assessment Centers

Research indicates that assessment centers have been successful in predicting a wide range of employee behavior (Arthur, Day, McNelly, & Edens, 2003; Gaugler, Rosenthal, Thornton, & Bentson, 1987; Hermelin, Lievens, & Robertson, 2007). Though assessment center scores are good predictors of performance, it has been argued that other methods can predict the same criteria better and less expensively than assessment centers (Schmidt & Hunter, 1998). Thus, even though an assessment center may be excellent in predicting certain aspects of employee behavior, other, less expensive methods may be as good if not better. Furthermore, there is some question regarding the ability of an assessment center developed at one location to predict performance in similar jobs at other locations (Schmitt, Schneider, & Cohen, 1990).

Though assessment centers were once thought to result in low levels of adverse impact, meta-analysis results (Dean, Roth, & Bobko, 2008) indicate that Black individuals score substantially lower ($d = .52$) and Hispanic individuals slightly lower ($d = .28$) on assessment centers than do White individuals. Women score slightly higher than men ($d = .19$).

5-6 Predicting Performance Using Prior Experience

Applicant experience is typically measured in one of four ways: experience ratings of application/résumé information, biodata, reference checks, and interviews. Because interviews were discussed extensively in Chapter 4 and reference checking was discussed earlier in this chapter, only experience ratings and biodata will be discussed here.

Experience Ratings

The basis for experience ratings is the idea that past experiences will predict future experience. As intuitive as this idea may be, meta-analytic results indicate that prior experience is a weak predictor of future work performance, training performance, and turnover (Van Iddekinge, Arnold, Frieder, & Roth, 2019). In giving credit for experience, one must consider the amount of experience, the level of performance demonstrated during the previous experience, and how related the experience is to the current job. That is, experience by itself is not enough. Having 10 years of low-quality unrelated experience is not the same as 10 years of high-quality related experience. Sullivan (2000) suggests that there be a cap on credit for experience (e.g., no credit for more than five years of experience) because knowledge obtained through experience has a shelf life, and paying for experience is expensive. For example, given the rapid changes in technology, would a computer programmer with 20 years of experience actually have more relevant knowledge than one with 5 years of experience?

Biodata

Biodata A method of selection involving application blanks that contain questions that research has shown will predict job performance.

Biodata is a selection method that considers an applicant's life, school, military, community, and work experience. Meta-analyses have shown that biodata is a good predictor of job performance, as well as the best predictor of future employee tenure (Beall, 1991; Schmidt & Hunter, 1998). Biodata has also been successful in predicting student academic performance and student activity accomplishments (Zhang & Kuncel, 2020).

In a nutshell, a biodata instrument is an application blank or questionnaire containing questions that research has shown measure the difference between successful and unsuccessful performers on a job. Each question receives a weight that indicates how well it differentiates poor from good performers. The better the differentiation, the higher the weight. Biodata instruments have several advantages:

- Research has shown that they can predict work behavior in many jobs, including sales, management, clerical, mental health counseling, hourly work in processing plants, grocery clerking, fast-food work, and supervising.
- They have been able to predict criteria as varied as supervisor ratings, absenteeism, accidents, employee theft, loan defaults, sales, and tenure.
- Biodata instruments result in higher organizational profit and growth (Terpstra & Rozell, 1993).
- Biodata instruments are easy to use, quickly administered, inexpensive, and not as subject to individual bias as interviews, references, and résumé evaluation.

Development of a Biodata Instrument

File approach The gathering of biodata from employee files rather than by questionnaire.

In the first step, information about employees is obtained in one of two ways: the file approach or the questionnaire approach. With the **file approach**, we obtain information from personnel files on employees' previous employment, education, interests, and demographics. As mentioned in the discussion of archival research in Chapter 1, the major disadvantage of the file approach is that information is often missing or incomplete.

Questionnaire approach The method of obtaining biodata from questionnaires rather than from employee files.

Second, we can create a biographical questionnaire that is administered to all employees and applicants. An example is shown in Figure 5.7. The major drawback to the **questionnaire approach** is that information cannot be obtained from employees who have quit or have been fired.

After the necessary information has been obtained, an appropriate criterion is chosen. As will be discussed in detail in Chapter 7, a criterion is a measure of work behavior such as quantity, absenteeism, or tenure. It is essential that a chosen criterion be relevant, reliable, and fairly objective. To give an example of developing a biodata instrument with a poor criterion, I was once asked to help reduce absenteeism in an

Figure 5.7
Biodata Questionnaire

1. Member of high school student government?
   ☐ No   ☐ Yes

2. Number of jobs in past 5 years?
   ☐ 1   ☐ 2   ☐ 3–5   ☐ More than 5

3. Length of time at present address?
   ☐ Less than 1 year   ☐ 1–3 years
   ☐ 4–5 years   ☐ More than 5 years

4. Transportation to work:
   ☐ Walk   ☐ Bike   ☐ Own car
   ☐ Bus   ☐ Ride with a friend   ☐ Other

5. Education:
   ☐ Some high school
   ☐ High school diploma or GED
   ☐ Some college
   ☐ Associate's degree
   ☐ Bachelor's degree
   ☐ Master's degree
   ☐ Doctoral degree

organization by selecting applicants who had a high probability of superior future attendance. When initial data were gathered, it was realized that absenteeism was not an actual problem for this company. Less than half of the workforce had missed more than one day in six months; but the company perceived a problem because a few key workers had missed many days of work. Thus, using biodata (or any other selection device) to predict a nonrelevant criterion would not have saved the organization any money.

Criterion groups Division of employees into groups based on high and low scores on a particular criterion.

Once a criterion has been chosen, employees are split into two **criterion groups** based on their criterion scores. For example, if tenure is selected as the criterion measure, employees who have worked for the company for at least one year might be placed in the "long tenure" group, whereas workers who quit or were fired in less than one year would be placed in the "short tenure" group. If enough employees are available, the upper and lower 27% of performers can be used to establish the two groups (Hogan, 1994).

Vertical percentage method For scoring biodata in which the percentage of unsuccessful employees responding in a particular way is subtracted from the percentage of successful employees responding in the same way.

Once employee data have been obtained and the criterion and criterion groups chosen, each piece of employee information is compared with criterion group membership. The purpose of this stage is to determine which pieces of information will distinguish the members of the high criterion group from those in the low criterion group. Traditionally, the **vertical percentage method** has been used to do this. Percentages are calculated for each group on each item. The percentage of a particular response for the low group is subtracted from the percentage of the same response in the high group to obtain a weight for that item. An example of this weighting process is shown in Table 5.1. It is important to ensure that the weights make rational sense. Items that make sense are more face valid and thus easier to defend in court than items that are empirically valid but don't make rational sense (Stokes & Toth, 1996).

Table 5.1 Biodata Weighting Process

Variable	Long Tenure (%)	Short Tenure (%)	Differences in Percentages	Unit Weight
Education				
High school	40	80	−40	−1
Bachelor's	59	15	+44	+1
Master's	1	5	−4	0

Once weights have been assigned to the items, the information is weighted and then summed to form a composite score for each employee. Composite scores are then correlated with the criterion to determine whether the newly created biodata instrument will significantly predict the criterion. Although this procedure sounds complicated, it actually is fairly easy, although time-consuming.

A problem with creating a biodata instrument is *sample size.* To create a reliable and valid biodata instrument, it is desirable to have data from thousands of employees. For most organizations, however, such large sample sizes are difficult if not impossible to obtain. In creating a biodata instrument with a small sample, the risk of using items that do not really predict the criterion increases. This issue is important because most industrial psychologists advise that employees should be split into two samples when a biodata instrument is created: One sample, the **derivation sample**, is used to form the weights; the other sample, the **hold-out sample**, is used to double-check the selected items and weights. Although this sample splitting sounds like a great idea, it may not be practical when dealing with a small or moderate sample size.

Research by Schmitt, Coyle, and Rauschenberger (1977) suggests that there is less chance of error when a sample is not split. Discussion on whether to split samples is bound to continue in the years ahead, but the majority opinion of I/O psychologists is that a hold-out sample should be used.

A final issue to consider is the sample used to create the biodata instrument. Responses of current employees can be used to select the items and create the weights that will be applied to applicants. Stokes, Hogan, and Snell (1993) found that incumbents and applicants respond in very different ways, indicating that the use of incumbents to create and scale items may reduce validity.

Derivation sample A group of employees who were used in creating the initial weights for a biodata instrument.

Hold-out sample A group of employees who are not used in creating the initial weights for a biodata instrument but instead are used to double-check the accuracy of the initial weights.

Criticisms of Biodata

Even though biodata does a good job of predicting future employee behavior, it has been criticized on two major points. The first holds that the validity of biodata may not be stable—that is, its ability to predict employee behavior decreases with time. For example, Wernimont (1962) found that only three questions retained their predictive validity over the five-year period from 1954 to 1959. Similar results were reported by Hughes, Dunn, and Baxter (1956).

Other research (Brown, 1978), however, suggests that declines in validity found in earlier studies may have resulted from small samples in the initial development of the biodata instrument. Brown used data from more than 10,000 life insurance agents to develop his biodata instrument, but data from only 85 agents were used to develop the biodata instrument that was earlier criticized by Wernimont (1962). Brown compared the validity of his original sample (1933) with those from samples taken 6 years later (1939) and 38 years later (1971). The results indicated that the same items that significantly predicted the criterion in 1933 predicted at similar levels in 1971.

A study of the use of a biodata instrument created in one organization and used in 24 others found that the validity generalized across all organizations (Carlson, Scullen, Schmidt, Rothstein, & Erwin, 1999). Thus, biodata may be more stable across time and locations than was earlier thought (Rothstein, Schmidt, Erwin, Owens, & Sparks, 1990; Schmidt & Rothstein, 1994).

The second criticism is that some biodata items may not meet the legal requirements stated in the federal *Uniform Guidelines*, which establish fair hiring methods. Of greater concern is that certain biodata items might result in adverse impact. For example, consider the biodata item "distance from work." Applicants who live close to work might get more points than applicants who live farther away. The item may result in adverse impact if the organization is located in an area where the population predominantly consists of White individuals. However, if the item predicts such employee behaviors as tenure or absenteeism, it would not be illegal. If an item resulting in adverse impact can be removed without reducing the validity of the biodata questionnaire, it should probably not be retained.

To make biodata instruments less disagreeable to critics, Gandy and Dye (1989) developed four standards to consider for each potential item:

1. The item must deal with events under a person's control (e.g., a person would have no control over birth order but would have control over the number of speeding tickets they received).
2. The item must be job-related.
3. The answer to the item must be verifiable (e.g., a question about how many jobs an applicant has had is verifiable, but a question about the applicant's favorite type of book is not).
4. The item must not invade an applicant's privacy (asking why an applicant quit a job is permissible; asking about an applicant's sex life is not).

Even though these four standards eliminated many potential items, Gandy and Dye (1989) still obtained a validity coefficient of .33. Just as impressive as the high validity coefficient was that the biodata instrument showed good prediction for Black, White, and Hispanic individuals.

The third criticism is that biodata can be faked, a charge that has been made against every selection method except work samples and ability tests. Research indicates that applicants do in fact respond to items in socially desirable ways (Stokes et al., 1993). To reduce faking, several steps can be taken, including:

- warning applicants of the presence of a lie scale (Kluger & Colella, 1993);
- using objective, verifiable items (Becker & Colquitt, 1992; Shaffer, Saunders, & Owens, 1986); and
- asking applicants to elaborate on their answers or to provide examples (Schmitt & Kunce, 2002). For example, if the biodata question asked, "How many leadership positions did you have in high school?," the next part of the item would be, "List the position titles and dates of those leadership positions."

By including bogus items—items that include an experience that does not actually exist (e.g., Conducted a Feldspar analysis to analyze data)—attempts to fake biodata can be detected (Kim, 2008). When including bogus items in a biodata instrument, it is important that the items be carefully researched to ensure that they don't represent activities that might actually exist (Levashina, Morgeson, & Campion, 2008). For example, a bogus item of, "Have you ever conducted a Paradox analysis of a computer system?," might be interpreted by an applicant as, "Have you ever used the actual computer program, Paradox?"

A study by Ramsay, Kim, Oswald, Schmitt, and Gillespie (2008) provides an excellent example of how endorsing a bogus item might be due more to confusion than to actual lying. In their study, Ramsay et al. found that only 3 out of 361 subjects said they had operated a rhetaguard (this machine doesn't exist), yet 151 of the 361 said they had resolved disputes by isometric analysis. Why the difference? It may be that most people know the word *isometric* and most people have resolved disputes. They may not be sure if they ever used an isometric analysis to resolve their dispute, so many indicated that they had. With the rhetaguard, no applicant would have heard of it so they were probably sure they had not used it. Not surprisingly, using job performance as a criterion, items on a biodata questionnaire that are verifiable have been shown to have higher validity than items that are not verifiable (Harold, McFarland, & Weekley, 2006).

Interestingly, bright applicants tend not to fake biodata items as often as applicants lower in cognitive ability. But when they do choose to fake, they are better at doing it (Levashina et al., 2008). Not surprisingly, applicants who fake biodata instruments are also likely to fake personality inventories and integrity tests (Carroll, 2008).

5-7 Predicting Performance Using Personality, Interest, and Character

Personality Inventories

Personality inventory A psychological assessment designed to measure various aspects of an applicant's personality.

Although an applicant's personality can be measured by several of the selection methods discussed in this chapter (e.g., biodata, interviews, situational judgement tests, assessment centers), **personality inventories** are the most common (Hough & Dilchert, 2017). Personality inventories are becoming increasingly popular as an employee selection method, in part because they predict performance better than was once thought, and in part because they result in less adverse impact than do ability tests. Research indicates that personality inventories predict a wide variety of work behaviors and attitudes such as performance, job satisfaction, unsafe behavior, customer service, organizational citizenship behaviors, and counterproductive work behavior (Hough & Dilchert, 2017).

Personality inventories fall into one of two categories based on their intended purpose: measurement of types of normal personality or measurement of psychopathology. Although these two categories were once considered to be distinct, recently there has been considerable discussion that the line between the two might not be as bright as once thought (Melson-Silimon, Harris, Shoenfelt, Miller, & Carter, 2019).

Tests of Normal Personality

Tests of normal personality measure the traits exhibited by normal individuals in everyday life. Examples of such traits are extraversion, shyness, assertiveness, and friendliness.

Determination of the number and type of personality dimensions measured by an inventory can usually be (1) based on a theory, (2) statistically based, or (3) empirically based. The number of dimensions in a *theory-based* test is identical to the number postulated by a well-known theorist. For example, the Myers-Briggs Type Indicator has four scales and is based on the personality theory of Carl Jung, whereas the

Edwards Personal Preference Schedule, with 15 dimensions, is based on a theory by Henry Murray. The number of dimensions in a *statistically based* test is determined through a statistical process called factor analysis. The most well-known test of this type, the 16PF (Personality Factor) test, was created by Raymond Cattell and, as its name implies, contains 16 dimensions. The number and location of dimensions under which items fall in an *empirically based* test is determined by grouping answers given by people known to possess a certain characteristic. For example, in developing the **Minnesota Multiphasic Personality Inventory—2 (MMPI-2)**, hundreds of items were administered to groups of psychologically healthy people and to people known to have certain psychological conditions such as paranoia. Items that were endorsed more often by patients diagnosed with paranoia than healthy individuals were keyed under the paranoia dimension of the MMPI-2.

Minnesota Multiphasic Personality Inventory-2 (MMPI-2) The most widely used objective test of psychopathology.

Although there are hundreds of personality inventories that measure hundreds of traits, there is general agreement that most personality traits can be placed into one of five broad personality dimensions. Popularly known as the "Big Five," or the *five-factor model*, these dimensions are

- openness to experience (bright, inquisitive);
- conscientiousness (reliable, dependable);
- extraversion (outgoing, friendly);
- agreeableness (works well with others, a team player); and
- emotional stability (not anxious, tense).

In recent years there has been considerable discussion whether these five factors are too broad, and that individual sub-dimensions within the five broad factors might be better predictors of employee behavior than the broad factors themselves. Researchers have proposed that there are either six (Costa & McCrae, 1992) or two (DeYoung, Quilty, & Peterson, 2007) subfactors for each of the Big Five factors. As an example, let's look at the Big Five factor of extraversion. The two subfactor model postulates that extraversion consists of two main subfactors: enthusiasm and assertiveness. The six subfactor model postulates that there are six main subfactors: gregariousness, warmth, positive emotions, excitement-seeking, activity, and assertiveness.

To test whether the number of subfactors really matters, Judge, Rodell, Klinger, Simon, and Crawford (2013) conducted a meta-analysis and found that a combination of the six individual subfactors, used separately, was a better predictor of employee behavior than when the individual subfactors are simply added to form the broad factor.

Examples of common measures of normal personality used in employee selection include the Hogan Personality Inventory, the California Psychological Inventory, the NEO-PI (Neuroticism Extraversion Openness Personality Inventory), Employee Personality Profile and the 16PF.

That objective personality inventories are useful in predicting performance in the United States and Europe is indicated in meta-analyses by Tett, Jackson, and Rothstein (1991); Barrick and Mount (1991); Tett, Jackson, Rothstein, and Reddon (1994); Salgado (1997); Hurtz and Donovan (2000); and Judge et al. (2013). Though there is some disagreement across the various meta-analyses, probably the best interpretation is that:

- personality can predict performance at low but statistically significant levels;
- personality inventories can add incremental validity to the use of other selection tests;
- conscientiousness is the best predictor in most occupations and for most criteria; and

- the validity of the other four personality dimensions is dependent on the type of job and criterion for which the test is being validated. For example, a meta-analysis of predictors of police performance found that openness was the best personality predictor of academy performance; conscientiousness was the best predictor of supervisor ratings of performance; and emotional stability was the best predictor of disciplinary problems (Aamodt, 2004). In contrast, a meta-analysis of predictors of sales performance found that conscientiousness was the best predictor of both supervisor ratings and actual sales performance (Vinchur et al., 1998).

One of the concerns about using personality inventories for employee selection is that, because they are self-reports, they are relatively easy to fake. Research indicates that applicants can fake personality inventories but do so less often than thought. When they do fake, it has minimal effect on the validity of the test results (Morgeson et al., 2007).

Because people often act differently at work than they do in other contexts, it has been suggested that personality inventories ask the applicant about their work personalities rather than their personality in general. A meta-analysis by Shaffer and Postlethwaite (2012) found that the validity of personality inventories asking about work personality was higher than that of the personality inventories asking about personality in general.

In recent years, there has been considerable interest in investigating the relationship between certain "aberrant" personality types and employee behavior. Aberrant personality types are "peculiarities that do not necessarily lead to a clinically impaired function (like personality disorders), but that may affect daily functioning (at work) in such ways that they deserve further attention" (Wille, De Fruyt, & De Clercq, 2013). Three such aberrant types, referred to as the "Dark Triad," are Machiavellianism, narcissism, and psychopathy (Paulhus & Williams, 2002). Employees with these traits tend to be manipulative, self-centered, and lack concern for others' well-being.

The results of a meta-analysis by O'Boyle, Forsyth, Banks, and McDaniel (2012) found that employees scoring high in Machiavellianism or narcissism were more likely to engage in counterproductive work behaviors than were employees scoring low on these traits. The correlations between the Dark Triad and job performance were very small as was the correlation between psychopathy and counterproductive work behaviors. Other aberrant personality types such as borderline, schizotypal, obsessive-compulsive, and avoidant have been negatively linked to various aspects of career success whereas antisocial and narcissistic personalities have actually been positively linked to certain aspects of career success (Wille et al., 2013).

Tests of Psychopathology

Tests of psychopathology determine whether individuals have serious psychological problems such as depression, bipolar disorder, and schizophrenia. Though used extensively by clinical psychologists, these tests are seldom used by I/O psychologists except in the selection of law enforcement officers. Because the courts consider tests of psychopathology to be "medical exams," they can be administered only after a conditional offer of employment has been made to an applicant.

Tests of psychopathology are generally scored in one of two ways: objectively or projectively. **Projective tests** provide the respondent with unstructured tasks such as describing ink blots and drawing pictures. Common tests in this category also include the **Rorschach Inkblot Test** and the **Thematic Apperception Test (TAT)**. Because projective tests are of questionable reliability and validity (Lilienfeld, Wood, & Garb,

Projective tests A subjective test in which a subject is asked to perform relatively unstructured tasks, such as drawing pictures, and in which a psychologist analyzes their responses.

Rorschach Inkblot Test A projective personality test.

Thematic Apperception Test (TAT) A projective personality test in which test-takers are shown pictures and asked to tell stories. It is designed to measure various need levels.

2001), and are time-consuming and expensive, they are rarely used in employee selection. However, an interesting review of the projective testing literature, Carter, Daniels, and Zickar (2013) concluded that I/O psychologists may have been too quick in giving up on projective tests and that further research should continue.

Objective tests are structured so that the respondent is limited to a few answers that will be scored by standardized keys. By far the most popular and heavily studied test of this type is the MMPI (MMPI, MMPI-2, MMPI-3). Other tests in this category are the Millon Clinical Multiaxial Inventory (MCMI-III) and the Personality Assessment Inventory (PAI).

As mentioned previously, although personality tests and tests of psychopathology were once thought to be very different types of tests, more recent research suggests that the Big Five dimensions and the dark triad are correlated with measures of several personality disorders (Melson-Silimon et al., 2019). Thus, some practitioners are concerned that using personality tests as part of the employee selection process might violate the Americans with Disabilities Act (ADA) though others believe that such a concern is exaggerated (Dilchert, Ones, & Krueger, 2019; Gonzalez, Capman, Martin, Johnson, Theys, & Boyce, 2019).

Interest Inventories

As the name implies, these tests are designed to tap vocational interests. The most commonly used **interest inventory** is the **Strong Interest Inventory (SII)**, which asks individuals to indicate whether they like or dislike 291 items such as bargaining, repairing electrical wiring, and taking responsibility. The answers to these questions provide a profile that shows how similar a person is to people already employed in 130 occupations that have been classified into 30 basic interest scales and 6 general occupational themes. The theory behind these tests is that an individual with interests similar to those of people in a particular field will more likely be satisfied in that field than in a field composed of people whose interests are dissimilar. However, the use of the Strong Interest Inventory has been criticized as some researchers have found the presence of adverse impact amongst genders and race (Einarsdóttir & Rounds, 2009; Carter & Swanson, 1990). Other popular interest inventories include the Minnesota Vocational Interest Inventory, the Occupational Preference Inventory, the Kuder Occupational Interest Survey, the Kuder Preference Record, and the California Occupational Preference System.

The relationship between scores on interest inventories can be complex. An early meta-analyses investigating the relationships between scores on individual interest dimensions and job performance concluded that the relationship between interest inventory scores and employee performance is minimal (Schmidt & Hunter, 1998). Two subsequent meta-analyses, however, found that the relationship between scores on individual interest scales and performance was moderate (Nye, Su, Rounds, & Drasgow, 2012; Van Iddekinge, Roth, Putka, & Lanivich, 2011). However, a meta-analysis investigating whether employees' interests matched those of their jobs found that employees whose interests matched the nature of their jobs were more satisfied with their jobs and performed at higher levels than did employees whose interests did not match the nature of their jobs (Morris & Campion, 2003; Nye, Su, Rounds, & Drasgow, 2017).

Interest inventories are useful in **vocational counseling** (helping people find the careers for which they are best suited). Conducted properly, vocational counseling uses a battery of tests that, at a minimum, should include an interest inventory and a series of ability tests. The interest inventory scores suggest careers for which the individual's interests are compatible; the ability tests will tell them if they have the necessary abilities to enter those careers. If interest scores are high in a particular occupational

Objective tests A type of personality test that is structured to limit the respondent to a few answers that will be scored by standardized keys.

Interest inventory A psychological test designed to identify vocational areas in which an individual might be interested.

Strong Interest Inventory (SII) A popular interest inventory used to help people choose careers.

Vocational counseling The process of helping an individual choose and prepare for the most suitable career.

area but ability scores are low, the individual is advised about the type of training that would best prepare them for a career in that particular area.

Integrity Tests

Integrity tests (also called *honesty tests*) tell an employer the probability that an applicant would steal money, time, or merchandise. Approximately 19% of employers use integrity tests to select employees for at least some jobs (Seitz, 2004). Such extensive use seems justified by a 2013 survey by Kessler International that found that 37.5% of employees admitted to stealing from their employer. One study estimates that 50% of employees with access to cash steal from their employers (Wimbush & Dalton, 1997). The 2011 National Retail Security Survey found that 44% of retail shrinkage is due to employee theft, 36% to shoplifting, and 20% to administrative error or vendor fraud. According to the 25th Annual Retail Theft Survey, 1 in every 40 retail employees is apprehended for theft by their employer (Jack L. Hayes International, 2013). With increases in employee theft and identify theft, it is not surprising that integrity tests are commonly used.

Prior to the 1990s, employers used both electronic and paper-and-pencil integrity tests to screen applicants. In 1988, however, the U.S. Congress passed the Employee Polygraph Protection Act making general use of electronic integrity tests, such as the **polygraph** and the **voice stress analyzer**, illegal for employee selection purposes except in a few situations involving law enforcement agencies and national security.

The law did, however, allow the use of paper-and-pencil integrity tests, which are either (1) overt or (2) personality-based. **Overt integrity tests** are based on the premise that a person's attitudes about theft as well as their previous theft behavior will accurately predict their future honesty. They measure attitudes by asking the test taker to estimate the frequency of theft in society, how harsh penalties against thieves should be, how easy it is to steal, how often they have personally been tempted to steal, how often their friends have stolen, and how often they personally have stolen. **Personality-based integrity tests** are more general in that they tap a variety of personality traits (e.g., conscientiousness, risk taking) thought to be related to a wide range of counterproductive behavior such as theft, absenteeism, and violence. For example, researchers have identified the use of moral character as an indication of how likely a potential employee will commit delinquent behavior such as theft in the workplace (Cohen, Panter, Turan, Morse, & Kim, 2014). A meta-analysis found that personality-based tests have slightly higher validity coefficients than do overt integrity tests (Van Iddekinge, Roth, Raymark, & Odle-Dusseau et al., 2012).

There is general agreement among testing experts that integrity tests predict a variety of employee behaviors including work performance, counterproductive work behavior, training performance, and absenteeism (Ones et al., 1993; Van Iddekinge et al., 2012). Furthermore, integrity tests tend to result in low levels of adverse impact against underrepresented groups (Ones & Viswesvaran, 1998). Where experts disagree, is *how well* integrity tests predict these various employee behaviors (Sackett & Schmitt, 2012). The earlier meta-analysis by Ones et al. (1993) found much higher validity coefficients than did the more recent meta-analysis by Van Iddekinge et al. (2012).

The difference in the findings of the two meta-analyses is probably explained by the criteria used to determine which studies to include. Van Iddekinge and his colleagues only included studies that predicted *individual employee behavior*, whereas Ones and her colleagues included studies validating integrity tests against such criteria as polygraph results, self-admissions of theft, shrinkage (the amounts of goods lost by a store), and known groups (e.g., *priests* vs. *convicts*). Unfortunately, few studies have attempted to correlate test scores with actual theft.

Unfortunately, all of these measures have problems. If polygraph results are used, the researcher is essentially comparing integrity test scores with the scores of a test—the polygraph—that has been made illegal for most employment purposes partly because of questions about its accuracy. If self-admissions are used, the researcher is relying on dishonest people to be honest about their criminal history. If **shrinkage** is used, the researcher does not know which of the employees is responsible for the theft or, for that matter, what percentage of the shrinkage can be attributed to employee theft as opposed to customer theft or incidental breakage. Even if actual employee theft is used, the test may predict only employees who *get caught* stealing, as opposed to those who steal and do not get caught. The problems with known-group comparisons will be discussed in great detail in Chapter 6.

Predicting actual theft from an integrity test can be difficult because not all theft is caused by a *personal tendency* to steal (Bassett, 2008). Normally honest people might steal from an employer due to *economic pressure* caused by factors such as high debts or financial emergencies or by an organizational culture in which it is considered *normal to steal* (e.g., "It's OK because everyone takes food home with them"). Employee theft can also be the result of a *reaction to organizational policy* such as layoffs or a change in rules that employees perceive as unfair. To reduce theft caused by situational factors, nontesting methods such as increased security, explicit policy, and availability of appeal and suggestion systems are needed.

Although integrity tests are inexpensive and may be useful in predicting a wide variety of employee behaviors, they also have serious drawbacks. The most important disadvantage might be that men have higher failure rates than do women and younger people have higher failure rates than do older people. Adverse impact on these two groups pose little legal threat. However, telling the parents of a 17-year-old that their teen has just failed an honesty test is not the best way to foster good public relations. Failing an integrity test has a much more deleterious psychological impact than failing a spatial relations test. Another drawback to integrity tests is that, not surprisingly, applicants don't think highly of them (Anderson, Salgado, & Hülsheger, 2010).

Conditional Reasoning Tests

A problem with self-report measures such as personality inventories and integrity tests is that applicants may not provide accurate responses. This inaccuracy could be due to either the applicant *faking* responses to appear to be honest or to have a "better" personality or the applicant not actually being *aware* of their own personality or values. **Conditional reasoning tests** were initially developed by James (1998) to reduce these inaccurate responses and get a more accurate picture of a person's tendency to engage in aggressive or counterproductive behavior.

Conditional reasoning tests provide test takers with a series of statements and then ask the respondent to select the reason that best justifies or explains each of the statements. The type of reason selected by the individual is thought to indicate their aggressive biases or beliefs. Aggressive individuals tend to believe (LeBreton, Barksdale, Robin, & James, 2007) that:

- most people have harmful intentions behind their behavior (hostile attribution bias);
- it is important to show strength or dominance in social interactions (potency bias);
- it is important to retaliate when wronged rather than try to maintain a relationship (retribution bias);
- powerful people will victimize less powerful individuals (victimization bias);

Shrinkage The amount of goods lost by an organization as a result of theft, breakage, or other loss.

Conditional reasoning tests Test designed to reduce faking by asking test-takers to select the reason that best explains a statement.

- evil people deserve to have bad things happen to them (derogation of target bias); and
- social customs restrict free will and should be ignored (social discounting bias).

As a result of these biases, aggressive individuals will answer conditional reasoning questions differently than less aggressive individuals. For example, a test taker might be given the following statement, "A senior employee asks a new employee if they would like to go to lunch." The test taker would then be asked to select which of the following statements best explains why the senior employee asked the new employee to lunch: (a) The senior employee was trying to make the new employee feel more comfortable or (b) the senior employee was trying to get the new employee on their side before the other employees had a chance to do the same thing. Selecting the first option would suggest an altruistic tendency whereas selecting the second option represents hostile attribution bias and would suggest a more aggressive tendency.

A meta-analysis by Berry, Sackett, and Tobares (2010) indicates that conditional reasoning tests of aggression predict counterproductive behaviors ($r = .16$) and job performance ($r = .14$) at statistically significant yet low levels. Even more promising is that conditional reasoning tests are more difficult to fake than are integrity tests (LeBreton et al., 2007).

Though more research is needed, a study by Bing, Stewart, Davison, Green, McIntyre, and James (2007) found that counterproductive behavior is best predicted when conditional reasoning tests (implicit aggression) are combined with self-reports of aggressive tendencies (explicit aggression). That is, people who hold the six beliefs discussed previously and report that they have aggressive personalities tend to engage in counterproductive behavior to a much greater extent than those who score highly in only implicit or explicit aggression.

Credit History

According to a 2019 survey by HireRight, 25% of employers conduct credit checks for at least some jobs. These credit checks are conducted for two reasons: (1) Employers believe that people who owe money might be more likely to steal or accept bribes, and (2) employees with good credit are more responsible and conscientious and thus will be better employees. On the basis of limited research, it appears that the use of credit histories may result in adverse impact against Latinx and Black applicants as well as low validity coefficients in predicting supervisor ratings ($r = .15$) and discipline problems ($r = .10$; Aamodt, 2014). Further research on organizations that use credit checks have uncovered a process called "moral storytelling" (Kiviat, 2019). In this process, employers either infer or contact the applicant in question with queries about their credit history to gain an understanding of whether any credit problems were a result of personal decisions, or life situations that were unavoidable. Such delineation can point to whether a potential employee was acting in bad faith and might continue to do so in the workplace, or if they could be expected to act differently based on a different situation.

Employers who use an external consumer reporting agency to obtain a person's credit history are subject to the **Fair Credit Reporting Act (FCRA)**. FCRA requires employers to (Guerin & Barreiro, 2019):

- Notify an applicant or employee that they are requesting a credit history.
- Get the applicant's or employee's permission to obtain the credit history.
- Notify the applicant or employee that it will be taking an adverse action against the applicant or employee based upon the credit history.
- Allow the person to challenge the finding.

Fair Credit Reporting Act (FCRA) A federal law that provides people with certain rights regarding the collection and use of credit history reports.

In addition to FCA, several states and localities have enacted legislation limiting the use of credit histories for employment purposes and the U.S. Congress is considering doing the same.

Criminal History

According to the same 2019 survey by HireRight mentioned previously, 93% of organizations check an applicant's criminal history for at least some jobs. If an organization is going to consider an applicant's criminal history, it first needs to determine the extent to which a prior criminal conviction is related to the job being applied for. That is, a prior conviction for theft might be relevant for a job as a bank teller but might not be relevant for a job as an assembler.

Exclusionary period The amount of time that must pass since conviction or release from prison before the conviction is no longer considered as being relevant to the hiring decision.

If an applicant's prior criminal history is not related to the job in question, the employer cannot consider it as part of the hiring process. If it is, the employer must determine an **exclusionary period**, the amount of time that must pass since conviction or release from prison before the conviction is no longer considered. The more serious the crime, the longer the exclusionary period will be. For certain crimes and jobs, there may not be an exclusionary period. For example, a person convicted of sexually abusing children will likely never be hired by a school system. Most exclusionary periods will be from one to eight years, with the longer exclusionary periods for felonies and the shorter exclusionary periods for misdemeanors. The U.S. Equal Employment Opportunity Commission has also released clear guidelines about using criminal history in the hiring process as it pertains to Title VII. Employers must be cautious about using this method as it has been determined to be a factor in hiring decisions and might lead to adverse impact. Research has shown that employers are one-half to one-third less likely to consider an applicant with a criminal background, and at the time that the research was conducted, that nearly 10 % of Black men between 25 and 29 are incarcerated (Pager 2003).

The best practices for a criminal history policy include:

- Do not have a policy that the organization will never hire applicants with criminal records;
- Consider only convictions, not arrests;
- Don't ask about an applicant's criminal history until after a conditional offer of hire; and
- As mentioned previously, only consider an applicant's criminal history if it is relevant to the job in question.

Graphology

Graphology Also called handwriting analysis, a method of measuring personality by looking at the way in which a person writes.

An interesting method to select employees is handwriting analysis, or **graphology**. The idea behind handwriting analysis is that the way people write reveals their personality, which in turn should indicate work performance. Contrary to popular belief, graphology is not a commonly used selection method in Europe (Bangerter, König, Blatti, & Salvisberg, 2009) and European employees react as poorly to it as do their American counterparts (Anderson & Witvliet, 2008).

To analyze a person's handwriting, a graphologist looks at the size, slant, width, regularity, and pressure of a writing sample. From these writing characteristics, information about temperament and mental, social, work, and moral traits is obtained.

Research on graphology has revealed interesting findings. First, graphologists are consistent in their judgments about script features but not in their interpretation about what these features mean (Driver, Buckley, & Frink, 1996). Second, trained graphologists are no more accurate or reliable at interpreting handwriting samples than are untrained undergraduates (Rafaeli & Klimoski, 1983) or psychologists (Ben-Shakhar, Bar-Hillel, Bilu, Ben-Abba, & Flug, 1986). Most importantly, the small body of scientific literature on the topic concludes that graphology is not a useful technique in employee selection (Simner & Goffin, 2003). Graphology predicts best when the writing sample is autobiographical (the applicants write an essay about themselves), which means that graphologists are making their predictions more on the *content* of the writing than on the quality of the *handwriting* (Simner & Goffin, 2003).

5-8 Predicting Performance Limitations Due to Medical and Psychological Problems

As mentioned in Chapter 3, the Americans with Disabilities Act (ADA) limits the consideration of medical and psychological problems to those that keep the employee from performing essential job functions.

Drug Testing

Drug testing Tests that indicate whether an applicant has recently used a drug.

Drug testing certainly is one of the most controversial testing methods used by HR professionals. The reason for its high usage is that, according to the 2019 National Survey on Drug Use and Health, 20.8% of people in the United States admit to using illicit drugs in the past year and HR professionals believe not only that illegal drug use is dangerous but also that many employees are under the influence of drugs at work. Their beliefs are supported by research indicating that compared with non–drug users, illegal drug users are more likely to miss work (Bahls, 1998; Larson et al., 2007; Normand, Salyards, & Mahoney, 1990), are 16 times as likely to use health-care benefits (Bahls, 1998), are more likely to be fired and quit their jobs (Larson et al., 2007; Normand et al., 1990), and have 3.6 times as many accidents on the job (Cadrain, 2003). Though the few available studies conclude that applicants testing positive for drugs will engage in some counterproductive behaviors, some authors (e.g., Morgan, 1990) believe that these studies are terribly flawed.

Because of such statistics, organizations are increasing their drug testing before applicants are hired. According to the Quest Diagnostics' Drug Testing Index, the increase in drug testing has resulted in fewer applicants testing positive for drugs; 4.5% in 2019 compared to 13.6% in 1988. With the legalization of marijuana in several states, and the consideration of legalization in other states, it will be interesting to see if these percentages increase in the coming years.

According to large surveys by the Substance Abuse and Mental Health Services Administration (Larson et al., 2007; SAMHSA, 2013),

- 49% of U.S. employers test applicants for drug use (HireRight, 2019);
- 8.9% of full-time American employees admitted to using drugs in the previous month and 29.9% reported to recent alcohol misuse;
- men, Black individuals, people without college degrees, the unemployed, people on parole, and employees with low-paying jobs were the most likely to have recently used drugs; and

- food preparation workers (17.4%), restaurant servers (15.4%), construction workers (15.1%), and writers, athletes, and designers (12.4%) are the most common users of drugs, whereas protective services (3.4%), social services (4.0%), and people working in education (4.1%) were the least common users of drugs.

In general, applicants seem to accept drug testing as being reasonably fair (Mastrangelo, 1997; Truxillo, Normandy, & Bauer, 2001). Not surprisingly, compared with people who have never tried drugs, current drug users think drug testing is less fair, and previous drug users think drug testing is less fair if it results in termination but not when the consequence for being caught is rehabilitation (Truxillo et al., 2001). Regardless of their popularity, drug testing programs appear to reduce employee drug use (French, Roebuck, & Alexandre, 2004).

Companies with a federal contract of $100,000 or more are required to comply with the **Drug-Free Workplace Act of 1988**. This act requires that federal contractors (Steingold, 2019):

Drug-Free Workplace Act of 1988 A federal law that requires federal contractors with a contract of at least $100,000 to maintain a drug-free workplace.

- Communicate to employees that using or being under the influence of illegal drugs in the workplace is prohibited;
- Establish a drug awareness program;
- Require employees to notify the organization of any conviction for workplace drug use; and
- Take remedial actions on employees convicted of workplace drug use.

Drug testing usually is done in two stages. In the first, an employee or applicant provides a urine, saliva, or hair sample that is subjected to an initial screening test. For urine or saliva, employers can use an on-site "instant" screener that provides results in seconds or they can send the employee to a drug testing lab. Hair samples must be sent to a lab for testing. Although hair samples are less convenient and more expensive than urine or saliva samples, they have the advantage of measuring drug use occurring further back than is the case for urine or saliva samples. If the initial test for drugs is positive, then the second-stage testing is done by a medical review officer (MRO) at a testing lab to ensure that the initial results were accurate.

When both stages are used, testing is very accurate in detecting the presence of drugs. But drug tests are not able to determine whether an individual is impaired by drug use. An employee smoking marijuana on Saturday night will test positive for the drug on Monday, even though the effects of the drug have long since gone away. The length of time since use that a drug can be detected depends on a variety of factors such as the type of drug, the amount of the drug taken, frequency of use, hydration level, body mass and weight, the method used to test for drugs. Most drugs can be detected two to three days after they have been used. The exceptions are the benzodiazepines, which can be detected for 4 to 6 weeks after use; PCP, which can be detected for 2 to 4 weeks; and marijuana, which can be detected up to 30 days in a urine test and up to 90 days in a hair follicle test. Testing conducted on hair follicles rather than urine samples can detect drug usage over longer periods, whereas testing using blood, saliva, or perspiration samples detect drug usage over shorter periods of time. A disadvantage to testing hair follicles is that it takes a few days before drugs will be detected in the hair; thus, it is not a good method to determine whether an employee is currently under the influence.

In the public sector or in the union environment, however, drug testing becomes complicated when it occurs after applicants are hired. Testing of employees usually takes one of three forms:

1. All employees or randomly selected employees are tested at predetermined times.
2. All employees or randomly selected employees are tested at random times.
3. Employees who have been involved in an accident or disciplinary action are tested following the incident.

The second form is probably the most effective in terms of punishing or preventing drug usage, but the third form of testing is legally the most defensible.

Psychological Exams

In jobs involving public safety (e.g., law enforcement, nuclear power, transportation), it is common for employers to give psychological exams to applicants after a conditional offer of hire has been made. If the applicant fails the exam, the offer is rescinded. Psychological exams usually consist of an interview by a clinical psychologist, an examination of the applicant's life history, and the administration of one or more of the psychological tests discussed earlier in this chapter. It is important to keep in mind that psychological exams are not designed to predict employee performance. Therefore, they should only be used to determine if a potential employee is a danger to themselves or others.

Medical Exams

In jobs requiring physical exertion, many employers require that a medical exam be taken after a conditional offer of hire has been made. In these exams, the physician is given a copy of the job description and asked to determine if there are any medical conditions that will keep the employee from safely performing the job.

5-9 Comparison of Techniques

After reading this chapter, you are probably asking the same question that industrial psychologists have been asking for years: Which method of selecting employees is best?

Validity

As shown in Table 5.2, it is clear that the unstructured interview, education, interest inventories, and some personality traits are not good predictors of future employee performance for most jobs. It is also clear that ability, work samples, biodata, and structured interviews do a fairly good job of predicting future employee performance. Over the past few years, researchers have been interested in determining which *combination* of selection tests is best. Though much more research is needed on this topic, it appears that the most valid selection battery includes a cognitive ability test and either a work sample, an integrity test, or a structured interview (Schmidt & Hunter, 1998).

Even though some selection techniques are better than others, *all* techniques are potentially useful methods for selecting employees. In fact, a properly constructed selection battery usually contains a variety of tests that tap different dimensions of a job. Take, for example, the job of police officer. We might use a cognitive ability test to ensure the applicant will understand the material presented in the academy, physical

Table 5.2 Validity of Selection Techniques

Criterion/Selection Technique	Validity		K	N	Meta-Analysis
	Observed	Corrected			
Performance					
Cognitive ability (U.S.)	.39	.51			Schmidt and Hunter (1998)
Biodata	.36	.51	22	20,905	Beall (1991)
Structured interviews	.34	.57	60	6,723	Huffcutt and Arthur (1994)
Work samples (verbal)	.34	.48	58	4,220	Hardison, Kim, and Sackett (2005)
Work samples (motor)	.31	.43	32	2,256	Hardison et al. (2005)
Behavioral description interviews	.31	.51	22	2,721	Huffcutt et al. (2003)
Cognitive ability (Europe)	.29	.62	93	9,554	Salgado et al. (2003)
Assessment centers	.28	.38	258	83,761	Arthur et al. (2003)
Situational interviews	.26	.43	32	2,815	Huffcutt et al. (2003)
Work samples	.26	.39	54	10,469	Roth et al. (2005)
Spatial-mechanical ability (Europe)	.23	.51	40	3,750	Salgado et al. (2003)
Job knowledge tests	22	.45	164	19,769	Dye et al. (1993)
Criminal history	-.21		8	1,982	Aamodt (2014)
Personality (conscientiousness)	.21	.26	74	41,939	Judge et al. (2013)
Situational judgment tests	.20	.26	118	24,756	McDaniel et al. (2007)
Personality (self-efficacy)	.19	.23	10	1,122	Judge and Bono (2001)
References	.18	.29	30	7,419	Aamodt and Williams (2005)
Personality (self-esteem)	.18	.26	40	5,145	Judge and Bono (2001)
In-basket	.16	.42	31	3,958	Whetzel et al. (2014)
Personality (extraversion)	.16	.20	63	19,868	Judge et al. (2013)
Grades	.16	.32	71	13,984	Roth et al. (1996)
Graphology (autobiographical)	.16	.22	17	1,084	Simner and Goffin (2003)
Credit history	.15		4	674	Aamodt (2014)
Personality (locus of control)	.14	.22	35	4,310	Judge and Bono (2001)
Integrity tests	.13	.18	74	13,706	Van Iddekinge et al. (2012)
Personality (agreeableness)	.13	.17	40	14,321	Judge et al. (2013)
Education	.13	.18	7	1,562	Ng and Feldman (2009)
Personality (overall)	.12	.17	97	13,521	Tett et al. (1994)
Unstructured interview	.11	.20	15	7,308	Huffcutt and Arthur (1994)
Interest inventories	.10	.13			Hunter and Hunter (1984)
Graphology (nonautobiographical)	.09	.12	6	442	Simner and Goffin (2003)
Personality (emotional stability)	.08	.10	55	17,274	Judge et al. (2013)
Personality (psychopathy)	−.08	−.10	68	10,227	O'Boyle et al. (2012)
Personality (Machiavellianism)	−.06	−.07	57	9,297	O'Boyle et al. (2012)
Personality (openness)	.06	.08	47	16,068	Judge et al. (2013)

Table 5.2   Validity of Selection Techniques (*Continued*)

Criterion/Selection Technique	Validity		K	N	Meta-Analysis
	Observed	**Corrected**			
Experience	.05	.06	44	11,785	Van Iddekinge et al. (2019)
Personality (narcissism)	−.02	−.03	18	3,124	O'Boyle et al. (2012)
Counterproductive Work Behavior					
Personality (narcissism)	.28	.32	16	4,424	Grijalva & Newman (2015)
Integrity tests	.26	.32	65	19,449	Van Iddekinge et al. (2012)
Personality (Machiavellianism)	.20	.25	13	2,546	O'Boyle et al. (2012)
Credit history	.10		8	9,341	Aamodt (2014)
Criminal history	.07		13	19,844	Aamodt (2014)
Personality (psychopathy)	.06	.07	27	6,058	O'Boyle et al. (2012)
Tenure					
Biodata	.28		27	70,737	Beall (1991)
References	.08		3	2,131	Aamodt and Williams (2005)
Integrity tests	.07	.09	20	24,808	Van Iddekinge et al. (2012)
Training Proficiency					
Cognitive ability (U.S.)		.56			Hunter and Hunter (1984)
Work samples (verbal)	.39	.44	50	3,161	Hardison et al. (2005)
Work samples (motor)	.36	.41	38	7,086	Hardison et al. (2005)
Cognitive ability (Europe)	.28	.54	97	16,065	Salgado et al. (2003)
Job knowledge tests	.27	.47	338	343,768	Dye et al. (1993)
Spatial-mechanical ability (Europe)	.20	.40	84	15,834	Salgado et al. (2003)
Biodata		.30			Hunter and Hunter (1984)
Personality (extraversion)	.15	.26	17	3,101	Barrick and Mount (1991)
Personality (openness)	.14	.25	14	2,700	Barrick and Mount (1991)
Integrity tests	.13	.16	8	1,530	Van Iddekinge et al. (2012)
Personality (conscientiousness)	.13	.23	17	3,585	Barrick and Mount (1991)
References		.23			Hunter and Hunter (1984)
Education		.20			Hunter and Hunter (1984)
Vocational interest		.18			Hunter and Hunter (1984)
Experience	.09	.11	21	8,176	Van Iddekinge et al. (2019)
Personality (emotional stability)	.04	.07	19	3,283	Barrick and Mount (1991)
Personality (agreeableness)	.04	.06	19	3,685	Barrick and Mount (1991)

Note: Observed = mean observed validity, Corrected = observed validity corrected for study artifacts; k = number of studies in the meta-analysis; N = total number of subjects in the meta-analysis.

ability test to make sure the applicant has the strength and speed necessary to chase suspects and defend themselves, a situational interview to tap their decision-making ability, a personality inventory to ensure that they have the traits needed for the job, and a background check to determine whether they have a history of antisocial behavior.

Legal Issues

As you might recall from Chapter 3, methods used to select employees are most prone to legal challenge when they result in adverse impact, invade an applicant's privacy, and do not appear to be job-related (lack face validity). As shown in Table 5.3, cognitive ability and GPA will result in the highest levels of adverse impact, whereas integrity tests, references, and personality inventories will result in the lowest levels (in viewing this table, you might want to review the concept of d scores and effect sizes discussed in Chapter 1). In terms of face validity, applicants perceive interviews, work samples/simulations, and résumés as being the most job-related/fair, and they view graphology, integrity tests, and personality tests as being the least job-related/fair (Anderson et al., 2010).

Table 5.3 Racial and Ethnic Differences in Scores of Selection Techniques

| | d score | | | |
Selection Technique	White-Black	White-Hispanic	Male-Female	Meta-Analysis
Cognitive ability (all jobs)	0.99	0.83		Roth et al. (2001)
Low complexity jobs	0.86			Bobko & Roth (2013)
Moderate complexity jobs	0.72			Bobko & Roth (2013)
GPA	0.78			Roth & Bobko (2000)
Work samples				
Applicants	0.73			Roth, Bobko, McFarland, & Buster (2008)
Incumbents — civilian	0.53			Roth, Bobko, McFarland, & Buster (2008)
Incumbents – military	0.03			Roth, Bobko, McFarland, & Buster (2008)
Assessment centers	0.52	0.28	−0.19	Dean, Roth, & Bobko (2008)
Job sample/job knowledge	0.48	0.47		Roth, Huffcutt, & Bobko (2003)
Situational judgment tests	0.38	0.24	−.11	Whetzel, McDaniel, & Nguyen (2008)
Biodata	0.33			Bobko, Roth, & Potosky (1999)
Structured interview	0.23		.14	Huffcutt & Roth (1998); Alonso et al. (2017)
Interest – conventional	−0.23			Jones, Newman, Su, & Rounds (2021)
Interest – realistic	0.18			Jones, Newman, Su, & Rounds (2021)
Personality – extraversion	0.16	0.02		Foldes, Duehr, & Ones (2008)
Interest – Social	−0.15			Jones, Newman, Su, & Rounds (2021)
Personality — openness	0.10	0.02		Foldes, Duehr, & Ones (2008)
Interrest – enterprising	−0.11			Jones, Newman, Su, & Rounds (2021)
Interest – investigative	0.11			Jones, Newman, Su, & Rounds (2021)
Personality — emotional stability	0.09	−0.03		Foldes, Duehr, & Ones (2008)
References	0.08		−0.01	Aamodt & Williams (2005)
Integrity tests	0.07	−0.05		Ones & Viswesvaran (1998)
Personality — agreeableness	0.03	0.05		Foldes, Duehr, & Ones (2008)
Personality — conscientiousness	−0.07	−0.08		Foldes, Duehr, & Ones (2008)
Interest – artistic	0.00			Jones, Newman, Su, & Rounds (2021)

5-10 Rejecting Applicants

Once a decision has been made regarding which applicants will be hired, those who will not be hired must be notified. Rejected applicants should be treated well because they are potential customers and potential applicants for other positions that might become available in the organization (Koprowski, 2004; Waung & Brice, 2003). In fact, Aamodt and Peggans (1988) found that applicants who were rejected "properly" were more likely to continue to be a customer at the organization and to apply for future job openings.

A good example of this was provided in a letter to the editor of *HR Magazine* by HR professional Jim Reitz, who was treated poorly on two different occasions when applying for a job with an employment agency. When he became an HR manager with a large company, one of the first things he did was contact the employment agency to notify it that his company would not be doing business with it due to the way in which he had been treated as an applicant. Reitz pointed out that his new company spends over a million dollars on temps and the employment agency would get none of it.

Rejection letter A letter from an organization to an applicant informing the applicant that they will not receive a job offer.

What is the best way to reject an applicant? The most interesting **rejection letter** I have seen came from Circuit City about 40 years ago. At the bottom of the letter was a sentence stating that you could take the rejection letter to any Circuit City store within the next 30 days and get a 10% discount. Imagine the clerk calling for assistance over the store intercom; "We have a rejected applicant on register four, could a manager please come and approve the discount?"

I remember getting a rejection letter from a graduate school stating that they had 400 people apply and that my application lacked the quality to get past the department clerk! They were kind enough to wish me success in my career.

Clearly the above two examples are not best practices. So, what is? Aamodt and Peggans (1988) found that rejection letters differ to the extent that they contain the following types of responses:

- A personally addressed and signed letter
- The company's appreciation to the applicant for applying for a position with the company
- A compliment about the applicant's qualifications
- A comment about the high qualifications possessed by the other applicants
- Information about the individual who was actually hired
- A wish of good luck in future endeavors
- A promise to keep the applicant's résumé on file

Though research has not clearly identified the best way to write a rejection letter, the following guidelines are probably a good place to start:

- Send rejection letters or emails to applicants. Though most organizations do not do this (Brice & Waung, 1995), failure to send a letter or email results in applicants feeling negatively toward an organization (Waung & Brice, 2000). Excuses about not having the time or funds to notify applicants are probably not justified when one considers the ill feelings that may result from not contacting applicants.
- Don't send the rejection letter immediately. The surprising results of a study by Waung and Brice (2000) suggest that applicants react more positively if there is a delay in receiving the letter. Though these findings seem to go against the thought that applicants can better manage their job searches if they know they have been rejected, it may be that too quick a rejection makes applicants feel as if they are such a loser that the organization quickly discarded them (e.g., the graduate school

whose clerk rejected my application). However, Cortini, Galanti, and Barattuci (2019) found that applicants receiving a rejection letter after two weeks thought the selection process was fairer than those who received the letter after two months.

- Be as personable and as specific as possible in the letter. With the use of automated applicant tracking systems, it is fairly easy to individually address each letter, express the company's appreciation for applying, and perhaps explain who was hired and what their qualifications were. In general, "friendly" letters result in better applicant attitudes (Aamodt & Peggans, 1988; Feinberg, Meoli-Stanton, & Gable, 1996).
- Including a statement about the individual who received the job can increase applicant satisfaction with both the selection process and the organization (Aamodt & Peggans, 1988; Gilliland et al., 2001).
- Do not include the name of a contact person. Surprisingly, research has shown that including such a contact decreases the probability that a person will reapply for future jobs or use the company's products (Waung & Brice, 2000).

Perhaps the most important thing to consider when writing a letter of rejection is to be honest. Do not tell applicants that their résumés will be kept on file if the files for each job opening will not be used. A study by Brice and Waung (1995) supports these ideas, as most organizations either never formally reject applicants, or when they do, take an average of almost a month to do so.

On the Job — Applied Case Study

City of New London, Connecticut, Police Department

The City of New London, Connecticut, was developing a system to select police officers. One of the tests it selected was the Wonderlic Personnel Test, a cognitive ability test that was mentioned in this chapter. For each occupation, the Wonderlic provides a minimum score and a maximum score. For police officers, the minimum score is 20 and the maximum is 27. Robert J. Jordan applied for a job as a police officer but was not given an interview because his score of 33 (equivalent to an IQ of 125) made him "too bright" to be a cop. New London's reasoning was that highly intelligent officers would get bored with their jobs and would either cause trouble or would quit. The New London deputy police chief was quoted as saying, "Bob Jordan is exactly the type of guy we would want to screen out. Police work is kind of mundane. We don't deal in gunfights every night. There's a personality that can take that." Turnover was a great concern, as the city spent about $25,000 sending each officer through the academy.

The police department in neighboring Groton, Connecticut, also uses the Wonderlic but tries to hire the highest scorers possible—a policy with which most I/O psychologists would agree.

When New London's policy received national publicity, the city became the butt of many jokes and the policy became a source of embarrassment to many of the residents. According to one resident, "I'd rather have them hire the right man or woman for the job and keep replacing them than have the same moron for twenty years." Another commented, "Your average dunderhead is not the person you want to try to solve a fight between a man and his wife at two a.m." The ridicule got so bad that another city ran an ad asking, "Too smart to work for New London? Apply with us"; San Francisco police chief Fred Lau encouraged Jordan to apply to the San Francisco Police Department; and host Jay Leno rewrote the theme song for the television show to include, "Dumb cops, dumb cops, whatcha gonna do with a low IQ?"

Jordan filed a lawsuit but lost. The judge ruled, "Plaintiff may have been disqualified unwisely but he was not denied equal protection."

- Do you agree with New London's reasoning about being "too bright"?
- Do you agree with the judge's decision that it was not discriminatory to not hire people who are highly intelligent? Why or why not?
- How would you have determined the cognitive ability requirements for this job?

Information about this case can be found by following the web links in the text website.

In this chapter, you learned that personality testing for selection purposes has become increasingly popular, particularly those that measure normal personality. As with any other selection test (i.e., cognitive ability, physical agility), an applicant has no choice but to complete the test or otherwise risk not being considered for a position. So, applicants are asked to share a bit of who they are, rather than what they can do and how well they can do it.

As long as these tests aren't used to discriminate against protected classes, they are not illegal to use in the selection process. But opponents of personality inventories wonder just how ethical these tests are. First, the personality inventories can be considered a violation of privacy: many of these inventories ask questions about how a person feels or thinks about a particular concept or situation. For example, the online Jung Typology test (www.humanmetrics.com) asks a test taker to answer yes or no to such questions as: You often think about humankind and its destiny; You trust reason more than feelings; You feel involved when you watch TV soap operas. If these questions don't pertain to the actual job a person will be doing, what business is it of a company to know that information? Supporters of personality inventories will say, "It might show us whether a candidate is an introvert or extrovert." But what right do employees have to know whether a candidate is an introvert or extrovert as long as the applicant can do the job well?

Second, just how well do these tests predict work performance in a particular job? That is, if your personality score shows you are low in creativity, is it saying that you will be a poor performer in a position that requires a certain level of creativity?

And, third, the results of some of these tests can be impacted by how the test taker is feeling that day. If the test taker is feeling sad or tired, how they rate themselves on a question that asks about how much they like to be around other people may be different than how the test taker really feels on a normal or usual day. So, rather than using these tests to make crucial hiring decisions based on test results, critics believe they should only be used as icebreakers, as exercises in employee training programs, or for counseling purposes. The testing industry is basically unregulated, although there have been some attempts to introduce legislation preventing or better regulating these, as well as any other employment tests. The Association of Test Publishers continues to fight off such legislative challenges preventing the use of these tests for selection purposes. The Association contends, as do companies that use personality inventories, that using personality inventories in conjunction with other selection methods increases the validity of the selection process. Interviews and other types of tests show the skill and knowledge of an applicant. Personality inventories will show how well an applicant might fit into the organizational culture and get along with others, which is just as important as the applicant's other competencies. So, why shouldn't the personality inventory be part of the selection process?

What Do You Think?

- Take the free personality test at 16personalities.com/infj -personality.com. After you do, consider whether or not you want your potential job performance to be judged based on the results of such a test. Would you say that this test would fairly predict your ability to perform in certain jobs?

- Does it accurately portray how you would fit into an organization's culture or how you would get along with others? If it doesn't accurately portray you, would you then say such a test is unethical?

- Should the tests be better regulated? Are companies right in using them in their selection process?

- Do you see any other ethical concerns related to using personality tests?

- Is there a fairer and more ethical way for companies to determine if applicants will fit into the organizational culture and get along with others?

Chapter Summary

In this chapter you learned:

- References typically are not good predictors of performance due to such factors as leniency, poor reliability, fear of legal ramifications, and a variety of extraneous factors.
- Reliability, validity, cost, and potential for legal problems should be considered when choosing the right type of employment test for a particular situation.

- Cognitive ability tests, job knowledge tests, biodata, work samples, and assessment centers are some of the better techniques in predicting future performance. Personality inventories, interest inventories, references, and graphology are not highly related to employee performance.
- Drug testing and medical exams are commonly used to screen employees prior to their starting a job.
- Writing a well-designed rejection letter can have important organizational consequences.

Key Terms

Reference check   (152)

Reference   (152)

Letter of recommendation   (152)

Résumé fraud   (152)

Negligent hiring   (154)

Validity coefficient   (155)

Corrected validity   (155)

Negligent reference   (157)

Reliability   (158)

Job knowledge tests   (161)

Ability   (161)

Cognitive ability   (162)

Cognitive ability tests   (162)

Wonderlic Personnel Test   (163)

Perceptual ability   (163)

Psychomotor ability   (166)

Physical ability   (166)

Assessment center   (169)

Unproctored internet-based
    testing   (170)

In-basket technique   (170)

Simulations   (171)

Work samples   (171)

Leaderless group discussion   (171)

Business simulation game   (171)

Gamification   (172)

Biodata   (173)

File approach   (173)

Questionnaire approach   (173)

Criterion groups   (174)

Vertical percentage method   (174)

Derivation sample   (175)

Hold-out sample   (175)

Personality inventory   (177)

Minnesota Multiphasic Personality
    Inventory-2 (MMPI-2)   (178)

Projective tests   (179)

Rorschach Inkblot Test   (180)

Thematic Apperception Test   (180)

Objective tests   (180)

Interest inventory   (180)

Strong Interest Inventory (SII)   (180)

Vocational counseling   (180)

Integrity test   (181)

Polygraph   (181)

Voice stress analyzer   (181)

Overt integrity test   (181)

Personality-based integrity test   (181)

Shrinkage   (182)

Conditional reasoning test   (182)

Fair Credit Reporting Act (FCRA)   (183)

Exclusionary period   (184)

Graphology   (184)

Drug testing   (185)

Drug-Free Workplace Act of 1988   (186)

Rejection letter   (191)

Questions for Review

1. Should an organization provide reference information for former employees? Why or why not?
2. What should be the most important factors in choosing a selection method? Explain your answers.
3. What selection methods are most valid?
4. Should employers test employees for drugs? Why or why not?
5. Are integrity tests fair and accurate? Explain your answer.

Chapter

6

Evaluating Selection Techniques and Decisions

Learning Objectives

6-1 Determine the reliability of a test and understand the factors that affect test reliability.

6-2 Recognize the five ways to validate a test.

6-3 Find information about tests.

6-4 Determine the utility of a selection test.

6-5 Evaluate a test for potential legal problems.

6-6 Use test scores to make personnel selection decisions.

In Chapter 3, you learned that many laws and regulations affect the employee selection methods. In Chapters 4 and 5, you learned about the ways in which to recruit and select employees. In this chapter, you will learn how to evaluate whether a particular selection method is useful and how to use test scores to make a hiring decision. Throughout this chapter, you will encounter the word *test*. Though this word often conjures up an image of a paper-and-pencil test, in industrial/organizational (I/O) psychology, the word "test" refers to any technique used to evaluate someone. Thus, employment tests include such methods as references, interviews, and assessment centers.

6-1 Characteristics of Effective Selection Techniques

Effective selection techniques have five characteristics—they are reliable, valid, cost-efficient, fair, and legally defensible.

Reliability

Reliability The extent to which a score from a test or from an evaluation is consistent and free from error.

Reliability is the extent to which a score from a selection measure is stable and free from error. If a score from a measure is not stable or error-free, it is not useful. For example, suppose we are using a ruler to measure the lengths of boards that will be used to build a doghouse. We want each board to be 4 feet long, but each time we measure a board, we get a different number. If the ruler does not yield the same number each time the same board is measured, the ruler cannot be considered reliable and thus is of no use. The same is true of selection methods. If applicants score differently each time they take a test, we are unsure of their actual scores. Consequently, the scores from the selection measure are of little value. Therefore, reliability is an essential characteristic of an effective measure (Spearman, 1904; Guttman, 1945). Test reliability is determined in four ways: test-retest reliability, alternate-forms reliability, internal reliability, and scorer reliability.

Test-Retest Reliability

Test-retest reliability The extent to which repeated administration of the same test will achieve similar results.

Temporal stability The consistency of test scores across time.

With the **test-retest reliability** method, several people take the same test twice. The scores from the first administration of the test are correlated with scores from the second to determine whether they are similar. If they are, then the test is said to have **temporal stability**: The test scores are stable across time and not highly susceptible to such random daily conditions as illness, fatigue, stress, or uncomfortable testing conditions. There is no standard amount of time that should elapse between the two administrations of the test. However, the time interval should be long enough so that the specific test answers have not been memorized, but short enough so that the person has not changed significantly.

For example, if three years have elapsed between administrations of a personality inventory, there may be a very low correlation between the two sets of scores; but the low correlation may not be the result of low test reliability. Instead, it could be caused by personality changes of the people in the sample over time (Kaplan & Saccuzzo, 2018). Likewise, if only 10 minutes separate the two administrations, a very high correlation between the two sets of scores might occur. This high correlation may represent only what the people remembered from the first testing rather than what they actually believe. Typical time intervals between test administrations range from 3 days to 3 months. Usually, the longer the time interval, the lower the reliability coefficient. The typical test-retest reliability coefficient for tests used by organizations is .86 (Hood, 2001).

Test-retest reliability is not appropriate for all kinds of tests. It would not make sense to measure the test-retest reliability of a test designed to measure short-term moods or feelings. For example, the State–Trait Anxiety Inventory measures two types of anxiety. *Trait anxiety* refers to the amount of anxiety that an individual normally has all the time, and *state anxiety* is the amount of anxiety an individual has at any given moment. For the test to be useful, it is important for the measure of trait anxiety, but not the measure of state anxiety, to have temporal stability.

Alternate-Forms Reliability

With the **alternate-forms reliability** method, two forms of the same test are constructed. As shown in Table 6.1, a sample of 100 people are administered both forms of the test; half of the sample first receive Form A and the other half first receive Form B. This **counterbalancing** of test-taking order is designed to eliminate any effects that taking one form of the test first may have on scores on the second form.

The scores on the two forms are then correlated to determine whether they are similar. If they are, the test is said to have **form stability**. Why would anyone use this method? If there is a high probability that people will take a test more than once, two forms of the test are needed to reduce the potential advantage to individuals who take the test a second time or who cheat. This situation might occur in police department examinations. To be promoted in most police departments, an officer must pass a promotion exam. If the officer fails the exam one year, the officer can retake the exam the next year. If only one form of the test were available, the officer retaking the test for the seventh time could remember many of the questions and possibly score higher than an officer taking the test for the first time. Likewise, applicants who fail a credentialing exam (e.g., the Bar Exam for attorneys or the SHRM Certified Senior Professional certification for human resources professionals) would be likely to retake the exam.

Will retaking an exam actually result in higher test scores? A meta-analysis by Hausknecht, Halpert, Di Paolo, and Moriarty Gerard (2007) found that applicants retaking the same cognitive ability test will increase their scores about twice as much ($d = .46$) as applicants taking an alternate form of the cognitive ability test ($d = .24$). Not surprisingly, the longer the interval between the two test administrations, the lower the gain in test scores. It should be noted that the Hausknecht et al. meta-analysis was limited to cognitive ability tests. It appears that with knowledge tests, retaking the test will still increase test scores, but the increase is at the same level whether the second test is the same test or an alternate form of the same test (Raymond, Neustel, & Anderson, 2007).

Multiple forms also might be used in large groups of test takers where there is a possibility of cheating. Perhaps one of your professors has used more than one form of the same test to discourage cheating. If you have ever taken a written driver's test, multiple forms probably were used, just as they were when you might have taken the SAT or ACT to be admitted to a college. As you can see, multiple forms of a test are common. Alternate forms are most important for knowledge and ability tests and least important for biodata and personality inventories (Johnson & Oswald, 2017).

Recall that with test-retest reliability, the time interval between administrations usually ranges from three days to three months. With alternate-forms reliability, however, the time interval should be as short as possible. If the two forms are administered three weeks apart and a low correlation results, the cause of the low reliability is difficult to determine. That is, the test could lack either form stability or temporal stability. Thus, to determine the cause of the unreliability, the interval needs

Table 6.1 Design for Typical Alternate Forms Reliability Study

Subjects	Administration Order	
	First	**Second**
1–50	Form A	Form B
51–100	Form B	Form A

Table 6.2   Example of Two Parallel but Nonequivalent Forms

Subjects	Test Scores Form A	Test Scores Form B
1	6	8
2	9	11
3	11	13
4	12	14
5	12	14
6	17	19
7	18	20
8	19	21
9	21	23
10	24	26
Average Score	14.9	16.9

to be short. The average correlation between alternate forms of tests used in industry is .89 (Hood, 2001).

In addition to being correlated, two forms of a test should also have the same mean and standard deviation (Clause, Mullins, Nee, Pulakos, & Schmitt, 1998). The test in Table 6.2, for example, shows a perfect correlation between the two forms. People who scored well on Form A also scored well on Form B. But the average score on Form B is two points higher than on Form A. Thus, even though the perfect correlation shows that the scores on the two forms are parallel, the difference in mean scores indicates that the two forms are not equivalent. In such a case, either the forms must be revised, or different standards (norms) must be used to interpret the results of the test.

Any changes in a test potentially change its reliability, validity, difficulty, or all three. Such changes might include the order of the items, examples used in the questions, method of administration, and time limits. Though alternate-form differences potentially affect the test outcomes, most of the research indicates that these effects are either nonexistent or rather small. For example, meta-analyses suggest that computer administration (Dwight & Feigelson, 2000; Kingston, 2009) or PowerPoint administration (Larson, 2001) of cognitive ability or knowledge tests results in scores equivalent to paper-and-pencil administration. However, a quasi-experimental study by Ployhart, Weekley, Holtz, and Kemp (2003) found that personality inventories and situational judgment tests administered on the web resulted in lower scores and better **internal reliability** than the same tests administered in the traditional paper-and-pencil format. Interestingly, research suggests that Black individuals, but not White individuals, score higher on video-based tests than on traditional paper-and-pencil tests (Chan & Schmitt, 1997).

Internal reliability   The extent to which responses to test items measuring the same construct are consistent.

Internal Reliability

A third way to determine the reliability of a test or inventory is to look at the consistency with which an applicant responds to items measuring a similar dimension or construct (e.g., personality trait, ability, area of knowledge). The extent to which similar items are answered in similar ways is referred to as *internal consistency* and measures **item stability**.

Item stability   The extent to which responses to the same test items are consistent.

In general, the longer the test, the higher its internal consistency—that is, the agreement among responses to the various test items. To illustrate this point, let us look at the final exam for this course. If the final exam was based on three chapters, would you want a test consisting of only three multiple-choice items? Probably not. If you made a careless mistake in marking your answer or fell asleep during part of the lecture from which a question was taken, your score would be low. But if the test had 100 items, one careless mistake or one missed part of a lecture would not severely affect your total score.

Another factor that can affect the internal reliability of a test is **item homogeneity**. That is, do all of the items measure the same thing, or do they measure different constructs? The more homogeneous the items, the higher the internal consistency. To illustrate this concept, let us again look at your final exam based on three chapters.

If we computed the reliability of the entire exam, it would probably be relatively low. Why? Because the material assessed by the test questions is not homogeneous. The questions are measuring knowledge from three topic areas (three chapters), two sources (lecture and text), and two knowledge types (factual and conceptual). If we broke the test down by chapter, source, and item type, the reliability of the separate test components would be higher, because we would be looking at groups of homogeneous items.

When reading information about internal consistency in a journal article or a test manual, you will encounter three terms that refer to the method used to determine internal consistency: split-half, coefficient alpha, and **Kuder-Richardson formula 20 (K-R 20)**. The **split-half method** is the easiest to use, as items on a test are split into two groups. Usually, all of the odd-numbered items are in one group and all the even-numbered items are in the other group. The scores on the two groups of items are then correlated. Because the number of items in the test has been reduced, researchers have to use a formula called the **Spearman-Brown prophecy formula** to adjust the correlation.

Cronbach's **coefficient alpha** (Cronbach, 1951) and the K-R 20 (Kuder & Richardson, 1937) are more popular and accurate methods of determining internal reliability, although they are more complicated to compute. Essentially, both the coefficient alpha and the K-R 20 represent the reliability coefficient that would be obtained from all possible combinations of split halves. The difference between the two is that the K-R 20 is used for tests containing dichotomous items (e.g., yes-no, true-false), whereas the coefficient alpha can be used not only for dichotomous items but also for tests containing interval and ratio items such as five-point rating scales. The median internal reliability coefficient found in the research literature is .81, and coefficient alpha is by far the most commonly reported measure of internal reliability (Hogan, Benjamin, & Brezinski, 2003).

Scorer Reliability

A fourth way of assessing reliability is **scorer reliability**. A test or inventory can have homogeneous items and yield heterogeneous scores and still not be reliable if the person scoring the test makes mistakes. Scorer reliability is especially an issue in projective or subjective tests in which there is no one correct answer, but even tests scored with the use of keys suffer from scorer mistakes. For example, Allard, Butler, Faust, and Shea (1995) found that 53% of hand-scored personality tests contained at least one scoring error, and 19% contained enough errors to alter a clinical diagnosis. Goddard, Simons, Patton, and Sullivan (2004) found that 12% of hand-scored interest inventories contained scoring or plotting errors, and of that percentage, 64% would have changed the career advice offered.

Item homogeneity The extent to which test items measure the same construct.

Kuder-Richardson Formula 20 (K-R 20) A statistic used to determine internal reliability of tests that use items with dichotomous answers (yes/no, true/false).

Split-half method A form of internal reliability in which the consistency of item responses is determined by comparing scores on half of the items with scores on the other half of the items.

Spearman-Brown prophecy formula Used to correct reliability coefficients resulting from the split-half method.

Coefficient alpha A statistic used to determine internal reliability of tests that use interval or ratio scales.

Scorer reliability The extent to which two people scoring a test agree on the test score, or the extent to which a test is scored correctly.

When human judgment of performance is involved, scorer reliability is discussed in terms of *interrater reliability*. That is, will two interviewers give an applicant similar ratings, or will two supervisors give an employee similar performance ratings? If you are a fan of the television shows *American Idol* or *The Voice*, how would you rate the interrater reliability among the judges?

Evaluating the Reliability of a Test

In the previous section, you learned that it is important that scores on a test be reliable and that there are four common methods for determining reliability. When deciding whether a test demonstrates sufficient reliability, two factors must be considered: the magnitude of the reliability coefficient and the people who will be taking the test.

The reliability coefficient for a test can be obtained from your own data, the test manual, journal articles using the test, or test compendia that will be discussed later in the chapter. To evaluate the coefficient, you can compare it with reliability coefficients typically obtained for similar types of tests. For example, if you were considering purchasing a personality inventory and saw in the test manual that the test-retest reliability was .60, a comparison with the coefficients shown in Table 6.3 would show that the reliability for the test you are considering is lower than what is normally found for that *type* of test.

The second factor to consider is the people who will be taking your test. For example, if you will be using the test for managers, but the reliability coefficient in the test manual was established with high school students, you would have less confidence that the reliability coefficient would generalize well to your organization. A good example of this was the meta-analysis of the reliability of the NEO personality scales. In that meta-analysis, Caruso (2003) found that the reliability was lower on samples of men and students than on samples of women and adults. The Career Workshop Box gives a summary of evaluating tests.

Table 6.3   Comparison of Typical Test Reliability Coefficients

Test Type	Reliability Type			Meta-Analysis
	Combined	Internal	Test-Retest	
Cognitive ability			.83	Salgado et al. (2003)
Integrity tests		.81	.85	Ones, Viswesvaran, and Schmidt (1993)
Overt		.83		Ones et al. (1993)
Personality based		.72		Ones et al. (1993)
Interest inventories		.92		Barrick, Mount, and Gupta (2003)
Personality inventories	.76			Barrick and Mount (1991)
Openness		.80	.73	Viswesvaran and Ones (2003)
Conscientiousness		.83	.76	Viswesvaran and Ones (2003)
Extraversion		.81	.78	Viswesvaran and Ones (2003)
Agreeableness		.74	.75	Viswesvaran and Ones (2003)
Stability		.82	.73	Viswesvaran and Ones (2003)
Situational judgment tests	.80			McDaniel et al. (2001)

Validity

Validity The degree to which inferences from test scores are justified by the evidence.

Validity is the degree to which inferences from scores on tests or assessments are justified by the evidence. As with reliability, a test must be valid to be useful. But just because a test is reliable does not mean it is valid. For example, suppose that we want to use height requirements to hire computer programmers. Our measure of height (a ruler) would certainly be a reliable measure; most adults will get no taller, and two people measuring an applicant's height will probably get very similar measurements. It is doubtful, however, that height is related to programming performance. Thus, a ruler would be a reliable measure of height, but height would not be a valid measure of programming performance.

Even though reliability and validity are not the same, they are related. The potential validity of a test is limited by its reliability. Thus, if a test has poor reliability, it cannot have high validity. But as we saw in the example above, a test's reliability does not imply validity. Instead, we think of reliability as having a *necessary but not sufficient relationship* with validity.

There are five common strategies to investigate the validity of scores on a test: content, criterion, construct, face, and known group.

Content Validity

Content validity The extent to which tests or test items sample the content that they are supposed to measure.

One way to determine a test's validity is to look at its degree of **content validity**—the extent to which test items sample the content that they are supposed to measure. Again, let us use your final exam as an example. Your instructor tells you that the final exam will measure your knowledge of Chapters 8, 9, and 10. Each chapter is of the same length, and your instructor spent three class periods on each chapter. The test will have 60 questions. For the test to be content valid, the items must constitute a representative sample of the material contained in the three chapters; therefore, there should be some 20 questions from each chapter. If there are 30 questions each from Chapters 8 and 9, the test will not be content valid because it left out Chapter 10. Likewise, if there are questions from Chapter 4, the test will not be content valid because it requires knowledge that is outside of the appropriate domain.

In industry, the appropriate content for a test or test battery is determined by the job analysis. A job analysis should first determine the tasks and the conditions under which they are performed. Next the KSAOs (knowledge, skills, abilities, and other characteristics) needed to perform the tasks under those particular circumstances are determined. All of the important dimensions identified in the job analysis should be covered somewhere in the selection process, at least to the extent that the dimensions (constructs) can be accurately and realistically measured. Anything that was not identified in the job analysis should be left out.

One way to test the content validity of a test is to have subject matter experts (e.g., experienced employees, supervisors) rate test items on the extent to which the content and level of difficulty for each item are related to the job in question. These subject matter experts should also be asked to indicate if there are important aspects of the job that are not being tapped by test items.

The readability of a test is a good example of how tricky content validity can be. Suppose we determine that conscientiousness is an important aspect of a job. We find a personality inventory that measures conscientiousness, and we are confident that our test is content valid because it measures a dimension identified in the job analysis. But the personality inventory is very difficult to read (e.g., containing such words as *meticulous, extraverted, gregarious*) and most of our applicants are only high school

At some point in your career, there may be a time when you are asked to purchase a test or other form of assessment for use in your organization. For example, your company might want to use a personality inventory to hire employees or purchase a job-satisfaction inventory to conduct an attitude survey of employees. Here are some important questions to ask the assessment vendor:

- Do you have data to show evidence that the scores are reliable? The vendor should be able to provide this information and the reliability coefficients should be above .70.

- Have you conducted validity studies? The vendor should make these available to you. You want to see criterion validity studies related to your particular job or type of organization. Recall research on minimum sample sizes for validity studies as well. You want to be certain that the validity studies have been conducted with adequate sample sizing for an accurate measure of a test's validity.

- Do scores on the test have adverse impact on women or minorities? If they do, it doesn't mean you can't use the test. It instead increases the need for good validity studies and also lets you know that you could be in for a legal challenge.

- Has the test been challenged in court? What were the results?

graduates. Is our test content valid? No, because it requires a high level of reading ability, and reading ability was not identified as an important dimension for our job. Therefore, the test was measuring two constructs (conscientiousness and reading ability), instead of just conscientiousness (its intended use).

Criterion Validity

Criterion validity The extent to which a test score is related to some measure of job performance.

Criterion A measure of job performance, such as attendance, productivity, or a supervisor rating.

Concurrent validity A form of criterion validity that correlates test scores with measures of job performance for employees currently working for an organization.

Predictive validity A form of criterion validity in which test scores of applicants are compared at a later date with a measure of job performance.

Restricted range A narrow range of performance scores that makes it difficult to obtain a significant validity coefficient.

Another measure of validity is **criterion validity**, which refers to the extent to which a test score is statistically related to some measure of job performance called a **criterion** (criteria will be discussed more thoroughly in Chapter 7). Commonly used criteria include supervisor ratings of performance, objective measures of performance (e.g., sales, number of complaints, number of arrests made), attendance (tardiness, absenteeism), tenure, training performance (e.g., police academy grades), and discipline problems.

Criterion validity is established using one of two research designs: concurrent or predictive. With a **concurrent validity** design, a test is given to a group of employees who are already on the job. The scores on the test are then correlated with a measure of the employees' current performance.

With a **predictive validity** design, the test is administered to a group of job applicants who are going to be hired. The test scores are then compared with a future measure of job performance. In the ideal predictive validity situation, every applicant (or a random sample of applicants) is hired, and the test scores are hidden from the people who will later make performance evaluations. If every applicant is hired, a wide range of both test scores and employee performance is likely to be found, and the wider the range of scores, the higher the validity coefficient. But because it is rarely practical to hire every applicant, the ideal predictive design is not often used. Instead, most criterion validity studies use a concurrent design.

Why is a concurrent design weaker than a predictive design? The answer lies in the homogeneity of performance scores. In a given employment situation, very few employees are at the extremes of a performance scale. Employees who would be at the bottom of the performance scale either were never hired or have since been terminated. Employees who would be at the upper end of the performance scale often get promoted. Thus, the **restricted range** of performance scores makes obtaining a significant validity coefficient more difficult.

Validity generalization (VG) The extent to which inferences from test scores from one organization can be applied to another organization.

A major issue concerning the criterion validity of tests focuses on a concept known as **validity generalization (VG)**—the extent to which a test found valid for a job in one location is valid for the same job in a different location. It was previously thought that the job of typist in one company was not the same as that in another company, the job of police officer in one small town was not the same as that in another small town, and the job of retail store supervisor was not the same as that of supervisor in a fast-food restaurant.

Research indicates that a test valid for a job in one organization is also valid for the same job in another organization (e.g., Schmidt, Gast-Rosenberg, & Hunter, 1980; Schmidt & Hunter, 1998; Schmidt, Hunter, Pearlman, & Hirsh, 1985). Schmidt, Hunter, and their associates have tested hundreds of thousands of employees to arrive at their conclusions. They suggest that previous thinking resulted from studies with small sample sizes, and the test being valid in one location but not in another was the product primarily of sampling error. With large sample sizes, a test found valid in one location probably will be valid in another, providing that the jobs actually are similar and are not merely two separate jobs sharing the same job title.

The two building blocks for validity generalization are meta-analysis, discussed in Chapter 1, and job analysis, discussed in Chapter 2. Meta-analysis can be used to determine the average validity of specific types of tests for a variety of jobs. For example, several studies have shown that cognitive ability is an excellent predictor of police performance. If we were to conduct a meta-analysis of all the studies looking at this relationship, we would be able to determine the average validity of cognitive ability in predicting police performance. If this validity coefficient is significant, then police departments similar to those used in the meta-analysis could adopt the test without conducting criterion validity studies of their own. This would be especially useful for small departments that have neither the number of officers necessary to properly conduct criterion validity studies nor the financial resources necessary to hire professionals to conduct such studies. Validity generalization should be used only if a job analysis has been conducted, the results of which show that the job in question is similar to those used in the meta-analysis. Though validity generalization is generally accepted by the scientific community, federal enforcement agencies such as the Office of Federal Contract Compliance Programs (OFCCP) seldom accept validity generalization as a substitute for a local validation study if a test is shown to have adverse impact.

Synthetic validity A form of validity generalization in which validity is inferred on the basis of a match between job components and tests previously found valid for those job components.

A technique related to validity generalization is **synthetic validity**. Synthetic validity assumes that tests that predict a particular component (e.g., customer service) of one job (e.g., a call center for a bank) should predict performance on the same job component for a different job (e.g., a receptionist at a law office). Thus, if studies show that a particular test predicts customer service performance, it follows logically that a company should be able to use that test if its own job analyses indicate that customer service is important to the job in question. The key difference between validity generalization and synthetic validity is that with validity generalization we are trying to generalize the results of studies conducted on a particular job to the same job at another organization, whereas with synthetic validity, we are trying to generalize the results of studies of different jobs to a job that shares a common component (e.g., problem solving, customer-service skills, mechanical ability). The concept of synthetic validity has been reinforced in the Uniform Guidelines (1978), and scientists have argued for the use of various techniques such as the Guion approaches and J-coefficient. Nevertheless, more research must be conducted on this topic before it can become an established method in personnel selection (Mossholder & Arvey, 1984).

Construct Validity

Construct validity is the most theoretical of the validity types. Basically, it is defined as the extent to which a test measures the construct that it purports to measure. Construct validity is concerned with inferences about test scores, in contrast to content validity, which is concerned with inferences about test construction.

Perhaps a good example of the importance of construct validity is a situation I encountered during graduate school. We had just completed a job analysis of the entry-level police officer position for a small town. One of the important dimensions (constructs) that emerged was honesty. Almost every officer insisted that a good police officer was honest, so we searched for tests that measured honesty and quickly discovered that there were many types of honesty—a conclusion also reached by Rieke and Guastello (1995). Some honesty tests measured theft, some cheating, and others moral judgment. None measured the honesty construct as it was defined by these police officers: not taking bribes and not letting friends get away with crimes. No test measured that particular construct, even though all of the tests measured "honesty."

Construct validity is usually determined by correlating scores on a test with scores from other tests. Some of the other tests measure the same construct (convergent validity), whereas others do not (discriminant validity). For example, suppose we have a test that measures knowledge of psychology. One hundred people are administered our Knowledge of Psychology Test as well as another psychology knowledge test, a test of reading ability, and a test of general intelligence. If our test really measures the construct that we say it does—knowledge of psychology—then it should correlate highest with the other test of psychology knowledge (convergent validity) but not very highly with the other two tests (discriminant validity). If our test correlates highest with the reading ability test, our test may be content valid (it contained psychology items), but not construct valid because scores on our test are based more on reading ability than on knowledge of psychology.

Another method of measuring construct validity is **known-group validity** (Hattie & Cooksey, 1984). This method is not common and should be used only when other methods for measuring construct validity are not practical. With known-group validity, a test is given to two groups of people who are "known" to be different on the trait in question.

For example, suppose we wanted to determine the validity of our new honesty test. The best approach might be a criterion validity study in which we would correlate our employees' test scores with their dishonest behavior, such as stealing or lying. The problem is, how would we know who stole or who lied? We could ask them, but would dishonest people tell the truth? Probably not. Instead, we decide to validate our test by administering it to a group known as honest (priests) and to another group known as dishonest (criminals).

After administering the test to both groups, we find, sure enough, that the priests score higher on honesty than do the criminals. Does this mean our test is valid? Not necessarily. It means that the test has known-group validity but not necessarily other types of validity. We do not know whether the test will predict employee theft (criterion validity), nor do we know whether it is even measuring honesty (construct validity). It is possible that the test is actually measuring another construct on which the two groups differ (e.g., intelligence). Because of these problems, the best approach to take with known-group validity is this: If the known groups do not differ on test scores, consider the test invalid. If scores do differ, one still cannot be sure of its validity.

Even though known-group validity usually should not be used to establish test validity, it is important to understand because some test companies use known-group validity studies to sell their tests, claiming that the tests are valid. Personnel analyst Jeff Rodgers once was asked to evaluate a test his company was considering for selecting bank tellers. The test literature sounded impressive, mentioning that the test was "backed by over 100 validity studies." Rodgers was suspicious and requested copies of the studies. After several months of "phone calls and teeth pulling," he obtained reports of the validity studies. Most of the studies used known-group methodology and compared the scores of groups such as monks and priests. Not one study involved a test of criterion validity to demonstrate that the test could actually predict bank teller performance. Thus, if you hear that a test is valid, it is important to obtain copies of the research reports.

Choosing a Way to Measure Validity

With three common ways of measuring validity, one might logically ask which of the methods is the "best" to use. As with most questions in psychology, the answer is that "it depends." In this case, it depends on the situation as well as what the person conducting the validity study is trying to accomplish. If it is to decide whether the test will be a useful predictor of employee performance, then content validity will usually be used, and a criterion validity study will also be conducted if there are enough employees and if a good measure of job performance is available.

In deciding whether content validity is enough, I advise organizations to use the "next-door-neighbor rule." That is, ask yourself, "If my next-door neighbor were on a jury and I had to justify the use of my test, would content validity be enough?" For example, suppose you conducted a job analysis of a clerical position and find that typing, filing, and answering the phone are the primary duties. So, you purchase a standard typing test and a filing test. The link between these tests and the duties performed by our clerical worker is so obvious that a criterion validity study is probably not essential to convince a jury of the validity of the two tests. However, suppose your job analysis of a police officer indicates that making decisions under pressure is an important part of the job. To tap this dimension, you choose the Gandy Critical Thinking Test. Because the link between your test and the ability to make decisions under pressure is not so obvious, you may need a criterion validity study.

Why not always conduct a criterion validity study? Having the significant validity coefficient is great, but the danger is in conducting the validity study. If you conduct a criterion validity study and do not get a significant validity coefficient, that failure could be problematic if your test were to be challenged in court. To get a significant validity coefficient, many things have to go right. You need a good test, a good measure of performance, and a decent sample size. Furthermore, most validity coefficients are small (in the .20 to .30 range). Though assessment experts understand the utility of such small correlations, it can be difficult to convince a jury or governmental agencies to share your excitement after you explain that the range for a correlation coefficient is 0 to 1, you got a correlation of .20, and your test explains 4% of the variance.

Finally, a test itself can never be valid. When we speak of validity, we are speaking about the validity of the *test scores* as they relate to a particular job. A test may be a valid predictor of tenure for counselors but not of performance for shoe salespeople. Thus, when we say that a test is valid, we mean that it is valid for a particular job and a particular criterion. No test will ever be valid for all jobs and all criteria.

Face Validity

Although face validity is not one of the three major methods of determining test validity cited in the federal *Uniform Guidelines on Employee Selection Procedures*, it is still important. **Face validity** is the extent to which a test appears to be job related. This perception is important because if a test or its items do not appear valid, the test takers and administrators will not have confidence in the results. If job applicants do not think a test is job related, their perceptions of its fairness decrease, as does their motivation to do well on the test (Hausknecht, Day, & Thomas, 2004). Likewise, if employees involved in a training session on interpersonal skills take a personality inventory and are given the results, they will not be motivated to change or to use the results of the inventory unless the personality profile given to them seems accurate.

The importance of face validity has been demonstrated in a variety of research studies. For example, Chan, Schmitt, DeShon, Clause, and Delbridge (1997) found that face-valid tests resulted in high levels of test-taking motivation, which in turn resulted in higher levels of test performance. Thus, face validity motivates applicants to do well on tests. Face-valid tests that are accepted by applicants decrease the chance of lawsuits (Rynes & Connerley, 1993), reduce the number of applicants dropping out of the employment process (Thornton, 1993), and increase the chance that an applicant will accept a job offer (Hoff Macan, Avedon, & Paese, 1994). The one downside to a face-valid test, however, is that applicants might be tempted to fake the test because the correct answers are obvious. For example, if you are applying to a graduate school and you are asked to take a test that clearly measures academic motivation, it would be very tempting to appear highly motivated in your responses. A study found that the higher the face validity of a test (in this case, a test measuring dependency) wherein participants were able to identify what construct the test was measuring, the higher the chance that participants would select the more "socially desirable" responses on the test (Bornstein, Rossner, Hill, & Stepanian, 1994).

The face validity and acceptance of test results can be increased by informing the applicants about how a test relates to job performance (Lounsbury, Bobrow, & Jensen, 1989) and by administering the test in a multimedia format (Richman-Hirsch, Olson-Buchanan, & Drasgow, 2000). Acceptance of test results also increases when applicants receive honest feedback about their test performance and are treated with respect by the test administrator (Gilliland, 1993).

But just because a test has face validity does not mean it is accurate or useful (Jackson, O'Dell, & Olson, 1982). For example, have you ever read a personality description based on your astrological sign and found the description to be quite accurate? Does this mean astrological forecasts are accurate? Not at all. If you also have read a personality description based on a different astrological sign, you probably found it to be as accurate as the one based on your own sign. Why is this? Because of something called **Barnum statements** (Dickson & Kelly, 1985)—statements so general that they can be true of almost everyone. For example, if I described you as "sometimes being sad, sometimes being successful, and at times not getting along with your best friend," I would probably be very accurate. However, these statements describe almost anyone. So, face validity by itself is not enough.

Finding Reliability and Validity Information

Over the previous pages, we have discussed different ways to measure reliability and validity. But even though most of you will eventually be involved with some form of employee testing, few of you will actually conduct a study on a test's reliability and validity. Consequently, where do you get information about these? There are many excellent sources containing reliability and validity information in the reference section of most university libraries.

Perhaps the most common source of test information is the *Twenty-First Mental Measurements Yearbook (MMY)* (Carlson, Geisinger, & Jonson, 2021), which contains information on over 2,700 psychological tests as well as reviews by test experts. Your library probably has online access to the *MMY*. Another excellent source of information is a compendium entitled *Tests in Print IX* (Anderson, Schlueter, Carlson, & Geisinger, 2016).

Cost-Efficiency

If two or more tests have similar validities, then cost should be considered. For example, in selecting police officers, it is common to use a test of cognitive ability such as the Wonderlic Personnel Test or the Wechsler Adult Intelligence Scale (WAIS). Both tests have similar reliabilities and validities, yet the Wonderlic costs only a few dollars per applicant and can be administered to groups of people in only 12 minutes. The WAIS must be administered individually at a time cost of at least an hour per applicant and a financial cost of more than $100 per applicant. Given the similar validities, it doesn't take a rocket scientist (or an I/O psychologist) to figure out which is the better deal. In situations that are not so clear, the utility formula discussed later in this chapter can be used to determine the best test.

A particular test is usually designed to be administered either to individual applicants or to a group of applicants. Certainly, group testing is usually less expensive and more efficient than individual testing, although important information may be lost in group testing. For example, one reason for administering an individual intelligence test is to observe the *way* in which a person solves a problem or answers a question. With group tests, only the answer can be scored.

As mentioned in Chapter 5, an increasing number of organizations are administering their tests over the Internet or at remote testing locations. With **unproctored internet-based testing (UIT)**, an applicant takes a test online or through a mobile platform, the test is automatically scored, and the results of the test and interpretation are immediately available. Because online testing can lower testing costs, decrease feedback time, and yield results in which the test takers can have great confidence, many public and private employers are switching to this method. Many state governments have found considerable cost savings in allowing applicants to take a computerized test from home rather than having them travel great distances to take a test at a central location. This increase in efficiency does not come at the cost of decreased validity because, as mentioned previously, tests administered electronically seem to yield results similar to those administered through the traditional paper-and-pencil format.

An increasingly common use of computer testing is **computer-adaptive testing (CAT)**. In fact, you might have taken the SAT in a computer-adaptive format. With CAT, the computer "adapts" the next question to be asked based on how the test taker responded to the previous question or questions. For example, if the test taker successfully answered three multiplication questions in a row, the computer would move to another type of math rather than wasting time by asking seven more multiplication questions. When taking a CAT, the computer starts by asking questions of average difficulty. If the test taker answers these correctly, the computer asks more difficult questions. If the test taker answers these questions incorrectly, the computer asks easier questions. The logic behind CAT is that if a test taker can't answer easy questions (e.g., addition and subtraction), it doesn't make sense to ask questions about algebra and geometry. The advantages to CAT is that fewer test items are required, tests take less time to complete, finer distinctions in applicant ability can be made, test takers can receive immediate feedback, and test scores can be interpreted not only on the number of questions answered correctly, but on which questions were correctly answered. However, a potential disadvantage to CAT that still needs to be further investigated is how test takers with specific disability subtypes might be affected, particularly disabilities that manifest through divergent knowledge patterns (Stone & Davey, 2011).

6-2 Establishing the Usefulness of a Selection Device

Even when a test is both reliable and valid, it is not necessarily useful. At first, this may not make much sense, but consider a test that has been shown to be valid for selecting employees for a fast-food restaurant chain. Suppose there are 100 job openings and 100 job seekers apply for those openings. Even though the test is valid, it will have no impact because the restaurant chain must hire every applicant if it wanted to fill every opening.

As another example, imagine an organization that already has a test that does a good job of predicting performance. Even though a new test being considered may be valid, the old test may have worked so well that the current employees are all successful or the organization may have such a good training program that current employees are all successful. Thus, a new test (even though it is valid) may not provide any improvement.

To determine how useful a test would be in any given situation, several formulas and tables have been designed. Each formula and table provides slightly different information to an employer. The *Taylor-Russell tables* provide an estimate of the percentage of total new hires who will be successful employees if a test is adopted (organizational success); both *expectancy charts* and the *Lawshe tables* provide a probability of success for a particular applicant based on test scores (individual success); and the *utility formula* provides an estimate of the amount of money an organization will save if it adopts a new testing procedure.

Taylor-Russell Tables

Taylor-Russell tables A series of tables based on the selection ratio, base rate, and test validity that yield information about the percentage of future employees who will be successful if a particular test is used.

Taylor-Russell tables (Taylor & Russell, 1939) are designed to estimate the percentage of future employees who will be successful on the job if an organization uses a particular test. The philosophy behind the Taylor-Russell tables is that a test will be useful to an organization if (1) the test is valid, (2) the organization can be selective in its hiring because it has more applicants than openings, and (3) there are plenty of current employees who are not performing well, thus there is room for improvement. To use the Taylor-Russell tables, three pieces of information must be obtained.

The first information needed is the test's *criterion validity coefficient.* There are two ways to obtain this coefficient. The best would be to actually conduct a criterion validity study with test scores correlated with some measure of job performance. Often, however, an organization wants to know whether testing is useful before investing time and money in a criterion validity study. This is where validity generalization comes into play. Based on findings by researchers such as Schmidt and Hunter (1998), we have a good idea of the typical validity coefficients that will result from various methods of selection. To estimate the validity coefficient that an organization might obtain, one of the coefficients from Table 5.2 in the previous chapter is used. The higher the validity coefficient, the greater the possibility the test will be useful.

Selection ratio The percentage of applicants an organization hires.

The second piece of information that must be obtained is the **selection ratio**, which is simply the percentage of people an organization must hire. The ratio is determined by the following formula:

$$\text{Selection ratio} = \frac{\text{number hired}}{\text{number of applications}}$$

Referring back to the initial example of 100 job openings and 100 job seekers, a test (no matter how valid) would not be effective. Thus, the lower the selection ratio, the greater the potential usefulness of the test.

The final piece of information needed is the **base rate** of current performance—the percentage of employees currently on the job who are considered successful. This figure is usually obtained in one of two ways. The first method is the simplest but the least accurate. Employees are split into two equal groups based on their scores on some criterion such as tenure or performance. The base rate using this method is always .50 because one-half of the employees are considered satisfactory.

The second and more meaningful method is to choose a criterion measure score above which all employees are considered successful. For example, at one real estate agency, any agent who sells more than $700,000 of properties makes a profit for the agency after training and operating expenses have been deducted. In this case, agents selling more than $700,000 of properties would be considered successes because they made money for the company. Agents selling less than $700,000 of properties would be considered failures because they cost the company more money than they brought in. In this example, there is a clear point at which an employee can be considered a success. Most of the time, however, there are no such clear points. In these cases, managers will subjectively choose a point on the criterion that they feel separates successful from unsuccessful employees.

After the validity, selection ratio, and base rate figures have been obtained, the Taylor-Russell tables are consulted (Table 6.4). To understand how they are used, let us take the following example. Suppose we have a test validity of .40, a selection ratio of .30, and a base rate of .50. Locating the table corresponding to the .50 base rate, we look along the top of the chart until we find the .30 selection ratio. Next, we locate the validity of .40 on the left side of the table. We then trace across the table until we locate the intersection of the selection ratio column and the validity row; we have found .69. If the organization uses that particular selection test, 69% of future employees are likely to be considered successful. This figure is compared with the previous base rate of .50, indicating a 38% increase in successful employees (.19 ÷ .50 = .38).

Proportion of Correct Decisions

Determining the **proportion of correct decisions** is easier to do but less accurate than the Taylor-Russell tables. The only information needed to determine the proportion of correct decisions is employee test scores and the scores on the criterion. The two scores from each employee are graphed on a chart similar to that in Figure 6.1. Lines are drawn from the point on the y-axis (criterion score) that represents a successful applicant, and from the point on the x-axis that represents the lowest test score of a hired applicant. As you can see, these lines divide the scores into four quadrants. The points located in quadrant I represent employees who scored poorly on the test but performed well on the job. Points located in quadrant II represent employees who scored well on the test and were successful on the job. Points in quadrant III represent employees who scored high on the test, yet did poorly on the job, and points in quadrant IV represent employees who scored low on the test and did poorly on the job.

If a test is a good predictor of performance, there should be more points in quadrants II and IV because the points in the other two quadrants represent "predictive failures." That is, in quadrants I and III no correspondence is seen between test scores and criterion scores.

To estimate the test's effectiveness, the number of points in each quadrant is totaled, and the following formula is used:

Points in quadrants I and IV ÷ Total points in all quadrants

Base rate Percentage of current employees who are considered successful.

Proportion of correct decisions A utility method that compares the percentage of times a selection decision was accurate with the percentage of successful employees.

Table 6.4 Taylor-Russell Tables

Employees Considered Satisfactory	r	Selection Ratio										
		.05	.10	.20	.30	.40	.50	.60	.70	.80	.90	.95
10%	.00	.10	.10	.10	.10	.10	.10	.10	.10	.10	.10	.10
	.10	.14	.13	.13	.12	.12	.11	.11	.11	.11	.10	.10
	.20	.19	.17	.15	.14	.14	.13	.12	.12	.11	.11	.10
	.30	.25	.22	.19	.17	.15	.14	.13	.12	.12	.11	.10
	.40	.31	.27	.22	.19	.17	.16	.14	.13	.12	.11	.10
	.50	.39	.32	.26	.22	.19	.17	.15	.13	.12	.11	.11
	.60	.48	.39	.30	.25	.21	.18	.16	.14	.12	.11	.11
	.70	.58	.47	.35	.27	.22	.19	.16	.14	.12	.11	.11
	.80	.71	.56	.40	.30	.24	.20	.17	.14	.12	.11	.11
	.90	.86	.69	.46	.33	.25	.20	.17	.14	.12	.11	.11
20%	.00	.20	.20	.20	.20	.20	.20	.20	.20	.20	.20	.20
	.10	.26	.25	.24	.23	.23	.22	.22	.21	.21	.21	.20
	.20	.33	.31	.28	.27	.26	.25	.24	.23	.22	.21	.21
	.30	.41	.37	.33	.30	.28	.27	.25	.24	.23	.21	.21
	.40	.49	.44	.38	.34	.31	.29	.27	.25	.23	.22	.21
	.50	.59	.52	.44	.38	.35	.31	.29	.26	.24	.22	.21
	.60	.68	.60	.50	.43	.38	.34	.30	.27	.24	.22	.21
	.70	.79	.69	.56	.48	.41	.36	.31	.28	.25	.22	.21
	.80	.89	.79	.64	.53	.45	.38	.33	.28	.25	.22	.21
	.90	.98	.91	.75	.60	.48	.40	.33	.29	.25	.22	.21
30%	.00	.30	.30	.30	.30	.30	.30	.30	.30	.30	.30	.30
	.10	.38	.36	.35	.34	.33	.33	.32	.32	.31	.31	.30
	.20	.46	.43	.40	.38	.37	.36	.34	.33	.32	.31	.31
	.30	.54	.50	.46	.43	.40	.38	.37	.35	.33	.32	.31
	.40	.63	.58	.51	.47	.44	.41	.39	.37	.34	.32	.31
	.50	.72	.65	.58	.52	.48	.44	.41	.38	.35	.33	.31
	.60	.81	.74	.64	.58	.52	.47	.43	.40	.36	.33	.31
	.70	.89	.62	.72	.63	.57	.51	.46	.41	.37	.33	.32
	.80	.96	.90	.80	.70	.62	.54	.48	.42	.37	.33	.32
	.90	1.00	.98	.90	.79	.68	.58	.49	.43	.37	.33	.32
40%	.00	.40	.40	.40	.40	.40	.40	.40	.40	.40	.40	.40
	.10	.48	.47	.46	.45	.44	.43	.42	.42	.41	.41	.40
	.20	.57	.54	.51	.49	.48	.46	.45	.44	.43	.41	.41
	.30	.65	.61	.57	.54	.51	.49	.47	.46	.44	.42	.41
	.40	.73	.69	.63	.59	.56	.53	.50	.48	.45	.43	.41
	.50	.81	.76	.69	.64	.60	.56	.53	.49	.46	.43	.42
	.60	.89	.83	.75	.69	.64	.60	.55	.51	.48	.44	.42
	.70	.95	.90	.82	.76	.69	.64	.58	.53	.49	.44	.42
	.80	.99	.96	.89	.82	.75	.68	.61	.55	.49	.44	.42
	.90	1.00	1.00	.97	.91	.82	.74	.65	.57	.50	.44	.42
50%	.00	.50	.50	.50	.50	.50	.50	.50	.50	.50	.50	.50
	.10	.58	.57	.56	.55	.54	.53	.53	.52	.51	.51	.50
	.20	.67	.64	.61	.59	.58	.56	.55	.54	.53	.52	.51

Table 6.4 Taylor-Russell Tables (Continued)

Employees Considered Satisfactory	r	.05	.10	.20	.30	.40	.50	.60	.70	.80	.90	.95
	.30	.74	.71	.67	.64	.62	.60	.58	.56	.54	.52	.51
	.40	.82	.78	.73	.69	.66	.63	.61	.58	.56	.53	.52
	.50	.88	.84	.76	.74	.70	.67	.63	.60	.57	.54	.52
	.60	.94	.90	.84	.79	.75	.70	.66	.62	.59	.54	.52
	.70	.98	.95	.90	.85	.80	.75	.70	.65	.60	.55	.53
	.80	1.00	.99	.95	.90	.85	.80	.73	.67	.61	.55	.53
	.90	1.00	1.00	.99	.97	.92	.86	.78	.70	.62	.56	.53
60%	.00	.60	.60	.60	.60	.60	.60	.60	.60	.60	.60	.60
	.10	.68	.67	.65	.64	.64	.63	.63	.62	.61	.61	.60
	.20	.75	.73	.71	.69	.67	.66	.65	.64	.63	.62	.61
	.30	.82	.79	.76	.73	.71	.69	.68	.66	.64	.62	.61
	.40	.88	.85	.81	.78	.75	.73	.70	.68	.66	.63	.62
	.50	.93	.90	.86	.82	.79	.76	.73	.70	.67	.64	.62
	.60	.96	.94	.90	.87	.83	.80	.76	.73	.69	.65	.63
	.70	.99	.97	.94	.91	.87	.84	.80	.75	.71	.66	.63
	.80	1.00	.99	.98	.95	.92	.88	.83	.78	.72	.66	.63
	.90	1.00	1.00	1.00	.99	.97	.94	.88	.82	.74	.67	.63
70%.	.00	.70	.70	.70	.70	.70	.70	.70	.70	.70	.70	.70
	.10	.77	.76	.75	.74	.73	.73	.72	.72	.71	.71	.70
	.20	.83	.81	.79	.78	.77	.76	.75	.74	.73	.71	.71
	.30	.88	.86	.84	.82	.80	.78	.77	.75	.74	.72	.71
	.40	.93	.91	.88	.85	.83	.81	.79	.77	.75	.73	.72
	.50	.96	.94	.91	.89	.87	.84	.82	.80	.77	.74	.72
	.60	.98	.97	.95	.92	.90	.87	.85	.82	.79	.75	.73
	.70	1.00	.99	.97	.96	.93	.91	.88	.84	.80	.76	.73
	.80	1.00	1.00	.99	.98	.97	.94	.91	.87	.82	.77	.73
	.90	1.00	1.00	1.00	1.00	.99	.98	.95	.91	.85	.78	.74
80%	.00	.80	.80	.80	.80	.80	.80	.80	.80	.80	.80	.80
	.10	.85	.85	.84	.83	.83	.82	.82	.81	.81	.81	.80
	.20	.90	.89	.87	.86	.85	.84	.84	.83	.82	.81	.81
	.30	.94	.92	.90	.89	.88	.87	.86	.84	.83	.82	.81
	.40	.96	.95	.93	.92	.90	.89	.88	.86	.85	.83	.82
	.50	.98	.97	.96	.94	.93	.91	.90	.88	.86	.84	.82
	.60	.99	.99	.98	.96	.95	.94	.92	.90	.87	.84	.83
	.70	1.00	1.00	.99	.98	.97	.96	.94	.92	.89	.85	.83
	.80	1.00	1.00	1.00	1.00	.99	.98	.96	.94	.91	.87	.84
	.90	1.00	1.00	1.00	1.00	1.00	1.00	.99	.97	.94	.88	.84
90%	.00	.90	.90	.90	.90	.90	.90	.90	.90	.90	.90	.90
	.10	.93	.93	.92	.92	.92	.91	.91	.91	.91	.90	.90
	.20	.96	.95	.94	.94	.93	.93	.92	.92	.91	.91	.90
	.30	.98	.97	.96	.95	.95	.94	.94	.93	.92	.91	.91
	.40	.99	.98	.98	.97	.96	.95	.95	.94	.93	.92	.91

Table 6.4   Taylor-Russell Tables (*Continued*)

Employees Considered Satisfactory		Selection Ratio										
	r	**.05**	**.10**	**.20**	**.30**	**.40**	**.50**	**.60**	**.70**	**.80**	**.90**	**.95**
	.50	1.00	.99	.99	.98	.97	.97	.96	.95	.94	.92	.92
	.60	1.00	1.00	.99	.99	.99	.98	.97	.96	.95	.93	.92
	.70	1.00	1.00	1.00	1.00	.99	.99	.98	.97	.96	.94	.93
	.80	1.00	1.00	1.00	1.00	1.00	1.00	.99	.99	.97	.95	.93
	.90	1.00	1.00	1.00	1.00	1.00	1.00	1.00	1.00	.99	.97	.94

Source: "The relationship of validity coefficients to the practical effectiveness of tests in selection: Discussion and tables," by H. C. Taylor and J. T. Russell, 1939, *Journal of Applied Psychology*, 23, 565–578.

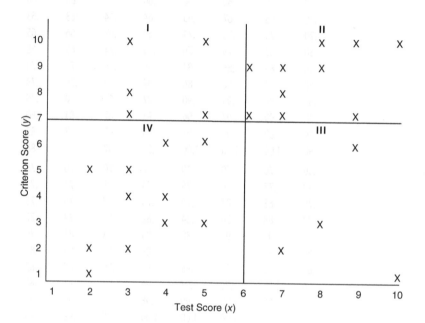

Figure 6.1

Determining the Proportion of Correct Decisions

The resulting number represents the percentage of time that we expect to be accurate in making a selection decision in the future. To determine whether this is an improvement, we use the following formula:

Points in quadrants I and II ÷ Total points in all quadrants

If the percentage from the first formula is higher than that from the second, our proposed test should increase selection accuracy. If not, it is probably better to stick with the selection method currently used.

As an example, look again at Figure 6.1. There are 5 data points in quadrant I, 10 in quadrant II, 4 in quadrant III, and 11 in quadrant IV. The percentage of time we expect to be accurate in the future would be:

$$\frac{\text{II} + \text{IV}}{\text{I} + \text{II} + \text{IV}} = \frac{10 + 11}{5 + 10 + 4 + 11} = \frac{21}{30} = .70$$

To compare this figure with the test we were previously using to select employees, we compute the satisfactory performance baseline:

$$\frac{I + II}{I + II + III + IV} = \frac{5 + 10}{5 + 10 + 4 + 11} = \frac{15}{30} = .50$$

Using the new test would result in a 40% increase in selection accuracy [.70 − .50 = .20 ÷ .50] over the selection method previously used.

Lawshe Tables

Lawshe tables Tables that use the base rate, test validity, and applicant percentile on a test to determine the probability of future success for that applicant.

The Taylor-Russell tables were designed to determine the overall impact of a testing procedure. But we often need to know the probability that a *particular applicant* will be successful. The **Lawshe tables** (Lawshe, Bolda, Brune, & Auclair, 1958) were created to do just that. To use these tables, three pieces of information are needed. The validity coefficient and the base rate are found in the same way as for the Taylor-Russell tables. The third piece of information needed is the applicant's test score. More specifically, did the person score in the top 20%, the next 20%, the middle 20%, the next lowest 20%, or the bottom 20%?

Once we have all three pieces of information, the Lawshe tables, as shown in Table 6.5, are examined. For our example, we have a base rate of .50, a validity of .40, and an applicant who scored third highest out of 10. First, we locate the table with the base rate of .50. Then we locate the appropriate category at the top of the chart. Our applicant scored third highest out of 10 applicants, so they would be in the second category, the next highest one-fifth, or 20%. Using the validity of .40, we locate the intersection of the validity row and the test score column and find 59. This means that the applicant has a 59% chance of being a successful employee.

Expectancy Charts

Expectancy charts Charts that indicate the chance of success for each test score range.

A simple way to demonstrate the effectiveness of a test is with an **expectancy chart**. Similar to the Lawshe tables, expectancy charts indicate the probability of being a successful employee given a particular test score. Unlike the Lawshe tables, expectancy charts are based on raw data distributions rather than correlation coefficients. Expectancy charts are especially effective for a nontechnical audience but can be misleading if the sample size in the study is small (Cucina, Berger, & Busciglio, 2017).

To create an expectancy chart, we begin by placing applicants into groups based on their test scores. These groups can be based on quartiles (i.e., four equally sized groups) or on ranges of scores (e.g., <60, 60−69, 70−79, 80−89, 90+). For each group of scores the expectancy chart would indicate the percentage of applicants that became successful employees. To demonstrate, imagine a study in which we create a biodata instrument to predict employee tenure. Any employee that is still employed after one year is considered a success. As shown in Figure 6.2, only 5% of applicants with the lowest scores were still employed a year late compared to 50% of the applicants with the highest scores.

Brogden-Cronbach-Gleser Utility Formula

Utility formula Method of ascertaining the extent to which an organization will benefit from the use of a particular selection system.

Another way to determine the value of a test in a given situation is by computing the amount of money an organization would save if it used the test to select employees. Fortunately, I/O psychologists have devised a fairly simple **utility formula** to estimate

Table 6.5   Lawshe Individual Prediction Tables

Percentage of Current Employees Considered Satisfactory	Applicant Scores on Selection Test					
	r	Top 20%	Next 20%	Middle 20%	Next 20%	Bottom 20%
30%	.20	40	34	29	26	21
	.30	46	35	29	24	16
	.40	51	37	28	21	12
	.50	58	38	27	18	09
	.60	64	40	26	15	05
40%	.20	51	45	40	35	30
	.30	57	46	40	33	24
	.40	63	48	39	31	19
	.50	69	50	39	28	14
	.60	75	53	38	24	10
50%	.20	61	55	50	45	39
	.30	67	57	50	43	33
	.40	73	59	50	41	28
	.50	78	62	50	38	22
	.60	84	65	50	35	16
60%	.20	71	63	60	56	48
	.30	76	66	61	54	44
	.40	81	69	61	52	37
	.50	86	72	62	47	25
	.60	90	76	62	47	25
70%	.20	79	75	70	67	59
	.30	84	78	71	65	54
	.40	88	79	72	63	49
	.50	91	82	73	62	42
	.60	95	85	74	60	36

Note: Percentages indicate probability that applicant with a particular score will be a successful employee.

Source: "Expectancy charts II: Their theoretical development," C. H. Lawshe and R. A. Brune, 1958, *Personnel Psychology*, 11, 545–599.

the monetary savings to an organization. To use this formula, five items of information must be known.

1. Number of employees hired per year (*n*). This number is easy to determine: It is simply the number of employees who are hired for a given position in a year.

Figure 6.2

Example of an expectancy chart

Tenure The length of time an employee has been with an organization.

2. Average tenure (*t*). This is the average amount of time that employees in the position tend to stay with the company. The number is computed by using information from company records to identify the time that each employee in that position stayed with the company. The number of years of **tenure** for each employee is then summed and divided by the total number of employees.

3. Test validity (*r*). This figure is the criterion validity coefficient that was obtained through either a validity study or validity generalization.

4. Standard deviation of performance in dollars (SDy). For many years, this number was difficult to compute. Research has shown, however, that for jobs in which performance is normally distributed, a good estimate of the difference in performance between an average and a good worker (one standard deviation away in performance) is 40% of the employee's annual salary (Hunter & Schmidt, 1982). The 40% rule yields results similar to more complicated methods and is preferred by managers (Hazer & Highhouse, 1997). To obtain this, the total salaries of current employees in the position in question should be averaged.

5. Mean standardized predictor score of selected applicants (*m*). This number is obtained in one of two ways. The first method is to obtain the average score on the selection test for both the applicants who are hired and the applicants who are not hired. The average test score of the nonhired applicants is subtracted from the average test score of the hired applicants. This difference is divided by the standard deviation of all the test scores.

For example, we administer a test of mental ability to a group of 100 applicants and hire the 10 with the highest scores. The average score of the 10 hired applicants was 34.6, the average test score of the other 90 applicants was 28.4, and the standard deviation of all test scores was 8.3. The desired figure would be:

$$\frac{34.6 - 28.4}{8.3} = \frac{6.2}{8.3} = .747$$

The second way to find *m* is to compute the proportion of applicants who are hired and then use a conversion table such as that in Table 6.6 to convert the proportion into a standard score. This second method is used when an organization plans to use a test and knows the probable selection ratio based on previous hirings but does not

Table 6.6   Selection-Ratio Conversion Table for Utility Formula

Selection Ratio	m
1.00	0.00
.90	0.20
.80	0.35
.70	0.50
.60	0.64
.50	0.80
.40	0.97
.30	1.17
.20	1.40
.10	1.76
.05	2.08

know the average test scores because the organization has never used the test. Using the previous example, the proportion of applicants hired would be:

$$\frac{\text{number of applications hired}}{\text{total number of applicants}} = \frac{10}{100} = .10$$

From Table 6.6, we see that the standard score associated with a selection ratio of .10 is 1.76. To determine the savings to the company, we use the following formula:

Savings = $(n)\ (t)\ (r)\ (SD_y)\ (m)$ − cost of testing (# of applicants × the cost per applicant)

As an example, suppose we hire 10 auditors per year, the average person in this position stays two years, the validity coefficient is .30, and the average annual salary for the position is $30,000, and we have 50 applicants for 10 openings. Thus,

$n = 10$
$t = 2$
$r = .30$
$SD_y = \$30,000 \times .40 = \$12,000$
$m = 10/50 = .20 = 1.40$ (.20 is converted to 1.40 by using Table 6.6)
cost of testing = (50 applicants × $10)

Using the above formula, we would have:

$$(10)\ (2)\ (.30)\ (12,000)\ (1.40) - (50)\ (10) = \$100,300$$

This means that after accounting for the cost of testing, using this particular test instead of selecting employees by chance will save a company $100,300 over the two years that auditors typically stay with the organization. Because a company seldom selects employees by chance, the same formula should be used with the validity of the test (interview, psychological test, references, etc.) that the company currently uses. The result of this computation should then be subtracted from the first.

This final figure, of course, is just an estimate based on the assumption that the highest-scoring applicants accept the job offer. To be most accurate, it must be adjusted by such factors as variable costs, discounting, corporate tax rates, and changes in strategic goals (Boudreau, 1983; Russell, Colella, & Bobko, 1993). Because utility estimates are often in the millions of dollars, there has been concern that managers may not believe the estimates (Cascio & Scott, 2017). However, research indicates that managers positively view utility estimates, and thus these estimates can be used to support the usefulness of testing (Carson, Becker, & Henderson, 1998; Hoff Macan & Foster, 2004). When one considers the costs of constant poor performance, the size of these estimates should not be surprising. The high estimated savings are even more believable when one considers the cost of one employee's mistake. For example:

- An employee of Oxford Organics Inc. mislabeled an artificial vanilla flavoring sent to General Mills, resulting in $150,000 in damaged cake frosting.
- A U.S. Navy mechanic left a 5-inch wrench inside the wheel compartment of a jet, causing the $33 million plane to crash.
- A typo in a letter by a car dealer told customers to call a 900 number instead of an 800 number. The 900 number turned out to be a sex line, and the dealership had to send out an additional 1,000 letters to apologize and correct the mistake.

Thus, the cost of daily poor performance, combined with the cost of occasional mistakes such as these, provides support for the validity of high utility estimates.

Though utility formulas are useful means for decision making, it should be noted that not all managers trust the results of utility formulas and thus other means for demonstrating validity might be needed. Such methods include benchmarking studies to show that what your organization is doing is a "best practice"; studies looking at applicant and employee reactions to demonstrate that your "clients" feel comfortable with your testing practices (face validity); data indicating that your new hires are successful (e.g., performance ratings, tenure, supervisor comments); data indicating that the results of hiring decisions are consistent with the organization's affirmative action and diversity goals; and data indicating that the hiring process is meeting the organization's goals for filling positions in a timely manner with competent employees.

6-3   Determining the Fairness of a Test

Once a test has been determined to be reliable and valid and to have utility for an organization, the next step is to ensure that the test is fair and unbiased. Although there is disagreement among I/O psychologists regarding the definition of test fairness, most professionals agree that one must consider potential race, gender, disability, and cultural differences in both the content of the test (measurement bias) and the way in which scores from the test predict job performance (predictive bias; Meade & Tonidandel, 2010).

Measurement Bias

Measurement bias refers to technical aspects of a test. A test is considered to have measurement bias if there are group differences (e.g., gender, race, or age) in test scores that are unrelated to the construct being measured. For example, if race differences on a test of logic are due to vocabulary words found more often in White than Black culture,

Measurement bias Group differences in test scores that are unrelated to the construct being measured.

Adverse impact An employment practice that results in members of a protected class being negatively affected at a higher rate than members of the majority class. Adverse impact is usually determined by the four-fifths rule.

but these same words are not important to the performance of the job in question, the test might be considered to have measurement bias and thus not be fair in that particular situation. The statistical methods for determining measurement bias can be very complicated and are certainly beyond the scope of this text. However, from a legal perspective, if differences in test scores result in one group (e.g., men) being selected at a significantly higher rate than another (e.g., women), **adverse impact** is said to have occurred and the burden is on the organization using the test to prove that the test is valid. (Refer back to Chapter 3 if you need a refresher on adverse impact.)

Predictive Bias

Predictive bias A situation in which the predicted level of job success falsely favors one group over another.

Single-group validity The characteristic of a test that significantly predicts a criterion for one class of people but not for another.

Predictive bias refers to situations in which the predicted level of job success falsely favors one group (e.g., men) over another (e.g., women). That is, a test would have predictive bias if men scored higher on the test than women, but the job performance of women was equal to or better than that of men.

One form of predictive bias is **single-group validity**, meaning that the test will significantly predict performance for one group and not others. For example, a test of reading ability might predict performance of White clerks but not of Black clerks.

To test for single-group validity, separate correlations are computed between the test and the criterion for each group. If both correlations are significant, the test does not exhibit single-group validity and it passes this fairness hurdle. If, however, only one of the correlations is significant, the test is considered fair for only that one group.

Single-group validity is very rare (O'Connor, Wexley, & Alexander, 1975) and is usually the result of small sample sizes and other methodological problems (Schmidt, 1988; Schmidt & Hunter, 1978). Where it occurs, an organization has two choices. It can disregard single-group validity because research indicates that it probably occurred by chance or it can stop using the test. Disregarding single-group validity probably is the most appropriate choice, given that most I/O psychologists believe that single-group validity occurs only by chance. As evidence of this, think of a logical reason a test would predict differently for Black individuals than for White individuals or differently for men than for women. That is, why would a test of intelligence predict performance for men but not for women? Or why would a personality inventory predict performance for Black employees but not for White employees? There may be many cultural reasons why two groups *score* differently on a test (e.g., educational opportunities, socioeconomic status), but finding a logical reason that the test would *predict* differently for two groups is difficult.

Differential validity The characteristic of a test that significantly predicts a criterion for two groups, such as both minorities and nonminorities, but predicts significantly better for one of the two groups.

A second form of predictive bias is **differential validity**. With differential validity, a test is valid for two groups but more valid for one than for the other. Single-group validity and differential validity are easily confused, but there is a big difference between the two. Remember, with single-group validity, the test is valid only for one group. With differential validity, the test is valid for both groups, but it is more valid for one than for the other.

Like single-group validity, differential validity is also rare (Katzell & Dyer, 1977; Mattern & Patterson, 2013; Schmidt & Hunter, 1981), although some researchers believe much more research is needed on this topic (Aguinis, Culpepper, & Pierce, 2016), and other researchers believe that examining biases of selection methods require much more than just the use of differential validity (Linn, 1978). When it does occur, it is usually in occupations dominated by a single sex, tests are most valid for the dominant sex and the tests overpredict minority performance (Rothstein & McDaniel, 1992; Saad & Sackett, 2002). If differential-group validity occurs, the organization has two choices. The first is not to use the test. Usually, however, this is not a good option. Finding a test that is valid is difficult; throwing away a good test would be a shame.

The second option is to use the test with separate regression equations for each group. Because applicants do not realize that the test is scored differently, there are not the public relations problems that occur with use of separate tests. However, the 1991 Civil Rights Act prohibits score adjustments based on race or gender. As a result, using separate equations may be statistically acceptable but would not be legally defensible.

Another important aspect of test fairness is the *perception* of fairness held by the applicants taking the test. That is, a test may not have measurement or predictive bias, but applicants might perceive the test itself or the way in which the test is administered as not being fair. Factors that might affect applicants' perceptions of fairness include the difficulty of the test, the amount of time allowed to complete the test, the face validity of the test items, the manner in which hiring decisions are made from the test scores (this will be discussed in detail in the next section), policies about retaking the test, and the way in which requests for testing accommodations for disabilities were handled.

6-4 Making the Hiring Decision

After valid and fair selection tests have been administered to a group of applicants, a final decision must be made as to which applicant or applicants to hire. At first, this may seem to be an easy decision—hire the applicants with the highest test scores. But the decision becomes more complicated as both the number and variety of tests increase.

If more than one criterion-valid test is used, the scores on the tests must be combined. Usually, this is done by a statistical procedure known as **multiple regression**, with each test score weighted according to how well it predicts the criterion. **Linear** approaches to hiring usually take one of four forms: unadjusted top-down selection, rules of three, passing scores, or banding.

Multiple regression A statistical procedure in which the scores from more than one criterion-valid test are weighted according to how well each test score predicts the criterion.

Linear A straight-line relationship between the test score and the criterion of measurement.

Top-down selection Selecting applicants in straight rank order of their test scores.

compensatory approach A method of making selection decisions in which a high score on one test can compensate for a low score on another test. For example, a high GPA might compensate for a low GRE score.

Unadjusted Top-Down Selection

With **top-down selection**, applicants are rank-ordered based on their test scores. Selection is then made by starting with the highest score and moving down until all openings have been filled. For example, for the data in Table 6.7, if we had four openings, we would hire the top four scorers, who, in this case, would be Ferguson, Letterman, Fallon, and Kimmel. Note that all four are men. If, for affirmative action purposes, we wanted to hire two women top-down selection would not allow us to do so.

The advantage to top-down selection is that by hiring the top scorers on a valid test, an organization will gain the most utility (Schmidt, 1991; Schmitt, Arnold, & Nieminen, 2017). The disadvantages are that this approach can result in high levels of adverse impact and it reduces an organization's flexibility to use nontest factors such as references or organizational fit.

In a **compensatory approach** to top-down selection, the assumption is that if multiple test scores are used, the relationship between a low score on one test can be compensated for by a high score on another (Aiken & Hanges, 2017). For example, a student applying to a graduate school might have a low GRE score but have a high undergraduate grade point average (GPA). If the GPA is high enough, it would compensate for the low GRE score. To determine whether a score on one test can compensate for a score on another, multiple regression is used in which each test score

Table 6.7 Hypothetical Testing Information

Applicant	Sex	Test Score
Ferguson	M	99
Letterman	M	98
Fallon	M	91
Kimmel	M	90
Winfrey	F	88
Lopez	M	87
Leno	M	72
Hasselbeck	F	70 Passing Score
Banks	F	68
Stewart	M	62
Colbert	M	60
Gifford	F	57
Jones	F	54
O'Brien	M	49
Maher	M	31

is weighted according to how well it predicts the criterion. When considering the use of a compensatory approach, it is essential that a high score on one test would actually compensate for a low score on another. For example, in a recent audit, the OFCCP argued that the organization being audited should let a high score on a personality inventory compensate for a low score on a physical ability exam. OFCCP's reasoning was that because men and women scored similarly on the personality inventory, adverse impact would be reduced. However, the argument doesn't make sense as personality will not compensate for the inability to be able to lift a heavy package.

Rule of Three

Rule of three A variation on top-down selection in which the names of the top three applicants are given to a hiring authority who can then select any of the three.

A technique often used in the public sector is the **rule of three** (or rule of five), in which the names of the top three scorers are given to the person making the hiring decision (e.g., police chief, HR director). This person can then choose any of the three based on the immediate needs of the employer. This method ensures that the person hired will be well qualified but provides more choice than does top-down selection. Interestingly, some states had rejected the "Rule of Three" in considering applicants for government jobs, including Virginia, California, Minnesota, citing an increase in discretion of hiring authorities; others suggested a "Rule of Ten" instead (Lasky, 1999).

Passing Scores

Passing score The minimum test score that an applicant must achieve to be considered for hire.

Passing scores are a means for reducing adverse impact and increasing flexibility. With this system, an organization determines the lowest score on a test that is associated with acceptable performance on the job. For example, we would assume that a student scoring 1,300 on the SAT will probably have better grades in college than a student scoring 800. But what is the lowest score on the SAT that we can accept and still be confident that the student will be able to pass classes and eventually graduate?

Notice the distinct difference between top-down selection and passing scores. With top-down selection, the question is, "Who will perform the *best* in the future?" With passing scores, the question becomes, "Who will be able to perform at an *acceptable level* in the future?"

As you can imagine, passing scores provide an organization with much flexibility. Again, using Table 6.7 as an example, suppose we determine that any applicant scoring 70 or above will be able to perform adequately the duties of the job in question. If we set 70 as the passing score, we can fill our four openings with any of the eight applicants scoring 70 or better. Because, for affirmative action reasons, we would like two of the four openings to be filled by women we are free to hire Winfrey and Hasselbeck. Use of passing scores allows us to reach our affirmative action goals, which would not have been met with top-down selection. By hiring applicants with lower scores, however, the performance of our future employees will be lower than if we used top-down selection (Schmidt, 1991).

Though the use of passing scores appears to be a reasonable step toward reaching affirmative action goals, determining the actual passing score can be a complicated process full of legal pitfalls (Biddle, 1993). The most common methods for determining passing scores (e.g., the Angoff and Nedelsky methods) require job experts to read each item on a test and provide an estimation about the percentage of minimally qualified employees that could answer the item correctly. The passing score then becomes the average of the estimations for each question. Legal problems can occur when unsuccessful applicants challenge the validity of the passing score.

If there is more than one test for which we have passing scores, a decision must be made regarding the use of a **multiple-cutoff approach** or a multiple-hurdle approach. Both approaches are used when one score can't compensate for another or when the relationship between the selection test and performance is not linear. With a multiple-cutoff approach, the applicants would be administered all of the tests at one time. If they failed any of the tests (fell below the passing score), they would not be considered further for employment.

For example, suppose that our job analysis finds that a good police officer is intelligent, has a college degree, is confident, can lift 50 pounds, and does not have a criminal record. Our validity study indicates that the relationships of both intelligence and confidence with job performance are linear: The smarter and more confident the officer, the better they perform. Because the relationships between strength, not having a criminal record, and having a college degree are not linear, we would use a multiple-cutoff approach in which applicants would need to pass the background check, have a college degree, and be able to lift 50 pounds. If they meet all three requirements, their confidence levels and cognitive ability test scores are used to determine who will be hired.

One problem with a multiple-cutoff approach is the cost. If an applicant passes only three out of four tests, he will not be hired, but the organization has paid for the applicant to take all four tests.

To reduce the costs associated with applicants failing one or more tests, **multiple-hurdle approaches** are often used. With a multiple-hurdle approach, the applicant is administered one test at a time, usually beginning with the least expensive. Applicants who fail a test are eliminated from further consideration and take no more tests. Applicants who pass all of the tests are then administered the linearly related tests; the applicants with the top scores on these tests are hired.

Multiple-cutoff approach A selection strategy in which applicants must meet or exceed the passing score on more than one selection test.

Multiple-hurdle approach Selection practice of administering one test at a time so that applicants must pass that test before being allowed to take the next test.

To clarify the difference between a multiple-cutoff and a multiple-hurdle approach, let us look at the following example. Suppose we will use four pass/fail tests to select employees. The tests have the following costs and failure rates:

Test	Test Cost	Failure Rate
Background check	$25	10%
Psychological screen	$50	10%
Medical exam	$100	10%
Physical ability test	$5	10%
Total per applicant	$180	

If the tests cost $180 per applicant and 100 applicants apply for a position, a multiple-cutoff approach would cost our organization $18,000 (100 applicants x $180 each) to administer the tests to all applicants. But with a multiple-hurdle approach, we can administer the cheapest test (the strength test) to all 100 applicants. Because 10% of the applicants will fail this test, we can then administer the next cheapest test to the remaining 90. This process continues until all tests have been administered. A savings of $3,900 will result, based on the following calculations:

Test	Test Cost	Applicants	Total Cost
Physical ability test	$5	100	$500
Background check	$25	90	$2,250
Psychological screen	$50	81	$4,050
Medical exam	$100	73	$7,300
Total cost			$14,100

If a multiple-hurdle approach is usually less expensive, why is it not *always* used instead of a multiple-cutoff approach? First, many of the tests cited above take time to conduct or score. For example, it might take a few weeks to run a background check or a few days to interpret a psychological screening. Therefore, the tests usually must be administered on several occasions, and an applicant would have to miss several days of work to apply for a particular job. Because people often cannot or will not take more than one day off from one job to apply for another, many potentially excellent applicants are lost before testing begins.

Second, research has shown that in general the longer the time between submission of a job application and the hiring decision, the smaller the number of Black applicants who will remain in the applicant pool (Arvey, Gordon, Massengill, & Mussio, 1975). Black individuals have higher unemployment rates than White individuals and people who are unemployed are more hurried to obtain employment than people with jobs. Thus, because the multiple-hurdle approach takes longer than multiple-cutoff, it may bring an unintended adverse impact, and affirmative action goals may not be met.

Third, research suggests that a compensatory approach does a better job of predicting performance than does a multiple-hurdle approach (Ock & Oswald, 2018).

Banding

Banding A statistical technique based on the standard error of measurement that allows similar test scores to be grouped.

As mentioned previously, a problem with top-down hiring is that the process results in the highest levels of adverse impact. On the other hand, use of passing scores decreases adverse impact but reduces utility. As a compromise between top-down hiring and passing scores, **banding** attempts to hire the top test scorers while still allowing some flexibility for affirmative action (Campion et al., 2001).

Banding takes into consideration the degree of error associated with any test score. Thus, even though one applicant might score two points higher than another, the two-point difference might be the result of chance (error) rather than actual differences in ability. The question then becomes, "How many points apart do two applicants have to be before we say their test scores are significantly different?"

Standard error of measurement (SEM) The number of points that a test score could be off due to test unreliability.

We can answer this question using a statistic called the **standard error of measurement (SEM)**. To compute this statistic, we obtain the reliability and standard deviation (SD) of a particular test either from the test catalog or we can compute it ourselves from the actual test scores. This information is then plugged into the following formula:

$$SEM = SD\sqrt{1 - \text{reliability}}$$

For example, suppose we have a test with a reliability of .90 and a standard deviation of 13.60. The calculation of the standard error would be:

$$SEM = 13.60\sqrt{1 - .90}$$
$$SEM = 13.60\sqrt{.10}$$
$$SEM = 13.60 \times .316$$
$$SEM = 4.30$$

Bands are typically—but do not have to be—determined by multiplying the standard error by 1.96 (the standard score associated with a 95% level of confidence). Because the standard error of our test is 4.30, test scores within 8.4 points (4.3 × 1.96) of one another would be considered statistically the same. If we take this concept a bit further, we can establish a hiring bandwidth of 8.4. For example, using our standard error of 4.3 and our bandwidth of 8.4 (8), look at the applicants depicted in Table 6.7. Suppose that we have four openings and would like to hire at least two women if possible. Because the highest scoring woman in our example is Winfrey at 88, a top-down approach would not result in any women being hired. With a nonsliding band, we are free to hire anyone whose scores fall between the top score (Ferguson at 99) and 91 (99 − 8.4). As with top-down selection, use of a nonsliding band in this example would not result in any women being hired. With a sliding band, however, we start with the highest score (Ferguson at 99) and subtract from it the bandwidth (8.4). In this case, 99 − 8.4 = 90.6, meaning that all applicants scoring between 91 and 99 are considered statistically to have the same score. Because no woman female falls within this band, we hire Ferguson and then consider the next score of Letterman at 98. Our next band of 98 through 90 (98 − 8.4) still does not contain a woman, so we hire Letterman and then consider the next score of Fallon at 91. Our new band of 94 to 86 contains four applicants, one of whom is a woman. Because we are free to hire anyone within a band, we would probably hire Winfrey to meet our affirmative action goals. We would then hire Fallon as our fourth person. With banding, one more woman was hired than would have occurred under a top-down system. Note, however, that our goal to hire two women was not reached, as it was when we used passing scores.

Though the concept of banding has been approved in several court cases (*Bridgeport Guardians v. City of Bridgeport*, 1991; *Chicago Firefighters Union Local No. 2 v. City of Chicago*, 1999; *Officers for Justice v. Civil Service Commission*, 1992), only selecting members of an underrepresented group in a band would be illegal. Instead, affirmative action goals must be considered as only one factor in selecting applicants from a band. For example, by allowing some flexibility in hiring, the use of banding might allow a police chief to hire a lower-scoring Spanish-speaking applicant or an applicant with computer skills over a higher-scoring applicant without these desired, but not required, skills.

Though banding seems to be a good compromise between top-down hiring and passing scores (Zedeck, Cascio, Goldstein, & Outtz, 1996), it is not without its critics (Campion et al., 2001). Research indicates that banding can result in lower utility than top-down hiring (Schmidt, 1991), that it may not actually reduce adverse impact in any significant way (Gutman & Christiansen, 1997), and that its usefulness in achieving affirmative action goals is affected by such factors as the selection ratio and the percentage of minority applicants (Sackett & Roth, 1991).

To complicate matters even more, it has been suggested that the SEM formula traditionally used in banding is incorrect and that the standard error of estimate (SEE) should be used instead of the standard error of measurement (Gasperson, Bowler, Wuensch, & Bowler, 2013). If Gasperson and his colleagues are correct, the bands resulting from the use of SEE will be smaller than those resulting from the use of SEM, thus, diminishing the already questionable usefulness of banding as a means of reducing adverse impact.

On the Job ▶ **Applied Case Study**

Thomas A. Edison's Employment Test

In Chapter 1, we mentioned that in 1920, inventor Thomas Edison created a 163-item test that he used to hire managers and scientists. All applicants were given two hours to answer a basic set of questions covering geography, science, history, and literature, and then, depending on the position applied for, some questions specific to their field. Edison created the test because he wanted to hire the best employees and he didn't trust college graduates. This distrust can be seen in his quote, "Men who have gone to college I find to be amazingly ignorant. They don't seem to know anything."

To pass the test, an applicant had to get 90% of the questions correct, a score thought to be comparable to an IQ of 180 (although there is no proof of this). According to Edison, of the first 718 men who took the test (there were no applicants who were women), only 57 (7.9%) had a grade of at least 70% (a passing score in college) and only 32 (4.5%) scored above 90%, Edison's passing score to be considered "Class A" men. What were some of the questions?

- What countries bound France?
- Where is the finest cotton grown?
- What city in the United States leads in making laundry machines?
- What has the greater area, Greenland or Australia?

As you can imagine, the test was not popular with applicants. Edison scored the test himself and, not only did he not share the test scores with the applicants, he had a rule that forbade applicants from communicating the questions to others. At least two applicants leaked the test results to the media, and on May 11, 1929, the *New York Times* published 141 of the questions that one of the unsuccessful applicants, Charles Hansen, could remember (you must be pretty bright to remember 141 questions verbatim!). The media challenged Edison by giving him pop quizzes like the one he created. He averaged 95% on these pop quizzes! Interestingly, Edison's son, Theodore, didn't pass the test, although he had a bachelor's degree in physics from the Massachusetts Institute of Technology.

Due to the criticism that his test placed too much emphasis on rote memory of trivial details, Edison defended his test in the October 23, 1921, issue of the *New York Times* with the following quotes:

- "If a man cannot remember things well in general, he cannot remember where to turn for them and how to look them up quickly and effectively. The man who tries to substitute a research method for a memory cannot act decisively and safely in an emergency."
- "It costs too much to learn whether a man is a good executive by trying him out on the job."
- "When I call upon any of my men for a decision, I want it right away. When his department calls on him for a decision, it wants it right away. It's all very well to say that you have got to look up the data on which the decision will be based, that you

know just where to look. But I want the decision now, and the department wants the decision now. It isn't convenient for me to wait."

- You can take a short version of Edison's test at www.nps.gov/edis/forteachers/the-edison-test.htm
- What do you think of Edison's test considering everything you have learned about validity in this chapter?
- Do you agree with his reasoning about the importance of memory?
- How would you have set the passing score for the test?
- If the test were used today, would it be considered legal? Biased? Fair?

Focus on Ethics   Diversity Efforts

In this chapter, you learned that employment tests must be valid and fair to pass legal scrutiny. You also learned that such methods as passing scores, rules of three, and banding can provide some flexibility in who gets hired—flexibility that often is used to reduce adverse impact. Almost every topic in this chapter has potential ethical issues associated with it. From an ethical perspective, should an employer care about issues such as adverse impact? How far should an organization go to increase diversity? Over the years, I have had many discussions with colleagues who thought that their organization either wasn't doing enough to ensure fairness in its testing process or was

going so far to the extreme that members of underrepresented groups and women were being favored.

What Do You Think?

- Is it ethical to hire a person with a lower test score because they seem to be a better personality fit for an organization?
- If an I/O psychologist is employed by a company that appears to be discriminating against Hispanic individuals is it ethical for them to stay with the company? What ethical obligations do they have?

Chapter Summary

In this chapter you learned:

- There are three ways to measure reliability: (a) the test-retest method, which measures temporal stability; (b) the alternate-forms method, which measures forms stability; and (c) the internal consistency method (split-half, K-R 20, and coefficient alpha), which measures item homogeneity.
- Tests can be validated using five approaches: content, criterion, construct, known-group, and face.
- Information about tests can be obtained from such sources as the *Mental Measurements Yearbook* and *Tests in Print.*

- The utility of a test can be determined using the Taylor-Russell tables, the Lawshe tables, proportion of correct decisions, expectancy tables, and utility formulas.
- The fairness of a test can be determined by testing for adverse impact, single-group validity, and differential validity.
- Selection decisions can be made in four ways: top-down, rule of three, top-down with banding, or passing scores.

Key Terms

Reliability (196)
Test-retest reliability (196)
Temporal stability (196)
Alternate-forms reliability (197)
Counterbalancing (197)
Form stability (197)
Internal reliability (198)
Item stability (198)
Item homogeneity (199)
Kuder-Richardson Formula 20
    (K-R 20) (199)
Split-half method (199)
Spearman-Brown prophecy formula (199)
Coefficient alpha (199)
Scorer reliability (199)
Validity (201)
Content validity (201)
Criterion validity (202)
Criterion (202)
Concurrent validity (202)
Predictive validity (202)
Restricted range (202)
Validity generalization (VG) (203)
Synthetic validity (203)
Construct validity (204)
Known-group validity (204)
Face validity (206)
Barnum statements (206)
Mental Measurements Yearbook
    (MMY) (206)

Unproctored internet-based testing
    (UIT) (207)
Computer-adaptive testing (CAT) (207)
Taylor-Russell tables (208)
Selection ratio (208)
Base rate (209)
Proportion of correct decisions (209)
Lawshe tables (213)
Expectancy charts (213)
Utility formula (213)
Tenure (215)
Measurement bias (217)
Adverse impact (218)
Predictive bias (218)
Single-group validity (218)
Differential validity (218)
Multiple regression (219)
Linear (219)
Top-down selection (219)
Compensatory approach (219)
Rule of three (220)
Passing score (220)
Multiple-cutoff approach (221)
Multiple-hurdle approach (221)
Banding (223)
Standard error of measurement
    (SEM) (223)

Questions for Review

1. What is the difference between reliability and validity?
2. What method of establishing validity is the best?
3. Why is the concept of test utility so important?
4. What is the difference between single-group and differential validity?
5. Why should we use anything other than top-down selection? After all, shouldn't we always—hire the applicants with the highest scores?

Learning Objectives

7-1 Create a performance appraisal instrument.

7-2 Administer a performance appraisal system.

7-3 Describe the problems associated with performance ratings.

7-4 Conduct a performance appraisal review.

7-5 Explain how to legally terminate an unproductive employee.

7-6 Determine the legality of a performance appraisal system.

Have you ever received a grade that you did not think was fair? Perhaps you had an 89.6 and the instructor would not "round up" to an A (a 90). Perhaps the test contained questions that had nothing to do with the class? If so, you were probably upset with the way your professor appraised your performance. In this chapter, we will discuss the process of evaluating and appraising employee performance, which is similar to evaluating a student's performance.

As shown in Figure 7.1, the performance appraisal process can be divided into 10 interrelated steps. Each of these steps will serve as a major section in this chapter.

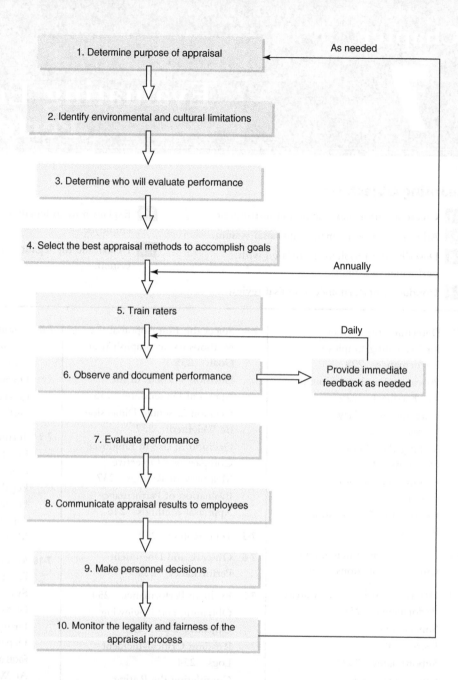

Figure 7.1
The Performance Appraisal Process

7-1 Determine the Reason for Evaluating Employee Performance

The first step in the performance appraisal process is to determine the reasons your organization wants to evaluate employee performance. That is, does the organization want to use the results to improve performance? Give raises based on performance? This determination is important because the various performance appraisal techniques are appropriate for some purposes but not for others. For example, a performance appraisal method—the **forced-choice rating scale** (see Appendix at the end of the chapter)—is excellent for determining compensation but terrible for training purposes. Likewise, the use of 360-degree feedback is an excellent source for improving employee performance but is not appropriate for determining salary increases. Surprisingly, most organizations do not have specific goals for their performance appraisal systems. As a result, it probably comes as no surprise that many performance appraisal systems are not successful (Pulakos, Mueller-Hanson, Arad, & Moye, 2015).

Though there are many uses and goals for performance appraisal, the most common include providing employee feedback and training, determining salary increases, making promotion decisions, making termination decisions, and conducting personnel research.

Providing Employee Training and Feedback

By far, the most important use of performance evaluation is to improve employee performance by providing feedback about what employees are doing right and wrong. Even though employee training should be an ongoing process (see Chapter 8), the **performance appraisal review** is an excellent time to meet with employees to discuss their strengths and weaknesses. But more important, it is the time to determine how weaknesses can be corrected. This process is thoroughly discussed later in the chapter. The importance of providing feedback can be seen by the increasing number of organizations that have moved away from one annual performance appraisal review to a focus on daily feedback (O'Connell, 2020).

Determining Salary Increases

As mentioned in Chapter 2, a job's worth is determined by many factors, including the degree of responsibility and level of education required to perform the job. But the difference in compensation between two individuals within the same job is a function of both tenure and job performance. That is, it would not seem fair to pay a poor-performing employee the same amount as an excellently performing one. Thus, one important reason for evaluating employee performance is to provide a fair basis on which to determine an employee's salary increase. If performance appraisal results are to be used to determine salary increases, a numerical rather than narrative format is probably needed. Additionally, it is important to keep in mind that when considering using performance appraisals for compensation, research has demonstrated potential issues associated with this method, such as introducing competition to the workplace (Solmon & Podgursky, 2000), or a perception of a lack of fairness (Swiercz, Icenogle, Bryan, & Renn, 1993).

Making Promotion Decisions

Another reason for evaluating performance is to determine which employees will be promoted. Even though promoting employees based on performance or tenure seems fair, it may not always be smart. The best employee at one level is not always the best at the next level. Promoting the best or most senior employee often results in the so-called **Peter Principle**—the promotion of employees until they reach their highest

Forced-choice rating scale A method of performance appraisal in which a supervisor is given several behaviors and is forced to choose which of them is most typical of the employee.

Performance appraisal review A meeting between a supervisor and a subordinate for the purpose of discussing performance appraisal results.

Peter Principle The idea that organizations tend to promote good employees until they reach the level at which they are not competent—in other words, their highest level of incompetence.

level of incompetence. If performance evaluations are used to promote employees, care should be taken to ensure that the employee is evaluated thoroughly on the job dimensions that are similar to those of the new position, instead of the job dimensions of their current position.

For example, the five important job dimensions of a salesperson might be sales, communication skills, attention to detail, client rapport, and responsibility. The four important job dimensions of sales manager would be communication skills, attention to detail, motivational ability, and employee rapport. The salesperson with the highest scores on the overlapping dimensions, which, in this case, are communication skills and attention to detail, should be the one promoted. Sales volume might not even be used as a factor in this decision.

Another use of performance appraisal data is in training needs analysis, which will be discussed in greater detail in Chapter 8. If many employees score poorly on a performance appraisal dimension, an increase or change in training is probably necessary for all employees. If only a few employees have low scores, training at an individual level is indicated. Thus, performance appraisal can provide useful information about an organization's strengths and weaknesses.

Making Termination Decisions

Unfortunately, providing feedback, counseling, and training to employees does not always increase performance or reduce discipline problems. When performance management techniques are not successful, the results of a performance review might suggest that the best course of action is to terminate the employee. Methods for doing this and the legal issues that surround such decisions will be discussed in great detail at the end of this chapter.

Conducting Organizational Research

A final reason for evaluating employees is for organizational research. As discussed in previous chapters, employment tests must be validated, and one way this can be done is by correlating test scores with some measure of job performance. To do this, however, an accurate and reliable measure of job performance must be available. The same is true in evaluating the effectiveness of training programs. To determine effectiveness, an accurate measure of performance must be available for use in determining whether performance increases because of training.

Although not the most important reason for evaluating employee performance, organizational research is still important, especially in organizations in which union contracts forbid the use of performance evaluations in personnel decisions. In those situations, performance evaluations are still needed for effective organizational research.

7-2 Identify Environmental and Cultural Limitations

The second step in the performance appraisal process is to identify the environmental and cultural factors that could affect the system. For example, if supervisors are highly overworked, an elaborate, time-consuming performance appraisal system could not be successfully conducted. In an environment in which there is no money available for merit pay, developing a numerically complex system will become frustrating, and the results of the evaluation may not be taken seriously. In an environment in which employees are very cohesive, the use of peer ratings might reduce the cohesiveness.

7-3 Determine Who Will Evaluate Performance

Traditionally, employee performance has been evaluated solely by only one person, normally the employee's supervisor (Fleenor, Taylor, & Chappelow, 2020). Organizations, however, have realized that supervisors observe only certain aspects of an employee's behavior. For example, as shown in Figure 7.2, a branch manager might observe only 30% of a teller's work behavior; the rest is observed by customers, peers, and support staff in other parts of the bank. Furthermore, the teller might behave very differently around their supervisor than around other people. Consequently, to obtain an accurate view of the teller's performance, these other sources can be used to provide feedback. The buzzwords for using multiple sources to appraise performance are **360-degree feedback** and **multiple-source feedback**. About 34% of large U.S. organizations use some form of multiple-source feedback (Mercer Consulting, 2013). It is important to note that 360-degree feedback is primarily used as a source of training and employee development and is seldom used in the appraisal process to determine salary increases or to make promotion and termination decisions. Sources of relevant information about employee performance include supervisors, peers, subordinates, customers, and self-appraisal. As shown in Table 7.1, often there is little agreement in the way two supervisors evaluate an employee or a supervisor and a peer might rate an employee.

360-degree feedback A performance appraisal system in which feedback is obtained from multiple sources such as supervisors, subordinates, and peers.

Multiple-source feedback performance appraisal strategy in which an employee receives feedback from sources (e.g., clients, subordinates, peers) other than just their supervisor.

Supervisors

By far the most common source of performance appraisal is the supervisor rating. In fact, a 2013 Survey by the Society for Human Resource Management (SHRM) found

Figure 7.2
Who Observes
Employee
Performance?

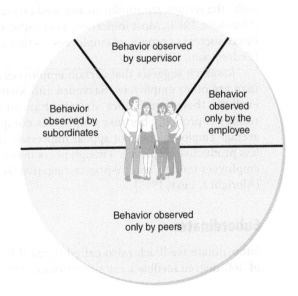

Table 7.1   Correlations Between Raters

Agreement Between	Correlation Coefficient
Two supervisors	.50
Two peers	.37
Two subordinates	.30
Supervisors and peers	.34
Supervisor and subordinates	.22
Supervisor and self	.22
Peers and subordinates	.22
Peers and self	.19

Source: Adapted from Conway & Huffcutt (1997).

that in 74% of organizations, the direct supervisor is the sole source of an employee's evaluation. Though supervisors may not see every minute of an employee's behavior, they do see the result. A supervisor may not actually see a teller sign up customers for Visa cards but will review the daily sales totals. Likewise, a professor does not see a student actually research and write a paper but infers the levels of these behaviors by viewing the results—the finished term paper.

Peers

Whereas supervisors see the *results* of an employee's efforts, peers often see the actual *behavior*. Peer ratings usually come from employees who work directly with an employee; a nurse could be rated by other nurses. However, other employees in the organization, those who often come in contact with the employee, can also provide useful information. For example, a nurse could be rated by employees from the laboratory or radiation departments.

Research has shown that peer ratings are fairly reliable only when the peers who make the ratings are similar to and well acquainted with the employees being rated (Mumford, 1983). Most important, peer ratings have been successful in predicting the future success of promoted employees, as they correlate highly with supervisor ratings (Cederbloom, 1989).

Research suggests that certain employees are more lenient in their peer ratings than are other employees. Saavedra and Kwun (1993) found that high performers evaluate their peers more strictly than do low performers. This difference in ratings is probably because employees compare others to themselves. Thus, the average employee does not appear impressive to a high performer but may do so to a less productive employee. Though peers may provide a unique view of performance, employees tend to react worse to negative feedback from peers than from experts (Albright & Levy, 1995).

Subordinates

Subordinate feedback (also called upward feedback) is an important component of 360-degree feedback, as subordinates can provide a very different view about a supervisor's behavior. Subordinate ratings can be difficult to obtain because employees fear a backlash if they unfavorably rate their supervisor, especially when a supervisor has only one or two subordinates. For example, when the supervisors at one mental health facility gave poor performance ratings to their boss, each was criticized for having the audacity to rate the boss poorly. After such a reaction, what do you think is the probability the subordinates will be honest in the future? Subordinates' feedback can be encouraged if supervisors appear open to employee comments (Baumgartner, 1994); if the ratings are made anonymously (Antonioni, 1994); if the ratings are used for developmental purposes (Avis & Kudisch, 2000); and if the employee feels competent to make the rating, feels there will be no retaliation for making honest ratings, and will somehow benefit by providing honest ratings (Smith & Fortunato, 2008).

Does multisource feedback help improve performance? A meta-analysis (Smither, London, & Reilly, 2005) found that although the effect was small, feedback from direct reports ($d = .24$) resulted in greater performance changes than did feedback from peers ($d = .12$) or supervisors ($d = .14$). Another meta-analysis found that multisource feedback was successful in increasing physician performance (Al Ansari, Donnon, Al Khalifa, Darwish, & Violato, 2014). However, contrary research has argued a lack of sustained changes due to multisource feedback from supervisors ($d = .1$) and peers ($d = .04$) (Ashworth, Champlain, & Kain, 2021). Multisource feedback is most effective when the feedback indicates that the employee needs to change their behavior, the employee perceives that the changes are feasible, and the employee is open to receiving constructive feedback (Smither et al., 2005). Performance increases can be enhanced when the feedback is provided in a workshop conducted by a feedback facilitator rather than by a direct supervisor (Seifert, Yukl, & McDonald, 2003). Though supervisor performance might increase from upward feedback, such feedback does not appear to improve the overall performance or stock value of an organization (Pfau & Kay, 2002a).

Customers

Although it would be unlikely that an organization would ask customers to fill out a performance appraisal instrument on an employee, organizations do value customer feedback. Informally, customers provide feedback on employee performance by filing complaints or complimenting a manager about one of their employees. Formally, customers provide feedback by completing evaluation cards such as that shown in Figure 7.3 or completing online surveys. Examples of formal customer feedback include statements on receipts from stores and restaurants that the customer can receive a free gift (e.g., large fries) if they complete an online survey, a request at the end of a customer service call to "stay on the line" and complete a short survey, or an email from a doctor's office asking the patient to evaluate their office visit. Organizations have also attempted to take advantage of the prevalence of smartphones, with the development of survey tools on mobile applications (Mourtzis, Vlachou, Zogopoulos, Gupta, Belkadi, Debbache, & Bernard, 2018).

Organizations also seek customer feedback in the form of *secret shoppers*—current customers who have been enlisted by a company to periodically evaluate the service they receive. In exchange for their ratings, secret shoppers get a few dollars and a free meal. For years, I was "employed" by a national marketing company to eat at local restaurants and secretly complete a rating of the quality of food and service.

Figure 7.3
Customer Evaluation
Card

The compensation is only $5 per visit plus reimbursement for the meal, but it is a fun experience. I only wish they would have granted my request for sunglasses and a trench coat!

Self-Appraisal

Allowing an employee to evaluate their own behavior and performance is a technique used by an increasing number of organizations. A 2013 SHRM survey found that 72% of organizations include an employee self-evaluation compared to just over half in a similar survey from 2000. In Bismarck, North Dakota, self-ratings account for 25% of city employees' evaluations (peer ratings account for 25% and supervisor ratings 50%).

Research on self-appraisal has found what we might expect to find—employee self-appraisals tend to suffer from leniency (Beehr, Ivanitskaya, Hansen, Erofeev, & Gudanowski, 2001) and correlate only moderately with actual performance (Zell & Krizan, 2014) and poorly with subordinate (Conway & Huffcutt, 1997) and management ratings (Beehr et al., 2001). Research has also demonstrated small detrimental sustained behavioral changes from self-assessment feedback ($d = -.03$) (Smither, London, & Reilly, 2005). However, when evaluations are made with clear rating standards and social comparison information, agreement is increased between self- and supervisor-ratings (Keeping & Sulsky, 1996; Schrader & Steiner, 1996). When peer ratings are lower than self-ratings, employees react negatively to, and question the accuracy of, negative feedback (Brett & Atwater, 2001).

The leniency found in the self-ratings of U.S. workers may not generalize to other countries. Self-ratings of Japanese, Korean, and Taiwanese workers suffer from modesty rather than leniency, whereas self-ratings from workers in the United States, mainland China, India, Singapore, and Hong Kong are characterized by leniency (Barron & Sackett, 2008). Further research is still needed to investigate potential cultural differences in self-ratings.

Self-appraisals of performance appear to be most accurate when the self-appraisal will not be used for such administrative purposes as raises or promotions (Atwater, 1998). They are also more accurate when employees understand the performance appraisal system (Williams & Levy, 1992) and when employees believe that an objective record of their performance is available with which the supervisor can compare the self-appraisal (Farh & Werbel, 1986).

7-4 Select the Best Appraisal Methods to Accomplish Your Goals

The next step in the performance appraisal process is to select the performance criteria and appraisal methods that will best accomplish your goals for the system. *Criteria* are ways of defining employee success. For example, it might be decided that attendance, quality of work, and safety are the three most important criteria for a successful employee. Now the methods for measuring the criteria must be chosen and created. That is, how can we measure attendance, quality, and safety?

Prior to developing the actual performance appraisal instrument, two important decisions must be made: the focus of the performance appraisal dimensions and whether to use rankings or ratings.

Decision 1: Focus of the Appraisal Dimensions

As shown in Table 7.2, the appraisal dimensions can focus on traits, competencies, task types, or goals.

Table 7.2   Four Ways to Focus Performance Dimensions

Competency Focus	Task Focus
Report-writing skills	Crime prevention
Driving skills	Arrest procedures
Public-speaking skills	Court testimony
Knowledge of the law	Use of vehicle
Decision-making skills	Radio procedures
Physical ability skills	Following rules and regulations
Goal Focus	**Trait Focus**
Prevent crimes from occurring	Honesty
Arrest/cite law breakers	Courtesy
Finish shift without personal injury	Responsibility
Have arrests and citations stand-up in court	Dependability
Minimize citizen complaints	Assertiveness
Ensure public safety	Cooperation

Trait-Focused Performance Dimensions

A trait-focused system concentrates on such employee attributes as dependability, honesty, and courtesy. Though commonly used, trait-focused performance appraisal instruments are not a good idea because they provide poor feedback and thus will not result in employee development and growth. For example, think of a performance-review meeting in which the supervisor tells an employee that they received low ratings on responsibility and friendliness. Because traits are personal, the employee is likely to become defensive. Furthermore, the employee will want specific examples the supervisor may not have available. The only developmental advice the supervisor can offer would be to "be more responsible and friendly." Such advice is not specific enough for the employee to change their behavior. Additionally, trait-based scales require an appraiser to make a subjective conclusion of an employee's trait based on their work performance, which could be easily challenged from a legal standpoint (Kline & Sulsky, 2009).

Competency-Focused Performance Dimensions

Rather than concentrating on an employee's traits, competency-focused dimensions concentrate on the employee's knowledge, skills, and abilities. For example, competency-focused dimensions might include writing skills, oral presentation skills, and driving skills. The advantage to organizing dimensions by competencies is that it is easy to identify problems, provide feedback, and suggest the steps necessary to correct deficiencies. That is, if an employee is evaluated as having poor writing skills, the obvious corrective measure would be for the employee to take a writing course.

Task-Focused Performance Dimensions

Task-focused dimensions are organized by the similarity of tasks that are performed. For a police officer, such dimensions might include *following radio procedures* or *court testimony*. Note that a task-focused dimension usually includes several competencies. For example, to receive a high rating on the dimension of *court testimony*, the officer would need the competencies of public speaking, organization, and knowledge of the law. The advantage of this approach is that because supervisors are concentrating on tasks that occur together and can thus visualize an employee's performance, it is often easier to evaluate performance than with the other dimensions. The disadvantage is that it is more difficult to offer suggestions for how to correct the deficiency if an employee scores low on a dimension. That is, is the low score on *court testimony* due to a lack of knowledge or to poor public-speaking skills?

Goal-Focused Performance Dimensions

The fourth type of performance dimension is to organize the appraisal based on goals to be accomplished by the employee. Sticking with our police officer example, goals might include preventing crimes from occurring, finishing the shift without personal injury, and minimizing the number of citizen complaints. The advantage of a goal-focused approach is that it makes it easier for an employee to understand why certain behaviors are expected. Take, for example, the behavioral expectations of having a police officer wear a seat belt and body armor. If these expectations were listed under the dimension of *Following Department Policy*, the officer might not be too concerned with changing behavior about following "some stupid rule." If, however, these two expectations were listed under the goal of *staying alive*, it would be clearer that they are there for an important purpose. Additionally, along with competency-focused performance dimensions and task-focused performance dimensions, goal-focused performance dimensions are also easier to identify and are more legally defensible than the trait-focused performance dimension.

Contextual Performance

In the above discussion, the four ways to focus performance dimensions all concentrated on the technical aspects of performing a job. Many organizations also value and measure *contextual performance*, that is, the effort an employee makes to get along with peers, improve the organization, and perform tasks that are needed but are not necessarily an official part of the employee's job description. Many organizations include rating scales addressing the technical aspects of the job as well as the contextual aspects. That is, they want employees who will be not only effective performers but good organizational citizens as well. In academia, it is not uncommon to deny tenure to a faculty member who is technically competent but does not "play well with others."

Contextual performance is important because not only are these prosocial organizational behaviors important to the success of an organization, but they also tend to be similar across jobs, whereas the dimensions involved in task performance differ across jobs (Borman & Motowidlo, 1997). Furthermore, the selection tests that might best predict task performance (e.g., cognitive ability, job knowledge) are not the same tests that might predict contextual performance (e.g., integrity tests, personality inventories).

Decision 2: Should Dimensions Be Weighted?

Once the type of dimension has been determined, the next decision is whether the dimensions should be weighted so that some are more important than others. Grading systems in the classes you have taken provide good examples of weighting dimensions. For example, you may have had a class where the final exam was given more weight than other exams or a class in which a particular project carried more weight than others.

Weighting dimensions makes good philosophical sense, as some dimensions might be more important to an organization than others. For example, the dimension of patient care would be more important for a nurse than would be keeping a professional appearance. Though both are important parts of the job, providing poor patient care has more of an impact for the organization than not wearing the proper clothing. Another advantage to differentially weighting dimensions is that it may reduce racial and other biases (McFarland, Wolf, & Nguyen, 2005).

Though differential weighting of dimensions makes sense and has some advantages, many organizations choose to weight all performance dimensions equally because it is administratively easier to compute and to explain to employees, avoiding potential issues with perceptions of fairness.

Decision 3: Use of Employee Comparisons, Objective Measures, or Ratings

Once the types of dimensions have been considered, the next decision is whether to evaluate performance by comparing employees with one another (ranking), using objective measures such as attendance and number of units sold, or having supervisors rate how well the employee has performed on each of the dimensions.

Table 7.3   Ranking Method of Evaluating Performance

Employee	Dimension			
	Knowledge	**Dependability**	**Quality**	**Total**
VanderWaal	1	1	1	1.00
Farmer	2	3	2	2.33
Lim	3	2	3	2.67
Lee	4	5	4	4.33
Leake	5	4	5	4.67

Employee Comparisons

To reduce leniency, employees can be compared with one another instead of being rated individually on a scale. The easiest and most common of these methods is the **rank order**. In this approach, employees are ranked in order by their judged performance for each relevant dimension. As Table 7.3 shows, the ranks are then averaged across each dimension to yield an overall rank.

Rank orders are easily used when there are only a few employees to rank, but they become difficult to use with larger numbers. Ranking the top few and bottom few employees is relatively easy; however, deciding which 2 of 50 employees should be placed at the 30th and 31st ranks is more difficult.

To make this process easier, **paired comparisons** can be used. This method involves comparing each possible pair of employees and choosing which one of each pair is the better employee. An example is shown in Figure 7.4.

Even though comparing one pair of employees at a time is easier than simultaneously comparing many employees, it does have its drawbacks. With large numbers of employees, the time necessary to make all the comparisons becomes prohibitive. For example, to determine how many comparisons must be made, we can use the following formula:

$$\text{number of comparisons} = \frac{n(n-1)}{2},$$

where $n =$ the number of employees. Thus, if we have 10 employees to compare:

$$\text{number of comparisons} = \frac{10(10-1)}{2} = \frac{10(9)}{2} = \frac{90}{2} = 45.$$

Thus, we would need to make 45 comparisons for each performance dimension. Although this number is not extreme, evaluating 100 employees would result in 4,950 separate comparisons! And with five performance dimensions, some unfortunate supervisor would have to make almost 25,000 separate comparisons! Obviously, the supervisor would not favor such a task.

The final type of employee comparison system is called the **forced distribution method**. With this method, a predetermined percentage of employees are placed in each of the five categories shown in Table 7.4. Forced distribution systems are used by more than 20% of Fortune 1000 companies (Bates, 2003a). Also called "rank and yank" or "stack ranking," forced distributions were a favorite method of Jack Welch,

Rank order A method of performance appraisal in which employees are ranked from best to worst.

Paired comparison A form of ranking in which a group of employees to be ranked are compared one pair at a time.

Forced distribution method A performance appraisal method in which a predetermined percentage of employees are placed into a number of performance categories.

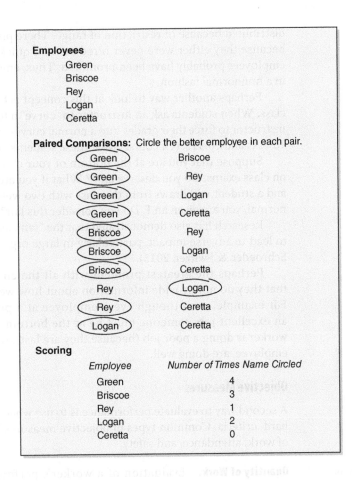

Figure 7.4
Example of Paired-Comparison Method

the former chief executive officer of General Electric, who required managers to fire the bottom-performing 10% of their employees each year. Though such systems seem harsh, the limited research on the topic suggests that rank-and-yank systems result in increased levels of organizational productivity, especially during the first few years in which the system is in place (Scullen, Bergey, & Aiman-Smith, 2005). Employees, however, consider forced distribution scales to be the least fair method of performance appraisal (Roch, Sternburgh, & Caputo, 2007) and most large organizations (e.g., Microsoft, Ford, Goldman Sachs) no longer use this method.

Forced distribution systems are much easier to use than the other two employee comparison methods, but they also have a drawback. To use the method, one must assume that employee performance is normally distributed, that is, that there are certain percentages of employees who are poor, average, and excellent. As will be discussed in more detail in Chapter 8, employee performance probably is not normally

Table 7.4   Forced-Distribution Method of Performance Appraisal

Moss	Davis, Pompeo	Kidman, Blunt, Streep, McCarthy	Gadot, Jolie	Vergara
10%	20%	40%	20%	10%
Terrible	Below average	Average	Good	Excellent

distributed because of restriction of range. There probably are few terrible employees because they either were never hired or were quickly fired. Likewise, truly excellent employees probably have been promoted. Thus, employee performance is distributed in a nonnormal fashion.

Perhaps another way to look at this concept is by examining the grades given in a class. When students ask an instructor to "curve" a test, technically they are asking the instructor to force their grades into a normal curve—that is, there will be approximately 10% As and 10% Fs. (Of course, what these students are often asking for is extra points.)

Suppose that you are at the bottom of your class, yet you still have a 75% average on class exams. Do you deserve an F? What if you are the last person in the D category and a student withdraws from the class with two weeks to go? To keep the distribution normal, you are given an F. Do you consider this fair?

Research has also demonstrated that the "rank and yank" method has the potential to lead to adverse impact, particularly in large organizations ($N = 10,000$)(Giumetti, Schroeder, & Switzer, 2015).

Perhaps the greatest problem with all the employee-comparison methods is that they do not provide information about how well an employee is actually doing. For example, even though every employee at a production plant might be doing an excellent job, someone must be at the bottom. Thus, it might appear that one worker is doing a poor job (because they are last), when in fact they, and every other employee, are doing well.

Objective Measures

A second way to evaluate performance is to use what are commonly called objective, or hard, criteria. Common types of objective measures include quantity of work, quality of work, attendance, and safety.

Quantity of Work. Evaluation of a worker's performance in terms of **quantity** is obtained by simply counting the number of relevant job behaviors that take place. For example, we might judge a salesperson's performance by the number of units they sell, an assembly line worker's performance by the number of bumpers they assemble, or a police officer's performance by the number of arrests they make.

Although quantity measures appear to be objective measures of performance, they are often misleading. As shown in Figure 7.5, it is important to realize that many factors determine quantity of work other than an employee's ability and performance.

Quantity A type of objective criterion used to measure job performance by counting the number of relevant job behaviors that occur.

Figure 7.5
Factors Affecting Performance

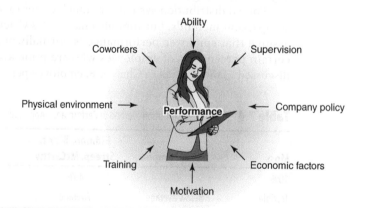

Furthermore, for many people's jobs it might not be practical or possible to measure quantity; computer programmers, doctors, and firefighters are examples. I once conducted a salary equity study for a large hospital. During the analysis we found that the best predictor of a physician's pay was the amount of revenue generated by the physician. What complicated the analysis was that women physicians had lower revenue levels than did men physicians. When I mentioned this to the client, their response was that they were aware of this difference and that the difference was due to the women physicians spending more time with each of their patients. I remember thinking, "Isn't that good thing?" In this case, the hospital seemed to value quantity over quality. A study published in 2020 confirmed that women primary care physicians do, in fact, spend more time with their patients: about 15% more (Ganguli et al., 2020).

Quality of Work.   Another method to evaluate performance is by measuring the quality of the work that is done. **Quality** is usually measured in terms of **errors**, which are defined as deviations from a standard. Thus, to obtain a measure of quality, there must be a standard against which to compare an employee's work. For example, a textile worker's quality would be judged by how their work compares with a "model" shirt; a medical coder might be judged on the percentage of medical procedures that they correctly coded; and a cook's quality might be judged by how their food resembles a standard as measured by size, temperature, and ingredient amounts.

Kentucky Fried Chicken, for example, evaluates the quality of its franchises' food by undercover inspectors. These inspectors purchase food, drive down the road, and after parking, use a thermometer to see whether the food has been served at a standard acceptable temperature and a scale to determine whether the weight of the mashed potatoes is within the acceptable range.

Note that the definition of an error is *any* deviation from a standard. Thus, errors can even be work quality that is higher than a standard. Why is this an error?

Quality A type of objective criterion used to measure job performance by comparing a job behavior with a standard.

Error Deviation from a standard of quality; also a type of response to communication overload that involves processing all information but processing some of it incorrectly.

Quality is a relevant criterion for many jobs.

AP Images/Midland Daily News, Nina Greipel

Suppose a company manufactures shirts that are sold for $30. To keep down the manufacturing cost of its shirts, the company probably uses cheaper material and has its workers spend less time per shirt than does a company that manufactures $150 shirts. Thus, if an employee sews a shirt with 15 stitches per inch instead of the standard 10, the company will lose money in material cost and employee time because of higher quality!

When I was working my way through school, I held a summer job at an amusement park. The job involved wearing a pink and purple uniform and cooking prefabricated pizza. The standard for the large pepperoni pizza was 2 handfuls of cheese and 15 pieces of pepperoni. Now most pizza lovers recognize this to be a barren pizza. The cooks thus tried to increase the pizza quality by tripling the number of pepperoni pieces. The management quickly explained to the young "gourmet chefs" that exceeding the standards was considered poor work performance and that employees who did so would be fired.

A similar situation developed at a factory that produced parts for telephones. Most of the employees were older and took great pride in their work quality and in the fact that their parts had the lowest percentage of errors in the company. They were told, however, that their quality was too high and that the parts were lasting so long that the company was not getting much repeat business. Quality errors can occur in many strange ways!

Attendance.   A common method for objectively measuring one aspect of an employee's performance is by looking at attendance (this is discussed in greater detail in Chapter 10). Attendance can be separated into three distinct criteria: absenteeism, tardiness, and tenure. Both absenteeism and tardiness have obvious implications for the performance appraisal process. The weight that each has in the overall evaluation of the employee largely depends on the nature of the job.

Tenure as a criterion, however, is used mostly for research purposes when evaluating the success of selection decisions. For example, in a job such as food preparer at McDonald's, due to standardization there is probably little difference in the quantity and quality of hamburgers or French fries that are cooked. But an employee might be considered "successful" if they stay with the company for at least four months and "unsuccessful" if they leave before that time. In fact, the importance of tenure can be demonstrated by noting that several major fast-food restaurants and convenience stores have established bonus systems to reward long-tenure employees—that is, those who have worked for a company at least six months. For each hour the employee works, the company places a specified amount of money into an account that can be used by the employee to pay such education expenses as books and tuition.

Safety.   Another method used to evaluate the success of an employee is safety. Obviously, employees who follow safety rules and who have no occupational accidents do not cost an organization as much money as those who break rules, equipment, and possibly their own bodies (where employees might file for worker's compensation if they are injured on the job). As with tenure, safety is usually used for research purposes, but it can also be used for employment decisions such as promotions and bonuses.

Ratings of Performance

The most commonly used option in evaluating performance is to have supervisors rate how well the employee performed on each dimension. Though there are many variations of how these rating scales can be created, the two most common are the graphic rating scale and the behavioral checklist.

Table 7.5 Example of a Graphic Rating Scale

Initiative	Poor	1	2	3	4	5	Excellent
Cooperation	Poor	1	2	3	4	5	Excellent
Dependability	Poor	1	2	3	4	5	Excellent
Attendance	Poor	1	2	4	4	5	Excellent

Graphic rating scale A method of performance appraisal that involves rating employee performance on an interval or ratio scale.

Graphic Rating Scale. The most common rating scale is the **graphic rating scale**. An example is shown in Table 7.5. As you can tell, such scales are fairly simple, with 5 to 10 dimensions accompanied by words such as *excellent* and *poor* anchoring the ends of the scale.

The obvious advantage of graphic rating scales is their ease of construction and use, but they have been criticized because of their susceptibility to such rating errors as halo and leniency, which are discussed later in this chapter.

Behavioral Checklists. As shown in Figure 7.6, behavioral checklists consist of a list of behaviors, expectations, or results for each dimension. This list is used to force the supervisor to concentrate on the relevant behaviors that fall under a dimension.

Figure 7.6

Example of a
Behavioral Checklist

Radio Procedures

Behavioral Elements

_____ Uses proper codes and signals when sending information
_____ Understands codes and signals when receiving information
_____ Voice is clear and easy-to-understand in normal situations
_____ Voice is clear, easy-to-understand, and does not indicate panic in high-stress situations
_____ Follows proper radio procedures
_____ Monitors the proper channels
_____ Knows the location of all district officers
_____ Never communicates improper information over the radio
_____ Keeps dispatch informed of current status
_____ Treats communications officers with respect and courtesy

Dimension Rating

_____ 5 Consistently exceeds requirements, no improvements needed
_____ 4 Exceeds most requirements
_____ 3 Usually meets requirements, acceptable performance
_____ 2 Usually meets most requirements, but needs improvement
_____ 1 Does not meet minimum requirements, needs immediate and extensive improvement

Comments

_____
_____
_____
_____

Behavioral checklists are constructed by taking the task statements from a detailed job description (e.g., "Types correspondence") and converting them into behavioral performance statements representing the level at which the behavior is expected to be performed (e.g., "Correspondence does not contain spelling or grammatical errors").

When creating the statements for each dimension, one should carefully consider whether to write the statements in the form of behaviors or in the form of results. Examples of behavior-based statements for a bank teller might include "Properly greets each customer," "Knows customers' names," and "Thanks customer after each transaction." The obvious advantage to a behavior-focused system is the increased amount of specific feedback that can be given to each employee.

Result-focused statements concentrate on what an employee *accomplished* as a result of what they did. For example, "Distributed at least 25 Visa applications each month"; "Teller drawer was not short at the end of the day"; and "Completed annual report on time." Result-focused systems are tempting because they evaluate employees on their contribution to the bottom line: Did their behavior on the job result in a tangible outcome for the organization?

A problem with result-focused statements is that an employee can do everything asked of them by an organization and still not get the desired results due to factors outside of their control. These factors are referred to as **contamination**. In banking, a teller might not be successful in getting customers to sign up for Visa cards because the bank's interest rate is not competitive. In law enforcement, a police officer might not write many traffic citations because they patrol an area in which there is little traffic. In retail, a salesperson might have poor sales because of their geographic location. For example: Two salespersons work in different locations. Mary Anderson sells an average of 120 air conditioners per month, whereas Tamika Johnson averages 93. Is this criterion free from contamination? Definitely not.

The number of sales is based not only on the skills of the salesperson but also on such factors as the number of stores in the sales territory, the average temperature in the territory, and the relations between the previous salesperson and the store owners. Thus, if we used only the number of sales, Mary Anderson would be considered our top salesperson. But if we take into account that sales are contaminated by the number of stores in the territory, we see that Mary Anderson sold 120 air conditioners in 50 possible stores, whereas Tamika Johnson sold 93 air conditioners in 10 stores. Thus, Mary Anderson sold an average of 2.4 air conditioners per store in an area with an average temperature of 93 degrees; Tamika Johnson sold an average of 9.3 air conditioners per store in an area with an average temperature of 80 degrees. By considering the potential areas of contamination, a different picture emerges of relative performance. As this example clearly shows, factors other than actual performance can affect criteria. Therefore, it is essential to identify as many sources of contamination as possible and to determine ways to adjust performance ratings to account for these contamination sources.

After considering the behaviors in the checklist, a supervisor provides an overall rating of the employee's performance on each dimension. As shown in Figure 7.7, employees can be rated in three ways: how they compared with other employees; the frequency with which they performed certain behaviors; and the extent to which the behaviors met the expectations of the employer.

Comparison with Other Employees. Supervisors can rate performance on a dimension by comparing the employee's level of performance with that of other employees. It is important to note that when such scale anchors as "below average," "average," and

Contamination The condition in which a criterion score is affected by things other than those under the control of the employee.

Figure 7.7

Examples of Three Scales to Measure Behavior

Comparison of Other Employees

Refers to customers by name
_____ Much better than other tellers
_____ Better than other tellers
_____ The same as other tellers
_____ Worse than other tellers
_____ Much worse than other tellers

Frequency

Refers to customers by name
_____ Always
_____ Almost always
_____ Often
_____ Seldom
_____ Never

Extent to Which Organizational Expectations Were Met

Refers to customers by name
_____ Greatly exceeds expectations
_____ Exceeds expectations
_____ Meets expectations
_____ Falls below expectations
_____ Falls well below expectations

"above average" are used, the evaluation involves rating employee performance in comparison with other employees. Though this approach will reduce such problems as overly lenient or overly strict ratings, it potentially forces a supervisor to rate employees who are performing well as being worse than other employees even if their performance is acceptable.

Frequency of Desired Behaviors. Behaviors can be rated based on the frequency with which they occur. For example, we expect our production workers to follow safety guidelines. As part of our performance appraisal system, supervisors are asked to decide whether their employees "always," "almost always," "often," "seldom," or "never" follow the rules. As you can imagine, it is often difficult for a supervisor to distinguish between levels such as "almost always" and "often." Supervisor appraisals could also be affected by ratings they have made of employees before or after the current employee they are appraising.

Extent to Which Organizational Expectations Are Met. Perhaps the best approach is to rate employees on the extent to which their behavior meets the expectations of the organization. Such an approach allows for high levels of feedback and can be applied to most types of employee behavior. Some behaviors, however, are not suitable for such a scale. Take, for example, the expectation that a police officer always wears their seat belt. If they wear it all the time, they have *met* expectations (a rating of 3): There is no way to get a higher rating because one cannot wear a seat belt more often than always and thus cannot ever exceed expectations. When such a situation is possible, the scale can be adjusted to be similar to that shown in Figure 7.8.

Use of Weapons and Vehicle

Behaviors that can meet or exceed expectations

_____ Effectively handled vehicle in pursuit or emergency situations

_____ Demonstrated marksmanship above minimum requirements

_____ Demonstrated appropriate judgment in determining the use of force

_____ Demonstrated appropriate judgment in making pursuit decisions

Behaviors that can only meet expectations

_____ Weapons ratings are current and meet minimum requirements

_____ Weapons were carried in an appropriate manner

_____ When weapons were used, reports were filed on time

_____ When weapons were used, reports contained accurate information

_____ When driving, seat belts were always worn

_____ Carried only weapons issued and/or authorized by the Department

_____ Applied force only when use of force was justified

Dimension Rating

_____ 5 Consistently exceeds requirements, no improvements needed

_____ 4 Exceeds most requirements

_____ 3 Usually meets requirements, acceptable performance

_____ 2 Usually meets most requirements, but needs improvement

_____ 1 Does not meet minimum requirements, needs immediate and extensive improvement

---

Figure 7.8

Rating Behaviors
That Can Only Meet
Expectations

As shown in Figures 7.9 through 7.11, in addition to graphic rating scales and behavioral checklists, a variety of methods to rate performance are available, including behaviorally anchored rating scales (BARS), mixed-standard scales, and forced-choice scales. Because these scales are not commonly used, but are historically and psychometrically interesting, information about them has been included in the Appendix to this chapter.

Whichever rating method is used, care should be taken to word the anchors in way that their meaning is clear and will not upset the employee. Figure 7.12 contains sample anchors that I have encountered over the years from a variety of organizations. Are there any that you think are particularly good or bad?

Evaluation of Performance Appraisal Methods

In the previous pages and in the chapter appendix, several methods for evaluating employee performance are offered. Of course, we might now ask: Is any one of these methods the best? Probably not. Research has shown that such complicated techniques as BARS, forced-choice scales, and mixed-standard scales are only occasionally superior to the inexpensive and uncomplicated graphic rating scale (Murphy, 2008).

Although techniques such as behavioral checklists are only slightly more psychometrically sound, they still have some advantages over graphic rating scales. Because employees are directly involved in creating them, they tend to see performance-evaluation results as being fairer. Furthermore, many supervisors who make such ratings prefer many of the behavioral approaches (Dickenson & Zellinger, 1980).

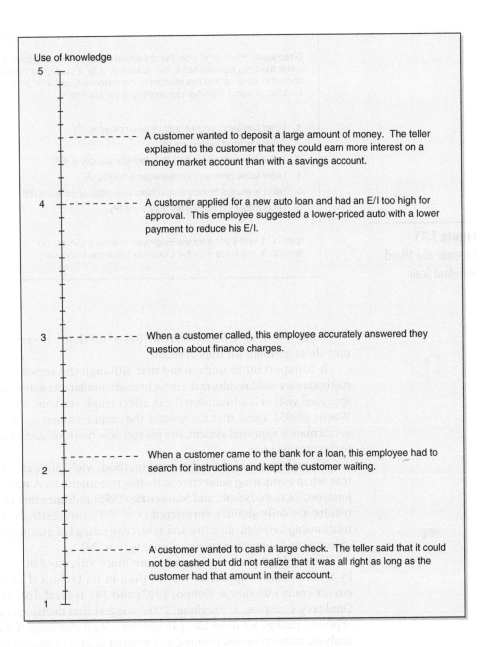

Use of knowledge

5

A customer wanted to deposit a large amount of money. The teller explained to the customer that they could earn more interest on a money market account than with a savings account.

4 — A customer applied for a new auto loan and had an E/I too high for approval. This employee suggested a lower-priced auto with a lower payment to reduce his E/I.

3 — When a customer called, this employee accurately answered they question about finance charges.

2 — When a customer came to the bank for a loan, this employee had to search for instructions and kept the customer waiting.

A customer wanted to cash a large check. The teller said that it could not be cashed but did not realize that it was all right as long as the customer had that amount in their account.

1

Figure 7.9
Example of a
Behaviorally Anchored
Rating Scale

Directions: In each of the following items, check the one statement that is *most like* the teller being rated and the one statement that is *least like* the teller being rated.

Most   Least

1. a) ✔ _____   _____   Teller is always on time (neutral).
   b) _____   _____   Teller is never short at end of day (poor).
   c) _____   ✔ _____   Teller smiles at each customer (excellent).

2. a) _____   ✔ _____   Teller usually cross-sells (excellent).
   b) ✔ _____   _____   Teller keeps work area neat and orderly (poor).
   c) _____   _____   Teller is friendly to other employees (neutral).

Figure 7.10
Example of a Forced-
Choice Rating Scale

Directions: Place a "+" after the statement if the typical behavior of the teller is usually better than that represented in the statement, a "0" if the typical behavior of the teller is about the same as that represented in the statement, and a "−" if the typical behavior of the teller is worse than that represented in the statement.

Rating

1. Teller constantly argues with other employees (P). _____
2. Teller smiles at customers (A). _____
3. Teller asks customers how their families are doing (E). _____
4. Teller helps other employees when possible (A). _____
5. Teller is always friendly to and talks with other employees (E). _____
6. Teller asks customers what they want (P). _____

Items 1, 4, and 5 are from the Employee Relations Dimension.
Items 2, 3, and 6 are from the Customer Relations Dimension.

Figure 7.11
Example of a Mixed-Standard Scale

Finally, feedback from behavior-based methods is easier to give and to use to provide suggestions for improvement.

It is important to understand that although the various performance appraisal methods may yield results that are technically similar, the way in which the performance appraisal system is administered can affect employee trust and satisfaction. Gaby and Woehr (2005) found that the greater the employee perception of the fairness of the performance appraisal system, the greater was their job satisfaction and commitment to the organization.

Though many of the behavioral methods yield similar results, the same is not true when comparing subjective and objective methods. A meta-analysis by Bommer, Johnson, Rich, Podsakoff, and Mackenzie (1995) indicates that objective and subjective results are only slightly correlated ($r = .39$). Interestingly, there was a stronger relationship between objective and subjective ratings of quantity ($r = .38$) than between objective and subjective ratings of quality ($r = .24$).

From a legal perspective, courts are more interested in the due process afforded by a performance appraisal system than in its technical aspects. Reviews of 295 circuit court (Werner & Bolino, 1997) and 145 federal district court cases (Foster, Dunleavy, Campion, & Steubing, 2008) suggest that decisions based on performance appraisal ratings are most likely to survive a legal challenge if they are based on a job analysis, raters received training and written instructions, raters had the opportunity to actually observe the performance of the employee, performance standards had been communicated to the employee, employees were allowed to review and comment on the appraisal results, employees were warned of performance problems and given a chance to improve their performance, and ratings from multiple raters are consistent. Interestingly, an analysis of appellate court cases suggests that conservative courts (e.g., Fourth Circuit) are more likely to base their decisions on the validity and accuracy of the performance appraisal instrument, whereas liberal courts (e.g., Ninth Circuit) are more likely to base their decisions on fairness issues (Lee, Havighurst, & Rassel, 2004).

Lower Performance

- Rating of 1
  - Not meeting expectations
  - Poor performance
  - Major improvement needed
  - Unsatisfactory
  - Did not meet expectations
  - Unacceptable
  - Did not achieve results
  - Fails to meet expectations

- Rating of 2
  - Some improvement needed
  - Inconsistent performance
  - Met most expectations
  - Needs improvement
  - Still building performance
  - Needs development
  - Partially achieved expected results
  - Generally acceptable performance
  - Minimally successful

Middle Performance

- Rating of 3
  - Meets expectations
  - Fully meets expectations
  - Successfully met expectations
  - Fully competent
  - Effective
  - Achieves
  - Solid performance
  - Average
  - Satisfactory
  - Good solid performance
  - Fully successful

Higher Performance

- Rating of 4
  - Often exceeds expectations
  - Highly effective
  - Highly successful
  - Exceeded expectations
  - Above average
  - Strong performance
  - Frequently exceeded expectations
  - Achieved more than expected
  - Good performance
  - High performance
- Rating of 5
  - Consistently exceeds expectations
  - Significantly exceeded expectations
  - Far exceeds expectations
  - Exceptional
  - Exemplary
  - Leading performance
  - Exceptional achievement
  - Outstanding
  - Game changer

Figure 7.12
Examples of Rating
Anchors Used by
Organizations

7-5 Train Raters

Although training supervisors to evaluate performance is essential to a sound and legal performance appraisal system, a 2010 ERC survey found that few organizations spend the time and resources necessary to do this properly. This lack of training is surprising given that research has indicated that training supervisors to become aware of the various rating errors and how to avoid them often increases accuracy and reduces rating errors (Hauenstein, 1998), increases the validity of tests validated against the ratings (Pursell, Dossett, & Latham, 1980), and increases employee satisfaction with the ratings (Ivancevich, 1982). This is especially true when the training technique uses discussion, practice in rating, and feedback about rating accuracy rather than lecture (Smith, 1986). These training effects, however, are short-lived unless additional training and feedback are provided (Noble, 1997), and they can even reduce the accuracy of ratings by substituting new errors (Bernardin & Pence, 1980).

Frame-of-reference training A method of training raters in which the rater is provided with job-related information, a chance to practice ratings, examples of ratings made by experts, and the rationale behind the expert ratings.

The effectiveness of rater training also is a function of training format. **Frame-of-reference training** provides raters with job-related information, practice in rating, and examples of ratings made by experts as well as the rationale behind those expert ratings (Hauenstein & Foti, 1989). The goal of frame-of-reference training is to communicate the organization's definition of effective performance and to then get raters to consider only relevant employee behaviors when making performance evaluations (Uggerslev & Sulsky, 2008). Research on frame-of-reference training indicates that it increases rater accuracy and reduced rater errors (Gorman & Rentsch, 2009; Hauenstein & McCusker, 2017; Roch & O'Sulivan, 2003; Roch, Woehr, Mishra, & Kieszczynska, 2012).

Though training raters is certainly important, it is also important to explain the performance appraisal system to employees. Not surprisingly, the better that those employees understand the performance appraisal system, the greater is their satisfaction with the system (Whiting, Kline, & Sulsky, 2008).

7-6 Observe and Document Performance

Critical incidents A method of performance appraisal in which the supervisor records employee behaviors that were observed on the job and rates the employee on the basis of that record.

The next step in the performance appraisal process is for supervisors to observe employee behavior and document **critical incidents** as they occur. Critical incidents are examples of excellent and poor employee performance. Such documentation is usually written in a critical incident log—formal accounts of excellent and poor employee performance that were observed by the supervisor. Critical incidents should be communicated to the employee at the time they occur (details on how to provide feedback will occur later in this chapter as well as in Chapter 9). Documentation is important for four reasons. First, documentation forces a supervisor to focus on employee behaviors rather than traits and provides behavioral examples to use when reviewing performance ratings with employees.

Second, documentation helps supervisors recall behaviors when they are evaluating performance. As shown in Figure 7.13, without documentation, instead of recalling all of an employee's behavior or at least a representative sample of behavior,

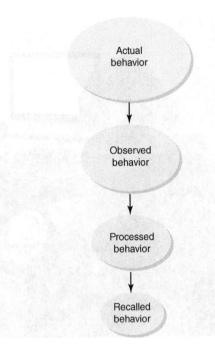

Figure 7.13
Information Loss in the Performance Appraisal System

supervisors tend to recall only a small percentage of an employee's actual behavior. Supervisors tend to remember the following:

- *First impressions.* Research from many areas of psychology indicates that we remember our first impression of someone (primacy effect) more than we remember later behaviors. Consequently, supervisors recall behaviors that are consistent with their first impression of an employee, even though those first behaviors may not have been representative of the employee's typical performance. Being aware of first impressions is important because performance can be *dynamic,* meaning that a person who is the top performer one year may not be the top performer during another year (Reb & Greguras, 2008).
- *Recent behaviors.* In addition to first impressions, supervisors tend to recall the most recent behavior that occurred during the evaluation period (recency effect).
- *Unusual or extreme behaviors.* Supervisors tend to remember unusual behaviors more than they remember common behaviors. For example, if an average-performing police officer captures an important suspect, the officer's performance evaluations are likely to be inappropriately high. Likewise, a good officer who makes one terrible mistake is likely to receive inappropriately low ratings.
- *Behavior consistent with the supervisor's opinion.* Once we form an opinion of someone, we tend to look for behaviors that confirm that opinion (confirmation bias). If a supervisor likes an employee, the supervisor will probably recall only behaviors consistent with that opinion. The opposite would be true for a supervisor who disliked an employee. Once you get on someone's bad side, it is hard to get off of it.

Third, documentation provides examples to use when reviewing performance ratings with employees. Instead of telling an employee that they are constantly getting

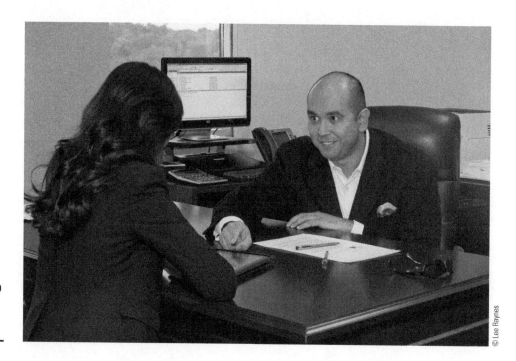

The performance review is the final step in the performance appraisal process.

© Lee Raynes

into arguments with customers, a supervisor can use documented critical incidents to show the employee the specific incidents and behaviors that are problematic.

Fourth, documentation helps an organization defend against legal actions taken against it by an employee who was terminated or denied a raise or promotion. As will be discussed later in this chapter, the courts closely examine the accuracy of the performance ratings upon which personnel decisions are based. Judges and juries are not likely to accept a supervisor's rating as proof of poor performance. Instead, they want to see proof of the behaviors that caused the supervisor to rate the employee poorly. Without documentation, employers will seldom win lawsuits filed against them (Foster, 2002). The courts' need for documentation is supported by research indicating that when evaluators must justify their performance ratings, their ratings are more accurate (Mero & Motowidlo, 1995).

To use critical incidents to document performance, a supervisor maintains a log of all the critical behaviors they observe their employees performing. These behaviors are then used during the performance appraisal review process to assign a rating for each employee. The log refreshes the supervisor's memory of their employees' performance and provides justification for each performance rating. The use of logbooks to record behaviors not only provides an excellent source of documentation but also results in more accurate performance appraisals (Bernardin & Walter, 1977). This is especially true if the logs are organized by employee rather than maintained as only a random collection of incidents observed on the job (DeNisi & Peters, 1996).

A more formal method for using critical incidents in evaluating performance was developed by Flanagan and Burns (1955) for use by General Motors. Called the **Employee Performance Record**, this method consists of a two-color form similar to that shown in Table 7.6. Half of the sheet is used to record examples of good behaviors, and the other half to record examples of poor behaviors. On each side,

Employee Performance Record A standardized use of the critical-incident technique developed at General Motors.

Table 7.6   Employee Performance Record

Dimension	Type of Performance	
	Poor	**Excellent**
Knowledge	1/17/22 *Could not answer client's question regarding EEOC policy on adverse impact* 7/28/22 *Used the wrong formula to calculate adverse impact during an audit* 11/06/22 *Could not explain the difference between criterion and content validity to a client*	1/3/22 *Went out of his way to learn about some new changes being made by OFCCP that would affect our work with clients. Ron shared these new changes at our staff meeting*
Teamwork	10/12/22 *Took credit for the work done by all members of his team*	2/4/22 *Another employee was swamped with work and Ron volunteered to help with her workload* 5/7/22 *Praised his work group for their excellent work on an OFCCP audit* 9/2/22 *Stayed late to help another employee finish an analysis that was due the next day*
Customer relations		1/4/22 *Called all his clients to wish them a happy New Year and to see if they were aware of some new changes in OFCCP policy* 3/6/22 *I received a call from one of Ron's clients stating how much they enjoyed working with him and how helpful he had been* 8/12/22 *I received an email from one of Ron's clients praising him for his excellent work ethic and attitude*
Accuracy of work	4/12/22 *Report sent to client had several typos* 6/7/22 *Left out several pages of a report that was sent to a client*	

there are columns for each of the relevant performance dimensions. Supervisors have a separate record for each employee and at the end of the day can record the observed behaviors.

The advantage of this format is that supervisors are allowed to record only job-relevant behaviors. At the end of the performance appraisal period (every six months), the supervisor has a record of job-relevant behaviors recorded in an organized fashion. The Employee Performance Record had several positive effects for General Motors. The number of disciplinary warnings declined, suggestions in the company suggestion box increased, and productivity increased. When the use of critical incidents was first announced, supervisors at General Motors were opposed, thinking it would take too much time. The actual time per day spent on recording the incidents, however, was only five minutes.

7-7 Evaluate Performance

Obtaining and Reviewing Objective Data

When it is time to appraise an employee's performance, a supervisor should first obtain and review the objective data relevant to the employee's behavior. For example, a police sergeant might review the numbers of tickets an officer wrote, arrests made, and citizen complaints received. A production supervisor might review the number of days an employee was absent, number of units produced, and the tons of material wasted. These data, when combined with critical-incident logs, provide a solid basis on which to rate an employee. As mentioned earlier in the chapter and shown in Figure 7.5, when reviewing objective data, it is essential that potential sources of contamination (e.g., shift, equipment, training, coworkers, geographic area) be considered.

Reading Critical-Incident Logs

After obtaining objective data, the supervisor should go back and read all of the critical incidents written for an employee. Reading these incidents should reduce errors of primacy, recency, confirmation bias, and attention to unusual information.

Completing the Rating Form

Once critical-incident logs have been read and objective data reviewed, the supervisor is ready to assign performance appraisal ratings. While making these ratings, the supervisor must be careful not to make common rating errors involving distribution, halo, proximity, and contrast.

Distribution Errors

Distribution errors Rating errors in which a rater will use only a certain part of a rating scale when evaluating employee performance.

Leniency error A type of rating error in which a rater consistently gives all employees high ratings, regardless of their actual levels of performance.

A common type of error in evaluating employee performance involves the distribution of ratings on a rating scale; such errors are known as **distribution errors**. Distribution errors are made when a rater uses only one part of a rating scale. For example, on a five-point scale, a supervisor might rate all their employees a 4 or a 5. One kind of distribution error is called **leniency error**, because certain raters tend to rate every employee at the upper end of the scale regardless of the actual performance of the employee. For example, on our five-point scale, the supervisor rates everyone a 4 or 5. Leniency error can in part be explained by the discomfort felt by supervisors about giving low ratings. That is, supervisors who are uncomfortable about how employees react to a low rating are more likely to be lenient than supervisors who are comfortable with negative employee reactions (Canali et al., 2005). Rater characteristics such as personality and cognitive ability do not seem to be related to leniency or strictness tendencies (Dewberry, Davies-Muir, & Newell, 2013). Another partial explanation for leniency is that supervisors don't really know the difference between good and bad performance, so they err on the positive side. Conducting frame of reference training should help reduce leniency in supervisors that don't know the difference between good and bad performance. In addition to fairness consideration, leniency error can pose legal problems if an organization terminates an employee who has a history of high performance ratings.

Central tendency error A type of rating error in which a rater consistently rates all employees in the middle of the scale, regardless of their actual levels of performance.

Strictness error A type of rating error in which a rater consistently gives all employees low ratings, regardless of their actual levels of performance.

A related error is **central tendency error**, which results in a supervisor rating every employee in the middle of the scale. For example, in our five-point scale, the supervisor rates everyone a 3. Still another error, **strictness error**, rates every employee at the low end of the scale. For example, on our five-point scale, our supervisor rates everyone a 1 or 2. You may have encountered such errors in your academic career when you took classes from "easy graders" or "hard graders."

These types of errors pose problems for an organization because two employees doing equal work will receive different ratings if one employee is supervised by a lenient rater and another by a strict rater. This problem can be partially eliminated by having several people rate each employee, although this is not often feasible, especially in small branch offices with only one manager or supervisor. There are times when distribution errors are caused by company policy—whether official or unofficial. In many organizations, there is pressure to not give an employee the highest rating. Such pressure is due either to an attempt to save money on raises or a cultural belief that "no one is perfect."

Halo Errors

Halo error A type of rating error that occurs when raters allow either a single attribute or an overall impression of an individual to affect the ratings that they make on each relevant job dimension.

A *halo error* occurs when a rater allows either a single attribute or an overall impression of an individual to affect the ratings that they make on each relevant job dimension. For example, a teacher might think that a student is highly creative. Because of that, the teacher might rate the student as being intelligent and industrious when, in fact, the student's grades are below average. In this case, the instructor has allowed the student's creativity to cloud their judgment of the student's other abilities. Halo effects occur especially when the rater has little knowledge of the job and is less familiar with the person being rated (Kozlowski, Kirsch, & Chao, 1986). Halo error is also more common in peer ratings than in supervisor ratings of subordinates (Viswesvaran, Schmidt, & Ones, 2005).

Usually, halo error is statistically determined by correlating the ratings for each dimension with those for the other dimensions. If they are highly correlated, halo error is often said to have occurred. As one might expect, there are explanations other than halo error for the high correlation among rating dimensions. Some psychologists have argued that consistent ratings across several dimensions might indicate actual consistencies in employee performance across dimensions rather than rating error (Murphy, Cleveland, & Hanscom, 2019). Thus, a teacher who is rated highly in classroom teaching, ability to work with students, knowledge, and fairness of grading actually may excel in those things. At this time, the best explanation for the consistency across rating dimensions is that some of the consistency is due to actual performance and some to halo and other rating errors (Viswesvaran et al., 2005).

Examples of halo, leniency, central tendency, and strictness errors are shown in Figure 7.14.

Proximity Errors

Proximity error A type of rating error in which a rating made on one dimension influences the rating made on the dimension that immediately follows it on the rating scale.

Proximity errors occur when a rating made on one dimension affects the rating made on the dimension that immediately follows it on the rating scale. For example, a supervisor gives an employee a rating of 5 on the first dimension. Because the second dimension is *physically located* on the rating form next to the first, there is a tendency to provide the same rating on both the first and second dimensions even if the employee might not actually perform at the same level on the second dimension.

Figure 7.14
Examples of Rating Errors

Leniency

Gil Grissom		Catherine Willows	
Cooperation	1 2 3 4 **5**	Cooperation	1 2 3 4 **5**
Knowledge	1 2 3 4 **5**	Knowledge	1 2 3 4 **5**
Leadership	1 2 3 4 **5**	Leadership	1 2 3 4 **5**

Warrick Brown		Nick Stokes	
Cooperation	1 2 3 4 **5**	Cooperation	1 2 3 4 **5**
Knowledge	1 2 3 4 **5**	Knowledge	1 2 3 4 **5**
Leadership	1 2 3 4 **5**	Leadership	1 2 3 4 **5**

Strictness

Gil Grissom		Catherine Willows	
Cooperation	**1** 2 3 4 5	Cooperation	**1** 2 3 4 5
Knowledge	**1** 2 3 4 5	Knowledge	**1** 2 3 4 5
Leadership	**1** 2 3 4 5	Leadership	**1** 2 3 4 5

Warrick Brown		Nick Stokes	
Cooperation	**1** 2 3 4 5	Cooperation	**1** 2 3 4 5
Knowledge	**1** 2 3 4 5	Knowledge	**1** 2 3 4 5
Leadership	**1** 2 3 4 5	Leadership	**1** 2 3 4 5

Central Tendency

Gil Grissom		Catherine Willows	
Cooperation	1 2 **3** 4 5	Cooperation	1 2 **3** 4 5
Knowledge	1 2 **3** 4 5	Knowledge	1 2 **3** 4 5
Leadership	1 2 **3** 4 5	Leadership	1 2 **3** 4 5

Warrick Brown		Nick Stokes	
Cooperation	1 2 **3** 4 5	Cooperation	1 2 **3** 4 5
Knowledge	1 2 **3** 4 5	Knowledge	1 2 **3** 4 5
Leadership	1 2 **3** 4 5	Leadership	1 2 **3** 4 5

Halo

Gil Grissom		Catherine Willows	
Cooperation	1 2 3 4 **5**	Cooperation	1 2 **3** 4 5
Knowledge	1 2 3 4 **5**	Knowledge	1 2 **3** 4 5
Leadership	1 2 3 4 **5**	Leadership	1 2 **3** 4 5

Warrick Brown		Nick Stokes	
Cooperation	1 2 3 4 **5**	Cooperation	**1** 2 3 4 5
Knowledge	1 2 3 4 **5**	Knowledge	**1** 2 3 4 5
Leadership	1 2 3 4 **5**	Leadership	**1** 2 3 4 5

The difference between this error and halo error is in the cause of the error and the number of dimensions affected. With halo error, all dimensions are affected by an overall impression of the employee. With proximity error, only the dimensions physically located nearest a particular dimension on the rating scale are affected; the reason for the effect, in fact, *is* the close physical proximity of the dimension rather than an overall impression.

Contrast Errors

The performance rating one person receives can be influenced by the performance of a previously evaluated person (Bravo & Kravitz, 1996). For example, a bank manager has six employees who are evaluated twice a year—on February 5 and again on August 5. The manager makes the evaluations in alphabetical order, starting with Joan Carr and then going to Donna Chan. Joan Carr is the best employee the bank has ever had, and she receives the highest possible rating on each dimension. After evaluating Carr, the manager then evaluates Chan. When compared with Carr, Chan is not nearly as effective an employee. Thus, Chan receives lower ratings than she might normally receive simply because she has been evaluated immediately after Carr. Her performance has been contrasted to Carr's performance rather than to some objective standard.

Such **contrast errors** can also occur between separate performance evaluations of the same person. That is, the ratings received on one performance appraisal will affect the ratings made on an appraisal six months later. For example, an employee's performance during the first six months of the year is "excellent," and they receive outstanding performance ratings. For some reason, the employee's actual behavior

Contrast error A type of rating error in which the rating of the performance level of one employee affects the ratings given to the next employee being rated.

in the next six months is only "good." What type of performance ratings will they receive? Based on the results of a study by Murphy, Gannett, Herr, and Chen (1986), the answer probably is that their ratings will be less than "good." In contrast to their initial excellent performance, the employee's subsequent performance (which may indeed have been "good") appeared to be lower than it actually was. Contrast effects occur only when the person making the evaluation actually sees the employee perform (Smither, Reilly, & Buda, 1988) and rates the employee (Summer & Knight, 1996) during both rating periods.

If a new supervisor reads that an employee's previous evaluations were excellent but they observe poor performance by the employee, the supervisor will probably continue to give excellent ratings—even though the employee's performance deteriorated. Smither and his colleagues call this rating error **assimilation**.

Low Reliability Across Raters

As shown back in Table 7.1, two people rating the same employee seldom agree with each other (Conway & Huffcut, 1997; Viswesvaran, Ones, & Schmidt, 1996). There are three major reasons for this lack of reliability. First, raters often commit the rating errors previously discussed (e.g., halo, leniency). Thus, if one rater engages in halo error and another in contrast error, it is not surprising that their ratings of the same employee are different.

Second, raters often have very different standards and ideas about the ideal employee. For example, I once conducted a performance appraisal workshop for a police department. After viewing a video clip of an officer handling a disturbance call, one sergeant rated the officer's performance as excellent; another rated the officer's performance as being terrible. When asked about their different ratings, one sergeant indicated that he thought officers should be aggressive and take command of a situation, whereas the other sergeant thought officers should be more citizen oriented. Thus, the same employee behavior elicited two very different ratings because each sergeant had a different "prototype" of the ideal cop.

Third, two different raters may actually observe very different behaviors by the same employee. For example, in law enforcement, a desk sergeant may encounter more administrative and paperwork behaviors while with the employee in the office, whereas a field sergeant may encounter more law enforcement behaviors while with the employee out in the field. Thus, different ratings by the two sergeants may simply reflect the fact that each has observed the same officer perform in very different situations. As mentioned earlier, one way to reduce the number of rating errors and increase reliability is to train the people who will be making the performance evaluations.

Sampling Problems

Recency Effect. Performance appraisals are typically conducted once a year. The evaluation is designed to cover all of the behaviors that have taken place during the previous six months to a year. Research has demonstrated, however, that recent behaviors are given more weight in the performance evaluation than behaviors that occurred during the first few months of the evaluation period (Steiner & Rain, 1989). Such an effect penalizes workers who performed well during most of the period but tailed off toward the end, and it rewards workers who saved their best work until just before the evaluation.

Assimilation A type of rating error in which raters base their rating of an employee during one rating period on the ratings the rater gave during a previous period.

Recency effect The tendency for supervisors to recall and place more weight on recent behaviors when they evaluate performance.

It seems that students are well aware of the recency effect when they argue that the high score on their final exam should carry more weight than the lower scores on previous exams!

Infrequent Observation. As shown back in Figure 7.2, another problem that affects performance appraisals is that many managers or supervisors do not have the opportunity to observe a representative sample of employee behavior. **Infrequent observation** occurs for two reasons. First, managers are often so busy with their own work that they have no time to "walk the floor" and observe their employees' behavior. Instead, they make inferences based on completed work or employee personality traits (Feldman, 1981). A good example involves a teacher who completes a reference form for a student. Reference forms commonly ask about characteristics such as the applicant's ability to cooperate or to get along with others. The teacher must base their evaluation on the term papers that they have read and the student's test grades. Rarely do they have the opportunity to observe the student "get along with" or "cooperate with others." Instead, because a group project was turned in on time and received an excellent grade, the teacher surmises that the student must have cooperated and gotten along well with other group members. However, it may be that the student does not cooperate well with others, and based on the infrequent opportunities to observe the student, the teacher gave an inaccurate rating on this dimension.

Due to the problem of infrequent observation, general managers at each Costco warehouse are required to take daily "walks" in which they and their assistant managers go through each section of the warehouse and talk to employees about the layout of the section as well as the sales numbers for each section.

Employees often act differently around a supervisor than around other workers, which is the second reason managers usually do not make accurate observations. When the supervisor is absent, an employee may break rules, show up late, or work slowly. But when the boss is around, the employee becomes a model worker. In the eyes of the supervisor, the employee is doing an excellent job; the other workers, however, know better.

As discussed earlier in the chapter, this problem can be alleviated somewhat by having several raters evaluate the employee. Other raters can be other supervisors, fellow workers (peer ratings), and even customers. A meta-analysis by Conway and Huffcutt (1997) indicated that supervisor ratings on the average correlate .34 with peer ratings. Thus, even though the two groups somewhat agree, the agreement is certainly not perfect.

Unfortunately, ratings from these sources are often subject to more errors than the uninformed ratings made by a supervisor. For example, customers may complain about a worker even though the employee is following policy, and a worker may provide low evaluations of their coworkers so that the worker will receive a higher raise. Even with these problems, multiple raters remain a good idea.

Cognitive Processing of Observed Behavior

Observation of Behavior. As shown in Figure 7.15, just because an employee's behavior is observed does not guarantee that it will be properly remembered or recalled during the performance appraisal review. In fact, research indicates that raters recall those behaviors that are consistent with their general impression of an employee (Cooper, 1981a; Feldman, 1981; Martell, Guzzo, & Willis, 1995), and the

Infrequent observation The idea that supervisors do not see most of an employee's behavior.

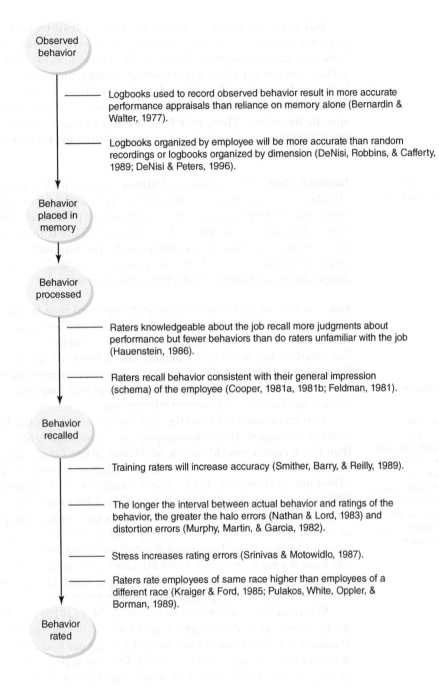

Figure 7.15
Factors Affecting
Information Loss

Observed
behavior

Logbooks used to record observed behavior result in more accurate performance appraisals than reliance on memory alone (Bernardin & Walter, 1977).

Logbooks organized by employee will be more accurate than random recordings or logbooks organized by dimension (DeNisi, Robbins, & Cafferty, 1989; DeNisi & Peters, 1996).

Behavior
placed in
memory

Behavior
processed

Raters knowledgeable about the job recall more judgments about performance but fewer behaviors than do raters unfamiliar with the job (Hauenstein, 1986).

Raters recall behavior consistent with their general impression (schema) of the employee (Cooper, 1981a, 1981b; Feldman, 1981).

Behavior
recalled

Training raters will increase accuracy (Smither, Barry, & Reilly, 1989).

The longer the interval between actual behavior and ratings of the behavior, the greater the halo errors (Nathan & Lord, 1983) and distortion errors (Murphy, Martin, & Garcia, 1982).

Stress increases rating errors (Srinivas & Motowidlo, 1987).

Raters rate employees of same race higher than employees of a different race (Kraiger & Ford, 1985; Pulakos, White, Oppler, & Borman, 1989).

Behavior
rated

greater the time interval between the actual behavior and the performance rating, the greater the probability that rating errors will occur (Murphy, Martin, & Garcia, 1982; Nathan & Lord, 1983). Furthermore, raters who are familiar with the job being evaluated recall more judgments about performance but fewer behaviors than do raters who are unfamiliar with the job (Harriman & Kovach, 1987; Hauenstein, 1986). The decrease in memory accuracy over time can be reduced if several raters, rather than one, are used to evaluate performance (Martell & Borg, 1993).

But even though memory-based ratings lead to more distortion, in many circumstances they are more accurate than ratings made immediately after the behaviors occur (Murphy & Balzer, 1986). The reason for these increases in halo and accuracy is not yet clear. Supervisors perhaps realize that it will be a long interval between observation of employee behavior and the formal evaluation of that behavior and that they will not be able (without great effort or the use of logbooks) to remember specific behaviors. Thus, they form an overall impression of the employee and an overall impression of an ideal and a poor employee and evaluate the employee based on comparison with the ideal.

Stress Perceived psychological pressure.

Emotional State. The amount of **stress** under which a supervisor operates also affects their performance ratings. Srinivas and Motowidlo (1987) found that raters who were placed in a stressful situation produced ratings with more errors than raters who were not under stress did. This finding is important because performance evaluations are often conducted hurriedly, as supervisors evaluate employee performance so they can return to their "real" work. Methods for reducing this problem will be discussed later in this chapter.

Bias. Raters who like the employees being rated may be more lenient (Lefkowitz, 2000; Sutton, Baldwin, Wood, & Hoffman, 2013) and less accurate in their ratings than would raters who neither like nor dislike their employees (Cardy & Dobbins, 1986). But this does not mean that a person who is liked will always receive higher ratings than someone who is disliked. The rater may overcompensate in an effort to be "fair." The rater's feelings, or **affect**, toward an employee may interfere with the cognitive processing of actual performance information.

Affect Feelings or emotion.

Racial bias The tendency to give members of a particular race lower evaluation ratings than are justified by their actual performance or to give members of one race lower ratings than members of another race.

Two meta-analyses investigating the presence of **racial bias** in performance evaluations suggests that White employees receive slightly higher performance ratings than Black employees (McKay & McDaniel, 2006; Roth, Huffcutt, & Bobko, 2003). Race accounts for about 1.7% of the variability in performance ratings (Murphy, Cleveland, & Hanscom, 2019). A meta-analysis of 74 studies by Kraiger and Ford (1985) found a racial similarity bias in that White raters gave higher performance ratings to White employees, and Black raters gave higher ratings to Black employees. Interestingly, this bias occurred only with studies involving real organizations—laboratory research seldom revealed racial bias in performance ratings. Complicating this issue is a study by Stauffer and Buckley (2005) arguing that much of the research in this area is flawed and that when the proper method (repeated measures) is used, evidence of racial bias in performance ratings exists.

Meta-analyses by Roth, Purvis, and Bobko (2012) and by Bowen, Swim, and Jacobs (2000), as well as a large data set of 360-degree feedback ratings by Church, Rogelberg, and Waclawski (2000) suggest that gender bias does not seem to be an issue in performance ratings. In fact, gender differences in performance ratings have become smaller and slightly favor women employees (Roth et al., 2012). Meta-analysis results also indicate that age is not related to performance ratings (Ng & Feldman, 2008).

7-8 Communicate Appraisal Results to Employees

As was stated in the beginning of this chapter, perhaps the most important use of performance-evaluation data is to provide feedback to the employees and assess their strengths and weaknesses so that further training can be implemented.

Although this feedback and training should be an ongoing process, the semiannual evaluation might be the best time to formally discuss employee performance. A 2018 study conducted by Robert Half Talent Solutions found that 28% of organizations conducted semiannual performance evaluations, and 40% of organizations conducted annual performance evaluations (Kong, 2018). Furthermore, holding a formal review interview places the organization on better legal ground in the event of a lawsuit (Foster et al., 2008; Malos, 1998).

Normally, in most organizations a supervisor spends a few minutes with employees each year to *tell* them about the scores they received during the most recent evaluation period. This process is probably the norm because most managers do not like to judge others; because of this dislike, they try to complete the evaluation process as quickly as possible (Grensing-Pophal, 2001b).

Furthermore, seldom does evaluating employees benefit the supervisor. The best scenario is to hear no complaints, and the worst scenario is a lawsuit. In fact, one study demonstrated that dissatisfaction and a decrease in organizational commitment occurs even when an employee receives an evaluation that is "satisfactory" but not "outstanding" (Pearce & Porter, 1986). Finally, in the "tell and sell" approach to performance appraisal interviews, a supervisor "tells" an employee everything they have done poorly and then "sells" them on ways they can improve. This method, however, accomplishes little (Winsor, 1984).

Research suggests that certain techniques can be used to make the performance appraisal interview more effective: time, scheduling, and preparation.

Prior to the Interview

Allocating Time

Both the supervisor and the employee must have time to prepare for the review interview. Both should be allowed at least an hour to prepare before an interview and at least an hour for the interview itself.

Scheduling the Interview

The interview location should be in a neutral place that ensures privacy and allows the supervisor and the employee to face one another without a desk between them as a communication barrier. Performance-appraisal review interviews should be scheduled at least once every six months for most employees and more often for new employees. As mentioned previously, a growing trend is for organizations to provide frequent feedback rather than waiting until the annual performance review. Review interviews are commonly scheduled six months after an employee begins working for the organization. If this date comes at a bad time (such as during the holidays, or a busy time for retail stores), the interview should be scheduled for a more convenient time. It is important to note that although the *formal* performance appraisal review occurs only once or twice a year, informal "progress checks" should be held throughout the year to provide feedback.

Preparing for the Interview

While preparing for the interview, the supervisor should review the ratings they have assigned to the employee and the reasons for those ratings, and is where detailed critical incidents will be very helpful for discussing performance. This step is important because the quality of feedback given to employees will affect their satisfaction with the entire performance appraisal process (Mount, 1983).

Furthermore, employees perceive and react to the amount of time that a supervisor uses to prepare for the interview.

Meanwhile, the employee should rate their own performance using the same format as the supervisor (Roberts, 2003). The employee also should write down specific reasons and examples that support the ratings they give themself, as well as ideas for personal development.

During the Interview

Because employees and supervisors are often anxious about performance reviews, it is a good idea to begin the interview with some small talk until the jitters go away. Once the employee and supervisor are feeling as comfortable as they are going to get, the supervisor should communicate the following: (1) the role of performance appraisal—that making decisions about salary increases and terminations is not its only purpose; (2) how the performance appraisal was conducted; (3) how the evaluation process was accomplished; (4) the expectation that the appraisal interview will be interactive; and (5) the goal of understanding and improving performance.

The review process is probably best begun with the employee communicating their own ratings and their justification for them (Bacal, 2012). Research indicates that employees who are actively involved in the interview from the start will be more satisfied with the results (Gilliland & Langdon, 1998; Roberts, 2003).

The supervisor then communicates their ratings and the reasons for them. The supervisor should limit this communication to statements about behavior and performance rather than traits that are or are not possessed by the employee. Of course, it would be nice to avoid negative feedback because employees then are more satisfied with their reviews and don't develop negative attitudes toward management (Brett & Atwater, 2001). But few employees are perfect, and some negative feedback is inevitable. Because of this, positive feedback generally should be given first, followed by the negative feedback, and finishing with more positive feedback. This process is often referred to as the "feedback sandwich," in which the negative feedback is sandwiched between positive feedback. Liberal use of positive feedback not only helps employees accept the negative feedback, but also helps supervisors who tend to avoid providing negative feedback in an effort to reduce the chance of interpersonal conflict (Waung & Highhouse, 1997). Any major differences between the employee's self-ratings and those given by the supervisor should be discussed until both understand the differences.

The next step is perhaps the most important. Because few employees receive perfect evaluations, it is essential to discuss the reasons an employee's performance is not considered to be perfect. The employee may lack some knowledge as to how to perform the job properly, may have been assigned too many duties, or may have outside problems that affect their work performance.

The supervisor's acknowledgment that there may be external reasons for an employee's poor performance can increase the employee's satisfaction with the review and enable them to perceive the feedback and evaluation as accurate and helpful. In addition, it will help the employee understand and appreciate the supervisor's perceptions (Bannister, 1986). Research also confirms that employees are more inclined to perform helpful behaviors toward their organization if they perceive that their performance appraisal was fair (Thurston & McNall, 2010). Feedback should be candid, specific, and behavioral rather than personal. Awareness and acknowledgment of external factors for performance is especially important because we have a tendency, called the *fundamental attribution error*, to attribute others' failure or poor performance to personal rather than situational factors.

Once the problems have been identified, the next and most difficult task is to find solutions. What can the supervisor do to help? What can the organization do? What can the employee do? The idea here is that solutions to the problems result from joint effort. Too often, we attribute poor performance solely to the fault of the employee, when, in fact, performance is affected by many factors including ability, motivation, company policy, supervisor ability, organizational support, coworker attitudes, and the physical environment.

Because communicating appraisal results that will affect an employee's raise and providing feedback for improvement are very different processes and have different implications for an employee, a good practice is to separate the two into two different conversations. By communicating the appraisal results first, and then discussing strategies to improve performance at a later date, the employee can think about their performance ratings and be better able to discuss future options.

It has been suggested that instead of providing feedback, which is past-focused, a supervisor should provide *feedforward*, which is future-focused (Kluger & Nir, 2010). The feedforward interview concentrates on what the employee did well in the past year, what characteristics of the employee contributed to that success, and how the employee can use those characteristics to be successful in the future (Murphy, Cleveland, & Hanscom, 2019).

At the conclusion of the interview, goals should be mutually set for future performance and behavior, and both supervisor and employee should understand how these goals will be met. Goals and goal setting will be thoroughly discussed in Chapter 9. For now, however, we should keep in mind that goals should be concrete and reasonable and set by both employee and supervisor. The Career Workshop Box gives tips on how employees can help themselves in terms of performance appraisals.

7-9 Terminate Employees

As discussed in the preceding pages, the primary use of performance-appraisal results is to provide feedback to employees about their behavior. Performance-appraisal results are also used to make positive personnel decisions such as raises and promotions. Unfortunately, there are times when managers must terminate an employee's employment. Over the next few pages, we will discuss the legal aspects of terminating an employee.

Employment-at-Will Doctrine

Employment-at-will doctrine The opinion of courts in most states that employers have the right to hire and fire an employee at will and without any specific cause.

In the United States, there is a big difference between terminating an employee in the public sector and terminating an employee in the private sector. In the private sector, the **employment-at-will doctrine** in most states allows employers freedom to fire an employee without a reason—at will. In the public sector, an employee can be fired only for cause.

The idea behind employment at will is that because employees are free to quit their jobs at will, so too are organizations free to terminate an employee at will. Though employment-at-will is common in the United States, countries such as France enforce the restriction that no employee can be fired unless it is for cause.

There are some limitations to the employment-at-will doctrine (Falcone, 2017; Steingold, 2019):

- *State law.* States such as California, Montana, and New York have laws that an employee can be fired only for cause—for example, breaking a rule, demonstrating an inability to perform.
- *Provisions of federal or state law.* Employees cannot be fired for reasons protected by federal or state law. For example, an employer cannot fire an employee because of the employee's gender, race, ethnicity, or because the employee is over the age of 40.
- *Public policy/interest.* Employers cannot terminate an employee for exercising a legal duty such as jury duty or refusing to violate the law or professional ethics. For example, a large savings and loan institution ordered one of its appraisers to appraise homes higher than their actual values so that its customers could qualify to finance property. Citing federal regulations and professional ethics against inflating property values, the employee refused the company order. After being terminated, the employee successfully filed a lawsuit (one of more than 200 filed by employees against this institution) claiming that they had been fired for refusing to violate the law and the ethical standards of their profession.
- *Contracts.* Obviously, if an individual employee has a signed employment contract stipulating a particular period of employment, an organization cannot fire the employee without cause. Likewise, unions enter into collective bargaining agreements (contracts) with employers that also limit or negate employment-at-will.
- *Implied contracts.* Employment-at-will is nullified if an employer implies that an employee "has a job for life" or can be fired only for certain reasons. For example, if an interviewer tells an applicant, "At this company, all you have to do is keep your nose clean to keep your job," the employer will not be able to terminate the employee for minor rules infractions or for poor performance.
- *Covenants of good faith and fair dealing.* Though employers are generally free to hire and fire at will, the courts have ruled that employers must still act in good faith and deal fairly with an employee. These rulings have been based on an item in the *Uniform Commercial Code* (UCC) stating, "Every contract . . . imposes an obligation of good faith in its performance or enforcement," and the fact that courts consider employment decisions to be a form of a contract.

Employment-at-will statements Statements in employment applications and company manuals reaffirming an organization's right to hire and fire at will.

To protect their right to use a policy of employment-at-will, most organizations include **employment-at-will statements**, such as that shown in Figure 7.16, in their job applications and employee handbooks. These statements usually hold up in court.

Figure 7.16
Sample Employment-at-Will Statement

> I understand that, if employed, I have the right to end my employment with Sordi Industries. Likewise, I understand that my employment with Sordi industries is not for any definite period of time, and Sordi Industries has the right to terminate my employment with or without cause and with or without notice. I understand that no representative of Sordi Industries is authorized to imply any contract for permanent employment.

Legal Reasons for Terminating Employees

In situations not covered by employment-at-will, there are only four reasons that an employee can be legally terminated: probationary period, violation of company rules, inability to perform, and an economically caused reduction in force (layoffs).

Probationary Period

In many jobs, employees are given a probationary period in which to prove that they can perform well. Though most probationary periods last three to six months, those for police officers are usually a year, and the probationary period for assistant professors is six years! Employees can be terminated more easily during the probationary period than at any other time.

Violation of Company Rules

Courts consider five factors in determining the legality of a decision to terminate an employee for violating company rules. The first factor is that a rule against a particular behavior must actually exist. Though this may seem obvious, organizations often have "unwritten" rules governing employee behavior. These unwritten rules, however, will not hold up in court.

If a rule exists, a company must prove that the employee knew the rule. Rules can be communicated orally during employee orientation and staff meetings and in writing in handbooks, newsletters, bulletin boards, and paycheck stuffers. Rules communicated in handbooks are the most legally defensible. To prove that an employee knew a rule, organizations require employees to sign statements that they received information about the rule, read the rule, and understand the rule.

The third factor is the ability of the employer to prove that an employee actually violated the rule. Proof is accomplished through such means as witnesses, video recordings, and job samples. Human resources professionals almost must be detectives because proving rule violations is often not easy. For example, two supervisors saw an employee stagger into work and could clearly smell alcohol on their breath. The employee was terminated for violating the company rule against drinking. During their appeal of the termination, they claimed that they staggered because they had the flu and what the supervisors smelled was cough syrup rather than alcohol. The employee won the appeal. As a result of this case, the company now has an on-site nurse, and breathalyzer tests are administered to employees suspected of using alcohol at work.

The fourth factor considered by the courts is the extent to which the rule has been equally enforced. That is, if other employees violated the rule but were not terminated, terminating an employee for a particular rule violation may not be legal (*Huske v. Honeywell International*, 2004; *Pineda v. United Parcel Service*, 2003). This factor poses a dilemma for many organizations. Because courts look at consistency, lawyers advise organizations to fire any employee who violates a rule. To not fire a rule breaker sets a precedent, making termination of future rule breakers more difficult. There are many times when a good employee breaks a rule, a situation that normally would result in termination. However, because the employee is highly valued, the organization does not want to fire the employee.

The fifth and final factor is the extent to which the punishment fits the crime (Falcone, 2017). Employees in their probationary period (usually their first six months) can be immediately fired for a rule infraction. For more tenured employees, however, the organization must make a reasonable attempt to change the person's behavior through **progressive discipline**. The longer an employee has been with an organization, the greater the number of steps that must be taken to correct their behavior. Discipline can begin with something simple such as counseling or an oral warning, move on to a written warning or probation, and end with steps such as reduction in pay, demotion, or termination.

For violations of some rules, progressive discipline is not always necessary. It is probably safe to say that an employer can terminate an employee who steals money.

Progressive discipline Providing employees with punishments of increasing severity, as needed, in order to change behavior.

Inability to Perform

Employees can also be terminated for an inability to perform the job. To do so, though, an organization will need to prove that the employee could not perform the job and that progressive discipline was taken to give the employee an opportunity to improve. For an employer to survive a court challenge to terminating an underperforming employee, it must first demonstrate that a reasonable standard of performance was communicated to the employee. The organization must next demonstrate that there was a documented failure to meet the standard. Such documentation can include critical-incident logs and work samples (e.g., photos of dripped paint for a painter, improperly hemmed pants for a tailor).

A properly designed performance appraisal system is the key to legally terminating an employee (Martin, Bartol, & Kehoe, 2000). Legal performance appraisal systems (Smith, 1993):

- are based on a job analysis;
- have concrete, relevant standards that have been communicated to employees;
- involve multiple behavioral measures of performance;
- include several raters, each of whom has received training;
- are standardized and formal; and
- provide the opportunity for an employee to appeal.

Reduction in Force (Layoff)

Employees can be terminated if it is in the best economic interests of an organization to do so. Reductions in force, more commonly called layoffs, have been used by many Fortune 500 companies in the past few decades. In cases of large layoffs or plant closings, the Worker Adjustment and Retraining Notification Act (WARN) requires that organizations provide workers with at least 60 days' notice. Though layoffs are designed to save money, research indicates not only that force reductions have a devastating effect on employees (Leana & Feldman, 1992), such as a loss of medical insurance and reported negative impact on employees' physical and mental health, but that they often do not result in the desired financial savings (Cascio, 2002). Layoffs are extensively discussed in Chapter 14.

The Termination Meeting

Prior to the Meeting

Once a decision has been made to terminate an employee, certain steps should be taken to prepare for the meeting in which the decision will be communicated to the employee. The first step is to ensure that the legal process has been followed. For example, if an organization is about to terminate an employee for a rule violation, it must be sure that a rule actually existed, that the employee knew the rule, that the organization has proof that the rule was violated, that progressive discipline was used, and that the rule was applied equally to all employees. An important responsibility for human resources professionals is to ensure that a termination decision is legally defensible.

The next step is to determine how much help, if any, the organization wants to offer the employee. Forms of help can include references, severance pay, benefits, and outplacement assistance (Steingold, 2019). Usually, greater levels of help are given to employees who sign agreements not to sue the organization.

The final step is to schedule an appropriate place and time for the meeting to occur. The meeting should be held in a neutral, private location. To avoid potential damage caused by a hostile reaction to the termination decision, the meeting should not be held in a supervisor's office. Rather than late on Friday afternoon, as is traditional, the meeting should take place in the middle of the week so that the employee has an opportunity to seek advice and the organization has a chance to talk to its employees (Zetlin, 2019). When a termination is made on a Friday afternoon, the employee is unable to contact sources of help over the weekend. Likewise, the terminated employee has all weekend to get on the phone to tell their side of the story to other employees, whereas the organization must wait until Monday to refute the gossip.

During the Meeting

During the meeting, the supervisor should get to the point about terminating the employee. The employee usually knows why they have been called in, and there is no reason to prolong the agony. The supervisor should rationally state the reasons for the decision, express gratitude for the employee's efforts (if sincere) and offer whatever assistance the organization intends to provide. Administrative duties such as obtaining copies of keys and completing paperwork are then performed. Finally, the employee is asked to gather personal belongings and is escorted out the door.

I realize that this advice sounds cold. However, terminating an employee is a difficult task, and there is little that can be done to make it pleasant. If you have ever ended a romantic relationship, I think you might understand the feelings that go into terminating an employee. It is an emotional time, and the key is to be brief and professional.

After the Meeting

Once the meeting is over, the natural reaction of the supervisor is to feel guilty. To relieve some of this guilt, a supervisor should review the facts—the supervisor gave the employee every chance to improve, but the employee chose not to. A human resources professional for Valleydale Foods tells employees this: "Through your behavior, you fired yourself. I'm just completing the paperwork."

When an employee is fired, other employees will be tense. Consequently, it is important to be honest with the other employees about what happened; at the same time, negative statements about the terminated employee's character must be avoided.

7-10 Monitor the Legality and Fairness of the Appraisal System

Performance appraisal systems are subject to the same legal standards as are employment tests and other employment decisions. As such, performance ratings should be analyzed each rating period to determine if there are gender, race/ethnicity, or age differences that can't be explained by actual differences in performance. Likewise, the personnel decisions that are based on the performance appraisal ratings should be analyzed to ensure discrimination does not occur in the raises, bonuses, promotions, and terminations that result from the performance ratings. Questions that should be asked by the organization during this monitoring process include the following:

- Has the organization provided adequate training to supervisors regarding how to evaluate performance, communicate appraisal results, mentor underperforming employees, and make decisions based on the appraisal results?
- Are there gender, race, ethnicity, disability, or age differences in performance ratings? If so, are the differences supported by actual differences in performance?
- Do employees with similar performance ratings receive similar outcomes such as raises, promotions, discipline, training, or promotion (*Russell v. Principi*, 2001)?
- Are there gender, race, ethnicity, disability, or age differences in the opportunities given to improve performance (*Johnson v. Kroger*, 2003; *Mayer v. Nextel*, 2003)? That is, if a low-rated Asian employee is provided opportunities for improvement, is a similarly situated Hispanic or Latinx employee given the same opportunities?
- Are there employees who historically have received high ratings suddenly being given a low rating (*Shackelford v. Deloitte & Touche*, 1999)? If so, is the drop in ratings due to an actual performance decrease or to potential discrimination?

On the Job ▶ **Applied Case Study**

Firing an Employee at Kohl's Department Store

Three employees were fired from the Kohl's Department Store in Mechanicsville, Virginia, for violating the store policy about using coupons. The store sent each employee 11 15% off coupons as part of a "friends and family" sale: 1 coupon was for the employee and the other 10 were to be given to family and friends. There were a lot of extra coupons, so on a Saturday, 18-year-old Rikki Groves, Rebecca Hagen, and Katie Kombacher gave the coupons to customers who did not have one. They assumed that these coupons were similar to other sale coupons used by the store and that the cashier could scan an already used coupon for a customer who did not have a coupon. According to Groves, who had been with Kohl's for three months, none of the managers told employees that these coupons were different from those processed every day. A few days after the incident, the person in charge of store security called Groves into a closed-door meeting a few hours before the end of her shift. He began to interrogate Groves, telling her that he had observed her using the coupons through the store camera and that she would have to pay the store $1,000 to cover the coupons she gave

to customers, or the store would call the police and have her arrested for embezzlement. The head of store security then began taking pictures of her and required her to sign a document that barred her from returning to the store for the next year. Groves started making payments toward the $1,000 when the story was published in a local newspaper. After outraged citizens complained and threatened to cut up their Kohl's credit cards and stop patronizing the store, the store returned Groves's money and said she would not have to pay it back. The three women were not offered their jobs back, nor were they given an apology. A spokesperson for the local police department indicated that the threat of arrest used by Kohl's was incorrect because what Groves did was not a crime, but a matter of internal policy.

- How could the store have better handled the termination? Should the three employees have been fired?
- What could Kohl's have done to have prevented the situation in the first place?
- What could the employees have done differently?

As mentioned in this chapter, the employment-at-will doctrine has been around for a very long time. It is based on English Common law of the eighteenth century, which said that the length of employment was presumed to be for one year when there is work to be done and when there is not. A New York State treatise writer, Horace Gay Wood, in his book *Master and Servant* (1877), expanded on the doctrine, stating that a hiring with no definite ending date is a hiring at will. That is, unless both master and servant agree that service was to extend for a specified time, it should be considered an indefinite hiring, and it us up to the servant, should he be terminated, to prove otherwise. From what was then called "Wood's Rule" came the U.S. interpretation of employment law: an employer is free to discharge individuals at any time for cause or for no cause at all, and the employee is equally free to quit at any time for any reason.

Many debates have arisen over the years as to the fairness or ethics of such a doctrine. Critics have long feared that it gives too much power to businesses over the lives of their employees. To have such a rule that allows a company to fire even good employees whenever and for whatever reason is unfair and unethical. The doctrine provides little protection to employees who work hard and who work well. And there is little job security in an at-will company. Theoretically, employees can be fired just because a supervisor may not like them or because of how they dress or look. An excuse often given to employees who are terminated under "at-will" is, "You just aren't the right fit for this company." Then there was a case where an armored truck driver was fired for leaving his post even though he only did so to save someone's life (*Gardner v. Loomis Armored, Inc.*, April 4, 1996).

Opponents say that from a business perspective, the doctrine provides little incentive for people to work hard, because, if employees can be terminated no matter how hard they work, what's the benefit of putting in the extra effort? Motivation can even suffer if employees are working under "fear" of their jobs. Finally, because at-will employees are treated differently than "for just cause" employees, critics state that it is unfair and unequal treatment under the law, which violates the Fourteenth Amendment. Also, motivation can suffer when employees fear that they can be terminated at any time.

Supporters state that the doctrine provides equal fairness to both the employer and employee when it comes to termination of employment. They say it is only fair that if an employee can terminate employment at any time, then the employer should have that same right. They cite the limitations to the doctrine, outlined in this chapter, provide further protection to employees. Supporters further state that the doctrine is not totally free from lawsuits, as evidenced by the lawsuit filed and won by the defendant in the above *Gardner* case. Additionally, applicants don't have to work for or sign an employment at-will statement at an at-will company if they think the doctrine is unfair. They have the right to seek employment elsewhere.

What Do You Think?

- What are other ethical dilemmas in the at-will doctrine?

- Which argument do you agree with: that of critics of the doctrine or supporters?

- Are there other limitations that should be imposed on the doctrine, other than those outlined in your textbook, that would make the doctrine more ethical, and therefore, fairer?

- Do you agree that having different laws for public and private sector employees (at will versus for just cause) is fair?

Chapter Summary

In this chapter you learned:

- There are 10 steps in creating a performance-appraisal system: (1) determine the reasons for performance evaluation, (2) identify environmental and cultural limitations that might affect the success of an appraisal system, (3) determine who will evaluate performance, (4) create an instrument to evaluate performance, (5) explain the system to those who will use it, (6) observe and document performance, (7) evaluate employee performance, (8) review the results of the evaluation with the employee, (9) make personnel decisions such as giving raises or terminating employees, and (10) monitor the system for fairness and legal compliance.

- Common rating errors such as leniency, central tendency, strictness, halo, proximity, contrast, primacy, recency, confirmation bias, and infrequent observation of behavior hinder the accuracy of performance appraisal results.
- Important factors in the success of the performance appraisal review include scheduling the review to eliminate or minimize interruptions, letting the employee discuss their feelings and thoughts, and mutually setting goals for improvements in future performance.
- In organizations not subject to employment-at-will, employees can be terminated only for violating a company rule or inability to perform or as part of a force reduction.

Key Terms

Forced-choice rating scale   (229)
Performance appraisal review   (229)
Peter Principle   (229)
360-degree feedback   (231)
Multiple-source feedback   (231)
Contextual performance   (237)
Rank order   (238)
Paired comparison   (238)
Forced distribution method   (238)
Quantity   (240)
Quality   (241)
Error   (241)
Graphic rating scale   (243)
Contamination   (244)
Frame-of-reference training   (250)
Critical incidents   (250)
Employee Performance Record   (252)
Distribution errors   (254)
Leniency error   (254)

Central tendency error   (255)
Strictness error   (255)
Halo error   (255)
Proximity error   (255)
Contrast errors   (256)
Assimilation   (257)
Recency Effect   (257)
Infrequent observation   (258)
Stress   (260)
Affect   (260)
Racial bias   (260)
Employment-at-will doctrine   (264)
Employment-at-will statements   (264)
Progressive discipline   (266)
Behaviorally anchored rating scales
     (BARS)   (271)
Mixed-standard scales   (274)
Behavioral observation scales (BOS)   (274)
Prototypes   (276)

Questions for Review

1. What do you think is the most important purpose for performance appraisal? Why?
2. What problems might result from using a 360-degree feedback system?
3. The chapter mentioned a variety of ways to measure performance. Which one do you think is the best? Why?
4. What do you think is the best way to communicate performance-appraisal results to employees?
5. Is the employment-at-will doctrine a good idea? Why or why not?

Appendix Additional Types of Rating Scales

Behaviorally Anchored Rating Scales

Behaviorally anchored rating scales (BARS) A method of performance appraisal involving the placement of benchmark behaviors next to each point on a graphic rating scale.

To reduce the rating problems associated with graphic rating scales, Smith and Kendall (1963) developed **behaviorally anchored rating scales (BARS)**. As shown in Figure 7.9, BARS use critical incidents (samples of behavior) to formally provide meaning to the numbers on a rating scale. Although BARS are time-consuming to construct, the process is not overly complicated.

Creating BARS

Generation of Job Dimensions

In the first step in BARS construction, the number and nature of job-related dimensions are determined. If a job analysis has already been conducted, the dimensions can be obtained from the job analysis report. If for some reason a job analysis has not been conducted, a panel of some 20 job experts—the employees—is formed. This panel determines the important dimensions on which an employee's performance should be evaluated. If 15 to 20 employees are not available, several supervisors can meet and develop the job dimensions as a group (Shapira & Shirom, 1980). Usually, 5 to 10 dimensions are generated (Schwab et al., 1975).

Generation of Critical Incidents

Once the relevant job dimensions have been identified, employees are asked to generate examples of good, average, and bad behavior that they have seen for each dimension. Thus, if five dimensions have been identified, each employee is asked to generate 15 critical incidents—a good, an average, and a bad incident for each of the five dimensions. If the organization is fairly small, employees may need to generate more than one example of the three types of behavior for each dimension.

Sorting Incidents

To make sure that the incidents written for each job dimension are actually examples of behavior for that dimension, three job experts independently sort the incidents into each of the job dimensions. The dimension into which each incident has been sorted by each of the three sorters then is examined. If at least two sorters placed an incident in the same dimension, the incident becomes part of that dimension. But if each sorter has placed the incident in a different category, the incident is considered to be ambiguous and thus is discarded.

Three sorters achieve results similar to those for 100 sorters (Chapter 2). Many developers of BARS, however, use as many sorters as possible so that employees have a part in developing the scales. If many employees are involved, a 60% level of sorter agreement should be used to determine whether an incident is part of a dimension.

Rating Incidents

Another group of job experts is given the incidents and asked to rate each one on a scale that can have from 5 to 9 points as to the level of job performance that it represents (Bernardin, LaShells, Smith, & Alveres, 1976). The ratings from each rater for all of the incidents are then used to determine the mean rating and standard deviation for each incident (typically by computer).

Choosing Incidents

The goal of this step is to find one incident to represent each of the points on the scale for each dimension. To do so, the incidents whose mean ratings come closest to each of the scale points and whose standard deviations are small are kept (Maiorca, 1997). This procedure usually results in the retention of less than 50% of the incidents (Green, Sauser, Fagg, & Champion, 1981).

Creating the Scale

The incidents chosen in the previous step are then placed on a vertical scale such as that shown in Figure 7.9. Because the mean for each incident is unlikely to fall exactly on one of the scale points, they are often placed between the points, thus serving as anchors for future raters.

Using BARS

To use the scale when actually rating a performance, the supervisor compares the incidents they have recorded for each employee with the incidents on each scale. This can be done in one of two ways. The most accurate (and the most time-consuming) method compares each of the recorded incidents with the anchors and records the value of the incident on the scale that most closely resembles the recorded incident. This is done for each recorded incident. The value for each incident is summed and divided by the total number of incidents recorded for that dimension; this yields an average incident value, which is the employee's rating for that particular job dimension.

In the second method (easier, but probably less accurate), all of the recorded incidents are read to obtain a general impression of each employee. This general impression is compared with the incidents that anchor each scale point. The scale point next to the incident that most closely resembles the general impression gained from the incidents then becomes an employee's score for that dimension.

The third way to use BARS (and the least recommended) is to use the incidents contained in the BARS to arrive at a rating of the employee without recording actual incidents. Instead, the BARS are only used to provide meaning to the 5 scale points.

Forced-Choice Rating Scales

One problem with BARS is that supervisors often do not use the anchors when rating employees. Instead, they choose a point on the scale and then quickly glance to see which anchor is associated with the number. Because of this tendency, BARS do not often reduce leniency in ratings.

To overcome this problem, *forced-choice rating scales* have been developed. These scales use critical incidents and relevant job behaviors, as do BARS, but the scale points are hidden. An example of a forced-choice scale is shown in Figure 7.10.

In using the forced-choice scale to evaluate employee performance, the supervisor chooses the behavior in each item that appears most typical of that performed by a given employee. The supervisor's choices then are scored by a member of the personnel department to yield the employee's rating on each dimension. The scores on each of the dimensions can be summed to form an overall rating.

The development of a forced-choice rating scale is a long and complicated process, which partly explains why it is not commonly used. However, this method of evaluation does have its advantages. For example, because the supervisor must choose behaviors without knowing "the key," common rating errors such as leniency and halo are less likely. Consequently, performance evaluations should be more accurate.

Creating a Forced-Choice Scale

To create a forced-choice scale, the first step is similar to that for BARS: Critical incidents and relevant job behaviors are generated. These incidents, of course, are available only when a job analysis has been conducted.

In the second step, employees rate all of the behaviors on the extent to which successful employees perform them. After an approximately one-month interval, the employees again rate the items. This time, however, they rate the extent to which bad employees perform the behaviors. Finally, after another month, the employees again rate the behaviors, this time for their desirability.

In the third step, the actual items for the rating scale are created. This is done by computing a value for each behavior by subtracting the average rating given to each behavior that describes the bad employee from the average rating given to each behavior that describes the good employee. Behaviors with high positive values are considered to discriminate successful from unsuccessful employees, items with high negative values are considered to discriminate unsuccessful from successful employees, and behaviors with values near zero are considered neutral.

The next step in creating the items is to pick good, bad, and neutral behaviors that have similar desirability ratings. Thus, each rating item has three behaviors: One indicates good performance, one indicates poor performance, and one indicates neither good nor bad performance. Furthermore, all of the behaviors for an item have the same level of desirability. This process is repeated until several items have been constructed for each of the relevant job dimensions.

The disadvantages of the forced-choice scale probably outweigh its advantages. First, evaluations on forced-choice scales can be "faked." A supervisor who wants to give an employee a high rating need only think about a good employee when evaluating the employee in question. Second, supervisors often object to forced-choice scales because the scoring key is kept secret. Not only does this secrecy deprive a supervisor of any control over the rating process, but it can be seen by supervisors as a lack of trust in their abilities to evaluate their employees. Most important, however, because the key must be kept secret, forced-choice scales make feedback almost impossible. Thus, they should be used only when the major goal of the performance appraisal system is accurate employee evaluation for purposes such as promotion and salary increases.

Mixed-Standard Scales

To overcome some of the problems of forced-choice scales, Blanz and Ghiselli (1972) developed mixed-standard scales, an example of which is shown in Figure 7.11.

Table 7.7 Original Scoring System for Mixed-Standard Scales

	Statement Type		
Good	**Average**	**Poor**	**Dimension Score**
+	+	+	7
0	+	+	6
−	+	+	5
−	0	+	4
−	−	+	3
−	−	0	2
−	−	−	1

Mixed-standard scale A method of performance appraisal in which a supervisor reads the description of a specific behavior and then decides whether the behavior of the employee is better than, equal to, or poorer than the behavior described.

Mixed-standard scales are developed by having employees rate job behaviors and critical incidents on the extent to which they represent various levels of job performance. For each job dimension, a behavior or incident is chosen that represents excellent performance, average performance, and poor performance. These behaviors then are shuffled, and the end results look similar to those shown in Figure 7.11.

To evaluate an employee, a supervisor reads each behavior and places a plus (+), next to it when a particular employee's behavior is usually better than the behavior listed, a zero (0) if the employee's behavior is about the same as the behavior listed, or a minus (−) if the employee's behavior is usually worse than the behavior listed. To arrive at a score for each scale, the supervisor uses a chart like the one shown in Table 7.7. An overall score can be obtained by summing the scores from each of the scales.

Although mixed-standard scales are less complicated than forced-choice scales, they also have their drawbacks. The most important is that supervisors often make what are called "logical rating errors." For example, it would not make sense for a supervisor to rate an employee as better than the example of good performance or worse than the example of poor performance. Yet these types of errors are common. Logical rating errors can still be scored by using the revised scoring method developed by Saal (1979) (Table 7.8), but their existence alone casts doubt on the accuracy of the entire performance appraisal.

Behavioral Observation Scales

Behavioral observation scales (BOS) A method of performance appraisal in which supervisors rate the frequency of observed behaviors.

Behavioral observation scales (BOS), developed by Latham and Wexley (1977), are a more sophisticated method for measuring the frequency of desired behaviors. Even though BOS have no psychometric advantages over BARS (Bernardin & Kane, 1980), they are simpler to construct and easier to use (Latham, Fay, & Saari, 1979). BOS also provide high levels of feedback and are better than simple rating scales at motivating employees to change their behavior (Tziner, Kopelman, & Livnech, 1993).

The development of a BOS is relatively straightforward. The first few steps are the same as with a BARS: Critical incidents and behaviors are obtained from employees, the incidents are placed into categories, and each incident is rated as to the level of job performance it represents.

Table 7.8   Revised Scoring System for Mixed-Standard Scales

Good	Average	Poor	Dimension Score
+	+	+	7
0	+	+	6
+	+	0	6
+	0	+	6
−	+	+	5
+	+	−	5
+	0	0	5
+	−	+	5
0	+	0	5
0	0	+	5
+	−	0	4
+	0	−	4
0	+	−	4
0	0	0	4
0	−	+	4
−	+	0	4
−	0	+	4
+	−	−	3
0	−	0	3
0	0	−	3
−	+	−	3
−	−	+	3
−	0	0	3
−	−	0	2
0	−	−	2
−	0	−	2
−	−	−	1

Source: Adapted from Saal (1979).

As shown in Table 7.9, the behaviors are then listed. Supervisors read each behavior on the list and use the following scale to find the frequency for an employee performing that specific behavior:

1 = Employee engaged in behavior less than 65% of the time
2 = Employee engaged in behavior 65–74% of the time
3 = Employee engaged in behavior 75–84% of the time
4 = Employee engaged in behavior 85–94% of the time
5 = Employee engaged in behavior 95–100% of the time

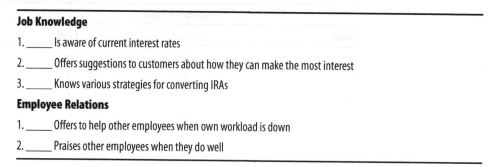

Table 7.9 Example of a Behavioral Observation Scale

Job Knowledge

1. _____ Is aware of current interest rates

2. _____ Offers suggestions to customers about how they can make the most interest

3. _____ Knows various strategies for converting IRAs

Employee Relations

1. _____ Offers to help other employees when own workload is down

2. _____ Praises other employees when they do well

After each employee has been rated on each behavior, the scores from each item in each dimension are summed to give the dimension score. Dimension scores are then summed to yield an overall score. The greatest advantage to BOS is that a supervisor can show employees the *specific behaviors* that they currently do correctly and the specific behaviors that they should do to receive higher performance evaluations.

Because many organizations conduct evaluations only once every six months or a year, BOS have been criticized for actually measuring only the *recall* of behaviors rather than measuring the actual *observation* of behaviors (Murphy et al., 1982). The importance of this distinction between recall and actual observation comes from research that has demonstrated that after some period of time, we cannot recall specific behaviors; instead, we "recall" behaviors that are consistent with sets of traits or **prototypes** we attribute to employees (Feldman, 1981). That is, we assign certain traits or prototypes to employees; six months later, we recall behaviors that are consistent with those traits or prototypes. Furthermore, the closer an employee's behavior is to the prototype, the more accurate the performance evaluations (Mount & Thompson, 1987). Thus, as objective and behavioral as BOS appear, they may not be as accurate as initially believed because of cognitive processing distortions.

Prototypes The overall image that a supervisor has of an employee.

Chapter

8

Designing and Evaluating Training Systems

Learning Objectives

8-1 Conduct a training needs analysis.

8-2 Explain the various training methods.

8-3 Develop a training program.

8-4 Apply the psychological theories behind successful training.

8-5 Evaluate the effectiveness of a training program.

Training A planned effort by an organization to facilitate the learning of job-related behavior on the part of its employees.

E mployee performance can be improved in many ways. In Chapters 4 and 5, you learned that one way to have high employee performance is to select employees with the necessary knowledge and skills. Another way to improve employee performance is to train employees who have the *ability* to perform the job, but might not have the *knowledge*, *skills*, or *motivation* to perform the job.

Training is the "systematic acquisition of skills, rules, concepts, or attitudes that result in improved performance" (Goldstein & Ford, 2002).

Training is essential for an organization because it ensures that employees have the knowledge and skills necessary to perform the job. In some cases, a lack of skill or knowledge is due to an organization having difficulty hiring applicants with the necessary knowledge and skills to perform a job. Thus, training compensates for the inability to select desired applicants. For example, ATK—one of the few American manufacturers of missile propellant—finds it almost impossible to find engineers with knowledge and experience in its niche field, so it hires outstanding engineers and then trains them in its specialty area. In other cases, an employee might have the necessary skills and knowledge when hired, but jobs, technology, and laws change. Thus, employees might have the necessary knowledge and skills one year but have deficiencies by the next.

In proactive organizations, training is used to teach knowledge and skills that, while not currently needed, will be needed in the future. For example, AT&T conducted an analysis of one of its jobs and determined that the field was changing so much that few of its employees had the skill that would be needed to perform the job five years in the future. Because of this, it provided training programs for employees to prepare them for the upcoming technology changes.

Collectively, organizations realize the importance of training by annually spending $1,308 per employee on training efforts (ATD, 2020), and requiring employees to complete an average of 47.6 hours of training (Industry Report, 2017). In some organizations, including the Palace Hotel in Inverness, Scotland, training is viewed as so valuable that employee training is mentioned in the hotel's mission statement.

Though most organizations value and provide organization-sponsored training, Netflix is an example of an organization that does not. It believes that employees should be responsible for their own training and professional development and thus leaves it to the employees to develop themselves (Grossman, 2010). One of the reasons Netflix can do this is that rather than hiring new college graduates, it tends to hire experienced employees who have already demonstrated their high-level skills and self-motivation.

8-1 Determining Training Needs

Needs analysis The process of determining the training needs of an organization.

Conducting a **needs analysis** is the first step in developing an employee training system (Noe, 2020). The purpose of needs analysis is to determine the types of training, if any, that are needed in an organization, as well as the extent to which training is a practical means of achieving an organization's goals. The importance of needs assessment was demonstrated by a meta-analysis indicating increased training effectiveness when a needs assessment had been done prior to the creation of the training program (Arthur, Bennett, Edens, & Bell, 2003). As shown in Figure 8.1, three types of needs analysis are typically conducted: organizational analysis, task analysis, and person analysis.

Organizational Analysis

Organizational analysis The process of determining the organizational factors that will either facilitate or inhibit training effectiveness.

The purpose of **organizational analysis** is to determine those organizational factors that either facilitate or inhibit training effectiveness. For example, an organization may view training as important but may not have the money to fund its training program, may be unable to afford the employee time away from work to be trained, or may not wish to spend money on training because employees leave

Figure 8.1
The Training Needs Assessment Process

the organization after a short period of time. A properly conducted organizational analysis will focus on the goals the organization wants to achieve, the extent to which training will help achieve those goals, the organization's ability to conduct training (e.g., finances, physical space, time), and the extent to which employees are willing and able to be trained (e.g., ability, commitment, motivation, stress) (McCabe, 2001).

A good example of the importance of organizational analysis comes from the AT&T business center previously mentioned. Employees at the center needed training due to the addition of new technology and a renewed company interest in customer service. However, because of recent layoffs and an increase in business, managers refused to let employees receive training "on the clock." As a result, an expensive series of newly developed training programs sat on the shelf. If an organizational analysis had been conducted, the organization would have concluded that its personnel did not view training as a priority at that point, and would have saved time and resources.

An organizational analysis should include a survey of employee readiness for training. For example, a large organization recently had several rounds of layoffs and had not given its employees salary increases in three years. When the organization introduced a new training program, it was surprised to find that the employees were so angry at the company that they were "not in the mood for training." As you can imagine, the training program wasn't successful. Thus, training will be effective only if the organization is willing to provide a supportive climate for training, it can afford an effective program, that employees want to learn, and the goals of a program are consistent with those of the organization (Broadwell, 1993). This powerful effect was demonstrated by two studies that illustrated a direct relationship between positive organizational climate and posttraining behavior, highlighting the importance of conducting an organizational analysis prior to implementing any training programs (Rouiller & Goldstein, 1993; Tracey, Tannenbaum, & Kavanagh, 1995).

Task Analysis

If the results of the organizational analysis indicate that a positive organizational climate for training exists, the next step is to conduct a task analysis. The purpose of a task analysis is to use the job analysis methods discussed in Chapter 2 to identify the tasks performed by each employee, the conditions under which these tasks are performed, and the competencies (knowledge, skills, abilities) needed to perform the tasks under the identified conditions. The most common job analysis methods used for this purpose include interviews, focus groups, observations, and task inventories. If an organization has detailed and current job descriptions already written, the task analysis process is fairly easy and does not take much time. If such job descriptions are not available, the task analysis process can be expensive and time-consuming.

Once the tasks and competencies for a job have been identified, the next step is to determine how employees learn to perform each task or obtain each competency. For example, due to a rigorous employee selection process, we might expect employees to be able to perform many of the tasks at the time they are hired. Some tasks might be so simple that they can be performed without the need of previous experience or future training. For other tasks, we might have formal training programs to teach employees the necessary competencies needed to perform them.

As shown in Figure 8.2, the task analysis process is usually conducted by listing tasks in one column and how the tasks are learned in a second column. The example shows that the hypothetical bank needs to develop training courses in dealing with difficult customers and in cross-selling, because these are competencies not tapped during the selection process nor learned in current bank training programs.

Person Analysis

Person analysis The process of identifying the employees who need training and determining the areas in which each individual employee needs to be trained.

The third and final step in the needs analysis process is determining which employees need training and in which areas. **Person analysis** is based on the recognition that not every employee needs further training for every task performed. For example, trainers at Applebee's restaurants test management trainees on essential on-the-job tasks. When the trainees demonstrate proficiency, the training ends. Thus, some trainees complete the management training program in half the time it takes others. A person analysis should also include an evaluation of an employee's readiness for the training. That is, does the employee have the ability and motivation to successfully complete the training?

Figure 8.2

Comparing Task Analysis Results with Training Programs

Task	How Task Is Learned
Answer customer questions about rates	Daily rate charts
Process customer transactions	Basic teller training
Calm irate customers	
Check loan applications for accuracy	Loan-processing course
Ask customers to complete Visa applications	
Input customer transactions into computer	Basic teller training
Answer customer questions about services	Basic teller training

To determine the individual training needs for each employee, person analysis uses performance appraisal scores, surveys, interviews, skill and knowledge tests, and/or critical incidents.

Performance Appraisal Scores

Performance appraisal score A rating representing some aspect of an employee's work performance.

Perhaps the easiest method of needs analysis is to use employees' **performance appraisal scores**. Low ratings on a particular dimension for most employees may indicate that additional training in that dimension is needed. Conversely, if most employees score high on a particular dimension, relatively little training time is needed. For example, as demonstrated in Table 8.1, the bank employees as a whole need little training in loan processing or data entry, but they do need further training in cross-selling, customer relations, and keeping accurate teller drawers. But even though most employees can accurately process loans, Fernandez needs further training in this area; both Abbott and Harrigan probably can skip the training in teller drawer accuracy.

Although using performance appraisal scores appears fairly easy as a method of needs assessment, three problems can interfere with their use. First, as discussed in the previous chapter, several types of rating errors can reduce the accuracy of performance appraisal scores. The most relevant here are leniency errors and strictness errors. If the performance appraisal scores are consistently high because of leniency error, a human resources professional might incorrectly conclude that employees are proficient in a particular area and thus need no training. Likewise, consistently low scores might be interpreted as a need for training when, in fact, the actual cause of the low scores is rater error.

The second problem is that rarely there are situations in which all employees score either high or low on a dimension. Instead, it is more common for only a few employees to score poorly. In this case, a person examining the average performance appraisal scores might conclude that training in a particular dimension is unnecessary. But that conclusion would be only partially correct. True, not everyone needs training in that dimension, but concluding that training should not be conducted would be incorrect. The correct interpretation is that training should be conducted for the few employees who scored low for that dimension.

Third, the current performance appraisal system may not provide the type of information needed to conduct a training needs analysis. As discussed in Chapter 7, performance appraisal systems must be specific to be useful.

Table 8.1 Using Performance Appraisal Scores for Training Needs Assessment

Performance Dimension	Employee					
	Abbott	**Finch**	**Osterman**	**Fernandez**	**Harrigan**	**Average**
Cross-selling	2	1	2	5	1	2.2
Loan processing	5	5	5	1	4	4.0
Data input accuracy	5	5	5	5	5	5.0
Customer relations	2	2	2	2	2	2.0
Teller drawer accuracy	5	3	1	2	5	3.2
Average	3.8	3.2	3.8	3.0	3.4	

Surveys

Another common approach to determine training needs is to design and administer a survey that asks employees what knowledge and skills they believe should be included in future training. **Surveys** offer several advantages. First, they eliminate the problems of performance rating errors, which were discussed previously. Second, employees often know their own strengths and weaknesses best. Thus, to determine what employees need, ask them. Finally, training needs can be determined with surveys, even when the organization has not previously made an effort to design an effective performance appraisal system or adequate job descriptions. The main disadvantages of surveys are that employees may not be honest, and the organization may not be able to afford the training suggested by the employees.

As with any type of survey, training needs surveys can be conducted in many ways. The most common method is a questionnaire that asks employees to list the areas in which they would like further or future training. Perhaps a better method is to provide a *list* of job-related tasks and components of knowledge and have employees rate the need for training on each. The results of these ratings are given to supervisors, who then "validate" the results. This process is used to determine whether the supervisors agree with their employees' perceptions and to prioritize training needs.

Interviews

The third method of needs analysis is the interview, which is usually done with a selected number of employees. Interviews are not used as extensively as surveys, but they can yield even more in-depth answers to questions about training needs (Patton & Pratt, 2002). The main advantage of interviews is that employee feelings and attitudes are revealed more clearly than with the survey approach. The main disadvantage of interviews is that interview data can be difficult to quantify and analyze.

Skill and Knowledge Tests

The fourth way to determine training needs is with a **skill test** or a **knowledge test**. Some examples of areas that could be tested to determine training needs include knowledge of lending laws for loan officers, knowledge of company policy for new employees, free-throw shooting for basketball players, and the dreaded midterm exam for this course.

If all employees score poorly on these tests, training across the organization is indicated. If only a few employees score poorly, they are singled out for individual training sessions. The greatest problem with using testing as a method to determine training needs is that relatively few tests are available for this purpose. An organization that wants to use this method will probably have to construct its own tests, and proper test construction is time-consuming and expensive.

Critical Incidents

The fifth method for determining training needs is the critical-incident technique discussed in Chapters 2, 4, and 7. Although not a commonly used method, it will be discussed here because it is relatively easy to use, especially if a proper job analysis is available. To use this technique for needs assessment, the critical incidents are sorted into dimensions and separated into examples of good and poor performance, as discussed in Chapter 2. Dimensions with many examples of poor performance are considered to be areas in which many employees are performing poorly and in which additional training is indicated.

8-2 Establishing Goals and Objectives

Once the needs analyses have been conducted, the next step is to establish the goals and objectives for the training. The importance of this process cannot be emphasized enough, as the training goals will determine the resources allocated to the training, the methods used to deliver the training, and the methods used to evaluate the success of the training. In setting goals, it is important to first determine what the organization wants to accomplish, given the time and resources that will be allocated to the training. For example, if an organizational analysis indicated that due to financial and time constraints a four-hour training session is all that the organization can afford to teach its supervisors conflict management skills, it would be unreasonable to establish the goal that supervisors be able to mediate conflicts between employees (a skill). Instead, a more reasonable goal might be that by the end of the four-hour training, supervisors will be able to identify the common causes of conflict (a knowledge). When the organization can afford several days of training, the goal of obtaining conflict mediation skills might be more obtainable.

Training goals and objectives should concretely state the following (Mager, 1997):

- what learners are expected to do;
- the conditions under which they are expected to do it; and
- the level at which they are expected to do it.

In other words, vague objectives such as "to be a better salesperson" should be replaced with specific objectives such as increasing customer contacts by 10% and increasing new accounts by 5%. Goal statements usually include an action word, an item, a condition, and a standard. For example:

- By the end of this training session, you will be able to answer (action word) customer questions about loan rates (item) without asking others (condition) 90% of the time (standard).
- By the end of this training session, you will be able to balance (action word) the teller drawer (item) without assistance (condition) in 30 minutes with no errors (standard).
- By the end of this training session, you will be able to compute (action word) adverse impact levels (item) using Microsoft Excel (condition) with no errors (standard).

8-3 Choosing the Best Training Method

Once goals and objectives have been established, the next step in developing a training program is to choose the training method—such as those shown in Table 8.2—that will best accomplish those goals and objectives. For example, if the goal is for employees to learn an actual skill, some type of hands-on training will be necessary (e.g., role-plays, simulations). Because most training programs have multiple goals and objectives, the best training programs often use a variety of methods so that employees will understand the reasons for doing a certain task, how it should be done, and in what situations it should be done (Lawson, 2000). In the following pages, several training methods will be discussed.

Table 8.2   Examples of Available Training Methods

Classroom Setting
- Lecture
- Case study
- Simulation
- Role-play
- Behavior modeling
- Video

Distance Learning
- Printed materials
- Video
- Interactive video
- Podcast
- Mobile learning (e.g., iPhone)
- Webinar
- Webcast
- Chat rooms and discussion boards

On-The-Job Learning
- Modeling
- Job rotation
- Apprentice training
- Coaching
- Mentoring
- Performance appraisal

Using Lectures to Provide Knowledge

Lectures are a good training source if the goal is for employees to obtain knowledge. Unless they are accompanied by such techniques as simulations and role-plays, however, they are not usually effective at teaching skills.

Putting together a lecture-based training program can take a great deal of time. The trainer must research a topic, develop a training outline, create visuals (e.g., Microsoft PowerPoint slides), create handouts, and obtain or create supporting materials such as video clips and role-play exercises. Though some authors use an estimate of 30 hours of preparation for every hour of training (Zemke, 1997) and others use 50 hours (Diekmann, 2001), I use an estimate of 16 hours of preparation for every hour of new training. Biech (2017) estimates that she spends between 70 and 100 hours to create and practice for a one-hour webinar! Of course, the actual time needed to develop a training seminar is a function of the trainer's knowledge of the topic, the amount of talking a trainer expects to do, and the ready availability of video clips, exercises, and role-plays related to the topic.

An important part of any training presentation is the handouts to the audience. The purpose of handouts is to provide material that the trainees can take back to their jobs. Providing comprehensive notes is important because people forget about half the training content once they leave the room and then forget another 25% within 48 hours (Nichols & Stevens, 1957). Handouts should include:

- a cover sheet with the title of the training program as well as the date and location in which the training took place;
- a list of goals and objectives;
- a schedule for the training (e.g., breaks, ending times);
- a biographical sketch of the trainer;
- the notes themselves in outline form, full text, or copies of the PowerPoint slides;
- activity sheets such as personality inventories, free writes, or group activity information;
- references and suggestions for further reading; and
- a form or a web link to evaluate the quality of the training program.

For financial, as well as environmentally conscious reasons, most organizations now provide "handouts" that can be downloaded to a trainee's laptop. Although such a practice has financial, environmental, and storage advantages, it does make it more difficult to take notes.

Although many lectures have been conducted virtually for years, almost all were conducted virtually during the COVID-19 pandemic. In fact, entire national conferences such as SIOP were conducted virtually in 2020 and 2021. One survey found that in a post-pandemic world, most employees want to have a blend of in-person and virtual training experiences (Harlow, 2021). These virtual training experiences are delivered through platforms such as Zoom and Teams and incorporate video, audio, screen share, interactive polls, and emoticons to increase interaction (Grochocki, 2021). Of course, if the training is presented virtually, such handouts as personality inventories and training assessments can be administered and scored online.

Using Case Studies to Apply Knowledge

Case study A training technique in which employees, usually in a group, are presented with a real or hypothetical workplace problem and are asked to propose the best solution.

Once employees have received the information they need through lecture, it is important that they be able to apply what they have learned. One way to do this is through the **case study**. Case studies are similar to leaderless group discussions and situational interview problems (which were discussed in Chapter 5) and are considered to be good sources for developing analysis, synthesis, and evaluation skills (Naidoo, 2021; Noe, 2020). Case studies also provide an open discourse for a diversity of views, allowing trainees to benefit from the various strengths and knowledge of each participant (Clark, 1985). With this method, the members of a small group each read a case, which is either a real or hypothetical situation typical of those encountered on the job. The group then discusses the case, identifies possible solutions, evaluates the advantages and disadvantages of each solution, and arrives at what it thinks is the best solution to the problem.

For case studies to be most successful, the cases should be taken from actual situations. For example, to make their case study more realistic, General Electric employees in New York use actual information about a problem within the company. Trainees not only discussed the problem but also interviewed employees to gather more information. This use of a **living case** was found to be superior to the typical case study. Not only was the problem relevant but also the solution could actually be used, thus providing an incentive for the trainees to take the training program seriously. One drawback to the living case study, however, is that trainees may not be the best individuals to solve the problem.

In addition to being realistic, case studies should be interesting. They are best when they are written in the form of a story, contain dialogue between the characters, use realistic details, are descriptive and easy to follow, contain all information necessary to solve the problem, and are difficult enough to be challenging (Owenby, 1992).

To increase the effectiveness of case studies, trainees should first be taught the principles involved in solving a particular type of problem, helped to use those principles in discussing the case, and then have the principles reinforced after reading the case study. If the key principles are not taught and reinforced, trainees tend to focus too much on the content of a particular case study when trying to solve future problems rather than using the key principles (Allen & Connelly, 2005).

Using Simulation Exercises to Practice New Skills

Whereas case studies are effective in applying knowledge and learning problem-solving skills, **simulation** exercises allow the trainee to practice newly learned skills. Simulations offer the advantage of allowing the trainee to work with equipment under actual working conditions without the consequences of mistakes. For example, using a cash register or taking a customer's order is easy to learn. But it is a much more difficult task with a long line of impatient customers or irritable coworkers. Simulation exercises allow the trainee to feel such pressure but without actually affecting the organization's performance.

Like all training methods, simulation exercises come in many different forms. Some, such as airline simulators, are extremely expensive and complex to use, but others, such as a simulated restaurant counter, are relatively inexpensive. For example, each week at the Salamander Restaurant in Cambridge, Massachusetts, servers role-play such situations as medical emergencies and computer breakdowns. Another good example of an inexpensive simulation exercise is that used by nurses to teach patients with diabetes how to administer their insulin shots—the patients practice by injecting water into oranges.

Whatever the method used, a simulation exercise can be effective only if it physically and psychologically simulates actual job conditions. For example, dummy simulators are a standard part of cardiopulmonary resuscitation (CPR) training provided by the American Red Cross. People practice CPR on the dummies, which simulate the human body and provide feedback on pressure and location of chest compressions. Although the use of these CPR simulators is better than lecture alone, there is some concern that the dummies do not adequately simulate the feel of the human chest. Even worse, practicing CPR on a dummy in front of fellow employees does not involve the pressure or environment that is often encountered in an actual emergency.

Although most simulators do not exactly replicate actual physical and psychological job conditions, they are still better than the single alternatives of either lecture or actual practice. Case in point, a meta-analysis by Sitzmann (2011) found

Living case A case study based on a real situation rather than a hypothetical one.

Simulation An exercise designed to place an applicant in a situation that is similar to the one that will be encountered on the job.

that employees trained with simulations learned more and retained more than did employee trained using such techniques as lecture or reading. Furthermore, training a pilot is cheaper on a simulator than on a passenger jet, and it is safer (for humans) for a medical student to practice on a pig than on a sick patient. Rapid advances in technology hold tremendous promise for trainers, including augmented reality, synthetic learning environments, and virtual reality. **Virtual reality** is defined as "any three-dimensional digital simulation that can imitate a physical presence, even if it is presented via a two-dimensional display" (Howard & Marshall, 2019, p. 349). Virtual reality is already being used to train soldiers, surgeons, air traffic controllers, and police officers. The day that we can exactly simulate real working conditions may not be far away. A *State of the Industry Report* published by the American Society for Training and Development noted a 27.5% increase of training methods in large companies conducted through the use of technology between 2005 and 2017 (Industry Report, 2017).

PwC, a professional services company, found that virtual reality was an effective way to provide training on diversity and inclusion. PwC employees found it less awkward to join in discussions through virtual reality than they did during in-person trainings (Thompson, 2021).

However, while simulation exercises offer a variety of advantages, experts caution organizations against needlessly creating simulation exercises using virtual reality or augmented reality technology, citing an emphasis on a thorough training needs analysis to identify the effectiveness of technology for each organization's use (Salas & Cannon-Bowers, 2001).

Practicing Interpersonal Skills Through Role-Play

Whereas simulations are effective for learning how to use new equipment or software programs, **role-play** allows the trainee to perform necessary interpersonal skills by acting out simulated roles. For example, when conducting seminars in conflict mediation, consultant Bobbie Raynes has her audience members participate as actors in predetermined situations. The participants are given a conflict situation and are told to use what they have learned to mediate the conflict. When Medtronic, a manufacturer of heart valves, decided to teach its sales force how to use video-based demonstrations, it began with an hour of classroom training and then used role-plays so that the salespeople could practice their new presentation skills.

Role-play is used in many types of training situations, from supervisors practicing performance appraisal reviews to salesclerks taking customer orders. One interesting variation of the role-play exercise has an employee playing the role of "the other person." For example, a supervisor might play the role of an employee, or a salesclerk might play the role of a customer who is frustrated with recently purchased merchandise. In this way, the employee can better understand the reasoning and feelings of the people with whom they work.

Though role-plays allow employees to practice what is being taught, they are not for everyone. Many employees feel uneasy and embarrassed about being required to "act." This reluctance can be reduced to some extent by using warm-up exercises and praising employees after they participate.

Farber (1994) thinks that role-play should be replaced by "real play," in which employees practice their skills on actual customers. For example, salespeople can be trained by having the sales staff sit around a conference table and take turns

Virtual reality Any three-dimensional digital simulation that can imitate a physical presence.

Role-play A training technique in which employees act out simulated roles.

making calls to actual/potential customers. The group then discusses the technique of the person making the call. However, the disadvantage with this method is that as it is not a simulation, but consists of direct contact with potential customers, any mistakes made during the "real play" session may have real consequences for the organization as well.

Increasing Interpersonal Skills Through Behavior Modeling

Behavior modeling A training technique in which employees observe correct behavior, practice that behavior, and then receive feedback about their performance.

One of the most successful training methods has been **behavior modeling** (Taylor, Russ-Eft, & Chan, 2005). Behavior modeling is similar to role-play, with the exception that trainees role-play ideal behavior rather than the behavior they might normally perform. The behavior modeling technique begins with a discussion of a problem, why it occurred, and the employee behaviors necessary to correct the problem. These behaviors are called *learning points* and are essentially rules to follow in solving a problem. Next, trainees view videos of employees correctly and incorrectly solving the problem. The trainees take notes during the video and are given an opportunity to ask questions.

After viewing the video, trainees mentally rehearse the solution to the problem in the way that the employee solved it on the video. Finally, employees role-play (behaviorally model) situations and receive feedback on their performances. Employees are also given the opportunity to play the role of the "other" person so that they will gain the same insight they would have by role-play training. Employees then discuss ways to apply their new skills on the job. By this procedure, employees will already have had experience dealing with the problem in the proper way when they encounter the same situation on the job. In other words, positive transfer of learning will have occurred.

Of course, for behavior modeling to be successful, the videos must represent commonly encountered problems and situations—thus demonstrating the importance of a thorough job analysis. By observing and interviewing employees and by collecting critical incidents, the necessary problems and situations can be obtained. An important and related issue is whether employees should be trained on specific situational skills or on generic skills that will cover any situation. For example, a specific situational skill would be handling a bank customer who is angry about a bounced check. The related generic skill would be calming *any* angry customer. Obviously, generic skills are more difficult to teach and require the modeling of many different types of behavior in many different situations.

Another issue involves the number and types of models that are viewed in the training video. Russ-Eft and Zucchelli (1987) conducted a study at Zenger-Miller, Inc. (Cupertino, California) in which employees viewed either one or two models. If the employees saw two models, they saw either two models performing correct behaviors or one model performing correctly and the other performing incorrectly. The study results indicated that viewing two models increased training performance more than viewing one but that the addition of a negative model was no more effective in increasing training performance than two positive models. When the proper procedures are followed, the results of a meta-analysis indicate that behavior modeling can significantly increase employee performance (Taylor, Russ-Eft, & Chan, 2005).

As technology advances and organizational cultures shift to an increase in remote jobs, behavior modeling can also offer a powerful method of training in multinational corporations. Researchers demonstrated an effective learning transfer through adding behavior modeling to their current cross-cultural management training program (Harrison, 1992).

Motivating Employees to Attend Training

Once the training program has been developed, the next step is to motivate employees to attend the training. The most obvious way to "motivate" employees to attend training is to *require* them to attend training "on the clock." However, many training opportunities are optional, and 10% of training opportunities take place on the employee's own time (Galvin, 2003). Here are some strategies to motivate employees to attend training:

- Relate the training to an employee's immediate job. Employees are more likely to attend when the material covered in training will directly affect their immediate job performance. For example, employees would be more motivated to attend a training session on a computer program that the organization will begin using in two weeks than a training session on "Future Trends in Office Automation." Thus, training should be provided "just in time" rather than "just in case."
- Make the training interesting. Employees are more likely to attend when they know they will have a good time as well as learn something useful.
- Increase employee buy-in. When employees play a role in choosing and planning the types of training offered, they are more likely to attend. Baldwin, Magjuka, and Loher (1991) found that employees given a choice about training programs were more motivated than employees not given a choice. Employees given a choice, but then not given the program they chose, were the least motivated.
- Provide incentives. Common incentives for attending training include certificates, money, promotion opportunities, and college credit. Microsoft increased employee participation in voluntary training by 2,000% when it created a program, "Ready, Set, Go," in which employees who participated in voluntary training received points that could be exchanged for merchandise, travel, and gift certificates (Renk, 2004).
- Provide food. Medeco Security Locks in Salem, Virginia, has optional monthly training sessions in which a topic is presented while the employees eat lunch provided by the company. Consultants Bobbie Raynes and GeGe Beall both have used free pizza as incentives to get employees to attend short training sessions during lunch or dinner.
- Reduce the stress associated with attending. Frequently, employees want to attend training but don't because they can't afford to take time away from their scheduled duties. To encourage employees to attend training, organizations should provide workload reductions or staffing assistance.

8-4 Delivering the Training Program

Once the training program has been created, there are three broad methods of delivering the training: in the classroom, through distance learning, and on the job.

Conducting Classroom Training

Initial Decisions

Prior to conducting classroom training, several decisions need to be made by an organization.

Who Will Conduct the Training?   Training seminars can be conducted by a variety of sources including in-house trainers who are employees of the organization, outside trainers who contract with the organization, videos, and local universities. In-house trainers are used when a training program will be presented too frequently to justify the cost of an outside trainer or when the training topic is so specific to the organization that finding outside trainers would be difficult.

External trainers are used when the trainers in an organization lack the expertise on a particular topic or when the cost of internally developing a training program exceeds the cost of contracting with an external trainer. For example, an organization needing two days of training in communication skills would be better served contracting with an external trainer at $3,500 a day than spending the $30,000 it would take to develop the training program on its own. However, if the training program were to be offered twice a week for two years, the organization might be better served using in-house trainers.

Tens of thousands of training consultants around the country offer seminars to industry. Needs analysis, however, must be used to determine whether such seminars are necessary. It is not unusual for human resource professionals to receive dozens of emails a week advertising various training seminars. Even though a seminar may sound interesting, it should be used only if it directly relates to some aspect of the job or to the people doing the job. For example, a seminar on communication skills may sound interesting, but it probably would not improve an electronics assembler's performance, whereas a seminar on electronics might. Likewise, a seminar on personal money management may not relate to the assembler's job, but it may be useful if it solves outside problems that affect their job performance or attendance.

Rather than using actual trainers, many organizations use videos as part of their training programs. Videos have a clear economic advantage over live lecture when the training session is to be repeated many times. With videos, organizations have the option of purchasing an actual copy of the video or downloading the video from the many vendors specializing in training videos.

Many organizations use local colleges and universities to handle their training needs. The advantages of using colleges and universities are lower costs, access to excellent training facilities, access to well-known faculty, and the potential for employees to receive college credit for completing the training (Martyka, 2001). Local universities are typically used for technical (e.g., electronics, computer programming) and leadership training and are most appropriate when only a few employees need training at any given time and the cost of setting up a training lab is prohibitive. A good example of an organization using a variety of training options can be found at an AT&T manufacturing plant: Seminars on problem solving are conducted by the training staff, seminars on communication skills are taught by an outside trainer, and classes on the principles of electronics are offered at a local community college.

Where Will the Training Be Held?   Training can be offered on-site, at an off-site location such as a hotel, university, or conference center, or virtually. The obvious advantage of conducting training on-site is that it is less expensive. However, many organizations have neither the space nor the equipment needed for on-site training. Holding training off-site has the advantage of getting the employees away from the work site and allowing them to concentrate on their training. In some cases, off-site training locations in Las Vegas, Miami, or San Diego are chosen as an incentive to get employees to attend training or as a reward for performing well at work.

How Long Should the Training Be?   Determining the length of a training session is an interesting dilemma. From a cost-efficiency perspective, it is better to conduct a weeklong training session rather than divide the training into 10 half-day sessions spread over a one-month period. However, from an interest perspective, few employees enjoy attending 40 hours of training in a week and employees might retain less information than if the sessions were spread over a longer period. From a practical perspective, it is difficult to pull employees off their jobs for an entire week.

For the highest level of learning, training material should be presented in small, easily remembered chunks distributed over a period of time (distributed learning) rather than learned all at once (massed learning). As shown in a meta-analysis by Donovan and Radosevich (1999), if too much training occurs at one time, employees will not be able to pay attention to all that is being taught or be able to remember that on which they did concentrate. Consequently, training performance will be lower when training is massed rather than distributed.

The best example of the principle of **massed practice** versus **distributed practice** is studying for exams. If we *distribute* the reading over several days, the material is relatively easy to learn. But if we wait until the night before the test to read three chapters—that is, *mass* the reading—we will not retain much at all.

Employers have begun using **microlearning** techniques, in which employees receive targeted training lasting only a few minutes. Microlearning works well when the goal is to update information the employees is already comfortable with, and the updated information is fairly simple (Paul, 2016).

Preparing for Classroom Training

Adjusting for the Audience.   The characteristics of the audience play an important role in developing a training program. A trainer must consider the size, demographics, and ability of the audience. For example, with a large audience, not only will the trainer need to use a microphone, but it becomes difficult to supplement lecture material with such exercises as role-play, simulation, and group discussions. An audience of women often will react differently to certain examples and types of exercises than will an audience of men. Likewise, examples used for a younger audience might not work on an older audience.

The ability level of the audience members is another important factor. If they are low on experience or ability, the training will need to proceed at a slower pace than if they were more experienced or more skilled. The toughest situation for a trainer is when the audience has mixed levels of ability. If the trainer sets a slow pace to help the lower-ability trainees, the higher-ability trainees become bored. If the trainer caters to the higher-ability trainees, the other trainees fall behind. For these reasons, most trainers present material at a moderate pace. Not surprisingly, the research evidence is clear that employees who perform well in training are bright, believe they can perform well (have high self-efficacy), are motivated, and are goal-oriented (Salas & Cannon-Bowers, 2001).

Massed practice Concentrating learning into a short period of time.

Distributed practice Learning a few things at a time.

Microlearning Training programs that are only a few minutes in length.

Delivering the Training Program

Introducing the Trainer and the Training Session. Training sessions usually begin with the introduction of the trainer. This can be done by the trainer introducing themself or by another person doing the introduction. The introduction should be short and should establish the credentials of the trainer. The length of the introduction depends on how much time is allocated for the training and the extent to which the audience already knows the trainer. If necessary, a more complete biography of the trainer can be placed in the training materials so that the audience can see the trainer's credentials without the trainer appearing to be bragging.

After the introduction of the trainer, the objectives of the training seminar, the training schedule (e.g., starting times, break times, mealtimes, quitting times), and seminar rules (e.g., turning off cell phones, not criticizing audience members) are covered. When possible, it is a good idea for the schedule to include a 10-minute break at the end of each hour and one and a half hours for lunch.

The Career Workshop Box gives tips on etiquette for audience members.

Using Icebreakers and Energizers. Following the introduction of the trainer, most training programs start with some sort of icebreaker, opener, or energizer. Types of icebreakers include the following:

- Introductions such as asking each trainee to introduce the person next to them, or having a scavenger hunt in which trainees are given a list of questions (e.g., "Who likes baseball?"; "Who has a daughter?") and are asked to mingle with the other trainees to obtain answers to the questions.
- Jokes or stories.
- Activities in which trainees, either individually or in small groups, are given a question or problem to solve.
- Open-ended questions to elicit audience response and encourage discussion.
- Free writes in which audience members are asked to write about the topic. For example, in a training seminar on sexual harassment, trainees were asked to write about a time when they either were harassed or saw another employee being harassed. In a training seminar on dealing with difficult customers, trainees were asked to write about an angry customer they had to deal with and how they handled the situation.

There are three considerations in choosing an icebreaker: the goal of the icebreaker, the length of the training session, and the nature of the audience.

For an icebreaker to be successful, it must accomplish a goal. The most common goals for icebreakers are to get people to know one another, to get them talking, to wake them up, and to get them thinking about the topic. For example, introductions work well when it is important that the audience members know one another, and free writes work well when the goal is to get the audience thinking about a topic. Having an icebreaker for the sake of having an icebreaker is not a good idea; for example, if participants already know each other and are comfortable with each other, an icebreaker may not be necessary.

If the training session will last only a few hours, the icebreaker should be short—if one is even used. If the training session will last an entire week, time should be spent on introductions and "group bonding" activities.

Certain types of icebreakers work better with some audiences than they do with others. For example, having a group of trainees introduce themselves by saying their name

Whether you are in class or attending a training workshop, your behavior as an audience member not only impacts the presenter and the other audience members but also gives others an impression of you as a professional. Here is some advice provided by consultant and trainer Bobbie Raynes:

- Get to the workshop on time so as not to disturb other audience members or the workshop presenter. It is a good idea to actually get there early, grab a good seat, and take advantage of the snacks that are often available.
- Come prepared. Have a pen and some paper or your laptop, so that you can take notes if necessary.
- If there are snacks, take only your share. Leave some for the other audience members.
- Turn off your cell phone (or at least put it on silent). If you must answer a call, do so outside of the training room.
- Try not to make unnecessary noises (e.g., cracking gum, rocking back and forth in your chair, constantly clicking a pen on and off). I can't tell you how many times I have had audience members complain about another person making noise!
- Stay awake! If you feel you are falling asleep, quietly leave the room.
- Let the presenter know you are listening by nodding your head, making an eye contact, or asking questions. This provides important feedback to the presenter. Based on the audience reaction, the presenter can change the way they do something, so that it better meets the needs of the audience.
- If you have a question, raise your hand and ask. Never feel shy about asking questions, because trainers like to get them, and if you are having trouble following something, you can be sure others are as well.
- Be courteous to other audience members and allow them to ask their questions, too. Don't do all the talking!
- If you disagree with something the presenter is saying, politely ask the presenter for a further explanation. If you still disagree, talk to the presenter after the workshop.
- Listen to other audience members without judging their comments. You can respond to them; but shooting down others' ideas and thoughts is not in good form.
- At the end of the workshop, introduce yourself to the presenter. If you enjoyed the workshop, say so.
- If the presenter asks you to evaluate the workshop when it is over, do so. This is the only way the presenter will know what to change or do differently and will provide important feedback for improvement. If there is room for comments, briefly explain why you liked or disliked something. The more specific you are, the more helpful the evaluation.
- Throw away your coffee cups, soda cans, or any other trash that you may have accumulated during the workshop.

and a trait starting with the first letter of their name (e.g., Friendly Fred, Timid Temea, Zany Zach) might not go over as well in a group with a strict organizational culture as it might with a group of restaurant employees with a more fun organizational culture.

Delivering the Presentation. Though this is not a public speaking text, here are some tips you might find useful in delivering a training presentation:

- Make eye contact with the audience.
- Use gestures effectively. That is, don't wave your hands or use other gestures unless they help make a point.
- Don't read your presentation. Use visuals such as your PowerPoint slides to guide you. If you know your material and have practiced your presentation, all you should need is the occasional reminder that can be provided by glancing at your PowerPoint slides projected on the screen.
- Don't hide behind the podium.
- Use a conversational style. A training presentation is not a speech, lecture, or sermon. Talk *with* your audience, not *at* them.

- Be confident. Avoid the use of fillers, speak at an appropriate volume, and don't brag about yourself. If you know your stuff, the audience will notice—you don't have to tell them how smart you are.
- Speak at a pace that is neither too fast nor too slow.
- Avoid swearing, making off-color or offensive remarks, and demeaning other people, groups, or organizations.
- Try to make the presentation interesting. This can be done by using fun (e.g., humor, stories) or a variety of activities (e.g., lecture, video, discussion, activity), creating energy either through the speaker's pace or through audience activity, and involving the audience by allowing them to share their opinions, stories, and expertise.
- Don't force humor. If you are a naturally funny person, it will show. When using humor, make sure it meets an objective such as demonstrating a point or keeping the audience awake during a dull topic. Otherwise, humor for the sake of humor can be distracting. Humor should never be at the expense of others—the only safe target is yourself (in moderation).
- When answering audience questions, repeat the question if the room is large. If you are unsure of the question, ask the audience member to repeat the question or try to paraphrase the question (e.g., "Is what you are asking …"). After answering the question, ask whether you have answered it sufficiently. If you don't know the answer to a question, don't bluff. You can ask if anyone in the audience knows the answer—9 out of 10 times they do.

As with college lectures, many activities can take place within a seminar, including lecture, the use of videos, discussion, and question-and-answer periods. Again, the choice of activities depends on the task or skill to be taught. If the skill is complicated, such as operating a machine or dealing with an angry customer, lecture alone will not be enough. The seminar should also include some type of practice or role-play. If the information is not complicated but involves such visual material as building locations, flowcharts, or diagrams, visual aids should be added to the lecture and be provided as handouts. If the material covered is not comprehensive or if the feelings of the employees toward the material are important, then discussion should be included. Discussion not only helps further learning but also allows employees to feel that their opinions are important.

Conducting Training Through Virtual Learning

Asynchronous technologies Distance learning programs in which employees can complete the training at their own pace and at a time of their choosing.

Synchronous technologies Distance learning programs that require employees to complete the training at the same time and at the same pace although they may be in different physical locations.

Although traditional classroom instruction is still the most common form of training (Ho, 2020), a disadvantage is that all employees must be taught at the same pace and in the same location. This is unfortunate because some employees learn more quickly or are more experienced than others and will be bored if a training seminar moves too slowly. Other employees, however, will become frustrated if the seminar goes too quickly. Thus, to allow employees to learn material at their own pace, at a time and place that is convenient to them, most organizations are using some form of virtual learning.

Virtual learning technologies can generally be placed into one of the two broad categories: **asynchronous** or **synchronous**. With asynchronous technologies, employees can complete the training at their own pace and at a time of their choosing. In contrast, synchronous technologies require employees to complete the training at the same time and at the same pace, although they may be in different physical locations.

Asynchronous Virtual Learning

With this method (also known as asynchronous distance learning or e-learning), employees are provided with media materials for learning the content, as well as with a series of exams that measure what they have learned from them. If employees do not pass the test at the end of each unit, they usually must reread the material and retake the test until they pass. In this way, employees can study at their own pace, and the exams ensure that employees understand the material. With asynchronous virtual learning, information can be provided to the employee in a variety of ways including printed materials, videos, and web-based programs. To increase the effectiveness of these programs and make them more interactive, trainees often can have access to an instructor or other trainees through email, messaging programs and message board forums.

The training program used by Life of Virginia is a good example. One problem encountered by the company was that more than 1,000 sales agents were spread over 140 offices throughout the country. Thus, to conduct a training program that would be both effective and practical, Life of Virginia used sales experts to create seven training modules: marketing and asking for referrals, calling for appointments, interviews, preparing the insurance recommendation, presenting the recommendation, delivering the insurance policy, and periodic review. Each module contained a 5- to 10-page reading assignment, a written exercise on the reading, a video showing models performing the appropriate behaviors, a situational problem, and a series of questions to be answered by each insurance agent. Agents study at their own pace, taking between two and four weeks per module. This training program resulted in a 25% annual increase in sales and a 10% decrease in turnover.

The H. E. Butt Grocery Company decided to use interactive video at its grocery stores because of the difficulty in getting employee schedules coordinated for group training. With **interactive video**, employees see a videotaped situation on a television, computer screen, phone, or iPad. At the end of each situation, employees choose their response to the situation and the computer selects a video that shows what would happen based on the employee's response. Butt's first interactive video training focused on food safety practices and included such features as a bacteria growth simulator. (Don't you wish you had one of those?)

Captain D's Seafood Kitchen provides another example of a company that successfully used a computer-based training program. Captain D's spent $2 million to develop its training programs and install computers in each of its 350 restaurants. As a result of this training, mystery-shopper ratings increased by 4% (Maurer, 2001).

In the public sector, many law-enforcement agencies are using training programs offered over the Internet. For example, the Federal Law Enforcement Training Center provides more than 1,700 courses through e-learning, and the U.S. Capitol Police provides its officers access to more than 2,100 web-based courses. Two law enforcement agencies in Florida saved $296,000 in travel-related expenses in one year by using e-learning. Because creating an e-learning training program can be expensive, most organizations contract with a learning portal, that is, a website containing a variety of e-courses.

Most asynchronous distance learning training takes advantage of the concept of **programmed instruction**. Programmed instruction is effective because it takes advantage of several important learning principles (Goldstein & Ford, 2002). First, learning is *self-paced*—that is, each trainee proceeds at their own pace. You might

Interactive video A training technique in which an employee is presented with a videotaped situation and is asked to respond to the situation and then receives feedback based on the response.

Programmed instruction A training method in which employees learn information at their own pace.

have been in classes in which the lecturer went too quickly and in others in which the lecturer went too slowly. When the presentation speed of the material does not parallel the comprehension speed of the learner, frustration occurs, and the material will not be learned as well as it might. This delivery method also allows trainees to revisit content as needed if they were having trouble comprehending a concept, as opposed to either having to ask a lecturer to explain a topic again (which oftentimes participants might be too shy to do so in a crowded classroom), or potentially miss a foundational concept for the rest of the training session.

Second, each trainee is *actively involved* in the learning. This contrasts sharply with the lecture method, where the employee might sit through two hours of lecture without being actively involved. Think of your favorite classes: The instructor probably allowed you to become involved and actually do things. (That is why some of the chapters in the text are so detailed. By making the text inclusive and complete, your instructor can spend class time on projects instead of straight lecture.)

Finally, programmed instruction presents information in *small units* or chunks, because learning smaller amounts of material is easier than learning larger amounts. To demonstrate this point, think of the exam for this class. Would your score on the test be higher if you read and reviewed one chapter each week or if you waited until the night before the test to read five chapters? (The answer should be obvious, and hopefully you did not answer the question from experience!) A meta-analysis by Allen, Mabry, Mattrey, Bourhis, Titsworth, and Burrell (2004) found that test scores for students in distance learning classes were no different than those earned by students in traditional courses.

To better engage the learner, an increasing number of training designers are including game elements such as progress bars and competition into their programmed instruction. This **gamification** is not so much a training method itself but a means to encourage employees to enroll in training and to complete the training program (Landers, Auer, Helms, Marin, & Armstrong, 2019).

Synchronous Distance Learning

Rather than using printed or prerecorded materials for distance learning, many training programs are conducted live where the trainer communicates to an audience that might be "attending" over the phone or through the Internet.

Fast-growing sources of synchronous distance learning are teleconferences, webinars, and webcasts. **Webinars** (short for web-based seminar) and **webcasts** are training programs transmitted over the web. The difference between the two is that a webinar is interactive whereas a webcast involves one-way communication from the trainer. With a teleconference, trainees are sent a PowerPoint presentation that they view on their computer while the trainer conducts the audio portion of the training over the phone. As with webinars, teleconferences can be interactive in nature. This interactivity is important as surveys suggest that trainees are increasingly expecting online learning to be interactive (Sternberg, 2020).

Another fast-growing source of synchronous distance learning is interactive, online communities of learning such as **blogs**, **wikis**, and **listservs**. With each of these methods, rather than waiting for an annual conference or scheduled training program, employees can ask questions, get immediate answers, post opinions, and share information with others in similar fields.

Meta-analysis results indicate that distance learning techniques are at least as effective as classroom training and their effectiveness increases when learners can

---

Gamification The application of game-like elements to traditional assessments.

Webinar Short for "web seminar," an interactive training method in which training is transmitted over the Internet.

Webcast A noninteractive training method in which the trainer transmits training information over the Internet.

Blog A website in which the host regularly posts commentaries on a topic that readers can respond to.

Wiki A collection of web pages in which users can create web pages on a topic and readers can freely edit those pages.

Listserv A program that automatically distributes email messages to a group of people who have a common interest.

control the pace of the learning and when feedback is given regarding the learner's progress (Sitzmann, Kraiger, Stewart, & Wisher, 2006).

Conducting On-The-Job Training

In the previous section, we discussed how employees can be trained in classroom settings and through distance learning. In this section, we will discuss how employees learn through on-the-job training (OJT), an important topic given that some researchers estimate that over 60% of employee training is OJT (DeRouin, Parrish, & Salas, 2005). Though there is some disagreement about what constitutes OJT, a good definition is that OJT is *informal training by experienced peers and supervisors that occurs on the job and during job tasks* (DeRouin et al., 2005). OJT works best for teaching skills that require supervision to learn, are best learned through repetition, and benefit from role modeling (Gallup & Beauchemin, 2000).

Learning by Modeling Others

Also called *social learning*, **modeling** is a vitally important method of learning for training in organizations. As the name implies, employees learn by watching how other employees perform, or model, a behavior.

Modeling Learning through watching and imitating the behavior of others.

Modeling as a learning technique is astoundingly pervasive and is the basis of the behavioral-modeling method of training discussed earlier. Think of how you first learned a sport such as baseball. You may have learned your batting stance by watching a favorite player. Or, you might have picked up how to drive a car by watching others drive before you were old enough to get behind the wheel. We are most likely to learn through modeling when we are unsure about how to behave. For example, in our first days on a new job, we watch how others act. Do they take only the allotted time on breaks? Do they treat customers politely? Do they pay attention to their work? We learn how to behave at work by watching others so that we will fit in. A theory of job satisfaction that will be discussed in Chapter 10 hypothesizes that we even decide how satisfied we will be in our job by matching our level of job satisfaction with the levels exhibited by other employees.

Modeling is most effective under certain conditions. These conditions mainly involve characteristics of the employee whose behavior is being duplicated and the characteristics of the person attempting to model that performance.

Characteristics of the Model. Of course, we do not model everyone else's behavior. Instead, we tend to model behavior of people who are similar to us, who are successful, and who have status. If we are going to model our golf swing after someone, who would it be? Almost certainly, we would choose someone on the professional tour because of their status and success. But which player would it be? It would not be one of the worst golfers on the tour. Instead, we probably would choose Tiger Woods, Nelly Korda, or another successful golfer. Finally, which successful golfer would it be? It would probably be the successful golfer who was most similar to us in terms of race, gender, hair color, hometown, style, and so on.

This raises an important point about models in industry. We tend to look for a model who is similar to us. For modeling to be effective, the appropriate role models for employees should be similar to them in significant ways. That is why it is essential that a school has a diverse faculty, that an organization has diverse managers, and that television shows portray all types of people in different occupational roles.

Characteristics of the Observer. For an employee to model another's behavior, three conditions are necessary (Bandura, 1977). First, the employee must pay attention to the behavior of other employees. All the role models in the world will be unable to affect a behavior change in an employee if the employee pays no attention to the role model.

Second, the employee must be able to *retain* the information that is being modeled. Have you ever watched a person dance, and then later tried the dance yourself? For most of us it is difficult to do if there are many steps to remember. (For some of us it is difficult to do even if there are only two steps to remember!) Thus, even though we might have been paying close attention, there were too many behaviors to recall or retain. That is why training techniques that use modeling concentrate on only a few behaviors at a time.

Finally, the employee must have the ability or skill to *reproduce* the behavior that is seen. For example, suppose a new employee observes a veteran employee winding coils. If the new employee does not have the proper dexterity, technique alone will not enable the employee to be as successful as the veteran. Thus, it is important to limit the scope of the behaviors being modeled, so that they are at a skill level that can be reproduced by the observing employee.

Learning Through Job Rotation

Job rotation A system in which employees are given the opportunity to perform several different jobs in an organization.

Another excellent on-the-job training method is **job rotation**, in which an employee performs several different jobs within an organization. Job rotation is especially popular for managerial training because it allows a manager trainee to experience and understand most, if not all, of the jobs within the organization that their subordinates will perform.

Across the United States, retail and supermarket corporations Kroger and Walmart train their assistant managers as clerks, stockers, and baggers before promotion to manager. Allstate, an American insurance company, trains its manager trainees in a similar fashion by having them spend a few months in sales, underwriting, personnel, cash control, and marketing. With job rotation, these organizations believe their managers will perform better by understanding more clearly how each employee performs their job. At Applebee's restaurants, executives exchange positions with restaurant employees so that the executives don't lose touch with routine problems. At Levy Restaurants in Chicago, 20 to 40 selected employees hoping to be managers spend four days at their normal job and one day working in a new area of the restaurant; 75% eventually get promoted. Also, chef trainees at Levy Restaurants spend their first week in the dining room, four weeks in the kitchen, and one week performing administrative tasks.

Job rotation is also commonly used to train nonmanagerial employees. Aside from increasing employee awareness, the main advantage of job rotation is that it allows for both lateral transfers within an organization and greater flexibility in replacing absent workers. For example, if two bank tellers are ill, an employee who normally approves loans can temporarily take over the tellers' tasks. Increased use of work teams is making job rotation, or **cross-training**, much more common.

Cross-training Teaching employees how to perform tasks traditionally performed by other employees.

Another advantage, which will be discussed in greater detail in Chapter 10, is that job rotation can improve job satisfaction by reducing the boredom that often comes with a task-repetitive job. Job rotation probably works best if a corporate trainer is assigned to supervise employees throughout the duration of their rotations. Such a situation provides more stability than would occur if the employee had a different supervisor for each rotation. Job rotation could also be helpful for physical jobs or ones that might lead to a higher rate of occupational injuries or illness. Researchers were able to develop a heuristic method for creating job rotation schedules that successfully decreased the number and severity of occupational injuries (Tharmmaphornphilas & Norman, 2007).

An interesting innovation is taking job rotation training outside the organization and encouraging employees to volunteer for worthwhile charities and nonprofit organizations. For example, Newell Rubbermaid has a Global Day of Service in which employees help Habitat for Humanity build houses, AppDynamics gives each of its employees five days off each year to perform volunteer activities, and Horizon Blue Cross Blue Shield of New Jersey employees participated in a Day of Caring and helped clean up Island Beach State Park. The United Way takes advantage of corporate volunteerism through its "Loaned Executive" program, in which organizations "lend" their executives to the United Way to help raise funds.

Employers report that volunteerism increases morale while also increasing employee communication, time management, and planning skills. Added benefits include increased respect for diversity, self-esteem, and social obligation (Caudron, 1994).

Learning Through Apprentice Training

Apprentice training is used by more than 350,000 people annually in the United States and is typically found in crafts and trades such as construction, manufacturing, and plumbing. With apprentice training, an individual takes a minimum of 144 hours of formal class work each year and works with an expert for several (usually four) years to learn a particular trade and perhaps become eligible to join a trade union. Although apprenticeships are usually formal agreements between labor and management and are regulated by the U.S. Department of Labor's Bureau of Apprenticeship and Training, as well as by state agencies, apprenticeships can also be less formal.

For example, an apprentice working with a plumber will initially help the plumber by carrying supplies, picking up parts from suppliers, and holding tools. But with time, the apprentice is taught the necessary knowledge and skills for plumbing. When the apprenticeship is complete, the apprentice can start their own business.

Apprenticeships are good for both the apprentice and the organization. The apprentice learns a valuable trade, and the organization can ensure that it will have highly trained employees for difficult to fill positions, employees that tend to stay with the employer long after the apprenticeship ends (Tyler, 2013). For example, Moog Components Group in Blacksburg, Virginia, developed an apprenticeship program to develop machinists. To complete the program, apprentices must complete 8,000 hours of on-the-job training and successfully complete seven classes taught by the local community college. To make the classes more convenient for the 34 apprentices, the community college holds the classes at the Moog facility.

Apprenticeships have become even more important now that most U.S. secondary schools have replaced shop classes with college prep classes (Tyler, 2013). Despite this increased popularity, however, apprenticeship programs have been criticized for two major reasons. First, the emphasis during the apprenticeship often is on the production of work as opposed to teaching new skills to the apprentice. Second, unions use apprenticeships to restrict entry into their trades, which results both in inflated wages caused by high demand and a lower supply of workers, and in unfair hiring practices of underrepresented groups. Employers often shun apprenticeships for fear that the apprentice will become a competitor or join a competing company.

Learning Through Coaching and Mentoring

Coaching A method of training in which a new employee receives on-the-job guidance from an experienced employee.

Coaching. **Coaching** is another popular method of training new employees and typically takes one of two forms: experienced employees working with new employees and professional coaches who work with all employees.

Experienced Employees as Coaches. In this form of coaching, a new employee is assigned to an experienced employee, who is told to "show the kid the ropes" (i.e., teach the new employee how to do the job). Coaching can be highly effective, allowing the new employee the chance to learn from a job expert. After all, who knows a job better than a person who has mastered it for several years? Coaching provides just-in-time training, flexible scheduling, customized training, and a smaller financial commitment than many other types of training (Leeds, 1996).

Coaching, however, has its own problems. First, good workers are not necessarily good trainers, and good trainers are not necessarily good workers. Being able to do a job is not the same as explaining it. For example, have you ever asked a great dancer to show you some dance steps, but they were unable to explain how they danced? In sports, the best coaches often have been terrible players. This is not to say, of course, that excellent employees or players will never be good teachers or coaches. For example, in the world of sports we have seen such successful basketball players as Doc Rivers, Larry Bird, and the late John Wooden become excellent coaches. In education, we see successful people leave industry to become fine educators. The key is finding a way to identify those workers who will be good coaches or trainers. One solution has been to establish "train-the-trainer" programs, in which future trainers or coaches are taught the skills they will need to train other employees.

A second problem with coaching is that it diminishes the expert's productivity (Wexley & Latham, 2002). That is, while the expert shows the new employee how to do the job, their own production declines. If they are on a bonus system, they may lose money as their production declines, as will the organization if the experienced employee is an outstanding worker. One solution to this problem is for the organization to reward workers who do well in training new employees.

Pass-through programs A formal method of coaching in which excellent employees spend a period of time in the training department learning training techniques and training employees.

Many organizations, such as Pitney-Bowes, an American technology company, have also adopted **pass-through programs**, in which experienced workers are temporarily assigned to the training department. These workers are taught training techniques and then spend several months training new employees before resuming their old jobs.

Professional Coaches. To overcome the problems mentioned here, many organizations are using "corporate coaches." Corporate coaches are similar to consultants, yet rather than working with the organization as a whole, they are hired to coach a particular employee, usually a manager. The job of a corporate coach goes beyond traditional training, as they also help employees identify strengths and weaknesses, set goals, and solve problems. Daimler AG (a German automotive corporation) is an example of an employer that uses coaches in its call centers. Each call center has a professional coach who works with employees and managers. For example, a manager may be having a problem with an employee who is short with customers. As a result, the manager goes to the coach for help. The coach might begin by listening to some of the employee's calls and then work with the manager on how to provide feedback to the employee. The coach might listen as the manager talks to the employee and provide additional feedback to the manager.

Mentoring. Mentoring is a form of coaching that has recently received much attention. A **mentor** is a veteran in the organization who takes a special interest in a new employee and helps them not only to adjust to the job but also to advance in the organization. Typically, mentors are older and at least one level or position above the employee being mentored. American Cytec agricultural products is a good example of an organization using mentoring. Cytec previously had its sales trainees spend six months in the classroom but has reduced classroom training to three months and now puts the trainees in the field with 1 of 31 "master reps" who serve as mentors. With time, trainees get greater responsibility until they can finally handle calls on their own. This change to mentoring is credited with a substantial increase in sales.

Mentor An experienced employee who advises and looks out for a new employee.

As with coaching, not all employees make good mentors; thus, both the mentor and the mentor-employee match must be carefully chosen. However, meta-analysis results indicate that, in general, having a mentor is beneficial to an employee's career (Eby, Allen, Evans, Ng, & DuBois, 2008; Kammeyer-Mueller & Judge, 2008). Interestingly, a study of 609 mentoring relationships found that mentoring was more effective when the relationship was informal rather than formal (Ragins & Cotton, 1999).

Performance Appraisal. As discussed in Chapter 7, one of the major uses for employee performance evaluation is training. One excellent method of on-the-job training is to have a supervisor meet with an employee to discuss their strengths and weaknesses on the job. Once the weaknesses have been identified, the supervisor and employee can determine what training methods would best help the employee to improve their job knowledge or skill.

But using performance appraisal for both training and determining raises and promotions can be difficult. As pointed out by Kirkpatrick (1986), three factors account for this difficulty. First, the focus on salary administration is on *past* behavior, whereas the focus for training is on *future* behavior. Second, performance appraisal for salary administration often is subjective and emotional, whereas such appraisal for training is objective and unemotional. Finally, salary administration looks at overall performance, whereas training looks at detailed performance. Because of these differences, Kirkpatrick (1986) suggests the use of two separate performance appraisal systems in an organization, one for salary administration and the other for training.

8-5 Motivating Employees to Learn During Training

Providing Incentives for Learning

Employees motivated to learn perform better in training than their less motivated counterparts (Mathieu, Tannenbaum, & Salas, 1992). This motivation is often related to the perception that there is an incentive (e.g., a pay raise or job advancement) to learning. That is, an electronics assembler who is taking a course in electronics will probably not study and learn unless he can see how that knowledge will improve their performance enough to result in a desirable outcome, such as a salary increase or chance of promotion. Types of incentives that can be used to motivate learning include money, job security, self-improvement, advancement, fun (e.g., an interesting training program), and opportunity to enter a new career. The incentives can be made contingent on a variety of factors, including completion of a training course, demonstration of new knowledge, demonstration of a new skill, or an increase in actual job performance.

A common financial incentive method is **skill-based pay**. With skill-based pay, an employee participates in a training program that is designed to increase a particular skill an employee needs either to be promoted or to receive a pay raise. For example, employees who are currently in the position of Assembler II must learn to solder wires before they can be promoted to Assembler III. The employees must be able to demonstrate their mastery of the newly taught skill rather than just attend training sessions. Similarly, in situations where promotion is not possible, pay increases alone are given to employees who master new skills. There are four common skill-based pay plans: *vertical skill plans* pay for skill in a single job; *horizontal skill plans* focus on skills used across multiple jobs; *depth skill plans* reward employees for learning specialized skills; and *basic skill plans* focus on such basic skills as math and English (Recardo & Pricone, 1996).

Skill-based pay not only provides incentives for employees to successfully complete training but also results in increased savings for an organization. For example, a General Foods plant in Kansas found a 92% decrease in its quality reject rate and a 33% decrease in fixed overhead costs after introducing a skill-based pay program.

Interest

Employees will be more motivated to learn when the training program is interesting. As a result, trainers who are not effective presenters do not last long. Some training topics are naturally interesting, and a trainer doesn't need to do much to spice up the material. For example, the topic of detecting deception is intrinsically interesting to most people, but the topic of performance appraisal is not. A topic can be made interesting by making it applicable to the employees' lives, having activities, including relevant anecdotes, using a variety of training techniques, using humor, and maximizing audience participation.

Feedback

Another essential aspect of motivating employees to learn is to provide **feedback**. With some tasks, feedback occurs naturally. For example, in baseball, a batter receives feedback on their swing by seeing how hard and far the ball travels. For other tasks, however, judging the correctness of a behavior without feedback is difficult. For example, if you write a term paper for this class and get a C, your next term paper will probably not improve unless you have been provided feedback about what was right and wrong with the previous paper.

The same is true for training in industry. Our electronics assembler needs feedback early in the training process to know if the winding of the coil is tight enough, if there is an easier way to wind the coil, or if the winding is equally distributed on the coil. A balance, however, must be maintained between giving too little and too much feedback. As shown in Figure 8.3, the employee will not learn if too little feedback is given. However, too much or overly detailed feedback causes frustration, and the employee will not learn at an optimal level.

A final consideration for feedback concerns what type of feedback to give. Research and common sense agree that positive feedback should be given when an employee correctly performs a task during training. Praise provides an incentive to continue correct behavior. But if an employee is not performing a task correctly, should they receive **negative feedback**? Probably yes, even though negative feedback is more

Figure 8.3
Relationship Between
Feedback Specificity
and Learning

Source: Adapted from Blum and Naylor (1968).

complicated than positive feedback. Negative feedback should focus on the incorrect actions instead of traits of the employee, and should probably also be accompanied by specific suggestions for how the employee can improve performance.

8-6 Ensuring Transfer of Training

Transfer of training The extent to which behavior learned in training will be performed on the job.

When an organization spends time and money on training, it expects that the knowledge and skills will be transferred to the job. Unfortunately, this is often not the case (Broad, 2000). There are several strategies for increasing the **transfer of training** to the workplace.

Use Realistic Training Programs

Research in learning has indicated that the more similar the training situation is to the actual job situation, the more effective training will be. This principle is extremely important when a training program is being chosen or designed. For example, if a restaurant is training its employees to wait on tables, the training will be more effective if the employees can practice in an environment that is similar to that encountered when they actually work. This realism might even include "customers" complaining and changing their orders.

An excellent example of making training more realistic comes from the French police. After examining the use of force by officers, Contournet (2004) found that officers most often use their weapons at night, when they are tired after many hours on their shift. Training in use of weapons, however, was conducted in the morning, when cadets first started their day. To ensure better transfer of training, shooting simulations are now being conducted during both the day and the evening hours.

Employees will also be motivated to apply what they learned in training if the training program has a reputation among them as being effective and useful (Switzer, Nagy, & Mullins, 2005). This is not surprising given that employees talk with one another about training, and when they find a training program useful (or not), they certainly pass that information on to other employees.

Have Opportunities to Practice Work-Related Behavior During the Training

Overlearning Practicing a task even after it has been mastered in order to retain learning.

Transfer of training is increased by having the trainee practice the desired behavior as much as possible. Such practice is especially important for tasks that will not be performed daily after training has been completed. For example, if a firefighter is learning to perform CPR, they must overlearn the task through constant practice. This **overlearning** is essential because it may be months before the firefighter will practice what they have learned. In contrast, once our electronics assembler learns a task during training, it is time for them to move to another task. Overlearning is not necessary for the coil winder because they will perform the task every hour once the training has been completed.

The term *overlearning* does not have the same meaning in training that it has on most college campuses. In training, overlearning means practicing a task, even after it has been successfully learned. Many students, however, think of overlearning as the negative consequence of "studying too hard." Although it is commonly believed that one can study too hard and "overlearn" the material, research does not support the conclusion that this type of overlearning occurs or has negative consequences. Therefore, no one will be hurt by studying a little longer. In fact, a meta-analysis by Driskell, Willis, and Copper (1992) indicates that overlearning significantly increases retention of training material, depending upon the extent of overlearning, the duration of retention period, and the type of task being trained.

Finally, to further increase the transfer of training, practice in as many different situations as possible should be provided. For example, we might have our electronics assembler wind coils as fast as possible, wind them slowly, and wind them in various sizes. In this way, the employee will be better able to deal with any changes that occur in the job.

Provide Employees with the Opportunity to Apply Their Training

For information learned in training to transfer to behavior on the job, employees must be given the opportunity and encouraged to apply what they have learned (Broad, 2000; Ford, Quiñones, Sego, & Sorra, 1992; Tracey, Tannenbaum, & Kavanagh, 1995). Employees are more likely to be given opportunities to perform what they learned if their supervisor perceives them to be competent and the organizational climate is supportive (Baldwin & Ford, 1988; Ford et al., 1992). Though this seems obvious, research indicates that many employers are neither supportive nor provide opportunities for employees to apply what is learned—especially if the training was in the form of employees going to school to work on a degree (Posner, Hall, & Munson, 1991). This lack of opportunity can have negative consequences: In a study of over 9,000 employees, Benson, Finegold, and Mohrman (2004) found that employees who were promoted after receiving a graduate degree (given the chance to use their new knowledge) were less likely to turn over than employees who completed their degrees but were not promoted.

One other method for getting employees to apply what they have learned in training is to train all the employees in a work area (team) at the same time. One advantage of doing this is that because all employees have been trained, they can help and encourage each other. That is, if one employee is not properly performing a task, they can be coached by another employee. Furthermore, if all employees are applying what they have learned, it sets the proper atmosphere for new employees as well as for employees tempted to go back to the old way of doing things.

Ensure Management Is Supportive of the Training

An important factor in employee motivation to apply training is the atmosphere set by management. That is, employees are most likely to apply their new knowledge and skills if supervisors encourage and reward them to do so.

A good example of the importance of management support can be found at a particular fast-food restaurant. The employees at two restaurants owned by the same company were given customer service training. At one of the restaurants, the training clearly had an effect, as customer complaints were down, and secret-shopper scores were up. At another of the restaurants, there were no changes in complaints or secret-shopper scores. What made the difference? At one restaurant, the supervisor set goals, provided feedback to the employees, actively encouraged them to use their training, and they themself modeled the behaviors learned in training. At the other restaurant, the manager hid in the back doing paperwork, a signal to employees that customer service was not important to their boss, regardless of what was emphasized in training.

Have Employees Set Goals

The use of knowledge and skills learned in training can also be encouraged by having employees set goals. For example, tellers at a credit union received two days of training on cross-selling new products. This training included information about new loans and new loan rates, types of retirement accounts, alternative savings plans, and the advantages of using a new "premium" credit card. Each teller might set a goal of daily asking four credit union members if they would like information about one of the new products. Goal setting works best when goals are individually set by each employee, are concrete rather than vague, and are high enough to be challenging but not so difficult as to be impossible. A more comprehensive discussion of goal setting is found in Chapter 9.

8-7 Putting It All Together

In this chapter, you have learned many factors that can affect the success of a training program. Before discussing how the success of a training program can be evaluated, let's recap what you have learned. As shown in Figure 8.4, the first issue to consider is whether training is the proper solution to a problem. That is, if employees already possess the necessary skills and knowledge but aren't performing well, the problem is probably one of motivation, communication, or work design rather than a lack of training.

If training is to be the desired intervention, several factors will affect its success:

- Employees must have the skills and abilities to complete the training successfully. For example, if an employee is not bright enough to learn a computer program or doesn't have the dexterity to perform intricate microelectronics assembly, no amount of training will improve their performance.

Figure 8.4
Determining the Success of a Training Program

- There should be minimal outside factors (e.g., work or family problems) that might distract the employee and keep them from concentrating on the training program.
- Employees must be motivated to learn. That is, they must perceive that training is needed, that the training program meets their expectations, that they can complete the training (self-efficacy), and that there will be some reward (e.g., pay, career advancement) for performing well.
- The training method (e.g., programmed instruction, behavioral modeling, lecture) must be a good match for the employee's learning style, ability, and personality.
- The training method must be a good match for the type of material being learned (e.g., knowledge vs. a physical skill).
- The training program must allow for goal setting, positive feedback, distributed practice, overlearning, and the chance to practice and apply the material learned (transfer of training).
- There must be an opportunity and encouragement to complete the training, and to use the newly acquired knowledge at work. This can be enhanced through a supportive organizational culture.

8-8 Evaluation of Training Results

As discussed in Chapter 1, one important characteristic of I/O psychology is its reliance on research. Evaluating training results is a good example of this reliance. Because training programs can be costly in both time and money, it is essential that they be evaluated to determine if they can be improved, should continue to be offered, and whether they significantly increase performance or affect positive changes in behavior (Kirkpatrick, 2000).

Research Designs for Evaluation

There are many ways to evaluate the effectiveness of a training program, and two factors differentiate the various methods. The first involves *practicality*, and the second is concerned with *experimental rigor*. Although scientifically rigorous research designs are preferred, their use is not always possible. Yet a practical research design without scientific rigor yields little confidence in research findings.

The most simple and practical of research designs implements a training program and then determines whether significant change is seen in performance of job knowledge. To use this method, performance or job knowledge must be measured twice. The first measurement, a **pretest**, is taken before the implementation of training. The second measurement, a **posttest**, is taken after the training program is complete. A diagram of this simple pretest-posttest design is as follows:

Pretest → Training → Posttest

Although this method is fairly simple, its findings are difficult to interpret because there is no control group against which the results can be compared. That is, suppose a significant difference in performance is seen between the pretest and the posttest. If a training program has occurred between the two tests, it would be

Pretest A measure of job performance or knowledge taken before the implementation of a training program.

Posttest A measure of job performance or knowledge taken after a training program has been completed.

tempting to credit the training for the increase. The increase, however, may have resulted from other factors, such as changes in job equipment, in motivation caused by nontraining factors, or in managerial style or philosophy.

Likewise, suppose no significant increase in performance is observed between pretest and posttest. The natural conclusion might be that the training program did not work. Without a control group, that interpretation is not necessarily correct. The same changes noted above for an increase may have caused a decrease in performance in this second case. Thus, it is possible that the training program actually did increase performance but that other factors reduced it, which resulted in no net gain in performance from training.

To overcome these problems, a control group should be established. For training purposes, a control group consists of employees who will be tested and treated in the same manner as the experimental group, except that they will not receive training. The control group will be subject to the same policy, job equipment, and economic conditions as the employees in the experimental group who receive training. The diagram for a pretest/posttest control group design looks like this:

Experimental group: Pretest → Training → Posttest
Control group: Pretest →   Posttest

The big advantage this second design has is that it allows a researcher to look at the training effect after controlling for outside factors. For example, after going through a training program, employees at RR Donnelley & Sons, an American communications company, increased their annual commissions by $22,000, and the company increased profits by $34 million. The company was obviously pleased but was worried that the increased performance could have been due to something other than training. It thus compared the results with a control group of employees who had not received training. The commissions of the control employees increased by $7,000 over the same period. Thus, the net effect of the training was still sizable—$15,000 per employee—but not as high as the $22,000 originally thought. The control group allowed the company to control for such factors as increased sales agent experience and new company promotions (Montebello & Haga, 1994).

Even though this design is an improvement on the first, it too has its drawbacks. First, except for training manipulation, it is almost impossible to treat a control group the same as the experimental group. Control groups often consist of workers at other plants or on other shifts at the same plant. Such groups are used because there often is no alternative. But the fact that they are in different environments reduces confidence in the research findings as different environments might introduce external factors that contribute to a difference in performance.

Even if employees in the same plant on the same shift can be randomly split into control and experimental groups, problems will still exist. The most glaring of these involves the possibility that because the two groups are close to one another, the training effect for the experimental group will spill over to the control group. Employees in the control group also may resent not being chosen for training. This resentment alone may lead to a decrease in motivation and performance by employees in the control group. Finally, it is possible that the untrained employees will pressure the newly trained employees to revert to the "old way" of doing things.

With both of these designs, the pretest itself presents a problem. That is, the mere taking of a test may itself lead to increases in performance. Because of this, a rather complicated method called the **Solomon four-groups design** can be used (Campbell & Stanley, 1963). With this design, one group will undergo training but will not take

Solomon four-groups design An extensive method of evaluating the effectiveness of training with the use of pretests, posttests, and control groups.

the pretest, a second group will undergo training but will take the pretest, a third group will not undergo training but will take the pretest, and a fourth group will neither undergo training nor take the pretest. The diagram for this design is as follows:

Group 1		Training →	Posttest
Group 2	Pretest →	Training →	Posttest
Group 3	Pretest →		Posttest
Group 4			Posttest

This design allows a researcher not only to control for outside effects but also to control for any pretest effect. This is the most scientifically rigorous of the research designs used to evaluate training, but even this has a serious drawback: It is often not practical. That is, four groups of employees must be used, two of which do not receive training. Thus, to use this design at one organization or plant, ideally a relatively large number of employees must be available and kept from discussing the training with one another.

Evaluation Criteria

In the previous section, we discussed research designs for evaluating training. In each design, a pretest and posttest were included. This section will discuss the types of criteria that can be used for these pretests and posttests. There are six levels at which training effectiveness can be measured: content validity, employee reactions, employee learning, application of training, business impact, and return on investment (Phillips & Stone, 2002).

Content Validity

At times, the only way that training can be evaluated is by comparing training content with the knowledge, skills, and abilities required to perform a job. In other words, the **content validity** of the training can be examined. For example, if a job analysis indicates that knowledge of electronic circuitry is necessary to perform a job, then a seminar that is designed to teach this knowledge would have content validity. Although content analysis may ensure that a training program is job related, it still does not indicate whether a particular training method is effective. But if a training program is content valid and is conducted by a professional trainer *documenting* previous success with the method in other organizations, it may be a safe assumption that the training program will be successful. Keep in mind, however, that making such an assumption is acceptable only when actually evaluating the effect of training is not possible because there are too few employees for a proper analysis or there are financial or political constraints on conducting a proper evaluation.

Employee Reactions

The most commonly used method to evaluate training is measuring **employee reactions** to the training (Sitzmann, Brown, Casper, Ely, & Zimmerman, 2008). Pioneered by Kirkpatrick in his seminal works, "Reactions" is the first level of training evaluation (Kiripatrick, 1959a). Employee reactions involve asking employees if they enjoyed the training and learned from the training. These ratings tend to be most influenced by the trainer's style and the degree of interaction in the training program but are also influenced by the motivation of the trainee prior to training as well as perceptions of organizational support for the training (Sitzmann et al., 2008).

Employee reactions are important because employees will not have confidence in the training and will not be motivated to use it if they do not like the training process. However, even though positive employee reactions are necessary for training to be successful, positive employee reactions do not mean that training will lead to changes in knowledge or performance (Pfau & Kay, 2002b).

Because trainee reactions constitute the lowest level of training evaluation, they can often be misleading. For example, most seminars conducted by outside consultants are informative and well presented, so employee reactions are almost always positive, even though the training may not actually affect knowledge or future performance. Reactions are generally guided by participant emotions and can be caused by many factors not directly related to the content. For example, as shown in Table 8.3, in a meta-analysis by Alliger, Tannenbaum, Bennett, Traver, and Shotland (1997), employee reactions had only a small correlation with learning and application of training.

Asking employees about their training experience provides an excellent opportunity to make the training process more enjoyable, efficient, and effective. Trainees should be asked for suggestions about how the training can be improved. Such suggestions might be related to the content of the training, the training process (e.g., length, mode, and pace), and the competence of the people conducting the training. If the training program is conducted virtually, trainees should be provided with a web link with which they can anonymously provide their feedback (Grochocki, 2021).

Employee Learning

Employee learning
Evaluating the effectiveness of a training program by measuring how much employees learned from it.

Formative test A test given during training to determine if a trainee is learning the material.

"Learning" is the second level of training evaluation (Kirkpatrick, 1959b). Instead of using employee reactions as the criterion in evaluating training performance, actual **employee learning** can usually be measured. That is, if a training program is designed to increase employee knowledge of communication techniques, then a test assessing knowledge of communication techniques can be used as a criterion of learning transfer. There are two main types of tests: formative and summative (Champagne, 2021). **Formative tests** are given during the training experience to determine

Table 8.3 Correlations Among Training Evaluation Criteria

	Employee Reactions		Measures of Learning			Application of Training
	E	U	IR	LTR	SD	AT
Employee Reactions						
Enjoyed the training (E)	(.82)	.34	.02		.03	.07
Thought it was useful (U)		(.86)	.26		.03	.18
Measures of Learning						
Immediate retention (IR)			(.77)	.35	.18	.11
Long-term retention (LTR)				(.58)	.14	.08
Skill demonstration (SD)					(.85)	.18
Application of Training (AT)						(.86)

Note: Reliabilities are in parentheses.
Source: Adapted from the meta-analysis by Alliger et al. (1997).

whether the trainee is learning the material. If the test scores are low, the trainer can re-present the material. If the training experience is virtual and asynchronous, the trainee must go over the material again and retake the test. Some trainers have found that adapting game shows such as Family Feud and Jeopardy allow an evaluation of trainee knowledge but in a more fun and interactive way than a traditional test (Douglas, 2021).

Summative tests are given at the end of the training program to evaluate the success of the training. Ideally, summative tests are administered before training and then again after the training has been completed. The measurements that will be used for the pretest and posttest, as with selection tests, must be both reliable and valid. Thus, if the purpose of a training program is to increase job knowledge, an appropriate job knowledge test must be constructed or purchased. A trainer can spend a great deal of time creating a training program and evaluating its effectiveness, but the whole training effort will be wasted if the measure used to evaluate effectiveness is no good.

The restaurant industry provides many examples of evaluating training effectiveness through employee learning. At Claim Jumper Restaurants, servers must pass a 100-item menu test before they are released from training. At Rock Bottom Restaurants, learning is measured by requiring new employees to obtain written statements from their peers verifying that they have mastered their new duties; however, 20% do not perform well enough to get the required verification. To make the testing process more fun, Bugaboo Creek Steak Houses hold scavenger hunts to ensure that trainees know where everything is located (Zuber, 1996).

Application of Training

Another criterion for evaluating the effectiveness of training is the degree of **application of training**, or the extent to which employees actually can use the learned material. Learning and memorizing new material is one thing, and applying it is another. In the Kirkpatrick Model, this is the third level, known as "Behavior" (Kirkpatrick, 1960a). For example, if employees learn how to deal with angry customers, their ability to apply this material can be measured by observing how they treat an angry customer while they are actually working. Application of training is often measured though supervisor ratings or using the secret shoppers discussed in Chapter 7.

Business Impact

The fifth criterion that can be used to evaluate a training program's effectiveness is **business impact**. Business impact is determined by evaluating whether the goals for training were met, and is the fourth and final level of the Kirkpatrick Model, "Results" (Kirkpatrick, 1960b). For example, a restaurant such as Buffalo Wild Wings conducts a training program designed to increase sales of top-shelf liquor. A week after the training, if sales of liquors such as Knob Creek bourbon and Absolut vodka (top-shelf liquor) increase, and sales of liquors such as Pepe Lopez tequila and Aristocrat vodka (bottom-shelf liquor) decrease, the training would be considered successful because it has had the desired business impact.

Return on Investment

The sixth criterion for evaluating the success of a training program is **return on investment (ROI)**. That is, after accounting for the cost of the training, did the organization actually save money? For example, imagine that a bank trains its tellers to cross-sell Visa cards. The tellers rate the training session as being enjoyable (employee reactions), all of the employees pass a test on sales techniques (knowledge), and sales *attempts* increase by 30% (application). The ROI approach would then ask, "If we spent $5,000 training the tellers, how much more revenue was brought in as a result of the training?" If the answer to the question is more than the amount spent on training, then the program would be considered a success. For example, Parry (2000) demonstrated that training employees how to conduct effective meetings at Southwest Industries cost $15,538 to implement but saved the organization $820,776 in the first year after the training.

On the Job | Applied Case Study

Training at Pal's Sudden Service

Headquartered in Kingsport, Tennessee, Pal's Sudden Service is a quick-service restaurant chain with over 30 locations. Pal's first franchise opened in 1956 with four items: Sauceburgers, Frenchie Fries, milk shakes, and coke. Customers walked up to the outside counter to place and receive their orders. Pal's first drive-through opened in 1985. Although certainly not as large as the McDonald's or Burger King chains, Pal's has a record of excellence including being the first restaurant to receive the prestigious Malcolm Baldrige National Quality Award and the first organization to win the Tennessee Excellence Award more than once. Pal's obsession with high quality might best be demonstrated by their use of the Hoshizaki ice cube shape that causes ice to melt more slowly so that their iced tea will stay cool all day. Pal's takes great pride in quickly getting orders to customers without mistakes. This is a difficult task given the fast pace of the business. Pal's created a unique training program that reduced employee errors from one error every 450 transactions to one error for every 3,360 transactions. Furthermore, service time was reduced from 23 seconds to 18 seconds. How did Pal's make such progress? Primarily through training, assessment, and feedback. Each hourly employee goes through 120 hours of training. This extensive training allows employees to be assigned to any of three positions so that they can easily fill in where most needed. The training program includes individual face-to-face training as well as e-learning. Trainees are assessed on their progress and go through additional training if they do not score high enough on the training tests. Training does not stop after the initial training period. Store managers constantly coach employees and every employee gets two or three pop quizzes at the beginning of their shift. The quizzes must be turned in by the end of the shift, and employees are allowed to look up information or ask other employees for answers. If they get less than a perfect score, they go through additional training.

- If you were in charge of training, how would you develop a training program that would reduce the number of transaction errors?
- How would you evaluate the success of your training program?

To read more about Pal's unique organizational climate, visit their website at www.palsweb.com.

As you learned in this chapter, role-plays are good teaching tools when training employees on what is called the "soft skills" of the workplace. "Soft skills" refer to the interpersonal skills, and include skills pertaining to such areas as conflict management, stress management, customer service skills, communication skills, and mediation skills.

The philosophy behind role-plays is that they should serve as a "rehearsal" of actual situations that could occur in the workplace. Trainees are given situations and asked to act them out in front of the other trainees. Sometimes, selected participants act out an example of the "wrong" way to do something, followed by a reenactment of the "right" way to do it. After the situation is done the "wrong" way, participants are usually asked what was wrong and how would they handle the situation differently. Then, the same situation would be acted out, only in the right way.

Sometimes, role-plays consist of trainees acting out a situation based on what they *think* is the right way. For example, when employees are being trained on how to manage conflict, the trainer will spend some time lecturing on the steps to take to manage conflict. Then, trainees are given a scenario to role-play and asked to apply what they have learned to that scenario. After it has been acted out, trainees are then asked to critique how well the role-player did and how that role-player could improve. The idea behind doing role-plays this way is that it gives people an opportunity to practice what they learn in a safe environment, before they have to actually use the skills in a real-life situation. Role-plays provide practice and immediate feedback from others that will improve the role-player's performance in actual situations.

The ethical concerns of using role-plays are these: In many training programs, participating in role-plays is mandatory. That is, the trainee cannot say "I don't want to do it." When the training is comprised of just a few participants, usually every participant is asked to act out a scenario in front of the others. Some people do not like to participate in role-plays because it makes them nervous and, at times, terrifies them. So critics would ask: Is it ethical to put people through something with such a negative impact?

Another ethical concern is that role-plays can often be somewhat challenging. For example, a professor at one university, when doing training in his management class, pretends that he is an employee who has a body odor problem. This is a situation that occurs in many organizations! Students are then asked to role-play how, if they were this person's supervisor, they would tell this person of their body odor and the impact it is having at work on other employees. The professor, in an attempt to make it even more real-life, often will yell and even physically push the student in "anger." His thought is that there are many times when employees do get very upset when given this type of evaluation. Many students come out of that role-play upset and even scared! Trainers who use this type of forceful role-play say that in order for people to get comfortable with using their soft skills, they must be faced with scenarios that have actually occurred in organizations and that may occur in one of the organizations in which they may work.

Proponents of role-plays ask how ethical it is NOT to make trainees practice these skills before using them. Merely sitting in a room listening to a trainer and doing exercises is not enough to properly prepare employees for what they might face in real-life situations. For example, just reading or listening how to manage an upset customer does not guarantee that trainees will be able to apply those skills once they leave the training. But, if you make them practice those skills via role-plays, that will better ensure that they will be able to handle the situation.

What Do You Think?

- What are some of the other ethical concerns of using role-plays to teach skills?

- Do you think organizations should implement policies on the type of strategies trainers can use when conducting training?

- Should role-plays be a mandatory part of training?

Chapter Summary

In this chapter you learned:

- The first step in the training process is to conduct a training needs assessment that includes an organizational analysis, task analysis, and person analysis.
- Training methods take many forms. Classroom learning techniques include seminars, audiovisual aids, programmed instruction, case studies, and critical

incidents. Sample job performance techniques include simulation, role-play, behavior modeling, and job rotation. Informal training techniques include apprentice training, coaching, and performance appraisal.

- Such psychological principles as modeling, distributed practice, and transfer of training must be considered when conducting a training program.
- It is important to evaluate training success by measuring trainee attitudes, knowledge, ability to apply newly learned material, improved performance, and return on investment.

Key Terms

Training (277)
Needs analysis (278)
Organizational analysis (278)
Person analysis (280)
Performance appraisal score (281)
Surveys (282)
Skill test (282)
Knowledge test (282)
Case study (285)
Living case (286)
Simulation (286)
Virtual reality (287)
Role-play (287)
Behavior modeling (288)
Massed practice (291)
Distributed practice (291)
Microlearning (291)
Asynchronous technologies (294)
Synchronous technologies (294)
Interactive video (295)
Programmed instruction (295)
Gamification (296)
Webinar (296)
Webcast (296)
Blog (296)

Wiki (296)
Listserv (296)
Modeling (297)
Job rotation (298)
Cross-training (298)
Apprentice training (299)
Coaching (300)
Pass-through programs (300)
Mentor (301)
Skill-based pay (302)
Feedback (302)
Negative feedback (302)
Transfer of training (303)
Overlearning (304)
Pretest (307)
Posttest (307)
Solomon four-groups design (308)
Employee reactions (309)
Employee learning (310)
Formative test (310)
Summative test (311)
Application of training (311)
Business impact (311)
Return on investment (ROI) (312)

Questions for Review

1. In what type of situations is training most useful? Least useful?
2. What motivates employees to learn during training sessions?
3. What would be the best training technique for teaching computer skills? What would be the best technique for customer service skills?
4. Do all new employees model the behavior of more experienced employees? Why or why not?
5. Why would measures of employees' attitudes about a training program and measures of actual learning be different?

Learning Objectives

9-1 Identify the types of people who tend to be more motivated than others.

9-2 Motivate employees through goal setting.

9-3 Realize the importance of providing feedback.

9-4 Use operant conditioning principles to motivate employees.

9-5 Treat employees fairly.

9-6 Choose the types of individual and organizational incentives that best motivate employees.

Motivation The force that drives an employee to perform well.

Once an organization has selected and trained its employees, it is important that employees be both motivated by and satisfied with their jobs. I/O psychologists generally define **motivation** as the internal force that drives a worker to action as well as the external factors that encourage that action (Locke & Latham, 2002). Ability and skill determine whether a worker *can* do the job, but motivation determines whether the worker *will* do it properly.

Because basic abilities don't change greatly over time, changes in work behavior are thought to be affected by the amount of effort employees apply to their work rather than applying that effort to other aspects of life such as family or hobbies. Thus, when we discuss work motivation, we are really talking about the factors that cause a person to apply their effort to work rather than on something else. Likewise, a person's overall level of work motivation might not change, but the effort spent on various tasks at work might change. That is, in a given year, a professor might be highly motivated to teach during the fall semester and thus direct their energy on preparing lectures. In the spring, they might shift their energy to conducting research. The theories discussed in this chapter will try to address why one employee directs a higher percentage of their effort to work than does another employee as well as why employees direct their energies to certain work tasks but not others.

As you can imagine, measuring actual levels of motivation can be difficult. As a result, other than *asking* employees about their motivation levels, researchers use behaviors such as those listed in Table 9.1 that *imply* high levels of motivation. There are, of course, problems with using such behaviors as proxies for motivation. For example, an employee might be highly motivated but have a low performance level because they lack the ability to do the job. Likewise, an employee might be highly motivated to attend work but suffers an illness that keeps them from attending.

Actually testing the relationship between motivation and performance is also difficult, because there are various types of motivation (internal and external) and

Table 9.1   Work Behaviors That Imply Motivation

High Performance Level
  Excellent supervisor ratings
  High productivity
  High quality
  Low levels of wasted materials
  Salary
  Number of promotions
Exemplary Attendance
  Not missing work
  Arriving to work early
  Staying late at work
Organizational Citizenship
  Volunteering for extra duties
  Helping coworkers
  Making suggestions for organizational improvement
  Skipping lunch to complete a project
Self-Improvement Efforts
  Attending voluntary training
  Participating during training
  Accepting performance feedback

various factors that affect motivation. However, psychologists generally agree that increased worker motivation results in increased job performance (Lăzăroiu, 2015).

In this chapter, we will explore several theories that seek to explain why workers are motivated by their jobs. None of the theories completely explains motivation, but each is valuable in that it suggests ways to increase employee performance. Thus, even though a theory itself may not be completely supported by research, the resulting suggestions have generally led to increased performance. As you will see in this chapter, the various theories suggest that employees will be highly motivated if:

- they have a personality that predisposes them to be motivated;
- their expectations have been met;
- the job and the organization are consistent with their values;
- the employees have been given achievable goals;
- the employees receive feedback on their goal attainment;
- the organization rewards them for achieving said goals;
- the employees perceive they are being treated fairly; and
- their coworkers demonstrate a high level of motivation.

9-1 Is an Employee Predisposed to Being Motivated?

Psychologists have postulated that some employees are more predisposed to being motivated than are others. That is, some employees come to most jobs with a tendency to be motivated, whereas others come with the tendency to be unmotivated. You can probably think of people you know who always appear to be motivated and you can probably think of others whom no amount of money would motivate. Researchers have found four individual differences that are most related to work motivation: personality, self-esteem, an intrinsic motivation tendency, and need for achievement.

Organizational citizenship behaviors (OCBs) Behaviors that are not part of an employee's job but which make the organization a better place to work (e.g., helping others, staying late).

Personality

If you recall from Chapter 5, most psychologists believe that there are five main personality dimensions: Openness to experience, conscientiousness, extraversion, agreeableness, and stability. As shown in Table 9.2, meta-analyses have found that several of these dimensions are related to behaviors suggesting high levels of motivation. Conscientiousness is the best personality predictor of work performance, **organizational citizenship behavior (OCB)**, and academic performance; stability is most associated with salary and setting high goals; and extraversion is most highly correlated with the number of promotions received.

Self-esteem The extent to which a person views themself as a valuable and worthy individual.

Self-Esteem

Consistency theory Korman's theory that employees will be motivated to perform at levels consistent with their levels of self-esteem.

Self-esteem is the extent to which a person views themself as valuable and worthy. In the 1970s, Korman (1970, 1976) theorized that employees high in self-esteem are more motivated and will perform better than employees low in self-esteem. According to Korman's **consistency theory**, there is a positive correlation between self-esteem and performance. That is, employees who feel good about themselves are motivated to perform better at work than employees who do not feel that they are valuable and worthy people.

Table 9.2 Relationship Between Big Five Personality Dimensions and Behaviors That Suggest Motivation

Dimension	Potential Indicator of Motivation						
	Performance	**Salary**	**Promotions**	**Attendance**	**OCB**	**Academic Performance**	**Goal Setting**
Stability	0.15[b]	0.12[d]	0.11[d]	−0.04[c]	.12[e]	.02[f]	.29[a]
Extraversion	0.09[b]	0.10[d]	0.18[d]	−0.08[c]		−.01[f]	.15[a]
Openness	0.06[b]	0.04[d]	0.01[d]	−0.00[c]		.12[f]	.18[a]
Agreeableness	0.12[b]	−0.10[b]	−0.05[d]	−0.04[c]	.13[e]	.07[f]	−.29[a]
Conscientiousness	0.24[b]	0.07[d]	0.06[d]	0.06[c]	.18[e]	.22[f]	.28[a]

[a]Judge and Ilies (2002).
[b]Hurtz and Donovan (2000).
[c]Salgado (2002).
[d]Ng, Eby, Sorensen, and Feldman (2005).
[e]Lodi-Smith and Roberts (2007).
[f]Poropat (2009).

Chronic self-esteem The positive or negative way in which a person views himself or herself as a whole.

Situational self-esteem The positive or negative way in which a person views him or herself in a particular situation.

Socially influenced self-esteem The positive or negative way in which a person views him or herself based on the expectations of others.

Organization-based self-esteem The level of an employee's competence and self-worth as a member of an organization.

Consistency theory takes the relationship between self-esteem and motivation one step further by stating that employees with high self-esteem actually *desire* to perform at high levels and employees with low self-esteem desire to perform at low levels. In other words, employees try to perform at levels consistent with their self-esteem level. This desire to perform at levels consistent with self-esteem is compounded by the fact that employees with low self-esteem tend to underestimate their actual ability and performance (Lindeman, Sundvik, & Rouhiainen, 1995). Thus, low self-esteem employees will desire to perform at lower levels than their actual abilities would allow.

The theory becomes somewhat complicated in that there are three types of self-esteem. **Chronic self-esteem** is a person's overall feeling about themselves. **Situational self-esteem** (also called *self-efficacy*) is a person's feeling about themselves in a particular situation such as repairing vehicles or providing customer service. **Socially influenced self-esteem** is how a person feels about themselves based on the expectations of others. All three types of self-esteem are important to job performance. For example, an employee might be low in chronic self-esteem but high in situational self-esteem. That is, a software programmer might believe they are a terrible person whom nobody likes (low chronic self-esteem) but feel that they can program software better than anyone else (high situational self-esteem). A type of situational self-esteem that is of particular interest to I/O psychologists is **organization-based self-esteem** (OBSE). OBSE is the level of an employee's competence and self-worth as a member of an organization, and research has found that OBSE is a strong predictor of job performance (Gardner & Pierce, 1998).

If consistency theory is true, we should find that employees with high self-esteem are more motivated, perform better, and rate their own performance as being higher than employees with low self-esteem. Research supports these predictions: Ilardi, Leone, Kasser, and Ryan (1993) found significant correlations between self-esteem and motivation, and meta-analyses by Bowling, Eschleman, Wang, Kirkendall, and Alarcon (2010) and by Judge and Bono (2001) found a significant relationship between self-esteem and job performance. The Bowling et al. (2010) meta-analysis found that organization-based self-esteem tended to be a better predictor of many employee behaviors and attitudes than general self-esteem.

Based on consistency theory, we should be able to improve performance by increasing an employee's self-esteem, and the results of a meta-analysis of 43 studies indicate that interventions designed to increase self-esteem or self-efficacy can greatly increase performance (McNatt, Campbell, & Hirschfeld, 2005). Organizations can theoretically do this in three ways: self-esteem workshops, experience with success, and supervisor behavior.

Self-Esteem Workshops

To increase self-esteem, employees can attend workshops or complete online trainings in which they are given insights into their strengths. It is thought that these insights raise self-esteem by showing employees that they have several strengths and are good people. For example, in one self-esteem training program, participants spend 10 days learning to sail on the *Spirit of New Zealand*. During the cruise, they not only learn how to sail, but engage in activities designed to provide opportunities for learning, teamwork, success, and positive reinforcement as well. Research indicates that compared to controls who did not to on the cruise, participants had significant increases in self-esteem; increases that were still present 12 months later (Hunter et al., 2013).

Outdoor experiential training (challenge courses) is another approach to increasing self-esteem. In training programs such as Outward Bound or the "ropes course," participants learn that they are emotionally and physically strong enough to be successful and to meet challenges. Meta-analysis results indicate that such programs increase both self-esteem and self-efficacy (Gillis & Speelman, 2008).

Experience with Success

Self-fulfilling prophecy The idea that people behave in ways consistent with their self-image.

Galatea effect When high self-expectations result in higher levels of performance.

With the experience-with-success approach, employees are given a task so easy that they will almost certainly succeed. It is thought that this success increases self-esteem, which should increase performance, which further increases self-esteem, which further increases performance, and so on. This method is based loosely on the principle of the **self-fulfilling prophecy**, which states that individuals will perform as well or as poorly as they expect to perform. In other words, if an individual believes they are intelligent, they should do well on tests. If they think they are not very intelligent, they should do poorly. So, if an employee believes they will always fail, the only way to break the vicious cycle is to ensure that they perform well on a task. This relationship between self-expectations and performance is called the **Galatea effect**.

Supervisor Behavior

Pygmalion effect The idea that if people believe that something is true, they will act in a manner consistent with that belief.

Golem effect When negative expectations of an individual cause a decrease in that individual's performance.

Another approach to increasing employee self-esteem is to train supervisors to communicate a feeling of confidence in an employee. The idea here is that if employees feel that a manager has confidence in them, their self-esteem will increase, as will their performance. Such a process is known as the **Pygmalion effect** and has been demonstrated in situations as varied as elementary school classrooms, the workplace, courtrooms, and the military (Rosenthal, 2002). The Pygmalion effect has been portrayed in several motion pictures, such as *My Fair Lady*, *Trading Places*, and *Ruby Sparks*. In contrast, the **Golem effect** occurs when negative expectations of an individual cause a decrease in that individual's actual performance (Babad, Inbar, & Rosenthal, 1982; Davidson & Eden, 2000). This effect often leads to a more overbearing management style, in which supervisors might assign an employee more routine tasks, or monitor the employee more frequently. Such actions convey a lack of trust and confidence on the supervisor's part, which in turn, lead to a decrease in motivation and job performance on the employee's part.

Two meta-analyses have shown that the Pygmalion effect greatly influences performance. The meta-analysis by McNatt (2000) found an overall effect size of 1.13, and the meta-analysis by Kierein and Gold (2001) found an overall effect size of 0.81. If you recall the discussion in Chapter 1, effect sizes of this magnitude are considered to be very large. The Pygmalion and Golem effects can be explained by the idea that our expectations of others' performance will lead us to treat them differently (Rosenthal, 1994). That is, if we think someone will do a poor job, we will probably treat that person in ways that bring about that result. If a supervisor thinks an employee is intrinsically motivated, they treat the employee in a less controlling way. The result of this treatment is that the employee actually becomes more intrinsically motivated (Pelletier & Vallerand, 1996). Thus, when employees become aware of others' expectations and matches their own expectations with them, they will perform in a manner that is consistent with those expectations (Oz & Eden, 1994; Tierney, 1998).

Though we know that the Pygmalion effect is true, efforts to teach supervisors to communicate positive expectations have not been successful. Based on seven field experiments, Eden and colleagues (2000) concluded that there was little support for the notion that teaching the "Pygmalion leadership style" would change the way supervisors treated their employees and thus increase employee self-esteem. Additionally, this effect has been shown to lack generalizability to women in supervisory roles, highlighting an important topic requires further investigation (White & Locke, 2000).

Given that consistency theory does have some reasonable research support, the next concern is how it can be used to increase employee performance. If employees do indeed respond to their managers' expectations, then it becomes reasonable to predict that managers who communicate positive and optimistic feelings to their employees will lead employees to perform at higher levels. A good example of such management behavior can be found in a study that increased the self-expectations of a group of auditors employed in four accounting firms (McNatt & Judge, 2004). Half of the new auditors (the experimental group) interviewed with a company representative who told them that they had been selected from a competitive applicant pool, praised them for being highly skilled, and reminded them of their previous accomplishments. The other half of the new auditors (the control group) did not receive this information. The results of the study indicated that the positive interview increased self-efficacy levels, motivation, and job performance, although the effect on performance went away after three months.

Intrinsic Motivation

Intrinsic motivation Work motivation in the absence of such external factors as pay, promotion, and coworkers.

When people are **intrinsically motivated**, they will seek to perform well because they either enjoy performing the actual tasks or enjoy the challenge of successfully completing the task. When they are extrinsically motivated, they may not necessarily enjoy the tasks but are motivated to perform well to receive some type of reward or to avoid negative consequences (Deci & Ryan, 1985). People who are intrinsically motivated don't need external rewards such as pay or praise. In fact, being paid for something they enjoy may reduce their satisfaction and intrinsic motivation (Deci, Koestner, & Ryan, 1999).

An interesting debate has formed between researchers who believe that rewards reduce intrinsic motivation and those who don't. A meta-analysis by Cameron, Banko, and Pierce (2001) added clarity to the debate by showing that the relationship between rewards and intrinsic motivation is complicated. In low interest tasks, rewards increase intrinsic motivation. In high interest tasks, verbal rewards positively affect intrinsic motivation but tangible rewards that are offered prior to performing the task negatively affect intrinsic motivation.

Individual orientations toward intrinsic and **extrinsic motivation** can be measured by the **Work Preference Inventory (WPI)** (Amabile, Hill, Hennessey, & Tighe, 1994). The WPI yields scores on two dimensions of intrinsic motivation (enjoyment, challenge) and two dimensions of extrinsic motivation (compensation, outward orientation).

9-2 Are Employees Effectively Involved in Self-Regulating Behavior?

As mentioned in the previous section, individuals differ greatly in their degree of general motivation and energy. Given whatever general level of motivation they have, what is the process by which individuals decide how they will direct their energy and effort? That is, why does one person choose to spend 12 hours a day at work while another person leaves work exactly when the clock hits five o'clock? Why does another person dedicate hours to community service whereas another spends their off-work time playing sports?

Most psychologists believe that the answer comes from the process of **self-regulation**: a person's ability to select, set, and modify goals to adapt to changing conditions. Self-regulation is a four-step process in which people

1. choose their goals and set levels for each goal;
2. plan how they will accomplish those goals;
3. take action toward accomplishing the goals (goal striving); and
4. evaluate progress toward goal attainment and either maintain, revise, or abandon a goal.

For example, suppose that an employee has a goal of completing a 100-page report in two weeks. If there are 10 working days in the two-week period, the employee might determine that they should complete 10 pages a day. After two days, the employee counts the number of pages written and compares it with where they thought they should be after two days (20 pages). If they have written only 10 pages, they have some choices to make. Should they change their goal to give themself more time to complete the report, or perhaps change the goal so that the report will be shorter? Should they change their behavior so that they quit working on other projects and concentrate only on the report? Should they work longer hours or get more help so they can complete the report in two weeks?

Though this example describes self-regulation of a specific task (writing a report), employees obviously have many goals, some of which are complex and some that might compete with other goals. For example, an employee might have goals of increasing their job knowledge (learning goal orientation), performing at a high level (performance goal orientation), making a lot of money, advancing within the organization, having a full social life, and spending quality time with the family. If the employee wanted to attend a weeklong seminar to increase their skills, would it come at the expense of their goals to perform at a high level and to spend time with their family? With multiple complex goals, self-regulation becomes more difficult, and employees must make a conscious effort to be aware of their goals, monitor their goal progress, and set priorities so that decisions can be made when encountering competing goals.

The extent to which an employee will be successful depends on the employee's ability to wisely select and set goals as well as their ability to monitor and adjust goals. In the following pages, we will discuss several theories that can influence an employee's self-regulation process.

9-3 Have the Employee's Values and Expectations Been Met?

The extent to which we might select a work goal and apply energy toward that goal is influenced by the discrepancy between what we *want*, *value*, and *expect* and what the job actually provides. For example, if you enjoy working with people but your job involves working with data, you are not likely to be motivated by or satisfied with your job. Likewise, if you value helping others, yet your job involves selling things people don't really need, you will probably not be motivated to perform well.

Potential discrepancies between what employees want and what the job gives them affect how motivated and satisfied employees will be with their jobs (Knoop, 1994). For example, imagine that Jane most values money and Akeem most values flexibility. Both are in jobs that pay well but have set hours and a standard routine. Though the job and the company are the same, one employee (Jane) will be motivated and the other (Akeem) will not be.

Because one's values often change over time, it is not surprising that an employee, who is motivated by their job one year, may not be so motivated in the next year. For example, an unmarried employee might value money and not mind working late hours at a high-paying job, but if they get married and start a family, their values might shift to their family and thus want a job in which they have a more structured schedule and allows them time to be with their family.

Job Expectations

A discrepancy between what an employee expected a job to be like and the reality of the job can affect motivation and satisfaction. For example, a recruiter tells an applicant how much fun employees have at a particular company and about the "unlimited potential" for advancement. After three months on the job, however, the employee has yet to experience the fun and can't find any signs of potential advancement opportunities. Because these expectations have not been met, the employee will probably feel unmotivated.

Employees compare what the organization promised to do for them (e.g., provide a computer, support continued education) with what the organization actually does. If the organization does less than it promised, employees will be less motivated to perform well and will retaliate by doing less than they promised (Morrison & Robinson, 1997). This relationship was explored further in a study that pinpointed work-related boredom as a factor in intrinsic motivation (Gkorezis & Kastritsi, 2017). If employee expectations about a new job are unmet, they will experience boredom on the job, which leads to a decline in intrinsic motivation.

As you can guess from these examples, it is important that applicants be given a **realistic job preview (RJP)** (a concept that you no doubt remember from Chapter 4). Though being honest about the negative aspects of a job may reduce the applicant pool, it decreases the chances of hiring a person who will later lose motivation or become dissatisfied.

A good example of this comes from an employee who works for a public mental health agency. Prior to accepting her current job, she had worked in the public sector for 10 years in a variety of administrative positions. She was excited about her new opportunity because it was a newly created position with what appeared to be an excellent opportunity for personal growth. After a year, however, it became clear that the position was clerical, had no opportunity for advancement, and the most important decision she could make involved whether to order pizza or sandwiches for executive meetings. To make matters worse, this aspiring professional was asked to shop for food to serve at meetings and then serve the food to the managers. As you can imagine, she was deeply disappointed and angry at having been misled. Because her role as a single parent did not allow her to quit her job, she vented her dissatisfaction by buying stale doughnuts for breakfast meetings, letting the coffee get cold, and "forgetting" to bring mayonnaise for her supervisor's sandwich—behaviors that could not get her fired but allowed her in a passive-aggressive manner to maintain some form of control in her work life.

Job Characteristics

According to **job characteristics theory**, employees desire jobs that are *meaningful*, provide them with the opportunity to be personally responsible for the outcome of their work (*autonomy*), and provide them with *feedback* of the results of their efforts (Hackman & Oldham, 1976). If there is a discrepancy between the extent to which a job provides these three outcomes and an employee's need for these outcomes, the employee will be less motivated.

According to job characteristics theory, jobs will have *motivation potential* if they allow employees to use a variety of skills (*skill variety*) and to connect their efforts to an outcome (*task identification*) that has meaning, is useful, or is appreciated by coworkers as well as by others in society (*task significance*). Take, for example, a job in which a factory worker stitches the company logo on shirts that were created by other workers and in which the quality of the shirts and the logo stitching are evaluated by employees in the quality control department. Because the job does not involve a variety of skills (lacks skill variety), someone else checks the quality of their work (no feedback, low task identification), putting logos on a shirt is probably not appreciated by society (low task significance), and the employee is closely supervised (low autonomy), the job would be considered to have low motivation potential. As shown in Table 9.3, meta-analysis results demonstrate that jobs with a high motivating potential score result in higher levels of employee satisfaction and performance, and lower levels of absenteeism (Fried & Ferris, 1987).

Age has surfaced as a complicated factor as well when considering the motivation potential of a job. Researchers have identified that older employees who have higher intrinsic motivation also have jobs with a higher motivating potential score (Boumans, De Jong, & Janssen, 2011). Younger employees, however, tend to have jobs with a higher motivating potential score when they view that their jobs offer more career growth.

Table 9.3 Results of the Fried and Ferris (1987) Meta-Analysis

Job Characteristic	Satisfaction	Performance	Absenteeism
Skill variety	.45	.09	−.24
Task identity	.26	.13	−.15
Task significance	.35	.14	.14
Autonomy	.48	.18	−.29
Job feedback	.43	.22	−.19
Motivating potential score	.63	.22	−.32

Source: Fried, Y., & Ferris, G. R. (1987). The validity of the job characteristics model: A review and meta-analysis. *Personnel Psychology*, 40, 287–322.

Needs, Values, and Wants

A discrepancy between an employee's needs, values, and wants and what a job offers can also lead to low levels of motivation and satisfaction (Morris & Campion, 2003). Three theories focus on employees' needs and values: Maslow's needs hierarchy, ERG (existence, relatedness, and growth) theory, and two-factor theory.

Maslow's Needs Hierarchy

Hierarchy A system arranged by rank.

Perhaps the most famous theory of motivation was developed by Abraham Maslow (1954, 1970). Maslow believed that employees would be motivated by and satisfied with their jobs at any given point in time if certain needs were met. As Table 9.4 shows, Maslow believed that there are five major types of needs and that these needs are hierarchical—that is, lower-level needs must be satisfied before an individual will be concerned with the next level of needs. It is helpful to look at a **hierarchy** as if it were a staircase that is climbed one step at a time until the top is reached. The same is true of Maslow's hierarchy. Each level is taken one step at a time, and a higher-level need cannot be reached until a lower-level need is satisfied. Maslow's five major needs are discussed next.

Basic biological needs The first step in Maslow's needs hierarchy, concerning survival needs for food, air, water, and the like.

Basic Biological Needs.   Maslow thought that an individual first seeks to satisfy **basic biological needs** for food, air, water, and shelter. In our case, an individual who does not have a job, is experiencing homelessness, and is on the verge of starvation will be satisfied with any job as long as it provides for these basic needs. When asked how well they enjoy their job, people at this level might reply, "I can't complain, it pays the bills."

Safety Needs.   After basic biological needs have been met, a job that merely provides food and shelter will no longer be satisfying. Employees then become concerned about

Table 9.4 Comparison of the Maslow, ERG, and Herzberg Theories

Maslow	ERG	Herzberg
Self-actualization	Growth	Motivators
Ego		
Social	Relatedness	
Safety	Existence	Hygiene factors
Physical		

Safety needs The second step in Maslow's hierarchy, concerning the need for security, stability, and physical safety.

meeting their **safety needs**. That is, they may work in an unsafe coal mine to earn enough money to ensure their family's survival, but once their family has food and shelter, they will remain satisfied with their jobs only if the workplace is safe.

Safety needs have been expanded to include psychological as well as physical safety. Psychological safety—often referred to as job security—can certainly affect job motivation. For example, public-sector employees often list job security as a main benefit to their jobs—a benefit so strong that they will stay in lower-paying public-sector jobs rather than take higher-paying less secure jobs in the private sector.

Social needs The third step in Maslow's hierarchy, concerning the need to interact with other people.

Employee resource groups A group of employees with similar interests, experiences, or demographics who meet to discuss those experiences.

Social Needs.   Once the first two need levels have been met, employees will remain motivated by their jobs only when their social needs have been met. **Social needs** involve working with others, developing friendships, and feeling needed. Organizations attempt to satisfy their employees' social needs in a variety of ways. Company cafeterias provide workers with a place and an opportunity to socialize and meet other employees, company picnics allow families to meet one another, **employee resource groups** allow employees with similar interests or experiences to meet and discuss those interests and experiences, and company sports programs such as bowling teams and softball games provide opportunities for employees to play together in a neutral environment.

It is important that an organization make a conscious effort to satisfy these social needs when a job itself does not encourage social activity. For example, janitors or night security officers encounter few other people while working. Thus, the chance of having their social needs met are small.

A good friend of mine worked in a large public agency before becoming a writer and working out of her home. Prior to working at home, she had seldom accepted invitations to attend parties or socialize. In her words, "Once I get home, I don't want to see another person." However, now that her only social contact during the day is a one-sided conversation with a neurotic dog, she socializes every chance she gets.

Ego needs The fourth step in Maslow's hierarchy, concerning the individual's need for recognition and success.

Ego Needs.   When social needs have been satisfied, employees concentrate next on meeting their **ego needs**. These are needs for recognition and success, and an organization can help to satisfy them through praise, awards, promotions, salary increases, publicity, and many other ways. For example, former *Tonight Show* host Johnny Carson once commented that the most prestigious sign at NBC was not the salary of the television star or producer, but rather whether the person had their own parking space. Likewise, many organizations use furniture to help satisfy ego needs. The higher the employee's position, the better the office furniture. Similarly, at one engineering firm in Louisville, Kentucky, engineers are not allowed to mount their diplomas or awards on the wall until they receive their professional certification. At the university where I worked, faculty, department chairs, deans, and vice presidents were given furniture that is "commensurate with their status." Perhaps this explains the card table and folding chairs in my office!

Self-actualization needs The fifth step in Maslow's hierarchy, concerning the need to realize one's potential.

Self-Actualization Needs.   Even when employees have friends, have earned awards, and are making a relatively high salary, they may not be completely motivated by their jobs because their **self-actualization needs** may not have been satisfied yet. These needs are the fifth and final level of Maslow's needs hierarchy (the top level in Table 9.4). Self-actualization might be best defined by the U.S. Army's former recruiting slogan "Be all that you can be." Employees striving for self-actualization want to reach their full potential in every task. Thus, employees who have worked with the same machine for 20 years may become dissatisfied with and less motivated by their jobs. They have accomplished all that can be accomplished with that particular machine and now search for a new challenge. If none is available, they may become dissatisfied and unmotivated.

With some jobs, satisfying self-actualization needs is easy. For example, a college professor always has new research to conduct, new classes to teach, and new clients to consult. Thus, the variety of tasks and the new problems encountered provide a constant challenge that can lead to higher motivation.

Other jobs, however, may not satisfy self-actualization needs. A good example is an employee who solders parts on an assembly line. For 8 hours a day, 40 hours a week, they perform only one task. Boredom and the realization that the job will never change begin to set in. It is no wonder that the employee becomes dissatisfied and loses motivation.

The Characteristics of Self-Actualization Scale (CSAS), developed by Kaufman (2018), demonstrated an association between high self-actualization scores and motivation by personal growth and exploration. The scale also predicted work-related outcomes such as job performance.

Evaluation of Maslow's Theory

Needs theory A theory based on the idea that employees will be satisfied with jobs that satisfy their needs.

Although Maslow's **needs theory** makes good intuitive sense and has always been popular with managers and marketing analysts, it lost popularity with academicians in the 1970s before making a resurgence in the new millennium (Latham & Pinder, 2005). The lack of popularity was due to three potential problems with the theory. The first concern was that Maslow's five levels may be too many, and that there are actually only two or three levels (Aldefer, 1972). However, some research (Ronen, 2001) suggests that five might actually be the correct number.

A second problem with the theory is that some people do not progress up the hierarchy as Maslow suggests they do. That is, most people move up from the basic biological needs level to safety needs to social needs and so on. Some people, however, have been known to skip levels. For example, bungee jumpers obviously skip the safety-needs level and go straight to satisfying their ego needs. Thus, when exceptions to the hierarchical structure occur, the theory loses support.

Another problem is that the theory predicts that once the needs at one level are satisfied, the next needs level should become most important. Research, however, has shown that this does not necessarily happen (Salancik & Pfeffer, 1977).

Even though Maslow's theory has not been supported by research, it may still be useful. Some of the theory's specific assertions may not be true, but it still provides guidelines that organizations can follow to increase motivation and satisfaction. Providing recognition, enrichment, and a safe workplace *does* increase employee motivation. The validity of this recommendation is probably why Maslow's theory still is widely used by human resources professionals, even though it is not popular with academicians and researchers who prefer more complicated models.

A situation at a major university provides an example of how Maslow's general principles can be used. After years of increasing enrollment and prestige, a scandal at the university caused a rapid decline in enrollment, financial backing, and staff morale. To fix these problems, a new president was hired. His first acts were to announce a "spirit day" each Friday on which employees could dress casually, an increased emphasis on diversity issues, and his intention to start a new sports team. Employee satisfaction and motivation continued to drop, faculty left in great numbers, and millions of dollars were cut from the budget. What went wrong? Among many things, the president's proposals were aimed at Maslow's level three and above, whereas the employees' needs were at level two—that is, "Will this university survive?" and "Will I still have a job next year?"

ERG Theory

ERG theory Aldefer's needs theory, which describes three levels of satisfaction: existence, relatedness, and growth.

Because of the technical problems with Maslow's hierarchy, Aldefer (1972) developed a needs theory that has only three levels. As shown in Table 9.4, the three levels are existence, relatedness, and growth—hence the name **ERG theory**.

Other than the number of levels, the major difference between Maslow's theory and ERG theory is that Aldefer suggested that a person can skip levels. By allowing for such movement, Aldefer has removed one of the biggest problems with Maslow's theory.

Furthermore, Aldefer's theory explains why a higher-level need sometimes does not become more important once a lower-level need has been satisfied. Aldefer believes that for jobs in many organizations, advancement to the next level is not possible because of such factors as company policy or the nature of the job. Thus, the path to the next level is blocked, and the employee becomes frustrated and places more importance on the previous level. Perhaps that is why some unions demand more money and benefits for their members rather than job enrichment. They realize that the jobs will always be tedious and that little can be done to improve them. Thus, the previous needs level becomes more important. This idea has received at least some empirical support (Hall & Nougaim, 1968; Salancik & Pfeffer, 1977).

Two-Factor Theory

Two-factor theory Herzberg's needs theory, postulating that there are two factors involved in job satisfaction: hygiene factors and motivators.

Hygiene factors In Herzberg's two-factor theory, job-related elements that result from but do not involve the job itself.

Motivators In Herzberg's two-factor theory, elements of a job that concern the actual duties performed by the employee.

As shown in Tables 9.4 and 9.5, Herzberg (1966) believed that job-related factors could be divided into two categories—hygiene factors and motivators—thus the name **two-factor theory**. **Hygiene factors** are those job-related elements that result from but do not involve the job itself. For example, pay and benefits are consequences of work but do not involve the work itself. Similarly, making new friends may result from going to work, but it is also not directly involved with the tasks and duties of the job.

Motivators are job elements that *do* concern actual tasks and duties. Examples of motivators would be the level of responsibility, the amount of job control, and the interest that the work holds for the employee. Herzberg believes that hygiene factors are necessary but not sufficient for job satisfaction and motivation. That is, if a hygiene factor is not present at an adequate level (e.g., the pay is too low), the employee will be dissatisfied and less motivated. But if all hygiene factors are represented adequately, the employee's level of satisfaction and motivation will only be neutral. Only the presence of both motivators and hygiene factors can bring job satisfaction and motivation.

Thus, an employee who is paid a lot of money but has no control or responsibility over their job will probably be neither motivated nor unmotivated. But an employee who is not paid enough *will* be unmotivated, even though they may have tremendous control and responsibility over their job. Finally, an employee who is paid well and has control and responsibility will probably be motivated.

Again, Herzberg's is one of those theories that makes sense but has not yet received strong research support. In general, researchers have criticized the theory because of the methods used to develop the two factors—the idea that factors such as pay can be both hygiene factors and motivators, and the fact that few independent research studies have replicated the findings obtained by Herzberg and his colleagues (Rynes, Gerhart, & Parks, 2005). For example, an empirical study conducted by Ewen, Smith, and Hulin (1966) was unable to find any evidence supporting the theory; however, Alfayad and Arif (2017) were able to confirm that a motivator (in this case, employee voice) lead to job satisfaction, and did not reduce job dissatisfaction. This study was conducted in the middle east and brings into question cultural connotations that may not be replicable

Table 9.5 Examples from Herzberg's Two-Factor Theory

Hygiene Factors	Motivators
Pay	Responsibility
Security	Growth
Coworkers	Challenge
Working conditions	Stimulation
Company policy	Independence
Work schedule	Variety
Supervisors	Achievement
	Control
	Interesting work

Need for achievement According to trait theory, the extent to which a person desires to be successful.

in other parts of the world. Nevertheless, while the latter study lends some support to the Herzberg Theory, further investigation is still needed.

Needs for Achievement, Affiliation, and Power

Need for affiliation The extent to which a person desires to be around other people.

Need for power According to trait theory, the extent to which a person desires to be in control of other people.

A theory developed by McClelland (1961) suggests that employees differ in the extent to which they are motivated by the need for achievement, affiliation, and power. Employees who have a strong **need for achievement** are motivated by jobs that are challenging and over which they have some control, whereas employees who have minimal achievement needs are more satisfied when jobs involve little challenge and have a high probability of success. In contrast, employees who have a strong **need for affiliation** are motivated by jobs in which they can work with and help other people. Finally, employees who have a strong **need for power** are motivated by a desire to influence others rather than simply to be successful.

9-4 Needs for Competency, Autonomy, and Relatedness

Self-determination theory A theory that postulates that people have an innate need for three things: competence, autonomy, and relatedness.

Competence The need from self-determination theory to be able to successfully perform the tasks that are important to us.

Self-determination theory was developed by Ryan and Deci (2000) and proposes that people have innate needs for three things: competency, autonomy, and relatedness. **Competency** is the need to feel that we have the ability to perform the tasks that are important to us. **Autonomy** is the need to have the freedom to make decisions about what we are going to do and how we are going to do it. **Relatedness** is the need to feel connected to others. Based on this theory, we are going to be most motivated by jobs in which we are confident that we can successfully perform the tasks, are given the freedom to make decisions, and allow us to feel that we are part of a group.

Drives to Acquire, Bond, Learn, and Defend

Similar to self-determination theory, the **Four Drive Theory of Human Nature** (Lawrence & Nohria, 2002) postulates that employees are influenced by four drives:

acquiring, bonding, learning, and defending. Employees will be motivated to perform well and remain in a job if each of these drives is met (Podmoroff, 2016). Lawrence and Nohia (2002) define these four drives as follows:

Drive to acquire: a drive to seek, take, control, and retain objects and personal experiences that humans value.

Drive to bond: a drive to form social relationships and develop mutual caring commitments with other humans.

Drive to learn: a drive to satisfy curiosity, to know, to comprehend, to appreciate, to develop understandings or representations of their environment and of themselves through a reflective process.

Drive to defend: a drive to defend themselves and their valued accomplishments whenever they perceive them to be endangered.

These four drives are innate and independent of one another: satisfying one drive will not satisfy the others. Based on this theory, if an organization can develop jobs, systems, and a culture that allows each of these drives to be met, it will have a motivated workforce.

9-5 Do Employees Have Achievable Goals?

Goal setting A method of increasing performance in which employees are given specific performance goals to aim for.

To increase motivation, goal setting should be used. With **goal setting**, each employee is given a goal such as increasing attendance, selling more products, or reducing the number of grammar errors in reports. The first goal-setting study that caught the interest of industrial psychologists was conducted by Latham and Blades (1975). Their study was brought about because truck drivers at a logging mill were not completely filling their trucks before making deliveries. Empty space in the trucks cost the company money. To increase each delivery's load, the drivers were given specific weight goals and were told that they would be neither punished nor rewarded for reaching the goal. A significant increase in the average load per delivery resulted. Although this is the most celebrated study, goal setting has been shown to be effective in a wide variety of situations.

For goal setting to be most successful, the goals themselves should possess certain qualities represented by the acronym SMART: specific, measurable, attainable, relevant, and time-bound (O'Farrell, 2020).

Specific

Properly set goals are concrete and specific (Locke & Latham, 2013). A goal such as "I will respond to as many emails as I can" will not be as effective as "I will respond to 15 emails in the next hour." The more specific the goal, the greater the productivity. To underscore this point, we will use an example involving pushups. If a person says they will do as many pushups as they can, does that mean they will do as many as they can until they tire? As many as they can before they begin to sweat? As many as they did the last time? The problem with such a goal is its ambiguity and lack of specific guidelines.

Though setting specific goals makes sense, it is not always easy to do. Microsoft found that nearly 25% of the goals set by employees as part of their performance plans were not specific (Shaw, 2004). The results of focus groups investigating this lack of specificity found that employees believed that with a constantly changing environment, it was difficult to set specific goals because the goals would need constant adjustment.

Measurable

Properly set goals are measurable. That is, if one's goal is to improve performance or increase customer service, can performance or customer service be measured? The purpose of setting goals is to identify a specific target to reach. If the target cannot be specified, then there would be little use in setting goals. In the Microsoft study mentioned in the previous paragraph, only 40% of the goals set by employees were measurable (Shaw, 2004).

Difficult but Attainable

Properly set goals are high but attainable. If a restaurant employee regularly washes 300 plates an hour and sets a goal of 250 plates, performance is certainly not going to increase. Conversely, if the goal becomes 1,000 plates, it will also not be effective because the employee will quickly realize that they cannot meet the goal and will become demotivated, or might even quit trying.

A good example of goals set too high comes from the academic retention program at one university. This program is designed to help special students who are having academic trouble and whose grade point averages (GPAs) have fallen below the minimum needed to stay in school. The program involves tutoring, study skills, and goal setting. Although it has generally been a success, many students have failed to improve their academic performance. A brief investigation revealed that the goal-setting process was one of the reasons for these failures. Students were allowed to set their own GPA goals for the semester—and students with GPAs of 1.0 were setting goals of 4.0! Obviously, few of the students were able to reach this goal. The problem typically came when students did poorly on their first test and lost their chance for an A in the class, and thus had no chance of making a 4.0 GPA for the semester. Because their goals could not be attained, the students felt they had failed and quit trying.

Though setting higher goals generally leads to better performance than does setting lower goals, the level of goal difficulty will most affect the performance when employees are committed to reaching the goal (Klein, Wesson, Hollenbeck, & Alge, 1999; Locke & Latham, 2013). For example, if a police chief sets a high goal for a police officer to write traffic citations, the officer will not increase the number of citations they write unless they are committed to the goal. That is, if they believe they can accomplish the goal, agree that the goal is worthwhile, and will be rewarded for achieving the goal, their commitment to achieve the goal is likely to be high.

Interestingly, setting goals that are too difficult to be accomplished can result not only in decreased performance, but in an increase in unethical behavior as well. When employees feel pressure to reach a goal that they realize can't be met, they at times will engage in unethical behaviors in attempts to reach the goal or to "cook the books" (i.e., falsify records) to make it look as if the goals have been met (Schweitzer, Ordóñez, & Douma, 2004).

Not surprisingly, people differ in the extent to which they set high goals. Optimists tend to set higher goals than do pessimists (Ladd, Jagacinski, & Stolzenberg, 1997). In the Big 5 schema, people scoring high in conscientiousness, extraversion, and openness and low in agreeableness and neuroticism also tend to set high goals (Judge & Ilies, 2002).

Relevant

Properly set goals are also relevant. Setting a goal about increasing public speaking skills will not be as motivating to a person working in a landfill as it would be to a police officer who often testifies in court.

Time-Bound

Goals work best when there is a time frame for their completion. For example, a goal to clean one's office would be more motivating if the goal included a date by which the office would be cleaned.

Employee Participation

Until recently, it was generally thought that a goal would lead to the greatest increase in productivity if it was set at least in part by the employee. That is, although performance would increase if the supervisor set the employee's goal, it would increase even more if the employee participated. However, several meta-analyses have indicated that participating in goal setting does not increase performance (Mento, Steel, & Karren, 1987; Tubbs, 1986; Zetik & Stuhlmacher, 2002). However, a meta-analysis indicates that employee participation in goal setting increases the commitment to reaching a goal (Klein et al., 1999).

9-6 Are Employees Receiving Feedback on Their Goal Progress?

To increase the effectiveness of goal setting, feedback should be provided to employees on their progress in reaching their goals (Locke & Latham, 2002; Stajkovic & Luthans, 2003). Feedback is so important that in one survey, 24% of employees said that ineffective feedback is a reason that they would change jobs (Yoh, 2018). Unfortunately, a survey by Officevibe found that 28% of employees reported that they didn't receive enough feedback to help them improve their performance (St. Aubin, 2020). Feedback can include verbally telling employees how they are doing, placing a chart on a wall, or using nonverbal communication such as smiles, glares, and pats on the back. Feedback best increases performance when it is positive and informational rather than negative and controlling (Zhou, 1998). To encourage employees to ask for feedback, supervisors should indicate their willingness to provide feedback and then reinforce employees who seek it (Williams, Miller, Steelman, & Levy, 1999).

Feedback is constructive when it is given positively with the goal of encouraging and reinforcing positive behavior. For feedback to be effective, it must be given when employees do things properly, not just when they make mistakes. It is also received more positively when given immediately and frequently (Kuvaas, Buch, & Dysvik, 2017). Some tips for providing effective feedback can be found in the Career Workshop Box.

9-7 Are Employees Rewarded for Achieving Goals?

An essential strategy for motivating employees is to provide an incentive for employees to accomplish the goals set by an organization. As a result, organizations offer incentives for a wide variety of employee behaviors, including working overtime or on weekends, making suggestions, referring applicants, staying with the company (length-of-service awards), coming to work (attendance bonuses), not getting into accidents,

During your career there will be many times when you need to provide feedback to coworkers, subordinates, and others. Here are some tips for providing effective feedback:

- Ensure that you are delivering this feedback in private.
- Identify the employee's behavior and focus on it rather than on the employee's personality. For example, if an employee is often late for work, a supervisor might say, "In the past two weeks, you have been late five times" rather than "We are having a problem with your lack of responsibility and commitment to your job."
- Explain how the behavior is impacting others. For example, "When you arrive to work ten minutes late, customers become angry because there is no one to help them with their purchases. When other employees cover the register for you, it causes them to get behind on their work, resulting in their missing part of their lunch break or being forced to work overtime."
- Ask the employee for suggestions on how the behavior can be changed. If the employee has none to offer, the

supervisor can provide some. A sample conversation might go something like this:

Employee: I know I shouldn't be missing work, but I'm so tired in the morning and often don't hear the alarm.

Supervisor: Can you think of things you can do so that you will not be so tired in the morning?

Employee: I could go to bed earlier, but I love to watch Jimmy Fallon and then Sports Center on ESPN.

Supervisor: Could you try watching the early edition of Sports Center and record the Jimmy Fallon show so that you can watch it when you get home from work?

Employee: I guess I could give that a try.

- After arriving at a solution, the supervisor and the employee should then set a specific goal. For example, they could agree that the employee will be on time every day for the next week.

After an agreed-upon time, the supervisor and the employee should meet to see if the goal has been met and to set new goals.

Operant conditioning A type of learning based on the idea that humans learn to behave in ways that will result in favorable outcomes and learn not to behave in ways that result in unfavorable outcomes.

and performing at a high level. The basis for these incentive systems are **operant conditioning** principles, which state that employees will engage in behaviors for which they are rewarded and avoid behaviors for which they are punished. Thus, if employees are rewarded for not making errors, they are more likely to produce high-quality work. If employees are rewarded for work done, they will place less emphasis on quality and try to increase their quantity. Finally, if employees are not rewarded for any behavior, they will search for behaviors that will be rewarded. Unfortunately, these might include absenteeism (which is rewarded by going fishing) or carelessness (which is rewarded by spending more time with friends).

Research and applied literature abound with studies demonstrating the effectiveness of reinforcement. For example:

- Slowiak (2014) used a combination of task clarification, goal setting, feedback, and rewards at a medical clinic to achieve a 38% increase in customer service employees using a proper greeting and a 22% increase in their using a friendly tone.
- Myers, McSween, Medina, Rost, and Alvero (2010) used a combination of employee involvement, feedback, and recognition to reduce injuries in a petroleum refinery by 81%.
- Austin, Kessler, Riccobono, and Bailey (1996) provided daily feedback and weekly monetary reinforcement to employees in a roofing crew. This intervention resulted in a 64% labor cost reduction and an 80% improvement in safety.

- Kortick and O'Brien (1996) devised the "World Series of Quality Control" at a package delivery company in New York. The 104 employees were divided into 13 teams of 8 employees each and competed against one another to have the best shipping accuracy and quantity. Performance information and team standings were posted each week, with the winning team receiving pizzas. At the end of each month, the winning received individual plaques and dinner at a local restaurant. The intervention resulted in promising increases in shipping accuracy.

Though the research is clear that rewarding employees will often lead to increased motivation and performance, six factors must be considered in determining the effectiveness of incentive programs:

1. Timing of the incentive
2. Contingency of the consequences
3. Type of incentive used
4. Use of individual-based versus group-based incentives
5. Use of positive incentives (rewards) versus negative incentives (punishment)
6. Fairness of the reward system (equity)

Timing of the Incentive

Research indicates that a *reinforcer* or a *punisher* is most effective if it occurs soon after the performance of the behavior. Unfortunately, if the timing of the incentive is too long, the effectiveness of the incentive to improve performance will be hindered. For example, a restaurant employee learning how to wait on tables performs many behaviors while serving a customer. A tip is usually left by the customer after the meal, which provides immediate feedback about the employee's performance. However, if the tip is small, the employee is not sure which particular behavior caused the customer's displeasure. Likewise, if the tip is large, the employee is unsure which particular behavior or behaviors initiated the large tip. Thus, the timing of the consequence by itself may not be enough.

Contingency of Consequences

If it is not possible to immediately reward or punish a behavior, it should at least be made clear that the employee understands the behaviors that brought reward or punishment. To return to our example of the restaurant server, if they are told the reason for the size of their tip, they will be better able to change their behavior. Have you ever given a restaurant server a large tip even though the service was terrible? Most of us have. When this happens, however, the server is reinforced for poor performance and has no incentive to improve unless poor performance has its own consequence. In a similar fashion, if the server has done an outstanding job but has received a small tip, the probability of their repeating their outstanding performance is reduced. Furthermore, when tips are pooled at restaurants so that each employee gets a share of all tips received, an individual employee's rewards are not as contingent on their own behavior as when tips are not pooled.

The point of these examples is that reward and punishment must be made contingent upon performance, and this contingency of consequence must be clear to employees if we want them to be motivated (Podsakoff, Bommer, Podsakoff, & MacKenzie, 2006).

If the reward or punishment cannot be administered immediately, the employee must be told the purpose of the consequence so that the link between behavior and outcome is clear.

Type of Incentive Used

Obviously, it is important to reward employees for productive work behavior. But, as you learned in the discussion of Maslow's hierarchy, different employees have different values, which is why supervisors should have access to and be trained to administer different types of reinforcers. For example, some employees can be rewarded with praise, others with awards, others with interesting work, and still others with money. In fact, a meta-analysis by Stajkovic and Luthans (1997) found that financial, nonfinancial, and social rewards all resulted in increased levels of performance. It is important to conduct periodic employee surveys about what employees want because supervisors and employees often have different ideas about what is rewarding and important (Babcock, 2005).

A good example of the use of a variety of incentives can be found at La Porte Hospital. As part of their award-winning "Caught You Caring" program, La Porte uses public recognition, gift certificates, small gifts, and a variety of other awards to reward employees who engage in excellent patient care. This use of rewards is one of the reasons that La Porte has a turnover rate of only 4% in an industry that has an 18% national turnover rate (Renk, 2004).

The need for variety in rewards is also true of punishment. Threatening an employee with a three-day suspension will be effective only if they need the money or don't like being off work; yelling at an employee will be effective only if the employee does not like being yelled at; and threatening to not promote an employee will be effective only if the employee values promotions and perceives they have a reasonable chance of getting one.

Premack Principle

Premack Principle The idea that reinforcement is relative both within an individual and between individuals.

Reinforcement hierarchy A rank-ordered list of reinforcers for an individual.

An interesting method of providing incentives that meet the individual needs of each employee stems from the **Premack Principle** (Premack, 1963), which states that reinforcement is relative and that a supervisor can reinforce an employee with something that on the surface does not appear to be a reinforcer. The best way to explain this principle is to construct a **reinforcement hierarchy** on which an employee lists their preferences for a variety of reinforcers.

As Figure 9.1 shows, our hypothetical employee most desires money and time off from work and least desires typesetting and cleaning the press. Our employee can enjoy and do a better job of cleaning the press if we give them money for each time they properly complete the task, but such a reward system can become expensive. Thus, according to the Premack Principle, we can get our employee to clean their press properly by allowing them to do one of the activities they like more than cleaning. From their reinforcement hierarchy, we can see that they rank throwing out oily rags as more enjoyable because they can take a short break by walking outdoors to the disposal area. Thus, all we need for a reward is to let them dispose of the rags.

The Premack Principle may sound silly; but think of the reinforcers you have used to reward yourself for studying. After reading a certain number of pages, you might allow yourself a trip to the water fountain. Certainly, getting a drink of water is hardly anyone's idea of a good time, but it may be more interesting than studying and so can become a reinforcer to increase studying.

Figure 9.1
Premack Principle

When I was in high school, I worked at a printing plant that produced stock reports. All entry-level employees were "collators," whose job was to place 500 copies of a book page on a piece of wood strapped to their necks and then walk around a room placing a piece of paper in each of the 500 slots. This process was repeated about 300 times until a complete book was put together. As you can imagine, the job was extremely boring. To motivate us, our supervisor would "reward" the fastest collators by allowing them to take out the trash, to go pick up lunch (it was kind of cool ordering 100 Whoppers and 100 fries and watching the Burger King employees' expressions), or to move the paper carts from one end of the building to the other. I didn't realize until 10 years later that my boss was using the Premack Principle—rewarding performance of a very boring task by allowing us to perform a less boring task.

As another example, my previous boss (the department chair) was a master at using the Premack Principle. Because salary raises are small in size and never a certainty, it is difficult to motivate faculty to do the "little things" by offering financial rewards. Instead, my boss rewarded good departmental citizenship by giving the best faculty their most desired schedule, their favorite classes, and their favorite committee assignments. From what I have seen, these reinforcers work better than money!

Of course, my boss was successful in using the Premack Principle because he had a good sense of every faculty member's reinforcement hierarchy. For example, I hate serving on committees, whereas a colleague of mine gets her entire self-worth by chairing department and university committees. So, my boss reinforced my colleague by putting her on committees and reinforced me by giving me some data to play with. Likewise, some faculty love early morning classes, whereas others would rather teach at night.

In an example from the research literature, Welsh, Bernstein, and Luthans (1992) demonstrated the effectiveness of the Premack Principle with employees at a fast-food restaurant. Employees whose errors decreased in a given day were rewarded by being allowed to work at their favorite workstation (e.g., cooking fries versus flipping burgers). This use of the Premack Principle resulted in a decrease in employee errors.

Financial Rewards

Financial incentives can be used to motivate better worker performance either by making variable pay an integral part of an employee's compensation package or by using financial rewards as a "bonus" for accomplishing certain goals. As shown in Figure 9.2, a compensation plan should include base pay and a benefits package to provide employees with security; salary adjustments to cover such conditions as

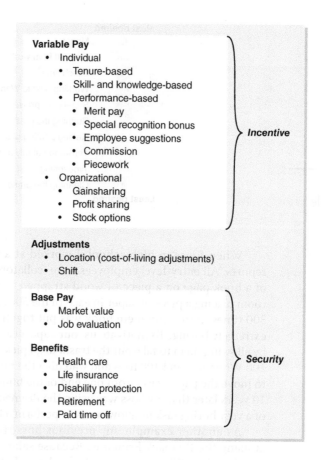

Figure 9.2
Compensation Plan

undesirable shifts and geographic areas with high costs of living; and variable pay to provide an incentive to perform better. Though incentive systems often result in higher levels of performance, when designed poorly they can result in such negative outcomes as increased stress and decreased performance.

Financial incentives in the form of bonuses or prizes are also used to motivate employees. For example, fast-food restaurants Chick-fil-A and McDonald's have scholarship programs for their employees; Banker Steel in Lynchburg, Virginia, provides productivity bonuses; and Abuelo's, the Mexican-food restaurant chain, gives "reward pesos" to employees who demonstrate "Xtraordinary" performance. These "pesos" can be exchanged for merchandise from the company store.

Recognition

Rather than providing financial incentives, many organizations reward employee behavior through recognition programs. Successful recognition programs are genuine, spontaneous, personal, specific, timely, and public (Podmoroff, 2016). For example:

- United Airlines holds a special ceremony each year in which employees are given service emblems for each year of service.
- Norton Healthcare created the "N Recognition of You" program to recognize its employees for a wide range of behaviors ranging from performance on a given day to performance on a long-term project. Employees can send N-cards

or N-buttons to thank or compliment another employee. Over 100,000 N-cards, N-buttons, or award nominations are sent each year.

- Supermarket chain Dierbergs in St. Louis has initiated a program called Extra Step, which recognizes employees who meet customers' needs. Over a five-year period, the Extra Step program resulted in a decline in turnover from 47% to 25%.
- Organizations such as Best Buy, Kohl's, and Helen Keller Hospital give employees of the month a personal parking space.

In some organizations, recognition awards are given by peers. For example, employees at the Angus Barn Restaurant in Raleigh, North Carolina, choose peers to receive the "People's Choice" award, employees at Oakland Mercy Hospital in Nebraska vote for the Staff Member of the Year, and at Fairmont Hotels and Resorts, employees give employee-of-the-month awards to their peers.

Informal recognition programs, called **social recognition**, can prove to be tremendous sources of employee motivation. Social recognition consists of personal attention, signs of approval (e.g., smiles, head nods), and expressions of appreciation (Stajkovic & Luthans, 2001).

Social recognition A motivation technique using such methods as personal attention, signs of approval, and expressions of appreciation.

Travel

Many organizations are offering travel awards rather than financial rewards. For example, every executive at McDonald's is allowed to nominate high-performing employees for a chance to spend a week in one of the company's condos in Hawaii, Florida, or Lake Tahoe, Nevada. At Effective Environmental, five employees each year are awarded an all-inclusive family vacation. At Chick-fil-A, sales teams compete for a vacation in Hawaii. At Motorola, managers can nominate employees for travel awards. In an unusual application of using travel as a reward, candy manufacturer Just Born promised its sales force a trip to Hawaii if they increased company sales by 4% and a January trip to Fargo, North Dakota, if they didn't reach their goal.

Individual Versus Group Incentives

Incentives can be given for either individual performance or group performance.

Individual Incentive Plans

Individual incentive plans are designed to make high levels of individual performance financially worthwhile, and the research is clear that monetary incentives increase performance over the use of a guaranteed hourly salary (Bucklin & Dickinson, 2001). Individual incentives help reduce such group problems as social loafing, which is discussed in Chapter 13. There are three main problems associated with individual incentive plans. The first is the difficulty in measuring individual performance. Not only are objective measures difficult to find, but supervisors are reluctant to evaluate employees, especially when the outcome determines the amount of money an employee will receive (Schuster & Zingheim, 1992).

The second problem is that individual incentive plans can foster competition among employees. Though competition is not always bad, it is seldom consistent with the recent trend toward a team approach to work, and can lead to a negative workplace environment. When done right, however, team environments and individual incentive programs can coexist and result in high levels of employee performance (Steers & Porter, 1991). The third

Pay for performance A system in which employees are paid on the basis of how much they individually produce.

Merit pay An incentive plan in which employees receive pay bonuses based on performance appraisal scores.

problem is that for an incentive plan to effectively motivate employees, it is essential that employees understand the incentive system. Surprisingly, only 40% of employees report that they understand how their pay is determined (Grensing-Pophal, 2003).

The two most common individual incentive plans are **pay for performance** and **merit pay**.

Pay for Performance. Also called *earnings-at-risk* (EAR) plans, pay-for-performance plans pay employees according to how much they individually produce. Simple pay-for-performance systems with which you are probably familiar include commission (being paid for each unit of something sold) and piecework (being paid for each unit of something produced).

The first step in creating more complicated pay-for-performance plans is to determine the average or standard amount of production. For example, the average number of envelopes sorted by mail clerks might be 300 per hour. The next step is to determine the desired average amount of pay. We might decide that on average, our mail clerks should earn $12 an hour. We then compute the piece rate by dividing hourly wage by the number of envelopes sorted (12/300), which is .04. Thus, each correctly sorted envelope is worth 4 cents. If a mail clerk is good and sorts 400 envelopes per hour, they will make $16 per hour. If our clerk is not a good worker and can sort only 200 pieces per hour, they will make $8 per hour. To protect workers from the effects of external factors, minimum-wage laws ensure that even the worst employee will make enough money to survive. As suggested in Figure 9.2, most organizations provide a base salary to ensure that employees will have at least minimal financial security. In fact, research indicates that employees paid a flat hourly rate plus a performance bonus perform at levels equal to employees who are paid on a piece-rate plan (Dickinson & Gillette, 1993).

A good example of such a plan comes from the Superior Court Records Management Center in Phoenix, Arizona (Huish, 1997). After conducting a study that showed a negative correlation between employee salary and productivity ($r = -.49$), the clerk of the court decided to try a pay-for-performance system. Each employee was given a base salary of $7.20 per hour and, based on the quantity and quality of their work, could earn incentive pay. This pay-for-performance intervention resulted in an average increase in employee pay of $2.60 per hour, a reduction in cost per unit (a unit was a court document page transferred to microfilm) from 39 cents to 21 cents, and a decreased need for storage space.

Tharaldson Enterprises in Fargo, North Dakota, changed its compensation system for the housekeepers employed in its 300 hotels. Rather than being paid by the hour, the housekeepers were paid by the number of rooms they cleaned. This change saved the company $2 million per year and resulted in the housekeepers making more money and working fewer hours than under the old hourly rate system (Tulgan, 2001).

Union National Bank in Little Rock, Arkansas, has had tremendous success by paying its workers for the number of customers they serve, the number of new customers gained, the amount of time taken to balance accounts at the end of the day, and so on. The bank's pay-for-performance program has resulted in the average employee making 25% more in take-home pay, and the bank itself has almost doubled its profits.

Though pay-for-performance plans appear to be successful for both the employee and the employer, some research suggests that employees are not satisfied with such plans (Brown & Huber, 1992). Interestingly, research has also found that for employees with values that are not aligned with an organization, a pay-for-performance plan also disincentivizes organizational citizenship behaviors, or behaviors that go above and beyond what an employee has been tasked with (Deckop, Mangel, & Cirka, 1999).

Merit Pay. The major distinction between *merit pay* and *pay for performance* is that merit pay systems base their incentives on performance appraisal scores rather than on such objective performance measures as sales and productivity. Thus, merit pay is a potentially good technique for jobs in which productivity is difficult to measure.

The actual link between performance appraisal scores and the amount of merit pay received by an employee varies greatly around the United States. In the merit pay system used by one nonprofit mental health agency, each employee's performance appraisal rating is divided by the total number of performance points possible, and this percentage is then multiplied by the maximum 3% merit increase that can be received by an employee. With this system, an employee must receive a perfect rating to receive the full 3% increase. Most employees receive between 2% and 2.5%.

The merit pay system used by a California public transit system is similar to that used by the mental health agency, with the exception that the merit increase becomes part of an employee's base salary for the next pay period. Thus, increases are perpetuated each year, unlike the mental health system's one-time reward. In Bismarck, North Dakota, a computer program uses employee self-ratings (25%), peer ratings (25%), and supervisor ratings (50%) to calculate an employee's merit pay. Bismarck does not award cost-of-living or automatic annual increases (also called *step increases*).

Research on merit pay has brought mixed reviews. Some research has shown that employees like the idea of merit pay, but other research has found that it is not popular with all employees and that many do not consider the merit ratings to be fair (Siegall & Worth, 2001). Not surprisingly, employees are most satisfied with merit pay if they help develop the system (Gilchrist & White, 1990).

One of merit pay's biggest problems is that increases are based on subjective performance appraisals. Aware of this, some supervisors will inflate performance appraisal scores to increase their employees' pay and thus increase the positive feelings of employees toward their supervisors. Managers have also been known to inflate performance appraisal ratings when they believe the base salaries for certain positions are too low.

Another problem with merit pay is that its availability or amount often changes with each fiscal year. Thus, excellent performance one year might result in a large bonus, but the same performance another year might bring no bonus at all. This is especially true in the public sector. For merit pay to be successful, funding must be consistently available, and the amount must be great enough (about 7%) to motivate employees (Bhakta & Nagy, 2005; Heneman & Coyne, 2007).

Group Incentive Plans

The idea behind group-based, or organization-based, incentive plans is to get employees to participate in the success or failure of the organization. Rather than encouraging individual competition, these plans reward employees for reaching group goals. The problems with group incentive plans are that they can encourage social loafing and can get so complicated that they become difficult to explain to employees. Despite these potential problems, meta-analysis results indicate that team-based incentive programs result in better performance ($d = 1.40$) than do individual-based programs ($d = .55$, Condly, Clark, & Stolovitch, 2003).

Profit sharing A group incentive method in which employees get a percentage of the profits made by an organization.

Profit Sharing. Profit sharing was developed in the United States by Albert Gallatin way back in 1794 (Henderson, 2006). As its name implies, profit-sharing programs provide employees with a percentage of *profits* above a certain amount. For example, in addition to their base salary, employees might receive 50% of the profits a company makes above 6%. Organizations will usually not share the initial 5% or so of profits, as that money is needed for research and development and as a safety net for unprofitable years. The profits to be shared can be paid directly to employees as a bonus (cash plans) or placed into the employees' retirement fund (deferred plans). Profit sharing will motivate employees only if they understand the link between performance and profits and believe that the company has a reasonable chance of making a profit. Research indicates that profit sharing results in greater employee commitment (Fitzgibbons, 1997; Bayo-Moriones & Larraza-Kintana, 2009).

Gainsharing A group incentive system in which employees are paid a bonus based on improvements in group productivity.

Gainsharing. **Gainsharing** ties groupwide financial incentives to *improvements* (gains) in organizational performance. Though the first gainsharing program was developed back in 1935 by the Nunn-Bush Shoe Company in Milwaukee, gainsharing has become popular only since the 1970s (Gowen, 1990). Gainsharing programs consist of three important elements: a cooperative/participative management philosophy, incentives based on improvement, and a group-based bonus formula (Gomez-Mejia, Welbourne, & Wiseman, 2000; Hanlon & Taylor, 1992).

Baseline The level of productivity before the implementation of a gainsharing plan.

The typical gainsharing program works as follows. First, the company monitors performance measures over some period of time to derive a **baseline**. Then productivity goals above the baseline are set, and the employees are told that they will receive bonuses for each period that the goal is reached. To make goal setting more effective, constant feedback is provided to employees on how current performance is in relation to the goal. At the end of each reporting period, bonuses are paid on the basis of how well the group did.

An excellent example of a successful gainsharing program can be found at the Dana Corporation Spicer Heavy Axle Division facility in Ohio. Employees at the Dana plant receive a financial bonus when productivity surpasses the baseline. The gainsharing program has dramatically increased the number of employee suggestions, product quality, and productivity. Employees' bonuses average 14% above their normal pay each month, with year-end bonuses between 11% and 16%.

As another example, Southern California Edison employees agreed to surrender 5% of their base pay. In return, they were given the opportunity to earn 10% to 15% of their base pay in a gainsharing plan. In one year alone, this plan generated $96 million in savings—$40 million of which was passed on to the employees.

In general, gainsharing plans seem to be effective. A review of gainsharing studies indicates improvements in productivity, increased employee and union satisfaction, and declines in absenteeism (Gowen, 1990). As with any incentive plan, gainsharing is most effective when employees are formally involved in the design and operation (Bullock & Tubbs, 1990) when there is not a long delay between performance and the financial payoff (Mawhinney & Gowen, 1990), transparency between the organization and employees is maintained, and the goal of the plan is in line with the organization's goals (Roy & Dugal, 2005).

Stock options A group incentive method in which employees are given the option of buying stock in the future at the price of the stock when the options were granted.

Stock Options. Although **stock options** represent the most complicated organizational incentive plan, a 2019 WorldatWork survey indicates they are offered to private sector employees by more than 19% of companies. With stock options, employees are given the opportunity to purchase stock in the future, typically at the market price on the day the options were granted. Stock options usually vest over a certain period of time and must be exercised within a maximum time frame. The idea is that as a company does well, the value of its stock increases, as does the employee's profit. For example, suppose AT&T stock is selling for $55 per share on June 1, and the company gives employees the option of purchasing the stock for $55 per share anytime in the next 10 years. Ten years later, the stock is worth $75 per share and the employee can purchase the stock for the $55 per share option price-a $20 per share profit. However, if the stock had fallen from $55 to $45, the employee would not exercise their option to purchase the stock at $55 per share.

Stock options allow employees to share in the long-term success of an organization. In fact, such organizations as GTE, United Airlines, Home Depot, and Foldcraft Company report not only that their employees are making good money through their stock ownership, but also that organizational productivity has improved as well. At times, stock options may not be good motivators because employees have trouble understanding the concept of stock and because the incentive (profit made on the selling of stock) is psychologically well removed from day-to-day performance. However, having partial ownership in a company can increase performance. For example, in a study of hotel managers, Qian (1996) found a significant correlation between the amount of manager ownership and the hotel's profit margin.

Expectancy Theory

An influential theory of worker motivation that integrates many of the factors discussed previously in this chapter is **expectancy theory**, which was first proposed by Vroom (1964) and then modified by others, including Porter and Lawler (1968). This theory has three components, the definitions of which vary with each modification of the theory. The following definitions are combinations of those suggested by others and make the theory easier to understand:

- **Expectancy (E):** The perceived relationship between the amount of effort an employee puts in and the resulting outcome.
- **Instrumentality (I):** The extent to which the outcome of a worker's performance, if noticed, results in a particular consequence.
- **Valence (V):** The extent to which an employee values a particular consequence.

To understand or predict an employee's level of motivation, these components are used in the following formula:

$$\text{Motivation} = E(I \times V)$$

Thus, all possible outcomes of a behavior are determined, the valence of each is multiplied by the probability that it occurs at a particular performance level, and then the sum of these products is multiplied by the expectancy of an employee putting in the effort to attain the necessary level of performance. As can be seen from this formula, the higher the score on each component, the greater the employee's motivation. To expound on this, let us examine each component in more detail.

In terms of *expectancy*, if employees believe that no matter how hard they work they will never reach the necessary level of performance, then their motivation will probably be low. For *instrumentality*, employees will be motivated only if their behavior results in some specific consequence. That is, if the employees work extra hours, they expect to be rewarded, or if they are inexcusably absent from work, they expect to be punished. For a behavior to have a desired consequence, two events must occur. First, the employee's behavior must be noticed. If employees believe they are able to attain the necessary level of performance but that their performance will not be noticed, then their level of motivation will be low. Second, noticed behavior must be rewarded. If no rewards are available, then, again, motivation will be low. As discussed earlier in this chapter, if appropriate behavior does not have positive consequences or if inappropriate

Expectancy theory Vroom's theory that motivation is a function of expectancy, instrumentality, and valence.

Instrumentality In expectancy theory, the perceived probability that a particular level of performance will result in a particular consequence.

Valence In expectancy theory, the perceived desirability of a consequence that results from a particular level of performance.

behavior does not have negative consequences, the probability that a worker will continue undesired behaviors increases, and the probability that an employee will continue desired behaviors decreases.

For *valence*, if an employee is rewarded, the reward must be something they value. If good performance is rewarded by an award, then the employee will be motivated only if they value awards. Likewise, if we punish an employee by suspending them, the punishment will be effective only if the employee needs the money. If they do not particularly like their job and would rather spend a few days at the lake, the suspension will obviously not be effective. In an applied study, Fox, Scott, and Donohue (1993) found that in a pay-for-performance environment, pay served as an incentive only for employees with a high monetary valence. This theory can be used to analyze the situation experienced by one bank in Virginia. Concerned that the bank's tellers were averaging only three new Visa card customers each month, the management sought to increase the number of Visa card applications taken by each teller. Tellers were expected to ask each customer if they had a Visa card. If not, the teller was to give the customer an application. A teller would receive $5 extra per month if they increased the number of new Visa customers per month to 25.

The program was a flop, much to management's surprise. Applying expectancy theory, however, would have led an industrial/organizational psychologist to predict the program's lack of success. First, let us look at the expectancy component. If the tellers currently averaged only three new Visa card customers each month, they probably did not believe that even working hard, they would be able to generate 25 new customers. Thus, the expectancy probability for the program was low.

Second, most tellers probably did not place much value on an extra $5 per month, so the valence component also was low. Thus, with two of three components having low values, the program was destined to fail from the start. The bank later reduced the monthly number of new Visa cards to 10 and increased the teller reward to $20. These simple changes brought about the desired increase in new Visa card customers.

In addition to predicting employee effort, expectancy theory has been applied successfully to predict speeding by drivers and cheating by students. To demonstrate this last behavior, imagine the typical examination in a typical college class.

First, look at the expectancy component. We might ask what the probability is for catching a cheater. Students who cheat most likely believe that it is very low. To determine the instrumentality component, we might ask what the probability is for some negative consequence if a cheater is caught. In many universities, this probability is low. Not only is it difficult to prove that a student cheated, but if it is the first time a student is caught, punishment usually results in no more than a few days' suspension.

Finally, we examine the valence component. Even if a student *was* caught and suspended, how terrible would that be? For many students, a few days of vacation may not seem so terrible. Thus, when combining the three components, we should not be surprised that cheating often occurs.

Expectancy theory can also be used to suggest ways to change employee motivation. As we saw with the bank, motivation was increased by making the performance standard more reasonable and by increasing the value of the consequence. Similarly, if we wanted to apply the theory to decrease cheating, we would increase the probability of catching cheaters, make convicting a person who has cheated easier, and make the consequences for cheating more severe.

Although expectancy theory is an interesting and useful method of predicting and increasing employee motivation, some researchers have criticized it. The major criticism involves the components equation. As it is now written, all of the components are multiplied. Some researchers have suggested that perhaps the addition of some components would be more appropriate than their multiplication (Schmidt, 1973). This is because when the components are multiplied, a zero in any component results in a prediction of zero motivation, even when ratings in the other components are high.

A second criticism involves the values assigned to each component (Ilgen, Nebeker, & Pritchard, 1981). Research has indicated that even though valence and instrumentality can be reliably measured (Mitchell, 1974), the theory is most predictive when people behave rationally (Stahl & Harrell, 1981), which they often do not, and have an **internal locus of control** (Lied & Pritchard, 1976), which may not always be the case. Despite problems with the equation, however, the theory is still one of the most useful for predicting employee behavior.

Internal locus of control The extent to which people believe that they are responsible for and in control of their success or failure in life.

Reward Versus Punishment

Rather than rewarding desired behaviors, we can change employee performance by punishing undesired behaviors. That is, instead of rewarding employees who do not miss work, we punish those who do. Instead of providing monetary incentives for high levels of performance, we suspend employees for low levels of performance. Though many psychologists advise against punishment, it is common, and managers generally believe it to be effective (Butterfield, Trevino, & Ball, 1996).

Proponents of using punishment to change employee behavior argue that if applied properly, punishment not only reduces undesired behaviors in a particular employee but also sets an example for other employees. Opponents of punishment argue that punishment changes behavior only in the short run, does not teach an employee appropriate behaviors, and causes resentment. Furthermore, punishment causes employees to learn new methods to break rules, rather than teaching them not to break rules. A meta-analysis comparing the reward and punishment behaviors of leaders found that although both reward and punishment behaviors affect employee behavior and attitudes, the magnitude of the effect is stronger for rewards (Podsakoff, Bommer, Podsakoff, & MacKenzie, 2006).

For punishment to be effective, an employee must understand why they are being punished and be shown alternative ways of behaving that will result in some type of desired reinforcement. The punishment must also "fit the crime" in that too severe a punishment will cause resentment and too lenient a punishment will not motivate a change in behavior. As one would imagine, punishment should usually be done in private rather than in front of other employees. Supervisors should also be aware of the effect a punishment might have on an employee's self-worth, and might consider having employees participate in self-restorative activities to maintain their self-worth (Wiesenfeld, Brockner, & Martin, 1999).

9-8 Are Rewards and Resources Given Equitably?

Equity theory A theory of job satisfaction stating that employees will be satisfied if their ratio of effort to reward is similar to that of other employees.

Another factor related to motivation and job satisfaction is the extent to which employees perceive that they are being treated fairly. The first theory on this topic was equity theory (Adams, 1965). **Equity theory** is based on the premise that our levels of motivation and job satisfaction are related to how fairly we believe we are treated in comparison with others. If we believe we are treated unfairly, we attempt to change our beliefs or behaviors until the situation appears to be fair. Three components are involved in this perception of fairness: inputs, outputs, and input/output ratio.

Inputs In equity theory, the elements that employees put into their jobs.

Outputs In equity theory, what employees get from their jobs.

Input/output ratio The ratio of how much employees believe they put into their jobs to how much they believe they get from their jobs.

Inputs are those personal elements that we put into our jobs. Obvious elements are time, effort, education, and experience. Less obvious elements include money spent on childcare and distance driven to work.

Outputs are those elements that we receive from our jobs. A list of obvious outputs includes pay, benefits, challenge, and responsibility. Less obvious outputs are benefits such as friends and office furnishings.

According to the theory, employees subconsciously list all their outputs and inputs and then compute an **input/output ratio** by dividing output value by input value. By itself, this ratio is not especially useful. But employees then compute the input/output ratios for other employees and for previous work experiences and compare them with their own. For example, imagine that Brad is paid $80,000 as a nurse at County General Hospital. He works 40 hours each week, mostly in the evening and on weekends. He is considered to be one of the most skilled nurses at the hospital and, as a result, is often assigned to the most difficult patients. He has 15 years of nursing experience. Tom is also a nurse at County General making $80,000 a year. He works 9:00 a.m. to 5:00 p.m. and has 10 years of nursing experience. When comparing inputs and outputs, Brad would realize that he receives the same outputs as Tom, but has more inputs (worse schedule, more years of experience); thus, his ratio would be lower than Tom's. So, what will Brad do? According to equity theory, when an employee's ratio is lower than those of others, they will become dissatisfied and be motivated to make the ratios equal in one or more ways.

First, employees can seek greater outputs by such means as asking for a raise or for more responsibility. Second, employees can make the ratio more equal by reducing their inputs. Thus, they might not work as hard or might reduce their attendance.

A less practical way of equalizing the ratios would be to change the ratios of other employees. For example, employees might try to get another employee to work harder and thus increase that employee's inputs. Or they might try to reduce the outputs of another employee by withholding friendship or finding a way to reduce the other employee's bonuses. Fortunately, however, strategies to equalize input/output ratios seldom involve reducing others' outputs. Employees can also restore equity by rationalizing the input/output ratio differences, changing the person with whom they are comparing themselves, or leaving the organization.

In general, research has supported the idea that our motivation decreases when our input/output ratios are lower than others' (Feight, Ferguson, Rodriguez, & Simmons, 2006). For example, research on major league baseball players (Hauenstein & Lord, 1989; Lord & Hohenfeld, 1979) found that players who either had their salary cut during their first year of free agency or lost an arbitration case performed at lower levels the following year. Thus, the players who thought that their *output* (salary) was too low, responded by reducing their *inputs* (performance). In a study of professional basketball players, Harder (1992) found that overpaid players responded by being more team oriented (e.g., passing the ball, rebounding), whereas underpaid players responded by being more selfish (e.g., taking shots).

In an interesting study, O'Reilly and Puffer (1989) found that employees' motivation increased when coworkers received appropriate sanctions for their behavior. That is, when a high-performing group member was rewarded or a poor-performing group member was punished, the satisfaction and motivation of the group increased.

The degree of inequity that an employee feels when underpaid appears to be a function of whether the employee chose the actions that resulted in underpayment (Cropanzano & Folger, 1989). That is, if an employee chooses to work harder than others who are paid the same, they will not feel cheated, but if they are pressured into working harder for the same pay, they will be unhappy.

An interesting prediction from this theory is a situation in which an employee's input/output ratio is *higher* than the ratio of others. Because the theory is based on equity, the prediction would be that the employee would still strive for equal ratios by either increasing their inputs or decreasing their outputs. In other words, the employee would either work harder or ask to be paid less. In fact, research has indicated that employees often do respond to being "overpaid" by feeling guilty (Lapidus & Pinkerton, 1995) or working harder (Adams & Rosenbaum, 1962; Pritchard, Dunnette, & Jorgenson, 1972). But feelings of inequity caused by being "overpaid" do not last long and probably do not produce long-term changes in behavior (Carrell & Dittrich, 1978).

Though equity theory has some theoretical problems, it was the springboard for modern research in **organizational justice**. Though this topic will be discussed in greater detail in Chapter 10, the idea behind organizational justice is that if employees are treated fairly, they will be more satisfied and motivated. Whereas equity theory was limited to work outcomes such as pay and promotions, organizational justice theory has focused on the fairness of many aspects of work such as the *process* of how decisions are made (procedural justice), the *outcomes* of the decisions (distributive justice), and the ways in which decisions and other information are *communicated* to employees (interactional justice). Table 9.6 summarizes the findings of equity theory research.

Organizational justice A theory that postulates that if employees perceive they are being treated fairly, they will be more likely to be satisfied with their jobs and motivated to do well.

9-9 Are Other Employees Motivated?

Employees observe the levels of motivation and satisfaction of other employees and then model those levels. Thus, if an organization's older employees work hard and talk positively about their jobs and their employer, new employees will model this behavior and be both productive and satisfied. The reverse is also true: If veteran employees work slowly and complain about their jobs, so too will new employees. The importance

Table 9.6   Equity Theory Research

When an employee's inputs are greater than their outputs (underpayment), they
▪ work less hard (Hauenstein & Lord, 1989)
▪ become more selfish (Harder, 1992)
▪ have lower job satisfaction (Carr, McLoughlin, Hodgson, & MacLachlan, 1996; Griffeth & Gaertner, 2001)

When an employee's outputs are greater than their inputs (overpayment), they
▪ are less likely to be persuaded by his underpaid peers (Stewart & Moore, 1992)
▪ do not feel guilty (Lapidus & Pinkerton, 1995)
▪ work harder (Adams & Rosenbaum, 1962; Pritchard, Dunnette, & Jorgenson, 1972)
▪ become more team oriented (Harder, 1992)

of this type of modeling was demonstrated in a study of 187 employees that found that employees who observed other employees engage in antisocial behavior began to act in a similar fashion (Robinson & O'Leary-Kelly, 1998).

9-10 Integration of Motivation Theories

As shown in Figure 9.3, people come to a job with a predisposition toward motivation. That is, some people, such as those with high self-esteem, are generally more motivated than others. In this chapter, we discussed many theories of work motivation. Let's review what we have learned:

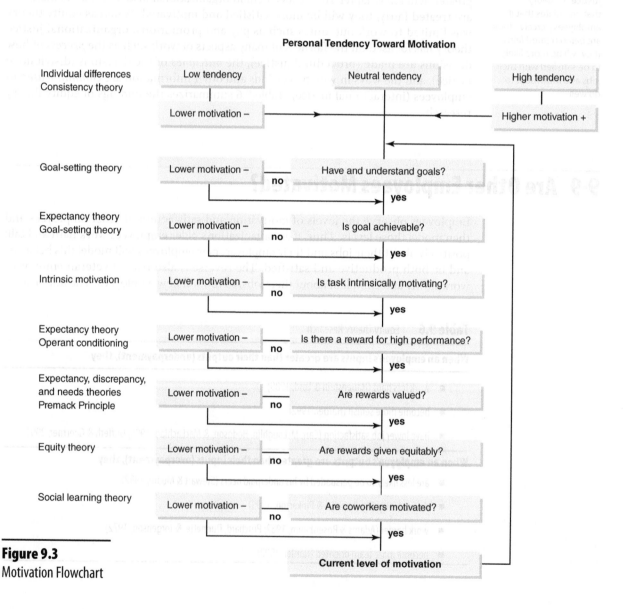

Figure 9.3
Motivation Flowchart

- From the discrepancy and needs theories, we will be motivated in our jobs if the job itself and the organization meet our expectations and values and satisfy our needs.
- From goal-setting theory, we find that employees who have, understand, and agree to goals will be more motivated than those without goals or with unclear goals.
- From expectancy theory and goal-setting theory, we know that the goals must be challenging but reasonable.
- From operant learning and expectancy theories, it is clear that extrinsically motivated people will be more motivated if behavior results in a reward.
- From these same two theories plus discrepancy theory, the needs theories, and the Premack Principle, we know that the rewards must have value to the employee to be motivating. Because different people value different rewards, care must be taken to ensure that a variety of rewards are available and that the rewards are aligned with what the employees value.
- From equity theory, we know that rewards that are valued will be motivating only if they are given in an equitable way. As discussed previously in the chapter, *perceptions* of equity are as important as the *reality* of equity.
- Social influence theory tells us that if other employees are motivated, there is an increased probability that we will model their behavior and be motivated.

On the Job ▶ Applied Case Study

Faster Service at Taco Bueno Restaurants

Taco Bueno is a fast-casual Mexican-food restaurant chain. It opened its first restaurant in 1967 in Abilene, Texas, and now has over 185 locations throughout Texas, Oklahoma, Nebraska, Missouri, Louisiana, Kansas, Indiana, New Mexico, and Arkansas. Taco Bueno emphasizes fresh quality food, affordable prices, and fast service times. Rather than bringing in prepared food, items such as salsa, guacamole, and seasoned beef are prepared fresh at each location, a policy that increases the food preparation time but results in higher-quality food. Menu items include burritos, tacos, muchacos, nachos, tostadas, quesadillas, and salads. Customers can order food inside the restaurant or through the drive-thru lane. Both cash and credit cards are accepted.

Five principles constitute the "Bueno Way":

- Integrity: We base our actions and words on the highest level of honesty.
- Customer focus: We strive to deliver 100% guest satisfaction.

- Teamwork: We act as one, encourage communication, and respect diversity.
- Accountability: We see it, own it, and take charge!
- Spirit: We have fun, celebrate victories, and share our success.

The goal of the restaurant is to get the orders to the customers within 60 seconds of their pulling up to the cashier. To meet or better this goal, Taco Bueno wanted to improve the time spent taking and completing orders in the drive-thru lanes at its 185 + restaurant locations. The restaurant's reasoning is that fast delivery speeds not only increase the average number of cars that can be served in an hour, but also reduces the number of people who might not patronize the restaurant if they see long, slow-moving lines.

Taking into consideration what you learned in this chapter on motivation, how would you motivate employees to improve the drive-thru speed at Taco Bueno? .

In 2001, a Hooters chain in Panama City Beach, Florida, came up with the idea of having a beer-selling contest to motivate its servers to sell as much beer as possible in the month of April. The top-selling waitress from each Hooters in the area had her name entered into a drawing. The waitress whose name was drawn would win the prize. Based on what the managers at each Hooters told their staff, the competing waitresses thought they would be winning a new Toyota automobile. The competition was a success: Most of the Hooters in the area seemed to have increased their sales of beer.

Jodee Berry was the winning waitress. On the day she was told she was the winner, she was blindfolded and led to the restaurant parking lot. However, instead of receiving a new Toyota car, she was presented with a Yoda doll. Inside the restaurant, the manager and other staff were laughing.

Ms. Berry didn't think it was so funny. She worked hard to win this contest. Her motivation level was high because of the thought of winning a Toyota, not a *toy Yoda*. So, she sued Gulf Coast Wings, Inc., owners of the restaurant, alleging breach of contract and fraudulent misrepresentation. She was seeking as compensation the cost of a new Toyota *car*. The case was settled out of court for an undisclosed amount.

As you read in this chapter, organizations come up with creative ways to try to motivate employees to work harder, work safer, or to cut costs. But the question is: Should there be any limits on the type of motivator that is used? Is it okay to use any motivational strategy just as long as it has the desired results?

Another example of creative motivation is the one employed by a manager of one corporation who bought 10 golden bonsai trees and held a "Save a Tree" competition. Each month, the 10 lowest users of paper would receive one of the bonsai trees, which could be displayed for the coming month. It did the trick! Employees were motivated to save paper. Apparently, the bonsai tree had a certain appeal to these employees. Everyone wanted one!

In another company, the motivator for working harder was a nice steak dinner at a nice restaurant; the losers of the competition also got to go to the restaurant, but they had to sit at a lousy table and eat beans. After dinner, the winners got to rip the shirts off the back of the losers! This type of motivator, like the Hooters and "Save a Tree" competitions, was also successful. It did what it set out to do: increase sales for the department.

A professor at a small college motivates his students by promising $100 to the student who makes the highest test grade. If more than one student has the same grade, they split the $100 between them. There are three tests per semester. So, theoretically, a student could end the semester $300 richer! Another professor at a different college offers gift cards to various stores and restaurants to the top classroom performers. The thinking behind these motivators is that it will encourage students to study harder.

Proponents of such motivation techniques say that competition increases motivation, which leads to desired results. Critics say that these types of competition are unethical because they pit employee against employee, encourage cheating or unsafe shortcuts, and can often lead to bullying and the use of fear tactics by some employees against others as a form of intimidating them into losing the competition. They also say that it rewards people for using bad behavior to achieve a goal set by the company. It doesn't motivate them to do better at their job. And finally, it treats people differently and unfairly.

What Do You Think?

- Although there were some legal ramifications for what Hooter's did, do you think what they did to the waitress was also unethical?

- Do you think that the waitresses were lied to? If so, do you think lying to employees is unethical?

- What do you think about the motivating strategy of allowing employees to rip off the shirts of other employees? Is humiliating employees ethical?

- Is it ethical to promise money or other monetary compensation to students for studying hard? What if the losing students actually studied harder than the winner, but the winner only did well because they just happened to be brighter? Would giving that student the money be fair to the students who studied hard but didn't do as well as the winner?

- Does the fact that these motivation techniques had the desired result by increasing sales or decreasing the use of paper outweigh any negative consequences of such motivators?

The results of these factors are summed to indicate an employee's current level of motivation. As conditions change, so will the motivation level.

Chapter Summary

In this chapter you learned:

- Employees who have high self-esteem, a high need for achievement, and intrinsic motivation and who are expected to perform well by others are more motivated than their counterparts with low self-esteem and low achievement need who are extrinsically motivated.
- Goals are most effective if they are concrete and specific, are of high but reasonable difficulty, and are set with the input of the employee.
- Providing feedback on goal attainment and performance levels will increase performance.
- Operant conditioning principles can be used to motivate employees.
- It is important to treat employees fairly.
- Common individual incentive plans include pay for performance and merit pay.
- Common organizational incentive plans include profit sharing, gainsharing, and stock options.

Key Terms

Motivation (315)
Organizational citizenship behaviors (OCBs) (317)
Self-esteem (317)
Consistency theory (317)
Chronic self-esteem (318)
Situational self-esteem (318)
Socially influenced self-esteem (318)
Organization-based self-esteem (318)
Self-fulfilling prophecy (319)
Galatea effect (319)
Pygmalion effect (319)
Golem effect (319)
Intrinsic motivation (320)
Extrinsic motivation (321)
Work Preference Inventory (WPI) (321)
Self-regulation (321)
Realistic job preview (RJP) (323)
Job characteristics theory (323)
Hierarchy (324)
Basic biological needs (324)
Safety needs (325)
Social needs (325)
Employee resource groups (325)
Ego needs (325)
Self-actualization needs (325)
Needs theory (326)
ERG theory (327)
Two-factor theory (327)

Hygiene factors (327)
Motivators (327)
Need for achievement (328)
Need for affiliation (328)
Need for power (328)
Self-determination theory (328)
Competence (328)
Autonomy (329)
Relatedness (329)
Goal setting (329)
Operant conditioning (332)
Premack Principle (334)
Reinforcement hierarchy (334)
Social recognition (337)
Pay for performance (338)
Merit pay (338)
Profit sharing (339)
Gainsharing (340)
Baseline (340)
Stock options (340)
Expectancy theory (341)
Instrumentality (341)
Valence (341)
Internal locus of control (343)
Equity theory (343)
Inputs (344)
Outputs (344)
Input/output ratio (344)
Organizational justice (345)

Questions for Review

1. Does getting paid for a task that one enjoys performing reduce intrinsic motivation? Why or why not?
2. If the right techniques are used, can everyone be motivated to perform well? Why do you think that?
3. Which of the individual incentive plans is most effective? Why?
4. Which of the theories in the chapter would be most useful for managers? Why?
5. Is the threat of punishment an effective motivator? Why or why not?

Chapter

10

Employee Satisfaction and Commitment

Learning Objectives

Imagine the following situations:

- Jean Davis and Maria McDuffie have worked as customer service representatives at Fuller Technologies for the past two years. Jean loves her job and wants to stay with Fuller until she retires in 10 years. Maria hates her job, uses all her available sick days, and would leave in a heartbeat if she could only find a job that paid as well.

- Rhonda Beall recently met with a career adviser to chart a new course for her life. She hates her current job and has hated every job she has ever had. She is hoping that the career adviser can find "*the* job" for her.
- David Chan loves his job and can't wait to get to work in the morning. He loves to work, loves his current job, and has loved every job he has ever had.
- Darnell Washington, human resources (HR) director for Simmons Enterprises, is frustrated because his company has the highest turnover rate in the area. Even more frustrating is that employees stay with Simmons just long enough to gain experience and then leave for lower pay with Raynes Manufacturing, another local employer.

Job satisfaction The attitude employees have toward their jobs.

Organizational commitment The extent to which an employee identifies with and is involved with an organization.

Why does Jean Davis love her job and Maria McDuffie hate the same job? Why do Rhonda Beall and David Chan have such different attitudes about their jobs and careers? What is Raynes Manufacturing doing better than Simmons Enterprises? This chapter will help you answer these questions about **job satisfaction**—the attitude an employee has toward her job—and **organizational commitment**—the extent to which an employee identifies with and is involved with an organization.

10-1 Why Should We Care About Employee Attitudes?

Many job-related attitudes have been studied by psychologists, but the two most studied are job satisfaction and organizational commitment. Though job satisfaction and organizational commitment are different work-related attitudes, they will be discussed together in this chapter because they are highly correlated and result in similar employee behaviors. As shown in Table 10.1, meta-analyses indicate that satisfied employees tend to be committed to an organization (Cooper-Hakim & Viswesvaran, 2005), and employees who are satisfied and committed are more likely to attend work (Hackett, 1989), stay with an organization (Griffeth, Hom, & Gaertner, 2000), arrive at work on time (Koslowsky, Sagie, Krausz, & Singer, 1997), perform well (Judge, Thoresen, Bono, & Patton, 2001), engage in behaviors helpful to the organization (LePine, Erez, & Johnson, 2002), not behave in counterproductive ways (Dalal, 2005), and engage in ethical behavior (Kish-Gephart, Harrison, & Treviño, 2010) than are employees who are not satisfied or committed. Job satisfaction is also positively related to physical and mental health (Faragher, Cass, & Cooper, 2005).

The relationship between job satisfaction and performance is not consistent across people or jobs. For example, for complex jobs, there is a stronger relationship between job satisfaction and performance than for jobs of low or medium complexity (Judge et al., 2001). For employees who have strong, consistent beliefs about their level of job satisfaction (called *affective-cognitive consistency*), the relationship between job satisfaction and performance is much stronger than it is for employees whose job satisfaction attitudes are not so well developed (Schleicher, Watt, & Greguras, 2004).

Though the relationships between job satisfaction and organizational commitment and attendance, performance, tardiness, and turnover are not as large as one would expect, it is important to note that there are many other factors affecting work behavior (Judge et al., 2001). For example, a dissatisfied employee may want to quit their job but cannot because no other jobs are available. Likewise, a dissatisfied employee may want to miss work but realizes that they will lose pay if they do. Thus, we often find that job satisfaction and organizational commitment are related more to a *desire* to quit, miss work, or reduce effort than they are to actual behaviors.

Table 10.1 Meta-Analysis Results of the Relationships Among Job Satisfaction, Performance, Turnover, Commitment, and Absenteeism

	Performance	Turnover	Absenteeism Frequency	Absenteeism Duration	Commitment Organizational	Commitment Occupational	Intrinsic Motivation	Lateness	Job Satisfaction	Job Involvement	Counterproductive Behavior
Job Satisfaction											
Facet											
Pay	.05[f]	−.17[f]	.08[c]	−.07[c]	.34[l]	.23[e]	.29[j]	−.22[k]		.09[n]	
Supervision	.19[a]	−.13[f]	−.13[c]	−.08[c]	.45[l]		.39[j]			.22[n]	
Coworkers	.12[a]	−.13[f]	−.07[c]	−.07[c]		.23[e]		−.16[k]		.17[n]	
Work	.21[a]		−.21[c]	−.14[c]		.53[e]				.42[n]	
Promotion	.15[a]		−.09[c]	−.07[c]						.19[n]	
Type											
Intrinsic	.23[a]		−.25[c]	−.01[c]							
Extrinsic	.18[a]		−.24[c]	−.21[c]							
Overall satisfaction	.30[d]	−.28[w]	−.15[c]	−.23[c]	.59[m]	.44[e]	.59[j]	−.11[k]		.37[n]	−.37[o]
Turnover											
Intent to leave	−.12[s]	.56[w]			−.57[m]	−.62[e]		.46[k]		−.10[n]	
Occupation		.45[l]				−.30[e]				−.24[n]	
Organization											
Actual turnover	−.19[f]	.26[w]			−.29[w]	−.21[e]		.07[k]	−.22[f]		
Absenteeism	−.29[g]	.14[w]			−.23[b]		−.25[c]	.26[v]			
Lateness	−.21[k]	.01[v]			−.29[q]				−.11[k]		
Tardiness											
Performance		.21[w]			.17[m]				.30[d]	.07[n]	
Supervisor ratings			−.32[g]	−.26[g]						.07[n]	
Performance measures			−.22[g]	−.28[g]				−.21[k]		.04[n]	
Job involvement					.42[n]						
Organizational citizenship behavior	.60[b]	−.13[b]	−.13[b]		.25[p]				.24[l]		−.32[b]
Ethical behavior									.23[a]		
Counterproductive behavior					−.36[o]				−.37[o]		

[a]Iaffaldano & Muchinsky (1985); [b]Podsakoff, Whiting, Podsakoff, & Blume (2009) (2006); [c]Hackett (1989); [d]Judge, Thoresen, Bono, & Patton (2001); [e]Lee, Carswell, & Allen (2000); [f]Griffeth, Hom, & Gaertner (2000); [g]Bycio (1992); [h]Farrell & Stamm (1988); [i]Mathieu & Zajac (1990); [j]Oldham, Hackman, & Stepina (1978); [k]Koslowsky, Sagie, Krausz, & Singer (1997); [l]LePine, Erez, & Johnson (2002); [m]Cooper-Hakim & Viswesvaran (2005); [n]Brown (1996); [o]Dalal (2005); [p]Riketta (2002); [q]Tubré & Collins (2000); [r]Abramis (1994); [s]Darnold and Zimmerman (2006); [t]Williams, McDaniel, and Nguyen (2006); [u]Kish-Gephart, Harrison, & Trevino (2010); [v]Berry, Lelchook, & Clark (2012); [w]Rubenstein et al. (2018).

10-2 What Causes Employees to Be Satisfied with and Committed to Their Jobs?

This chapter will explore several theories that seek to explain why workers are satisfied with and committed to their jobs, but none of the theories completely explains these job-related attitudes. Each is valuable, however, because it suggests ways to increase employee satisfaction and commitment. Thus, even though a theory itself may not be completely supported by research, the resulting suggestions have generally led to increased performance or longer tenure.

Before discussing various theories, it is important to note that both work-related attitudes are multifaceted. That is, employees may be satisfied with one facet of work (e.g., their pay) but not another (e.g., their coworkers). The most studied facets of job satisfaction are pay, supervision, coworkers, work, and promotion opportunities. Many other facets such as satisfaction with equipment, the work facility, the worksite, and company policy are also important but have not received as much research attention.

Affective commitment The extent to which an employee wants to remain with an organization and cares about the organization.

It is thought that there are three motivational facets to organizational commitment (Meyer & Allen, 1997). **Affective commitment** is the extent to which an employee wants to remain with the organization, cares about the organization, and is willing to exert effort on its behalf. For example, an employee of the Red Cross might like their coworkers and their boss, share the altruistic goals of the organization, and realize that their efforts will result in better organizational performance.

Continuance commitment The extent to which employees believe they must remain with an organization due to the time, expense, and effort they have already put into the organization.

Continuance commitment is the extent to which an employee believes they must remain with the organization due to the time, expense, and effort that they have already put into it or the difficulty they would have in finding another job. Take, for example, a chamber of commerce director who spent 10 years making business contacts, getting funding for a new building, and earning the trust of the local city council. Though they could take a new job with a chamber in a different city, they would need to spend another 10 years with that chamber just to make the gains they have already made. As another example, an employee might hate their job and want to leave but realizes that no other organization would hire them or give them the salary they desire.

Normative commitment The extent to which employees feel an obligation to remain with an organization.

Normative commitment is the extent to which an employee feels obligated to the organization and, because of this obligation, must remain with the organization. A good example of normative commitment would be an employee who was given their first job by an organization, was mentored by their manager, and was trained at great cost to the organization. The employee may feel that they are ethically obligated to remain with the organization because of its extensive investment in them.

Research on the three facets of organizational commitment has found that affective commitment enhances organizational effectiveness the most, and a subcomponent of continuance commitment (low perceived alternatives) is detrimental to organizational effectiveness (Iverson & Buttigieg, 1999).

What Individual Differences Affect Job Satisfaction?

As shown in Figure 10.1, one of the factors (called *antecedents*) that influence levels of job satisfaction and commitment is our personal predisposition to be satisfied. Going back to our examples at the beginning of the chapter, what would explain why David Chan loves his current job and Rhonda Beall hates hers? According to theories involving individual differences, the key to the answer is the fact that David has been satisfied at every job he has had, whereas Rhonda has never been satisfied with a job.

Figure 10.1
Antecedents and
Consequences of
Job Satisfaction
and Organizational
Commitment

Individual difference theory postulates that some variability in job satisfaction is due to an individual's personal tendency across situations to enjoy what they do. Thus, certain types of people will generally be satisfied and motivated regardless of whatever job they hold. This idea also makes intuitive sense. We all know people who constantly complain and whine about every job they have, and we also know people who are motivated and enthusiastic about their every job or task.

For individual-difference theory to be true, it would be essential that job satisfaction be consistent across time and situations. Research seems to support this notion, as meta-analysis results indicate that the average correlation between job satisfaction levels, measured an average of three years apart, is .50 (Dormann & Zapf, 2001).

Because there seems to be at least some consistency in job satisfaction across time and jobs, the next question concerns the types of people that seem to be consistently satisfied with their jobs. Research in this area has focused on genetic predispositions (Lykken & Tellegen, 1996), core self-evaluations (Judge, Locke, Durham, & Kluger, 1998), and life satisfaction (Tait, Padgett, & Baldwin, 1989).

Genetic Predispositions

An interesting and controversial set of studies (Arvey, Bouchard, Segal, & Abraham, 1989; Arvey, McCall, Bouchard, Taubman, & Cavanaugh, 1994; Keller, Bouchard, Arvey, Segal, & Dawis, 1992) suggests that job satisfaction not only may be fairly stable across jobs but also may in part be genetically determined. Arvey and his colleagues arrived at this conclusion by comparing the levels of job satisfaction of 34 sets of identical twins who were separated from each other at an early age. If job satisfaction is purely environmental, there should be no significant correlation between levels of job satisfaction for identical twins who were raised in different environments and who are now working at different types of jobs. But if identical twins have similar levels of job satisfaction despite being reared apart and despite working at dissimilar jobs, then a genetic predisposition for job satisfaction is likely.

Based on their three studies, Arvey and his colleagues found that approximately 30% of job satisfaction appears to be explainable by genetic factors. Such a finding does not of course mean that there is a "job satisfaction gene." Instead, inherited personality traits such as negative affectivity (the tendency to have negative emotions such as fear, hostility, and anger) are related to our tendency to be satisfied with jobs (Ilies & Judge, 2003). Genetic factors play a more important role in job satisfaction earlier in life: Li,

Stanek, Zhang, Ones, and McGue (2016) found that genetics accounted for 31% of job satisfaction at age 21 but only 20% at age 30.

What are the implications of these findings? It may be that some people will probably not be satisfied with any job, and supervisors should not lose sleep over the fact that these employees are not happy or motivated. Furthermore, one way to increase the overall level of job satisfaction in an organization would be to hire only those applicants who show high levels of overall job and life satisfaction. Because these findings are controversial and have received some criticism (Cropanzano & James, 1990), more research is needed before firm conclusions can be drawn.

Core Self-Evaluations

Whether the consistency in job satisfaction is due to genetic or environmental factors, a series of personality variables appear to be related to job satisfaction. That is, certain types of personalities are associated with the tendency to be satisfied or dissatisfied with one's job. Judge, Locke, and Durham (1997) have hypothesized that four personality variables are related to people's predisposition to be satisfied with their life and jobs: emotional stability, self-esteem, self-efficacy (perceived ability to master their environment), and **internal locus of control** (perceived ability to control their environment). That is, people prone to be satisfied with their jobs and with life in general have high self-esteem and a feeling of being competent, are emotionally stable, and believe they have control over their lives, especially their work lives. This view is supported by several meta-analyses and studies:

As shown in Table 10.2, a meta-analysis by Judge and Bono (2001) found these four variables to be related to both job satisfaction and job performance.

- Judge, Locke, Durham, and Kluger (1998) found a significant correlation between a combination of these four variables and job satisfaction ($r = .41$) and life satisfaction ($r = .41$).
- Meta-analyses by Connolly and Viswesvaran (2000) and by Bowling, Hendricks, and Wagner (2008) indicate that overall job satisfaction, as well as different facets of job satisfaction, is related to affectivity. That is, people with a tendency to have positive emotions (positive affectivity) tend to be more satisfied with their jobs than do people with a tendency to have negative emotions (negative affectivity).
- A meta-analysis by Judge, Heller, and Mount (2002) concluded that emotional stability and extraversion were significantly related to job and life satisfaction.

Culture

As shown in Table 10.3, workers in different countries have different levels of job satisfaction. The 2019 Randstad Workmonitor found that, of 34 countries surveyed, employees in India, Mexico, and Turkey were the most satisfied and employees in Singapore, Hong Kong, and Japan the least. U.S. employees ranked 5th in the survey employees in Canada and the United Kingdom were tied for 9th. Employees in collectivistic cultures tend to experience more job satisfaction than employees in individualistic cultures (Hui, Yee, & Eastman, 1995).

Intelligence

In 1997, a police department in New London, Connecticut, created controversy when it announced that applicants who were "too smart" would not be hired (see the Chapter 5 On the Job Box). The police chief's reasoning was that highly intelligent people would be

---

Internal locus of control The extent to which people believe that they are responsible for and in control of their success or failure in life.

Table 10.2   Correlations Between Individual Difference Variables and Satisfaction and Work Behavior

Individual Difference	Satisfaction	Performance	Turnover	Absenteeism	OCB	CWB	Aggression
Affectivity							
Positive	.49[e]	.19[d]	.05[d]		.23[d]	−.34[l]	
Negative	−.33[e]	−.15[d]	−.16[d]		−.10[d]	.30[d]	.29[h]
Core Self-Evaluation							
Self-esteem	.26[b]	.26[b]				-.13[j]	
Self-efficacy	.45[b]	.23[b]					
Internal locus of control	.32[b]	.22[b]					
General locus of control	.22[i]						
Work locus of control	.34[i]						
Emotional stability	.24[b]	.19[b]	−.19[g]	.04[f]		−.06[f]	
Personality							
Openness	.02[c]	.06[a]	.14[g]	.00[f]		.14[f]	
Conscientiousness	.26[c]	.24[a]	−.16[g]	−.06[f]		−.26[f]	
Extraversion	.25[c]	.09[a]	.02[g]	.08[f]		.01[f]	
Agreeableness	.17[c]	.12[a]	−.08[g]	.04[f]		−.20[f]	
Stability	.29[c]	.15[a]	−.19[g]	.04[f]		−.06[f]	

[a]Hurtz & Donovan (2000); [b]Judge & Bono (2001); [c]Judge, Heller, & Mount (2002); [d]Kaplan et al. (2009); [e]Connolly & Viswesvaran (2000); [f]Salgado (2002); [g]Rubenstein et al. (2018); [h]Hershcovis et al. (2007); [i]Wang; Bowling, & Eschleman (2010); [j]Whelpley & McDaniel (2011); [k]Chiaburu et al. (2011); [l]Shockley, Ispas, Rossi, & Levine (2012).

bored and have low job satisfaction. Though there has been little research on the topic, a study by Ganzach (1998) suggests that employees higher in intelligence have slightly lower job satisfaction than do employees lower in intelligence in jobs that are not complex. In complex jobs, the relationship between intelligence and satisfaction is negligible. A meta-analysis of seven studies by Griffeth, Hom, and Gaertner (2000) found that intelligence and turnover were not significantly related.

Are Employees Satisfied with Other Aspects of Their Lives?

Judge et al. (1998), Judge and Watanabe (1993), and Tait et al. (1989) have theorized not only that job satisfaction is consistent across time but that the extent to which a person is satisfied with all aspects of life (e.g., marriage, friends, job, family, and geographic location) is consistent as well. Furthermore, people who are satisfied with their jobs tend to be satisfied with life. These researchers found support for their theory, as their data indicate that job satisfaction is significantly correlated with life satisfaction. Thus, people happy in life tend to be happy in their jobs and vice versa.

In an interesting study, Judge and Watanabe (1994) found that for about two-thirds of participants, high levels of life satisfaction are associated with high levels of job satisfaction. In other words, satisfaction with one's job "spills over" into other aspects of life, and satisfaction with other aspects of life spills over into satisfaction with one's job. For the remaining 30% or so of the population, either there is no relationship between life and job satisfaction or there is a negative relationship.

Table 10.3 International Differences in the Percentage of Employees
Satisfied with Their Jobs in 2019 (Randstad Survey)

Country	% Satisfied
India	89
Mexico	88
Turkey	80
Norway	79
United States	78
Denmark	78
Spain	77
United Kingdom	74
Canada	74
Brazil	74
China	74
Malaysia	73
Poland	73
Chile	73
Austria	72
Belgium	71
Germany	71
Romania	70
The Netherlands	70
Luxemburg	70
Argentina	70
Italy	69
New Zealand	68
Portugal	68
France	68
Sweden	66
Greece	65
Czech Republic	64
Hungary	64
Singapore	61
Hong Kong	49
Japan	42

That life satisfaction can influence job satisfaction in most people is an important finding. In the twenty-first century, managers are being asked to work miracles in making even the worst of jobs satisfying (think about some of the jobs portrayed on the Discovery Channel's reality TV show *Dirty Jobs*, which are listed in Table 10.4). Perhaps a more realistic approach is what I refer to as the "John Travolta method." If you will

Table 10.4 Dirty Jobs: Would You Be Satisfied with Any of These Jobs?

Sewer inspector	Shark-suit tester
Pigeon-poop cleaner-upper	Salmon carcass counter
Baby chicken sexer	Dump-truck cleaner
Sludge recycler	Odor eater
Bug breeder	Owl vomit collector

recall from those classic films *Saturday Night Fever* and *Urban Cowboy*, John Travolta, an American actor, had boring jobs (as a paint store employee in *Fever* and as an oil refinery worker in *Urban Cowboy*) but made his life meaningful through his dancing. Now I'm not suggesting that disco and line dancing are the solutions to life's problems (although they are a good start). I am instead suggesting that an employee's needs can be met in a variety of nonwork activities such as hobbies and volunteer work. A mistake we have made for years has been to assume that a job must satisfy all of a person's needs. Instead, an organization should work toward fulfilling those needs that it can and should help employees find alternative avenues to meet their other needs.

Judge's (1993) interesting study demonstrates the importance of individual differences. Judge had more than 200 nurses in a medical clinic complete a questionnaire tapping their propensity to gripe about things in everyday life and asking them to indicate how satisfied they were with their jobs. Judge then compared the nurses' levels of job satisfaction with whether they quit their jobs with the clinic over the next 10 months. The results of this study indicated that for the people who griped about everything in life, there was no significant relationship between satisfaction and turnover ($r = .05$); however, for the nurses who were not chronic gripers, satisfaction was significantly correlated with turnover ($r = .39$). In other words, people who are unhappy in life and unhappy on their jobs will not leave their jobs, because they are used to being unhappy. But for people who are normally happy in life, being unhappy at work is seen as a reason to find another job.

Are Employees' Job Expectations Being Met?

As was discussed in Chapter 9, employees come to a job with certain needs, values, and expectations. If there is a discrepancy between these needs, values, and expectations and the reality of the job, employees will become dissatisfied and less motivated. In a test of this *discrepancy theory*, a meta-analysis by Wanous, Poland, Premack, and Davis (1992) concluded that when an employee's expectations are not met, the results are lower job satisfaction ($r = .39$), decreased organizational commitment ($r = .39$), and an increased intent to leave the organization ($r = .29$). These results support the importance of ensuring that applicants have realistic job expectations. Though the meta-analysis results supported the "met expectations" theory, Irving and Meyer (1994) criticized the studies that were included in the meta-analysis. In their own study, Irving and Meyer found that an employee's experiences on the job were most related to job satisfaction and that the *difference* between their expectations and experiences was only minimally related to job satisfaction. More studies using methods like Irving and Meyer's are needed to clarify this issue.

In a related meta-analysis, Zhao, Wayne, Glibkowski, and Bravo (2007) investigated the effect of employees perceiving that an organization has not fulfilled its promises and obligations (called *psychological contracts*) to an employee. When such psychological contract breaches occur, job satisfaction and organizational commitment go down and employee intentions to leave the organization increase. The results of these two meta-analyses support the importance of ensuring not only that applicants have realistic job expectations but that any promises made to employees must be kept.

Is the Employee a Good Fit with the Job and the Organization?

When employees consider how well they "fit" with a job or an organization, they consider the extent to which their values, interests, personality, lifestyle, and skills match those of their *vocation* (e.g., a career such as nursing, law enforcement, or psychology), *job* (its particular tasks), *organization, coworkers*, and *supervisor* (Kristof-Brown, Zimmerman, & Johnson, 2005). In addition to these five aspects of fit, Cable and DeRue (2002) believe that needs/supplies fit is also important. Needs/supplies fit is the extent to which the rewards, salary, and benefits received by employees are perceived to be consistent with their efforts and performance.

As shown in Table 10.5, the meta-analysis by Kristof-Brown et al. (2005) clearly demonstrates the importance of fit. Employees who perceive a good fit with their organization, job, coworkers, and supervisor tend to be satisfied with their jobs, identify with the organization, remain with the organization, perform better, and engage in organizational citizenship behaviors (OCBs). A meta-analysis by Hoff, Song, Wee, Phan, and Rounds (2020) found that employees whose jobs matched their interests had higher levels of job satisfaction than did employees whose jobs did not match their interests.

Another "fit" factor that has been shown to be related to job satisfaction and commitment is the extent to which employees' desire for a particular work schedule (e.g., shift, number of hours) matches their actual schedule. As one would expect, the better the fit between an employee's desired schedule and their actual schedule, the greater an employee's job satisfaction, organizational commitment, performance, and the likelihood to remain with the organization (Holtom, Lee, & Tidd, 2002). As organizations shift to incorporate more remote work schedules, this has also shown to increase job satisfaction through higher perceived autonomy, greater work-life balance, and higher telecommuting intensity (Schall, 2019).

Branham (2012) believes that there are certain signs to which an organization should pay attention that indicate a job/person mismatch. Some of these signs are that the employee:

- does not seem excited when first hired or assigned to a job;
- starts asking for some tasks to be given to other employees;
- applies for other jobs in the organization;
- begins to ask for new projects; and
- appears bored or unchallenged.

Are the Tasks Enjoyable?

The SHRM 2017 Employee Job Satisfaction and Engagement survey found that 51% of employees indicated that the nature of the work itself was a very important factor in their level of job satisfaction. Given that the nature of the work itself was ranked as the seventh most important factor, employers should take innovative steps to make work more interesting. What were the top three factors? Opportunity for the employer to use their skills and abilities, job security, and compensation/pay.

Table 10.5 Kristof-Brown, Zimmerman, and Johnson (2005) Meta-Analysis Results

	Employee Fit with			
Attitude or Behavior	**Organization**	**Group**	**Supervisor**	**Job**
Job satisfaction	.44	.31	.44	.56
Commitment	.51	.19	.09	.47
Performance	.07	.19	.18	.20
Actual turnover	−.14			−.08
Turnover intentions	−.35			−.46
Absenteeism	−.05			

Source: Kristof-Brown, Zimmerman, and Johnson (2005).

Do Employees Enjoy Working with Supervisors and Coworkers?

Research indicates that people who enjoy working with their supervisors and coworkers will be more satisfied with their jobs (Mossholder, Settoon, & Henagan, 2005; Repetti & Cosmas, 1991). Such findings certainly make sense. We all have had coworkers and supervisors who made our jobs unbearable, and we all have had coworkers and supervisors who made our jobs fun to have. In a study of 500 employees at an apparel manufacturing plant, Bishop and Scott (1997) found that satisfaction with supervisors and coworkers was related to organizational and team commitment, which in turn resulted in higher productivity, lower intent to leave the organization, and a greater willingness to help. Additionally, accounting for sex differences in the workplace, researchers were unable to find an association between sex and job satisfaction, and sex and satisfaction with coworkers and supervisors (Sauser & York, 1978).

Are Coworkers Outwardly Unhappy?

Social information processing theory States that employees model their levels of satisfaction and motivation from other employees.

Social learning theory States that employees model their levels of satisfaction and motivation from other employees.

Social information processing theory, also called **social learning theory**, postulates that employees observe the levels of motivation and satisfaction of other employees and then model those levels (Salancik & Pfeffer, 1977). Thus, if an organization's long-term employees work hard and talk positively about their jobs and their employer, new employees will model this behavior and be both productive and satisfied. The reverse is also true: If veteran employees work slowly and complain about their jobs, so will new employees.

To test this theory, Weiss and Shaw (1979) had subjects view a training video in which assembly line workers made either positive or negative comments about their jobs. After viewing the videotape, each subject was given an opportunity to perform the job. The study found that those subjects who had seen the positive tape enjoyed the task more than did the subjects who viewed the negative tape. In a similar study conducted by Mirolli, Henderson, and Hills (1998), subjects performed a task with two experimenters pretending to be other subjects (these are called confederates). In one condition, the confederates made positive comments about the task (e.g., "Gee, this is fun."); in a second condition, they made negative comments about the task (e.g., "This sucks."); and in the control condition, they did not make any comments. Consistent with social information processing theory, actual subjects exposed to the confederates' positive comments rated the task as more enjoyable than did the subjects exposed to negative comments.

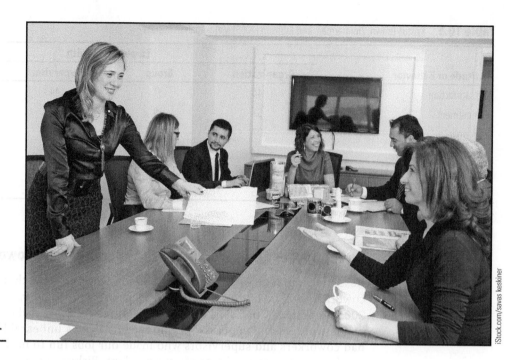

One's coworkers can affect job satisfaction.

In general, the research on social information processing theory supports the idea that the social environment does influence employees' attitudes and behaviors (Pollock, Whitbred, & Contractor, 2000; Robinson & O'Leary-Kelly, 1998). As with all of the theories in this chapter, it plays a role in job satisfaction but does not play the only role. One of the appeals of social information processing theory is that it certainly makes intuitive sense. Think of courses you have taken in which one student participated more than anyone else. After a while, the student's level of participation probably decreased to be more in line with the rest of the class. In work as in school, social pressures force individuals to behave in ways that are consistent with the norm, even though the person may privately believe something different (Nail, 1986).

An IT company in Germany, Nutzwerk, believed so strongly in this theory that it made new employees sign a contract agreeing not to whine and complain. The policy was created after employees started complaining about a woman who kept complaining! So far, two employees have been fired for excessive whining.

Are Rewards and Resources Given Equitably?

One factor related to both job satisfaction and employee motivation is the extent to which employees perceive that they are being treated fairly. As you probably recall from Chapter 9, **equity theory** is based on the premise that our levels of job satisfaction and motivation are related to how fairly we believe we are treated in comparison with others. If we believe we are treated unfairly, we attempt to change our beliefs or behaviors until the situation appears to be fair.

One of the greatest problems with the equity and justice theories is that despite their rational sense, they are difficult to implement. That is, based on equity and justice theories, the best way to keep employees satisfied would be to treat them all fairly, which would entail paying the most to those employees who contributed the most. Although few of us would disagree with this approach, it is difficult to implement for several reasons.

Equity theory A theory of job satisfaction stating that employees will be satisfied if their ratio of effort to reward is similar to that of other employees.

The first is *practicality*. An organization certainly can control such variables as salary, hours worked, and benefits, but it cannot easily control other variables, such as how far an employee lives from work or the number of friends an employee makes on the job.

The second reason that equity is difficult to achieve is that the employee's *perception* of inputs and outputs determines equity, not the *actual* inputs and outputs. For example, two students of equal ability receive the same grade on an exam. Sara knows that she studied 10 hours for the exam but never saw the other student attend the online study sessions. Sara may feel that the scores are unfair because she studied harder but received the same grade as the student she never saw study. Of course, the other student may have studied 20 hours and not needed to attend the study sessions, but Sara would not know that. In this case, the student's perception of input level may not match reality.

It is important that employees base their judgments on factual information. Of course, this may be easier said than done. In two national surveys, only 40% of employees stated that they understood how their pay was determined (Grensing-Pophal, 2003). This is an important finding because another survey found that 74% of employees who understood how their pay was determined were satisfied with their jobs compared with only 42% of employees who did not understand the basis for their pay (Grensing-Pophal, 2003). The results of these surveys suggest that to increase perceptions of equity, organizations need to do a better job of explaining their compensation systems.

Another way to increase perceptions of equity would be to allow employees access to the salaries of other employees. In the public sector, employee salaries are available to the public, although most public agencies certainly do not go out of their way to publicize salary information. In the private sector, most organizations keep such information confidential. Such policies, however, encourage employees to speculate about how much other people make. This speculation usually results in employees thinking the worst and believing that others make more than they do.

Even if an organization were able to maintain complete internal equity, employees would then compare their ratios with those of employees from other organizations.

The problem with such comparisons is that an organization has little or no control over another's policies. Furthermore, perceptions of wages and benefits at other organizations most likely will be more distorted than internal perceptions. Thus, even if equity theory were completely accurate, maintaining a high level of employee satisfaction would still be difficult.

The third reason that implementing the equity theory is difficult is that people have varying levels of equity sensitivity. As defined by Huseman, Hatfield, and Miles (1987), equity sensitivity postulates that while individuals react consistently *after* recognizing an unfair difference in treatment, individuals have varying levels of what they consider to be unfair treatment. That is to say, one employee will be prompted to act at a much lower level of perceived unequal treatment than another employee. Thus, accounting for employees' equity sensitivity introduces more complications when implementing theories in the workplace.

Although equity theory is historically interesting, a more useful approach to fairness issues has been the study of three aspects of **organizational justice**: distributive justice, procedural justice, and interactional justice. **Distributive justice** is the perceived fairness of the actual decisions made in an organization. For example, did one manager get a higher budget than another? Was the higher raise received by one employee justified? Did the right employee get promoted? **Procedural justice** is the

Organizational justice A theory that postulates that if employees perceive they are being treated fairly, they will be more likely to be satisfied with their jobs and motivated to do well.

Distributive justice The perceived fairness of the decisions made in an organization.

Procedural justice The perceived fairness of the methods used by an organization to make decisions.

perceived fairness of the methods used to arrive at the decision. Take, for example, a situation in which an employee was fired for breaking the rules but was never given the opportunity to explain what happened. Or, imagine a situation in which an excellent employee was given a promotion, but no other employees were allowed to compete for the promotion. In both situations, an employee might not completely disagree with the *outcome*, but they might be upset with the *process*.

Interactional justice is the perceived fairness of the interpersonal treatment employees receive. That is, a supervisor might spend substantial time talking with, mentoring, and socializing with some employees while completely ignoring others. It is thought that there are two components to interactional justice: informational justice and interpersonal justice. **Informational justice** is the extent to which a supervisor or coworker is open and transparent is sharing information and **interpersonal justice** is the extent to which a supervisor or coworker adequately treats an employee (Martinez-Tur, Moliner, & Maniezki, 2021). An interesting example of a problem with interactional justice comes from an organization in which a regional manager took women branch managers to breakfast at McDonald's to discuss sales but took men managers to dinner at a nice restaurant. Although the quality of the restaurant is certainly an issue, the 30 minutes spent with the women managers over an Egg McMuffin does not provide the amount or quality of the interaction spent eating steak and having drinks at a strip club (this is where the regional manager actually took the men managers).

As shown in Table 10.6, meta-analysis results indicate that perceived justice is related to several important factors, including job satisfaction, organizational commitment, performance, trust, withdrawal (e.g., turnover, absenteeism), and negative employee reactions (e.g., theft, sabotage). Because the relationships between perceptions of justice and employee attitudes and behavior are so strong, it is essential that employers be open about how decisions are made, take time to develop fair procedures, involve employees in the process of how decisions will be made, provide feedback to employees who might not be happy with decisions that are made, and allow a process for appealing decisions.

Is There a Chance for Growth and Challenge?

For many employees, job satisfaction is affected by opportunities for challenge and growth. As discussed in Chapter 9, Maslow thought that the need for growth and challenge, which he labeled as *self-actualization*, is important only after low-level needs (e.g., safety, social) have been met. To help satisfy employee self-actualization needs, organizations can do many things. The easiest and most common are **job rotation, job enlargement**, and **job enrichment**. With job rotation and job enlargement, an employee learns how to use several different machines or conduct several different tasks within an organization. With job rotation, the employee is given the same number of tasks to do at one time, but the tasks change from time to time. With job enlargement, an employee is given more tasks to do at one time.

A job can be enlarged in two ways: knowledge used and tasks performed. With knowledge enlargement, employees are allowed to make more complex decisions. With task enlargement, they are given more tasks of the same difficulty level to perform. As one might imagine, satisfaction increases with knowledge enlargement and decreases with task enlargement (Campion & McClelland, 1993).

Job rotation and job enlargement accomplish two main objectives. First, they challenge employees by requiring them to learn to operate several different machines or perform several different tasks. Thus, once employees have mastered one task or machine, they can work toward mastering another.

Interactional justice The perceived fairness of the interpersonal treatment that employees receive in an organization.

Informational justice The extent to which a supervisor is open and transparent in sharing information.

Interpersonal justice The extent to which a supervisor adequately treats an employee.

Job rotation A system in which employees are given the opportunity to perform several different jobs in an organization.

Job enlargement A system in which employees are given more tasks to perform at the same time.

Job enrichment A system in which employees are given more responsibility over the tasks and decisions related to their job.

Table 10.6 Organizational Justice Meta-Analysis Results: Corrected Correlations

	Organizational Justice Dimension				
	Procedural	**Distributive**	**Interactional**	**Interpersonal**	**Informational**
Job Satisfaction	.62[a]	.56[a]			
Commitment					
Organizational	.57[a]	.51[a]			
Affective	.53[d]	.49[d]		.41[d]	.38[d]
Normative	.31[c]	.31[c]	.52[c]		
Continuance	−.14[c]	−.06[c]	−.16[c]		
Performance—employee level	.24[d]	.26[d]		.16[d]	.16[d]
Performance—unit level	.32[e]	.50[e]	.34[e]		
Attitudes—unit level	.41[e]	.55[e]	.64[e]		
Absenteeism	−.46[a]	−.50[a]			
Aggression	−.20[b]	−.13[b]			
Organizational citizenship behaviors	.30[d]	.21[d]		.43[d]	.42[d]
Counterproductive work behaviors	−.28[d]	−.28[d]		−.24[d]	−.29[d]

[a]Colquitt et al. (2001); [b]Hershcovis et al. (2007); [c]Meyer et al. (2002); [d]Colquitt et al. (2013);
[e]Whitman, Caleo, Carpenter, Horner, & Bernerth (2012).

Second, job rotation helps to alleviate boredom by allowing an employee to change tasks. Thus, if an employee welds parts one day, assembles bumpers on another, and tightens screws on a third, the boredom caused by performing the same task every day should be reduced.

Perhaps an even better way to satisfy self-actualization needs is through job enrichment. The main difference between job rotation and job enrichment is that with job rotation an employee performs different tasks, and with job enrichment the employee assumes more responsibility over the tasks.

In their **job characteristics theory** that was discussed in Chapter 9, Hackman and Oldham (1975, 1976) theorized that enriched jobs are the most satisfying. Enriched jobs allow a variety of skills to be used, allow employees to complete an entire task (e.g., process a loan application from start to finish) rather than parts of a task, involve tasks that have meaning or importance, allow employees to make decisions, and provide feedback about performance. Hackman and Oldham developed the **Job Diagnostic Survey (JDS)** to measure the extent to which these characteristics are present in a given job.

If we look again at the job of college professor, job enrichment is clearly an inherent part of the job. That is, the professor decides what they will research and what they will teach in a particular course. This authority to make decisions about one's own work leads to higher job satisfaction.

With an assembly line worker, however, responsibility is something that must be added because the employee has minimal control over the way a job is done. After all, bumpers must be assembled in the same way each time and welded to the same place. So what can be done to enrich the typical factory worker's job?

Job characteristics theory The theory proposed by Hackman and Oldham that suggests that certain characteristics of a job will make the job more or less satisfying, depending on the particular needs of the worker.

Job Diagnostic Survey (JDS) A measure of the extent to which a job provides opportunities for growth, autonomy, and meaning.

One method is to give workers more responsibility over their jobs. For example, when an employee first begins working for a company, their work is checked by a quality control inspector. After they have been with the company long enough for the first four needs levels to be satisfied, they are given responsibility for checking their own quality. Likewise, more control can be given to the employee about where and when they will eat lunch, when they will take vacation time, or how fast they will accomplish their work. At one Kaiser Aluminum production plant, for example, time clocks were removed so that the workers could assume more responsibility for their performance by keeping track of their own hours.

Even when increased decision-making responsibilities are not possible, job enrichment ideas can still be implemented. For example, many organizations have or work with credit unions whose credit committees and boards of directors consist of company employees. These committees and boards provide excellent opportunities to increase employees' decision-making powers even though the decisions are not directly related to their jobs.

Another method to increase job enrichment levels is showing employees that their jobs have meaning and that they are meeting some worthwhile goal through their work (Hackman & Oldham, 1975). At some automobile factories, for example, this is accomplished by having employees work in teams to build cars. Instead of an employee performing a single task all day, they perform several tasks, as do the other employees in their group. At the end of the day, the employee can see a completed car that they have had a major role in building.

A plant that manufactures transformers provides another example. The training department realized that even though employees spent eight hours a day manufacturing the product, few understood what it did, who used it, and what would happen if it were not manufactured correctly. To correct this problem, the employees participated in a training session in which they were shown how the transformer was used, who used it, and the consequences that resulted from poor manufacturing.

Self-directed teams *See Quality circles.*

Quality circles Employee groups that meet to propose changes that will improve productivity and the quality of work life.

The final method for increasing employees' self-actualization needs that we will discuss here is the use of **self-directed teams**, or **quality circles**. With quality circles, employees meet as a group to discuss and make recommendations about work issues. These issues range from something as trivial as the music played in the work area to something as important as reducing waste or improving productivity. Meta-analysis results indicate that quality circles increase job satisfaction ($d = .25$) and commitment ($d = .22$) for employees in the private sector but not for those in public agencies (Pereira & Osburn, 2007).

In an extensive review of the literature, Wagner (1994) concluded that allowing employees to participate in decision-making results in small but significant increases in performance and job satisfaction. Arthur (1994) found lower turnover in steel mills that allowed employees to make decisions on their own than in steel mills with a more controlling style. Rentsch and Steel (1998) found that job enrichment resulted in decreased absenteeism.

Though team approaches are popular, there is considerable debate about their effectiveness. Most quality improvement programs using a team approach fail to provide the desired results (Zemke, 1993).

Integration of Theories

In this chapter, we discussed many theories of job satisfaction. Besides "When does this chapter end?," the question you must be asking is, "How, then, do we satisfy employees?" Unfortunately, the answer to this question is complex and depends on a variety of factors. We can, however, use the theories to design an organizational climate that is more conducive to motivation and satisfaction.

As shown in Figure 10.2, individual-difference theories say that each of us brings to a job an initial tendency to be satisfied with life and its various aspects such as work. A person with a low tendency toward satisfaction might *start* a job with only 6 hypothetical satisfaction points, a person with a neutral tendency might start with 10 hypothetical points, and a person with a high tendency might bring 14 points.

For example, research indicates that in addition to genetics, such traits as conscientiousness, emotional stability, and extraversion (Judge, Heller, & Mount, 2002); internal locus of control (Judge & Bono, 2001), Type A behavior, patience/tolerance (Bluen, Barling, & Burns, 1990), and social trust (Liou, Sylvia, & Brunk, 1990) are related to our tendency to be satisfied with work. Demographically, men and women are equally satisfied with work, White employees are more satisfied than Black employees, and older workers are slightly more satisfied and committed than younger workers (Ng & Feldman, 2010).

Personal Tendency Toward Satisfaction

Figure 10.2
Satisfaction Flowchart

Surrette and Harlow (1992) found that people will be most satisfied with a job if they had the *option to choose* that job from other alternatives rather than the particular job being their only choice. Once people are employed at a job, however, they are most satisfied when they don't have other career alternatives (Pond & Geyer, 1987).

During our years at work, certain events and conditions occur that can add to or decrease our initial level of satisfaction that was due to personal predispositions.

According to discrepancy theories, we will remain satisfied with our job if it meets our various needs, wants, expectations, and values. As discussed previously in the chapter, individuals vary greatly in their needs for such things as achievement, status, safety, and social contact. Thus, not every job can satisfy the needs of every employee during every period of their life. By being aware of employee needs, however, we can select the employees whose needs are consistent with the requirements and characteristics of the job. The Career Workshop Box provides some strategies for those who may be unhappy with their jobs.

According to the intrinsic satisfaction theory and job characteristics theory, we will be more satisfied with our jobs if the tasks themselves are enjoyable to perform. What makes a task enjoyable varies across individuals. For some, working on a computer is fun, whereas for others, nothing could be more boring. Some people enjoy making decisions, solving conflicts, and seeing a project through from start to finish, whereas others don't.

Overall satisfaction can be affected by our satisfaction with individual facets of the job. For example, an incompetent boss, terrible coworkers, low pay, or limited opportunities for advancement can lessen overall job satisfaction. Even trivial things can lessen job satisfaction. I once worked at a job where the vending machines never worked and supplies such as paper and pens were often not available. These factors were irritants for most employees—enough to lessen job satisfaction but certainly not enough to make any of us *dissatisfied* with the job. According to social learning theory, we will be more satisfied if our coworkers are satisfied. If everyone else is whining and complaining, it is difficult to be the only person at work who loves their job.

No matter how much we intrinsically like our work, equity and justice theories predict that we will become dissatisfied if rewards, punishments, and social interactions are not given equitably. If you work harder than a coworker, yet they receive a bigger raise, you are less likely to be satisfied even though money may not be the reason you are working.

Based on job characteristics theory and Maslow's level of self-actualization, lack of opportunity for growth, challenge, variety, autonomy, and advancement will decrease satisfaction for many people.

The results of these factors are summed to indicate an employee's current level of satisfaction. As conditions change, so too will the level of satisfaction.

10-3 Measuring Job Satisfaction and Commitment

This chapter has discussed several theories that seek to explain job satisfaction and commitment. But one important issue that remains is how an employee's level of job satisfaction or commitment is measured. Generally, job satisfaction is measured in one of two ways: standard job satisfaction inventories or custom-designed satisfaction inventories. Commitment is usually measured through standard commitment inventories.

What to Do If You Are Unhappy with Your Job

In this chapter, you learned the reasons why employees are dissatisfied with their jobs and interventions that organizations can engage in to increase employee satisfaction. Unfortunately, many organizations will not be proactive in their approach to job satisfaction. That means that you must take responsibility for your own level of happiness and satisfaction. What can you do?

- During the initial employment interview, ask questions about the job and the organization. Ask to meet other employees and perhaps watch how the job is done. Remember that two causes of job dissatisfaction are expectations not being met and a poor person/job fit. The more you know prior to accepting the job offer, the greater opportunity you will have to communicate your expectations to the organization, find out what they expect from you, and assess how well the job and organization fit with your needs, values, and personality.

- Just because your coworkers are constantly complaining about the job or the organization doesn't mean that you have to as well. Change the topic or remain silent. Try to socialize with employees who have a better attitude. The longer you hang around the whiners, the worse your attitude will become.

- If you don't think you are being treated fairly or are not being appreciated, say something. Rationally explain to your supervisor why you think you are being treated unfairly, provide examples, and discuss what you need. A fact of life at work is that supervisors are rarely in touch with their employees' feelings, and if you don't speak up, they will never know. If the behavior continues after your discussion, you may need to think about options such as talking to a higher-level manager, ignoring your feelings (easier said than done), or changing jobs. However, remember that there is some truth to clichés such as "Life is rough" and "The grass is always greener on the other side of the hill." If you leave an organization to find one where "nobody plays politics," you will probably be disappointed.

- During your annual performance appraisal, discuss your needs for challenge and growth. If you want to advance in the organization, find out what you need to do and work with your supervisor to develop a plan for you to get the necessary training or experience. Again, don't wait for someone to come to you. You need to take charge of your own career.

- If you are unhappy, keep it to yourself. This advice may seem a bit harsh, but the reality is that other employees don't want to hear your complaints, and if they do, they will probably use your words against you at some point. Identify the reasons you are unhappy at work and create a plan for change. Whining without rational action will not help your career or make you any happier.

Commonly Used Standard Inventories
Measures of Job Satisfaction

Faces Scale A measure of job satisfaction in which raters place a mark under a facial expression that is most similar to the way they feel about their jobs.

Job Descriptive Index (JDI) A measure of job satisfaction that yields scores on five dimensions.

Minnesota Satisfaction Questionnaire (MSQ) A measure of job satisfaction that yields scores on 20 dimensions.

One of the first methods for measuring job satisfaction was developed by Kunin (1955) and is called the **Faces Scale** (a simulation is shown in Figure 10.3). Although the scale is easy to use, it is no longer commonly administered, partly because it lacks sufficient detail, lacks construct validity, and because some employees believe it is so simple that it is demeaning.

The most commonly used scale today is the **Job Descriptive Index (JDI)** (Figure 10.4). The JDI, developed by Smith, Kendall, and Hulin in 1969 and most recently revised in 2009, consists of 72 job-related adjectives and statements that are rated by employees. The scales yield scores on five dimensions of job satisfaction: supervision, pay, promotional opportunities, coworkers, and the work itself.

A similar measure of job satisfaction is the **Minnesota Satisfaction Questionnaire (MSQ)**, which was developed by Weiss, Dawis, England, and Lofquist (1967). The MSQ contains 100 items that yield scores on 20 scales. To get experience taking a satisfaction inventory, complete the short form of the MSQ in Figure 10.5.

Place a check under the face that expresses how you feel about your job in general.

Figure 10.3
Simulation of
Faces Scale of Job
Satisfaction

The fact that the JDI has five scales and the MSQ 20 underscores the point that job satisfaction is not easy to measure. This is especially true when one considers that employees' responses on the JDI are not highly correlated with their responses on the MSQ (Gillet & Schwab, 1975). Because both the JDI and the MSQ measure specific aspects of job satisfaction, Ironson, Smith, Brannick, Gibson, and Paul (1989) developed the **Job in General (JIG) Scale**. The JIG is useful when an organization wants to measure the overall level of job satisfaction rather than specific aspects. Both the JIG and the JDI are available for free at https://webapp.bgsu.edu/jdi.

Job in General (JIG) Scale A measure of the overall level of job satisfaction.

Nagy (1996) criticized many of the standard measures of job satisfaction because these measures ask only if employees are satisfied with a particular aspect of their job, but not how important that job aspect is to them. Recall from our previous discussion on discrepancy theories that people differ about what is important to them. With this in mind, imagine that both Juan and Temea think their salaries are lower than they should be. Juan is a real social climber and thinks that salary is a measure of one's status in life. Temea, however, has inherited plenty of money and works because she enjoys keeping busy. Although both Juan and Temea think their pay is low, Nagy (1996) argues that only Juan would be dissatisfied. To understand these differences, Nagy (1995) created the Nagy Job Satisfaction Scale, which includes two questions per facet: one asking how important the facet is to the employee and the other asking how satisfied the employee is with the facet.

Measures of Commitment

Most measures of organizational commitment are relatively short and tap aspects similar to affective commitment, continuance commitment, and normative commitment. Perhaps the most commonly used measure of organizational commitment is that developed by Allen and Meyer (1990). The Allen and Meyer survey has 24 items, 8 each for the 3 factors of affective, continuance, and normative commitment. Examples of questions are as follows:

Affective commitment

- I would be very happy to spend the rest of my career in this organization.
- I really feel as if this organization's problems are my own.

Continuance commitment

- It would be very hard for me to leave my organization right now, even if I wanted to.
- I believe that I have too few options to consider leaving this organization.

Normative commitment

- I would feel guilty if I left my organization now.
- This organization deserves my loyalty.

Think of your present work. What is it like most of the time? In the blank beside each word given below, write

___Y___ for "Yes" if it describes your work
___N___ for "No" if it does NOT describe it
___?___ if you cannot decide

Work on Present Job

_____ Routine
_____ Satisfying
_____ Good
_____ On your feet

Think of the pay you get now. How well does each of the following words describe your present pay? In the blank beside each word, put

___Y___ for "Yes" if it describes your pay
___N___ for "No" if it does NOT describe it
___?___ if you cannot decide

Present Pay

_____ Income adequate for normal expenses
_____ Insecure
_____ Less than I deserve
_____ Highly paid

Think of the opportunities for promotion that you have now. How well does each of the following words describe these? In the blank beside each word put

___Y___ for "Yes" if it describes your opportunities for promotion
___N___ for "No" if it does NOT describe them
___?___ if you cannot decide

Opportunities for Promotion

_____ Promotion on ability
_____ Dead-end job
_____ Unfair promotion policy
_____ Regular promotions

Think of the kind of supervision that you get on your job. How well does each of the following words describe this supervision? In the blank beside each word below, put

___Y___ if it describes the supervision you get on your job
___N___ if it does NOT describe it
___?___ if you cannot decide

Supervision on Present Job

_____ Impolite
_____ Praises good work
_____ Influential
_____ Doesn't supervise enough

Think of the majority of the people that you work with now or the people you meet in connection with your work. How well does each of the following words describe these people? In the blank beside each word below, put

___Y___ if it describes the people you work with
___N___ if it does NOT describe them
___?___ if you cannot decide

People on Your Present Job

_____ Boring
_____ Responsible
_____ Intelligent
_____ Talk too much

Source: *The measurement of satisfaction in work and retirement,* by P. C. Smith, L. M. Kendall, and C. L. Hulin (1969), Chicago: Rand McNally. The Job Descriptive Index is copyrighted by Bowling Green State University. The complete forms, scoring key, instructions, and norms can be requested from Dr. Patricia Smith.

Figure 10.4

Sample Items from the Job Descriptive Index

Other measures include the following:

- **Organizational Commitment Questionnaire (OCQ):** A 15-item questionnaire developed by Mowday, Steers, and Porter (1979) to measure three commitment factors: acceptance of the organization's values and goals, willingness to work to help the organization, and a desire to remain with the organization. Although the questions tap three factors, most people using the scale combine the factors to yield one overall commitment score (Kacmar, Carlson, & Brymer, 1999).

Figure 10.5

Minnesota Satisfaction Questionnaire Short Form

Ask yourself: How **satisfied** am I with this aspect of my job?

Very Sat. means I am very satisfied with this aspect of my job.

Sat. means I am satisfied with this aspect of my job.

N means I can't decide whether I am satisfied or not with this aspect of my job.

Dissat. means I am dissatisfied with this aspect of my job.

Very Dissat. means I am very dissatisfied with this aspect of my job.

On my present job, this is how I feel about . . .	Very Dissat.	Dissat.	N	Sat.	Very Sat.
1. Being able to keep busy all the time	☐	☐	☐	☐	☐
2. The chance to work alone on the job	☐	☐	☐	☐	☐
3. The chance to do different things from time to time	☐	☐	☐	☐	☐
4. The chance to be "somebody" in the community	☐	☐	☐	☐	☐
5. The way my boss handles employees	☐	☐	☐	☐	☐
6. The competence of my supervisor in making decisions	☐	☐	☐	☐	☐
7. Being able to do things that don't go against my conscience	☐	☐	☐	☐	☐
8. The way my job provides for steady employment	☐	☐	☐	☐	☐
9. The chance to do things for other people	☐	☐	☐	☐	☐
10. The chance to tell people what to do	☐	☐	☐	☐	☐
11. The chance to do something that makes use of my abilities	☐	☐	☐	☐	☐
12. The way company policies are put into practice	☐	☐	☐	☐	☐
13. My pay and the amount of work I do	☐	☐	☐	☐	☐
14. The chances for advancement on this job	☐	☐	☐	☐	☐
15. The freedom to use my own judgment	☐	☐	☐	☐	☐
16. The chance to try my own methods of doing the job	☐	☐	☐	☐	☐
17. The working conditions	☐	☐	☐	☐	☐
18. The way my coworkers get along with each other	☐	☐	☐	☐	☐
19. The praise I get for doing a good job	☐	☐	☐	☐	☐
20. The feeling of accomplishment I get from the job	☐	☐	☐	☐	☐
	Very Dissat.	Dissat.	N	Sat.	Very Sat.

- **Organizational Commitment Scale (OCS):** A nine-item survey developed by Balfour and Wechsler (1996) that measures three aspects of commitment: identification, exchange, and affiliation. Sample questions include, "I felt like a part of the family at this organization," and "What this organization stands for is important to me."

Custom-Designed Inventories

Though most research on job satisfaction is conducted using one or more of the previously mentioned standard inventories, most organizations tap their employees' levels of job satisfaction by using custom-designed inventories. The advantage to custom-designed inventories is that an organization can ask employees questions specific to their organization and job tasks. For example, a local agency recently restructured many of its jobs and wanted to tap how satisfied its employees were with the changes. To do this, they hired a consultant who designed questions that specifically tapped employees' thoughts and feelings about the changes. Using one of the standard inventories would not have provided the needed information.

10-4 Consequences of Dissatisfaction and Other Negative Work Attitudes

Absenteeism

As discussed earlier in this chapter and depicted in Figure 10.1, when employees are dissatisfied or not committed to the organization, they are more likely to miss work and leave their jobs than are satisfied or committed employees. In the remaining two sections of the chapter, absenteeism and turnover will be discussed and methods to decrease these negative employee behaviors will be presented.

Data from the Bureau of Labor Statistics indicates that in 2020, U.S. workers missed 3% of scheduled work hours, a statistic that translates to about 7.8 days per year. Although comparable international data are difficult to come by, a 2019 survey by Direct Health Solutions found that the average employee in Australia missed 11.2 days per year. In Europe, 2019 data from Mitrefinch indicate that employees from Bulgaria (22.0), Germany (18.3), Czech Republic (15.4), and Norway (14.6) missed the most days of work and employees from Switzerland (1.6), Ukraine (4.1), Malta (4.2), and the United Kingdom (4.4) missed the fewest number of days. Data from the Statistics Canada indicate that the average Canadian employee missed 11.6 days in 2020.

Including absences due to holidays, sickness, and parental leave, the average employee in Iran received took 53 days off work in 2019 (OECD, 2020). Comparing U.S. absenteeism rates with those in other countries can be difficult because many countries require employers to provide paid days off for absenteeism whereas the United States has no such laws. In fact, data from the U.S. Department of Labor indicate that 80% of low-paid or part-time employees do not get a single day of paid absence.

Organizations throughout the world are concerned with absenteeism, not only because of its high monetary cost, but also because absenteeism is moderately correlated with turnover ($p = .25$; Berry, Lelchook, & Clark, 2012) and thus might be a warning sign of intended turnover.

Because of the high costs of absenteeism and turnover, organizations are expending great effort to reduce the number of unscheduled absences. For these efforts to be effective, it is important that we understand why employees miss work. That is, punishment will reduce absenteeism only if employees make conscious decisions about attending. Likewise, wellness programs will increase attendance only if absenteeism is mostly the result of illness. In a 2017 survey of 3,697 employees by CareerBuilder.com, 40% of employees admitted to taking at least one "sick day" off each year even though they weren't sick. The top treasons for taking the time off were as follows:

- Doctor's appointment (30%)
- Not feeling like going to work (23%)
- Needing to relax (20%)
- Getting more sleep (15%)
- Running errands (14%)

Some of the more creative excuses reported by employers were that the employee's fake eye kept falling out of its socket; there was a bear in the employee's back yard and they were scared to come outside; the employee bit their tongue and couldn't talk; the employee left their clothes at the laundry mat; or that someone glued the employee's doors and windows shut so they couldn't leave the house to come to work.

Linking Attendance to Consequences

The basis behind rewarding attendance and punishing absenteeism is that employees make a decision each day as to whether they will not attend work. Although the decision-making process is not clearly understood, it probably includes weighing the consequences of going to work (or to class) against the consequences of not going. For example, imagine that you have an 8:00 a.m. class and are deciding whether you will attend this morning. By missing class, you can sleep a few hours longer, watch the *Today Show*, and stay out of the rain. By attending class, you will get the notes that you know will be on the test but aren't in the book, get to listen to the instructor's terrific sense of humor, and get to sit next to the great-looking student you think is interested in you. If a good test grade and a chance at a date are more important, you will attend class. If sleep is more important, you will miss class.

If in fact employees make conscious decisions about attending work, attendance can be increased in several ways: rewarding attendance, disciplining absenteeism, and keeping accurate attendance records.

Rewards for Attending

Attendance can be increased using financial incentives, time off, and recognition programs.

Well pay A method of absenteeism control in which employees are paid for their unused sick leave.

Financial Incentives. Financial incentive programs use money to reward employees for achieving certain levels of attendance. One of these programs, **well pay**, involves paying employees for their unused sick leave. Some employers reward the employee by paying the equivalent of the employee's daily salary, whereas others might split the savings by paying the employee an amount equal to half their daily salary for each unused sick day.

Financial bonus A method of absenteeism control in which employees who meet an attendance standard are given a cash reward.

A second method provides a **financial bonus** to employees who attain a certain level of attendance. With this method, an employee with perfect attendance over a year might receive a $1,000 bonus, and an employee who misses 10 days might receive nothing. For example, at Steel Warehouse in Memphis and Chattanooga, employees can earn $700 a year if they have perfect attendance. At United Airlines, employees with perfect attendance for six months are entered into a drawing for a chance to win one of 18 new cars (Woodward, 2013).

Games An absenteeism control method in which games such as poker and bingo are used to reward employee attendance.

A third financial incentive method is to use **games** to reward employees who attend work. There are many examples. One company used poker as its game, giving a playing card each day to employees who attended. At the end of the week, employees with five cards compared the value of their hands, and the winning employee would be given a prize such as dinner for two at the best restaurant in town or a gas barbecue grill. Although some studies have reported success in using such games, the meta-analysis by Wagner (1990) found that the mean effect size for games was close to zero.

Paid time off program (PTO) An attendance policy in which all paid vacations, sick days, holidays, and so forth are combined.

Time Off. Another approach is the **paid time off program (PTO)**, or paid-leave bank (PLB). With this style of program, vacation, personal, holiday, and sick days are combined into one category—paid time off. For example, in a traditional system, an employee might be given 10 vacation days, 3 personal days, 5 holidays, and 10 sick days, for a total of 28 days. With a PTO program, the employee might be given 26 days in total for the year—companies adopting PTO programs usually offer slightly fewer days off than under their old system (Frase, 2010). An employee who is seldom sick has more days to use for vacation and is protected in case of a long-term illness, and the organization saves money by reducing the total number of unscheduled absences. As shown in Table 10.7, human resources (HR) directors rate buy-back programs, paid-leave banks, and disciplinary action as the most effective absence control methods.

In 37% of PTO programs, an employee can "bank" time off to use later, and 17% of organizations with a PTO program allow employees to donate unused leave to a leave bank for employees who are stricken by a catastrophic illness such as cancer (CCH, 2004). My neighbor provides an excellent example of a PTO in which employees can bank their time off. She works for a hospital and has not missed a day of work in five years. Consequently, she now has three months' extra vacation time, which she plans to spend with her newborn son.

Recognition Programs. One other way that we can make work attendance more rewarding is through recognition and praise. Formal recognition programs provide employees with perfect-attendance certificates, coffee mugs, plaques, lapel pins, watches, and so forth. As shown in Table 10.7, HR directors do not perceive these programs to be as effective as many of the other programs. Though incentive programs can be an effective means of increasing attendance, many organizations have eliminated perfect-attendance incentives out of a concern that such programs might violate the Family Medical Leave Act (Tyler, 2001).

Table 10.7   CCH Surveys of Absenteeism Control Policies

Absence Control Policy	Percent Using Method					Effectiveness Rating				
	2000	2004	2005	2006	2007	2000	2004	2005	2006	2007
Disciplinary action	88	91	90	90	89	3.5	3.5	3.4	3.3	3.4
Performance appraisal	58	79	79	82	82	3.2	3.0	3.0	2.9	2.9
Verification of illness		76	76	79	74		3.0	3.2	2.9	3.2
Paid-leave bank	21	63	67	70	60	3.9	3.5	3.5	3.7	3.6
Personal recognition	62	59	66	68	57	3.1	2.6	2.6	2.7	2.6
No-fault systems	31	59	63	67	59	3.7	2.9	3.0	2.8	2.9
Bonus programs	21	49	57	61	51	3.1	3.2	3.3	3.3	3.3
Buy-back programs	17	48	58	59	53	3.4	3.3	3.5	3.4	3.4

Source: CCH Annual Unscheduled Absence Surveys.

Discipline for Not Attending

Absenteeism can be reduced by punishing or disciplining employees who miss work. Discipline can range from giving a warning or a less popular work assignment to firing an employee. As shown in Table 10.7 discipline works fairly well, especially when combined with some positive reinforcement for attending.

Clear Policies and Better Record Keeping

Another way to increase the negative consequences of missing work is through policy and record keeping. Most organizations measure absenteeism by counting the number of days missed, or *frequency*. Perhaps a better method would be to record the number of *instances* of absenteeism rather than the number of days. For example, instead of giving employees 12 days of sick leave, they are given 3 or 4 instances of absenteeism. Missing one day or three consecutive days each counts as one instance of absenteeism.

As shown in Figure 10.6, the number of days missed and the instances of absenteeism often yield different results. By decreasing the number of times that a person can miss work, the odds increase that the employee will use sick leave only for actual illness. These odds can further be increased by requiring a doctor's excuse for missing a certain number of consecutive days.

Absenteeism can be decreased by setting attendance goals and by providing feedback on how well the employees are reaching those goals. An interesting study by Harrison and Shaffer (1994) found that almost 90% of employees think their attendance is above average and estimate the typical absenteeism of their coworkers at a level two times higher than the actual figures. Similar results were found by Johns (1994). Thus, one reason employees might miss work is that they incorrectly believe that their attendance is at a higher level than their coworkers'. Providing feedback to employees about their absenteeism levels may be one way to reduce absenteeism.

Figure 10.6

Frequency and Instance Methods of Measuring Absenteeism

Frequency Method				
Patricia Austin				
Days missed:	March	4		
	April	9		
	May	2		
	May	30	Days Missed	= 8
	June	7	Instances	= 8
	July	2		
	Sept	3		
	Nov	24		
Instance Method				
Christine Evert				
Days missed:	April	3		
	April	4		
	April	5		
	July	15	Days Missed	= 8
	July	16	Instances	= 3
	Dec	2		
	Dec	3		
	Dec	4		

Increasing Attendance by Reducing Employee Stress

Absenteeism can be reduced by removing the negative factors employees associate with going to work. One of the most important of these factors is *stress*. The greater the job stress, the lower the job satisfaction and commitment, and the greater the probability that most people will want to skip work. As will be discussed in greater detail in Chapter 15, there are many sources of stress at work including physical danger, boredom, overload, conflict, and bad management practices.

To increase attendance, negative factors must be eliminated. The first step in this elimination, of course, is to become aware of the negative factors that bother employees. These can be determined by asking supervisors or by distributing employee questionnaires. Once the problems are known, it is important that management diligently work to eliminate the identified problems from the workplace. As will also be discussed in Chapter 15, employers engage in a variety of programs designed to reduce job-related stress as well as stress from family and personal issues. Meta-analysis results indicate that these programs are successful in reducing employee stress levels but have only a negligible effect on reducing absenteeism (Richardson & Rothstein, 2008).

To help employees cope with stress and personal problems, 79% of employers offer some form of employee assistance program (EAP) (SHRM, 2019). EAPs use professional counselors to deal with employee problems. An employee with a problem can either choose to see a counselor on their own or be recommended by their supervisor. Some large organizations have their own EAP counselors, but most use private agencies, which are often run through local hospitals.

The motivation for EAPs may be good, but little if any empirical evidence supports their effectiveness. Still, many organizations have used EAPs and have been quite pleased with them. Independently operated EAPs typically claim a three to one return on the dollars invested through increased productivity and reduced absenteeism and turnover.

Organizations also have implemented interesting initiatives to reduce stress, such as free meals or free rides into work by the mobile app development company, Appster. Other organizations offer employees stress reduction tools, such as a one-on-one session with a stress management coach, or meditation and mindfulness classes.

Increasing Attendance by Reducing Illness

Over the years, CCH surveys indicate that about 35% of absenteeism is due to employee illness—a percentage that mirrors that of college students missing class. Kovach, Surrette, and Whitcomb (1988) asked more than 500 general psychology students to anonymously provide the reason for each day of class they missed. Less than 30% of the missed days were the result of illness!

To reduce absenteeism related to illness, organizations are implementing a variety of wellness programs. According to the 2019 SHRM Employee Benefits Survey (SHRM, 2019):

- 58% have some form of wellness program
- 60% provide on-site flu vaccinations
- 39% have a smoking cessation program
- 32% subsidize the cost of off-site fitness center dues
- 31% have on-site health screening (e.g., blood pressure, cholesterol)
- 29% offer a weight-management program
- 29% have on-site fitness centers
- 13% offer on-site stress reduction programs
- 4% offer on-site nap room

To reduce both absenteeism and health care costs, many employers are rewarding employees whose body mass index, cholesterol levels, and blood pressure levels are within acceptable ranges based on benchmarks from organizations such as the American Diabetes Association (ADA) and American Heart Association (AHA). Typically, the reward comes in the form of a reduction in the employee's monthly health care premium. Other organizations take a more punitive approach and increase the premiums of unhealthy employees. For example, beginning in 2009, Clarian Health in Indianapolis, Indiana, began reducing the pay by 10 dollars per paycheck for employees whose body mass index was greater than 29.9. Under the 2014 Affordable Care Act (ACA), employers can legally charge an employee and additional 30% of the cost of health benefits if the employee does not meet certain wellness benchmarks.

Two meta-analyses suggest that worksite fitness programs have a small but significant effect on reducing *absenteeism*. The meta-analysis of 11 studies by Parks and Steelman (2008) found an effect size of $-.30$; the meta-analysis by Wolkove and Layman (2006) found an effect size of $-.37$. Parks and Steelman further found that wellness programs increase job satisfaction ($d = .42$). Results found by Erfurt, Foote, and Heirich (1992) did not support the effectiveness of wellness programs in reducing health problems.

Reducing Absenteeism by Not Hiring "Absence-Prone" Employees

An interesting theory of absenteeism postulates that one reason people miss work is the result of a particular set of personality traits they possess. That is, certain types of people are more likely to miss work than other types. In fact, in one study, only 25% of the employees were responsible for all of the unavoidable absenteeism (Dalton & Mesch, 1991).

Although little research has tested this theory, two meta-analyses have produced conflicting findings. Salgado (2002) found very low correlations between personality and absenteeism but Ones, Viswesvaran, and Schmidt (2003) found that scores on personality-based integrity tests—which seem to measure a combination of conscientiousness, agreeableness, and emotional stability (Ones, 1993)—significantly predicted employee absenteeism. Why the difference between the two meta-analyses? Ones et al. (2003) believe that at least part of the explanation is that integrity tests were designed to predict employee behavior whereas the personality inventories included in the Salgado (2002) meta-analyses were not. If more research supports the Ones et al. findings, then a new strategy for increasing employee attendance might be to screen out "absence-prone people" during the selection stage.

Uncontrollable Absenteeism Caused by Unique Events

Many times an individual will miss work because of events or conditions that are beyond management's control. One study estimated that 40% of absenteeism is unavoidable (Dalton & Mesch, 1991). For example, bad weather is one reason absenteeism is higher in the Northeast than in the South. Although an organization can do little to control the weather, the accessibility of the plant or office can be considered in the decision of where to locate. In fact, this is one reason many organizations have started in or moved to the so-called Sunbelt in the last several decades. Organizations may also want to offer some type of shuttle service for their employees to avoid not only weather problems but also any resulting mechanical failures of employees' automobiles.

Bad weather can certainly be a legitimate reason for an employee to miss work, but one study found that job satisfaction best predicted attendance on days with poor weather. That is, in good weather, most employees attended, but in inclement weather, only those employees with high job satisfaction attended. Thus, even in bad weather, the degree to which an employee likes their job will help to determine their attendance. As the late industrial psychologist Dan Johnson has asked: "How come we hear about employees not being able to get to work and students not being able to attend class because of bad weather, yet we don't ever hear about an employee or a student who can't get home because of bad weather?" It certainly makes one think!

Turnover

Cost of Turnover

As mentioned previously in this chapter and depicted in Table 10.1, employees with low job satisfaction and low organizational commitment are more likely to quit their jobs and change careers than are employees with high job satisfaction and high organizational commitment. Though turnover rates fluctuate from year to year, about 1.4% of an organization's employees leave each month (16.8% per year). Though some sources estimate that the cost of turnover can exceed 100% of the employee's annual salary (Allen, Bryant, & Vardaman, 2010; Bliss, 2001; Cascio, 2013), a review of 30 case studies suggests that the actual cost is probably closer to 20% of the annual salary for the position (Boushey & Glynn, 2012). Both visible and hidden costs determine this estimate. Visible costs of turnover include advertising charges, employment agency fees, referral bonuses, recruitment travel costs, salaries and benefits associated with the employee time spent processing applications and interviewing candidates, and relocation expenses for the new employee. Hidden costs include the loss of productivity associated with the employee leaving—other employees trying to do extra work, no productivity occurring from the vacant position—and the lower productivity associated with a new employee being trained. Additional hidden costs include overtime of employees covering the duties of the vacant position and training costs once the replacement is hired. The actual cost of turnover for any given position can be more accurately estimated using a formula such as one of those found on the text website.

In terms of turnover in an organization, there are four views on the effect of performance on such factors as safety, productivity, and profitability:

- There is a negative correlation such that higher turnover rates will result in lower organizational performance.
- Because some turnover is healthy for an organization, there is a U-shaped relationship between turnover and performance such that very low or very high levels of turnover will result in lower organizational performance, but a moderate amount of turnover will result in higher performance.
- The negative effect of turnover is strongest when an organization's turnover rate is low, and this effect then diminishes as turnover rates climb.
- The effect of turnover on organizational performance is mediated by the strength of an organization's HR efforts. Turnover will most likely affect organizations that don't invest in their employees and will least affect organizations that spend time and money to develop their employees.

Though all four theories make good sense, research seems to support the idea that an employee leaving an organization will most affect an organization's performance when the monthly turnover rate for the organization is low and will have a diminishing effect on performance when the turnover rate is high (Shaw, Gupta, & Delery, 2005).

Reducing Turnover

The first step in reducing turnover is to find out why your employees are leaving. This is usually done by administering attitude surveys to current employees and conducting exit interviews with employees who are leaving. Salary surveys can also be useful because they allow you to compare your organization's pay and benefit practices with those of other organizations. Surveys are important because there appears to be a real disconnect between the reasons managers think employees leave and the actual reasons: 89% of managers believe employees leave for more money, yet 88% of employees say they left for other reasons, such as career growth opportunities or negative relationships with coworkers or supervisors (Branham, 2012).

It is important to understand that employee turnover is a *process* of disengagement from the organization that can take days, weeks, or months (Branham, 2012). So, employees don't awaken one day and just decide to leave. Instead, they have been thinking about it for a period of time, which means that better communication between employees and management might prevent the ultimate decision to leave. Employees typically leave their jobs for one of five reasons: unavoidable reasons, advancement, unmet needs, escape, or unmet expectations.

Unavoidable Reasons. Unavoidable turnover includes such reasons as school starting (e.g., quitting a summer job) or ending (e.g., a student quits their job as a part-time receptionist because they graduated and will be moving), the job transfer of a spouse, employee illness or death, or family issues (e.g., employees staying home to raise their children or take care of their parents). Though employers are taking steps to reduce turnover due to family issues, there is little an organization can do to prevent turnover due to the other reasons.

Advancement. Employees often leave organizations to pursue promotions or better pay. When an organization has few promotion opportunities, there is little it can do to reduce turnover for those employees who are seeking advancement. One solution used by an increasing number of police departments who have limited promotion opportunities is to allow officers with extensive experience and skills to advance to status positions such as master officer or senior officer. Such positions have no supervisory responsibility but do bring an increase in pay and status.

At times, employers can reduce turnover by offering more pay; however, this will work only if a low compensation or an inadequate benefits package is the prime reason for employees leaving the organization. Furthermore, any increase in pay must be a meaningful amount. That is, if an organization increases pay by $3,000, yet other organizations are paying $6,000 more, the increase in pay most probably will not decrease turnover.

Unmet Needs. Employees whose needs are unmet will become dissatisfied and perhaps leave the organization. For example, if an employee has high social needs and the job involves little contact with people, or if an employee has a need for appreciation and recognition that is not being met by the organization, the employee might leave to find a job in which their social needs can be met. To reduce turnover caused by unmet needs, it is important that an organization considers the **person/organization fit** when selecting employees. That is, if an applicant has a need for structure and close supervision, but the culture of the organization is one of independence, full of "free

Person/organization fit The extent to which an employee's personality, values, attitudes, philosophy, and skills match those of the organization.

spirits," the applicant should not be hired because there would be a poor fit between the employee's need and the organization.

Escape. A common reason employees leave an organization is to escape from people, working conditions, and stress. When conflict between an employee and their supervisor, a coworker, or customers becomes unbearable, the employee may see no option other than to leave the organization. Therefore, it is important to effectively deal with conflict when it occurs (this is covered in detail in Chapter 13). Likewise, if working conditions are unsafe, dirty, boring, too strenuous, or too stressful, there is an increased likelihood that the employee will seek employment in an organization with better working conditions. Providing a mentor to help the employee deal with workplace problems (Payne & Huffman, 2005) and having a formal dispute resolution program such as mediation (Heavey, Holwerda, & Hausknecht, 2013) may help to reduce turnover.

Unmet Expectations. Employees come to an organization with certain expectations about a variety of issues, such as pay, working conditions, opportunity for advancement, and organizational culture. When reality does not match these expectations, employees become less satisfied and, as a result, are more likely to leave the organization (Griffeth et al., 2000). As discussed in Chapter 5, turnover due to unmet expectations can be reduced by providing applicants with realistic job previews.

To summarize, organizations can reduce turnover in one of the following ways:

- Conduct realistic job previews during the recruitment stage.
- Select employees who have been referred by a current employee, who have friends and/or family working for the organization, and who did not leave their previous job after only a short tenure (Barrick & Zimmerman, 2005).
- Look for a good person/organization fit during the selection interview.
- Meet employee needs (e.g., safety, social, growth).
- Mediate conflicts between employees and their peers, supervisors, and customers.
- Provide a good work environment.
- Provide a competitive pay and benefits package.
- Provide opportunities to advance and grow.

There are many times when employees remain with an organization even though characteristics of their jobs suggest that they would leave. Lee, Mitchell, Sablynski, Burton, and Holtom (2004) suggest that the extent to which an employee is embedded in the organization or the community might explain this lack of turnover. **Embeddedness** is described as the extent to which employees have links to their jobs and community, the importance of these links, and the ease with which these links could be broken and reestablished elsewhere. That is, if an employee has many friends at work or in the community, is actively involved in community organizations, and has a spouse who also has an excellent job; it would be difficult to leave an organization if the only alternative was to relocate to another community. Ramesh and Gelfand (2010) have expanded the concept of embeddedness to include the extent to which an employee fits with the culture of the organization and community, the employee's links to people in the organization and the community, and the sacrifices an employee would make if they left the organization or the community. As expected, a meta-analysis by Jiang, Liu, McKay, Lee, and Mitchell (2012) found that higher

Embeddedness The extent to which employees have links to their jobs and community, the importance of these links, and the ease with which they can be broken and replaced at another job.

levels of embeddedness result in lower levels of employee turnover. Higher levels of embeddedness are also related to higher levels of commitment and performance (Halvorsen, Radford, Chapman, & Nikolic, 2021).

Counterproductive Behaviors

As discussed previously, employees who are unhappy with their jobs miss work, are late to work, and quit their jobs at higher rates than employees who are satisfied with their jobs and are committed to the organization. Dissatisfied employees, especially those who are unable to change jobs, also engage in a variety of other counterproductive behaviors in organizations. These counterproductive behaviors can be separated into two types of behaviors: those aimed at individuals and those aimed at the organization (Berry, Ones, & Sackett, 2007). Behaviors aimed at individuals include gossip, playing negative politics, harassment, incivility, workplace violence, and bullying. Behaviors aimed at the organization include theft and sabotage. Though such behaviors are not limited to unhappy employees, they provide ways for employees to "get back" at the organization or the coworkers they believe are responsible for their lack of happiness.

For example, Cropanzano and Greenberg (1997) found that employees who were unhappy with the way in which they were treated by their supervisors had an increased likelihood of stealing from their employers. The interesting finding of this study was that the employees tended to take things that were of value to the organization but not to them. That is, they didn't steal because they wanted an item, they stole because they wanted to hurt the organization.

Dissatisfied employees often act out.

Personality types also contribute to whether an employee is more likely to engage in counterproductive behaviors in the workplace. For example, meta-analysis results investigating the Big Five personality dimensions found that conscientiousness predicted turnover and deviant behaviors and that extroversion, agreeableness, openness, and emotional stability predicted turnover (Salgado, 2002). Researchers also found a positive relationship between narcissism and counterproductive behaviors (Penney & Spector, 2002).

Lack of Organizational Citizenship Behaviors

Organizational citizenship behaviors (OCBs) Behaviors that are not part of an employee's job but that make the organization a better place to work (e.g., helping others, staying late).

Employees who engage in **organizational citizenship behaviors (OCBs)** are motivated to help the organization and their coworkers by doing the "little things" that they are not required to do. Examples of OCBs include staying late to get a project done, helping a coworker who is behind in their job, mentoring a new employee, volunteering for committees, and flying in coach when the employee might be entitled to first class.

As one would expect, a meta-analysis has demonstrated that job satisfaction is related to OCBs. That is, employees who are satisfied with their jobs and committed to the organization are more likely to "go the extra mile" than are employees who are dissatisfied with their jobs (LePine et al., 2002). Also not surprisingly, meta-analysis results show that there is a negative correlation between OCBs and employee counterproductive behavior (Dalal, 2005).

On the Job ▶ **Applied Case Study**

Reducing Turnover at Bubba Gump Shrimp Co.

Following the success of the motion picture *Forrest Gump*, the Bubba Gump Shrimp Company opened its first restaurant in 1996 on Cannery Row in Monterey, California. Today, they have grown to over 30 locations worldwide. The importance of employee relations at the restaurant chain is demonstrated by awards such as the 2005 *Nation's Restaurant News* NRAEF Spirit Award for excellence in hiring, training, retaining, and developing employees; *Chain Leader's* Best Places to Work in 2006 and being named by the *OC Metro Magazine* as the "2006 Best Company to Work for in Orange County." As one would imagine from the name, Bubba Gump specializes in shrimp but also has items such as fish and chips, mahimahi, and ribs. Each restaurant also contains a store in which customers can purchase Forrest Gump souvenirs as well as seafood to prepare at home.

In addition to traditional benefits, the kitchen staff receive a free meal each shift, and all employees receive 50% off meals for themselves and up to three

guests when they are not working. Managers receive two weeks of vacation to start, and four weeks after 10 years. They are also part of a bonus program that allows them to earn up to 200% of their potential. The company uses salary surveys to ensure that their pay and bonus package is competitive.

The president of Bubba Gump Shrimp Company believes that one of the secrets to success is to have minimal management turnover. In fact, this focus on turnover has been so successful that he did not have a general manager leave in three years, and he decreased management turnover from 36% to 16% in two years.

- Based on what you learned in this chapter, what interventions would you make to reduce management turnover?
- How would these interventions be different if you were trying to reduce nonmanagerial turnover?

In a small rural school division in Virginia, a superintendent, with the support of his school board, adopted an attendance reward program for teachers. Teachers with perfect attendance receive a $500 bonus at the end of the school year. Teachers who miss only one day receive $250. The superintendent believes that the program will increase teachers' commitment to the students, parents, and community by rewarding them for not taking days off from work.

This chapter discussed that one of the consequences of low commitment and job dissatisfaction is high absenteeism. In the school mentioned above, absenteeism had significantly risen over the past few years. The superintendent believed that the increase was because of a lack of commitment by the teachers. After all, if the teachers were committed, they would try harder not to miss school. "It's human nature," he said, "when you know you might lose your sick days at the end of the year to take those days even when you are not sick. By rewarding good attendance, the school division will increase commitment from these teachers and, consequently, reduce absenteeism." If you talk to the teachers, however, many will say that the school division would rather "buy" their good attendance than determine and fix why teachers choose to be absent in the first place, which is in response to unethical practices by management and the poor treatment of teachers by the administration.

Critics of such incentives say that it is unethical to "buy" commitment. They believe that it is only an excuse for leaders not doing what they should do: change how they treat employees. Many believe that organizational commitment and loyalty comes from how much employees identify with the organization's goals, mission, and leaders. And it comes from variety in work, the freedom to make decisions, and the freedom to make mistakes without losing their jobs. It is when employees don't believe in what management is doing or when they feel management is mistreating them that their commitment

decreases. And, say these critics, you can't get that commitment back simply by "bribing" them with bonuses, incentives, or pay increases. The leaders of today, the critics say, don't want to give more freedom to employees to make decisions; they find it easier to fire employees for mistakes than offering them additional training to perform better, and leaders don't want to take the time to learn better management techniques, because, to them, time away from work means money out of their own pockets.

Supporters of such incentives say that part of organizational commitment is getting better performance out of employees, reducing absenteeism, and reducing turnover. They see nothing wrong in rewarding employees for doing a good job, being at work, and staying at work. Ultimately, these incentives meet the goal they are intended for. So, if such incentives work, why not use them? Proponents counter the argument that management uses incentives instead of finding better ways to treat employees by arguing that incentives are one way of treating employees better.

What Do You Think?

- Do you think that incentives are a form of bribery? If so, do you think it's unethical for companies to do this?

- What would keep you at a company for a longer period? Would incentives such as an Attendance Reward Program or end-of-the-year bonuses make a difference in whether you left a job?

- Do you think that using such incentives is a way for leaders to ignore what they should be doing to make things better for the employees?

- What are some other ethical dilemmas that might occur by offering incentives to increase commitment or job satisfaction?

Chapter Summary

In this chapter you learned:

- Satisfied and committed employees are more likely to have better performance, have lower turnover, miss fewer days of work, be more motivated, engage in organizational citizenship behaviors, and be less likely to engage in counterproductive work behaviors.

- Employees are more likely to be satisfied with their jobs if there is a good fit between their needs and what the job and organization offers, if they are treated fairly, if their coworkers are satisfied, and if the job is not stressful.

- Absenteeism is a problem both in the United States and in other countries.
- Absenteeism can be reduced using financial incentives and recognition programs, reducing job-related stress, having clear policies, disciplining employees who miss work, and using wellness programs to reduce illness.
- Employees are likely to leave an organization if they lack advancement opportunities, have needs or expectations that are not met, are not treated fairly, or want to escape from negative working conditions.

Key Terms

Job satisfaction (352)
Organizational commitment (352)
Affective commitment (354)
Continuance commitment (354)
Normative commitment (354)
Internal locus of control (356)
Social information processing
    theory (361)
Social learning theory (361)
Equity theory (362)
Organizational justice (363)
Distributive justice (363)
Procedural justice (363)
Interactional justice (364)
Informational justice (364)
Interpersonal justice (364)
Job rotation (364)
Job enlargement (364)
Job enrichment (364)
Job characteristics theory (365)

Job Diagnostic Survey (JDS) (365)
Self-directed teams (366)
Quality circles (366)
Faces Scale (369)
Job Descriptive Index (JDI) (369)
Minnesota Satisfaction Questionnaire
    (MSQ) (369)
Job in General (JIG) Scale (370)
Organizational Commitment
    Questionnaire (OCQ) (371)
Organizational Commitment
    Scale (OCS) (372)
Well pay (374)
Financial bonus (374)
Games (374)
Paid time off program (PTO) (375)
Person/organization fit (380)
Embeddedness (381)
Organizational citizenship behaviors
    (OCBs) (383)

Questions for Review

1. Are some employees "destined" to always be dissatisfied with their job? Why or why not?
2. What do most employees value and need in a job?
3. Is it possible to treat all employees equitably? Why or why not?
4. What is the best way to improve employee attendance?
5. Which measure of job satisfaction is best? Why?

Chapter

11

Organizational Communication

Learning Objectives

11-1 Recognize the types of organizational communication.

11-2 Explain why interpersonal communication often is not effective.

11-3 Increase your listening effectiveness.

11-4 Improve your communication skills.

P icture the following situations:

- A male employee cannot understand why he was reprimanded for referring to female employees as the "girls in the office."
- A supervisor has tried everything to communicate with their employees, but the employees still seem unsure of what they should do.
- Customers don't like Sheila because she appears cold and aloof, although she is actually a very caring person.
- A supervisor is frustrated because their employees never read the notices posted on the bulletin board in the break room.

All four situations represent common communication problems. This chapter looks at the ways employees communicate within an organization, problems in the communication process, and the ways communication can be improved.

11-1 Types of Organizational Communication

To be an effective employee, manager, client, or consultant, it is essential to communicate effectively with others. Having ideas, knowledge, or opinions is useless unless you can communicate those concepts to others. Most communication in organizations can be classified into four types: upward communication, downward communication, business communication, and informal communication.

Upward Communication

Upward communication Communication within an organization in which the direction of communication is from employees up to management.

Upward communication is communication of subordinates to superiors or of employees to managers. Of course, in ideal upward communication, employees speak directly to management in an environment with an "open door" policy. In fact, the quality of upward communication is a significant factor in employee job satisfaction (Miles, Patrick, & King, 1996). Such a policy, however, is often not practical for several reasons—perhaps the most important being the potential volume of communication if every employee communicated with a specific manager. Direct upward communication also may not be workable because employees often feel threatened by managers and may not be willing to openly communicate bad news or complaints.

Serial communication Communication passed consecutively from one person to another.

To minimize the number of different people communicating with the top executive, many organizations use **serial communication**. With serial communication, the message is relayed from an employee to their supervisor, who relays it to their supervisor, who, in turn, relays it to their supervisor, and so on until the message reaches the top. Although this type of upward communication relieves the top executive of excessive demands, it suffers several serious drawbacks.

The first is that the content and tone of the message change as it moves from person to person. As will be discussed later in the chapter, messages are seldom received the way they were sent—especially if the message is being passed orally from person to person.

MUM (minimize unpleasant messages) effect The idea that people prefer not to pass on unpleasant information, with the result that important information is not always communicated.

The second drawback to serial communication is that bad news and complaints are seldom relayed, in part due to the stress associated with delivering bad news (McKee & Ptacek, 2001). Rosen and Tesser (1970) have labeled this reluctance to relay bad news the **MUM (minimize unpleasant messages) effect**. The MUM effect negatively affects the organization by keeping important information from reaching the upper levels. But for an employee, the MUM effect is an excellent survival strategy—no one wants to be the bearer of bad news. Interestingly, people have no problem passing on bad news to peers, especially when the organizational climate is generally negative (Heath, 1996).

Communication channel The medium by which a communication is transmitted.

Proximity Physical distance between people.

Serial communication's third drawback, especially with informal **communication channels**, is that it is less effective the farther away two people are from one another. That is, a supervisor is more likely to pass along a message to another supervisor if the two are in close physical **proximity**. It is unlikely, therefore, that an informal message originating with an employee at a plant in Atlanta will reach another employee at the corporate office in Phoenix. The importance of physical proximity cannot be overstated. In fact, a major source of power often comes from being physically near an executive. Seasoned executives have been known to place rising executives in distant offices to reduce their potential power. And going to lunch with coworkers has long been recognized as a means of obtaining new information and increased power.

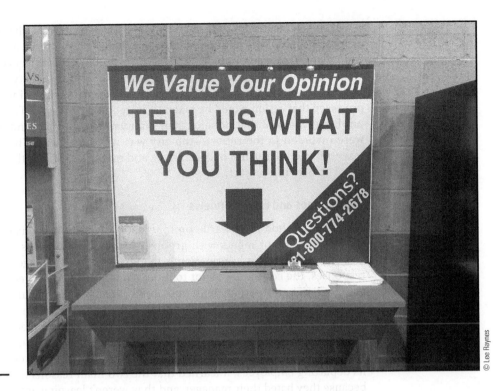

© Lee Raynes

Suggestion boxes are a common source of upward communication.

As one would imagine, proximity does not play a role when messages are communicated virtually through such means as email, texts, social media, and cloud-based team collaboration software such as Microsoft Teams.

Because of these problems with serial communication, organizations use several other methods to facilitate upward communication: attitude surveys, focus groups, suggestion boxes, and third parties.

Attitude Surveys

Attitude survey A form of upward communication in which a survey is conducted to determine employee attitudes about an organization.

Attitude surveys are usually conducted annually by an outside consultant who administers a questionnaire asking employees to rate their opinions on such factors as satisfaction with pay, working conditions, and supervisors. Employees are also given the opportunity to list complaints or suggestions that they want management to read. The consultant then tabulates the responses and reports the findings to management.

SurveyMonkey conducted a study to determine which organizations employees are most excited to work for. At least three of the top ten—Microsoft, Alphabet (Google), and Intel—had one thing in common: they extensively surveyed their employees to determine how the employees felt about topics such as their managers, the company, and pay and benefits.

Although attitude surveys are commonly used, they are useful only if an organization takes the results seriously. If an organization finds that its employees are unhappy and does nothing to address the problem areas, the survey results will not be beneficial. Additionally, this could even have detrimental effects if employees convey that they are unhappy through the attitude surveys and then do not perceive that the organization has adequately addressed their concerns. Furthermore, to increase trust, an organization should share survey results with its employees.

If survey results are to be shared, then management must share *all* of them. While proposing a project to a local police department, I encountered a great deal of hostility from many of the senior officers. After a little probing, the officers revealed that several years earlier they had completed an attitude survey for the city. A few months later, the results were made public. The city cited five main complaints by the officers and promised that action would be taken to solve these problems. The officers were happy until they realized that none of their complaints about pay and working conditions were included in the report—the city was ignoring them. The officers became so resentful and mistrustful of consultants and management that they vowed never again to participate in a project.

Focus Groups and Exit Interviews

A second method of upward communication is to hold focus groups, in which an outside consultant meets with groups of current employees to get their opinions and suggestions. This information is then passed on to management. To spur candid responses, the consultant is not told the names of the employees in the focus group, and no direct quotes that could potentially identify a particular employee are passed on. Exit interviews with employees voluntarily leaving an organization also provide an excellent source of information. Although these interviews can be emotionally charged, an organization can learn much by listening to the "real" reason that an employee is leaving the organization. For example, when Netscape conducted exit interviews of its departing employees, it learned that the two main reasons the employees left were because they hated their manager, and they weren't learning any new skills (Horowitz, 2014). Research shows that employees are more likely to be honest in an exit interview if they perceive that they have been treated fairly by the organization, and if they believe that their interests are aligned with the organization's (Giacalone, Knouse, & Montagliani, 1997).

Suggestion Boxes

A third method for facilitating upward communication is the use of **suggestion boxes** or **complaints boxes**. Theoretically, these two boxes should be the same, but a box asking for suggestions is not as likely to get complaints as a box specifically labeled *complaints* and vice versa. The biggest advantage of these boxes is that they allow employees to immediately communicate their feelings in an anonymous fashion. Suggestion boxes provide a safe voice for subordinates and customers and essential feedback to the organization. Furthermore, suggestion boxes help engage employees by making them feel the organization values their input (Randhawa, 2014). Although some small organizations still use physical suggestion and complaint boxes, larger organizations with multiple locations utilize such online suggestion boxes as Brightidea, Idea Box, and Ideawake that allow employees to submit suggestions and complaints, notify management when a comment has been received, and keep the employee informed of the progress and outcome of their suggestion.

Some organizations take suggestions quite seriously and reward employees who provide useful ideas. For example, Texas Industries in Dallas provides bonuses that can reach 20% of an employee's salary, IBM provides a reward equal to 25% of the savings resulting from an idea (up to $150,000), and Ingersoll-Rand gives plaques to employees who submit cost-saving ideas that are ultimately adopted by the company. In a study of organizations encouraging suggestions, the Employee Involvement Association found that over 30% of employees submitted at least one suggestion, approximately 37% of suggestions were adopted, and the value of the typical suggestion was 10 times greater than the cost of rewarding the suggestion (Wells, 2005). Successful products that were the result of employee suggestion programs include Post-It Notes, Gmail, the Sony PlayStation, and Amazon Prime.

Third-Party Facilitators

Liaison A person who acts as an intermediary between employees and management, or the type of employee who both sends and receives most grapevine information.

Ombudsperson A person who investigates employees' complaints and solves problems.

The use of a third party such as a **liaison** or an **ombudsperson** is another method that can increase upward communication. Both are responsible for taking employee complaints and suggestions and personally working with management to find solutions. The advantage of this system is that the ombudsperson is neutral and works for a solution that is acceptable to both employees and management. Furthermore, the ombudsperson is typically supervised at the vice presidential level, so they are not concerned about being fired if they step on a few toes while looking for a solution.

Unfortunately, the ombudsperson method is often not used because organizations do not want the expense of an employee who "does not produce." To overcome this problem, Moore Tool Company in Springdale, Arkansas, started its "Red Shirt" program, in which selected senior employees wear red shirts that identify them as informal ombudspeople. If an employee has a problem, they can seek help from a Red Shirt, who has the authority to help find a solution. This system not only opens communication channels but also provides job enrichment for an employee who works at an otherwise boring job.

Union steward An employee who serves as a liaison between unionized employees and management.

In organizations that have their employees represented by unions, the job of the ombudsperson is typically handled by the **union steward**. But management–union relationships are often adversarial, so the union steward has a difficult time solving problems because they are not perceived by management or union members as being neutral.

Downward Communication

Downward communication Communication within an organization in which the direction of communication is from management to employees.

Downward communication is that of superior to subordinate or management to employees. The downward communication process in organizations has changed greatly over the years. Originally, downward communication involved newsletters designed to bolster employee morale by discussing happy events such as the "three B's"—babies, birthdays, and ball-game scores. Now, however, downward communication is considered a key method not only of keeping employees informed but of communicating vital information needed by employees to perform their jobs. Such communication can be accomplished in many ways, including bulletin boards, policy manuals, newsletters, and intranets.

Bulletin Boards

Bulletin board A method of downward communication in which informal or relatively unimportant written information is posted in a public place.

The next time you visit an organization, look around for **bulletin boards**. You will see them everywhere. Their main use, however, is to communicate nonwork-related opportunities such as scholarships, optional meetings, and items for sale. Important information is seldom seen because the bulletin board is not the appropriate place to post a change of policy or procedure. Still, bulletin boards have the advantage of low costs and wide exposure to both employees and visitors. This is especially true if the boards are placed in high-traffic areas such as outside restrooms and cafeterias or near time clocks. Electronic bulletin boards, also called *in-house message networks*, allow the display of even more current information.

Policy Manuals

The **policy manual** is the place for posting important changes in policy or procedure. This manual contains all the rules under which employees must operate. Most manuals are written in highly technical language, although they should be written in a less technical style to encourage employees to read them, as well as to make them easier to understand. Furthermore, the contents of these manuals are considered binding contracts by courts, so the manuals must be updated each time a policy changes.

Sosnin (2001) advises that policy manuals should contain the following six disclaimers:

1. Employment with the organization is at-will (refer to Chapter 7 for a discussion of employment-at-will).
2. The handbook does not create either an expressed or an implied contract.
3. The handbook is a set of guidelines and should not be considered all-inclusive.
4. The material in the present handbook supersedes material in previous handbooks.
5. The handbook can be changed only in writing by the president of the organization, and it can be changed unilaterally at any time.
6. Employees are subject to provisions of any amendments, deletions, and changes in the handbook.

The typical company manual is hundreds of pages long, so it is not surprising that many employees do not want to read it. To reduce length problems, most organizations have two types of company manual. The first, called a *policy manual*, is very specific and lengthy, containing all of the rules and policies under which the organization operates. The second type, usually known as the *employee handbook*, is much shorter and contains only the most essential policies and rules, as well as general summaries of less important rules.

An example that supports the need for two manuals involved security guards at a manufacturing plant. The security guards were paid minimum wage and had an average tenure of about three months before quitting. The company became concerned for two reasons. First, three months was not enough time for the guards to learn all of the policies in the 300-page emergency procedures manual. Second, the manual was written by an engineer, and none of the security guards were able to understand the writing. The organization thus had I/O psychology graduate-student interns develop a short, easy-to-read procedure manual that could be read and understood in a day or two. Tips for effective writing that also apply to manuals are shown in Table 11.1.

Newsletters

As mentioned earlier, **newsletters** are designed to bolster employee morale by discussing happy or innocuous events such as the three B's (babies, birthdays, and ball-game scores). Newsletters are good sources of information for celebrating employee successes, providing feedback on how well the organization is doing, introducing a new employee, and providing reminders about organizational changes. Though some organizations still provide newsletters in print format, most post them electronically through either email or an intranet.

Table 11.1 Tips for Effective Writing

Rather Than	Try
Trying to impress someone with your vocabulary	Using a more conversational style
Personnel	Employees
Utilize	Use
Urban mass-transit vehicle	Bus
Cognizant	Aware
Writing in generalities	Writing what you mean
I wasn't gone long	I was gone for five minutes
A survey said that most of our employees . . .	A survey said that 54% of our employees . . .
Using an entire phrase	Using a single word
Enclosed please find . . .	Enclosed is . . .
Motivation is the idea that . . .	Motivation is . . .
Should it come to pass that you . . .	If you . . .

Intranets

To replace bulletin boards, newsletters, and company manuals, most organizations use **intranets,** which are organization-wide versions of the Internet. Intranets are currently common resources for:

- online employee handbooks;
- answers to FAQs (frequently asked questions);
- employee activity calendars;
- forms that can be completed online;
- programs to write job descriptions or performance appraisals;
- job postings;
- online benefits information;
- training courses; and
- information about reward and incentive programs (Grensing-Pophal, 2001a).

Business Communication

Business communication is the transmission of business-related information among employees, management, and customers. Business communication methods include telephone and video calls, email, texts, and voice mail.

Telephone Calls and Video Conferencing

One method of business communication is the *telephone call*. An advantage of telephone calls over methods such as email and texting is that both parties can hear the other's voice inflection, making it easier to understand the tone of the message. Whereas spontaneously picking up the phone and calling a coworker was common 10 years ago, the current trend is to rely more on email and texting for most communication and to schedule calls in advance.

Though videoconferencing is a great improvement over the traditional phone call, it is still important to pay attention to etiquette. Consider the following advice:

- Although you may be working from home, wear clothing that is appropriate to your audience. A casual shirt might be appropriate for talking with your coworkers, it may not be appropriate for a video conference with a potential client.
- Start the call on time and end a few minutes early. If you have a 2:00 call, start the call-in process a minute or two prior to the actual call time so that you will be logged in and ready to go at 2:00.
- Be aware of your background, especially when working from home. Keep in mind that the background can be visual (your dirty laundry) and audio (e.g., dogs barking, the TV). If you are going to use a virtual background, be sure to use one that is appropriate for business. Again, a background that might be appropriate for a call with coworkers (e.g., an ocean scene) may not be appropriate for a call with a client or upper management.
- Mute yourself when not speaking but remember to unmute yourself when you are ready to talk.
- Do not multitask during the meeting.
- Be careful about your nonverbal. It is easy to forget that people can see you and eye rolling and shaking your head will not go over well.

One limitation of phone calls, of course, is that nonverbal cues are not available. Thus, a major portion of the message is often not communicated. As a result, video-enhanced teleconferencing (videoconferencing) has generally replaced telephone calls in most large organizations. A second limitation to phone calls is that, depending on the organization, conversations might not be documented. For example, one department recently had a problem with an administrator who continually provided incorrect information over the phone or at meetings, denied that they had done so, and then blamed another department for errors that resulted from the use of the information. To correct this problem, employees quit talking to the administrator over the phone and stuck to email, where every "conversation" was documented. Some advice on proper videoconferencing etiquette is provided in the Career Workshop Box.

Email and Voice Mail

Most business communication involves *email*, *texting*, and *voice mail*. These methods are used primarily to exchange general and/or *timely* information and ask questions; they are not meant as substitutes for important conversation. The advantages to email and voice mail include a reduction in the use and filing of paper and time saved by avoiding "small talk" when communicating a short message by phone.

On the downside, voice mail often results in "phone tag," and email, texting, and voice mail reduce opportunities for personal contact. Well-designed voice mail systems are limited to simple tasks, have short menus, and allow a caller to talk to a real person at any time during the call.

Email has many advantages over voice mail, including the ability to easily document the sending and receiving of email, the opportunity to communicate with many people at one time, and the potential for quick response times, especially when some form of instant messaging is used. Employees are also able to access their email in situations where they might not be near an office phone. The drawbacks to email include misinterpretations due to the absence of paralanguage, the tendency to be too informal, the increased likelihood of expressing negative emotions ("flaming") that might not have been communicated in person, and the tendency to not proofread messages (O'Kane, Palmer, & Hargie, 2007).

Before writing an email message, decide if email is the appropriate communication channel. Email is appropriate for preparing people for meetings, scheduling meetings, communicating common news, and summarizing a conversation (Poe, 2001). Because email eliminates such factors as body language and tone, it is easy to misinterpret the meaning of an email message.

A good rule is to never put something in an email that you would not want to see published. Examples of material better left unsent include comments about other people, complaints, and offensive jokes. Because of the increased use and misuse of email, many organizations send their employees through email training. Casperson (2002) and Poe (2001) offer the following email etiquette commonly provided in such training:

- Include a greeting (e.g., "Hi, Mark") and a closing (e.g., "Take care").
- Include a detailed subject line.
- Don't write in all caps. It is difficult to read and comes across as if you are screaming.
- If you are going to forward an email message, change the original subject line and delete the long list of previous messages or names of people to whom the email had been previously forwarded.
- Take the same care in writing (e.g., spelling, grammar) that you would take in writing a formal memo.
- Don't spend company time on personal email unless your organization specifically allows you to do so.
- Allow ample time for the receiver to respond; not everyone considers email to require an immediate response.

When leaving a message on someone's voice mail, follow these guidelines:

- Speak slowly.
- Give your name at the beginning of the message and then repeat it at the end of the message.
- Spell your name if the person is not familiar with you or if your name is difficult to spell.
- Leave your phone number, even if you think the person already has it.
- To avoid phone tag, indicate some good times that the person can return your call.
- Don't ramble. Anticipate the possibility of getting voice mail rather than talking to the actual person and have a short message ready.
- Don't include information that you don't want other people to hear.

Business Meetings

As will be discussed in more detail in Chapter 13, a common method of business communication is the dreaded committee meeting. Research indicates that the typical employee spends an average of 4.35 hours attending 3.34 meetings each week (Rogelberg, Leach, Warr, & Burnfield, 2006). Supervisors attended even more meetings (5.0) and spent more time in these meetings (6.6 hours), and estimates show that senior managers spend nearly 23 hours weekly in meetings (Rogelberg, Scott, & Kello, 2007). Though meetings offer several advantages over email, memos, and phone calls, their time demands can result in negative employee attitudes (Rogelberg et al., 2006).

A 2021 survey by Fellow found that the five biggest meeting problems reported by employees were: going off topic, lack of preparation, no clear takeaways, time management, and status updates. What makes a great meeting? A clear purpose, a prepared agenda, psychological safety, active collaboration, and actionable takeaways.

Office Design

To facilitate employee communication, 70% of organizations have adopted what is formally called an "open" or "landscaped" office design, and informally called a "cube farm" (Grossman, 2002). Originally developed by furniture manufacturers in West Germany, the design uses large, open office areas without walls. Individual work units are separated into cubicles by such items as plants, bookcases, desks, and partitions. The idea behind this design is that employees will communicate better with one another and be easier to supervise and help without the physical barriers of walls (Poe, 2000). When it consolidated its many offices into one central location in Minneapolis, Allina Health System was so sold on the idea of an open office environment that even the CEO had a cubicle!

There are three common designs for open or landscaped offices (Martinez, 1990). In a *freestanding design* (also called a *bullpen design*), all desks are placed in a large area that is completely open. With *uniform plans*, desks are placed at uniform distances and are separated by panels into cubicle areas. *Free-form workstations* use a combination of designs so that the different needs of each worker can be accommodated.

Two interesting trends in office design are "boulevards" and portable offices. A boulevard is a wide hallway that runs through several departments. A boulevard's width allows space for impromptu employee communication, and a boulevard's path through, rather than around, departments encourages employee interaction. Because landscaped, or open, office environments reduce privacy, many organizations have "portable offices" containing an employee's computer, files, and supplies that can be wheeled into a walled office or cubicle when privacy is needed.

The landscaped office may be appealing, but research has not generally been supportive. Landscaped offices can increase contact and communication and are less expensive than regular offices, but often they can lessen productivity and job satisfaction (Brennan, Chugh, & Kline, 2002; De Been & Beijer, 2014). In a study of more than 500 employees in 14 organizations, O'Neill (1994) found that storage space and the ability to adjust or control one's office space were the best predictors of satisfaction with workspace. Variables such as partition type, panel height, and square footage were not related to satisfaction or performance. Other research on landscaped office has also concluded that variables such as occupancy of coworkers in the same space and desk ownership contribute to productivity and employee well-being (Babapour, 2019; Cordero, 2019).

Informal communication Communication among employees in an organization that is not directly related to the completion of an organizational task.

Grapevine An unofficial, informal communication network.

Informal Communication

An interesting type of organizational communication is **informal communication**. Often, informal information is transmitted through the **grapevine**, a term that can be traced back to the Civil War, when loosely hung telegraph wires resembled grapevines. The communication across these lines was often distorted. Because unofficial employee communication is also thought to be distorted, the term has become synonymous with an informal communication network (Davis, 1977). Grapevines are common because they provide employees with information, power, and entertainment (Kurland &

Pelled, 2000). Not surprisingly, the prevalence of email, texting, and social media has increased the importance of the grapevine.

Davis (1953) studied the grapevine and established the existence of four grapevine patterns: single strand, gossip, probability, and cluster. As Figure 11.1 shows, in the **single-strand grapevine**, Jones passes a message to Smith, who passes the message to Brown, and so on until the message is received by everyone or someone "breaks the chain." This pattern is similar to the children's game of "telephone" in which the first person in the line whispers a phrase to the next person, and this continues until it reaches the last person in the line. In the **gossip grapevine**, Jones passes the message to only a select group of people. Notice that with this pattern only one person passes the message along, and not everyone has a chance to receive, or will receive, it. In the **probability grapevine**, Jones tells the message to a few other employees, and they in turn randomly pass the message along to other employees. In the **cluster grapevine**, Jones tells only a few select employees, who in turn tell a few select others.

Research on the grapevine has supported several of Davis's (1953) findings. Sutton and Porter (1968) studied 79 employees in a state tax office and reached several interesting conclusions. They found that employees could be placed into one of three categories. **Isolates** were employees who received less than half of the information, liaisons were employees who both received most of the information and passed it on to others, and **dead-enders** were those who heard most of the information but seldom passed it on to other employees.

Managers tended to be liaisons because they had heard 97% of the grapevine information and most of the time passed it on. Nonmanagerial employees heard 56% of the grapevine information but seldom passed it on. Only 10% of nonmanagerial employees were liaisons; 57% were dead-enders; and 33% were isolates.

Although most people consider the grapevine to be inaccurate, research has shown that information in the grapevine often contains a great deal of truth, though it is often incomplete. A review of rumors in organizations indicates that organizational rumors are about 80% accurate (DiFonzo & Bordia, 2006). Such a statistic, however, can be

Figure 11.1
Grapevine Patterns

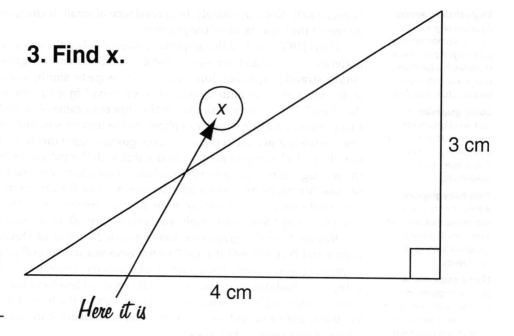

3. Find x.

3 cm

4 cm

Here it is

As shown in this answer to a geometry test, directions should be specific to get the desired results.

misleading. Consider the following hypothetical example: A message travels through the grapevine that "the personnel director will fire 25 people on Monday morning at nine o'clock." The truth, however, is that the personnel director will *hire* 25 people on Monday morning at nine o'clock. Thus, even though four out of five parts of the message (80%) are correct, the grapevine message paints a picture quite different from reality.

The grapevine contains two types of information: gossip and rumor. Although both gossip and rumor contain poorly substantiated information, **gossip** is primarily about individuals and the content of the message lacks significance to the people gossiping. **Rumor**, however, contains information that is significant to the lives of those communicating the message and can be about individuals or other topics (DiFonzo & Bordia, 2006). Usually, rumor will occur when the available information is both interesting and ambiguous. Thus, rumor serves the function of helping to make sense of ambiguous information and of helping manage potential threats, whereas gossip serves to entertain and supply social information (DiFonzo & Bordia, 2007). The most common topics for rumor are personnel changes, job security, and the external reputation of the organization (DiFonzo & Bordia, 2007). Rumor and gossip are often ways in which employees can relieve stress and anxiety, respond to perceived organizational wrongs in a nonaggressive way, maintain a sense of control, and increase their power in an organization (DiFonzo & Bordia, 2006, 2007; Kurland & Pelled, 2000).

Certainly, not all horizontal communication is informal. Employees at the same level often exchange job-related information on such topics as customers and clients, the status of projects, and information necessary to complete a particular task. To increase the amount of job-related horizontal communication, many organizations have adopted the practice of self-managed work groups.

For example, at Columbia Gas Development in Houston, Texas, 12-person drilling teams were formed. The team approach greatly increased communication among geologists, engineers, and other staff members who had previously been located in

Gossip Poorly substantiated information and insignificant information that is primarily about individuals.

Rumor Poorly substantiated information that is passed along the grapevine.

separate departments. As another example, the use of teams at Meridian Insurance in Indianapolis increased communication and efficiency so much that a 29-step process for handling paperwork was reduced to 4 steps.

11-2 Interpersonal Communication

Interpersonal communication
Communication between two individuals.

Interpersonal communication involves the exchange of a message across a communication channel from one person to another. As shown in Figure 11.2, the interpersonal communication process begins with a sender encoding and transmitting a message across a communication channel (e.g., by memo, orally, nonverbally) and ends with another person (the receiver) receiving and decoding the message. Although this seems like a simple process, there are three main problem areas where things can go wrong and interfere with the accurate transmission or reception of the message.

Problem Area 1: Intended Message Versus Message Sent

For effective communication, the sender must know what they want to say and how they want to say it. Interpersonal communication problems can occur when the message a person sends is not the message they intended. There are three solutions to this problem: thinking about what you want to communicate, practicing what you want to communicate, and learning better communication skills.

Thinking About What You Want to Communicate

Often the reason we don't say what we mean is that we are not really sure what we want to say. For example, think of using the drive-thru window at a fast-food restaurant. As soon as you stop, but before you have a chance to read the menu board, a voice crackles, "Can I take your order?" You intelligently reply something like, "*Uhhhhhhh*, could you hang on a minute?," and then quickly try to place an order as the pressure builds. As you drive off, you realize that you did not really order what you wanted.

Does this scenario sound familiar? If so, you are not alone. Foster and his colleagues (1988) found that many fast-food restaurant customers have so little time

Figure 11.2
The Interpersonal Communication Process

Sender — Encodes message "What I want to say." — Transmits message "What I say." — Communication Channel — Noise — Receives message "I hear her say." — Receiver — Decodes message "I think she means."

to think about their order that they make ordering mistakes. They found that placing a menu sign before the ordering station gave customers more time to think about their orders and that this decreased average ordering times from 28 seconds to 6 seconds and ordering errors from 29% to 4%.

As another example, think about calling a friend and unexpectedly getting their voice mail recording. Have you ever left a message in which the first few sentences sounded reasonably intelligent? Did the first sentence again begin with "*Uhhhhhhhhh*"? Or have you ever made a call expecting to get the voice mail recording and instead had an actual person answer the phone? These examples show the importance of thinking about what you want to communicate.

Practice What You Want to Communicate

Even though you may know what you want to say, communication errors can occur if you do not actually say what you meant to say. Thus, when communication is important, it should be practiced. Just as consultants practice before giving a training talk and actors rehearse before a performance, you too need to practice what you want to say in important situations. Perhaps you can remember practicing how you were going to ask a person out on a date: changing the tone of your voice, altering your first line, or thinking of topics to discuss so that you would appear spontaneous.

Learn Better Communication Skills

Even if you know what you want to say and how you want to say it, communication errors can still occur if you do not have the proper communication skills. It is essential to take courses in public speaking, writing, and interpersonal communication so that you will be better prepared to communicate effectively. Because of the importance of communication skills, many organizations offer a wide range of communication training programs for their employees.

Problem Area 2: Message Sent Versus Message Received

Even though an individual knows what they want to say and says it exactly as they planned, as shown in Figure 11.3, many factors affect how that message is received.

The Actual Words Used

A particular word may mean one thing in one situation but something else in another. Take the word *fine* as an example. If you were told that you had "*fine* jewelry," you would probably take the statement as a compliment. If the word were used to describe the weather—"The weather here in California is just *fine*"—it would still have a positive connotation. However, if a spouse asked, "How was the dinner I cooked?," or, "How did you like our evening of romance?," an answer of "fine" would probably result in a very lonely evening.

A particular word may also mean one thing to one person and something different to another. For example, an 80-year-old man with a rural background may use the word *girl* as a synonym for *female*. He may not understand why the women at work get upset when he refers to them as the "girls in the office." When I conduct training sessions for police officers, we discuss how such words as *boy*, *son*, and *pretty little lady* can be emotionally charged and should thus be avoided.

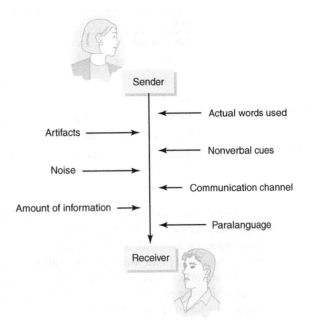

Figure 11.3
Factors Affecting the
Message Sent Versus
the Message Received

Even within English-speaking countries, a particular word can have different meanings. Take, for example, if someone said, "He was pissed." In the United States, we would interpret that the person was angry, yet people in Ireland would interpret that the person was drunk. If someone in Ireland said, "Where is the crack?," then they would be asking the location of a party, not asking about drugs.

Vague words or phrases can also cause problems. For example, you need a set of data by the end of the day, so you tell your assistant that you need the data immediately. At the end of the day, however, the data are not there. The next morning, the employee proudly brings you the data that they have compiled in "less than a day" and is confused about why you are angry. In this example, you encoded the message as "I need it by five o'clock," you transmitted the message as, "I need it immediately," and the employee decoded it as "They need it tomorrow."

If someone told you, "I won't be gone long," when would you expect them back? When I ask this question of my classes or seminar audiences, the answers usually range from 10 minutes to 3 hours. Interestingly, at one seminar I conducted, a woman responded that her husband said that very phrase and came back four days later.

As the previous examples demonstrate, it is important to be concrete in the words we use. Why, then, are we often vague in the way we communicate? One reason is that we want to avoid confrontations. If a person tells their spouse that they will be gone for four days, they may know that the spouse will object. By being vague, they avoid the initial confrontation and hope that the spouse will not notice how long they have actually been gone.

Another reason for vagueness is that it gives us a chance to "test the water" and see what a person's initial reaction might be before we say what we really want. Asking someone out on a date is a perfect example. Instead of being direct and saying, "Do you want to go out this Friday?," we often say something such as, "So, what are you up to this weekend?" If the response is positive, we become a bit bolder.

Men	Women
Talk about major global events	Talk about daily life
Tell the main point	Provide details
Are more direct	Are more indirect
Use "uh-huh" to agree	Use "uh-huh" to listen
Are comfortable with silence	Are less comfortable with silence
Concentrate on the words spoken	Concentrate on meta-messages
Sidetrack unpleasant topics	Focus on unpleasant topics

Figure 11.4
Gender Differences in Communication

Gender is another factor related to the use of words. As shown in Figure 11.4, Deborah Tannen (1995, 2001) believes that men and women speak very different languages and have different communication styles. By understanding these differences, communication in the workplace as well as in the home can be dramatically improved.

Communication can be improved if we choose our words carefully and ask, "How might the other person interpret what I am about to say?" If I use a particular word, will anyone be upset? If so, what word could I use that would be better?

Communication Channel

Problems in communication can occur because of the communication channel through which the message is transmitted. Information can be communicated in a variety of ways, such as orally, nonverbally, through a second party, or through a written medium such as a letter or memo. The same message can be interpreted in different ways based on the channel used to communicate it. For example, an employee being reprimanded will receive the message very differently if it is communicated in an email rather than face to face. A miffed employee who gives the cold shoulder to a coworker will receive a different response than if they yelled at the coworker or discussed the anger with them.

Another example of the channel's importance is a supervisor criticizing an employee in front of other employees. The employee might be so embarrassed and angered that they would not hear the content of the message. Again, transmitting a message through an inappropriate channel interferes with the message's meaning and accurate interpretation.

Often, the communication channel is the message itself. For example, if top management sends a "gofer" (i.e., someone that usually does every little task no matter how big or small) to deliver a message, it is essentially communicating that either the message or the receiver is not important. A colleague at another university talks about a former boss who always personally delivered good news (e.g., promotions, raises) as well as doughnuts on Friday. But lower-level management always had to communicate the bad news, a practice that was resented by employees.

Perhaps the worst choice of a communication channel occurred in 2006, when Radio Shack *emailed* 400 of its workers in their Fort Worth, Texas, headquarters that they would be losing their jobs. Even worse than the choice of communication channel was the actual wording of the communication, "the work force reduction notification is currently in progress. Unfortunately your position is one that has been eliminated." Employees were given boxes and plastic bags to pack their personal belongings and given 30 minutes to leave. What message do you think this sent to the employees?

Noise

The **noise** surrounding a transmission channel can also affect the way a message is received. *Noise* can be defined as any interference that affects proper reception of a message. An obvious example is actual auditory noise, such as the sound of a subway or elevated train interfering with conversation. Other examples are the appropriateness of the channel, the reputation of the person sending the message, and other information being received at the same time.

Nonverbal Cues

Much of what we communicate is conveyed by nonverbal means. Our words often say one thing, but our actions say another. For example, a supervisor may tell an employee that they are interested in hearing the employee's opinions, while at the same time the supervisor is frowning and looking out the window or responding to a text on their cell phone. The verbal message from the supervisor may be "I care," but the nonverbal message is "I'm bored." Which message will the employee pay attention to? Most likely, it will be the nonverbal one, even though nonverbal cues often lead to incorrect impressions. Nonverbal cues can be divided into five categories: body language, paralanguage, use of space, use of time, and artifacts.

Body Language. How we move and position our body—our *body language*—communicates much to other people. For example:

- When one's body faces another person, it is often interpreted as a sign of liking, whereas when a person's body is turned away from another, it is often interpreted as a sign of dislike or lack of interest.
- Superiority is communicated by interrupting others, leaning back in a chair, moving closer to someone, or sitting while others stand.
- Making eye contact implies interest. In a casual conversation, increased eye contact is interpreted as a sign of liking, in a bar it may be a sign of flirting, and on a football field it may be interpreted as a sign of aggression. Lack of eye contact can mean many things, including disinterest, discomfort, or embarrassment. A person who makes eye contact while speaking but not while listening is often perceived as being powerful or dominant.
- Raising or lowering the head or the shoulders may indicate superiority or inferiority, respectively.
- Touching someone usually indicates liking, friendship, or nurturance. In fact, a review of several studies indicated that servers who touch their customers will receive a larger tip than those who do not (Azar, 2007). Another study found that library clerks who briefly touched patrons as they were being handed books were rated by the patrons as being better employees than clerks who did not touch (Fisher, Rytting, & Heslin, 1976). Men initiate contact more often than women (Major, Schmidlin, & Williams, 1990).
- A meta-analysis by DePaulo et al. (2003) found that when people lie, they are more likely to purse their lips, raise their chin, fidget, and show nervousness than when they are not telling a lie.

As one might expect, gender differences occur in the use of nonverbal cues. For example, Dolin and Booth-Butterfield (1993) found that women use nonverbal cues such as head nodding to show attention more often than do men. In social situations, women touch, smile, and make eye contact more than men do (DePaulo, 1992).

Not surprisingly, there are many cultural differences in nonverbal communication. Here are a few examples:

- In the United States, a thumbs-up indicates agreement. In Australia, it is considered a rude gesture.
- In Japan, bowing is preferred to shaking hands.
- In the United States, people point at objects with their index finger. Germans point with their little finger, and Japanese point with the entire hand. In Japan and the Middle East, pointing with your index finger is considered rude.
- Showing the soles of one's feet is common in the United States but is considered offensive in Thailand and Saudi Arabia.
- Sitting with one's legs crossed shows relaxation in the United States but is considered offensive in Ghana and Turkey.
- Prolonged eye contact is the norm in Arabic cultures, but it shows a lack of respect in many African, Latin American, and Caribbean countries.
- Touching another person is common in Latin and Middle Eastern countries, but not in northern European or Asian countries.

Research has shown that body language can affect employee behavior. For example, a meta-analysis by Barrick, Shaffer, and DeGrassi (2009) found that the use of appropriate nonverbal communication is highly correlated with interview scores.

Though body language can be a useful source of information, it is important to understand that the same nonverbal cue can mean different things in different situations and cultures. So, be careful and try not to read too much into a particular nonverbal cue.

Use of Space. The ways people make use of space also provides nonverbal cues about their feelings and personality. Dominant people or those who have authority are given more space by others and at the same time take space from others. For example, people stand farther away from such status figures as executives and police officers (and even college professors) and stand in an office doorway rather than directly enter such a person's office. These same status figures, however, often move closer as a show of power. Police officers are taught that moving in close is one method of intimidating a person.

On the other hand, status figures also increase space to establish differences between themselves and the people with whom they are dealing. A common form of this use of distance is for an executive to place a desk between themself and another person. An interesting story is told by a sports agent who was negotiating a player's contract with George Steinbrenner, the late owner of the New York Yankees. When the agent arrived at Steinbrenner's office, he noticed that Steinbrenner sat at one end of a long desk. At the other end was a small chair in which the agent was to sit. Recognizing the spatial arrangement to be a power play, the agent moved his chair next to Steinbrenner's. As the story goes, the Yankee owner was so rattled by this ploy that the agent was able to negotiate an excellent contract for his player client.

Four major spatial distance zones in the United States have been recognized and defined (Hall, 1963): intimacy, personal distance, social distance, and public distance.

The **intimacy zone** extends from physical contact to 18 inches away from a person and is usually reserved for close relationships such as dates, spouses, and family. When this zone is entered by strangers in crowded elevators and the like, we generally feel uncomfortable and nervous. The **personal distance zone** ranges from 18 inches to 4 feet away from a person and is the distance usually reserved for friends

Intimacy zone A distance zone within 18 inches of a person, where only people with a close relationship to the person are allowed to enter.

Personal distance zone A distance zone from 18 inches to 4 feet from a person that is usually reserved for friends and acquaintances.

and acquaintances. The **social distance zone** is from 4 feet to 12 feet away and is the distance typically observed when dealing with businesspeople and strangers. Finally, the **public distance zone** ranges from 12 feet to 25 feet away and is characteristic of such large group interactions as lectures and seminars.

The way an office is furnished also communicates a lot about that person. As mentioned earlier, certain desk placements indicate openness and power; visitors and subordinates prefer not to sit before a desk that serves as a barrier (Davis, 1984). People whose offices are untidy are perceived as being busy, and people whose offices contain plants are perceived as being caring and concerned.

Use of Time. The way people make use of time is another element of nonverbal communication. If an employee is supposed to meet with a supervisor at 1:00 and the supervisor shows up at 1:10, the supervisor is communicating an attitude about the employee, the importance of the meeting, or both. Tardiness is more readily accepted from a higher-status person than from a lower-status person. Dean Smith, the great former basketball coach at the University of North Carolina, suspended any player who was even a minute late for a practice because he believed that tardiness was a sign of arrogance and worked against the team concept.

In a similar fashion, a supervisor sets aside 30 minutes for a meeting and tells others that they are not to be disturbed because they are in conference. A definitive message thus is conveyed, one that is likely to prevent constant interruptions by telephone calls or people stopping by to say hello because they saw an open door.

Care must be taken when considering how others use time, as there are tremendous cultural differences in such things as being late and keeping to time schedules. For example, punctuality is important in the United States, Austria, Canada, and Japan but not a priority in Brazil, France, Mexico, and Saudi Arabia (Olofsson, 2004).

Paralanguage

Paralanguage involves the way we say things and consists of variables such as tone, tempo, volume, number and duration of pauses, and rate of speech. A message that is spoken quickly will be perceived differently from one that is spoken slowly. In fact, research has shown that people with fast speech rates are perceived as more intelligent, friendly, and enthusiastic (Hecht & LaFrance, 1995) than people with slow rates of speech. People who use many "uh-hums," "ers," and "ahs" are also considered less intelligent. People telling lies talk less, provide fewer details, repeat words and phrases more often, have more uncertainty and vocal tension in their voice, and speak in a higher pitch than do people telling the truth (DePaulo et al., 2003).

Simple changes in the tone used to communicate a message can change the entire meaning of the message. To demonstrate this point, consider this sentence: "I didn't say Bill stole your car." At first reading, it does not seem unusual, but what does it actually mean? As Figure 11.5 shows, if we emphasize the first word, *I*, the implication is that *someone else* said, "Bill stole your car." But if we emphasize the word *Bill*, the meaning changes to "Someone else stole your car." And so on. Thus, a simple written message can be interpreted in seven different ways. As you can see, many messages are better communicated orally than in writing.

Artifacts

A final element of nonverbal communication concerns the objects, or **artifacts**, that a person wears or with which they surround themself. A person who wears bright and

Inflected Sentences	Meaning
I did not say Bill stole your car.	**Someone else** said Bill stole your car.
I **did not** say Bill stole your car.	I **deny** I said Bill stole your car.
I did not **say** Bill stole your car.	I **implied** that Bill stole your car.
I did not say **Bill** stole your car.	**Someone else** stole your car.
I did not say Bill **stole** your car.	He **borrowed** your car.
I did not say Bill stole **your** car.	Bill stole **someone else's** car.
I did not say Bill stole your **car.**	Bill stole **something else** of yours.

Figure 11.5
Inflection Changes and Meaning

colorful clothes is perceived differently from a person who wears conservative white or gray clothing. Similarly, the manager who places all of their awards on their office wall, the executive with a large and expensive chair, and the student who carries a briefcase rather than a backpack are all making nonverbal statements about themselves.

Research on visitors' perceptions of certain office characteristics has resulted in several interesting but not necessarily surprising findings. One line of research examined the perceptions of visitors to offices that used either open or closed desk arrangements. An **open desk arrangement** faces a desk against a wall so that a visitor can sit next to the person who sits behind the desk. A **closed desk arrangement** places a desk so that a visitor must sit across from the person behind the desk.

Visitors to offices that use open rather than closed desk arrangements perceive the offices to be more comfortable, and their occupants as friendlier and more trustworthy, open, interested, and extraverted (Campbell, 1979; Knapp, Hall, & Horgan, 2014; McElroy, Morrow, & Wall, 1983). Visitors rate people with messy offices as being active and busy, those with clean offices as being organized and introverted, and those with organized offices (lots of papers placed in stacks) as being active and achievement-oriented (McElroy et al., 1983; Morrow & McElroy, 1981). Finally, visitors rate offices with plants and posters as more comfortable, inviting, and hospitable than offices without plants and posters (Campbell, 1979).

Thinking about the placement of desks in an office has gone beyond the simple concept of visitor reactions. Office decorating experts (e.g., Too, 2009) using the concepts of *feng shui*—the Chinese art of placement and design—advise that, to properly use the energy of a room, desks:

- should never be placed directly across from a doorway;
- should always face away from a wall; and
- should never be placed in the center of the room.

Research on office design is not only interesting but also important. A supervisor with a messy office and a closed desk arrangement is sending the message that they do not want to be bothered. This may not be the supervisor's intended message, but it is the one perceived by their subordinates. Thus, if this supervisor wants to be more open and improve communication with his employees, they might start by changing the appearance of their office.

Clearly, people make judgments about others based on their offices, and the next logical step is to determine whether people with different types of offices actually have different types of personalities. Limited research, in fact, does seem to show that the appearance of an office provides insight into the personality of the occupant.

Open desk arrangement An office arranged so that a visitor can sit adjacent to rather than across from the person behind the desk.

Closed desk arrangement An office arranged so that a visitor must sit across from the person behind the desk.

Feng shui The ancient Chinese practice of arranging objects to maximize positive energy and improve the quality of life.

McElroy, Morrow, and Ackerman (1983) looked at the personalities of faculty members who had open desk arrangements and those who had closed desk arrangements and found that those with open desk arrangements were more extraverted and "people oriented" than their closed desk counterparts. Furthermore, faculty members who used open desk arrangements had lower external locus of control and scored higher on the Least-Preferred Coworker (LPC) Scale, which is discussed in Chapter 12.

In another study, Zweigenhaft (1976) compared desk placement using several variables and found that older, higher-status faculty members used closed desk arrangements more than did younger members. Even more interesting was the finding that faculty members who used closed desk arrangements were also evaluated less favorably in the classroom. Thus, desk placement was able to partially predict the effectiveness of a faculty member, providing support for the idea that different types of people arrange their offices in different ways.

In a study of personnel managers, Cochran, Kopitzke, and Miller (1984) compared the office characteristics used by managers with their personalities. They found that dominant, achievement-oriented managers did not decorate their offices with anything other than standard furniture; more outgoing managers had photographs of their vacations to remind them of good times and a clock to let them know when it was quitting time; introverted managers had plants and paintings so that their office would remind them of home; and organized managers had cartoons to show that even though they were neat and compulsive, they also had a sense of humor.

The presence of windows is another factor that seems to affect the way an office is decorated. Heerwagen and Orians (1986) examined the ways people decorated both windowed and windowless offices and found that occupants of windowless offices used twice as many decorative items such as posters, pictures, and paintings. Not surprisingly, the posters in windowless offices contained more landscapes and fewer cityscapes than did offices with windows.

Amount of Information

The amount of information contained in a message can affect the accuracy with which it is received. When a message contains more information than we can hold in memory, the information becomes leveled, sharpened, and assimilated. For example, suppose a friend told you the following message over the phone:

> John Atoms worked in Detroit for the automobile manufacturer General Floaters Corporation. He came to work on Tuesday morning wearing a brown shirt, plaid pants, white socks, and dark shoes. He leaned forward, barfed all over the floor, and then passed out. He was obviously intoxicated. He had worked for the company for 13 years, so they didn't want to fire him, but they had to do something. The company decided to suspend him for a few days and place him on probation. They were especially sensitive to his problems because he was on his eighth marriage.

What would the story sound like if you passed it on to a friend? When you **level** some of the information, unimportant details are removed. For example, information about the color of the employee's shirt and socks would probably not be passed along to the next person. When you **sharpen** the information, interesting and unusual information is kept. In the example here, the employee's "barfing" and his eight marriages would probably be the story's main focus as it is passed from you to your

Leveled Describes a message from which unimportant informational details have been removed before the message is passed from one person to another.

Sharpened Describes a message in which interesting and unusual information has been kept in the message when it is passed from one person to another; *see Leveled.*

friend. When you **assimilate** the information, it is modified to fit your existing beliefs and knowledge. Most of us have probably never heard of the last name Atoms, but we probably have known someone named "Adams." Likewise, "General Floaters" might be passed along as General Motors. You might use the word *drunk* rather than *intoxicated*.

Reactions to Communication Overload

With many jobs, communication overload can occur when an employee receives more communication than they can handle. When an employee is overloaded, they can adapt or adjust in one of several ways to reduce the stress: omission, error, queuing, escape, using a gatekeeper, or using multiple channels.

Omission.   One way to manage communication overload is **omission**: a conscious decision not to process certain types of information. For example, a busy supervisor may let the phone ring without answering it so that they can finish their paperwork. Although this technique can work if the overload is temporary, it will be ineffective if an employee misses an important communication.

Error.   In the **error** type of response, the employee attempts to deal with every message they receive. But in so doing, each processed message includes reception error. The processing errors are not intentional but result from processing more than can be handled.

Perhaps a good example of this would be a student who has two hours in which to study four chapters for a test. A student using the error method would attempt to read and memorize all four chapters in two hours. Obviously, their test score will probably indicate that even though they did all of the reading, much of it was not remembered or not remembered correctly.

The probability of error occurring can be reduced in two ways. First, the message can be made *redundant*. That is, after communicating an important message over the telephone, it is a good idea to write a memo to the other person summarizing the major points of the conversation. Furthermore, after sending an important memo, it is wise to call its recipient to ensure that the memo was not only received but also read.

Second, error can be reduced by having the recipient *verify* the message. Ask the person to repeat the message or to acknowledge that they have read and understood it. For example, after a customer has placed an order at the drive-thru window of a fast-food restaurant, the employee repeats the order to the customer to make sure they heard it correctly.

Queuing.   Another method of dealing with communication overload is **queuing**—placing the work into a *queue*, or waiting line. The order of the queue can be based on such variables as the message's importance, timeliness, or sender. For example, an email sent by the company president will probably be placed near or at the beginning of the queue, as will an emergency phone message. A message to return the phone call of a salesperson, however, most likely will go at the end of the queue.

With this method of handling communication overload, all of the work will usually get done. However, queues are effective only if the communication overload is temporary. If the employee is constantly overloaded, they will never reach the messages at the end of the queue.

Escape.   If communication overload is prolonged, a common employee response is to **escape**, usually through absenteeism and ultimately through resignation. This response certainly is not beneficial to an organization, but it can be beneficial to an employee if it protects their mental and physical health by relieving stress.

An example of the escape response is often seen with students who withdraw from college courses. A student may enroll in six classes and realize after two months that they do not have enough time to do all of the reading and writing required for six classes. Rather than choosing the error or omission strategy, either of which would result in lower grades, the student withdraws from one of the classes to reduce their overload.

Use of a Gatekeeper. A response to communication overload used by many executives is the use of a **gatekeeper**, a person who screens potential communication and allows only the most important to go through. Receptionists and administrative assistants are the most obvious examples of gatekeepers.

Use of Multiple Channels. The final coping response to communication overload is the use of **multiple channels**. With this strategy, an organization reduces the amount of communication going to one person by directing some of it to another. For example, in a small restaurant, all of the problems involving customers, employees, finances, and vendors are handled by the owner. But as the business grows, the owner may not be able to handle all of the communication and thus may hire others to deal with finances (a bookkeeper) and vendors (an assistant manager).

Knowing and understanding this list of responses to communication overload is important. When communication overload occurs, employees will react in ways that reduce the increased stress. Some of these strategies (omission, error, escape) result in negative consequences for the organization. Thus, the organization must recognize when overload occurs and aggressively adopt an acceptable strategy to deal with it.

Problem Area 3: Message Received Versus Message Interpreted

Even though a person knows what they want to say and says it the way they want, and even though another individual properly receives the intended message, its meaning can change depending on the way in which the receiver interprets the message. As shown in Figure 11.6, this interpretation is affected by a variety of factors, such as listening skills, listening style, emotional state, cognitive ability, and personal biases.

Listening Skills

Listening is probably the most important communication skill that a supervisor should master. In a study of managers, Nichols and Stevens (1957) found that 70%

Gatekeeper A person who screens potential communication for someone else and allows only the most important information to pass through.

Multiple channels A strategy for coping with communication overload in which an organization reduces the amount of communication going to one person by directing some of it to another person.

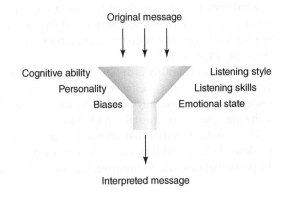

Figure 11.6
Factors Affecting the Message Received Versus the Message Interpreted

of the white-collar workday is spent communicating. Of that, 9% is spent in writing, 16% in reading, 30% in speaking, and 45% in listening. Thus, a manager spends more time listening than doing any other single activity. This is an important point for two reasons.

First, listening is a skill, and our formal education in high school and college often does not prepare us for managerial communication (Burley-Allen, 2001). We are required to take English courses to improve our reading and writing and are usually required to take one speech course to improve our oral communication skills, but we spend little, if any, time learning how to listen. Thus, the amount of time spent learning about various types of communication is inversely related to the actual amount of time spent by managers on the job.

Second, listening effectiveness is poor. It has been estimated that immediately after a meeting, we retain only 50% of the material we have heard and only 25% of the material 48 hours later (Nichols & Stevens, 1957). Although much of this loss can be attributed to poor memory practices, some is the result of poor listening habits.

Styles of Listening

What can be done to increase listening effectiveness? Perhaps the most important thing we can do is to recognize that every person has a particular "listening style" that serves as a communication filter. Geier and Downey (1980) have developed a test, the **Attitudinal Listening Profile**, to measure an employee's listening style. Their theory postulates six main styles of listening: leisure, inclusive, stylistic, technical, empathic, and nonconforming (LISTEN).

Leisure listening is practiced by "good-time" people who listen only for words that indicate pleasure. For example, a student who is a leisure listener will pay attention only when the teacher is interesting and tells jokes. As an employee, they are the last one to "hear" that employees are needed to work overtime.

Inclusive listening is the style of the person who listens for the main ideas behind any communication. In an hour-long meeting full of details and facts about a decline in sales, the only information this type of listener will "hear" is the main point that sales are down and that things had better improve. This listening style can be an advantage when cutting through a jungle of detail, but it can be a disadvantage when detail is important.

Stylistic listening is practiced by the person who listens to the *way* the communication is presented. Stylistic listeners will not listen unless the speaker's style is appropriate, the speaker "looks the part," or both. For example, when speaking to a stylistic listener, a lecturer on finance will find an attentive ear only if they wear a nice suit. After all, this listener reasons, if the lecturer cannot afford a nice suit, why listen to what they have to say about investing money? Similarly, if the speaker says that an event will be fun, they must *sound* as if they mean it. And if an employee calls in sick to a manager who is a stylistic listener, they had better "sound" sick if this message has been conveyed verbally.

Technical listening is the style practiced by the "Jack Webbs" of the listening world—those who want "just the facts, ma'am." The technical listener hears and retains large amounts of detail, but they do not hear the *meaning* of those details. In the earlier example of the meeting in which employees are told that sales have decreased, the technical listener will hear and remember that sales last year were 12.3% higher than this year, that profits are down by 21%, and that six employees will probably be laid off. However, they will miss the point that unless sales improve, they could be one of those six.

Attitudinal Listening Profile A test developed by Geier and Downey that measures individual listening styles.

Leisure listening The listening style of a person who cares about only interesting information.

Inclusive listening The listening style of a person who cares about only the main points of a communication.

Stylistic listening The listening style of a person who pays attention mainly to the way in which words are spoken.

Technical listening The listening style of a person who cares about only facts and details.

Empathic listening The listening style of a person who cares primarily about the feelings of the speaker.

Nonconforming listening The listening style of a person who cares about only information that is consistent with their way of thinking.

Empathic listening tunes in to the feelings of the speaker and, of the six listening types, is the most likely to pay attention to nonverbal cues. Thus, an empathic listener will listen to an employee complain about their boss and is the only one of the six types of listeners who will not only pay attention but also understand that the employee's complaints indicate true frustration and unhappiness.

Nonconforming listening is practiced by the individual who attends only to information that is consistent with their way of thinking. If the nonconforming listener does not agree with a speaker, they will not listen to what the speaker says. Furthermore, the nonconforming listener will pay attention only to those people they consider to be strong or to have authority.

How Listening Styles Affect Communication

The following example will demonstrate the importance of the six listening styles in a work setting. Suppose an employee approaches a supervisor and tells the supervisor that they have a temperature of 108 degrees. How would each of the six listeners react?

The leisure listener would pay little attention to the employee because they do not like to hear about unpleasant things, and illness certainly is not pleasant. The inclusive listener would probably tell a story about when they had a high temperature, thinking that the topic of conversation is fever. You may have friends who often say things that are not related to your conversation; as this example points out, they are probably inclusive listeners who mistake the main points of a conversation. In this case, the employee is communicating that they do not feel well; they are not discussing "temperatures I have had."

The stylistic listener would pay attention only if the employee sounded and looked ill. You may have also called a professor or a date and tried to sound ill in order to cancel an appointment or a date (e.g., fake a cough, or a stuffed nose). Few people actually sound ill even when they are, but we understand the importance of style in listening and behave accordingly.

The technical listener would hear every word but would not realize their meaning. That is, 10 minutes later, when another employee asked whether Sue is sick, the supervisor would respond, "She didn't say. She has a temperature of 108, but I'm not sure how she is feeling."

The nonconforming listener would pay little attention to the employee. After all, if the employee actually had a temperature of 108 degrees, they would be dead, and because they are not dead, they must be lying. Of course, the employee exaggerated their temperature because they were emphasizing the point that they are sick. But the nonconforming listener would not "hear" anything once they recognized that an initial statement was incorrect.

In this example, the empathic listener would be the only one who would understand the real point of the communication. The employee is mentioning their temperature because they do not feel well and want to go home.

Understanding each of the six styles can make communication more effective in two ways. First, becoming aware of your own style allows you to understand the filter you use when listening to others. For example, a student who uses a leisure style may need to recognize that if they listen only to lectures that they find interesting, they probably will miss a lot of important information. They might want to learn how to concentrate on lectures even when they are boring. Second, understanding the six styles can lead to better communication with others. For example, when speaking to an inclusive listener, we must either write down relevant details that we want them to remember or have them repeat the details. Otherwise, the inclusive listener will remember only the main point: "I know there is a party tonight, but I'm not sure when or where." On the other hand, when we speak to a technical listener, it is important to tell them what the details mean. For example, if you tell a technical listener there will be a party at your house on Thursday at 8:00 p.m., you should also add that they are invited, or they will understand only that there is a party, and not that they have been invited.

Of course, the million-dollar question is, "How can we tell what style of listener is listening to us?" The best way might be to test the listener on the Attitudinal Listening Profile mentioned earlier, but this is hardly practical. The most practical method is to use the person's *speaking* style as an indicator of listening style. If the person usually mentions how they feel about things, they are probably an empathic listener, but if they speak with a lot of detail, they are probably a technical listener.

Someone speaking to a group, of course, must relate to all styles of listeners. The best communicators will have something for everyone. A good instructor will provide jokes and humorous stories for leisure listeners, use an outline format and provide main points for inclusive listeners, provide specific facts and details for technical listeners, discuss their feelings about the topic for empathic listeners, have good speaking skills and appropriate dress for stylistic listeners, and be confident and accurate for nonconforming listeners.

Tips for Effective Listening

In addition to understanding how your listening style serves as a filter, you can improve your listening effectiveness in many other ways. Following is a summary of tips taken from a variety of sources:

- Don't dominate the conversation.
- Let the other person finish speaking.
- Focus on what the person is saying rather than on how well they are saying it, what your next response will be, or what you will eat for lunch. Try to understand what the other person is *trying* to say.
- Ask questions to make sure you understand the person's point, but don't ask so many questions that they distract the speaker.
- Be patient and keep an open mind. If you disagree, you can always do so after the person is finished talking.
- Show the speaker you want to listen by using nonverbal cues such as making eye contact and nodding your head.
- Remove or resist distractions that will keep you from listening.
- Be silent for a few seconds after the person has finished speaking. This will encourage the person to continue to talk, you will be sure when they have finished talking, and it will give you time to respond calmly.

Emotional State

The interpretation of a message can certainly be affected by the receiver's emotional state. When we are mad, anxious, depressed, elated, or upset, we do not think as clearly as when our moods are more moderate. Think of the last time you had an argument with someone. How rational and intelligent was your conversation? After the argument was over, did both of you remember what was said in the same way?

Likewise, have you ever attended a class when your mind was somewhere else? My guess is that neither your attention span nor your comprehension of the material was as high as normal.

Bias

Our biases obviously affect our ability to interpret information we receive. For example, we can hate a political candidate so much that we can refuse to process any of the positive information we hear about them. We do, however, process every piece of information that is consistent with our opinion.

11-3 Improving Employee Communication Skills

Organizations are always looking for employees with excellent communication skills. The difficulty in finding such employees was exemplified by the experience of a national insurance company. The company was having difficulty with a position that required employees to respond to customer complaints. The company had hired expensive consultants to teach its employees how to write effective emails, but performance had not improved. The company then constructed sample emails so that an employee could read a customer complaint, find a standard response form, and add a few personal lines. This also did not work. Finally, the company tried using a standardized writing test before hiring its employees. This test predicted success for some employee groups but not for others. Thus, the question remains: How can an organization increase the communication skills of its employees?

Would this be an example of good communication?

Interpersonal Communication Skills

One of the most common methods used to increase interpersonal communication skills is the training workshop conducted by an outside consultant or a company trainer. In these workshops, employees learn about many of the topics discussed in this chapter. Although many consultants lead communication workshops, such workshops often bring only short-term improvement in skills.

An example of an organization investing in its employees' interpersonal skills is a case study conducted on its information technology department, consisting of about 1,300 employees. Through the use of external vendors, the organization was able to achieve anecdotal success and recommended the use of case studies and real-life examples as training strategies (Hynes, 2012).

Written Communication Skills

Attempts to improve the quality of written communication have generally taken two paths. One approach concentrates on improving the writer's skills and the other concentrates on making material easier to read.

Improving Writing

With increased use of informal email and texting, effective writing skills are more essential than ever. It is difficult for an organization to overcome an employee's lack of formal training in writing (or to change bad writing habits). Several consulting firms, however, specialize in the improvement of employee writing by teaching employees the most important concepts of writing. For example, Broadbent (1997) advises that writing can be improved when writers value what they write, set personal standards and goals (e.g., vocabulary usage at a 12th-grade reading level, no grammar errors, each document proofread twice), and spend considerable time doing their own editing as well as getting others to edit the document. Employees need to analyze their audience: If a written communication is intended for employees that are not likely to have attended college, then the readability must be kept simple. If the intended audience is a busy executive, the message must be kept short.

Readability

Written communication can break down when material is too difficult for many employees to read. Here are some examples:

- Federal Aviation Administration regulations and many airline-company pilots' association agreements are too difficult for pilots to read (Blumenfeld, 1985).
- Corporate annual reports are too difficult for most adults to understand (Courtis, 1995).
- The Position Analysis Questionnaire (the job analysis instrument discussed in Chapter 2) is also too difficult for most job incumbents to read (Ash & Edgell, 1975).

Thus, providing employees with important material to read will be an effective communication form only if the employees can understand what is written. In a study of written communication at a restaurant chain, Smith and Christensen (2007) found a wide range of readability levels in written materials given to employees. Though most communication was written at a ninth-grade level, a memo to cooks was written at the

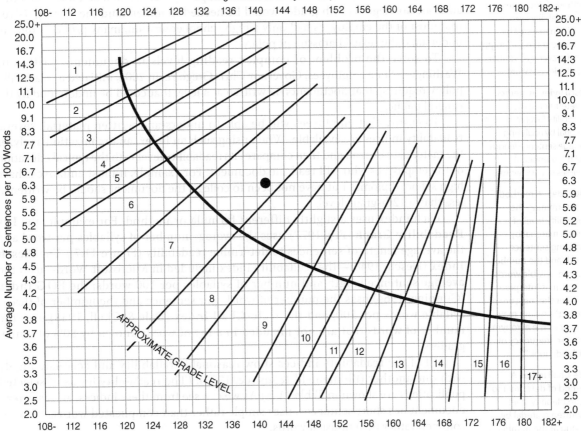

Average Number of Syllables per 100 Words

Expanded Directions for Working Readability Graph

1. Randomly select three sample passages and count out exactly 100 words each, beginning with the beginning of a sentence. Do count proper nouns, initializations, and numerals.
2. Count the number of sentences in the 100 words, estimating length of the fraction of the last sentence to the nearest one-tenth.
3. Count the total number of syllables in the 100-word passage. If you don't have a hand counter available, simply put a mark above every syllable over one in each word. Then when you get to the end of the passage, count the number of marks and add 100. Small calculators can also be used as counters by pushing numeral 1, then pushing the + sign for each word or syllable when counting.
4. Enter graph with *average* sentence length and *average* number of syllables; plot dot where the two lines intersect. Area where dot is plotted will give you the approximate grade level.
5. If a great deal of variability is found in syllable count or sentence count, putting more samples into the average is desirable.
6. A word is defined as a group of symbols with a space on either side; thus *Joe, IRA, 1945,* and *&* are each one word.
7. A syllable is defined as a phonetic syllable. Generally, there are as many syllables as vowel sounds. For example, *stopped* is one syllable and *wanted* is two syllables. When counting syllables for numerals and initializations, count one syllable for each symbol. For example, *1945* is four syllables, *IRA* is three syllables, and *&* is one syllable.

Figure 11.7
Graph for Estimating Readability

Fry Readability Graph A method of determining the readability level of written material by analyzing sentence length and the average number of syllables per word.

Flesch Index A method of determining the readability level of written material by analyzing average sentence length and the number of syllables per 100 words.

FOG Index A method of determining the readability level of written material by analyzing sentence length and the number of three-syllable words. (The term is interpreted as either the measure of the "fog" a reader may be in or as the acronym FOG, for "frequency of gobbledygook.")

Dale-Chall Index A method of determining the readability level of written material by looking at the number of commonly known words used in the document.

fourth-grade level and the sexual harassment policy was written at a level such that an associate degree (14th grade) would be needed to understand the writing. Given that most of the employees had only a high school education, many probably did not understand the sexual harassment policy.

To solve the problem of complex reading levels in documents written by Washington State employees, Governor Chris Gregoire, in 2004, initiated a "plain talk" policy requiring that documents be written at a level that could be understood by the general public.

To ensure that employees will be able to understand written material, several readability indices are available. When using such an index, an organization analyzes the material to be read and then compares its readability level with the typical education of the employees who will read the document. For example, if most employees have high school diplomas but have not been to college, the document should be written at less than a 12th-grade level.

Each index uses a slightly different formula or method. For example, the **Fry Readability Graph** (Fry, 1977) uses the average number of syllables per word and the average length of sentences to determine readability (Figure 11.7). The **Flesch Index** (Flesch, 1948)—the readability index included in Microsoft Word—uses the average sentence length and number of syllables per 100 words; the **FOG Index** (Gunning, 1964) uses the number of words per sentence and the number of three-syllable words per 100; and the **Dale-Chall Index** (Dale & Chall, 1948) uses the number of words that are not included in a list of words known by 80% of fourth graders.

All of the readability indices show reasonable reliability and correlate highly with one another (Blumenfeld & Justice, 1975). (The readability levels of selected publications are shown in Table 11.2.) As we can see from these indices, an easily read document has short sentences, uses simple rather than complicated words, and uses common rather than unusual words.

Table 11.2 Readability Levels of Selected Publications

Document	Readability Level
FAA regulations	Graduate student
Position Analysis Questionnaire	College graduate
Harvard Law Review	College graduate
Airline Pilot magazine	College student
Study of Values	12th grade
Time magazine	11th grade
Newsweek	11th grade
Washington Post	11th grade
USA Today	10th grade
Otis Employment Test	9th grade
Ladies' Home Journal	8th grade
Reader's Digest	8th grade
Minnesota Multiphasic Personality Inventory—2	8th grade
Most comic books	6th grade

Applied Case Study

As mentioned in this chapter, ordering errors are common at the drive-thru windows of quick-service restaurants such as Hardee's, McDonald's, Burger King, and Wendy's. One of the reasons for these errors is that order takers are distracted and thus do not listen properly. That is, while taking one customer's order, an employee is simultaneously taking money and counting change for another customer, filling drinks, and assembling food orders. Another reason is that some customers may not speak the same language as the person taking the order.

- From what you learned in this chapter, what could a quick-service restaurant do to increase order accuracy?
- What are the advantages and disadvantages to your plan?

To find out how some McDonald's and Hardee's franchises reduced ordering errors, use the link found on your text webpage.

Focus on Ethics — Ethical Communication

Transparent communication is when there is open and honest communication between employees and management regarding work-life issues. But how transparent should a company be in situations that may have a negative impact on both the company and employees?

For example, a large insurance company in Maryland is going through some difficult times. The company has not done well financially for about two or three years. As a result, management is considering whether to lay off some employees in the coming year.

When supervisors asked management if they should tell employees of possible layoffs, the supervisors were told not to. The reason was twofold: management is not absolutely sure layoffs would be necessary, and if employees heard such news, it might start a panic. This panic might encourage some employees to look for and take positions in other companies. Management wants to make sure they did not lose any of their good staff. Management also said that not communicating this information would "protect" employees from unnecessary stress caused by worrying about something that may never happen. Management feels it is more ethical not to communicate this news until they are absolutely sure the layoffs would occur.

But not communicating this information could, instead of "protecting" employees, cause problems for some. Employees who are about to make some kind of financial decisions, such as buying a house or a car or spending a large amount of money on a vacation, may make a completely different decision if they know they may be laid off in the near future. Additionally, employees who may have already been offered jobs in another

company and are deciding whether to stay or quit may make a different decision if they know about pending layoffs in their current company.

A 2008 survey done by Ethics and Workplace Survey done by Deloitte, LLP, an independent consulting firm, reported that 84% of employees said that transparent communication leads to a more ethical workplace. These employees may believe that communicating about possible layoffs is more ethical than trying to protect employees from the stress of worrying about something that may never happen.

The other side of transparent communication is the ethical responsibility of *employees* to communicate certain information to their supervisors. For example, there are times when people, while employed in one company, search for other jobs. Usually, those employees will not let their managers know that they are looking for other jobs. The thinking behind not doing that is that if the supervisor finds out, they may get upset and retaliate in some way against that employee. If the employee is able to get another position, the usual amount of notice given to the current manager is two weeks.

For some organizations, it may be difficult and/or time-consuming to find someone to replace an employee who has taken a position in another organization. If managers know ahead of time that one of their employees is job searching, the company could start the recruitment process for a replacement. Even if the current employee does not leave after all, the company would at least have names of potential candidates who, in the future, may fill a position should it become vacant. But when a company is not aware that an employee in a

(Continued)

hard-to-fill position may leave and is only given two weeks' notice that the employee will be quitting, that company could go months before finding a suitable replacement. This could potentially cause financial hardships to the company, as well as increase the workloads of other employees who must take up the slack after a position is vacated.

What Do You Think?

- Do you agree that companies should communicate any and all information that may pertain to employees?
- Would there ever be a time where it would be more ethical to hold back information from employees?

- If you were an employee in the insurance company, what would you consider to be the ethical step to take: inform employees of the possibilities of layoffs or keep that information confidential until the company is absolutely sure layoffs might happen?
- What would be the best, most ethical, channel to use when communicating bad news such as layoffs?
- Do you think it is unethical not to tell your boss that you are looking for another job? What are the situations in which employees have an ethical obligation to provide this information to their managers or supervisors?

Chapter Summary

In this chapter you learned:

- There are three types of organizational communication: upward, downward, and horizontal.
- There are three main problem areas in interpersonal communication: the intended message versus the message actually sent, the message sent versus the message received, and the message received versus the message interpreted.
- Interpersonal communication can be improved with more effective listening skills, understanding the six different styles of listening (leisure, inclusive, stylistic, technical, empathic, and nonconforming), and considering the emotional state, cognitive ability, and personal biases of the sender and the receiver.
- Written communication can be improved by learning better writing skills and by writing organizational documents at a reading level that matches the reading level of most employees.

Key Terms

Upward communication (388)
Serial communication (388)
MUM (minimize unpleasant messages) effect (388)
Communication channel (388)
Proximity (388)
Attitude survey (389)
Suggestion box (390)
Complaint box (390)
Liaison (391)
Ombudsperson (391)
Union steward (391)
Downward communication (391)

Bulletin board (391)
Policy manual (392)
Newsletters (392)
Intranet (393)
Business communication (393)
Informal communication (396)
Grapevine (396)
Single-strand grapevine (397)
Gossip grapevine (397)
Probability grapevine (397)
Cluster grapevine (397)
Isolate (397)
Dead-enders (397)

Questions for Review

1. Why do people hate to communicate bad news?
2. When is email an inappropriate method of communication?
3. What is the best way to stop a rumor?
4. Which is most important: nonverbal cues, paralanguage, or the actual words chosen to communicate? Why?
5. Can people be taught to be effective listeners? Explain your answer.

Chapter

12

Leadership

Learning Objectives

12-1 Identify the types of people that become good leaders.

12-2 Explain the importance of leaders adapting their behavior to each situation.

12-3 Recognize the skills that are essential for effective leadership.

12-4 Differentiate among the theories of leadership.

12-5 Explain how leaders use power and influence.

Imagine a company with thousands of workers that has seen sales drop in each of the past five years. The president of the company steps down, and a new president is installed. Several years later, the company makes a profit, and everyone hails the new president as the reason for the improvement.

Now imagine a football team with a winning record in each of the last 10 years. The team's coach leaves for another school, and the team loses the majority of its games in the next few years.

In both of these examples, a new leader took over. In the first example, the organization became more successful, whereas in the second example, the team went into decline. How much of the organization's performance can be attributed to the leader? If the leader *was* the major cause of the changes in performance, why was one leader successful and the other a failure? These types of questions will be addressed in this chapter.

12-1 An Introduction to Leadership

Many different theories about leadership have been developed over the last few decades. Although none of the theories "tells the whole story" about leadership, each has received at least some empirical support. Understanding the theories and research behind leadership is important because the theory that company executives believe about leadership will, for the most part, determine how an organization selects or develops its managers.

For example, if we believe that certain people are "born leaders" because of their personal traits, needs, or orientation, then managers could be selected partially based on their scores on certain tests. But if we believe that leadership consists of specific skills or behaviors, then theoretically we should be able to train any employee to become an outstanding leader. If we believe that good leadership is the result of an interaction between certain types of behaviors and particular aspects of the situation, then we might choose certain types of people to be leaders at any given time, or we might teach leaders how to adapt their behavior to meet the situation.

The following pages provide brief explanations of the most popular leadership theories. When reading about each theory, think about what the theory would imply regarding the selection or development of leaders for an organization. In addition, think of how you manage and the type of leader you wish to be.

12-2 Personal Characteristics Associated with Leadership

In the last 100 years, many attempts have been made to identify the personal characteristics associated with leader emergence and leader performance.

Leader Emergence

Leader emergence A part of trait theory that postulates that certain types of people will become leaders and certain types will not.

Leader emergence is the idea that people who *become* leaders possess traits or characteristics different from people who do not become leaders. That is, people who become leaders—such as U.S. presidents George W. Bush and Barack H. Obama and CEOs Mary Barra and Sundar Pichai—share traits that your neighbor or a food preparer at McDonald's does not. If we use your school as an example, we would predict that the students in your student government would be different from students who do not participate in leadership activities. In fact, research indicates that to some extent, people are "born" with a desire to lead or not lead, as somewhere between 17% (Ilies, Gerhardt, & Le, 2004) and 30% (Arvey, Rotundo, Johnson, Zhang, & McGue, 2006) of leader emergence has a genetic basis.

Does that mean that there is a "leadership gene" that influences leader emergence? Probably not. Instead, we inherit certain traits and abilities that might influence our decision to seek leadership. Though early reviews of the literature suggested that the relationship between traits and leader emergence is not very strong, as shown in Table 12.1, more recent reviews suggest that:

- people high in openness, conscientiousness, extraversion, masculinity, creativity, and authoritarianism and low in neuroticism are more likely to emerge as leaders than their counterparts (Ensari, Riggio, Christian, & Carslaw, 2011; Judge, Bono, Ilies, & Gerhardt, 2002);

- people who score higher in narcissism are more likely to emerge as leaders, a relationship that has been explained by extraversion (Grijalva, Harms, Newman, Gaddis, & Fraley, 2015);
- high self-monitors (people who adapt their behavior to the social situation) emerge as leaders more often than low self-monitors (Day & Schleicher, 2006; Day, Schleicher, Unckless, & Hiller, 2002);
- people higher in cognitive ability are more likely to emerge as leaders than are people lower in cognitive ability (Ensari et al., 2011; Judge, Colbert, & Ilies, 2004); and
- looking at *patterns* of abilities and personality traits is more useful than looking at *single* abilities and traits (Foti & Hauenstein, 2007).

It is especially perplexing that some of the early reviews concluded that specific traits are seldom related to leader emergence because both anecdotal evidence and research suggest that leadership behavior has some stability (Law, 1996). To illustrate this point, think of a friend you consider to be a leader. In all probability, that person is a leader in many situations. That is, they might influence a group of friends about what movie to see, make decisions about what time everyone should meet for dinner, and "take charge" when playing sports. Conversely, you probably have a friend who has never assumed a leadership role in their life. Thus, it appears that some people consistently emerge as leaders in a variety of situations, whereas others never emerge as leaders.

Perhaps one explanation for the lack of agreement on a list of traits consistently related to leader emergence is that the motivation to lead is more complex than originally thought. In a study using a large international sample, Chan and Drasgow (2001) found that the motivation to lead has three aspects (factors): affective identity, noncalculative, and social-normative motivation. People with an **affective identity motivation** become leaders because they enjoy being in charge and leading others. Of the three leadership motivation factors, people scoring high on this one tend to have the most leadership experience and are rated by others as having high leadership potential. Those with a **noncalculative motivation** seek leadership positions when they perceive that such positions will result in personal gain. For example, becoming a leader may result in an increase in status or in pay. People with a **social-normative motivation** become leaders out of a sense of duty. For example, a member of the Kiwanis Club

Affective identity motivation The motivation to lead as a result of a desire to be in charge and lead others.

Noncalculative motivation Those who seek leadership positions because they will result in personal gain.

Social-normative motivation The desire to lead out of a sense of duty or responsibility.

Table 12.1 Summary of Meta-Analyses of Leader Emergence and Performance

Trait	Leader Emergence		Leader Performance		Meta-Analysis
	K	p	K	p	
Personality					
Neuroticism	30	−.24	18	−.22	Judge et al. (2002)
Extraversion	37	.33	23	.24	Judge et al. (2002)
Openness	20	.24	17	.24	Judge et al. (2002)
Agreeableness	23	.05	19	.21	Judge et al. (2002)
Conscientiousness	17	.33	18	.16	Judge et al. (2002)
Self-monitoring	23	.21			Day et al. (2002)
Intelligence	65	.25	151	.27	Judge et al. (2004)
Need for achievement			11	.23	Argus and Zajack (2008)

might agree to be the next president because it is "their turn," or a faculty member might agree to chair a committee out of a sense of commitment to the university.

Individuals with high leadership motivation tend to obtain leadership experience and have confidence in their leadership skills (Chan & Drasgow, 2001). Therefore, after researching the extent to which leadership is consistent across life, it makes sense that Bruce (1997) concluded that the best way to select a chief executive officer (CEO) is to look for leadership qualities (e.g., risk taking, innovation, vision) and success early in a person's career. As support for this proposition, Bruce cites the following examples:

- Harry Gray, the former chair and CEO of United Technologies, demonstrated vision, risk taking, and innovation as early as the second job in his career.
- Ray Tower, former president of FMC Corporation, went way beyond his job description as a salesperson in his first job to create a novel sales-training program. Tower continued to push his idea despite upper management's initial lack of interest.
- Lee Iacocca, known for his heroics at Ford and Chrysler, pioneered the concept of new car financing. His idea of purchasing a 1956 Ford for monthly payments of $56 ("Buy a '56 for $56") moved his sales division from last in the country to first. What is most interesting about this success is that Iacocca didn't even have the authority to implement his plan—but he did it anyway.

The role of gender in leader emergence is complex. Meta-analyses indicate that, in general, men emerge as leaders more often than do women (Badura, Grijalva, Newman, Yan, & Jeon, 2018). This is especially true in lab settings (d = .43) and less true in business settings (d = .17). Men are most likely to emerge as leaders when the length of the group interaction is low and the social complexity of the task is low. When the length of the group interaction is high and the social complexity of the task is high, gender differences in leader emergence are small (Badura et al., 2018).

Though women often emerge as leaders, historically they have been excluded from the highest levels of leadership and power in politics and business. Thus, it is said that there is a "glass ceiling" for women in leadership and management. This glass ceiling is slowly breaking, as many women leaders at the highest levels have achieved their positions since 1990 (Carli & Eagly, 2001). For example, although the gains have been slow, 47% of newly appointed members to Fortune 500 company Boards of Directors in 2020 were women, compared to 21% in 2010 (Spencer Stuart, 2020).

Leader Performance

Leader performance A part of trait theory that postulates that certain types of people will be better leaders than will other types of people.

In contrast to leader emergence, which deals with the likelihood that a person will *become* a leader, **leader performance** involves the idea that leaders who *perform well* possess certain characteristics that poorly performing leaders do not. For example, an excellent leader might be intelligent, assertive, friendly, and independent, whereas a poor leader might be shy, aloof, and calm. Research on the relationship between personal characteristics and leader performance has concentrated on three areas: traits, needs, and orientation.

Traits

As shown in Table 12.1, a meta-analysis by Judge et al. (2002) found that extraversion, openness, agreeableness, and conscientiousness were positively related to leader performance and that neuroticism was negatively related to leader performance.

Similar results were found in a meta-analysis by Do and Minbashian (2020) although they argued that a higher order trait that combines each of the Big 5 personality factors, General Factor of Personality, is a better predictor of leadership performance than the individual Big 5 factors. However, while people high in narcissism were more likely to emerge as leaders, that same positive relationship was not found between narcissism and leader performance (Grijalva et al., 2015). A meta-analysis by Youngjohn and Woehr (2001) also found that management, decision making, and oral-communication skills were highly correlated with leadership effectiveness.

As was the case with leader emergence, high self-monitors tend to be better leaders than do low self-monitors (Day & Schleicher, 2006; Day et al., 2002). The concept of **self-monitoring** is especially interesting, as it focuses on what leaders *do* as opposed to what they *are*. For example, a high self-monitoring leader may possess the trait of shyness and not truly want to communicate with other people. They know, however, that talking to others is an important part of their job, so they say hello to their employees when they arrive at work, and at least once a day stops and talks with each employee. Thus, our leader has the trait of shyness but adapts their outward behavior to appear to be outgoing and confident.

An interesting extension of the trait theory of leader performance suggests that certain traits are necessary requirements for leadership excellence but that they do not guarantee it (Simonton, 1987). Instead, leadership excellence is a function of the right person being in the right place at the right time. The fact that one person with certain traits becomes an excellent leader while another with the same traits flounders may be no more than the result of timing and chance.

For example, Lyndon Johnson and Martin Luther King, Jr., were considered successful leaders because of their strong influence on improving civil rights in the United States. Other people prior to the 1960s had had the same thoughts, ambitions, and skills as King and Johnson, yet they had not become successful civil rights leaders, perhaps because the time had not been right.

Cognitive Ability

A meta-analysis of 151 studies by Judge et al. (2004) found a moderate but significant corrected correlation ($p = .27$) between cognitive ability and leadership performance. The meta-analysis further discovered that cognitive ability is most important when the leader is not distracted by stressful situations and when the leader uses a more directive leadership style. In studies investigating the performance of U.S. presidents, it was found that the presidents rated by historians as being the most successful were smart and open to experience, had high goals, and interestingly, had the ability to bend the truth (Dingfelder, 2004; Rubenzer & Faschingbauer, 2004). Sternberg (2007) has expanded on the importance of cognitive ability by theorizing that the key to effective leadership is the *synthesis* of three variables: wisdom, intelligence (academic and practical), and creativity.

Needs

A personal characteristic that has received some support pertains to a leader's **need for power**, **need for achievement**, and **need for affiliation**. In fact, as shown in Table 12.1, a meta-analysis by Argus and Zajack (2008) found a significant relationship between need for achievement and leader performance. Research by McClelland and Burnham (1976) and McClelland and Boyatzis (1982) demonstrates that high-performance managers have a **leadership motive pattern**, which is a high need for power and a low need for affiliation. The need is not for personal power but for organizational power.

Self-monitoring A personality trait characterized by the tendency to adapt one's behavior to fit a particular social situation.

Need for power According to trait theory, the extent to which a person desires to be in control of other people.

Need for achievement According to trait theory, the extent to which a person desires to be successful.

Need for affiliation The extent to which a person desires to be around other people.

Leadership motive pattern The name for a pattern of needs in which a leader has a high need for power and a low need for affiliation.

This pattern of needs is thought to be important because it implies that an effective leader should be concerned more with results than with being liked. Leaders who need to be liked by their subordinates will have a tough time making decisions. A decision to make employees work overtime, for example, may be necessary for the organization's survival, but it will probably be unpopular with employees. Leaders with high affiliation needs may decide that being liked is more important than being successful, causing conflict with their decision.

This theory would also explain why internal promotions often do not work. Consider, for example, a person who worked for six years as a loan officer. They and 10 coworkers often went drinking together after work and went away on weekends. One day the loan officer was promoted to manager, and they had to lead the same people with whom they had been friends. The friendships and their need to be liked hindered the new manager when giving orders and disciplining employees. When they tried to separate themself from their friends, they were quickly thought of as being "too good" for them—a tough situation with no apparent solution, according to this theory.

This does not mean that a leader should not be friendly and care about subordinates. But successful leaders will not place their need to be liked above the goals of the organization. President Richard Nixon was thought to have a high need to be liked. He would often make a tough decision and then apologize for it because he wanted to be liked by both the public and the press.

Needs for power, achievement, and affiliation can be measured through various psychological tests. The most commonly used is the **Thematic Apperception Test (TAT)**. The TAT is a projective test in which a person is shown a series of pictures and asked to tell a story about what is happening in each. A trained psychologist then analyzes the stories, identifying the needs themes contained within them. Obviously, this technique is time-consuming and requires a great deal of training.

Another commonly used measure is the **Job Choice Exercise (JCE)**, developed by Stahl and Harrell (1982). With the JCE, the person reads descriptions of jobs that involve varying degrees of power, achievement, and affiliation needs and rates how desirable he finds each particular job. These ratings are then subjected to a complicated scoring procedure that uses regression analysis to reveal scores on the three needs categories.

Another method to determine leaders' needs is to examine the themes that occur in their writing and speeches. In one interesting use of this method, it was found that U.S. presidents Franklin Roosevelt, Kennedy, and Reagan had high needs for power; Presidents Harding, Truman, and Nixon had high needs for affiliation; and Presidents Wilson, Hoover, and Carter had high needs for achievement (Winter, 1988).

Gender

As with leader emergence, meta-analyses suggest that the role of gender in leader effectiveness is complex. When all studies are combined, men and women appear not to differ in leadership effectiveness (Eagly, Karau, & Makhijani, 1995). However, men were more effective as leaders in situations traditionally defined in masculine terms and in situations in which the majority of subordinates were men. Women were more effective as leaders in situations traditionally defined in less masculine terms. Though men and women appear to be equally effective leaders, a meta-analysis of leadership styles indicated that women were more likely than men to engage in behaviors associated with high-quality leadership (Eagly, Johannesen-Schmidt, & van Engen, 2003). Additionally, Paustian-Underdahl, Walker, and Woehr (2014) conducted a meta-analysis as an

---

Thematic Apperception Test (TAT) A projective personality test in which test takers are shown pictures and asked to tell stories. It is designed to measure various need levels.

Job Choice Exercise (JCE) An objective test used to measure various need levels.

extension to Eagly et al.'s (1995) meta-analysis and found contradictory support for the moderating effects of subordinate gender. Interestingly, researchers also found that rating source also affected leadership effectiveness rating scores, in which women scored significantly higher in leadership effectiveness from ratings from other people, and men scored significantly higher in leadership effectiveness from self-ratings.

Task Versus Person Orientation

Over the years, three major schools of thought—Ohio State Studies (Fleishman, Harris, & Burtt, 1955), Theory X (McGregor, 1960), and **Managerial Grid** (Blake & Mouton, 1984)—have postulated that differences in leader performance can be attributed to differences in the extent to which leaders are task versus person oriented. As shown in Figure 12.1, though the three schools of thought use different terms, they say similar things.

Person-oriented leaders such as **country club leaders**, **Theory Y leaders**, and leaders high in consideration act in a warm and supportive manner and show concern for their subordinates. Person-oriented leaders believe that employees are intrinsically motivated, seek responsibility, are self-controlled, and do not necessarily dislike work. Because of these assumptions, person-oriented leaders consult their subordinates before making decisions, praise their work, ask about their families, do not look over their shoulder, and use a more "hands-off" approach to leadership. Under pressure, person-oriented leaders tend to become socially withdrawn (Bond, 1995).

Task-oriented leaders such as **task-centered leaders**, **Theory X leaders**, and leaders high in **initiating structure** define and structure their own roles and those of their subordinates to attain the group's formal goals. Task-oriented leaders see their employees as lazy, extrinsically motivated, wanting security, undisciplined, and shirking responsibility. Because of these assumptions, task-oriented leaders tend to manage or lead by giving directives, setting goals, and making decisions without consulting their subordinates. Under pressure, they become anxious, defensive, and dominant (Bond, 1995). Interestingly, task-oriented leaders tend to produce humor (e.g., tell jokes and stories), whereas person-oriented leaders tend to appreciate humor (e.g., listen to others' jokes) (Philbrick, 1989). As shown in Figure 12.2, when using the terms from Figure 12.1, the best leaders (**team**) are both task and person oriented, whereas the worst (**impoverished**) are neither task nor person oriented. Some leaders (**middle-of-the-road**) have moderate amounts of both orientations.

Meta-analyses by Judge, Piccolo, and Ilies (2004) and by DeRue, Nahrgang, Wellman, and Humphrey (2011) found that higher scores on consideration or on initiating structure were associated with such positive leadership criteria as follower satisfaction and group performance. The relationships between person orientation (consideration) and follower satisfaction, follower motivation, and ratings of leadership effectiveness were stronger than the relationships between task orientation (initiating structure) and these same three leadership criteria. Perhaps the reason for the weaker relationships involving task orientation is that once an employee receives the desired amount of structure from a supervisor, the "excess" structure becomes irritating whereas the excess consideration may not have the same irritating effect (Lambert, Tepper, Carr, Holt, & Barelka, 2012).

Managerial Grid A measure of leadership that classifies a leader into one of five leadership styles.

Country club leaders A style of leadership in which the leader is concerned about the well-being of employees but is not task oriented.

Theory Y leaders Leaders who believe that employees are intrinsically motivated and thus lead with a "hands-off" or a participative approach.

Task-centered leaders Leaders who define and structure their roles as well as the roles of their subordinates.

Theory X leaders Leaders who believe that employees are extrinsically motivated and thus lead by giving directives and setting goals.

Initiating structure The extent to which leaders define and structure their roles and the roles of their subordinates.

Team leadership A leadership style in which the leader is concerned with both productivity and employee well-being.

Impoverished leadership A style of leadership in which the leader is concerned with neither productivity nor the well-being of employees.

Middle-of-the-road leadership A leadership style reflecting a balanced orientation between people and tasks.

Figure 12.1

Relationship Between Managerial Grid (MG) Theory, Theory X, and Ohio State (OS) Theory

A leader's task or person orientation can be measured by several instruments, two of which are the **Leadership Opinion Questionnaire (LOQ)** and the **Leader Behavior Description Questionnaire (LBDQ)**. The LOQ is filled out by supervisors or leaders who want to know their own behavioral style. The LBDQ is completed by subordinates to provide a picture of how they perceive their leader's behavior. A meta-analysis by Eagly and Johnson (1990) indicated that in laboratory studies, women were more likely to have a person orientation and less likely to have a task orientation than were men. They did not find any such difference in studies that were conducted in actual organizations. They did, however, find small gender differences, such as that women were more likely to use a more participative approach and that men were more likely to use a more autocratic approach.

As depicted in Figure 12.2, theoretically, person-oriented leaders should have satisfied employees, whereas task-oriented leaders should have productive employees. Leaders scoring high in both (called *team leadership*) should have satisfied and productive employees, whereas leaders scoring low in both (called *impoverished leadership*) should have unhappy and unproductive employees (Fleishman & Harris, 1962; Hutchison, Valentino, & Kirkner, 1998; Korman, 1966; Pool, 1997).

Although these predictions certainly make sense, the meta-analysis by Judge and his colleagues (2004) found that consideration scores (person orientation) were more strongly correlated with follower satisfaction, follower motivation, and ratings

Figure 12.2

Consequences of Leader Orientation

of leadership effectiveness than were initiating structure scores (task orientation). Correlations with the performance of the work group were similar in magnitude for both consideration and initiating structure.

To complicate matters further, the relationship between person and task orientation is probably more complex than was first thought. Several studies have shown that leader experience and knowledge and such external variables as time pressures and work importance tend to moderate the relationship between person-orientation scores and satisfaction and between task-orientation scores and subordinate performance.

Unsuccessful Leaders

The traits and behaviors of unsuccessful leaders are not necessarily the opposite of those of successful leaders (Hackman & Wageman, 2007). In a departure from research to identify characteristics of successful leaders, Hogan (1989) attempted to identify traits of unsuccessful leaders. Hogan was interested in investigating poor leaders because, according to both empirical research and anecdotal accounts, most employees report that one of the greatest sources of stress in their jobs is their supervisors' poor performance, strange behavior, or both. This finding should come as no surprise: You can probably quickly recall many examples of poor performance or strange behavior with current or former supervisors.

Lack of Training. Based on years of research, Hogan, Raskin, and Fazzini (1990) concluded that poor leader behavior has three major causes. The first is a *lack of leadership training* given to supervisors. The armed forces are among the few organizations that require supervisors to complete leadership training before taking charge of groups of people. The norm for most organizations, however, is either to promote a current employee or hire a new employee and place them directly into a leadership role. If training is ever provided, it is usually after the promotion and well after the supervisor has begun supervising. The serious consequences of this lack of training can best be understood if we imagine allowing doctors to perform surgery without training, or truck drivers to drive on the highways without first learning how to drive.

Cognitive Deficiencies. The second cause of poor leadership stems from *cognitive deficiencies*. Hogan et al. (1990) believe that poor leaders are unable to learn from experience and are unable to think strategically—they consistently make the same mistakes and do not plan ahead. Support for this concept comes from the meta-analysis by Judge et al. (2004), which found a significant relationship between cognitive ability and leader performance.

The manager of a local convenience store that I frequent is an example of a person who does not learn from their mistakes. The manager did not give employees their work schedules until one or two days before they had to work. The employees complained because the hours always changed and they could not schedule their personal, family, and social lives. But the manager continued to do it their way, and most of the employees quit. Eight years later, the manager still does it their way, and their employees still leave at a high rate.

Personality. The third, and perhaps most important, source of poor leadership behavior involves the *personality* of the leader. Hogan et al. (1990) believed that many unsuccessful leaders are insecure and adopt one of three personality types: the paranoid/passive-aggressive type, the high-likability floater type, and the narcissist type.

The source of insecurity for leaders who are paranoid, passive-aggressive, or both is some incident in their life in which they felt betrayed. This *paranoid/passive-aggressive* leader has deeply rooted, but perhaps unconscious, resentment and anger.

On the surface, these leaders are charming, quiet people who often compliment their subordinates and fellow workers. But they resent the successes of others and are likely to act against subordinates in a passive-aggressive manner; that is, on the surface they appear to be supportive, but at the same time they will "stab" another person in the back (i.e., betray someone's trust).

The type of leader who is insecure and seldom rocks the boat or causes trouble is known as a *high-likability floater*. This person goes along with the group, is friendly to everyone, and never challenge anyone's ideas. Thus, they travel through life with many friends and no enemies. The reason they have no enemies is because they never do anything, challenges anyone, or stand up for the rights of their employees. Such leaders will be promoted and never fired because even though they make no great performance advances, they are well liked. Their employees have high morale but show relatively low performance.

Narcissists are leaders who overcome their insecurity by overconfidence. They like to be the center of attention, promote their own accomplishments, and take most, if not all, of the credit for the successes of their group—but they avoid all blame for failure. Researchers have postulated that there exists a curvilinear relationship (more specifically, an inverted-U shape) where there is an optimal level of narcissism that promotes leadership performance, and as such, can be extrapolated that an unsuccessful leader would either be high or low in narcissism (Grijalva et al., 2015).

Rather than concentrate on *traits*, Rasch, Shen, Davies, and Bono (2008) collected critical incidents of ineffective leader *behavior* and found that such behavior fell under 10 basic dimensions:

- Engaging in illegal and unethical behavior
- Avoiding conflict and people problems
- Demonstrating poor emotional control (e.g., yelling and screaming)
- Overcontrolling (e.g., micromanaging)
- Demonstrating poor task performance
- Poor planning, organization, and communication
- Starting or passing on rumors or sharing confidential information
- Procrastinating and not meeting time commitments
- Failing to accommodate the personal needs of subordinates
- Failing to nurture and manage talent

12-3 Interaction Between the Leader and the Situation

As already indicated, a leader's effectiveness often depends not only on the traits they possess but also on the particular situation in which the leader finds themself (Hackman & Wageman, 2007). In the past few decades, several theories have emerged that have sought to explain the situational nature of leadership.

Situational Favorability

The best-known and most controversial situational theory was developed by Fred Fiedler in the mid-1960s (Fiedler, 1967). Fiedler believed that an individual's leadership style is the result of a lifetime of experiences and thus is extremely difficult to change. **Fiedler's contingency model** holds that any individual's leadership style is effective only in certain situations. Thus, Fiedler would argue that rather than teaching people to change their leadership styles, leadership training should concentrate on helping people understand their style of leadership and learn how to manipulate a situation so that the two match. To help people understand their leadership style, Fielder developed the **Least-Preferred Coworker (LPC) Scale**.

To complete the LPC Scale, leaders identify the subordinate or employee with whom they would least want to work. Leaders then rate that person on several semantic differential scales that range from *nice* to *nasty* and from *friendly* to *unfriendly*. The higher the leaders rate their least preferred coworker, the higher the LPC score. This score is then compared with the favorableness of the situation to determine leader effectiveness. Low-scoring LPC leaders tend to be task oriented, whereas high-scoring LPC leaders tend to be more concerned with interpersonal relations (DuBrin, 2013; Fiedler, 1978). High-LPC leaders would fall in the same quadrant in Figure 12.1 as Theory Y and consideration leaders. Low-LPC leaders would fall in the same quadrant as Theory X and initiating-structure leaders.

The favorableness of a situation is determined by three variables. The first is **task structuredness**. Structured tasks have goals that are clearly stated and known by group members, have only a few correct solutions to a problem, and can be completed in only a few ways. The more structured the task, the more favorable the situation.

The second variable is **leader position power**. That is, the greater the position or legitimate power of the leader, the more favorable the situation. Thus, a group or organizational setting in which there is no assigned leader is not considered to be a favorable leadership situation. The third variable is **leader–member relations**. The more the subordinates like their leader, the more favorable the situation will be. The leader–member relationship is considered the most important of the three variables.

As shown in Figure 12.3, the relationship between LPC scores and group performance is complex. Basically, low-scoring LPC leaders (those who rate their least-preferred coworker low) function best in situations that are either favorable or unfavorable, whereas high-scoring LPC leaders function best when the situation is only of moderate favorability.

Despite psychometric problems with the LPC Scale (Kennedy, Houston, Korsgaard, & Gallo, 1987; Stewart & Latham, 1986), research generally has supported Fiedler's theory. Strube and Garcia (1981) conducted a meta-analysis of 145 independent studies that investigated Fiedler's model as well as 33 of Fiedler's own studies and concluded that the ideas were well supported by the research. Schriesheim, Tepper, and Tetrault (1994) found support for the general predictions of leader behavior but not for some of the specific predictions.

Fiedler's training program, called **Leader Match**, has also been supported by research (Strube & Garcia, 1981). This program is based on Fiedler's belief that an individual's leadership style is not easily changed. Thus, to improve their abilities, leaders learn through four-hour workshops how to diagnose situations and then change these situations to fit their particular leadership styles (Csoka & Bons, 1978). Leader Match is probably the only training program in the country concentrating on changing the situation rather than the leader.

Fiedler's contingency model A theory of leadership that states that leadership effectiveness is dependent on the interaction between the leader and the situation.

Least-Preferred Coworker (LPC) Scale A test used in conjunction with Fiedler's contingency model to reveal leadership style and effectiveness.

Task structuredness The variable in Fiedler's contingency model that refers to the extent to which tasks have clear goals and problems can be solved.

Leader position power The variable in Fiedler's contingency model that refers to the extent to which a leader, by the nature of their position, has the power to reward and punish subordinates.

Leader–member relations The variable in Fiedler's contingency model that refers to the extent to which subordinates like a leader.

Leader Match A training program that teaches leaders how to change situations to match their leadership styles.

Figure 12.3
Relationship Between LPC Scores and Group Success

	Low	Moderate	High
High LPC Score	Low performance	High performance	Low performance
Low LPC Score	High performance	Low performance	High performance

Situation Favorability

Organizational Climate

IMPACT theory A theory of leadership that states that there are six styles of leadership (in-formational, magnetic, position, affiliation, coercive, and tactical) and that each style will be effective only in one of six organizational climates.

Informational style A style of leadership in which the leader leads through knowledge and information; most effective in a climate of ignorance.

Ignorance An organizational climate in which important information is not available.

Another situational theory, known as **IMPACT theory**, was developed by Geier, Downey, and Johnson (1980), who believed that each leader has one of six behavioral styles: *i*nformational, *m*agnetic, *p*osition, *a*ffiliation, *c*oercive, or *t*actical. Each style is effective in only a particular situation, or in what the researchers call an *organizational climate*. As shown in Table 12.2, the six styles are similar to the five bases of power suggested many years ago by French and Raven (1959; Raven, 1965).

Informational Style in a Climate of Ignorance

The leader who has an **informational style** provides information in a climate of **ignorance**, where important information is missing from the group. For example, if a car containing four college professors and a mechanic broke down on the side of the road, who would become the leader? Almost certainly it would be the mechanic because he would probably be the one who had the most knowledge or information needed to solve the problem.

For many years in the U.S. Senate, John Warner was one of the most powerful and respected congressional leaders. He became powerful because of his expertise in defense matters, an area that was important and that few in Congress knew much about. Thus, Warner used an informational style in a climate of ignorance to become a powerful leader.

Table 12.2 Comparison of IMPACT Styles and Bases of Power

IMPACT Style[a]	Base of Power[b]
Informational	Expert
Magnetic	Referent
Position	Legitimate
Affiliation	
Coercive	Coercive/Reward
Tactical	

[a]Geier et al. (1980); [b]French & Raven (1959).

IMPACT = informational, magnetic, position, affiliation, coercive, or tactical.

Source: Geier, J. G., Downey, D. E., & Johnson, J. B. (1980). Climate impact profile. Minneapolis, MN: Performax Systems International; French, J. R. P., & Raven, B. H. (1959). The bases of social power. In D. Cartwright (Ed.), Studies in social power (pp. 150–167). Ann Arbor: University of Michigan Press.

Magnetic Style in a Climate of Despair

A leader with a **magnetic style** leads through energy and optimism and is effective only in a climate of **despair**, which is characterized by low morale. Ronald Reagan is perhaps the best example of a magnetic leader. As President of the United States, he was optimistic and well liked, even by people who may not have agreed with him politically. He was elected at a time when the national mood was depressed because of high inflation, high unemployment, and the Iran hostage situation. The chances of successful leadership increase in a situation of general despair when a magnetic or charismatic individual assumes control (Latham, 1983).

Position Style in a Climate of Instability

A person who uses the **position style** leads by virtue of the power inherent in that position. Such a person might lead through statements like, "As your captain, I am ordering you to do it," or "Because I am your mother—that's why." Individuals who use a position style will be effective only in climates of **instability**. This style is especially effective during corporate mergers, particularly when people are not sure what actions to take. However, there are often questions about a leader's legitimate scope of power (Yukl & Gardner, 2020).

Affiliation Style in a Climate of Anxiety

A person with an **affiliation style** leads by liking and caring about others. This style is similar to that of the person-oriented leader discussed previously. A leader using affiliation will be most effective in a climate of **anxiety** or when worry predominates. Former U.S. president Jimmy Carter provides an excellent example of the affiliation style. Carter was elected president shortly after the Watergate affair, when many voters were worried that they could not trust politicians or their government. Carter campaigned successfully with statements such as "I care" and "I'm not part of that Washington crowd."

Coercive Style in a Climate of Crisis

A person using the **coercive style** leads by controlling reward and punishment and is most effective in a climate of **crisis**. Such a leader will often use statements such as, "Do it or you're fired," or, "If you can get the package there on time, I will have a little something for you." This style is typical in war. If soldiers disobey an order, an officer can have them discharged. Conversely, if soldiers behave with bravery and distinction, an officer can reward them with a medal or promotion.

Mulder, de Jong, Koppelaar, and Verhage (1986) found support for the situational appropriateness of coercive styles of leadership. They studied the behavior of bankers whose leadership styles had been measured by the Influence Analysis Questionnaire. Mulder and his colleagues found that in crisis situations, bankers tend to use more formal and coercive types of power than they do in noncrisis situations.

The importance of leaders' use of reward and punishment was best demonstrated in a series of studies by Komaki (1998). Komaki and her colleagues observed a wide range of managers/leaders including police sergeants, sailboat skippers, construction supervisors, and investment bankers and concluded that the best managers complimented and rewarded their employees/subordinates who performed well and sanctioned those who did not. Perhaps the most important finding was that the best managers/leaders spend considerable time gathering performance information from their subordinates, sometimes asking simple questions such as, "How is it going?"

Tactical Style in a Climate of Disorganization

Tactical style A leadership style in which a person leads through organization and strategy; most effective in a climate of disorganization.

Disorganization A climate in which the organization has the necessary knowledge and resources but does not know how to efficiently use the knowledge or the resources.

A leader with a **tactical style** leads using strategy and is most effective in a climate of **disorganization**. A good example is a class that breaks into small groups to complete an assignment. Ideally, every student knows the material well enough to complete the assignment, but normally there is a limited amount of time and too much work to do. The person who becomes the leader is the one who is best able to organize the group.

Becoming an Effective Leader According to IMPACT Theory

If IMPACT theory is correct, people can become effective leaders by one of the four methods shown in Table 12.3. The first is by finding a climate that is consistent with their behavioral style. This method, however, involves either a great deal of luck or a lot of patience, as the leader must be in the right place at the right time.

In the second method, leaders change their style to meet a particular climate. That is, if the climate is one of ignorance, individuals change their behavior and use information to lead. On the other hand, if the climate is one of despair, individuals become more outgoing and positive. Thus, people who are willing to adapt their behavior and who can "play" each of the six leadership styles should be effective leaders.

Although there is continual debate about whether a person can be trained to be a leader, a meta-analysis by Collins and Holton (2004) supports the effectiveness of leadership training. Another example of successful leadership training is provided by Dvir, Eden, Avolio, and Shamir (2002), in which researchers demonstrated an improvement in subordinate job performance after leaders completed leadership training. Thus, those who are willing to use different leadership styles can learn the necessary skills and behaviors through training programs.

The third method by which a person can become an effective leader is to change followers' perception of the climate so that the perception matches the leader's behavioral style. This tactic is common in politics, in which each candidate tries to convince the voting public that they are the best person for an office.

The fourth method by which a leader can become effective is by actually changing the climate itself rather than simply changing followers' perceptions of the climate. Obviously, this is difficult to do, but it is the strategy advocated in Fiedler's Leader Match training. Such a strategy is difficult but can be successful.

Subordinate Ability

An important influence on leader effectiveness is the abilities and attitudes of the leader's followers and how these abilities and attitudes interact with the style and characteristics of the leader (Hollander & Offermann, 1990). House (1971) believed

Table 12.3 Four Leadership Strategies

- Find a climate consistent with your leadership style.
- Change your leadership style to better fit the existing climate.
- Change your followers' perception of the climate.
- Change the actual climate.

a leader's behavior will be accepted by subordinates only to the extent to which the behavior helps the subordinates achieve their goals. Thus, leaders will be successful only if their subordinates perceive them as working with them to meet certain goals and if those goals offer a favorable outcome for the subordinates.

Because the needs of subordinates change with each new situation, supervisors must adjust their behavior to meet the needs of their subordinates. That is, in some situations, subordinates need a leader to be directive and to set goals; in others, they already know what to do and need only emotional support. Leaders who adapt their behavior to match the needs of their subordinates will be more effective than leaders who stick to one leadership style (Foster, 1999).

According to House's **path–goal theory**, a leader can adopt one of four behavioral leadership styles to handle each situation: instrumental, supportive, participative, or achievement-oriented.

The **instrumental-style** leader calls for planning, organizing, and controlling the activities of employees. The **supportive-style** leader shows concern for employees, the **participative-style** leader shares information with employees and lets them participate in decision making, and the leader who uses the **achievement-oriented style** sets challenging goals and rewards increases in performance.

Each style will work only in certain situations and depends on subordinates' abilities and the extent to which the task is structured. In general, the higher the level of subordinate ability, the less directive the leader should be. Likewise, the more unstructured the situation, the more directive the leader should be (Schriesheim & DeNisi, 1981).

House and Mitchell (1974) further advise that to be effective, a leader should:

- recognize the needs of subordinates and work to satisfy those needs;
- reward subordinates who reach their goals;
- help subordinates identify the best paths to take in reaching particular goals; and
- clear those paths so that employees can reach their goals.

Path–goal theory is intuitively appealing because it gives a manager direct advice about how to behave in certain situations. Furthermore, because it is behavior based rather than trait based, the theory could be used in training. Unfortunately, a meta-analysis of the research on path–goal theory has not supported its general effectiveness (Wofford & Liska, 1993). If path–goal theory is to have real impact, it will need further revision.

Another theory that focuses on the relationship between leader and follower is the **situational leadership theory** developed by Hersey and Blanchard (1988), who postulated that a leader typically uses one of four behavioral styles: delegating, directing, supporting, or coaching. Hersey and Blanchard termed the most important follower characteristic *follower readiness*, or the ability and willingness to perform a particular task. The degree of follower readiness can be measured by either the manager's rating form or the self-rating form developed by Hersey and Blanchard. Scores from these forms place followers into one of four categories, or readiness (R) levels:

R1: Unable and unwilling or insecure
R2: Unable but willing or confident
R3: Able but unwilling or insecure
R4: Able and willing or confident

Path–goal theory A theory of leadership stating that leaders will be effective if their behavior helps subordinates achieve relevant goals.

Instrumental style In the path–goal theory, a leadership style in which the leader plans and organizes the activities of employees.

Supportive style In the path–goal theory, a leadership style in which leaders show concern for their employees.

Participative style In the path–goal theory, a leadership style in which the leader allows employees to participate in decisions.

Achievement-oriented style In the path–goal theory, a leadership style in which the leader sets challenging goals and rewards achievement.

Situational leadership theory A theory of leadership stating that effective leaders must adapt their style of leadership to fit both the situation and the followers.

Figure 12.4

Appropriate
Situational Leadership
Styles Based on
Employee Ability and
Willingness

	Employee Ability Level	
	Unable	Able
Unwilling	Directing	Supporting
Employee Willingness Level	R1	R3
Willing	Coaching	Delegating
	R2	R4

As shown in Figure 12.4, for R1 followers, the most effective leader behavior is the *directing approach*. That is, the leader directs the follower by telling him what to do and how to do it. A *coaching approach* should be used with R2 followers because they are willing to do the work but are not sure *how* to do it. Leaders using this approach explain and clarify how work should be done. R3 followers are given plenty of emotional support as well as opportunities for two-way communication. This approach is successful because these followers already know what to do but are not sure whether they *want* to do it. R4 followers are most productive and happy when a delegating leadership style is used. These followers are both willing and able to perform the task. Thus, the only real job for the leader is to delegate specific tasks to subordinates and then let them complete those tasks with minimal supervision or guidance.

Under this theory, effective leaders first diagnose the competency and motivation levels of employees for each goal or series of tasks, and then adapt their leadership style to fit the employees' level. As an employee makes developmental progress, the leader changes styles and becomes less directive. It is important for leaders to discuss this strategy with each employee so that employees will understand why they are being treated a particular way (Blanchard, Zigarmi, & Zigarmi, 2013).

As with many theories of leadership, situational leadership theory has excellent intuitive appeal and has been successful in some organizational applications (Gumpert & Hambleton, 1979) but not others (Goodson, McGee, & Cashman, 1989; Norris & Vecchio, 1992), and research has highlighted a lack of support for the underlying assumptions of situational leadership theory (Blank, Green, & Weitzel, 1990). In general, however, meta-analyses by Shilobod, McMullen, and Raymark (2003) and Day et al. (2002) provide support for situational leadership theory by demonstrating a moderate relationship between leader adaptability and self-monitoring and leadership performance.

Relationships with Subordinates

Leader–member exchange (LMX) theory

Leader–member exchange (LMX) theory A leadership theory that focuses on the interaction between leaders and subordinates.

Vertical dyad linkage (VDL) theory A leadership theory that concentrates on the interaction between the leader and their subordinates.

Leader–member exchange (LMX) theory was developed by Dansereau, Graen, and Haga (1975) and was originally called **vertical dyad linkage (VDL) theory**. **LMX theory** is a unique situational theory that makes good intuitive sense. The situational theories discussed earlier concentrate on interactions between leaders and situations, and between leaders and employees with differing levels of ability. LMX theory, however, concentrates on the *interactions* between leaders and subordinates. These interactions are called leader–member exchanges (LMX). The theory originally took its name from the relationship between two people (a *dyad*), the position of the leader above the subordinate (*vertical*), and their interrelated behavior (*linkage*).

LMX theory states that leaders develop different roles and relationships with the people under them and thus act differently with different subordinates. Dansereau and his colleagues believed that subordinates fall into one of two groups—the *in-group*, characterized by a high-quality relationship with the leader, or the *out-group*, characterized by a low-quality relationship with the leader.

In-group subordinates are those who have developed trusting, friendly relationships with the leader. As a result, the leader deals with in-group members by allowing them to participate in decisions and by rarely disciplining them. Out-group subordinates are treated differently from those in the in-group and are more likely to be given direct orders and to have less say about how affairs are conducted (Graen & Uhl-Bien, 1995). As one would imagine, employees with a high-quality LMX are more satisfied with their jobs, perform better, are less likely to leave the organization, perform at higher levels, and engage in more organizational citizenship behaviors than do employees with a low-quality LMX (Colella & Varma, 2001; Griffeth, Hom, & Gaertner, 2000; Ilies, Nahrgang, & Morgeson, 2007). These findings seem to generalize to employees in most countries, although the relationships are usually stronger in individualistic cultures (e.g., U.S., Canada, Germany) than in collectivist cultures such as India, China, and South Korea (Rockstuhl, Dulebohn, Ang, & Shore, 2012).

To become members of the in-group, employees often engage in such ingratiating behaviors as complimenting their leader. The extent to which these ingratiation attempts work is a function of such factors as the number of employees being supervised (Schriesheim, Castro, & Yammarino, 2000) and whether the employee is disabled (Colella & Varma, 2001).

In general, research on LMX theory has been supportive (Erdogan & Enders, 2007). Though in-group employees often receive higher performance ratings than out-group employees, the relationship between performance and LMX is complicated. Supervisors and employees often have different perceptions of the leader–member exchange, and such factors as the number of employees being supervised and impression-management attempts by employees moderate the relationship between LMX and performance (Schriesheim et al., 2000).

To complicate matters further, supervisors can only help members of the in-group when the supervisors themselves have a good relationship with their bosses. That is, if a supervisor is well liked by their boss and feels supported by the organization, they are better able to help or hurt their subordinates (Erdogan & Enders, 2007; Tangirala, Green, & Ramanujam, 2007).

12-4 Specific Leader Skills

Another way to think about leadership is that excellent leaders possess specific *skills* or engage in *behaviors* that poor leaders do not. After observing thousands of leaders in a variety of situations, Yukl (1982), Carter (1952), Hemphill and Coons (1950), and Gibbs (1969) have proposed a behavioral "theory." According to these researchers, effective leaders do the following:

1. Initiate ideas.
2. Informally interact with subordinates.
3. Stand up for and support subordinates.

4. Take responsibility.
5. Develop a group atmosphere.
6. Organize and structure work.
7. Communicate formally with subordinates.
8. Reward and punish subordinates.
9. Set goals.
10. Make decisions.
11. Train and develop employee skills.
12. Solve problems.
13. Generate enthusiasm.

In a job analysis of first-line supervisors at the Maryland Department of Transportation, Cooper, Kaufman, and Hughes (1996) found the following skills to be essential:

- Organizing
- Analysis and decision making
- Planning
- Communication (oral and written)
- Delegation
- Work habits (high-quality work)
- Carefulness
- Interpersonal skills
- Job knowledge
- Organizational knowledge
- Toughness
- Integrity
- Development of others
- Listening

Management consultant Deseri Garcia (2019) has found that great leaders have nine characteristics in common:

- They provide clarity.
- They listen and allow others to be heard.
- They value conversations.
- They model desired behaviors.
- They encourage healthy conflict.
- They create an environment of emotional safety.
- They have high levels of self-awareness.
- They empower others.
- They welcome feedback.

This theory is not particularly exciting and is the least described in textbooks, but it is the way leadership is often practiced in organizations. If this theory is true, then leadership and management are something learned, usually through experience (McCall, 2010). Thus, if the specific behaviors and skills important for effective leadership can be identified, then most people can be trained to become effective leaders, especially if they are given the necessary learning experiences.

In addition to learning leadership skills through experience, many leadership skills can be taught in training programs. The city of San Diego has its own management academy that provides interested employees with the skills necessary to become managers. On weeknights and weekends, employees learn skills such as oral communication, report writing, decision making, conflict management, and performance appraisal. After an employee is trained and tested in each of these important skill areas, they receive a certificate of completion. Even though graduates of the management academy are not promised managerial positions, more often than not they are the employees who are promoted.

If you have ever attended a leadership conference, you probably have noticed that the training involves specific leadership skills such as time management, goal setting, persuasion, and communication. Such an agenda typifies the idea that leadership consists of specific and learnable skills and behaviors.

Not surprisingly, the trend toward more employees working virtually has resulted in the need for additional types of leadership skills. Three skills thought to be important in virtual leadership are facility in using virtual technology, awareness of the problems that can occur when communicating virtually, and the ability to be a role model for effectively and professionally communicating virtually (Bell, McAlpine, & Hill, 2019). Leadership experts believe that leading virtually is more difficult than leading face-to-face (Bell et al., 2019; Hoch, 2019), where task interdependence and team size are factors that complicate the success of a virtual leadership (Brown, Hill, & Lorinkova, 2021).

Although it is beyond the scope of this chapter to discuss each of the behaviors and skills listed in Table 12.4, many are covered throughout this text. A discussion of a few additional skills follows.

Table 12.4 Specific Behaviors Taught in Leadership Training Programs

Specific Behavior	Corresponding Chapter in This Text
Communication skills	11
Conflict management	13
Decision making skills	12, 14
Delegation	
Discipline	7, 10
Motivation	9
Persuasion	
Planning and organizing	
Problem solving	
Providing performance feedback	7
Public speaking, oral communication	8
Reward and punishment	9
Running a meeting	
Soothing and supporting	15
Stress management	15
Team building	13, 14
Time management	15
Training and mentoring	8
Understanding people	
Writing	

Leadership Through Decision Making

Decision making is a specific behavior or skill that is important for a leader to possess. Vroom and Yetton (1973), however, point out that previous research has shown that only in certain situations are decisions best made by the leader; in other situations, decisions are best made with the participation of a leader's subordinates, colleagues, or both. Because of this situational aspect to decision making, Vroom and Yetton believe that leadership performance can be improved by teaching leaders to become better decision makers. To aid this process, Vroom and Yetton developed a decision tree to help leaders decide when decisions should be made alone and when they should be made with the help of others. Of course, developing a chart that would tell a leader what to do in every possible situation is impossible. But the **Vroom–Yetton Model** does provide a flowchart that can tell a leader what *process* to go through to make a decision in a particular situation. This theory will be discussed in further detail in Chapter 14.

Vroom–Yetton Model A theory of leadership that concentrates on helping a leader choose how to make a decision.

Leadership Through Contact: Management by Walking Around

Management by walking around (MBWA) is another popular specific behavioral theory. This one holds that leaders and managers are most effective when they are out of their offices, walking around, and meeting with and talking to employees and customers about their needs and progress. Many industry leaders, such as the late Sam Walton of Walmart, have used this approach with great success. MBWA is thought to increase communication, build relationships with employees, and encourage employee participation (Streshly, Gray, & Frase, 2012).

Belyh (2020) believes that there are three key requirements to MBWA:

- The leader must take the time to walk around the organization.
- The leader must have actual conversations with employees, vendors, and customers.
- The conversations should result in stronger relationships with the leader and a feeling that open communication is encouraged.

As one would imagine, MBWA is more difficult when many of a leader's employees are working virtually. Managers, however, can virtually "walk around" using email, videoconference meetings, direct messaging systems, and phone calls to keep informal contact with their employees.

In an interesting series of studies by Komaki and her associates (Komaki, 1986; Komaki, Zlotnick, & Jensen, 1986), the behavior of bank managers was observed to determine the differences between effective and ineffective managers. The results of the investigations indicated that the main difference between the two was that effective managers spent more time walking around and monitoring the behavior and performance of their employees. Empirical evidence thus seems to support the MBWA concept.

Leadership Through Power

Another strategy leaders often use is management by power. Power is important to a leader because as it increases so does the leader's potential to influence others (Nesler, Aguinis, Quigley, Lee, & Tedeschi, 1999). Leaders who have power can obtain more resources, dictate policy, and advance farther in an organization than those who have little or no power.

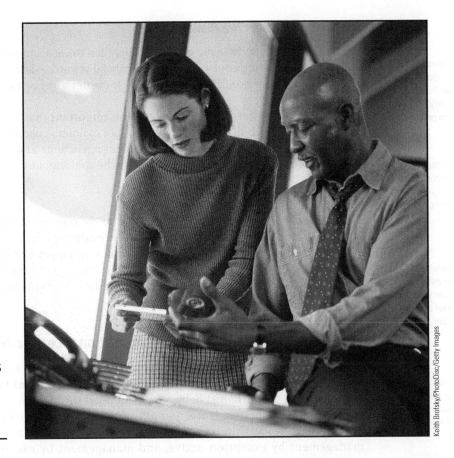

Adapting to the needs of subordinates is an essential component of leadership.

Keith Brofsky/PhotoDisc/Getty Images

Earlier in this chapter, French and Raven's bases of power were alluded to in terms of their relationships to Geier et al.'s IMPACT theory. These authors (French & Raven, 1959; Raven, 2008) identified five basic types of power: expert, legitimate, reward, coercive, and referent.

Expert Power

As mentioned earlier in the chapter, in certain situations, leaders who know something useful—that is, have expert knowledge—will have power. But there are two requirements for **expert power**. First, the knowledge must be something that others in an organization need. In a university's psychology department, a researcher with an excellent grasp of statistics has power over those who do not. Similarly, a soldier who knows how to get around the military bureaucracy has more power than those who know only to follow established channels and procedures.

Second, others must be aware that the leader knows something. Information is powerful only if other people know that the leader has it or if the leader uses it.

Expert power Power that individuals have because they have knowledge.

Legitimate Power

Leaders obtain **legitimate power** based on their positions. For example, a sergeant has power over a corporal, a vice president has power over a supervisor, and a coach has power over players on a football team. Leaders with legitimate power are best able to get employees to comply with their orders (Rahim & Afza, 1993) but have low follower satisfaction (Rahim, 1989).

Legitimate power The power that individuals have because of their elected or appointed position.

Reward and Coercive Powers

Leaders also have power to the extent that they can reward and punish others. **Reward power** involves having control over both financial rewards—salary increases, bonuses, or promotions—and nonfinancial rewards—praise or more favorable work assignments (Ward, 2001).

For a leader to have **coercive power**, it is important that others believe they are willing to use their ability to punish; they cannot maintain coercive power if employees believe they are bluffing. Punishment includes such actions as firing or not promoting and the more subtle action of giving someone the cold shoulder.

Referent Power

Another source of power for a leader may lie in the positive feelings that others hold for him. Leaders who are well liked can influence others even in the absence of reward and coercive power. Leaders can obtain such **referent power** by complimenting others, doing favors, and generally being friendly and supportive (Raven, 2008). Employees of leaders with referent power are most committed to their organizations and satisfied with their jobs (Rahim & Afza, 1993).

Leadership Through Vision: Transformational Leadership

In the past few decades, it has become popular to separate leadership styles into two types: transactional and transformational. **Transactional leadership** consists of many of the task-oriented behaviors mentioned throughout this chapter—setting goals, monitoring performance, and providing a consequence to success or failure. Transactional leadership is thought to have three dimensions: contingent reward, management by exception-active, and management by exception-passive. The contingent reward dimension refers to leaders who reward followers for engaging in desired activity. *Management by exception-active* refers to leaders who actively monitor performance and take corrective action when needed. *Management by exception-passive* refers to leaders who do not actively monitor follower behavior and who take corrective action only when problems are serious.

Transformational leadership focuses on changing or transforming the goals, values, ethics, standards, and performance of others (Northouse, 2019). Transformational leaders are often labeled as being "visionary," "charismatic," and "inspirational." They lead by developing a vision, changing organizations to fit this vision, and motivating employees to reach the vision or long-term goal. Transformational leaders are confident, have a need to influence others, and hold a strong attitude that their beliefs and ideas are correct (Bryman, 1992). They innovate, challenge the status quo, focus on people, are flexible, look to the future, carefully analyze problems, act in an ethical manner, and trust their intuition (Avolio & Yammarino, 2013; Bass & Riggio, 2006; Yukl, 1994). Transformational leadership is most related to the personality dimension of extraversion; is positively related to agreeableness, conscientiousness, and openness to experience; and is negatively related to neuroticism (Bono & Judge, 2004).

It is believed that there are three highly related dimensions to transformational leadership: charisma (idealized influence, inspirational motivation), intellectual stimulation, and individual consideration. *Charisma* refers to leaders with high moral and ethical standards who have a strong vision of where they want their followers to go and who use enthusiasm to motivate their followers. *Intellectual stimulation* refers to leaders who encourage change and open thinking, challenge the status quo, and appreciate diversity. *Individual consideration* refers to leaders who encourage individual growth and take the time to mentor and coach their followers.

A good example of a transformational leader is Herb Kelleher, cofounder, chairman emeritus, and former CEO who turned Southwest Airlines into one of the top airlines in the world. Kelleher is charismatic (on one occasion he settled a dispute by arm wrestling, on another he came to work dressed as the American singer, Elvis Presley); employee oriented (his employees come first, the customers second); visionary (his concept of a low-cost airline was designed to compete as much with ground transportation as with other airlines); and a great motivator of people.

Interestingly, the meta-analysis by Eagly et al. (2003) found that women leaders engaged in transformational behaviors slightly more often than men leaders. Though men leaders generally engage in more transactional and laissez-faire leadership behaviors than do women leaders, women are more likely to use reward to motivate employees.

Yukl (1994) offered the following guidelines for transformational leadership:

- Develop a clear and appealing vision.
- Develop a strategy for attaining the vision.
- Articulate and promote the vision.
- Act confident and optimistic.
- Express confidence in followers.
- Use early success in small steps to build confidence.
- Celebrate successes.
- Use dramatic, symbolic actions to emphasize key values.
- Lead by example.
- Create, modify, or eliminate such cultural forms as symbols, slogans, and ceremonies.

The research on transformational leadership has yielded positive results. The meta-analysis by Judge et al. (2004) found strong correlations between transformational leadership and several aspects of leader effectiveness, such as follower satisfaction, follower motivation, and group performance. Further research on transformational leadership suggests that it is used on every continent and is best liked by employees (Bass, 1997).

After studying a variety of successful and unsuccessful leaders, Hunt and Laing (1997) concluded that too much effort has been expended in trying to label leaders as "transformational" or "charismatic." Instead, they proposed that excellent leadership should be defined by exemplar—that is, does a leader have characteristics similar to successful leaders and dissimilar to unsuccessful leaders? Support for this notion comes from the meta-analysis by Judge et al. (2004), which, although supporting the effectiveness of transformation leadership, found similar results for transactional leadership.

Based on their research, Hunt and Laing (1997) hypothesized that good leaders possess five characteristics not shared by poor leaders: vision, differentiation, values, transmission, and flaws.

Vision

Consistent with the notion of transformational leadership, good leaders have a vision of where they want the organization to go and provide direction toward that end. Hunt and Laing (1997) found that 72% of high-performing leaders were described by their subordinates as being visionary compared with only 34% of the least successful leaders.

Differentiation

Successful leaders are somehow different from their followers. In some cases, the difference might be one of personality; in others, it might be one of charisma, knowledge, or skill. Though successful leaders are somehow different from their followers, they are also similar enough to relate to and empathize with them. A good example of this can be found in presidential elections. Candidates travel the country trying to relate to the people by wearing regional attire (e.g., a cowboy hat in Texas, a John Deere cap in Iowa) but still trying to "look presidential."

Values

Successful leaders have strong values. For example, Walmart founder Sam Walton strongly valued customer service, whereas retired Southwest Airlines CEO Herb Kelleher strongly valued employee relations.

Transmission of Vision and Values

Successful leaders can communicate their vision and values to others. In a study of speeches given by U.S. presidents, it was found that presidents who communicated their messages using imagery were considered more charismatic and had higher ratings of "greatness" than presidents who engaged in content-based rhetoric (Emrich, Brower, Feldman, & Garland, 2001).

Flaws

Interestingly, successful leaders typically have a major flaw, and they know it. This flaw makes the leader more human and provides a target that followers can focus on when they are upset with the leader. A look at the more recent U.S. presidents shows many with flaws: Jimmy Carter "lusted in his heart," Ronald Reagan tended to ramble and forget, Bill Clinton had his affairs, George W. Bush mangled the English language, Barack Obama smoked cigarettes behind the White House, Donald Trump had his Tweets, and Joe Biden forgot his words. Our attention to these flaws often kept us from criticizing these presidents on more important problems (e.g., ethics, economy, foreign relations).

Leadership Through Authenticity

In 2003, former Medtronic CEO Bill George published a book on leadership that criticized common beliefs about projecting a certain leadership *image* and constantly adapting one's leadership style to fit a given situation. Instead, George (2003) advocated for **authentic leadership**, in which leaders reflect on their own ethics, core beliefs, and values and, rather than leading by copying the leadership style of others, lead by being themselves and acting in accordance with their heartfelt ethics, beliefs, and values to create a positive environment. Rather than leading out of a desire for profit or fame, the authentic leader desires to serve others and leads in a manner that empowers others. Former EEOC chair Cari Dominguez calls this style "leading with your heart" (Dominguez & Sotherlund, 2010) whereas Whitney and Trosten-Bloom (2012) call it "appreciative leadership."

Self-awareness is an important aspect of authentic leadership. For leaders to be successful, they need to understand who they are, recognize and accept their weaknesses, and take steps to correct those weaknesses. Authentic leaders have a

Authentic leadership A leadership theory stating that leaders should be honest and open and lead out of a desire to serve others rather than a desire for self-gain.

high self-esteem that gives them the confidence to be courageous and do the right thing as well as the willingness to accept criticism and make personal changes when necessary.

Authentic leadership has been emphasized as a "root construct" (Avolio, Gardner, Walumbwa, Luthans, & May, 2004) and rather than differentiating it from other leadership theories, researchers have clarified that it is a foundational basis for other types of positive leadership and can incorporate other forms, such as charismatic or transformational leadership (Avolio & Gardner, 2005).

12-5 Cultural Differences in Leadership: Project Globe

An extensive international project involving approximately 150 researchers has been undertaken to study cultural differences in leadership. This endeavor, called Project GLOBE (Global Leadership and Organizational Behavior Effectiveness), has two goals: (1) discover differences and similarities in cultures and (2) determine why these differences exist (House, Javidan, Hanges, & Dorfman, 2002). Project GLOBE researchers have concluded that cultures can differ on these nine dimensions:

- *Uncertainty avoidance*: the extent to which a culture avoids uncertainty by using social norms and rituals
- *Power distance*: the extent to which power is unequally shared
- *Social collectivism*: the extent to which a culture encourages collective distribution of resources
- *In-group collectivism*: the extent to which individuals express pride in their organizations and families
- *Gender egalitarianism*: the extent to which a culture tries to minimize differences in gender roles and prevent discrimination
- *Assertiveness*: the extent to which individuals in a culture are assertive and challenging in social relationships
- *Future orientation*: the extent to which a culture plans for and invests in the future
- *Performance orientation*: the extent to which a culture encourages and rewards improvement in performance
- *Humane orientation*: the extent to which a culture encourages and rewards people for being fair, caring, and giving

A comparison of data from 61 nations revealed that each nation could be placed into 1 of 10 clusters (Gupta, Hanges, & Dorfman, 2002). These clusters are shown in Table 12.5.

Project GLOBE researchers also determined that six main leadership styles distinguish cultures: charismatic, self-protective, humane, team oriented, participative, and autonomous (Den Hartog, House, Hanges, Ruiz-Quintanilla, & Dorfman, 1999). A *charismatic* style involves vision, inspiration, integrity, and a performance orientation. A *self-protective* style involves following procedure, emphasizing status differences, being self-centered, and saving face. A *humane* style involves being modest and helping others. A *team-oriented* style involves being collaborative, building teams, and being diplomatic. A *participative* style involves getting the opinions and help of others. An *autonomous* style involves being independent and individualistic and making one's own decisions.

© Pete Sousa/Whitehouse.gov

Are there cultural
differences in
leadership?

Table 12.5   Project GLOBE: Cultural Differences in Leadership

	Leadership Style Raw Scores					
	Charisma	**Team**	**Self-Protective**	**Participative**	**Humane**	**Autonomous**
All Countries						
Mean	5.83	5.76	3.45	5.35	4.77	3.86
Standard deviation	0.33	0.26	0.41	0.41	0.38	0.45
Latin Europe (Israel, Italy, Portugal, Spain, France, French-speaking Switzerland)	5.74	5.83	3.19	5.48	4.24	3.70
Eastern Europe (Hungary, Russia, Greece, Poland, Georgia, Slovenia, Albania, Kazakhstan)	5.73	5.50	3.67	5.09	4.75	4.18
Germanic Europe (Austria, Switzerland, Netherlands, Germany)	5.93	5.62	3.03	5.85	4.71	4.16
Arab Cultures (Qatar, Morocco, Turkey, Egypt, Kuwait)	5.35	5.55	3.79	4.98	4.80	3.69
Anglo Cultures (United States, England, Australia, Canada, New Zealand, Ireland, South Africa [White sample])	6.04	5.74	3.82	5.72	5.08	3.82
Southern Asia (India, Indonesia, Philippines, Malaysia, Thailand, Iran)	5.97	5.86	3.82	5.06	5.68	3.99
Latin America (Argentina, Bolivia, Brazil, Colombia, Costa Rica, Ecuador, El Salvador, Guatemala, Mexico, Venezuela)	5.91	5.91	3.65	5.25	4.85	3.68
Sub-Sahara Africa (Namibia, Zambia, Zimbabwe, Nigeria, South Africa [Black sample])	5.63	5.57	3.74	5.19	5.22	3.69
Confucian Asia (Taiwan, Singapore, Hong Kong, South Korea, China, Japan)	5.64	5.62	3.73	4.99	5.04	4.03
Nordic Europe (Denmark, Finland, Sweden)	5.88	5.76	2.77	5.64	4.59	3.97

Culture Cluster	Leadership Style Standard Scores					
	Charisma	**Team**	**Self-Protective**	**Participative**	**Humane**	**Autonomous**
Latin Europe	−0.27	0.27	−0.63	0.32	−1.39	−0.36
Eastern Europe	−0.30	−1.00	0.54	−0.63	−0.05	0.71
Germanic Europe	0.30	−0.54	−1.02	1.22	−0.16	0.67
Arab Cultures	−1.45	−0.81	0.83	−0.90	0.08	−0.38
Anglo Cultures	0.64	−0.08	0.90	0.90	0.82	−0.09
Southern Asia	0.42	0.38	0.90	−0.71	2.39	0.29
Latin America	0.24	0.58	0.49	−0.24	0.21	−0.40
Sub-Sahara Africa	−0.61	−0.73	0.71	−0.39	1.18	−0.38
Confucian Asia	−0.58	−0.54	0.68	−0.88	0.71	0.38
Nordic Europe	0.15	0.00	−1.66	0.71	−0.47	0.24

GLOBE = Global Leadership and Organizational Behavior Effectiveness.

Project GLOBE researchers found that the 10 culture clusters differed on the six main leadership styles. For example, compared with other clusters, leaders from countries in the Anglo cluster are more self-protective and participative, leaders from countries in the Nordic Europe cluster are more participative and less self-protective, and leaders from the Southern Asia cluster are more humane and less participative.

12-6 Leadership: Where Are We Today?

Most of this chapter has described leadership theories. Of course, when several theories address the same topic, the question comes to mind: "Which of the theories is (are) true?" The answer probably is that each is somewhat true and that the best "theory" about leadership is some combination.

As Figure 12.5 shows, if we combine all of the theories discussed in this chapter, leadership emerges as a set of interactions: between a leader's traits and skills, between a situation's demands and characteristics, and between followers' needs and characteristics. If we begin with a leader's traits and skills, a summary of the theories would suggest that individuals would be more likely to be successful leaders if they

- have received leadership training and mastered the skills listed in Table 12.4;
- are high self-monitors;
- are high in both task and person orientations;
- have the leadership motive pattern (high need for power, low need for affiliation);
- are intelligent;
- are emotionally stable (don't possess such problematic personality traits as those of the high-likability floater, the narcissist, or the passive-aggressive person); and
- possess the skills and personality to be a transformational leader.

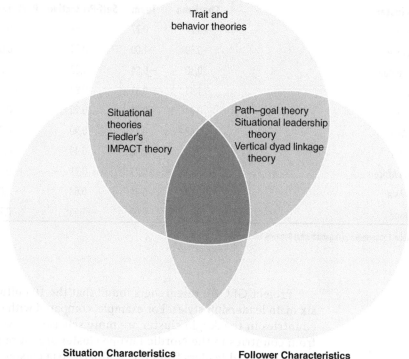

Trait and
behavior theories

Situational
theories
Fiedler's
IMPACT theory

Path–goal theory
Situational leadership
theory
Vertical dyad linkage
theory

Situation Characteristics

Follower Characteristics

Figure 12.5

Effective Leadership:
Interaction of Leader,
Situation, and Follower
Characteristics

If individuals have these skills and traits, their leadership performance will depend on the characteristics of the situation. Thus, as shown in Figure 12.6, certain people will be effective leaders in certain situations when particular types of people are followers. For example, in a structured situation in which the leader has both legitimate and referent power (a highly favorable situation), a low-LPC leader will perform better than a high-LPC leader. If subordinates are unwilling and unable to perform a task, a directive leadership style will work better than a supportive style. If there is a climate of despair and the leader has referent power, a magnetic leadership style will work better than an informational style. Unfortunately, we are not yet at the stage where we can determine the exact matches that result in the best leadership for every situation. But it is probably safe to make the following assumptions.

First, because different situations require different leadership styles and skills, individuals who have a wide variety of relevant skills will be best able to be effective leaders in a larger variety of situations. That is, a person who has only excellent planning skills will be an effective leader only in situations that require planning. But a leader who has excellent skills in planning, persuasion, people, goal setting, and motivation will be able to lead in many different types of situations.

The advice that flows from this assumption is obvious. As Table 12.6 shows, an individual interested in becoming an effective leader should obtain as many leadership skills as possible. By attending leadership conferences, taking college courses, and gaining a variety of experiences, a leader can gain most of these skills. The Career Workshop Box offers such a comprehensive strategy.

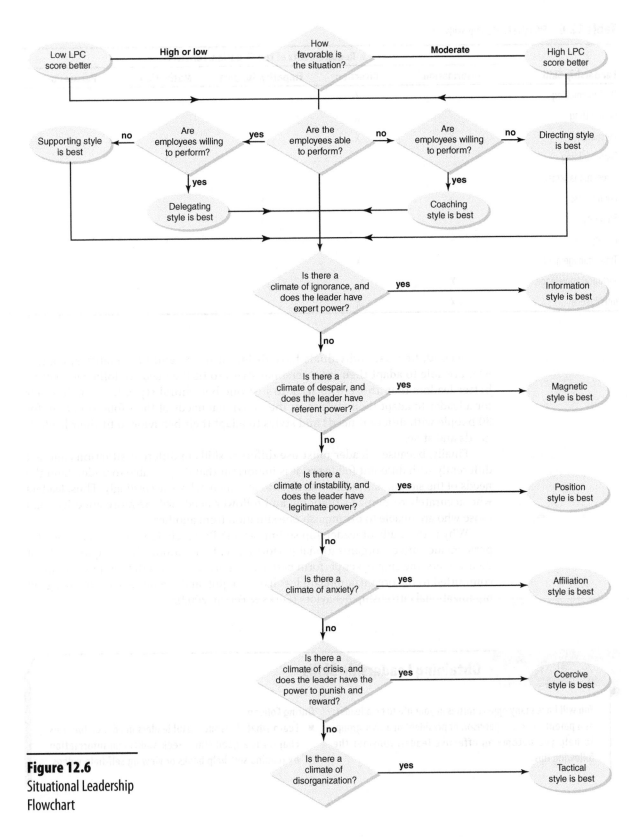

Figure 12.6
Situational Leadership
Flowchart

Table 12.6 Effective Leadership Skills

Leadership Skill	Requirements of the Situation/Follower				
	Information	**Direction**	**Empathy/Support**	**Motivation**	**Persuasion**
Decision making		X			
Goal setting		X			
Persuasion	X	X		X	X
Team building			X	X	
Stress management			X		
Friendliness			X	X	
Empathy			X		
Energy				X	
Time management		X			
Technical knowledge	X				
Intelligence	X	X			

Second, because individuals have different needs and personalities, leaders who are able to adapt their interpersonal styles to fit the needs of followers will be better leaders than those who stick to just one behavioral style. It is much easier for a leader to adapt their style to fit the individual needs of their followers than for 30 people with different needs and styles to adapt their behavior to fit their leader's needs and style.

Finally, because a leader must use different skills in different situations and act differently with different followers, it is important that they be able to understand the needs of the situation, the follower, or both and then behave accordingly. Thus, leaders who accurately recognize situational and follower needs will be more effective than those who are unable to distinguish one situation from another.

Why is the study of leadership so important? Research demonstrates that leader performance affects organizational performance. In addition, when employees trust their leaders, the employees perform better, are more satisfied with their jobs, are more committed to the organization, are less likely to quit, and are more likely to engage in organizational citizenship behaviors (Dirks & Ferrin, 2002).

Career Workshop **Obtaining Leadership Skills**

You will have many opportunities in your life to be a leader: as a parent, coach, supervisor, or president of a civic group. To help you become an effective leader, consider the following tips.

During College

- Learn what skills successful leaders need. Reading this chapter is a good start. Seek additional information by reading self-help books or viewing self-help videos.

Then, seek out opportunities where you can practice and build these skills, such as becoming an officer in a club on campus. The more you use a skill, the better you become.

- Identify and acknowledge the skills you lack. Successful leaders are willing to acknowledge their weaknesses and then do what it takes to improve. If you aren't sure how strong your skills are, ask someone you trust and who you know will be honest to tell you.

- Many colleges provide guest speakers on leadership or provide leadership workshops. Learn when these trainings will be scheduled and make it a point to enroll.

- Get a part-time job in an organization where you can quickly advance to a supervisory role. Being a lifeguard may be more fun but getting job-related leadership experience will be much more beneficial.

- Enroll in a conflict management course, whether it is offered by the college or by a training program outside of the college. An important skill that a successful leader needs to know is how to successfully manage conflict.

- Identify someone on campus or at work who you think is a successful leader. Observe their behavior and the reaction of others to that behavior. Is it a behavior that you want to model? Or is it one that you discover should not be used? Ask the leader questions about how they do things and why they do it that way.

- If you are strong in a particular subject, volunteer to tutor other college students. This will help build your coaching skills.

After College

- When you get your first job, identify someone you think is a successful leader. Do what you did in college: Observe their behavior and ask them questions.

- Enroll in leadership development seminars. You may find that your organization will pay for these.

- Join professional organizations and volunteer for committee positions. Eventually you can move into leadership positions such as committee chair or president.

- Volunteer to head committees or teams. You will learn how to better organize people and events, strategic planning, public speaking, dealing with conflict, motivating, and working in teams.

- Volunteer for extra assignments that will provide you with new skills. Others will see that you have initiative and are willing to learn new information and skills.

- Be honest with your coworkers and others at work. One of the biggest factors in successful leadership is the ability to be trusted by others.

On the Job ▶ Applied Case Study

Developing Leaders at Claim Jumper Restaurants

One of the major success factors for any restaurant is the quality of the people managing it. They must enjoy what they do, be technical experts, and have the leadership qualities to manage restaurant employees. Claim Jumper Restaurants, a California-based casual dining chain, developed an interesting program for hiring and developing its restaurant managers.

The first Claim Jumper restaurant opened in Los Angeles in 1977 and there are currently 28 restaurants, most of which are in western states. Each restaurant features Douglas fir logs, natural stone, and natural wood beams to promote a "gold rush" theme. The restaurant is open for lunch and dinner and has a wide menu, including ribs, chicken, steak, seafood, and pasta.

The restaurant chain uses two strategies to hire managers: hiring from the outside and promoting current employees. In 2001, they created a new program to select and develop internal candidates for management positions. Interested employees are first screened to determine if they would make good managers. If they seem to be a good fit, they are enrolled in the Expeditor Program to learn management skills and gain management experience. If they don't seem like a good fit, they are given feedback on what they can do to increase their readiness for the program.

(Continued)

Employees in the Expeditor Program, now called "Expeditors," work closely with restaurant managers, receive management training and experience, and are provided with feedback on their progress.

- If you were in charge of hiring and developing managers for Claim Jumper Restaurants, what competencies and experiences would you look for?

- Based on what you learned in this chapter, how much emphasis would you place on *hiring* the right people as opposed to *developing* current employees into good leaders?

Focus on Ethics — Ethics and Leadership

Imagine the following four situations:

- A professor with a policy of failing students who miss more than six days of class in one semester decides not to fail one particular student with high absenteeism, even though two other students were failed in the same semester because of their high absenteeism. If the professor fails that third student, the professor knows that the student will be unable to graduate. If the student can't graduate, they won't be able to enter their master's program in the fall.

- A director of a mental health agency overrepresents the number of clients their agency served for the previous year. The agency gets funds from the state based on how many clients it serves each year. The director knows that if they were to report the correct number of clients, the agency would get significantly less money to use for the next year. A reduction in funds would mean that some staff would have to be laid off, causing the agency to help even fewer clients.

- A supervisor allows their staff to take an hour for lunch even though company policy allows only 30-minute lunch breaks. The supervisor's philosophy is that as long as their employees get their work done, it won't make a difference if they are allowed an hour for lunch instead of 30 minutes.

- A big brother raised in a family who believes that honesty is always the best policy tells his little sister that she looks great in her new dress, even though he thinks she looks terrible.

The examples above involve people in leadership positions. A leader is someone people look up to and are willing to follow; it is a person who is able to get others to reach a goal, who is in a position to guide and influence others' behavior and professional and personal lives; and it is a person of integrity. So based on that definition, any one of us can be, and have been, leaders at one time or another. A professor is a leader in their classroom; a director is the leader of an agency; a supervisor is the leader of their department; and an older sibling is, or should be, a leader of their younger siblings.

What the leaders in the above examples have in common is that they are bending the rules. Bending the rules means going against policy, regulations, or rules, whether they are set by the leader, as in the professor's classroom policy of failing students with poor attendance, or set by an organization, such as the policy of 30-minute lunch breaks for all employees. There are two thoughts about this concept of "bending the rules": one is that it is unethical and the other is that it is necessary. Those who believe it is necessary to bend the rules will say that all rules are meant to be broken.

Proponents of bending the rules say that it's a moral cop-out when leaders choose not to bend the rules in situations in which bending the rules, going against policy, is actually the right and ethical thing to do. For example, in the first situation above, the reason why that one student missed so many days during the semester is because they had cancer and their treatments often made them too sick to come to class. In this case, say the supporters of bending the rules, for the professor to say, "I must abide by my policy," would be a moral cop-out against doing the responsible thing. Sometimes, they say, a leader has to bend the rules for the bigger good.

However, critics of leaders who bend the rules say that a policy is a policy—it's there for a reason and should be followed at all times. If a leader doesn't like the policy or rule, that leader should do what is necessary to change the policy so that they won't have to bend it. So, these critics might say in the previous example that the professor, in their policy, should state that allowances should be made for students who miss classes due to a long-term illness. If that wasn't stated in their policy, then it would be unethical for them to break the policy, no matter the reason. Bending the rules breaks trust with others. Critics hold leaders to a higher standard than other employees. Because leaders are, or should be, role models, anything they do is often accepted and copied by others. So, if a leader breaks a policy, what they are saying to others is that it is okay to bend the rules and break policies.

What Do You Think?

- In the first situation, do you think it is unethical for the professor to bend the rules under those circumstances? If you were one of the students failed because of high absenteeism and you found out that the professor didn't fail another student for their high absenteeism, would you think you were being treated unfairly? What would you do?

- Do you think what the leaders did in the other examples was ethical? Why or why not?

- In the example with the brother, is it okay to lie in this situation? Do you consider lying as unethical? Are there ever times when lying is better than telling the truth?

- What are some situations in which bending the rules might be more ethical than following policy?

Chapter Summary

In this chapter you learned:

- Intelligence, interpersonal adjustment, self-monitoring, a leadership motive pattern (high power, low affiliation), and the combination of a task and person orientation are related to high levels of leadership performance.
- Leadership effectiveness is also a function of the interaction between the leader and the situation. Important situational aspects include situational favorability (Fiedler), organizational climate (IMPACT theory), subordinate ability (path–goal theory, situational leadership theory), and the relationship between leaders and their subordinates (vertical dyad linkage, LMX theory).
- Effective leaders possess specific skills—such as persuasion, motivation, and decision making—that ineffective leaders do not.

Key Terms

Leader emergence   (422)
Affective identity motivation   (423)
Noncalculative motivation   (423)
Social-normative motivation   (423)
Leader performance   (424)
Self-monitoring   (425)
Need for power   (425)
Need for achievement   (425)
Need for affiliation   (425)
Leadership motive pattern   (425)

Thematic Apperception Test (TAT)   (426)
Job Choice Exercise (JCE)   (426)
Managerial Grid   (427)
Country club leaders   (427)
Theory Y leaders   (427)
Task-centered leaders   (427)
Task-centered leaders   (427)
Theory X leaders   (427)
Initiating structure   (427)
Team leadership   (427)

Questions for Review

1. Do those who seek leadership roles, those who emerge as leaders, and those who are successful leaders share similar traits?
2. Which of the situational theories seems to provide the best explanation for successful leadership?
3. Hogan identified three main reasons for unsuccessful leadership. Are there others that he did not mention?
4. Can effective leadership actually be taught?
5. How can a leader be more persuasive?

Chapter

13

Group Behavior, Teams, and Conflict

Learning Objectives

13-1 Define what constitutes a group and a team.

13-2 Explain why people join groups.

13-3 Increase group performance.

13-4 Explain how teams operate.

13-5 Decide when groups perform better than individuals.

13-6 Decide when the team approach is not always the best.

13-7 Identify the causes of conflict.

13-8 Reduce conflict.

With few exceptions, most employee behavior takes place in groups or teams. Firefighters work together when fighting fires, managers make decisions in committee meetings, and bank tellers work together to deal with customers. Because employees tend to work in groups or teams, it is important for a manager or a leader to understand group dynamics. This understanding is especially important considering the continuing use of teams by organizations.

13-1 Group Dynamics

Definition of a Group

In reviewing the books written on group dynamics, it quickly becomes clear that there is no agreed-upon definition of a group. Some experts use a general definition that basically defines a group as two or more people who *perceive* themselves as a group and *interact* in some way. Other definitions require that a group must involve some degree of structure and permanency. I prefer the definition used by Gordon (2001), who believes that for a collection of people to be called a group, the following four criteria must be met: (a) The members of the group must see themselves as a unit; (b) the group must provide rewards to its members; (c) anything that happens to one member of the group affects every other member; and (d) the members of the group must share a common goal.

Multiple Members Who Perceive Themselves as a Unit

The first criterion is that the group must have multiple members. Obviously, one person does not constitute a group (even if they have multiple personalities). Therefore, at least two people are necessary to form a group. Usually we refer to 2 people as a *dyad*, to 3 people as a *triad*, and to 4 to 20 people as a *small group* (Forsyth, 2019). To be considered a group, these two or more people must also see themselves as a unit. Thus, three individuals walking down the sidewalk would be considered a group only if they knew one another and were together. Eight separate customers shopping at a store would not be considered a group.

Group Rewards

The second group criterion is that membership must be rewarding for each individual in the group. In the next section, we will discuss the reasons people join groups, but for now it is important to remember that people will join or form a group only if it provides some form of reward.

To demonstrate this point, imagine four students studying for an exam. If the four study in separate rooms and do not share information, they are not a group. Likewise, consider if the same four people sat at one desk in the library. If each person studies the book separately and never communicates with the other three, then the four still will not be a group because none of the individuals is rewarded by being with the others. But if none of the four would have otherwise studied independently, then the four students would be considered a group because being together was rewarding. Even though they did not talk with one another during their time in the library, the fact that they were together provided the structure for each of them to study.

Corresponding Effects

Corresponding effects An event that affects one member of a group will affect the other group members.

The third group criterion is that an event that affects one group member should affect all group members. That is, if something significant happens to one person and does not affect any of the other people gathered with her, then the collection of people cannot be considered a group. This requirement is called **corresponding effects**. For example, suppose five accounting clerks work side by side, and one clerk becomes ill and goes home. If the activities of the other four change because of one clerk leaving, the five might be considered a group. But if the activities of the other four do not change after one clerk leaves, then the accounting clerks cannot be considered a group.

Common Goals

Common goal An aim or purpose shared by members of a group.

The fourth and final criterion is that all members must have a **common goal**. In the accounting clerk example, if the goal of one of the clerks is to do as little work as possible and the goal of another clerk is to ensure high quality output, the clerks are not considered to be a group because they work in different ways and for different reasons.

Why do we care if a collection of people meets the technical definition of a group? The answer lies within your ability to change employee performance. Over the course of this chapter, you will learn many factors affecting group performance. If you apply what you learn, you will be effective in changing performance only if the collection of individuals is actually a *group*.

Reasons for Joining Groups

Assignment

In the workplace, the most common reason for joining groups is that employees are assigned to them. For example, a new employee might be assigned to a department with 5 other employees, 5 employees might be appointed to serve on a committee, and 10 employees are scheduled for the same training class.

Physical Proximity

One especially strong reason that a person might join a particular group, especially if the group is informal, is physical proximity (Forsyth, 2019). That is, people tend to form groups with people who either live or work nearby. For example, think of the intramural teams on your campus. Most teams consist of students who live in the same residence halls or have classes together. At work, employees tend to form groups that consist of those who work in the same general area. And some employees seek close physical proximity to people in power, hoping they will become part of an elite group.

The "bomber wing" provides an interesting example of how physical proximity can create an unlikely group. The bomber wing was a small section of the federal maximum-security prison in Florence, Colorado, whose 1999 residents included Ted Kaczynski (the Unabomber), Ramzi Yousef (the World Trade Center bomber), and Timothy McVeigh (the Oklahoma City bomber). Though the three had access to one another for only two hours a week and had to shout across the hall to communicate, they formed quite the social group. Without this proximity, it is unlikely that the three would ever have belonged to the same group (Chua-Eoan, 1999).

Affiliation

Affiliation A leadership style in which the individual leads by caring about others and that is most effective in a climate of anxiety.

Affiliation involves our need to be with other people. Thus, one reason people join groups is to be near and talk to other people. Research has demonstrated that our need for affiliation is very strong. Mayo (1946), for example, found that employees at a textile plant who worked separately from other employees were not as satisfied with their jobs as were employees at the same plant who had the opportunity to work with others. Likewise, McLaughlin and Cheatham (1977) found that "outside" bank tellers who were isolated from their "inside" coworkers had lower job satisfaction.

Perhaps the most interesting demonstrations of the strength of the human affiliation need come from the writings of Schein (1956) and Naughton (1975). These researchers were interested in the reasons American prisoners of war (POWs) in World War II behaved so differently from those in the Korean and Vietnam conflicts. POWs in World War II made more escape attempts, suffered fewer deaths, and provided information less frequently to the enemy than did their counterparts in Korea and Vietnam. Although the American public attributed the differences to a postwar decline in the American character (Hampton, Summer, & Webber, 1978), both Schein and Naughton pointed out the differences from a perspective of group dynamics. In World War II, the POWs were kept in groups that remained together for long periods of time. Thus, these POWs were able to receive emotional support from one another, they could work together to plan escapes, they were able to hear what each POW said to the enemy, and they knew about and supported a strong group norm about not talking to the enemy. In the two post–World War II Asian conflicts, the situations were entirely different. Rather than living in groups, these POWs were isolated and not allowed to communicate with one another. Naughton (1975) reports that the POWs were so in need of contact and communication with others that they scraped their cell walls to make noise and establish contact and informal communication with one another. This behavior is similar to that reported by hostages held in Beirut and Syria.

If people are not allowed the opportunity for affiliation, they make attempts to secure at least minimal contact. When even minimal contact is not possible, morale and perhaps even the will to live are lessened. Such is the concern about the use of supermaximum prisons (prisons with the highest level of security) built for individuals who behave violently while incarcerated. In these prisons, incarcerated persons spend 23 hours a day alone in concrete stalls without air conditioning. There are no books, magazines, or television and only minimal contact with guards. During the remaining hour each day, the incarcerated persons are placed alone in an 18-by-20-foot cage where they can pace or toss a basketball at an iron hoop. As one might imagine, incarcerated persons' rights advocates are concerned about the long-term effects of such isolation. Similar concerns were expressed after several suspected al-Qaeda terrorists housed in Guantanamo Bay, Cuba, attempted suicide in February 2003.

Because people are not equal in their desire or need to affiliate with others (Ray & Hall, 1995), it is important to consider the need for affiliation and the negative consequences of isolation given such trends as having employees work from home (telecommuting) and sending employees to work in different countries (expatriates).

Identification

Identification The need to associate ourselves with the image projected by other people, groups, or objects.

Another reason we join groups is our desire for **identification** with some group or cause. There are many examples of this need to identify with others. In the 1960s and 1970s, young men wore their hair long; although some thought it attractive and comfortable, many others grew long hair because it helped them identify with other men of their generation and separated them from adult men of previous generations. Many of us still know a man who wears their hair long and makes references to the 1960s and 1970s, thus identifying themself with an earlier period. In the 1980s and 1990s, so-called punk and grunge styles of hair and clothes were worn by students in much the same way that long hair and tie-dyed shirts were worn by people in the 1960s. In the current decade, tattoos and body piercing seem to be the mode of expression. For each generation, the purpose of the "odd" self-expression may have been to separate oneself from a previous generation and identify with a new, "better" generation.

Around your school you may notice that many students wear T-shirts with logos or messages. Students wearing "BTS," "Los Angeles Lakers," or "Spring Break Cancun 2023" shirts are all identifying with particular groups and thus are making statements about themselves.

In an interesting study of how clothing is used as a means of identification, Cialdini and his colleagues (1976) observed the number of students at several universities who wore school-related clothing such as T-shirts and sweatshirts on the Monday following a school football game. They found that following a football victory, many more students wore school-related clothing than on Mondays following football losses. In a second study, Cialdini et al. also asked students who won the football game. As we might expect, when the football team won, the students answered by saying, "We won." When the team lost, the students answered by saying, "They lost." Based on these two studies, Cialdini called this identification process "basking in reflected glory."

Another example of the identification process comes from a major manufacturing plant in Virginia. Several months before union contract talks began, the company gave each employee several nice shirts with the company name printed on the front. The company did this because it had previously noticed that in the months before contract negotiations began, the employees began to wear more union caps and shirts. The company believed that this clothing helped increase the employees' level of identification with the union. To counter this effect, the company hoped that its shirts would influence the negotiation process. Although we cannot determine the exact effect of this strategy, that year was the only one in a decade in which union members did not strike.

Emotional Support

We also join groups to obtain emotional support. Alcoholics Anonymous, Gamblers Anonymous, and Weight Watchers are good examples of groups that provide emotional support for their members. A quick perusal of ads in the local paper or a quick surfing of the Internet will demonstrate the importance of this need, as there are hundreds of different types of support groups.

Assistance or Help

People often join groups to obtain assistance or help. For example, students having problems with an algebra class might form a study group. Or, on the reality show *Survivor*, contestants might form alliances to increase the odds of not being voted off the island.

Common Interests

People often join groups because they share a common interest. At school, students joining a geology club share an interest in geology, students joining a fraternity share an interest in socializing, and students joining a service club such as Circle K or Alpha Phi Omega share an interest in helping people.

It is an interesting side note that most campus clubs based on common academic interests, such as a psychology club or a Latin club, are smaller and less active than other campus groups. Apparently, college students have many needs, and common academic interests are usually not as strong as the social needs satisfied by the Greek organizations. For example, a service club on the Radford University campus was having difficulty attracting members, so several advisors suggested that it increase its number of social activities to attract people who had both community service and social needs. This slight change in activities increased membership from 15 to 45.

Common Goals

People who join political parties exemplify being in pursuit of a common goal. These people may also share common interests, but their primary purpose is to get a particular person or members of a particular party elected to office. Another example of people who join a group in pursuit of common goals are unions. Employees may form or join a union to obtain better job benefits or improve safety standards.

13-2 Factors Affecting Group Performance

Group Cohesiveness

Group cohesiveness The extent to which members of a group like and trust one another.

Group cohesiveness is the extent to which group members like and trust one another, are committed to accomplishing a team goal, and share a feeling of group pride (Beal, Cohen, Burke, & McLendon, 2003). In general, the more cohesive the group, the greater its

- performance (Castaño, Watts, & Tekleab, 2013);
- decision quality (Lohan, Acton, & Conboy, 2014; Mullen, Anthony, Salas, & Driskell, 1994);
- member satisfaction (Brawley, Carron, & Widmeyer, 1993; Deluga & Winters, 1991);
- creativity and innovation (Hülsheger, Anderson, &Salgado, 2009);
- member interaction (Shaw & Shaw, 1962); and
- employee courtesy (Kidwell, Mossholder, & Bennett, 1997).

In its 1989 strike against Pittston Coal Company, the United Mine Workers union realized the importance of cohesiveness and identification needs by adopting a unique strategy. Each union member as well as their family members and supportive friends wore camouflage shirts and fatigues as a sign of unity. Every time miners looked around, they saw others dressed alike. The union members thus developed a sense of unity and cohesiveness that helped them last through a lengthy strike. Groups such as the Girl Scouts and the Guardian Angels also wear uniforms to increase group cohesiveness.

But cohesiveness can also lower group performance, especially in a work setting. When employees become too cohesive, they often lose sight of organizational goals. For example, it is common for restaurant employees to put the needs of other employees above those of their customers. Similarly, police departments tend to be highly cohesive—so much so that anyone who is not a police officer is considered an outsider, which can make community relations difficult.

Although the majority of research supports the conclusion that cohesiveness results in better group performance, it is not always necessary for ultimate group success. For example, the Oakland A's in the early 1970s and the Los Angeles Lakers in 2002 were sports teams that won championships despite constant fighting among the players.

Research has also demonstrated that employees in cohesive work groups will conform to a norm of lower production even though they are capable of higher performance (Forsyth, 2019). An excellent example of this conformity to a group norm involved the Hollywood Division of the Los Angeles Police Department in the early 1980s. Many of the division's officers and detectives were extensively involved in property crimes. They would break into various retail stores and radio that they were responding to the ringing burglar alarms. They then placed the stolen goods in their car trunks and proceeded as if they were investigating the break-ins. The officers later met at specific locations to hide and sell the stolen goods. Officers who did not participate in the crimes saw the merchandise and knew what was going on, but they did not report the offenders. Instead, they put their loyalty to their fellow officers above their loyalty to the city or the police department.

Group Homogeneity

The homogeneity of a group is the extent to which its members are similar. A **homogeneous group** contains members who are similar in some or most ways, whereas a **heterogeneous group** contains members who are more different than alike. Of course, the difficulty in determining the homogeneity of a group comes from the many ways in which people are different. Group members might be demographically similar (e.g., age, gender, race) but be very different in personality, attitudes, values, and competencies.

An important question for a leader to consider when developing a group is which composition—homogeneous or heterogeneous—will lead to the best group performance. Many research studies have sought to answer this question, but only mixed results have been found, with some studies finding homogeneous groups most effective and others finding heterogeneous groups most effective (Bowers, Pharmer, & Salas, 2000; Stewart, 2006). Aamodt, Kimbrough, and Alexander (1983) hypothesized that previous research yielded mixed results because the compositions of the best-performing groups were actually somewhere between completely homogeneous and completely heterogeneous. These authors labeled them **slightly heterogeneous groups**. For example, in a five-person group, a group with five men would be considered as homogeneous, one with three men and two women as heterogeneous, and one with four men and one woman as slightly heterogeneous. A meta-analysis by Mascio, Rainey, and Zinda (2008) offered some support for the superiority of slightly heterogeneous groups, as slightly heterogeneous groups performed somewhat better than did homogeneous ($d = .17$) and heterogeneous ($d = .12$) groups.

Thus, it appears that the best working groups consist primarily of similar people but have a dissimilar person adding tension and a different vantage point. But it is not yet clear which variable is most important in terms of determining group composition. For example, a group might be homogeneous in terms of race but heterogeneous in gender. Researchers have studied race, gender, personality, intelligence, attitudes, and background, but more research is needed to clarify this issue. For example, one meta-analysis found that heterogeneity in group member skills was related to better group performance, but demographic heterogeneity did not influence group performance (Horwitz & Horwitz, 2007). Other meta-analyses indicate, however, that homogeneous groups result in higher member satisfaction, higher levels of communication and interaction, and lower turnover (Nolan, Lee, & Allen, 1997; Roberson & Colquitt, 2005).

Another meta-analysis (Stahl, Maznevski, Voight, & Jonsen, 2009) found that cultural heterogeneity had no overall effect on group performance because cultural heterogeneity resulted in both process gains and losses. That is, cultural heterogeneity not only resulted in increased group creativity and satisfaction (process gains) but also increased conflict and decreased social integration (process losses).

Although group performance is best in slightly heterogeneous groups, the group member who is "different" (e.g., the only man, the only Black employee, the only introvert) may not have the same level of satisfaction as the rest of the group members.

Homogeneous groups Groups whose members share the same characteristics.

Heterogeneous groups Groups whose members share few similarities.

Slightly heterogeneous groups Groups in which a few group members have different characteristics from the rest of the group.

In fact, in a study of more than 255,000 employees at quick-service restaurants, it was found that employees who were the statistical minority in a restaurant in terms of race, gender, or age were more likely to leave the organization than were employees who were in the statistical majority (Sacco & Schmitt, 2005).

Another factor that might influence how group homogeneity affects group performance is the type of group. A meta-analysis by Stewart (2006) found that heterogeneous project teams (temporary teams working together to complete an assignment) performed slightly better than homogeneous project teams, whereas homogeneous production teams (teams working together to produce a product) performed slightly better than heterogeneous production teams.

Stability of Membership

Stability The extent to which the membership of a group remains consistent over time.

The greater the **stability** of the group, the greater the cohesiveness. Thus, groups in which members remain for long periods of time are more cohesive and perform better than groups that have high turnover (Bell, 2005), and groups whose members have previously worked together perform better than groups whose members are not familiar with one another (Harrison, Mohammed, McGrath, Florey, & Vanerstoep, 2003).

A good example again can be found on a college campus. At most colleges, fraternities and sororities usually are the most active organizations and have high levels of performance; professional clubs and honorary societies such as Psi Chi and Lambda Alpha Beta tend to be the least active. Why is this? Certainly, it cannot be the abilities of the members—honorary societies have members with higher IQs than do most fraternities and sororities. Instead, the answer might be in the stability of the groups. Students tend to join Greek organizations in their freshman or sophomore years, whereas students tend to join professional clubs in their junior year and honorary societies in their senior year, often to help "pad" (i.e., improve) their résumés. The Greek organizations thus have more stable memberships than the other organizations.

Isolation

Isolation The degree of physical distance of a group from other groups.

Physical **isolation** is another variable that tends to increase a group's cohesiveness. Groups that are isolated or located away from other groups tend to be highly cohesive.

Outside Pressure

Outside pressure The amount of psychological pressure placed on a group by people who are not members of the group.

Groups that are pressured by outside forces also tend to become highly cohesive. To some degree, this response to **outside pressure** can be explained by the phenomenon of *psychological reactance* (Brehm, 1966). When we believe that someone is trying to intentionally influence us to take some particular action, we often react by doing the opposite. Consider, for example, a teenaged dating couple. As the teen arrives to pick up their date, the other teens father notices the young man's beard and Harley-Davidson motorcycle and forbids his child to go out with him. Before this order, the child may not have been especially interested in the young man, but after being told they cannot go on the date, they react by liking the young man more.

An interesting example of psychological reactance comes from a study by Ruback and Juieng (1997), who observed drivers leaving their parking spots at a local mall. There were four conditions in the study. In the control condition, the researchers timed how long it took from the moment the driver opened their door to the moment they completely left the parking space when no other cars were present. In the distraction condition, they noted how much time was taken when a car drove past the parking space. In the low-intrusion condition, an experimenter pulled up next to the parking spot, indicating that they were waiting for the spot. In the high-intrusion condition, the waiting driver honked their horn. Consistent with psychological reactance, when a driver honked, it took 42.75 seconds for the parked driver to leave versus 26.47 seconds when there was no driver waiting for the spot (control) and 31.09 seconds when a car drove by (distraction).

On a larger scale, such reactions are commonly seen in labor negotiations. Company managements and unions tend to disagree with and criticize one another. But often such criticism backfires because attacking another group may serve to strengthen that group. In fact, if a company or group wants to increase the cohesiveness of its membership, it can artificially create pressure and attribute it to another group. This tactic involves building a *straw man*—an opponent who does not actually exist but to whom negative statements about the group can be attributed.

Group Size

Group size The number of members in a group.

Groups are most cohesive when **group size** is small but perform slightly better when group size is larger. Studies have shown that large groups have slightly higher productivity (Stewart, 2006), are more innovative (Hulsheger, Anderson, & Salgado, 2009), have lower levels of coordination and morale (Frank & Anderson, 1971), are less active (Indik, 1965), less cohesive (Carron, 1990), and more critical (Valacich, Dennis, & Nunamaker, 1992) than smaller groups. In fact, research suggests that groups perform best (Kaplan, 2002; Manners, 1975) and have greatest member satisfaction (Hackman & Vidmar, 1970) when they consist of approximately five members. Thus, a large organization probably works best when work groups contain approximately five people.

Additive tasks Tasks for which the group's performance is equal to the sum of the performances of each individual group member.

Although small groups usually increase cohesiveness, high performance is seen with only certain types of tasks. **Additive tasks** are those for which the group's performance is equal to the sum of the performances by each group member. Examples of groups performing additive tasks include bowling teams and typing pools. In groups working on additive tasks, each member's contribution is important, and larger groups will probably be better than smaller groups. **Conjunctive tasks** are those for which the group's performance depends on the least effective group member (a chain is only as strong as its weakest link). Examples of conjunctive tasks include an assembly line and friends going hiking (you can walk only as fast as the slowest hiker). Because success on a conjunctive task is limited by the least effective member, smaller groups are usually best. **Disjunctive tasks** are those for which the group's performance is based on the most talented group member. Examples of disjunctive tasks include problem solving, brainstorming, and a captain's choice golf tournament (each person plays the best shot of the four golfers). As with additive tasks, larger groups are probably better at disjunctive tasks than are smaller groups.

Conjunctive tasks Tasks for which the group's performance is dependent on the performance of the least effective group member.

Disjunctive tasks Tasks for which the performance of a group is based on the performance of its most talented member.

Social impact theory States that the addition of a group member has the greatest effect on group behavior when the size of the group is small.

The addition of more members has its greatest effect when the group is small. Latane (1981) first investigated this idea when he formulated **social impact theory**. Imagine that a four-person committee is studying safety problems at work. If the group is stable and cohesive, adding a fifth person may be disruptive. But in a factory of 3,000 employees, hiring 1 new employee is not likely to change the complexion of the company. That is why sports experts have observed that a single great player can turn around a poor basketball team—as occurred with Bill Walton and the Portland Trailblazers, David Robinson and the San Antonio Spurs, Jason Kidd and the New Jersey Nets, and Steve Nash and the Phoenix Suns—but not a football or baseball team.

Not surprisingly, research indicates that groups working virtually behave differently from groups working face to face. When working virtually, large groups appear to perform best and have the most satisfied members (Dennis & Williams, 2007; Dennis, Valacich, & Nunamaker, 1990; Valacich, Dennis, & Connolly, 1994; Valacich et al., 1992). Interestingly, when groups work virtually, members whose opinion is in the minority are more likely to *express* opinions than when the group meets face-to-face. However, these same minority members are more *persuasive* when the group meets face-to-face (McLeod, Baron, Marti, & Yoon, 1997).

Group Status

Group status The esteem in which the group is held by people not in the group.

The higher the group's status, the greater its cohesiveness. This is an important point: A group can be made more cohesive by increasing **group status**. The group does not actually have to *have* high status, but it is important that its members *believe* they have high status. An interesting caveat to this point is that communication between group members tends to increase as a group decreases in perceived status, and vice versa (Thibaut, 1950).

Again, look around campus and notice the methods used by various groups to artificially increase their status. On our campus, one fraternity advertises itself as the "Porsche of fraternities"; another claims to be the "fraternity of distinction." Of course, there is little difference between the actual status and performance of most campus organizations, so effective leaders try to increase the cohesiveness of group members by claiming high status—and apparently it works.

One way leaders can increase their group's status is by increasing the perception that the group is difficult to join but that, once in, members will find that the group's activities are special. In most high schools, "two-a-day" practices are typical during the week before football practice begins. During this period, each prospective team member is worked close to exhaustion. Coaches have such "hell weeks" to increase the team's status and thus its cohesion and performance. Obviously, a player cannot get into shape in a week, so the purpose of two-a-day practices is not conditioning—it is to build the status of the group members who survive the week. A similar approach is taken by the U.S. Marine Corps. By its tough basic training, the Corps builds the status of its enlistees so that marines and non-marines alike will believe that the Corps consists of just a few elite fighters.

Fraternities and sororities are also notorious for hazing during their pledge weeks, in which new members are often put through dangerous and humiliating tasks. Aside from the illegality and cruelty of this behavior, hazing serves the purpose of increasing the effort required for a potential member to join, thus increasing the group's cohesiveness and status. Football players, marines, and fraternity or sorority members are not likely to quit a group that they have worked so hard to join.

Group Ability and Confidence

Not surprisingly, groups consisting of high-ability members outperform those with low-ability members (Devine & Phillips, 2001). Furthermore, groups whose members believe that their team can be successful both at a specific task (high team efficacy) and at tasks in general (high team potency) perform better than groups whose members aren't as confident about their probability for success (Gully, Incalcaterra, Joshi, & Beaubien, 2002).

Personality of the Group Members

An important factor affecting group performance is the personality of the group members. Meta-analysis results indicate that in general, groups whose members have task-related experience and score high in the personality dimensions of openness to experience and emotional stability will perform better than groups whose members do not have these characteristics (Bell, 2007). In addition, groups working on intellectual tasks will do better if their group members are bright, and groups working on physical tasks (e.g., sports teams) will do better if their group members score high in the personality dimensions of conscientiousness, extraversion, and agreeableness (Bell, 2005).

A fascinating study reported by Wilson (2007) demonstrates the importance of personality to group performance—in chickens! A company was trying to determine ways to increase the egg production of chickens kept together in small cages and explored two breeding strategies. One was to take the highest producing *individual* chicken in each of the cages and breed them for six generations. The other strategy was to take the highest producing *group* of chickens and let them breed. When the offspring of the nine-highest-producing individual chickens were placed in a group, they became aggressive and six were killed. It seemed that the reason the individual chickens were so productive is that they did so by lowering the production of the other chickens. The offspring of the best group of chickens, however, were not aggressive and produced at a high rate. Thus, there seems to be a genetic predisposition for being an effective group member.

Communication Structure

Communication structure The manner in which members of a group communicate with one another.

Another variable that can affect a group's performance is its **communication structure**, or network. For a group to perform successfully, good communication among members is essential. As shown in Figure 13.1, a variety of communication networks can be used by small groups, and even more complex networks are possible with larger groups. Each network has its advantages and disadvantages, but the best networks depend on the situations and goals of their groups. For example, if the goals of fraternities and

Figure 13.1
Possible Communication Networks for Small Groups

singles clubs are to encourage members to get to know one another, then a centralized structure will be less conducive than a completely open one. Conversely, if the goal of a group is to solve a problem as quickly as possible, then the centralized network will be the best structure. A good leader carefully chooses the communication network that best facilitates the goals of their group.

Group Roles

Another factor that affects the performance of a group is the extent to which its members assume different roles. For a group to be successful, its members' roles must fall into one of two categories: task oriented and social oriented (Stewart, Fulmer, & Barrick, 2005). *Task-oriented roles* involve behaviors such as offering new ideas, coordinating activities, and finding new information. *Social-oriented roles* involve encouraging cohesiveness and participation.

A third category—the *individual role*—includes blocking group activities, calling attention to oneself, and avoiding group interaction. Individual roles seldom result in higher group productivity.

Group members will often naturally assume these roles based on their individual personalities and experiences. For example, people high in conscientiousness tend to fill task-oriented roles, and people high in agreeableness tend to fill social-oriented roles (Stewart et al., 2005). When roles are not naturally filled by group members, leaders must assign roles to certain individuals. For example, if a leader notices that every group member is filling a task-oriented role, they may either recruit a new group member or assign a current member to fill a social role. Additionally, with telecommuting becoming more common, virtual teams may require group members to be flexible with their roles and adapt to changing group requirements.

Presence of Others: Social Facilitation and Inhibition

At the turn of the nineteenth century, researcher Norman Triplett (1898) noticed that cyclists rode faster when competing against other cyclists than when competing against a clock. Intrigued by this observation, Triplett conducted a study in which children completed a task either alone or while competing against other children. As expected, Triplett found that children who worked against others completed their tasks faster than did children who worked alone.

Since that first study, psychologists have studied what we now call *social facilitation* and *social inhibition*. **Social facilitation** involves the positive effects of the presence of others on an individual's behavior; **social inhibition** involves the negative effects of others' presence. Social facilitation and social inhibition can be further delineated by audience effects and coaction.

Social facilitation
The positive effects that occur when a person performs a task in the presence of others.

Social inhibition The negative effects that occur when a person performs a task in the presence of others.

Audience effects The effect on behavior when one or more people passively watch the behavior of another person.

Audience Effects. The phenomenon of audience effects takes place when a group of people passively watch an individual. An example would be a sporting event held in an arena.

The strength of the effect of having an audience present is a function of at least three factors (Latane, 1981): an audience's size, its physical proximity to the person or group, and its status. Thus, groups are most likely to be affected by large audiences of experts who are physically close to them. Not surprisingly, meta-analysis results indicate that the presence of others increases performance in people who are extraverts and have high self-esteem and decreases performance in people with low self-esteem and who score high in neuroticism (Uziel, 2007).

Coaction The effect on behavior when two or more people are performing the same task in the presence of each other.

Coaction.   The effect on behavior when two or more people are performing the same task in the presence of one another is called **coaction**. Examples would be two runners competing against each other without a crowd present, or two mail clerks sorting envelopes in the same room. Shalley (1995) found that coaction decreased creativity and productivity. There are many studies demonstrating interesting examples of coaction-influenced behavior. For example:

- Rockloff and Dyer (2007) found that gamblers placed larger bets and lost more money when gambling near others than when gambling alone.
- Sommer, Wynes, and Brinkley (1992) found that when people shopped in groups, they spent more time in a store and purchased more goods than when alone. Similar results were not found by Lee and Martin (2001).
- A meta-analysis by Ruddock, Brunstrom, Vartanian, and Higgs (2019) discovered that people eat more food when dining with others than when dining alone.

Explaining Social Facilitation Effects.   More than 200 studies of social facilitation have indicated that performance does not always increase in the presence of others. Performance increases only when the task being performed is easy or well learned; performance decreases when the task is difficult or not well learned (Bond & Titus, 1983; Platania & Moran, 2001). Social facilitation and coaction effects occur not only with humans but also with cockroaches running a maze (Zajonc, Heingartner, & Herman, 1969), chickens eating food (Tolman, 1968), and ants building nests (Chen, 1937). Some research examples are shown in Table 13.1.

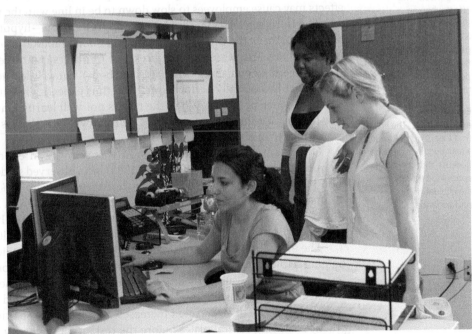

Evaluation apprehension can cause performance to drop when trying to learn a new task.

Table 13.1 Tasks Affected by Social Facilitation and Social Inhibition

Skill Level	Facilitation: Increased Performance	Inhibition: Decreased Performance
Well learned	Bicycle racing	
	Pool shooting	
	Simple mathematics	
	Shopping	
	Eating	
	Jogging	
Novice		Pool shooting
		Learning nonsense syllables
		Completing a maze
		Complex mathematics
		New drivers taking a driving test

Mere presence Theory stating that the very fact that others happen to be present naturally produces arousal and thus may affect performance.

Comparison The effect when an individual working on a task compares their performance with that of another person performing the same task.

Evaluation apprehension The idea that a person performing a task becomes aroused because they are concerned that others are evaluating their performance.

Although researchers have not agreed on the exact reason for these findings, four explanations have each received some empirical support. The first explanation holds that the **mere presence** of others naturally produces arousal (Zajonc, 1980). This arousal, or increase in energy, helps an individual perform well-learned tasks but hinders them in performing poorly learned or unpracticed tasks.

The second explanation states that a coacting audience provides a means for **comparison**. If an individual is working on a task with another individual, he can directly compare their performance with the other person's. In some jobs, this comparison effect may increase competition and production quantity, whereas in other jobs, comparison effects may cause employees to slow down to be in line with the working norm.

The third explanation—**evaluation apprehension**—hypothesizes that judgment by others causes the differential effects of social facilitation (Cottrell, 1972). That is, individuals are aware that the presence of others can be rewarding (e.g., when a crowd cheers) or punishing (when a crowd boos). On well-learned tasks, the individual knows that he normally performs well and thus expects a rewarding experience when in the presence of others. When the task is not well learned, however, the individual may believe that they will not perform well and will be embarrassed; thus they perform even worse than if they were alone.

One example of this phenomenon was seen in an experiment by Michaels, Blommel, Brocato, Linkous, and Rowe (1982), who observed students shooting pool and found that good players increased their shot accuracy from 71% to 80% when watched by an audience, whereas poor players' accuracy decreased from 36% to 25% when they were watched. Thombs, Beck, and Mahoney (1993) found that high-intensity drinkers were more likely than low-intensity drinkers to drink in social situations.

The evaluation-apprehension explanation has special application to industry and training settings. Imagine a server who must carry five plates of food to a table. For a new server, this is not a well-learned task, and in the presence of others they are likely to be anxious. When the lack of practice in carrying plates is combined with a large restaurant crowd, the chance of an accident increases. So what is the solution? The server should practice carrying several plates before the restaurant opens. Evaluation apprehension also occurs when performance is being monitored electronically rather than in person

(Davidson & Henderson, 2000). Thus, supervisors who remotely monitor virtual employee performance must be aware of the potential effects on performance.

The fourth explanation proposes that the presence of others is **distracting** to the individual who is trying to perform a task (Sanders, 1981). On well-learned tasks, the individual can perform despite the distraction because the behaviors are almost automatic. On a novel or complicated task, however, the distraction caused by other people's presence keeps the individual from concentrating and learning the task. For example, Baxter, Manstead, Stradling, and Campbell (1990) found that drivers with passengers were less likely to signal than were drivers without anyone else in the car, and a meta-analysis by Caird, Willness, Steel, and Scialfa (2008) found that drivers using cell phones had slower reaction times than drivers not using cell phones while driving.

An example that demonstrates the effects emphasized by both the evaluation-apprehension and distraction theories is that of coaching children in sports. In a typical Little League practice, one coach must teach an eight-year-old how to bat while 10 other children stand in the field and wait for a ball to be hit to them. Each time the child at the plate fails to hit the ball, the others tease the batter. After a while, the children in the field are bored and begin to throw rocks and talk with one another. What is the probability of success in teaching this child to hit under these circumstances? For the coach to be successful, they must teach the child alone and away from other children.

Effects of social facilitation also have been examined in sports by investigating the advantage that a team might have by playing its game at home. In general, having a home crowd behind a team or an individual athlete such as a wrestler increases the probability of winning (Jamieson, 2010; McAndrew, 1993).

Social Loafing. Whereas the social facilitation versus social inhibition theory explains increases and decreases in performance when others are present and either watching the individual or working with them, the **social loafing** theory considers the effect on individual performance when people work together on a task. Social loafing was first investigated by Ringleman (reported in Moede, 1927) in a study in which subjects singly pulled as hard as possible on a rope while he measured their exerted force. Ringleman then had his subjects perform the task in pairs. He expected the force exerted by two subjects to be approximately twice that exerted by a single subject, but to his surprise he found that both subjects exerted less force than when they worked alone.

Additional research has supported the theory and has found that social loafing occurs with many tasks (Karau & Williams, 1993). For example, Parrett (2006) found that restaurant customers left a higher tip percentage when they dined alone than when they dined with others. This explains why gratuities often are automatically added to a bill when six or more people dine at a table.

Although it is clear that social loafing occurs, especially in poor performers (Hardy & Crace, 1991), it is not clear *why* it occurs. One theory is that because group members realize that their individual efforts will not be noticed, there is little chance of individual reward. A second theory, called the *free-rider theory* (Kerr & Bruun, 1983), postulates that when things are going well, a group member realizes that their effort is not necessary and thus does not work as hard as they would if they were alone. Support for this theory comes from meta-analysis results showing that people don't socially loaf when their individual inputs are unique and can't be performed by other group members (Karau & Williams, 1993).

The third theory, called the *sucker effect* (Kerr, 1983), hypothesizes that social loafing occurs when a group member notices that other group members are not working hard and thus are "playing them for a sucker." To avoid this situation, the individual lowers their work performance to match those of the other members. This theory, however, does not explain the loafing of other members.

Given that working with others can both increase performance (social facilitation) and decrease performance (social loafing, social inhibition), how does a manager know whether to assign employees to a group or have the employees work alone? The answer seems to be that if the task is complex or not well learned, employees should work alone. If the task is easy or well learned, and each individual's performance can be identified, working in groups might be best (Aiello & Douthitt, 2001). Social loafing can be reduced by evaluating employees on their individual contributions to the group (Karau & Williams, 1993), posting performance results (Lount & Wilk, 2014), explaining the link between individual effort and group performance (Shepperd & Taylor, 1999), and rewarding those who achieve (George, 1995; Shepperd, 1993). Punishing social loafers has unpredictable effects—sometimes it works, sometimes it doesn't (George, 1995; Miles & Greenberg, 1993).

Individual Dominance

Individual dominance When one member of a group dominates the group.

Another variable that can affect group performance is **individual dominance** by a leader or single group member. If the leader or group member has an accurate solution to a problem the group is trying to solve, the group will probably perform at a high level. But if the leader or group member has an inaccurate solution, they will lead the group astray, and it will perform poorly. For example, a study by LePine, Hollenbeck, Ilgen, and Hedlund (1997) found that a group of highly intelligent members perform poorly when its leader is not very intelligent. The same relationship was found for the personality variable of conscientiousness.

Groupthink

Groupthink A state of mind in which a group is so concerned about its own cohesiveness that it ignores important information.

The term **groupthink** was coined by Janis (1972) after studying the disastrous Bay of Pigs invasion of 1961. The Bay of Pigs was the Cuban landing site for 1,400 Cuban exiles who sought to overthrow the government of Fidel Castro. The plan called for the U.S. Navy and Air Force to covertly protect the invasion force and its supply ships. The invaders, however, were met unexpectedly by 20,000 Cuban troops and were quickly killed or captured. The help promised by the U.S. government never appeared. Janis (1972) proposed the concept of groupthink to explain how some of the nation's brightest people could hatch such an ill-conceived plan.

With groupthink, members become so cohesive and like-minded that they make poor decisions despite contrary information that might reasonably lead them to other options. Groupthink most often occurs when the group

- is cohesive;
- is insulated from qualified outsiders;
- has an illusion of invulnerability, infallibility, or both;
- believes that it is morally superior to its adversaries;
- is under great pressure to conform;
- has a leader who promotes a favorite solution; and
- has gatekeepers who keep information from other group members.

Groupthink can be reduced in several ways. First, the group leader should not state their own position or beliefs until late in the decision-making process.

Second, the leader should promote open discussion and encourage group members to speak. Third, a group or committee can be separated into subgroups to increase the chance of disagreement. Finally, one group member can be assigned the job of **devil's advocate**—one who questions and disagrees with the group. Research has also postulated that the effects of groupthink can be lessened by introducing gender diversity (Kamalnath, 2017).

Devil's advocate A group member who intentionally provides an opposing opinion to that expressed by the leader or the majority of the group.

As with most things in psychology, the potential for groupthink is complicated. Though cohesive groups with strong leaders often result in groupthink, there are situations in which these two characteristics result in high levels of group performance (Kerr & Tinsdale, 2004).

13-3 Individual Versus Group Performance

When several people individually work on a problem but do not interact, they are called a **nominal group**. When several individuals interact to solve a problem, they are called an **interacting group**. An important decision a leader must make is when to assign tasks to individuals, nominal groups, or interacting groups. After decades of research investigating group effectiveness, the consensus appears to be that interacting groups will usually outperform one individual, but interacting groups do not outperform nominal groups (Kerr & Tinsdale, 2004).

Nominal group A collection of individuals whose results are pooled but who never interact with one another.

Interacting group A collection of individuals who work together to perform a task.

The importance of the difference between nominal and interacting groups can be found in an interesting study by Liden et al. (1999). Liden and his colleagues had managers, nominal groups of employees, and interacting groups of employees read

Employees wearing company-provided clothing can increase group identification.

© Lee Raynes

scenarios about a group member's poor performance and then determine how the employee should be disciplined. The interacting groups and the managers decided on more severe levels of discipline than did the nominal groups.

If the task involves *creating* ideas, individuals should be asked to independently create them and then meet as a group. Although **brainstorming** is a commonly used technique, it is not an effective one. In brainstorming, group members are encouraged to say aloud any and all ideas that come to mind and are not allowed to comment on the ideas until all have been given. When research compares a brainstorming group's creativity with that of a single individual, the brainstorming group will almost always be more creative. However, when comparing the number and quality of ideas created by nominal groups with the quality and number of ideas created by an interacting group in a brainstorming session, the ideas of nominal groups are more creative and of higher quality than ideas of the interacting group (Kerr & Tinsdale, 2004). This difference may partially be due to interacting groups setting lower goals than individuals (Larey & Paulus, 1995).

Due to the increasing cost of travel, it is increasingly common for groups to "meet" virtually rather than face to face. In fact, in my own consulting, it has become rare to fly to a company to participate in a meeting; almost everything is handled through email and video conferences. The results of meta-analyses by DeRosa, Smith, and Hantula (2007) and Dennis and Williams (2007) suggest that such a practice is not only cost effective but also results in more effective performance than face-to-face group meetings. DeRosa et al. found that virtual brainstorming groups outperform face-to-face interacting groups. The comparison with nominal groups is more complicated. Overall, virtual brainstorming groups and nominal groups appear to perform at equal levels when the groups are small, but virtual groups are superior when the group is large.

The superiority of nominal groups over interacting groups may depend on the type of task. Brophy (1996) found nominal groups to be most effective with a single brainstorming problem and interacting groups to be most effective with complex problems. Similar results were reported by Davis and Harless (1996), who found that with complex problems, interacting groups take better advantage of feedback and learning and thus outperform nominal groups.

An interesting aspect of interacting groups is the tendency for groups to take more extreme positions than the positions of individual members. This tendency, called group polarization, suggests that group members will shift their beliefs to a more extreme version of what they already believe individually, that is, if individual group members are on the risky side, the group will make highly risky decisions. If, however, the individual members are conservative or cautious, the group as a whole will be extremely cautious (Isenberg, 1986). The American electorate is a good example of group polarization. Researchers have documented the inclination of partisans to express increased hostility to partisans of a different political affiliation even regarding nonpolitical behaviors (Iyengar & Westwood, 2015).

The tendency to make more risky decisions was demonstrated in a particularly interesting piece of research by Cromwell, Marks, Olson, and Avary (1991) who found that burglars committed more crimes when working as part of a group than when working alone. Another example of increased group riskiness comes from a brokerage firm that was interested in getting its brokers to make riskier but higher yielding investments. A consulting firm was asked to develop a way to select such brokers. Using its knowledge of group dynamics, the consulting firm told the brokerage company that it could obtain better results by having its brokers make investment decisions in groups rather than individually. Implementing this suggestion, the company later reported that its brokers were indeed making riskier investments.

Brainstorming A technique in which ideas are generated by people in a group setting.

Although the research seems to conclude that interacting groups offer no performance improvement over nominal groups, Wilson (2007) has criticized this conclusion because it flies in the face of evolutionary research that demonstrates the value of groups in most species. He believes that a problem with previous group research is that the tasks were too easy and that when a task is difficult, interacting groups are superior to nominal groups.

13-4 Teams

Now that you have a good understanding of group dynamics, let's focus on a specific type of group behavior that occurs in work teams. The concept of employee work teams has been around for decades (they were often called "quality circles" in the 1970s), but their use greatly increased in the 1990s and continue to be commonly used today.

Unfortunately, this increase in the use of teams is often the result of "keeping up with the Joneses" (an idiom that refers to using one's neighbors as a benchmark of socio-economic status) rather than a strategically planned method of organization development. As with any type of organizational intervention, teams can improve performance in some, but not all, situations. Teams work best in situations in which (a) the job requires high levels of employee interaction, (b) a team approach will simplify the job, (c) a team can do something an individual cannot, and (d) there is time to create a team and properly train team members (Kriegel & Brandt, 1996).

What Is a Work Team?

According to Devine, Clayton, Philips, Dunford, and Melner (1999), a work team is "a collection of three or more individuals who interact intensively to provide an organizational product, plan, decision, or service" (p. 681). At times, putting employees into teams fails because the team is really a "group" or a "committee" rather than a true team. In fact, according to a survey of practitioners who work with teams, only 48% of work groups would be officially classified as a team (Offermann & Spiros, 2001). Before calling a group of individuals a team, several factors should be considered (Donnellon, 1996).

Identification

Identification is the extent to which group members identify with the team rather than with other groups. For example, suppose a committee was created composed of one representative from each of five different departments (e.g., accounting, engineering, human resources). During the meetings, members use such statements as "Our department won't agree," "This committee just doesn't like those of us in engineering," or, "We didn't even want to be on this committee." Notice that the use of *we*, *our*, and *us* refers to their departments rather than to the committee. According to Donnellon (1996), for the committee to be considered a team, those same words would need to refer to the committee: for example, "How can we convince the accounting department?" or "Our solution is a good one."

Interdependence

In a team, members need and desire the assistance, expertise, and opinions of the other members. If a team member can perform her job without the assistance of others, the team would not meet the definition of a group. For example, some teams,

Interdependence The extent to which team members need and rely on other team members.

such as a surgical team in a hospital, have very high task **interdependence** in that what one member does greatly influences what another member does. Other teams (most committees) have low task interdependence in that each member completes a task and the separate parts are then compiled. Though each part is important in completing the final product, the completion of each part is not dependent on another group member. The importance of task interdependence was demonstrated by Liden, Wayne, and Bradway (1996), who found that empowerment increased the performance of teams with high task interdependence (e.g., team members had to get information from each other, worked together on projects) but decreased the performance of teams with low task interdependence (e.g., did their work separately, did not have to rely on others).

Power Differentiation

Power differentiation The extent to which team members have the same level of power and respect.

In a team, members try to decrease **power differentiation** by treating others as equals and taking steps to ensure equality. In groups that are not teams, members challenge, correct, and interrupt each other, give orders, and use sarcasm. For example, I worked with one organization that had an "administrative team." What I discovered, however, was that one individual in that team was treated differently, had less authority, and had no voting power. Consequently, rather than being a "team," they were a "committee."

In teams, members apologize for overstepping their roles, ask indirect questions to avoid challenges, and are polite to one another (Donnellon, 1996). For example, in a team, a member might disagree with another member by saying something like, "I don't know your field as well as you do, but what if we tried . . ."; whereas, in a nonteam, a member might disagree by saying, "That's so stupid. I'll tell you what will work."

Social Distance

Social distance The extent to which team members treat each other in a friendly, informal manner.

In a team, members try to decrease **social distance** by being casual, using nicknames, and expressing liking, empathy, and common views. Nonteam members use formal language and forms of address, excessive politeness, and impersonal conversations. For example, team members would use such phrases as "Hey, how's it going?" "Thanks, my friend," and "I understand your feelings on that." Nonteam members might address another member as "Mr. Jones" rather than "Bob" or agree with someone by saying, "I concur with your opinion" rather than "I'm right with you on that one."

Conflict Management Tactics

Team members respond to conflict by collaborating, whereas nonteam members respond by forcing and accommodating (these terms will be discussed later in the chapter). In nonteams, members react to conflict by threatening, directing, or giving in. In teams, members try to understand the others' views, make attempts to compromise, and use nonthreatening tones (Donnellon, 1996).

Negotiation Process

In teams, members negotiate in a win–win style in which the goal is for every person to come out ahead. In nonteams, members negotiate so that they win and the other members lose.

On the basis of the six factors just discussed, Donnellon (1996) placed teams into one of five categories: collaborative teams, emergent teams, adversarial teams, nominal teams, and doomed teams. Collaborative teams and emergent teams are what I have referred to as true teams, whereas nominal teams and doomed teams are what I have referred to as nonteams. Adversarial teams are somewhere in between a true team and a nonteam.

Permanency The extent to which a team will remain together or be disbanded after a task has been accomplished.

Proximity Physical distance between people.

Virtual teams Teams that communicate through email rather than face to face.

Though not affecting the extent to which a group is officially a team, teams differ in two other ways. Teams differ as to their **permanency**. That is, some teams are designed to work together permanently, whereas others are formed to solve a particular problem and then are expected to dissolve. For example, I was appointed to a university task force designed to create a new system for students to use to evaluate faculty. Once the system was created, our team disbanded.

Teams can also differ in the **proximity** of their members. Members of surgical teams, baseball teams, and the cast of a Broadway play not only are task interdependent but also work physically close to one another. In many instances, however, members of teams may be located across several cities, states, or countries. Because of the expense of bringing such teams to the same location, such companies as IBM, Google, and Intel use **virtual teams**, whose members carry out their team functions through email and videoconferencing (Lepsinger & DeRosa, 2010). Though virtual teams can certainly be productive, they tend to struggle with building trust, creating synergy, and overcoming feelings of isolation (Kirkman, Rosen, Gibson, Tesluk, & McPherson, 2002).

Types of Teams

Teams come in many shapes and sizes based on the factors discussed earlier in the chapter. For example, Devine et al. (1999) surveyed organizations and determined that teams differ on two major characteristics: temporal duration (ad hoc versus ongoing) and product type (project versus production). For this chapter, teams will be classified into the four categories determined by Cohen and Bailey (1997): work teams, parallel teams, project teams, and management teams.

Work Teams

Work teams Groups of employees who manage themselves, assign jobs, plan and schedule work, make work-related decisions, and solve work-related problems.

Work teams consist of groups of employees who manage themselves, assign jobs, plan and schedule work, make work-related decisions, and solve work-related problems (Kirkman & Shapiro, 2001). They are typically formed to produce goods, provide service, or increase the quality and cost-effectiveness of a product or system. For example, work teams at

- Monarch Marking Systems in Dayton, Ohio, reduced past-due shipments by 70% and doubled productivity;
- GTE Directories in Dallas increased the production of telephone directories by 158%, reduced errors by 48%, and reduced the time to respond to customer complaints from 18.8 days to 2.9 days; and
- Xerox in Webster, New York, saved $266,000 by discovering the cause of high failure rates in one of its products.

As shown in Figure 13.2, the traditional method of manufacturing a product is to have employees specialize in performing one particular task. For example, a company might have a supervisor, sorter, assembler, solderer, and quality inspector. The sorter places parts on the assembly line, the assembler puts the parts together, the solderer solders the parts, and the quality control inspector makes sure the part is properly assembled.

In a team approach, there would be no supervisor. Each of the production workers would be called a "team member" and be cross-trained to perform all of the tasks. In this way, if parts were assembled faster than they could be soldered, the sorter might spend some time soldering rather than sorting or waiting. The team would be responsible for checking its own quality, and one of the production workers would probably be

Traditional Approach

Supervisor

Sorter | Assembler | Solderer | Quality Inspector

Team Approach

Team Member I ⟷ Team Member III

Team Member II

Figure 13.2
Traditional Versus
Team Approaches

appointed as a team leader. The use of production teams saves money by removing management layers and making the team responsible for its own production.

Customer service teams are commonly found in restaurants and retail stores. In the traditional customer service model at a restaurant, each employee is assigned specific tasks (e.g., serving, cooking, busing tables) in specific areas. With the team approach, each employee may still be assigned a primary duty and area but is expected to "do what it takes" to satisfy customers. For example, suppose that Ken is your server at a very busy restaurant. You want another drink, but Ken is at another table. The closest person to you is Barbie, who is clearing tables. In the traditional system, a request of another drink from Barbie would result in a response such as "I only clear tables; you'll have to wait for your server." In the team approach, Barbie would have been cross-trained in serving beverages and would be able to comply with your request.

Webber and Klimoski (2004) believe that not all work teams are alike and that an important type of work team is the *crew*. Crews are groups of "expert specialists [who each] have specific role positions, perform brief events that are closely synchronized with each other, and repeat these events across different environmental conditions" (Webber and Klimoski, 2004, p. 265). Examples of crews would include a group of firefighters, a flight crew (pilots, navigators, flight attendants, etc.), and a motion picture production crew (director, cameraman, key grip, etc.). Because crews include highly trained specialists and often rely on technology, they are affected less by changes in membership than are other work teams.

Parallel Teams

Parallel teams, also called **cross-functional teams**, consist of representatives from various departments (functions) within an organization (Keller, 2001). For example, a team formed to reduce the time to ship a product might include members from the sales, shipping, production, and customer service departments. For cross-functional teams to be successful, it is important that they have a clear purpose, receive support from each functional area, and take steps to increase the trust levels of committee members. Building trust in cross-functional teams is especially important, as members

Parallel teams Also called *cross-functional teams*, they consist of representatives from various departments (functions) within an organization.

Cross-functional teams Teams consisting of representatives from various departments (functions) within an organization.

are often torn between representing the interests of their function and doing what is best for the organization as a whole.

Project Teams

Project teams Groups formed to produce onetime outputs such as creating a new product, installing a new software system, or hiring a new employee.

Project teams are formed to produce onetime outputs such as creating a new product, installing a new software system, or hiring a new employee. Once the team's goal has been accomplished, the team is dismantled. The temporary nature of project teams is what distinguishes them from parallel and work teams. The environmental consulting firm of Camp Dresser and McKee provides an excellent example of a project team. The company needed to replace its human resource information system (HRIS), which tracks employment information for its 3,500 employees. Because such a system was used by a wide variety of departments, Camp Dresser and McKee formed a 40-person team to select and implement the new system. Once the system was in place, the team disbanded (Jossi, 2001b).

Management Teams

Management teams Teams that coordinate, manage, advise, and direct employees and teams.

Management teams coordinate, manage, advise, and direct employees and teams. Whereas work, parallel, and project teams are responsible for directly accomplishing a particular goal, management teams are responsible for providing general direction and assistance to those teams.

How Teams Develop

Forming stage The first stage of the team process, in which team members "feel out" the team concept and attempt to make a positive impression.

In an influential theory of team development, Tuckman (1965) proposed that teams typically go through four developmental phases: *forming, storming, norming,* and *performing.* In the **forming stage**, team members get to know each other and decide what roles each member will play. During the early part of this stage, team members are on their best behavior as they try to impress and get along with the other team members. Team members are often excited about the potential to accomplish something but are also anxious about working with others in a team. During the latter part of this stage, the team concentrates on clarifying its mission, determining the goals it wants to accomplish, deciding on the tasks to be done to accomplish their goals, setting rules and procedures, and developing alternative courses of action to reach their goals (Marks, Mathieu, & Zaccaro, 2001). A meta-analysis by Salas, Mullen, Rozell, and Driskell (1997) indicates that formal team building (training on how to be a team) that focuses on role clarification will slightly improve team performance.

Storming stage The second stage in group formation in which group members disagree and resist their team roles.

During the **storming stage**, the good behavior disappears. On an individual level, team members often become frustrated with their roles, show the stress of balancing their previous duties with their new team responsibilities, and question whether they have the ability to accomplish the goals set in the forming stage. Interpersonally, team members begin to disagree with one another and to challenge each other's ideas. It is from this tension and conflict that the team often gets the energy to perform well in later stages.

Norming stage The third stage of the team process, in which teams establish roles and determine policies and procedures.

During the **norming stage**, the team works toward easing the tension from the storming stage. Team members begin to acknowledge the reality of the team by accepting the team leader and working directly with other team members to solve difficulties. At this point, team members have either accepted their initial roles or made adjustments to roles for which they are better suited. Team members also begin developing shared mental models that contribute to the effectiveness of the team in the last stage (Neuman & Wright, 1999).

In the **performing stage**, the team begins to accomplish its goals. Group members make innovative suggestions, challenge one another without defensive responses, and participate at high levels. During this stage, the team continually monitors its progress toward goals, determines additional resources that might be needed, provides assistance and feedback to team members, and makes necessary strategic adjustments (Marks et al., 2001).

Although this theory of team development is commonly used, as one would imagine, there is tremendous variation in how a given team will develop. Various limitations of Tuckman's model were identified, including an assumption of generalizability beyond the research, and a lack of explanation of how groups transform over time (Bonebright, 2010). An alternate theory, called *punctuated equilibrium*, suggests that rather than forming in stages, teams develop direction and strategy in the first meeting, follow this direction for a period of time, and then drastically revise their strategy about halfway through the life of the team (Gersick, 1988).

Why Teams Don't Always Work

Given that the scientific literature suggests that teams are seldom more effective than individuals (Allen & Hecht, 2004), there has been an abundance of advice in the literature about how to create successful teams. In a study investigating this advice, Hyatt and Ruddy (1997) found that customer service teams were most effective when they received the necessary support from management (e.g., information, technology, training), had confidence in their ability to complete their tasks; were customer oriented; exhibited an open, supportive, and professional communication style; had set appropriate goals; and followed an agreed-upon group process. Moran, Musselwhite, and Zenger (1996) identified 12 common problems encountered by teams. Let's look at the six most important ones.

The Team Is Not a Team

Consistent with the previous discussion, teams often aren't successful because they are teams in name only.

Excessive Meeting Requirements

A common problem with teams is that they either meet too infrequently or meet so often that they waste time when they do meet. The key to successful team meetings is to limit the topics to be discussed and to meet only when the entire team is needed to contribute. Furthermore, teams often feel the need to meet for the entire time for which a meeting is scheduled, even though the necessary business could be conducted in much less time. This tendency to "stretch" a meeting can reduce the motivation and enthusiasm of a team.

As an example of the tendency to meet too often, I was placed on one of several teams whose task it was to address specific problems facing the university. Our team leader (committee chair) wanted us to meet every Wednesday at two o'clock until our task was completed. Because of the nature of our task, weeks might pass before we had anything new to bring to the group. Yet we still met every Wednesday. After four weeks, attendance at the meetings dropped to about 50%. When our angry team leader confronted our team members, they were shocked to hear such comments as, "These weekly meetings are a waste of time" and "I always attend the important meetings, just not the worthless ones."

I was on another committee that demonstrated the tendency to stretch meetings. The committee comprised 25 people and met one Friday a month from 3:00 p.m. to 4:30 p.m. When the dean ran the meetings, they always ended at exactly 4:30 p.m. When the dean was out of town, the committee's vice-chair (the second in command, not the person in charge of vice) would start the meetings by saying, "Let's do our business and get out of here." On these occasions, we never stayed past 3:45 p.m.

Lack of Empowerment

Many teams are formed to solve problems but are not given sufficient authority to conduct their business. According to Moran et al. (1996), teams aren't empowered because managers worry that the job won't be done correctly, the teams are moving too fast, and the teams will overstep their boundaries such that other parts of the organization will be affected. This last managerial concern is especially important because as teams work to solve problems, their solutions often involve many different departments. If the teams are not properly empowered, they will lack the authority to overcome the political resistance of each affected department.

Though empowerment is essential for the success of most teams, it is not uncommon for team members to reject their empowered status. After all, with the advantages of empowerment come the risks of making mistakes and getting others angry. To many employees, these risks override the benefits of empowerment.

Lack of Skill

It is assumed that members assigned to a team have the skills necessary to effectively carry out their assignment. Unfortunately, this is often not the case (Yandrick, 2001). What is most common is for team members to lack either the skills needed to work in a team (e.g., communication, problem solving) or the expertise to solve the problem itself. As an example, universities typically form committees whose membership consists of representatives from various colleges (e.g., arts and sciences, education) and departments (e.g., history, psychology, economics). Such a membership strategy makes sense if the issue is one on which various departments might differ. That is, a committee asked to determine general education requirements or summer school offerings should have representatives from each department. However, a committee formed to develop fund-raising strategies would be better served with a membership of marketing and psychology faculty rather than history and music faculty.

Research on the personal characteristics of team members has revealed some interesting findings. Teams whose members are bright, conscientious, extraverted, and emotionally stable perform better than teams whose members do not possess such characteristics (Barrick, Stewart, Neubert, & Mount, 1998; Devine & Phillips, 2001).

Distrust of the Team Process

Many teams don't succeed because management doesn't trust the concept of teams. A study by the consulting firm Zenger-Miller found that in organizations in which top management was not enthusiastic about the team approach, only 49% of teams made satisfactory progress. However, in teams with supportive management, 84% made satisfactory progress (Moran et al., 1996). Some of this distrust comes from managers being unwilling to give up any authority. Managers, too, need to be trained in the team process if the team concept is going to survive.

Team members must also be receptive to the team process. Research indicates that job satisfaction and organizational commitment are reduced when members are not receptive to the team process (Kirkman & Shapiro, 2001). Another source of team distrust is that not all work is appropriate for teams (Drexler & Forrester, 1998). That is, some tasks (e.g., data input) are better done individually, and others, such as performing a surgery, are performed better with the help of others.

Unclear Objectives

Teams work best when they know why they were formed, what they are expected to accomplish (what the team's "charge" is), and when they are supposed to be finished. Though this would all seem obvious, you would be surprised at how many teams aren't sure what they are supposed to do. As an example, I was on a university committee entitled "Committee on Student Evaluation of Faculty." We spent most of the time during our first few meetings asking, "What are we supposed to do?," "Are we supposed to design a new evaluation instrument?," and "Do we make decisions or do we just make recommendations?" It took almost a month to get clarification, and during that time the committee made no progress, its members became frustrated, and attendance dropped.

13-5 Group Conflict

When individuals work together in groups or in formal teams, there is always potential for conflict. In fact, in one survey, 85% of employees said that they experience conflict on their jobs and 22% said they have missed work due to the conflict (Tyler, 2010). Even working remotely doesn't seem to reduce workplace conflict as a 2021 survey by MyPerfectResume found that 80% of remote workers experienced conflict on the job: 65% with coworkers and 19% with their boss.

Conflict The psychological and behavioral reaction to a perception that another person is keeping you from reaching a goal, taking away your right to behave in a particular way, or violating the expectancies of a relationship.

Conflict is the psychological and behavioral reaction to a perception that another person is keeping you from reaching a goal, taking away your right to behave in a particular way, or violating the expectancies of a relationship. For example, Bob might perceive that Lakisha is trying to get the promotion that is "rightfully his" (keeping him from his goal), Andrea might perceive that Jon is trying to pressure her to hire a particular applicant (taking away the right to behave in a particular way), or Carlos might perceive that when Jill goes to lunch with her men colleagues she is violating their agreement not to date other people (violation of a relationship expectation).

It is important to note that one of the key components to conflict is *perception*. For example, two people may share the same goals, but if one person perceives that their goals are different, the possibility of conflict increases. Thus, conflict is often the result of one person's misperception of another's goals, intentions, or behavior. Because conflict can often be attributed to misperceptions, an important part of conflict resolution is for each party to discuss their perceptions of a situation.

The level of conflict that occurs is a function of the importance of the goal, behavior, or relationship. That is, one person's behavior may force a change in another's, but if the change in behavior is not important to the individual (e.g., waiting in line for a few minutes), conflict will be less severe than in a situation in which the change is important (e.g., a promotion or a person's reputation).

Dysfunctional conflict Conflict that keeps people from working together, lessens productivity, spreads to other areas, or increases turnover.

On the basis of a meta-analysis by De Dreu and Weingart (2003), we are pretty safe in saying that most conflict results in lower team performance and lower member satisfaction. This **dysfunctional conflict** keeps people from working together, lessens productivity, spreads to other areas, and increases turnover. Dysfunctional conflict usually occurs when one or both parties feel a loss of control due to the actions of the other party and has its greatest effect on team performance when the task being performed is complex. Though most conflict is dysfunctional, there are times when a moderate degree of conflict can result in better performance. Called **functional conflict**, moderate levels of conflict can stimulate new ideas, increase friendly competition, and increase team effectiveness (Jehn & Mannix, 2001; Jeong, 2008). Furthermore, moderate conflict can reduce the risk of much larger conflicts.

Why should an organization be concerned with dysfunctional conflict? Employees react to conflict by missing work, leaving the organization, forming unions, and filing lawsuits (SHRM, 2021c).

Types of Conflict
Interpersonal Conflict

Interpersonal conflict occurs between two individuals. In the workplace, interpersonal conflict might occur between two coworkers, a supervisor and a subordinate, an employee and a customer, or an employee and a vendor.

Individual–Group Conflict

Conflict can occur between an individual and a group just as easily as between two individuals. **Individual–group conflict** usually occurs when the individual's needs are different from the group's needs, goals, or norms. For example, a marine might want more independence than the Corps will give them, a basketball player might want to shoot when the team needs them to set picks, a faculty member might be more interested in teaching when their university wants them to publish, and a store employee might be more interested in customer relations when the store wants them to concentrate on sales.

Group–Group Conflict

The third type of conflict occurs between two or more groups. In academia, such **group–group conflict** occurs annually as departments fight for budget allocations and space. In industry, company divisions often conflict for the same reasons. A good example of group–group conflict occurred between two branches of the same bank located in the same town. The branches competed for customers not only with other banks but also with each other. To make matters worse, the two branches were to be consolidated, so their staffs were involved in even more conflict as they tried to establish who would be in charge of the new and unified branch.

Causes of Conflict
Competition for Resources

In the marketplace, when customer demand exceeds product supply, prices increase. Similarly, in groups, when demand for a resource exceeds its supply, conflict occurs. This is often true in organizations, especially when there is not enough money, space, personnel, or equipment to satisfy the needs of every person or every group.

A good example of this cause of conflict, **competition for resources**, occurs annually when the U.S. Congress decides on the nation's budget. With only limited tax revenues and many worthy programs, tough choices must be made. But often, instead of working together to solve the country's problems, the state representatives come into conflict over whose favorite programs will be funded.

Functional conflict Conflict that results in increased performance or better interpersonal relations.

Interpersonal conflict Conflict between two people.

Individual–group conflict Conflict between an individual and the other members of a group.

Group–group conflict Conflict between two or more groups.

Competition for resources A cause of conflict that occurs when the demand for resources is greater than the resources available.

Another example of this competition occurs in colleges and universities across the country. There are probably few universities where parking and office spaces are not a problem. Faculty and students argue about who gets the parking spaces, and once that argument is settled, seniors and juniors argue over what is left.

I once belonged to an organization that initially had no conflict over resources because there were none to fight over. There were no extra offices, no equipment, and no supplies. Organization members even had to supply their own paper! After several years, however, the organization received a large amount of money and a new building with plenty of space. But as expected, conflict increased. All the employees wanted more space, their own printers, and so on. What had once been a very cohesive group was now characterized by conflict because of competition for new resources.

Task Interdependence

Task interdependence A potential source of conflict that arises when the completion of a task by one person affects the completion of a task by another person.

Another cause of conflict, **task interdependence**, comes when the performance of some group members depends on the performance of other group members. For example, a group is assigned to present a research report. The person who is assigned to type the report cannot do their job unless they can read what others have written, the person assigned to write the conclusion cannot do so until others have written their sections, and no member of the group is finished until every member has completed the assigned work.

Conflict caused by task interdependence is especially likely when two groups who rely on each other have conflicting goals. For example, the production department in a factory wants to turn out a high volume of goods, whereas the quality control department wants the goods to be of high quality. Neither department can do its job without the help of the other, yet a production department with high quantity goals probably will have lower quality standards than those desired by quality control. By insisting on high quality, the quality control department is forcing the production department to slow down. When this happens, conflict is likely to occur.

Jurisdictional Ambiguity

Jurisdictional ambiguity Conflict caused by a disagreement about geographical territory or lines of authority.

A third cause of conflict, **jurisdictional ambiguity**, is found when geographical boundaries or lines of authority are unclear. For example, two employees might argue over whose job it is to get the mail, two supervisors might fight over who is in charge when the vice president is out of town, or two administrative assistants might disagree about who controls the conference room. When lines of authority are not clear, conflict is most likely to result when new situations and relationships develop. Thus, to some extent, turf wars can be avoided through the use of thorough job descriptions and up-to-date organizational charts.

On an international level, jurisdictional ambiguity is a cause for many wars and conflicts. For example, in the 2020s, India and Pakistan continue to fight over the disputed territory of Kashmir; in 2014, Russia invaded Crimea in part over disputed territory; in the early 1990s Iraq invaded Kuwait under the pretense that Kuwait actually belonged to Iraq; and in the 1980s, England and Argentina fought over who had the right to the Falkland Islands. In cities, jurisdictional ambiguity is often a cause for gang wars.

Communication Barriers

Communication barriers Physical, cultural, and psychological obstacles that interfere with successful communication and create a source of conflict.

Communication barriers are the fourth cause of conflict. The barriers to interpersonal communication can be *physical*, such as separate locations on different floors or in different buildings; *cultural*, such as different languages or different customs; or *psychological*, such as different styles or personalities. An in-depth discussion of the communication process can be found in Chapter 11.

Beliefs

A fifth cause of conflict is the belief systems of individuals or groups. Conflict is most likely to occur when individuals or groups believe that they

- are superior to other people or groups;
- have been mistreated by others;
- are vulnerable to others and are in harm's way;
- cannot trust others; and/or
- are helpless or powerless (Eidelson & Eidelson, 2003).

Personality

A sixth cause of conflict can be found in the **personalities** of the people involved. Conflict is often the result of people with incompatible personalities who must work together. For example, a person who is very quality oriented will probably have conflicts with a person who is very quantity oriented. Likewise, a "big picture" person is likely to have conflicts with a "nuts and bolts" person.

Though it is probably true that most of the conflict attributable to personality is the result of incompatibility, it is also very true that certain people are generally more difficult to work with than others. For example, it has been suggested that people who are dogmatic and authoritarian and have low self-esteem are involved in conflict more often than open-minded people who feel good about themselves (Bramson, 1981; Brinkman & Kirschner, 2012). Little research has gone into investigating "difficult people" who are most likely to cause conflict, but a fair amount has been written about the topic in the popular press. For example, Bernstein and Rozen (1992) describe in great detail three types of "Neanderthals at work"—rebels, believers, and competitors—and how conflict with each can be managed.

The most commonly referred to classification of difficult people was developed by Bramson (1981) and enhanced by Brinkman and Kirschner (2012). The latter postulated that abnormally high needs for control, perfection, approval, or attention form the basis for the difficult personality.

People with high needs for *control* are obsessed with completing a task and take great pride in getting a job done *quickly*. Among such personality types are the *Tank*, who gets things done quickly by giving orders, being pushy, yelling, and at times being too aggressive; the *Sniper*, who controls people by using sarcasm, embarrassment, and humiliation; and the *Know-It-All*, who controls others by dominating conversations, not listening to others' ideas, and rejecting arguments counter to their position.

People with high needs for *perfection* are obsessed with completing a task *correctly*. They seldom seem satisfied with anyone or any idea. These personality types include the *Whiner*, who constantly complains about the situation but never tries to change it; the *No Person*, who believes that nothing will ever work and thus disagrees with every suggestion or idea; and the *Nothing Person*, who responds to difficult situations by doing and saying nothing—they simply give up or retreat.

People with high needs for *approval* are obsessed with being liked. Their behavior is often centered on gaining approval rather than completing a task correctly or quickly. The *Yes Person* agrees to everything and, as a result, often agrees to do so much that they cannot keep their commitments. The Yes Person seldom provides feedback to others because they are afraid of getting someone mad at them. The *Maybe Person* avoids conflicts by never taking a stand on any issue. They delay making decisions, seldom offers opinions, and seldom commits to any course of action.

People with high needs for *attention* are obsessed with being appreciated. They behave in a manner that will get them noticed. When they don't feel appreciated, the *Grenade* throws a tantrum: They yell, swear, rant, and rave. The *Friendly Sniper* gets attention by poking fun at others. Unlike the Sniper, the Friendly Sniper aims to get attention rather than control. The *Think-They-Know-It-All* exaggerates, lies, and gives unwanted advice to gain attention.

Do you recognize any of these people? A summary of how to deal with each type of difficult person can be found in Table 13.2. Though early writings on difficult people suggested that their behavior is due to low self-esteem or a high need for control, a study by Raynes (2001) indicated that the cause is much more complicated. For example, Raynes found that *high* self-esteem and confidence were correlated with behaviors associated with the Think-They-Know-It-All and the No Person; the personality variable of extraversion was correlated with gossiping; and a high level of work interest was positively correlated with behaviors associated with the Yes Person and negatively correlated with whining. Advice on how to be a good group member is given in the Career Workshop Box.

Conflict Styles

It is generally believed that most people have a particular style they use when faced with conflict. Although a variety of names are assigned to these styles, the consensus among experts is that five are common: avoiding, accommodating, forcing, collaborating, and compromising (Hocker & Wilmot, 2018).

Avoiding style The conflict style of a person who reacts to conflict by pretending that it does not exist.

Avoiding Style

Employees using an **avoiding style** choose to ignore the conflict and hope it will resolve itself. When conflicts are minor and infrequent, this style may be fine, but obviously it is not

Table 13.2 Types of Difficult People

Type	Need	Obsession	Description	Best Way to Handle
Tank	Control	Task completion	Pushes, yells, gives orders, intimidates	Don't counterattack or offer excuses, hold your ground.
Sniper	Control	Task completion	Uses sarcasm, criticizes, humiliates others	Call them on their sarcasm and have them explain what was really behind their comment.
Know-It-All	Control	Task completion	Dominates conversations, doesn't listen	Acknowledge their knowledge, make your statements appear as if they are in agreement.
Whiner	Perfection	Task quality	Constantly complains	Focus their complaints on specifics and solutions.
No Person	Perfection	Task quality	Disagrees with everything	Don't rush them or argue; acknowledge their good intentions.
Nothing Person	Perfection	Task quality	Doesn't do anything	Be patient and ask them open-ended questions.
Yes Person	Approval	Being liked	Agrees to everything	Talk honestly and let the person know it is safe to disagree with you.
Maybe Person	Approval	Being liked	Won't commit or make a decision	Help them learn a decision-making system, and then reassure about the decisions they make.
Grenade	Attention	Being appreciated	Throws tantrums	Don't show anger, acknowledge their complaint, and give them a chance to cool down.
Friendly Sniper	Attention	Being appreciated	Uses jokes to pick on people	Give them attention when they are not making fun of you.
Think-They-Know-It-All	Attention	Being appreciated	Exaggerates, lies, gives advice	Give them attention and ask them for specifics; don't embarrass them.

Whether you are a member of a team or committee, or just part of an office group, the following tips will help you be a better member:

- Don't gossip or engage in talk about other people. That is, if another employee comes to you with some gossip or a complaint about another employee, politely tell them that you don't feel comfortable talking behind another person's back. Also, suggest that if that person has concerns about someone, it would be best to share them directly with that employee. Being respected is very important to being perceived as a good group or team member. This is one of the best ways to build that respect!

- If you or your team is given an assignment or project, be sure that you fully understand the goal of that assignment and what is expected of you. To do this, go to your manager or another colleague to get clarification. Ask about the goal and the expectations. Will you and/or your team be responsible just for gathering and submitting information? Will you serve as an advisory group, giving recommendations or suggestions? Or do you have full authority to carry out all decisions regarding the project or assignment?

- Confront conflict as it occurs. Don't wait, thinking that "it will go away." If you have concerns with another person, speak to that person about how you feel. Don't be accusatory. Just explain how you interpreted the events and then ask if you and the other person could discuss how to resolve the situation. Be willing to ask for mediation, if necessary. When two or more members of a group or team are in conflict, everyone suffers, and you get a bad reputation for being a poor group/team member.

- Make sure you understand what your role is in the office or the team. This is where a good job description helps! One of the fastest ways to get a bad reputation as a colleague or team member is when others "perceive" that you are stepping into their territory. Again, if you aren't sure what tasks you should be performing, ask someone before you do them, to avoid stepping on toes.

- Don't share personal information about yourself. You may find one group or team member willing to listen to issues that are occurring in your personal life, but most employees may not want to hear it. Also, you may run into a problem with information you want "kept secret" getting out to others, which may cause problems for you.

- Participate as much as you feel comfortable in group activities. That is, if employees are putting together a birthday party for another employee, offer to help. This will show your desire to be a good group or team member.

- Be a good listener. You don't want to participate in office gossip; however, there will be times when someone may just want to "vent." Show them that you can keep confidences and that they can feel safe talking to you. As stated above, if they are venting about another person, suggest that they share those concerns with that individual. Some good listening skills include good eye contact, acknowledgment that you are listening by asking questions or merely by nodding your head and asking open-ended questions.

- In meetings, when everyone is asked for their input, be willing to make suggestions. Don't continually just sit at meetings, refusing to share or discuss ideas. You will quickly get the reputation of being a "difficult team member or difficult employee." On the other hand, don't whine about what's going wrong, don't monopolize the entire meeting with your grievances, and don't brag about how great you are. Give credit where credit is due. Compliment your teammates when they offer a good suggestion or have successfully completed a project.

- Recognize when you are in a bad mood or upset. Be sure not to take out on others how you are feeling on any particular day. If there is someone in the group or team that you trust, share your feelings with this person. They may help brighten the day.

- There are times when you may have to be the leader because of your expertise or knowledge. Or perhaps you are the only person in the office or on a team with the ability to manage conflict. Be willing to step out of your usual role and take on another role as needed. Don't do what many employees and/or team members do and walk away from that new or additional responsibility. If necessary, attend workshops on how to better lead groups/teams, or how to better manage conflict. This will build credibility, trust, and respect.

Withdrawal An approach to handling conflict in which one of the parties removes themself from the situation to avoid the conflict.

Triangling An employee discusses a conflict with a third-party such as a friend or supervisor. In doing so, the employee hopes that the third party will talk to the second party and that the conflict will be resolved without the need for the two parties to meet.

Accommodating style The conflict style of a person who tends to respond to conflict by giving in to the other person.

Forcing style The conflict style of a person who responds to conflict by always trying to win.

Winning at all costs An approach to handling conflict in which one side seeks to win regardless of the damage to the other side.

Collaborating style The conflict style of a person who wants a conflict resolved in such a way that both sides get what they want.

the best way to handle every type of conflict. When conflict occurs, **withdrawal** from the situation is one of the easiest ways to handle it. A person can leave a difficult marriage by divorce, an employee can avoid a work conflict by quitting the organization, or a manager can avoid a turf battle by letting another manager win. Common withdrawal behaviors include avoiding the source of conflict, quitting, talking behind the other person's back, and forming alliances with others (Martin & Bergmann, 1996). Even though withdrawal can make one feel better, often it only postpones conflict rather than prevents it.

An interesting form of avoidance, called **triangling**, occurs when an employee discusses the conflict with a third party, such as a friend or supervisor. In doing so, the employee hopes that the third party will talk to the second party and that the conflict will be resolved without the need for the two parties to meet. When triangling occurs, supervisors are advised to have the two parties meet to resolve the issue or to use a formal third-party approach such as mediation.

Accommodating Style

When a person is so intent on settling a conflict that they give in and risk hurting themself, they have adopted the **accommodating style**. People who use this style when the stakes are high are usually viewed as cooperative but weak. I observed an example of this style at a self-serve gas station. Two drivers parked their cars next to the same pump at roughly the same time. Both drivers got out of their cars and simultaneously reached for the only pump. Obviously, one person had to give in to avoid conflict and would have to wait five minutes longer than the other. Yet one driver quickly told the other to "go ahead." Why did this person so quickly accede to the other? Probably because they had an accommodating reaction to potential conflict and because, in this case, the stakes were low.

Forcing Style

A person with a **forcing style** handles conflict in a win–lose fashion and does what it takes to win, with little regard for the other person. This style is appropriate in emergencies or when there is the potential for a violation on policy, ethical, or legal grounds if the other party does not agree to your proposal. Though this style can be effective in winning, it also can damage relations so badly that other conflicts will result. This strategy of **winning at all costs** occurs especially when a person regards their side as correct and the other person is regarded as the enemy whose side is incorrect. This reaction often occurs when each side needs a victory to gain or retain status. Union–management conflicts provide good examples of this need for status. For a union to survive, its members must perceive it as being useful. Thus, during contract negotiations, union leadership must force management to "give in" or run the risk of losing status with its membership.

But the problem with putting status on the line is that it makes backing down to resolve a conflict very difficult. As a conflict escalates, each side "digs in" and becomes less willing to compromise. Unless one side has the resources to clearly win, the win-at-all-costs reaction is likely to prolong conflict. Thus, this strategy is appropriate only if the position holder is actually correct and if winning the conflict is in fact more important than the probable damage to future relationships.

Collaborating Style

An individual with a **collaborating style** not only wants to win but also wants to see the other person win. These people seek win–win solutions—that is, ways in which both sides get what they want. Though this style is probably the best to use whenever possible, it can be time-consuming and may not be appropriate in emergencies (e.g., determining how best to treat a person having a heart attack).

Compromising Style

Compromising style A style of resolving conflicts in which an individual allows each side to get some of what it wants.

The final strategy is the **compromising style**. The user of this type adopts give-and-take tactics that enable each side to get some of what it wants but not everything it wants. Most conflicts are resolved through some form of compromise so that a solution benefits both sides. Compromising usually involves a good deal of **negotiation and bargaining**. The negotiation process begins with each side making an offer that asks for much more than it really wants. For example, union leaders might demand $30 an hour, whereas management offers $15 an hour. Each side understands what the other is doing, so the union might lower its demand to $26 and management might raise its offer to $20. This process continues until an acceptable compromise has been reached.

Negotiation and bargaining A method of resolving conflict in which two sides use verbal skill and strategy to reach an agreement.

An *acceptable compromise* is one that falls within the settlement range for both sides (Acuff, 2008). According to Acuff, a settlement range is between the **least acceptable result (LAR)** and the **maximum supportable position (MSP)** for each side. The LAR is the lowest settlement that a person is willing to accept; it must be realistic and satisfy the person's actual needs. The MSP is the best possible settlement that a person can ask for and still reasonably support with facts and logic. The MSP is usually the negotiator's initial offer. A short-order cook's proposal for $40 an hour would not be reasonably supportable and thus would not be a proper MSP.

Least acceptable result (LAR) The lowest settlement that a person is willing to accept in a negotiated agreement.

Maximum supportable position (MSP) The highest possible settlement that a person could reasonably ask for and still maintain credibility in negotiating an agreement.

As shown in Figure 13.3, negotiations usually begin with each side offering its MSP as an opening bid. The actual negotiating territory is the area between both sides' LARs. Each side then bargains for a settlement closest to its own MSP and the other's LAR. The final settlement will be a function of the skill of each negotiator as well as of time pressures. Such pressures may be exerted by customers who cannot wait for a settlement or by union members who cannot financially afford prolonged negotiations.

An important influence on the outcome of a negotiation is what is called the *best alternative to a negotiated agreement* (BATNA). A BATNA is the best alternative that negotiators have if they can't reach an agreement. For example, if I am buying a car and I already have an offer of $36,500 from one dealer (my BATNA), my least acceptable result when I negotiate with a new dealer will be less than the $36,500. If the dealer won't go lower, I can walk away knowing I already have a better deal. If the dealer is aware of my BATNA, it will reduce their initial offer because they know that an initial offer greater than my BATNA will not be effective (Buelens & Van Poucke, 2004).

Figure 13.3
Negotiating Territory and Conflict Resolution

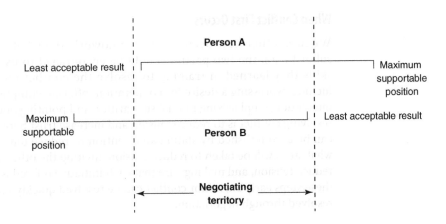

Seltz and Modica (1980) have suggested four indicators that tell when negotiations are coming to an end so that each side can prepare its final offer:

1. The number of counterarguments is reduced.
2. The positions of the two sides appear closer together.
3. The other side talks about final arrangements.
4. The other side appears willing to begin putting things in writing.

Although this conflict resolution strategy appears to be the best approach to take, it often is not. Sometimes, compromise results in a bad solution. For example, if a school superintendent wants to include $30 million in the county l budget to construct a new secondary school and the board of supervisors wants to budget only $10 million, then the two are likely to agree on a median figure such as $20 million. But if the project cannot be completed for less than $30 million, then the compromise may waste millions of dollars that could be spent elsewhere.

As with individuals, organizations seem to also have a conflict resolution style. Gelfand, Leslie, Keller, and de Dreu (2012) studied 97 separate branches of a large bank and found that each branch tended to have one of three styles for handling conflict: Collaborative, dominating, and avoidant. Those with a collaborative style had more positive work outcomes than did the dominating or avoidant cultures.

Determining Conflict Styles

A person's method of dealing with conflict at work can be measured by the Rahim Organizational Conflict Inventory II (Rahim & Magner, 1995) or the Cohen Conflict Response Inventory (Cohen, 1997).

Resolving Conflict
Prior to Conflict Occurring

An organization should have a formal policy on how conflict is to be handled. Usually such a policy will state that employees should first try to resolve their own conflicts, and if that is not successful, they can utilize a third-party intervention. Employees should receive training on the causes of conflict, ways to prevent conflict, and strategies for resolving conflict. For example, at the Timken plant in Alta Vista, Virginia, all employees received 12 hours of training on how to resolve conflicts, which included role-plays to practice what they learned. Similarly, the City of Plano, Texas, offered employees an optional 40-hour training program in conflict mediation and facilitation.

When Conflict First Occurs

When conflict first occurs between coworkers or between a supervisor and a subordinate, the two parties should be encouraged to use the conflict resolution skills they learned in training to resolve the conflict on their own. These skills include expressing a desire for cooperation, offering compliments, avoiding negative interaction, emphasizing mutual similarities, and pointing out common goals. A key to resolving conflict is to reduce tension and increase trust between the two parties. This can be accomplished by stating an intention to reduce tension, publicly announcing what steps will be taken to reduce tension, inviting the other side also to take action to reduce tension, and making sure that each initiative offered is unambiguous. By taking these steps early on, minor conflict can be resolved quickly, and serious conflict can be resolved through negotiation.

The two parties meet in a private location to address the problem—prior to this meeting, the two parties should not talk to others about the problem. When the two parties actually do sit down together, the employee who arranged the meeting explains their perception of the problem, when it occurred, and the impact that it has had on them (e.g., anxiety, anger, depression, lower productivity). For example, an employee might say, "When you made fun of my accent at lunch last week, it made me feel that you were putting me down and didn't respect me." Or an employee might tell a supervisor, "When the promotion was given to John instead of me, I thought it was because he is a man and I am a woman." It is important that the employee address the behavior of the other person rather than such aspects as the person's values, personality, and ability. For example, an employee would not want to say, "You demonstrated what a racist you are by giving the promotion to Henry instead of me." In other words, the focus should not be on who an employee *is* but rather what the employee has *done*.

The second party then responds to what was said by the first party. If the second party agrees, they might apologize and then agree to stop the behavior. If the second party doesn't agree, they would explain their perception of what happened. The two parties would then exchange views and suggestions until they have reached an agreement on how to resolve the issue. If the two can't agree, the conflict is labeled a **dispute**, and the parties should seek third-party intervention.

An interesting aspect of this idea is called **cooperative problem solving**. An example of this approach is when the president of an organization forms a task force or committee with representatives from all of the departments or divisions that will be affected by the solution. Together these representatives work to define the problem, identify possible solutions, and arrive at the best one.

This process doesn't always go smoothly, but it is important that employees try to resolve their own conflicts before seeking help from a third party. Employees who resolve their own conflicts are more likely to buy into a resolution than employees who use a third party. Furthermore, bringing in a supervisor makes it more difficult for employees to admit that they have done something wrong. Of course, employees should not be forced to try to resolve all conflicts on their own. When emotions are high, alcohol or drugs are involved, or one party feels threatened by the other, a third-party intervention is in order.

Third-Party Intervention

If conflict cannot be resolved by the parties involved, it is often a good idea to seek help—that is, to ask for **third-party intervention**. This third party usually is provided through mediation, and if that doesn't work, through arbitration.

Mediation. With **mediation**, a neutral third party is asked to help both parties reach a mutually agreeable solution to the conflict. Mediators are not there to make decisions. Instead, their role is to facilitate the communication process by providing the parties with a safe and equitable venue so that they are more willing and able to reach a solution. Mediators can be employees of the organization (e.g., team leader, supervisor, human resource manager) or professional mediators who work with a variety of organizations. Mediators are most successful when two parties do not trust one another (Ross & Wieland, 1996), and they provide the best results when both sides consider the mediator to be competent and trustworthy. For mediation to be successful, both parties must agree that there is a conflict and that a solution can be found by working together.

Dispute A situation when two parties do not agree.

Cooperative problem solving A method of resolving conflict in which two sides get together to discuss a problem and arrive at a solution.

Third-party intervention When a neutral party is asked to help resolve a conflict.

Mediation A method of resolving conflict in which a neutral third party is asked to help the two parties reach an agreement.

Mediation has been effective in resolving even the most difficult conflicts. For example, in 2020, 69.4% of the employment discrimination claims that were sent to mediation by the Equal Employment Opportunity Commission were resolved. Furthermore, the mediation process took 147 days—substantially less time than did the typical lawsuit. As a result of the EEOC's successful experience in mediation, the Office of Federal Contract Compliance Programs (OFCCP) has increased its use of mediation to resolve disagreements with federal contractors regarding charges of discrimination.

According to Lovenheim and Guerin (2004), mediation is better than filing a lawsuit when

- you need to solve a problem with a person with whom you do not want to end your relationship (e.g., coworker, boss, neighbor);
- you don't want your problems publicized in the media;
- you want to save the costs associated with paying a lawyer; or
- you want to settle your dispute promptly.

Arbitration A method of resolving conflicts in which a neutral third party is asked to choose which side is correct.

Arbitration. With **arbitration**, a neutral third party listens to both sides' arguments and then makes a decision. Within an organization, this neutral party is often the manager of the two employees in conflict. However, if that manager just served as a mediator, then an HR director might be used.

Organizations are increasingly using outside arbitrators to handle discrimination claims by employees. This increase in the use of arbitrators represents organizational attempts to avoid the negative publicity associated with discrimination suits and to reduce the costs that come with lengthy litigation. In 2001, the U.S. Supreme Court ruled that employers can require employees to use arbitration rather than litigation (*Circuit City Stores v. Adams*, 2001). However, arbitration works best when it is provided as an option rather than being a requirement.

Though mandatory arbitration can be effective, arbitration is more expensive than mediation; so much so that mandatory arbitration policies discourage employees from making formal disputes or cause financial hardships if they do (Armour, 2001). Additionally, literature has highlighted three major critiques of mandatory arbitration: its nonconsensual nature, the potential for employers to gain an unfair advantage over employees that participate in the arbitration and its questionable application to statutory claims (e.g., Title VII) (Levinson, 2019).

Arbitration decisions can be either *binding* or *nonbinding*. If the decision is binding, the two sides have agreed to abide by the arbitrator's decision regardless of how displeased one or both sides may be with that decision. If the decision is nonbinding, then one or both sides can reject an unfavorable decision. Even though arbitration can end conflicts quickly, usually neither side is as satisfied with the outcome as both would have been if they had settled the conflict themselves or used mediation. Employees are most willing to use arbitration when they perceive that a conflict was the result of intentional behavior by another, resolution of the conflict has important consequences, and the conflicting employees are of equal power (Arnold & Carnevale, 1997).

Some research suggests that performance may drop (Shirreffs & Sommers, 2006; Sommers, 1993) and turnover increase (Bretz & Thomas, 1992) because of an arbitrator's decision. As you might imagine, an individual's performance is most likely to drop after losing and most likely to improve after winning an arbitration hearing (Hauenstein & Lord, 1989).

Applied Case Study

Conflict at Work

The director of a nonprofit agency has asked you for help. He has 13 employees and feels that there are a lot of interpersonal issues going on that are causing them to be unhappy and not do a good job of serving the needs of their clients. He senses that there is a lot of tension and has noticed that the employees are reluctant to attend group meetings. When they do attend, there is tension and anger.

- What could be the cause of this problem?
- What would you do to reduce the conflict?

Focus on Ethics   Group Hazing

A new employee is locked in a meat freezer for 15 minutes before being let out. Dog food is put in a new firefighter's dinner without their knowledge. A new employee at a jail is asked to get on the intercom and page Jack Meoff. Are these examples of practical jokes and a form of initiation for new employees? Or is it something else?

One of the best-kept secrets of the workplace is workplace hazing. Critics opposed to stunts like the ones above say that those would fall under hazing. And they say it is unethical because it is intentional humiliation of a person and has no purpose other than to show that employee their place in the organization. And it could be dangerous. As evidenced by some of the hazing done in colleges, stunts that start as practical jokes can often be deadly. What if the new employee in the meat locker had been left in it a minute too long? What if there was something in the dog food that the new firefighter had been allergic to? Would it still have been considered harmless initiation or would it have been considered hazing?

Supporters of such antics say that it is not a form of hazing but of harmless practical jokes by groups of employees who have been in the organization for a while and who, themselves, have been subjected to the same practical jokes. And, according to these proponents, such a practice does serve a purpose. Anytime a new person enters a group, the group becomes temporarily unstable while the new group member attempts to learn the rules and the existing group members learn to trust the new one. So, these practical jokes can build cohesion between employees who must often work together to get a job done.

In this chapter, you learned that for a group to be effective and perform well, it must be cohesive. Your text lists several ways to build cohesion. Proponents of workplace initiation say that such practical jokes will build cohesion. It is a way for employees to get to know each other better and establish a common bond. Natasha Josefowitz, from San Diego State University, and Herman Gadon, from the University of California–San Diego, explain that it ensures that new employees learn and respect the rules of the group. They further state that membership in a group should be earned and considered a privilege. When employees successfully handle a practical joke, they earn the right to be part of a particular group. Without such initiation practices, it may take longer for employees to be accepted, or they may not become accepted at all. So initiation practices such as those stated above actually have positive benefits for new employees.

Critics believe that the only benefit such jokes have is to those employees carrying out the joke. For those employees, it establishes a hierarchy of who is in charge, who not to cross, and who has the most power. It establishes dominance and fear. And it becomes even more unethical when supervisors or managers know that such practices go on and do nothing about it, such as warn new employees or punish those employees who pull the practical jokes.

What Do You Think?

- Do you think the stunts described above are harmless jokes or a form of hazing? If you consider it to be hazing, are they unethical?
- Are practical jokes ever acceptable in the workplace? Are some less ethical than others?
- Do you think it is ethical for management to support such practical jokes?
- Is it unethical for a manager not to warn new employees that they may be subject to a practical joke as part of an initiation process?

Chapter Summary

In this chapter you learned:

- Groups consist of multiple members who perceive themselves as a unit and share a common goal or goals.
- People join groups due to a need for affiliation, a need to identify with success, a need for emotional support, a need for assistance, common goals, physical proximity, and assignment.
- Factors that influence a group's success include its level of cohesiveness, the composition and stability of its membership, and the group's size, status, and communication structure.
- Teams go through four developmental stages: forming, storming, norming, and performing.
- The team approach is not always the best.
- Conflict usually results from factors such as competition for resources, task interdependence, jurisdictional ambiguity, communication barriers, and personality.
- People react to conflict by ignoring it through withdrawal, trying to win at all costs, trying to persuade the other side to resolve the conflict in their favor, bargaining for an agreement, or asking for third-party help.

Key Terms

Corresponding effects   (456)
Common goal   (457)
Affiliation   (457)
Identification   (458)
Group cohesiveness   (460)
Homogeneous groups   (461)
Heterogeneous groups   (461)
Slightly heterogeneous groups   (461)
Stability   (462)
Isolation   (462)
Outside pressure   (462)
Group size   (463)
Additive tasks   (463)
Conjunctive tasks   (463)
Disjunctive tasks   (463)
Social impact theory   (463)
Group status   (464)
Communication structure   (465)
Social facilitation   (466)
Social inhibition   (466)
Audience effects   (466)
Coaction   (467)
Mere presence   (468)
Comparison   (468)
Evaluation apprehension   (468)
Distracting   (469)
Social loafing   (469)

Individual dominance   (470)
Groupthink   (470)
Devil's advocate   (471)
Nominal group   (471)
Interacting group   (471)
Brainstorming   (472)
Interdependence   (474)
Power differentiation   (474)
Social distance   (474)
Permanency   (475)
Proximity   (475)
Virtual teams   (475)
Work teams   (475)
Parallel teams   (476)
Cross-functional teams   (476)
Project teams   (477)
Management teams   (477)
Forming stage   (477)
Storming stage   (477)
Norming stage   (477)
Performing stage   (478)
Conflict   (480)
Dysfunctional conflict   (480)
Functional conflict   (481)
Interpersonal conflict   (481)
Individual–group conflict   (481)
Group–group conflict   (481)

Competition for resources (481)
Task interdependence (482)
Jurisdictional ambiguity (482)
Communication barriers (482)
Personality (483)
Avoiding style (484)
Withdrawal (486)
Triangling (486)
Accommodating style (486)
Forcing style (486)
Winning at all costs (486)

Collaborating style (486)
Compromising style (487)
Negotiation and bargaining (487)
Least acceptable result (LAR) (487)
Maximum supportable position
   (MSP) (487)
Dispute (489)
Cooperative problem solving (489)
Third-party intervention (489)
Mediation (489)
Arbitration (490)

Questions for Review

1. How can you use the knowledge of why people join groups to increase group effectiveness?
2. When are interacting groups better than nominal groups or individuals?
3. Why does the presence of others cause increased performance in some situations and decreased performance in others?
4. When can a group be too cohesive?
5. How do we build effective teams?
6. How are mediation and arbitration different?

Learning Objectives

Y ou learned about increasing an individual employee's skills through training in Chapter 8. In this chapter, you will learn about organization development—the process of improving organizational performance by making *organization-wide*, rather than *individual*, changes (Burke, 2018). Though there are many aspects to organization development, this chapter will focus on four major issues: managing change, empowering employees, implementing innovative work schedules, and downsizing.

14-1 Managing Change

In organizations, change occurs for many reasons and takes on many forms. Some changes are due to such organization development efforts as downsizing, reorganization, or the introduction of teams. Some changes are the result of external mandates like managed care or new government regulations. Still other changes occur due to new leadership or new personnel.

Sacred Cow Hunts

Sacred cow hunt The first step in organizational change, in which employees look for practices and policies that waste time and are counterproductive.

Perhaps the first step toward organizational change is what Kriegel and Brandt (1996) called a **sacred cow hunt**. Organizational sacred cows are practices that have been around for a long time and invisibly reduce productivity. A sacred cow hunt, then, is an organization-wide attempt to get rid of practices that serve no useful purpose. Merck Pharmaceutical and Tractor Supply Stores have periodic sacred cow hunts in which cow bells are rung when a sacred cow is found, monthly sacred cow barbecues are held, and employees receive awards and money for finding a sacred cow. In a sacred cow hunt, an organization looks at all of its practices and policies and asks questions like these:

- Why are we doing it? Does it add value, quality, service, or productivity?
- What if it didn't exist?
- Is it already being done by someone else?
- How and when did we start doing this?
- Can it be done better by another person, department, or company?

According to Kriegel and Brandt, common types of sacred cows include the paper cow, the meeting cow, and the speed cow.

The Paper Cow

Paper cow Unnecessary paperwork generated within organizations out of force of habit.

Paper cows are unnecessary paperwork—usually forms and reports that cost organizations money to prepare, distribute, and read. To determine if something is a paper cow, consider the extent to which the paperwork increases efficiency, productivity, or quality. Ask if anyone actually reads the paperwork. A unique strategy tried by employees at one company was to stop sending a monthly report that had been distributed for years. The employees' thinking was that if the report was actually needed, they would receive complaints. Three months and three missing reports later, no one had complained.

Steve Kerr, an executive at Goldman Sachs, provides an interesting example of how to combat paper cows. The organization issued rubber stamps to managers that said, "Why am I receiving this?" to be used if a manager received a report that they did not need. The person sending the report could then get feedback on how many managers were actually using the report. In one situation, every copy of the report was returned with the stamp, *Why am I receiving this*? (Kerr, 2009).

Kerr also recalled a practice in which people generating a report had to indicate the total numbers of hours spent writing the report. When the CEO of a company discovered that 1,015 hours were spent on a trivial report that they requested, they altered their practice of asking for such reports on short notice.

A good annual practice is to review all forms and reports and determine whether they are still needed and, if they are, whether they are needed in their current format. To demonstrate the importance of this practice, review the forms used by your university or organization. How many of them are a third of a page or a quarter of a page? Probably none. There seems to be an unwritten rule that all forms must ask questions until the bottom of the page is reached. I was preparing contracts for our graduate assistants and noticed that I was being asked questions about the university from which the students had received their undergraduate degrees, their undergraduate grade point average, and their work histories. Note that these were contracts, not application forms, where this information was already contained. So, in the spirit of a good sacred cow hunt, I called the graduate college to ask why this information was necessary. Their reply? No one knew. Did anyone actually need this information? No. Will you change the form for next year? No. This is an example of a sacred cow hunt—but no sacred cow barbecue.

The Meeting Cow

Another area ripe for change is the number and length of meetings. Think about meetings you have attended recently. How much meeting time was spent doing business as opposed to socializing? Was the meeting really necessary? To reduce the number and length of meetings, some organizations ask the person calling the meeting to determine the cost of the meeting (e.g., one hour's salary of each attendee, cost of meeting room, cost of refreshments and supplies) and consider whether the cost will exceed the potential benefits. In some of these organizations, the meeting costs are actually posted at the beginning of the meeting! Needless to say, when people are forced to consider the benefits of meetings against their cost, most meetings will not be held.

The Speed Cow

Unnecessary deadlines are another source for potential change. Requiring work to be done "by tomorrow" is sometimes necessary. However, unnecessary deadlines cause employees to work at a faster than optimal pace, resulting in decreased quality, increased stress, and increased health problems. An example of eliminating the **Speed Cow** was demonstrated by a Big 5 accounting firm (Kriegel & Brandt, 2008). The chief information officer was perplexed by a hefty $45,000 FedEx bill for delivering a time sensitive report using same-day delivery. After further investigation, they found out that the report did not get read the minute the person received it, and thus cut the cost in half by sending it through second-day delivery.

Kriegel and Brandt (1996) suggest that in addition to sacred cow hunts, effective change can be encouraged by using these strategies:

- Think like a beginner: Ask stupid questions, constantly ask "why" things are being done a certain way, and don't assume that anything makes sense.
- Don't be complacent with something that is working well. Keep looking for ways to improve, new markets to enter, new products to introduce.
- Don't play by everyone else's rules; make your own. Domino's Pizza is a great example of this type of thinking. Although all the other pizza chains competed for ways to increase the number of customers entering their restaurants, Domino's decided to change the rules and bring the restaurant to the people rather than bringing the people to the restaurant.
- Rather than penalizing mistakes, reward employees for making the attempt to change or to try something new.

Employee Acceptance of Change

Though change can be beneficial to organizations, employees are often initially reluctant to change. This reluctance is understandable, as employees are comfortable doing things the old way. They may fear that change will result in less favorable working conditions and economic outcomes than they are used to. Employees may also fear that their skills may not be valued in the future, and they might worry about whether they can adapt to the new changes (Cummings & Worley, 2015).

Stages

Over the years, there have been many theories regarding the change process. Most of these theories postulate that the change process occurs in between three (Lewin, 1958) and seven (Lippitt, Watson, & Westley, 1958) stages or phases, depending on whether the focus of the theory is the organization (Lewin, 1958), the change agent (Lippitt et al., 1958), or the employee (Carnall & By, 2014). The difference between a stage and a phase is that stages are distinct time periods, whereas phases can overlap with one another (Burke, 2018).

Lewin (1958) theorized that *organizations* go through three stages: unfreezing, moving, and refreezing. In the unfreezing stage, the organization must convince employees and other stakeholders (e.g., shareholders, the community) that the current state of affairs is unacceptable and that change is necessary. In the moving stage, the organization takes steps (e.g., training, new work processes) to move the organization to the desired state. In the refreezing stage, the organization develops ways to keep the new changes in place, such as formalizing new policy and rewarding employees for behaving in a manner consistent with the new change.

Carnall and By (2014) suggest that *employees* typically go through five stages during major organizational changes: denial, **defense**, **discarding**, **adaptation**, and **internalization**.

Stage 1: Denial.   During this initial stage, employees deny that any changes will actually take place, try to convince themselves that the old way is working, and create reasons why the proposed changes will never work (e.g., "We tried that before and it didn't work. Something like that won't work in a company like ours.").

Stage 2: Defense.   When employees begin to believe that change will actually occur, they become defensive and try to justify their positions and ways of doing things. The idea here is that if an organization is changing the way in which employees perform, there is an inherent criticism that the employees must have previously been doing things wrong.

Stage 3: Discarding.   At some point, employees begin to realize not only that the organization is going to change but also that the employees are going to have to change as well. That is, change is inevitable, and it is in the best interest of the employee to discard the old ways and start to accept the change as the new reality.

Stage 4: Adaptation.   At this stage, employees test the new system, learn how it functions, and begin to make adjustments in the way they perform. Employees spend tremendous energy at this stage and can often become frustrated and angry.

Stage 5: Internalization.   In this final stage, employees have become immersed in the new culture and comfortable with the new system and have accepted their new coworkers and work environment.

Defense The second stage of change, in which employees accept that change will occur but try to justify the old way of doing things.

Discarding The third stage of change, in which employees accept that change will occur and decide to discard their old ways of doing things.

Adaptation The fourth stage of change, in which employees try to adapt to new policies and procedures.

Internalization The fifth and final stage of organizational change, in which employees become comfortable with and productive in the new system.

Important Factors

The extent to which employees readily accept and handle change is dependent on the reason behind the change, the leader making the change, and the personality of the person being changed.

The Type of Change.   Organization change expert Warner Burke (2018) distinguishes two types of change: evolutionary and revolutionary. The vast majority of change is *evolutionary*, that is the continual process of upgrading or improving processes; for example, the unpopular changes from Windows XP to Vista and Windows 7 to Windows 8, a change in the supervisor to whom one reports, or a change in how to submit travel receipts for reimbursement. Burke defines *revolutionary* change as a "real jolt to the system" that drastically changes the way things are done. Examples might include developing a brand-new product line that requires a vastly different skill set, completely changing the organizational structure, or organizational misconduct (e.g., Enron, Adelphia, Arthur Andersen) that causes an organization to completely change its ethical policies and behavior. Clearly, revolutionary change is more difficult than is evolutionary change.

The Reason Behind the Change.   Employee acceptance of change is often a function of the reason behind the change. For example, employees understand (but don't necessarily like) change that is due to financial problems, external mandates, or attempts to improve the organization. Acceptance is lower when employees perceive the change to be in organizational philosophy, a whim on the part of the person making the change ("Hey, let's use Microsoft Teams for our chats and videoconferences"), or a change because everyone else is changing ("Everyone else has teams, so we need to create them now before we get left behind"). Employees are least likely to accept change if they don't understand or were not told the reasons behind the change.

The Person Making the Change.   Another factor affecting employee acceptance of change is the person making or suggesting the change. Not surprisingly, workers are more positive about change when the source of change is within the work group rather than an external source (Griffin, Rafferty, & Mason, 2004). Changes proposed by leaders who are well liked and respected and who have a history of success are more likely to be accepted than changes proposed by leaders whose motives are suspect (Dirks, 2000; Lam & Schaubroeck, 2000). Let me provide two very different examples.

- In the first example, the head of a small consulting firm decided to change the focus of their business from delivering training seminars to helping companies switch from a traditional organizational approach to a flatter, team-based approach. Though the consultant's employees were apprehensive about the change in focus, they quickly accepted the change because the consultant was well respected for their knowledge, treated their employees as family, and had on a prior occasion changed the company's focus, resulting in a 30% increase in revenue.
- In the second example, due to financial and regulatory reasons, a local mental health agency was forced to move its 120 employees from their current buildings to a new location. A management committee was formed to determine the location for the new building. When the new location was announced, the employees were very upset. The new building was expensive, in a highly congested traffic area, and located far away from most of the agency's clients.

The employees' unhappiness was not due to the relocation but to the choice of buildings. It just didn't make sense. That is, it didn't make sense until several of the employees realized that the new building was only five minutes from where each of the deciding committee members lived. I don't think I have to finish the story for you to understand the importance of motive.

The differences in these two stories are clear. In the first, employees quickly accepted change because they trusted the person making the change. In the second, the employees did not accept the change because the decision makers were not well respected and acted in a manner inconsistent with the well-being of the majority of employees.

For organizational change of any type to work, it is essential that employees trust the organization as a whole as well as the specific individuals making the change. Viking Glass in Sioux Falls, South Dakota, realized the importance of trust when it decided to change the organization to foster more employee participation. Viking Glass spent more than a year laying the foundation to increase the extent to which its employees trusted the company. After gaining employees' trust, the company successfully increased the level of employee empowerment.

The Person Being Changed. As one would imagine, there is considerable variability in the way in which people instigate or react to change. **Change agents** are people who enjoy change and often make changes just for the sake of it. A change agent's motto might best be expressed as "If it ain't broke, break it." Though many people like to call themselves change agents, it may not be such a compliment. That is, reasoned change is good, but change for the sake of change is disruptive.

Let me give you an example. When I was about 30, I was president of our local Kiwanis Club. Now before you get too impressed, I was asked to be president because I was the only person in the club who had not yet been president and one of only five or so members who was under the age of 60. My first act as president was to restructure all of the committees and create an impressive-looking matrix to depict these changes. When I presented this matrix at our board meeting, each member just stared at me (some were already asleep), until one person said, "Mike, you can't change committees. It's in the national bylaws." My response was to say "oops" and move on to the next topic. Though this story is not an example of good leadership skills, it is a perfect example of being a change agent. By the way, with some maturity, I hope I have become a change analyst.

Change analysts are not afraid to change or make changes but want to make changes only if the changes will improve the organization. Their motto might be "If it ain't broke, leave it alone; if it's broke, fix it." Change analysts are people who constantly ask such questions as "Why are we doing this?" and "Is there a better way we could be doing this?" But in contrast to the change agent, they are not driven by a need to change constantly.

Receptive changers are people who probably will not instigate change but are willing to change. Their motto is "If it's broke, I'll help fix it." Receptive changers typically have high self-esteem and optimistic personalities and believe they have control over their own lives (Wanberg & Banas, 2000). Receptive changers are essential for any major organizational change to be successful.

Reluctant changers will certainly not instigate or welcome change, but they will change if necessary. Their motto is "Are you sure it's broken?" **Change resisters** hate change, are scared by it, and will do anything they can to keep change from occurring. Their motto is "It may be broken, but it's still better than the unknown." Research shows that the relationship between a change agent promoting a change, and a change

Change agent A person who enjoys change and makes changes for the sake of it.

Change analyst A person who is not afraid of change but makes changes only when there is a compelling reason to do so.

Receptive changer A person who is willing to change.

Reluctant changer A person who will initially resist change but will eventually go along with it.

Change resister A person who hates change and will do anything to keep change from occurring.

resister can either hinder or help their efforts depending on how divergent this change is from the institutional status quo (Battilana & Casciaro, 2013).

Implementing Change

Another important factor in employee acceptance of change is the way the change is implemented. That is, how and when will details be communicated? How long will the implementation take? Does the organization have the right personnel for the change? What types of training needs does the organization have?

When organizations are planning change, they intend the change process to be linear in that they begin with Phase 1, move to Phase 2, and so forth until the change is complete. Typically, there is an initial timeline for each phase. As you read the following "steps" to implementing change, it is important to understand that the change process seldom (perhaps never) goes as planned and that setbacks will occur, resulting in the need to make revisions to the change process (Burke, 2018).

Creating an Atmosphere for Change

One of the first steps in organizational change is to create the proper atmosphere (Denton, 1996). This process begins by creating dissatisfaction with the current system. Employees should be surveyed to determine how satisfied they are with the current system. If things go as normal, the results of the survey will indicate that many employees are unhappy with the way things are currently done and have suggestions for improvement. By sharing these results with employees, an organization can protect itself from employees reacting to change by remembering the "good old days." Instead, they will focus on the "bad old days" and be more willing to change.

Perhaps a good example of this comes from some friends of mine who had been dating for several years. For the last few months of their relationship, each of the two would privately tell me how stale their relationship had become and say that it was time for a change. Jill made the decision to end the relationship and told Jack of her decision on a Friday night. The following week, Jill was energetic and enthusiastic, talked of dating new people, and even asked if I knew any good-looking single guys. Jack, however, whined all week about how good a relationship he and Jill had had and how he would never be able to find another woman he would love so much. What accounted for the sudden difference in their attitudes? Jill kept the "bad old days" in mind when she made the decision to end the relationship, and Jack remembered only the "good old days" after the relationship ended.

Some of this pining for the good old days seems inevitable. A colleague of mine had been complaining for years about their college president. The president eventually was fired and replaced by a new president who made many strange changes. It didn't take a year before my colleague lamented about how much they missed their former boss. It took only a few reminders of the horror stories my colleague had told me about their previous boss to quiet this lamenting.

After creating dissatisfaction with the status quo, Denton (1996) advises organizations to work hard to reduce the fear of change by providing emotional support, allowing employees to vent and discuss their feelings, and providing employees with a safety net that allows them to make mistakes during the transition period. Fear can also be reduced by having someone in the organization describe the benefits of change.

Communicating Details

Employees are most responsive to change when they are kept well informed (Wanberg & Banas, 2000). Unless there is a need for secrecy (e.g., a merger), employees should be aware of and involved in all aspects of the change, from initial planning to final implementation. If employees are kept in the dark until the very end, they usually suspect that something bad is happening. It seems to be human nature to think the worst when we don't know something. After undergoing a major restructuring, staff at Educational Testing Service (ETS) in Princeton, New Jersey, reported that poor communication was responsible for many of the difficulties encountered in the change process (Wild, Horney, & Koonce, 1996). During their restructuring, ETS learned these important lessons:

1. *Communicating change is hard work.* Early in the change process, ETS thought it had done a good job communicating the reasons for and details of its restructuring. However, a change readiness survey that ETS administered to its employees indicated that many employees didn't understand the change or were still resisting it. The survey results told ETS that it still had a long way to go in communicating important information to its employees.

2. *Training is needed.* The employees who were given the responsibility for communicating the change had not been properly trained in such areas as dealing with employee hostility and resistance.

3. *Two-way communication is essential.* Employees must have the opportunity to provide feedback to the people making the changes.

4. *Honesty is the best policy.* Be honest with employees and tell them information as it arises rather than waiting until all aspects of the change are completed.

Time Frame

Most successful organizational changes occur in a timely fashion. The longer it takes to change, the greater the opportunity for things to go wrong and the greater the chance that employees will become disillusioned. Many consultants advise that organizations should not remain in a "change mode" for longer than two years.

Training Needs

After an organization has made a major change, it is often necessary to train employees. For example, if an organization changes to a new computer system, all employees will need to be trained in the use of the new system. Likewise, if an organization is changing to a self-directed team environment, employees will need to be trained in such areas as goal setting, teamwork, presentation skills, and quality analysis. An organization must take great care to prepare employees for upcoming trainings and emphasize the importance of participation.

Organizational Culture

Organizational culture The shared values, beliefs, and traditions that exist among individuals in an organization.

Another important consideration in organizational change is organizational culture (Cameron & Green, 2020). Often referred to as *corporate culture* or corporate climate, **organizational culture** comprises the shared values, beliefs, and traditions that exist among individuals in organizations (Anderson, 2020). It is this culture that establishes workplace norms of appropriate behavior (what's wrong or right) and defines roles and expectations that employees and management have of each other (Nwachukwu & Vitell, 1997; Sackman, 1991). Most cultures have a subculture. For example, the environment in which you were raised is a subculture of a bigger culture, for example, the American culture for those born and raised in the United States.

Though organizational change can be traumatic for employees, it can also be exciting and full of new opportunities. Organizational-change expert Price Pritchett (2008) offered the following advice to employees involved in organizational change. This advice can be communicated by management to other employees throughout the organization.

Speed Up

- It is natural for people faced with a new situation to be cautious and want to take things slowly (Kotter & Cohen, 2002). However, Pritchett advises employees to get involved, increase the pace of their work, and not get left behind. This advice is analogous to paddling a canoe: If you move faster than the current, you can control where you are going. If you slow down or remain at the same speed as the current, you will be swept wherever the current takes you.

Take the Initiative

- Instead of waiting for instructions and for people to tell you what to do, chart your own course. Show initiative, try to solve problems, make suggestions. Don't be afraid to take risks, and don't be afraid to make mistakes. As hockey star Wayne Gretzky once said, "You miss a hundred percent of the shots you don't take."

Spend Energy on Solutions

- Instead of spending energy complaining and resisting change, accept change, and then spend your energy trying to solve problems and make the new system work. Take personal responsibility for fixing what doesn't work and for making suggestions for ways the system can be improved.

To remove the stress associated with change, some psychologists suggest that organizations do innovative things to make work more fun (Brotherton, 1996). Consultant Matt Weinstein offers these suggestions to managers:

- Post baby pictures of managers so that employees can laugh at them and realize that the people making the change weren't always in powerful positions.
- Create a stress-free zone where employees can go to relax for a few moments. The Brookstar Corporation in Michigan went so far as to put a punching bag in a room so that employees could take out their frustration on the bag rather than on each other.
- Give employees a surprise hour off. Store managers at Crate & Barrel tell one employee each week to take an hour and have fun, go shopping, or take a nap.
- Other suggestions include holding an ugly tie contest, giving employees stuffed animals, and designing personalized fortune cookies.

Though we certainly have no scientific evidence that any of these techniques will work, the idea is that managers should realize the stress inherent in change and take creative measures to reduce that stress.

In organizations, each department or office can be a subculture with norms of behaviors that may be different from those of the overall organization. How each department reacts to change is a result of that subculture. Most major changes, such as changing management philosophies, will require a cultural and a subcultural change to support the implementation of new ideas throughout the entire organization. This topic is discussed in more detail later in this section.

Think of your university as an organization with its own culture and your classroom as a subculture. Your university probably has created a culture of honesty and trust in which each student is expected to adhere to honor codes. To enforce or maintain that culture, it uses sanctions such as taking you before the Judicial Board if you are caught cheating or violating some other rule.

From the first day of class, norms such as good attendance and participation in class have been established, creating a subculture. These norms were probably established by rules that your professor orally communicated or that were written in your class syllabus. If you know that the classroom culture is one where you may be expected to discuss your reading material, you are more likely to read your text each week prior to class. Your professor may use certain rewards (such as giving points for classroom participation) or sanctions (such as taking off points) to maintain the culture. Eventually, this culture, which includes the expectations of the professor, gets communicated to other students, who at that point decide whether they want to be members of that culture. In other words, if the class and expectations are too hard, the students will sign up for a different class with a more compatible culture.

Culture and norms also result from observing, or modeling, the behaviors of others. Just like your individual personal cultures, which contained role models such as your parents, clergy, friends, and teachers who significantly influenced you over the years, organizational culture also has role models who influence your work behavior and teach you norms (Nwachukwu & Vitell, 1997). Going back to the classroom example, if you observe your professor coming in late every class or several of your classmates consistently arriving late or leaving early without negative consequences, this may begin to create a culture of irresponsibility or unaccountability. You may eventually become one of those students with poor attendance because this has become the accepted "norm." To transform that culture into one of accountability and responsibility, the leader (your professor) needs to model appropriate behavior and to use some strategy (such as taking off points for tardiness) to maintain the better culture.

As you can see, organizational culture can aid employees in behaving optimally. However, it can also be a contributing factor in many undesirable behaviors such as unethical decision making. For example, if an organization's top management consistently engages in unethical behaviors and decision making, it is likely that its employees will learn those norms and incorporate them into their own professional value system and behave accordingly (Chen, Sawyers, & Williams, 1997). To change that behavior, the cultural norms that hinder change must be eliminated (e.g., unethical supervisors, positive consequences of unethical behavior such as financial rewards).

As important as it is, organizational culture has traditionally been ignored during restructuring and other changes. This is either because there is a general belief that culture can't be changed or because many organizations do not know how to change their cultures. Without such knowledge, changes in the way the company operates, and thus, the way its employees behave, will not be long lasting. Consequently, it is important that an organization knows how to include culture in its change process.

Changing Culture

Making organizational changes doesn't necessarily mean that everything about the existing culture must change. According to one manager, "The change process includes holding on to the successful elements of the present culture and adding new elements that are important" (Laabs, 1996, p. 56). Consequently, the first step in changing culture is assessing the desired culture and comparing it with the existing one to determine what needs to change. Two additional steps are creating dissatisfaction with the current culture to create support for the new one and maintaining the new culture.

Assessing the New Culture

Assessment of the new culture involves a great deal of discussion and analysis and should include the following steps (Sherriton & Stern, 1997).

Step 1: Needs Assessment.   Because parts of the existing culture may actually support certain organizational changes, the current culture must be analyzed and compared with the desired culture to determine what might need to change. For example, if an organization wants to move from a traditional hierarchical management philosophy to a more empowering one where employees share more decision-making responsibilities, there will have to be a change in systems, procedures, and policies to fully support the new culture. Areas such as role expectations, job descriptions identifying the new decision-making responsibilities, accountability, rewards, and employee selection systems must be reviewed. Data for an analysis are usually collected through observations, review of existing documentation, and employee interviews and surveys consisting of questions that ask for potential recommendations of changes.

Step 2: Determining Executive Direction. Management must then analyze the needs assessment to determine the decisions or actions that will reinforce the culture and to assess the feasibility of certain changes. Using the previous example, if most of the supervisors and managers in an organization are unwilling to share their decision-making authority, a true "empowering" culture cannot be maintained. Consequently, that may be a change that will not be reinforced by the culture. In fact, according to research, it takes the wholehearted support of top management to implement an empowering philosophy (Schuster et al., 1997). Addressing possible obstacles to culture change during the transformation process can usually minimize unintended consequences.

Step 3: Implementation Considerations. This area addresses how the new culture will be implemented. Will committees or ad hoc groups be set up to carry out changes or will management execute the changes? If the organization's desired culture includes encouragement of more input by employees, they should be allowed to participate in implementing the empowering organization in order to support the new culture.

Step 4: Training. Culture change means a change of philosophy, and that ultimately means different role expectations. As with any new skill, all organizational members must be trained in a new philosophy for the new culture to thrive and be long lasting. This has often been the biggest barrier in organizations that have declared that their members are now empowered to share in decisions. Employees, both management and lower level, are typically not trained in what that means. As explained later in this chapter, management and employees have different interpretations of what empowerment culture means and how to carry it out. Training can reduce such ambiguity and confusion.

Step 5: Evaluation of the New Culture. As with any changes, an evaluation mechanism must be established to review the new culture. Issues such as whether the change actually has occurred or whether old norms and procedures still exist should be addressed. If change has not occurred, additional strategies must be identified to establish and support the new culture.

Now that the ideal culture has been determined, the next step is implementing it. This is done by creating dissatisfaction with the existing culture.

Creating Dissatisfaction with Existing Culture

Just as creating dissatisfaction with the status quo in general is necessary to promote change, for employees to accept a new culture, the existing culture and status quo must be "upset." This might mean communicating to employees the future impact of continuing to "do business as usual." For example, many organizations share data that show technological trends and the financial performance of the company. If employees see this information as negatively affecting either them or the organization as a whole, this can create the necessary displeasure with the status quo and be the catalyst for developing a new business strategy.

Another way to create dissatisfaction is to distribute attitude surveys that ask people how satisfied they are with the organization's goal and to suggest ideas for changes. The results of the survey are distributed throughout the organization so that people can see the dissatisfaction level and will begin to buy into a new culture and other organizational changes.

The key at this point is to seek input from employees in the process. A successful cultural transformation requires commitment from all levels of the organization. When employees have an opportunity to be an actual part of the change, they are more likely to be committed to it. Once you have started the process of transformation, it is important that it be maintained.

Maintaining the New Culture

If the new culture is expected to last, developing new reward systems and selection methods should occur. Rewarding current employees for successfully participating and cooperating with the new system is imperative (Kotter & Cohen, 2002). These rewards can include pay for performance in jobs that have increased responsibilities due to the new culture or other changes. But they also go beyond financial rewards and can include employee recognition and meaningful work.

Selection of Employees

Future employees should be selected based on how well they epitomize the new culture. For example, if the new culture is one of team decision making, new employees should have not only the ability but also the willingness and personality to perform in such an environment. As current employees are replaced by new ones, the new culture can become "frozen" into the desired system selected by the leadership (Lewin, 1951). However, continuing to hire employees who prefer a more structured management philosophy and who work better alone will eventually cause the organization to revert to its old culture.

Organizational socialization The process whereby new employees learn the behaviors and attitudes they need to be successful in an organization.

Finally, the socialization process of new employees must reinforce the new culture. **Organizational socialization** is the process whereby new employees learn the behaviors and attitudes they need to be successful in the organization. It also helps any newcomer to the organization define their role and what is expected of them in their position (Morrison, 1993). Both informal and formal strategies can help with this process. Informal strategies of socialization include such things as hearing the same stories repeated by several different employees. For example, you have probably listened to people in the workforce talk about getting the best stories by hanging around the water cooler or the copier. Usually stories about some "bad decisions" are discussed. New employees who hear stories consistently repeated will get an understanding of the type of culture the organization has. If the discussions are negative, the new employee will begin to believe that the organization is incompetent, mistreats its employees, or is unethical.

Rituals Procedures in which employees participate to become "one of the gang."

Symbols Organizational behaviors or practices that convey messages to employees.

There are also formal ways in which organizations can influence the socialization process. One way is through establishing rituals. **Rituals** are procedures in which employees participate to become "one of the gang." Activities such as annual awards, banquets, or staff picnics are rituals that reinforce the impression of a "caring" organization. Another ritual is requiring all new employees to go through a probationary period before being considered a permanent employee.

Finally, symbols that represent certain attitudes of the organization can be used. **Symbols** are communication tools that convey certain messages to employees. For example, establishment of an on-site wellness center conveys the organization's interest in health. In addition, communication techniques such as the use of mission and value statements can help acculturate the new person to their environment.

14-2 Empowerment

As discussed in Chapter 10, many employees are more satisfied with their jobs if they feel they have some control over what they do. As a result, many organizations are "empowering" employees to participate in and make decisions. As you will see in the following pages, empowering employees can range from asking them for their opinions to giving them complete decision-making control. However, before discussing ways to empower employees—which I will refer to as ways to increase "levels of employee input"—it might be best to first discuss why and when employees should be involved in decision making.

Making the Decision to Empower
Factors in Making the Decision to Empower

Employees need to be involved in decisions in circumstances in which the quality of the decision is important, the decision affects employees, the supervisor doesn't have the knowledge to make the decision, or the employees don't trust the supervisor. As shown in Figure 14.1, Vroom and Yetton (1973) developed a flowchart to help determine when employees should be involved in making decisions. The flowchart uses the seven factors discussed next.

Importance of Decision Quality.   The first factor to be considered in making a decision is whether one decision will be better than another. For example, if a supervisor is trying to decide whether to sign a letter with blue ink or black ink, their decision probably will not make any difference to the organization. Thus, the importance of the decision quality is low, and little time or effort should be spent making it.

Leader Knowledge of the Problem Area.   The second factor in decision making involves the extent to which leaders have sufficient information to make the decision alone. If they do, then consultation with others is desired only if leaders want their subordinates to feel involved. If leaders lack sufficient knowledge to make a decision, then consultation is essential. For example, it would be difficult for managers to select a benefit package without first asking their employees about the types of benefits they need.

Structure of the Problem.   The third factor of concern in decision making is the extent to which a leader knows what information is needed and how it can be obtained—that is, the problem's structure. If the leader does not know how to obtain this information, the decision-making process will require other people, and the decision will take longer to reach.

Importance of Decision Acceptance.   The fourth decision-making factor involves the degree to which it is important that the decision be accepted by others. For example, for a supervisor to decide what hours each employee will work, it is important that the employees agree with and have input into the decision-making process.

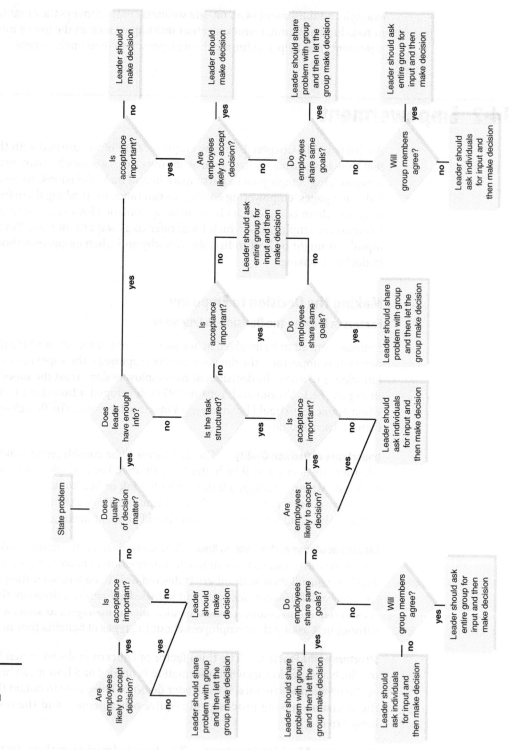

Figure 14.1
The Vroom–Yetton
Decision-Making
Flowchart

However, if the supervisor is deciding what they want for lunch, whether others agree with or have input into the decision is not important (unless, of course, the choices involve onions or garlic).

Probability of Decision Acceptance. The fifth decision-making factor is subordinate acceptance. If the leader feels that they can make the decision themself but that subordinates accepting the decision is important, they must determine whether their subordinates will accept it. If the leader is popular and viewed as being competent, their subordinates will probably accept and follow the decision. But if the leader is not popular, powerful, and competent, they will probably want help from their subordinates and colleagues in making the decision, even though they have the ability to make the decision themself. This is why leaders often ask subordinates and colleagues for their opinions. The leader may already know what they will decide, but gaining the support of others by eliciting opinions and comments increases the chances that they will accept the leader's decision when it is announced.

A colleague told me a story that provides an example of the importance of considering the need for subordinate acceptance. At my colleague's university, the graduate college changed the way in which it administered and awarded graduate assistantships. The assistant dean was placed in charge of developing and implementing the new system. A week prior to the end of school, the new system was announced, and the graduate faculty went crazy. The awarding of the assistantships came too late to recruit students, the new application forms did not provide the information needed by departments to make decisions, and the deadlines for paperwork were convenient for the graduate college but not for the students or the departments.

What went wrong? If we look at the Vroom–Yetton model, two problems stand out. First, the assistant dean did not have the information necessary to make the decision. They had never taught a class, been a graduate student, or been involved in the financial aid process. Despite this lack of experience and information, they chose not to consult any of the stakeholders (e.g., faculty, department chairs, graduate students) who would be affected by the decisions. Second, although acceptance of their decision was certainly important, they made no attempt to communicate the reasons for their decisions or to work with the departments to increase acceptance. Furthermore, the staff at the graduate college was viewed by faculty as being incompetent, not trustworthy, and making decisions beneficial to the dean's career but not always in the best interest of the students, faculty, or university as a whole.

Subordinate Trust and Motivation. The sixth factor in the decision-making process is the extent to which subordinates are motivated to achieve the organizational goals and thus can be trusted to make decisions that will help the organization. For example, suppose a marketing survey indicates that a bank will attract more customers if it is open on Saturdays. If the branch manager allows the employees to decide whether the branch should be open on Saturdays, can the manager trust the employees to make the decision based on what is best for the bank and its customers rather than what is best for the employees? If the answer is no, the branch manager will need to make the unpopular decision after receiving input from their subordinates.

Probability of Subordinate Conflict. The final factor for our consideration in the decision-making process involves the amount of conflict that is likely among the subordinates when various solutions to the problem are considered. If there are many possible solutions and the employees are likely to disagree about which is best, the leader will be best served by gathering information from employees and then, as in the previous situation, making the decision themself.

Decision-Making Strategies Using the Vroom–Yetton Model

Answering the questions in the flowchart shown in Figure 14.1 will lead to one of five possible decision-making strategies: Autocratic I, Autocratic II, Consultative I, Consultative II, or Group I.

With the **Autocratic I strategy**, leaders use the available information to make the decision without consulting their subordinates. This is an effective strategy when the leader has the necessary information and when acceptance by the group either is not important or is likely to occur regardless of the decision.

With the **Autocratic II strategy**, leaders obtain the necessary information from their subordinates and then make their own decisions. The leader may or may not tell the subordinates about the nature of the problem. The purpose of this strategy is for leaders to obtain information they need to make a decision even though acceptance of the solution by the group is not important.

Leaders using the **Consultative I strategy** share the problem on an individual basis with some or all of their subordinates. After receiving their input, the leader makes a decision that may or may not be consistent with the thinking of the group. This strategy is especially useful in situations in which it is important for the group to accept the decision but in which the group members may not agree regarding the best decision.

Leaders using the **Consultative II strategy** share the problems with their subordinates as a group. After receiving the group's input, the leader makes a decision that may or may not be acceptable to the group. The main difference between this strategy and the Consultative I strategy is that with Consultative II the entire group is involved, whereas in Consultative I only a few employees are asked to provide input. This strategy is used when acceptance of the decision by the group is important and when the individual group members are likely to agree with one another about the best solution.

With the **Group I strategy**, the leader shares the problem with the group and lets the group reach a solution. The role of the leader is merely to assist in the decision-making process. This strategy is effective when group acceptance of the decision is important and when the group can be trusted to arrive at a decision that is consistent with the goals of the organization.

Although relatively little research has been conducted on the Vroom–Yetton model, the results of a few studies have been encouraging (Bass & Bass, 2008). For example, Field and House (1990) and Jago and Vroom (1977) found that managers who used the decision-making strategy recommended by the model made better-quality decisions than managers who used decision-making strategies that the model would not have recommended.

Levels of Employee Input

When employers talk about "empowering" employees, they seldom intend to let employees make all of the decisions affecting an organization. Instead, they most often want to give employees "more say" in day-to-day activities. Unfortunately, when employees are told that they are being "empowered," they often apply a different meaning to the word than that intended by the employer. In fact, one organization that went through a change spent two full meetings with employees to hash out what

---

Autocratic I strategy Leaders use available information to make a decision without consulting their subordinates.

Autocratic II strategy Leaders obtain necessary information from their subordinates and then make their own decision.

Consultative I strategy Leaders share the problem on an individual basis with their subordinates and then make a decision that may or may not be consistent with the thinking of the group.

Consultative II strategy Leaders share the problem with the group as a whole and then make a decision that may or may not be consistent with the thinking of the group.

Group I strategy Leaders share the problem with the group and let the group reach a decision or solution.

empowerment should and would mean in that organization! Thus, it might be useful to set aside the word *empowerment* and talk instead of levels of employee input and control. Let me provide two examples of why *levels of input* might be a better choice of term than *empowerment*.

Several years ago, I was hired by a large poultry company to help them design a system to empower their employees. In such situations, my first question is always, "Why do you want to empower your employees?" In this case, the response was that they were implementing a total quality management (TQM) system and were at the stage in which they were supposed to empower employees. In other words, the organization was making a change because the managers thought they were "supposed to do it" rather than because something was actually going wrong. When I asked them if they wanted to actually "empower" their employees to make most of the decisions about their jobs, the company responded that it did not. When I asked what they meant by *empower*, their response was that they were not sure. I conducted a training workshop in which I discussed the concept of empowerment and the levels of employee input examined in the following paragraphs. At the end of the workshop, I told them to discuss what they had just learned and make a decision about what level of employee input they wanted their employees to have. It took just a short time for the managers to reach consensus that they wanted their employees at the advisory level, that their employees already had one of the best suggestion/advisory systems in the nation, and that there was no real need to change. In other words, the organization was already "empowering" its employees at the optimal level for that particular industry.

The second example comes from a university setting in which a new president appointed a number of committees to study such issues as summer school and student recruitment, and "empowered" these committees to make changes to improve the current system. The committees worked diligently for several months and then presented their new systems to the president. After a week of consideration, the president thanked the committees and told them that the committee's hard work was appreciated but the president had decided not to follow any of their recommendations. The committee members were shocked at this response, because, to them, being told they were "empowered" meant that their decisions were final and thus would become the new policy. The president responded by saying that they had empowered the committee to "study" the issues and make "recommendations." The president's intent had never been to allow a committee to make a final decision.

As these two examples demonstrate, *empowerment* means many things to many people. As shown in Figure 14.2, there are five main levels of employee input and control.

Following

Employees at the *following* level have no real control over their jobs. They are given instructions about what to do, when to do it, and how it should be done. Furthermore, their work is often checked by other employees (e.g., quality control) or by their supervisor. Employees at this level can be those who are new or inexperienced to the work being performed or those with weak decision-making skills.

Ownership of Own Product

At this level, employees are still told what to do but are solely responsible for the quality of their output. For example, an employee working on an assembly line would follow a set of procedures in assembling a product but would decide whether the quality of the assembled product was good enough. Likewise, an administrative

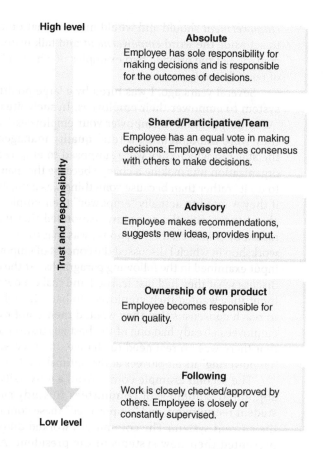

High level

Absolute
Employee has sole responsibility for making decisions and is responsible for the outcomes of decisions.

Shared/Participative/Team
Employee has an equal vote in making decisions. Employee reaches consensus with others to make decisions.

Advisory
Employee makes recommendations, suggests new ideas, provides input.

Ownership of own product
Employee becomes responsible for own quality.

Following
Work is closely checked/approved by others. Employee is closely or constantly supervised.

Low level

Trust and responsibility

Figure 14.2
Levels of Employee Input

assistant might type a report the way it was submitted by their boss but would be responsible for ensuring that there were no grammatical errors.

In essence, this level removes what psychologist Rick Jacobs (1997) calls "redundant systems." With a redundant human system, every person's work is checked by another person. In some organizations, a single piece of work might even be checked by several different people. The logic behind redundant systems is that with more than one person checking quality, there is less chance of a poor-quality product reaching a consumer. Furthermore, in many cases, an employee might not have the skill level necessary to check their own work. For example, a medical assistant might do an excellent job of preparing prescription requests but not have sufficient knowledge of pharmaceuticals to catch transcription errors caused by the physician's poor handwriting.

Though redundant systems make sense in many cases, they do have their drawbacks. The most relevant of these to this chapter are that satisfaction, motivation, and performance can be lessened when others check our work. Let me provide you with a prime example. At my university, graduate students must submit a program of studies covering the courses they intend to take during their two years in graduate school. The student completes the program form, signs it, and then gets their advisor to sign it. The advisor must then get the department chair to sign the form, and the department chair must then get the graduate dean to sign the form. Now keep in mind that because 11 of our 12 classes are required and thus standard for all industrial/organizational (I/O) psychology graduate students, theoretically there should be little room for error in choosing courses. However, as an advisor, I often see mistakes made by my students, who then tell me that they didn't bother to read the catalog because they figured that I would catch their mistakes. The problem is that I seldom read the forms because I figure that if there are any mistakes, my department chair will catch them. The department chair never reads the forms because they figure that the dean will catch them. Thus, the very redundant system designed to prevent errors is actually the cause of errors!

As one can imagine, making employees responsible for their own output does a number of things. It motivates employees to check their work more carefully, provides them with a sense of "ownership" in their product, and provides a greater sense of autonomy and independence. In the former Saturn division of General Motors, employees received feedback on problems that drivers encountered with the cars assembled by a particular group of employees. This feedback helped employees gauge their quality control efforts, and it affected the size of their bonus.

Advisory

At the advisory level, employees are asked to provide feedback, suggestions, and input into a variety of organizational concerns. The key at this level is that there is no guarantee that an organization will follow the advice given by the employees; the only guarantee is that the organization will seriously consider the advice.

The idea behind this level is that employees often have the best knowledge about their jobs, so getting their input makes good business sense. As previously discussed, though employees often have the knowledge to make a decision, they are placed at an advisory level because they may not have the "motivation" to make the best decision. In such situations, an organization will ask employees for their opinions and preferences to better understand the employees' positions but will reserve the right to make the actual decision.

Shared/Participative/Team

The fourth level of employee input and control allows an employee to make a decision. However, this decision is made at a group level. For example, an organization might put a team together to find better ways to market its projects or to determine what type of benefits package employees will receive. This level differs from the previous level (advisory) in that only in very rare circumstances will the team's decision *not* be implemented. At this level, employees must not only be well trained in decision making but also be willing to take on the responsibility of making decisions.

Absolute

The final level of employee input and control gives an employee the absolute authority to make a decision on their own—no group consensus, no supervisory approval. It is important to point out, however, that they are also responsible for the consequences of that decision. So if they make the wrong decision, they may be reprimanded or fired. Because of these potential consequences, many employees are leery about being given absolute power. Thus, it is important in many circumstances to remove the potential for a negative sanction.

For example, Four Seasons Hotels and Resorts empowered each of its employees to take any reasonable means necessary to satisfy a customer. This decision was made so that an unhappy guest can have their problem solved immediately rather than passed on to a manager. So if a guest complains to a housekeeper that there were not enough towels in their room, the housekeeper is empowered to deal with the situation. The housekeeper might opt to apologize, or they might opt to take $25 off the night's stay. Let's imagine that a particular housekeeper "comps" ("compensates," or gives for free) a night's lodging for each of 10 people who complained about not having enough towels.

The manager thinks that this decision was excessive and fires the housekeeper. What effect will the firing have on future employee decisions?

When employees are empowered to make decisions, they must first receive some training in how to make them. Rather than punishing an employee who makes a bad decision, it is better for the organization to discuss with the employee what might have been a better decision and to explain why the employee's decision was improper. Without such training and coaching, employees are not likely to enthusiastically accept their newly empowered status, especially if their new level of authority is not accompanied by an increase in pay.

Empowerment Charts

Organizations never have just one level of employee input and control that applies to every employee. Instead, levels will differ by employee as well as by task. For example, a bank teller might be placed at the *absolute* level to decide when they will take their breaks, at the *advisory* level when it comes to hiring new employees, and at the *following* level when it comes to waiving check fees. To reduce confusion, it is a good idea for organizations to develop what I call individual employee **empowerment charts**. An example of such a chart is shown in Figure 14.3.

In the chart, notice that for each task, a range of control/input is allowed. For example, the task of opening new accounts can be performed at the *following, ownership,* or *advisory* level. Our new employee, Jane (J), is at the *following* level, whereas our experienced teller, Emily (E), is at the *advisory* level. In most organizations, a new employee would most likely be placed at the *following* level until they have demonstrated mastery in performing the task. Individual employee empowerment charts reduce confusion and provide a systematic plan for providing employees with more autonomy as their skills and experience increase.

Empowerment chart A chart made for each employee that shows what level of input the employee has for each task.

Job Component	Following	Ownership	Advisory	Participative	Absolute
Job-Related Tasks					
Opening new accounts	[----J---E----]				
Approving loans	[----J---E----]				
Waiving check fees	[----J--E----]				
Scheduling Issues					
Taking breaks	[---J-E--------------]				
Taking vacations	[---J-E--------------]				
Scheduling hours	[---J-E----]				
Personnel Issues					
Hiring new staff			[-----E----]		
Innovation Issues					
Changing procedures/methods			[-----E----]		
Developing new products			[-----E----]		

J = Jane; E = Emily.

Figure 14.3

Example of an Employee Empowerment Chart

Table 14.1 Consequences to Empowerment

Personal
1. Increased job satisfaction for most
2. Stress
   a. Decreased stress due to greater control
   b. Increased stress due to greater responsibility

Financial
1. Bonuses
2. Pay increases

Career
1. Increased job security
2. Promotions
3. Increased marketability
4. Increased chance of being terminated

Consequences of Empowerment

As shown in Table 14.1, being at a higher level of control/input has many positive aspects. For example, research indicates that increased empowerment typically results in increased job satisfaction for employees in the United States, Mexico, and Poland but not for employees in India (Robert, Probst, Martocchio, Drasgow, & Lawler, 2000). The increased responsibility can result in higher skill levels, which in turn can result in higher pay, increased job security, and increased potential to find other employment. However, empowerment can have its downside. With increased responsibility comes increased stress. With the power to make decisions comes the risk of making bad ones and thus being fired or denied a promotion. Thus, it is not surprising that some employees resist efforts to empower them or their teams (Maynard, Mathieu, Marsh, & Ruddy, 2007).

One of the things that is true throughout life is that people are different, and not everything affects everyone the same way. For example, imagine that we place all of the employees in a fast-food restaurant at the *absolute* level in making decisions such as when to comp drinks or a meal if the service is slow or the food is bad or when to allow customers to make substitutions. For many of these employees, this authority will be welcome, as it reduces the time taken to get permission from a supervisor and provides them with a sense of power. However, for some employees, the increased stress of making acceptable decisions far outweighs any feelings of so-called empowerment.

14-3 Flexible Work Arrangements

A popular organization development intervention is to provide employees with flexibility in the hours they work. As shown in Table 14.2, such flexibility might involve the number of hours worked, the times in which the hours are worked, or where the work itself is performed. Employers who allow flexible work arrangements generally see such positive outcomes as lower absenteeism and turnover, higher productivity, and more highly satisfied employees (Baltes, Briggs, Huff, Wright, & Neuman, 1999).

Table 14.2 Flexible Work Schedules Can Lead to Positive Outcomes Under the Right Conditions

Flexible Work Arrangements		Positive Outcomes		The Employee Wants Flexibility
Flextime				
Compressed Workweeks		Lower Absenteeism		
Reduced Hours		Lower Turnover		Management is supportive
Part-Time Work	**Result In**	Higher Productivity	**If**	The job itself allows for flexibility
Peak-Time Pay		Higher Job Satisfaction		
Casual Work		Better Work–Life Balance		
Job Sharing		Lower Commuting Costs		
Work from Home				

In addition, the employees themselves benefit by having a better work–life balance and lower commuting costs. However, flexible work arrangements have also been postulated to contribute to work-family conflict due to work-family role blurring, although research shows that allowing employees to have greater control over their schedule weakens this relationship (Schieman & Young, 2010).

Interventions involving flexible work arrangements typically follow one of four strategies: Full-time work with the employee selecting the actual work hours, full-time work compressed into fewer than five days, part-time work, and full- or part-time work from home.

Strategy 1: Full-Time Work, Flexible Hours

Flextime A work schedule that allows employees to choose their own work hours.

To accommodate the family lives and personal preferences of employees, 57% of U.S. organizations provide **flextime**, a work schedule in which employees have some flexibility in the hours they work (SHRM, 2019). At Unilever, all 100,000 employees, except production workers, can work any hours they want at any location they want (e.g., workplace, home), if they get their work done (SHRM, 2021b). In the United Kingdom, employees with children under 6 or a disabled child under the age of 18 have the legal right to request flexible work hours and the organization must seriously consider the request. In 2004, 14% of U.K. employees requested flexible hours and 81% of these requests were granted (Holt & Grainger, 2005). Though family issues typically drive the use of flextime today, flextime actually originated in West Germany as a way to alleviate traffic problems by staggering the hours people worked. The plan then spread to North America, where it was used first in Canada and then in the United States in the mid-1970s.

With flextime, employees are given greater control over the hours they work. It is believed that this increase in control and flexibility has many advantages for employees. First, an employee can take care of personal tasks such as going to the doctor, picking up children from school, and even sleeping in after a rough night. Furthermore, this increased control should enrich the employee's job, thus theoretically resulting in increased job satisfaction (see Chapter 10).

In a review of flexible work hours, Dale (2021) reports that flexible work schedules can

- increase job satisfaction;
- reduce stress;

- provide a better work-life balance;
- reduce commute times;
- reduce absenteeism;
- reduce turnover; and
- increase employee and organizational performance.

Although there are many advantages to flexible work schedules, some employees are reluctant to ask for a flexible schedule out of concern that other employees and managers will think that they aren't dedicated to their jobs (Auerbach, 2021).

Flextime can be arranged in many ways, but all share the same three basic components: *bandwidth*, *core hours*, and *flexible hours*. As shown in Table 14.3, the **bandwidth** is the total number of potential hours available for work each day. For example, employees can work their 8 hours anytime in the 12-hour bandwidth between 6:00 a.m. and 6:00 p.m. PRO Group, a marketing company in Denver, has a 10-hour bandwidth, in which employees can choose to start the day at either 6:30 a.m. or 7:30 a.m. and finish at 3:30 p.m. or 4:30 p.m. These 10-hour bands are the most common (used by 45% of organizations), followed by 12-hour bands (Clark, 2001).

Core hours are those that everyone must work and typically consist of the hours during which an organization is busiest with its outside contacts. For example, a restaurant might have core hours between 11:00 a.m. and 1:00 p.m. to cover its lunchtime business, whereas a bank might have core hours from 12:00 noon to 1:00 p.m. and from 5:00 p.m. to 6:00 p.m. to cover the periods of highest customer volume. In the example from PRO Group given above, the core hours would be between 7:30 a.m. and 3:30 p.m.

Finally, **flexible hours** are those that remain in the bandwidth and in which the employee has a choice of working. For example, if the bandwidth is the 12-hour period from 6:00 a.m. to 6:00 p.m. and the core hours are from 11:00 a.m. to 1:00 a.m., then the employee can schedule the remaining 6 hours (including lunch hour) anywhere from 6:00 a.m. to 10:00 a.m. and from 2:00 p.m. to 6:00 p.m. The actual degree to which these hours are truly flexible depends on the specific flextime program used by the organization.

The most flexible of these schedules is called **gliding time**. With this system, an employee can choose their own hours without advance notice or scheduling. Employees can come and go as they please as long as they work 8 hours each day and 40 hours each week. With gliding time, there are no core hours. For example, at 5W Public Relations in New York, employees can work their hours anytime between 7:00 a.m. and 11:00 p.m. Such a flexible schedule, however, will work only where it is not necessary to always have an employee working, as in typing or accounting. In an organization such as a retail store or a restaurant, such a system would mean that at any given time there might not be *any* employee present—which, of course, is probably not the best way to conduct these types of businesses.

Bandwidth The total number of potential work hours available each day.

Core hours The hours in a flextime schedule during which every employee must work.

Flexible hours The part of a flextime schedule in which employees may choose which hours to work.

Gliding time A flextime schedule in which employees can choose their own hours without any advance notice or scheduling.

Table 14.3 Diagram of a Bank's Flextime Program

Hours												
Flex					Core			Flex			Core	
6	7	8	9	10	11	12	1	2	3	4	5	6
			A.M.						P.M.			

Most flexible working schedules are categorized as **flexitour** or **modified flexitour**, with the employee enjoying greater flexibility in working hours, although the hours must be scheduled in advance. With a flexitour system, the employee must submit a schedule on a weekly, biweekly, or monthly basis, depending on the organization. In a modified flexitour, the employee must schedule their hours in advance but can change these hours daily with some advance notice.

Flexible working schedules are popular with employees and beneficial to organizations. Many employees opt to start work earlier in the day and come home earlier so that they can beat traffic and spend more time with their children. As mentioned previously, meta-analyses by Estes (1990) and Baltes et al. (1999) found that flextime resulted in less absenteeism, less overtime, higher job satisfaction, less role conflict, and increased productivity. The effects of flexible working schedules on work–family conflict are more complicated. A meta-analysis by Allen, Johnson, Kimburz, and Schockley (2013) found that flexible working arrangements are associated with a small, but statistically significant, reduction in work interfering with family life but no reduction in family life interfering with work. Given the positive impact that flexible working hours have on employees, it is not surprising that a meta-analysis by Combs, Liu, Hall, and Ketchen (2006) found that flexible working schedules increased organizational performance.

Interestingly, with employees on flextime often starting work earlier in the day, restaurants such as Burger King and Starbucks began opening earlier in the morning to accommodate the early commuters. In urban areas, many mass transit systems are also beginning service or seeing peak ridership earlier in the morning (Armour, 2004).

An innovative approach to flextime is the FlexYear option offered by tax firms RSM McGladrey, Inc. and McGladrey & Pullen LLP (Hopke, 2010). Rather than working parts of days, employees approved for FlexYear work certain parts of the year (during tax season, when their services would be most in demand) and take the remainder of the year off. Also called term-time flex, employees under these schedules usually work most of the year but take extended time off during the holidays (Auerbach, 2021). Such schedules are common with teachers who often have summers off but are fairly unusual in industry.

Strategy 2: Compressed Workweeks

Although the vast majority of people still work eight hours a day, five days a week, there is a trend toward working fewer days a week but more hours per day. These deviations from the typical five-day workweek are called **compressed workweeks** and usually involve either 10 hours a day for four days or 12 hours a day for three days. At a Motorola plant in East Kilbride, Scotland, production workers work four 12-hour shifts one week and then three 12-hour shifts the following week.

In Europe, some organizations use a "nine-day fortnight" in which 80 hours of work are performed over 9 working days every two weeks rather than the traditional 10 days (i.e., five days a week). Such a schedule provides flexibility without the demand of working the 12-hour shifts previously described (Dale, 2021).

The first formal use of a compressed workweek was in 1940, when both Mobil Oil and Gulf Oil had their truck drivers work 10 hours a day for four days and then take three days off. The "explosion" in organizations using compressed schedules came in the early 1970s after Riva Poor (1970) published the first book on the topic. In 2019, 32% of organizations surveyed by the Society for Human Resource Management (SHRM) offered compressed workweeks (SHRM, 2019).

The potential advantages of compressed workweeks are obvious from the employees' perspective. They get more vacation days, have more time to spend with their families, have increased opportunities to moonlight, and have reduced commuting costs and times. Furthermore, if parents have different compressed schedules, child-care costs are greatly reduced.

Because it appears obvious that the employee's non-work-related life will improve with a compressed schedule, the important question becomes, "What is the effect of a compressed schedule on an employee's performance at work?" Most people answer that a worker will be more tired, causing more mistakes and accidents.

The research thus far, however, does not support such speculation. Although research generally indicates that workers do feel moderately more fatigued, their work behavior and work attitudes generally *improve* once a compressed weekly work schedule has been adopted. The results of two meta-analyses (Baltes et al., 1999; Moores, 1990) suggest that compressed schedules generally bring a moderate reduction in absenteeism, a small increase in productivity, a large increase in job satisfaction, and a moderate increase in fatigue. Furthermore, based on data from 3,800 employees in six studies, Moores (1990) concluded that almost 90% of employees who worked compressed schedules were satisfied with them.

Regarding employee health, Williamson, Gower, and Clarke (1994) found that employees who worked 12-hour shifts were healthier than those working 8-hour shifts. There were no differences in productivity or turnover. Duchon, Keran, and Smith (1994) found even more positive results with underground mine workers. Mine workers changing from an 8- to 12-hour shift reported higher satisfaction, improved sleep, and no negative health or performance changes.

In addition to these empirically verified benefits to employees, an organization that adopts compressed workweeks may realize other advantages. Perhaps the greatest of these is the reduction in start-up and cleanup times associated with many jobs. For example, a printer spends considerable time inking and setting up a press before beginning work. At the end of the day, the printer must also spend time cleaning the press and putting supplies away. If these beginning and ending activities together take an hour, then at least an hour a week can be saved if the printer works four days rather than five. Extended across a year and multiplied by the number of employees in a company, such savings can be substantial.

A word of caution should be made regarding the length of shifts. Though employees seem to suffer few problems with 12-hour shifts, there is probably an upper limit in shift length. For example, Knauth, Keller, Schindele, and Totterdell (1995) found a 14-hour shift for firefighters to be too long. Frei (2018) reports that resident doctors working long on-call shifts were five times more likely to make errors and three times more likely to make serious mistakes that resulted in patient fatalities!

To help reduce fatigue associated with long working hours, most organizations provide 20 to 40 minutes of paid breaks during the workday. Research suggests that providing four 9-minute breaks is superior to two 15-minute breaks or twelve 3-minute breaks (Dababneh, Swanson, & Shell, 2001). Interestingly, 5% of employers provide a place where their employees can take a nap (SHRM, 2018). For example, Google provides "napping pods" that its employees can use, and Arizona-based technology company Jawa allows its employees to use two napping rooms—one with a napping pod and the other with a couch. Such a practice may be a good idea, because in a study of Italian police, Garbarino (2004) found that properly scheduled naps prior to working the night shift resulted in a 28% reduction in automobile accidents.

A study by Barnes and Wagner (2009) provides another good example of the negative effects related to lack of sleep. On Mondays directly following the change to daylight saving time, there were more workplace injuries than other days. Furthermore, workers reported sleeping 40 minutes less that night than on other nights.

Not surprisingly, lack of sleep lowers performance on many cognitive tasks. A meta-analysis by Lim and Dinges (2010) found that short-term sleep deprivation resulted in lower levels of attention, lower cognitive response times, and decreases in memory.

Strategy 3: Reducing Work Hours

A third strategy to increase worker flexibility is to allow employees to work fewer hours. While still uncommon, four-day workweeks have been offered by 15% of surveyed organizations, in which employees work 32 hours or less. This strategy has resulted in no reported impact on productivity or revenue (SHRM, 2019). Additionally, though part-time work has been a common practice for many years, two programs—peak-time pay and job-sharing—provide examples of the strategic use of part-time work.

Peak-Time Pay

Peak-time pay A system in which part-time employees who work only during peak hours are paid at a higher hourly rate than all-day, full-time employees.

With **peak-time pay**, certain employees are encouraged to work only part time but are paid at a higher hourly rate for those hours than employees who work full time. Thus, an employee will make more per hour than their full-time counterpart, although they will make less money per day.

The concept of peak-time pay came from the banking and fast-food industries, both of which face unique problems. Both types of organizations need to be open during the entire day yet have only approximately four hours per day that are busy. For example, a McDonald's restaurant might need 20 employees to cover its lunchtime crowd but need only 5 employees from 2:00 p.m. until 5 p.m., at which time the dinner crowd begins for another two-hour peak period. Rather than paying 20 employees to sit around for most of the day, it would be better to have 15 employees work for three hours a day during peak time and only 5 employees work the full eight hours.

Unfortunately, few people want to work only three hours a day at $12 an hour. And those who would be willing, such as students, are often not available during the most crucial hours. Thus, with peak-time pay, 15 people may be paid $16 or $16 per hour to work only the three peak hours. Thus, the employee makes a reasonable amount of money per day, and the organization still saves money over what it would have spent had its employees worked the entire eight hours.

Casual work A scheduling practice in which employees work on an irregular or as-needed basis.

A practice related to peak-time pay is **casual work**. With casual work, an employee works on an irregular or as-needed basis. For example, a theme park might hire employees for only three months during the summer or a concert hall might hire security guards and janitors only during the nights there is a concert. Organizations also use casual workers to fill-in for absent employees. Take, for example, a hospital that needs two additional registered nurses (RNs) to work on a given Friday night. It communicates the availability of the two shifts to its casual RN pool. The first two members of the pool that respond are assigned to work the shift. Such an arrangement provides tremendous flexibility to employees and ensures that the employer will always be able to fill its staffing needs with experienced workers. As with peak-time work, casual workers usually receive a higher hourly rate of pay than do their full-time counterparts.

Job Sharing

Job sharing A work schedule in which two employees share one job by splitting the work hours.

Job sharing is offered by 9% of organizations (SHRM, 2018) and involves two employees who share their work hours. Rather than one person working 40 hours each week, two employees combine their hours so that they total 40. At first glance, job sharing may seem to be little more than part-time work. There are, however, big psychological, if not administrative, differences.

First, part-time work usually involves lower-level jobs such as those found in the retail and restaurant industries. But job sharing allows people in such complex occupations as teaching and accounting to enjoy the advantages of fewer work hours.

Second, with part-time work, the performance of one employee rarely affects the performance of another. That is, the work completed by two part-time employees results from two separate jobs. But with job sharing, the work may be done by two different employees who share one job title and one position. Poor-quality work by one employee must be corrected by the other. Furthermore, in job sharing, the employees, rather than the organization, are responsible for covering the hours when one of the employees is sick or on vacation (Dale, 2021).

From a psychological standpoint, the main difference between job sharing and part-time employment is the level of employee commitment, both to the organization and to the other employee. Job-sharing programs are often targeted at employees who have family responsibilities. Thus, an organization can attract a highly qualified employee who would not be able to work full time. Although there are many advantages to job sharing, some supervisors prefer to have one employee rather than two in a job as job sharing increases the number of employees they must train, supervise, and evaluate (Dale, 2021).

Strategy 4: Working from Home

Some employees set their own work schedules by working at home rather than at the workplace. Although working at home has recently received increased attention, especially following the COVID-19 pandemic, it is certainly not a new concept. For more than a century, employees have sewn garments at home and then sold them to factories for piece-rate prices. Today, with the technology advances, other types of work can also be done in the home. Many types of homework are completed with little or no contact with a central office or factory. With **telecommuting**, however, an employee virtually interacts with other employees, clients, customer, and vendors. Other terms commonly used for telecommuting are *virtual work, telework,* and *mobile working.* Though there are many estimates of the frequency of telecommuting, in the United States, prior to the COVID-19 pandemic, one survey found that 69% of organizations offer some form of telecommuting (SHRM, 2019). BLS data indicate that due to the COVID-19 pandemic, the percentage of employees working at home increased from 22% in 2019 to 42% in 2020. This relatively high percentage is not surprising, as a meta-analysis on telecommuting found that telecommuters have less work–family conflict, better relationships with their supervisor, higher job satisfaction, less role stress, lower intention to turnover, and higher performance levels than their non-telecommuting colleagues (Gajendran & Harrison, 2007).

Telecommuting Working at home rather than at the office by communicating with managers and coworkers via phone, computer, fax machine, and other off-site media.

A 2021 survey (SHRM, 2021a) found that employees reported that the greatest advantage to working at home was:

- Reduced commuting time (44%)
- Better ability to balance home and work responsibilities (14%)

- Getting to spend more time with those who live with me (14%)
- Flexible hours (9%)

The same survey found that the biggest challenges of working at home were:

- Lack of in-person collaboration with colleagues (21%)
- It's hard to unplug at the end of the day (17%)
- More distractions and interruptions (13%)
- It's too easy to raid the fridge (13%)
- Juggling both my work and my children's schoolwork (12%)

Working at home has many advantages for both the employee and the employer. For the employee, it offers the opportunity to avoid or minimize child-care and commuting costs, while allowing flexibility and comfort in working conditions. For the employer, money is saved on both office space and utilities.

But with the advantages come certain disadvantages, which is why many unions oppose working from home. First, it is difficult for a union to organize workers when they are scattered around many locations. Second, it is difficult for the government to enforce safety and fair treatment standards when employees are not in a central location. Third, employees cannot be easily supervised when they work at home.

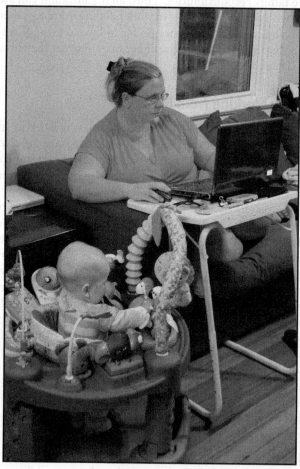

Many employees work from home in order to balance work and family demands.

© Lee Raynes

Finally, employees, especially those working full-time from home, can feel isolated from their coworkers and that the lack of in-person contact with their managers could negatively impact their opportunities to advance in the organization (Beauregard, Basile, & Canonico, 2019).

Although many organizations offer the opportunity to work from home, one survey found that new college graduates want to work in the office (Maurer, 2021). Only 2% of the 500 college seniors surveyed indicated that they want to work remotely on a full-time basis; 98% said they would prefer a hybrid arrangement in which they work most of the time in the office and some of the time remotely.

14-4 Downsizing

When organizations restructure, the result is often a decrease in the size of their workforce (Figure 14.4). For example, the discontinuation of the space shuttle program in 2011 resulted in 2,600 fewer jobs at United Space Alliance. In 2021, Expedia cut 3,000 jobs and General Mills cut 1,400 jobs in efforts to streamline operations. Such reductions in force are the result of a variety of factors, including economic difficulties, loss of large contracts, pressure by stockholders for quick profits, mergers, new technology replacing humans, and employee empowerment programs resulting in less need for managers. Interestingly, 81% of downsizing organizations were profitable the year prior to downsizing (Cascio, 1995). Thus, economics is not always the major force driving downsizing. For example, the number of layoffs in 2001 and 2002 rose tremendously due primarily to the fallout of the September 11, 2001, terrorist attacks and accounting scandals at such organizations as Enron and WorldCom.

Reducing the Impact of Downsizing
Signs of Problems

Short of a catastrophe, organizations usually have some warning that there may be an impending need to downsize. Steps taken at this stage can greatly reduce the need for, or size of, future downsizing (Cascio, 2002).

A strategy taken by many organizations at this stage is to freeze the hiring of new permanent employees and either not fill vacancies caused by employees leaving or retiring or fill vacancies with **temporary employees** (temps). Typically, these temps are hired through temporary employment agencies such as Kelly Services, Allegis, Adecco, or Robert Half International. The advantage to using a temporary agency is that temps are not considered employees of the company and thus have no expectation of a future with the company. If business declines, the company can cancel its contract with the temporary agency. If business remains at a good level, the temp remains with the company.

Temporary employees Also called "temps"—employees hired through a temporary employment agency.

Figure 14.4
What's in a Word? No Matter What We Call It, Losing One's Job Is Painful

Laid off	Restructured	Fired
Downsized	Dejobbed	Separated
Rightsized	Terminated	Canned
Wrongsized	Axed	Given the boot
Reengineered	Furloughed	RIFfed (reduction in force)

If temps are going to stay with the organization for a long time, it is essential that they be treated like other employees. That is, they should be given the proper training, receive incentives for excellent performance, be given the supplies they need to do their jobs, and be invited to participate in informal activities such as going to lunch or attending a wedding shower (Vines, 1997).

A related strategy used by many organizations is **outsourcing**—using outside vendors to provide services previously performed internally. For example, many organizations have found that it is more cost-efficient and productive to hire an outside vendor to manage their data-processing system than it is to keep five full-time data-processing employees on their payroll. Commonly outsourced functions include employee assistance/wellness programs, benefits and payroll administration, training, data processing, housekeeping, and landscaping.

Outsourcing The process of having certain organizational functions performed by an outside vendor rather than an employee in the organization.

Another strategy that can be taken at this stage is to encourage employees to change careers and then help these employees learn the skills needed to make the career change. An excellent example of this strategy, called the Alliance for Employee Development and Growth, was developed in the 1980s as a joint venture between AT&T and its union, the CWA (Communication Workers of America). In the 1980s and 1990s, AT&T realized that it would need to lay off many of its employees. To reduce the number of layoffs, the Alliance was created to encourage employees to look at their future, decide whether they would be happier in another career, and then take steps toward changing careers. To help this change, the Alliance provided current employees with $2,250 per year to take classes or receive training in any legitimate career area. Thus, an assembly line worker could receive funding to learn to be a cosmetologist, a paralegal, or a computer programmer. Though the Alliance cost AT&T about $15 million per year, the money was easily recovered in decreased downsizing costs when employees left voluntarily, or increased productivity resulting from a better-trained workforce.

A fourth strategy for reducing the need for layoffs is to offer early retirement packages. The idea here is to make it financially worthwhile for an employee to retire earlier than planned. For example, in 2020, Ford Motor Company offered employees, depending on their years of service with the company, between three months and nine months of salary to retire early. In the public sector, in 2020 the San Diego Unified School District employees 55 years of age or older and with at least 15 years of service $25,000–$75,000 if they agreed to retire at the end of the year.

A fifth option to layoffs is to ask employees to take pay cuts or defer salary increases. This strategy is based on the idea that most economic recessions last less than a year. If an organization lays off a significant number of its employees, it can take years to get production back to normal when the economy recovers. To get employees to agree to a pay cut, many organizations offer them company stock worth more than the pay cut. When the economy recovers, the employees are financially better off, and the company has employees who are more committed to the success of the organization. As you can imagine, employees aren't keen on being asked to take pay cuts. Over the past few years, the airline industry asked employees to take pay cuts so that the airlines could survive. Though employees at most airlines agreed, the mechanics at Northwest Airlines went on strike rather than take lower pay, and some airline employees who accepted the salary reduction took it out on passengers by displaying a surly attitude.

A final strategy involves adjusting work schedules. Many organizations try to avoid layoffs by restricting overtime, implementing job sharing, encouraging employees to work at home, implementing payless holidays or a shortened workweek, and reducing their employees' pay.

Employees can also reduce the effect of downsizing by monitoring their organization's economic health. According to Beyer, Pike, and McGovern (1993), signs of possible trouble include use of any of the workforce reduction strategies previously mentioned, rumors of corporate acquisitions or mergers, loss of a major contract, and increases in the number of "secret" managerial meetings.

Beyer et al. also advised employees to take stock of their personal standing at work to help determine their vulnerability to being laid off. Here are some important questions employees should ask themselves:

- Have I kept up with the latest changes in technology? Have I changed with the times?
- Have I received excellent performance appraisals? Do I actually contribute to the organization? Do I have a lot of downtime in which I do nothing?
- Do I hate my job? Does my dissatisfaction show? Does it affect my performance?
- Am I well liked? Do others, especially my manager, include me in both trivial and important decisions? Have I kept a good enough attitude that it would be emotionally difficult for my boss to get rid of me?

Selecting the Employees to Be Laid Off

Should the above measures not be sufficient and a layoff becomes necessary, the next step is to choose the positions that will be eliminated. The proper mindset is that work is being eliminated, not people (Alvey & Robbins, 2009). If there is more than one employee in that position, the next step is to select which employees will leave the organization. Criteria used to make this decision might include seniority, performance, salary level, and organizational need. To reduce the chances of legal problems, the committee deciding which employees will leave should be diverse in terms of race, sex, and age (Segal, 2001). The committee's decisions should be analyzed to determine potential adverse impact against protected classes (e.g., race, sex) or intentional discrimination against older workers.

The Announcement

The way in which the layoff is announced can affect the success of future programs designed to help employees. Layoff announcements are best done in person. Some organizations opt for a general announcement, whereas others prefer that supervisors notify their employees on a one-to-one basis. At this time, it is essential that employees receive concrete information. A mistake made by many organizations is to announce a downsizing but not to have answers to the hundreds of employee questions and concerns that are bound to follow. Employees need answers to questions like these:

- Why are the layoffs needed?
- Isn't there any alternative?
- When will the layoffs take place?
- Who will be laid off?
- What type of financial assistance will be available?
- Will we get help writing our résumés?
- How will this affect my pension?

When answers to employees' questions are not available, employees become anxious, angry, and resentful and tend to develop their own answers (rumors).

Outplacement Programs

To help layoff victims move on with their lives, many organizations have some type of outplacement program (Alvey & Robbins, 2009). These programs typically include emotional counseling, financial counseling, career assessment and guidance, and job search training.

Emotional Counseling. After receiving word of being laid off, employees go through four stages that are similar to the stages of change: denial, anger, fear, and acceptance. In the **denial stage**, employees deny that a layoff will actually occur. They make statements like "I'm sure the company will come to its senses," "There is no way they will actually lay off a person with my seniority," and "This can't be happening." For some employees, this stage will last a few hours; for others, it can last until the minute they are no longer working. When employees are in the denial stage, they will not participate in the organization's efforts to help them (e.g., help with résumé writing or interview skills) because they don't see a need to participate in something that is not going to happen.

In the **anger stage**, employees realize that they will be losing their jobs, and they become angry at the organization, their supervisors, and even their coworkers, especially those who will not be losing their jobs. At this stage it is important that employees be given an appropriate avenue through which to vent their anger and frustration. It is not uncommon to have "support groups" for layoff victims, and the first few meetings of these groups are usually spent venting.

After the anger has subsided, employees move to the **fear stage**. During this third stage, employees start to worry about how they are going to pay bills, feed their families, and find new jobs. At this stage, the emotional counseling moves from a listening stage to one that is more empathic and soothing.

Though layoff victims remain fearful for much of the layoff period, they eventually move to the **acceptance stage**. At this stage, the victims accept that the layoff will occur and are now ready to take steps to secure their future. It is at this last stage that employees are ready for specific offers of assistance.

Financial Counseling. As layoff victims move through the fear stage into the acceptance stage, financial counseling is needed. They are under tremendous stress as they worry about how to make their rent, mortgage, and loan payments and how to pay for utilities, insurance, food, tuition, and medical and dental costs. Most banks and credit unions have certified financial counselors who are well trained in helping people with these concerns. The financial counseling process should include the issues of severance pay, unemployment insurance, medical insurance, and any special programs that might be available to help the layoff victims.

Career Assessment and Guidance. Though many layoff victims will search for jobs similar to the ones that they left, many will need to consider other careers. Psychologists involved in this process will administer a battery of tests that tap an individual's basic abilities (e.g., math, grammar), transferable skills (e.g., woodworking, typing), career interests, and work values (e.g., status, independence, leadership). In discussing potential careers, consideration must be given to such life realities as financial needs, time constraints (e.g., "I can't take four years to earn a degree"), and geographic constraints (e.g., "I want to stay near my family," or "My spouse has a good job and I can't leave the immediate area"). For employees willing and able to relocate or go back to school, finding a new job is not as difficult as it is for employees who are limited to a particular geographic area and are not able or willing to be retrained.

Denial stage The first stage in the emotional reaction to change or layoffs, in which an employee denies that an organizational change or layoff will occur.

Anger stage The second stage of emotional reaction to downsizing, in which employees become angry at the organization.

Fear stage The third emotional stage following the announcement of a layoff, in which employees worry about how they will survive financially.

Acceptance stage The fourth and final stage of emotional reaction to downsizing, in which employees accept that layoffs will occur and are ready to take steps to secure their future.

A major issue that arises during this process is the ability of a layoff victim to obtain new training. Jobs in the twenty-first century require higher levels of skill than did their earlier counterparts. So retraining is often necessary to get a new job. However, barriers such as funding and day-care problems, the lack of relevant training sites, and fear of going back to school can keep layoff victims from getting the new training they so desperately need.

To help layoff victims find new employment, workshops are conducted on such topics as understanding the job market, finding potential job openings, writing résumés, performing well in the employment interview, and making decisions about job offers.

Effects of Downsizing

Victims

Research is clear that there are many negative consequences to losing one's job. From a health perspective, **victims** of downsizing report increases in headaches, stomach upsets, sleeping problems, cholesterol levels, physical illness, hospitalization rates, heart trouble, hypertension, ulcers, vision problems, and shortness of breath. Emotionally, victims report high levels of stress, increased drug and alcohol misuse, more marital problems, and feelings of depression, unhappiness, anger, frustration, and dissatisfaction with life. Socially, victims are reluctant to share their feelings with friends, avoid family and friends due to feelings of embarrassment and shame, and avoid social situations and entertainment requiring money.

Shlosberg (2010) lists the following sources of "aggravation" that might be felt by a layoff victim:

- Loss of income
- Feelings of betrayal
- Feelings of personal failure
- Feelings of uncertainty about the future
- Feelings of disrespect.
- Feelings of unfair treatment

To reduce the effects of downsizing, Beyer and colleagues (1993) have these advices for layoff victims:

1. Immediately tell families.
2. Evaluate the reasons for the job loss. That is, was the loss inevitable due to problems with the organization, or could better performance, more current skills, or a better attitude have allowed the employee to keep their job?
3. Deal with the emotions that accompany a layoff (e.g., anger, disbelief, guilt, shame) and get help if necessary.
4. Prepare for departure by doing such things as securing references, negotiating a severance package, and taking advantage of outplacement opportunities.
5. Take a vacation or a short rest period to help prepare for the journey ahead.
6. Plan a new course of action and go forward with confidence.

Survivors

At first, one might think that an organization need not worry about **survivors**—those employees not laid off. After all, these are people who still have their jobs. However, research indicates not only that survivors suffer psychological trauma but also that their future productivity is related to the way in which they and their not-so-fortunate counterparts are treated during the downsizing process (Shlosberg, 2010). Research (Cascio, 2002; Marks, 2003) indicates that survivors

- become afraid of taking risks and are more apprehensive and narrow-minded;
- are more stressed, anxious, secretive, skeptical, cynical, and distrustful;
- have greater role conflict and ambiguity;
- lose confidence in themselves and in management;
- have lower levels of morale and job satisfaction; and
- feel a loss of control.

Survivors will be more productive and feel more secure if they are allowed to participate in decisions and make suggestions, are given a moderate level of job security, are supported by supervisors and the organization, and if the layoff victims were treated well (Kernan & Hanges, 2002; Preston, 2003). It is important that the organization talk positively about the layoff victims, keep an open two-way communication policy with survivors, and communicate the company vision to the survivors. To reduce the negative effects on survivors, organizations must ensure that the procedure used to determine layoffs is fair and clearly communicated to both victims and survivors (Sadri, 1996).

Local Community

Though not often considered, layoffs and plant closings have a tremendous impact on the local community. Local governments suffer as their tax base and revenues are reduced, local charities such as the United Way get fewer donations and often have increased demands for their services, retail stores lose business, banks have greater numbers of loan defaults, crime rates increase, and social problems (e.g., drinking, divorce) increase. On the positive side, layoffs result in an increase in the quality of the available workforce. This increased quality can help other employers and may even result in attracting new industry.

The Organization

Though many organizations continue to downsize, it is not clear that downsizing produces the desired increases in organizational effectiveness. For example:

- Cascio (2002) reports that organizations that downsized between 1982 and 2000 did not improve the financial success of their organizations.
- Henkoff (1990) surveyed almost 1,500 downsized organizations and found that half reported lower productivity.
- A Wyatt Company (1993) survey found that only 46% of downsized organizations reduced expenses, 22% increased productivity, and 9% improved quality.
- De Meuse, Bergmann, Vanderheiden, and Roraff (2004) found that Fortune 100 firms that downsized had lower performance than nondownsizing firms for the first two years following the downsizing. After two years, there were no significant differences between the two groups.

Managing Change at Carlson Restaurants

Carlson Restaurants is an international restaurant chain whose flagship restaurant is TGI Fridays. When Richard Snead took over as CEO, he wanted to focus on diversity issues and make diversity an important part of the culture at Carlson Restaurants. Such a focus was not new to Snead, as he had successfully implemented diversity initiatives at LensCrafters and Burger King prior to coming to Carlson. Snead strongly believed that diversity was essential if an organization was going to have restaurants in different countries and in cities and states with different cultures.

The diversity effort focused on three separate areas: hiring, training, and employee development.

The implementation phase included conducting a needs and culture assessment, creating a high-level diversity team that sought input from employees and managers, and evaluating each location and manager on its diversity efforts and success.

- What factors would you advise the CEO to consider when implementing such a change in organizational culture?

- What should he do to increase employee acceptance of the change?

To find out how Snead managed this change in culture, use the link found on your text webpage.

In today's business world, change is inevitable. Changes in technology occur almost every day (or so it seems). Newer and better companies spring up, forcing other organizations to reevaluate how they do business and to do what's necessary in order to remain competitive or become more so. Fluctuations in the economy also cause change, as companies find ways to deal with lower profit margins. This may mean mergers, downsizing, reorganizations, or even bankruptcies. Whatever the cause for the change, as you read in this chapter, change must be well planned, well managed, and well executed in order to be ethical and successful.

Many companies, when making decisions for change, operate under the philosophy of "the ends will justify the means." The "ends" is the result that the company wants from the change. The "means" is the action taken in order to achieve those results. Critics interpret this philosophy as suggesting that a good result excuses any wrongs committed to attain it. This, they say, is unethical because no excuses are acceptable for committing any wrongs. In the controversial situation of first testing new drugs on animals, critics say that the ends do not justify the means. It is wrong to harm any living being, whether animal or human.

Proponents of animal testing, however, say that whenever implementing any change in an organization, the cost must be weighed against the result. Sometimes a few must be hurt for the good of society. In the example of drug testing on animals, proponents of the philosophy would say that the ends do justify the means because it is done for the good of society: The successful development of important life-saving drugs justifies testing the drugs on animals.

Following are two situations. After reading them, answer the questions under "What do you think?"

Situation A: A small consulting firm was struggling to survive after 9/11. The company got most of its revenue from doing supervisory trainings and other human resources consulting. Almost all organizations within and outside of the United States were financially impacted by 9/11. One of the first places that companies cut back was in their training budget. So, the consulting firm had to make some changes in order to survive or else they would go bankrupt and many people would be out of work. The company operated under the "ends justify the means" philosophy: their goal was to increase revenue, and in order to do that, they had to make changes that negatively impacted on some employees. This is what they did: Employees were no longer reimbursed for mileage, no matter how far they had to go to provide consulting services. All employees had to pay for their own airfare if they had to travel out of state or the country. All employees had to take one week off without pay, regardless of whether they were salaried or wage employees. The company had a wellness program where they paid for the membership fees for all employees. The company no longer paid the membership. If the employees wanted to continue going, they had to pay the membership themselves.

By taking these steps, the company was able to save a significant amount of money over the next few years. In the past two years, they have been able to give small salary increases to employees.

Situation B: A large manufacturing company, to reduce turnover and thereby increase productivity and revenue, decided to make a major organizational change: It was going to decentralize its decision making. Decentralizing is when a company allows each department to make decisions on that department's product, service, and budget. When it was centralized, all decisions went through the CEO and other administrators. Departments had to complete a lot of paperwork and often would have to wait weeks to get a decision on something as simple as which applicant to hire for a particular position. This caused a lot of stress and bad feelings, which led to managers and their employees quitting, often without notice. With decentralization, departments could recruit, interview, and select personnel; prepare yearly budgets; make decisions on purchases for the department and staff; and take disciplinary actions—all without checking with the CEO or administrative staff. The thought of the company was that this increased decision-making power would make managers and their employees more willing to stay with the company. This, in turn, would help increase profits.

One manager was excited about this change in management style. They would finally be able to do some things that they thought would help increase the profitability of their department, and subsequently, the entire company. They felt that the more profitable the company was, the better

it would be for all employees. So, after being empowered to make more decisions on their own, they decided to fire the department administrative assistant. Although the administrative assistant had been with the company for eight years and had done a good job, it was the manager's opinion that the assistant was not attractive enough. One of the duties of the administrative assistant was to give a sales pitch to potential customers who came in and asked about the company's products. The manager believed the department would get more customers with an attractive administrative assistant assisting them because the customers would be more willing to listen to a sales pitch from an attractive person rather than an unattractive one.

What Do You Think?

- In situation A, did you see any ethical problems? If so, what were they and why do you say that? What would you do differently, if anything, if you faced this situation as a leader?

- What was the "end" in this case and what was the "means"? That is, what was the change the company wanted to make and what steps did they take to make the change? Did the end justify the means?

- In situation B, were there any ethical problems? If so, what were they and why do you think that?

- What was the "end" in case B and what was the "means"? That is, what was the change the company wanted to make and what steps did they take? Did the ends justify the means? What would you do, as a leader, if you faced this situation?

- What was the change that the department manager wanted to make and how did they do it? Did the end justify the means?

Chapter Summary

In this chapter you learned:

- Employees react to change by going through the stages of denial, defense, discarding, adaptation, and finally, internalization.
- Employees best accept change if the reason behind the change makes sense and the person making the change is trusted and respected.
- Change is best implemented by creating an atmosphere for change, communicating details, making the change over a reasonable period of time, and training employees. Employees can best accept change if they speed up, take initiative, and spend energy on solutions rather than complaining.

- The five levels of employee input are following, ownership of own product, advisory, shared, and absolute.
- Layoffs can be avoided by using temporary employees, outsourcing, offering early retirement programs, and creating alternative work schedules.
- There is a proper way to conduct a layoff.
- Layoffs have negative effects on victims, survivors, the organization, and the community.
- Compressed work schedules and flextime increase job satisfaction and decrease absenteeism.

Key Terms

Sacred cow hunt   (496)
Paper cow   (496)
Meeting cow   (497)
Speed cow   (497)
Defense   (498)
Discarding   (498)
Adaptation   (498)
Internalization   (498)
Change agent   (500)
Change analyst   (500)
Receptive changer   (500)
Reluctant changer   (500)
Change resister   (500)
Organizational culture   (502)
Organizational socialization   (506)
Rituals   (506)
Symbols   (506)
Autocratic I strategy   (510)
Autocratic II strategy   (510)
Consultative I strategy   (510)
Consultative II strategy   (510)
Group I strategy   (510)

Empowerment chart   (514)
Flextime   (516)
Bandwidth   (517)
Core hours   (517)
Flexible hours   (517)
Gliding time   (517)
Flexitour   (518)
Modified flexitour   (518)
Compressed workweeks   (518)
Peak-time pay   (520)
Casual work   (520)
Job sharing   (521)
Telecommuting   (521)
Temporary employees   (523)
Outsourcing   (524)
Denial stage   (526)
Anger stage   (526)
Fear stage   (526)
Acceptance stage   (526)
Victims   (527)
Survivors   (527)

Questions for Review

1. Why are employees reluctant to change?
2. How important is organizational culture in organization development?
3. When organizations talk about "empowering employees," what do they actually mean?
4. Is downsizing a good idea? Why or why not?
5. What factors determine the effectiveness of flexible work schedules?

Chapter

15

Stress Management: Dealing with the Demands of Life and Work

Learning Objectives

15-1 State the definition of stress.

15-2 Name common stressors.

15-3 Explain the common consequences of stress (strains).

15-4 Identify the effects of stress on behavior.

15-5 Recognize ways to reduce stress.

15-6 Know the importance of child-care and elder-care programs.

15-7 Explain how stress can at times result in workplace violence.

A factor that influences your behavior and thus your relations with others at work is stress: Over 70% of workers in the United States consider their jobs to be stressful (Clay, 2011). Not only does stress affect your interpersonal style, but it can also have serious health implications if ignored and not properly managed. To properly manage stress, you must first identify and understand what causes your stress and then learn ways to handle it. This chapter will identify some of the sources of stress and suggest ways for successfully dealing with it.

15-1 Stress Defined

Though psychologists cannot agree on one definition for the word *stress* (Greenberg, 2017; Sulsky & Smith, 2005), it will be defined for the purpose of this chapter as the psychological and physical reaction to certain life events or situations. The stress process begins with life events or situations that cause stress. These life events are called *stressors* and include such things as weddings, job interviews, dentist appointments, basketball games, deadlines, and traffic jams. If we perceive these events as being stressful, our bodies respond in many ways, including elevated blood pressure, increased heart rate, muscle tension, and perspiration. These reactions are called stress reactivity. If these physical reactions occur for periods longer than our body can tolerate, negative physical and psychological consequences can occur (Greenberg, 2017). These consequences are called *strains*.

As you may have already discovered in your life, an event that is a stressor to you may not be stressful to another person. For example, a human resource (HR) director told me a story about an applicant going through what the interview panel had designed to be a stress interview. They grilled the applicant for two hours on such topics as statistical analysis, employment laws, and job analysis. Toward the end of the interview, one panel member asked the applicant, "Are you enjoying this?" To which the applicant replied, "This is fun. We're not through, are we?" The response stunned the panel because previous applicants had reacted to the interview by shaking, crying, and perspiring. This applicant smiled the entire time. What does the story demonstrate? Contrary to popular belief, not all stress is bad (Cunningham & Black, 2021).

Eustress (from the root *eu-*, meaning something that is proper) occurs when stressors result in feelings of challenge or achievement—the feelings of stress get converted into positive energy and actually become motivating. You might say it is a desirable outcome of stress. An example of positive stress is the anxiety you feel before taking a test. If you felt no anxiety at all, you might not have the motivation and energy to spend the necessary time studying for the exam. Thus, some stress in this situation is probably helpful. However, if you are too stressed, your performance will decline. This is what is known as the **optimal level of arousal** or inverted-U theory. As shown in Figure 15.1, according to the inverted-U theory, having little arousal or too much arousal results in poor performance, whereas a moderate level results in the highest levels of performance (Muse, Harris, & Field, 2003). Of course, the optimal level of arousal is different for each person.

Bad or negative stress, known as **distress**, happens when there is too much stress and when nothing is done to eliminate, reduce, or counteract its effects. Distress usually occurs in situations or at events on which you place great importance (e.g., interviewing for a job), that put great demands on you, and over which you eventually perceive you have little or no control. For example, having to wait in line to drop or add a class may be irritating, but it's usually not a big enough deal to cause distress. But interviewing for a new job or a new position that you really need for financial reasons can be a big source of stress, particularly if you feel you have little control over whether you get the job. Quite simply, negative stress occurs when we perceive that there is an imbalance between the demands (stressors) placed on us and our ability to meet those demands.

The distinction between eustress and distress is important because when employees report being stressed, their performance will not necessarily diminish. For example, in a study of more than 1,800 U.S. managers, the amount of eustress

Eustress Stress that results in positive energy and improvements in performance and health.

Optimal level of arousal The idea that performance is best with moderate levels of arousal.

Distress Stress that results in negative energy and decreases in performance and health.

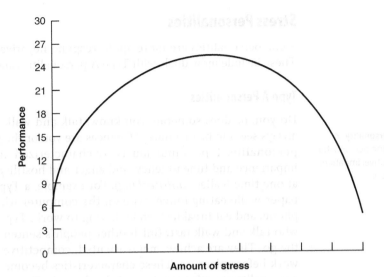

Figure 15.1
The Optimal Level of Arousal

(called *challenge-related stress* by the researchers) had no relationship to job satisfaction or attempts to leave the organization. However, managers with high levels of distress (hindrance-related stress) were less satisfied with their jobs, left their jobs more often, and made more attempts to find a new job than did managers with low levels of distress (Cavanaugh, Boswell, Roehling, & Boudreau, 2000). Similar findings were reported in a meta-analysis by Podsakoff, LePine, and LePine (2007).

As will be discussed in more detail later in the chapter, when people feel stressed, the engage in behaviors to recover from stress. According to Cunningham and Black (2021), these behaviors fall into one of four main strategies. With *psychological detachment*, the employee distances them self and disconnects from the work-related demand. That is, an employee might miss work for two days or quit their job to get away from the source of stress. With *mastery experiences*, the employee develops new skills and competencies to overcome the demand. For example, an employee feeling overwhelmed by video conferencing software might view a video tutorial on how to use Zoom or Microsoft Teams. With *control*, the employee decides what tasks they perform and when they will perform them. For example, an employee who feels overworked may decide to postpone a few tasks and ignore a few tasks until their workload gets under control. With *relaxation*, the employee might take a walk, engage in breathing exercises, or meditate to remove the negative feelings associated with the stress.

15-2 Predisposition to Stress

There appear to be individual differences in the extent to which people are susceptible to stress or are predisposed to tolerate stressors. For example, rates of coronary heart disease, exacerbated by stress, are higher for divorced persons than married people. Married people report higher satisfaction and less stress than unmarried people, top corporation executives have lower mortality rates than second-level executives, and people who live in suburban environments have more stress-related illness than people who live in rural environments. These individual tolerances can be explained by the following factors.

Stress Personalities

Some personalities are more apt to respond negatively to stressors than are others. These include individuals with Type A personalities and neurotics.

Type A Personalities

Type A personality A stress-prone person who is competitive, impatient, and hurried.

Do you, or does someone you know, talk and walk fast, get impatient easily, and always seem to be in a hurry? Chances are you or the person you know has a **Type A personality**. Type A individuals are characterized mainly by achievement striving, impatience and time urgency, and anger and hostility. They tend to do many things at one time (called *multitasking*). For example, a Type A individual would read the paper while eating lunch, type on the computer while talking to someone on the phone, and eat breakfast while driving to work. Type A's are fast-paced individuals who talk and walk fast, finish other people's sentences, and always seem to be on the go. They are achievement-oriented, competitive individuals who tend to place work before pleasure. These characteristics become exaggerated when the Type A personality experiences stress (Schaubroeck, Ganster, & Kemmerer, 1994). Type A employees under stress are more likely than others to exhibit high blood pressure and high levels of stress-related hormones. In addition, Type A individuals are slower to recover after the stressor is removed (Schaubroeck et al., 1994).

Type B personality A non-stress-prone person who is relaxed and agreeable.

Type B personalities seem to be more laid-back. That is, when a potentially stress-producing event occurs, they are better able to keep it in perspective and use more positive ways to deal with it. They are more relaxed and more agreeable.

Type D personality A person with an inclination to experience negative emotions.

The **Type D personality** is a less-known construct and is identified as the "distressed" personality. Type D individuals are described as having the inclination to experience negative emotions, as well as to suppress the emotions and avoid social contact (Sher, 2005). In the workplace context, individuals with this personality have a tendency to perceive their workplace as more stressful and are more likely to experience stress in the form of burnout, emotional exhaustion, and decreased personal accomplishment (Oginska-Bulik, 2006).

Neuroticism

Neuroticism A personality trait characterized by a tendency to experience such negative emotions as anxiety, anger, tension, and moodiness.

Although research over the years has identified several individual personality traits related to stress (e.g., pessimism, negative affectivity, reduced hardiness, and low self-esteem), research indicates that these individual traits fall under the general trait of **neuroticism**. Individuals high in neuroticism are anxious, often depressed, pessimistic, and lack hopefulness. They are more likely to perceive events as being stressful and more likely to have negative reactions to stressful events than are people who are more emotionally stable (Conard & Matthews, 2008).

Gender, Ethnicity, and Race

Much of the research on gender and stress is conflicting. Many studies suggest that women have more stress than men and that depression is twice as common among them. Other studies claim that gender is not a contributor to stress. Presently, perhaps the best interpretation of the research on gender and stress is that women may experience certain stressors more often than men (e.g., sexual harassment, work–family conflict), and men and women may react differently to certain types of stressors (Sulsky & Smith, 2005).

Though there is not much research on the topic, it appears that members of underrepresented groups have higher levels of stress than do White individuals , but this difference becomes nonsignificant after controlling for such demographic variables as age, education, and income (Cohen & Janicki-Deverts, 2012). Furthermore, racial and ethnic differences mostly concern physical reactions to stress. For example, due to a variety of physiological (e.g., vitamin D3 deficiency, type 2 diabetes) and lifestyle factors (e.g., high salt intake, smoking, stress), Black individuals experience higher rates of hypertension than other ethnic groups (Walker, 2011).

Stress Sensitization

The amount of stress you have experienced throughout your life seems to affect how you will handle future stress. For instance, if you are exposed to high levels of stress (such as abuse) over a long duration, studies suggest that you are likely to react more quickly and more negatively to situations that are potentially stress producing because, in a sense, you have become "trained" to respond in such a way. That is, if you are used to being jumpy because of the stress you experienced earlier in your life, you are more likely to react that way with future stress. This, of course, has implications for your future health and your stress behaviors. Desensitization can occur through learning new behaviors to handle stress and working through your feelings about past stress.

15-3 Sources of Stress

Many events and factors could be considered stressors, and, as previously stated, what is stressful for one person may not be for stressful another. Again, what determines whether something will be a stressor depends a great deal on its importance and the amount of perceived controllability. Stressors can be grouped under two broad categories: personal and occupational. Table 15.1 lists common personal and occupational sources of stress.

Personal Stressors

Personal sources of stress deal with such nonwork issues as family and intimate relationships, marriage, divorce, health issues, financial problems, and raising children. Difficult and angry people are also sources of stress because of the conflict they cause in our personal and work lives. In addition, having to deal with life's changes can be enormously stressful. In fact, many stressors can be considered as our reaction to change, whether the change is moving to a new home, ending or beginning a new relationship, or changing ourselves.

Fear

When we voluntarily or involuntarily leave a stage of our lives that has become comfortable and predictable, we enter another stage in which we don't know what will happen. The challenge and potential excitement from the change can produce eustress in people who thrive on unpredictability. But to many of us, fear of the unknown produces distress. For example, when you were a senior in high school, did you think a lot about what the future would hold? Although eager to move out of the

Table 15.1 Most Common Causes of Stress

1. Money
2. Work
3. The economy
4. Family responsibilities
5. Relationships
6. Concerns about personal health
7. Housing costs
8. Job stability
9. Concerns about family health
10. Personal safety

Source: Clay (2011).

nest and be on their own, many students respond that they are terrified of what could happen. These students don't know if they will be successful in life—they aren't even sure that they can get a job to support themselves. They are certain that they will fail in college, which they feel means failing in life!

Other students respond that they are "psyched" about the thought of moving out and trying a new life! For those of you who are more fearful than challenged by change, you are probably already recognizing that the key to handling "fear of the unknown" is seeing that there aren't the monsters you thought there would be if you made the change. In other words, handling your fears in the future means realizing that most changes do not end up being as bad as you first imagined.

Resistance

Let's face it—some of us just don't want to leave the security and structure of that which is known. We like the predictability in our lives, no matter how boring. We like knowing what is going to happen from day to day, and telling us that we have to change our routine can throw us into a tailspin. Something as minor as having to change brands of toothpaste can be too much for us to handle and send us into a determined stubbornness not to change! A good illustration of resistance to change is holding on to old traditions that are no longer feasible. For example, I met a person at a conference who said that for many years after their divorce they still expected to spend Christmases with their former in-laws! It had been a tradition for them for more than 15 years, and they didn't understand why that tradition should stop just because they were no longer legally part of the family. They continued to call their ex-spouse for several Christmases after the divorce, asking to join in the festivities. Of course, they were turned down, and the continued stress from this rejection and their refusal to change eventually led them to seek counseling. They seem to be doing better now and has even begun trying to start their own holiday traditions with the new partner in their life. Resisting change doesn't allow people to cope with inevitable changes that come from living. This resistance leads to stress.

Resentment

Finally, changes that are forced on us, particularly those that we feel we had no control over or input into, can cause resentment. If we don't want the change, don't understand why we have to make the change, and don't like how the change makes us feel (e.g., scared and confused), it raises feelings of resentment. Later in this chapter, we will discuss more about how to deal with life's changes.

Occupational Stressors

Occupational stressors can be grouped under two broad categories: job characteristics and organizational characteristics (Cordes & Dougherty, 1993).

Job Characteristics

Role conflict The extent to which an employee's role and expected role are the same.

Three main job characteristics cause stress: role conflict, role ambiguity, and role overload.

Role conflict occurs when our work expectations and what we think we should be doing don't match up with the work we actually have to do. For example, someone who was hired as assistant to the chief executive officer (CEO) of one particular organization was informed upon hire that they would be handling such administrative duties as policy development, participating as an equal partner in management meetings, and serving as a liaison between the CEO and the public. However, after they had been on the job for a while, they heard themself referred to as a "secretary" not only by the CEO but also by other department heads too. In fact, the work they ended up doing consisted of mainly taking minutes at various meetings, ensuring that there was food at those meetings, and doing other routine clerical work such as answering the phone and routing interoffice mail. What they expected from the position was incompatible with what they were actually required to do. This role conflict caused the employee a great deal of stress, and, consistent with research on the effects of role conflict (e.g., Griffeth, Hom, & Gaertner, 2000; Rahim & Psenicka, 1996), they eventually quit that job.

Role conflict can also occur when an employee has competing roles or conflicting roles. For example, an employee's role as manager may require them to work on a Saturday, but their role as a parent requires them to attend their child's soccer game on the same day.

Role ambiguity The extent to which an employee's roles and expectations are unclear.

Role ambiguity occurs when an individual's job duties and performance expectations are not clearly defined. In the preceding example about the assistant to the CEO, the assistant experienced not only role conflict but also role ambiguity because what their boss expected them to do was different from what the other staff expected them to do. Although their boss referred to them as a "secretary," a job title that clearly denotes certain duties, their boss felt that they should have an equal say in certain decisions affecting the organization. The other directors, however, did not consider them their peer and did not feel that they should have the same power or authority that they had. Because the director did not, in the four years the assistant worked there, ever settle that issue, they were never sure just how they were supposed to act at committee meetings. Needless to say, each day brought more and more stress as they struggled to find out, on their own, just what their job responsibilities should be. Consistent with the research of Frone, Russell, and Cooper (1995), the stress of this role ambiguity caused them to become depressed, and consistent with the meta-analysis by Abramis (1994), their job satisfaction decreased.

Role overload The extent to which an employee is able to psychologically handle the number of roles and tasks assigned.

Role overload develops when individuals either feel they lack the skills or workplace resources to complete a task or perceive that the task cannot be done in the required amount of time. Not surprisingly, role overload is highly correlated with stress (Bolino & Turnley, 2005) and negative health outcomes (Shultz, Wang, & Olson, 2010), especially when employees have little control over their jobs (Karasek & Theorell, 1990;

Parker & Sprigg, 1999). Furthermore, employees perceiving role overload, role ambiguity, or role conflict are less likely to engage in organizational citizenship behaviors (Eatough, Chang, Miloslavic, & Johnson, 2011).

The key to minimizing the stress that comes from role conflict, ambiguity, and overload is to get clarification about your job duties. Although you are given a job description upon hire, make sure you sit down with your boss to ensure that you know just what they expect from you. In fact, it is wise to discuss the particulars of the job description prior to hire so that you are clear about work expectations. If you have been assigned a project you don't fully understand or feel you can't complete, let your employer know. Further, if possible, suggest that you be allowed to participate in training that can help you complete the project. Finally, it is sometimes beneficial if your boss explains your job responsibilities to other staff. This explanation should reduce any misunderstanding about your role in the organization.

Organizational Stressors

Organizational characteristics that are likely to cause stress include such factors as person-organization fit, organizational rules and policies, supervisory relationships, and organizational change.

Person-Organization Fit

Person-organization fit The extent to which an employee's personality, values, attitudes, philosophy, and skills match those of the organization.

The term **person-organization fit** refers to how well such factors as your skills, knowledge, abilities, expectations, personality, values, and attitudes match those of the organization. At one time, organizations were concerned primarily that applicants had the necessary skills and knowledge to perform certain jobs. Now, organizations, as well as workers, realize that there are other areas in which compatibility is critical for an employee to "fit" into an organization and perform well. For example, a pro-life individual may not work well in an organization such as Planned Parenthood, a non-smoker may not feel comfortable working for Philip Morris, and an environmentally conscious person may be unhappy working for Exxon because the philosophies of the individual and the organization are not the same. As shown in Table 15.2, meta-analysis results indicate that this incompatibility in philosophies and values can cause stress, lower job satisfaction, and increase turnover (Kristof-Brown, Zimmerman, & Johnson, 2005).

The management philosophy of an organization may not meet the expectations of some individuals. A person who works best in a very structured environment (e.g., the military) in which everyone must follow a chain of command may not work well in a team-oriented environment in which the workers have the opportunity to make and enforce policy. Incompatibilities between personal and management philosophies can quickly become a stressor. Other stressors include the relationships between supervisors and employees. If an employee's expectation of that relationship differs from the supervisor's, not only will stress result but also conflict between the parties will inevitably arise.

Change

As discussed in Chapter 14, a major contributor to organizational stress is change, which occurs most often from downsizing and restructuring (Robinson & Griffiths, 2005). Realizing the amount of stress accompanying change, organizations are placing increasing emphasis on workplace wellness by offering programs that teach employees how to cope with change and manage stress.

Table 15.2 Correlations with Employee Stress

	Corrected Correlation	Meta-Analysis
Cause		
Organizational politics	.45	Miller, Rutherford, and Kolodinsky (2008)
Job insecurity	.19	Sverke, Hellgren, and Naswall (2002)
Lack of fit		
Person-job	.28	Kristof-Brown et al. (2005)
Person-organization	.27	Kristof-Brown et al. (2005)
Lack of support		
Coworkers	.18	Viswesvaran, Sanchez, and Fisher (1999)
Supervisors	.24	Viswesvaran et al. (1999)
Consequence		
Performance	−.13	Podsakoff et al. (2007)
Absenteeism		
Turnover		
Actual	.13	Podsakoff et al. (2007)
Intended	.41	Podsakoff et al. (2007)
Organizational citizenship behavior	−.16	Chang, Johnson, and Yang (2007)
Satisfaction	−.34	Podsakoff et al. (2007)
Commitment	−.31	Podsakoff et al. (2007)

Relations with Others

Our coworkers and customers can be a major source of workplace stress (see Chapter 13). Though I don't want to rehash material you learned in previous chapters, it is important to understand the stress associated with conflict, working with difficult people, dealing with angry customers, and feeling that you are not being treated fairly. An employee I met at one organization provides a perfect example of this stress. The employee worked at a job they enjoyed, and their personal life was more fulfilling than it had been in years. Despite the positive aspects of their job and life, they had trouble sleeping, lacked energy, and was depressed. What was the source of these strains? A difficult coworker who constantly yelled, used sarcasm, and belittled everyone. Such a story is not unusual and demonstrates the important role that interpersonal relationships can play in causing stress. In fact, a study of more than 15,000 employees over a four-year period found that stress from interpersonal conflict at work resulted in a number of severe psychiatric problems (Romanov, Appelberg, Honkasalo, & Koskenvuo, 1996).

Organizational Politics

Meta-analyses by Chang, Rosen, and Levy (2009) and Miller et al. (2008) found that an important source of employee stress is the perceived use of organizational politics. Organizational politics are self-serving behaviors employees use to increase the probability of obtaining positive outcomes in organizations. *Positive politics* are behaviors designed to influence others with the goal of helping both the organization and the person playing the politics (Holden, 1998; Horan & Seldman, 2012). Examples of positive politics include portraying a professional image, publicizing one's accomplishments, volunteering, and complimenting others. *Negative politics* are manipulative behaviors designed to achieve personal gain at the expense of others and the organization (Holden, 1998). Examples of negative politics include backstabbing, withholding important information from others, and spreading rumors. In addition to increasing stress, negative organizational politics results in lower performance, lower levels of job satisfaction, and higher amounts of turnover (Chang et al., 2009; Miller et al., 2008). Research has also demonstrated a difference in how negative politics are processed between genders, specifically between men and women (Webster, Adams, Maranto, & Beehr, 2018). They found that women experienced heightened levels of threat when exposed to negative politics than when compared to men, and ultimately, increased workplace stress in the form of negative emotions.

Stressors in the Physical Work Environment
Noise

If you have ever been upset when someone played their music too loudly while you were studying, then you can understand why psychologists are interested in studying the effects of workplace noise on employee stress. If the "obvious" were true, we could start and end our discussion of noise by stating that high levels of noise increase stress, reduce performance, and make workers unhappy. But as Figure 15.2 shows, the relationship between noise and worker behavior is much more complicated than we might first think.

To understand this relationship, we must first realize that not all noise is the same. Two sounds with the same level of loudness can have different frequencies. For example, the sound of a tugboat whistle is much lower in frequency than a train whistle. Lower frequencies do not affect employee performance as much as higher frequencies.

Furthermore, sounds that have the same frequency, intensity, and loudness can differ in their *pleasantness*. For example, noise levels at concerts and nightclubs are certainly loud, yet some of us enjoy the sound enough to pay money to hear it. We would probably not pay money to hear a jet engine producing the same sound levels as a rock concert. This difference provides an excellent example of why the definition of noise is unwanted sound (Smith, 2013).

Figure 15.2
Factors Determining Possible Noise Effects

This effect can be seen with an employee who listens to music through headphones at work. The noise level of the music is often greater than that of the machines in the environment, but it is considered to be more pleasant. Keep in mind, however, that even though the music may be more interesting than the machine noise, the noise level has the same potential effects: Hearing loss can occur just as easily from music as it can from factory noise.

Noises also differ in whether they are continuous or intermittent (Szalma & Hancock, 2011). Constant noise has less effect on employee behavior, so environments with steady noise levels are not as disrupting as those in which either noise frequency or noise intensity changes.

Another factor that affects the relationship between noise and employee behavior is the *type of the task*. Noise affects tasks that involve cognitive skills or communication more than it affects tasks involving perception (Szalma & Hancock, 2011).

Individual differences in people also determine the degree to which noise will affect performance. Extraverts, who tend to be underaroused, are affected less by noise than are introverts, who tend to be overaroused (Smith, 2013). Weinstein (1978) examined individual differences in noise sensitivity in college students and found that noise-sensitive students had lower academic performance, were less comfortable in the presence of others, and became more disturbed than their less noise-sensitive peers. Melamed, Harari, and Green (1993) found that Type A personalities' blood pressure and heart rate increased under conditions of high noise but not under conditions of low noise. Individuals with misophonia (a condition which causes negative reactions to common sounds) might also experience irritation and difficulty concentrating because of repetitive noises in the workplace, such as clicking of a pen or the humming of fluorescent lights.

The effect of noise also depends on the *necessity* for and *familiarity* of the noise. When certain noises cannot be avoided—for example, the sound of a machine in a manufacturing plant—they are less irritating than unnecessary noises such as an employee talking too loudly or a roommate playing their music at full volume (Kjellberg, Landstrom, Tesarz, & Soderberg, 1996).

Likewise, familiar noise is less irritating than unfamiliar noise, probably for two reasons. First, a familiar noise is less distracting or meaningful than the one that we hear for the first time. For example, the regular passing of a train outside an office produces less distracting noise than a suddenly dropped glass. Even though the train is louder, it is expected and familiar and thus not as distracting. Soldiers with war experience have often reported they were able to sleep through artillery explosions but would awaken instantly at the sounds of snapped twigs or close footsteps.

Familiar sounds may also be less distracting because our hearing loses sensitivity to loud sounds. For example, on first entering a factory, the noise levels are often very high and distracting. After a few minutes, however, the noise is less noticeable because we have become temporarily less sensitive to it.

Finally, noise affects certain *types* of employee behaviors in different ways. Noise is more likely to decrease the *quality* of performance rather than its quantity (Szalma & Hancock, 2011), to cause people to walk faster and make less eye contact (Korte & Grant, 1980), to decrease job satisfaction (Sundstrom, Town, Rice, Osborn, & Brill, 1994), and to decrease performance on cognitive tasks (Smith & Jones, 1992). But perhaps the greatest effects of noise are not on performance but on employee health and morale.

As Figure 15.3 shows, research indicates that in addition to hearing loss, continued exposure to high levels of noise (measured in decibels [db]) can raise blood pressure of employees (van Kempen et al., 2002), increase worker illness (Cohen, 1972), cause people to be less helpful (Fisher, Bell, & Baum, 1984), and produce more aggression and irritability (Quigley, Leonard, & Collins, 2003). Even low levels of office noise have been found to increase employee stress and reduce task motivation (Evans & Johnson, 2000).

Noise also causes people to narrow their focus of attention so that they concentrate only on the most important stimuli. In one experiment, Korte and Grant (1980) placed unusual objects (e.g., a brightly colored balloon tied to a lamppost) and people (a woman wearing a large pink hat) along the sidewalk of a busy shopping district. Korte and Grant then asked shoppers if they had seen anything unusual and read them a list of the unusual people and things they could have seen. When traffic noise was high, only 35% of the shoppers noticed the items, compared with more than 50% when the noise was low. Although such narrowing of attention may decrease the performance levels of employees for whom it is important to notice many stimuli (e.g., police officers or safety inspectors), it may help the performance of employees who need focus on only a few different stimuli (Broadbent, 1971).

Noise Reduction

Given that noise affects employee morale, health, and perhaps performance, employers have attempted to solve or minimize the problem of noise by several methods. One has been by setting legal time limits on the exposure to noise at different decibel levels.

Figure 15.3
Effects of Noise at Different Levels

Cause of Noise	Loudness of Noise (in decibels)	Effect of Noise
Rocket launch	180	
	170	
	160	
	150	
Gunshot blast	140	
Jet takeoff	130	Brief exposure can result in permanent deafness (Trahiotis & Robinson, 1979)
	125	
Disco	120	
Riveting machine	115	Maximum legal exposure to noise
Power lawn mower	110	A person cannot speak over a sound at this level
	105	
Textile-weaving plant	100	Blood pressure increases (Burns, 1979)
Food blender	95	Cognitive performance is reduced (Hockey, 1970)
		Employees report more illness and somatic complaints (Cohen, 1972)
	93	Angry people become more aggressive (Donnerstein & Wilson, 1976)
		Driving performance decreases (Finkelman, Zeitlin, Filippi, & Friend, 1977)
City traffic	90	Legal acceptable noise limit for eight-hour day (OSHA guidelines)
Computer card verifier	85	Helping behavior decreases (Mathews & Canon, 1975)
Train (100 feet away)	80	Reaction time decreases by 3% (Lahtela, Niemi, Kunsela, & Hypen, 1986)
Car	75	
Noisy restaurant	70	Telephone use is difficult
	68	Reduced detection of grammatical errors during proofreading (Weinstein, 1977)
	65	Hearing loss can occur in sensitive individuals
Normal speech	60	
	50	
Normal noise at home	40	
Soft whisper	30	
	20	
	10	
Breathing	0	

As you can see from Table 15.3, the legal limits set by the Occupational Safety and Health Administration (OSHA) are not as stringent as those recommended by the National Institute for Occupational Safety and Health (NIOSH).

A second method is to change the environment by using carpeting and acoustically treated ceilings (Sundstrom et al., 1994).

A third method is to reduce the amount of unwanted noise that reaches an employee. Examples have included employees wearing protective earplugs and muffs or working in soundproof areas away from the sources of noise. In one study, use of hearing protection devices in a noisy factory reduced workers' hostile behaviors (Rabinowitz, Melamed, Feiner, & Weisberg, 1996). Although these methods may limit the effects on employee health, they may also decrease performance in jobs that require detection of or attention to certain types of noise (Mershon & Lin, 1987).

Another method used to limit the problem of noise has been through engineering technology—that is, by reducing the actual amount of noise emitted. For example, rubber pads on machines reduce noise by reducing vibration, and belt drives instead of gears reduce the noise made by many types of machines. In one study, using white noise to mask office noise improved performance on a cognitive task. However, the white-noise group still performed worse than the no-noise group (Loewen & Suedfeld, 1992). In offices, airflow from ventilation systems can serve as a source of white noise.

This discussion has concentrated on the potential harmful effects of noise, but noise can also be beneficial in the working environment, especially as a warning method. For example, loud noises alert workers that a forklift is backing up, loud whistles tell workers when it is time to go home, and alarms tell workers when a machine has malfunctioned.

Temperature

Another important issue concerning the working environment is the effect of temperature on employee stress, performance, and health. Many jobs, such as those in the construction and in the steel industry, involve working in intense heat, and others, such as rescue squad work and meatpacking, often involve working in extreme cold.

Table 15.3 Maximum Legal Exposure to Noise

	Maximum Noise Level (in decibels)	
Hours of Exposure	OSHA Limits	NIOSH Recommendations
8	90	85
7	91	
6	92	
5	93	
4	95	88
3	97	
2	100	91
1.5	102	
1	105	94
0.5	110	97
0.25	115	100

OSHA = U.S. Occupational Safety and Health Administration; NIOSH = National Institute for Occupational Safety and Health (Centers for Disease Control and Prevention).

Perhaps the best place to begin a discussion of the effects of temperature is by describing how the human body tries to maintain an ideal temperature. When body temperature is above normal, we cool down in one of two ways. The first is through **radiation**, with the excess heat radiating away from the body. The second way is by **evaporation**, or by sweating away excess heat.

When body temperature is below normal, blood vessels constrict. Although this process helps protect against cold, it also produces numbness by reducing circulation. That is why our feet and hands are the first parts of the body to feel numb when we are cold. Police officers patrolling their assigned territory can often be seen stomping their feet in cold temperatures to stimulate circulation.

We must next understand how different factors affect what is called the **effective temperature**, or how hot or cold our environment feels to us. In theory, effective temperature has four components—air temperature, humidity, airflow, and temperature of objects in the environment—but it is usually computed by considering only air temperature and humidity. Note that effective temperature is more than simple air temperature. A 90-degree day in the Nevada desert feels cooler than a 90-degree day in a Georgia swamp. As Table 15.4 shows, the higher the humidity, the warmer the air temperature feels, and thus the higher the effective temperature.

In addition to humidity, airflow is also important. Many of us can probably recall the feeling of relief from a breeze coming off a lake or the ocean. The air temperature probably did not change, but discomfort decreased along with the effective temperature. Likewise, we might recall a "biting wind" that made a winter day seem so cold.

Finally, the effective temperature is affected by the heat that radiates from other objects in the environment. For example, the field-level temperature of outdoor sports stadiums that use artificial turf is usually much higher than the air temperature in the stands because heat radiates from the artificial turf. Other examples of this radiation effect include how much hotter it feels when sitting with a group of people than when sitting alone or how much hotter it feels when lying on the sand at the beach than when sitting up.

I can remember many summer days in Los Angeles when the air temperature was already more than 100 degrees but was combined with heat radiating from the sidewalk adding 15 degrees more, thus making walking uncomfortable. Similarly, a manager who thinks that their outdoor salespeople will be fine in an 85-degree temperature must also account for the effective temperature caused by radiating heat. An air temperature of 85 degrees above a concrete sidewalk is not the same as 85 degrees above a dirt road.

Both air temperature and humidity interact with the body's ability to cool down through radiation and evaporation. When air temperature is higher than body

Radiation One way our bodies maintain a normal temperature, by the emission of heat waves.

Evaporation One way our bodies maintain a normal temperature, in which perspiration reduces excess heat.

Effective temperature The combination of air temperature, humidity, airflow, and heat radiation that determines how hot or cold the environment feels.

Table 15.4 Effective Temperature as a Function of Air Temperature and Humidity

Humidity (%)	Air Temperature (°F)					
	41	**50**	**59**	**68**	**77**	**86**
100	41	52	64	78	96	120
80	41	52	63	75	90	111
60	40	51	62	73	86	102
40	40	51	61	72	83	96
20	39	50	60	70	81	91
0	39	50	59	69	77	86

temperature, we are unable to radiate heat. When humidity is high, it is more difficult to lose body heat through evaporation. Thus, high air temperature and high humidity make the body's "natural cooling system" less effective.

The relevant question here, of course, is what happens when the effective temperature in the working environment is high or low? As shown in Figure 15.4, the answer is that performance usually deteriorates. The degree of deterioration, however, depends on several factors, including the type of task, the workload, and the number and frequency of rest periods that are allowed.

Figure 15.4
Effects of Various Temperatures on Employee Behavior

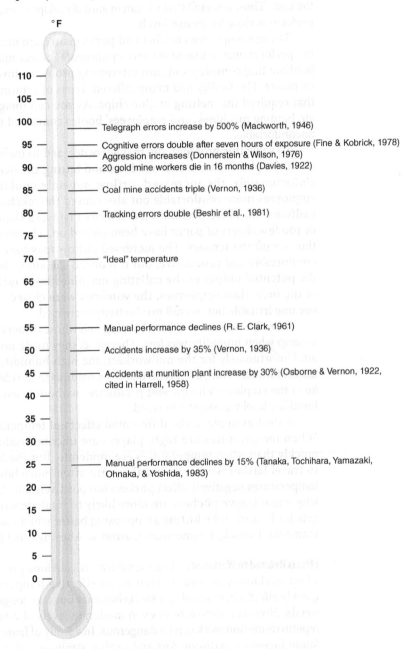

°F

110 —

105 —

100 — ———— Telegraph errors increase by 500% (Mackworth, 1946)

95 — ———— Cognitive errors double after seven hours of exposure (Fine & Kobrick, 1978)
———— Aggression increases (Donnerstein & Wilson, 1976)

90 — ———— 20 gold mine workers die in 16 months (Davies, 1922)

85 — ———— Coal mine accidents triple (Vernon, 1936)

80 — ———— Tracking errors double (Beshir et al., 1981)

75 —

70 — ———— "Ideal" temperature

65 —

60 —

55 —

50 — ———— Manual performance declines (R. E. Clark, 1961)

45 — ———— Accidents increase by 35% (Vernon, 1936)

40 — ———— Accidents at munition plant increase by 30% (Osborne & Vernon, 1922, cited in Harrell, 1958)

35 —

30 —

25 — ———— Manual performance declines by 15% (Tanaka, Tochihara, Yamazaki, Ohnaka, & Yoshida, 1983)

20 —

15 —

10 —

5 —

0 —

Effects on Tasks. Research indicates that extremely high or low temperatures can affect performance on cognitive, physical, and perceptual tasks. A meta-analysis by Pilcher, Nadler, and Busch (2002) found that performance dropped by 13.9% when temperatures rose above 90 degrees and by 14.9% when temperatures fell below 50 degrees. Hot temperatures had their greatest effect on reaction time and on performance of attentional, perceptual, and mathematical tasks. Cold temperatures had their greatest effect on reasoning, memory, and learning tasks. Interestingly, extreme temperatures seem to have their greatest effect on tasks when only a small amount of time is spent on the task. Thus, it seems that we can eventually adapt to extreme cold temperatures and perform at close to normal levels.

Though employee comfort and performance are important, heat can also affect the performance of machines and equipment. For example, a California printing and bookbinding company ran into interesting problems involving the airflow in one of its plants. The facility had many different types of printing presses, as well as binders that required the melting of glue chips. As you can imagine, the heat from summer air, binding machines, and employees' bodies combined to make working conditions uncomfortable.

To solve this problem, the managers decided to increase the airflow by opening all of the plant's doors and windows and letting the ocean breezes cool the plant. Unfortunately, the increased airflow not only cooled the plant and made the employees more comfortable but also caused the mechanical collating machines to malfunction. These machines use sensors that warn their operators when too many or too few sheets of paper have been picked up. The breezes ruffled the sheets and thus set off the sensors. The increased airflow may have made the employees more comfortable and productive, but it reduced the equipment's productivity. Because the potential output of the collating machines was much greater than the outputs of the individual employees, the windows were closed. As a result, the employees became irritable but overall productivity increased.

A similar case occurred at a knitting mill whose owners discovered that yarn tended to snap when humidity was low. Therefore, they made no attempt to dehumidify the air. Unfortunately for the millworkers, the high humidity made working conditions uncomfortable. Thus, a decision had to be made as to the ideal humidity level that would keep the employees happy and productive without causing the yarn to snap. So the humidity level was slightly lowered.

A final example of the differential effects of temperature comes from baseball. When temperatures are high, players are uncomfortable, and pitchers tire more quickly than when temperatures are moderate. But the hotter air allows a baseball to travel farther when hit, and there are often more home runs. Thus, the higher temperatures negatively affect pitchers but positively affect batters. This might explain why major league pitchers are more likely to retaliate when one of their teammates gets hit by a pitch by hitting an opposing batter when the temperature is hot rather than cold (Larrick, Timmerman, Carton, & Abrevaya, 2011).

Effects Related to Workload. High temperatures obviously most affect work performance when workloads are heavy. That is, an effective temperature of 95 degrees would quickly affect a person using a sledgehammer but take longer to affect a person pulling weeds. However, exposure to even moderate levels of heat while performing "light" repetitive-motion work can be dangerous. In a study of laundry workers, Brabant (1992) found increases in discomfort and cardiac strain—results that were not immediately dangerous but had the potential for future health problems.

Rest Periods.   Temperature will have the greatest effect on performance when work activity is continuous. With rest breaks, the effects of either heat or cold can be greatly reduced. For example, NIOSH work/rest schedules, most people can work for approximately 120 minutes at 90 degrees without impaired performance or health risk. At 100 degrees, however, the maximum time for continued performance is approximately 30 minutes. Thus, in temperatures of 90 degrees, rest breaks scheduled at a maximum of two hours apart will help keep performance (and the employee) from deteriorating. At 100 degrees, rest breaks must occur at intervals of less than 30 minutes. The Center for Disease Control (CDC) recommends that the actual temperature be adjusted for environmental conditions and the humidity level. These recommended adjustments are:

Environmental Conditions

- Full sun (add 13°F)
- Partly clouded (add 7°F)
- No shadows visible, in the shade, at night (no adjustment)

Humidity

- 40% humidity (add 3°F)
- 50% humidity (add 6°F)
- 60% humidity or more (add 9°F)

Thus, if it is 90°F, partly cloudy, and 50% humidity, the adjusted temperature would be 90 + 7 + 6 = 103°F.

An interesting problem developed at a large amusement park when its employees were exposed to summer heat. The park had several employees dress in theme costumes, which we will call "gnomes" to protect the park's reputation. The thick and heavy gnome costumes were worn even during summer when temperatures were almost always in the 90s and 100s. The job of each costumed employee was to walk around the park and greet customers, especially children. Problems, however, began when children punched the gnomes and knocked them over (a rolling gnome was actually a fairly funny sight). Normally, the gnomes kept their sense of humor and laughed, but after an hour in costume in 100-degree temperatures, they sometimes lost their humor and began punching back. And when they were not hitting children, the gnomes were passing out from the heat. Obviously, something had to be done.

To solve the problem, the park's management had the gnomes work four-hour shifts instead of eight. As we might expect from the previous discussion, this solution was ineffective. Why? Because the outside temperature was 100 degrees and the effective temperature inside the costume was at least 20 degrees higher. At such high temperatures, continuous activity brought decreased performance in less than 30 minutes. The solution that worked, of course, was to have the gnomes work for 20 minutes and then take short breaks in an air-conditioned room, thus taking advantage of what we know about exposure limits to heat as well as frequency of breaks.

An interesting adaptation to extreme temperature can be found at ICEHOTEL, located above the Arctic Circle in Sweden. ICEHOTEL is a fascinating structure made completely of ice—the walls, floors, beds, chairs, and even the chandeliers! During the winter, the temperature outside the hotel falls to 30 degrees below zero and the inside temperature stays at a constant 30 degrees. How do the employees and guests handle these temperatures? By wearing snowsuits, gloves, and hats while indoors, everyone stays rather toasty. Because the people at the reception desk are exposed to the bitter outside cold each time someone opens the door, the receptionists work

30 minutes at the reception desk and then 30 minutes in a "warmer" part of the hotel before rotating back to the reception desk for another 30 minutes. Thus, through the use of proper clothing and rest periods, ICEHOTEL is able to keep its employees safe and productive.

Stress Caused by Work Schedules
Shift Work

Even though most people work from 8:00 a.m. or 9:00 a.m. to 5:00 p.m., data from the Bureau of Labor Statistics indicate that approximately 16% of all U.S. employees work evening or late-night shifts due to economic and safety factors. Police officers and nurses must work around the clock because neither crime nor illness stops at 5:00 p.m.; retail employees must work late hours to accommodate people who are able to shop only late in the day; and factory workers work shifts because one plant can be three times as productive if it operates round the clock.

Because shift work is necessary and affects approximately 16% of all employees in the United States, research has attempted to identify its effects as well as ways to reduce any effects that might be negative. A review of the research on shift work (Smith, Folkard, Tucker, & Evans, 2011) clearly indicates that working evening ("swing") and late-night/overnight ("graveyard") shifts has many work and health-related negative effects, including

- sleep problems;
- chronic fatigue;
- accidents and injuries;
- gastrointestinal disorders (e.g., constipation, heartburn, gas);
- cardiovascular disorders (Lin et al., 2015);
- increased cancer mortality (Lin et al., 2015);
- increased mortality from all causes (Lin et al., 2015);
- increased problems during pregnancy (Cai et al., 2019);
- increased odds of abdominal obesity (Sun et al., 2017);
- increased absenteeism from work (Jamal, 1981);
- lowered low satisfaction (Jamal, 1981);
- lower job performance (Smith, Totterdell, & Folkard, 1995); and
- increased social and family problems (Jamal, 1981; Presser, 2000).

Circadian rhythm The hour cycle of physiological functions maintained by every person.

Many of these negative effects are thought to occur because of disruptions in **circadian rhythms**, the 24-hour cycles of physiological functions maintained by every person. For example, most people sleep at night and eat in the morning, at noon, and in the evening. Although there are individual differences in the exact times for each function (such as eating or sleeping), people generally follow the same pattern. Working evening and late-night shifts disrupts this pattern and often causes digestive, appetite, sleeping, and other health problems (Frei, 2018; Price, 2011). Unfortunately, we don't "get used to" shift work, and these effects get worse with continued exposure to night shifts (Folkard, 2008; Kaliterna, Vidacek, Prizmic, & Radosevic-Vidacek, 1995). For example, Garbarino (2004) found that Italian police working shifts had more sleep disorders than non-shift workers and that the greater the number of years spent working shifts, the worse the sleep disorders.

Frei (2018) suggests that the negative effects of shift work can be reduced by moving the "drowsy phase" of the circadian rhythm from the normal nighttime to the morning or afternoon. This movement can be accomplished by keeping the sleeping environment dark, having lot of light in the work area while working at night, taking naps, using a reasonable amount of caffeine, and taking melatonin,

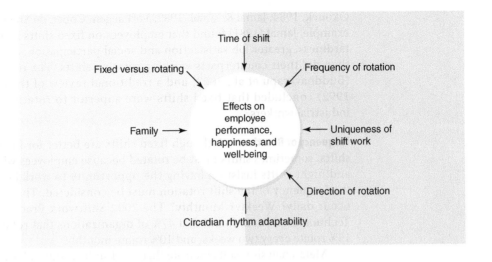

Figure 15.5
Factors Influencing
Shift Work Effects

Many of the psychological and social effects of shift work are caused by the incompatibility of an employee's schedule with the schedules of other people. That is, a person who works nights and sleeps mornings may be ready to socialize in the afternoon. Unfortunately, fewer people are around. And when the family is active, the employee is sleeping, and thus requires quiet.

As Figure 15.5 shows, many factors influence the degree to which shift work will affect an employee. For example, employees who live with families are affected more than employees who live alone because the former must adjust their sleeping schedules to those of others in the household (Smith & Folkard, 1993). Other important factors are uniqueness of shift, whether a shift is fixed or rotating, frequency of rotation, and individual differences.

Uniqueness of Shift.   The social effects of shift work can be greatly reduced if other organizations in the geographical area also use other shifts. The higher the percentage of organizations with shifts, the greater the number of stores and restaurants that are open during the evening and the greater the number of other people available with whom to socialize.

Fixed shift A shift schedule in which employees never change the shifts they work.

Fixed Versus Rotating Shifts.   Shifts can be either fixed or rotated. With **fixed shifts**, separate groups of employees permanently work the day shift, swing shift, and night shift. Rotating shifts are those in which an employee rotates through all three shifts, working the day shift for a while, then switching to the swing shift, then working the night shift, and so on. Although the vast majority of employees prefer fixed shifts, a survey of 623 U.S. and Canadian companies using shifts found that 66% used rotating rather than fixed shifts (Circadian Technologies, 2002).

The rationale for rotating shifts is that the negative effects of working swing and night shifts can be lessened if each employee is allowed to work the day shift part of the time. With fixed shifts, even though two-thirds of all workers will have hours that are not compatible with their circadian rhythms, staying permanently on the same shifts will allow them to physically adjust better than if they change shifts, especially when considering that about two days are needed to adjust to each shift change.

Research on shift rotation has strongly suggested that fixed shifts result in fewer performance, sleep, physical, and psychological problems than do rotating shifts (Buddhavarapu, Borys, Hormant, & Baltes, 2002; Chang & Peng, 2021; Frese &

Okonek, 1984; Jamal & Jamal, 1982; Verhaegen, Cober, de Smedt, & Dirkx, 1987). For example, Jamal (1981) found that employees on fixed shifts had less absenteeism and tardiness, greater job satisfaction and social participation, and better mental health than did their counterparts working rotating shifts. The results of a meta-analysis (Buddhavarapu et al., 2002) and a traditional review of the literature (Wilkinson, 1992) concluded that fixed shifts were superior to rotating shifts, especially for industrial workers.

Frequency of Rotation.   Although fixed shifts are better for individuals than rotating shifts, sometimes shifts must be rotated because employees who feel stuck on swing and night shifts insist on having the opportunity to workdays. In such situations, the frequency of the shift rotation must be considered. That is, should the rotation occur daily? Weekly? Monthly? The 2002 Shiftwork Practices Survey (Circadian Technologies, 2002) found that 47% of organizations that rotate shifts do so weekly, 15% rotate every two weeks, and 10% rotate monthly.

Meta-analysis results indicate that fixed shifts result in fewer sleep problems than rotating shifts and that slowly rotating shifts result in fewer sleep problems than do faster rotating shifts (Pilcher, Lambert, & Huffcutt, 2000). If shifts are to be rotated, the rotation should be clockwise (Circadian Technologies, 2002), with later starting times for the morning shift (Barton & Folkard, 1993; Knauth, 1996). Rest periods of at least two days between shift rotations can lessen the negative effects of the rotations (Totterdell, Spelten, Smith, Barton, & Folkard, 1995).

Individual Differences.   The final factor concerning the effects of shift work involves individual differences in employees. Obviously, not all employees will react to shift work in the same way because of the differences in their biological time clocks. In fact, we have all probably known people who claimed to be "night people" or to "prefer the morning." These individual differences in time preference are called *chronotypes*.

Several questionnaires have been developed to distinguish so-called morning people from evening people. Perhaps the best of these was developed by Smith, Reilly, and Midkiff (1988), which contains the 13 most reliable and valid questions from three other available scales (Reilly & Smith, 1988). Such a questionnaire can be used to select and place employees in their optimal shifts. Extraverts tend to be evening people more than do introverts (Schröeder, 2010). Men adapt to shift work better than do women, and shift work affects older workers more than younger workers (Oginska, Pokorski, & Oginski, 1993).

Moonlighting

Moonlighting Working more than one job.

As mentioned previously, one of the concerns with compressed workweeks is the possibility of employee fatigue. The same concern applies to employees working more than one job, or **moonlighting**. For example, an employee might work the day shift as a machine operator for Ford Motor Company and then work the night shift as a store clerk for a 7-Eleven convenience store. People typically moonlight because they want or need to earn extra money. Alboher (2007) distinguishes between moonlighters who work for extra money, and employees whom she refers to as having "slash" careers (e.g., attorney/landscaper). People with slash careers work a second job because they enjoy the second career rather than because they need extra money. Between 5% and 7% of U.S. employees work more than one job (Krell, 2010). Both moonlighting and slash employees raise concerns about the effects of extra work on performance and absenteeism for these employees' primary jobs.

Few studies have investigated the effects of moonlighting. Jamal (1981) and Jamal and Crawford (1984) surveyed more than 400 workers at six organizations and found that moonlighters were no different from non-moonlighters in terms of mental health, quality of life, job performance, and intention to leave their companies. But moonlighters did miss about one day more of work per year than did non-moonlighters.

Arcuri and Lester (1990), Miller and Sniderman (1974), and Mott, Mann, McLoughlin, and Warwick (1965) did not find any negative effects for moonlighting. In fact, Mott and colleagues found that moonlighters were better adjusted and more active in the community than were their non-moonlighting counterparts. Because there seem to be few negative effects to moonlighting, few organizations prohibit it. In fact, in most states it may be illegal to do so. Instead, most organizations have policies that prohibit moonlighting that might be a conflict of interest (e.g., working for a competitor), that uses company equipment in the outside job, or that requires performing outside jobs during company time.

Other Sources of Stress
Minor Frustration

Minor frustration is stress we encounter in our daily lives, and it might include irritations such as waiting in traffic or not being able to get some information from the library. Minor frustrations may try our patience, but in and of themselves they may not be a problem and usually last for only a short duration, such as an hour or a few hours. If we do not have a healthy outlet for our frustrations, they may build up over time until they control us. These short-term frustrations may then carry over to the next day and then the next, until finally they become long-term stressors.

Perspective taking Rating a potential stressor by asking how bad it really is compared with all things considered or with a worst-case scenario.

Minor frustrations can be managed through perspective taking. **Perspective taking** means rating the frustration on a scale of 1 to 10, with 10 meaning the situation is worthy of high levels of irritation. A friend of mine rates everything on a scale of life and death. He says that during potential stress-producing situations, he asks himself the following question: "How bad is this in relation to death?" Because he served in Vietnam, faced death often, and in fact saw many of his buddies killed, most of the situations he confronts get a very low rating. Consequently, he is basically a very peaceful and laid-back individual. Now, most of us can't relate to life's situations on that basis because we have never come close to experiencing death. But we can still ask ourselves: "In the scheme of things, just how important was that incident? Is it important enough for me to have a bad day, increase my chances of a heart attack, or die for?" See how perspective taking works? Making sure you don't make "mountains out of molehills" (an idiom referring to overreacting to a minor issue) can keep you from having to deal with the long-term effects of stress.

Forecasting

Forecasting Constant worrying about the future.

The stress from **forecasting** develops from our constantly worrying about the future and wasting time and energy on "What ifs?" This continuous fretting about things over which we may have no control (such as the end of the universe from aliens!) or that may never even happen can become very emotionally and physically draining, not to mention debilitating. Forecasting very quickly becomes long-term stress as we continue to keep our minds and bodies in a fearful and anxious state. Learning how to recognize those areas you can't control and ceasing to worry about them is the key to eliminating stress from forecasting.

Residual Stress

Residual stress is stress that is carried over from previous stressful situations that we refuse to "let go." Minor frustrations can become residual stress if we don't handle those daily problems effectively and rehash them over and over again. Many people continue to carry grudges, hurt, or anger from past situations that keep them in a constant state of stress. For example, have you ever been in a relationship that ended unexpectedly? If you didn't want the relationship to end, you may have been very hurt and then become angry. Now, every time you think of that situation, you get angry and hurt all over again. Many people continue to dredge up those bad feelings long after the relationship is over. All this does is recycle the stress process. Residual stress is almost always long term: If not dealt with, it chips away at our physical and emotional well-being until we become prisoners to its effects. This type of stress eventually leads individuals to therapy and counseling to learn positive ways, such as forgiveness, to cope with past negative experiences.

15-4 Consequences of Stress

Personal Consequences

How we respond to stress can have devastating consequences. For instance, responding with anger or rage can lead to family members being hurt, the loss of jobs, and perhaps trouble with the law. Responding with the use of alcohol and drugs can lead to addiction, broken relationships, and even death. Financially, the impaired decisions we make while under stress can have negative consequences. In an interesting study, Repetti and Wood (1997) examined the effects of work stress on the relationships between 30 working mothers and their preschool children. The results of the study indicated that on highly stressful workdays, mothers spoke less often to their children and had fewer expressions of affection.

As shown in Figure 15.6, there are numerous physical responses to stress. Some people sweat under extreme stress. For example, many people report that interviewing for a job is very stressful and causes them to sweat. Headaches and body aches are also symptoms of stress. If you are prone to migraines, you may find that your migraines occur more often during stressful situations. Body aches often are the result of tensing up during stressful times. Many people report that when they awake in the morning, their back, neck, shoulders, and legs are very sore, which can be attributed to tensing during sleep. Extreme physical responses to stress include hair loss. Although we are supposed to lose 50 to 100 strands of hair a day, which are replaced by new hair, hair that falls out in clumps is often your body's way of signaling high amounts of stress.

Stress has been labeled the "silent killer" because, as you have already read, it can quietly chip away at your immune system, thereby weakening your body's ability to prevent or fight off illnesses and diseases. It is often the source of escalating blood pressure, heart attacks, strokes, or worse: death. Stress may also increase the symptoms of rheumatoid arthritis because the hormones released in response to stress can cause swelling in the joints (Carpi, 1996). In fact, research suggests that 50% to 70% of all illnesses, such as coronary heart disease, can be attributed at least in part to stress. Even minor ailments such as recurring colds can be attributed to recent stressful events.

Depression is another health problem associated with stress. Most of us experience some form of depression from time to time. Usually, a good night's sleep or being with friends and family will lift that depression. Sometimes a few visits to

Stressors	Strains	Behaviors
Personal	**Psychological**	**Health**
Marital problems	Depression	Smoking
Family problems	Anxiety	Drinking
Health problems	Anger	Drug abuse
Financial problems	Sleep problems	
Daily hassles		**Work Related**
Residual stress	**Physical**	Absenteeism
	Illness	Turnover
Occupational	Cardiovascular problems	Lower productivity
Job Characteristics	Headaches	Workplace violence
Role conflict	Joint pain	
Role ambiguity		
Role overload		
Organizational Characteristics		
Person-organization fit		
Work environment		
Change		
Relations with others		
Coworker problems		
Supervisor problems		
Difficult and angry		
customers		
Lack of Empowerment		
Personality/Habits		
Type A		
Pessimism		
Tendency to forecast		
Diet		
Exercise		

Figure 15.6
The Stress Process

a counselor who can help us sort out our feelings and put things in perspective is helpful. Long-term stress, however, can eventually lead to clinical depression, which often requires medical treatment. In addition, prolonged depression is related to health problems such as hypertension (Meng, Chen, Yang, Sheng, & Hui, 2012). Early diagnosis and treatment of depression is the key to managing it. If you feel you are suffering from depression, you may want to consult the counseling center at your college. Or, if your town has a public mental health agency, contact them. Any visit you make to a counselor is confidential.

Organizational Consequences
Job Performance

Studies show that in general, high levels of stress reduce performance on many tasks. However, as mentioned earlier, a curvilinear relationship between stress and job performance may exist in that moderate stress levels actually improve productivity, increase energy levels, and heighten creativity (Muse et al., 2003).

Burnout

Burnout The psychological state of being overwhelmed with stress.

Burnout, the state of being overwhelmed by stress, is usually experienced by highly motivated professionals faced with high work demands. Initial studies on burnout targeted people in the health-care field as employees most likely to experience burnout. But over the years, the definition has expanded to include other types of workers who become emotionally exhausted and no longer feel they have a positive impact on

Table 15.5 Signs of Burnout

■ Less energy	■ Apathy
■ Lower productivity	■ Dread of coming to work
■ Consistently late for work	■ Feelings of little impact on coworkers or the organization
■ Complaining and negativity	■ Feeling overwhelmed
■ Decreased concentration	■ Tension and frustration
■ Forgetfulness	

other people or their job. People who feel burned out lack energy and are filled with frustration and tension. Emotional symptoms of burnout include a loss of interest in work, decreased work performance, feelings of helplessness, and trouble sleeping. As shown in Table 15.5, behavioral signs may include cynicism toward coworkers, clients, and the organization. People who are burned out display detachment toward the people (e.g., clients) with whom they work. Eventually, they may become depressed and respond to burnout through absenteeism, turnover, and lower performance (Parker & Kulik, 1995).

Absenteeism and Turnover

Absenteeism and turnover, resulting in loss of productivity and subsequently revenues, are highest during times of burnout and increased stress as employees struggle to deal with physical and emotional ailments. About 2.3% of the workforce is absent each day in the United States and 13% of absenteeism is attributed to stress (Commerce Clearing House, 2007). With this in mind, the question then becomes: Is this absenteeism due to illness brought about by stress or does it represent "mental health days," in which employees miss work to take a break from stress? From a study by Heaney and Clemans (1995), it appears that the stress–illness relationship best explains absenteeism. Such absenteeism costs employers billions of dollars a year in lost productivity and is thought to be a warning sign of intended turnover (Berry, Lelchook, & Clark, 2012).

Interestingly, even when employees take a "mental health day," the strategy apparently is not highly effective. In a study of hospital nurses, Hackett and Bycio (1996) found that stress was lowered immediately following a day of absence but that taking a day off had no longer-term effects.

Drug and Alcohol Misuse

Unfortunately, as stress levels rise and anger increases, often so does the misuse of drugs and alcohol. Most incidents of domestic and other types of violence occur after an individual has been drinking or using drugs. This doesn't excuse the violator's behavior, but it does indicate the relationship of drugs and alcohol to anger and rage. And there are an increasing number of news reports of violence occurring in the workplace. Of those violent events, many are carried out by employees who have misused drugs and alcohol.

Because of the increasing problems of drug and alcohol misuse in organizations, many companies have set up employment assistance programs (EAPs) to which they refer employees suspected of drug or alcohol misuse, as well as those who are depressed and experiencing other problems. EAPs use professional counselors to deal with employee problems. Some large companies have their own EAP counselors, but most use private agencies, which are often run through local hospitals.

Many organizations also offer stress management programs that help people learn how to cope with stress. Having such organizational programs that can be used as a positive outlet for stress and the problems that come from it can often be beneficial to employees' regaining control over their lives.

Because many of our behavioral responses to stress are learned, the negative ones can be unlearned. Stress management teaches us positive and healthy behavioral responses. The key is to acknowledge the occasions on which you use destructive methods and take measures to correct them. If you don't, you won't like the consequences that result from improperly managed stress.

As organizations recognize the consequences of stress, they are beginning to take better precautions against it. For example, free voluntary counseling is made available by many organizations to all employees exhibiting emotional or discipline problems and particularly to those who have been terminated or laid off.

Health-Care Costs

One other organizational, as well as personal, consequence of stress is an increase in health insurance premiums. Because of the high use of medical facilities and options by others suffering from illnesses caused by stress, organizations that at one time paid the full cost for health insurance benefits are passing the increases on to the employees. This additional financial burden to some employees can be a new source of stress! The answer is to reduce the number of ailments causing stress, thereby decreasing the need to seek medical attention.

15-5 Managing Stress

Managing stress, or better yet, changing your behavior to healthfully respond to stress, should occur before, during, and after stress (Tyler, 2003). Managing stress before it happens means incorporating daily practices (e.g., exercise) that will prepare your mind and body to handle the effects of stress. During stress you should continue with your prestress management techniques (such as reducing caffeine), as well as incorporate some others. Finally, after the stressor is eliminated (if that's even possible!), continue to proactively manage your stress. In addition, there are some other things you should consider. Let's examine some techniques for before, during, and after stress.

Planning for Stress

Some of the techniques that are suggested to proactively reduce stress should also be considered during times you are actually engaged in stress. These are discussed in the following sections.

Exercise

Exercising not only keeps your heart strong and resistant to the effects of stress but can also help reduce your stress levels during particular stressful moments. It is a good idea to incorporate some kind of exercise program into your life at least three or four times a week for 20 minutes. You can reap great benefits from walking, swimming, running, playing sports, or climbing stairs because these strengthen your cardiovascular system, thereby making you more resistant to the effects of stress. Even such household chores as mowing the lawn, vacuuming, or washing your car can help your cardiovascular system. The good news is that not all exercise has to be strenuous. Certain good prestress relaxation techniques (explained later in this section) can be used during and after stress.

To begin an exercise program, start with "baby steps." For instance, instead of taking the elevator at work or school, walk up the stairs. Or consider this: Stop driving around the mall parking lot 20 times looking for the perfect parking spot! Instead, make a conscious effort to park farther away and walk the distance. At work, Hasson and Butler (2020) provide the following additional "baby steps":

- Walk to talk to someone instead of calling, emailing, or texting.
- Organize walking meetings in which you can walk while you talk.
- Stand-up and stretch while on the phone or reading.
- Drink more water, but don't keep the water bottle or your snacks at your desk. Instead, put them somewhere where you have to stand up and walk to get them.

From these baby steps, make the transition into a more serious exercise routine. Just remember to pick a program that works for you, which might not be the one your friends use. If you don't like running, don't do it. There is no need to add to your stress by choosing exercises that you absolutely can't tolerate. As a good example, many of my graduate students lift weights to reduce stress. They have repeatedly asked me to join them, but I decline because I know that their plan of "We're going to work on abs for an hour this morning and then shoulders for an hour this evening" involves more time than is practical for my Type A personality. Instead, I stick to the trusty Bullworker I purchased in the 1970s (they actually still make the Bullworker—a piece of isometric exercise equipment).

Organizations realize how important exercise is to managing the effects of stress, as evidenced by the increase in work-site fitness and health programs over the past 15 years. According to the president of SHRM, 58% of surveyed organizations offered a general wellness program in 2018 (Taylor, 2021). Research shows that exercise can reduce coronary heart disease by reducing blood pressure and lowering cholesterol (Pattyn, Cornelissen, Eshghi, & Vanhess, 2013). In addition, meta-analysis results indicate that employee wellness programs, which often include exercise, result in lower levels of absenteeism and perhaps higher levels of performance (DeGroot & Kiker, 2003).

A good example of the effectiveness of wellness programs can be found at the Emergency Medical Services (EMS) in Catawba County, North Carolina. Prior to initiation of its wellness program, the EMS was losing an average of two paramedics a year to work-related injuries. To increase wellness, the EMS conducted medical screenings and offered memberships to a local gym. After one year, absenteeism dropped from an average of 78 hours per employee to 57 hours; two employees quit smoking; and 47% of the employees lost body fat (Bradley, 2004).

Laughter

Humor has been shown to buffer stress in several ways (Deshpande, 2012; Singer, 2000). First, it can help you put a new perspective on a stressful situation. You have probably heard many jokes about death—many of which are told by police officers, doctors, and morticians! The purpose of such jokes is not to hurt feelings or show callousness but to better deal with an uncomfortable topic that we all must face sooner or later. It is better to laugh at it than to dwell over what we can't control. But be careful when telling such jokes: Not everyone will appreciate the humor, and a little sensitivity and common sense should be exercised before sharing it.

Second, when you are upset and in what seems to be a difficult situation, going to a funny movie, listening to a comedian, or watching a funny television show can help distance you from the situation until you have calmed down enough to begin thinking rationally again.

Physically, laughter can reduce your blood pressure. Studies show that laughing through a funny movie can increase cardiovascular health (Sugawara, Tarumi, & Tanaka, 2010). So next time you have the opportunity to go to a funny movie, go! Or, if you have a favorite comedy show that comes on more than once a week, try to watch as many episodes as possible (but don't forget to study for this class).

Though much has been written about the potential stress reduction benefits of humor, a qualitative literature review by Martin (2001) suggests that more research is needed to determine whether humor is as useful as thought to be. Martin's review does not conclude that humor is not useful, but instead concludes that the jury is still out.

Diet

Foods that have been shown to counteract the effects of stress include fresh fruits and vegetables, whole grains, and nonfat yogurt, which contains the B vitamin considered to be lost during high-stress periods of time (Posner & Hlivka, 2009). A daily dose of one or more of these can help you meet stress head-on! To help reduce the effects of stress, many organizations are including healthier items in their vending machines.

A popular experiment conducted by Google successfully demonstrated how to promote a healthy diet among its employees (Black, 2020). The company completely redesigned its foodscape, including placing fresh fruits and vegetables first in the buffet line, increasing the distance between the coffee machines and the snack table, and keeping sugary drinks behind frosted glass to avoid tempting its employees. This led to many impressive results, such as an increase from 0 to 2,300 breakfast salads being served within two years.

Drinking water helps keep your body hydrated and able to cope with daily stressors (maybe all that running to the bathroom is an added bonus to reducing stress and keeping you fit!). Caffeine use should be gradually reduced. Be aware of just how much caffeine you are getting. You may be getting more than you think. It's not just cola and coffee products that contain caffeine; chocolate and many types of medicines and other foods have caffeine as well. If you decide to reduce caffeine from your diet, do it gradually. Most people who are used to large amounts of daily caffeine experience withdrawal symptoms such as nausea, severe headaches, and fatigue if they go "cold turkey."

Smoking Reduction

Though many smokers say smoking decreases their feelings of stress, research indicates that smoking increases the physiological characteristics associated with stress (Kassel, Stroud, & Paronis, 2003). This is an important finding because research also indicates that smokers increase their smoking when they feel stressed (McCann & Lester, 1996). Thus, smoking and stress become a vicious cycle in which people smoke because they are stressed and then become more stressed because they smoke.

Sleep

There is no one study that says absolutely just how much individuals need to sleep. What studies show is that sleep deprivation or lack of sleep can cause negative behavior such as irritability, fatigue, lack of concentration, and even depression.

Alcohol can severely affect your sleep, although it may seem that it helps you go to sleep. Studies show that the sleep of people who have had as little as two drinks before bed is interrupted several times a night. In addition, stay away from caffeine at least six hours before going to bed.

Support Network

Studies show that people who have someone to talk to, such as a family member or a friend, are better able to manage their stress. You may have already experienced this. When you feel you aren't doing well in class, do you talk to someone about your feelings? Do you feel better afterward? Sometimes talking to someone we trust helps put things in perspective. So if you don't have a good support system, seek one out. This may mean joining certain college groups where you can meet people. Attend campus lectures where meeting friends is possible. And for extreme situations, familiarize yourself with the type of professional help that is available on or off campus that can give you the support you need during stressful times.

Self-Empowerment

In Chapter 14, you learned about empowerment. Most of the literature on empowerment is approached from an organizational, managerial perspective. That is, the literature explains how management can empower employees by giving them more control over important decisions that affect their lives. This has become important to organizations because research suggests that not having input into matters that affect us can be a big source of stress.

What most of the literature doesn't discuss is how employees can and need to learn to empower themselves. Ninety percent of workers think employers must act to reduce stress. But because employees cannot control what organizations do, it is more important for them to find their own ways to reduce stress. This is another form of self-empowerment. In addition, instead of complaining about how they don't get to participate in organizational decision making, employees need to take the initiative to volunteer to participate in committees or in group projects; this is one way to take back some control they perceive they have lost.

Individuals can also empower themselves in their personal lives. Instead of playing the victim who believes that life has singled them out to play dirty tricks on, individuals must learn to find ways to gain control over those situations they can control. This means taking an active role in finding out why something didn't turn out the way they wanted and making changes to prevent the event from occurring again. Chronic complaining about how everyone mistreats you is, to most people, a behavioral response to what is perceived as lack of control in your life. Most victimization is from learned behavior that we see modeled by family members, friends, coworkers, and even people we don't know, such as those in the news. To break that behavior, attending workshops on assertiveness and decision making can be beneficial. These types of workshops are usually offered through colleges, churches, and community groups. If you are interested in attending such training, check with your university to see what may be available.

Coping Skills

Improving your coping skills often means learning how to deal with conflict. It also means learning how to accept what you can't change. I often tell workers who participate in stress management classes that they can't change the fact that their organizations are downsizing or that restructuring is the trend for today's companies. Spending energy and time worrying about it or being angry is a waste of time. The best solution for them is to find areas that they can control to meet organizational change. This includes returning to college or taking technical training to make themselves marketable should they be laid off.

This is good advice for you as a college student as well. Worrying about whether you will graduate with a 4.0 GPA is both emotionally and physically stressful. Though setting a goal of high achievement is admirable, worrying about it for the entire four years you are in college is unproductive. Check out the Career Workshop Box for a summary of relaxation strategies.

15-6 Stress Reduction Interventions Related to Life/Work Issues

As shown in Table 15.6, due to the combination of an increasing number of dual-income and single-parent families, a tight job market, and a trend toward longer workdays, many organizations have made efforts to ensure that their employees maintain a balance between work and private life. Such efforts are important, as research suggests that employees with work–family conflicts are several times more likely to develop mood, anxiety, and substance-misuse disorders than are employees without such conflicts (Frone, 2000). Though organizational efforts to reduce private life–work conflicts are designed to help employees reduce their stress levels and thus increase their mental and physical health, they are also motivated by the fact that employees with such outside concerns as child-care and care for older adults are more prone to miss work and are less productive than employees without such concerns. Meta-analysis results suggest that employers who have work–family support policies will have employees that are more satisfied, more committed to the organization, and less likely to leave than organizations that do not have such policies (Butts, Casper, & Yang, 2013).

Easing the Child-Care Burden

On-site child-care facility A child-care center that is located on the site of the organization employing the parent.

Data from the Bureau of Labor Statistics (BLS) indicate that more than 40% of employees in the labor force have children under the age of 18 and thus have a variety of child-care needs. To help employees meet these needs, an increasing number of organizations have become involved with child-care issues. This increase is due in part to research demonstrating that the lack of regular child-care options causes employees with children to miss an additional eight days of work per year and costs an organization with 250 employees an average of $75,000 per year in lost work time (Reed & Clark, 2004; Woodward, 1999). Organizational child-care programs usually fall into one of three categories: on-site care, voucher systems, and referral services. In the first category, organizations such as Aflac Insurance, Discovery Communications, SAS Institute, and Meridian Health built **on-site child-care facilities**. In the United States, less than 1% of organizations have on-site child-care centers, 4% subsidize off-site programs, 25% allow employees to bring a sick child to work, and 11% offer a child-care referral service (SHRM, 2019). Although less than 1% of U.S. companies have on-site child-care centers, almost one-third of the companies in *Money* magazine's Top 100 Companies to Work For had on-site child-care centers in 2012.

Some organizations fully fund the cost of child-care, whereas others charge the employee the "going rate." There are advantages to both the employee and the organization that pays the full cost of a child enrolled in its facility. For example, the child-care cost can be used as a benefit, meaning that neither the employee nor the organization will have to pay taxes on the amount. Of course, tax laws may eventually change the situation, but until that time, calculating child-care as an employee benefit is financially rewarding for both the employee and the organization.

Although the employee response to such on-site programs has been overwhelmingly positive, on-site centers are expensive to start to maintain. Because of such high costs, it is important to determine whether these centers "pay off" by reducing such problems as employee turnover and absenteeism. According to Scarr (1998), secure child-care results in reduced levels of absenteeism and tardiness. Positive evidence has been provided from six sources:

- Intermedics, in Freeport, Texas, reported a 23% decrease in turnover and absenteeism.
- Prudential Insurance in Newark, New Jersey, reported $80,000 in annual savings due to their child-care center.
- Bristol-Myers Squibb found that users of its on-site child-care center had fewer intentions to leave the company than did other employees.
- Banc One Corporation in Chicago found that users of on-site child-care centers had seven fewer days of absenteeism than nonusers.
- Scott and Markham (1982) reported an average decrease of 19% in absenteeism for organizations that established on-site centers.
- Tioga Sportswear in Fall River, Massachusetts, found a 50% decrease in turnover.

As one can imagine, it is difficult to conduct a well-controlled study on the effects of on-site child-care centers, as researchers need measures of absenteeism, turnover, and so on before and after the implementation of the child-care center, as well as a control group with which to compare users of the child-care center. Unfortunately, there have been few such studies. Even more unfortunate is that these few studies suggest that on-site child-care centers do not reduce absenteeism or increase performance (e.g., Goff, Mount, & Jamison, 1990; Miller, 1984).

A second avenue that can be taken with child-care, one that is especially popular in the United Kingdom, is to provide employees with *vouchers* to be used with private day-care centers. From the perspective of the organization, **voucher systems** alleviate both the high start-up costs and the high costs of liability insurance associated with on-site centers. From an employee's perspective, this approach reduces the cost of private child-care.

Unfortunately, there are several reasons this approach probably does not reduce employee turnover or absenteeism. First, an employee must still leave work to visit a sick child or to attend parent conferences. Although the Family and Medical Leave Act (FMLA) discussed in Chapter 3 allows an employee to take up to 12 weeks of unpaid leave to care for a sick family member, employees who leave work to care for their families leave a void that organizations may find difficult to fill. Furthermore, because only 24% of organizations provide paid family leave (SHRM, 2019), the financial loss to the employee can create tremendous stress and hardship. A second reason off-site

Voucher system Child-care policy in which an organization pays all or some of its employees' child-care costs at private child-care centers by providing the employees with vouchers.

In this chapter you learned that stress can have many negative effects. Following are some tips for dealing with stress.

Use Relaxation Techniques

Abdominal breathing is especially helpful for emotional calming. This requires that you get into a comfortable position, either sitting or lying on your back. Close your eyes and place your left hand on your abdomen and your right hand on your chest. Breathe normally, mentally counting from 1 to 4 as you inhale through your nose. Pause for two counts. Then open your mouth and mentally count from 1 to 6 as you exhale through your mouth. After several minutes of slow, rhythmic breathing, let your hands slowly move to your sides as your abdomen continues to move freely in and out with each breath. When you are finished, open your eyes and sit quietly.

Progressive muscle relaxation is used to relax the body. In a sitting or prone position, close your eyes and tense the following muscle groups: hands and arms, face, neck and shoulders, stomach and abdomen, buttocks and thighs, calves, and feet. Tense each group separately for a few seconds while breathing normally. Slowly release the tension as you focus on the pleasant contrast between tight and relaxed muscles.

Meditation is helpful for quieting a chaotic mind. Sit in a comfortable position and close your eyes. Breathe slowly from the abdomen. Focus your mind on a single word (e.g., *calm*), phrase ("*peace, love, joy*"), or sound ("*ooommm*"). Mentally repeat the chosen sound over and over. Adopt a passive attitude toward the process. When intruding thoughts occur, as they will, slowly and gently redirect your mind back to your repetitive sound. After 15 to 20 minutes, slowly open your eyes.

Your local library or hospital has additional information about relaxation methods. This is a good place to begin if you are interested in finding out more.

Engage in Time Management

Because a general feeling of being out of time can be a big source of stress, using time-management techniques before and during stress can be helpful (Jex & Elacqua, 1999). Here is a small sample of the many time-management techniques suggested by Mayer (1990):

- Take several hours to clean your desk. I have a ritual in which at the end of the semester, I take almost a full day to clean my desk and office. For the two or three weeks that they stay uncluttered, I feel much more relaxed—as do the visitors to my office.
- Place a dollar amount on your time and then determine if any activity is worth the money. For example, if you value your time at $100 per hour and you spend 30 minutes each morning gossiping with a coworker, ask yourself, "Was the conversation worth $50?" If the answer is no, the conversation was a time waster.
- Make "to-do" lists, and cross out tasks once they have been accomplished.
- Keep a daily time log in which you schedule your appointments, even appointments for yourself. For example, you might schedule 10:00 a.m. to 11:00 a.m. to return phone calls or to read your mail. Treat these self-appointments as you would any other meeting, and don't let people interrupt you.
- To avoid waiting in line, do things at times when nobody else is doing them. For example, eat lunch at 11:00 a.m. rather than noon, go to the bank in the middle of the week rather than on Friday, or do your grocery shopping in the evening rather than right after work or on Saturday morning.

Though many of these suggestions seem reasonable, the empirical literature is unclear regarding the actual stress-reduction benefits of such time-management techniques as making lists (Adams & Jex, 1999).

---

child-care facilities aren't optimal is that most private child-care centers operate from 7:00 a.m. to 6:00 p.m. Thus, employees who work swing or night shifts are not helped. Finally, there is a shortage of quality child-care in many areas. Some corporations, such as the Fayetteville, Arkansas, branch of Levi Strauss, donate large sums of money to local child-care centers to expand hours or services. Others, such as Time Warner and SunTrust Bank, contract with outside vendors to provide emergency child-care services for children who are ill. Because it can be difficult to find child-care centers

Table 15.6   Percentage of Employers Offering Stress-Reducing Practices

Stress-Reducing Practice	2019 SHRM Survey
Provide alternative work schedules	
Telecommuting of any type	69
Flextime	57
Compressed workweek	32
Four-day workweek	15
Assist with child-care	
On-site lactation room	51
Allow employee to bring child to work during emergencies	25
Provide a child-care referral service	11
Subsidize cost of child-care	4
Assist with elder care	
Provide an elder-care referral service	10
Provide emergency elder care	<1
Increase employee wellness	
Provide wellness information	64
Provide health screening program	43
Offer a smoking cessation program	39
Subsidize fitness center dues	32
Offer a weight-loss program	29
Provide on-site fitness center	29
Offer a stress-reduction program	13
On-site nap room	4
Assist with daily chores	
Legal assistance	32
Provide dry-cleaning service	7

Source: Society for Human Resource Management (SHRM) 2019 Benefits Survey.

that will take sick children, employers such as the Principal Financial Group in Des Moines, Iowa, have contracted with local health-care agencies to provide in-home care for their employees' sick children. Twenty-five percent of organizations allow their employees to bring their children to work in emergency situations in which child-care is not available (SHRM, 2019).

Referral service A system of child-care in which an employer maintains a list of certified child-care centers that can be used by its employees.

The final avenue taken by organizations is to provide a **referral service** to quality child-care centers. This approach has been taken by both IBM and Digital Corporation. Although this is certainly a useful service, nothing about it would suggest that it would reduce either absenteeism or turnover.

Hallmark Cards, Inc. is an excellent example of a company with progressive child-care and family benefits. Hallmark allows employees to take six months of unpaid maternity and paternity leave, reimburses employees up to $5,000 for the cost of adopting a child, helps employees locate care for children and aged parents, provides care for mildly ill children, holds parenting seminars, and provides alternative care arrangements for children out of school during holidays, inclement weather, or teacher workdays.

Easing the Care of the Older Population Burden

In 2019, 16.5% of the people in the United States were 65 or older, a percentage that is projected to increase to 22% by 2050. As the number of older individuals increases, so too does the need for care for the older adults. According to the 2013 American Time Use Survey, more than 40 million adults are providing unpaid care to an older relative; 64% of the people providing care for an older adult also work full- or part-time jobs, and 41% also care for children (O'Toole & Ferry, 2002). According to statistics generated by the National Council on Aging, 50% of employees taking care of an older relative were absent from work, arrived at work late, or left work early to care for the relative. Six percent quit working to spend the necessary care time for the older adult. Given the negative impact on emotional health of working and providing elder care (Lee, Walker, & Shoup, 2001), such statistics are not surprising.

In spite of the great demand for care for older adults, organizational efforts on this front have lagged behind child-care efforts. According to a survey by the Society for Human Resource Management (SHRM, 2019), only 10% of organizations provide referral services for care for older adults, and a less than 1% offer a company-sponsored or on-site care facility. The most common care programs provided by employers include flexible work schedules, resource and referral programs, long-term care insurance, expanded FMLA benefits, flexible spending and dependent care accounts, adult day care, seminars, and support groups. Such companies as AstraZeneca, Freddie Mac, Raytheon, Nike, and Intel offer seminars to employees to teach them how to care for their older relatives as well as deal with the stress that goes with such care. The Federal National Mortgage Association, or "Fannie Mae," is an excellent example of an employer that understands the potential crisis surrounding care for the older population. After a survey of its employees revealed that 70% expected to take on responsibilities for caring for the older population within five years, Fannie Mae hired a licensed clinical social worker to help employees coordinate this care. Fannie Mae estimates that it saves $1.50 in absenteeism and turnover costs for every $1.00 it spent on its care for older adults. Most important, 28% of the employees said that they would have quit their jobs had they not had the company-provided help (Wells, 2000).

Easing the Daily-Chore Burden

With work, child-care, and older adult-care responsibilities, many employees find it increasingly difficult to complete such basic chores as going to the dentist, getting the car inspected, and picking up dry cleaning. As a result, organizations have implemented a variety of strategies to ease this burden. Popular among these are increasing the use of flexible working hours, increasing the number of paid personal days off, and providing essential services on-site.

By providing essential services on site, employers assume that employees will work more hours because they will not have to take time away from work to complete common chores. For example, Analytical Graphics of Exton, Pennsylvania, provides its employees with free on-site breakfasts, lunches, and dinners so that employees don't have to leave the building to eat. Not only do employees feel appreciated and save money, but the company also gets an additional 30 to 45 minutes of work out of them each day because they can eat while they work.

Providing Rest Through Paid Time Off

Working long hours is a major factor in employee stress, as a 2013 survey by the Families and Work Institute found that one-third of U.S. employees feel that they are overworked and 54% indicated that they were overwhelmed at least once in the past month. These long hours are compounded by the fact that, according to a 2012 survey by Right Management, 28% of employees rarely take time off for lunch and another 39% eat lunch at their desks. A 2019 survey by Allianz Global Assistance found that 51% of people in the United States had not taken a vacation in the past year. Likewise, a 2013 survey by the American Psychological Association (APA) found that 44% of employees check their work email and phone messages while on vacation.

To help employees balance life and work, the majority of employers provide paid time off, usually in the form of vacations, holidays, sick days, and rest periods. The amount of paid time off varies across organizations, and some organizations do not provide any paid vacation days for hourly employees. In contrast to the United States, where organizations are not legally mandated to provide paid vacations, many countries do. For example, the legal minimum number of vacation days is 25 in Austria, Sweden, and France; 20 in Australia, Iraq, Ireland, Italy, and the United Kingdom; and 10 in Canada, Jamaica, and Japan. The country with the highest minimum number of vacation days is Andorra with 31 days for all employees along with an additional 11 public holidays. In Luxembourg, public employees younger than 50 get 32 days of vacation, employees aged 50–54 get 34 days, and employees 55 or older get 36 days. Russia is complicated in that most employees receive a minimum of 28 days of vacation but employees in the north territories receive 52 days of vacation.

In addition to paid vacation days, most countries also have legally required paid public holidays. These paid holidays range from a low of 3 in Chad and 5 in Uruguay to a high of 27 in Cambodia and Iran. Although many organizations in the United States provide paid national holidays (e.g., Memorial Day, Labor Day), they are not required by law to do so.

To reduce stress and establish a good work-life balance, Hasson and Butler (2020) advise employees, when possible, to:

- Set a firm cutoff time to leave work. Schedule activities (e.g., cook dinner, exercise) right after work that provides an incentive to leave work on time.
- Take a break for lunch and get away from your desk.
- Disconnect from work when you get home. Leave your phone and laptop for several hours.
- Set boundaries. Let others know that you don't do business calls or regularly check your mail in the evening, on weekends, or when you are on vacation.
- Use all of your vacation days.

Organizations are also increasingly offering unlimited paid time off as another method of managing employee stress and attracting talent. This strategy has been received positively as demonstrated by a 2019 MetLife study, which revealed that 72% of surveyed employees were interested in receiving unlimited paid time off (Metlife, 2019). However, while unlimited paid time off may seem attractive, it comes with understandable concerns, such as overuse and more surprisingly, underuse. Experts emphasize that the ideal strategy to implement unlimited paid time off is to have senior employees model taking time off, as well as establishing a set minimum hours of required paid time off (Sammer, 2021).

15-7 Measuring Stress

In this chapter we discussed many causes and consequences of stress. A logical question, then, is how do we know when a person is stressed? In research, the most common measures of stress are self-report questionnaires in which people are asked a series of questions about their current level of stress. Commonly used measures of work-related stress and strain include the Occupational Stress Inventory, Job Stress Inventory, Maslach Burnout Inventory, Interpersonal Conflict at Work Scale, Organizational Constraints Scale, Quantitative Workload Inventory, and Physical Symptoms Inventory. Examples of questions found in stress questionnaires can be found in Table 15.7.

The problem with self-reports, of course, is that people may not know they are stressed or may not be truthful in their answers. So, in addition to self-report inventories, physiological and biochemical measures of stress can be used. Physiological measures include blood pressure, perspiration, heart rate, and muscle tension, and biochemical measures include cortisol and catecholamine levels (Sulsky & Smith, 2005).

15-8 Workplace Violence

The issue of workplace violence has received considerable interest from psychologists and HR professionals. In part this interest has been spurred by statistics such as these:

- In 2019, 454 employees were murdered at work in the United States (Lebron, 2021).
- In 2019, 20,974 employees in the United States were injured in workplace violence. This is an increase from 11,690 in 2011 (Lebron, 2021).
- In 2019, 8.5% of fatal workplace injuries in the United States were the result of homicide.
- In 2019, 20,870 employees were injured as a result of workplace violence.
- Twenty-five percent of workers in the United Kingdom were victims of some form of bullying at work in the past five years.

Table 15.7 Examples of Questions on Self-Reported Stress Questionnaires

- Do you frequently get angry or irritable?
- Do you take on too many responsibilities at work?
- I have trouble sleeping at night (true/false).
- I feel tense and on edge (true/false).
- Are you sad a lot and don't know why?
- Are you more forgetful (missing appointments, losing things)?
- I have to make important snap judgments and decisions (true/false).
- I am not consulted about what happens on my job (true/false).

Though the issue of workplace violence has received considerable interest, the number of workplace homicides had declined steadily from 1,080 in 1994 to a low of 404 in 2013, but increased to 453 in 2018 and 454 in 2019. From 2010–2019, 9.3% of workplace fatalities were the result of homicide compared to 16% in the 1990s.

Though more than 86% of homicide victims at work in 2019 were men, homicide was only the fifth most common cause of fatal workplace injuries among men (traffic accidents, falls, contact with objects, and exposure to harmful substances are the first four), but was the second most common cause of fatal workplace injuries among women (traffic accidents were the most common). The gender differences in workplace violence can be explained by the fact that men traditionally work in higher-risk occupations such as mining that have high levels of fatalities caused by such other means as driving and construction accidents.

Though these figures are certainly attention getting, from an HR perspective they can be misleading, as a relatively small portion of the homicides are committed by current or former employees. Incidents of workplace violence can be placed into one of four categories. The first category, representing the majority of job-related homicides, is violence against an employee occurring as a result of a *crime* being committed. The most common examples are employees assaulted during the commission of a robbery. Work situations that pose greater risk of this type of workplace violence include

- jobs that involve the exchange of money;
- jobs involved in the delivery of passengers or goods;
- working late at night;
- working alone;
- working in high-crime areas; and
- working is health-care settings.

In 2018, the occupations with the most workplace homicides were:

- Restaurants and bars (60)
- Law enforcement (51)
- Gas stations (35)
- Grocery and convenience stores (23)
- Health care (22)
- Security guards (18)
- Taxi drivers (14)
- Landlords (10)

The second category is violence against an employee perpetrated by a customer or client. For example, in 2021, an angry customer attacked an employee at a Los Angeles area McDonalds's restaurant. After the attack, the employees went on strike, asking for more security as the restaurant employees called 911 an average of once every four days due to attacks by customers or other individuals (Meisenzahl, 2021).

The third category is violence against an employee or supervisor as an act of *anger or vengeance* by another employee. It is this category of violence that most involves HR professionals and has captured the imagination of the public.

Employee violence against other employees is usually the result of interpersonal disagreements. For example, in 2011, an employee of Fast Cuts Barber Shop in Miami, Florida killed a coworker following an argument at work. In another 2011 shooting at a barbershop, a former employee of Belle View Barber Shop in Alexandria, Virginia, killed a former coworker with whom he had been arguing when he was employed.

However, coworkers can be assaulted when employees take out their anger against a supervisor. Thirteen percent of workplace-violence incidents involve employees seeking revenge against a supervisor as a result of being fired, laid off, or subjected to some form of negative personnel action. Here are some examples:

- In 2021, a disgruntled employee of the Santa Clara Valley Transportation Authority in San Jose, California fatally shot nine coworkers as they were changing shifts. The shooter, Samuel James Cassidy, was unhappy because he felt that his work assignments were unfair.
- An employee at the Connecticut State Lottery was upset with his supervisors for "not listening to him," and the employee killed four coworkers before killing himself. Suicide is done by 36% of employees committing workplace violence.
- A Tulsa, Oklahoma, Wendy's employee, angry because his boss asked him to start work early, fired 12 shots from a .380-caliber handgun, wounding his supervisor and five other employees.
- Gregory Gray, a former case manager for Conrad House Community Services in San Francisco, killed a former coworker because he was angry about being fired. Gray brought a handgun, shotgun, and ax to his former place of employment, and had his handgun not jammed, more people would have been killed.
- After receiving notice that he would be fired, Nathaniel Brown, a janitor at Ohio State University, killed a supervisor and wounded another before fatally shooting himself.
- Omar Thornton killed eight employees and then himself after he left a disciplinary hearing in which he was accused of stealing beer from his employer, Hartford Distributors in Connecticut.
- After being suspended from her job at Kraft Foods in Philadelphia, Yvonne Hiller returned to work and killed two employees and wounded another.

The fourth category is violence against an employee by a person who does not work at the place of employment but has a personal relationship with one or more of the employees. For example, in 2021, a 38-year-old server at a Bob Evans restaurant in Canton, Ohio, in the United States, was fatally shot by an ex-boyfriend who had a criminal record, including convictions for domestic violence (Krane, 2021).

Psychologists have expanded their studies of workplace violence to include behaviors referred to as *mobbing* and *bullying*. Mobbing and bullying consist of hostile, alienating, and unethical behavior among employees. Bullying is defined as "offensive, intimidating, malicious or insulting behavior, an abuse or misuse of power through means that undermine, humiliate, denigrate or injure the recipient" (Hasson & Butler, 2020). Examples of such behavior include intimidating a person, excluding or isolating someone socially, spreading malicious gossip that is not true, yelling at a person, using profanity, and belittling a person's opinions or work. This expanded definition of workplace violence has been adopted by the Canadian Centre for Occupational Health and Safety, whose definition of workplace violence includes the following actions:

- Threatening behavior
- Physical attacks
- Verbal abuse
- Verbal or written threats
- Harassment (any behavior that demeans, embarrasses, humiliates, annoys, alarms, or verbally abuses a person)

A 2021 survey by the Workplace Bullying Institute found that workplace bullying is common in the United States (Namie, 2021):

- 30% of employees report currently being bullied or had been bullied in the past.
- 19% of employees reported that although they had not been bullied, they had witnessed it the workplace.
- Most of the bullies are men (67%) as are most of the targets of bullies (51%). Men are more likely to bully other men and women are more likely to bully other women.
- Hispanic or Latinx employees (35.5%) were most likely to report having been bullied followed by White employees (30.1%), Black employees (26.3%), and Asian employees (11.7%).
- Most employees were bullied by a person of a higher rank (65%), followed by coworkers/peers (21%) and employees of a lower rank (14%).
- Remote workers were more likely to get bullied (43.2%) than workers who never worked remotely (20.6%). Of those bullied, 50% were bullied in virtual meetings and 9% in email.

Surveys in countries such as Australia, Canada, India, Japan, and the United Kingdom indicate that workplace bullying is not a problem limited to the United States.

Perpetrators of Workplace Violence

Though many types of people commit workplace violence, the typical *employee* who engages in workplace violence in the United States (Glotz & Ruotolo, 2006; Turner & Gelles, 2003) has the following profile:

- Is a man (80%) between the ages of 20 and 50 (usually in their 40s)
- Has their self-esteem tied to their job and perceives that they have been disrespected or unfairly treated
- Feels that they have no other way of resolving this mistreatment other than violence
- Has demonstrated a recent pattern of problems at work (increased absenteeism, violations of company policy, verbal threats to coworkers, decreased attention to appearance and personal hygiene)
- Has tried to get others to take their dilemma seriously by threatening, harassing, intimidating, yelling, and threatening to file grievances and lawsuits
- Has begun showing signs of paranoid thinking, delusions of persecution, and other bizarre thought patterns
- Has become isolated and withdrawn
- Has ready access to guns

Reducing Workplace Violence

Acts of workplace violence cannot completely be eliminated, but they can be reduced through security measures, employee screening, and management awareness.

Security Measures

Increased security measures can decrease the probability of workplace violence (Fowler, 2013). These measures can include such physical changes as adding surveillance cameras, silent alarms, bright external lighting, bulletproof barriers, sophisticated lock systems, and security guards; making high-risk areas more visible; and using drop safes and posting signs stating that only limited cash is kept on the premises. Staffing changes can include increasing the number of staff on duty; closing during the higher-risk late night and early hours of the morning; and training employees in how to deal with robberies, conflicts, and angry customers.

Employee Screening

Though the security measures mentioned here are aimed primarily at reducing workplace violence resulting from other crimes such as robbery, they can also aid in reducing violence caused by current and former employees. Another method of reducing violence committed by current and former employees is to use psychological tests, reference checks, and background checks to screen applicants for violence potential.

Background and reference checks can provide information about an applicant's history of violence. These checks are important because employees who engage in workplace violence are chronically disgruntled, have a history of causing trouble, and frequently change jobs. Dietz (1994) provides two interesting examples. An applicant at a California maintenance company was hired despite a history of domestic violence and burglary convictions. He later set fire to a bookkeeper who wouldn't give him his paycheck. Another organization was sued because an employee who had killed a coworker was rehired by the same company in an effort to employ ex-cons. After a short period on the job, the employee killed another coworker.

It is important to note that ex-cons cannot categorically be denied employment. An organization must take into account the length of time that has passed since the crime was committed, the seriousness of the crime, and the relevance of the crime to the job in question.

Psychological tests such as the Minnesota Multiphasic Personality Inventory (MMPI-2) and a variety of integrity tests discussed in Chapter 5 can potentially predict violence in people without a history of violence. However, an empirical link between scores on these tests and workplace violence has yet to be made (Tonowski, 1993), in part because the violent event being predicted usually occurs many years after the preemployment testing. Furthermore, incidents of workplace violence are an interaction between a high-risk employee, an organization with poor management for which the employee works, and a stressful event attributed by the employee to the organization (Habeeb & Prencipe, 2001). Thus, a high-risk employee will be violent only under certain circumstances, which constantly change and are difficult to measure. Testing for high-risk employees is made even more difficult because the Americans with Disabilities Act provides limitations to the use of tests designed to determine psychological problems.

Management Awareness

Workplace violence can be greatly reduced by making managers aware of high-risk situations and empowering them to take immediate action. Most experts on workplace violence (e.g., Warren, Mullen, & McEwan, 2014) believe that *berserkers*—employees who "go crazy" and shoot people—give indications that they are going to commit future violence. Such indications include threats, acts of violence, comments about wanting to get even, excessive talk of guns, and comments about famous serial killers and mass murderers.

Take, for example, Thomas McIlvane, a fired postal worker who shot eight former coworkers, killing four. Prior to a union hearing appealing his termination, he stated that if he lost his grievance, he would make a shooting incident in Oklahoma that took the lives of 14 postal workers "look like a tea party." As another example, prior to being fired and then killing his supervisors, Larry Hansel was reprimanded for excessively talking about a postal worker who killed two coworkers in Escondido, California. Jennifer San Marco, who killed five postal workers in California in January 2006 before taking her own life, had already been placed on medical leave because of her clearly unstable behavior at the postal facility.

Mohandie (2014) advises "zero tolerance" for threats and violence. That is, one act and the employee is terminated (fired, not killed). Turner and Gelles (2003) suggest that employees whose behavior makes others feel scared should be screened for violence potential. This screening includes interviews with coworkers and supervisors as well as meetings with a clinical psychologist. From these interviews and meetings, Turner and his associates place the employee into one of five risk categories:

1. High violence potential, qualifies for arrest/hospitalization
2. High violence potential, does not qualify for arrest/hospitalization
3. Insufficient evidence for violence potential, but sufficient evidence for *intentional* infliction of emotional distress upon coworkers
4. Insufficient evidence for violence potential, but sufficient evidence for *unintentional* infliction of emotional distress upon coworkers
5. Insufficient evidence for violence potential, and insufficient evidence for infliction of emotional distress upon coworkers

The potential for workplace violence can also be reduced through careful handling of terminations and layoffs. Refer to the discussion in Chapter 7 for specific ways to fairly evaluate and terminate employees. In addition to these techniques, free voluntary counseling should be made available to all employees, especially those exhibiting emotional, interpersonal, or discipline problems (Silbergeld & Jan, 2004).

On the Job ▶ **Applied Case Study**

Reducing Stress at a Manufacturing Company

Mira Sermanissian is the human resources director for a manufacturer of airline parts in Montreal. The environment of the company is one of high stress, due in part to the necessity to produce parts with no errors. Because the company operates in a "just-in-time" environment, there is no inventory and the parts not only must be perfect, but they must also be produced on demand. This need for precision and timeliness has resulted in an environment that some employees compare to that of brain surgery. As a result of this tension, Sermanissian realized that she needed to

take steps to ensure that stress would not affect the physical and psychological health of the firm's employees.

- If you were Sermanissian, what would you do to help prevent the effects of stress?

- If stress is not reduced, what are the potential consequences for the employees and for the organization?

To find out how Sermanissian prepared her employees for stress, use the link found on your text webpage.

In October of 2007, the American Psychological Association (APA) released a study on stress in the United States. The study reported that one-third of Americans experience extreme stress. Seventy-four percent cite work as their number one stressor. Stressors such as reorganizations, constant changes in the way companies do business, having to learn new technology, mergers, layoffs, and being asked to work longer hours can be blamed on workplace stress. And, in answer to the demands placed on workers, 50% of those surveyed in the APA report say that they do not use their allotted vacation time because of too much work. All work and no play, as the saying goes, increases stress and leads to potential health problems.

Negative stress (also called distress), as you learned in this chapter, has significant physiological, physical, and psychological consequences on employees. Distress can raise cholesterol and blood pressure levels, which can lead to heart attacks and strokes. It can make it harder to control diabetes and cause panic attacks. In the APA study, three-fourths of employees surveyed reported severe headaches, fatigue, and upset stomachs. Fifty percent reported that they did not sleep well, which can lead to accidents in the workplace. Forty-three percent report they have bad diets and will overeat and/or drink to make themselves feel better. All of these factors cause dangerous health problems for employees.

In their 2007/2008 Staying@Work report, Watson Wyatt Worldwide, an international consulting firm, reported that 48% of employers surveyed agreed that the stress levels in their companies were high, but only 5% of them said that they were doing anything to help reduce employee stress. Even though stress-related illness costs businesses an estimated $300 billion a year that comes from turnover, layoffs, low productivity, work-related accidents, high insurance premiums, and legal fees, companies don't make the project of reducing workplace stress a top priority.

The question becomes, whose responsibility is it to reduce, or at least better manage workplace stress? Should the employee be held accountable for finding ways to reduce their stress and the negative impact it has on them? Or, ethically, is it the responsibility of companies to find ways to reduce employee stress and keep employees healthy?

Many people would say that, because of the dangerous health issues caused by high stress, businesses should be doing more to help reduce it or to help employees better manage it. In March 2008, the APA recognized five organizations that did believe it was companies' responsibility to promote employee health and well-being. These companies believe that they have an ethical responsibility to reduce the chances of any employee having to suffer the debilitating effects of extreme, long-term stress. They recognize that because of the demands placed on workers by companies and because workers have no control over what is expected of them, companies should do whatever they can to make work less stressful or less unhealthy.

Others say that it is the responsibility of individuals to find ways to decrease or better manage their stress. Employees have options: there are fitness centers they can join, or they can stop smoking, reduce their consumption of alcohol or caffeinated drinks, or read self-help books. They can seek help from counselors or other health professionals. Companies are in the business of making money, not of ensuring that people are healthy. Companies can't make and shouldn't be expected to make people take better care of themselves. And because what is stressful to one person may not be stressful to another, it is impossible to find and offer any one solution that's going to help everyone who is feeling stressed out because of the demands of their jobs. It would be too costly to companies to offer enough stress-reducing alternatives that would address the needs of all employees.

What do you think?

- Do you think companies have an ethical responsibility to offer solutions for employees that will help reduce stress?

- Do you think companies are to blame for the high stress levels in the workplace?

- What are some things that companies can offer or do for their employees?

- Do you think employees have any responsibility for ensuring they stay healthy under stressful conditions? If so, what are some things that employees can do for themselves?

Chapter Summary

In this chapter you learned:

- Stress is a psychological and physical reaction to certain life events or situations.
- Common sources of stress include personal stressors and such occupational stressors as job characteristics (role conflict, role ambiguity, role overload), organizational characteristics, work environment (noise and temperature), change, and relationships with others (e.g., conflict, difficult people, angry customers).
- At a personal level, stress can affect marriages and relationships with others. At a health level, stress results in a number of psychological (e.g., anxiety, depression) and physical disorders (e.g., joint pain, cardiovascular problems). At an organizational level, stress results in burnout, increased drug and alcohol use, lower job satisfaction, increased absenteeism, and increased turnover.
- Type A individuals, Type D individuals, and pessimists are more prone to stress than Type B individuals and optimists.
- Such techniques as exercise, laughter, a healthy diet, not smoking, getting plenty of sleep, joining support groups, self-empowerment, and time management can reduce stress.
- Workplace violence can result from employee stress.

Key Terms

Eustress (534)
Optimal level of arousal (534)
Distress (534)
Type A personality (536)
Type B personality (536)
Type D personality (536)
Neuroticism (536)
Role conflict (539)
Role ambiguity (539)
Role overload (539)
Person-organization fit (540)
Radiation (546)

Evaporation (546)
Effective temperature (546)
Circadian rhythm (550)
Fixed shift (551)
Moonlighting (552)
Perspective taking (553)
Forecasting (553)
Residual stress (554)
Burnout (555)
On-site child-care facility (561)
Voucher system (562)
Referral service (564)

Questions for Review

1. Why are some people more affected by stress than others?
2. What job characteristics are most likely to result in high levels of stress?
3. Why should organizations be concerned about employee stress?
4. How much attention should organizations pay to noise and temperature?
5. Do stress management techniques actually work? Why or why not?
6. Why does workplace violence occur?

Appendix Working Conditions and Human Factors

Ergonomics and *human factors* are areas of study in which psychologists and engineers try to produce products and systems that are easy to use, are safe, maximize efficiency, and minimize physical and psychological strain. While there are many areas involved in ergonomics and human factors, only four will be highlighted in this appendix: injury reduction, product design, system efficiency, and transportation.

Preventing Repetitive Stress Injuries

As a result of the amount of precision and computer work that employees perform, hand and wrist injuries commonly occur at work. The most common of these repetitive-stress injuries (RSIs) or cumulative trauma disorders (CTDs) are carpal tunnel syndrome (CTS) and tendonitis. According to the 2021 Liberty Mutual Workplace Safety Index, RSIs are the tenth most common injury affecting U.S. workers and annually cost employers over $1.6 billion in workers' compensation claims.

RSIs are the result of physical stress placed on the tendons and nerves that pass through a tunnel connecting the wrists and hands. The normal stress associated with repeated finger and hand movements is complicated by the awkward angle at which many employees must hold their wrists. Early symptoms of RSI include numbness and tingling in the hands and forearms. Later stages involve pain severe enough to make opening a door or holding a pen difficult if not impossible.

Forms of CTS treatment include taking anti-inflammatory drugs, wearing wrist braces, and undergoing surgery. Many RSIs can be prevented by learning ergonomically proper work techniques, performing warm-up exercises, using wrist rests and special keyboards, taking breaks, and stopping work when numbness or pain begins.

A good example of an intervention to reduce RSIs is provided by Pratt & Whitney in Middletown, Connecticut. After employees complained of the physical stress caused by repetitively using their finger to open plastic bags containing machine parts, the company placed a small letter opener on the top of the carts used to move the parts. The cost for this intervention was only $3 a cart. A more complicated intervention was implemented at a Gold Kist plant in Alabama. To eliminate the need for employees to repetitively push crates of chicken along a series of rollers, the company installed a moving conveyor belt (Grossman, 2000). Automating manually performed tasks is another common intervention to reduce RSIs (Newton, 2021).

Organizations that have trained employees on ways to prevent RSIs have seen excellent results (Smith, 2003). For example, Mitsubishi reported a 45% decrease in RSIs over a two-year period following training, and 3M reported that its training program resulted in a 50% decrease in workers' compensation claims (Tyler, 1998). The training provided by 3M not only reduced the number of worker's compensation claims by 50%, but also decreased absenteeism by 13% (Tyler, 1998). Due to employer awareness of RSIs, data from the annual Liberty Mutual Workplace Safety Index indicate that the number of RSI-related workman's compensation claims continues to drop. As an example, after implementing its WorkingWell program, Amazon found that musculoskeletal disorders decreased by 32% from 2019 to 2020 (Rosenbaum, 2021).

Product Design

Human-factors psychologists are often employed by organizations to improve the "user friendliness" of products. Examples might include determining the best layout for a computer keyboard, choosing the optimal size for the finger holes in a pair of scissors, or designing an automobile dashboard to reduce the distance a driver needs to reach to play the car stereo.

A good example of product design comes from a study by Dempsey et al. (1996), who were asked to help design the ideal satchel to be carried by postal workers. To do this, they tested four different satchels to determine which one was most comfortable, worked best in diverse climates, was easiest to use, and provided the best protection against attacking dogs. The results of their study indicated that the most comfortable bag also provided the worst protection against attacking dogs and had some problems with ease of mail retrieval.

A similar study was conducted by Pascoe, Pascoe, Wang, Shim, and Kim (1997) in designing book bags. Pascoe and his colleagues compared the effect that three types of bags—the two-strap backpack, the one-strap backpack, and the one-strap athletic bag—had on the posture and gait of the student wearing the book bag. When compared with no book bag, all three types reduced stride length and increased stride frequency. Furthermore, the one-strap backpack and the one-strap athletic bag resulted in uncomfortable changes in posture. However, the two-strap backpack did not result in such changes. Thus, the practical aspects of this study suggest that students should buy a backpack with two straps and, even though it is not as cool as slinging one strap over one shoulder, use both straps.

The search for the ideal work glove provides another example of product design studies. This search took two paths: one that investigated the effects of wearing gloves and another that compared the advantages of certain types of gloves over others. Though gloves clearly increase worker safety, their effect on work performance depends on the type of task performed. For example, researchers have found that wearing gloves increases muscle fatigue (Willms, Wells, & Carnahan, 2009), reduces the ability to hold on to a handle (Hur, Motawar, & Seo, 2012), reduces dexterity (Dianat, Haslegrave, & Stedmon, 2010; Yao et al., 2018), and decreases the amount of turning force (the authors of the study called this "maximum volitional torque exertion of supination") that can be exerted by a worker (Shih & Wang, 1997) but does not affect the ability to discriminate weights (Shih & Wang, 1996).

Acknowledging that gloves reduce the force that can be exerted with the bare hand, Kovacs, Splittstoesser, Maronitis, and Marras (2002) compared nine different types of gloves to determine which type had the least effect on force. Their results indicated that surgical gloves had the least decline in force and leather gloves the greatest decline in force.

An example of a study searching for the optimal glove comes from Nelson and Mital (1995), who investigated the optimal thickness for examination gloves used by physicians (ouch!). Their study was conducted because although thicker gloves provide greater protection against needle sticks, they might also reduce the ability of the physician to perform sensitive work. The researchers tested five gloves ranging in thickness from 0.21 mm to 0.83 mm. Nelson and Mital found that the 0.83 mm glove not only resisted routine impacts but also provided the same level of dexterity and tactility as a bare hand. Though neither bags nor gloves are particularly exciting topics, these examples show the meticulous human-factors research that goes into the development of good products.

System Efficiency

A major human-factors area, at times referred to as "time and motion studies," is making systems more efficient. These studies usually begin with a job analysis to determine how employees perform their jobs. These job analyses tend to be much more specific than the ones you learned about back in Chapter 2. For example, suppose you were trying to reduce the time it took for a counterperson at a fast-food restaurant to perform their job. As shown in Figure A.1, the employee reached for ketchup packets 150 times, pepper packets 10 times, french-fry containers 140 times, and french fries 140 times. What is wrong with the current layout? As you probably guessed, one of the most frequently retrieved items (ketchup) is farthest away, and the least frequently retrieved item (pepper) is closest. Also note from the correlation table that each time the employee retrieved a french-fry container, they also retrieved french fries, yet the two are in different areas. To improve efficiency, the most often retrieved items should be moved closer to the employee, and items that are retrieved together would be located near one another.

As another example, due to the high number of musculoskeletal complaints (e.g., back pain or sore wrists) by grocery store cashiers, extensive research has gone into designing a checkout stand that is both efficient and comfortable. According to a literature review and new data by Grant and Habes (1995), these are the features of the ideal checkout stand:

- The cashier would face the customer.
- The height of the work surface would be no taller than the cashier's elbows.
- The scanner and keyboard would be in front of the cashier and the cash drawer to their side (less than 18 inches away).
- Groceries would be presented to the cashier on a conveyor belt that is narrow (to reduce reach) and that runs from the scanner to the back of the checkout stand.
- Stools, footrests, and antifatigue mats would be present to allow the cashier the choice of sitting or standing.

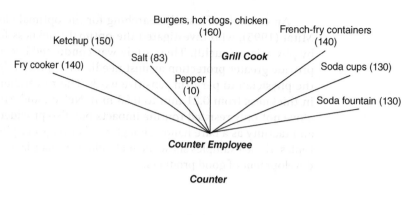

Fry cooker (140) Ketchup (150) Salt (83) **Grill Cook** Burgers, hot dogs, chicken (160) French-fry containers (140) Soda cups (130)

Pepper (10) Soda fountain (130)

Counter Employee

Counter

Customers

Movement Correlation Chart								
	(F)	(FC)	(K)	(G)	(P)	(S)	(D)	(DC)
Fries (F)	1.00	.86	.70	.10	.30	.63	.63	
Fry containers (FC)			.86	.70	.10	.30	.63	.63
Ketchup (K)				.70	.30	.60	.45	.45
Grilled food (G)					.10	.40	.65	.65
Pepper (P)						.50	.20	.20
Salt (S)							.29	.29
Drinks (D)								1.00
Drink cups (DC)								

Figure A.1

Layout of a Fast-Food Counter (The numbers indicate the number of times the counter-person walked to get a particular item.)

Transportation

Putting the Brakes on Rear-End Collisions

The goal of human-factors research in this area is to make driving safer and easier. For example, human-factors researchers have conducted several studies to reduce rear-end collisions. The first step is to study the driving process and create a process chart that diagrams the events that take place, the order in which they occur, and their duration. Such a chart might show that the amount of time needed to avoid a collision is a function of (1) the time it takes for the lead driver to scan the environment, determine if there is a reason to brake, make the decision to brake, and then apply the brake and that (2) the time it takes for the trailing driver to notice cues (brake lights, turn indicators, slowing of speed), distinguish one cue from another, make a decision to brake, and then apply the brakes. To reduce rear-end collisions, human-factors psychologists look for ways to reduce the processing time at each of the steps shown in the process chart. For example, talking on a cellular phone (Caird, Willness, Steel, & Scialfa, 2008); texting (Caird, Johnston, Willness, Ashbridge, & Steel, 2014); listening to loud music (Febriandirza, Chaozhong, Zhong, Hu, & Zhang, 2017; Turner, Fernandez, & Nelson, 1996); or talking to a passenger (Young & Stanton, 2007) while driving increases the time it takes to notice such cues as brake lights and traffic signals. Sivak, Flannagan,

Sato, and Traube (1994) found that neither neon nor LED brake lights resulted in better reaction times than either standard or enhanced incandescent lights.

Researchers in another study focused on the step of distinguishing one cue from another. They hypothesized that because both your brake lights and your turn indicators are red, a driver following behind you must spend fractions of a second interpreting whether you are braking or using your turn signal (Luoma, Flannagan, Sivak, Aoki, & Traube, 1997). These fractions of a second could be the difference in avoiding an accident in the case of an immediate stop. Luoma and his research team found that changing the color of the turn signal from red to yellow reduced the time taken to react to a brake signal. This study supports the European and Japanese requirements that turn signals be yellow (in the United States, both red and yellow are allowed). In another study focusing on the ability to discriminate brake lights from other lights, Theeuwes and Alferdinck (1995) found that a brake light mounted in the rear window is more effective if it is located higher on the window rather than toward the bottom of the window.

Another study sought to reduce the time between the lead driver taking their foot off the accelerator and moving it to the brake. To do this, Shinar (1995) developed an advance brake warning (ABW) system in which a sudden release in the accelerator pedal would activate the brake light for one second. If the driver hit the brake pedal, the brake light would stay on. If the driver did not brake, then the brake light would go off. Though this system provides an early warning system, it could potentially result in false alarms. To study this possibility, Shinar (1995) studied 95,394 times in which six drivers applied their brakes. The ABW was activated during 820 of the 95,394 instances of braking and provided a following driver an average of one-fifth of a second more warning. The false alarm rate was 23% of ABW activations but accounted for only 2% of all brake light activations of less than a second. Thus, the extra warning time did not appear to result in an excessive number of false alarms.

Reducing Speeding

Human-factors experts have also conducted research to determine ways to reduce speeding by changing the driving environment. For example, De Waard, Jessurun, Steyvers, Raggatt, and Brookhuis (1995) hypothesized that drivers would speed less often if speeding were made perceptually uncomfortable (as opposed to traffic citations, making speeding financially uncomfortable). To do this, De Waard et al. removed the white lines on the right side of a single-lane road and replaced them with intermittent chippings that made noise when run over by a speeding car. The idea behind this intervention was that speeding drivers often touch the lines on each side of the lane because they are going too fast to keep their vehicles in the center of the lane. "Penalizing" the speeding driver with a noxious noise reduced average speeds by three kilometers per hour—enough of a reduction to increase safety. Speeding can also be reduced by elevating the road surface using speed humps and raised pedestrian crossings or changing the directness of the road by adding roundabouts or chicanes (serpentine curves built into a road to slow traffic rather than to go around a geographic barrier such as a hill or river; Turner, Job, & Mitra, 2021).

In another attempt to reduce speeding, one group of researchers believed that some instances of speeding were the result of drivers being unaware of the speed limit. To reduce this possibility, three researchers at the University of Helsinki in Finland (Lajunen, Hakkarainen, & Summala, 1996) tested three different types of signs telling drivers to slow down as they were entering a "built-up" (densely populated) area, in

Figure A.2
Some Highway Signs are Easier to Understand than Others.

which the national speed limit was 50 kilometers per hour. The first sign contained the symbol for the built-up area, the second the built-up area symbol plus the symbol for danger, and the third the built-up area symbol plus the number 50 in a circle. As you might expect, drivers reduced their speed most often with the sign that showed the explicit speed limit number and least often with the two signs in which one had to simply know the speed limit in a built-up area. In the United States, these findings might be generalized to replace signs that say "School Zone" with ones that say "School Zone: Speed Limit 25 MPH."

Although this study seems to suggest that signs with text are superior to those with icons and symbols, this is not usually the case. Research indicates that icon/symbol highway signs are easier to read and result in lower reaction times than do text-based highway signs (Long & Kearns, 1996). Why the contradictory findings? Icon/symbol signs are easier to read than signs containing text. However, seeing a symbol and understanding its meaning are two different things. Refer to the highway signs shown in Figure A.2. All of them are easy to read, yet some of them may not be familiar to you. If you aren't familiar with the meaning, or if you are familiar with the meaning ("slow down" in Figure A.2) but don't know what you are supposed to do (not exceed 25 mph), the benefit of the increased viewing distances of the iconic signs may be nullified by the increased time to interpret them.

This use of icons will be effective only if people have knowledge about the meaning of the icons. Let me provide you with a great example of this point. The interstate highway system in the United States is actually very well designed and very well marked in most locations. However, many people can't take full advantage of these well-designed and well-marked highways because they aren't familiar with the codes appearing on the signs. For example, suppose you were driving on I-81 or I-77. That both of these highways end in an odd number tells you that the highway runs north and south; even-numbered highways run east and west. Likewise, a route that goes

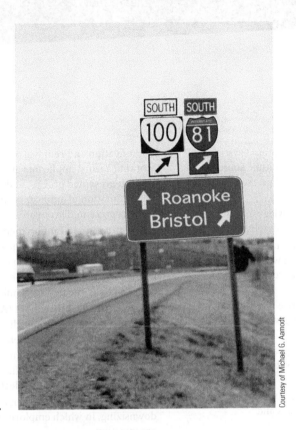

Courtesy of Michael G. Aamodt

What lane should you get in to travel to Roanoke?

from an Interstate highway into a major city will have three digits and begin with an odd number (e.g., I-395 goes from I-95 *into* Washington, D.C.) whereas one that goes around a major city will have three digits and begin with an even number (e.g., I-495 goes from I-95 *around* Washington, D.C.).

The color of the traffic sign also provides valuable information. According to a guide published by the Iowa Department of Transportation:

- Red signs indicate you should stop, yield, or do what is stated on the sign.
- Green signs provide directional information such as where a place is, or how far a place is from your current location (e.g., Los Angeles – 50 miles).
- Blue signs provide information on services for travelers such as rest areas, hotels, or hospitals.
- Brown signs identify recreation and cultural points of interest such as parks and recreational areas.
- Orange signs warn about temporary road conditions such as road construction or temporary traffic control adjustments.
- Yellow signs provide general warnings such as a no passing zone or a narrow bridge.

How many people do you think know these rules?

Glossary

360-degree feedback A performance appraisal system in which feedback is obtained from multiple sources such as supervisors, subordinates, and peers.

Ability A basic capacity for performing a wide range of different tasks, acquiring knowledge, or developing a skill.

Acceptance stage The fourth and final stage of emotional reaction to downsizing, in which employees accept that layoffs will occur and are ready to take steps to secure their future.

Accommodating style The conflict style of a person who tends to respond to conflict by giving in to the other person.

Achievement-oriented style In path–goal theory, a leadership style in which the leader sets challenging goals and rewards achievement.

Adaptation The fourth stage of change, in which employees try to adapt to new policies and procedures.

Additive tasks Tasks for which the group's performance is equal to the sum of the performances of each individual group member.

Adverse impact An employment practice resulting in members of a protected class being negatively affected at a higher rate than members of the majority class. Adverse impact is usually determined by the four-fifths rule.

AET An ergonomic job analysis method developed in Germany (*Arbeitswissenschaftliches Erhebungsverfahren zur Tätigkeitsanalyse*).

Affect Feelings or emotion.

Affective commitment The extent to which an employee wants to remain with an organization and cares about the organization.

Affective identity motivation The motivation to lead as a result of a desire to be in charge and lead others.

Affiliation style A leadership style in which the individual leads by caring about others and that is most effective in a climate of anxiety.

Affirmative action The process of ensuring proportional representation of employees based on variables such as race and gender. Affirmative-action strategies include intentional recruitment of applicants from underrepresented groups, identification and removal of employment practices working against applicants and employees from underrepresented groups, and preferential hiring and promotion of applicants and employees from underrepresented groups.

Age Discrimination in Employment Act (ADEA) A federal law that, with its amendments, forbids discrimination against an individual who is over the age of 40.

Alternate-forms reliability The extent to which two forms of the same test are similar.

Americans with Disabilities Act (ADA) A federal law, passed in 1990, that forbids discrimination against the physically and mentally disabled.

Ammerman technique A job analysis method in which a group of job experts identifies the objectives and standards to be met by the ideal worker.

Anger stage The second stage of emotional reaction to downsizing, in which employees become angry at the organization.

Anxiety An organizational climate in which worry predominates.

Application of training Measurement of the effectiveness of training by determining the extent to which employees apply the material taught in a training program.

Apprentice training A training program, usually found in the craft and building trades, in which employees combine formal coursework with formal on-the-job training.

Arbitration A method of resolving conflicts in which a neutral third party is asked to choose which side is correct.

Archival research Research that involves the use of previously collected data.

Army Alpha An intelligence test developed during World War I and used by the army for soldiers who can read.

Army Beta An intelligence test developed during World War I and used by the army for soldiers who cannot read.

Artifacts The things people surround themselves with (clothes, jewelry, office decorations, cars, etc.) that communicate information about the person.

Assessment center   A method of selecting employees in which applicants participate in several job-related activities, at least one of which must be a simulation, and are rated by several trained evaluators.

Assimilated   A description of a message in which the information has been modified to fit the existing beliefs and knowledge of the person sending the message before it is passed on to another person.

Assimilation   A type of rating error in which raters base their rating of an employee during one rating period on the ratings the rater gave during a previous period.

Asynchronous technologies   Distance-learning programs in which employees can complete the training at their own pace and at a time of their choosing.

Attitude survey   A form of upward communication in which a survey is conducted to determine employee attitudes about an organization.

Attitudinal Listening Profile   A test developed by Geier and Downey that measures individual listening styles.

Audience effects   The effect on behavior when one or more people passively watch the behavior of another person.

Authentic leadership   A leadership theory stating that leaders should be honest and open and lead out of a desire to serve others rather than a desire for self-gain.

Autocratic I strategy   Leaders use available information to make decisions without consulting their subordinates.

Autocratic II strategy   Leaders obtain necessary information from their subordinates and then make their own decision.

Autonomy   The need from self-determination theory to decide what we want to do and how we are going to do it.

Averaging versus adding model   A model proposed by Anderson that postulates that our impressions are based more on the average value of each impression than on the sum of the values for each impression.

Avoiding style   The conflict style of a person who reacts to conflict by pretending that it does not exist.

Banding   A statistical technique based on the standard error of measurement that allows similar test scores to be grouped.

Bandwidth   The total number of potential work hours available each day.

Barnum statements   Statements, such as those used in astrological forecasts, that are so general that they can be true of almost anyone.

Base rate   Percentage of current employees who are considered successful.

Baseline   The level of productivity before the implementation of a gainsharing plan.

Basic biological needs   The first step in Maslow's needs hierarchy, concerning survival needs for food, air, water, and the like.

Behavior modeling   A training technique in which employees observe correct behavior, practice that behavior, and then receive feedback about their performance.

Behavioral observation scales (BOS)   A method of performance appraisal in which supervisors rate the frequency of observed behaviors.

Behaviorally anchored rating scales (BARS)   A method of performance appraisal involving the placement of benchmark behaviors next to each point on a graphic rating scale.

Benchmark answers   Standard answers to interview questions, the quality of which has been agreed on by job experts.

Binding arbitration   A method of resolving conflicts in which a neutral third party is asked to choose which side is correct and in which neither party is allowed to appeal the decision.

Biodata   A method of selection involving application blanks that contain questions that research has shown will predict job performance.

Blog   A website in which the host regularly posts commentaries on a topic that readers can respond to.

Bona fide occupational qualification (BFOQ)   A selection requirement that is necessary for the performance of job-related duties and for which there is no substitute.

Brainstorming   A technique in which ideas are generated by people in a group setting.

Bridge publication   A publication with the goal of bridging the gap between the research conducted by academics and the practical needs of practitioners.

Bulletin board   A method of downward communication in which informal or relatively unimportant written information is posted in a public place.

Burnout   The psychological state of being overwhelmed with stress.

Business communication   Transmitting business-related information among employees, management, and customers.

Business simulation game   An exercise, usually found in assessment centers, that is designed to simulate the business and marketing activities that take place in an organization.

Business impact   A method of evaluating the effectiveness of training by determining whether the goals of the training were met.

Case law The interpretation of a law by a court through a verdict in a trial, setting precedent for subsequent court decisions.

Case study A training technique in which employees, usually in a group, are presented with a real or hypothetical workplace problem and are asked to propose the best solution.

Casual work A scheduling practice in which employees work on an irregular or as-needed basis.

Cause-and-effect relationship The result of a well-controlled experiment about which the researcher can confidently state that the independent variable caused the change in the dependent variable.

Central tendency error A type of rating error in which a rater consistently rates all employees in the middle of the scale, regardless of their actual levels of performance.

Change agent A person who enjoys change and makes changes for the sake of it.

Change analyst A person who is not afraid of change but makes changes only when there is a compelling reason to do so.

Change resister A person who hates change and will do anything to keep change from occurring.

Chronic self-esteem The positive or negative way in which a person views themselves as a whole.

Circadian rhythm The 24-hour cycle of physiological functions maintained by every person.

Clarifier A type of structured interview question that clarifies information on the résumé or application.

Closed desk arrangement An office arranged so that a visitor must sit across from the person behind the desk.

Cluster grapevine A pattern of grapevine communication in which a message is passed to a select group of people who each in turn pass the message to a few select others.

Coaching A method of training in which a new employee receives on-the-job guidance from an experienced employee.

Coaction The effect on behavior when two or more people are performing the same task in the presence of each other.

Coefficient alpha A statistic used to determine internal reliability of tests that use interval or ratio scales.

Coercive power Leadership power that comes from the leader's capacity to punish others.

Coercive style A leadership style in which the individual leads by controlling reward and punishment; most effective in a climate of crisis.

Cognitive ability Abilities involving the knowledge and use of information such as math and grammar.

Cognitive ability test Tests designed to measure the level of intelligence or the amount of knowledge possessed by an applicant.

Collaborating style The conflict style of a person who wants a conflict resolved in such a way that both sides get what they want.

Common goal An aim or purpose shared by members of a group.

Communication barriers Physical, cultural, and psychological obstacles that interfere with successful communication and create a source of conflict.

Communication channel The medium by which a communication is transmitted.

Communication structure The manner in which members of a group communicate with one another.

Comparison The effect when an individual working on a task compares their performance with that of another person performing the same task.

Compensable job factors Factors, such as responsibility and education requirements, that differentiate the relative worth of jobs.

Compensatory approach A method of making selection decisions in which a high score on one test can compensate for a low score on another test. For example, a high GPA might compensate for a low GRE score.

Competence The need from self-determination theory to be able to successfully perform the tasks that are important to us.

Competencies The knowledge, skills, abilities, and other characteristics needed to perform a job.

Competition for resources A cause of conflict that occurs when the demand for resources is greater than the resources available.

Complaint box A form of upward communication in which employees are asked to place their complaints in a box.

Compressed workweeks Work schedules in which 40 hours are worked in less than the traditional five-day workweek.

Compromising style A style of resolving conflicts in which an individual allows each side to get some of what it wants.

Computer-adaptive testing (CAT) A type of test taken on a computer in which the computer adapts the difficulty level of questions asked to the test-taker's success in answering previous questions.

Concurrent validity A form of criterion validity that correlates test scores with measures of job performance for employees currently working for an organization.

Conditional reasoning test Tests designed to reduce faking by asking test-takers to select the reason that best explains a statement.

Conflict The psychological and behavioral reaction to a perception that another person is either keeping you from reaching a goal, taking away your right to behave in a particular way, or violating the expectancies of a relationship.

Conjunctive tasks Tasks for which the group's performance is dependent on the performance of the least effective group member.

Consideration The degree to which leaders act in a warm and supportive manner toward their subordinates.

Consistency theory Korman's theory that employees will be motivated to perform at levels consistent with their levels of self-esteem.

Construct validity The extent to which a test actually measures the construct that it purports to measure.

Consultative I strategy Leaders share the problem on an individual basis with their subordinates and then make a decision that may or may not be consistent with the thinking of the group.

Consultative II strategy Leaders share the problem with the group as a whole and then make a decision that may or may not be consistent with the thinking of the group.

Contamination The condition in which a criterion score is affected by things other than those under the control of the employee.

Content validity The extent to which tests or test items sample the content that they are supposed to measure.

Contextual performance The effort employees make to get along with their peers, improve the organization, and "go the extra mile."

Continuance commitment The extent to which employees believe they must remain with an organization due to the time, expense, and effort they have already put into the organization.

Contrast effect When the performance of one applicant affects the perception of the performance of the next applicant.

Contrast error A type of rating error in which the rating of the performance level of one employee affects the ratings given to the next employee being rated.

Control group A group of employees who do not receive a particular type of training so that their performance can be compared with that of employees who do receive training.

Convenience sample A nonrandom research sample that is used because it is easily available.

Cooperative problem solving A method of resolving conflict in which two sides get together to discuss a problem and arrive at a solution.

Core hours The hours in a flextime schedule during which every employee must work.

Corrected validity A term usually found with meta-analysis, referring to a correlation coefficient that has been corrected for predictor and criterion reliability and for range restriction. Corrected validity is sometimes called "true validity."

Correlation A statistical procedure used to measure the relationship between two variables.

Correlation coefficient A statistic, resulting from performing a correlation, that indicates the magnitude and direction of a relationship.

Corresponding effects An event that affects one member of a group will affect the other group members.

Cost per applicant The amount of money spent on a recruitment campaign divided by the number of people that subsequently apply for jobs as a result of the recruitment campaign.

Cost per qualified applicant The amount of money spent on a recruitment campaign divided by the number of qualified people that subsequently apply for jobs as a result of the recruitment campaign.

Counterbalancing A method of controlling for order effects by giving half of a sample Test A first, followed by Test B, and giving the other half of the sample Test B first, followed by Test A.

Country club leaders A style of leadership in which the leader is concerned about the well-being of employees but is not task oriented.

Cover letter A letter that accompanies a résumé or job application.

Crisis A critical time or climate for an organization in which the outcome to a decision has extreme consequences.

Criterion A measure of job performance, such as attendance, productivity, or a supervisor rating.

Criterion group Division of employees into groups based on high and low scores on a particular criterion.

Criterion validity The extent to which a test score is related to some measure of job performance.

Critical Incident Technique (CIT) The job analysis method developed by John Flanagan that uses written reports of good and bad employee behavior.

Critical incidents A method of performance appraisal in which the supervisor records employee behaviors that were observed on the job and rates the employee based on that record.

Cross-functional teams Teams consisting of representatives from various departments (functions) within an organization.

Cross-training   Teaching employees how to perform tasks traditionally performed by other employees.

Cutoff approach   A method of hiring in which an applicant must score higher than a particular score to be considered for employment.

Dale-Chall Index   A method of determining the readability level of written material by looking at the number of commonly known words used in the document.

Dead-enders   Employees who receive much grapevine information but who seldom pass it on to others.

Debriefing   Informing the subject in an experiment about the purpose of the study in which they were a participant and providing any other relevant information.

Defense   The second stage of change, in which employees accept that change will occur but try to justify the old way of doing things.

Denial stage   The first stage in the emotional reaction to change or layoffs, in which an employee denies that an organizational change or layoff will occur.

Dependent variable   The measure of behavior that is expected to change as a result of changes in the independent variable.

Derivation sample   A group of employees who were used in creating the initial weights for a biodata instrument.

Desirability   The extent to which a trait or behavior is valued as being good in society.

Despair   An organizational climate characterized by low morale.

Devil's advocate   A group member who intentionally provides an opposing opinion to that expressed by the leader or the majority of the group.

***Dictionary of Occupational Titles* (DOT)**   A directory that was published by the federal government that supplied information for almost 30,000 jobs. It has been replaced by O*NET.

Difference score   A type of effect size used in meta-analysis that is signified by the letter d and indicates how many standard deviations separate the mean score for the experimental group from the control group.

Differential validity   The characteristic of a test that significantly predicts a criterion for two groups, such as both minorities and nonminorities, but predicts significantly better for one of the two groups.

Direct compensation   The amount of money paid to an employee (does not count benefits, time off, etc.).

Direct mail   A method of recruitment in which an organization sends out mass mailings of information about job openings to potential applicants.

Discarding   The third stage of change, in which employees accept that change will occur and decide to discard their old ways of doing things.

Disjunctive tasks   Tasks for which the performance of a group is based on the performance of its most talented member.

Disorganization   A climate in which the organization has the necessary knowledge and resources but does not know how to efficiently use the knowledge or the resources.

Dispute   A situation when two parties do not agree.

Disqualifier   A type of structured interview question in which a wrong answer will disqualify the applicant from further consideration.

Dissertation   A formal research paper required of most doctoral students to graduate.

Distracting   The idea that social inhibition occurs because the presence of others provides a distraction that interferes with concentration.

Distress   Stress that results in negative energy and decreases in performance and health.

Distributed practice   Learning a few things at a time.

Distribution errors   Rating errors in which a rater will use only a certain part of a rating scale when evaluating employee performance.

Distributive justice   The perceived fairness of the decisions made in an organization.

Downward communication   Communication within an organization in which the direction of communication is from management to employees.

Drive to acquire   A drive to seek, take, control, and retain objects and personal experiences that humans value.

Drive to bond   A drive to form social relationships and develop mutual caring commitments with other humans.

Drive to defend   A drive to defend themselves and their valued accomplishments whenever they perceive them to be endangered.

Drive to learn   A drive to satisfy curiosity, to know, to comprehend, to appreciate, to develop understandings or representations of their environment and of themselves through a reflective process.

Drug-Free Workplace Act of 1988   A federal law that requires federal contractors with a contract of at least $100,000 to maintain a drug-free workplace.

Drug testing   Tests that indicate whether an applicant has recently used a drug.

Dysfunctional conflict   Conflict that keeps people from working together, lessens productivity, spreads to other areas, or increases turnover.

Effect size   Used in meta-analysis, a statistic that indicates the amount of change caused by an experimental manipulation.

Effective temperature   The combination of air temperature, humidity, airflow, and heat radiation that determines how hot or cold the environment feels.

Ego needs   The fourth step in Maslow's hierarchy, concerning the individual's need for recognition and success.

Embeddedness   The extent to which employees have links to their jobs and community, the importance of these links, and the ease with which they can be broken and replaced at another job.

Empathic listening   The listening style of a person who cares primarily about the feelings of the speaker.

Employee learning   Evaluating the effectiveness of a training program by measuring how much employees learned from it.

Employee Performance Record   A standardized use of the critical-incident technique developed at General Motors.

Employee reactions   A method of evaluating training in which employees are asked their opinions of a training program.

Employee referral   A method of recruitment in which a current employee refers a friend or family member for a job.

Employee resource groups   A group of employees with similar interests, experiences, or demographics who meet to discuss those experiences.

Employment agency   An organization that specializes in finding jobs for applicants and finding applicants for organizations looking for employees.

Employment-at-will doctrine   The opinion of courts in most states that employers have the right to hire and fire an employee at will and without any specific cause.

Employment-at-will statements   Statements in employment applications and company manuals reaffirming an organization's right to hire and fire at will.

Employment interview   A method of selecting employees in which an interviewer asks questions of an applicant and then makes an employment decision based on the answers to the questions as well as the way in which the questions were answered.

Empowerment chart   A chart made for each employee that shows what level of input the employee has for each task.

Equal Employment Opportunity Commission (EEOC)   A branch of the Department of Labor charged with investigating and prosecuting complaints of employment discrimination.

Equity theory   A theory of job satisfaction stating that employees will be satisfied if their ratio of effort to reward is similar to that of other employees.

ERG theory   Aldefer's needs theory, which describes three levels of satisfaction: *existence*, *relatedness*, and *growth*.

Error   Deviation from a standard of quality; also a type of response to communication overload that involves processing all information but processing some of it incorrectly.

Escape   A response to communication overload in which the employee leaves the organization to reduce the stress.

Eustress   Stress that results in positive energy and improvements in performance and health.

Evaluation apprehension   The idea that a person performing a task becomes aroused because they are concerned that others are evaluating their performance.

Evaporation   One way our bodies maintain a normal temperature, in which perspiration reduces excess heat.

Exclusionary period   The amount of time that must pass since conviction or release from prison before the conviction is no longer considered as being relevant to the hiring decision.

Executive search firms   Employment agencies, often also called headhunters, that specialize in placing applicants in high-paying jobs.

Expectancy   In expectancy theory, the perceived probability that a particular amount of effort will result in a particular level of performance.

Expectancy charts   Charts that indicate the chance of success for each test score range.

Expectancy theory   Vroom's theory that motivation is a function of expectancy, instrumentality, and valence.

Expectation-lowering procedure (ELP)   A form of RJP that lowers an applicant's expectations about the various aspects of the job.

Experiment   A type of research study in which the independent variable is manipulated by the experimenter.

Experimental group   In an experiment, the group of subjects that receives the experimental treatment of interest to the experimenter.

Expert power   Power that individuals have because they have knowledge.

External equity   The extent to which employees within an organization are paid fairly compared with employees in other organizations.

External recruitment   Recruiting employees from outside the organization.

External validity   The extent to which research results can be expected to hold true outside the specific setting in which they were obtained.

Extrinsic motivation   Work motivation that arises from such nonpersonal factors as pay, coworkers, and opportunities for advancement.

Face validity   The extent to which a test appears to be valid.

Faces Scale   A measure of job satisfaction in which raters place a mark under a facial expression that is most similar to the way they feel about their jobs.

Fair Credit Reporting Act (FCRA)   A federal law that provides people with certain rights regarding the collection and use of credit history reports.

Family and Medical Leave Act (FMLA)   Passed in 1993, the FMLA provides 12 weeks of unpaid leave for birth, adoption, or serious illness of a child, parent, spouse, or the employee. All organizations that physically employ 50 or more people within a 70-mile radius of one another are covered by the act.

Fear stage   The third emotional stage following the announcement of a layoff, in which employees worry about how they will survive financially.

Feedback   Providing employees with specific information about how well they are performing a task or series of tasks.

Feng shui   The ancient Chinese practice of arranging objects to maximize positive energy and improve the quality of life.

Fiedler's contingency model   A theory of leadership that states that leadership effectiveness is dependent on the interaction between the leader and the situation.

Field research   Research conducted in a natural setting as opposed to a laboratory.

Fifth Amendment   The amendment to the U.S. Constitution that mandates that the federal government may not deny a person equal protection under the law.

File approach   The gathering of biodata from employee files rather than by questionnaire.

Financial bonus   A method of absenteeism control in which employees who meet an attendance standard are given a cash reward.

Fixed shift   A shift schedule in which employees never change the shifts they work.

Fleishman Job Analysis Survey (F-JAS)   A job analysis method in which jobs are rated based on the abilities needed to perform them.

Flesch Index   A method of determining the readability level of written material by analyzing average sentence length and the number of syllables per 100 words.

Flexible hours   The part of a flextime schedule in which employees may choose which hours to work.

Flexitour   A flextime schedule in which employees have flexibility in scheduling but must schedule their work hours at least a week in advance.

Flextime   A work schedule that allows employees to choose their own work hours.

FOG Index   A method of determining the readability level of written material by analyzing sentence length and the number of three-syllable words. (The term is interpreted as either the measure of the "fog" a reader may be in or as the acronym FOG, for "frequency of gobbledygook.")

Forced-choice rating scales   A method of performance appraisal in which a supervisor is given several behaviors and is forced to choose which of them is most typical of the employee.

Forced distribution method   A performance appraisal method in which a predetermined percentage of employees are placed into various performance categories.

Forcing style   The conflict style of a person who responds to conflict by always trying to win.

Forecasting   Constant worrying about the future.

Form stability   The extent to which the scores on two forms of a test are similar.

Formative test   A test given during training to determine if a trainee is learning the material.

Forming stage   The first stage of the team process, in which team members "feel out" the team concept and attempt to make a positive impression.

Four-fifths rule   When the selection ratio for one group (e.g., women) is less than 80% (four-fifths) of the selection ratio for another group (e.g., men), adverse impact is said to exist.

Fourteenth Amendment   The amendment to the U.S. Constitution that mandates that no state may deny a person equal protection under the law.

Fourth Amendment   The amendment to the U.S. Constitution that protects against unreasonable search or seizure; the amendment has been ruled to cover such privacy issues as drug testing, locker and office searches, psychological testing, and electronic surveillance.

Frame-of-reference training   A method of training raters in which the rater is provided with job-related information, a chance to practice ratings, examples of ratings made by experts, and the rationale behind the expert ratings.

Fry Readability Graph   A method of determining the readability level of written material by analyzing sentence length and the average number of syllables per word.

Functional conflict Conflict that results in increased performance or better interpersonal relations.

Functional Job Analysis (FJA) A job analysis method developed by Fine that rates the extent to which a job incumbent is involved with functions in the categories of data, people, and things.

Future-focused question A type of structured interview question in which applicants are given a situation and asked how they would handle it.

Gainsharing A group incentive system in which employees are paid a bonus based on improvements in group productivity.

Galatea effect When high self-expectations result in higher levels of performance.

Games An absenteeism control method in which games such as poker and bingo are used to reward employee attendance.

Gamification The application of game-like elements to traditional assessments.

Gatekeeper A person who screens potential communication for someone else and allows only the most important information to pass through.

Generalizability Like external validity, the extent to which research results hold true outside the specific setting in which they were obtained.

Gliding time A flextime schedule in which employees can choose their own hours without any advance notice or scheduling.

Goal setting A method of increasing performance in which employees are given specific performance goals to aim for.

Golem effect When negative expectations of an individual cause a decrease in that individual's performance.

Gossip Poorly substantiated information and insignificant information that is primarily about individuals.

Gossip grapevine A pattern of grapevine communication in which a message is passed to only a select group of individuals.

Grade A cluster of jobs of similar worth.

Graduate Record Exam (GRE) A standardized admission test required by most psychology graduate schools.

Grapevine An unofficial, informal communication network.

Graphic rating scale A method of performance appraisal that involves rating employee performance on an interval or ratio scale.

Graphology Also called handwriting analysis, a method of measuring personality by looking at the way in which a person writes.

Grievance system A process in which an employee files a complaint with the organization and a person or committee within the organization makes a decision regarding the complaint.

Group cohesiveness The extent to which members of a group like and trust one another.

Group–group conflict Conflict between two or more groups.

Group I strategy Leaders share the problem with the group and let the group reach a decision or solution.

Group size The number of members in a group.

Group status The esteem in which the group is held by people not in the group.

Groupthink A state of mind in which a group is so concerned about its own cohesiveness that it ignores important information.

Halo error A type of rating error that occurs when raters allow either a single attribute or an overall impression of an individual to affect the ratings that they make on each relevant job dimension.

Hawthorne effect When employees change their behavior due solely to the fact that they are receiving attention or are being observed.

Hawthorne studies A series of studies, conducted at the Western Electric plant in Hawthorne, Illinois, that have come to represent any change in behavior when people react to a change in the environment.

Heterogeneous groups Groups whose members share few similarities.

Hierarchy A system arranged by rank.

Hold-out sample A group of employees who are not used in creating the initial weights for a biodata instrument but instead are used to double-check the accuracy of the initial weights.

Homogeneous groups Groups whose members share the same characteristics.

Hostile environment A type of harassment characterized by a pattern of unwanted conduct related to gender that interferes with an individual's work performance.

Human factors A field of study concentrating on the interaction between humans and machines.

Hygiene factors In Herzberg's two-factor theory, job-related elements that result from but do not involve the job itself.

Hypothesis An educated prediction about the answer to a research question.

Identification The need to associate ourselves with the image projected by other people, groups, or objects.

Ignorance An organizational climate in which important information is not available.

IMPACT theory   A theory of leadership that states that there are six styles of leadership (*i*nformational, *m*agnetic, *p*osition, *a*ffiliation, *c*oercive, and *t*actical) and that each style will be effective only in one of six organizational climates.

Impoverished leadership   A style of leadership in which the leader is concerned with neither productivity nor the well-being of employees.

In-basket technique   An assessment center exercise designed to simulate the types of information that daily come across a manager's or employee's desk in order to observe the applicant's responses to such information.

Inclusive listening   The listening style of a person who cares about only the main points of a communication.

Independent variable   The manipulated variable in an experiment.

Individual dominance   When one member of a group dominates the group.

Individual–group conflict   Conflict between an individual and the other members of a group.

Industrial/organizational (I/O) psychology   A branch of psychology that applies the principles of psychology to the workplace.

Informal communication   Communication among employees in an organization that is not directly related to the completion of an organizational task.

Informational justice   The extent to which a supervisor is open and transparent in sharing information.

Informational style   A style of leadership in which the leader leads through knowledge and information; most effective in a climate of ignorance.

Informed consent   The formal process by which subjects give permission to be included in a study.

Infrequent observation   The idea that supervisors do not see most of an employee's behavior.

Initiating structure   The extent to which leaders define and structure their roles and the roles of their subordinates.

Input/output ratio   The ratio of how much employees believe they put into their jobs to how much they believe they get from their jobs.

Inputs   In equity theory, the elements that employees put into their jobs.

Instability   An organizational climate in which people are not sure what to do.

Institutional review board   A committee designated to ensure the ethical treatment of research subjects.

Instrumental style   In path–goal theory, a leadership style in which the leader plans and organizes the activities of employees.

Instrumentality   In expectancy theory, the perceived probability that a particular level of performance will result in a particular consequence.

Integrity test   Also called an honesty test; a psychological test designed to predict an applicant's tendency to steal.

Interacting group   A collection of individuals who work together to perform a task.

Interactional justice   The perceived fairness of the interpersonal treatment that employees receive in an organization.

Interactive video   A training technique in which an employee is presented with a videotaped situation and is asked to respond to the situation and then receives feedback based on the response.

Interdependence   The extent to which team members need and rely on other team members.

Interest inventory   A psychological test designed to identify vocational areas in which an individual might be interested.

Internal locus of control   The extent to which people believe that they are responsible for and in control of their success or failure in life.

Internal pay equity   The extent to which employees within an organization are paid fairly compared with other employees within the same organization.

Internal recruitment   Recruiting employees already employed by the organization.

Internal reliability   The extent to which responses to test items measuring the same construct are consistent.

Internalization   The fifth and final stage of organizational change, in which employees become comfortable with and productive in the new system.

Internship   A situation in which a student works for an organization, either for pay or as a volunteer, to receive practical work experience.

Interpersonal communication   Communication between two individuals.

Interpersonal conflict   Conflict between two people.

Interpersonal justice   The extent to which a supervisor adequately treats an employee.

Intervening variable   A third variable that can often explain the relationship between two other variables.

Intimacy zone   A distance zone within 18 inches of a person, where only people with a close relationship to the person are allowed to enter.

Intranet   A computer-based employee communication network used exclusively by one organization.

Intrinsic motivation   Work motivation in the absence of such external factors as pay, promotion, and coworkers.

Isolate   An employee who receives less than half of all grapevine information.

Isolation   The degree of physical distance of a group from other groups.

Item homogeneity   The extent to which test items measure the same construct.

Item stability   The extent to which responses to the same test items are consistent.

Job Adaptability Inventory (JAI)   A job analysis method that taps the extent to which a job involves eight types of adaptability.

Job analysis   The process of identifying how a job is performed, the conditions under which it is performed, and the personal requirements it takes to perform the job.

Job analysis interview   Obtaining information about a job by talking to a person performing it.

Job analyst   The person conducting the job analysis.

Job characteristics theory   The theory proposed by Hackman and Oldham that suggests that certain characteristics of a job will make the job more or less satisfying, depending on the particular needs of the worker.

Job Choice Exercise (JCE)   An objective test used to measure various need levels.

Job Components Inventory (JCI)   A structured job analysis technique that concentrates on worker requirements for performing a job rather than on specific tasks.

Job crafting   A process in which employees unofficially change their job duties to better fit their interests and skills.

Job description   A written summary of the tasks performed in a job, the conditions under which the job is performed, and the requirements needed to perform the job.

Job Descriptive Index (JDI)   A measure of job satisfaction that yields scores on five dimensions.

Job Diagnostic Survey (JDS)   A measure of the extent to which a job provides opportunities for growth, autonomy, and meaning.

Job Elements Inventory (JEI)   A structured job analysis technique developed by Cornelius and Hakel that is similar to the Position Analysis Questionnaire (PAQ) but easier to read.

Job enlargement   A system in which employees are given more tasks to perform at the same time.

Job enrichment   A system in which employees are given more responsibility over the tasks and decisions related to their job.

Job evaluation   The process of determining the monetary worth of a job.

Job fair   A recruitment method in which several employers are available at one location so that many applicants can obtain information at one time.

Job in General (JIG) Scale   A measure of the overall level of job satisfaction.

Job knowledge test   A test that measures the amount of job-related knowledge an applicant possesses.

Job participation   A job analysis method in which the job analyst actually performs the job being analyzed.

Job related   The extent to which a test or measure taps a knowledge, skill, ability, behavior, or other characteristic needed to successfully perform a job.

Job rotation   A system in which employees are given the opportunity to perform several different jobs in an organization.

Job satisfaction   The attitude employees have toward their jobs.

Job sharing   A work schedule in which two employees share one job by splitting the work hours.

Job specifications   A relatively dated term that refers to the knowledge, skills, and abilities needed to successfully perform a job. *Competencies* is the more common term used today.

Job Structure Profile (JSP)   A revised version of the Position Analysis Questionnaire (PAQ) designed to be used more by the job analyst than by the job incumbent.

Jobs for Veterans Act   A law passed in 2002 that increased the coverage of VEVRA to include disabled veterans, veterans who have recently left the service, and veterans who participated in a U.S. military operation for which an Armed Forces Service Medal was awarded.

Journal   A written collection of articles describing the methods and results of new research.

Jurisdictional ambiguity   Conflict caused by a disagreement about geographical territory or lines of authority.

Key-issues approach   A method of scoring interview answers that provides points for each part of an answer that matches the scoring key.

Knowledge   A body of information needed to perform a task.

Knowledge test   A test that measures the level of an employee's knowledge about a job-related topic.

Known-group validity   A form of validity in which test scores from two contrasting groups "known" to differ on a construct are compared.

KSAOs   *K*nowledge, *s*kills, *a*bilities, and *o*ther characteristics required to perform a job.

Kuder-Richardson Formula 20 (K-R 20)   A statistic used to determine internal reliability of tests that use items with dichotomous answers (yes/no, true/false).

Laboratory research Research that is conducted in a laboratory setting that can be controlled more easily than research conducted in a field setting.

Lawshe tables Tables that use the base rate, test validity, and applicant percentile on a test to determine the probability of future success for that applicant.

Leader Behavior Description Questionnaire (LBDQ) A test used to measure perceptions of a leader's style by their subordinates.

Leader emergence A part of trait theory that postulates that certain types of people will become leaders and certain types will not.

Leader Match A training program that teaches leaders how to change situations to match their leadership styles.

Leader performance A part of trait theory that postulates that certain types of people will be better leaders than will other types of people.

Leader position power The variable in Fiedler's contingency model that refers to the extent to which a leader, by the nature of their position, has the power to reward and punish subordinates.

Leaderless group discussion A selection technique, usually found in assessment centers, in which applicants meet in small groups and are given a problem to solve or an issue to discuss.

Leader–member exchange (LMX) theory A leadership theory that focuses on the interaction between leaders and subordinates.

Leader-member relations The variable in Fiedler's contingency model that refers to the extent to which subordinates like a leader.

Leadership motive pattern The name for a pattern of needs in which a leader has a high need for power and a low need for affiliation.

Leadership Opinion Questionnaire (LOQ) A test used to measure a leader's self-perception of their leadership style.

Least acceptable result (LAR) The lowest settlement that a person is willing to accept in a negotiated agreement.

Least-Preferred Coworker (LPC) Scale A test used in conjunction with Fiedler's contingency model to reveal leadership style and effectiveness.

Legitimate power The power that individuals have because of their elected or appointed position.

Leisure listening The listening style of a person who cares about only interesting information.

Leniency error A type of rating error in which a rater consistently gives all employees high ratings, regardless of their actual levels of performance.

Letter of recommendation A letter expressing an opinion regarding an applicant's ability, previous performance, work habits, character, or potential for success.

Leveled Describes a message from which unimportant informational details have been removed before the message is passed from one person to another.

Liaison A person who acts as an intermediary between employees and management, or the type of employee who both sends and receives most grapevine information.

Linear A straight-line relationship between the test score and the criterion of measurement.

Listserv A program that automatically distributes e-mail messages to a group of people who have a common interest.

Living case A case study based on a real situation rather than a hypothetical one.

Magazine An unscientific collection of articles about a wide range of topics.

Magnetic style A style of leadership in which the leader has influence because of their charismatic personality; most effective in a climate of despair.

Management teams Teams that coordinate, manage, advise, and direct employees and teams.

Managerial Grid A measure of leadership that classifies a leader into one of five leadership styles.

Manipulation The alteration of a variable by an experimenter in expectation that the alteration will result in a change in the dependent variable.

Massed practice Concentrating learning into a short period of time.

Maximum supportable position (MSP) The highest possible settlement that a person could reasonably ask for and still maintain credibility in negotiating an agreement.

Mean effect size Used in meta-analysis, a statistic that is the average of the effect sizes for all studies included in the analysis.

Measurement bias Group differences in test scores that are unrelated to the construct being measured.

Mediation A method of resolving conflict in which a neutral third party is asked to help the two parties reach an agreement.

Meeting cow An unnecessary or unnecessarily long meeting scheduled out of force of habit.

Mental Measurements Yearbook **(MMY)** The name of a book containing information about the reliability and validity of various psychological tests.

Mentor An experienced employee who advises and looks out for a new employee.

Mere presence   Theory stating that the very fact that others happen to be present naturally produces arousal and thus may affect performance.

Merit pay   An incentive plan in which employees receive pay bonuses based on performance appraisal scores.

Meta-analysis   A statistical method for cumulating research results.

Microlearning   Training programs that are only a few minutes in length.

Middle-of-the-road leadership   A leadership style reflecting a balanced orientation between people and tasks.

Minnesota Multiphasic Personality Inventory-2 (MMPI-2)   The most widely used objective test of psychopathology.

Minnesota Satisfaction Questionnaire (MSQ)   A measure of job satisfaction that yields scores on 20 dimensions.

Mixed-standard scale   A method of performance appraisal in which a supervisor reads the description of a specific behavior and then decides whether the behavior of the employee is better than, equal to, or poorer than the behavior described.

Modeling   Learning through watching and imitating the behavior of others.

Modified flexitour   A flextime schedule in which employees have flexibility in scheduling but must schedule their work hours a day in advance.

Moonlighting   Working more than one job.

Motivation   The force that drives an employee to perform well.

Motivators   In Herzberg's two-factor theory, elements of a job that concern the actual duties performed by the employee.

Multiple channels   A strategy for coping with communication overload in which an organization reduces the amount of communication going to one person by directing some of it to another person.

Multiple-cutoff approach   A selection strategy in which applicants must meet or exceed the passing score on more than one selection test.

Multiple-hurdle approach   Selection practice of administering one test at a time so that applicants must pass that test before being allowed to take the next test.

Multiple regression   A statistical procedure in which the scores from more than one criterion-valid test are weighted according to how well each test score predicts the criterion.

Multiple-source feedback   A performance appraisal strategy in which an employee receives feedback from sources (e.g., clients, subordinates, peers) other than just their supervisor.

MUM (minimize unpleasant messages) effect   The idea that people prefer not to pass on unpleasant information, with the result that important information is not always communicated.

Need for achievement   According to trait theory, the extent to which a person desires to be successful.

Need for affiliation   The extent to which a person desires to be around other people.

Need for power   According to trait theory, the extent to which a person desires to be in control of other people.

Needs analysis   The process of determining the training needs of an organization.

Needs theory   A theory based on the idea that employees will be satisfied with jobs that satisfy their needs.

Negative feedback   Telling employees what they are doing incorrectly to improve their performance of a task.

Negative-information bias   The fact that negative information receives more weight in an employment decision than does positive information.

Negligent hiring   An organization's failure to meet its legal duty to protect its employees and customers from potential harm caused by its employees.

Negligent reference   An organization's failure to meet its legal duty to supply relevant information to a prospective employer about a former employee's potential for legal trouble.

Negotiation and bargaining   A method of resolving conflict in which two sides use verbal skill and strategy to reach an agreement.

Neuroticism   A personality trait characterized by a tendency to experience such negative emotions as anxiety, anger, tension, and moodiness.

Newsletters   A method of downward communication typically used to communicate organizational feedback and celebrate employee success.

Noise   Any variable concerning or affecting the channel that interferes with the proper reception of a message.

Nominal group   A collection of individuals whose results are pooled but who never interact with one another.

Nonbinding arbitration   A method of resolving conflicts in which a neutral third party is asked to choose which side is correct but in which either party may appeal the decision.

Noncalculative motivation   Those who seek leadership positions because they will result in personal gain.

Nonconforming listening   The listening style of a person who cares about only information that is consistent with their way of thinking.

Nonverbal communication   Factors such as eye contact and posture that are not associated with actual words spoken.

Normative commitment   The extent to which employees feel an obligation to remain with an organization.

Norming   The third stage of the team process, in which teams establish roles and determine policies and procedures.

Objective tests   A type of personality test that is structured to limit the respondent to a few answers that will be scored by standardized keys.

Observation   A job analysis method in which the job analyst watches job incumbents perform their jobs.

Occupational Information Network (O*NET)   The job analysis system used by the federal government that has replaced the Dictionary of Occupational Titles (DOT).

Ombudsperson   A person who investigates employees' complaints and solves problems.

Omission   A response to communication overload that involves the conscious decision not to process certain types of information.

On-site childcare facility   A childcare center that is located on the site of the organization employing the parent.

Open desk arrangement   An office arranged so that a visitor can sit adjacent to rather than across from the person behind the desk.

Operant conditioning   A type of learning based on the idea that humans learn to behave in ways that will result in favorable outcomes and learn not to behave in ways that result in unfavorable outcomes.

Optimal level of arousal   The idea that performance is best with moderate levels of arousal.

Organization-based self-esteem   The level of an employee's competence and self-worth as a member of an organization.

Organizational analysis   The process of determining the organizational factors that will either facilitate or inhibit training effectiveness.

Organizational citizenship behaviors (OCBs)   Behaviors that are not part of an employee's job but that make the organization a better place to work (e.g., helping others, staying late).

Organizational commitment   The extent to which an employee identifies with and is involved with an organization.

Organizational Commitment Questionnaire (OCQ)   A 15-item questionnaire that taps three organizational commitment dimensions.

Organizational Commitment Scale (OCS)   A nine-item survey that taps three aspects of organizational commitment.

Organizational culture   The shared values, beliefs, and traditions that exist among individuals in an organization.

Organizational-fit questions   A type of structured-interview question that taps how well an applicant's personality and values will fit with the organizational culture.

Organizational justice   A theory that postulates that if employees perceive they are being treated fairly, they will be more likely to be satisfied with their jobs and motivated to do well.

Organizational psychology   The field of study that investigates the behavior of employees within the context of an organization.

Organizational socialization   The process whereby new employees learn the behaviors and attitudes they need to be successful in an organization.

Other characteristics   Such personal factors as personality, willingness, and interest that are not knowledge, skills, or abilities.

Outputs   In equity theory, what employees get from their jobs.

Outside pressure   The amount of psychological pressure placed on a group by people who are not members of the group.

Outsourcing   The process of having certain organizational functions performed by an outside vendor rather than an employee in the organization.

Overlearning   Practicing a task even after it has been mastered to retain learning.

Overt integrity test   A type of honesty test that asks questions about applicants' attitudes toward theft and their previous theft history.

Paid time off program (PTO)   An attendance policy in which all paid vacations, sick days, holidays, and so forth are combined.

Paired comparison   A form of ranking in which a group of employees to be ranked are compared one pair at a time.

Paper cow   Unnecessary paperwork generated within organizations out of force of habit.

Paralanguage   Communication inferred from the tone, tempo, volume, and rate of speech.

Parallel teams   Also called *cross-functional teams*, they consist of representatives from various departments (functions) within an organization.

Participative style   In path–goal theory, a leadership style in which the leader allows employees to participate in decisions.

Passing score   The minimum test score that an applicant must achieve to be considered for hire.

Pass-through programs   A formal method of coaching in which excellent employees spend a period of time in the training department learning training techniques and training employees.

Past-focused question   A type of structured-interview question that taps an applicant's experience.

Path–goal theory   A theory of leadership stating that leaders will be effective if their behavior helps subordinates achieve relevant goals.

Patterned-behavior description interview (PBDI)   A structured interview in which the questions focus on behavior in previous jobs.

Pay for performance   A system in which employees are paid based on how much they individually produce.

Peak-time pay   A system in which part-time employees who work only during peak hours are paid at a higher hourly rate than all-day, full-time employees.

Perceptual ability   Measure of facility with such processes as spatial relations and form perception.

Performance appraisal review   A meeting between a supervisor and a subordinate for the purpose of discussing performance appraisal results.

Performance appraisal score   A rating representing some aspect of an employee's work performance.

Performing   The fourth and final stage of the team process, in which teams work toward accomplishing their goals.

Permanency   The extent to which a team will remain together or be disbanded after a task has been accomplished.

Person analysis   The process of identifying the employees who need training and determining the areas in which each individual employee needs to be trained.

Personal distance zone   A distance zone from 18 inches to 4 feet from a person that is usually reserved for friends and acquaintances.

Personality   Relatively stable traits possessed by an individual.

Personality-based integrity test   A type of honesty test that measures personality traits thought to be related to antisocial behavior.

Personality inventory   A psychological assessment designed to measure various aspects of an applicant's personality.

Personality-Related Position Requirements Form (PPRF)   A new job analysis instrument that helps determine the personality requirements for a job.

Personnel psychology   The field of study that concentrates on the selection and evaluation of employees.

Person-organization fit   The extent to which an employee's personality, values, attitudes, philosophy, and skills match those of the organization.

Perspective taking   Rating a potential stressor by asking how bad it really is compared with all things considered or with a worst-case scenario.

Peter Principle   The idea that organizations tend to promote good employees until they reach the level at which they are not competent—in other words, their highest level of incompetence.

Physical ability tests   Tests that measure an applicant's level of physical ability required for a job.

Point-of-purchase method   A recruitment method in which help-wanted signs are placed so that they can be viewed by people who visit the organization.

Policy manual   A formal method of downward communication in which an organization's rules and procedures are placed in a manual; legally binding by courts of law.

Polygraph   An electronic test intended to determine honesty by measuring an individual's physiological changes after being asked questions.

Position Analysis Questionnaire (PAQ)   A structured job analysis method developed by McCormick.

Position style   A leadership style in which the leaders influence others by virtue of their appointed or elected authority; most effective in a climate of instability.

Posttest   A measure of job performance or knowledge taken after a training program has been completed.

Power differentiation   The extent to which team members have the same level of power and respect.

Practical significance   The extent to which the results of a study have actual impact on human behavior.

Practicum   A paid or unpaid position with an organization that gives a student practical work experience.

Predictive bias   A situation in which the predicted level of job success falsely favors one group over another.

Predictive validity   A form of criterion validity in which test scores of applicants are compared at a later date with a measure of job performance.

Pregnancy Discrimination Act   A 1978 federal law protecting the rights of pregnant women.

Premack Principle   The idea that reinforcement is relative both within an individual and between individuals.

Pretest   A measure of job performance or knowledge taken before the implementation of a training program.

Primacy effect   The fact that information presented early in an interview carries more weight than information presented later.

Probability grapevine   A pattern of grapevine communication in which a message is passed randomly among all employees.

Procedural justice   The perceived fairness of the methods used by an organization to make decisions.

Profit sharing A group incentive method in which employees get a percentage of the profits made by an organization.

Programmed instruction A training method in which employees learn information at their own pace.

Progressive discipline Providing employees with punishments of increasing severity, as needed, to change behavior.

Project teams Groups formed to produce onetime outputs such as creating a new product, installing a new software system, or hiring a new employee.

Projective tests A subjective test in which a subject is asked to perform relatively unstructured tasks, such as drawing pictures, and in which a psychologist analyzes their responses.

Proportion of correct decisions A utility method that compares the percentage of times a selection decision was accurate with the percentage of successful employees.

Protected class Any group of people for whom protective legislation has been passed.

Prototype The overall image that a supervisor has of an employee.

Proximity Physical distance between people.

Proximity error A type of rating error in which a rating made on one dimension influences the rating made on the dimension that immediately follows it on the rating scale.

Psychomotor ability Measure of facility with such processes as finger dexterity and motor coordination.

Public distance zone Distance greater than 12 feet from a person that is typical of the interpersonal space allowed for social interactions such as large group lectures.

Public employment agency An employment service operated by a state or local government, designed to match applicants with job openings.

Pygmalion effect The idea that if people believe that something is true, they will act in a manner consistent with that belief.

Qualified workforce The percentage of people in a given geographic area who have the qualifications (skills, education, etc.) to perform a certain job.

Quality A type of objective criterion used to measure job performance by comparing a job behavior with a standard.

Quality circles Employee groups that meet to propose changes that will improve productivity and the quality of work life.

Quantity A type of objective criterion used to measure job performance by counting the number of relevant job behaviors that occur.

Quasi-experiment Research method in which the experimenter either does not manipulate the independent variable or in which subjects are not randomly assigned to conditions.

Questionnaire approach The method of obtaining biodata from questionnaires rather than from employee files.

Queuing A method of coping with communication overload that involves organizing work into an order in which it will be handled.

Quid pro quo A type of sexual harassment in which the granting of sexual favors is tied to an employment decision.

Race According to Congress, the four races are African American, European American, Asian American, and Native American Indian.

Racial bias The tendency to give members of a particular race lower evaluation ratings than are justified by their actual performance or to give members of one race lower ratings than members of another race.

Radiation One way our bodies maintain a normal temperature by the emission of heat waves.

Random assignment The random, unbiased assignment of subjects in a research sample to the various experimental and control conditions.

Random sample A sample in which every member of the relevant population had an equal chance of being chosen to participate in the study.

Rank order A method of performance appraisal in which employees are ranked from best to worst.

Realistic job preview (RJP) A method of recruitment in which job applicants are told both the positive and the negative aspects of a job.

Recency effect The tendency for supervisors to recall and place more weight on recent behaviors when they evaluate performance.

Receptive changer A person who is willing to change.

Recruitment The process of attracting employees to an organization.

Reference The expression of an opinion, either orally or through a written checklist, regarding an applicant's ability, previous performance, work habits, character, or potential for future success.

Reference check The process of confirming the accuracy of résumé and job application information.

Referent power Leadership power that exists when followers can identify with a leader and the leader's goals.

Referral service A system of childcare in which an employer maintains a list of certified childcare centers that can be used by its employees.

Reinforcement hierarchy   A rank-ordered list of reinforcers for an individual.

Rejection letter   A letter from an organization to an applicant informing the applicant that they will not receive a job offer.

Relatedness   The need from self-determination theory to feel that we are part of a group.

Reliability   The extent to which a score from a test or from an evaluation is consistent and free from error.

Reluctant changer   A person who will initially resist change but will eventually go along with it.

Residual stress   Stress that is carried over from previous stressful situations.

Restricted range   A narrow range of performance scores that makes it difficult to obtain a significant validity coefficient.

Résumé   A formal summary of an applicant's professional and educational background.

Résumé fraud   The intentional placement of untrue information on a résumé.

Return on investment (ROI)   The amount of money an organization makes after subtracting the cost of training or other interventions.

Reward power   Leadership power that exists to the extent that the leader has the ability and authority to provide rewards.

Right/wrong scoring   A method of scoring interview questions in which the answer is either right or wrong (e.g., What is the legal drinking age in Virginia?).

Rituals   Procedures in which employees participate to become "one of the gang."

Role ambiguity   The extent to which an employee's roles and expectations are unclear.

Role conflict   The extent to which an employee's role and expected role are the same.

Role overload   The extent to which an employee is able to psychologically handle the number of roles and tasks assigned.

Role-play   A training technique in which employees act out simulated roles.

Rorschach Inkblot Test   A projective personality test.

Rotating shift   A shift schedule in which employees periodically change the shifts that they work.

Rule of three   A variation on top-down selection in which the names of the top three applicants are given to a hiring authority who can then select any of the three.

Rumor   Poorly substantiated information that is passed along the grapevine.

Sacred cow hunt   The first step in organizational change, in which employees look for practices and policies that waste time and are counterproductive.

Safety needs   The second step in Maslow's hierarchy, concerning the need for security, stability, and physical safety.

Salary survey   A questionnaire sent to other organizations to see how much they are paying their employees in positions similar to those in the organization sending the survey.

Scientist-practitioner model   A teaching model in which students are trained first to be scientists and second to be able to apply the science of their field to find solutions to real-world problems.

Scorer reliability   The extent to which two people scoring a test agree on the test score, or the extent to which a test is scored correctly.

Selection ratio   The percentage of applicants an organization hires.

Self-actualization needs   The fifth step in Maslow's hierarchy, concerning the need to realize one's potential.

Self-determination theory   A theory that postulates that people have an innate need for three things: Competence, autonomy, and relatedness.

Self-directed teams   *See Quality circles.*

Self-esteem   The extent to which a person views themselves as a valuable and worthy individual.

Self-fulfilling prophecy   The idea that people behave in ways consistent with their self-image.

Self-monitoring   A personality trait characterized by the tendency to adapt one's behavior to fit a particular social situation.

Self-regulation theory   Postulates that employees can be motivated by monitoring their own progress toward the goals they set and adjusting their behavior to reach those goals.

Serial communication   Communication passed consecutively from one person to another.

Sharpened   Describes a message in which interesting and unusual information has been kept in the message when it is passed from one person to another.

Shrinkage   The amount of goods lost by an organization as a result of theft, breakage, or other loss.

Simulation   An exercise designed to place an applicant in a situation that is similar to the one that will be encountered on the job.

Single-group validity   The characteristic of a test that significantly predicts a criterion for one class of people but not for another.

Single-strand grapevine   A pattern of grapevine communication in which a message is passed in a chainlike fashion from one person to the next until the chain is broken.

Situational leadership theory   A theory of leadership stating that effective leaders must adapt their style of leadership to fit both the situation and the followers.

Situational question   A structured-interview technique in which applicants are presented with a series of situations and asked how they would handle each one.

Situational self-esteem   The positive or negative way in which a person views themselves in a particular situation.

Skill   Proficiency to perform a particular task.

Skill-based pay   Compensating an employee who participates in a training program designed to increase a particular job-related skill.

Skill-level determiner   A type of structured-interview question designed to tap an applicant's knowledge or skill.

Skill test   A test that measures an employee's level of some job-related skill.

Slightly heterogeneous groups   Groups in which a few group members have different characteristics from the rest of the group.

SME conference   A group job analysis interview consisting of subject-matter experts (SMEs).

Social distance   The extent to which team members treat each other in a friendly, informal manner.

Social distance zone   An interpersonal distance from 4 to 12 feet from a person that is typically used for business and for interacting with strangers.

Social facilitation   The positive effects that occur when a person performs a task in the presence of others.

Social information processing theory   States that employees model their levels of satisfaction and motivation from other employees.

Social impact theory   States that the addition of a group member has the greatest effect on group behavior when the size of the group is small.

Social inhibition   The negative effects that occur when a person performs a task in the presence of others.

Social learning theory   States that employees model their levels of satisfaction and motivation from other employees.

Social loafing   The fact that individuals in a group often exert less individual effort than they would if they were not in a group.

Social needs   The third step in Maslow's hierarchy, concerning the need to interact with other people.

Social-normative motivation   The desire to lead out of a sense of duty or responsibility.

Social recognition   A motivation technique using such methods as personal attention, signs of approval, and expressions of appreciation.

Socially influenced self-esteem   The positive or negative way in which a person views themselves based on the expectations of others.

Solomon four-groups design   An extensive method of evaluating the effectiveness of training with the use of pretests, posttests, and control groups.

Spearman-Brown prophecy formula   Used to correct reliability coefficients resulting from the split-half method.

Speed cow   The tendency for organizations to require employees to work faster and produce work sooner than needed.

Split-half method   A form of internal reliability in which the consistency of item responses is determined by comparing scores on half of the items with scores on the other half of the items.

Stability   The extent to which the membership of a group remains consistent over time.

Standard deviation (SD)   A statistic that indicates the variation of scores in a distribution.

Standard error of measurement (SEM)   The number of points that a test score could be off due to test unreliability.

Stock options   A group incentive method in which employees are given the option of buying stock in the future at the price of the stock when the options were granted.

Storming   The second stage in group formation in which group members disagree and resist their team roles.

Stress   Perceived psychological pressure.

Stressors   Events that cause stress.

Stretch assignment   A training method in which employees are placed in new assignments that allow them to "stretch" their skill set.

Strictness error   A type of rating error in which a rater consistently gives all employees low ratings, regardless of their actual levels of performance.

Strong Interest Inventory (SII)   A popular interest inventory used to help people choose careers.

Structured interviews   Interviews in which questions are based on a job analysis, every applicant is asked the same questions, and there is a standardized scoring system so that identical answers are given identical scores.

Stylistic listening   The listening style of a person who pays attention mainly to the way in which words are spoken.

Subject-matter experts (SMEs)   Sources such as supervisors and incumbents who are knowledgeable about a job.

Suggestion box   A form of upward communication in which employees are asked to place their suggestions in a box.

Summative test   A test given at the end of a training program to evaluate the success of the training program.

Supportive style   In path–goal theory, a leadership style in which leaders show concern for their employees.

Surveys   Questionnaires asking employees about the areas in which they feel they need training.

Survivors   Employees who retain their jobs following a downsizing.

Symbols   Organizational behaviors or practices that convey messages to employees.

Synchronous technologies   Distance learning programs that require employees to complete the training at the same time and at the same pace, although they may be in different physical locations.

Synthetic validity   A form of validity generalization in which validity is inferred based on a match between job components and tests previously found valid for those job components.

Tactical style   A leadership style in which a person leads through organization and strategy; most effective in a climate of disorganization.

Task analysis   The process of identifying the tasks for which employees need to be trained.

Task-centered leaders   Leaders who define and structure their roles as well as the roles of their subordinates.

Task interdependence   A potential source of conflict that arises when the completion of a task by one person affects the completion of a task by another person.

Task inventory   A questionnaire containing a list of tasks each of which the job incumbent rates on a series of scales such as importance and time spent.

Task structuredness   The variable in Fiedler's contingency model that refers to the extent to which tasks have clear goals and problems can be solved.

Taylor-Russell tables   A series of tables based on the selection ratio, base rate, and test validity that yield information about the percentage of future employees who will be successful if a particular test is used.

Team leadership   A leadership style in which the leader is concerned with both productivity and employee well-being.

Technical listening   The listening style of a person who cares about only facts and details.

Telecommuting   Working at home rather than at the office by communicating with managers and coworkers via phone, computer, fax machine, and other offsite media.

Temporal stability   The consistency of test scores across time.

Temporary employees   Also called "temps"—employees hired through a temporary employment agency.

Tenure   The length of time an employee has been with an organization.

Terminal master's degree programs   Graduate programs that offer a master's degree but not a Ph.D.

Test-retest reliability   The extent to which repeated administration of the same test will achieve similar results.

Thematic Apperception Test (TAT)   A projective personality test in which test-takers are shown pictures and asked to tell stories. It is designed to measure various need levels.

Theory   A systematic set of assumptions regarding the cause and nature of behavior.

Theory X leaders   Leaders who believe that employees are extrinsically motivated and thus lead by giving directives and setting goals.

Theory Y leaders   Leaders who believe that employees are intrinsically motivated and thus lead with a "hands-off" or a participative approach.

Third-party intervention   When a neutral party is asked to help resolve a conflict.

Threshold Traits Analysis (TTA)   A 33-item questionnaire developed by Lopez that identifies traits necessary to successfully perform a job.

Top-down selection   Selecting applicants in straight rank order of their test scores.

Trade magazine   A collection of articles for those "in the biz," about related professional topics, seldom directly reporting the methods and results of new research.

Training   A planned effort by an organization to facilitate the learning of job-related behavior on the part of its employees.

Transactional leadership   Leadership style in which the leader focuses on task-oriented behaviors.

Transfer of training   The extent to which behavior learned in training will be performed on the job.

Transformational leadership   Visionary leadership in which the leader changes the nature and goals of an organization.

Triangling   An employee discusses a conflict with a third-party such as a friend or supervisor. In doing so, the employee hopes that the third party will talk to the second party and that the conflict will be resolved without the need for the two parties to meet.

Two-factor theory   Herzberg's needs theory, postulating that there are two factors involved in job satisfaction: hygiene factors and motivators.

Type A personality   A stress-prone person who is competitive, impatient, and hurried.

Type B personality   A non–stress-prone person who is relaxed and agreeable.

Typical-answer approach   A method of scoring interview answers that compares an applicant's answer with benchmark answers.

Uniform Guidelines   Federal guidelines used to guide an employer in establishing fair selection methods.

Union steward   An employee who serves as a liaison between unionized employees and management.

Unproctored internet-based testing (UIT)   An assessment method that can be taken virtually at any time and place and on the device of the applicant's choosing.

Unstructured interview   An interview in which applicants are not asked the same questions and in which there is no standard scoring system to score applicant answers.

Upward communication   Communication within an organization in which the direction of communication is from employees up to management.

Utility formula   Method of ascertaining the extent to which an organization will benefit from the use of a particular selection system.

Valence   In expectancy theory, the perceived desirability of a consequence that results from a particular level of performance.

Validity   The degree to which inferences from scores on tests or assessments are justified by the evidence.

Validity coefficient   The correlation between scores on a selection method (e.g., interview, cognitive ability test) and a measure of job performance (e.g., supervisor rating, absenteeism).

Validity generalization (VG)   The extent to which inferences from test scores from one organization can be applied to another organization.

Vertical dyad linkage (VDL) theory   A leadership theory that concentrates on the interaction between the leader and their subordinates.

Vertical percentage method   For scoring biodata in which the percentage of unsuccessful employees responding in a particular way is subtracted from the percentage of successful employees responding in the same way.

Victims   Employees who lose their jobs due to a layoff.

Vietnam-Era Veterans Readjustment Assistance Act (VEVRAA)   A 1974 federal law that mandates that federal government contractors and subcontractors take affirmative action to employ and promote Vietnam-era veterans.

Virtual job fair   A job fair held on campus in which students can "tour" a company virtually, ask questions of recruiters, and electronically send résumés.

Virtual reality   Any three-dimensional digital simulation that can imitate a physical presence.

Virtual teams   Teams that communicate through email rather than face-to-face.

Vocational counseling   The process of helping an individual choose and prepare for the most suitable career.

Vocational Rehabilitation Act of 1973   Federal act passed in 1973 that prohibits federal government contractors or subcontractors from discriminating against the physically or mentally handicapped.

Voice stress analyzer   An electronic test to determine honesty by measuring an individual's voice changes after being asked questions.

Voucher system   Childcare policy in which an organization pays all or some of its employees' childcare costs at private child-care centers by providing the employees with vouchers.

Vroom-Yetton Model   A theory of leadership that concentrates on helping a leader choose how to make a decision.

Wage trend line   A line that represents the ideal relationship between the number of points that a job has been assigned (using the point method of evaluation) and the salary range for that job.

Webcast   A noninteractive training method in which the trainer transmits training information over the Internet.

Webinar   Short for "web seminar," an interactive training method in which training is transmitted over the Internet.

Well pay   A method of absenteeism control in which employees are paid for their unused sick leave.

Wiki   A collection of web pages in which users can create web pages on a topic and readers can freely edit those pages.

Winning at all costs   An approach to handling conflict in which one side seeks to win regardless of the damage to the other side.

Withdrawal   An approach to handling conflict in which one of the parties removes themselves from the situation to avoid the conflict.

Wonderlic Personnel Test   The cognitive ability test that is most commonly used in industry.

Work Preference Inventory (WPI)   A measure of an individual's orientation toward intrinsic versus extrinsic motivation.

Work sample   A method of selecting employees in which an applicant is asked to perform samples of actual job-related tasks.

Work teams   Groups of employees who manage themselves, assign jobs, plan and schedule work, make work-related decisions, and solve work-related problems.

References

Aamodt, M. G. (1986). *Validity of expert advice regarding the employment interview.* Paper presented at the annual meeting of the International Personnel Management Association Assessment Council, San Francisco.

Aamodt, M. G. (2004). *Research in law enforcement selection.* Boca Raton, FL: BrownWalker.

Aamodt, M. G. (2008). Reducing misconceptions and false beliefs in police and criminal psychology. *Criminal Justice and Behavior, 35*(10), 1231–1240.

Aamodt, M. G. (2014). Using background checks in the employee selection process. In C. Hanvey and K. Sady (Eds.), *Practitioners guide to legal issues in organizations.* New York: Springer.

Aamodt, M. G., & Carr, K. (1988). Relationship between recruitment source and employee behavior. *Proceedings of the 12th Annual Meeting of the International Personnel Management Association Assessment Council, 143–146.*

Aamodt, M. G., Kimbrough, W. W., & Alexander, C. J. (1983). A preliminary investigation of the relationship between team racial heterogeneity and team performance in college basketball. *Journal of Sports Sciences, 1,* 131–133.

Aamodt, M. G., Kimbrough, W. W., Keller, R. J., & Crawford, K. (1982). Relationship between sex, race, and job performance level and the generation of critical incidents. *Educational and Psychological Research, 2,* 227–234.

Aamodt, M. G., & Peggans, D. (1988). Tactfully rejecting job applicants. *Personnel Administrator, 33,* 58–60.

Aamodt, M. G., Reardon, C., & Kimbrough, W. W. (1986). The Critical Incident Technique revisited. *Journal of Police and Criminal Psychology, 2,* 48–59.

Aamodt, M. G., Surrette, M. A., & Cohen, D. (2010). *Understanding statistics in I/O psychology and human resource management* (2nd ed.). Belmont, CA: Wadsworth Publishing.

Aamodt, M. G., & Williams, F. (2005, April). *Reliability, validity, and adverse impact of references and letters of recommendation.* Paper presented at the 20th annual meeting of the Society for Industrial and Organizational Psychology, Los Angeles, CA.

Abramis, D. J. (1994). Work role ambiguity, job satisfaction, and job performance: Meta-analyses and review. *Psychological Reports, 75*(3), 1411–1433.

Acuff, F. (2008). *Negotiate anything with anyone anywhere around the world.* New York: AMACOM.

Adams, G. A., & Jex, S. M. (1999). Relationships between time management, control, work-family conflict, and strain. *Journal of Occupational Health Psychology, 4*(10), 72–77.

Adams, J. S. (1965). Inequity in social change. In L. Berkowitz (Ed.), *Advances in experimental social psychology* (Vol. 2, pp. 267–299). New York: Academic Press.

Adams, J. S., & Rosenbaum, W. B. (1962). The relationship of worker productivity to cognitive dissonance about wage inequities. *Journal of Applied Psychology, 46,* 161–164.

Adler, S., Boyce, A. S., Martin, N. R., & Dreibelbis, R. C. (2019). The state of technology enabled simulations. In R. N. Landers (Ed.), *The Cambridge handbook of technology and employee behavior* (pp. 208–231). Cambridge: Cambridge University Press.

Aguinis, H., Culpepper, S. A., & Pierce, C. A. (2016). Differential prediction generalization in college admissions testing. *Journal of Educational Psychology, 108*(7), 1045–1059.

Aiello, J. R., & Douthitt, E. A. (2001). Social facilitation from Triplett to electronic performance monitoring. *Group Dynamics: Theory, Research, and Practice, 5*(3), 163–180.

Aiken, J. R., & Hanges, P. J. (2017). The sum of the parts: Methods of combining assessments for employment decisions. In J. L. Farr & N. T. Tippins (Eds.), *Handbook of employee selection* (pp. 388–396). New York: Routledge.

Al Ansari, A., Donnon, T., Al Khalifa, K., Darwish, A., & Violato, C. (2014). The construct and criterion validity of the multi-source feedback process to assess physician performance: A meta-analysis. *Advances in Medical Education and Practice, 5*(1), 39–51.

Alboher, M. (2007). *One person/multiple careers: A new model for work/life success.* NY: Business Plus.

Albright, M. D., & Levy, P. E. (1995). The effects of source credibility and performance rating discrepancy on reactions to multiple raters. *Journal of Applied Social Psychology, 25*(7), 577–600.

Aldefer, C. P. (1972). *Existence, relatedness, and growth: Human needs in organizational settings.* New York: Free Press.

Alfayad, Z., & Arif, L. S. M. (2017). Employee voice and job satisfaction: An application of Herzberg two-factor theory. *International Review of Management and Marketing, 7*(1), 150–156.

Allard, G., Butler, J., Faust, D., & Shea, T. M. (1995). Errors in hand scoring objective personality tests: The case of the Personality Diagnostic Questionnaire. *Professional Psychology: Research & Practice, 26*(3), 304–308.

Allen, D. G., Bryant, P. C., & Vardaman, J. M. (2010). Retaining talent: Replacing misconceptions with evidence-based strategies. *Academy of Management Perspectives, 24,* 48–64.

Allen, D. G., Mahto, R. V., & Otondo, R. F. (2007). Web-based recruitment: Effects of information, organizational brand, and attitudes toward a web site on applicant attraction. *Journal of Applied Psychology, 92,* 1696–1708.

Allen, M., Mabry, E., Mattrey, M., Bourhis, J., Titsworth, S., & Burrell, N. (2004). Evaluating the effectiveness of distance learning: A comparison using meta-analysis. *Journal of Communication, 54*(3), 402–420.

Allen, M. T., & Connelly, M. S. (2005, April). *Case features and individual attributes in case-based training.* Poster presented at the 20th annual meeting of the Society for Industrial and Organizational Psychology, Los Angeles, CA.

Allen, N. J., & Hecht, T. D. (2004). The "romance of teams": Toward an understanding of its psychological underpinnings and implications. *Journal of Occupational and Organizational Psychology, 77*(4), 439–461.

Allen, T. D., Johnson, R. C., Kimburz, K. M., & Shockley, K. M. (2013). Work-family conflict and flexible work arrangements: Deconstructing flexibility. *Personnel Psychology, 66*(2), 345–376.

Allen, T. D., & Meyer, J. P. (1990). The measurement and antecedents of affective, continuance, and normative commitment to the organization. *Journal of Occupational Psychology, 63*(1), 1–18.

Alliger, G. M., Tannenbaum, S. I., Bennett, W., Traver, H., & Shotland, A. (1997). A meta-analysis of the relations among training criteria. *Personnel Psychology, 50*(2), 341–358.

Alonso, P., Moscoso, M., & Salgado, J. F. (2017). Structured behavioral interview as a legal guarantee for ensuring equal employment opportunities for women: A meta-analysis. *The European Journal of Psychology Applied to the Legal Context, 9*, 15–23.

Alvey, S., & Robbins, S. (2009). *Laying off employees.* Boston, MA: Harvard Business Press.

Amabile, T. M., Hill, K. G., Hennessey, B. A., & Tighe, E. M. (1994). The Work Preference Inventory: Assessing intrinsic and extrinsic motivational orientations. *Journal of Personality and Social Psychology, 66*(5), 950–967.

Ammerman, H. L. (1965). *A model of junior officer jobs for use in developing task inventories* (HumRRO Tech. Rep. 65–10). Alexandria, VA: Human Resources Research Organization.

Anderson, D. L. (2020). *Organization development: The process of leading organizational change (5th ed.).* Thousand Oaks, CA: Sage.

Anderson, N. H. (1965). Adding versus averaging as a stimulus combination rule in impression formation. *Journal of Experimental Psychology, 70*, 394–400.

Anderson, N., Salgado, J. F., & Hülsheger, U. R. (2010). Applicant reactions in selection: Comprehensive meta-analysis into reaction generalization versus situational specificity. *International Journal of Selection & Assessment, 18*(3), 291–304.

Anderson, N., Schlueter, J. E., Carlson, J. F., & Geisinger, K. F. (2016). *Tests in print IX.* Lincoln, NE: Buros Center for Testing.

Anderson, N., & Witvliet, C. (2008). Fairness reactions to personnel selection methods: An international comparison between the Netherlands, the United States, France, Spain, Portugal, and Singapore. *International Journal of Selection & Assessment, 16*(1), 1–13.

Andersson, B. E., & Nilsson, S. G. (1964). Studies in the reliability and validity of the critical incident technique. *Journal of Applied Psychology, 48*, 398–403.

Andrews, L. W. (2005). Hiring people with intellectual disabilities. *HR Magazine, 50*(7), 72–77.

Anseel, F., Lievens, F., Schollaert, E., & Choragwicka, B. (2010). Response rates in organizational science, 1995–2008: A meta-analytic review and guidelines for survey researchers. *Journal of Business and Psychology, 25*(3), 335–349.

Ansoorian, A. E., & Shultz, K. S. (1997). *The influence of expertise and gender on physical effort ratings.* Poster presented at the 12th annual conference of the Society for Industrial and Organizational Psychology, St. Louis, MO.

Antonioni, D. (1994). The effects of feedback accountability on upward appraisal ratings. *Personnel Psychology, 47*(2), 349–356.

Arcuri, A. E., & Lester, D. (1990). Moonlighting and stress in police officers. *Psychological Reports, 66*, 350.

Argus, K., & Zajack, M. (2008, April). *Need for achievement and leader effectiveness: A meta-analysis.* Poster presented at the 23rd annual conference of the Society for Industrial and Organizational Psychology, San Francisco, CA.

Armour, S. (2001, June 12). Arbitration's rise raises fairness issue. *USA Today*, p. B1–B2.

Armour, S. (2004, December 6). Working 9-to-5 no longer: More choose flexible hours on the job. *USA Today*, p. B1–B2.

Arnold, J. A., & Carnevale, P. J. (1997). Preferences for dispute resolution procedures as a function of intentionality, consequences, expected future interaction, and power. *Journal of Applied Social Psychology, 27*(5), 371–398.

Arthur, J. B. (1994). Effects of human resource systems on manufacturing performance and turnover. *Academy of Management Journal, 37*(3), 670–687.

Arthur, W., Bennett, W., Edens, P. S., & Bell, S. T. (2003). Effectiveness of training in organizations: A meta-analysis of design and evaluation features. *Journal of Applied Psychology, 88*(2), 234–243.

Arthur, W., Day, E. A., McNelly, T. L., & Edens, P. S. (2003). A meta-analysis of the criterion-related validity of assessment center dimensions. *Personnel Psychology, 56*(1), 125–154.

Arthur, W., Keiser, N. L., & Doverspike, D. (2018). An information processing-based conceptual framework of the effects of unproctored internet-based testing devices on scores on employment-related assessments and tests. *Human Performance, 31*(1), 1–32.

Arthur, W., & Traylor, Z. (2019). Mobile assessment in personnel testing. In R. N. Landers (Ed.), *The Cambridge handbook of technology and employee behavior* (pp. 179–207). Cambridge: Cambridge University Press.

Arvey, R. D., & Begalla, M. E. (1975). Analyzing the homemaker job using the PAQ. *Journal of Applied Psychology, 60*, 513–517.

Arvey, R. D., Bouchard, T. J., Segal, N. L., & Abraham, L. M. (1989). Job satisfaction: Environmental and genetic components. *Journal of Applied Psychology, 74*, 187–192.

Arvey, R. D., Gordon, M. E., Massengill, D. P., & Mussio, S. J. (1975). Differential report rates of minority and majority job candidates due to time lags between selection procedures. *Personnel Psychology, 28*(2), 175–180.

Arvey, R. D., McCall, B. P., Bouchard, T. J., Taubman, P., & Cavanaugh, M. A. (1994). Genetic influences on job satisfaction and work values. *Personality and Individual Differences, 17*(1), 21–33.

Arvey, R. D., Rotundo, M., Johnson, W., Zhang, Z., & McGue, M. (2006). The determinants of leadership role occupancy: Genetic and personality factors. *Leadership Quarterly, 17*(1), 1–20.

Ash, R. A., & Edgell, S. A. (1975). A note on the readability of the Position Analysis Questionnaire (PAQ). *Journal of Applied Psychology, 60*, 765–766.

Ash, R. A., Levine, E. L., Higbee, R. H., & Sistrunk, F. (1982). *Comparisons of task ratings from subject matter experts versus job incumbents.* Paper presented at the annual meeting of the Southeastern Psychological Association, New Orleans, LA.

Ashworth, N., De Champlain, A. F., & Kain, N. (2021). A review of multi-source feedback focusing on psychometrics, pitfalls and some possible solutions. *SN Social Sciences, 1*(1), 1–12.

ATD. (2020). *2020 State of the industry.* Alexandria, VA: Association for Talent Development.

Atwater, L. E. (1998). The advantages and pitfalls of self-assessment in organizations. In J. W. Smither (Ed.), *Performance appraisal: State of the art in practice* (pp. 331–369). San Francisco: Jossey-Bass.

Auerbach, A. (2021). *Flex: Reinventing work for a smarter, happier life.* London: HQ.

Austin, J., Kessler, M. L., Riccobono, J. E., & Bailey, J. S. (1996). Using feedback and reinforcement to improve the performance and safety of a roofing crew. *Journal of Organizational Behavior Management, 16*(2), 49–75.

Avery, D. R., & McKay, P. F. (2006). Target practice: An organizational impression management approach to attracting minority and female job applicants. *Personnel Psychology, 59,* 157–187.

Avis, J., & Kudisch, J. (2000). *Factors influencing subordinates' willingness to participate in an upward feedback system.* Paper presented at the 21st annual Graduate Student Conference in Industrial-Organizational Psychology and Organizational Behavior, Knoxville, TN.

Avolio, B. J., & Gardner, W. L. (2005). Authentic leadership development: Getting to the root of positive forms of leadership. *The Leadership Quarterly, 16*(3), 315–338.

Avolio, B. J., Gardner, W. L., Walumbwa, F. O., Luthans, F., & May, D. R. (2004). Unlocking the mask: A look at the process by which authentic leaders impact follower attitudes and behaviors. *The Leadership Quarterly, 15*(6), 801–823.

Avolio, B. J., & Yammarino, F. J. (2013). *Transformational and charismatic leadership: The road ahead* (2nd ed.). Bingley, England: Emerald Group Publishing.

Awad, G. H. (2013). Does policy name matter? The effect of framing on the evaluations of African American applicants. *Journal of Applied Social Psychology, 43*(S2), E379–E387.

Azar, O. H. (2007). The social norm of tipping: A review. *Journal of Applied Social Psychology, 37*(2), 380–402.

Babad, E. Y., Inbar, J., & Rosenthal, R. (1982). Pygmalion, Galatea, and the Golem: Investigations of biased and unbiased teachers. *Journal of Educational Psychology, 74,* 459–474.

Babapour, M. (2019). *The quest for the room of requirement.* Gothenburg, Sweden: Chalmers University of Technology.

Babar, T. (2021). 10 effective ways to make your boss like you. Retrieved May 1, 2021, from https://www.lifehack.org/articles/work/10-effective-ways-make-your-boss-like-you.html.

Babcock, L., & Laschever, S. (2008). *Ask for it: How women can use the power of negotiation to get what they really want.* New York: Bantam.

Babcock, P. (2005). Find what workers want. *HR Magazine, 50*(4), 51–56.

Bacal, R. (2012). *Performance management* (2nd ed.). New York: McGraw-Hill.

Badura, E., Grijalva, D. A., Newman, D. A., Yan, T. T., & Jeon, G. (2018). Gender and leadership emergence: A meta-analysis and explanatory model. *Personnel Psychology, 71*(3), 335–367.

Bahls, J. E. (1998). Drugs in the workplace. *HR Magazine, 43*(2), 81–87.

Bal, A. C., Reiss, A. E. B., Rudolph, C. W., & Baltes, B. (2011). Examining positive and negative perceptions of older workers: A meta-analysis. *The Journals of Gerontology, 66B*(6), 687–698.

Baldridge, D. C., & Veiga, J. F. (2001). Toward a greater under-standing of the willingness to request an accommodation: Can requesters' beliefs disable the Americans with Disabilities Act? *Academy of Management Review, 26*(1), 85–99.

Baldwin, T. T., & Ford, J. K. (1988). Transfer of training: A review and directions for future research. *Personnel Psychology, 41,* 63–105.

Baldwin, T. T., Magjuka, R. J., & Loher, B. T. (1991). The perils of participation: Effects of choice of training on trainee motivation and learning. *Personnel Psychology, 44,* 51–65.

Balfour, D. L., & Wechsler, B. (1996). Organizational commitment: Antecedents and outcomes in public organizations. *Public Productivity and Management Review, 29,* 256–277.

Baltes, B. B., Briggs, T. E., Huff, J. W., Wright, J. A., & Neuman, G. A. (1999). Flexible and compressed workweek schedules: A meta-analysis of their effects on work-related criteria. *Journal of Applied Psychology, 84*(4), 496–513.

Bandura, A. (1977). *Social learning theory.* Englewood Cliffs, NJ: Prentice Hall.

Bangerter, A., König, C. J., Blatti, S., & Salvisberg, A. (2009). How widespread is graphology in personnel selection practice? A case study of a job market myth. *International Journal of Selection and Assessment, 17*(2), 219–230.

Banks, M. H., Jackson, P. R., Stafford, E. M., & Warr, P. B. (1983). The Job Components Inventory and the analysis of jobs requiring limited skill. *Personnel Psychology, 36,* 57–66.

Banks, M. H., & Miller, R. L. (1984). Reliability and convergent validity of the Job Components Inventory. *Journal of Occupational Psychology, 57,* 181–184.

Bannister, B. D. (1986). Performance outcome feedback and attributional feedback: Interactive effects on recipient responses. *Journal of Applied Psychology, 71,* 203–210.

Barnes, C. W., & Wagner, D. T. (2009). Changing to daylight saving time cuts into sleep and increases workplace injuries. *Journal of Applied Psychology, 94*(5), 1305–1317.

Barrick, M. R., & Mount, M. K. (1991). The big five personality dimensions and job performance: A meta-analysis. *Personnel Psychology, 44*(1), 1–26.

Barrick, M. R., Mount, M. K., & Gupta, R. (2003). Meta-analysis of the relationship between the five-factor model of personality and Holland's occupational types. *Personnel Psychology, 56*(1), 45–74.

Barrick, M. R., Shaffer, J. A., & DeGrassi, S. W. (2009). What you see may not be what you get: Relationships among self-presentation tactics and ratings of interview and job performance. *Journal of Applied Psychology, 94,* 1394–1411.

Barrick, M. R., Stewart, G. L., Neubert, M. J., & Mount, M. K. (1998). Relating member ability and personality to work-team processes and team effectiveness. *Journal of Applied Psychology, 83*(3), 377–391.

Barrick, M. R., Swider, B. W., & Stewart, G. L. (2010). Initial evaluations in the interview: Relationships with subsequent interview evaluations and employment offers. *Journal of Applied Psychology, 95*(6), 1163–1172.

Barrick, M. R., & Zimmerman, R. D. (2005). Reducing voluntary, avoidable turnover through selection. *Journal of Applied Psychology, 90*(1), 159–166.

Barron, L. G., & Sackett, P. R. (2008). Asian variability in performance rating modesty and leniency bias. *Human Performance, 21*, 277–290.

Barton, J., & Folkard, S. (1993). Advancing versus delaying shift systems. *Ergonomics, 36*(1), 59–64.

Bass, B. M. (1997). Does the transactional-transformational leadership paradigm transcend organizational and national boundaries? *American Psychologist, 52*(2), 130–139.

Bass, B. M., & Bass, R. (2008). *The Bass handbook of leadership: Theory, research, and managerial applications.* New York: Free Press.

Bass, B. M., Klubeck, S., & Wurster, C. R. (1953). Factors influencing reliability and validity of leaderless group discussion assessment. *Journal of Applied Psychology, 37*(1), 26–30.

Bass, B. M., & Riggio, R. E. (2006). *Transformational leadership.* Mahwah, NJ: Erlbaum.

Bassett, J. W. (2008). *Solving employee theft.* Charleston, SC: BookSurge Publishing.

Bates, S. (2003a). Forced ranking. *HR Magazine, 48*(6), 62–68.

Bates, S. (2003b). Performance appraisals: Some improvement needed. *HR Magazine, 48*(4), 12.

Battilana, J., & Casciaro, T. (2013). Overcoming resistance to organizational change: Strong ties and affective cooptation. *Management Science, 59*(4), 819–836.

Baumgartner, J. (1994). Give it to me straight. *Training & Development Journal, 48*(6), 49–51.

Baxter, J. S., Manstead, A. S., Stradling, S. G., & Campbell, K. A. (1990). Social facilitation and driving behavior. *British Journal of Psychology, 81*(3), 351–360.

Bayo-Moriones, A., & Larraza-Kintana, M. (2009). Profit-sharing plans and affective commitment: Does the context matter? *Human Resource Management, 48*(2), 207–226.

Beal, D. J., Cohen, R. R., Burke, M. J., & McLendon, C. L. (2003). Cohesion and performance in groups: A meta-analytic clarification of construct relations. *Journal of Applied Psychology, 88*(6), 989–1004.

Beall, G. E. (1991). Validity of the weighted application blank across four job criteria. *Applied H.R.M. Research, 2*(1), 18–26.

Beatty, G. O. (1996). *Job analysis sample size: How small is large enough?* Poster presented at the annual meeting of the Society for Industrial and Organizational Psychology, San Diego, CA.

Beauregard, T. A., Basile, K. A., & Canonico, E. (2019). Telework: Outcomes and facilitators for employees. In R. N. Landers (Ed.), *The Cambridge handbook of technology and employee behavior* (pp. 511–543). Cambridge: Cambridge University Press.

Becker, T. E., & Colquitt, A. L. (1992). Potential versus actual faking of a biodata form: An analysis along several dimensions of item type. *Personnel Psychology, 45*, 389–406.

Beehr, T. A., Ivanitskaya, L., Hansen, C. P., Erofeev, D., & Gudanowski, D. M. (2001). Evaluation of 360-degree feedback ratings: Relationships with each other and with performance and selection predictors. *Journal of Organizational Behavior, 22*, 775–788.

Beerepoot, N., & Lambregts, B. (2015). Competition in online job marketplaces: Towards a global labour market for outsourcing services? *Global Networks, 15*(2), 236–255.

Bell, B. S., McAlpine, K. L., & Hill, N. S. (2019). Leading from a distance: Advancements in virtual leadership research. In R. N. Landers (Ed.), *The Cambridge handbook of technology and employee behavior* (pp. 387–418). Cambridge: Cambridge University Press.

Bell, S. T. (2005, April). *The relationship between team composition variables and team performance: A comprehensive meta-analysis.* Paper presented at the 20th annual meeting of the Society for Industrial and Organizational Psychology, Los Angeles, CA.

Bell, S. T. (2007). Deep-level composition variables as predictors of team performance: A meta-analysis. *Journal of Applied Psychology, 92*(3), 595–615.

Belyh, A. (2020). *Management by walking around: The essential guide.* https://www.cleverism.com/management-by-walking-around-mbwa/

Ben-Shakhar, G., Bar-Hillel, M., Bilu, Y., Ben-Abba, E., & Flug, A. (1986). Can graphology predict occupational success? Two empirical studies and some methodological ruminations. *Journal of Applied Psychology, 71*, 645–653.

Benson, G. S., Finegold, D., & Mohrman, S. A. (2004). You paid for the skills, now keep them: Tuition reimbursement and voluntary turnover. *Academy of Management Journal, 47*(3), 315–331.

Bernardin, H. J., & Kane, J. S. (1980). A second look at behavioral observation scales. *Personnel Psychology, 33*, 809–814.

Bernardin, H. J., LaShells, M. B., Smith, P. C., & Alvares, K. M. (1976). Behavioral expectation scales: Effects of developmental procedures and formats. *Journal of Applied Psychology, 61*, 75–79.

Bernardin, H. J., & Pence, E. C. (1980). Effects of rater training: Creating new response sets and decreasing accuracy. *Journal of Applied Psychology, 65*, 60–66.

Bernardin, H. J., & Walter, C. S. (1977). Effects of rater training and diary-keeping on psychometric error in ratings. *Journal of Applied Psychology, 62*, 64–69.

Bernstein, A. J., & Rozen, S. C. (1992). *Neanderthals at work.* New York: Ballantine.

Berry, C. M., Lelchook, A. M., & Clark, M. A. (2012). A meta-analysis of the interrelationships between employee lateness, absenteeism, and turnover: Implications for models of withdrawal behavior. *Journal of Organizational Behavior, 33*(5), 678–699.

Berry, C. M., Ones, D. S., & Sackett, P. R. (2007). Interpersonal deviance, organizational deviance, and their common correlates: A review and meta-analysis. *Journal of Applied Psychology, 92*(2), 410–424.

Berry, C. M., Sackett, P. R., & Tobares, V. (2010). A meta-analysis of conditional reasoning tests of aggression. *Personnel Psychology, 63*(2), 361–384.

Beshir, M. Y., El-Sabagh, A. S., & El-Nawawi, M. A. (1981). Time on task effect on tracking performance under heat stress. *Ergonomics, 24*, 95–102.

Beyer, C., Pike, D., & McGovern, L. (1993). *Surviving unemployment.* New York: Henry Holt.

Bhakta, M., & Nagy, M. S. (2005). Are higher pay increases necessarily better? *Applied H.R.M. Research, 10*(1), 1–12.

Biddle, R. E. (1993). How to set cutoff scores for knowledge tests used in promotion, training, certification, and licensing. *Public Personnel Management, 22*(1), 63–79.

Biech, E. (2017). *The art and science of training.* Alexandria, VA: ATD Press.

Bing, M. N., Stewart, S. M., Davison, H. K., Green, P. D., McIntyre, M. D., & James, L. R. (2007). An integrative typology of personality assessment for aggression: Implications for predicting counterproductive workplace behavior. *Journal of Applied Psychology, 92*(3), 722–744.

Bishop, J. W., & Scott, K. D. (1997). How commitment affects team performance. *HR Magazine, 42*(2), 107–111.

Black, J. (2020). *How Google got its employees to eat their vegetables.* Medium. https://onezero.medium.com/how-google-got-its-employees-to-eat-their-vegetables-a2206820d90d.

Blake, R. R., & Mouton, J. S. (1984). *The managerial grid III.* Houston: Gulf.

Blakley, B. R., Quiñones, M. A., Crawford, M. S., & Jago, I. A. (1994). The validity of isometric strength tests. *Personnel Psychology, 47*(2), 247–274.

Blanchard, K. H., Zigarmi, P., & Zigarmi, D. (2013). *Leadership and the one minute manager: Increasing effectiveness through situational leadership II.* New York: William Morrow.

Blank, W., Green, S. G., & Weitzel, J. R. (1990). A test of the situational leadership theory. *Personnel Psychology, 43*(3), 579–597.

Blanz, F., & Ghiselli, E. E. (1972). The mixed standard scale: A new rating system. *Personnel Psychology, 25,* 185–200.

Bliss, W. G. (2001). Cost of employee turnover can be staggering. *Fairfield County Business Journal, 40*(19), 20.

Bluen, S. D., Barling, J., & Burns, W. (1990). Predicting sales performance, job satisfaction, and depression using the Achievement Strivings and Impatience-Irritability dimensions of Type A behavior. *Journal of Applied Psychology, 75,* 212–216.

Blum, M. L., & Naylor, J. C. (1968). *Industrial psychology: Its theoretical and social foundations* (3rd ed.). New York: Harper and Row.

Blumenfeld, W. S. (1985). Appropriateness of readability of a Federal Aviation Agency regulation, a flight crew manual, and a company pilot labor agreement for an airline's pilots. *Perceptual and Motor Skills, 61,* 1189–1190.

Blumenfeld, W. S., & Justice, B. M. (1975). Six replicated investigations of the relationship between Flesch and Gunning readability indices. *Perceptual and Motor Skills, 40,* 110.

Bobko, P., & Roth, P. L. (2013). Reviewing, categorizing, and analyzing the literature on black-white mean differences for predictors of job performance: Verifying some perceptions and updating/correcting others. *Personnel Psychology, 66*(1), 91–126.

Bobko, P., Roth, P. L., & Buster, M. A. (2005). Work sample selection tests and expected reduction in adverse impact: A cautionary note. *International Journal of Selection and Assessment, 13*(1), 1–11.

Bobko, P., Roth, P. L., & Potosky, D. (1999). Derivation and implications of a meta-analytic matrix incorporating cognitive ability, alternative predictors, and job performance. *Personnel Psychology, 52*(3), 561–589.

Bocketti, S., Hamilton, M., & Maser, S. (2000). *Comparing the effect of negative information on resumes and interviews.* Paper presented at the 21st annual Graduate Student Conference in Industrial-Organizational Psychology and Organizational Behavior, Knoxville, TN.

Bolino, M. C., & Turnley, W. H. (2005). The personal costs of citizenship behavior: The relationship between individual initiative and role overload, job stress, and work-family conflict. *Journal of Applied Psychology, 90*(4), 740–748.

Bolles, R. N. (2020). *What color is your parachute? 2021: A practical manual for job-hunters and career-changers.* Berkeley, CA: Ten Speed Press.

Bommer, W. H., Johnson, J. L., Rich, G. A., Podsakoff, P. M., & Mackenzie, S. B. (1995). On the interchangeability of objective and subjective measures of employee performance: A meta-analysis. *Personnel Psychology, 48*(3), 587–605.

Bond, C. F., & Titus, L. J. (1983). Social facilitation: A meta-analysis of 241 studies. *Psychological Bulletin, 94,* 265–292.

Bond, G. E. (1995). *Leadership behavior: How personality, stress, and gender affect leader behavior.* Unpublished doctoral dissertation, University of Washington, Seattle, WA.

Bonebright, D. A. (2010). 40 years of storming: A historical review of Tuckman's model of small group development. *Human Resource Development International, 13*(1), 111–120.

Bono, J. E., & Judge, T. A. (2004). Personality and transformational and transactional leadership: A meta-analysis. *Journal of Applied Psychology, 89*(5), 901–910.

Bordens, K. S., & Abbott, B. B. (2014). *Research design and methods: A process approach* (9th ed.). New York: McGraw-Hill.

Borman, W. C., & Motowidlo, S. J. (1997). Task performance and contextual performance: The meaning for personnel selection research. *Human Performance, 10*(2), 99–109.

Bornstein, R. F., Rossner, S. C., Hill, E. L., & Stepanian, M. L. (1994). Face validity and fakability of objective and projective measures of dependency. *Journal of Personality Assessment, 63*(2), 363–386.

Boudreau, J. W. (1983). Economic considerations in estimating the utility of human resource productivity improvement programs. *Personnel Psychology, 36,* 551–576.

Boumans, N. P., De Jong, A. H., & Janssen, S. M. (2011). Age-differences in work motivation and job satisfaction. The influence of age on the relationships between work characteristics and workers' outcomes. *The International Journal of Aging and Human Development, 73*(4), 331–350.

Boushey, H., & Glynn, S. J. (2012). *There are significant business costs to replacing employees.* Washington, DC: Center for American Progress.

Bowen, C. C., Swim, J. K., & Jacobs, R. R. (2000). Evaluating gender biases on actual job performance of real people: A meta-analysis. *Journal of Applied Social Psychology, 30*(10), 2194–2215.

Bowers, C. A., Pharmer, J. A., & Salas, E. (2000). When member homogeneity is needed in work teams. *Small Group Research, 31*(3), 305–327.

Bowling, N. A., Eschleman, K. J., Wang, Q., Kirkendall, C., & Alarcon, G. (2010). A meta-analysis of the predictors and consequences of organization-based self-esteem. *Journal of Occupational and Organizational Psychology, 83*(3), 601–626.

Bowling, N. A., Hendricks, E. A., & Wagner, S. H. (2008). Positive and negative affectivity and facet satisfaction: A meta-analysis. *Journal of Business and Psychology, 22,* 115–125.

Brabant, C. (1992). Heat exposure standards and women's work: Equitable or debatable? *Women and Health, 18*(3), 119–130.

Bradley, D. (2004). Catawba county, N.C. Emergency Medical Services (EMS) wellness program. *IPMA-HR News,* pp. 6–7.

Bramson, R. (1981). *Coping with difficult people.* New York: Anchor.

Branham, L. (2012). *The 7 hidden reasons employees leave* (2nd ed.). New York: AMACOM.

Bravo, I. M., & Kravitz, D. A. (1996). Context effects in performance appraisals: Influence of target value, context polarity, and individual differences. *Journal of Applied Social Psychology, 26*(19), 1681–1701.

Brawley, L. R., Carron, A. V., & Widmeyer, W. N. (1993). The influence of the group and its cohesiveness on perceptions of group goal-related variables. *Journal of Sport and Exercise Psychology, 15*(3), 245–260.

Breaugh, J. A. (1981). Relationships between recruitment sources and employee performance, absenteeism, and work attitudes. *Academy of Management Journal, 24,* 261–267.

Breaugh, J. A. (2008). Employee recruitment: Current knowledge and important areas for future research. *Human Resource Management Review, 18*(3), 103–118.

Breaugh, J. A., & Mann, R. B. (1984). Recruiting source effects: A test of two alternative explanations. *Journal of Occupational Psychology, 57,* 261–267.

Brehm, J. W. (1966). *A theory of psychological reactance.* New York: Academic Press.

Brennan, A., Chugh, J. S., & Kline, T. (2002). Traditional versus open office design. *Environment and Behavior, 34*(3), 279–299.

Brett, J. F., & Atwater, L. E. (2001). 360-degree feedback: Accuracy, reactions, and perceptions of usefulness. *Journal of Applied Psychology, 86*(5), 930–942.

Bretz, R. D., & Judge, T. A. (1998). Realistic job previews: A test of the adverse self-selection hypothesis. *Journal of Applied Psychology, 83*(2), 330–337.

Bretz, R. D., & Thomas, S. L. (1992). Perceived equity, motivation, and final offer arbitration. *Journal of Applied Psychology, 77*(3), 280–287.

Brice, T. S., & Waung, M. (1995). Applicant rejection letters: Are businesses sending the wrong message? *Business Horizons, 38*(2), 59–62.

Brinkman, R., & Kirschner, R. (2012). *Dealing with people you can't stand* (3rd ed.). New York: McGraw-Hill.

Broad, M. (2000). Ensuring transfer of learning to the job. In G. M. Piskurich, P. Beckschi, & B. Hall (Eds.), *The ASTD handbook of training design and delivery: A comprehensive guide to creating and delivering training programs, instructor-led, computer-based, or self-directed* (pp. 430–452). New York: McGraw-Hill.

Broadbent, B. (1997). Writing for the 90's. *Training & Development, 51*(3), 11–12.

Broadbent, D. E. (1971). *Decision and stress.* New York: Academic Press.

Brodin, M. S. (2018). Discriminatory job knowledge tests, police promotions, and what Title VII can learn from tort law. *Boston College Law Review, 59*(7), 2319–2375.

Broadwell, M. M. (1993). Seven steps to building better training. *Training, 30*(10), 75–81.

Brophy, D. R. (1996). *Matching individual and group creativity to different types of problems.* Poster presented at the 11th annual conference of the Society for Industrial and Organizational Psychology, San Diego, CA.

Brotherton, P. (1996). The company that plays together. . . . *HR Magazine, 41*(12), 76–82.

Brown, D. L. (1993). Target stores settle out of court in Soroka v. Dayton Hudson. *The Industrial Organizational Psychologist, 31*(2), 88–89.

Brown, K. A., & Huber, V. L. (1992). Lowering floors and raising ceilings: A longitudinal assessment of the effects of an earnings-at-risk plan on pay performance. *Personnel Psychology, 45*(2), 279–311.

Brown, M., Setren, E., & Topa, G. (2013). *Do informal referrals lead to better matches? Evidence from a firm's employee referral system.* Federal Reserve Bank of New York Staff Reports, no. 568.

Brown, S. G., Hill, N. S., & Lorinkova, N. N. M. (2021). Leadership and virtual team performance: A meta-analytic investigation. *European Journal of Work and Organizational Psychology,* 1–14.

Brown, S. H. (1978). Long-term validity of a personal history item scoring procedure. *Journal of Applied Psychology, 63,* 673–676.

Brown, S. P. (1996). A meta-analysis and review of organizational research on job involvement. *Psychological Bulletin, 120*(2), 235–255.

Bruce, H. J. (1997). Looking for a CEO? Look for early career signs of "leadership without portfolio." *Directors & Boards, 21*(2), 20–21.

Bryman, A. (1992). *Charisma & leadership.* Newbury Park, CA: Sage.

Buchner, L. M. (1990). Increases in interrater reliability of situational interviews as a function of the number of benchmark answers. *Applied H.R.M. Research, 1*(2), 27–31.

Buckley, M. R., Jackson, K. A., Bolino, M. C., Veres, J. G., & Feild, H. S. (2007). The influence of relational demography on panel interview ratings: A field experiment. *Personnel Psychology, 60*(3), 627–646.

Buckley, M. R., Mobbs, T. A., Mendoza, J. L., Novicevic, M. M., Carraher, S. M., & Beu, D. S. (2002). Implementing realistic job previews and expectation-lowering procedures: A field experiment. *Journal of Vocational Behavior, 61,* 263–278.

Bucklin, B. R., & Dickinson, A. M. (2001). Individual monetary incentives: A review of different types of arrangements between performance and pay. *Journal of Organizational Behavior Management, 21*(3), 45–137.

Buddhavarapu, S., Borys, J., Homant, M., & Baltes, B. (2002). *The twenty-four hour dilemma: A meta-analytic review of shift work.* Paper presented at the 17th annual conference of the Society for Industrial and Organizational Psychology, Toronto, Canada.

Buelens, M., & Van Poucke, D. (2004). Determinants of a negotiator's initial opening offer. *Journal of Business and Psychology, 19*(1), 23–35.

Bullock, R. J., & Tubbs, M. E. (1990). A case meta-analysis of gainsharing plans as organization development interventions. *Journal of Applied Behavioral Science, 26*(3), 383–404.

Burke, W. W. (2018). *Organization change: Theory and practice* (5th ed.). Thousand Oaks, CA: Sage.

Burks, S. V., Cowgill, B., Hoffman, M., & Housman, M. (2015). The value of hiring through employee referrals. *The Quarterly Journal of Economics, 130*(2), 805–839.

Burley-Allen, M. (2001). Listen up. *HR Magazine, 46*(11), 115–120.

Burnett, J. R., & Motowidlo, S. J. (1998). Relations between different sources of information in the structured selection interview. *Personnel Psychology, 51*(4), 963–983.

Burns, W. (1979). Physiological effects of noise. In C. M. Harris (Ed.), *Handbook of noise control* (pp. 15-1–15-23). New York: McGraw-Hill.

Butterfield, K. D., Trevino, L. K., & Ball, G. A. (1996). Punishment from the manager's perspective: A grounded investigation and inductive model. *Academy of Management Journal, 39*(6), 1479–1512.

Butts, M. M., Casper, W. J., & Yang, T. S. (2013). How important are work-family support policies? A meta-analytic investigation of their effects on employee outcomes. *Journal of Applied Psychology, 98*(1), 1–25.

Bycio, P. (1992). Job performance and absenteeism: A review and meta-analysis. *Human Relations, 45*(2), 193–220.

Cable, D. M., & DeRue, D. S. (2002). Convergent and discriminant validity of subjective fit perceptions. *Journal of Applied Psychology, 87*(5), 875–884.

Cadrain, D. (2003). Are your employee drug tests accurate? *HR Magazine, 48*(1), 40–45.

Cadrain, D. (2004). Job detectives dig deep for defamation. *HR Magazine, 49*(10), 34–36.

Cai, C., Vandermeer, B., Khurana, R., Nerenberg, K., Featherstone, R., Sebastianski, M., & Davenport, M. H. (2019). The impact of occupational shift work and working hours during pregnancy on health outcomes: A systematic review and meta-analysis. *American Journal of Obstetrics and Gynecology, 221*(6), 563–576.

Caird, J. K., Johnston, K. A., Willness, C. R., Asbridge, M., & Steel, P. (2014). A meta-analysis of the effects of texting on driving. *Accident Analysis & Prevention, 71*, 311–318.

Caird, J. K., Willness, C. R., Steel, P., & Scialfa, C. (2008). A meta-analysis of the effects of cell phones on driver performance. *Accident Analysis and Prevention, 40*, 1282–1293.

Caldwell, C., Thornton, G. C., & Gruys, M. L. (2003). Ten classic assessment center errors: Challenges to selection validity. *Public Personnel Management, 32*(1), 73–88.

Caldwell, D. F., & Burger, J. M. (1998). Personality characteristics of job applicants and success in screening interviews. *Personnel Psychology, 51*(1), 119–136.

Caleo, S., & Heilman, M. E. (2019). What could go wrong? Some unintended consequences of gender bias interventions. *Archives of Scientific Psychology, 7*(1), 71–80.

Callinan, M., & Robertson, I. V. (2001). Work sample testing. *International Journal of Selection and Assessment, 8*(4), 248–260.

Cameron, E., & Green, M. (2020). *Making sense of change management* (5th ed.). New York: Kogan Page.

Cameron, J., Banko, K. M., & Pierce, W. D. (2001). Pervasive negative effects of rewards on intrinsic motivation: The myth continues. *The Behavior Analyst, 24(1)*, 1–44.

Campbell, D. E. (1979). Interior office design and visitor response. *Journal of Applied Psychology, 64*, 648–653.

Campbell, D. T., & Stanley, J. C. (1963). *Experimental and quasi-experimental designs in research.* Chicago: Rand McNally.

Campion, J. E., Greener, J., & Wernli, S. (1973). Work observation versus recall in developing behavioral examples for rating scales. *Journal of Applied Psychology, 58*, 286–288.

Campion, M. A., Campion, J. E., & Hudson, J. P. (1994). Structured interviewing: A note on incremental validity and alternative question types. *Journal of Applied Psychology, 79*(6), 998–1002.

Campion, M. A., & McClelland, C. L. (1993). Follow-up and extension of the interdisciplinary costs and benefits of enlarged jobs. *Journal of Applied Psychology, 78*(3), 339–351.

Campion, M. A., Outtz, J. L., Zedeck, S., Schmidt, F. L., Kehoe, J. F., Murphy, K. R., et al. (2001). The controversy over score banding in personnel selection: Answers to 10 key questions. *Personnel Psychology, 54*(1), 149–185.

Campion, M. A., Palmer, D. K., & Campion, J. E. (1997). A review of structure in the selection interview. *Personnel Psychology, 50*(3), 655–702.

Canali, K. G., Alton, S., Perreault, N. E., Rusbasan, D., Reese, A. L., & Barnes-Farrell, J. L. (2005, April). *Understanding performance appraisal leniency: Antecedents and consequences of rating discomfort.* Poster presented at the 20th annual meeting of the Society for Industrial and Organizational Psychology, Los Angeles, CA.

Cardy, R. L., & Dobbins, G. H. (1986). Affect and appraisal accuracy: Liking as an integral dimension in evaluating performance. *Journal of Applied Psychology, 71*, 672–678.

Carli, L. L., & Eagly, A. H. (2001). Gender, hierarchy, and leadership: An introduction. *Journal of Social Issues, 57*(4), 629–636.

Carlson, J. F., Geisinger, K. F., & Jonson, J. L. (2021). *Twenty-first mental measurements yearbook.* Lincoln, NE: Buros Center for Testing.

Carlson, K. D., Scullen, S. E., Schmidt, F. L., Rothstein, H., & Erwin, F. (1999). Generalizable biographical data validity can be reached without multi-organizational development and keying. *Personnel Psychology, 52*(3), 731–755.

Carnall, C. A., & By, R. T. (2014). *Managing change in organizations* (6th ed.). New York: Pearson.

Carpi, J. (1996). Stress: It's worse than you think. *Psychology Today*, Jan/Feb, pp. 34–42.

Carr, S. C., McLoughlin, D., Hodgson, M., & MacLachlan, M. (1996). Effects of unreasonable pay discrepancies for under- and overpayment on double demotivation. *Genetic, Social, and General Psychology Monographs, 122*(4), 475–494.

Carrell, M. R., & Dittrich, J. E. (1978). Equity theory: The recent literature, methodological considerations, and new directions. *Academy of Management Review, 3*, 202–210.

Carroll, S. A. (2008, April). Detecting faking using a bogus knowledge test: Relationships with impression management, personality, and deviant behavior. In J. Levashina & M.

A. Campion (Co-Chairs), *That can't be true! Detecting faking using bogus items.* Symposium presented at the 23rd annual meeting of the Society for Industrial-Organizational Psychology, San Francisco, CA.

Carron, A. V. (1990). Group size in sport and physical activity: Social psychological and performance consequences. *International Journal of Sport Psychology, 21*(4), 286–304.

Carson, K. P., Becker, J. S., & Henderson, J. A. (1998). Is utility really futile? A failure to replicate and an extension. *Journal of Applied Psychology, 83*(1), 84–96.

Carson, P. P., Lanier, P. A., Carson, K. D., & Guidry, B. N. (2000). Clearing a path through the management fashion jungle: Some preliminary trailblazing. *Academy of Management Journal, 43*(6), 1143–1158.

Carter, J. H. (1952). Military leadership. *Military Review, 32,* 14–18.

Carter, N. T., Daniels, M. A., & Zickar, M. J. (2013). Projective testing: Historical foundations and uses for human resources management. *Human Resource Management Review, 23,* 205–218.

Carter, R. T., & Swanson, J. L. (1990). The validity of the Strong Interest Inventory with Black Americans: A review of the literature. *Journal of Vocational Behavior, 36*(2), 195–209.

Caruso, J. C. (2003). Reliability generalization of the NEO personality scales. In B. Thompson (Ed.), *Score reliability: Contemporary thinking on reliability issues.* Thousand Oaks, CA: Sage Publications.

Cascio, W. F. (1995). Whither industrial and organizational psychology in a changing world of work? *American Psychologist, 50*(11), 928–939.

Cascio, W. F. (2002). *Responsible restructuring: Creative and profitable alternatives to layoffs.* San Francisco, CA: Berrett-Koehler.

Cascio, W. F. (2002). Strategies for responsible restructuring. *Academy of Management Executive, 16*(3), 80–91.

Cascio, W. F. (2013). *Managing human resources: Productivity, quality of work life, profits* (9th ed.). Burr Ridge, IL: McGraw-Hill/Irwin.

Cascio, W. F., & Scott, J. C. (2017). The business value of employee selection. In J. L. Farr & N. T. Tippins (Eds.), *Handbook of employee selection* (pp. 226–248). New York: Routledge.

Casperson, D. M. (2002, December). E-mail etiquette: How to make sure your message gets across. *IPMA News,* p. 25.

Castano, N., Watts, T., & Tekleab, A. G. (2013). A reexamination of the cohesion-performance relationship meta-analysis: A comprehensive approach. *Group Dynamics: Theory Research and Practice, 17*(4), 207–231.

Caudron, S. (1994). Volunteer efforts offer low cost training options. *Personnel Journal, 73*(6), 38–44.

Caughron, J. J., Mumford, M. D., & Fleishman, E. A. (2012). The Fleishman job analysis survey: Development, validation, and applications. In M. A. Wilson, W. Bennett Jr., S. G. Gibson, & G. M. Alliger (Eds.), *The handbook of work analysis: Methods, systems, applications and science of work measurement in organizations* (pp. 231–246). New York, NY: Routledge Taylor & Francis Group.

Cavanaugh, M. A., Boswell, W. R., Roehling, M. V., & Boudreau, J. W. (2000). An empirical examination of self-reported work stress among U.S. managers. *Journal of Applied Psychology, 85*(1), 65–74.

Ceci, S. J., & Peters, D. (1984). Letters of reference: A naturalistic study of the effects of confidentiality. *American Psychologist, 39,* 29–31.

Cederbloom, D. (1989). Peer and supervisor evaluations: An underused promotion method used for law enforcement. *Proceedings of the 13th Annual Meeting of the International Personnel Management Association Assessment Council.*

Cellar, D. F., Curtis, J. R., Kohlepp, K., Poczapski, P., & Mohiuddin, S. (1989). The effects of rater training, job analysis format and congruence of training on job evaluation ratings. *Journal of Business and Psychology, 3*(4), 387–401.

Chambers, B. A., & Arnold, J. D. (2015). Using technology to improve the interview as a selection tool. *Personnel Assessment and Decisions, 1*(1), 57–64.

Champagne, J. (2021). Is it assessment or evaluation? *TD: Talent Development, 75*(2), 20–23.

Chan, D., & Schmitt, N. (1997). Video-based versus paper-and-pencil method of assessment in situational judgment tests: Subgroup differences in test performance and face validity perceptions. *Journal of Applied Psychology, 82*(1), 143–159.

Chan, D., Schmitt, N., DeShon, R. P., Clause, C. S., & Delbridge, K. (1997). Reactions to cognitive ability tests: The relationship between race, test performance, face validity perceptions, and test-taking motivation. *Journal of Applied Psychology, 82*(2), 300–310.

Chan, K. Y., & Drasgow, F. (2001). Toward a theory of individual differences and leadership: Understanding the motivation to lead. *Journal of Applied Psychology, 86*(3), 481–498.

Chang, C. H., Johnson, R. E., & Yang, L. Q. (2007). Emotional strain and organizational citizenship behaviors: A meta-analysis and review. *Work & Stress, 21*(4), 312–332.

Chang, C. H., Rosen, C. C., & Levy, P. E. (2009). The relationship between perceptions of organizational politics and employee attitudes, strain, and behavior: A meta-analysis. *Academy of Management Journal, 52*(4), 779–801.

Chang, W. P., & Peng, Y. X. (2021). *Influence of rotating shifts and fixed night shifts on sleep quality of nurses of different ages: A systematic literature review and meta-analysis.* Chronobiology International, DOI: 10.1080/07420528.2021.1931273

Chapman, D. S., Uggerslev, K. L., Carroll, S. A., Piasentin, K. A., & Jones, D. A. (2005). Applicant attraction to organizations and job choice: A meta-analytic review of the correlates of recruiting outcomes. *Journal of Applied Psychology, 90*(5), 928–944.

Chapman, D. S., & Webster, J. (2003). The use of technologies in the recruiting, screening, and selection processes for job candidates. *International Journal of Selection and Assessment, 11*(2-3), 113–120.

Chapman, D. S., & Zweig, D. I. (2005). Developing a nomological network for interview structure: Antecedents and consequences of the structured selection interview. *Personnel Psychology, 58*(3), 673–702.

Chen, A. Y., Sawyers, R. B., & Williams, P. F. (1997). Reinforcing ethical decision making through corporate culture. *Journal of Business Ethics, 16,* 855–865.

Chen, S. C. (1937). Social modification of the activity of ants in nest-building. *Physiological Zoology, 10,* 420–436.

Chiaburu, D. S., Oh, I., Berry, C. M., Li, N., & Gardner, R. G. (2011). The five-factor model of personality traits and organizational citizenship behaviors: A meta-analysis. *Journal of Applied Psychology, 96*(6), 1140–1166.

Christian, M. S., Edwards, B. D., & Bradley, J. C. (2010). Situational judgment tests: Constructs assessed and a meta-analysis of their criterion-related validities. *Personnel Psychology, 63*(1), 83–117.

Chua-Eoan, H. (1999, March 22). The bomber next door: What are the most dangerous men in America talking about at the Supermax prison in Colorado? *Time, 153*(11), 55.

Church, A. H. (2001). Is there a method to our madness? The impact of data collection methodology on organizational survey results. *Personnel Psychology, 54*(4), 937–969.

Church, A. H., Rogelberg, S. G., & Waclawski, J. (2000). Since when in no news good news? The relationship between performance and response rates in multirater feedback. *Personnel Psychology, 53*(2), 435–451.

Cialdini, R. B., Borden, R., Thorne, A., Walker, M., Freeman, S., & Sloane, L. T. (1976). Basking in reflected glory: Three (football) field studies. *Journal of Personality and Social Psychology, 34,* 366–375.

Circadian Technologies. (2002). *2002 shiftwork practices survey.* Lexington, MA: Circadian Technologies, Inc.

Clark, M. M. (2001). More companies offering flextime: Are scheduling options flexible enough? *HR News, 20*(6), pp. 1–10.

Clark, R. E. (1961). *The limiting hand skin temperature for unaffected manual performance in the cold.* Natwick, MA: Quartermaster Research and Engineering Command, Technical Re. EP-147.

Clark, V. N. (1985). The effectiveness of case studies in training principals, using the deliberative orientation. *Peabody Journal of Education, 63*(1), 187–195.

Clause, C. S., Mullins, M. E., Nee, R., Pulakos, E. D., & Schmitt, N. (1998). Strictly parallel test forms: A development procedure and example. *Personnel Psychology, 51*(1), 193–208.

Clay, R. A. (2011). Is stress getting to you? *Monitor on Psychology, 42*(1), 58–63.

Clevenger, J., Pereira, G. M., Wiechmann, D., Schmitt, N., & Harvey, V. S. (2001). Incremental validity of situational judgment tests. *Journal of Applied Psychology, 86*(3), 410–417.

Cochran, A., Kopitzke, K., & Miller, D. (1984). *Relationship between interviewer personality and interior office characteristics.* Paper presented at the 5th annual Graduate Student Conference in Industrial/Organizational Psychology and Organizational Behavior, Norfolk, VA.

Cohen, A. (1972, September). *The role of psychology in improving worker safety and health under the Worker Safety and Health Act.* Paper presented at the annual meeting of the American Psychological Association, Honolulu, HI.

Cohen, D. B. (1997). *Cohen Conflict Response Inventory.* Washington, DC: Author.

Cohen, D. B., Aamodt, M. G., & Dunleavy, E. M. (2010). *Technical advisory committee report on best practices in adverse impact analyses.* Washington, DC: Center for Corporate Equality.

Cohen, D. B., & Scott, D. (1996). *Construct validity of a situational interview and patterned behavior description interview.* Paper presented at the 17th annual Graduate Student Conference in Industrial/Organizational Psychology and Organizational Behavior, Toledo, OH.

Cohen, J. (1988). *Statistical power analysis for the behavioral sciences* (2nd ed.). Hillsdale, NJ: Lawrence Erlbaum.

Cohen, P. (1984). College grades and adult achievement. *Research in Higher Education, 20,* 281–293.

Cohen, S. G., & Bailey, D. E. (1997). What makes teams work: Group effectiveness research from the shop floor to the executive suite. *Journal of Management, 23*(3), 239–290.

Cohen, S., & Janicki-Deverts, D. (2012). Who's stressed? Distributions of psychological stress in the United States in probability samples from 1983, 2006, and 2009. *Journal of Applied Social Psychology, 42*(6), 1320–1334.

Cohen, T. R., Panter, A. T., Turan, N., Morse, L., & Kim, Y. (2014). Moral character in the workplace. *Journal of Personality and Social Psychology, 107*(5), 943–963.

Colella, A., & Varma, A. (2001). The impact of subordinate disability on leader-member exchange relationships. *Academy of Management Journal, 44*(2), 304–315.

Collins, D. B., & Holton, E. F. (2004). The effectiveness of managerial leadership development programs: A meta-analysis of studies from 1982 to 2001. *Human Resource Development Quarterly, 15*(2), 217–248.

Colquitt, J. A., Conlon, D. E., Wesson, M. J., Porter, O. L. H., & Ng, K. Y. (2001). Justice at the millennium: A meta-analytic review of 25 years of organizational justice research. *Journal of Applied Psychology, 86*(3), 425–445.

Colquitt, J. A., Scott, B. A., Rodell, J. B., Long, D. M., Zapata, C. P., Conlon, D. E., & Wesson, M. J. (2013). Justice at the millennium, a decade later: A meta-analytic test of social exchange and affect-based perspectives. *Journal of Applied Psychology, 98*(2), 199–236.

Combs, G. M., & Nadkarni, S. (2005). The tale of two cultures: Attitudes toward affirmative action in the United States and India. *Journal of World Business, 40*(2), 158–171.

Combs, J., Liu, Y., Hall, A., & Ketchen, D. (2006). How much do high-performance work practices matter? A meta-analysis of their effects on organizational performance. *Personnel Psychology, 59,* 501–528.

Commerce Clearing House (2004). 2004 CCH unscheduled absenteeism survey. Riverwoods, IL: Author.

Commerce Clearing House. (2007). *2007 CCH unscheduled absenteeism survey.* Riverwoods, IL: Author.

Conard, M. A., & Ashworth, S. D. (1986). *Recruiting source effectiveness: A meta-analysis and re-examination of two rival hypotheses.* Paper presented at the 1st annual meeting of the Society for Industrial and Organizational Psychology, Chicago, IL.

Conard, M. A., & Matthews, R. A. (2008). Modeling the stress process: Personality trumps stressors in predicting strain. *Personality and Individual Differences, 44*(1), 171–181.

Condly, S. J., Clark, R. E., & Stolovitch, H. D. (2003). The effects of incentives on workplace performance: A meta-analytic review of research studies. *Performance Improvement Quarterly, 16*(3), 46–63.

Conley, P. R., & Sackett, P. R. (1987). Effects of using high- versus low-performing job incumbents as sources of job analysis information. *Journal of Applied Psychology, 72*(3), 434–437.

Connolly, J. J., & Viswesvaran, C. (2000). The role of affectivity in job satisfaction: A meta-analysis. *Personality and Individual Differences, 29*(2), 265–281.

CONSAD Research Corporation (2009). *An analysis of the reasons for the disparity in wages between men and women.* Pittsburgh, PA: CONSAD Research Corporation.

Contournet, G. (2004, October). *Maintenance of order: Legal and psycho-sociological aspects.* Paper presented at the annual meeting of the Society for Police and Criminal Psychology, Rome, Italy.

Conway, J. M., & Huffcutt, A. I. (1997). Psychometric properties of multi-source performance ratings: A meta-analysis of subordinate, supervisor, peer, and self-ratings. *Human Performance, 10*(4), 331–360.

Cooper, M., Kaufman, G., & Hughes, W. (1996, December). Measuring supervisory potential. *IPMA News*, pp. 8–9.

Cooper, W. H. (1981a). Conceptual similarity as a source of illusory halo in job performance ratings. *Journal of Applied Psychology, 66,* 302–307.

Cooper, W. H. (1981b). Ubiquitous halo. *Psychological Bulletin, 90,* 218–244.

Cooper-Hakim, A., & Viswesvaran, C. (2005). The construct of work commitment: Testing an integrative framework. *Psychological Bulletin, 131*(2), 241–259.

Cordero, A. C. (2019). *Office Landscapes for Well-Being. Interrelations between Employee, Activities, Spatial Attributes and Context* (Doctoral dissertation, Chalmers Tekniska Hogskola (Sweden)).

Cordes, C. L., & Dougherty, T. W. (1993). Review and integration of research on job burnout. *Academy of Management Review, 18*(4), 621–656.

Cornelius, E. T., & Hakel, M. D. (1978). *A study to develop an improved enlisted performance evaluation system for the U.S. Coast Guard.* Washington, DC: Department of Transportation.

Cornelius, E. T., Hakel, M. D., & Sackett, P. R. (1979). A methodological approach to job classification for performance appraisal purposes. *Personnel Psychology, 32,* 283–297.

Cornelius, E. T., & Lyness, K. S. (1980). A comparison of holistic and decomposed judgment strategies in job analysis by job incumbents. *Journal of Applied Psychology, 65,* 155–163.

Cortina, J. M., Goldstein, N. B., Payne, S. C., Davison, H. K., & Gilliland, S. W. (2000). The incremental validity of interview scores over and above cognitive ability and conscientiousness scores. *Personnel Psychology, 53*(2), 325–351.

Cortini, M., Galanti, T., & Barattucci, M. (2019). The effect of different rejection letters on applicants' reactions. *Behavioral Sciences, 9,* 1–15.

Costa, P. T., Jr., & McCrae, R. R. (1992). *The NEO-PI-R professional manual.* Odessa, FL: Psychological Assessment Resources.

Cottrell, J. M., Newman, D. A., & Roisman, G. I. (2015, April 13). Explaining the Black–White gap in cognitive test scores: Toward a theory of adverse impact. *Journal of Applied Psychology, 100*(6), 1713–1736.

Cottrell, N. B. (1972). Social facilitation. In C. G. McClintock (Ed.), *Experimental social psychology* (pp. 185–236). New York: Holt, Rinehart & Winston.

Courtis, J. K. (1995). Readability of annual reports: Western versus Asian evidence. *Accounting, Auditing and Accountability, 8*(2), 4–17.

Courtright, S. H., McCormick, B. W., Postlethwaite, B. E., Reeves, C. J., & Mount, M. K. (2013). A meta-analysis of sex differences in physical ability: Revised estimates and strategies for reducing differences in selection contexts. *Journal of Applied Psychology, 98*(4), 623–641.

Crispin, G., & Mehler, M. (2013). *Sources of hire 2013: Perception is reality.* Retrieved December 28, 2013, from www .careerxroads.com/news/SourcesOfHire2013.pdf

Cromwell, P. F., Marks, A., Olson, J. N., & Avary, D. W. (1991). Group effects on decision-making by burglars. *Psychological Reports, 69*(2), 579–588.

Cronbach, L. J. (1951). Coefficient alpha and the internal structure of tests. *Psychometrika, 16,* 297–334.

Cronshaw, S. F. (2012). Functional job analysis. In M. A. Wilson, W. Bennett Jr., S. G. Gibson, & G. M. Alliger (Eds.), *The handbook of work analysis: Methods, systems, applications and science of work measurement in organizations* (pp. 265–280). New York, NY: Routledge Taylor & Francis Group.

Cropanzano, R., & Folger, R. (1989). Referent cognitions and task decision autonomy: Beyond equity theory. *Journal of Applied Psychology, 74,* 293–299.

Cropanzo, R., & Greenberg, J. (1997). Progress in organizational justice: Tunneling through the maze. In C. L. Cooper & I. T. Robertson (Eds.), *International review of industrial and organizational psychology* (Vol. 12, pp. 317–372). Chichester: Wiley.

Cropanzano, R., & James, K. (1990). Some methodological considerations for the behavioral genetic analysis of work attitudes. *Journal of Applied Psychology, 75,* 433–439.

Csoka, L. S., & Bons, P. M. (1978). Manipulating the situation to fit the leader's style: Two validation studies of leader match. *Journal of Applied Psychology, 63,* 295–300.

Cucina, J. M., Berger, J. L., & Busciglio, H. H. (2017). Communicating criterion-related validity using expectancy charts: A new approach. Personnel Assessment and Decisions, *3*(1), Article 1. Available at http://scholarworks .bgsu.edu/pad/vol3/iss1/1

Cucina, J. M., Vasilopoulos, N. L., & Sehgal, K. G. (2005). Personality-based job analysis and the self-serving bias. *Journal of Business and Psychology, 20*(2), 273–290.

Cummings, T. G., & Worley, C. G. (2015). *Organization development and change* (10th ed.). Stamford, CT: Cengage Learning.

Cunningham, C. J. L., & Black, K. J. (2021). *Essentials of occupational health psychology.* New York: Routledge.

Dababneh, A. J., Swanson, N., & Shell, R. L. (2001). Impact of added rest breaks on the productivity and well being of workers. *Ergonomics, 44*(2), 164–174.

Dalal, R. S. (2005). A meta-analysis of the relationship between organizational citizenship behavior and counterproductive work behavior. *Journal of Applied Psychology, 90*(6), 1241–1255.

Dale, E., & Chall, J. S. (1948). A formula for predicting readability. *Educational Research Bulletin, 27,* 37–54.

Dale, G. (2021). *Flexible working.* London: Kogan Page.

Dalton, D. R., & Mesch, D. J. (1991). On the extent and reduction of avoidable absenteeism: An assessment of absence policy provisions. *Journal of Applied Psychology, 76*(6), 810–817.

Dansereau, F., Graen, G., & Haga, W. J. (1975). *A vertical dyad linkage approach to leadership within the formal organization.* Unpublished report, State University of New York, Buffalo.

Darnold, T. C., & Zimmerman, R. D. (2006, May). *Performance and intent to quit: A meta-analysis and path model.* Poster presented at the annual meeting of the Society for Industrial-Organizational Psychology, Dallas, TX.

Davidson, O. B., & Eden, D. (2000). Remedial self-fulfilling prophecy: Two field experiments to prevent Golem effects among disadvantaged women. *Journal of Applied Psychology, 85*(3), 386–398.

Davidson, R., & Henderson, R. (2000). Electronic performance monitoring: A laboratory investigation of the influence of monitoring and difficulty on task performance, mood state, and self-reported stress levels. *Journal of Applied Social Psychology, 30*(5), 906–920.

Davies, E. (1922). *Transactions of the Institute of Mining Engineering, 63,* 326.

Davis, D. D., & Harless, D. W. (1996). Group v. Individual performance in a price-searching experiment. *Organizational Behavior and Human Decision Processes, 66*(2), 215–227.

Davis, K. (1953). Management communication and the grape-vine. *Harvard Business Review, 31*(5), 43–59.

Davis, K. (1977). *Human behavior at work.* New York: McGraw-Hill.

Davis, T. R. (1984). The influence of the physical environment in offices. *Academy of Management Review, 9,* 271–283.

Day, D. V., & Schleicher, D. J. (2006). Self-monitoring at work: A motive-based perspective. *Journal of Personality, 74*(3), 685–714.

Day, D. V., Schleicher, D. J., Unckless, A. L., & Hiller, N. J. (2002). Self-monitoring personality at work: A meta-analytic investigation of construct validity. *Journal of Applied Psychology, 87*(2), 390–401.

De Dreu, C. K. W., & Weingart, L. R. (2003). Task versus relationship conflict, team performance, and team member satisfaction: A meta-analysis. *Journal of Applied Psychology, 88*(4), 741–745.

Dean, M. A., Roth, P. L., & Bobko, P. (2008). Ethnic and gender subgroup differences in assessment center ratings: A meta-analysis. *Journal of Applied Psychology, 93*(3), 685–691.

Deane, C. (1999, January 10). Don't worry, we've got your number. *The Washington Post,* p. C4.

Deci, E. L., Koestner, R., & Ryan, R. M. (1999). A meta-analytic review of experiments examining the effects of extrinsic rewards on intrinsic motivation. *Psychological Bulletin, 125*(6), 627–668.

Deci, E. L., & Ryan, R. M. (1985). *Intrinsic motivation and self-determination in human behavior.* New York: Plenum.

Deckop, J. R., Mangel, R., & Cirka, C. C. (1999). Getting more than you pay for: Organizational citizenship behavior and pay-for-performance plans. *Academy of Management Journal, 42*(4), 420–428.

DeGroot, T., & Kiker, D. S. (2003). A meta-analysis of the non-monetary effects of employee health management programs. *Human Resource Management, 42*(1), 53–69.

DeGroot, T., & Motowidlo, S. J. (1999). Why visual and vocal interview cues can affect interviewers' judgments and predict job performance. *Journal of Applied Psychology, 84*(6), 986–993.

Deluga, R. J., & Winters, J. J. (1991). Why the aggravation? Reasons students become resident assistants. *Journal of College Student Development, 32*(6), 546–552.

De Been, I., & Beijer, M. (2014). The influence of office type on satisfaction and perceived productivity support. *Journal of Facilities Management, 12*(2), 142–157.

De Mauro, A., Greco, M., Grimaldi, M., & Ritala, P. (2018). Human resources for Big Data professions: A systematic classification of job roles and required skill sets. *Information Processing and Management, 54*(5), 807–817.

De Meuse, K. P., Bergmann, T. J., Vanderheiden, P. A., & Roraff, C. E. (2004). New evidence regarding organizational downsizing and a firm's financial performance: A long-term analysis. *Journal of Managerial Issues, 16*(2), 155–177.

Dempsey, P. G., Ayoub, M. M., Bernard, T. M., Endsley, M. R., Karwowski, W., & Lin, C. J. (1996). Ergonomic investigation of letter-carrier satchels: Part I. Field study. *Applied Ergonomics, 27*(5), 303–313.

Den Hartog, D. N., House, R. J., Hanges, P. J., Ruiz-Quintanilla, S. A., & Dorfman, P. W. (1999). Culture specific and cross culturally generalizable implicit leadership theories: Are attributes of charismatic/transformational leadership universally endorsed? *Leadership Quarterly, 10*(2), 219–256.

De Mauro, A., Greco, M., Grimaldi, M., & Ritala, P. (2018). Human resources for Big Data professions: A systematic classification of job roles and required skill sets. *Information Processing and Management, 54*(5), 207–817.

DeNisi, A. S., & Peters, L. H. (1996). Organization of information in memory and the performance appraisal process: Evidence from the field. *Journal of Applied Psychology, 81*(6), 717–737.

DeNisi, A. S., Robbins, T., & Cafferty, T. P. (1989). Organization of information used for performance appraisals: Role of diary-keeping. *Journal of Applied Psychology, 74,* 124–129.

Dennis, A. R., Valacich, J. S., & Nunamaker, J. F. (1990). An experimental investigation of the effects of group size in an electronic meeting environment. *IEEE Transactions on Systems, Man, and Cybernetics, 20*(5), 1049–1057.

Dennis, A. R., & Williams, M. L. (2007). A meta-analysis of group size effects in electronic brainstorming: More heads are better than one. In N. F. Kock (Ed.), *Emerging E-collaboration concepts and applications: Volume 1.* Hershey, PA: CyberTech Publishing.

Denton, D. K. (1996). 9 ways to create an atmosphere for change. *HR Magazine, 41*(10), 76–81.

DePaulo, B. M. (1992). Nonverbal behavior and self-presentation. *Psychological Bulletin, 111,* 203–243.

DePaulo, B. M., Lindsay, J. J., Malone, B. E., Muhlenbruck, L., Charlton, K., & Cooper, H. (2003). Cues to deception. *Psychological Bulletin, 129*(1), 74–118.

DeRosa, D. M., Smith, C. L., & Hantula, D. A. (2007). The

medium matters: Mining the long-promised merit of group interaction in creative idea generation tasks in a meta-analysis of the electronic group brainstorming literature. *Computers in Human Behavior, 23*(3), 1549–1581.

DeRouin, R. E., Parrish, T. J., & Salas, E. (2005). *On-the-job training: A review for researchers and practitioners*. Poster session presented at the 20th annual conference of the Society for Industrial and Organizational Psychology, Los Angeles, CA.

DeRue, D. S., Nahrgang, J. D., Wellman, N., & Humphrey, S. E. (2011). Trait and behavioral theories of leadership: An integration and meta-analytic test of their relative validity. *Personnel Psychology, 64*, 7–52.

Deshpande, R. C. (2012). A healthy way to handle workplace stress through yoga, meditation and soothing humor. *International Journal of Environmental Sciences, 2*(4), 2143–2154.

Devine, D. J., Clayton, L. D., Philips, J. L., Dunford, B. B., & Melner, S. B. (1999). Teams in organizations: Prevalence, characteristics, and effectiveness. *Small Group Research, 30*(6), 678–711.

Devine, D. J., & Philips, J. L. (2001). Do smarter teams do better: A meta-analysis of cognitive ability and team performance. *Small Group Research, 32*(5), 507–532.

Dew, A. F., & Steiner, D. D. (1997). *Inappropriate questions in selection interviews: Interviewer knowledge and applicant reactions*. Poster presented at the 12th annual conference of the Society for Industrial and Organizational Psychology, St. Louis, MO.

De Waard, D., Jessurun, M., Steyvers, F. J., Raggatt, P. T., & Brookhuis, K. A. (1995). Effect of road layout and road environment on driving performance, drivers' physiology, and road appreciation. *Ergonomics, 38*(7), 1395–1407.

Dewberry, C., Davies-Muir, A., & Newell, S. (2013). Impact and causes of rater severity/leniency in appraisals without postevaluation communication between raters and rates. *International Journal of Selection and Assessment, 21*(3), 286–293.

DeYoung, C. G., Quilty, L. C., & Peterson, J. B. (2007). Between facets and domains: 10 aspects of the Big Five. *Journal of Personality and Social Psychology, 93*, 880–896.

Dianat, I., Haslegrave, C. M., & Stedmon, A. (2010). Short and longer duration effects of protective gloves on hand performance capabilities and subjective assessments in a screwdriving task. *Ergonomics, 53*(12), 1468–1483.

Dickenson, T. L., & Zellinger, P. M. (1980). A comparison of the behaviorally anchored rating and mixed standard scale format. *Journal of Applied Psychology, 65*, 147–154.

Dickinson, A. M., & Gillette, K. L. (1993). A comparison of the effects of two individual monetary incentive systems on productivity and piece rate pay versus base pay plus incentives. *Journal of Organizational Behavior Management, 14*(1), 63–82.

Dickson, D. H., & Kelly, I. W. (1985). The "Barnum Effect" in personality assessment: A review of the literature. *Psychological Reports, 57*, 367–382.

DiClemente, D. F., & Hantula, D. A. (2000). John Broadus Watson, I-O psychologist. *The Industrial-Organizational Psychologist, 37*(4), 47–55.

Diekmann, F. J. (2001, July 23). Everything you wanted to know about e-learning (But didn't know where to log on to ask). *Credit Union Journal, 5*(30), 6–7.

Dierdorff, E. C. (2012). Using secondary sources of work information to improve work analysis. In M. A. Wilson, W. Bennett Jr., S. G. Gibson, & G. M. Alliger (Eds.), *The handbook of work analysis: Methods, systems, applications and science of work measurement in organizations* (pp. 81–92). New York, NY: Routledge Taylor & Francis Group.

Dierdorff, E. C., & Rubin, R. S. (2007). Carelessness and discriminability in work role requirement judgments: Influences of role ambiguity and cognitive complexity. *Personnel Psychology, 60*, 597–625.

Dierdorff, E. C., & Wilson, M. A. (2003). A meta-analysis of job analysis reliability. *Journal of Applied Psychology, 88*(4), 635–646.

Dietz, P. E. (1994). *Overview of workplace violence*. Roanoke, VA: Seminar presented to the Society for Human Resource Management.

DiFonzo, N., & Bordia, P. (2006). Rumor in organizational contexts. In R. L. Rosnow & D. A. Hantula (Eds.), *Advances in social and organizational psychology*. Hillsdale, NJ: Lawrence Erlbaum.

DiFonzo, N., & Bordia, P. (2007). *Rumor psychology: Social and organizational approaches*. Washington, DC: American Psychological Association.

Dilchert, S., Ones, D. S., & Krueger, R. F. (2019). Personality assessment for work: Legal, I-O, and clinical perspective. *Industrial and Organizational Psychology, 12*(2), 143–150.

Dineen, B. R., Ling, J., Ash, S. R., & DelVecchio, D. (2007). Aesthetic properties and message customization: Navigating the dark side of web recruitment. *Journal of Applied Psychology, 92*(2), 356–372.

Dingfelder, S. F. (2004). A presidential personality. *Monitor on Psychology, 35*(10), 26–28.

Dipboye, R. L., Stramler, C. S., & Fontenelle, G. A. (1984). The effects of the application on recall of information from the interview. *Academy of Management Journal, 27*, 561–575.

Dirks, K. T. (2000). Trust in leadership and team performance: Evidence from NCAA basketball. *Journal of Applied Psychology, 85*(6), 1004–1012.

Dirks, K. T., & Ferrin, D. L. (2002). Trust in leadership: Meta-analytic findings and implications for research and practice. *Journal of Applied Psychology, 87*(4), 611–628.

Do, M. H., & Minbashian, A. (2020). Higher-order personality factors and leadership outcomes: A meta-analysis. *Personality and Individual Differences, 163*, 110058.

Dolin, D. J., & Booth-Butterfield, M. (1993). Reach out and touch someone: Analysis of nonverbal comforting responses. *Communication Quarterly, 41*(4), 383–393.

Dominguez, C. M., & Sotherlund, J. (2010). *Leading with your heart: Diversity and ganas for inspired inclusion*. Alexandria, VA: Society for Human Resource Management.

Donnellon, A. (1996). *Team talk: The power of language in team dynamics*. Boston, MA: Harvard Business School Press.

Donnerstein, E., & Wilson, D. W. (1976). Effects of noise and perceived control on ongoing and subsequent aggressive behavior. *Journal of Personality and Social Psychology, 34*, 774–781.

Donovan, J. J., & Radosevich, D. J. (1999). A meta-analytic review of the distribution of practice effect: Now you see it, now you don't. *Journal of Applied Psychology, 84*, 795–805.

Dormann, C., & Zapf, D. (2001). Job satisfaction: A meta-analysis of stabilities. *Journal of Organizational Behavior, 22*, 483–504.

Dougherty, T. W., Turban, D. B., & Callender, J. C. (1994). Confirming first impressions in the employment interview: A field study of interviewer behavior. *Journal of Applied Psychology, 79*(5), 659–665.

Douglas, J. (2021). Easily adapt familiar games for learning. *TD: Talent Development, 75*(1), 18–19.

Drexler, A. B., & Forrester, R. (1998). Teamwork—not necessarily the answer. *HR Magazine, 43*(1), 55–58.

Driskell, J. E., Willis, R. P., & Copper, C. (1992). Effect of overlearning on retention. *Journal of Applied Psychology, 77*(5), 615–623.

Driver, R. W., Buckley, M. R., & Frink, D. D. (1996). *Should we write off Graphology? International Journal of Selection and Placement, 4*(2), 78–86.

DuBrin, A. J. (2013). *Leadership: Research, findings, practice and skills.* Mason, OH: South-Western.

Duchon, J. C., Keran, C. M., & Smith, T. J. (1994). Extended workdays in an underground mine: A work performance analysis. *Human Factors, 36*(2), 258–268.

Dvir, T., Eden, D., Avolio, B. J., & Shamir, B. (2002). Impact of transformational leadership on follower development and performance: A field experiment. *Academy of Management Journal, 45*(4), 735–744.

Dwight, S. A., & Feigelson, M. E. (2000). A quantitative review of the effect of computerized testing on the measurement of social desirability. *Educational and Psychological Measurement, 60*(3), 340–360.

Dye, D. A., & Reck, M. (1989). College grade point average as a predictor of adult success: A reply. *Public Personnel Management, 18*(2), 239–240.

Dye, D. A., Reck, M., & McDaniel, M. A. (1993). The validity of job knowledge measures. *International Journal of Selection and Assessment, 1*(3), 153–157.

Dye, D. A., Reck, M., & McDaniel, M. A. (2007). The validity of job knowledge measures. *International Journal of Selection and Assessment, 1*(3), 153–157.

Eagly, A. H., Johannesen-Schmidt, M. C., & van Engen, M. L. (2003). Transformational, transactional, and laissez-faire leadership styles: A meta-analysis comparing men and women. *Psychological Bulletin, 129*(4), 569–591.

Eagly, A. H., & Johnson, B. T. (1990). Gender and leadership style: A meta-analysis. *Psychological Bulletin, 108*(2), 233–256.

Eagly, A. H., Karau, S. J., & Makhijani, M. G. (1995). Gender and the effectiveness of leaders: A meta-analysis. *Psychological Bulletin, 117*(1), 125–145.

Earnest, D. R., Allen, D. G., & Landis, R. S. (2011). Mechanisms linking realistic job previews with turnover: A meta-analytic path analysis. *Personnel Psychology, 64*(4), 865–897.

Eatough, E. M., Chang, C.-H., Miloslavic, S. A., & Johnson, R. E. (2011). Relationships of role stressors with organizational citizenship behaviors: A meta-analysis. *Journal of Applied Psychology, 96*(3), 619–632.

Eby, L. T., Allen, T. D., Evans, S. C., Ng, T., & DuBois, D. L. (2008). Does mentoring matter? A multidisciplinary meta-analysis comparing mentored and non-mentored individuals. *Journal of Vocational Behavior, 72*(2), 254–267.

Eden, D., Geller, D., Gewirtz, A., Gordon-Terner, R., Inbar, I., Liberman, M., Pass, Y., Salomon-Segev, I., & Shalit, M. (2000). *Leadership Quarterly, 11*(2), 171–210.

Eidelson, R. J., & Eidelson, J. I. (2003). Dangerous ideas: Five beliefs that propel groups toward conflict. *American Psychologist, 58*(3), 182–192.

Einarsdóttir, S., & Rounds, J. (2009). Gender bias and construct validity in vocational interest measurement: Differential item functioning in the Strong Interest Inventory. *Journal of Vocational Behavior, 74*(3), 295–307.

EmployeeScreenIQ (2014). *The unvarnished truth: 2014 top trends in employment background checks.* Cleveland, OH: EmployeeScreenIQ.

Emrich, C. G., Brower, H. H., Feldman, J. M., & Garland, H. (2001). Images in words: Presidential rhetoric, charisma, and greatness. *Administrative Science Quarterly, 46*(3), 527–560.

Ensari, N., Riggio, R. E., Christian, J., & Carslaw, G. (2011). Who emerges as a leader? Meta-analyses of individual differences as predictors of leadership emergence. *Personality and Individual Differences, 51*(4), 532–536.

Erdogan, B., & Enders, J. (2007). Support from the top: Supervisors' perceived organizational support as a moderator of leader-member exchange to satisfaction and performance relationships. *Journal of Applied Psychology, 92*(2), 321–330.

Erfurt, J. C., Foote, A., & Heirich, M. A. (1992). The cost-effectiveness of worksite wellness programs for hypertension control, weight loss, smoking cessation, and exercise. *Personnel Psychology, 45*(1), 5–28.

Estes, R. (1990). Effects of flexi-time: A meta-analytic review. *Applied H.R.M. Research, 1*(1), 15–18.

Eurich, T. L., Krause, D. E., Cigularov, K., & Thornton, G. C. (2009). The current use of assessment center programs in the U.S. *Journal of Business and Psychology, 24*, 387–407

Evans, G. W., & Johnson, D. (2000). Stress and open-office noise. *Journal of Applied Psychology, 85*(5), 779–783.

Ewen, R. B., Smith, P. C., & Hulin, C. L. (1966). An empirical test of the Herzberg two-factor theory. *Journal of Applied Psychology, 50*(6), 544–550.

Falcone, P. (2017). *101 sample write-ups for documenting employee performance problems* (3rd ed.). New York: American Management Association.

Faragher, E. B., Cass, M., & Cooper, C. L. (2005). The relationship between job satisfaction and health: A meta-analysis. *Occupational and Environmental Medicine, 62*, 105–112.

Farber, B. J. (1994). Sales managers: Get real! Real play, not role play, is the best training you can give your salespeople. *Sales & Marketing Management, 146*(10), 25–26.

Farh, J., & Werbel, J. D. (1986). Effects of purpose of the appraisal and expectation of validation on self-appraisal leniency. *Journal of Applied Psychology, 71*, 527–529.

Farr, J. L. (1973). Response requirements and primacy-recency effects in a simulated selection interview. *Journal of Applied Psychology, 57*(3), 228–232.

Farrell, D., & Stamm, C. I. (1988). Meta-analysis of the correlates of employee absence. *Human Relations, 41*, 211–227.

Febriandirza, A., Chaozhong, W., Zhong, M., Hu, Z., & Zhang, H. (2017). The effect of natural sounds and music on driving performance and physiological. *Engineering Letters, 25*(4), 455–463.

Feight, L., Ferguson, G., Rodriguez, C., & Simons, C. (2006, February). *Can't get no satisfaction: A meta-analysis of equity theory and its effects on satisfaction and motivation.* Paper presented at the annual Graduate Student Conference in Industrial-Organizational Psychology and Organizational Behavior, Fairfax, VA.

Feinberg, R. A., Meoli-Stanton, J., & Gable, M. (1996). Employment rejection and acceptance letters and their unintended consequences on image, self-concept, and intentions. *Journal of Business and Psychology, 11*(1), 63–71.

Feitosa, J., & Sim, J. (2021). I-O psychology around the world: A snapshot of historical roots. In L. Koppes Bryan, *Historical perspectives in industrial and organizational psychology* (2nd Ed.) (pp. 63–82). New York: Routledge.

Feldblum, C. R., & Lipnic, V. A. (2016). *Select task force on the study of harassment in the workplace: Report of cochairs.* Washington, DC: Equal Employment Opportunity Commission.

Feldman, J. (1981). Beyond attribution theory: Cognitive processes in performance appraisal. *Journal of Applied Psychology, 66*, 127–148.

Ferreter, J. M., Goldstein, H. W., Scherbaum, C. A., Yusko, K. P., & Jun, K. (2008). *Examining adverse impact using a nontraditional cognitive ability assessment.* Poster session presented at the 23rd annual meeting of the Society for Industrial-Organizational Psychology, San Francisco, CA.

Fiedler, F. (1967). *A theory of leadership effectiveness.* New York: McGraw-Hill.

Fiedler, F. (1978). Recent developments in research on the contingency model. In L. Berkowitz (Ed.), *Group processes* (pp. 207–223). New York: Academic Press.

Field, R. H., & House, R. J. (1990). A test of the Vroom-Yetton model using manager and subordinate reports. *Journal of Applied Psychology, 75*(3), 362–266.

Fine, S. A. (1955). What is occupational information? *Personnel and Guidance Journal, 33*, 504–509.

Fine, B. J., & Kobrick, J. L. (1978). Effects of altitude and heat on complex cognitive tasks. *Human Factors, 20*, 115–122.

Finkelman, J. M., Zeitlin, L. R., Filippi, J. A., & Friend, M. A. (1977). Noise and driver performance. *Journal of Applied Psychology, 80*, 652–663.

Fisher, J. D., Bell, P. N., & Baum, A. (1984). *Environmental psychology.* New York: Holt, Rinehart & Winston.

Fisher, J. D., Rytting, M., & Heslin, R. (1976). Hands touching hands: Affective and evaluative effects of an interpersonal touch. *Sociometry, 39*, 416–421.

Fisher, S. L., & Greenis, J. L. (1996). *The customer in job analysis.* Poster presented at the 11th annual conference of the Society for Industrial and Organizational Psychology, San Diego, CA.

Fitzgibbons, A. (1997). Employees' perceived importance of profit sharing plays a role in profit sharing's organizational impact.

Proceedings of the 18th Annual Graduate Conference in Industrial/Organizational Psychology and Organizational Behavior, 18, 43–44.

Flanagan, J. C. (1954). The critical incident technique. *Psychological Bulletin, 51*, 327–358.

Flanagan, J. C., & Burns, R. K. (1955). The employee performance record: A new appraisal and development tool. *Harvard Business Review, 33*, 95–102.

Fleenor, J., Taylor, S., & Chappelow, C. (2020). *Leveraging the impact of 360-degree feedback* (2nd ed.). Oakland, CA: Berrett-Koehler.

Fleishman, E. A., & Harris, E. F. (1962). Patterns of leadership behavior related to grievances and turnover. *Personnel Psychology, 15*(2), 43–56.

Fleishman, E. A., Harris, E. F., & Burtt, H. E. (1955). *Leadership and supervision in industry.* Columbus: Ohio State University Press.

Flesch, R. (1948). A new readability yardstick. *Journal of Applied Psychology, 32*, 221–233.

Fletcher, J., Friedman, L., McCarthy, P., McIntyre, C., O'Leary, B., & Rheinstein, J. (1993). *Sample sizes required to attain stable job analysis inventory profiles.* Poster presented at the 8th annual meeting of the Society for Industrial and Organizational Psychology, San Francisco, CA.

Foldes, H. J., Duehr, E. E., & Ones, D. S. (2008). Group differences in personality: Meta-analyses comparing five U.S. racial groups. *Personnel Psychology, 61*(3), 579–616.

Folkard, S. (2008). Do permanent night workers show circadian adjustment? A review based on the endogenous melatonin rhythm. *Chronobiology International, 25*, 183–198.

Ford, D., Truxillo, D. M., Wang, M., & Bauer, T. (2008, April). *Individual differences and the quality of job analysis ratings.* Poster session presented at the 23rd annual meeting of the Society for Industrial-Organizational Psychology, San Francisco, CA.

Ford, J. K., Quiñones, M. A., Sego, D. J., & Sorra, J. S. (1992). Factors affecting the opportunity to perform trained tasks on the job. *Personnel Psychology, 45*, 511–527.

Forsyth, D. R. (2019). *Group dynamics* (7th ed.). Boston, MA: Cengage.

Foster, D. A. (1999). *A leader-subordinate fit model of the path-goal theory of leadership.* Unpublished doctoral dissertation, George Washington University, Washington, DC.

Foster, J., Gaddis, B., & Hogan, J. (2012). Personality-based job analysis. In M. A. Wilson, W. Bennett Jr., S. G. Gibson, & G. M. Alliger (Eds.), *The handbook of work analysis: Methods, systems, applications and science of work measurement in organizations* (pp. 247–264). New York, NY: Routledge Taylor & Francis Group.

Foster, M. (1990). A closer look at the relationship between interviewer-interviewee similarity and ratings in a selection interview. *Applied H.R.M. Research, 1*(1), 23–26.

Foster, N., Dingman, S., Muscolino, J., & Jankowski, M. A. (1996). Gender in mock hiring decisions. *Psychological Reports, 79*(1), 275–278.

Foster, P. (2002). Performance documentation. *Business Communication Quarterly, 65*(2), 108–114.

Foster, R. S., Aamodt, M. G., Bodenmiller, J. A., Rodgers, J. G., Kovach, R. C., & Bryan, D. A. (1988). Effect of menu sign position on customer ordering times and number of food-ordering errors. *Environment and Behavior, 20*(2), 200–210.

Foster, T. C., Dunleavy, E., Campion, J., & Steubing, K. (2008, April). *Understanding performance appraisal litigation: Does justice explain wrongful discharge rulings?* Poster session presented at the 23rd annual meeting of the Society for Industrial and Organizational Psychology, San Francisco, CA.

Foti, R. J., & Hauenstein, N. M. A. (2007). Pattern and variable approaches in leadership emergence and effectiveness. *Journal of Applied Psychology, 92*(2), 347–355.

Fowler, D. (2013). *Violence in the workplace: Education, prevention, and mitigation.* Couer d' Alene, ID: Personal Safety Training, Inc.

Fowler-Hermes, J. (2001). The beauty and the beast in the workplace: Appearance-based discrimination claims under EEO laws. *Florida Bar Journal, 75*(4), 32–46.

Fox, J. B., Scott, K. D., & Donohue, J. M. (1993). An investigation into pay valence and performance in a pay-for-performance field setting. *Journal of Organizational Behavior, 14*, 687–693.

Frank, C. L., & Hackman, J. R. (1975). Effects of interviewer-interviewee similarity on interviewer objectivity in college admissions interviews. *Journal of Applied Psychology, 60*, 356–360.

Frank, F., & Anderson, L. R. (1971). Effects of task and group size upon group productivity and member satisfaction. *Sociometry, 34*, 135–149.

Frase, M. (2010). Taking time off to the bank. *HR Magazine, 55*(3), 41–46.

Frei, S. (2018). *Making night shift work: A practical guide for the night worker.* Columbia, SC: Steve Frei.

Freiberger, P. (2013). *When can you start? Ace the interview and get hired.* San Mateo, CA: Career Upshift Productions.

French, J. R. P., & Raven, B. H. (1959). The bases of social power. In D. Cartwright (Ed.), *Studies in social power* (pp. 150–167). Ann Arbor: University of Michigan Press.

French, M. T., Roebuck, C. M., & Alexandre, P. K. (2004). To test or not to test: Do workplace drug testing programs discourage employee drug use? *Social Science Research, 33*(1), 45–63.

Frese, M., & Okonek, K. (1984). Reasons to leave shiftwork and psychological and psychosomatic complaints of former shiftworkers. *Journal of Applied Psychology, 69*, 509–514.

Fried, Y., & Ferris, G. R. (1987). The validity of the job characteristics model: A review and meta-analysis. *Personnel Psychology, 40*, 287–322.

Frone, M. R. (2000). Work-family conflict and employee psychiatric disorders: The national comorbidity survey. *Journal of Applied Psychology, 85*(6), 888–895.

Frone, M. R., Russell, M., & Cooper, M. L. (1995). Job stressors, job involvement, and employee health: An identity theory. *Journal of Occupational and Organizational Psychology, 68*(1), 1–11.

Fry, E. (1977). Fry's Readability Graph: Clarifications, validity, and extension to level 17. *Journal of Reading, 21*, 243–252.

Gaby, S. H., & Woehr, D. J. (2005, April). *Development and evaluation of a 'Climate for Performance Appraisal' measure.* Poster presented at the 20th annual meeting of the Society for Industrial and Organizational Psychology, Los Angeles, CA.

Gael, S. (1988). Subject matter expert conferences. In S. Gael (Ed.), *The job analysis handbook for business, industry, and government* (Vol. 1, p. 434). New York: Wiley.

Gajendran, R. S., & Harrison, D. A. (2007). The good, the bad, and the unknown about telecommuting: Meta-analysis of psychological mediators and individual consequences. *Journal of Applied Psychology, 92*(6), 1524–1541.

Gallup, D. A., & Beauchemin, K. V. (2000). On-the-job training. In G. M. Piskurich, P. Beckschi, & B. Hall (Eds.), *The ASTD handbook of training design and delivery.* New York: McGraw-Hill.

Galvin, T. (2003). 2003 Industry report. *Training Magazine, 40*(9), 21–45.

Gandy, J. A., & Dye, D. A. (1989). Development and initial validation of a biodata inventory in a merit system context. *Proceedings of 13th Annual Meeting of the International Personnel Management Association Assessment Council*, 138–142.

Ganguli, I., Sheridan, B., Gray, J., Chernew, M., Rosenthal, M. B., & Neprash, H. (2020). Physician work hours and the gender pay gap: Evidence from primary care. *New England Journal of Medicine, 383*, 1349–1357. DOI: 10.1056/NEJMsa2013804.

Ganzach, Y. (1998). Intelligence and job satisfaction. *Academy of Management Journal, 41*(5), 526–539.

Garbarino, S. (2004). *Shift-work: Sleep disorders, car accidents, and officer performance.* Paper presented at the annual meeting of the Society for Police and Criminal Psychology, Rome, Italy.

Garcia, D. (2019, August 14). *9 things great presidents and leaders have in common.* https://vidaaventura.net/common-presidential-leadership-qualities/

Gardner, D. G., & Pierce, J. L. (1998). Self-esteem and self-efficacy within the organizational context: An empirical examination. *Group & Organization Management, 23*(1), 48–70.

Gasperson, S. M., Bowler, M. C., Wuensch, K. L., & Bowler, J. L. (2013). A statistical correction to 20 years of banding. *International Journal of Selection and Assessment, 21*(1), 46–56.

Gaugler, B. B., Rosenthal, D. B., Thornton, G. C., & Bentson, C. (1987). Meta-analysis of assessment center validity. *Journal of Applied Psychology, 72*, 493–511.

Gebhardt, D. L., & Baker, T. A. (2017). Physical performance tests. In J. L. Farr & N. T. Tippins (Eds.), *Handbook of Employee Selection* (pp. 277–297). Routledge.

Geier, J. G., & Downey, D. E. (1980). *Attitudinal listening profile system.* Minneapolis, MN: Performax Systems International.

Geier, J. G., Downey, D. E., & Johnson, J. B. (1980). *Climate impact profile.* Minneapolis, MN: Performax Systems International.

Gelbart, M. (2001, October 30). 425 hopefuls attend Philadelphia job fair for airline workers. *Philadelphia Inquirer.*

Gelfand, M. J., Leslie, L. M., Keller, K., & de Dreu, C. (2012). Conflict cultures in organizations: How leaders shape conflict cultures and their organizational-level consequences. *Journal of Applied Psychology, 97*(6), 1131–1147.

George, J. M. (1995). Asymmetrical effects of rewards and punishments: The case of social loafing. *Journal of Occupational and Organizational Psychology, 68*(4), 327–338.

George, W. (2003). *Authentic leadership: Rediscovering the secrets to creating lasting value.* San Francisco: Jossey-Bass.

Georgiou, K., Gouras, A., & Nikolaou, I. (2019). Gamification in employee selection: The development of a gamified assessment. *International Journal of Selection and Assessment, 27*(2), 91–103.

Gere, D., Scarborough, E. K., & Collison, J. (2002). *SHRM/Recruit Marketplace 2002 recruiter budget/cost survey.* Alexandria, VA: Society for Human Resource Management.

Gersick, C. J. G. (1988). Time and transition in work teams: Toward a new model of group development. *Academy of Management Journal, 31*(1), 9–41.

Giacalone, R. A., Knouse, S. B., & Montagliani, A. (1997). Motivation for and prevention of honest responding in exit interviews and surveys. *The Journal of Psychology, 131*(4), 438–448.

Gibbs, C. A. (1969). Leadership. In G. Lindzey & E. Aronson (Eds.), *Handbook of social psychology* (pp. 205–282). Reading, MA: Addison-Wesley.

Gilchrist, J. A., & White, K. D. (1990). Policy development and satisfaction with merit pay: A field study in a university setting. *College Student Journal, 24*(3), 249–254.

Gillespie, J. Z., & Ryan, A. M. (2012). Gender-based preferential selection: Influences of perceptions of procedurally unfair advantage on performance and self-evaluations. *Journal of Applied Social Psychology, 42*(S1), E150–E179.

Gillet, B., & Schwab, D. P. (1975). Convergent and discriminant validities of corresponding Job Descriptive Index and Minnesota Satisfaction Questionnaire scales. *Journal of Applied Psychology, 60,* 313–317.

Gilliland, S. W. (1993). The perceived fairness of selection systems: An organizational justice perspective. *Academy of Management Review, 18,* 694–734.

Gilliland, S. W., Groth, M., Baker, R. C., Dew, A. F., Polly, L. M., & Langdon, J. C. (2001). Improving applicants' reactions to rejection letters: An application of fairness theory. *Personnel Psychology, 54*(3), 669–703.

Gilliland, S. W., & Langdon, J. C. (1998). Creating performance management systems that promote perceptions of fairness. In J. W. Smither (Ed.), *Performance appraisal: State of the art in practice* (pp. 209–243). San Francisco: Jossey-Bass.

Gilliland, S. W., & Steiner, D. D. (1997). *Challenge #6: Interactional and procedural justice.* Paper presented at the 12th annual meeting of the Society for Industrial and Organizational Psychology, St. Louis, MO.

Gillis, H. L., & Speelman, E. (2008). Are challenge (ropes) courses an effective tool? A meta-analysis. *Journal of Experiential Education, 31*(2), 111–135.

Gilmore, D. C. (1989). Applicant perceptions of simulated behavior description interviews. *Journal of Business and Psychology, 3,* 279–288.

Giluk, T., Stewart, G. L., & Shaffer, J. (2008, April). Interviewer decision making: The role of judgments during rapport building. In M. R. Barrick (Chair), *The role of unstructured information in the employment interview.* Symposium presented at the 23rd annual meeting of the Society for Industrial-Organizational Psychology, San Francisco, CA.

Giumetti, G. W., Schroeder, A. N., & Switzer III, F. S. (2015). Forced distribution rating systems: When does "rank and yank" lead to adverse impact? *Journal of Applied Psychology, 100*(1), 180.

Gkorezis, P., & Kastritsi, A. (2017). Employee expectations and intrinsic motivation: Work-related boredom as a mediator. *Employee Relations, 39*(1), 100–111.

Glotz, B., & Ruotolo, C. (2006). *Profiling the workplace killer.* Paper presented at the annual Graduate Conference in Industrial-Organizational Psychology and Organizational Behavior, Fairfax, VA.

Goddard, R., Simons, R., Patton, W., & Sullivan, K. (2004). Psychologist hand-scoring error rates on the Rothwell-Miller Interest Blank: A comparison of three job allocation systems. *Australian Journal of Psychology, 56*(1), 25–32.

Goff, S. J., Mount, M. K., & Jamison, R. L. (1990). Employer supported child care, work/family conflict, and absenteeism: A field study. *Personnel Psychology, 43*(4), 793–809.

Goldman, B., Pearsall, M. J., Gilliland, S. W., & Shapiro, D. L. (2007). An investigation of organizational reluctance to mediate employment disputes. In *Academy of Management Proceedings* (Vol. 2007, No. 1, pp. 1–6). Briarcliff Manor, NY: Academy of Management.

Goldstein, C. H. (2000, July). Employee drug testing in the public sector. *IPMA News,* pp. 13–16.

Goldstein, I. L., & Ford, J. K. (2002). *Training in organizations* (4th ed.). Belmont, CA: Wadsworth.

Gomez-Mejia, L. R., Welbourne, T. M., & Wiseman, R. M. (2000). The role of risk sharing and risk taking under gainsharing. *Academy of Management Review, 25*(3), 492–507.

Gomm, K. (2005, February 1). EU agism law could put an end to 'milk round' campus recruitment. *Computer Weekly,* p. 36.

Gonzalez, M. F., Capman, J. F., Martin, N. R., Johnson, T. M., Theys, E. R., & Boyce, A. S. (2019). Personality and the ADA: Ameliorating fairness concerns and maintaining utility. *Industrial and Organizational Psychology, 12*(2), 151–156.

Goodson, J. R., McGee, G. W., & Cashman, J. F. (1989). Situational leadership theory: A test of leadership prescriptions. *Group and Organization Studies, 14*(4), 446–461.

Gordon, J. R. (2001). *Organizational behavior: A diagnostic approach* (7th ed.). Englewood Cliffs, NJ: Prentice Hall.

Gordon, R. A., & Arvey, R. D. (2004). Age bias in laboratory and field settings: A meta-analytic investigation. *Journal of Applied Social Psychology, 34*(3), 468–492.

Gorman, C. A., & Rentsch, J. R. (2009). Evaluating frame-of-reference rater training effectiveness using performance schema accuracy. *Journal of Applied Psychology, 94*(5), 1336–1344.

Gowen, C. R. (1990). Gainsharing programs: An overview of history and research. *Journal of Organizational Behavior Management, 11*(2), 77–99.

Graen, G., & Uhl-Bien, M. (1995). Relationship-based approach to leadership: Development of leader-member exchange (LMX) theory of leadership over 25 years: Applying a multi-level multi-domain perspective. *Leadership Quarterly, 6,* 219–247.

Grant, K. A., & Habes, D. J. (1995). An analysis of scanning postures among grocery cashiers and its relationship to checkstand design. *Ergonomics, 38*(10), 2078–2090.

Green, S. B., Sauser, W. I., Fagg, F. N., & Champion, C. H. (1981). Shortcut methods for deriving behaviorally anchored rating scales. *Educational and Psychological Measurement, 41,* 761–775.

Green, S. B., & Stutzman, T. (1986). An evaluation of methods to select respondents to structured job-analysis questionnaires. *Personnel Psychology, 39,* 543–564.

Greenberg, J. S. (2017). *Comprehensive stress management* (14th ed.). New York: McGraw-Hill.

Grensing-Pophal, L. (2001a). *HR and the corporate intranet: Beyond brochureware.* Alexandria, VA: Society for Human Resource Management.

Grensing-Pophal, L. (2001b). Motivate managers to review performance. *HR Magazine, 46*(3), 45–48.

Grensing-Pophal, L. (2003). Communication pays off. *HR Magazine, 48*(5), 77–82.

Griffeth, R. W., & Gaertner, S. (2001). A role for equity theory in the turnover process: An empirical test. *Journal of Applied Social Psychology, 31*(5), 1017–1037.

Griffeth, R. W., Hom, P. W., & Gaertner, S. (2000). A meta-analysis of antecedents and correlates of employee turnover: Update, moderator tests, and research implications for the next millennium. *Journal of Management, 26*(3), 463–488.

Griffin, M. A., Rafferty, A. E., & Mason, C. M. (2004). Who started this? Investigating different sources of organizational change. *Journal of Business and Psychology, 18*(4), 555–570.

Griffiths, R. F., & McDaniel, Q. P. (1993). Predictors of police assaults. *Journal of Police and Criminal Psychology, 9*(1), 5–9.

Grijalva, E., Harms, P. D., Newman, D. A., Gaddis, B. H., & Fraley, R. C. (2015). Narcissism and leadership: A meta-analytic review of linear and nonlinear relationships. *Personnel Psychology, 68*(1), 1–47.

Grochocki, L. K. (2021). Modern technology and measurement are key in the era of less. *TD: Talent Development, 75*(2), 18–20.

Grossman, R. J. (2000). Make ergonomics. *HR Magazine, 45*(4), 36–42.

Grossman, R. J. (2002). Space: Another HR frontier. *HR Magazine, 47*(9), 28–34.

Grossman, R. J. (2010). Tough love at Netflix: The movie rental company minimizes policies but demands high performance. *HR Magazine, 55*(4), 36–41.

Grote, C. L., Robiner, W. N., & Haut, A. (2001). Disclosure of information in letters of recommendation: Writers' intentions and readers' experiences. *Professional Psychology-Research and Practice, 32*(6), 655–661.

Guerin, L., & Barreiro, S. (2019). *The essential guide to federal employment laws* (6th ed.). Berkeley, CA: NOLO.

Gully, S. M., Incalcaterra, K. A., Joshi, A., & Beaubien, J. M. (2002). A meta-analysis of team-efficacy, potency, and performance: Interdependence and level of analysis as moderators of observed relationships. *Journal of Applied Psychology, 87*(5), 819–832.

Gumpert, R. A., & Hambleton, R. K. (1979). Situational leadership: How Xerox managers fine-tune managerial styles to employee maturity and task needs. *Management Review, 12,* 9.

Gunning, R. (1964). *How to take the FOG out of writing.* Chicago: Dartnell Corp.

Gupta, V., Hanges, P. J., & Dorfman, P. (2002). Cultural clusters: Methodology and findings. *Journal of World Business, 37,* 11–15.

Gutman, A. (2004). Grutter goes to work. The 7th Circuit Court's ruling in Petit v. City of Chicago. *The Industrial-Organizational Psychologist, 41*(1), 71–77.

Gutman, A. (2005). Sexual harassment: Here, there, and everywhere Part 1: English-speaking countries. *The Industrial-Organizational Psychologist, 42*(4), 55–67.

Gutman, A., & Christiansen, N. (1997). Further clarification of the judicial status of banding. *The Industrial-Organizational Psychologist, 35*(1), 75–81.

Gutman, A., & Dunleavy, E. M. (2012). Documenting work analysis projects: A review of strategy and legal defensibility for personnel selection. In M. A. Wilson, W. Bennett Jr., S. G. Gibson, & G. M. Alliger (Eds.), *The handbook of work analysis: Methods, systems, applications and science of work measurement in organizations* (pp. 139–167). New York, NY: Routledge Taylor & Francis Group.

Guttman, L. (1945). A basis for analyzing test-retest reliability. *Psychometrika, 10*(4), 255–282.

Guzzo, R. A., Jette, R. D., & Katzell, R. A. (1985). The effects of psychologically based intervention programs on worker productivity: A meta-analysis. *Personnel Psychology, 38,* 275–291.

Habeeb, K., & Prencipe, L. W. (2001). Avoiding workplace violence. *InfoWorld, 23*(6), 63.

Hackett, R. D. (1989). Work attitudes and employee absenteeism: A synthesis of the literature. *Journal of Occupational Psychology, 62*(3), 235–248.

Hackett, R. D., & Bycio, P. (1996). An evaluation of employee absenteeism as a coping mechanism among hospital nurses. *Journal of Occupational and Organizational Psychology, 69*(4), 327–338.

Hackman, J. R., & Oldham, G. R. (1975). Development of the job diagnostic survey. *Journal of Applied Psychology, 60,* 159–170.

Hackman, J. R., & Oldham, G. R. (1976). Motivation through the design of work: Test of a theory. *Organizational Behavior and Human Performance, 16,* 250–279.

Hackman, J. R., & Vidmar, N. (1970). Effects of size and task type on group performance and member reactions. *Sociometry, 33,* 37–54.

Hackman, J. R., & Wageman, R. (2007). Asking the right questions about leadership: Discussions and conclusions. *American Psychologist, 62*(1), 43–47.

Hall, D. T., & Nougaim, K. E. (1968). An examination of Maslow's need hierarchy in an organizational setting. *Organizational Behavior and Human Performance, 3,* 12–35.

Hall, E. T. A. (1963). A system for the notation of promemic behavior. *American Anthropologist, 65,* 1003–1026.

Halvorsen, B., Radford, K., Chapman, G., & Nikolic, B. (2021). Job embeddedness. In V. I. Sessa & N. A. Bowling (Eds.), *Essentials of job attitudes and other workplace psychological constructs* (pp. 184–206). New York: Routledge.

Hammer, L. B., & Brady, J. M. (2021). The evolution of worker well-being and work-life issues. In L. Koppes Bryan (Ed.), *Historical perspectives in industrial and organizational psychology* (2nd Ed.) (pp. 270–291). New York: Routledge.

Hampton, D. R., Summer, C. E., & Webber, R. A. (1978). *Organizational behavior and the practice of management.* Glenview, IL: Scott, Foresman.

Hanlon, S. C., & Taylor, R. R. (1992). How does gainsharing work? Some preliminary answers following application in a service organization. *Applied H.R.M. Research, 3*(2), 73–91.

Harder, J. W. (1992). Play for pay: Effects of inequity in a pay-for-performance context. *Administrative Science Quarterly, 37,* 321–335.

Hardison, C. M., Kim, D., & Sackett, P. R. (2005, April). *Meta-analysis of Work Sample Criterion Related Validity: Revisiting Anomalous Findings.* Paper presented at the 20th annual conference of the Society for Industrial-Organizational Psychology, Los Angeles, CA.

Hardy, C. J., & Crace, R. K. (1991). The effects of task structure and teammate competence on social loafing. *Journal of Sport and Exercise Psychology, 13*(4), 372–381.

Harlow, J. (2021). Virtual training is here to stay. *TD: Talent Development, 75*(3), 10–11.

Harold, C. M., McFarland, L. A., & Weekley, J. A. (2006). The validity of verifiable and non-verifiable biodata items: An examination across applicants and incumbents. *International Journal of Selection and Assessment, 14*(4), 336–346.

Harriman, T. S., & Kovach, R. (1987). The effects of job familiarity on the recall of performance information. *Proceedings of the 8th Annual Graduate Conference in Industrial/Organizational Psychology and Organizational Behavior,* 49–50.

Harris, B. (1979). What ever happened to little Albert? *American Psychologist, 34*(2), 151–160.

Harrison, D. A., Kravitz, D. A., Mayer, D. M., Leslie, L. M., & Lev-Arey, D. (2006). Understanding attitudes toward affirmative action programs in employment: Summary and meta-analysis of 35 years of research. *Journal of Applied Psychology, 91*(5), 1013–1036.

Harrison, D. A., Mohammed, S., McGrath, J. E., Florey, A. T., & Vanerstoep, S. W. (2003). Time matters in team performance: Effects of member familiarity, entrainment, and task discontinuity on speed and quality. *Personnel Psychology, 56*(3), 633–669.

Harrison, D. A., & Shaffer, M. A. (1994). Comparative examinations of self-reports and perceived absenteeism norms: Wading through Lake Wobegon. *Journal of Applied Psychology, 79*(2), 240–256.

Harrison, J. K. (1992). Individual and combined effects of behavior modeling and the cultural assimilator in cross-cultural management training. *Journal of Applied Psychology, 77*(6), 952–962.

Harvey, R. J., Friedman, L., Hakel, M. D., & Cornelius, E. T. (1988). Dimensionality of the Job Element Inventory, a simplified worker-oriented job analysis questionnaire. *Journal of Applied Psychology, 73,* 639–646.

Harvey, R. J., & Wilson, M. A. (2000). Yes Virginia, there is an objective reality in job analysis. *Journal of Organizational Behavior, 21,* 829–854.

Hasson, G., & Butler, D. (2020). *Mental health and wellbeing in the workplace.* Chichester, West Sussex: Wiley-Capstone.

Hattie, J., & Cooksey, R. W. (1984). Procedures for assessing the validities of tests using the "known-groups" method. *Applied Psychological Measurement, 8,* 295–305.

Hauenstein, N. M. A. (1986). *A process approach to ratings: The effects of ability and level of processing on encoding, retrieval, and rating outcomes.* Unpublished doctoral dissertation, University of Akron, Akron, OH.

Hauenstein, N. M. A. (1998). Training raters to increase the accuracy of appraisals and the usefulness of feedback. In J. W. Smither (Ed.), *Performance appraisal: State of the art in practice* (pp. 404–442). San Francisco: Jossey-Bass.

Hauenstein, N. M. A., & Foti, R. J. (1989). From laboratory to practice: Neglected issues in implementing frame-of-reference rater training. *Personnel Psychology, 42,* 359–378.

Hauenstein, N. M. A., & Lord, R. G. (1989). The effects of final-offer arbitration on the performance of major league baseball players: A test of equity theory. *Human Performance, 2*(3), 147–165.

Hauenstein, N. M. A., & McCusker, M. E. (2017). Rater training: Understanding effects of training content, practice ratings, and feedback. *International Journal of Selection and Assessment, 25,* 253–266.

Hausknecht, J. P., Day, D. V., & Thomas, S. C. (2004). Applicant reactions to selection procedures: An updated model and meta-analysis. *Personnel Psychology, 57*(3), 639–683.

Hausknecht, J. P., Halpert, J. A., Di Paolo, N. T., & Moriarty Gerard, M. O. (2007). Retesting in selection: A meta-analysis of coaching and practice effects for tests of cognitive ability. *Journal of Applied Psychology, 92*(2), 373–385.

Hazer, J. T., & Highhouse, S. (1997). Factors influencing managers' reactions to utility analysis: Effects of SD_y method, information frame, and focal intervention. *Journal of Applied Psychology, 82*(1), 104–112.

Heaney, C. A., & Clemans, J. (1995). Occupational stress, physician-excused absences, and absences not excused by a physician. *American Journal of Health Promotion, 10*(2), 117–124.

Heath, C. (1996). Do people prefer to pass along good or bad news? Valence and relevance of news as predictors of transmission propensity. *Organizational Behavior and Human Decision Processes, 68*(2), 79–94.

Heavey, A. L., Holwerda, J. A., & Hausknecht, J. P. (2013). Causes and consequences of collective turnover: A meta-analytic review. *Journal of Applied Psychology, 98*(3), 412–453.

Hecht, M. A., & LaFrance, M. (1995). How (fast) can I help you? Tone of voice and telephone operator efficiency in interactions. *Journal of Applied Social Psychology, 25*(23), 2086–2098.

Heerwagen, J. H., & Orians, G. H. (1986). Adaptations to windowlessness: A study of the use of visual decor in windowed and windowless offices. *Environment & Behavior, 18,* 604–622.

Heilman, M. E., & Alcott, V. B. (2001). What I think of me: Women's reactions to being viewed as beneficiaries of preferential selection. *Journal of Applied Psychology, 86*(4), 574–582.

Heilman, M. E., Block, C. J., & Lucas, J. A. (1992). Presumed incompetent? Stigmatization and affirmative action efforts. *Journal of Applied Psychology, 77*(4), 536–544.

Heilman, M. E., Block, C. J., & Stathatos, P. (1997). The affirmative action stigma of incompetence: Effects of performance information ambiguity. *Academy of Management Journal, 40*(3), 603–625.

Heilman, M. E., Kaplow, S. R., Amato, M. G., & Stathatos, P. (1993). When similarity is a liability: Effects of sex-based preferential selection on reactions to like-sex and different-sex others. *Journal of Applied Psychology, 78*(6), 917–927.

Hemphill, J. K., & Coons, A. E. (1950). *Leader behavior description.* Columbus: Personnel Research Board, Ohio State University.

Henderson, N. D., Berry, M. W., & Matic, T. (2007). Field measures of strength and fitness predict firefighters performance on physically demanding tasks. *Personnel Psychology, 60*(2), 431–473.

Henderson, R. I. (2006). *Compensation management in a knowledge-based world* (10th ed.). Englewood Cliffs, NJ: Prentice Hall.

Heneman, R. L., & Coyne, E. E. (2007). *Implementing total rewards strategies.* Alexandria, VA: SHRM Foundation.

Henkoff, R. (1990, June 17). Cost cutting: How to do it right. *Fortune,* p. 73.

Henle, C. A., Dineen, B. R., & Duffy, M. K. (2019). Assessing intentional resume deception: Development and nomological network of a resume fraud measure. *Journal of Business and Psychology, 34*(1), 87–106.

Hermelin, E., Lievens, F., & Robertson, I. T. (2007). The validity of assessment centres for the prediction of supervisory performance ratings: A meta-analysis. *International Journal of Selection & Assessment, 15*(4), 405–411.

Hersey, P., & Blanchard, K. H. (1988). *Management of organizational behavior* (5th ed.). Englewood Cliffs, NJ: Prentice Hall.

Hershcovis, M. S., Turner, N., Barling, J., Arnold, K. A., Dupré, K. E., Inness, M., et al. (2007). Predicting workplace aggression: A meta-analysis. *Journal of Applied Psychology, 92*(1), 228–238.

Herzberg, F. (1966). *Work and the nature of man.* Cleveland: World.

Highhouse, S. (2021). The dubious legacy of early "O"-side interventions. In L. Koppes Bryan, *Historical perspectives in industrial and organizational psychology* (2nd Ed.) (pp. 184–202). New York: Routledge.

HireRight (2019). *Employment screening benchmark report.* Irvine, CA: HireRight.

Ho, M. (2020). Learning technology is trending up. *TD: Talent Development, 74*(12), 28–33.

Hoch, J. E. (2019). Managing distributed work: Theorizing an IPO framework. In R. N. Landers (Ed.), *The Cambridge handbook of technology and employee behavior* (pp. 419–440). Cambridge: Cambridge University Press.

Hocker, J. L., & Wilmot, W. W. (2018). *Interpersonal conflict* (10th ed.). New York: McGraw-Hill.

Hockey, G. R. (1970). Signal probability and spatial locations as possible bases for increased selectivity in noise. *Journal of Experimental Psychology, 22,* 37–42.

Hoff, K. A., Song, Q. C., Wee, C. J. M., Phan, W. M. J., & Rounds, J. (2020). Interest, fit and job satisfaction: A systematic review and meta-analysis. *Journal of Vocational Behavior, 123,* 103503. https://doi.org/10.1016/j.jvb.2020.103503.

Hoff Macan, T., Avedon, M., & Paese, M. (1994). *The effects of applicants' reactions to cognitive ability tests and an assessment center.* Paper presented at the 9th annual conference of the Society for Industrial and Organizational Psychology, Nashville, TN.

Hoff Macan, T., & Foster, J. (2004). Managers' reactions to utility analysis and perceptions of what influences their decisions. *Journal of Business and Psychology, 19*(2), 241–253.

Hogan, J. B. (1994). Empirical keying of background data measures. In G. S. Stokes, M. D. Mumford, & W. A. Owens (Eds.), *Biodata handbook* (pp. 69–107). Palo Alto, CA: CPP Books.

Hogan, J., & Quigley, A. (1994). Effects of preparing for physical ability tests. *Public Personnel Management, 23*(1), 85–104.

Hogan, R. (1989). *The darker side of charisma.* Paper presented at the 13th annual meeting of the International Personnel Management Association Assessment Council, Orlando, FL.

Hogan, R., Raskin, R., & Fazzini, D. (1990). The dark side of charisma. In K. E. Clark & M. B. Clark (Eds.), *Measures of leadership* (pp. 343–354). West Orange, NJ: Leadership Library of America.

Hogan, T. P., Benjamin, A., & Brezinski, K. L. (2000). Reliability methods: A note on the frequency and use of various types. In B. Thompson (Ed.), *Score reliability: Contemporary thinking on reliability issues.* Thousand Oaks, CA: Sage Publications.

Holden, M. (1998). *Positive politics: Overcoming office politics and fast-track your career.* Warriewood, Australia: Business & Professional Publishing.

Hollander, E. P., & Offermann, L. R. (1990). Power and leadership in organizations: Relationships in transition. *American Psychologist, 45*(2), 179–189.

Holt, H. & Grainger, H. (2005). *Results of the second flexible working employee survey.* London: Department of Trade and Industry.

Holtom, B. C., Lee, T. W., & Tidd, S. T. (2002). The relationship between work status congruence and work-related attitudes and behaviors. *Journal of Applied Psychology, 87*(5), 903–915.

Hood, D. (2001). *A meta-analysis of the reliability levels for selection tests used in industry.* Paper presented at the 22nd annual Graduate Conference in Industrial-Organizational Psychology and Organizational Behavior, State College, PA.

Hoover, L. T. (1992). Trends in police physical ability selection testing. *Public Personnel Management, 21*(1), 29–40.

Hopke, T. (2010). Go ahead, take a few months off. *HR Magazine, 55*(9), 71–74.

Horan, J., & Seldman, M. (2012). *I wish I'd known that earlier in my career: The power of positive workplace politics.* Singapore: John Wiley & Sons.

Horowitz, B. (2014). *The hard thing about hard things: Building a business when there are no easy answers.* NY: HarperCollins.

Horwitz, S. K., & Horwitz, I. B. (2007). The effect of team diversity on team outcomes: A meta-analytic review of team demography. *Journal of Management, 33*(6), 987–1015.

Hosoda, M., Stone-Romero, E. F., & Coats, G. (2003). The effects of physical attractiveness on job-related outcomes: A meta-analysis of experimental studies. *Personnel Psychology, 56*(2), 431–462.

Hough, L., & Dilchert, S. (2017). Personality: Its measurement and validity for employee selection. In J. L. Farr & N. T. Tippins (Eds.) *Handbook of employee selection* (pp. 298–325). New York: Routledge.

Hough, L. M., Oswald, F. L., & Ployhart, R. E. (2001). Determinants, detection and amelioration of adverse impact in personnel selection procedures: Issues, evidence, and lessons learned. *International Journal of Selection and Assessment, 9*(1/2), 152–194.

House, R. J. (1971). A path-goal theory of leader effectiveness. *Administrative Science Quarterly, 9*, 321–332.

House, R. J., Javidan, M., Hanges, P., & Dorfman, P. (2002). Understanding cultures and implicit leadership theories across the globe: An introduction to Project GLOBE. *Journal of World Business, 37*, 3–10.

House, R. J., & Mitchell, T. R. (1974, Autumn). Path-goal theory of leadership. *Journal of Contemporary Business, 3*, 81–98.

Howard, J. L., & Ferris, G. R. (1996). The employment interview context: Social and situational influences on interviewer decisions. *Journal of Applied Social Psychology, 26*(2), 112–136.

Howard, M. C., & Marshall, C. J. (2019). Virtual reality training in organizations. In R. N. Landers (Ed.), *The Cambridge handbook of technology and employee behavior* (pp. 347–383). Cambridge: Cambridge University Press.

Huffcutt, A. I., & Arthur, W. (1994). Hunter and Hunter (1984) revisited: Interview validity for entry-level jobs. *Journal of Applied Psychology, 79*(2), 184–190.

Huffcutt, A. I., Conway, J. M., Roth, P. L., & Stone, N. J. (2001). Identification and meta-analytic assessment of psychological constructs measured in employment interviews. *Journal of Applied Psychology, 86*(5), 897–913.

Huffcutt, A. I., Culbertson, S. S., & Weyhrauch, W. S. (2013). Employment interview reliability: New meta-analytic estimates by structure and format. *International Journal of Selection and Assessment, 21*(3), 264–276.

Huffcutt, A. I., & Roth, P. L. (1998). Racial group differences in employment interview evaluations. *Journal of Applied Psychology, 83*(2), 179–189.

Huffcutt, A. L., Roth, P. L., Conway, J. M., & Klehe, U. C. (2003). *Moderators of situational and behavior description interview validity*. Poster presented at the 18th annual meeting of the Society for Industrial and Organizational Psychology, Orlando, FL.

Huffcutt, A. I., Roth, P. L., Conway, J. M., & Klehe, U. C. (2004). The impact of job complexity and study design on situational and behavior description interview validity. *International Journal of Selection and Assessment, 12*(2), 262–273.

Huffcutt, A. I., Weekley, J. A., Wiesner, W. H., DeGroot, T. G., & Jones, C. (2001). Comparison of situational and behavioral description interview questions for higher-level positions. *Personnel Psychology, 54*(3), 619–644.

Huffcutt, A. I., & Woehr, D. J. (1999). Further analyses of employment interview validity: A quantitative evaluation of interviewer-related structuring methods. *Journal of Organizational Behavior, 20*(4), 549–560.

Hughes, J. F., Dunn, J. F., & Baxter, B. (1956). The validity of selection instruments under operating conditions. *Personnel Psychology, 9*, 321–324.

Hui, C. H., Yee, C., & Eastman, K. L. (1995). The relationship between individualism—collectivism and job satisfaction. *Applied Psychology, 44*(3), 276–282.

Huish, G. B. (1997, August). Piece-rate play plan in clerk's office motivates quantum leap in quality productivity. *IPMA News*, pp. 22–27.

Hulsheger, U. R., Anderson, N., & Salgado, J. F. (2009). Team-level predictors of innovation at work: A comprehensive meta-analysis spanning three decades of research. *Journal of Applied Psychology, 94*(5), 1128–1145.

Hunt, J. W., & Laing, B. (1997). Leadership: The role of the exemplar. *Business Strategy Review, 8*(1), 31–42.

Hunter, J. A., Hayhurst, J., Kafka, S., Boyes, M., Ruffman, T., O'Brien, K. O., & Stringer, M. (2013). Elevated self-esteem 12 months following a 10-day developmental voyage. *Journal of Applied Social Psychology, 43*, 1956–1961.

Hunter, J. E., & Hunter, R. F. (1984). Validity and utility of alternative predictors of job performance. *Psychological Bulletin, 96*(1), 72–98.

Hunter, J. E., & Schmidt, F. L. (1982). Fitting people to jobs: The impact of personnel selection on national productivity. In M. D. Dunnette & E. D. Fleishman (Eds.), *Human performance and productivity: Vol. 1 Human capacity assessment* (pp. 233–284). Hillsdale, NJ: Lawrence Erlbaum.

Hur, P., Motawar, B., & Seo, N. J. (2012). Hand breakaway strength model: Effects of glove use and handle shapes on a person's hand strength to hold onto handles to prevent fall from elevation. *Journal of Biomechanics, 45*, 958–964.

Hurtz, G. M., & Donovan, J. J. (2000). Personality and job performance: The Big Five revisited. *Journal of Applied Psychology, 85*(6), 869–879.

Hurtz, G. M., & Wright, C. W. (2012). Designing work descriptions to maximize the utility of employee recruitment efforts. In M. A. Wilson, W. Bennett Jr., S. G. Gibson, & G. M. Alliger (Eds.), *The handbook of work analysis: Methods, systems, applications and science of work measurement in organizations* (pp. 347–364). New York, NY: Routledge Taylor & Francis Group.

Huseman, R. C., Hatfield, J. D., & Miles, E. W. (1987). A new perspective on equity theory: The equity sensitivity construct. *Academy of Management Review, 12*(2), 222–234.

Hutchison, S., Valentino, K. E., & Kirkner, S. L. (1998). What works for the gander does not work as well for the goose: The effects of leader behavior. *Journal of Applied Social Psychology, 28*(2), 171–182.

Hyatt, D. E., & Ruddy, T. M. (1997). An examination of the relationship between work group characteristics and performance: Once more into the breach. *Personnel Psychology, 50*(3), 533–585.

Hynes, G. E. (2012). Improving employees' interpersonal communication competencies: A qualitative study. *Business Communication Quarterly, 75*(4), 466–475.

Iaffaldano, M. T., & Muchinsky, P. M. (1985). Job satisfaction and job performance: A meta-analysis. *Psychological Bulletin, 97*, 251–273.

Ilardi, B. C., Leone, D., Kasser, T., & Ryan, R. M. (1993). Employee and supervisor ratings of motivation: Main effects and discrepancies associated with job satisfaction and adjustment in a factory setting. *Journal of Applied Social Psychology, 23*(21), 1789–1805.

Ilgen, D. R., & Bell, B. S. (2001a). Informed consent and dual purpose research. *American Psychologist, 56*(12), 1177.

Ilgen, D. R., & Bell, B. S. (2001b). Conducting industrial and organizational psychology research: Review of research in work organizations. *Ethics and Behavior, 11*, 395–412.

Ilgen, D. R., Nebeker, D. M., & Pritchard, R. D. (1981). Expectancy theory measures: An empirical comparison in an experimental simulation. *Organizational Behavior and Human Performance, 28*, 189–223.

Ilies, R., Gerhardt, M. W., & Le, H. (2004). Individual differences in leadership emergence: Integrating meta-analytic findings and behavioral genetics estimates. *International Journal of Selection and Assessment, 12*(3), 207–219.

Ilies, R., & Judge, T. A. (2003). On the heritability of job satisfaction: The mediating role of personality. *Journal of Applied Psychology, 88*(4), 750–759.

Ilies, R., Nahrgang, J. D., & Morgeson, F. P. (2007). Leader-member exchange and citizenship behaviors: A meta-analysis. *Journal of Applied Psychology, 92*(1), 269–277.

Imrhan, S. N., Imrhan, V., & Hart, C. (1996). Can self-estimates of body weight and height be used in place of measurements for college students? *Ergonomics, 39*(12), 1445–1453.

Indik, B. P. (1965). Organization size and member participation: Some empirical tests of alternate explanations. *Human Relations, 15*, 339–350.

Industry Report (2017). *Training Magazine.* Retrieved from https://trainingmag.com/trgmagarticle/2017-training-industry-report

International Task Force on Assessment Center Guidelines (2015). Guidelines and ethical considerations for assessment center operations: International task force on assessment center guidelines. *Journal of Management, 41*(4), 1244–1273.

Ironson, G. H., Smith, P. C., Brannick, M. T., Gibson, W. M., & Paul, K. B. (1989). Construction of a job in general scale: A comparison of global, composite, and specific measures. *Journal of Applied Psychology, 74*, 193–200.

Irving, P. G., & Meyer, J. P. (1994). Reexamination of the met-expectations hypothesis: A longitudinal analysis. *Journal of Applied Psychology, 79*(6), 937–949.

Isenberg, D. J. (1986). Group polarization: A critical review and meta-analysis. *Journal of Personality and Social Psychology, 50*(6), 1141–1151.

Ivancevich, J. M. (1982). Subordinates' reactions to performance appraisal interviews: A test of feedback and goal-setting techniques. *Journal of Applied Psychology, 67*, 581–587.

Iverson, R. D., & Buttigieg, D. M. (1999). Affective, normative and continuance commitment: Can the "right kind" of commitment be managed? *Journal of Management Studies, 36*(3), 307–333.

Iyengar, S., & Westwood, S. J. (2015). Fear and loathing across party lines: New evidence on group polarization. *American Journal of Political Science, 59*(3), 690–707.

Jack Hayes International, Inc. (2013). *25th annual retail theft survey.* Wesley Chapel, FL: Jack L. Hayes International, Inc.

Jackson, D. E., O'Dell, J. W., & Olson, D. (1982). Acceptance of bogus personality interpretations: Face validity reconsidered. *Journal of Clinical Psychology, 38*, 588–592.

Jackson, T. W. (2008). Apprenticeships: Creating new work-forces. *Blue Ridge Business Journal, 20*(12), 18–19.

Jacobs, J. A., & Kearns, C. N. (2001). Responding effectively to a claim of sexual harassment in the workplace. *Association Management, 53*(11), 19–20.

Jacobs, R. (1997). *Organizational effectiveness: Downsizing, one of many alternatives.* Keynote address presented at the 18th annual Graduate Student Conference in Industrial Organizational Psychology and Organizational Behavior, Roanoke, VA.

Jago, A. G., & Vroom, V. H. (1977). Hierarchical level and leadership style. *Organizational Behavior and Human Performance, 18*, 131–145.

Jamal, M. (1981). Shift work related to job attitudes, social participation, and withdrawal behavior: A study of nurses and industrial workers. *Personnel Psychology, 34*, 535–547.

Jamal, M., & Crawford, R. L. (1984). Consequences of extended work hours: A comparison of moonlighters, overtimers, and modal employees. *Human Resource Management, 4*, 18–23.

Jamal, M., & Jamal, S. M. (1982). Work and nonwork experiences of employees on fixed and rotating shifts: An empirical assessment. *Journal of Vocational Behavior, 20*, 282–293.

James, L. R. (1998). Measurement of personality through conditional reasoning. *Organizational Research Methods, 1*, 131–163.

Jamieson, J. P. (2010). The home field advantage in athletics: A meta-analysis. *Journal of Applied Social Psychology, 40*(7), 1819–1848.

Janis, I. L. (1972). *Victims of groupthink.* New York: Houghton Mifflin.

Janz, T., Hellervik, L., & Gilmore, D. C. (1986). *Behavior description interviewing.* Boston, MA: Allyn & Bacon.

Jehn, K. A., & Mannix, E. A. (2001). The dynamic nature of conflict: A longitudinal study of intragroup conflict and group performance. *Academy of Management Journal, 44*(2), 238–251.

Jeong, H. (2008). *Understanding conflict and conflict analysis.* Thousand Oaks, CA: Sage.

Jex, S. M., & Elacqua, T. C. (1999). Time management as a moderator of relations between stressors and employee strain. *Work & Stress, 13*(2), 182–191.

Jiang, K., Liu, D., McKay, P. F., Lee, T. W., & Mitchell, T. R. (2012). When and how is job embeddedness predictive of turnover? A meta-analytic investigation. *Journal of Applied Psychology, 97*(5), 1077–1096.

Job Accommodation Network (2020). *Workplace accommodations: Low cost, high impact.* Mograntown, WV: Job Accommodation Network.

Johns, G. (1994). Absenteeism estimates by employees and managers: Divergent perspectives and self-serving perceptions. *Journal of Applied Psychology, 79*(2), 229–239.

Johnson, J. W., & Oswald, F. L. (2017). Test administration and the use of test scores. In J. L. Farr & N. T. Tippins (Eds.), *Handbook of employee selection* (pp. 182–204). New York: Routledge.

Joiner, D. (2002). Assessment centers: What's new? *Public Personnel Management, 31*(2), 179–185.

Jones, K. S., Newman, D. A., Su, R., & Rounds, J. (2021). Black-White differences in vocational interests: Meta-analysis and boundary conditions. *Journal of Business and Psychology, 36*(4), 589–607.

Jossi, F. (2001). Teamwork aids HRIS decision process. *HR Magazine, 46*(6), 165–173.

Judge, T. A. (1993). Does affective disposition moderate the relationship between job satisfaction and voluntary turnover? *Journal of Applied Psychology, 78*(3), 395–401.

Judge, T. A., & Bono, J. E. (2001). Relationship of core self-evaluations traits—self-esteem, generalized self-efficacy, locus of control, and emotional stability—with job satisfaction and job performance: A meta-analysis. *Journal of Applied Psychology, 86*(1), 80–92.

Judge, T. A., Bono, J. E., Ilies, R., & Gerhardt, M. W. (2002). Personality and leadership: A qualitative and quantitative review. *Journal of Applied Psychology, 87*(4), 765–780.

Judge, T. A., Colbert, A. E., & Ilies, R. (2004). Intelligence and leadership: A quantitative review and test of theoretical propositions. *Journal of Applied Psychology, 89*(3), 542–552.

Judge, T. A., Heller, D., & Mount, M. K. (2002). Five-factor model of personality and job satisfaction: A meta-analysis. *Journal of Applied Psychology, 87*(3), 530–541.

Judge, T. A., & Ilies, R. (2002). Relationship of personality to performance motivation: A meta-analytic review. *Journal of Applied Psychology, 87*(4), 797–807.

Judge, T. A., Locke, E. A., & Durham, C. C. (1997). The dispositional causes of job satisfaction: A core evaluations approach. *Research in Organizational Behavior, 19*(1), 151–188.

Judge, T. A., Locke, E. A., Durham, C. C., & Kluger, A. N. (1998). Dispositional effects on job and life satisfaction: The role of core evaluations. *Journal of Applied Psychology, 83*(1), 17–34.

Judge, T. A., Piccolo, R. F., & Ilies, R. (2004). The forgotten ones? The validity of consideration and initiating structure in leadership research. *Journal of Applied Psychology, 89*(1), 36–51.

Judge, T. A., Rodell, J. B., Klinger, R. L., Simon, L. S., & Crawford, E. R. (2013). Hierarchical representations of the Five-Factor Model of personality in predicting job performance: Integrating three organizing frameworks with two theoretical perspectives. *Journal of Applied Psychology, 98*(6), 875–925.

Judge, T. A., Thoresen, C. J., Bono, J. E., & Patton, G. K. (2001). The job satisfaction-job performance relationship: A qualitative and quantitative review. *Psychological Bulletin, 127*(3), 376–407.

Judge, T. A., & Watanabe, S. (1993). Another look at the job satisfaction—life satisfaction relationship. *Journal of Applied Psychology, 78*(6), 939–948.

Judge, T. A., & Watanabe, S. (1994). Individual differences in the nature of the relationship between job and life satisfaction. *Journal of Occupational and Organizational Psychology, 67*, 101–107.

Kacmar, K. M., Carlson, D. S., & Brymer, R. A. (1999). Antecedents and consequences of organizational commitment: A comparison of two scales. *Educational and Psychological Measurement, 59*(6), 976–994.

Kaess, W. A., Witryol, S. L., & Nolan, R. E. (1961). Reliability, sex differences, and validity in the leaderless group discussion technique. *Journal of Applied Psychology, 45*(5), 345–350.

Kaliterna, L., Vidacek, S., Prizmic, Z., & Radosevic-Vidacek, B. (1995). Is tolerance to shiftwork predictable from individual difference measures? *Work and Stress, 9*, 140–147.

Kamalnath, A. (2017). Gender diversity as the antidote to 'groupthink' on corporate boards. *Deakin Law Review, 22*, 85–106.

Kammeyer-Mueller, J. D., & Judge, T. A. (2008). A quantitative review of mentoring research: Test of a model. *Journal of Vocational Behavior, 72*(3), 269–283.

Kaplan, I. T. (2002, April). *Effects of group size and problem difficulty on decision accuracy.* Paper presented at the 17th annual meeting of the Society for Industrial and Organizational Psychology, Toronto, Canada.

Kaplan, R. M., & Saccuzzo, D. P. (2018). *Psychological testing* (9th ed.). Boston, MA: Cengage.

Kaplan, S., Bradley, J. C., Luchman, J. N., Haynes, D. (2009). On the role of positive and negative affectivity in job performance: A meta-analytic investigation. *Journal of Applied Psychology, 94*(1), 162–176.

Karasek, R., & Theorell, T. (1990). *Healthy work: Stress, productivity and the reconstruction of working life.* New York: Basic Books.

Karau, S., & Williams, K. (1993). Social loafing: A meta-analytic review and theoretical integration. *Journal of Personality and Social Psychology, 65*(4), 681–706.

Kassel, J. D., Stroud, L. R., & Paronis, C. A. (2003). Smoking, stress, and negative affect: Correlation, causation, and context across stages of smoking. *Psychological Bulletin, 129*(2), 270–304.

Kassin, S., Fein, S., & Markus, H. R. (2014). *Social psychology* (9th ed.). Belmont, CA: Cengage Learning.

Katzell, R. A., & Austin, J. T. (1992). From then to now: The development of industrial-organizational psychology in the United States. *Journal of Applied Psychology, 77*(6), 803–835.

Katzell, R. A., & Dyer, F. J. (1977). Differential validity revived. *Journal of Applied Psychology, 62*, 137–145.

Kaufman, S. B. (2018). Self-actualizing people in the 21st century: Integration with contemporary theory and research on personality and well-being. *Journal of Humanistic Psychology,* doi.org/10.1177/0022167818809187.

Keeping, L. M., & Sulsky, L. M. (1996). *Examining the quality of self-ratings of performance.* Poster presented at the 11th annual meeting of the Society for Industrial and Organizational Psychology, San Diego, CA.

Keller, L. M., Bouchard, T. J., Arvey, R. D., Segal, N. L., & Dawis, R. V. (1992). Work values: Genetic and environmental influences. *Journal of Applied Psychology, 77*(1), 79–88.

Keller, R. T. (2001). Cross-functional project groups in research and product development: Diversity, communications, job stress, and outcomes. *Academy of Management Journal, 44*(3), 547–555.

Kennedy, J. K., Houston, J. M., Korsgaard, M. A., & Gallo, D. D. (1987). Construct space of the Least Preferred Coworker (LPC) Scale. *Educational and Psychological Measurement, 47*(3), 807–814.

Kernan, M. C., & Hanges, P. J. (2002). Survivor reactions to reorganization: Antecedents and consequences of procedural, interpersonal, and informational justice. *Journal of Applied Psychology, 87*(5), 916–928.

Kerr, N. L. (1983). Motivation loss in small groups: A social dilemma analysis. *Journal of Personality and Social Psychology, 45,* 819–828.

Kerr, N. L., & Bruun, S. E. (1983). Dependability of member effort and group motivation loss: Free-rider effects. *Journal of Personality and Social Psychology, 44,* 78–94.

Kerr, N. L., & Tinsdale, R. S. (2004). Group performance and decisions making. *Annual Review of Psychology, 55,* 623–655.

Kerr, S. (2009). Some random thoughts on the false dichotomies, common coffee spots, and the portability of knowledge. *The Industrial-Organizational Psychologist, 47*(2), 11–24.

Kidwell, R. E., Mossholder, K. W., & Bennett, N. (1997). Cohesiveness and organizational citizenship behavior: A multilevel analysis using work groups and individuals. *Journal of Management, 23*(6), 775–793.

Kierein, N., & Gold, M. A. (2001). Pygmalion in work organizations: A meta-analysis. *Journal of Organizational Behavior, 21,* 913–928.

Kim, B. H. (2008, April). *Truth. Lies and everything in between: Bogus items response processes.* Presented in J. Levashina & M. A. Campion (Co-Chairs), That can't be true! Detecting faking using bogus items. Symposium presented at the 23rd annual meeting of the Society for Industrial-Organizational Psychology, San Francisco, CA.

Kimbrough, A., Durley, J., & Muñoz, C. (2005). TIP-TOPics for students. *The Industrial-Organizational Psychologist, 42*(3), 107–114.

Kingston, N. M. (2009). Comparability of computer- and paper-administered multiple-choice tests for K-12 populations: A synthesis. *Applied Measurement in Education, 22*(1), 22–37.

Kirkman, B. L., Rosen, B., Gibson, C. B., Tesluk, P. E., & McPherson, S. O. (2002). Five challenges to virtual team success: Lessons from Sabre, Inc. *Academy of Management Executive, 16*(3), 67–79.

Kirkman, B. L., & Shapiro, D. L. (2001). The impact of cultural values on job satisfaction and organizational commitment in self-managing work teams: The mediating role of employee resistance. *Academy of Management Journal, 44*(3), 557–569.

Kirkpatrick, D. L. (1959a). Techniques for evaluating training programs. *Journal of ASTD, 13,* 3–9.

Kirkpatrick, D. L. (1959b). Techniques for evaluating training programs: Part 2-Learning. *Journal of ASTD, 13,* 21–26.

Kirkpatrick, D. L. (1960a). Techniques for evaluating training programs: Part 3-Behavior. *Journal of ASTD, 14,* 13–18.

Kirkpatrick, D. L. (1960b). Techniques for evaluating training programs: Part 4-Results. *Journal of ASTD, 14,* 28–32.

Kirkpatrick, D. L. (1986). Performance appraisal: When two jobs are too many. *Training, 23*(3), 65–68.

Kirkpatrick, D. L. (2000). Evaluating training programs: The four levels. In G. M. Piskurich, P. Beckschi, & B. Hall (Eds.), *The ASTD handbook of training design and delivery* (pp. 133–146). New York: McGraw-Hill.

Kirnan, J. P., Farley, J. A., & Geisinger, K. F. (1989). The relationship between recruiting source, applicant quality, and hire performance: An analysis by sex, ethnicity, and age. *Personnel Psychology, 42*(2), 293–308.

Kish-Gephart, J. J., Harrison, D. A., & Trevino, L. K. (2010). Bad apples, bad cases, and bad barrels: Meta-analytic evidence about sources of unethical decisions at work. *Journal of Applied Psychology, 95*(1), 1–31.

Kiviat, B. (2019). The art of deciding with data: Evidence from how employers translate credit reports into hiring decisions. *Socio-Economic Review, 17*(2), 283–309.

Kjellberg, A., Landstrom, U., Tesarz, M., & Soderberg, L. (1996) The effects of nonphysical noise characteristics, ongoing task and noise sensitivity on annoyance and distraction due to noise at work. *Journal of Environmental Psychology, 16*(2), 123–136.

Kleiman, L. S., & White, C. S. (1991). Reference checking: A field survey of SHRM professionals. *Applied H.R.M. Research, 2*(2), 84–95.

Klein, H. J., Wesson, M. J., Hollenbeck, J. R., & Alge, B. J. (1999). Goal commitment and the goal-setting process: Conceptual clarification and empirical synthesis. *Journal of Applied Psychology, 84*(6), 885–896.

Kline, T. J., & Sulsky, L. M. (2009). Measurement and assessment issues in performance appraisal. *Canadian Psychology/ Psychologie Canadienne, 50*(3), 161–171.

Kluger, A. N., & Colella, A. (1993). Beyond the mean bias: The effect of warning against faking on biodata item variances. *Personnel Psychology, 46,* 763–780.

Kluger, A. N., & Nir, D. (2010). The feedforward interview. *Human Resource Management Review, 20,* 235–246.

Knapp, M. L., Hall, J. A., & Horgan, T. G. (2014). *Nonverbal communication in human interaction* (2nd ed.). Boston, MA: Wadsworth.

Knauth, P. (1996). Designing better shift systems. *Applied Ergonomics, 27*(1), 39–44.

Knauth, P., Keller, J., Schindele, G., & Totterdell, P. (1995). A 14-hour night-shift in the control room of a fire brigade. *Work and Stress, 9,* 176–186.

Knoop, R. (1994). The relationship between importance and achievement of work values and job satisfaction. *Perceptual and Motor Skills, 79*(1), 595–605.

Knouse, S. B. (1983). The letter of recommendation: Specificity and favorability of information. *Personnel Psychology, 36,* 331–341.

Komaki, J. L. (1986). Toward effective supervision: An operant analysis and comparison of managers at work. *Journal of Applied Psychology, 71,* 270–279.

Komaki, J. L. (1998). *Leadership from an operant perspective.* London: Routledge.

Komaki, J. L., Zlotnick, S., & Jensen, M. (1986). Development of an operant-based taxonomy and observational index of supervisory behavior. *Journal of Applied Psychology, 71,* 260–269.

Kong, C. (2018, December 12). *Time to Review the Performance Review?* Robert Half Talent Solutions. https://www .roberthalf.com/blog/management-tips/time-to-review-the-performance-review?utm_campaign=Press_Release&utm_ medium=Link&utm_source=Press_Release.

Kopelman, M. D. (1975). The contrast effect in the selection interview. *British Journal of Educational Psychology, 45*(3), 333–336.

Koppes, L. L. (1997). American female pioneers of industrial and organizational psychology during the early years. *Journal of Applied Psychology, 82*(4), 500–515.

Koppes, L. L., & Pickren, W. (2007). Industrial and organizational psychology: An evolving science and practice. In L. L.

Koppes (Ed.), *Historical perspectives in industrial and organizational psychology*. Mahwah, NJ: Lawrence Erlbaum.

Koprowski, G. J. (2004). Rude awakening. *HR Magazine, 49*(9), 50–55.

Korman, A. K. (1966). Consideration, initiating structure, and organizational criteria: A review. *Personnel Psychology, 19*, 349–361.

Korman, A. K. (1970). Toward a hypothesis of work behavior. *Journal of Applied Psychology, 54*, 31–41.

Korman, A. K. (1976). Hypothesis of work behavior revisited and an extension. *Academy of Management Review, 1*, 50–63.

Korte, C., & Grant, R. (1980). Traffic noise, environmental awareness, and pedestrian behavior. *Environment & Behavior, 12*, 408–420.

Kortick, S. A., & O'Brien, R. M. (1996). The world series of quality control: A case study in the package deliver industry. *Journal of Organizational Behavior Management, 16*(2), 77–93.

Koslowsky, M., Sagie, A., Krausz, M., & Singer, A. H. (1997). Correlates of employee lateness: Some theoretical considerations. *Journal of Applied Psychology, 82*(1), 79–88.

Kotter, J. P., & Cohen, D. S. (2002). *The heart of change*. Boston: Harvard Business School Press.

Kottke, J. L., Shultz, K. S., & Aamodt, M. G. (2020). Importance of applied experiences: Course projects, practica, simulations, and internships. In E. L. Shoenfelt (Ed.), *Mastering industrial-organizational psychology: Training issues for master's level I-O psychologists*. New York: Oxford University Press.

Kovach, R., Surrette, M. A., & Whitcomb, A. J. (1988, January). *Contextual, student, and instructor factors involved in college student absenteeism*. Paper presented at the 10th annual National Institute on the Teaching of Psychology, St. Petersburg, FL.

Kovacs, K., Splittstoesser, R., Maronitis, A., & Marras, W. W. (2002). Grip force and muscle activity differences due to glove type. *AIHA Journal, 63*, 269–274.

Kozlowski, S. W., Kirsch, M. P., & Chao, G. T. (1986). Job knowledge, ratee familiarity, conceptual similarity and halo error: An exploration. *Journal of Applied Psychology, 71*, 45–49.

Kraiger, K., & Ford, J. K. (1985). A meta-analysis of ratee race effects. *Journal of Applied Psychology, 70*, 56–65.

Krane, S. (2021). *Friends, family remember woman killed by ex-boyfriend at Bob Evans*. https://www.cleveland19 .com/2021/04/20/friends-family-remember-woman-killed-by-ex-boyfriend-bob-evans/

Kravitz, D. A., Harrison, D. A., Turner, M. E., Levine, E. L., Chaves, W., Brannick, M. T., et al. (1997). *A review of psychological and behavioral research on affirmative action*. Bowling Green, OH: Society for Industrial and Organizational Psychology.

Krell, E. (2010). Second jobs: Blessing or curse? *HR Magazine, 55*(3), 57–59.

Kriegel, R., & Brandt, D. (1996). *Sacred cows make the best burgers*. New York: Warner.

Kristof-Brown, A. L., Zimmerman, R. D., & Johnson, E. C. (2005). Consequences of individuals' fit at work: A meta-analysis of person-job, person-organization, person-group, and person-supervisor fit. *Personnel Psychology, 58*(2), 281–342.

Kruger, J., Wirtz, D., & Miller, D. T. (2005). Counterfactual thinking and the first instinct fallacy. *Journal of Personality and Social Psychology, 88*(5), 725–735.

Kuder, G. F., & Richardson, M. W. (1937). The theory of estimation of test reliability. *Psychometrika, 2*, 151–160.

Kugler, K. G., Tamara, K., Reif, J., & Brodbeck, F. C. (2014). *Gender differences in the propensity to initiate negotiations: A meta-analysis*. Poster presented at the 29th Annual Meeting of the Society for Industrial and Organizational Psychology, Honolulu, Hawaii.

Kuncel, N. R., Credé, M., & Thomas, L. L. (2005). The validity of self-reported grade point averages, class ranks, and test scores: A meta-analysis and review of the literature. *Review of Educational Research, 75*(1), 63–82.

Kuncel, N. R., Hezlett, S. A., & Ones, D. S. (2001). A comprehensive meta-analysis of the predictive validity of the Graduate Record Examination: Implications for graduate student selection and performance. *Psychological Bulletin, 127*(1), 162–178.

Kuncel, N. R., Klieger, D. M., Connelly, B. S., & Ones, D. S. (2013). Mechanical versus clinical data combination in selection and admission decisions: A meta-analysis. *Journal of Applied Psychology, 98*(6), 1060–1072.

Kunin, T. (1955). The construction of a new type of attitude measure. *Personnel Psychology, 8*, 65–78.

Kurland, N. B., & Pelled, L. H. (2000). Passing the word: Toward a model of gossip and power in the workplace. *Academy of Management Review, 25*(2), 428–438.

Kutcher, E. J., & Bragger, J. N. (2004). Selection interviews of overweight job applicants: Can structure reduce the bias? *Journal of Applied Social Psychology, 34*(10), 1993–2022.

Kuvaas, B., Buch, R., & Dysvik, A. (2017). Constructive supervisor feedback is not sufficient: Immediacy and frequency is essential. *Human Resource Management, 56*(3), 519–531.

Laabs, J. J. (1996, July). Expert advice on how to move forward with change. *Personnel Journal*, 54–63.

Lachnit, C. (2001). Employee referral saves time, saves money, delivers quality. *Workforce, 80*(6), 67.

Ladd, D., Jagacinski, C., & Stolzenberg, K. (1997). Differences in goal level set for optimists and defensive pessimists under conditions of encouragement. *Proceedings of the 18th Annual Graduate Conference in Industrial/Organizational Psychology and Organizational Behavior, 18*, 85–86.

Lahtela, K., Niemi, P., Kuusela, V., & Hypen, K. (1986). Noise and visual choice reaction time. *Scandinavian Journal of Psychology, 27*, 52–57.

Lajunen, T., Hakkarainen, P., & Summala, H. (1996). The ergonomics of road signs: Explicit and embedded limits. *Ergonomics, 39*(8), 1069–1083.

Lam, S. S. K., & Schaubroeck, J. (2000). A field experiment testing frontline opinion leaders as change agents. *Journal of Applied Psychology, 85*(6), 987–995.

Lambert, L. S., Tepper, B. J., Carr, J. C., Holt, D. T., & Barelka, A. J. (2012). Forgotten but not gone: An examination of fit between leader consideration and initiating structure needed and received. *Journal of Applied Psychology, 97*(5), 913–930.

Landers, R. N. (2018, February 26). *Journal popularity among I-O psychology academics*. http://neoacademic.com/2018/02/26/journal-popularity-io-academics/

Landers, R. N., Auer, E. M., Helms, A. B., Marin, S., & Armstrong, M. B. (2019). Gamification of adult learning: Gamifying employee training and development. In R. N. Landers (Ed.), *The Cambridge handbook of technology and employee behavior* (pp. 271–295). Cambridge: Cambridge University Press.

Landers, R. N., & Behrend, T. S. (2015). An inconvenient truth: Arbitrary distinctions between organizational, Mechanical Turk, and other convenience samples. *Industrial and Organizational Psychology, 8*(2), 142–164.

Landy, F. J., & Bates, F. (1973). Another look at contrast effects in the employment interview. *Journal of Applied Psychology, 58*(1), 141–144.

Landy, F. J., & Vasey, J. (1991). Job analysis: The composition of SME samples. *Personnel Psychology, 44*, 27–50.

Langdale, J. A., & Weitz, J. (1973). Estimating the influence of job information on interviewer agreement. *Journal of Applied Psychology, 57*(1), 23–27.

Lantz, C. (2001). Essential skills for international careers. *Planning Job Choices: 2002*, 42–44.

Lapidus, R. S., & Pinkerton, L. (1995). Customer complaint situations: An equity theory perspective. *Psychology and Marketing, 12*(2), 105–122.

Larey, T. S., & Paulus, P. B. (1995). Social comparison and goal setting in brainstorming groups. *Journal of Applied Social Psychology, 25*(18), 1579–1596.

Larrick, R. P., Timmerman, T. A., Carton, A. M., & Abrevaya, J. (2011). Temper, temperature, and temptation: Heat-related retaliation in baseball. *Psychological Science, 22*(4), 423–428.

Larson, J. J. (2001). *A comparison of performance and attitudes of college students on computer-based versus paper-and-pencil testing.* Paper presented at the 22nd annual Graduate Conference in Industrial-Organizational Psychology and Organizational Behavior, Pennsylvania State University, PA.

Larson, S. L., Eyerman, J., Foster, M. S., & Gfroerer, J. C. (2007). *Worker substance use and workplace policies and programs.* Washington, DC: Department of Health and Human Services.

Lasky, J. W. (1999). Loosen the Shackles on Pennsylvania local government's hiring authority: An argument for banding. *Duquesne Law Review, 37*, 445–463.

Latane, B. (1981). The psychology of social impact. *American Psychologist, 36*, 343–356.

Latham, G. P., & Blades, J. J. (1975). The practical significance of Locke's theory of goal setting. *Journal of Applied Psychology, 60*, 122–124.

Latham, G. P., & Budworth, M. H. (2021). The study of work motivation. In L. Koppes Bryan (Ed.), *Historical Perspectives in industrial and organizational psychology* (2nd Ed.) (pp. 203–226). New York: Routledge.

Latham, G. P., Fay, C. H., & Saari, L. M. (1979). The development of behavioral observation scales for appraising the perfor-mance of foremen. *Personnel Psychology, 32*, 299–311.

Latham, G. P., & Pinder, C. C. (2005). Work motivation theory and research at the dawn of the twenty-first century. *Annual Review of Psychology, 56*, 485–516.

Latham, G. P., & Wexley, K. N. (1977). Behavioral observation scales for performance appraisal purposes. *Personnel Psychology, 30*, 225–268.

Latham, G. P., & Wexley, K. N. (1994). *Increasing productivity through performance appraisal.* Reading, MA: Addison Wesley.

Latham, V. M. (1983). Charismatic leadership: A review and proposed model. *Proceedings of the 4th Annual Graduate Conference in Industrial/Organizational Psychology and Organizational Behavior.*

Law, J. R. (1996). *Rising to the occasion: Foundations, processes, and outcomes of emergent leadership.* Unpublished doctoral dissertation, University of Texas, Austin, TX.

Lawshe, C. H., Bolda, R. A., Brune, R. L., & Auclair, G. (1958). Expectancy charts II: Their theoretical development. *Personnel Psychology, 11*, 545–559.

Lawrence, P. R., & Nohria, N. (2012). *Driven: How human nature shapes our choices.* San Francisco: Jossey-Bass.

Lawson, K. (2000). Making training active. In G. M. Piskurich, P. Beckschi, & B. Hall (Eds.), *The ASTD handbook of training design and delivery* (pp. 42–53). New York: McGraw-Hill.

Lăzăroiu, G. (2015). Employee motivation and job performance. *Linguistic and Philosophical Investigations,* (14), 97–102.

Leana, C. R., & Feldman, D. C. (1992). *Coping with job loss.* New York: Lexington.

LeBreton, J. M., Barksdale, C. D., Robin, J., & James, L. R. (2007). Measurement issues associated with conditional reasoning tests: Indirect measurement and test faking. *Journal of Applied Psychology, 92*(1), 1–16.

Lebron, A. (2021, February 9). *The latest on workplace violence statistics.* https://www.ravemobilesafety.com/blog/latest-workplace-violence-statistics

Lee, J. A., Havighurst, L. C., & Rassel, G. (2004). Factors related to court references to performance appraisal fairness and validity. *Public Personnel Management, 33*(1), 61–77.

Lee, J. A., Walker, M., & Shoup, R. (2001). Balancing elder care responsibilities and work: The impact on emotional health. *Journal of Business and Psychology, 16*(2), 277–289.

Lee, K., Carswell, J. J., & Allen, N. J. (2000). A meta-analytic review of occupational commitment: Relations with person- and work-related variables. *Journal of Applied Psychology, 85*(5), 799–811.

Lee, L. J., & Martin, A. L. (2001). Influence of social facilitation and gender on purchasing behavior of consumers in a mall. *Modern Psychological Studies, 8*(1), Article 6. Available at: https://scholar.utc.edu/mps/vol8/iss1/6

Lee, T. W., Mitchell, T. R., Sablynski, C. J., Burton, J. P., & Holtom, B. C. (2004). The effects of job embeddedness on organizational citizenship, job performance, volitional absences, and voluntary turnover. *Academy of Management Journal, 47*(5), 711–722.

Leeds, D. (1996). Training one-on-one. *Training & Development, 50*(9), 42–44.

Lefkowitz, J. (2000). The role of interpersonal affective regard in supervisory performance ratings: A literature review and proposed causal model. *Journal of Occupational and Organizational Psychology, 73*(1), 67–85.

Leonard, D. C., & France, A. H. (2003, May–June). Workplace monitoring: Balancing business interests with employee privacy rights. *SHRM Legal Report*, pp. 3–7.

LePine, J. A., Erez, A., & Johnson, D. E. (2002). The nature and dimensionality of organizational citizenship behavior: A critical review and a meta-analysis. *Journal of Applied Psychology, 87*(1), 52–65.

LePine, J. A., Hollenbeck, J. R., Ilgen, D. R., & Hedlund, J. (1997). Effects of individual differences on the performance of hierarchical decision-making teams: Much more than *g. Journal of Applied Psychology, 82*(5), 803–811.

Lepsinger, R., & DeRosa, D. (2010). *Virtual team success: A practical guide for working and leading from a distance.* San Francisco, CA: Jossey-Bass.

Leslie, L. M., Mayer, D. M., & Kravitz, D. A. (2014). The stigma of affirmative action: A stereotyping-based theory and meta-analytic test of the consequences for performance. *Academy of Management Journal, 57*(4), 964–989.

Levashina, J., Hartwell, C. J., Morgeson, F. P., & Campion, M. A. (2014). The structured employment interview: Narrative and quantitative review of the research literature. *Personnel Psychology, 67*(1), 241–293.

Levashina, J., Morgeson, F. P., & Campion, M. A. (2008, April). They don't do it often, but they do it well: Exploring the relationship between applicant mental abilities and faking. In J. Levashina & M. A. Campion (Co-Chairs), *That can't be true! Detecting faking using bogus items.* Symposium presented at the 23rd annual meeting of the Society for Industrial-Organizational Psychology, San Francisco, CA.

Levine, E. L., Ash, R. A., & Bennett, N. (1980). Exploratory comparison study of four job analysis methods. *Journal of Applied Psychology, 65*, 524–535.

Levine, E. L., Ash, R. A., Hall, H., & Sistrunk, F. (1983). Evaluation of job analysis methods by experienced job analysts. *Academy of Management Journal, 26*, 339–348.

Levine, J. D., & Oswald, F. L. (2012). O*NET: The Occupational Information Network. In M. A. Wilson, W. Bennett, S. G. Gibson, & G. M. Alliger (Eds.), *The handbook of work analysis* (pp. 281–301). New York: Routledge.

Levine, S. P., & Feldman, R. S. (2002). Women and men's nonverbal behavior and self-monitoring in a job interview setting. *Applied H.R.M. Research, 7*(1), 1–14.

Levinson, M. (2019). Mandatory arbitration: How the current system perpetuates sexual harassment cultures in the workplace. *Santa Clara L. Rev., 59*(2), 485–524.

Levit, A. (2008). *Success for hire: Simple strategies to find and keep outstanding employees.* Alexandria, VA: ASTD Press.

Lewin, K. (1951). *Field theory in social science.* New York: Harper & Row.

Lewin, K. (1958). Group decision and social change. In E. E. Maccoby, T. M. Newcomb, & E. L. Hartley (Eds.), *Readings in social psychology* (pp. 197–211). New York: Holt, Rinehart & Lewis, G. Winston. (2020). *6 recruiting trends that will shape 2021.* LinkedIn. https://www.linkedin.com/business/talent/blog/talent-strategy/future-of-recruiting.

Li, W.-D., Stanek, K. C., Zhang, Z., Ones, D. S., & McGue, M. (2016). Are genetic and environmental influences on job satisfaction stable over time? A three-wave longitudinal twin study. *Journal of Applied Psychology, 101*(11), 1598–1619.

Liden, R. C., Wayne, S. J., & Bradway, L. (1996). Connections make the difference. *HR Magazine, 41*(2), 73–79.

Liden, R. C., Wayne, S. J., Judge, T. A., Sparrowe, R. T., Kraimer, M. L., & Franz, T. M. (1999). Management of poor performance: A comparison of manager, group member, and group disciplinary decisions. *Journal of Applied Psychology, 84*(6), 835–850.

Lied, T. L., & Pritchard, R. D. (1976). Relationship between personality variables and components of the expectancy-valence model. *Journal of Applied Psychology, 61*, 463–467.

Lievens, F., & Patterson, F. (2011). The validity and incremental validity of knowledge tests, low-fidelity simulations, and high-fidelity simulations for predicting job performance in advanced-level high-stakes selection. *Journal of Applied Psychology, 96*(5), 927–940.

Lilienfeld, S. O., Wood, J. M., & Garb, H. N. (2001, May). What's wrong with this picture? *Scientific American*, 80–87.

Lim, J., & Dinges, D. F. (2010). A meta-analysis of the impact of short-term sleep deprivation on cognitive variables. *Psychological Bulletin, 136*(3), 375–389.

Lin, X., Chen, W., Wei, F., Ying, M., Wei, W., & Xie, X. (2015). *Sleep Medicine, 16*(11), 1381–1387.

Lindell, M. K., Clause, C. S., Brandt, C. J., & Landis, R. S. (1998). Relationship between organizational context and job analysis task ratings. *Journal of Applied Psychology, 83*(5), 769–776.

Lindeman, M., Sundvik, L., & Rouhiainen, P. (1995). Under- or overestimation of self? Person variables and self-assessment accuracy in work settings. *Journal of Social Behavior and Personality, 10*(1), 123–134.

Linn, R. L. (1978). Single-group validity, differential validity, and differential prediction. *Journal of Applied Psychology, 63*(4), 507–512.

Liou, K. T., Sylvia, R. D., & Brunk, G. (1990). Non-work factors and job satisfaction revisited. *Human Relations, 43*, 77–86.

Lippitt, R., Watson, J., & Westley, B. (1958). *Dynamics of planned change.* New York: Harcourt Brace.

Liu, O. L., Minsky, J., Ling, G., & Kyllonen, P. (2009). Using the standardized letters of recommendation in selection: Results from a multidimensional Rasch model. *Educational and Psychological Measurement, 69*, 475–492.

Locke, E. A., & Latham, G. P. (2002). Building a practically useful theory of goal setting and task motivation. *American Psychologist, 57*(9), 705–717.

Locke, E. A., & Latham, G. P. (2013). Goal setting theory, 1990. In E. A., Locke & G. P. Latham (Eds.), *New developments in goal setting and task performance* (pp. 3–15). New York: Routledge.

Lodi-Smith, J., & Roberts, B. W. (2007). Social investment and personality: A meta-analysis of the relationship of personality traits to investment in work, family, religion, and volunteerism. *Personality and Social Psychology Review, 11*(1), 68–86.

Loewen, L. J., & Suedfeld, P. (1992). Cognitive arousal effects of masking office noise. *Environment and Behavior, 24*(3), 381–395.

Lohan, G., Acton, T. & Conboy, K. (2014). *An investigation into time pressure, group cohesion and decision making in software development groups.* Paper presented at the 25th

Australasian Conference on Information Systems, Auckland, New Zealand.

Loher, B. T., Hazer, J. T., Tsai, A., Tilton, K., & James, J. (1997). Letters of reference: A process approach. *Journal of Business and Psychology, 11*(3), 339–355.

Long, G. M., & Kearns, D. F. (1996). Visibility of text and icon highway signs under dynamic viewing conditions. *Human Factors, 38*(4), 690–701.

Lopez, F. M., Kesselman, G. A., & Lopez, F. E. (1981). An empirical test of a trait-oriented job analysis technique. *Personnel Psychology, 34*, 479–502.

Lopez, F. E., Rockmore, B. W., & Kesselman, G. A. (1980). The development of an integrated career planning program at Gulf Power Company. *Personnel Administrator, 25*(10), 21–29.

Lord, R. G., & Hohenfeld, J. A. (1979). Longitudinal field assessment of equity effects in the performance of major league baseball players. *Journal of Applied Psychology, 64*, 19–26.

Lounsbury, J. W., Bobrow, W., & Jensen, J. B. (1989). Attitudes toward employment testing: Scale development, correlates, and "known group" validation. *Professional Psychology: Research and Practice, 20*(5), 340–349.

Lount, R. B., & Wilk, S. L. (2014). Working harder or hardly working? Posting performance eliminates social loafing and promotes social laboring in workgroups. *Management Science, 60*, 1098–1106.

Lovenheim, P., & Guerin, L. (2004). *Mediate, don't litigate: Strategies for successful mediation.* Berkley, CA: Nolo.

Luoma, J., Flannagan, M. J., Sivak, M., Aoki, M., & Traube, E. C. (1997). Effects of turn-signal colour on reaction times to brake signals. *Ergonomics, 40*(1), 62–68.

Lykken, D. T., & Tellegen, A. (1996). Happiness is a stochastic phenomenon. *Psychological Science, 7*(3), 186–189.

Lyons, P. (2008). The crafting of jobs and individual differences. *Journal of Business and Psychology, 23*(1/2), 25–36.

Mackworth, N. H. (1946). Effects of heat on wireless telegraphy operators hearing and receiving Morse messages. *British Journal of Industrial Medicine, 3*, 145.

Madera, J. M., Hebl, M. R., & Martin, R. C. (2009). Gender and letters of recommendation for academia: Agentic and communal differences. *Journal of Applied Psychology, 94*(6), 1591–1599.

Mager, R. F. (1997). *Preparing instructional objectives* (3rd ed.). Atlanta, GA: Center for Effective Performance.

Mailhot, E. K. (1996). *Incumbents as job experts: Effects of individual and group characteristics on job analysis results.* Unpublished doctoral dissertation, University of Connecticut.

Maiorca, J. (1997). How to construct behaviorally anchored rating scales (BARS) for employee evaluations. *Supervision, 58*(8), 15–18.

Major, B., Schmidlin, A. M., & Williams, L. (1990). General patterns in social touch: The impact of setting and age. *Journal of Personality and Social Psychology, 58*, 634–643.

Malos, S. B. (1998). Current legal issues in performance appraisal. In J. W. Smither (Ed.), *Performance appraisal: State of the art in practice* (pp. 49–94). San Francisco: Jossey-Bass.

Manners, G. E. (1975). Another look at group size, group problem solving, and member consensus. *Academy of Management Journal, 18*, 715–724.

Manning, R., Levine, M., & Collins, A. (2007). The Kitty Genovese murder and the social psychology of helping. *American Psychologist, 62*(6), 555–562.

Marks, M. A., Mathieu, J. E., & Zaccaro, S. J. (2001). A temporally based framework and taxonomy of team processes. *Academy of Management Review, 26*(3), 356–376.

Marks, M. L. (2003). *Charging back up the hill: Workplace recovery after mergers, acquisitions, and downsizings.* San Francisco: Jossey-Bass.

Martell, R. F., & Borg, M. R. (1993). A comparison of the behavioral rating accuracy of groups and individuals. *Journal of Applied Psychology, 78*(1), 43–50.

Martell, R. F., Guzzo, R. A., & Willis, C. E. (1995). A methodological and substantive note on the performance-cue effect in ratings of work-group behavior. *Journal of Applied Psychology, 80*(1), 191–195.

Martin, C. L., & Nagao, D. H. (1989). Some effects of computerized interviewing on job applicant responses. *Journal of Applied Psychology, 74*, 72–80.

Martin, D. C., Bartol, K. M., & Kehoe, P. E. (2000). The legal ramifications of performance appraisal: The growing significance. *Public Personnel Management, 29*(3), 379–405.

Martin, G. E., & Bergmann, T. J. (1996). The dynamics of response to conflict in the workplace. *Journal of Occupational and Organizational Psychology, 69*(41), 377–387.

Martin, R. A. (2001). Humor, laughter, and physical health: Methodological issues and research findings. *Psychological Bulletin, 127*(4), 504–519.

Martinez, A. D., Laird, M. D., Martin, J. A., & Ferris, G. R. (2008). Job title inflation. *Human Resource Management Review, 18*(1), 19–27.

Martinez-Tur, V., Moliner, C., & Maniezki, A. (2021). Organizational justice. In V. I. Sessa & N. A. Bowling (Eds.), *Essentials of job attitudes and other workplace psychological constructs* (pp. 45–70). New York: Routledge.

Martinez, M. N. (1990). In search of a productive design. *HR Magazine, 35*(2), 36–39.

Martinez, A. D., Laird, M. D., Martin, J. A., & Ferris, G. R. (2008). Job title inflation. *Human Resource Management Review, 18*(1), 19–27.

Martocchio, J. J. (2017). *Strategic compensation: A human resource management approach* (9th ed.). Upper Saddle River, NJ: Prentice-Hall.

Martyka, J. (2001, June 8). Colleges customize employee training. *Minneapolis-St. Paul City Business, 19*(1), 17–18.

Mascio, C., Rainey, R., & Zinda, M. (2008, March). *Effect of group composition on group performance: Are slightly-heterogeneous groups the answer to the homogeneity vs. heterogeneity puzzle?* Poster presentation at the annual Graduate Student Conference in Industrial-Organizational Psychology and Organizational Behavior (IOOB), Denver, Colorado.

Maslow, A. H. (1954; 1970). *Motivation and personality.* New York: Harper & Row.

Mastrangelo, P. M. (1997). Do college students still prefer companies without employment drug testing? *Journal of Business and Psychology, 11*, 325–337.

Mathews, K. E., & Canon, L. K. (1975). Environmental noise level as a determinant of helping behavior. *Journal of Personality and Social Psychology, 32*, 571–577.

Mathieu, J. E., Tannenbaum, S. I., & Salas, E. (1992). Influences of individual and situational characteristics on measures of training effectiveness. *Academy of Management Journal, 35*(4), 828–847.

Mathieu, J. E., & Zajac, D. M. (1990). A review and meta-analysis of the antecedents, correlates, and consequences of organizational commitment. *Psychological Bulletin, 108*(1), 171–194.

Mattern, K. D., & Patterson, B. F. (2013). Test of slope and intercept bias in college admissions: A response to Aguinis, Culpepper, and Pierce (2010). *Journal of Applied Psychology, 98*(1), 134–147.

Maurer, R. (2021). *The class of 2021 wants to work in the office.* https://www.shrm.org/resourcesandtools/hr-topics/talent-acquisition/pages/the-class-of-2021-wants-to-work-in-the-office-hybrid-flexible-salaries.aspx

Maurer, S. A. (2001). Logging on to learn. *Chain Leader, 6*(7), 49–52.

Maurer, T. J., Solamon, J. M., Andrews, K. D., & Troxtel, D. D. (2001). Interviewee coaching, preparation strategies, and response strategies in relation to performance in situational employment interviews: An extension of Maurer, Solamon, and Troxtel (1998). *Journal of Applied Psychology, 86*(4), 709–717.

Maurer, T. J., Solamon, J. M., & Troxtel, D. D. (1998). Relationship of coaching with performance in situational job interviews. *Journal of Applied Psychology, 83*(1), 128–136.

Maurer, T. J., & Tross, S. (2000). SME committee vs. field job analysis ratings: Convergence, cautions, and a call. *Journal of Business and Psychology, 14*(3), 489–499.

Mawhinney, T. C., & Gowen, C. R. (1990). Gainsharing and the law of effect as the matching law: A theoretical framework. *Journal of Organizational Behavior Management, 11*(2), 61–75.

Mayer, J. J. (1990). *If you haven't got the time to do it right, when will you find the time to do it over?* New York: Simon & Schuster.

Maynard, M. T., Mathieu, J. E., Marsh, W. M., & Ruddy, T. M. (2007). A multilevel investigation of the influences of employees' resistance to empowerment. *Human Performance, 20*(2), 147–171.

Mayo, E. (1946). *The human problems of an industrial civilization.* Cambridge, MA: Harvard University Press.

McAndrew, F. T. (1993). The home advantage in individual sports. *Journal of Social Psychology, 133*(3), 401–403.

McCabe, M. J. (2001). The money pit. *The RMA Journal, 83*(10), 18–19.

McCalips, R. (2001). What recent court cases indicate about English-only rules in the workplace: A critical look at the need for a Supreme Court ruling on the issue. *U. Pa. J. Lab. & Emp. L., 4*, 417.

McCall, M. W. (2010). Recasting leadership development. *Industrial and Organizational Psychology: Perspectives on Science and Practice, 3*(1), 3–19.

McCandless, K. (2002). Circuit City Stores, Inc. v. Adams: The debate over arbitration Agreements in the employment context rages on. *Denver University Law Review, 80*, 225.

McCann, N., & Lester, D. (1996). Smoking and stress: Cigarettes and marijuana. *Psychological Reports, 79*(2), 366.

McCarthy, J. M., & Goffin, R. D. (2001). Improving the validity of letters of recommendation: An investigation of three standardized reference forms. *Military Psychology, 13*(4), 199–222.

McCarthy, J. M., & Goffin, R. (2004). Measuring job interview anxiety: Beyond weak knees and sweaty palms. *Personnel Psychology, 57*(3), 607–637.

McCarthy, J. M., & Saks, A. M. (2008, April). Rapport building in job interviews: Implications for interviewee anxiety and interview performance. In M. R. Barrick (Chair), *The role of unstructured information in the employment interview.* Symposium presented at the 23rd annual meeting of the Society for Industrial-Organizational Psychology, San Francisco, CA.

McCarthy, J. M., Van Iddekinge, C. H., & Campion, M. A. (2010). Are highly structured job interviews resistant to demographic similarity effects? *Personnel Psychology, 63*(2), 325–359.

McClelland, D. C. (1961). *The achieving society.* Princeton, NJ: Van Nostrand.

McClelland, D. C., & Boyatzis, R. E. (1982). Leadership motive pattern and long-term success in management. *Journal of Applied Psychology, 67*, 737–743.

McClelland, D. C., & Burnham, D. H. (1976). Power is the great motivator. *Harvard Business Review, 54*(2), 102–104.

McCormick, E. J., Jeanneret, P. R., & Mecham, R. C. (1969). *Position analysis questionnaire.* West Lafayette, IN: Purdue Research Foundation.

McCormick, E. J., Jeanneret, P. R., & Mecham, R. C. (1972). A study of job characteristics and job dimensions as based on the Position Analysis Questionnaire (PAQ). *Journal of Applied Psychology, 56*, 347–368.

McDaniel, M. A., Hartman, N. S., Whetzel, D. L., & Grubb, W. L. (2007). Situational judgment tests, response instructions, and validity: A meta-analysis. *Personnel Psychology, 60*(1), 63–91.

McDaniel, M. A., Morgeson, F. P., Finnegan, E. B., Campion, M. A., & Braverman, E. P. (2001). Use of situational judgment tests to predict performance: A clarification of the literature. *Journal of Applied Psychology, 86*(4), 730–740.

McDaniel, M. A., Whetzel, D. L., Schmidt, F. L., & Maurer, S. D. (1994). The validity of employment interviews: A comprehensive review and meta-analysis. *Journal of Applied Psychology, 79*(4), 599–616.

McElroy, J. C., Morrow, P. C., & Ackerman, R. J. (1983). Personality and interior office design: Exploring the accuracy of visitor attributions. *Journal of Applied Psychology, 68*, 541–544.

McElroy, J. C., Morrow, P. C., & Wall, L. C. (1983). Generalizing impact of object language to other audiences: Peer response to office design. *Psychological Reports, 53*, 315–332.

McFarland, L. A., Ryan, A. M., Sacco, J. M., & Kriska, S. D. (2004). Examination of structured interview ratings across time: The effects of applicant race, rater race, and panel composition. *Journal of Management, 30*, 435–452.

McFarland, L. A., Wolf, P. P., & Nguyen, J. D. (2005, April). *Does weighting criteria by job importance reduce racial differences in performance ratings?* Poster presented at the 20th annual meeting of the Society for Industrial and Organizational Psychology, Los Angeles, CA.

McGregor, D. (1960). *The human side of enterprise.* New York: McGraw-Hill.

McKay, P. F., & McDaniel, M. A. (2006). A reexamination of Black-White mean differences in work performance: More data, more moderators. *Journal of Applied Psychology, 91*(3), 538–554.

McKee, T. L., & Ptacek, J. T. (2001). I'm afraid I have something bad to tell you: Breaking bad news from the perspective of the giver. *Journal of Applied Social Psychology, 31*(2), 246–273.

McLaughlin, M. L., & Cheatham, T. R. (1977). Effects of communication isolation on job satisfaction of bank tellers: A research note. *Human Communication Research, 3*(2), 171–175.

McLeod, P. L., Baron, R. S., Marti, M. W., & Yoon, K. (1997). The eyes have it: Minority influence in face-to-face and computer-mediated group discussion. *Journal of Applied Psychology, 82*(5), 706–718.

McManus, M. A., & Baratta, J. E. (1992). *The relationship of recruiting source to performance and survival.* Paper presented at the annual meeting of the Society for Industrial and Organizational Psychology, Montreal, Canada.

McNatt, D. B. (2000). Ancient Pygmalion joins contemporary management: A meta-analysis of the result. *Journal of Applied Psychology, 85*(2), 314–322.

McNatt, D. B., Campbell, S., & Hirschfeld, R. R. (2005, April). *Building self-confidence: A meta-analysis of the effectiveness of self-efficacy interventions.* Poster presented at the 20th annual conference of the Society for Industrial and Organizational Psychology, Los Angeles, CA.

McNatt, D. B., & Judge, T. A. (2004). Boundary conditions of the Galatea effect: A field experiment and constructive replication. *Academy of Management Journal, 47*(4), 550–565.

Meade, A. W., & Tonidandel, S. (2010). Not seeing clearly with Cleary: What test bias analyses do and do not tell us. *Industrial and Organizational Psychology, 3*(2), 192–205.

Meehan, B. T. (1994, January 16). Ice star, bodyguard a pair who didn't fit in. *Roanoke Times and World News,* pp. A1–A8.

Mehrabian, A. (1965). Communication length as an index of communicator attitude. *Psychological Reports, 17,* 519–522.

Meisenzahl, M. (2021, August 4). *McDonald's workers in LA are striking after a violent attack by a customer reportedly left one employee bruised and beaten.* https://news.yahoo.com/mcdonalds-workers-la-striking-violent-145239991.html

Melamed, S., Harari, G., & Green, M. S. (1993). Type A behavior, tension, and ambulatory cardiovascular reactivity in workers exposed to noise stress. *Psychosomatic Medicine, 55*(2), 185–193.

Melson-Silimon, A., Harris, A. M., Shoenfelt, E. L., Miller, J. D., & Carter, N. T. (2019). Personality testing and the Americans with Disabilities Act: Cause for concern as normal and abnormal personality models are integrated. *Industrial and Organizational Psychology, 12*(2), 119–132.

Meng, L., Chen, D., Yang, Y., Zheng, Y., & Hui, R. (2012). Depression increases the risk of hypertension incidence: A meta-analysis of prospective cohort studies. *Journal of Hypertension, 30*(5), 842–851.

Mento, A. J., Steel, R. P., & Karren, R. J. (1987). A meta-analytic study of the effects of goal setting on task performance: 1966–1984. *Organizational Behavior and Human Decision Processes, 39,* 52–83.

Mercer Consulting (2013). *Mercer 2012/2013 Compensation Planning Survey.* New York: William M. Mercer, Inc.

Mero, N. P., & Motowidlo, S. J. (1995). Effects of rater accountability on the accuracy and the favorability of performance ratings. *Journal of Applied Psychology, 80*(4), 517–524.

Mershon, D. H., & Lin, L. (1987). Directional localization in high ambient noise with and without the use of hearing protectors. *Ergonomics, 30,* 1161–1173.

Metlife (2019). Thriving in the new work-life world. Metlife. *https://www.metlife.com/content/dam/metlifecom/us/ebts/pdf/MetLife-Employee-Benefit-Trends-Study-2019.pdf*

Meyer, J. P., & Allen, N. J. (1997). *Commitment in the workplace: Theory, research, and application.* Thousand Oaks, CA: Sage.

Meyer, J. P., Stanley, D. J., Herscovitch, L., & Topolnytsky, L. (2002). Affective, continuance, and normative commitment to the organization: A meta-analysis of antecedents, correlates, and consequences. *Journal of Vocational Behavior, 61*(1), 20–52.

Michaels, J. W., Blommel, J. M., Brocato, R. M., Linkous, R. A., & Rowe, J. S. (1982). Social facilitation and inhibition in a natural setting. *Replications in Social Psychology, 2,* 21–24.

Miles, J. A., & Greenberg, J. (1993). Using punishment threats to attenuate social loafing effects among swimmers. *Organizational Behavior and Human Decision Processes, 56*(2), 246–265.

Miles, E. W., Patrick, S. L., & King, W. C. (1996). Job level as a systematic variable in predicting the relationship between supervisory communication and job satisfaction. *Journal of Occupational and Organizational Psychology, 69*(3), 277–292.

Miller, B. K., Rutherford, M. A., & Kolodinsky, R. W. (2008). Perceptions of organizational politics: A meta-analysis of outcomes. *Journal of Business and Psychology, 22,* 209–222.

Miller, G. W., & Sniderman, M. S. (1974). Multi-job holding of Wichita public school teachers. *Public Personnel Management, 3,* 392–402.

Miller, T. I. (1984). Effects of employee-sponsored day care on employee absenteeism, turnover, productivity, recruitment or job satisfaction: What is claimed and what is known. *Personnel Psychology, 37,* 277–289.

Mirolli, K., Henderson, P., & Hills, D. (1998). *Coworkers' influence on job satisfaction.* Paper presented at the 19th annual Graduate Student Conference in Industrial/Organizational Psychology and Organizational Behavior, San Diego, CA.

Mirza, P. (2003). A bias that's skin deep. *HR Magazine, 48*(12), 62–67.

Mitchell, G. (2012). Revisiting truth or triviality: The external validity of research in the psychological laboratory. Perspectives on *Psychological Science, 7*(2), 109–117.

Mitchell, T. R. (1974). Expectancy models of job satisfaction, occupational preference, and effort: A theoretical, methodological, and empirical approach. *Psychological Bulletin, 81*, 1053–1077.

Moberg, J. L., & Moore, S. (2011). *I/O psychology versus M.B.A. programs.* Paper presented at the 32nd annual Industrial/Organizational Psychology and Organizational Behavior Graduate Student Conference, San Diego, CA.

Moede, W. (1927). Die Richtlinien der Leistungs-Psychologie. *Industrielle Pscyhotechnik, 4*, 193–207.

Mohandie, K. (2014). Threat assessment in schools. In J. R. Meloy & J. Hoffman (Eds.), *International handbook of threat assessment.* New York: Oxford University Press.

Montebello, H. R., & Haga, M. (1994). To justify training, test, test again. *Personnel Journal, 30*(1), 83–87.

Moores, J. (1990). A meta-analytic review of the effects of compressed work schedules. *Applied H.R.M. Research, 1*(1), 12–18.

Moran, L., Musselwhite, E., & Zenger, J. H. (1996). *Keeping teams on track.* Chicago: Irwin.

Morelli, N. A., & Illingworth, A. J. (2019). The next wave of internet-based recruitment. In R. N. Landers (Ed.), *The Cambridge handbook of technology and employee behavior* (pp. 59–99). Cambridge: Cambridge University Press.

Morgan, J. (1990, March). Test negative: A look at the "evidence" justifying illicit-drug tests. *Scientific American* 18–19.

Morgeson, F. P., Brannick, M. T., & Levine, E. L. (2020). *Job and work analysis (3rd ed.).* Thousand Oaks, CA: Sage.

Morgeson, F. P., Campion, M. A., Dipboye, R. L., Hollenbeck, J. R., Murphy, K., & Schmitt, N. (2007). Reconsidering the use of personality tests in personnel selection contexts. *Personnel Psychology, 60*(3), 683–729.

Morris, M. A., & Campion, J. E. (2003). *New use for an old tool: Vocational interests and outcomes.* Poster presented at the 18th annual meeting of the Society for Industrial and Organizational Psychology, Orlando, Florida.

Morrison, E. W. (1993). Newcomer information seeking: Exploring types, modes, sources, and outcomes. *Academy of Management Journal, 36*(3), 557–589.

Morrison, E. W., & Robinson, S. L. (1997). When employees feel betrayed: A model of how psychological contract violation develops. *Academy of Management Review, 22*(1), 226–256.

Morrow, P. C., & McElroy, J. C. (1981). Interior office design and visitor response: A constructive replication. *Journal of Applied Psychology, 66*, 646–650.

Mossholder, K. W., & Arvey, R. D. (1984). Synthetic validity: A conceptual and comparative review. *Journal of Applied Psychology, 69*(2), 322–333.

Mossholder, K. W., Settoon, R. P., & Henagan, S. C. (2005). A relational perspective on turnover: Examining structural, attitudinal, and behavioral predictors. *Academy of Management Journal, 48*(4), 607–618.

Mott, P. E., Mann, F. C., McLoughlin, Q., & Warwick, D. P. (1965). *Shift work.* Ann Arbor: University of Michigan Press.

Mount, M. K. (1983). Comparisons of managerial and employee satisfaction with a performance appraisal system. *Personnel Psychology, 36*, 99–110.

Mount, M. K., & Ellis, R. A. (1989). Sources of bias in job evaluation: A review and critique of research. *Journal of Social Issues, 45*(4), 153–167.

Mount, M. K., & Thompson, D. E. (1987). Cognitive categorization and quality of performance ratings. *Journal of Applied Psychology, 72*, 240–246.

Mourtzis, D., Vlachou, E., Zogopoulos, V., Gupta, R. K., Belkadi, F., Debbache, A., & Bernard, A. (2018). Customer feedback gathering and management tools for product-service system design. *Procedia Cirp, 67*, 577–582.

Mouw, T. (2002). Are black workers missing the connection? The effect of spatial distance and employee referrals on interfirm racial segregation. *Demography, 39*(3), 507–528.

Mowday, R., Steers, R., & Porter, L. (1979). The measurement of organizational commitment. *Journal of Vocational Behavior, 14*, 224–247.

Mueller, M., & Belcher, G. (2000). Observed divergence in the attitudes of incumbents and supervisors as subject matter experts in job analysis: A study of the fire captain rank. *Public Personnel Management, 29*(4), 529–555.

Mulder, M., de Jong, R. D., Koppelaar, L., & Verhage, J. (1986). Power, situation, and leaders' effectiveness: An organizational field study. *Journal of Applied Psychology, 71*, 566–570.

Mullen, B., Anthony, T., Salas, E., & Driskell, J. E. (1994). Group cohesiveness and quality of decision making: An integration of the groupthink hypothesis. *Small Group Research, 25*(2), 189–204.

Mullins, W. C. (1983). *Job analysis outcomes as a function of group composition.* Unpublished doctoral dissertation, University of Arkansas, Fayetteville.

Mullins, W. C. (1986). *A note on the efficacy of the spurious nature of relational causation.* Paper presented at the annual meeting of the Society of Police and Criminal Psychology, Little Rock, AR.

Mullins, W. C., & Kimbrough, W. W. (1988). Group composition as a determinant of job analysis outcomes. *Journal of Applied Psychology, 73*, 657–664.

Mumford, M. D. (1983). Social comparison theory and the evaluation of peer evaluations: A review and some applied implications. *Personnel Psychology, 36*, 867–881.

Munson, L. J., Hulin, C., & Drasgow, F. (2000). Longitudinal analysis of dispositional influences and sexual harassment: Effects on job and psychological outcomes. *Personnel Psychology, 53*(1), 21–46.

Munsterberg, H. (1913). *Psychology and industrial efficiency.* Boston: Houghton Mifflin.

Murphy, K. R. (2008). Explaining the weak relationship between job performance and ratings of job performance. *Industrial and Organizational Psychology: Perspectives on Science and Practice, 1*(2), 148–160.

Murphy, K. R., & Balzer, W. K. (1986). Systematic distortions in memory-based behavior ratings and performance evaluations: Consequences for rating accuracy. *Journal of Applied Psychology, 71*, 39–44.

Murphy, K. R., Cleveland, J. N., & Hanscom, M. E. (2019). *Performance appraisal and management.* Los Angeles: Sage.

Murphy, K. R., Gannett, B. A., Herr, B. M., & Chen, J. A. (1986). Effects of subsequent performance on evaluations of previous performance. *Journal of Applied Psychology, 71*, 427–431.

Murphy, K. R., Martin, C., & Garcia, M. (1982). Do behavioral observation scales measure observation? *Journal of Applied Psychology, 67,* 562–567.

Muse, L. A., Harris, S. G., & Field, H. S. (2003). Has the inverted-U theory of stress and job performance had a fair test? *Human Performance, 16*(4), 349–364.

Myers, W. V., McSween, T. E., Medina, R. E., Rost, K., & Alvero, A. M. (2010). The implementation and maintenance of a behavioral safety process in a petroleum refinery. *Journal of Organizational Behavioral Management, 30*(4), 285–307.

Nagy, M. S. (1995). *An integrated model of job satisfaction.* Unpublished doctoral dissertation, Louisiana State University, Louisiana.

Nagy, M. S. (1996, April). What to do when you are dissatisfied with job satisfaction scales: A better way to measure job satisfaction. *Assessment Council News,* pp. 5–10.

Nagy, M. S. (2005, April). *Practical suggestions in providing and asking for references and letters of recommendation.* Paper presented at the 20th annual meeting of the Society for Industrial and Organizational Psychology, Los Angeles, CA.

Nagy, M. S., Schroeder, B. W., & Aamodt, M. G. (2005). Educational training for master's degree programs in industrial-organizational psychology. *The Industrial-Organizational Psychologist, 43*(2), 89–96.

Naidoo, L. J. (2021). The case for cases. *The Industrial-Organizational Psychologist, 58*(4), https://www.siop.org/Research-Publications/Items-of-Interest/ArtMID/19366/ArticleID/5045/preview/true/Max-Classroom-Capacity-The-Case-for-Cases.

Nail, P. R. (1986). Toward an integration of some models and theories of social response. *Psychological Bulletin, 100*(2), 190–206.

Namie, G. (2021). *2021 WBI U.S. Workplace bullying survey.* Clarkston, WA: Workplace Bullying Institute.

Nathan, B., & Lord, R. (1983). Cognitive categorization and dimensional schemata: A process approach to the study of halo in performance ratings. *Journal of Applied Psychology, 68,* 102–114.

Naughton, R. J. (1975). Motivational factors of American prisoners of war in Vietnam. *Naval War College Review, 27*(4), 2–14.

Naughton, T. J. (1988). Effect of female-linked job titles on job evaluation ratings. *Journal of Management, 14*(4), 567–578.

Nelson, J. B., & Mital, A. (1995). An ergonomic evaluation of dexterity and tactility with increase in examination/surgical glove thickness. *Ergonomics, 38*(4), 723–733.

Nesler, M. S., Aguinis, H., Quigley, B. M., Lee, S. J., & Tedeschi, J. T. (1999). The development and validation of a scale measuring global social power based on French and Raven's power taxonomy. *Journal of Applied Social Psychology, 29*(4), 750–751.

Neuman, G. A., & Wright, J. (1999). Team effectiveness: Beyond skills and cognitive ability. *Journal of Applied Psychology, 84*(3), 376–389.

Newton, E. (2021). *Here's how automated packaging gives your e-commerce business a competitive edge.* https://www.roboticstomorrow.com/story/2021/08/heres-how-automated-packaging-gives-your-e-commerce-business-a-competitive-edge-/17322/

Ng, T. W. H., Eby, L. T., Sorensen, K. L., & Feldman, D. C. (2005). Predictors of objective and subjective career success: A meta-analysis. *Personnel Psychology, 58,* 367–408.

Ng, T. W. H., & Feldman, D. C. (2008). The relationship of age to ten dimensions of job performance. *Journal of Applied Psychology, 93*(2), 392–423.

Ng, T. W. H., & Feldman, D. C. (2009). How broadly does education contribute to job performance? *Personnel Psychology, 62*(1), 89–134.

Ng, T. W. H., & Feldman, D. C. (2010). The relationship of age with job attitudes: A meta-analysis. *Personnel Psychology, 63*(3), 677–718.

Ng, T. W. H., Sorensen, K. L., & Eby, L. T. (2006). Locus of control at work: A meta-analysis. *Journal of Organizational Behavior, 27,* 1057–1087.

Nichols, R. G., & Stevens, L. A. (1957). *Are you listening?* New York: McGraw-Hill.

Niebuhr, R. E., & Oswald, S. L. (1992). The impact of workgroup composition and other work unit/victim characteristics on perceptions of sexual harassment. *Applied H.R.M. Research, 3,* 30–47.

Noble, S. A. (1997). *Effects of a time delay on frame-of-reference training.* Poster presented at the 12th annual conference of the Society for Industrial and Organizational Psychology, St. Louis, MO.

Noe, R. (2020). *Employee training and development* (8th ed.). New York: McGraw-Hill.

Nolan, J., Lee, K., & Allen, N. (1997). *Work group heterogeneity, performance, and turnover: Some meta-analytic findings.* Poster presented at the 12th annual conference of the Society for Industrial and Organizational Psychology, St. Louis, MO.

Normand, J., Salyards, S. D., & Mahoney, J. J. (1990). An evaluation of preemployment drug testing. *Journal of Applied Psychology, 75*(6), 629–639.

Norris, W. R., & Vecchio, R. P. (1992). Situational leadership theory: A replication. *Group and Organization Management, 17*(3), 331–342.

Northouse, P. G. (2019). *Leadership: Theory and practice* (8th ed.). Thousand Oaks, CA: Sage Publications.

Nwachukwu, S. L., & Vitell, S. J. (1997). The influence of corporate culture on managerial ethical judgments. *Journal of Business Ethics, 16,* 757–776.

Nye, C. D., Su, R., Rounds, J., & Drasgow, F. (2012). Vocational interests and performance: A quantitative summary of 60 years of research. *Perspectives on Psychological Science, 7,* 384–403.

Nye, C. D., Su, R., Rounds, J., & Drasgow, F. (2017). Interest congruence and performance: Revisiting recent meta-analytic findings. *Journal of Vocational Behavior, 98,* 138–151.

O'Boyle, E. H., Forsyth, D. R., Banks, G. C., & McDaniel, M. A. (2012). A meta-analysis of the dark triad and work behavior: A social exchange perspective. *Journal of Applied Psychology, 97*(3), 557–579.

O'Connell, B. (2020). *Performance management evolves.* https://www.shrm.org/hr-today/news/all-things-work/pages/performance-management-evolves.aspx

O'Connor, E. J., Wexley, K. N., & Alexander, R. A. (1975). Single group validity: Fact or fallacy? *Journal of Applied Psychology, 60,* 352–355.

Ock, J., & Oswald, F. L. (2018). The utility of personnel selection decisions: Comparing compensatory and multiple-hurdle selection models. *Journal of Personnel Psychology, 17*(4), 172–182.

Oduwole, A., Morgan, A., & Bernardo, M. (2000). *A reexamination of contrast effects in the evaluation of job applicant resumes.* Paper presented at the 21st annual Graduate Student Conference in Industrial-Organizational Psychology and Organizational Behavior, Knoxville, TN.

O'Farrell, I. (2020). *SMART objective setting for managers: A roadmap.* Dublin, Ireland: Evolution Consulting.

Offermann, L. R., & Spiros, R. K. (2001). The science and practice of team development: Improving the link. *Academy of Management Journal, 44*(2), 376–392.

Oginska, H., Pokorski, J., & Oginski, A. (1993). Gender, aging, and shiftwork intolerance. *Ergonomics, 36*(1), 161–168.

Oginska-Bulik, N. (2006). Occupational stress and its consequences in healthcare professionals: The role of type D personality. *International Journal of Occupational Medicine and Environmental Health, 19*(2), 113–122.

O'Kane, P., Palmer, M., & Hargie, O. (2007). Workplace interactions and the polymorphic role of e-mail. *Leadership & Organization Development Journal, 28*(4), 308–324.

Oldham, G. R., Hackman, R. J., & Stepina, L. P. (1978). *Norms for the Job Diagnostic Survey.* Technical Report no. 16, School of Organization and Management, Yale University.

O'Leary, B. S., Rheinstein, J., & McCauley, D. E. (1990). *Job analysis for test development: Can it be streamlined?* Paper presented at the annual meeting of the American Psychological Association, Boston, MA.

Olofsson, G. (2004). *When in Rome or Rio or Riyadh: Cultural Q & As for successful business behavior around the world.* Yarmouth, ME: Intercultural Press.

Olson, R., Verley, J., Santos, L., & Salas, C. (2004). What we teach students about the Hawthorne Studies: A review of content within a sample of introductory I-O and OB textbooks. *The Industrial-Organizational Psychologist, 41*(3), 23–39.

O'Neill, M. J. (1994). Work space adjustability, storage, and enclosure as predictors of employee reactions and performance. *Environment and Behavior, 26*(4), 504–526.

Ones, D. S. (1993). *The construct validity of integrity tests.* Unpublished doctoral dissertation, University of Iowa.

Ones, D. S., Dilchert, S., Viswesvaran, C., & Salgado, J. F. (2017). Cognitive ability: Measurement and validity for employee selection. In J. L. Farr & N. T. Tippins (Eds.), *Handbook of employee selection* (pp. 251–276). New York: Routledge.

Ones, D. S., & Viswesvaran, C. (1998). Gender, age, and race differences on overt integrity tests: Results across four large-scale job applicant data sets. *Journal of Applied Psychology, 83*(1), 35–42.

Ones, D. S., Viswesvaran, C., & Schmidt, F. L. (1993). Comprehensive meta-analysis of integrity test validities: Findings for personnel selection and theories of job performance. *Journal of Applied Psychology, 78*(4), 679–703.

Ones, D. S., Viswesvaran, C., & Schmidt, F. L. (2003). Personality and absenteeism: A meta-analysis of integrity tests. *European Journal of Personality, 17,* S19–S38.

O'Reilly, C. A., & Puffer, S. M. (1989). The impact of rewards and punishments in a social context: A laboratory and field experiment. *Journal of Occupational Psychology, 62*(1), 41–53.

Osborne, E. E., & Vernon, H. M. (1952). The influence of temperature and other conditions on the frequency of industrial accidents. Cited in Harrell, T. W. (1958). *Industrial psychology.* New York: Rinehart.

O'Toole, R. E., & Ferry, J. L. (2002). The growing importance of elder care benefits for an aging workforce. *Compensation & Benefits Management, 18*(1), 40–44.

Overman, S. (2007). The quest for hidden talent. *Staffing Management, 3*(4), 16–20.

Owenby, P. H. (1992). Making case studies come alive. *Training, 29*(1), 43–46.

Owens, D. (2009). Treating employees like customers. *HR Magazine, 54*(10), 28–29.

Oz, S., & Eden, D. (1994). Restraining the Golem: Boosting performance by changing the interpretation of low scores. *Journal of Applied Psychology, 79*(5), 744–754.

Padgett, V. R. (1989). Empirical validation of firefighter vision standards. Paper presented at the *13th Annual Meeting of the International Personnel Management Association Assessment Council.*

Pager, D. (2003). The mark of a criminal record. *American Journal of Sociology, 108*(5), 937–975.

Parker, P. A., & Kulik, J. A. (1995). Burnout, self- and supervisor-related job performance, and absenteeism among nurses. *Journal of Behavioral Medicine, 18*(6), 581–599.

Parker, S. K., & Sprigg, C. A. (1999). Minimizing strain and maximizing learning: The role of job demands, job control, and proactive personality. *Journal of Applied Psychology, 84*(6), 925–939.

Parks, K. M., & Steelman, L. A. (2008). Organizational wellness programs: A meta-analysis. *Journal of Occupational Health Psychology, 13*(1), 58–68.

Parrett, M. (2006). An analysis of the determinants of tipping behavior: A laboratory experiment and evidence from restaurant tipping. *Southern Economic Journal, 73*(2), 489–514.

Parry, S. B. (2000). Measuring training's return on investment: A case in point. In G. M. Piskurich, P. Beckschi, & B. Hall (Eds.), *The ASTD handbook of training design and delivery* (pp. 147–157). New York: McGraw-Hill.

Pascoe, D. D., Pascoe, D. E., Wang, Y. T., Shim, D. M., & Kim, C. K. (1997). Influence of carrying book bags on gait cycle and posture of youths. *Ergonomics, 40*(6), 631–641.

Pass, J. J., & Robertson, D. W. (1980). *Methods to evaluate scales and sample size for stable task inventory information.* (Rep. No. NPRDC TR 80-28). San Diego, CA: Naval Personnel Research and Development Center.

Patrick, J., & Moore, A. K. (1985). Development and reliability of a job analysis technique. *Journal of Occupational Psychology, 58,* 149–158.

Patton, W. D., & Pratt, C. (2002). Assessing the training needs of high-potential managers. *Public Personnel Management, 31*(4), 465–484.

Pattyn, N., Cornelissen, V. A., Eshghi, S. R. T., & Vanhess, L. (2013). The effect of exercise on the cardiovascular risk factors constituting the metabolic syndrome: A meta-analysis. *Sports Medicine, 43*(1), 121–133.

Paul, A. M. (2016). Microlearning 101. *HR Magazine, 61*(4), 37–42.

Paulhus, D. L., & Williams, K. M. (2002). The Dark Triad of personality: Narcissism, Machiavellianism, and psychopathy. *Journal of Research in Personality, 36*, 556–563.

Paustian-Underdahl, S. C., Walker, L. S., & Woehr, D. J. (2014). Gender and perceptions of leadership effectiveness: A meta-analysis of contextual moderators. *Journal of Applied Psychology, 99*(6), 1129–1145.

Payne, S. C., & Huffman, A. H. (2005). A longitudinal examination of the influence of mentoring on organizational commitment and turnover. *Academy of Management Journal, 48*(1), 158–168.

Pearce, J. L., & Porter, L. W. (1986). Employee responses to formal performance appraisal feedback. *Journal of Applied Psychology, 71*, 211–218.

Peeters, M. A. G., Van Tuijl, H. F., Rutte, C. G., & Reymen, I. M. (2006). Personality and team performance: A meta-analysis. *European Journal of Personality, 20*, 377–396.

Pelletier, L. G., & Vallerand, R. J. (1996). Supervisors' beliefs and subordinates' intrinsic motivation: A behavioral confirmation analysis. *Journal of Personality and Social Psychology, 71*(2), 331–340.

Penney, L. M., & Spector, P. E. (2002). Narcissism and counterproductive work behavior: Do bigger egos mean bigger problems? *International Journal of Selection and Assessment, 10*(1–2), 126–134.

Pereira, G. M., & Osburn, H. G. (2007). Effects of participation in decision making on performance and employee attitudes: A quality circles meta-analysis. *Journal of Business and Psychology, 22*, 145–153.

Peter, L. J., & Hull, R. (1969). *The Peter Principle: Why things go wrong.* New York: Morrow.

Peterson, P. E., & West, M. R. (2015). Why do two good polls get different results? https://www.educationnext.org/why-do-two-good-polls-get-different-results/

Pfau, B., & Kay, I. (2002a). Does 360-degree feedback negatively affect company performance? *HR Magazine, 47*(6), 55–59.

Pfau, B., & Kay, I. (2002b). HR playing the training game and losing. *HR Magazine, 47*(8), 49–54.

Philbrick, K. D. (1989). *The use of humor and effective leadership styles.* Unpublished doctoral dissertation, University of Florida, Gainesville, FL.

Phillips, A. P., & Dipboye, R. L. (1989). Correlational tests of predictions from a process model of the interview. *Journal of Applied Psychology, 74*, 41–52.

Phillips, J. J., & Stone, R. D. (2002). *How to measure training results: A practical guide to tracking the six key indicators.* New York: McGraw-Hill.

Phillips, J. M. (1998). Effects of realistic job previews on multiple organizational outcomes: A meta-analysis. *Academy of Management Journal, 41*(6), 673–690.

Pilcher, J. J., Lambert, B. J., & Huffcutt, A. I. (2000). Differential effects of permanent and rotating shifts on self-report sleep length: A meta-analytic review. *Sleep, 23*(2), 155–163.

Pilcher, J. J., Nadler, E., & Busch, C. (2002). Effects of hot and cold temperature exposure on performance: A meta-analysis. *Ergonomics, 45*(10), 682–698.

Pine, D. E. (1995). Assessing the validity of job ratings: An empirical study of false reporting in task inventories. *Public Personnel Management, 24*(4), 451–460.

Pingitore, R., Dugoni, B. L., Tindale, R. S., & Spring, B. (1994). Bias against overweight job applicants in a simulated employment interview. *Journal of Applied Psychology, 79*(6), 909–917.

Platania, J., & Moran, G. P. (2001). Social facilitation as a function of the mere presence of others. *Journal of Social Psychology, 141*(2), 190–197.

Ployhart, R. E., Weekley, J. A., Holtz, B. C., & Kemp, C. (2003). Web-based and paper-and-pencil testing of applicants in a proctored setting: Are personality, biodata, and situational judgment tests comparable? *Personnel Psychology, 56*(3), 733–752.

Podmoroff, D. (2016). *365 ways to motivate and reward your employees every day.* Ocala, FL: Atlantic Publishing Group.

Podsakoff, N. P., LePine, J. A., & LePine, M. (2007) Differential challenge stressor-hindrance stressor relationships with job attitudes, turnover intentions, turnover, and withdrawal behavior: A meta-analysis. *Journal of Applied Psychology, 92*(2), 438–454.

Podsakoff, N. P., Whiting, S. W., Podsakoff, P. M., & Blume, B. D. (2009). Individual- and organizational-level consequences of organizational citizenship behaviors: A meta-analysis. *Journal of Applied Psychology, 94*(1), 122–141.

Podsakoff, P. M., Bommer, W. H., Podsakoff, N. P., & MacKenzie, S. B. (2006). Relationships between leader reward and punishment behavior and subordinate attitudes, perceptions, and behaviors: A meta-analytic review of existing and new research. *Organizational Behavior and Human Decision Processes, 99*(2), 113–142.

Poe, A. C. (2000). An office undivided. *HR Magazine, 45*(2), 58–64.

Poe, A. C. (2001). Don't touch that send button. *HR Magazine, 46*(7), 74–80.

Pollock, T. G., Whitbred, R. C., & Contractor, N. (2000). Social information processing and job characteristics: A simultaneous test of two theories with implications for job satisfaction. *Human Communication Research, 26*(2), 292–330.

Pond, S. B., & Geyer, P. D. (1987). Employee age as a moderator or the relationship between perceived work alternatives and job satisfaction. *Journal of Applied Psychology, 72*, 552–557.

Pool, S. W. (1997). The relationship of job satisfaction with substitutes of leadership, leadership behavior, and work motivation. *Journal of Psychology, 131*(3), 271–283.

Poor, R. (1970). *4 days, 40 hours.* Cambridge, MA: Bursk Poor.

Poropat, A. E. (2009). A meta-analysis of the five-factor model of personality and academic performance. *Psychological Bulletin, 135*(2), 322–338.

Porter, L. W., & Lawler, E. E. (1968). *Managerial attitudes and performance.* Homewood, IL: Dorsey.

Posner, B. Z., Hall, J. L., & Munson, J. M. (1991). A first look at the benefits of educational benefits programs. *Applied H.R.M. Research, 2*(2), 128–152.

Posner, R. B., & Hlivka, L. (2009). *Stress eater diet.* Great Falls, VA: LINX.

Pratt, A. K., Burnazi, L., LePla, L. A., Boyce, A. M., & Baltes, B. B. (2003). *Relationship between sexual harassment and negative outcomes: A meta-analysis.* Poster presented at the 18th annual meeting of the Society for Industrial and Organizational Psychology, Orlando, Florida.

Premack, D. (1963). Prediction of the comparative reinforcement values of running and drinking. *Science, 139,* 1062–1063.

Presser, H. B. (2000). Nonstandard work schedules and marital instability. *Journal of Marriage and the Family, 62*(1), 93.

Preston, L. A. (2003). *Coping with downsizing: A quantitative review.* Poster presented at the 18th annual meeting of the Society for Industrial and Organizational Psychology, Orlando, Florida.

Prewett-Livingston, A. J., Feild, H. A., Veres, J. G., & Lewis, P. M. (1996). Effects of race on interview ratings in a situational panel interview. *Journal of Applied Psychology, 81*(2), 178–186.

Price, M. (2011). The risks of night work. *Monitor on Psychology, 42*(1), 38–41.

Prien, K. O., Prien, E. P., & Wooten, W. (2003). Interrater reliability in job analysis: Differences in strategy and perspective. *Public Personnel Management, 32*(1), 125–141.

Pritchard, R. D., Dunnette, M. D., & Jorgenson, D. (1972). Effects of perceptions of equity on worker motivation and satisfaction. *Journal of Applied Psychology, 56*(1), 75–94.

Pritchett, P. (2008). *Culture shift: The employee handbook for changing corporate culture.* Dallas: Pritchett & Associates.

Pulakos, E. D., Arad, S., Donovan, M. A., & Plamondon, K. E. (2000). Adaptability in the workplace: Development of a taxonomy of adaptive performance. *Journal of Applied Psychology, 85*(4), 612–624.

Pulakos, E. D., Mueller-Hanson, R. A., Arad, S., & Moye, N. (2015). Performance management can be fixed: An on-the-job experimental learning approach for complex behavior change. *Industrial and Organizational Psychology: Perspectives on Science and Practice, 8,* 51–76.

Pulakos, E. D., & Schmitt, N. (1995). Experience-based and situational interview questions: Studies of validity. *Personnel Psychology, 48,* 289–308.

Pulakos, E. D., Schmitt, N., Whitney, D., & Smith, M. (1996). Individual differences in interviewer ratings: The impact of standardization, consensus discussion, and sampling error on the validity of a structured interview. *Personnel Psychology, 49*(1), 85–102.

Pulakos, E. D., White, L. A., Oppler, S. H., & Borman, W. C. (1989). An examination of race and sex effects on performance ratings. *Journal of Applied Psychology, 74,* 770–780.

Pursell, E. D., Dossett, D. L., & Latham, G. P. (1980). Obtaining valid predictors by minimizing rating errors in the criterion. *Personnel Psychology, 33,* 91–96.

Qian, Y. J. (1996). *Managers' stock ownership and performance in lodging industry.* Unpublished master's thesis, University of Nevada, Las Vegas.

Quigley, B. M., Leonard, K. E., & Collins, L. (2003). Characteristics of violent bars and bar patrons. *Journal of Studies on Alcohol, 64*(6), 765–772.

Rabinowitz, S., Melamed, S., Feiner, M., & Weisberg, E. (1996). Hostility and hearing protection behavior: The mediating role of personal beliefs and low frustration tolerance. *Journal of Occupational Health Psychology, 1*(4), 375–381.

Rafaeli, A., & Klimoski, R. J. (1983). Predicting sales success through handwriting analysis: An evaluation of the effects of training and handwriting sample content. *Journal of Applied Psychology, 68,* 212–217.

Ragins, B. R., & Cotton, J. L. (1999). Mentor functions and outcomes: A comparison of men and women in formal and informal mentoring relationships. *Journal of Applied Psychology, 84*(4), 529–550.

Rahim, M. A. (1989). Relationships of leader power to compliance and satisfaction with supervision: Evidence from a national sample of managers. *Journal of Management, 15*(4), 545–556.

Rahim, M. A., & Afza, M. (1993). Leader power, commitment, satisfaction, compliance, and propensity to leave a job among U.S. accountants. *Journal of Social Psychology, 133*(5), 611–625.

Rahim, M. A., & Magner, N. R. (1995). Confirmatory factor analysis of the styles of handling interpersonal conflict: First-order factor model and its invariance across groups. *Journal of Applied Psychology, 80*(1), 122–132.

Rahim, M. A., & Psenicka, C. (1996). A structural equations model of stress, locus of control, social support, psychiatric symptoms, and propensity to leave a job. *Journal of Social Psychology, 136*(1), 69–84.

Ramesh, A., & Gelfand, M. J. (2010). Will they stay or will they go? The role of job embeddedness in predicting turnover in individualistic and collectivist cultures. *Journal of Applied Psychology, 95*(5), 807–823.

Ramsay, L. J., Kim, B. H., Oswald, F. L., Schmitt, N., & Gillespie, M. A. (2008, April). Bogus items, their content, and responses under different situational constraints. In J. Levashina & M. A. Campion (Co-Chairs), *That can't be true! Detecting faking using bogus items.* Symposium presented at the 23rd annual meeting of the Society for Industrial-Organizational Psychology, San Francisco, CA.

Randhawa, J. (2014). *The bright idea box: A proven system to drive employee engagement and innovation.* Redwood City, CA: Ideal Employee Labs.

Rasch, R. L., Shen, W., Davies, S. E., & Bono, J. E. (2008). *The development of a taxonomy of ineffective leadership behaviors.* Paper presented at the 23rd annual meeting of the Society for Industrial-Organizational Psychology, San Francisco, CA.

Raven, B. H. (1965). Social influence and power. In I. D. Steiner & M. Fishbein (Eds.), *Current studies in social psychology* (pp. 371–382). New York: Holt, Rinehart & Winston.

Raven, B. H. (2008). The bases of power and the power/interaction model of interpersonal influence. *Analyses of Social Issues and Public Policy, 8*(1), 1–22.

Ray, J. J., & Hall, G. P. (1995). Need for affiliation and group identification. *Journal of Social Psychology, 135*(4), 519–521.

Raymark, P. H., Keith, M. K., Odle-Dusseau, H. N., Giumetti, G., Brown, B., & Van Iddekinge, C. H. (2008, April). *Snap decisions in the employment interview.* Paper presented at the 23rd annual Conference of the Society for Industrial and Organizational Psychology, San Francisco, CA.

Raymark, P. H., Schmit, M. J., & Guion, R. M. (1997). Identifying potentially useful personality constructs for employee selection. *Personnel Psychology, 50*(3), 723–736.

Raymond, M. R., Neustel, S., & Anderson, D. (2007). Retest effects on identical and parallel forms in certification and licensure testing. *Personnel Psychology, 60*(2), 367–396.

Raynes, B. L. (1997). Review of employee privacy issues: Implications for law enforcement and other public and private sector agencies. *Journal of Police and Criminal Psychology, 12*(2), 19–27.

Raynes, B. L. (2001). Predicting difficult employees: The relationship between vocational interests, self-esteem, and problem communication styles. *Applied HRM Research, 6*(1), 33–66.

Raynes, B. L. (2005, April). *Ethical issues involving employment and academic references.* Paper presented at the 20th annual meeting of the Society for Industrial and Organizational Psychology, Los Angeles, CA.

Reade, Q. (2005). Job offers scrapped as firms uncover fiddled applications. *Personnel Today,* p. 1.

Reb, J., & Greguras, G. J. (2008). Dynamic performance and the performance-performance rating relation. *Industrial and Organizational Psychology: Perspectives on Science and Practice, 1*(2), 194–196.

Recardo, R. J., & Pricone, D. (1996). Is skill-based pay for you? *SAM Advanced Management Journal, 61*(4), 16–21.

Reed, P. S., & Clark, S. M. (2004). *Improved organizational results and improved quality of life.* [A report prepared for the U.S. Department of Labor Women's Bureau.] Retrieved from http://choose2lead.org/Publications/Study%20on%20Win-Win%20Workplace%20Practices.pdf.

Reeve, C. L., & Schultz, L. (2004). Job-seeker reactions to selection process information in job ads. *International Journal of Selection and Assessment, 12*(4), 343–355.

Reichard, R. J., & Avolio, B. J. (2005). Where are we? The status of leadership intervention research: A meta-analytic summary. In W. L. Gardner, B. J. Avolio, & F. O. Walumbwa (Eds.), *Authentic leadership theory and practice: Origins, effects, and development* (pp. 203–226). Oxford, UK: Elsevier.

Reilly, C. E., & Smith, C. (1988). Effects of shiftwork and psychometric evaluation of shiftworker selection instruments. *Proceedings of 9th Annual Graduate Conference in Industrial/Organizational Psychology and Organizational Behavior.*

Renk, K. (2004). The power of incentive programs. *HR Magazine, 49*(9), 91–96.

Rentsch, J. R., Lowenberg, G., Barnes-Farrell, J., & Menard, D. (1997). Report on the survey of graduate programs in industrial/organizational psychology and organizational behavior/human resources. *The Industrial-Organizational Psychologist, 35*(1), 49–68.

Rentsch, J. R., & Steel, R. P. (1998). Testing the durability of job characteristics as predictors of absenteeism over a six-year period. *Personnel Psychology, 51*(1), 165–190.

Repetti, R. L., & Cosmas, K. A. (1991). The quality of the social environment at work and job satisfaction. *Journal of Applied Social Psychology, 21*(10), 840–854.

Repetti, R. L., & Wood, J. (1997). Effects of daily stress at work on mothers' interactions with preschoolers. *Journal of Family Psychology, 11*(1), 90–108.

Richardson, K. M., & Rothstein, H. R. (2008). Effects of occupational stress management intervention programs: A meta-analysis. *Journal of Occupational Health Psychology, 13*(1), 69–93.

Richman-Hirsch, W. L., Olson-Buchanan, J. B., & Drasgow, F. (2000). Examining the impact of administration medium on examinee perceptions and attitudes. *Journal of Applied Psychology, 85*(6), 880–887.

Riddle, D., & Foster, L. (1997). You know, I've been wondering. *The Industrial-Organizational Psychologist, 35*(2), 49–56.

Rieke, M. L., & Guastello, S. J. (1995). Unresolved issues in honesty and integrity testing. *American Psychologist, 50*(6), 458–459.

Riketta, M. (2002). Attitudinal organizational commitment and job performance: A meta-analysis. *Journal of Organizational Behavior, 23,* 257–266.

Roberson, Q. M., Collins, C. J., & Oreg, S. (2005). The effects of recruitment message specificity to applicant attraction to organizations. *Journal of Business and Psychology, 19*(3), 319–339.

Roberson, Q. M., & Colquitt, J. A. (2005). Shared and configural justice: A social network model of justice in teams. *Academy of Management Review, 30*(3), 595–607.

Robert, C., Probst, T. M., Martocchio, J. J., Drasgow, F., & Lawler, J. J. (2000). Empowerment and continuous improvement in the United States, Mexico, Poland, and India: Predicting fit on the basis of the dimensions of power distance and individualism. *Journal of Applied Psychology, 85*(5), 643–658.

Roberts, G. E. (2003). Employee performance appraisal system participation: A technique that works. *Public Personnel Management, 32*(1), 89–98.

Robertson, I. T., & Kandola, R. S. (1982). Work sample tests: Validity, adverse impact, and applicant reaction. *Journal of Occupational Psychology, 55,* 171–183.

Robinson, D. D. (1981). Content-oriented personnel selection in a small business setting. *Personnel Psychology, 34,* 77–87.

Robinson, O., & Griffiths, A. (2005). Coping with the stress of transformational change in a government department. *Journal of Applied Behavioral Science, 41*(2), 203–221.

Robinson, R. K., Allen, B. M., & Abraham, Y. T. (1992). Affirmative action plans in the 1990's: A double edged sword? *Public Personnel Management, 21*(2), 261–272.

Robinson, S. L., & O'Leary-Kelly, A. M. (1998). Monkey see, monkey do: The influence of work groups on the antisocial behavior of employees. *Academy of Management Journal, 41*(6), 658–672.

Roch, S. G. (2008). Data sources and publication in top journals: The hunt for participants. *The Industrial-Organizational Psychologist, 46*(1), 91–94.

Roch, S. G., & O'Sullivan, B. J. (2003). Frame of reference rater training issues: Recall, time, and behavior observation training. *International Journal of Training and Development, 7*(2), 93–107.

Roch, S. G., Sternburgh, A. M., & Caputo, P. M. (2007). Absolute vs relative performance rating formats: Implications for fairness and organizational justice. *International Journal of Selection and Assessment, 15*(3), 302–316.

Roch, S. G., & Williams, K. J. (2012). Building effective performance appraisals from an analysis of work. In M. A. Wilson, W. Bennett Jr., S. G. Gibson, & G. M. Alliger (Eds.), *The handbook of work analysis: Methods, systems, applications and science of work measurement in organizations* (pp. 419–436). New York, NY: Routledge Taylor & Francis Group.

Roch, S. G., Woehr, D. J., Mishra, V., & Kieszczynska, U. (2012). Rater training revisited: An updated meta-analytic review of frame-of-reference training. *Journal of Occupational and Organizational Psychology, 85,* 370–395.

Rockloff, M. K., & Dyer, V. (2007). An experiment on the social facilitation of gambling behavior. *Journal of Gambling Studies, 23*(1), 1–12.

Rockstuhl, T., Dulebohn, J. H., Ang, S., & Shore, L. M. (2012). Leader-Member Exchange (LMX) and culture: A meta-analysis of correlates of LMX across 23 countries. *Journal of Applied Psychology, 97*(6), 1097–1130.

Roehling, M. V., Pichler, S., & Bruce, T. A. (2013). Moderators of the effect of weight on job-related outcomes: A meta-analysis of experimental studies. *Journal of Applied Social Psychology, 43*(2), 237–252.

Rogelberg, S. G., Leach, D. J., Warr, P. B., & Burnfield, J. L. (2006). "Not another meeting!" Are meeting time demands related to employee well being? *Journal of Applied Psychology, 91*(1), 86–96.

Rogelberg, S. G., Scott, C., & Kello, J. (2007). The science and fiction of meetings. *MIT Sloan Management Review, 48*(2), 18–21.

Rohmert, W., & Landau, K. (1983). *A new technique for job analysis*. New York: Taylor & Francis.

Romanov, K., Appelberg, K., Honkasalo, M., & Koskenvuo, M. (1996). Recent interpersonal conflict at work and psychiatric morbidity: A prospective study of 15,530 employees aged 24-64. *Journal of Psychosomatic Research, 40*(2), 169–176.

Ronen, S. (2001). Self-actualization versus collectualization: Implications for motivation theories. In M. Erez, U. Kleinbeck, & H. Thierry (Eds.), *Work motivation in the context of a globalized economy*. Mahwah, NJ: Erlbaum.

Rosen, S., & Tesser, A. (1970). Reluctance to communicate undesirable information: The MUM effect. *Sociometry, 33*, 253–263.

Rosenbaum, E. (2001). *Amazon has a new plan to cut worker injuries by 50%*. https://www.cnbc.com/2021/05/17/relentless-amazon-has-new-plan-to-cut-worker-injuries-by-50percent-.html.

Rosenbaum, E. (2021, May). *Amazon has a new plan to cut worker injuries by 50%*. https://www.cnbc.com/2021/05/17/relentless-amazon-has-new-plan-to-cut-worker-injuries-by-50percent-.html

Rosenthal, R. (1994). Interpersonal expectancy effects: A 30 year perspective. *Current Directions in Psychological Science, 3*(6), 176–179.

Rosenthal, R. (2002). Covert communications in classrooms, clinics, courtrooms, and cubicles. *American Psychologist, 57*(11), 839–849.

Ross, W. R., & Wieland, C. (1996). Effectiveness of interpersonal trust and the pressure on managerial mediation strategy in a simulated organizational dispute. *Journal of Applied Psychology, 81*(3), 228–248.

Roth, P. L., BeVier, C. A., Bobko, P., Switzer, F. S., & Tyler, P. (2001). Ethnic group differences in cognitive ability in employment and educational settings: A meta-analysis. *Personnel Psychology, 54*(2), 297–330.

Roth, P. L., BeVier, C. A., Switzer, F. S., & Schippmann, J. S. (1996). Meta-analyzing the relationship between grades and job performance. *Journal of Applied Psychology, 81*(5), 548–556.

Roth, P. L., & Bobko, P. (2000). College grade point average as a personnel selection device: Ethnic group differences and potential adverse impact. *Journal of Applied Psychology, 85*(3), 399–406.

Roth, P. L., Bobko, P., & McFarland, L. A. (2005). A meta-analysis of work sample test validity: Updating and integrating some classic literature. *Personnel Psychology, 58*(4), 1009–1037.

Roth, P. L., Bobko, P., McFarland, L. A., & Buster, M. (2008). Work sample tests in personnel selection: A meta-analysis of black-white differences in overall and exercise scores. *Personnel Psychology, 61*(3), 637–662.

Roth, P. L., & Clarke, R. L. (1998). Meta-analyzing the relationship between grades and salary. *Journal of Vocational Behavior, 53*, 386–400.

Roth, P. L., Huffcutt, A. I., & Bobko, P. (2003). Ethnic group differences in measures of job performance: A new meta-analysis. *Journal of Applied Psychology, 88*(4), 694–706.

Roth, P. L., Purvis, K. L., & Bobko, P. (2012). A meta-analysis of gender group differences for measures of job performance in field studies. *Journal of Management, 38*(2), 719–739.

Rothstein, H. R., & McDaniel, M. A. (1992). Differential validity by sex in employment settings. *Journal of Business and Psychology, 7*(1), 45–62.

Rothstein, H. R., Schmidt, F. L., Erwin, F. W., Owens, W. A., & Sparks, C. P. (1990). Biographical data in employment selection: Can validities be made generalizable? *Journal of Applied Psychology, 75*, 175–184.

Rotundo, M., Nguyen, D. H., & Sackett, P. R. (2001). A meta-analytic review of gender differences in perceptions of sexual harassment. *Journal of Applied Psychology, 86*(5), 914–922.

Rouiller, J. Z., & Goldstein, I. L. (1993). The relationship between organizational transfer climate and positive transfer of training. *Human Resources Development Quarterly, 4*, 377–390.

Rouleau, E. J., & Krain, B. F. (1975). Using job analysis to design selection procedures. *Public Personnel Management, 4*, 300–304.

Roulin, N., Bangerter, A., & Yerly, E. (2011). The uniqueness effect in selection interviews. *Journal of Personnel Psychology, 10*(1), 43–47.

Rowe, P. M. (1989). Unfavorable information and interview decisions. In R. W. Eder & G. R. Ferris (Eds.), *The employment interview* (pp. 77–89). Newbury Park, CA: Sage.

Roy, M. H., & Dugal, S. S. (2005). Using employee gainsharing plans to improve organizational effectiveness. *Benchmarking: An International Journal, 12*(3), 250–259.

Ruback, R. B., & Juieng, D. (1997). Territorial defense in parking lots: Retaliation against waiting drivers. *Journal of Applied Social Psychology, 27*(9), 821–834.

Rubenstein, A. L., Eberly, M. B., Lee, T. W., & Mitchell, T. R. (2018). Surveying the forest: A meta-analysis, moderator investigation, and future-oriented discussion of the antecedents of voluntary employee turnover. *Personnel Psychology, 71*(1), 23–65.

Rubenzer, S. J., & Faschingbauer, T. R. (2004). *Personality, character, and leadership in the White House: Psychologists assess the presidents*. Washington, DC: Brassey's.

Rucci, A. J. (2008). I-O psychology's "core purpose": Where science and practice meet. *The Industrial-Organizational Psychologist, 46*(1), 17–34.

Ruddock, H. K., Brunstrom, J. M., Vartanian, L. R., & Higgs, S. (2019). A systematic review and meta-analysis of the social facilitation of eating. *American Journal of Clinical Nutrition, 110*(4), 842–861.

Rudolph, C. W., Wells, C. K., Weller, M. D., & Baltes, B. B. (2009). A meta-analysis of empirical studies of weight-based bias in the workplace. *Journal of Vocational Behavior, 74*(1), 1–10.

Rupert, G. (1989). Employee referrals as a source of recruitment and job performance. *Proceedings of the 10th Annual Graduate Conference in Industrial/Organizational Psychology and Organizational Behavior.*

Russ-Eft, D., & Zucchelli, L. (1987). When wrong is all right. *Training and Development Journal, 41*(11), 78–79.

Russell, C. J., Colella, A., & Bobko, P. (1993). Expanding the context of utility: The strategic impact of personnel selection. *Personnel Psychology, 46,* 781–801.

Ryan, A. M., & Lasek, M. (1991). Negligent hiring and defamation: Areas of liability related to pre-employment inquiries. *Personnel Psychology, 44,* 293–319.

Ryan, R. M., & Deci, E. L. (2000). Self-determination theory and the facilitation of intrinsic motivation, social development, and well being. *American Psychologist, 55*(1), 68–78.

Rynes, S. L., & Connerley, M. L. (1993). Applicant reactions to alternative selection procedures. *Journal of Business and Psychology, 7,* 261–277.

Rynes, S. L., Gerhart, B., & Parks, L. (2005). Personnel psychology: Performance evaluation and pay for performance. *Annual Review of Psychology, 56,* 571–600.

Rynes, S. L., Weber, C. L., & Milkovich, G. T. (1989). Effects of market survey rates, job evaluation, and job gender on job pay. *Journal of Applied Psychology, 74*(1), 114–123.

Saad, S., & Sackett, P. R. (2002). Investigating differential prediction by gender in employment-oriented personality measures. *Journal of Applied Psychology, 87*(4), 667–674.

Saal, F. E. (1979). Mixed standard rating scale: A consistent system for numerically coding inconsistent response combinations. *Journal of Applied Psychology, 64,* 422–428.

Saavedra, R., & Kwun, S. K. (1993). Peer evaluation in self-managing work groups. *Journal of Applied Psychology, 78*(3), 450–462.

Sacco, J. M., Scheu, C. R., Ryan, A. M., & Schmitt, N. (2003). An investigation of race and sex similarity effects in interviews: A multilevel approach to relational demography. *Journal of Applied Psychology, 88*(5), 852–865.

Sacco, J. M., & Schmitt, N. (2005). A dynamic multilevel model of demographic diversity and misfit effects. *Journal of Applied Psychology, 90*(2), 203–231.

Sackett, P. R., & Roth, L. (1991). A Monte Carlo examination of banding and rank order methods of test score use in personnel selection. *Human Performance, 4*(4), 279–295.

Sackett, P. R., & Schmitt, N. (2012). On reconciling conflicting meta-analytic findings regarding integrity test validity. *Journal of Applied Psychology, 97*(3), 550–556.

Sackman, S. (1991). Uncovering culture in organizations. *Journal of Applied Behavioral Science, 27*(3), 294–315.

Sadri, G. (1996). Reflections: The impact of downsizings on survivors—some findings and recommendations. *Journal of Managerial Psychology, 11*(4), 56–59.

Saks, A. M., Wiesner, W. H., & Summers, R. J. (1996). Effects of job previews and compensation policy on applicant attraction and job choice. *Journal of Vocational Behavior, 49*(1), 68–85.

Salancik, G., & Pfeffer, J. (1977). An examination of need-satisfaction models of job satisfaction and job attitudes. *Administrative Science Quarterly, 22,* 427–456.

Salas, E., & Cannon-Bowers, J. A. (2001). The science of training: A decade of progress. *Annual Review of Psychology,* 471–499.

Salas, E., Mullen, B., Rozell, D., & Driskell, J. E. (1997). *The effects of team building on performance: An integration.* Poster presented at the 12 annual conference of the Society for Industrial and Organizational Psychology, St. Louis, MO.

Salgado, J. F. (1997). The five-factor model of personality and job performance in the European community. *Journal of Applied Psychology, 82*(1), 30–43.

Salgado, J. F. (2002). The big five personality dimensions and counterproductive behaviors. *International Journal of Selection and Assessment, 10*(1/2), 117–123.

Salgado, J. F., Anderson, N., Moscoso, S., Bertua, C., & De Fruyt, F. (2003). International validity generalization of GMA and cognitive abilities: A European Community meta-analysis. *Personnel Psychology, 56,* 573–605.

Salkind, N. J. (2019). *Exploring research* (9th ed.). New York: Pearson.

Sammer, J. (2015, September). Take it or leave it: Should salary discussion be a one-way street? *HR Magazine, 60*(7), 35–39.

Sammer, J. (2021). *4 lessons about unlimited vacation.* SHRM. https://www.shrm.org/resourcesandtools/hr-topics/benefits/pages/4-lessons-about-unlimited-vacation.aspx.

Sanchez, J. I., & Fraser, S. L. (1992). On the choice of scales for task analysis. *Journal of Applied Psychology, 77,* 545–553.

Sanchez, J. I., Prager, I., Wilson, A., & Viswesvaran, C. (1998). Understanding the within-job title variance in job analytic ratings. *Journal of Business and Psychology, 12,* 407–419.

Sanders, G. S. (1981). Driven by distraction: An integrative review of social facilitation theory and research. *Journal of Experimental Social Psychology, 17,* 227–251.

Sauser W. I., Jr., & York, C. M. (1978). Sex differences in job satisfaction: A re-examination. *Personnel Psychology, 31*(3), 537–547.

Scarr, S. (1998). American child care today. *American Psychologist, 53*(2), 95–108.

Schall, M. A. (2019). *The relationship between remote work and job satisfaction: The mediating roles of perceived autonomy, work-family conflict, and telecommuting intensity.* Unpublished doctoral dissertation, San Jose State University.

Schaubroeck, J., Ganster, D. C., & Kemmerer, B. E. (1994). Job complexity, Type A behavior, and cardiovascular disorder: A prospective study. *Academy of Management Journal, 37*(2), 426–439.

Schein, E. (1956). The Chinese indoctrination program for prisoners of war. *Psychiatry, 19,* 149–177.

Schleicher, D. J., Watt, J. D., & Greguras, G. J. (2004). Reexamining the job satisfaction-performance relationship: The complexity of attitudes. *Journal of Applied Psychology, 89*(1), 165–177.

Schieman, S., & Young, M. (2010). Is there a downside to schedule control for the work-family interface? *Journal of Family Issues, 31*(10), 1391–1414.

Schmidt, F. L. (1973). Implications of a measurement problem for expectancy theory research. *Organizational Behavior and Human Performance, 10,* 243–251.

Schmidt, F. L. (1988). The problem of group differences in ability test scores in employment selection. *Journal of Vocational Behavior, 33*(3), 272–292.

Schmidt, F. L. (1991). Why all banding procedures in personnel selection are logically flawed. *Human Performance, 4,* 265–277.

Schmidt, F. L., Gast-Rosenberg, I., & Hunter, J. E. (1980). Validity generalization results for computer programmers. *Journal of Applied Psychology, 65,* 643–661.

Schmidt, F. L., & Hunter, J. E. (1978). Moderator research and the law of small numbers. *Personnel Psychology, 31,* 215–232.

Schmidt, F. L., & Hunter, J. E. (1981). Employment testing: Old theories and new research. *American Psychologist, 36,* 1128–1137.

Schmidt, F. L., & Hunter, J. E. (1998). The validity and utility of selection methods in personnel psychology: Practical and theoretical implications of 85 years of research findings. *Psychological Bulletin, 124*(2), 262–274.

Schmidt, F. L., Hunter, J. E., Pearlman, K., & Hirsh, H. R. (1985). Forty questions about validity generalization and meta-analysis. *Personnel Psychology, 38,* 697–798.

Schmidt, F. L., & Rader, M. (1999). Exploring the boundary conditions for interview validity: Meta-analytic validity findings for a new interview type. *Personnel Psychology, 52*(2), 445–464.

Schmidt, F. L., & Rothstein, H. R. (1994). Application of validity generalization to biodata scales in employment selection. In G. S. Stokes, M. D. Mumford, & W. A. Owens (Eds.), *Biodata handbook* (pp. 237–260). Palo Alto, CA: Consulting Psychologists Press.

Schmitt, N., Arnold, J. D., & Nieminen, L. (2017). Validation strategies for primary studies. In J. L. Farr & N. T. Tippins (Eds.). *Handbook of employee selection* (pp. 34–55). New York: Routledge.

Schmitt, N., & Cohen, S. A. (1989). Internal analyses of task ratings by job incumbents. *Journal of Applied Psychology, 74,* 96–104.

Schmitt, N., Coyle, B. W., & Rauschenberger, J. (1977). A Monte Carlo evaluation of three formula estimates of cross-validated multiple correlation. *Psychological Bulletin, 84,* 751–758.

Schmitt, N., & Kunce, C. (2002). The effects of required elaboration of answers to biodata questions. *Personnel Psychology, 55,* 569–587.

Schmitt, N., & Mills, A. E. (2001). Traditional tests and job simulations: Minority and majority performance and test validities. *Journal of Applied Psychology, 86*(3), 451–458.

Schmitt, N., Schneider, J. R., & Cohen, S. A. (1990). Factors affecting validity of a regionally administered assessment center. *Personnel Psychology, 43,* 1–12.

Schrader, B. W., & Steiner, D. D. (1996). Common comparison standards: An approach to improving agreement between self and supervisory performance ratings. *Journal of Applied Psychology, 81*(6), 813–820.

Schriesheim, C. A., Castro, S. L., & Yammarino, F. J. (2000). Investigating contingencies: An examination of the impact of span of supervision and upward controllingness on leader-member exchange using traditional and multivariate within- and between-entities analysis. *Journal of Applied Psychology, 85*(5), 659–677.

Schriesheim, C. A., & DeNisi, A. S. (1981). Task dimensions as moderators of the effects of instrumental leadership: A two-sample replicated test of path-goal leadership theory. *Journal of Applied Psychology, 66,* 589–597.

Schriesheim, C. A., Tepper, B. J., & Tetrault, L. A. (1994). Least Preferred Coworker score, situational control, and leadership effectiveness: A meta-analysis of contingency model performance predictions. *Journal of Applied Psychology, 79*(4), 561–573.

Schröeder, C. M. (2010). Social experience and personality affect resilience to sleep deprivation. *Sleep, 33*(11), 1433–1434.

Schuster, F. E., Morden, D. L., Baker, T. E., McKay, I. S., Dunning, K. E., & Hagan, C. M. (1997). Management practice, organization climate, and performance: An exploratory study. *Journal of Applied Behavioral Science, 33*(2), 209–226.

Schuster, J. R., & Zingheim, P. K. (1992). *The new pay.* New York: Lexington.

Schwab, D. P. (1982). Recruiting and organizational participation. In K. M. Rowland & G. R. Farris (Eds.), *Personnel management.* Boston, MA: Allyn & Bacon.

Schwab, D. P., Heneman, H. G., & DeCotiis, T. A. (1975). Behaviorally anchored rating scales: A review of the literature. *Personnel Psychology, 28,* 549–562.

Schweitzer, M. E., Ordóñez, L., & Douma, B. (2004). Goal setting as a motivator of unethical behavior. *Academy of Management Journal, 47*(3), 422–432.

Scott, K. D., & Markham, S. E. (1982). Absenteeism control methods: A survey of practice and results. *Personnel Administrator, 27*(6), 73–84.

Scullen, S. E., Bergey, P. K., & Aiman-Smith, L. (2005). Forced distribution rating systems and the improvement of workforce potential: A baseline simulation. *Personnel Psychology, 58*(1), 1–32.

Sears, D. O. (1986). College sophomores in the laboratory: Influences of a narrow database on social psychology's view of human nature. *Journal of Personality and Social Psychology, 51*(3), 515–530.

Segal, J. A. (2001). Workplace tribal councils. *HR Magazine, 46*(6), 197–209.

Seifert, C. F., Yukl, G., & McDonald, R. A. (2003). Effects of multisource feedback and a feedback facilitator on the influence behavior of managers towards subordinates. *Journal of Applied Psychology, 88*(3), 561–569.

Seitz, R. (2004). *Portland metropolitan area employee selection practices: Use of tests and assessments.* Portland, OR: SHAPE Consulting.

Seltz, D. D., & Modica, A. J. (1980). *Negotiating your way to success.* New York: Mentor.

Shadish, W. R., & Ragsdale, K. (1996). Random versus nonrandom assignment in controlled experiments: Do you get the same answer? *Journal of Consulting and Clinical Psychology, 64*(6), 1290–1305.

Shaffer, D. R., & Tomarelli, M. (1981). Bias in the ivory tower: An unintended consequence of the Buckley Amendment for graduate admissions. *Journal of Applied Psychology, 66,* 7–11.

Shaffer, G. S., Saunders, V., & Owens, W. A. (1986). Additional evidence for the accuracy of biographical data: Long-term retest and observer ratings. *Personnel Psychology, 39*(4), 791–809.

Shaffer, J. A., & Postlethwaite, B. E. (2012). A matter of context: A meta-analytic investigation of the relative validity of contextualized and noncontextualized personality measures. *Personnel Psychology, 65,* 445–494.

Shalley, C. E. (1995). Effects of coaction, expected evaluation, and goal setting on creativity and productivity. *Academy of Management Journal, 38*(2), 483–503.

Shapira, Z., & Shirom, A. (1980). New issues in the use of behaviorally anchored rating scales: Level of analysis, the effects of incident frequency, and external validation. *Journal of Applied Psychology, 65*, 517–523.

Shaw, J. D., Gupta, N., & Delery, J. E. (2005). Alternative conceptualizations of the relationship between voluntary turnover and organizational performance. *Academy of Management Journal, 48*(1), 50–68.

Shaw, K. N. (2004). Changing the goal-setting process at Microsoft. *Academy of Management Executive, 18*(4), 139–142.

Shaw, M. E., & Shaw, I. M. (1962). Some effects of social grouping upon learning in a second grade classroom. *Journal of Social Psychology, 57*, 453–458.

Shepperd, J. A. (1993). Productivity loss in performance groups: A motivation analysis. *Psychological Bulletin, 113*(1), 67–81.

Shepperd, J. A., & Taylor, K. M. (1999). Social loafing and expectancy-value theory. *Personality and Social Psychology Bulletin, 25*(9), 1147–1158.

Sher, L. (2005). Type D personality: The heart, stress, and cortisol. *QJM, 98*(5), 323–329.

Sherriton, J., & Stern, J. (1997). HR's role in culture change. *HR Focus, 74*(4), 27.

Shetzer, L., & Stackman, R. (1991). The career path component in realistic job previews: A meta-analysis and proposed integration. *Applied H.R.M. Research, 2*(2), 153–169.

Shih, Y. C., & Wang, M. J. (1997). The influence of gloves during maximum volitional torque exertion of supination. *Ergonomics, 40*(4), 465–475.

Shih, Y. C., & Wang, M. J. (1996). The effects of weight levels and gloves on the ability to discriminate weight differences. *Ergonomics, 39*(5), 729–739.

Shilobod, T. L., McMullen, L. J., & Raymark, P. H. (2003). *Situational leadership theory: A meta-analysis of the adaptability hypothesis.* Poster presented at the 18th annual meeting of the Society for Industrial and Organizational Psychology, Orlando, Florida.

Shinar, D. (1995). Field evaluation of an advance brake warning system. *Human Factors, 37*(4), 746–751.

Shirreffs, B. P., & Sommers, P. M. (2006). The effect of salary arbitration on NHL player performance. *International Advances in Economic Research, 12*, 142.

Shlosberg, M. (2010). *Letting people go: The people-centered approach to firing and laying off employees.* New York: Business Expert Press.

Shockley, K. M., Ispas, D., Rossi, M. E., & Levine, E. L. (2012). A meta-analytic investigation of the relationship between state affect, discrete emotions, and job performance. *Human Performance, 25*(5), 377–411.

Shoenfelt, E. L., & Pedigo, L. C. (2005). A review of court decisions on cognitive ability testing, 1992–2004. *Review of Public Personnel Administration, 5*(3), 271–287.

SHRM (2007). *Advances in e-recruiting: Leveraging the jobs domain.* Alexandria, VA: Society for Human Resource Management.

SHRM (2013). *SHRM survey findings: Employee recognition programs, spring 2013.* Alexandria, VA: Society for Human Resource Management.

SHRM (2017). *Employee job satisfaction and engagement.* Alexandria, VA: Society for Human Resource Management.

SHRM (2018). *SHRM employee benefits 2018.* Alexandria, VA: Society for Human Resource Management.

SHRM (2019). *SHRM employee benefits 2019.* Alexandria, VA: Society for Human Resource Management.

SHRM (2021a). *Full poll results: Telework in the Time of COVID-19.* https://www.shrm.org/hr-today/news/hr-news/pages/poll-telework-coronavirus-full-results.aspx

SHRM (2021b). *Managing flexible work arrangements.* https://www.shrm.org/resourcesandtools/tools-and-samples/toolkits/pages/managingflexibleworkarrangements.aspx

SHRM (2021c). *Managing workplace conflict.* https://www.shrm.org/resourcesandtools/tools-and-samples/toolkits/pages/managingworkplaceconflict.aspx

Shultz, K. S., Hoffman, C. C., & Reiter-Palmon, R. (2005). Using archival data for I-O research: Advantages, pitfalls, sources, and examples. *The Industrial-Organizational Psychologist, 42*(3), 31–37.

Shultz, K. S., Wang, M., & Olson, D. A. (2010). Role overload and underload in relation to occupational stress and health. *Stress & Health, 26*(2), 99–111.

Siegall, M., & Worth, C. (2001). The impacts of trust and control on faculty reactions to merit pay. *Personnel Review, 30*(5/6), 646–656.

Silbergeld, A. F., & Jan, G. C. (2004, November). Awareness and prevention of violence in the workplace. *IPMA-HR News*, 6–8.

SilkRoad (2017). 2017 *Annual recruiting survey.* Chicago, IL: SilkRoad Technology.

Silkroad (2018). *Sources of hire 2018.* Chicago, IL: SilkRoad Technology.

Simner, M. L., & Goffin, R. D. (2003). A position statement by the International Graphonomics Society on the use of graphology in personnel selection testing. *International Journal of Testing, 3*(4), 353–364.

Simonton, D. K. (1987). *Why presidents succeed: A political psychology of leadership.* New Haven, CT: Yale University Press.

Singer, B. W. (2000). Get goofy now! *Health, 14*(8), 76–79.

SIOP (2018). *Principles for the validation and use of personnel selection procedures.* Bowling Green, OH: Society for Industrial and Organizational Psychology.

SIOP (2020). *Income & employment report 2020.* Bowling Green, OH: Society for Industrial and Organizational Psychology.

Sitzmann, T. (2011). A meta-analytic examination of the instructional effectiveness of computer-based simulation games. *Personnel Psychology, 64*, 489–528.

Sitzmann, T., Brown, K. G., Casper, W. J., Ely, K., & Zimmerman, R. D. (2008). A review and meta-analysis of the nomological network of trainee reactions. *Journal of Applied Psychology, 93*(2), 280–295.

Sitzmann, T., Kraiger, K., Stewart, D., & Wisher, R. (2006). The comparative effectiveness of web-based and classroom instruction: A meta-analysis. *Personnel Psychology, 59*, 623–664.

Skinner, B. F. (1971). *Beyond freedom and dignity.* New York: Knopf.

Slowiak, J. M. (2014). "How may I help you?" Improving telephone customer service in a medical clinic setting. *Journal of Organizational Behavior Management, 34*(1), 39–51.

Smith, A. (2013). An update on noise and performance: Comment on Szalma and Hancock (2011). *Psychological Bulletin, 138*(6), 1262–1268.

Smith, A., & Jones, D. M. (1992). Noise and performance. In D. M. Jones & A. P. Smith (Eds.), *Handbook of human performance* (Vol. 1, pp. 1–28). London: Academic Press.

Smith, B. N., Hornsby, J. S., Benson, P. G., & Wesolowski, M. (1989). What is in a name: The impact of job titles on job evaluation results. *Journal of Business and Psychology, 3*(3), 341–351.

Smith, C. S., Folkard, S., Tucker, P., & Evans, M. S. (2011). Work schedules, health and safety. In J. C. Cambell & L. E. Tetrick (Eds.), *Occupational health psychology* (2nd ed., pp. 185–204). Washington, DC: American Psychological Association.

Smith, C. S., Reilly, C., & Midkiff, K. (1988, August). *Psychometric evaluation of circadian rhythm questionnaires with suggestions for improvement.* Paper presented at the annual meeting of the American Psychological Association, Atlanta, GA.

Smith, D. E. (1986). Training programs for performance appraisal: A review. *Academy of Management Review, 11,* 22–40.

Smith, F. R., & Fortunato, V. J. (2008). Factors influencing employee intentions to provide honest upward feedback ratings. *Journal of Business and Psychology, 22,* 191–207.

Smith, L., & Folkard, S. (1993). The perceptions and feelings of shift workers' partners. *Ergonomics, 36*(1-3), 299–305.

Smith, L., Totterdell, P., & Folkard, S. (1995). Shiftwork effects in nuclear power workers: A field study using portable computers. *Work and Stress, 9,* 235–244.

Smith, M. (2003, January). Repetitive motion injuries and workers' compensation. *IPMA News,* p. 9.

Smith, M. L. (1993). Defensible performance appraisals. *Journal of Management in Engineering, 9*(2), 128–135.

Smith, P., & Christensen, J. (2007). *The readability of common documents used in organizations.* Paper presented at the 28th annual Graduate Student Conference in Industrial-Organizational Psychology and Organizational Behavior (IOOB), Indianapolis, Indiana.

Smith, P. C., & Kendall, L. M. (1963). Retranslating expectations: An approach to the construction of unambiguous anchors for rating scales. *Journal of Applied Psychology, 47,* 149–155.

Smither, J. W., Barry, S. R., & Reilly, R. R. (1989). An investigation of the validity of expert true score estimates in appraisal research. *Journal of Applied Psychology, 74,* 143–151.

Smither, J. W., London, M., & Reilly, R. R. (2005). Does performance improve following multisource feedback? A theoretical model, meta-analysis, and review of empirical findings. *Personnel Psychology, 58*(1), 33–66.

Smither, J. W., Reilly, R. R., & Buda, R. (1988). Effect of prior performance information on ratings of recent performance: Contrast versus assimilation revisited. *Journal of Applied Psychology, 73,* 487–496.

Sollie, D., & Sollie, W. (1993). *Non-lethal weapons: An implementation study.* Paper presented at the annual Meeting of the Society of Police and Criminal Psychology, New Orleans, LA.

Solmon, L. C., & Podgursky, M. (2000). *The pros and cons of performance-based compensation.* https://files.eric.ed.gov/fulltext/ED445393.pdf

Sommer, R., Wynes, M., & Brinkley, G. (1992). Social facilitation effects in shopping behavior. *Environment and Behavior, 24*(3), 285–297.

Sommers, P. M. (1993). The influence of salary arbitration on player performance. *Social Science Quarterly, 74*(2), 439–443.

Song, I-Y., & Zhu, Y. (2015). Big data and data science: What should we teach? *Expert Systems, 33*(4), 364–373.

Sosnin, B. (2001). Packaging your policies. *HR Magazine, 46*(7), 66–72.

Sparks, C. P. (1988). Legal basis for job analysis. In S. Gael (Ed.), *The job analysis handbook for business, industry, and government* (Vol. 1, pp. 37–47). New York: Wiley.

Spearman, C. T. (1904). The proof and measurement of association between two things. *American Journal of Psychology, 15,* 72–101.

Spencer Stuart (2020). *2020 U.S. Spencer Stuart board index.* Chicago, IL: Spencer Stuart.

Spock, G., & Stevens, S. (1985). A test of Anderson's averaging versus adding model on resume evaluations. *Proceedings of the 6th Annual Graduate Conference in Industrial/Organizational Psychology and Organizational Behavior,* 95–96.

Spychalski, A. C., Quiñones, M. A., Gaugler, B. B., & Pohley, K. (1997). A survey of assessment center practices in organizations in the United States. *Personnel Psychology, 50,* 71–90.

Srinivas, S., & Motowidlo, S. J. (1987). Effects of rater's stress on the dispersion and favorability of performance ratings. *Journal of Applied Psychology, 72,* 247–251.

St.Albin, N. (2020). *Employee feedback demystified: A comprehensive guide for managers.* https://officevibe.com/guides/employee-feedback

Stafford, E. M., Jackson, P. R., & Banks, M. H. (1984). An empirical study of occupational families in the youth labor market. *Journal of Occupational Psychology, 57,* 141–155.

Stahl, G. K., Maznevski, M., Voight, A., Jonsen, K. (2009). Unraveling the effects of cultural diversity in teams: A meta-analysis of research on multicultural work groups. *Journal of International Business Studies,* 1–20. doi:10.1057/jibs.2009.85

Stahl, M. J., & Harrell, A. M. (1981). Modeling effort decisions with behavioral decision theory: Toward an individual differences model of expectancy theory. *Organizational Behavior and Human Performance, 27,* 303–325.

Stahl, M. J., & Harrell, A. M. (1982). Evolution and validation of a behavioral decision theory measurement approach to achievement, power, and affiliation. *Journal of Applied Psychology, 67,* 744–751.

Stajkovic, A. D., & Luthans, F. (1997). A meta-analysis of the effects of organizational behavior modification on task performance, 1975–1995. *Academy of Management Journal, 40*(5), 1122–1149.

Stajkovic, A. D., & Luthans, F. (2001). Differential effects of incentive motivators on work performance. *Academy of Management Journal, 44*(3), 580–590.

Stajkovic, A. D., & Luthans, F. (2003). Behavioral management and task performance in organizations: Conceptual background, meta-analysis, and test of alternative models. *Personnel Psychology, 56*(1), 155–194.

Stauffer, J. M., & Buckley, M. R. (2005). The existence and nature of racial bias in supervisory ratings. *Journal of Applied Psychology, 90*(3), 586–591.

Steers, R. M., & Porter, L. W. (1991). *Motivation and work behavior* (4th ed.). New York: McGraw-Hill.

Steggert, J., Chrisman, S., & Haap, N. (2006, February). *Beware of the eye of the beholder: A meta-analysis of the effects of physical attractiveness on employee selection and other personnel decisions.* Paper presented at the annual Graduate Conference in Industrial-Organizational Psychology and Organizational Behavior, Fairfax, VA.

Steiner, D. D., & Rain, J. S. (1989). Immediate and delayed primacy and recency effects in performance evaluation. *Journal of Applied Psychology, 74*(1), 136–142.

Steingold, F. S. (2019). *Employer's legal handbook* (14th ed.). Berkeley, CA: Nolo Press.

Sternberg, H. (2020). Don't leave online training tool selection to chance. *TD: Talent Development, 74*(11), 9.

Sternberg, R. J. (2007). A systems model of leadership: WICS. *American Psychologist, 62*(1), 34–42.

Stewart, D. W., & Latham, D. R. (1986). On some psychometric properties of Fiedler's contingency model of leadership. *Small Group Behavior, 17*(1), 83–94.

Stewart, G. L. (2006). A meta-analytic review of relationships between team design features and team performance. *Journal of Management, 32*(1), 29–54.

Stewart, G. L., Dustin, S., Shaffer, J., & Giluk, T. (2008, April). Antecedents to rapport building during the employment interview. In M. R. Barrick (Chair), *The role of unstructured information in the employment interview.* Symposium presented at the 23rd annual meeting of the Society for Industrial-Organizational Psychology, San Francisco, CA.

Stewart, G. L., Fulmer, I. S., & Barrick, M. R. (2005). An exploration of member roles as a multilevel linking mechanism for individual traits and team outcomes. *Personnel Psychology, 58*(2), 343–365.

Stewart, P. A., & Moore, J. C. (1992). Wage disparities and performance expectations. *Social Psychology Quarterly, 55*(1), 78–85.

Stewart, R., Ellenburg, G., Hicks, L., Kremen, M., & Daniel, M. (1990). Employee references as a recruitment source. *Applied H.R.M. Research, 1*(1), 1–3.

Stokes, G. S., Hogan, J. B., & Snell, A. F. (1993). Comparability of incumbent and applicant samples for the development of biodata keys: The influence of social desirability. *Personnel Psychology, 46*, 739–762.

Stokes, G. S., & Toth, C. S. (1996). Background data for personnel selection. In R. S. Barrett (Ed.), *Fair employment strategies in human resource management* (pp. 171–179). Westport, CT: Quorum.

Stone, E. & Davey, T. (2011). *Computer-adaptive testing for students with disabilities: A review of the literature.* Princeton, NJ: Educational Testing Service.

Stone, N. J., & Sanders, A. M. F. (2020). Applying to industrial-organizational master's programs. In E. L. Shoenfelt (Ed.), *Mastering industrial-organizational psychology.* New York: Oxford University Press.

Streshly, W. A., Gray, S. P., & Frase, L. E. (2012). *The new school management by wandering around.* Thousand Oaks, CA: Corwin.

Strube, M. J., & Garcia, J. E. (1981). A meta-analytic investigation of Fiedler's contingency model of leadership effectiveness. *Psychological Bulletin, 90*, 307–321.

Stuhlmacher, A. F., & Walters, A. E. (1999). Gender differences in negotiation outcome: A meta-analysis. *Personnel Psychology, 52*(3), 653–677.

Substance Abuse and Mental Health Services Administration. (2013). *Results from the 2012 National Survey on Drug Use and Health: Volume I. Summary of National Findings* (Office of Applied Studies, NSDUH Series H-38A, HHS Publication No. SMA 10-4586 Findings). Rockville, MD.

Sugawara, J., Tarumi, T. & Tanaka, H. (2010). Effect of mirthful laughter on vascular function. *The American Journal of Cardiology, 106*(6), 856–859.

Sullivan, J. (2000). Experience: It "Ain't what it used to be." *Public Personnel Management, 29*(4), 511–516.

Sulsky, L. M., & Smith, C. (2005). *Work stress.* Belmont, CA: Wadsworth.

Summer, H. C., & Knight, P. A. (1996). Assimilation and contrast effects in performance ratings: Effects of rating the previous performance on rating subsequent performance. *Journal of Applied Psychology, 81*(4), 436–442.

Sun, M., Feng, W., Want, F., Li, P., Li, M., Tse, G., Vlaanderen, J., Vermeulen, R., & Tse, L. A. (2017). Meta-analysis on shift work and risks of specific obesity types. *Obesity Reviews, 19*(1), 28–40.

Sundstrom, E., Town, J. P., Rice, R. W., Osborn, D. P., & Brill, M. (1994). Office noise, satisfaction, and performance. *Environment and Behavior, 26*(2), 195–222.

Surrette, M. A., Aamodt, M. G., & Johnson, D. L. (1990). Effect analyst training and amount of available information on job analysis ratings. *Journal of Business and Psychology, 4,* 439–451.

Surrette, M. A., & Harlow, L. L. (1992). Level of satisfaction and commitment to a decisional choice as mediated by locus of control. *Applied H.R.M. Research, 3*(2), 92–113.

Sutton, A. W., Baldwin, S. P., Wood, L., & Hoffman, B. J. (2013). A meta-analysis of the relationship between rater liking and performance ratings. *Human Performance, 26*(5), 409–429.

Sutton, H. W., & Porter, L. W. (1968). A study of the grapevine in a governmental organization. *Personnel Psychology, 21,* 223–230.

Sverke, M., Hellgren, J., & Näswall, K. (2002). No security: A meta-analysis and review of job insecurity and its consequences. *Journal of Occupational Health Psychology, 7*(3), 242–264.

Swaroff, P. G., Barclay, L. A., & Bass, A. R. (1985). Recruiting sources: Another look. *Journal of Applied Psychology, 70,* 720–728.

Swider, B. W., Barrick, M. R., & Harris, T. B. (2016). Initial impressions: What they are, what they are not, and how they influence structured interview outcomes. *Journal of Applied Psychology, 101*(5), 625–638.

Swiercz, P. M., Icenogle, M. L., Bryan, N. B., & Renn, R. W. (1993, August). Do perceptions of performance appraisal fairness predict employee attitudes and performance?. In *Academy* of *Management Proceedings* (Vol. 1993, No. 1, pp. 304–308). Briarcliff Manor, NY: Academy of Management.

Switzer, K. C., Nagy, M. S., & Mullins, M. E. (2005). The influence of training reputation, managerial support, and self-efficacy on pre-training motivation and perceived training transfer. *Applied H.R.M. Research, 10*(1), 21–34.

Szalma, J. L., & Hancock, P. A. (2011). Noise effects on human performance. A meta-analytic synthesis. *Psychological Bulletin, 137*(4), 682–707.

Tait, M., Padgett, M. Y., & Baldwin, T. T. (1989). Job and life satisfaction: A reexamination of the strength of the relationship and gender effects as a function of the date of the study. *Journal of Applied Psychology, 74,* 502–507.

Tanaka, M., Tochihara, Y., Yamazaki, S., Ohnaka, T., & Yoshida, K. (1983). Thermal reaction and manual performance during cold exposure while wearing cold-protective clothing. *Ergonomics, 26,* 141–149.

Tangirala, S., Green, S. G., & Ramanujam, R. (2007). In the shadow of the boss's boss: Effects of supervisors' upward exchange relationships on employees. *Journal of Applied Psychology, 92*(2), 309–320.

Tannen, D. (1995). *Talking 9 to 5.* New York: Harper.

Tannen, D. (2001). *You just don't understand: Women and men in conversation.* New York: Harper.

Tannenbaum, R. J., & Wesley, S. (1993). Agreement between committee-based and field-based job analyses: A study in the context of licensure testing. *Journal of Applied Psychology, 78,* 975–980.

Taylor, S. (2007). Red-carpet treatment: Creative staffing pros use everything from microwave ovens to day care centers to deck parties to woo candidates. *Staffing Management, 3*(4), 23–26.

Taylor, H. C., & Russell, J. T. (1939). The relationship of validity coefficients to the practical effectiveness of tests in selection: Discussion and tables. *Journal of Applied Psychology, 23,* 565–578.

Taylor, J. C. (2021). *Ask HR: How can organizations offer health and wellness benefits in 2021?* SHRM. https://www.shrm.org/resourcesandtools/hr-topics/organizational-and-employee-development/pages/ask-hr-how-can-organizations-offer-health-and-wellness-benefits-in-2021.aspx.

Taylor, M. S., & Schmidt, D. W. (1983). A process-oriented investigation of recruitment source effectiveness. *Personnel Psychology, 36,* 343–354.

Taylor, P. J., Pajo, K., Cheung, G. W., & Stringfield, P. (2004). Dimensionality and validity of a structured telephone reference check procedure. *Personnel Psychology, 57*(3), 745–772.

Taylor, P. J., Russ-Eft, D. F., & Chan, D. W. L. (2005). A meta-analytic review of behavior modeling training. *Journal of Applied Psychology, 90*(4), 692–709.

Terpstra, D. E., Mohamed, A. A., & Kethley, R. B. (1999). An analysis of federal court cases involving nine selection devices. *International Journal of Selection & Assessment, 7,* 26–34.

Terpstra, D. E., & Rozell, E. J. (1993). Relationship of staffing practices to organizational level measures of performance. *Personnel Psychology, 46,* 27–48.

Tett, R. P., Jackson, D. N., & Rothstein, M. (1991). Personality measures as predictors of job performance: A meta-analytic review. *Personnel Psychology, 44,* 703–742.

Tett, R. P., Jackson, D. N., Rothstein, M., & Reddon, J. R. (1994). Meta-analysis of personality-job performance relations: A

reply to Ones, Mount, Barrick, & Hunter (1994). *Personnel Psychology, 47*(1), 157–172.

Tharmmaphornphilas, W., & Norman, B. A. (2007). A methodology to create robust job rotation schedules. *Annals of Operations Research, 155*(1), 339–360.

Theeuwes, J., & Alferdinck, J. W. (1995). Rear light arrangements for cars equipped with a center-high mounted stop lamp. *Human Factors, 37*(2), 371–380.

Thibaut, J. (1950). An experimental study of the cohesiveness of underprivileged groups. *Human Relations, 3*(3), 251–278.

Thombs, D. L., Beck, K. H., & Mahoney, C. A. (1993). Effects of social context and gender on drinking patterns of young adults. *Journal of Counseling Psychology, 40*(1), 115–119.

Thompson, D. (2021). Is VR the solution for soft skills training? *TD: Talent Development, 75*(1), 10–11.

Thompson, D. E., & Thompson, T. A. (1982). Court standards for job analysis in test validation. *Personnel Psychology, 35,* 865–874.

Thorsteinson, T. J. (2018). *A meta-analysis of interview length on reliability and validity.* Poster presented at the annual meeting of the Society for Industrial and Organizational Psychology, Honolulu, Hawaii.

Thorsteinson, T. J., Palmer, E. M., Wulff, C., & Anderson, A. (2004). Too good to be true? Using realism to enhance applicant attraction. *Journal of Business and Psychology, 19*(1), 125–137.

Thurston, P. W., & McNall, L. (2010). Justice perceptions of performance appraisal practices. *Journal of Managerial Psychology, 25*(3), 201–228.

Tierney, P. (1998). *The role of the Pygmalion effect in employee creativity.* Poster presented at the annual meeting of the Society for Industrial and Organizational Psychology, Dallas, TX.

Tims, M., & Bakker, A. B. (2010). Job crafting: Towards a new model of individual job redesign. *South African Journal of Industrial Psychology, 36*(2), 1–9.

Tolman, C. W. (1968). The role of the companion in social facilitation of animal behavior. In E. C. Simmel, R. A. Hoppe, & G. A. Milton (Eds.), *Social facilitation and initiative behavior* (pp. 33–54). Boston: Allyn & Bacon.

Tonowski, R. F. (1993, September). Assessing a violent situation: Violence and personnel assessment practices in the U.S. Postal Service. *IPMAAC News,* pp. 3–5.

Too, L. (2009). *Quick & easy feng shui office.* Malaysia: Konsep Lagenda.

Totterdell, P., Spelten, E., Smith, L., Barton, J., & Folkard, S. (1995). Recovery from work shifts: How long does it take? *Journal of Applied Psychology, 80*(1), 43–57.

Tourangeau, R., & Yan, T. (2007). Sensitive questions in surveys. *Psychological Bulletin, 133*(5), 859–883.

Tracey, J. B., Tannenbaum, S. I., & Kavanagh, M. J. (1995). Applying trained skills on the job: The importance of the work environment. *Journal of Applied Psychology, 80*(2), 239–252.

Trahiotis, C., & Robinson, D. E. (1979). Auditory psychophysics. *Annual Review of Psychology, 30,* 31–61.

Triplett, N. (1898). The dynamogenic factors in pacemaking and competition. *American Journal of Psychology, 9,* 507–533.

Trix, F., & Psenka, C. (2003). Exploring the color of glass: Letters of recommendation for female and male medical faculty. *Discourse and Society, 14*, 191–220.

Truxillo, D. M., Normandy, J. L., & Bauer, T. N. (2001). Drug use history, drug test consequences, and the perceived fairness of organizational drug testing programs. *Journal of Business and Psychology, 16*(1), 87–99.

Truxillo, D. M., Paronto, M. E., Collins, M., & Sulzer, J. L. (2004). Effects of subject matter expert viewpoint no job analysis results. *Public Personnel Management, 33*(1), 33–46.

Tubbs, M. E. (1986). Goal setting: A meta-analytic examination of the empirical evidence. *Journal of Applied Psychology, 71*, 474–483.

Tubré, T. C., Bly, P. R., Edwards, B. D., Pritchard, R. D., & Simoneaux, S. (2001). Building a better literature review: References and information sources for I-O psychology. *The Industrial-Organizational Psychologist, 38*(4), 55–59.

Tubré, T. C., & Collins, J. M. (2000). Jackson and Schuler (1985) revisited: A meta-analysis of the relationships between role ambiguity, role conflict, and job performance. *Journal of Management, 26*(1), 155–169.

Tuckman, B. (1965). Developmental sequence in small groups. *Psychological Bulletin, 63*, 384–399.

Tulgan, B. (2001). Real pay for performance. *Journal of Business Strategy, 22*(3), 19–22.

Turner, B., Job, S., & Mitra, S. (2021). *Road safety interventions: Evidence of what works and what does not work*. Washington, DC: Global Road Safety Facility – World Bank.

Turner, M. L., Fernandez, J. E., & Nelson, K. (1996). The effect of music amplitude on the reaction to unexpected visual events. *The Journal of General Psychology, 123*(1), 51–62.

Turner, J. T., & Gelles, M. G. (2003). *Threat assessment: A risk management approach*. Binghamton, New York: Haworth Press.

Twomey, D. P., & Greene, S. (2020). *Labor and employment law* (16th Ed.). St. Paul, MN: West Academic Publishing.

Tyler, K. (1996). Employees can help recruit new talent. *HR Magazine, 41*(9), 57–60.

Tyler, K. (1998). Sit up straight. *HR Magazine, 43*(9), 124–128.

Tyler, K. (2000). Recruiting through religious organizations. *HR Magazine, 45*(9), 131–138.

Tyler, K. (2001). All present and accounted for? *HR Magazine, 46*(10), 101.

Tyler, K. (2007). Mediating a better outcome. *HR Magazine, 52*(11), 63–66.

Tyler, K. (2010). Helping employees cool it. *HR Magazine, 55*(4), 53–55.

Tyler, K. (2013). The American apprentice. *HR Magazine, 58*(11), 33–36.

Tziner, A., Kopelman, R. E., & Livnech, N. (1993). Effects of performance appraisal format on perceived goal characteristics, appraisal process satisfaction, and changes in rated job performance: A field experiment. *Journal of Psychology, 127*(3), 281–292.

Uggerslev, K. L., Fassina, N. E., & Kraichy, D. (2012). Recruiting through the stages: A meta-analytic test of predictors of applicant attraction at different stages of the recruiting process. *Personnel Psychology, 65*(3), 597–660.

Uggerslev, K. L., & Sulsky, L. M. (2008). Using frame-of-reference training to understand the implications of rater idiosyncrasy for rating accuracy. *Journal of Applied Psychology, 93*(3), 711–719.

Uniform Guidelines on Employee Selection Procedures. (1978). Retrieved February 10, 2011, from http://www.usdoj.gov/crt/emp/uniformguidelines.html

Uziel, L. (2007). Individual differences in the social facilitation effect: A review and meta-analysis. *Journal of Research in Personality, 41*(3), 579–601.

Valacich, J. S., Dennis, A. R., & Connolly, T. (1994). Idea generation in computer-based groups: A new ending to an old story. *Organizational Behavior and Human Decision Processes, 57*(3), 448–467.

Valacich, J. S., Dennis, A. R., & Nunamaker, J. F. (1992). Group size and anonymity effects on computer-mediated idea generation. *Small Group Research, 23*(1), 49–73.

Van De Water, T. J. (1997). Psychology's entrepreneurs and the marketing of industrial psychology. *Journal of Applied Psychology, 82*(4), 486–499.

Van Iddekinge, C. H., Arnold, J. D., Frieder, R. E., & Roth, P. L. (2019). A meta-analysis of the criterion-related validity of prehire work experience. *Personnel Psychology, 72*, 571–598.

Van Iddekinge, C. H., Roth, P. L., Putka, D. J., & Lanivich, S. E. (2011). Are you interested? A meta-analysis of relations between vocational interests and employee performance and turnover. *Journal of Applied Psychology, 96*, 1167–1194.

Van Iddekinge, C. H., Roth, P. L., Raymark, P. H., & Odle-Dusseau, H. N. (2012). The criterion-related validity of integrity tests: An updated meta-analysis. *Journal of Applied Psychology, 97*(3), 499–530.

van Kempen, E. E. M., Kruize, H., Boshuizen, H. C., Ameling, C. B., Staatsen, B. A. M., & de Hollander, A. E. M. (2002). The association between noise exposure and blood pressure and ischemic heart disease: A meta-analysis. *Environmental Health Perspectives, 110*, 307–317.

Vaughn, D., Petersen, N., & Gibson, C. (2019). The use of social media in staffing. In R. N. Landers (Ed.), *The Cambridge handbook of technology and employee behavior* (pp. 232–268). Cambridge: Cambridge University Press.

Veres, J. G., Green, S. B., & Boyles, W. R. (1991). Racial differences on job analysis questionnaires: An empirical study. *Public Personnel Management, 20*(2), 135–144.

Verhaegen, P., Cober, R., de Smedt, M., & Dirkx, J. (1987). The adaptation of night nurses to different work schedules. *Ergonomics, 30*, 1301–1309.

Vernon, H. M. (1936). *Accidents and their prevention*. London: Cambridge University Press.

Vincent, C., Rainey, R., Faulkner, D., Mascio, C., & Zinda, M. (2007, March). *How often should job descriptions be updated*. Poster presented at the annual graduate conference for Industrial-Organizational Psychology and Organizational Behavior, Indianapolis, IN.

Vinchur, A. J. (2021). A history of psychology applied to employee selection. In L. Koppes Bryan (Ed.), *Historical perspectives in industrial and organizational psychology* (2nd Ed.) (pp. 103–123). New York: Routledge.

Vinchur, A. J. (2018). *The early years of industrial and organizational psychology*. New York: Cambridge University Press.

Vinchur, A. J., & Koppes Bryan, L. (2021). Early contributors to the science and practice of industrial psychology. In L.

Koppes Bryan (Ed.), *Historical perspectives in industrial and organizational psychology* (2nd Ed.) (pp. 21–41). New York: Routledge.

Vinchur, A. J., Schippmann, J. S., Switzer, F. S., & Roth, P. L. (1998). A meta-analytic review of predictors of job performance for salespeople. *Journal of Applied Psychology, 83*(4), 586–597.

Vines, L. S. (1997). Make long-term temporary workers part of the team. *HR Magazine, 42*(1), 65–70.

Viswesvaran, C., & Ones, D. S. (2003). Measurement error in "big five factors" personality assessment. In B. Thompson (Ed.), *Score reliability: Contemporary thinking on reliability issues.* Newbury Park, CA: Sage Publications.

Viswesvaran, C., Ones, D. S., & Schmidt, F. L. (1996). Comparative analysis of the reliability of job performance ratings. *Journal of Applied Psychology, 81*(5), 557–574.

Viswesvaran, C., Sanchez, J. I., & Fisher, J. (1999). The role of social support in the process of work stress: A meta-analysis. *Journal of Vocational Behavior, 54,* 314–334.

Viswesvaran, C., Schmidt, F. L., & Ones, D. S. (2005). Is there a general factor in ratings of job performance? A meta-analytic framework for disentangling substantive and error influences. *Journal of Applied Psychology, 90*(1), 108–131.

Vroom, V. H. (1964). *Work and motivation.* New York: John Wiley.

Vroom, V., & Yetton, P. W. (1973). *Leadership and decision making.* Pittsburgh, PA: University of Pittsburgh Press.

Wagner, J. A. (1994). Participation effects on performance and satisfaction: A reconsideration of research evidence. *Academy of Management Review, 19*(2), 312–330.

Wagner, R. F. (1950). A study of the critical requirements for dentists. *University of Pittsburgh Bulletin, 46,* 331–339.

Wagner, T. L. (1990). A meta-analytic review of absenteeism control methods. *Applied H.R.M. Research, 1*(1), 23–26.

Walion, N. J., & Baker, T. (2018, April). *Same job, different job: Task differences between men and women in police work.* Poster presented at the 33rd annual meeting of the Society for Industrial and Organizational Psychology, Chicago, IL.

Walker, H. J., Feild, H. S., Giles, W. F., Armenakis, A. A., & Bernerth, J. B. (2009). Displaying employee testimonials on recruitment web sites: Effects of communication media, employee race, and job seeker race on organizational attraction and information credibility. *Journal of Applied Psychology, 94*(5), 1354–1364.

Wall, H. J. (2000, October). The gender wage gap and wage discrimination: Illusion or reality? *Regional Economist,* pp. 1–5.

Wanberg, C. R., & Banas, J. T. (2000). Predictors and outcomes of openness to changes in a reorganizing workplace. *Journal of Applied Psychology, 85*(1), 132–142.

Wang, Q., Bowling, N. A., & Eschleman, K. J. (2010). Meta-analytic examination of work and general locus of control. *Journal of Applied Psychology, 95*(4), 761–768.

Wanous, J. P. (1980). *Organizational entry: Recruitment, selection, and socialization of newcomers.* Reading, MA: Addison-Wesley.

Wanous, J. P., Poland, T. D., Premack, S. L., & Davis, K. S. (1992). The effects of met expectations on newcomer attitudes and behavior: A review and meta-analysis. *Journal of Applied Psychology, 77*(3), 288–297.

Ward, E. A. (2001). Social power bases of managers: Emergence of a new factor. *The Journal of Social Psychology, 141*(1), 144–147.

Warr, P. (2007). Some historical developments in I-O psychology outside the United States. In L. L. Koppes (Ed.), *Historical perspectives in industrial and organizational psychology* (pp. 81–107). Mahwah, NJ: Lawrence Erlbaum.

Warren, L., Mullen, P., & McEwan, T. (2014). Explicit threats of violence. In J. R. Meloy & J. Hoffmann (Eds.), *The international handbook of threat assessment* (pp. 18–38). New York: Oxford University Press.

Watson, C. (1987). Sex-linked differences in letters of recommendation. *Women and Language, 10,* 26–28.

Waung, M., & Brice, T. S. (2000). Communicating negative hire decisions to applicants: Fulfilling psychological contracts. *Journal of Business and Psychology, 15*(2), 247–263.

Waung, M., & Brice, T. S. (2003). *The impact of a rejection communication on rejected job applicants.* Poster presented at the 18th annual meeting of the Society for Industrial and Organizational Psychology, Orlando, Florida.

Waung, M., & Highhouse, S. (1997). *Feedback inflation: Empathic buffering or fear of conflict?* Poster presented at the 12th annual conference of the Society for Industrial and Organizational Psychology, St. Louis, MO.

Webber, S. S., & Klimoski, R. J. (2004). Crews: A distinct type of work team. *Journal of Business and Psychology, 18*(3), 261–279.

Webster, J. R., Adams, G. A., Maranto, C. L., & Beehr, T. A. (2018). "Dirty" workplace politics and well-being: The role of gender. *Psychology of Women Quarterly, 42*(3), 361–377.

Weidner, N., & Short, E. (2019). Playing with a purpose: The role of games and gamification in modern assessment practices. In R. N. Landers (Ed.), *The Cambridge handbook of technology and employee behavior* (pp. 151–178). Cambridge: Cambridge University Press.

Weins, A. N., Jackson, R. H., Manaugh, T. S., & Matarazzo, J. D. (1969). Communication length as an index of communicator attitude: A replication. *Journal of Applied Psychology, 53,* 264–266.

Weinstein, N. D. (1977). Noise and intellectual performance: A confirmation and extension. *Journal of Applied Psychology, 62,* 104–107.

Weinstein, N. D. (1978). A longitudinal study in a college dormitory. *Journal of Applied Psychology, 63,* 458–466.

Weiss, H. M., Dawis, R. V., England, G. W., & Lofquist, L. H. (1967). *Manual for the Minnesota Satisfaction Questionnaire.* Minneapolis: University of Minnesota, Industrial Relations Center.

Weiss, H. M., & Shaw, J. B. (1979). Social influences on judgments about tasks. *Organizational Behavior and Human Performance, 24,* 126–140.

Wells, S. J. (2000). The elder care gap. *HR Magazine, 45*(5), 39–46.

Wells, S. J. (2005). No results, no raise. *HR Magazine, 50*(5), 76–80.

Welsh, D. H., Bernstein, D. J., & Luthans, F. (1992). Application of the Premack Principle of reinforcement to the quality performance of service employees. *Journal of Organizational Behavior Management, 13*(1), 9–32.

Werner, J. M., & Bolino, M. C. (1997). Explaining U.S. Courts of Appeals decisions involving performance appraisal: Accuracy, fairness, and validation. *Personnel Psychology, 50*(1), 1–24.

Wernimont, P. F. (1962). Re-evaluation of a weighted application blank for office personnel. *Journal of Applied Psychology, 46*, 417–419.

Wexley, K. N., & Latham, G. A. (2002). *Developing and training human resources in organizations* (3rd ed.). Upper Saddle River, NJ: Prentice Hall.

Wexley, K. N., Sanders, R. E., & Yukl, G. A. (1973). Training interviewers to eliminate contrast effects in employment interviews. *Journal of Applied Psychology, 57*, 233–236.

Wexley, K. N., Yukl, G. A., Kovacs, S. Z., & Sanders, R. E. (1972). Importance of contrast effects in employment interviews. *Journal of Applied Psychology, 56*, 45–48.

Whelchel, B. D. (1985). Use of performance tests to select craft apprentices. *Personnel Journal, 65*(7), 65–69.

Whelpley, C. E., & McDaniel, M. A. (2011, April). *Self-esteem and counterproductive behaviors: A meta-analytic review.* Poster presented at the annual Meeting of the Society for Industrial-Organizational Psychology, Chicago, IL.

Whetzel, D. L., McDaniel, M. A., & Nguyen, N. T. (2008). Subgroup differences in situational judgment test performance: A meta-analysis. *Human Performance, 21*, 291–309.

Whetzel, D. L., Rotenberry, P. F., & McDaniel, M. A. (2014). In-basket validity: A systematic review. *International Journal of Selection and Assessment, 22*(1), 62–79.

White, S. S., & Locke, E. A. (2000). Problems with the Pygmalion effect and some proposed solutions. *The Leadership Quarterly, 11*(3), 389–415.

Whiting, H. J., Kline, T. J. B., & Sulsky, L. M. (2008). The performance appraisal congruency: An assessment of person-environment fit. *International Journal of Productivity and Performance Management, 57*(3), 223–236.

Whitman, D. S., Caleo, S., Carpenter, N. C., Horner, M. T., & Bernerth, J. B. (2012). Fairness at the collective level: A meta-analytic examination of the consequences and boundary conditions of organizational justice climate. *Journal of Applied Psychology, 97*(4), 776–791.

Whitney, D., & Trosten-Bloom, A. (2012). Positive power: Transforming possibilities through appreciative leadership. In C. S. Pearson (Ed.), *The transforming leader.* San Francisco: Berrett-Koehler.

Wiesenfeld, B. M., Brockner, J., & Martin, C. (1999). A self-affirmation analysis of survivors' reactions to unfair organizational downsizings. *Journal of Experimental Social Psychology, 35*, 441–460.

Wild, C., Horney, N., & Koonce, R. (1996). Cascading communications creates momentum for change. *HR Magazine, 41*(12), 94–100.

Wilkinson, R. T. (1992). How fast should the night shift rotate? *Ergonomics, 35*(12), 1425–1446.

Wille, B., De Fruyt, F., & De Clercq, B. (2013). Expanding and reconceptualizing aberrant personality at work: Validity of five-factor model aberrant personality tendencies to predict career outcomes. *Personnel Psychology, 66*(1), 173–223.

Williams, J. R., & Levy, P. E. (1992). The effects of perceived system knowledge on the agreement between self-ratings and supervisor ratings. *Personnel Psychology, 45*, 835–847.

Williams, J. R., Miller, C. E., Steelman, L. A., & Levy, P. E. (1999). Increasing feedback seeking in public contexts: It takes two (or more) to tango. *Journal of Applied Psychology, 84*(6), 969–976.

Williams, M. L., McDaniel, M. A., & Nguyen, N. T. (2006). A meta-analysis of the antecedents and consequences of pay level satisfaction. *Journal of Applied Psychology, 91*(2), 392–413.

Williamson, A. M., Gower, C. G. I., & Clarke, B. C. (1994). Changing the hours of shift work: A comparison of 8- and 12-hour shift rosters in a group of computer operators. *Ergonomics, 37*(2), 287–298.

Williamson, L. G., Campion, J. E., Malos, S. B., Roehling, M. V., & Campion, M. A. (1997). Employment interview on trial: Linking interview structure with litigation outcomes. *Journal of Applied Psychology, 82*(6), 900–912.

Willihnganz, M. A., & Myers, L. S. (1993). Effects of time of day on interview performance. *Public Personnel Management, 22*(4), 545–550.

Willms, K., Wells, R., & Carnahan, H. (2009). Glove attributes and their contribution to force decrement and increased effort in power grip. *Human Factors, 51*(6), 797–812.

Willness, C. R., Steel, P., & Lee, K. (2007). A meta-analysis of the antecedents and consequences of workplace sexual harassment. *Personnel Psychology, 60*(1), 127–162.

Wilson, D. S. (2007). *Evolution for everyone.* New York: Bantam Dell.

Wilson, M. A. (2012). Methodological decisions in work analysis: A theory of effective work analysis in organizations. In M. A. Wilson, W. Bennett, S. G. Gibson, & G. M. Alliger (Eds.), *The handbook of work analysis* (pp. 3–21). New York: Routledge.

Wilson, M. A., & Harvey, R. J. (1990). The value of relative-time-spent ratings in task-oriented job analysis. *Journal of Business and Psychology, 4*(4), 453–461.

Wimbush, J. C., & Dalton, D. R. (1997). Base rate for employee theft: Convergence of multiple methods. *Journal of Applied Psychology, 82*(5), 756–763.

Winsor, J. L. (1984). Effective appraisal systems. *Professional Communication in the Modern World: Proceedings of the Southeast Convention of the American Business Communication Association (31st, Hammond, LA, April 5–7, 1984),* 95–102.

Winter, D. G. (1988). What makes Jesse run? *Psychology Today, 22*(6), 20–24.

Wofford, J. C., & Liska, L. Z. (1993). Path-goal theories of leadership: A meta-analysis. *Journal of Management, 19*(4), 857–876.

Wolkove, M. P., & Layman, J. J. (2006, February). *Methods for controlling absenteeism in an organizational setting: A meta-analysis.* Paper presented at the annual Graduate Student Conference in Industrial-Organizational Psychology and Organizational Behavior, Fairfax, VA.

Woodward, N. H. (1999). In case of emergency break glass. *HR Magazine, 44*(8), 83–88.

Woodward, N. H. (2013). Being there: Companies take diverse approaches to attendance rewards programs. *HR Magazine, 58*(11), 44–46.

Wooten, W. (1993). Using knowledge, skill and ability (KSA) data to identify career pathing opportunities: An application of job analysis to internal manpower planning. *Public Personnel Management, 22*(4), 551–563.

WorldatWork (2016). Bonus programs and practices. Scottsdale, AZ: WorldatWork.

Wrzesniewski, A., & Dutton, J. E. (2001). Crafting a job: Revisioning employees as active crafters of their work. *Academy of Management Review, 26*(2), 179–201.

Wyatt Company (1993). *Best practices in corporate restructuring.* Washington, DC: Author.

Yandrick, R. M. (2001). A team effort. *HR Magazine, 46*(6), 136–141.

Yao, Y., Rakheja, S., Gauvin, C., Marcotte, P., & Hamouda, K. (2018). Evaluation of effects of anti-vibration gloves on manual dexterity. *Ergonomics, 61*(11), 1530–1544.

Yoh (2018). Yoh survey: Lack of respect, broken promises, and overworking employees are top issues with managers that would make employed Americans consider new job. Retrieved from https://www.globenewswire.com/news-release/2018/10/25/1627089/0/en/Yoh-Survey-Lack-of-Respect-Broken-Promises-and-Overworking-Employees-Are-Top-Issues-with-Managers-That-Would-Make-Employed-Americans-Consider-New-Jobs.htmls.

Young, M. S., & Stanton, N. A. (2007). Back to the future: Brake reaction times for manual and automated vehicles. *Ergonomics, 50*(1), 46–58.

Youngjohn, R. M., & Woehr, D. J. (2001, April). *A meta-analytic investigation of the relationship between individual differences and leader effectiveness.* Poster presented at the 16th annual conference of the Society for Industrial and Organizational Psychology, San Diego, CA.

Yukl, G. A. (1982, April). *Innovations in research on leader behavior.* Paper presented at the annual meeting of the Eastern Academy of Management, Baltimore, MD.

Yukl, G. A. (1994). *Leadership in organizations* (3rd ed.). Englewood Cliffs, NJ: Prentice Hall.

Yukl, G. A., & Gardner, W. L. (2020). *Leadership in organizations* (9th ed.). New York: Pearson.

Zaccaro, S. J., Day, D. V., & Hedrick, K. (2021). Leadership: A critical historical analysis of the influence of leader traits. In L. Koppes Bryan (Ed.), *Historical perspectives in industrial and organizational psychology* (2nd Ed.) (pp. 227–248). New York: Routledge.

Zajonc, R. B. (1980). Compressence. In P. B. Paulus (Ed.), *Psychology of group influence.* Hillsdale, NJ: Lawrence Erlbaum.

Zajonc, R. B., Heingartner, A., & Herman, E. M. (1969). Social enhancement and impairment of performance in the cockroach. *Journal of Personality and Social Psychology, 13,* 83–92.

Zedeck, S., Cascio, W. F., Goldstein, I., & Outtz, J. (1996). Sliding bands: An alternative to top-down selection. In R. Barrett (Ed.), *Fair employment strategies in human resource management* (pp. 222–234). Westport, CT: Quorum.

Zell, E., & Krizan, Z. (2014). Do people have insight into their abilities? A meta-synthesis. *Perspectives on Psychological Science, 9*(2), 111–125.

Zemke, R. (1993). Rethinking the rush to team-up. *Training, 30*(11), 55–61.

Zemke, R. (1997). How long does it take? *Training, 34*(5), 69–79.

Zetik, D. C., & Stuhlmacher, A. F. (2002). Goal setting and negotiation performance: A meta-analysis. *Group Processes and Intergroup Relations, 5*(1), 35–52.

Zetlin, M. (2019, May 29). *This is the best day of the week to fire an employee, according to HR experts.* https://www.inc.com/minda-zetlin/firing-employee-wednesday-best-day.html

Zhang, C., & Kuncel, N. R. (2020). Moving beyond the brag sheet: A meta-analysis of biodata measures predicting student outcomes. *Educational Measurement: Issues and Practice, 39*(3), 106–121.

Zhao, H., Wayne, S. J., Glibkowski, B. C., & Bravo, J. (2007). The impact of psychological contract breach on work-related outcomes: A meta-analysis. *Personnel Psychology, 60*(3), 647–680.

Zhou, J. (1998). Feedback valence, feedback style, task autonomy, and achievement orientation: Interactive effects on creative performance. *Journal of Applied Psychology, 83*(2), 261–276.

Zickar, M. J., & Gibby, R. E. (2021). Four persistent themes throughout the history of I-O psychology in the United States. In L. Koppes Bryan (Ed.), *Historical perspectives in industrial and organizational psychology* (2nd Ed.) (pp. 42–62). New York: Routledge.

Zimmerman, R. D., Triana, M. C., & Barrick, M. R. (2010). The criterion-related validity of a structured letter of reference using multiple raters and multiple performance criteria. *Human Performance, 23,* 361–378.

Zink, D. L. (2002). Chevron U.S.A., Inc. v. Echazabal: Has the Americans with Disabilities Act become a toothless tiger? *The Industrial-Organizational Psychologist, 40*(2), 70–75.

Zink, D. L., & Gutman, A. (2005, April). *Legal issues in providing and asking for references and letters of recommendation.* Paper presented at the 20th annual meeting of the Society for Industrial and Organizational Psychology, Los Angeles, CA.

Zottoli, M. A., & Wanous, J. P. (2000). Recruitment source research: Current status and future directions. *Human Resource Management Review, 10,* 435–451.

Zuber, A. (1996). Tapping a human resource: Restaurants fight labor crunch with training programs. *Nation's Restaurant News, 30*(26), 33–35.

Zweigenhaft, R. L. (1976). Personal space in the faculty office: Desk placement and the student-faculty interaction. *Journal of Applied Psychology, 61,* 529–532.

Name Index

Chall, J.S., 416
Chambers, B.A., 133
Champagne, J., 312
Champion, C.H., 273
Chan, D., 198, 206
Chan, D.W.L., 290
Chan, K.Y., 423, 424
Chang, C.H., 540, 541, 542
Chang, W., 551
Chao, G.T., 255
Chaozhong, W., 578
Chapman, D.S., 122, 134, 142
Chapman, G., 382
Chappelow, C., 231
Cheatham, T.R., 457
Chen, A.Y., 504
Chen, D., 555
Chen, J.A., 257
Chen, S.C., 467
Cheung, G.W., 159
Chiaburu, D.S., 357
Choragwicka, B., 24
Chrisman, S., 137
Christensen, J., 414
Christian, J., 422
Christian, M.S., 163
Christiansen, N., 224
Chua-Eoan, H., 457
Chugh, J.S., 396
Church, A.H., 24, 260
Cialdini, R.B., 459
Cigularov, K., 170
Cirka, C.C., 340
Clark, M.A., 353, 373, 556
Clark, M.M., 517
Clark, R.E., 341, 547
Clark, S.M., 561
Clark, V.N., 287
Clarke, B.C., 519
Clarke, P.L., 161
Clause, C.S., 53, 198, 206
Clay, R.A., 533, 538
Clayton, L.D., 473
Clemans, J., 556
Cleveland, J.N., 255, 263
Clevenger, J., 163
Clinton, W.J., 444
Coats, G., 137
Cober, R., 552
Cochran, A., 407
Cohen, A., 544
Cohen, D., 488
Cohen, D.B., 26, 94, 140
Cohen, D.S., 503, 506
Cohen, J., 26
Cohen, P., 161
Cohen, R.R., 460
Cohen, S., 537
Cohen, S.A., 46, 172
Cohen, S.G., 475, 543

Cohen, T.R., 181
Colbert, A.E., 423
Colella, A., 176, 217, 437
Collins, A., 18
Collins, C.J., 119
Collins, D.B., 434
Collins, J.M., 353
Collins, L., 544
Collins, M., 46
Collison, J., 119
Colquitt, A.L., 176
Colquitt, J.A., 365, 461
Combs, G.M., 109
Combs, J., 518
Conard, M.A., 131, 536
Conboy, K., 460
Condly, S.J., 341
Conley, P.R., 46
Conlon, D.E., 365
Connelly, B.S., 135
Connelly, M.S., 288
Connerley, M.L., 206
Connolly, J.J., 356, 357
Connolly, T., 464
Contournet, G., 305
Contractor, N., 362
Conway, J.M., 133, 134, 135,
    140, 232, 234, 257, 258
Cook, T., 74
Cooksey, R.W., 204
Coons, A.E., 437
Cooper, C.L., 352
Cooper, M., 438
Cooper, M.L., 539
Cooper, W.H., 258, 259
Cooper-Hakim, A., 352, 353
Copper, C., 306
Cordero, A.C., 396
Cordes, C.L., 539
Cornelissen, V.A., 558
Cornelius, E.T., 52, 57
Cortina, J.M., 134
Cortini, M., 192
Cosgrave, G., 7
Cosmas, K.A., 361
Costa, P.T., 178
Cotton, J.L., 303
Cottrell, J.M., 162
Cottrell, N.B., 468
Courtis, J.K., 414
Courtright, S.H., 168
Cowgill, B., 124
Coyle, B.W., 175
Coyne, E.E., 341
Crace, R.K., 469
Crawford, E.R., 178
Crawford, K., 46
Crawford, M.S., 168
Crawford, R.L., 553
Credé, M., 25

Crispin, D., 119
Cromwell, P.F., 472
Cronbach, L.J., 199
Cronshaw, S.F., 57
Cropanzano, R., 346, 356, 382
Csoka, L.S., 431
Cucina, J.M., 46, 213
Culbertson, S.S., 133
Culpepper, S.A., 218
Cummings, T.D., 498
Cunningham, C.J.L., 534, 535
Curtis, J.R., 41
Daanen, H.A.M., 547
Dababneh, A.J., 519
Dalal, R.S., 352, 353, 383
Dale, E., 416
Dale, G., 516, 518, 521
Dalton, D.R., 181, 378
Daniel, M., 124
Daniels, M.A., 180
Dansereau, F., 436
Darnold, T., 353
Darwish, A., 233
Davey, T., 207
Davidson, O.B., 321
Davidson, R., 469
Davies, E., 547
Davies, S., 430
Davies-Muir, A., 254
Davis, D.D., 472
Davis, K., 396, 397
Davis, K.S., 359
Davis, T.R., 404
Davison, H.K., 134, 183
Dawis, R.V., 355, 369
Day, D.V., 8, 206, 423, 425, 436
Day, E.A., 172
De Been, I., 396
De Champlain, A.F., 233
De Clercq, B., 179
de Dreau, C., 488
De Dreu, C.K.W., 480
De Fruyt, F., 179
De Jong, A.H., 325
de Jong, R.D., 433
De Mauro, A., 37, 44
De Meuse, K.P., 528
de Smedt, M., 552
De Waard, D., 579
Dean, M.A., 172, 190
Deane, C., 26
Debbache, A., 233
Deci, E.L., 322, 330
Deckop, J.R., 340
DeFruyt, F., 162
DeGrassi, S.W., 137, 404
DeGroot, T., 140, 142, 558
Del Vecchio, D., 126
Delbridge, K., 206
Delery, J.E., 379

Deluga, R.J., 460
Dempsey, P.G., 576
Den Hartog, D.N., 445
DeNisi, A.S., 252, 259, 435
Dennis, A.R., 463, 464, 472
Denton, D.K., 501
DePaulo, B.M., 403, 404
DeRosa, D. M., 472, 475
DeRouin, R.E., 299
DeRue, D.J., 360
DeRue, D.S., 427
DeShon, R.P., 206
Deshpande, R.C., 558
Devine, D.J., 464, 473, 475, 479
Dew, A.F., 135
Dewberry, C., 254
DeYoung, C.G., 178
Di Paolo, N.T., 197
Dianal, I., 576
DiBritto, F., 153
Dickenson, T.L., 246
Dickinson, A.M., 339, 340
Dickson, D.H., 206
DiClemente, D.F., 6
Diekmann, F.J., 286
Dierdorff, E.C., 49, 53, 65
Dietz, P.E., 571
DiFonzo, N., 397, 398
Dilchert, S., 162, 177, 180
Dineen, B.R., 126, 154
Dinges, D.F., 520
Dingfelder, S.F., 425
Dingman, S., 137
Dirks, K.T., 450, 499
Dirkx, J., 552
Dittrich, J.E., 347
DiVasto, P., 141, 142
Do, M.H., 425
Dobbins, G.H., 260
Dolin, D.J., 403
Dominguez, C.M., 444
Donnellon, A., 472, 473, 474
Donnerstein, E., 547
Donnon, T., 233
Donohue, J.M., 343
Donovan, J.J., 178, 293, 320,
    357
Donovan, M.A., 64
Dorfman, P.W., 445
Dormann, C., 355
Dossett, D.L., 250
Dougherty, T.W., 136, 539
Douglas, J., 313
Douma, B., 332
Douthitt, E.A., 470
Doverspike, D., 170
Downey, D.E., 410, 432
Drasgow, F., 101, 180, 206, 423,
    424, 513
Dreibelbis, R.C., 171

Krause, D.E., 170
Krausz, M., 352, 353
Kravitz, D.A., 108, 256
Krell, E., 552
Kremen, M., 124
Kriegel, R., 473, 496, 497
Kriska, S.D., 137
Kristof-Brown, A.L., 360, 361, 540, 541
Krizan, Z., 234
Krueger, R.F., 180
Kruger, J., 14
Kuder, G.F., 199
Kudisch, J., 233
Kugler, K.G., 71
Kulik, J.A., 556
Kunce, C., 176
Kuncel, N.R., 25, 135, 161, 173
Kunin, T., 369
Kurland, N.B., 396, 398
Kutcher, E.J., 138
Kuusela, V., 544
Kuvaas, B., 333
Kwun, S.K., 232
Kyllonen, P., 159
Laabs, J.J., 504
Lachnit, C., 124
Ladd, D., 332
LaFrance, M., 404
Lahtela, K., 544
Lahy, J.M., 7
Laing, B., 443
Laird, M.D., 39
Lajunen, T., 579
Lam, S.S.K., 499
Lambert, B.J., 552
Lambert, L.S., 427
Lambregts, B., 127
Landau, K., 59
Landers, R.N., 17, 28, 298
Landis, R.S., 53
Landstrom, U., 543
Landy, F.L., 46, 137
Langdale, J.A., 137
Langdon, J.C., 262
Lanier, P.A., 8
Lantz, C., 143
Lapidus, R.S., 347
Larey, T.S., 472
Larraza-Kintana, M., 342
Larrick, R.P., 548
Larson, J., 198
Larson, S.L., 185
Laschever, S., 71
Lasek, M., 157
LaShells, M.B., 273
Lasky, J.W., 220
Latane, B., 463, 466
Latham, G.A., 250, 274, 302, 317, 328, 331, 333

Latham, G.P., 8
Latham, V.M., 433
Law, J.R., 423
Lawler, E.E., 343
Lawler, J.J., 513
Lawrence, P.R., 330, 331
Lawshe, C.H., 213
Lawson, K., 285
Layman, J.J., 378
Lazaroiu, G., 319
Le, H., 422
Leach, D.J., 395
Leana, C.R., 267
LeBreton, J.M., 182
Lebron, A., 567
Lee, J.A., 248, 565
Lee, K., 101, 353, 461
Lee, L.J., 467
Lee, S.J., 440
Lee, T.W., 353, 360, 381
Leeds, D., 302
Lefkowitz, J., 260
Lelchook, A.M., 353, 373, 556
Leonard, D.C., 111
Leonard, K.E., 544
Leone, D., 320
LePine, J.A., 352, 353, 383, 470, 535
LePine, M., 535
LePla, L.A., 101
Lepsinger, R., 475
Leslie, L.M., 108, 488
Lester, D., 553, 559
Lev-Arey, D., 108
Levashina, J., 134, 176
Levine, E., 38, 45, 56, 57, 65
Levine, E.L., 357
Levine, J.D., 59
Levine, M., 18
Levine, S.P., 138
Levinson, M., 490
Levit, A., 119
Levy, P.E., 232, 235, 333, 541
Lewin, K., 498, 499, 506
Lewis, G., 118, 122
Li, N., 357
Li, W.D., 355
Liden, R.C., 471, 474
Lied, T.L., 345
Lievens, F., 24, 171, 172
Lilienfeld, S.O., 179
Lim, J., 520
Lin, L., 545
Lin, X., 550
Lindell, M.K., 53
Lindeman, M., 320
Ling, G., 159
Ling, J., 126
Linkous, R.A., 468
Linn, R.L., 218

Liou, K.T., 367
Lipmann, O., 7
Lipnic, V.A., 98
Lippitt, R., 498
Liska, L.Z., 435
Liu, D., 381
Liu, O.L., 159
Liu, Y., 518
Livnech, N., 274
Locke, E.A., 317, 322, 331, 333, 355, 356
Lodi-Smith, J., 320
Loewen, L.J., 545
Lofquist, L.H., 369
Lohan, G., 460
Loher, B.T., 158, 159, 291
London, M., 233, 234
Long, D.M., 365
Long, G.M., 580
Lopez, F.E., 62
Lopez, F.M., 62
Lord, R.G., 259, 346, 347, 490
Lorinkova, N.N.M., 439
Lounsbury, J.W., 206
Lount, R.B., 470
Lovenheim, P., 490
Lowenberg, G., 13
Lucas, J.A., 108
Luoma, J., 579
Luthans, F., 333, 336, 337, 339, 445
Lykken, D.T., 355
Lyness, K.S., 52
Lyons, P., 44
Mabry, E., 298
Mackenzie, S.B., 248, 336, 345
Mackworth, N.H., 547
MacLachlan, M., 347
Madera, J.M., 159
Mager, R.F., 285
Magjuka, R.J., 291
Magner, N.R., 488
Mahoney, C.A., 468
Mahoney, J.J., 185
Mahto, R.V., 126
Mailhot, E.K., 46
Maiorca, J., 273
Major, B., 403
Makihijani, M.J., 426
Malos, S.B., 134, 261
Manaugh, T.S., 159
Mangel, R., 340
Maniezki, A., 364
Mann, F.C., 553
Mann, R.B., 131
Manners, G.E., 463
Manning, R., 18, 19
Mannix, E.A., 481
Manstead, A.S., 469
Maranto, C.L., 542

Marcotte, P., 576
Marin, S., 298
Markham, S.E., 562
Marks, M.A., 476, 477
Marks, M.L., 528
Markus, H.R., 131
Maronitis, A., 576
Marras, W.W., 576
Marsh, W.M., 513
Marshall, C.J., 289
Martell, R.F., 258
Marti, M., 464
Martin, A., 6
Martin, A.L., 467
Martin, C., 345
Martin, C.L., 91, 137, 259
Martin, D.C., 267
Martin, G.E., 486
Martin, J.A., 39
Martin, N.R., 171, 180
Martin, R.A., 559
Martin, R.C., 159
Martinez, A.D., 39
Martinez, M.N., 396
Martinez-Tur, V., 364
Martocchio, J.J., 70, 513
Martyka, J., 292
Mascio, C., 44, 461
Maser, S., 137
Maslow, A.H., 326, 327
Mason, C.M., 499
Massengill, D.P., 222
Mastrangelo, P.M., 186
Matarazzo, J.D., 159
Mathews, K.E., 544
Mathieu, J.E., 303, 353, 476, 513
Matic, T., 169
Mattern, K.D., 218
Matthews, R.A., 536
Mattrey, M., 298
Maurer, R., 523
Maurer, S.A., 297
Maurer, T.J., 45, 133, 143
Mawhinney, T.C., 342
May, D.R., 445
Mayer, D.M., 108
Mayer, J.J., 563
Maynard, M.T., 513
Mayo, E., 457
Maznevski, M., 461
McAlpine, K.L., 439
McAndrew, F.T., 469
McCabe, M.J., 281
McCalips, R., 86
McCall, B.P., 355
McCall, M.W., 438
McCandless, K., 79
McCann, N., 559
McCarthy, J.M., 135, 143, 159
McCarthy, P.M., 45

Subject Index